Lecture Notes in Artificial Intelligence   6717

Edited by R. Goebel, J. Siekmann, and W. Wahlster

Subseries of Lecture Notes in Computer Science

T0190003

Weiru Liu (Ed.)

Symbolic and Quantitative Approaches to Reasoning with Uncertainty

11th European Conference, ECSQARU 2011
Belfast, UK, June 29 – July 1, 2011
Proceedings

 Springer

Series Editors

Randy Goebel, University of Alberta, Edmonton, Canada
Jörg Siekmann, University of Saarland, Saarbrücken, Germany
Wolfgang Wahlster, DFKI and University of Saarland, Saarbrücken, Germany

Volume Editor

Weiru Liu
Queen's University Belfast
School of Electronics, Electrical Engineering and Computer Science
Belfast, BT9 5BN, UK
E-mail: w.liu@qub.ac.uk

ISSN 0302-9743   e-ISSN 1611-3349
ISBN 978-3-642-22151-4   e-ISBN 978-3-642-22152-1
DOI 10.1007/978-3-642-22152-1
Springer Heidelberg Dordrecht London New York

Library of Congress Control Number: 2011930186

CR Subject Classification (1998): I.2, F.4.1, F.3-4, I.2.3, I.2.4, H.3-4

LNCS Sublibrary: SL 7 – Artificial Intelligence

Typesetting: Camera-ready by author, data conversion by Scientific Publishing Services, Chennai, India

Printed on acid-free paper

Springer is part of Springer Science+Business Media (www.springer.com)

Preface

The biennial ECSQARU conference is a major forum for advances in the theory
and practice of reasoning under uncertainty. Contributions are expected to come
from both researchers who are interested in advancing the technology and practi-
tioners who use uncertainty techniques in applications. The scope of ECSQARU
includes, but is not limited to, fundamental issues, representation, inference,
learning, and decision making in qualitative and numeric paradigms.

Previous ECSQARU conferences were held in Marseille (1991), Granada
(1993), Fribourg (1995), Bonn (1997), London (1999), Toulouse (2001), Aalborg
(2003), Barcelona (2005), Hammamet (2007), and Verona (2009).

The 11th European Conference on Symbolic and Quantitative Approaches to
Reasoning with Uncertainty (ECSQARU 2011) was held in Belfast, UK, from
June 29 to July 1, 2011, with a particular focus on unifying logic and uncer-
tainty reasoning approaches for solving complex problems. ECSQARU 2011 also
featured PhD Forum Posters and the Workshop on "Uncertainty Reasoning and
Multi-agent Systems for Sensor Networks (URMASSN 2011)".

The best paper from ECSQARU 2011, "Measuring Consistency Gain and
Information Loss in Stepwise Inconsistency Resolution" by John Grant and An-
thony Hunter, was chosen to represent ECSQARU in the Large Track of Best
Papers from Sister Conferences at IJCAI 2011.

The papers in this volume were selected from 108 submissions, after a strict
review process by the members of the Program Committee. In addition, the
volume contains three invited talks by three outstanding researchers in the field,
Didier Dubois, Dov Gabbay, and Joe Halpern.

I would like to thank all the members of the Program Committee and the
additional reviewers for their timely and valuable reviews. I would also like to
thank the members of the local Organizing Committee and the additional support team for their hard work and contribution to the success of the conference.
Finally, financial support from CSIT (Centre for Secure Information Technologies), the School of Electronics, Electrical Engineering and Computer Science at
Queen's University Belfast, and Belfast City Council is greatly appreciated.

April 2011   Weiru Liu

Organization

ECSQARU 2011 was organized by the School of Electronics, Electrical Engineering and Computer Science, Queen's University Belfast.

Executive Committee

Conference/Program Chairs	Weiru Liu	
Organizing Committee	David A. Bell	Michael Davis
	Jianbing Ma	Kevin McAreavey
	Paul Miller	Neil Montgomery
Additional Support	William Coey	Brian Fleming
	Tony McHale	Evelyn Milliken
	Lesley Moreland	Colette Tipping

Program Committee

Leila Amgoud (France)
Alessandro Antonucci (Switzerland)
David A Bell (UK)
Nahla Ben Amor (Tunisia)
Boutheina Ben Yaghlane (Tunisia)
Salem Benferhat (France)
Philippe Besnard (France)
Isabelle Bloch (France)
Richard Booth (Luxembourg/Thailand)
Gerd Brewka (Germany)
Claudette Cayrol (France)
Carlos Chesñevar (Spain)
Laurence Cholvy (France)
Giulianella Coletti (Italy)
Fabio Cozman (Brazil)
Fabio Cuzzolin (UK)
Adnan Darwiche (USA)
Cassio de Campos (Switzerland)
Luís Miguel de Campos (Spain)
Gert de Cooman (Belgium)
Thierry Denoeux (France)
Sébastien Destercke (France)
Marek Druzdzel (USA)
Didier Dubois (France)

Thomas Eiter (Austria)
Zied Elouedi (Tunisia)
Luis Enrique Sucar (Mexico)
Hélène Fargier (France)
Angelo Gilio (Italy)
Lluís Godo (Spain)
Andreas Herzig (France)
Eyke Hüllermeier (Germany)
Anthony Hunter (UK)
Van-Nam Huynh (Japan)
Audun Joang (Australia)
Gabriele Kern-Isberner (Germany)
Sébastien Konieczny (France)
Ivan Kramosil (Czech Republic)
Paul Krause (UK)
Rudolf Kruse (Germany)
Jérôme Lang (France)
Jonathan Lawry (UK)
Philippe Leray (France)
Churn-Jung Liau (Taiwan)
Paolo Liberatore (Italy)
Peter Lucas (The Netherlands)
Thomas Lukasiewicz (Italy/UK)
Jianbing Ma (UK)

Trevor Martin (UK)
Sally McClean (UK)
Pierre Marquis (France)
Khaled Mellouli (Tunisia)
Tommie Meyer (South Africa)
Serafín Moral (Spain)
Kedian Mu (P.R.China)
Thomas Dyhre Nielsen (Denmark)
Kristian G. Olesen (Denmark)
Ewa Orlowska (Poland)
Odile Papini (France)
Ramón Pino-Pérez (Venezuela)
David Poole (Canada)
Henri Prade (France)
Guilin Qi (P.R.China)
Maria Rifqi (France)
Silja Renooij (The Netherlands)

Sandra Sandri (Spain)
Torsten Schaub (Germany)
Johan Schubert (Sweden)
Qiang Shen (UK)
Romano Scozzafava (Italy)
Prakash P. Shenoy (USA)
Guillermo Simari (Argentina)
Claudio Sossai (Italy)
Milan Studeny (Czech Republic)
Enric Trillas (Spain)
Linda van der Gaag (The Netherlands)
Leon van der Torre (The Netherlands)
Barbara Vantaggi (Italy)
Emil Weydert (Luxembourg)
Mary-Anne Williams (Australia)
Dongmo Zhang (Australia)
Nevin L. Zhang (Hong Kong, China)

Additional Reviewers

Marco Baioletti
Sihem Belabbes
Yaxin Bi
Solon Carvalho
Weiwei Cheng
Wolfgang Dvorak
Sander Evers
Tommaso Flaminio
Corina Freitas
Perry Groot
Krystian Ji
Marie-Christine Lagasquie
Michel Lemaître
Jun Liu
Tengfei Liu
Arjen Hommersom

Christian Moewes
Irina Perfilieva
Anna Radzikowska
Gavin Rens
Matthias Steinbrecher
Minh Dao Tran
Georg Ruß
Gerardo Simari
Carlos Uzcategui
Serena Villata
Jiangou Zhang
Zhizheng Zhang
Junwu Zhu
Yi Wang

Sponsors

Belfast City Council
Center for Secure Information Technology (CSIT)
School of Electronics, Electrical Engineering and Computer Science, Queen's
University Belfast

Table of Contents

Invited Talks

Information Fusion and Revision in Qualitative and Quantitative
Settings: Steps Towards a Unified Framework 1
  Didier Dubois

Introducing Equational Semantics for Argumentation Networks 19
  Dov M. Gabbay

Constructive Decision Theory: Short Summary 36
  Joseph Y. Halpern

Argumentation

Strong Equivalence for Argumentation Semantics Based on
Conflict-Free Sets 38
  Sarah Alice Gaggl and Stefan Woltran

Backing and Undercutting in Defeasible Logic Programming 50
  Andrea Cohen, Alejandro J. García, and Guillermo R. Simari

Arguing with Valued Preference Relations 62
  Souhila Kaci and Christophe Labreuche

Arguing about the Trustworthiness of the Information Sources 74
  *Serena Villata, Guido Boella, Dov M. Gabbay, and
  Leendert van der Torre*

Two Roles of Preferences in Argumentation Frameworks 86
  Leila Amgoud and Srdjan Vesic

Bayesian Networks and Causal Networks

A Re-definition of Mixtures of Polynomials for Inference in Hybrid
Bayesian Networks 98
  Prakash P. Shenoy

Using Four Cost Measures to Determine Arc Reversal Orderings 110
  Cory J. Butz, Anders L. Madsen, and Kevin Williams

Using the Noisy-OR Model Can Be Harmful . . . But It Often Is Not ... 122
  Steven P.D. Woudenberg and Linda C. van der Gaag

Attaining Monotonicity for Bayesian Networks 134
   Merel T. Rietbergen and Linda C. van der Gaag

Importance Sampling on Bayesian Networks with Deterministic
Causalities 146
   Haohai Yu and Robert van Engelen

Bayesian Networks and the Imprecise Dirichlet Model Applied to
Recognition Problems 158
   Cassio P. de Campos and Qiang Ji

On Stopping Evidence Gathering for Diagnostic Bayesian Networks 170
   Linda C. van der Gaag and Hans L. Bodlaender

SemCaDo: A Serendipitous Strategy for Learning Causal Bayesian
Networks Using Ontologies 182
   Montassar Ben Messaoud, Philippe Leray, and Nahla Ben Amor

Scaling Up the Greedy Equivalence Search Algorithm by Constraining
the Search Space of Equivalence Classes 194
   *Juan I. Alonso-Barba, Luis de la Ossa, Jose A. Gámez, and
   Jose M. Puerta*

Extensions of Decision-Theoretic Troubleshooting: Cost Clusters and
Precedence Constraints 206
   Václav Lín

Locally Averaged Bayesian Dirichlet Metrics 217
   *Andrés Cano, Manuel Gómez-Olmedo, Andrés R. Masegosa, and
   Serafín Moral*

Mixture of Markov Trees for Bayesian Network Structure Learning
with Small Datasets in High Dimensional Space 229
   Sourour Ammar and Philippe Leray

Finding P–Maps and I–Maps to Represent Conditional
Independencies 239
   Marco Baioletti, Giuseppe Busanello, and Barbara Vantaggi

Marginalization without Summation: Exploiting Determinism in Factor
Algebra 251
   Sander Evers and Peter J.F. Lucas

Belief Functions

Independence and 2-Monotonicity: Nice to Have, Hard to Keep 263
   Sebastien Destercke

Constructing Dynamic Frames of Discernment in Cases of Large
Number of Classes 275
    Yousri Kessentini, Thomas Burger, and Thierry Paquet

On Consistent Approximations of Belief Functions in the Mass Space ... 287
    Fabio Cuzzolin

Generalized Information Theory Based on the Theory of Hints 299
    Marc Pouly

Towards an Alarm for Opposition Conflict in a Conjunctive
Combination of Belief Functions 314
    Éric Lefèvre, Zied Elouedi, and David Mercier

E2GK: Evidential Evolving Gustafsson-Kessel Algorithm for Data
Streams Partitioning Using Belief Functions 326
    Lisa Serir, Emmanuel Ramasso, and Noureddine Zerhouni

Evidential Markov Decision Processes 338
    Hélène Soubaras, Christophe Labreuche, and Pierre Savéant

Continuous Belief Functions to Qualify Sensors Performances 350
    *Pierre-Emmanuel Doré, Christophe Osswald, Arnaud Martin,
    Anne-Laure Jousselme, and Patrick Maupin*

Belief Revision and Inconsistency Handling

Measuring Consistency Gain and Information Loss in Stepwise
Inconsistency Resolution 362
    John Grant and Anthony Hunter

Relating Truth, Knowledge and Belief in Epistemic States 374
    Costas D. Koutras and Yorgos Zikos

How Strong Can an Agent Believe Reported Information? 386
    Laurence Cholvy

Logic-Based Fusion of Complex Epistemic States 398
    Amílcar Mata Díaz and Ramón Pino Pérez

Classification and Clustering

Latent Tree Classifier 410
    Yi Wang, Nevin L. Zhang, Tao Chen, and Leonard K.M. Poon

When Learning Naive Bayesian Classifiers Preserves Monotonicity 422
    Barbara F.I. Pieters, Linda C. van der Gaag, and Ad Feelders

Possibilistic Classifiers for Uncertain Numerical Data 434
    *Myriam Bounhas, Henri Prade, Mathieu Serrurier, and
    Khaled Mellouli*

Default Reasoning and Logics for Reasoning under Uncertainty

Relational Probabilistic Conditional Reasoning at Maximum Entropy ... 447
    Matthias Thimm, Gabriele Kern-Isberner, and Jens Fisseler

Probabilistic Approach to Nonmonotonic Consequence Relations 459
    Dragan Doder, Aleksandar Perović, and Zoran Ognjanović

Bridging the Gap between Reinforcement Learning and Knowledge
Representation: A Logical Off- and On-Policy Framework 472
    Emad Saad

Answer Set Programming for Computing Decisions under
Uncertainty 485
    Roberto Confalonieri and Henri Prade

Quasi Conjunction and Inclusion Relation in Probabilistic Default
Reasoning... 497
    Angelo Gilio and Giuseppe Sanfilippo

Handling Exceptions in Logic Programming without Negation as
Failure 509
    Roberto Confalonieri, Henri Prade, and Juan Carlos Nieves

Probabilistic Stit Logic 521
    Jan Broersen

Overriding Subsuming Rules 532
    Philippe Besnard, Éric Grégoire, and Sébastien Ramon

Foundations of Reasoning and Decision Making under Uncertainty

Pseudo-polynomial Functions over Finite Distributive Lattices 545
    Miguel Couceiro and Tamás Waldhauser

A Bridge between Probability and Possibility in a Comparative
Framework... 557
    Giulianella Coletti, Romano Scozzafava, and Barbara Vantaggi

Leximax Relations in Decision Making through the Dominance
Plausible Rule 569
    Franklin Camacho and Ramón Pino Pérez

Parameterized Uncertain Reasoning Approach Based on a
Lattice-Valued Logic 582
Shuwei Chen, Jun Liu, Hui Wang, and Juan Carlos Augusto

Fuzzy Sets and Fuzzy Logic

From Preference Relations to Fuzzy Choice Functions 594
Davide Martinetti, Ignacio Montes, and Susana Díaz

Fuzzy Relational Inequations and Equations in the Framework of
Control Problems 606
*Jorge Jiménez, Susana Montes, Branimir Šešelja, and
Andreja Tepavčević*

Fuzzy Autoepistemic Logic: Reflecting about Knowledge of Truth
Degrees.. 616
*Marjon Blondeel, Steven Schockaert, Martine De Cock, and
Dirk Vermeir*

Belief Functions on MV-Algebras of Fuzzy Events Based on Fuzzy
Evidence... 628
Tommaso Flaminio, Lluis Godo, and Enrico Marchioni

Order Compatible Fuzzy Relations and Their Elicitation from General
Fuzzy Partitions 640
Sandra Sandri and Flávia Toledo Martins-Bedé

Implementation and Applications of Uncertain Systems

Web Services and *Incerta Spiriti*: A Game Theoretic Approach to
Uncertainty 651
Joaquim Gabarro, Maria Serna, and Alan Stewart

Underwater Archaeological 3D Surveys Validation within the Removed
Sets Framework.. 663
*Julien Hué, Mariette Sérayet, Pierre Drap, Odile Papini, and
Eric Würbel*

Adaptive Dialogue Strategy Selection through Imprecise Probabilistic
Query Answering 675
Ian O'Neill, Anbu Yue, Weiru Liu, and Phil Hanna

Possibility Theory and Possibilistic Logic

Statistical Estimations of Lattice-Valued Possibilistic Distributions 688
Ivan Kramosil and Milan Daniel

Compiling Min-based Possibilistic Causal Networks: A Mutilated-Based
Approach 700
    Raouia Ayachi, Nahla Ben Amor, and Salem Benferhat

Possibilistic Evidence 713
    Henri Prade and Agnès Rico

Uncertainty in Databases

A Preference Query Model Based on a Fusion of Local Orders 725
    Patrick Bosc, Olivier Pivert, and Grégory Smits

Approximate Achievability in Event Databases 737
    Austin Parker, Gerardo I. Simari, Amy Sliva, and
    V.S. Subrahmanian

A Probabilistic Interpretation for a Geometric Similarity Measure 749
    Sebastian Lehrack and Ingo Schmitt

Author Index 761

Information Fusion and Revision
in Qualitative and Quantitative Settings
Steps Towards a Unified Framework

Didier Dubois

IRIT, CNRS and Université de Toulouse
dubois@irit.fr

Abstract. Fusion and revision are two key topics in knowledge representation and uncertainty theories. However, various formal axiomatisations of these notions were proposed inside specific settings, like logic, probability theory, possibility theory, kappa functions, belief functions and imprecise probability. For instance, the revision rule in probability theory is Jeffrey's rule, and is characterized by two axioms. The AGM axioms for revision are stated in the propositional logic setting. But there is no bridge between these axiomatizations. Likewise, Dempster rule of combination was axiomatized by Smets among others, and a logical syntax-independent axiomatization for merging was independently proposed by Koniezny and Pino-Perez, while a belief function can be viewed as a weighted belief set. Moreover the distinction between fusion and revision is not always so clear and comparing sets of postulates for each of them can be enlightening. This paper presents a tentative set of basic principles for revision and another set of principles for fusion that could be valid regardless of whether information is represented qualitatively or quantitatively. In short, while revision obeys a success postulate and a minimal change principle, fusion is essentially symmetric, and obeys a principle of optimism, that tries to take advantage of all sources of information. Moreover, when two pieces of information are consistent, revising one by the other comes down to merging them symmetrically. Finally, there is a principle of minimal commitment at work in all settings, and common to the two operations.

1 Introduction

A major issue in knowledge representation and reasoning is the modeling of the dynamics of information possessed by agents. This kind of topic has been triggered by works in probability kinematics [1], and also in logic-based artificial intelligence, starting with the AGM theory of belief revision [2], relying on previous considerations by Isaac Levi. More recently the issue of information fusion has also received a lot of attention [3]. The history of these developments has been somewhat shaky, with emphasis on axiomatic frameworks, but sometimes unconvincing rationale.

In the probabilistic area, conditioning is central to model the acquisition of new information. The prototypical revision operation in probability theory is

W. Liu (Ed.): ECSQARU 2011, LNAI 6717, pp. 1–18, 2011.
© Springer-Verlag Berlin Heidelberg 2011

Jeffrey's rule [4], that accepts probabilistic inputs and returns a new probability measure. It is often viewed as an extension of conditioning.

In the logical setting, one is interested in how a set of accepted beliefs changes when a new piece of information is received by an agent. Postulates that should drive the evolution of a set of beliefs have been convincingly advocated. Soon enough, it has been noticed that nothing is said in the AGM theory concerning the way the plausibility ranking changes with the arrival of new information. Various proposals have been made, and noticeably by Darwiche and Pearl [5] to address this problem, thus paving the way to a study of iterated belief revision. However, what iterated belief revision deals with and what can be a canonical example of it are often not very clear from reading papers on this topic. More generally the lack of prototypical scenarios for belief change has been noticed [6,7].

A special case of belief revision is when the input information does not contradict the prior information. This is called expansion in the AGM setting. Then the change operation becomes symmetric and comes down to a fusion operation. The fusion of information is again an area where various proposals exist independently in various settings. Moreover, it has also been extensively addressed in decision sciences where preference relations or utility functions are aggregated, rather than epistemic states. There is an extensive and scattered literature about fusion in probability theory [8,9], in possibility theory [10], in the theory of evidence[11,12], in logic [3,13], etc.

There is a clear need for a general framework that could account for fusion and revision of information, and that could cover both numerical and qualitative frameworks, in order to better understand what these operations are relevant for and what are the basic principles at work, beyond the particulars of the representation settings. This paper only takes modest steps to contribute to this research program. First, in Section 2, we question the notion of epistemic state, insisting on the difference between singular and generic information, a distinction that may shed light on how agents construct beliefs. Then, in Section 3, we recall the difference between combining pieces of information of the same nature, and constructing beliefs from generic knowledge and singular evidence. Section 4 describes general principles of information combination common to all frameworks. Section 5 provides preliminary comments on how these principles are at work in various settings. This paper owes much to on-going work with Weiru Liu, Jianbing Ma and Henri Prade.

2   Epistemic States

An *epistemic state* is understood as the information possessed by an agent. This term has been used in logic-based artificial intelligence to designate a simple subset of possible worlds one of which is the true one, thus representing incomplete information (sometimes called an OR-set). Other authors, especially in the belief revision camp, use this term to name a plausibility ranking of possible worlds, or, equivalently, a deductively closed set of propositions ordered by an epistemic entrenchment, the latter governing AGM revision processes. We have argued in the past [7] that the meaning of an epistemic state is not unique, and that it is important to distinguish between two types of information:

- **Generic knowledge:** it collects the agent's past experience about the world. It consists of a confidence relation between events depicting what is likely and what is not, based on frequency or typicality. It also often takes the form of if-then rules tainted with exceptions (sometimes called conditional assertions). The specificity of generic knowledge is that it refers to a population of situations, as stored in the agent's memory, not to the current world.
- **Singular evidence:** It collects all the information known by the agent about the current world, that is, information on which the agent relies to make decisions (here we do not consider the latter issue). Singular information consists of two parts:
  - *Observations*: This is the part of the information that comes from the outside world, as the result of measurements, testimonies, and the like. Of course, observations can be uncertain, or conflicting. However, such uncertainties and conflicts must be solved prior to being exploited properly.
  - *Beliefs*: This is the part of the information constructed by the agent himself, by means of generic knowledge and observations. Belief construction proceeds by restricting the generic knowledge to the subpopulation of situations for which the current observations are valid. Beliefs are tentative and likely to be questioned when new observations come in.

In the following, we adopt a semantic point of view in terms of possible worlds, where a proposition is understood as an event, and represented by a subset of possible worlds or situations. There are several reasons for this. First, it allows for the use of all representation frameworks we consider, that is, numerical or qualitative. Then, syntactic representations create additional problems, such as proving that two propositions are equivalent, not related to the understanding of the nature of belief change; syntactic representations are a matter of representation conciseness and easy computation. Moreover, most logical revision theories are construed as syntax-independent, and it looks paradoxical to couch belief revision axioms in a syntactic framework, while claiming syntax-independence. Finally we claim the meaning of postulates is much clearer at the semantic level.

Let S be a set of possible situations. Propositions are denoted by capitals $A, B, ...$ and are subsets of S. Conjunction, disjunction and negation connectives are denoted by set-theoretic operations, $\cap, \cup, (\cdot)^c$. We denote by $\succeq$ a weak ordering on S representing a plausibility ranking (with $\succ$ and $\sim$ respectively denoting its strict and equivalence parts); it corresponds to a well-ordered partition of S, $\mathcal{P}_{\succeq} = \{E_1, ... E_k\}$ [14], where E_i contains worlds that are more plausible than those in E_j if $j > i$. Let $Bel(\succeq) = E_1$ be the proposition representing the set of most plausible states according to $\succeq$. More generally, a confidence relation is a partial ordering $>$ of propositions (irreflexive and transitive) in agreement with classical deduction in the sense that [15]:

If $A \subset A', B' \subset B$ and $A > B$, then $A' > B'$.

$A > B$ means that A is more likely than B. An example of confidence relation is one that stems from a plausibility ranking: $A > B$ if and only if $\forall s \in B, \exists s' \in A, s \succ s'$, known as a comparative possibility relation [16]. Another example is the order induced by a probability measure.

Such orderings can be understood as generic knowledge or uncertain singular information. In the following we consider several popular settings: propositional logic, probability theory, possibility theory, Shafer belief functions, and imprecise probabilities.

1. In a logical framework, S is the set of interpretations of a language. This framework can encode observations and beliefs as propositions but cannot account for the difference between generic knowledge and singular evidence.
2. Possibility theory [17] encompasses various possible formal settings including Spohn's kappa functions [14], and the representation of relative plausibility in terms of simple weak orders on S (which is the most usual representation, derived from the belief revision axioms in the AGM theory). Using degrees of possibility, the generic knowledge is represented by means of a possibility distribution $\pi : S \to L$ where L is a possibility scale that may range from a finite totally ordered scale to the unit interval. In this setting, observations usually take the form of a proposition C. Believing B in the context C is then modelled by the fact that the most plausible worlds in C lie in B. On the other hand, a possibility distribution can represent uncertain evidence as well.
3. In probability theory, the generic knowledge is representing by a statistical probability distribution on S, possibly encoded as a Bayesian network; in this case the underlying population is usually well-defined. Observations usually take the form of a proposition C. And the construction of beliefs comes down to computing the conditional probability $P(B|C)$. Uncertain observations can be modelled attaching *subjective* probabilities to unique events, or simply defining a subjective probability distribution over S. But there is no formal difference between a subjective and a statistical probability.
4. In the theory of evidence, as presented by Shafer [11], there is no room for statistical knowledge. The available information consists in uncertain observations from which belief degrees are derived. Mathematically, a belief function is defined as a random OR-set where focal sets (having positive probability mass) stand for candidate propositions, one of which represents the available information.
5. In the theory of imprecise probability, there are two trends. One trend considers convex sets of probability functions (called *credal sets*) representing ill-known generic probabilistic models. This is a mere extension of the standard probabilistic setting where the problem is to derive probability bounds on events of interest, conditioned on the available evidence. In the subjectivist view of Walley [18] lower probabilities represent degrees of belief and more generally lower expectations of gambles represent the agent's willingness to buy them. This setting is the most general one, hence the most

expressive. A special case is the upper and lower probability framework proposed by Dempster [19], where lower probabilities coincide with Shafer's belief functions, but may have a statistical flavor.

It should be clear that belief functions and credal sets are a blend of set-valued and probabilistic representations, that is, they subsume both the propositional and the probabilistic settings. Numerical possibility measures are also a special case of Shafer plausibility functions (the consonant random set setting).

These close links between representations of information suggest that change operations should be studied in a broader framework than what has been studied so far, whereby each author focuses on a favorite language.

3   Plausible Inference vs. Prioritized Combination

Being cast in a rather poorly expressive language, the AGM revision concept [2] is arguably ambiguous. The input information consists of a single proposition I, the prior beliefs can be represented by another proposition E; the result of the change operation is another proposition $E * I$. In the propositional logic case, Katsuno and Mendelzon redefined the AGM axioms replacing belief sets by equivalent single propositions [20]:

- R1: $E *_r I \subseteq I$ (Success)
- R2: If $E \cap I \neq \emptyset$ then $E *_r I = E \cap I$ (Expansion)
- R3: If $I \neq \emptyset$, then $E *_r I \neq \emptyset$
- R4: If $E = E'$ and $I = I'$ then $E *_r I = E' *_r I'$
- R5: $(E *_r I_1) \cap I_2 \subseteq E *_r (I_1 \cap I_2)$
- R6: If $(E *_r I_1) \cap I_2 \neq \emptyset$, then $E *_r (I_1 \cap I_2) \subseteq (E *_r I_1) \cap I_2$

Axiom R3 forbids to get inconsistent outcomes from consistent inputs, but we do not consider inconsistent inputs here; and the 4th axiom is syntax-independence, which is vacuous. The AGM axiomatic framework enforces the existence of a confidence relation called epistemic entrenchment, that comes down to a plausibility ranking $\succeq_E$ on possible worlds that opaquely drives the revision process. This ordering is determined by E and is faithful, that is, $Bel(\succeq_E) = E$. Then $E * I$ gathers the most $\succeq_E$-plausible worlds in I. The meaning of this procedure may depend on the way the input information and/or the plausibility ranking is interpreted.

- *Plausible inference.* If $\succeq_E$ is viewed as encoding generic knowledge, and the input we denote by $I = C$ collects observations on the current world, then $E * I = Bel(\succeq_E | C)$ induces the set of beliefs in the context $I = C$. However, in this case, the prior belief E is the set of most plausible worlds by default, according to the generic knowledge $\succeq_E$, prior to receiving I, and the latter is a piece of singular information outlining a reference class C. In this case, E stems from the plausibility ranking $\succeq_E$, and not the converse. In other words, the notation $\succeq_E$ is questionable. The primitive information is made of generic knowledge $\succeq$ and singular observations C. What changes is the

body of singular information, and $E * I$ depends on $\succeq$ and I, not on E. This view is confirmed by Gärdenfors and Makinson[21] when they view belief revision as another way of explaining what nonmonotonic reasoning consists of. Note that in this operation, the plausibility ranking is left untouched, and $E * I$ is obtained by temporarily restricting $\succeq$ to the current context C.
 – *Prioritized combination.* In this case, $\succeq_E$ is viewed as describing uncertain evidence. The input information I is an additional piece of evidence, that is totally sure: in other words, the agent is told that the true world does not lie outside I, and this is taken for granted. E stands for the current set of most plausible worlds prior to receiving I. The revision consists in changing $\succeq_E$ into another plausibility ranking $\succeq_{E*I}$ obtained by down-grading possible worlds where I does not hold. The most drastic way is to let $\succeq_{E*I}=\succeq_E$ on I, $s \succ_{E*I} s'$ if $s \in I$, $s' \notin I$, and $s \sim_{E*I} s'$ if $s, s' \notin I$ (all non-I states become the least plausible ones). It corresponds to conditioning in possibility theory (see Dubois and Prade [22]).

The main difference between the two views of the AGM setting is that in the case of plausible inference (also called prediction in statistics) the input information and the epistemic entrenchment relation are not of the same nature. The entrenchment relation then does not change across plausible inference steps. Only beliefs about the current situation are modified. In some sense, generic knowledge is more stable than singular evidence. On the contrary in the case of prioritized combination, the plausibility ranking and the input information are of the same nature (here, singular[1]) even if the input is considered absolutely true.

In probability theory, the same ambiguity is present regarding the meaning of conditioning. If the prior probability measure P represents generic information, and the input I corresponds to the available singular information about the current situation, then $P(B|I)$ stands for the propensity of situations where I is true to satisfy B. This conditional probability is then interpreted as the degree of belief that B is true in the current situation, for which all that is known is I. On the contrary suppose that P is a subjective probability representing what is more or less probably the current world. Then the input information I indicates that I is definitely true. So, the uncertain prior beliefs, described by P are modified in the form of a new probability function P', whereby the prior degree of belief $P(B)$ is changed into $P'(B) = P(B|I)$, thus acknowledging the fact that $P'(I) = 1$.

4   Revision vs. Fusion

In the following we focus on the situation when the pieces of information to be combined are of the same nature. In the above discussion, whether in the Boolean or probabilistic setting, the combination process looks asymmetric. This asymmetry is basically due to the fact that even if both are of the same nature, the piece of information $\succeq_E$ displays shades of uncertainty, while I is a sure fact.

---

[1] In fact, both $\succeq_E$ and I could be generic knowledge.

Is such an asymmetry a basic feature? There is nothing compelling about it. Indeed, in the AGM setting, the combination process becomes symmetric (what is called *expansion*) when E and I are consistent. Viewing expansion as the natural mode of combining two consistent pieces of information, revision is then viewed as an asymmetric extension of the expansion to the case of inconsistent pieces of information, whereby priority is given to the input. A more general setting is when the input information also takes the form of a plausibility ranking $\succeq_I$ (or a probability measure P_I). The simplest case is the following. Let $\succeq_E$ be the least informative plausibility ranking faithful to E, that is,

$$s \sim_E s', \forall s \in E, s' \in E; s \sim_E s', \forall s \in E^c, s' \in E^c; s \succ_E s', \forall s \in E, s' \in E^c$$

and likewise for $\succeq_I$. These are the natural plausibility rankings, if nothing else is known but I and E. When $E \cap I \neq \emptyset$, the result is the least informative plausibility ranking faithful to $I * E = E * I = I \cap E$ due to R2. In the case of inconsistency, E is deleted and the least informative plausibility ranking faithful to I is kept. Namely we get the *basic revision rule*:

$$E *_r I = I \cap E \text{ if } I \cap E \neq \emptyset \tag{1}$$
$$= I \text{ otherwise} , \tag{2}$$

Alternatively, one may consider E and I on a par, even when inconsistent. In the latter case, the union rule is used since none of I and E is preferred. In that case, the most elementary scheme is the *basic fusion rule*:

$$A_1 *_f A_2 = A_2 \cap A_1 \text{ if } A_2 \cap A_1 \neq \emptyset \tag{3}$$
$$= A_2 \cup A_1 \text{ otherwise} . \tag{4}$$

denoting $A_1 = E, A_2 = I$, for the sake of symmetry.

The choice between symmetric and asymmetric extensions of expansion depends on the situation we wish to model. The asymmetric combination rule refers to the case of an agent modifying its epistemic state upon receiving new information. There is a prior state of information and a posterior state of information. The asymmetry is caused by the price attached by the agent to prior beliefs he or she is not willing to give up without reason. On the other hand, the symmetric combination of possibly inconsistent pieces of information, we call fusion, corresponds to one agent receiving information from two (or more) sources that play the same role, and where prior information is absent.

Revision and fusion should follow principles that remain valid across all representation frameworks. The two principles underlying any revision operation are *Success* and *Minimal Change*. The idea is that the input information is taken for granted by the agent, but changes to the prior beliefs are only made insofar as they are enforced by the input information. On the contrary, the basic principles of the fusion operation are *fairness*, since both pieces of information are on a par, and *optimism* in the sense that information sources should be trusted as much as possible. This means that as many pieces of information as possible should be retained from the sources, insofar as consistency can be maintained.

Of course, informativeness should be immune to arbitrariness, that is, the results of revision or fusion should be obey a *minimal commitment* principle forbidding to infer more information than actually available. Likewise, we assume only consistent pieces of information are combined $(I, E \neq \emptyset)$ and a consistent result should be obtained $(E * I \neq \emptyset)$. These requirements are not typical of belief change, that is, they apply in general.

4.1   Elementary Revision

It is easy to formally express the above requirements in the simple setting where all pieces of information take the form of sets. Namely, let $E \neq \emptyset$ be the prior information and $I \neq \emptyset$ be the input, and $*_r$ stands for revision

- **Success:** $E *_r I \subseteq I$.
- **Minimal Change:** $E *_r I \subseteq E$ if $E \cap I \neq \emptyset$.
- **Minimal commitment:** $E *_r I$ is the largest subset of possible worlds obeying Success and Minimal Change.

Under the minimal commitment principle, it is easy to see that the revision rule in this setting is the basic one (1). Indeed, if $E \cap I \neq \emptyset$ then Success and Minimal Change imply $E *_r I \subseteq E \cap I$, and minimal commitment enforces $E *_r I = E \cap I$. If $E \cap I = \emptyset$, then Minimal Change does not apply, and then minimal commitment enforces $E *_r I = I$ (there is no reason to be more specific, for a lack of additional information). It is the AGM revision rule based on the least informative plausibility ranking faithful to E.

It is interesting to compare the AGM axioms in the KM rendering to these elementary revision axioms. We borrow the success postulate R1 from them. The R2 axiom explicitly enforces expansion under consistency between E and I, hence follows from our three axioms. The revision rule (1) satisfies the KM-AGM axioms. Since this revision rule is enforced by our three revision axioms, we know that our revision axioms are stronger than the KM-AGM axioms. What makes them stronger is the minimal commitment principle, which, once omitted, leads to revision rules that may violate R5 and R6. Since $E *_r I_1 \subseteq I_1$, $(E *_r I_1) \cap I_2 \neq \emptyset$ implies $I_1 \cap I_2 \neq \emptyset$. Using a selection function, one may decide that under Success and Minimal Change, $E *_r I_1 = A \subset I_1$ and $E *_r (I_1 \cap I_2) = B \subset I_1 \cap I_2$ but $A \cap I_2 \neq B$. Axioms R5-R6 just say that if a subset of the most plausible elements in I_1 in the face of the prior information E lie in I_2, then this subset forms precisely the most plausible elements in $I_1 \cap I_2$ in the face of the prior information E. In other words, the selection function is based on some faithful plausibility ordering $\succeq_E$ attached to E. Axioms R5-R6 essentially enforce a specific uncertainty theory, that is, possibility theory [23]. However, one may argue these two axioms are not essential to revision.

4.2   Elementary Fusion

In the case of the fusion of pieces of information taking the form of OR-sets A_1, A_2, we denote by $*_f$ the corresponding operator; the basic principles of symmetry and optimism are more conveniently expressed via the following axioms:

- **Optimism:** $A_1 *_f A_2 \subseteq A_1 \cup A_2$, and if $A_2 \cap A_1 \neq \emptyset$, then both $A_1 *_f A_2 \subseteq A_1$ and $A_1 *_f A_2 \subseteq A_2$ hold.
- **Fairness:**
  1. *No Dismissal:* $(A_1 *_f A_2) \cap A_1 \neq \emptyset, (A_1 *_f A_2) \cap A_2 \neq \emptyset$.
  2. *No Favoritism:* If $A_2 \cap A_1 = \emptyset$, none of $(A_1 *_f A_2) \subseteq A_1, (A_1 *_f A_2) \subseteq A_2$ hold.
- **Minimal commitment:** $A_1 *_f A_2$ is the largest subset of possible worlds obeying Optimism and Fairness.

Under the minimal commitment rule it is clear that the Optimism axiom enforces the fusion rule (3), that neither dismisses nor favours any source. However the two first above axioms are independent. Without the minimal commitment principle, other results satisfy Optimism and Fairness (the result can be a single $s \in A_2 \cap A_1$ if possible and any set $\{s_2, s_1\}$ where $s_1 \in A_1, s_2 \in A_2$ otherwise).

Note that, under these axioms, and minimal commitment, fusion and revision do collapse into a symmetric conjunctive combination rule (an expansion) when the two pieces of information are consistent. The use of minimal commitment is already at work when defining the models of a set of propositional formulas: we consider the largest set of interpretations which satisfy all formulas. We just continue to use it for fusion and revision in the inconsistent case.

5   Revision and Fusion across Uncertainty Theories

An important issue on this basis is to try and unify existing axiomatic frameworks for revision and fusion of information in the various uncertainty theories. There should be a deep consistency between revision and fusion rules, beyond the difference in expressiveness of the various languages such as logic, probability, possibility or belief functions. The above purely set-based framework is very elementary. In order to be expanded to more general settings, several prerequisites are needed:

- A number of notions must be extended: we must explain what it means for two pieces of information to be consistent (generalizing the property $A_1 \cap A_2 \neq \emptyset$), and what it means for a piece of information to be more informative than another (generalizing the entailment relation $\subseteq$). In particular, we need to make it clear how to model vacuous information (it should be S), and to define what is the support of a piece of information, understood as the set of possible worlds not incompatible with it.
- We must check to what extent the basic postulates given above can be extended to other more expressive frameworks. Additional postulates may be added to account for specific features of more complex representation settings.
- In the case of the revision operation, the issue of iterated revision should be dealt with. Note that our stance to restrict revision to pieces of information of the same nature makes iteration possible (in contrast, we consider it makes little sense to revise, let alone iteratively, a generic plausibility ranking by a sequence of propositions representing singular evidence on the same case).

- In the case of the fusion operation, the set of axioms should be extended to $n > 2$ sources prior to envisaging more complex frameworks. Note that the natural generalisation of the minimal commitment rule consists in conjunctively aggregating information from maximal subsets of mutually consistent sources, and performing the disjunction of the partial results, an idea that dates back to Resher and Manor [24].

In the following we hint on extensions of the above framework to various theories of uncertainty.

5.1   Revision and Fusion of Comparative Possibilities

Suppose the prior information is made of a plausibility ranking $\succeq_\mathbb{E}$ on S as enforced by the AGM axioms, and the input information is likewise another plausibility ranking $\succeq_\mathbb{I}$. Let $\mathcal{P}_\mathbb{E} = \{E_1, \ldots E_k\}$ and $\mathcal{P}_\mathbb{I} = \{I_1, \ldots I_\ell\}$ be the associated well-ordered partitions. The iterated revision problem has been addressed by Darwiche and Pearl [5] when the input $\succeq_\mathbb{I}$ reduces to a proposition, and by Benferhat *et al.* [25] without this restriction.

In these approaches, plausibility orderings are not explicitly used in the postulates. Axioms basically bear on the belief sets E_1 and I_1 induced by abstract epistemic states. These belief sets are considered as the visible part of the epistemic states. Under this assumption, the KM axioms can be reconducted as such; but Darwiche and Pearl [5] weaken R4 using the equivalence between epistemic states $\succeq_\mathbb{E} = \succeq_{\mathbb{E}'}$ explicitly, in place of $Bel(\mathbb{E}) = Bel(\mathbb{E}')$. They complement KM axioms with other ones dedicated to iterated revision by successive input propositions. They then prove that the prior and posterior epistemic states can be represented by plausibility rankings $\succeq_\mathbb{E}$ and $\succeq_{\mathbb{E}*_r\mathbb{I}}$ that obey some minimal change properties. This kind of approach may be viewed as problematic for two reasons (apart from the questionable issue of revising a ranking by a formula):

- It uses a very weak notion of entailment between rankings: $\succeq_\mathbb{E} \models \succeq_\mathbb{I}$ just means $E_1 \subseteq I_1$. Likewise the two rankings are considered inconsistent if they do not have have common best elements.
- Like in the AGM theory, part of the revision axioms are only used to enforce the use of one uncertainty framework: comparative possibility theory.

One may think of more demanding notions of entailment between possibility rankings [26]:

- Refinement: $\succeq_\mathbb{E} \sqsubseteq \succeq_\mathbb{I}$ if and only if $\mathcal{P}_\mathbb{E}$ refines $\mathcal{P}_\mathbb{I}$;
- Specificity: $\succeq_\mathbb{E} \sqsubseteq_s \succeq_\mathbb{I}$ if and only if $\forall i = 1, \ldots, \min(k, \ell), \cup_{j=1 \ldots i} E_j \subseteq \cup_{j=1 \ldots i} I_j$

The specificity entailment is weaker than refinement but it introduces a kind of commensurateness between the weak order relations. Likewise a more demanding form of consistency between rankings is as follows: $\succeq$ is *strongly consistent* with $\succeq'$ if and only if $\nexists s_1, s_2, s_1 \succ s_2, s_2 \succ' s_1$. Then one may think of other extensions of the basic revision framework: let $\succeq_{\mathbb{E}*_r\mathbb{I}}$ be the posterior ranking. A strong set of postulates is as follows:

- **Success:** $\succeq_{E*_rI} \sqsubseteq \succeq_I$.
- **Minimal Change:** $\forall s_1, s_2$, if $s_1 \sim_I s_2$ and $s_1 \succeq_E s_2$ then $s_1 \succeq_{E*_rI} s_2$.
- **Minimal commitment:** $\succeq_{E*_rI}$ is the least refined plausibility ordering satisfying Success and Minimal Change.

Note that in particular, if $\succeq_E$ and $\succeq_I$ are strongly consistent, then the revision rule becomes symmetric since Minimal Change enforces $\succeq_{E*_rI} \sqsubseteq \succeq_E$ as well. Likewise, if $\succeq_E$ is already a refinement of $\succeq_I$, the revision has no effect, that is $\succeq_{E*_rI} = \succeq_E$. The above success postulate is stronger than what Darwiche & Pearl, and others, require. Our postulates enforce a known revision rule in this case:

- If $\succeq_E$ and $\succeq_I$ are strongly consistent, then $s_1 \succ_{E*_rI} s_2$ if and only if $s_1 \succ_E s_2$ or $s_1 \succ_I s_2$, and $s_1 \sim_{E*_rI} s_2$ otherwise.
- Else $s_1 \succ_{E*_rI} s_2$ if and only if either $s_1 \succ_I s_2$ or ($s_1 \sim_I s_2$ and $s_1 \succ_E s_2$).

It is clear that this revision rule is the lexicographic refinement of $\succeq_I$ by $\succeq_E$ (with priority to the former) used by Benferhat *et al.* [25], hence generalizes Papini's drastic revision [27], and it coincides with the prioritized fusion of Maynard-Reid and Shoham [28].

Similar considerations can be made for symmetric fusion operations. On the one hand, most existing axiomatizations (like Konieczny and Pino-Perez [29], Delgrande *et al.* [30]) in AI rely on belief sets again. On the other hand, it is not clear how to generalize the axioms of OR-set fusion to the symmetric fusion of plausibility rankings. Only Lehmann and Maynard-Reid [13] seem to address this issue. Of course, so doing one has to cope with Arrow's impossibility theorem from voting theory [31]. However, contrary to what many authors assert, it is not clear that the fusion of plausibility rankings is reducible to an instance of preference aggregation, as the aim of merging knowledge looks quite different.

5.2   Revision and Fusion of Probability Measures

In probability theory, an epistemic state is a probability distribution on possible worlds. There is a natural method for revising a prior probability P_E in the presence of new probabilistic information denoted by $\mathbb{I} = \{(I_i, p_i) : i = 1, ..., m\}$, where the I_i's form a partition of S, and $p_i = P_{\mathbb{I}}(I_i)$. The coefficients p_i sum to 1 and act as constraints on the posterior probability of elements I_i of the partition. Such an updating rule is proposed by Jeffrey in 1965 [4]. It provides an effective means to revise a prior probability distribution P_E into a posterior P_{E*_rI}. The input information and the prior probability are of the same nature, with priority given to the input. This rule satisfies revision axioms as follows:

- Success: $P_{E*_rI}(I_i) = p_i$.
- Minimal Change: $\forall I_i, \forall A, P_{E*_rI}(A|I_i) = P_E(A|I_i)$.

The interpretation of Minimal Change is that the revised probability measure P_{E*_rI} must preserve the conditional probability degree of any event A given uncertain event I_i. Besides, according to Success, it is clear that the coefficient p_i

represents what the probability of I_i should be, and not (for instance) uncertainty about the reliability of the input. Jeffrey's rule of conditioning is the unique revision method that satisfies these two properties (see, e.g.,[32]):

$$P_{\mathbb{E}*_r\mathbb{I}}(A) = \sum_{i=1}^{m} p_i \cdot \frac{P_{\mathbb{E}}(A \cap I_i)}{P_{\mathbb{E}}(I_i)}. \tag{5}$$

It respects the probability kinematics principle, whose objective is to minimize change, in the sense of an informational distance between probability distributions [1]: the posterior probability $P_{\mathbb{E}*_r\mathbb{I}}$ minimizes relative entropy with respect to the original distribution under the probabilistic constraints defined by the input $\mathbb{I}$. Note that no Minimal Commitment assumption is requested here: the two axioms are strong enough to ensure the unicity of the rule. This is because a probability measure conveys no incomplete information. In particular, if the input partition contains only singletons, the revision consists of a mere substitution of $P_{\mathbb{E}}$ by $P_{\mathbb{I}}$. It is noticeable that the above revision axioms are clearly numerical counterparts of the strong ones proposed in the previous section for plausibility orderings. Moreover the lexicographic change rule laid bare is an ordinal counterpart to Jeffrey's revision: the posterior plausibility ranking is the same as the input ordering on the well-ordered partition defined by the latter, and the prior ranking is preserved inside the partition elements.

There is a large literature on the fusion of probability measures, split in two schools. Under the Bayesian approach [9], the fusion process is in fact a combined revision/fusion process due to the presence of a prior probability. When parallel fusion is taken for granted (see for instance [8]), the result is often taken as a weighted average of original probabilities. A probability distribution is arguably the full-fledged opposite to an OR-set: it cannot represent incomplete knowledge faithfully. It is understood as a weighted collection of conflicting singletons. Contrary to the basic fusion of OR-sets that comes down to a conjunction or a disjunction, there is no such connectives in probability theory. Only the setting of evidence theory can shed light on what could be a conjunction or a disjunction of probability distributions.

5.3   Revision and Fusion of Possibility Distributions

Possibility distributions π map the set S to a plausibility scale L. This scale can be numerical or qualitative. Representations of epistemic states by possibility distributions do not have the same expressive power. In fact we can distinguish several representation settings according to the expressiveness of the scale used:

1. The qualitative finite setting (QUALFI for short) with possibility degrees in a finite totally ordered scale : $L = \{\alpha_0 = 1 > \alpha_1 > \cdots > \alpha_{m-1} > 0\}$. This setting is used in possibilistic logic [33].
2. The denumerable setting (DENUM for short), using a scale $L = \{\alpha^0 = 1 > \alpha^1 > \cdots > \alpha^i > \ldots 0\}$, for some $\alpha \in (0,1)^2$. This scale is quite expressive

---

^{2} As usual α^i stands for the ith power of α.

as it is equipped with semi-group operations min, max, product, and also division. This is isomorphic to the use of integers in so-called κ-functions by Spohn [14].

3. The dense ordinal setting (DORD for short) using $L = [0, 1]$, seen as an ordinal scale. In this case, the possibility distribution π is defined up to any monotone increasing transformation $f : [0, 1] \rightarrow [0, 1], f(0) = 0, f(1) = 1$. This setting is also used in possibilistic logic [33].

4. The dense absolute setting (DABS for short) where $L = [0, 1]$, seen as a genuine numerical scale equipped with product. In this case, a possibility measure can be viewed as special case of a Shafer [11] plausibility function, actually a consonant plausibility function, and $1 - \pi$ a potential surprise function in the sense of Shackle [34].

Revision rules in possibility theory look like Jeffrey's rule, and representation results continue to hold for the most part [35]. Two different but similar types of conditioning, in agreement with this conditional ordering and instrumental for revision purposes, have been defined in possibility theory. Let C be the conditioning event such that $\Pi(C) = \max_{s \in C} \pi(s) > 0$:

- In the ordinal setting, if $s \in C, \pi(s \mid_m C) = 1$ if $\pi(s) = \Pi(C)$ and $\pi(s)$ if $\pi(s) < \Pi(C)$ (and of course, 0 if $s \notin C$). This is the definition of *minimum-based conditioning*. It can be defined in any ordinal scale especially the QUALFI and DORD environments.

- In numerical settings such as DENUM or DABS, we can define $\pi(s \mid_p C) = \frac{\pi(s)}{\Pi(C)}$ and 0 if $s \notin C$. This is the definition of *product-based conditioning*, which is also a special case of Dempster rule of conditioning restricted to consonant belief functions [11]. In the DENUM setting, it also captures Spohn [14] conditioning of κ-functions [36].

These two definitions of conditioning satisfy an equation of the form

$$\Pi(A \cap C) = \Pi(A \mid_\otimes C) \otimes \Pi(C),$$

where $\otimes$ is min ($\mid_\otimes = \mid_m$) or the product ($\mid_\otimes = \mid_p$) respectively, which is similar to Bayesian conditioning. Besides, when $\Pi(C) = 0$, the above conditioning rules do not really apply, and we can then decide to replace π by 1_C. Note that these conditionings extend the basic revision rule for sets : the success postulate consists in noticing that the support $\pi(\cdot \mid_\otimes C)$ lies in C, the minimal change is absolute for the min-based conditioning (possibility degrees remain the same inside C, but for the largest ones) and relative for the product-based conditioning. Moreover when $\Pi(C) = 1$ (consistency with the input), the conditioning comes down to the fusion rule [22]: $\pi(\cdot \mid_\otimes C) = \min(\pi(\cdot), 1_C(\cdot))$.

More generally the input information can be a possibility distribution $\pi_\mathbb{I}$. We can model it by $\mathbb{I} = \{(I_i, \lambda_i) \ i = 1, ..., m\}$, where $\{I_1, ..., I_m\}$ is the well-ordered partition induced by $\pi_\mathbb{I}$ and $\lambda_i = \Pi_\mathbb{I}(I_i)$. So, $\max_{i=1,...,m} \lambda_i = 1$, and $\lambda_1 > \cdots > \lambda_m$. Therefore, revising a prior possibility distribution $\pi_\mathbb{E}$ with an input $\mathbb{I}$ can be achieved using the following Jeffrey-like revision [36]:

$$\forall (I_i, \lambda_i) \in \mathbb{I}, \forall s \models I_i, \pi_{\mathbb{E}*_r\mathbb{I}}(s \mid_\otimes \mathbb{I}) = \lambda_i \otimes \pi_\mathbb{E}(s \mid_\otimes I_i) \qquad (6)$$

where $\otimes$ is either min or the product, depending on whether conditioning is based on the minimum or the product operator, respectively. When $\otimes = $ product (resp. min) the possibilistic revision will be simply called product-based (resp. minimum-based) conditioning with partial epistemic states. These two natural ways of defining possibilistic revision based on Jeffrey's rule naturally extend the two forms of conditioning that exist in possibility theory. The Jeffrey-like revision rule (6) satisfies the following properties [35] in agreement with the elementary revision setting.

$\mathbf{A_1}$ **(Consistency):** $\pi_{\mathbb{E}*_r\mathbb{I}}$ should be normalized.

$\mathbf{A_2}$ **(Priority to Input):** $\forall i = 1, ..., m, \Pi_{\mathbb{E}*_r\mathbb{I}}(I_i) = \lambda_i$.

$\mathbf{A_3}$ **(Faithfulness):** $\forall s_1, s_2 \models I_i$ if $\pi_{\mathbb{E}}(s_1) \geq \pi_{\mathbb{E}}(s_2)$ then $\pi_{\mathbb{E}*_r\mathbb{I}}(s_1) \geq \pi_{\mathbb{E}*_r\mathbb{I}}(s_2)$.

$\mathbf{A_4}$ **(Inertia):** $\forall i = 1, ..., m$, if $\Pi(I_i) = \lambda_i$ then $\forall s \models I_i : \pi_{\mathbb{E}*_r\mathbb{I}}(s) = \pi_{\mathbb{E}}(s)$.

The two last axioms express minimal change. Note that like for the probabilistic Jeffrey's rule, if $\mathbb{I} = \{(S, 1)\}$ (ignorance), the revision preserves the prior epistemic state. We retrieve expansion-like operations in specific conditions:

- When $\otimes = $ min we get $\pi_{\mathbb{E}*_r\mathbb{I}}(s) = \min(\pi_{\mathbb{I}}(s), \pi_{\mathbb{E}}(s))$ if and only if $\Pi_{\mathbb{I}}(I_i) \geq \lambda_i, \forall i$, which says that the coarsening of $\pi_{\mathbb{E}}$ on the input partition is less informed than the input.
- When $\otimes = \cdot$, in the product case, we get $\pi_{\mathbb{E}*_r\mathbb{I}}(s) = \pi_{\mathbb{I}}(s) \cdot \pi_{\mathbb{E}}(s)$, if and only if $\Pi_{\mathbb{E}}(I_i) = 1, \forall i$, which says that the coarsening of $\pi_{\mathbb{E}}$ on the input partition is vacuous.

The axiomatisation of possibilistic fusion by means of optimism and fairness axioms is a question under study.

5.4 Belief Functions

In belief function theory, a mass function is represented as a "random" set, that is, a probability distribution $m_{\mathbb{E}}$ on the power set $2^S \setminus \{\emptyset\}$. The mass function $m_{\mathbb{E}}$ models an ill-known epistemic state, and $m_{\mathbb{E}}(E)$ represents the subjective probability that the correct epistemic state is E. The probability measure $P(A)$ is replaced by a pair $(Cr(A), Pl(A))$, where $Cr(A) = \sum_{E \subseteq A} m_{\mathbb{E}}(E)$ represents the degree of certainty of A understood as the probability of proving A from the ill-known epistemic state $\mathbb{E}$; $Pl(A) = \sum_{E \cap A \neq \emptyset} m_{\mathbb{E}}(E)$ represents the degree of plausibility of A understood as the probability that A is not inconsistent with the ill-known epistemic state $\mathbb{E}$. The modal duality between implication and logical consistency is retrieved as $Cr(A) = 1 - Pl(A^c)$. This approach encompasses probability and possibility measures. The latter are retrieved if the set of focal elements forms a nested sequence. In this so-called *consonant* case, the contour function $Pl(\{s\}) = \sum_{s \in E} m_{\mathbb{E}}(E)$ is a possibility distribution and $Pl(A) = \max_{s \in A} Pl(\{s\})$. Another important concept in evidence theory is the one of specialisation ordering, that generalizes inclusion and possibilistic specificity to mass functions. The *s-ordering* $m \sqsubseteq_s m'$ holds iff there exists a square matrix Σ with general term $\sigma(A, B) \in [0, 1]$, $A, B \in 2^S$ verifying

$$\sum_{A \subseteq S} \sigma(A, B) = 1, \forall B \subseteq S, \text{ where } \sigma(A, B) > 0 \Rightarrow A \subseteq B, \ A, B \subseteq S,$$

such that $m(A) = \sum_{B \subseteq S} \sigma(A, B) m'(B), \forall A \subseteq S$. The term $\sigma(A, B)$ may be seen as the proportion of the mass $m'(B)$ that flows down to its subset A.

Expansion and fusion. The use of the mass function makes it easy to generalize basic fusion and revision rules. Suppose new information comes in the form of another proposition I that is surely true. This is modelled by a mass function m_I such that $m_I(I) = 1$. Conditioning reassigns each mass $m_{\mathbb{E}}(E)$ to the set $E \cap I$, thus getting $m_{\mathbb{E}}(E|_u I) = \sum_{B: I \cap B = E} m_{\mathbb{E}}(B)$. It corresponds to an expansion, but $m(\emptyset|_u I) > 0$ is possible. To recover a standard mass function, a normalisation step is done (the so-called Dempster rule of conditioning):

$$m_{\mathbb{E}}(E|I) = \frac{\sum_{B: I \cap B = E} m_{\mathbb{E}}(B)}{Pl(I)}$$

so that $Cr(I|I) = 1$, recovering the success postulate. It is clear that when $I \cap E \neq \emptyset, \forall E, m_{\mathbb{E}}(E) > 0$, then $m_{\mathbb{E}}(\cdot|_u I) = m_{\mathbb{E}}(\cdot|I) \sqsubseteq_s m_{\mathbb{E}}$, thus generalizing the Minimal Change axiom of the basic revision rule.

The apparent dissymmetry of $m_{\mathbb{E}}(\cdot|I)$ is due to the fact that m_I is a sure fact I while the epistemic state is uncertain. Moreover, when $I \cap E = \emptyset, \forall E, m_{\mathbb{E}}(E) > 0$, the conditioning is undefined. To make it coherent with the basic revision rule one must complement it by a Success postulate $m_{\mathbb{E}}(\cdot|I) = m_I$, in this case.

The unnormalized conditioning $|_u$ symmetrically generalizes to the case of an input mass $m_{\mathbb{I}}$ as $m^u_{\mathbb{E} *_f \mathbb{I}}(E) = \sum_{E = F \cap G} m_{\mathbb{E}}(F) m_{\mathbb{I}}(G)$. It is Smets' conjunctive rule, which again may leave a positive mass $m^u_{\mathbb{E} *_f \mathbb{I}}(\emptyset)$ on the empty set. $m^u_{\mathbb{E} *_f \mathbb{I}}$ is the result of an expansion in the sense that $m^u_{\mathbb{E} *_f \mathbb{I}} \sqsubseteq_s m_{\mathbb{E}}$ and $m^u_{\mathbb{E} *_f \mathbb{I}} \sqsubseteq_s m_{\mathbb{I}}$ hold, but it is not the least committed one because there is a reinforcement effect between the two mass functions, due to an independence asumption, that cannot be expressed using pure propositional information. A unique least committed expansion may fail to exist [37], except when both mass functions are consonant, in which case the least committed expansion (in the sense of the inequality between contour functions) is given by the minimum rule of possibility theory..

Dempster conditioning is extended symmetrically into an associative combination rule called Dempster rule of combination merging two mass functions m_1 and m_2 into $m = m_1 \oplus m_2$ such that:

$$\forall E \neq \emptyset, m_D(E) = \frac{\sum_{E = F \cap G} m_1(F) m_2(G)}{\sum_{\emptyset \neq F \cap G} m_1(F) m_2(G)} \tag{7}$$

but the renormalisation term prevents it from being an expansion (neither $m_D \sqsubseteq_s m_{\mathbb{E}}$ nor $m_D \sqsubseteq_s m_{\mathbb{I}}$ hold generally). And this scheme is undefined under total conflict. A mass function fusion rule that directly extends the basic fusion rule was proposed by Dubois and Prade [38] as follows: $\forall E \neq \emptyset$,

$$m_f(E) = \sum_{F, G: E = F \cap G} m_1(F) m_2(G) + \sum_{F, G: E = F \cup G, F \cap G = \emptyset} m_1(F) m_2(G) \tag{8}$$

It is the application of the basic fusion rule to each pair of focal sets, and it coincides with Dempster's rule of combination and the conjunctive rule if and only if the two mass functions are strongly consistent, that is, $\forall F, m_1(F) > 0, \forall G, m_2(G) > 0, F \cap G \neq \emptyset$. This fusion rule satisfies the two postulates of optimism and fairness of the basic fusion rule (3), and the minimal commitment axiom is here replaced by a more demanding independence condition.

Revision. Non-symmetric extensions of Dempster conditioning that also generalize Jeffrey's rule were proposed by Ichihashi and Tanaka [39] and Smets [40]. Smets' proposal presupposes an input $m_{\mathbb{I}}$ defined on a partition of S, while the former authors considered general inputs. The idea of this revision rule is as follows: for each input focal subset $I \in \mathcal{F}_{\mathbb{I}}$, the mass $m_{\mathbb{I}}$ is shared among focal sets $E \in \mathcal{F}_{\mathbb{E}}$ of the prior $m_{\mathbb{E}}$ that have a non empty intersection with I, proportionally to $m_{\mathbb{E}}(E)$, and each such share bears on $I \cap E$. This scheme does not apply if $\exists I \in \mathcal{F}_{\mathbb{I}}$ such that $I \cap E = \emptyset, \forall E \in \mathcal{F}_{\mathbb{E}}$. This Jeffrey-like rule has been extended to encompass the basic revision rule as a special case as well, by allocating mass $m_{\mathbb{I}}(I)$ to subset I in the posterior mass $m_{\mathbb{E}*_r\mathbb{I}}$, when the original rule does not apply. This asymmetric Dempster-Jeffrey revision rule, recently studied by Ma *et al.* [41] in an extensive way, reads formally:

$$(m_{\mathbb{E}*_r\mathbb{I}})(C) = \sum_{E,I:E\cap I=C, Pl_{\mathbb{E}}(I)>0} \frac{m_{\mathbb{E}}(E)m_{\mathbb{I}}(I)}{Pl_{\mathbb{E}}(I)} + 1_{\{Pl_{\mathbb{E}}(C)=0\}}m_{\mathbb{I}}(C), \quad (9)$$

where $1_{\{Pl_{\mathbb{E}}(C)=0\}} = 1$ if $Pl_{\mathbb{E}}(C) = 0$ and 0 otherwise. By construction, the above revision rule and the fusion rule (8) and Smets conjunctive rule all coincide with Dempster's rule of combination when the input is strongly consistent with the prior mass function. They reduce to a mere expansion without renormalization. This does for the Minimal Change postulate. A restricted form of Jeffrey rule style Minimal Change principle still holds for $m_{\mathbb{E}*_r\mathbb{I}}$:

If $I \in \mathcal{F}_{\mathbb{I}}$ is such that $\forall A \in \mathcal{F}_{\mathbb{E}}$, either $A \subseteq I$ or $A \subseteq I^c$, and moreover $\forall F \neq I \in \mathcal{F}_{\mathbb{I}}, F \cap I = \emptyset$, then $\forall A \subseteq I, m_{\mathbb{E}*_r\mathbb{I}}(A|I) = m_{\mathbb{E}}(A|I)$

Moreover, $m_{\mathbb{E}*_r\mathbb{I}} \sqsubseteq_s m_{\mathbb{I}}$ (success postulate) does hold. So, revision and fusion rules in belief function theory rely on the postulates akin to the ones in the Boolean and probabilistic settings.

6 Conclusion

This paper is a preliminary attempt at organizing the literature on belief revision and fusion regardless of the chosen representation setting, starting from the assumption that basic principles independently put forward in logical and numerical settings on similar notions must have some relationship with one another. It is more a program of future research than a compendium of results. It is also very partial in its coverage, and important issues or landmark contributions have only been mentioned, and some omitted. Nevertheless, some core principles for revision and fusion are laid bare, assuming, like in the AGM theory, that in the case when pieces of information to be combined are consistent with each other, both operations come down to expansion, a symmetric operation that increases information content. Starting with the most elementary (set-theoretic) setting, and provisionally doing away with syntactic issues specific to logical languages, we have discussed existing revision and fusion rules in more elaborated representation frameworks, especially in the ordinal case, the probabilistic setting, possibility and evidence theories. Much work still needs to be done for sketching a coherent map of revision and fusion rules according to their axiomatic systems in different representation frameworks, showing their fundamental agreement and understanding their discrepancies.

References

1. Domotor, Z.: Probability kinematics and representation of belief change. Philosophy of Science 47, 284–403 (1980)
2. Alchourrón, C.E., Gärdenfors, P., Makinson, D.: On the logic of theory change: Partial meet functions for contraction and revision. Symbolic Logic 50, 510–530 (1985)
3. Konieczny, S., Pino-Pérez, R.: On the logic of merging. In: Procs. of KR 1998, pp. 488–498 (1998)
4. Jeffrey, R.: The logic of decision, 2nd edn. Chicago University Press, Chicago (1983)
5. Darwiche, A., Pearl, J.: On the logic of iterated belief revision. Artificial Intelligence 89, 1–29 (1997)
6. Friedman, N., Halpern, J.: Belief revision: A critique. In: Proceedings of KR 1996, pp. 421–631 (1996)
7. Dubois, D.: Three scenarios for the revision of epistemic states. Journal of Logic and Computation 18(5), 721–738 (2008)
8. Cooke, R.M.: Experts in Uncertainty. Oxford University Press, Oxford (1991)
9. Genest, C., Zidek, J.: Combining probability distributions: A critique and an annoted bibliography. Statistical Science 1(1), 114–135 (1986)
10. Benferhat, S., Dubois, D., Kaci, S., Prade, H.: Possibilistic merging and distance-based fusion of propositional information. Annals of Mathematics and Artificial Intelligence 34(1-3), 217–252 (2002)
11. Shafer, G.: A Mathematical Theory of Evidence. Princeton University Press, Princeton (1976)
12. Smets, P.: Analyzing the combination of conflicting belief functions. Information Fusion 8(4), 387–412 (2007)
13. Maynard-Reid II, P., Lehmann, D.: Representing and aggregating conflicting beliefs. In: Proceedings of KR 2000, pp. 153–164 (2000)
14. Spohn, W.: Ordinal conditional functions: A dynamic theory of epistemic states. Causation in Decision, Belief Change, and Statistics 2, 105–134 (1988)
15. Halpern, J.Y.: Defining relative likelihood in partially-ordered preferential structures. Journal of A.I. Research 7, 1–24 (1997)
16. Lewis, D.: Counterfactuals. Basil Blackwell, U.K (1973)
17. Dubois, D., Prade, H.: Possibility theory: qualitative and quantitative aspects. In: Handbook of Defeasible Reasoning and Uncertainty Management Systems, vol. 1, pp. 169–226. Kluwer, Dordrecht (1998)
18. Walley, P.: Statistical reasoning with imprecise Probabilities. Chapman and Hall, New York (1991)

19. Dempster, A.P.: Upper and lower probabilities induced by a multivalued mapping. The Annals of Statistics 28, 325–339 (1967)
20. Katsuno, H., Mendelzon, A.O.: Propositional knowledge base revision and minimal change. Artificial Intelligence 52, 263–294 (1991)
21. Gärdenfors, P., Makinson, D.: Nonmonotonic inference based on expectations. Artificial Intelligence 65, 197–245 (1994)
22. Dubois, D., Prade, H.: Belief change and possibility theory. In: Gärdenfors, P. (ed.) Belief Revision, pp. 142–182. Cambridge University Press, Cambridge (1992)
23. Dubois, D., Prade, H.: Epistemic entrenchment and possibilistic logic. Artificial Intelligence 50, 223–239 (1991)
24. Rescher, N., Manor, R.: On inference from inconsistent premises. Theory and Decision 1, 179–219 (1970)
25. Benferhat, S., Konieczny, S., Papini, O., Pérez, R.P.: Iterated revision by epistemic states: Axioms, semantics and syntax. In: Proc. of ECAI 2000, pp. 13–17 (2000)
26. Benferhat, S., Dubois, D., Prade, H.: Possibilistic and standard probabilistic semantics of conditional knowledge bases. Journal of Logic and Computation 9, 873–895 (1999)
27. Papini, O.: Iterated revision operations stemming from the history of an agentÕs observations. In: Rott, H., Williams, M.A. (eds.) Frontiers of Belief Revision, pp. 281–293. Kluwer Academic Publishers, Dordrecht (2001)
28. Maynard-Reid II, P., Shoham, Y.: Belief fusion: Aggregating pedigreed belief states. Journal of Logic, Language and Information 10(2), 183–209 (2001)
29. Konieczny, S., Pino Pérez, R.: Merging information under constraints: a qualitative framework. Journal of Logic and Computation 12(5), 773–808 (2002)
30. Delgrande, J., Dubois, D., Lang, J.: Iterated revision as prioritized merging. In: Proc. of KR 2006, pp. 210–220 (2006)
31. Chopra, S., Ghose, A.K., Meyer, T.A.: Social choice theory, belief merging, and strategy-proofness. Information Fusion 7(1), 61–79 (2006)
32. Chan, H., Darwiche, A.: On the revision of probabilistic beliefs using uncertain evidence. Artif. Intell. 163(1), 67–90 (2005)
33. Dubois, D., Lang, J., Prade, H.: Possibilistic logic. In: Gabbay, D., et al. (eds.) Handbook of Logic in Artificial Intelligence and Logic Programming, vol. 3, pp. 439–513. Oxford University Press, Oxford (1994)
34. Shackle, G.: Decision Order and Time In Human Affairs. Cambridge University Press, U.K (1961)
35. Benferhat, S., Dubois, D., Prade, H., Williams, M.: A framework for revising belief bases using possibilistic counterparts of Jeffrey's rule. Fundamenta Informaticae 11, 1–18 (2009)
36. Dubois, D., Prade, H.: A synthetic view of belief revision with uncertain inputs in the framework of possibility theory. Int. J. Approx. Reasoning 17(2-3), 295–324 (1997)
37. Destercke, S., Dubois, D.: Can the minimum rule of possibility theory be extended to belief functions? In: Sossai, C., Chemello, G. (eds.) ECSQARU 2009. LNCS, vol. 5590, pp. 299–310. Springer, Heidelberg (2009)
38. Dubois, D., Prade, H.: Representation and combination of uncertainty with belief functions and possibility measures. Computational Intelligence 4, 244–264 (1988)
39. Ichihashi, H., Tanaka, H.: Jeffrey-like rules of conditioning for the Dempster-Shafer theory of evidence. Int. J. of Approximate Reasoning 3, 143–156 (1989)
40. Smets, P.: Jeffrey's rule of conditioning generalized to belief functions. In: Proc. of UAI, pp. 500–505 (1993)
41. Ma, J., Liu, W., Dubois, D., Prade, H.: Revision rules in the theory of evidence. In: Procs. of ICTAI 2010, pp. 295–302. IEEE Press, Los Alamitos (2010)

Introducing Equational Semantics for Argumentation Networks

Dov M. Gabbay

[1] King's College London
dov.gabbay@kcl.ac.uk
[2] Bar Ilan University Israel
[3] University of Luxembourg

Abstract. This paper provides equational semantics for Dung's argumentation networks. The network nodes get numerical values in [0,1], and are supposed to satisfy certain equations. The solutions to these equations correspond to the "extensions" of the network.

This approach is very general and includes the Caminada labelling as a special case, as well as many other so-called network extensions, support systems, higher level attacks, Boolean networks, dependence on time, etc, etc.

The equational approach has its conceptual roots in the 19th century following the algebraic equational approach to logic by George Boole, Louis Couturat and Ernst Schroeder.

1 Introduction

This paper is a short version of [11], which expands (as promised) on our equational ideas introduced in pages 246–251 of [9]. The Equational approach has its conceptual roots in the 19th century following the algebraic equational approach to logic by George Boole [2], Louis Couturat [4] and Ernst Schroeder [13].

The equational algebraic approach was historically followed, in the first half of the 20th century by the Logical Truth (Tautologies) approach supported by giants such as G. Frege, D. Hilbert, B. Russell and L. Wittgenstein. In the second half of the twentieth Century the new current approach has emerged, which was to study logic through it consequence relations, as developed by A. Tarski, G. Gentzen, D. Scott and (for non-monotonic logic) D. Gabbay.

1.1 Aims of This Paper

We have several good reasons for writing [11], the full paper.

1. To provide a general computational framework for Dung's argumentation networks; a framework in which the logical aspects, computational aspects and the conceptual aspects involved in Dung's original proposal can be isolated, highlighted and analysed, and thus paving the way for orderly responsible generalisations.

    The logical aspects involve the question of what is the logical content of an argumentation network and what inferences we can draw from it, see [8]. The computational aspects have to do with viewing the abstract argumentation networks

W. Liu (Ed.): ECSQARU 2011, LNAI 6717, pp. 19–35, 2011.

as directed graphs or as finite models with binary relations on them and various algorithms for extracting subsets of such graphs or models. See for example our paper [12] on annotation theories. The conceptual aspect is the reason behind the computation, involving concepts such as admissibility and a variety of extensions.

At present Dung's networks are generalised in chaotic and incompatible ways by many capable researchers. Unfortunately, we have no general meta-level approach which the community can use for guidance and comparison.

2. To generalise Dung's argumentation networks in a natural way and connect and compare it with other networks communities, such as neural nets, Bayesian nets, biological–ecological nets, logical labelled deductive nets and more.

These networks have a different conceptual base but they look like abstract argumentation networks, i.e. they are directed graphs. We manipulate the the graphs differently because they come from different applications. So the question to ask is whether we can we find common grounds (such as an equational approach to such graphs) which will bring the applications together at least on the formal mathematical side?

3. To introduce in a natural way various meta operations on networks such as distributed networks (modal logic), time dependence and fibring which exist in other types of networks and logics.

4. To connect with pure mathematics, numerical analysis and computational algebra.

5. To show the argumentation community the extent of our own contributions to this area and the rationale and priority of these contributions.[1]

Dung's argumentation networks (see [6]) have the form (S, R_A) where S is a set of arguments, which for the current purposes we assume to be finite, and R_A is a binary attack relation on S. We are interested in subsets E of S of arguments which are admissible, that is self defending and conflict free, namely:

1. E is conflict free, namely for no x, y in E do we have that $xR_A y$.
2. E defends each of its elements: Whenever for some x, we have $xR_A y$ and y is in E, there is some z in E defending y, i.e. we have $zR_A y$. (E is self-defending.)
3. E is complete if E contains all the elements it defends.

The smallest such E is called the *grounded extension*, a maximal E (there may be several different such maximal sets) is called a *preferred extension*, and if we are lucky, we may also have a *stable extension* E, namely one which attacks anything not on it.

See [5; 12] for surveys.

Such extensions are preceived as indicating coherent logical positions which can defend themselves against attacks.

We make use of the Caminada labelling functions $\lambda : S \mapsto \{\text{in, out, undecided}\}$. λ satisfies the following condition

---

[1] The argumentation area has undergone phenomenal expansion, and many researchers are not aware of the full extent of research done in the area, resulting in a poor record in crediting and quoting each others' work.

(C1)   If $\lambda(a) =$ in and aR_Ab then $\lambda(b) =$ out.

(C2)   If for all $x, (xR_Ab \rightarrow \lambda(x) =$ out) then $\lambda(b) =$ in. (Note that this includes the case that b has no attackers.)

(C3)   If $\forall x(xR_Ab \rightarrow \lambda(x) \neq 1)]$ and $[\exists y(yR_Ab$ and $\lambda(y) =$ undecided)] then $\lambda(b) =$ undecided.

Every such λ gives a complete extension $E_\lambda = \{x|\lambda(x) =$ in$\}$, and vice versa. See [5].

1.2   Equational Examples

This subsection is intended to motivate the formal equation section, Section 2. We give here several examples of the equational approach.

Let (S, R_A) be a Dung network. So $R_A \subseteq S^2$ is the attack relation. We are looking for a function $\mathbf{f} : S \mapsto [0, 1]$ assigning to each $a \in S$ a value of $0 \leq \mathbf{f}(a) \leq 1$ such that the following holds.

1. $(S, R_A, \mathbf{f})$ satisfies the following equations for some family of functions $\{\mathbf{h}_a\}, a \in S$:
   (a) If a is not attacked (i.e. $\neg\exists x(xR_Aa)$) then $\mathbf{f}(a) = 1$.
   (b) If $x_1, \ldots, x_n$ are all the attackers of a (i.e. $\bigwedge_{i=1}^n x_iR_Aa \wedge \forall y(yR_Aa \rightarrow \bigvee_{i=1}^n y = x_i)$) then we have that $\mathbf{f}(a) = \mathbf{h}_a(\mathbf{f}(x_1), \ldots, \mathbf{f}(x_n))$.
   Let us take, for example the same $\mathbf{h}_a = \mathbf{h}$ for all a and let

$$\mathbf{h}(\mathbf{f}(x_1), \ldots, \mathbf{f}(x_n)) = \prod_{i=1}^n (1 - \mathbf{f}(x_i))$$

   The above equation we shall call Eq_{inverse}. We shall define other possible equations later on.
   Thus we get
   Eq_{inverse} for the function $\mathbf{f}$:

$$\mathbf{f}(a) = \prod_{i=1}^n (1 - \mathbf{f}(x_i)).$$

2. For any Caminada labelling λ of (S, R_A), there exists an $(S, R_A, \mathbf{f})$ such that

$$E_\mathbf{f} = \begin{cases} \text{If } \lambda(a) = \text{in then } \mathbf{f}(a) = 1 \\ \text{If } \lambda(a) = \text{out then } \mathbf{f}(a) = 0 \\ \text{If } \lambda(a) = \text{undecided then don't care what } \mathbf{f}(a) \text{ is} \\ \text{provided it satisfies the equations.} \end{cases}$$

Condition (1) above reads $\lambda(a) =$ in as $\mathbf{f}(a) = 1$ and $\lambda(a) =$ out as $\mathbf{f}(a) = 0$.
   Therefore the equation

$$\mathbf{f}(a) = \prod_{i=1}^n (1 - \mathbf{f}(x_i))$$

ensures that:

If one of x_i (x_i are the attackers of a) is in then a is out.
If all the attackers are out then a is in.

The question is what happens with the undecided cases. Here we have condition (2).

Any Dung extension can have a corresponding function **f** which agrees with the "in" and "out", though may be also more specific about the undecided.

So if the Dung extension says I don't know, the function **f** can say whatever it wants, provided it satisfies the equations.

Note that we can have a different function **h**. Time to give a formal definition.

Definition 1 (Possible equational systems). *Let (S, R_A) be a networks and let a be a node and let $x_1, \ldots, x_n$ be all of its attackers.*

We list below several possible equational systems, we write $Eq(\mathbf{f})$ to mean the equational system Eq applied to $\mathbf{f}$:

1. $Eq_{\text{inverse}}(\mathbf{f})$

$$\mathbf{f}(a) = \prod_i (1 - \mathbf{f}(x_i))$$

2. $Eq_{\text{geometrical}}(\mathbf{f})$

$$\mathbf{f}(a) = [\prod_i (1 - \mathbf{f}(x_i))]/[\prod_i (1 - \mathbf{f}(x_i)) + \prod_i x_i].$$

We call this equation $Eq_{\text{geometrical}}$ because it is connected to the projective geometry Cross Ratio, see our 2005 paper [1].

3. $Eq_{\text{max}}(\mathbf{f})$

$$\mathbf{f}(a) = 1 - \max(\mathbf{f}(x_i)).$$

4. $Eq_{\text{suspect}}(\mathbf{f})$

We shall see the difference in the examples. In fact we shall see that this new function gives exactly the Caminada labelling.

Let us further introduce a fourth system of equations which we call $Eq_{\text{suspect}}(\mathbf{f})$:

$$\mathbf{h}_a(\mathbf{f}(x_1), \ldots, \mathbf{f}(x_n)) = \prod_i (1 - \mathbf{f}(x_i)), \text{ if } \neg a R_A a \text{ holds}$$

and

$$\mathbf{h}_a(\mathbf{f}(x_1), \ldots, \mathbf{f}(x_n)) = \mathbf{f}(a) \prod_i (1 - \mathbf{f}(x_i)), \text{ if } a R_A a \text{ holds}.$$

Example 1. Let us do an example using all four options for equations, namely $Eq_{\text{geometrical}}, Eq_{\text{inverse}}, Eq_{\text{max}}$ and Eq_{suspect}.

Consider Figure 1. We are looking for **f** solving the equations. Let $\mathbf{f}(a) = \alpha, \mathbf{f}(b) = \beta, \mathbf{f}(c) = \gamma$.

I We use Eq_{inverse}:

The equations are

1. $\alpha = (1 - \alpha)(1 - \gamma)$
2. $\beta = (1 - \beta)(1 - \alpha)$
3. $\gamma = 1 - \beta$

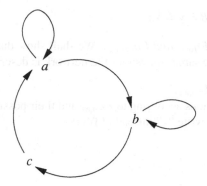

Fig. 1.

There are programs like Maple which can solve the equations of this sort and give all the solutions. We used one and got

$$\alpha = 1 - \frac{\sqrt{2}}{2}$$
$$\beta = \sqrt{2} - 1$$
$$\gamma = 2 - \sqrt{2}$$

The interest in this case is that we are getting all kinds of values which shows that these equations are sensitive to the nature of the loops involved!

II. We use Eq_{max}:

The equations are

1. $\alpha = 1 - \max(\alpha, \gamma)$
2. $\beta = 1 - \max(\beta, \alpha)$
3. $\gamma = 1 - \beta$

The only solution in this case is $\alpha = \beta = \gamma = \frac{1}{2}$.

III. We use $Eq_{suspect}$:

The equations are

1. $\alpha = \alpha(1 - \alpha) \cdot (1 - \gamma)$
2. $\beta = \beta(1 - \beta)(1 - \alpha)$
3. $\gamma = 1 - \beta.$

The solution is $\alpha = 0, \beta = 0, \gamma = 1$.

IV. We use $Eq_{geometrical}$.
   The equations are:

1. $\alpha = \frac{(1-\alpha)(1-\gamma)}{(1-\alpha)(1-\gamma)+\alpha\gamma}$
2. $\beta = \frac{(1-\alpha)(1-\beta)}{(1-\alpha)(1-\beta)+\alpha\beta}$
3. $\gamma = 1 - \beta.$

The only solution is $\alpha = \beta = \gamma = \frac{1}{2}$.:

Example 2 (Comparing Eq_{max} and $Eq_{inverse}$). We shall show that these two equational systems may not yield the same extensions. the network is described in Figure 2.

Extensions according to Eq_{max}.
Let us compute the equations according to Eq_{max} and their possible solutions.
  The equations are (we write "x" instead of $\mathbf{f}(x)$):

1. $a = 1 - b$
2. $b = 1 - \max(a, b)$
3. $c = 1 - \max(b, e)$
4. $d = 1 - c$
5. $e = 1 - d$.

Fig. 2.

We get two extensions

1. $\{a\}, (a = 1, b = 0, c = d = e = \frac{1}{2})$
2. $\phi, (a = \frac{1}{2}, b - \frac{1}{2}, c = d = e = \frac{1}{2})$

Compare this result with Theorem 2 below.

We now deal with Figure 2 using $Eq_{inverse}$. The equations are:

1. $a = 1 - b$
2. $b = (1 - b)(1 - a)$
3. $c = (1 - b)(1 - e)$
4. $d = 1 - c$
5. $e = 1 - d$.

We can have only one extension

$$\{a\}, (a = 1, b = 0, c = d = e = \frac{1}{2}).$$

2 Formal Theory of the Equational Approach to Argumentation Networks

In this section we formally develop our equational approach. Conceptually the nodes and the Equations attached to them is the network and the solutions to the equations are the complete extensions, as we have seen in the examples of Section 1.

Definition 2 (Real equational networks)

1. *An argumentation base is a pair* (S, R_A) *where* $S \neq \varnothing$ *is a finite set and* $R_A \subseteq S^2$.
2. *A real equation function in* k *variables* $\{x_1, \ldots, x_k\}$ *over the real interval* $[0, 1]$ *is a continuous function* $\mathbf{h} : [0, 1]^k \mapsto [0, 1]$ *such that*
   (a) $\mathbf{h}(0, \ldots, 0) = 1$
   (b) $\mathbf{h}(x_1, \ldots, 1, \ldots, x_k) = 0$
   Sometimes we also have condition (c) below, as in ordinary Dung networks, but not always.
   (c) $\mathbf{h}(x_1, \ldots, x_k) = \mathbf{h}(y_1, \ldots, y_k)$ *where* $\{y_j\} = \{x_i\}$ *are premutations of each other.*
3. *An equational argumentation network over* $[0, 1]$ *has the form* $(S, R_A, \mathbf{h}_a)$, $a \in S$ *where*
   (a) (S, R_A) *is a base*
   (b) For each $a \in S, \mathbf{h}_a$ *is a real equation function.*
   (c) If $\neg \exists y (y R_A a)$ *then* $\mathbf{h}_a \equiv 1$.
4. *An extension is a function* $\mathbf{f}$ *from* S *into* $[0, 1]$ *such that the following holds:*
   - $\mathbf{f}(a) = 1$ *if* $\neg \exists y (y R_a a)$
   - *If* $\{x_1, \ldots, x_k\}$ *are all the elements in* S *such that* $x_i R_A a$, *then* $\mathbf{h}_a$ *is a* k *variable function and* $\mathbf{f}(a) = \mathbf{h}_a(\mathbf{f}(x_1), \ldots, \mathbf{f}(x_k))$.

Theorem 1 (Existence theorem). *Let* $(S, R_A, \mathbf{h}_a), a \in S$ *be a network as in Definition 2. Then there exists an extension function* $\mathbf{f}$ *satisfying (4) of Definition 2.*

Proof. Let n be the number of elements of S. For each $a \in S$ consider $\mathbf{h}_a$ as a continuous function from $[0, 1]^S \mapsto [0, 1]$. Let $\mathbf{h}$ be the continuous function from $[0, 1]^S$ into $[0, 1]^S$ defined component wise by $\mathbf{h}(\alpha_1, \ldots, \alpha_n) = (\mathbf{h}_{a_1}(\alpha_1, \ldots, \alpha_n), \ldots, \mathbf{h}_{a_n}(\alpha_1, \ldots, \alpha_n))$.

This is a continuous function on a compact cube of n dimensional space and has therefore, by Brouwer's fixed point theorem, a fixed point $(x_1, \ldots, x_n) = \mathbf{h}(x_1, \ldots, x_n)$.

Let $\mathbf{f}$ be defined by $\mathbf{f}(a_i) = x_i$. Then we have that for each $a \in S$

$$\mathbf{f}(a) = \mathbf{h}_a(\mathbf{f}(a_1), \ldots, \mathbf{f}(a_k))$$

where a_i are all the points in S attacking a.

Remark 1. For Brouwer's fixed point theorem see Wikipedia.[2]

Lemma 1. *Let* (S, R_A) *be a Dung argumentation network. Let* $\lambda : S \mapsto \{in, out, undecided\}$ *be a legitimate Caminada labelling, yielding an extension* E_λ. *Consider the functions* $\mathbf{h}_a, a \in S$ *as follows:*

---

[2] See http://en.wikipedia.org/wiki/Brouwer_fixed_point_theorem and Sobolev, V. I., "Brouwer theorem", in Hazewinkel, Michiel, "Encyclopaedia of Mathematics, Springer, 2001.

1. $\mathbf{h}_a \equiv 0$ *if* $\lambda(a) = out$
2. $\mathbf{h}_a \equiv 1$ *if* $\lambda(a) = in.$
3. $\mathbf{h}_a$ *arbitrary real equation function, otherwise.*

Then there exists, by Theorem 1 an extension function $\mathbf{f}$ *such that for all* $a \in S$

$$\mathbf{f}(a) = \mathbf{h}_a(\mathbf{f}(x_1), \ldots, \mathbf{f}(x_k)),$$

where $\{x_i\}$ *are all the nodes attacking* $a.$

Note that we have argued in these examples that we get a good refinement of the undecided allocations.

To get exactly the Caminada labelling, we use the next theorem, Theorem 2.

Theorem 2 (Caminada labelling functions and $Eq_{\max}$**).** *Consider the function*

$$\mathbf{h}_{\max}(x_1, \ldots, x_n) = 1 - \max(x_1, \ldots, x_n).$$

This function is continuous in $[0, 1]^n \mapsto [0, 1]$ *and therefore falls under Definition 2.*

1. Let $(S, R_A, \mathbf{h}_{\max})$ *be an equational network with* $\mathbf{h}_{\max}$ *and let* $\mathbf{f}$ *be an extension, as in item 4 of Definition 2. Define a labelling* $\lambda_{\mathbf{f}}$ *dependent on* $\mathbf{f}$ *as follows*

$$\lambda_{\mathbf{f}}(a) = \begin{cases} in \text{ if } \mathbf{f}(a) = 1 \\ out \text{ if } \mathbf{f}(a) = 0 \\ undecided \text{ if } 0 < \mathbf{f}(a) < 1 \end{cases}$$

Then $\lambda_{\mathbf{f}}$ *is a proper Caminada extension of* $(S, R_A).$
2. Let λ *be a Caminada extension for* $(S, R_A).$ *Let* $\mathbf{f}_\lambda$ *be the real number function defined as follows*

$$\mathbf{f}_\lambda(a) = \begin{cases} 1 \text{ if } \lambda(a) = in \\ 0 \text{ if } \lambda(a) = out \\ \frac{1}{2} \text{ if } \lambda(a) = undecided. \end{cases}$$

Then $\mathbf{f}_\lambda$ *is a proper equational extension for* $(S, R_A, \mathbf{h}_{\max})$, *i.e.* $\mathbf{f}_\lambda$ *solves the equations* $\mathbf{f}_\lambda(a) = 1 - \max(\mathbf{f}_\lambda(x_1), \ldots, \mathbf{f}_\lambda(x_n))$ *where* x_i *are all the attackers of* $a.$

Proof.

1. We show that $\lambda_{\mathbf{f}}$ satisfies the Caminada conditions (C1)–(C3).
   Case C1 Assume x_1 attacks a and $\lambda_{\mathbf{f}}(x_1) = in$. This means that $\mathbf{f}(x_1) = 1$. Let $x_2, \ldots, x_n$ be the other attackers of a. Then $\mathbf{f}(a) = 1 - \max(\mathbf{f}(x_1), \ldots, \mathbf{f}(x_n))$ and hence $\mathbf{f}(a) = 0$ and hence $\lambda_{\mathbf{f}}(a) = out.$
   Caes C2 Assume a has no attackers then $\mathbf{f}(a) = 1$ and $\lambda_{\mathbf{f}}(a) = in.$
   Otherwise let as before $x_1, \ldots, x_n$ be all the attackers of a, and assume $\lambda_{\mathbf{f}}(x_i) = out$, for all i. This means $\mathbf{f}(x_i) = 0$ for all i. Hence $\max(\mathbf{f}(x_i)) = 0$ and hence $\mathbf{f}(a) = 1$ and hence $\lambda_{\mathbf{f}}(a) = in.$
   Case C3 Assume $\lambda_{\mathbf{f}}(x_i) = out$ or undecided, with say $\lambda_{\mathbf{f}}(x_1)$ at least is undecided. This means that $\mathbf{f}(x_i) < 1$ for all i and for at least x_1 we have $\mathbf{f}(x_1) > 0$. This means that $0 < \max(\mathbf{f}(x_i) < 1.$
   Hence $0 < 1 - \max(\mathbf{f}(x_i) < 1.$ Hence $0 < \mathbf{f}(a) < 1.$ Hence $\lambda_{\mathbf{f}}(a) = undecided.$

2. Let λ be a proper Caminada extension. We show that $\mathbf{f}_\lambda$ solves the equations with **h**.

   (a) If a has no attackers then $\lambda(a) = $ in and $\mathbf{f}_\lambda(a) = 1$.
   (b) Let $x_1,\ldots,x_n$ be all attackers of a.
       i. If for some i, $x_i = $ in then $\mathbf{f}_\lambda(x_i) = 1$.
          Also in this case $\lambda(a) = 0$ and so $\mathbf{f}_\lambda(a) = 0$.
          But $\max(\mathbf{f}(x_i)) = 1$ and hence indeed $\mathbf{f}_\lambda(a) = 1 - \max(\mathbf{f}(x_i))$.
       ii. If all $\lambda(x_i) = $ out then $\lambda(a) = $ in. So $\mathbf{f}_\lambda(a) = 1$ and $\mathbf{f}_\lambda(x_i) = 0$. Thus $\max(\mathbf{f}_\lambda(x_i)) = 0$. So indeed $\mathbf{f}_\lambda(a) = 1 - \max(\mathbf{f}_\lambda(x_i))$.
   (c) If all $\lambda(x_i)$ are either out or undecided with at least $\lambda(x_1) = $ undecided then $\lambda(a) = $ undecided and so all $\mathbf{f}_\lambda(x_i)$ are either 0 or $\frac{1}{2}$ with at least $\mathbf{f}_\lambda(x_1) = \frac{1}{2}$, and $\mathbf{f}_\lambda(a) = \frac{1}{2}$.
       Hence $\max(\mathbf{f}(x_i)) = \frac{1}{2}$ and indeed $\mathbf{f}_\lambda(a) = 1 - \max(\mathbf{f}_\lambda(x_i))$.

Remark 2 (Caminada labelling and $Eq_{inverse}$). Theorem 2 does not hold for $Eq_{inverse}$. This follows from Example 2.

Summary 3 (Advantages of the Equational Approach). *Time to list the advantages of our approach, see also Remark 3 below:*

First let us highlight the fact that given a traditional argumentation network with attacks only, we use equations as a conceptual framework. We no longer talk about concepts like defense, acceptability, admissible extensions, etc. etc., but talk instead about solutions to the equations.

Therefore conceptually we have

- *an extension is a solution to the equations and different extensions (grounded, preferred, stable, semi-stable, etc.) are characterised by further equations on these solutions functions using say Lagrange Multipliers see Section 6 below.*

Within this framework we note the following:

1. *To find all possible extensions we solve equations. We feed the equations into existing well known mathematical programs such as MAPLE or MATLAB or NSolve and get the solutions.*

   There are many papers which calculated computational complexity of finding various extensions, when we reduce the problem to that of solving equations in MAPLE or MATLAB or NSolve, complexity is not reduced, it can only increase. What do we gain then?
   - *A new uniform framework, not only for argumentation networks, but also for other types, Ecological, flow, etc., etc.*
   - *Possibility of finding different heuristics for equations which will work faster for most cases, giving an advantage over non-equational algorithms*
   - *Ordinary people such as lawyers etc., to the extent that they use argumentation at all and are not averse to formal logic, they may find that it is psychologically easier to plug the problem into the computer, go and make a cup of tea and then check the results.*

Furthermore, if we insist on certain arguments being in or out, we can experimentally feed this into the equations and test the effect on other arguments. MATLAB itself does not generate all the solutions automatically but requires initial input, which is an advantage if we have a special set of arguments in mind.

For example the question of whether a set of arguments belongs to some extension (being credulous) of a certain type or whether the set belongs to all extensions of a certain type (being sceptical) can very naturally be handled in the equational framework.

To generate all extensions we need to keep plugging initial conditions into MATLAB, i.e., plug in all possible candidates for extensions (this is exponential in the number of nodes but we show in the full paper [11] that any Boolean set of functions can be embedded in argumentation networks, and so the complexity is exponential anyway).

Another possibility is to use NSolve which does generate solutions, see `http://reference.wolfram.com/mathematica/ref/NSolve.html`.

Another disadvantage of this is that we might get approximate solutions. So if we get x = 0.999 we ask is this for real or is the solution supposed to be x = 1?

On the other hand an advantage of using such programs is that it makes it easy to incorporate argumentations feature into other larger AI programs, as almost anything allows for solving equations.

2. *We have a framework for introducing support discussed in the full paper [11].*

3   Numerical Calculations

This section deals with numerical and computational aspects of our equational models.

We begin with options for calculating extensions in ordinary Dung networks and their comparison with Caminada labelling. Our embarkation point is a table from Caminada and Gabbay [5].

See Table 1.

We now write equations whose solutions give the correct extensions. We assume a set of equations Eq which is sound for Dung semantics, such as offered in Definition 1.

Our network is (S, R_A).

Table 1. Argument labellings and Dung-style semantics

restriction complete labellings	Dung-style semantics	linked by def. and th. of paper [5]
no restrictions	complete semantics	Def. 5 and Th. 1
empty undec	stable semantics	Def. 8 and Th. 5
maximal in	preferred semantics	Def. 10 and Th. 7
maximal out	preferred semantics	Def. 10 and Th. 7
maximal undec	grounded semantics	Def. 9 and Th. 6
minimal in	grounded semantics	Def. 9 and Th. 6
minimal out	grounded semantics	Def. 9 and Th. 6
minimal undec	semi-stable semantics	Def. 11 and Th. 8

Case complete extensions
Solve the equations. Any solution **f** is an extension.

Case stable extensions
Add a new variable y such that $y \notin S$, and write the additional equation

$$\mathbf{f}(y) = \mathbf{h}_y = \sum_{x \in S} \mathbf{f}(x)(1 - \mathbf{f}(x)).$$

If the solution **f** to the new expanded set of equations is a stable extension, then $\mathbf{f}(x)(1 - \mathbf{f}(x))$ is 0 for all $x \in S$ and hence $\mathbf{f}(y) = 0$. Conversely, if $\mathbf{f}(y) = 0$ then **f** is stable. Thus to check for stable extensions, we check $\mathbf{f}(y)$.

Case of semi-stable extensions
This case minimises the undecided. We do the following.
    Consider the quantity

$$\mu = \sum_{\substack{a \in S \\ x_1, \ldots, x_n \in S \\ \text{are all} \\ \text{attackers of } a}} [a - \mathbf{h}_a(x_1, \ldots, x_n)]^2.$$

In μ we regard all elements of S as variables. The equation $\mu = 0$ has a solution. We regard $\mu = 0$ as a constraint and minimise the expression

$$v = \sum_{x \in S} x(1 - x)$$

subject to the constraint $\mu = 0$.
    This can be done using the method of Lagrange multipliers (see Wikipedia).

Case of grounded extensions
This is like the semi-stable case except that we minimise the expression $1 - v$.

Case of preferred extensions
This case is dealt with in the full paper. It is a bit involved and is of exponential complexity.

4   Equational Approach to Logic

We explain the general idea via some examples, and this would give the reader a better perspective on our equational approach to argumentation networks.

Example 3 (Disjunctive inference). Consider a simple inference:

1. $(p \lor q)$
2. $p \to r$
3. $q \to r$

From (1)–(3) we want to infer

4. r

We proceed as follows, assuming our logic satisfies the Deduction theorem:

$$E \text{ and } x \text{ proves } y \text{ iff } E \text{ proves } x \rightarrow y.$$

5.   1. Assume p
     2. Get r from (5.1) and (2) using modus ponens.
6.   1. Assume q
     2. Get r from 6.1 and (3), using modus ponens
7.   Get r from (1), (5-1–5.2) and (6.1–6.2) and the rule for disjunction elimination.

We now compare this with an equational approach.

   Note that the above proof theoretic inference is valid in many logics, such as classical logic, intuitionistic logic and Łukasiewicz infinite valued logic.

   When we write equations for the above inference, we have to choose in which logic we are operating. There will be different equations for different logics.

Definition 3 (Boolean negation disjunction network). *Let $(S, R_\neg, R_+)$ be a network with two binary relations and the following properties:*
   Let $R = R_\neg \cup R_+$. Then the following holds

1. $xR_\neg y \wedge xR_\neg y' \rightarrow y = y'$.
2. $\neg \exists y_1 y_2 (xR_\neg y_1 \wedge xR_+ y_2)$
3. $xR_+ y \rightarrow \exists! z (z \neq y \wedge xR_+ z)$.
4. $\neg xRx$.

We associate the following functions wth R_+ and $R_\neg$.

1. *If $xR_\neg y$ then $x = 1 - y$.*
2. *If $xR_+ y_1 \wedge xR_+ y_2$ then $x = [1 - (1 - y_1)(1 - y_2)]$.*

Example 4 (Equational approach to disjunctive inference in classical logic). Consider Figure 3. This is a construction tree for the wffs involved in Example 3 from the point of view of classical logic. In classical logic R_+ indicates disjunction.

   Let us apply our equational definition of Definition 3 to Figure 3. We get in terms of p, q, r the following equations

1. $u = [1 - (1 - p)(1 - q)]$
2. $z = [1 - p(1 - r)]$
3. $y = [1 - q(1 - r)]$

The disjunctive inference problem of Example 3 becomes the following equational problem

   – Given that $u = z = y = 1$, solve for r. $r = ?$

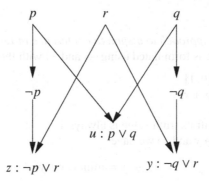

$$p \qquad r \qquad q$$

$$\neg p \qquad\qquad\qquad \neg q$$

$$u : p \vee q$$

$$z : \neg p \vee r \qquad\qquad y : \neg q \vee r$$

Fig. 3. F73

Let us see how to do it. We get

(*1) $(1 - p)(1 - q) = 0$
(*2) $p(1 - r) = 0$
(*3) $q(1 - r) = 0$

The way the proof procedure of Example 3 proceeds is to do case analysis. From (*1) either $p = 1$ or $q = 1$ and in each case from (*2) (resp. *3) we get $r = 1$.

This is not equational solving but reasoning about the equations to prove that $r = 1$.
We want to be more direct. Let us expand the equations.

(*1) $1 - p - q + pq = 0$
(*2) $p - pr = 0$
(*3) $q - qr = 0$

Add up all three equations and get

(*4) $1 + pq - pr - qr = 0$

or

(*5) $1 + pq = (p + q)r.$

Let us now add (*2) and (*3), we get

(*6) $p + q - pr - qr = 0$

or

(*7) $(p + q) = (p + q)r.$

We need to show that $p + q$ is not 0 so that we can divide by it.
From (*7) and (*5) we get

(*8) $1 + pq = p + q$

We can also deduce from (*8) that $p + q \neq 0$ and so we divide by $p + q$.
So from (*7) by dividing by $p + q$ we get

(*9) $r = 1$.

Example 5 (Equational approach to disjunctive inference in Łukasiewicz many valued logic). Łukasiewicz logic is formulated using $\to$ and $\neg$, with the following truth table:

1. atoms get values in $[0, 1]$
2. $x \to y = \min(1, 1 - x + y)$
3. $\neg x = 1 - x$
4. A wff is a tautology iff its truth value is always 1
5. Define $x \oplus y = \neg x \to y$ and so we have

$$\neg x \to y = \min(1, x + y)$$

We can define therefore

$$x_1 \oplus \ldots \oplus x_{n+1}$$

to be

$$\neg x_1 \to (\neg x_2 \to \ldots \to (\neg x_n \to x_{n+1}) \ldots)$$

and its table is

$$\min(1, x_1 + \ldots x_{n+1}).$$

Consider now the network of Definition 3. We use new functions for the case of $x R_+ y_1$ and $x R_+ y_2$, we let

$$x = \min(y_1 + y_2).$$

We note that in Łukasiewicz logic the disjunction $x \vee y$ has the table

$$x \vee y = \max(x, y)$$

and can be defined as

$$(x \to y) \to y.$$

We can define conjunction $x \wedge y$ but

$$x \wedge y = \neg(\neg x \vee \neg y)$$

we have:

$$x \wedge y = \min(x, y).$$

6. The consequence relation for Łukasiewicz logic can be defined in several ways. We use the options which allows for the Deduction theorem, because the disjunctive proof in Example 3 uses it.
   – $A_1, \ldots, A_n \vdash B$ iff $(A_1 \oplus \ldots \oplus A_n) \to B$ is a tautology.
   The above means that $\sum_i \mathrm{value}(A_i) \leq \mathrm{value}(B)$.
   Consider now the network of Figure 4.
   Note that R_+ in the figure indicates the connective $x \oplus y = \neg x \to y$, therefore we have

$$x \to y = (\neg x) \oplus y.$$

   and disjunction $x \vee y$ is defined as $(x \to y) \to y$, therefore

$$x \vee y = [\neg(\neg x) \oplus y)] \oplus y.$$

We ask the following question:

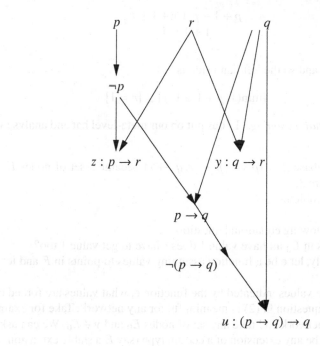

Fig. 4. F73a

- Given that $\min(1, u + z + y) \leq r$, what values can r have?

This means that given

$$\min(1, \max(p, q) + \min(1, 1 - p + r) + \min(1, 1 - q + r)) \leq r$$

what can r be?

Assume without loss of generality that $p \geq q$.

We ask can r be less than 1?

Assume $r < 1$ and get a contradiction.

Case 1

$r < q \leq 1$.

In this case we get

$$(p + 1 - p + r + 1 - q + r) \leq r$$

$$1 + 2r - q \leq r$$
$$2 + 2r \leq r + q$$

Since $r < q$ we get

$$2 + r + q \leq r + q$$
$$2 \leq 1$$

not possible.

Case 2

$1 > r \geq q$

We get

$$p + 1 - p + r + 1 \leq r$$
$$1 + 1 \leq 1$$

not possible.

Therefore $r = 1$ and so the left hand side is

$$[\min(1, p + 1 + 1_= 1] \leq [r = 1]$$

Remark 3 (Equational reasoning). Let us put on our meta-level hat and analyse what is happening here.

1. The logical database $\Delta = \{p \vee q, p \rightarrow r, q \rightarrow r\}$ became a set of nodes E_Δ in the network of Figure 3..
2. The inference problem
   - $\Delta \vdash ?r$

   becomes the following equational question
   - If the points in E_Δ all have value 1 does r have to get value 1 too?

   or more generally, let $\mathbf{e}$ be a function assigning values to points in E and let $y \notin E$. We can ask
   - If E gets the values indicated by the function $\mathbf{e}$, what values are forced on y?
3. The equational question in (2) is meaningful for any network. Take for example an argumentation network and take any set of nodes E_0 and $y \notin E_0$. We can ask
   - Let $E \supseteq E_0$ be any extension of a certain type (say E a stable extension) are we forced to have $y \in E$?

   In which case we can write
   - $E \Vdash y_{\text{stable}}$
4. What is the analogous feature in the case of logic to the notion of extension in argumentation networks?

   We know that any set of nodes corresponds to a database. So the algorithms generating extensions correspond to a way of generating databases.
5. The notion of "consistency" in logic corresponds to "having a solution" in an equational network.

   Let $\mathbf{e}$ be a function associating values to the points in E. Then $(\mathbf{e}, E)$ is equationally consistent, iff there exists a solution $\mathbf{f}$ to the equations such that $\mathbf{f} \restriction E = \mathbf{e}$.

5   Conclusion

We have shown the reader some of what the equational approach can do. The full paper (which may as well become a book) contains a lot more material, including:

1. Equations for higher level attacks (attacks from argument nodes to attack arrows of [10])
2. Equations for logic programs
3. Connections with fuzzy logic and fuzzy argumentation
4. Translation (critical faithful embedding) of Boolean networks (also known as abstract dialectical frameworks in [3]) into Dung networks
5. Time dependent networks and equations, including attacks arising from argument decay

6. Approximate admissible extensions (where we accept arguments whose value is almost 1) and their relation to weighted argument systems of [7]
7. Analysis of support
8. Equational characterisation of loops
9. General meta-level considerations
10. Comparison with related literature.

Acknowledgements

I am grateful to Martin Caminada, Nachum Dershowitz, Phan Minh Dung, David Makinson, Alex Rabinowich,and Serena Villata for helpful discussions.

References

1. Barringer, H., Gabbay, D.M., Woods, J.: Temporal dynamics of support and attack networks. In: Hutter, D., Stephan, W. (eds.) Mechanizing Mathematical Reasoning. LNCS (LNAI), vol. 2605, pp. 59–98. Springer, Heidelberg (2005)
2. Boole, G.: The Mathematical Analysis of Logic, Cambridge and London (1847)
3. Brewka, G., Woltran, S.: Abstract dialectical frameworks. In: Proc. KR 2010, pp. 102–111. AAAI Press, Menlo Park (2010)
4. Couturat, L.: The Algebra of Logic. Open Court (1914)
5. Caminada, M., Gabbay, D.M.: A logical account of formal argumentation. Studia Logica 93(2-3), 109–145 (2009)
6. Dung, P.M.: On the acceptability of arguments and its fundamental role in nonmonotonic reasoning, logic programming and n-person games. Artificial Intelligence 77, 321–357 (1995)
7. Dunne, P., Hunter, A., McBurney, P., Wooldridge, M.: Weighted argument systems. Artificial Intelligence 175, 457–486 (2011)
8. Gabbay, D.M.: Provability foundations for argumentation networks. Studia Logica 93(2-3), 181–198 (2009)
9. Gabbay, D.M.: Fibring argumentation frames. Studia Logica 93(2-3), 231–295 (2009)
10. Gabbay, D.M.: Semantics for higher level attacks in extended argumentation frames. Part 1: Overview. Studia Logica 93, 355–379 (2009)
11. Gabbay, D.M.: Equational approach to argumentation networks, 90pp (February 2011)
12. Gabbay, D.M., Szałas, A.: Annotation theories over finite graphs. Studia Logica 93(2-3), 147–180 (2009)
13. Schröder, E.: Vorlesungen über die Algebra die Logik, vol. 3, pp. 1890–1904. B. G. Tuebner, Leipzig; Reprints, Chelsea (1966); Thoemmes Press (2000)

Constructive Decision Theory: Short Summary*

Joseph Y. Halpern

Computer Science Department
Cornell University
Ithaca, NY 14853, USA
halpern@cs.cornell.edu

In almost all current approaches to decision making under uncertainty, it is assumed that a decision problem is described by a set of states and set of outcomes, and the decision maker (DM) has a preference relation on a rather rich set of *acts*, which are functions from states to outcomes. The standard representation theorems of decision theory give conditions under which the preference relation can be represented by a utility function on outcomes and numerical representation of beliefs on states. For example, Savage [4] shows that if a DM's preference order satisfies certain axioms, then the DM's preference relation can be represented by a probability Pr on the state space and a utility function mapping outcomes to the reals such that she prefers act a to act b iff the expected utility of a (with respect to Pr) is greater than that of b. Moreover, the probability measure is unique and the utility function is unique up to affine transformations. Similar representations of preference can be given with respect to other representations of uncertainty (see, for example, [2,5]).

Most interesting decision problems do not come with a state space and acts specified as functions on these states. Instead they are typically problems of the sort "Should I buy 100 shares of IBM or leave the money in the bank?" or "Should I attack Iraq or continue to negotiate?". To apply standard decision theory, the DM must first formulate the problem in terms of states and outcomes. But in complex decision problems, the state space and outcome space are often difficult to formulate. For example, what is the state space and outcome space in trying to decide whether to attack Iraq? And even if a DM could formulate the problem in terms of states and outcome, there is no reason to believe that someone else trying to model the problem would do it in the same way. For example, reasonable people might disagree about what facts of the world are relevant to the pricing of IBM stock. As is well known [3], preferences can be quite sensitive to the exact formulation. To make matters worse, a modeler may have access to information not available to the DM, and therefore incorrectly construe the decision problem from the DM's point of view.

We take a different view of acts here. The inspiration for our approach is the observation that objects of choice in an uncertain world have some structure to

---

* This is a short summary of a paper written with Lawrence Blume and David Easley [1]. Work supported in part by NSF under grants ITR-0325453, and IIS-0534064, by ONR under grants N00014-00-1-03-41 and N00014-01-10-511, and by the DoD Multidisciplinary University Research Initiative (MURI) program administered by the ONR under grant N00014-01-1-0795.

them. Individuals choose among some simple actions: "do x" or "do y". But they also perform various tests on the world and make choices contingent upon the outcome of these tests: "If the stock broker says t, do x; otherwise do y." We formalize this view by taking the objects of choice to be (syntactic) programs in a programming language. We then show that if the DM's preference relation on programs satisfies appropriate axioms, we, the modelers, can impute a state space, an outcome space, and an interpretation of programs as functions from states to outcomes such that the (induced) preferences on these functions have a subjective expected utility (SEU) representation, similar in spirit to that of Savage. Just as probability and utility are derived notions in the standard approach, and are tools that we can use to analyze and predict decisions, so too are the state space and outcome space in our framework.

This formulation of decision problems has several advantages over more traditional formulations. First, we can theorize (if we want) about only the actual observable choices available to the DM, without having states and outcomes, and without needing to view acts as functions from states to outcomes. Indeed, we can test whether a DM's behavior is consistent with SEU despite not having states and outcomes. The second advantage is more subtle but potentially quite profound. Representation theorems are just that; they merely provide an alternative description of a preference order in terms of numerical scales. Decision theorists make no pretense that these representations have anything to do with the cognitive processes by which individuals make choices. But to the extent that the programming language models the language of the DM, we have the ability to interpret the effects of cognitive limitations having to do with the language in terms of the representation. For instance, there may be limitations on the space of acts because some sequence of tests is too computationally costly to verify. We can also take into account a DM's inability to recognize that two programs represent the same function. Finally, the approach lets us take into account the fact that different DMs use different languages to describe the same phenomena.

References

1. Blume, L., Easley, D., Halpern, J.Y.: Redoing the foundations of decision theory. In: Principles of Knowledge Representation and Reasoning: Proc. Tenth International Conference (KR 2006), pp. 14–24 (2006); a longer version, with the title "Constructive decision theory", can be found at
   http://www.cs.cornell.edu/home/halpern/papers/behfinal.pdf
2. Gilboa, I., Schmeidler, D.: Maxmin expected utility with a non-unique prior. Journal of Mathematical Economics 18, 141–153 (1989)
3. Kahneman, D., Slovic, P., Tversky, A. (eds.): Judgment Under Uncertainty: Heuristics and Biases. Cambridge University Press, Cambridge (1982)
4. Savage, L.J.: Foundations of Statistics. Wiley, New York (1954)
5. Schmeidler, D.: Subjective probability and expected utility without additivity. Econometrica 57, 571–587 (1989)

Strong Equivalence for Argumentation Semantics Based on Conflict-Free Sets*

Sarah Alice Gaggl and Stefan Woltran

Vienna University of Technology, Austria

Abstract. Argumentation can be understood as a dynamic reasoning process, i.e. it is in particular useful to know the effects additional information causes with respect to a certain semantics. Accordingly, one can identify the information which does not contribute to the results no matter which changes are performed. In other words, we are interested in so-called *kernels* of frameworks, where two frameworks with the same kernel are then "immune" to all kind of newly added information in the sense that they always produce an equal outcome. The concept of *strong equivalence* for argumentation frameworks captures this intuition and has been analyzed for several semantics which are all based on the concept of admissibility. Other important semantics have been neglected so far. To close this gap, we give strong equivalence results with respect to naive, stage and *cf2* extensions, and we compare the new results with the already existing ones. Furthermore, we analyze strong equivalence for symmetric frameworks and discuss local equivalence, a certain relaxation of strong equivalence.

1 Introduction

The field of abstract argumentation became increasingly popular within the last decades and is nowadays identified as an important tool in various applications as inconsistency handling (see e.g. [2]) and decision support (see e.g. [1]). One of the key features abstract argumentation provides is a clear separation between logical content and non-classical reasoning (which is solely done over abstract entities, the arguments A, and a certain relationship R between those entities; forming so-called argumentation frameworks (AFs) of the form (A, R)). For abstract argumentation, many semantics have been proposed to evaluate such frameworks including Dung's famous original semantics [8], but also other semantics like the *cf2* semantics [4] or the stage semantics [13] received attention lately. The aim of argumentation semantics is to select possible subsets of acceptable arguments (the so-called extensions) from a given argumentation framework. Since the relation in such frameworks indicates possible conflicts between adjacent arguments, one basic requirement for an argumentation semantics is to yield sets which are *conflict-free*, i.e., arguments which attack each other never appear jointly in an extension. To get more adequate semantics, conflict-freeness is then augmented by further requirements. One such requirement is *admissibility* (a set S of arguments is admissible in some framework (A, R) if, S is conflict-free and, for each $(b, a) \in R$ with $a \in S$, there is a $c \in S$, such that $(c, b) \in R$) but also other requirements have

---

* Supported by the Vienna Science and Technology Fund (WWTF) under grant ICT08-028.

W. Liu (Ed.): ECSQARU 2011, LNAI 6717, pp. 38–49, 2011.

been used (maximality, or graph properties as covers or components). Properties of and relations between these semantics are nowadays a central research issue, see e.g. [3].

One such property is the notion of *strong equivalence* [12]. In a nutshell, strong equivalence between two AFs holds iff they behave the same under any further addition of arguments and/or attacks. In particular, this allows for identifying redundant patterns in AFs. As an example, consider the *stable semantics* (a set S of arguments is called stable in an AF F if S is conflict-free in F and each argument from F not contained in S is attacked by some argument from S). Here an attack (a, b) is redundant whenever a is self-attacking. This can be seen as follows; in case b is in a stable extension, removing (a, b) cannot change the extension (a cannot be in any stable extension due to (a, a), thus there is no change in terms of conflict-free sets); in case b is not in some stable extension S, then it is attacked by some $c \in S$. However, $c \neq a$ since a is self-attacking; thus b remains attacked, even when the attack (a, b) is dropped. In fact, the AF $F = (\{a, b\}, \{(a, a), (a, b)\})$ is strongly equivalent to the AF $G = (\{a, b\}, \{(a, a)\})$. In general, two AFs are strongly equivalent wrt. stable semantics, if their only syntactical difference is due to such redundant attacks as outlined above. More formally, this concept can be captured via so-called *kernels* (as suggested in [12]): The *stable kernel* of an AF $F = (A, R)$ is given by the framework (A, R^*) where R^* stems from R by removing all attacks (a, b) such that $a \neq b$ and (a, a) is in R. Then, F and G are strongly equivalent (wrt. stable semantics) iff F and G have the same such kernel.

In [12], such results have been given for several semantics, namely: stable, grounded, complete, admissible, preferred (all these are due to Dung [8]), ideal [9], and semi-stable [5]. Four different kernels were identified to characterize strong equivalence between these semantics. Interestingly, it turned out that strong equivalence wrt. admissible, preferred, semi-stable and ideal semantics is exactly the same concept, while stable, complete, and grounded semantics require distinct kernels. We complement here the picture by analyzing strong equivalence in terms of *naive, stage*, and *cf2 semantics*.

Strong equivalence not only gives an additional property to investigate the differences between argumentation semantics but also has some interesting applications. First, suppose we have modelled a negotiation between two agents via argumentation frameworks. Here, strong equivalence allows to characterize situations where the two agents have an equivalent view of the world which is moreover robust to additional information. Second, we believe that the identification of *redundant attacks* is important in choosing an appropriate semantics. Caminada and Amgoud outlined in [6] that the interplay between how a framework is built and which semantics is used to evaluate the framework is crucial in order to obtain useful results when the (claims of the) arguments selected by the chosen semantics are collected together. Knowledge about redundant attacks (wrt. a particular semantics) might help to identify unsuitable such combinations.

The main contributions and organization of the paper are as follows. In Section 2, we give the necessary background. The main results are then contained in Section 3, where characterizations for strong equivalence wrt. naive, stage, and *cf2* semantics are provided. As our results show, *cf2* semantics are the most sensitive ones in the sense that there are no redundant attacks at all (this is not the case for the other semantics which have been considered so far). In Section 4, we relate our new results to known results from [12] and draw a full picture how the different semantics behave in terms of strong equivalence. Finally, we also provide some results concerning local equivalence, a relaxation of strong equivalence proposed in [12], and symmetric frameworks [7].

2 Background

We first introduce the concept of abstract argumentation frameworks and the semantics we are mainly interested here.

Definition 1. *An* argumentation framework *(AF) is a pair* $F = (A, R)$, *where A is a finite set of arguments and* $R \subseteq A \times A$. *The pair* $(a, b) \in R$ *means that a attacks b. A set* $S \subseteq A$ *of arguments* **defeats** b *(in F), if there is an* $a \in S$, *such that* $(a, b) \in R$.

For an AF $F = (B, S)$ we use $A(F)$ to refer to B and $R(F)$ to refer to S. When clear from the context, we often write $a \in F$ (instead of $a \in A(F)$) and $(a, b) \in F$ (instead of $(a, b) \in R(F)$). For two AFs F and G, we define the union $F \cup G = (A(F) \cup A(G), R(F) \cup R(G))$ and $F|_S = ((A(F) \cap S), R(F) \cap (S \times S))$ as the *sub-framework* of F wrt S; furthermore, we also use $F - S$ as a shorthand for $F|_{A \setminus S}$.

A semantics σ assigns to each AF F a collection of sets of arguments. The following concepts underly such semantics.

Definition 2. *Let* $F = (A, R)$ *be an AF. A set S of arguments is*

- **conflict-free** *(in F), i.e.* $S \in cf(F)$, *if* $S \subseteq A$ *and there are no* $a, b \in S$, *such that* $(a, b) \in R$.
- **maximal conflict-free** *(in F), i.e.* $S \in mcf(F)$, *if* $S \in cf(F)$ *and for each* $T \in cf(F)$, $S \not\subset T$. *For the empty AF* $F_0 = (\emptyset, \emptyset)$, *let* $mcf(F_0) = \{\emptyset\}$.
- *a* **stable** *extension (of F), i.e.* $S \in stable(F)$, *if* $S \in cf(F)$ *and each* $a \in A \setminus S$ *is defeated by S in F.*
- *a* **stage** *extension (of F), i.e.* $S \in stage(F)$, *if* $S \in cf(F)$ *and there is no* $T \in cf(F)$ *with* $T_R^+ \supset S_R^+$, *where* $S_R^+ = S \cup \{b \mid \exists a \in S, \text{ such that } (a, b) \in R\}$.

When talking about semantics, one uses the terms stable, and respectively, stage semantics, as expected. For maximal conflict-free sets, the name *naive* semantics is also common; we thus use $naive(F)$ instead of $mcf(F)$.

We note that each stable extension is also a stage extension, and in case $stable(F) \neq \emptyset$ then $stable(F) = stage(F)$. This is due to the fact that for a stable extension S of (A, R), $S_R^+ = A$ holds. In general, we have the following relations for each AF F:

$$stable(F) \subseteq stage(F) \subseteq naive(F) \subseteq cf(F) \tag{1}$$

We continue with the *cf2* semantics [4] and use the characterization from [10]. We need some further terminology. By $SCCs(F)$, we denote the set of strongly connected components of an AF $F = (A, R)$ which identify the maximal strongly connected[1] subgraphs of F; $SCCs(F)$ is thus a partition of A. Moreover, we define $[[F]] = \bigcup_{C \in SCCs(F)} F|_C$. Let B a set of arguments, and $a, b \in A$. We say that b is reachable in F from a modulo B, in symbols $a \Rightarrow_F^B b$, if there exists a path from a to b in

---

[1] A directed graph is called *strongly connected* if there is a path from each vertex in the graph to every other vertex of the graph.

$F|_B$, i.e. there exists a sequence $c_1, \ldots, c_n$ $(n > 1)$ of arguments such that $c_1 = a$, $c_n = b$, and $(c_i, c_{i+1}) \in R \cap (B \times B)$, for all i with $1 \leq i < n$. Finally, for an AF $F = (A, R)$, $D \subseteq A$, and a set S of arguments, let

$$\Delta_{F,S}(D) = \{a \in A \mid \exists b \in S : b \neq a, (b, a) \in R, a \not\Rightarrow_F^{A \setminus D} b\}.$$

and $\Delta_{F,S}$ be the least fixed-point of $\Delta_{F,S}(\emptyset)$.

Proposition 1. *The cf2 extensions of an AF F can be characterized as follows:*
$cf2(F) = \{S \mid S \in cf(F) \cap mcf([[F - \Delta_{F,S}]])\}$.

Similar to relation (1), we have the following picture in terms of *cf2* extensions:

$$stable(F) \subseteq cf2(F) \subseteq naive(F) \subseteq cf(F') \tag{2}$$

However, there is no particular relation between stage and *cf2* extensions as shown by the following example.

Example 1. Consider the following AFs F (on the left side) and G (on the right side):

Here $\{a, c\}$ is the only stage extension of F (it is also stable). Concerning the *cf2* semantics, note that F is built from a single SCC. Thus, the *cf2* extensions are given by the maximal conflict-free sets of F, which are $\{a, c\}$ and $\{a, d\}$. Thus, we have $stage(F) \subset cf2(F)$.

On the other side the framework G is such that $cf2(G) \subset stage(G)$. G consists of two $SCCs$ namely $C_1 = \{a\}$ and $C_2 = \{b, c\}$. The maximal conflict-free sets of G are $E_1 = \{a\}$ and $E_2 = \{b\}$. In order to check whether they are also *cf2* extensions of G, we compute $\Delta_{G,E_1} = \{b\}$ and indeed $E_1 \in mcf(G - \{b\})$, whereas $\Delta_{G,E_2} = \emptyset$ and $E_2 \notin mcf(G')$, where $G' = [[G - \emptyset]] = (\{a, b, c\}, \{(b, c), (c, b)\})$. Thus, $cf2(G) = \{E_1\}$. On the other hand, $stage(G) = \{E_1, E_2\}$ is easily verified. $\Diamond$

Furthermore, it is easy to show that there is no particular relation between naive, stage, stable, and *cf2* semantics in terms of standard equivalence, which means that two frameworks possess the same extensions under a semantics. For more details we refer to an extended version [11] of this paper which contains some explanatory examples.

3   Characterizations for Strong Equivalence

In this section, we will provide characterizations for strong equivalence wrt. naive, stage, and *cf2* semantics. The definition is as follows.

Definition 3. *Two AFs F and G are* **strongly equivalent** *to each other wrt. a semantics σ, in symbols $F \equiv_s^\sigma G$, iff for each AF H, $\sigma(F \cup H) = \sigma(G \cup H)$.*

By definition we have that $F \equiv_s^\sigma G$ implies $\sigma(F) = \sigma(G)$, but the other direction is not true in general. This indeed reflects the nonmonotonic nature of most of the argumentation semantics.

Example 2. Consider the following AFs F and G.

For all semantics $\sigma \in \{stable, stage, cf2\}$, we have $\sigma(F) = \sigma(G) = \{\{a, b\}\}$. Whereas, if we add the AF $H = (\{a, b\}, \{(a, b)\})$, we observe $stable(F \cup H) = stage(F \cup H) = cf2(F \cup H) = \{\{a\}\}$ but $stable(G \cup H) = \emptyset$ and $stage(G \cup H) = cf2(G \cup H) = \{\{a\}, \{b\}\}$. As an example for the naive semantics let us have a look at the frameworks $T = (\{a\}, \emptyset)$ and $U = (\{a, b\}, \{(b, b)\})$ with $naive(T) = naive(U) = \{\{a\}\}$. By adding the AF $V = (\{b\}, \emptyset)$ we get $naive(T \cup V) = \{\{a, b\}\} \neq \{\{a\}\} = naive(U \cup V)$.   ◊

We next provide a few technical lemmas which will be useful later.

Lemma 1. *Let F and H be AFs and S be a set of arguments. Then, $S \in cf(F \cup H)$ if and only if, jointly $(S \cap A(F)) \in cf(F)$ and $(S \cap A(H)) \in cf(H)$.*

Proof. The only-if direction is clear. Thus suppose $S \notin cf(F \cup H)$. Then, there exist $a, b \in S$, such that $(a, b) \in F \cup H$. By our definition of "$\cup$", then $(a, b) \in F$ or $(a, b) \in H$. But then $(S \cap A(F)) \notin cf(F)$ or $(S \cap A(H)) \notin cf(H)$ follows.   □

Lemma 2. *For any AFs F and G with $A(F) \neq A(G)$, there exists an AF H such that $A(H) \subseteq A(F) \cup A(G)$ and $\sigma(F \cup H) \neq \sigma(G \cup H)$, for $\sigma \in \{naive, stage, cf2\}$.*

Proof. In case $\sigma(F) \neq \sigma(G)$, we just consider $H = (\emptyset, \emptyset)$ and get $\sigma(F \cup H) \neq \sigma(G \cup H)$. Thus assume $\sigma(F) = \sigma(G)$ and let wlog. $a \in A(F) \setminus A(G)$. Thus for all $E \in \sigma(F), a \notin E$. Consider the framework $H = (\{a\}, \emptyset)$. Then, for all $E' \in \sigma(G \cup H)$, we have $a \in E'$. On the other hand, $F \cup H = F$ and also $\sigma(F \cup H) = \sigma(F)$. Hence, a is not contained in any $E \in \sigma(F \cup H)$, and we obtain $F \not\equiv_s^\sigma G$.   □

Lemma 3. *For any AFs F and G such that $(a, a) \in R(F) \setminus R(G)$ or $(a, a) \in R(G) \setminus R(F)$, there exists an AF H such that $A(H) \subseteq A(F) \cup A(G)$ and $\sigma(F \cup H) \neq \sigma(G \cup H)$, for $\sigma \in \{naive, stage, cf2\}$.*

Proof. Let $(a, a) \in R(F) \setminus R(G)$ and consider the AF $H = (A, \{(a, b), (b, b) \mid a \neq b \in A\})$ with $A = A(F) \cup A(G)$. Then $\sigma(G \cup H) = \{a\}$ while $\sigma(F \cup H) = \{\emptyset\}$ for all considered semantics $\sigma \in \{naive, stage, cf2\}$. For example, in case $\sigma = cf2$ we obtain $\Delta_{G \cup H, E} = \{b \mid b \in A \setminus \{a\}\}$. Moreover, $\{a\}$ is conflict-free in $G \cup H$ and $\{a\} \in mcf(G')$, where $G' = (G \cup H) - \Delta_{G \cup H, E} = (\{a\}, \emptyset)$. On the other hand, $cf2(F \cup H) = \{\emptyset\}$ since all arguments in $F \cup H$ are self-attacking. The case for $(a, a) \in R(G) \setminus R(F)$ is similar.   □

3.1 Strong Equivalence wrt. Naive Semantics

We start with the naive semantics. As we will see, strong equivalence is only a marginally more restricted concept than standard equivalence, namely in case the two compared AFs are not given over the same arguments.

Theorem 1. *The following statements are equivalent: (1) $F \equiv_s^{naive} G$; (2) $naive(F) = naive(G)$ and $A(F) = A(G)$; (3) $cf(F) = cf(G)$ and $A(F) = A(G)$.*

Proof. (1) implies (2): basically by the definition of strong equivalence and Lemma 2.

(2) implies (3): Assume $naive(F) = naive(G)$ but $cf(F) \neq cf(G)$. Wlog. let $S \in cf(F) \setminus cf(G)$. Then, there exists a set $S' \supseteq S$ such that $S' \in naive(F)$ and by assumption then $S' \in naive(G)$. However, as $S \notin cf(G)$ there exists an attack $(a, b) \in R(G)$, such that $a, b \in S$. But as $S \subseteq S'$, we have $S' \notin cf(G)$ as well; a contradiction to $S' \in naive(G)$.

(3) implies (1): Suppose $F \not\equiv_s^{naive} G$, i.e. there exists a framework H such that $naive(F \cup H) \neq naive(G \cup H)$. Wlog. let now $S \in naive(F \cup H) \setminus naive(G \cup H)$. From Lemma 1 one can show that $(S \cap A(F)) \in naive(F)$ and $(S \cap A(H)) \in naive(H)$, as well as $(S \cap A(G) \notin naive(G)$. Let us assume $S' = S \cap A(F) = S \cap A(G)$, otherwise we are done yielding $A(F) \neq A(G)$. If $S' \notin cf(G)$ we are also done (since $S' \in cf(F)$ follows from $S' \in naive(F)$); otherwise, there exists an $S'' \supset S'$, such that $S'' \in cf(G)$. But $S'' \notin cf(F)$, since $S' \in naive(F)$. Again we obtain $cf(F) \neq cf(G)$ which concludes the proof. $\qquad\square$

3.2 Strong Equivalence wrt. Stage Semantics

In order to characterize strong equivalence wrt. stage semantics, we define a certain kernel which removes attacks being redundant for the stage semantics.[2]

Example 3. Consider the frameworks F and G:

They only differ in the attacks outgoing from the argument a which is self-attacking and yield the same single stage extension, namely $\{c\}$, for both frameworks. We can now add, for instance, $H = (\{a, c\}, \{(c, a)\})$ and the stage extensions for $F \cup H$ and $G \cup H$ still remain the same. In fact, no matter how H looks like, $stage(F \cup H) = stage(G \cup H)$ will hold. $\qquad\Diamond$

The following kernel reflects the intuition given in the previous example.

Definition 4. *For an AF $F = (A, R)$, define $F^{sk} = (A, R^{sk})$ where*

$$R^{sk} = R \setminus \{(a, b) \mid a \neq b, (a, a) \in R\}.$$

Theorem 2. *For any AFs F and G, $F \equiv_s^{stage} G$ iff $F^{sk} = G^{sk}$.*

Proof. Only-if: Suppose $F^{sk} \neq G^{sk}$, we show $F \not\equiv_s^{stage} G$. From Lemma 2 and Lemma 3 we know that in case the arguments or the self-loops are not equal in both frameworks, $F \equiv_s^{stage} G$ does not hold. We thus assume that $A = A(F) = A(G)$ and $(a, a) \in F$ iff $(a, a) \in G$, for each $a \in A$. Let thus wlog. $(a, b) \in F^{sk} \setminus G^{sk}$. We can conclude $(a, b) \in F$ and $(a, a) \notin F$, thus $(a, a) \notin G$ and $(a, b) \notin G$. Let c be a fresh argument and take

$$H = \{A \cup \{c\}, \{(b, b)\} \cup \{(c, d) \mid d \in A\} \cup \{(a, d) \mid d \in A \cup \{c\} \setminus \{b\}\}).$$

---

[2] As it turns out, we require here exactly the same concept of a kernel as already used in [12] to characterize strong equivalence wrt. stable semantics. We will come back to this point in Section 4.

Then, $\{a\}$ is a stage extension of $F \cup H$ (it attacks all other arguments) but not of $G \cup H$ (b is not attacked by $\{a\}$);

For the if-direction, suppose $F^{sk} = G^{sk}$. Let us first show that $F^{sk} = G^{sk}$ implies $cf(F \cup H) = cf(G \cup H)$, for each AF H. Towards a contradiction, let $T \in cf(F \cup H) \setminus cf(G \cup H)$. Since $F^{sk} = G^{sk}$, we know $A(F) = A(G)$. Thus there exist $a, b \subset T$ (not necessarily $a \neq b$) such that $(a, b) \in G \cup H$ or $(b, a) \in G \cup H$. On the other hand $(a, b) \notin F \cup H$ and $(b, a) \notin F \cup H$ hold since $a, b \in T$ and $T \in cf(F \cup H)$. Thus, in particular, $(a, b) \notin F$ and $(b, a) \notin F$ as well as $(a, b) \notin H$ and $(b, a) \notin H$; the latter implies $(a, b) \in G$ or $(b, a) \in G$. Suppose $(a, b) \in G$ (the other case is symmetric). If $(a, a) \in G$ then $(a, a) \in G^{sk}$, but $(a, a) \notin F^{sk}$ (since $a \in T$ and thus $(a, a) \notin F$). If $(a, a) \notin G, (a, b) \in G^{sk}$ but $(a, b) \notin F^{sk}$ (since $(a, b) \notin F$). In either case $F^{sk} \neq G^{sk}$, a contradiction.

We next show that $F^{sk} = G^{sk}$ implies $(F \cup H)^{sk} = (G \cup H)^{sk}$ for any AF H. Thus, let $(a, b) \in (F \cup H)^{sk}$, and assume $F^{sk} = G^{sk}$; we show $(a, b) \in (G \cup H)^{sk}$. Since, $(a, b) \in (F \cup H)^{sk}$ we know that $(a, a) \notin F \cup H$ and therefore, $(a, a) \notin F^{sk}$, $(a, a) \notin G^{sk}$ and $(a, a) \notin H^{sk}$. Hence, we have either $(a, b) \in F^{sk}$ or $(a, b) \in H^{sk}$. In the latter case, $(a, b) \in (G \cup H)^{sk}$ follows because $(a, a) \notin G^{sk}$ and $(a, a) \notin H^{sk}$. In case $(a, b) \in F^{sk}$, we get by the assumption $F^{sk} = G^{sk}$, that $(a, b) \in G^{sk}$ and since $(a, a) \notin H^{sk}$ it follows that $(a, b) \in (G \cup H)^{sk}$.

Finally we show that for any frameworks K and L such that $K^{sk} = L^{sk}$, and any $S \in cf(K) \cap cf(L)$, $S^+_{R(K)} = S^+_{R(L)}$. This follows from the fact that for each $s \in S$, (s, s) is neither contained in K nor in L. But then each attack $(s, b) \in K$ is also in K^{sk}, and likewise, each attack $(s, b) \in L$ is also in L^{sk}. Now since $K^{sk} = L^{sk}$, $S^+_{R(K)} = S^+_{R(L)}$ is obvious.

We thus have shown that, given $F^{sk} = G^{sk}$, the following relations hold for each AF H: $cf(F \cup H) = cf(G \cup H)$; $(F \cup H)^{sk} = (G \cup H)^{sk}$; and $S^+_{R(F \cup H)} = S^+_{R(G \cup H)}$ holds for each $S \in cf(F \cup H) = cf(G \cup H)$ (taking $K = F \cup H$ and $L = G \cup H$). Thus, $stage(F \cup H) = stage(G \cup H)$, for each AF H. Consequently, $F \equiv^{stage}_s G$. □

3.3 Strong Equivalence wrt. *cf2* Semantics

Finally, we turn our attention to *cf2* semantics. Interestingly, it turns out that for this semantics there are no redundant attacks at all. In fact, even in the case where an attack links two self-attacking arguments, this attack might play a role by glueing two components together. Having no redundant attacks means that strong equivalence has to coincide with syntactic equality. We now show this result formally.

Theorem 3. *For any AFs F and G, $F \equiv^{cf2}_s G$ iff $F = G$.*

Proof. We only have to show the only-if direction, since $F = G$ obviously implies $F \equiv^{cf2}_s G$. Thus, suppose $F \neq G$, we show that $F \not\equiv^{cf2}_s G$.

From Lemma 2 and Lemma 3 we know that in case the arguments or the self-loops are not equal in both frameworks, $F \equiv^{cf2}_s G$ does not hold. We thus assume that $A = A(F) = A(G)$ and $(a, a) \in R(F)$ iff $(a, a) \in R(G)$, for each $a \in A$. Let us thus suppose wlog. an attack $(a, b) \in R(F) \setminus R(G)$ and consider the AF

$$H = (A \cup \{d, x, y, z\},$$
$$\{(a, a), (b, b), (b, x), (x, a), (a, y), (y, z), (z, a), (d, c) \mid c \in A \setminus \{a, b\}\}).$$

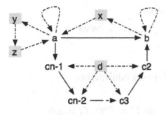

Fig. 1. $F \cup H$

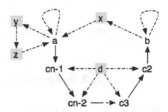

Fig. 2. $G \cup H$

Then, there exists a set $E = \{d, x, z\}$, such that $E \in cf2(F \cup H)$ but $E \notin cf2(G \cup H)$; see also Figures 1 and 2 for illustration. To show that $E \in cf2(F \cup H)$, we first compute $\Delta_{F \cup H, E} = \{c \mid c \in A \setminus \{a, b\}\}$. Thus, in the instance $[[(F \cup H) - \Delta_{F \cup H, E}]]$ we have two $SCCs$ left, namely $C_1 = \{d\}$ and $C_2 = \{a, b, x, y, z\}$. Furthermore, all attacks between the arguments of C_2 are preserved, and we obtain that $E \in mcf([[(F \cup H) - \Delta_{F \cup H, E}]])$, and as it is also conflict-free we have that $E \in cf2(F \cup H)$ as well. On the other hand, we obtain $\Delta_{G \cup H, E} = \{a\} \cup \{c \mid c \in A \setminus \{a, b\}\}$, and the instance $G' = [[(G \cup H) - \Delta_{G \cup H, E}]]$ consists of five $SCCs$, namely $C_1 = \{d\}$, $C_2 = \{b\}$, $C_3 = \{x\}$, $C_4 = \{y\}$ and $C_5 = \{z\}$, with b being self-attacking. Thus, the set $E' = \{d, x, y, z\} \supset E$ is conflict-free in G'. Therefore, we obtain $E \notin mcf(G')$, and hence, $E \notin cf2(G \cup H)$. $F \not\equiv_s^{cf2} G$ follows. $\qquad\square$

In other words, the proof of Theorem 3 shows that no matter which AFs $F \neq G$ are given, we can always construct a framework H such that $cf2(F \cup H) \neq cf2(G \cup H)$. In particular, we can always add new arguments and attacks such that the missing attack in one of the original frameworks leads to different $SCCs(F)$ in the modified ones and therefore to different $cf2$ extensions, when suitably augmenting the two AFs under comparison.

4   Relation between Different Semantics wrt. Strong Equivalence

In this section, we first compare our new results to known ones from [12] in order to get a complete picture about the difference between the most important semantics in terms of strong equivalence and redundant attacks. Then, we restrict ourselves to symmetric AFs [7]. Finally, we provide some preliminary results about local equivalence [12], a relaxation of strong equivalence, where no new arguments are allowed to be raised.

4.1   Comparing Semantics wrt. Strong Equivalence

Together with the results from [12], we now know how to characterize strong equivalence for the following semantics of abstract argumentation: admissible, preferred, complete, grounded, stable, semi-stable, ideal, stage, naive, and $cf2$. Let us briefly, rephrase the results from [12]. First of all, it turns out the concept of the kernel we used for stage semantics (see Definition 4) exactly matches the kernel for stable semantics in [12]. We thus get:

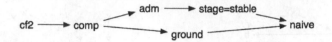

Fig. 3. Full picture of implication in terms of strong equivalence

Corollary 1. *For any AFs F and G, $F \equiv_s^{stable} G$ holds iff $F \equiv_s^{stage} G$ holds.*

Three more kernels for AFs $F = (A, R)$ have been found in [12]:

- $F^{ck} = (A, R \setminus \{(a, b) \mid a \neq b, (a, a) \in R, (b, b) \in R\})$;
- $F^{ak} = (A, R \setminus \{(a, b) \mid a \neq b, (a, a) \in R, \{(b, a), (b, b)\} \cap R \neq \emptyset\})$;
- $F^{gk} = (A, R \setminus \{(a, b) \mid a \neq b, (b, b) \in R, \{(a, a), (b, a)\} \cap R \neq \emptyset\})$.

As in Theorem 2, these kernels characterize strong equivalence in the sense that, for instance, F and G are strongly equivalent wrt. complete semantics, in symbols $F \equiv_s^{comp} G$, if $F^{ck} = G^{ck}$. Similarly, strong equivalence between F and G wrt. grounded semantics ($F \equiv_s^{ground} G$) holds, if $F^{gk} = G^{gk}$. Moreover, $F^{ak} = G^{ak}$ characterizes not only strong equivalence wrt. admissible sets ($F \equiv_s^{adm} G$), but also wrt. preferred, semi-stable, and ideal semantics.

Inspecting the respective kernels provides the following picture, for any AFs F, G:

$$F = G \Rightarrow F^{ck} = G^{ck} \Rightarrow F^{ak} = G^{ak} \Rightarrow F^{sk} = G^{sk}; \quad F^{ck} = G^{ck} \Rightarrow F^{gk} = G^{gk}$$

and thus strong equivalence wrt. *cf2* semantics implies strong equivalence wrt. complete semantics, etc.

To complete the picture, we also note the following observation:

Lemma 4. *If $F^{sk} = G^{sk}$ (resp. $F^{gk} = G^{gk}$), then $cf(F) = cf(G)$.*

Proof. If $F^{sk} = G^{sk}$ then $A = A(F) = A(G)$ and for each $a \in A$, $(a, a) \in R(F)$ iff $(a, a) \in R(G)$. Let $S \in cf(F)$, i.e. for each $a, b \in S$, we have $(a, b) \notin R(F)$. Then, $(a, b) \notin R(F^{sk})$ and by assumption $(a, b) \notin R(G^{sk})$. Now since $a \in S$, we know that $(a, a) \notin R(F)$ and thus $(a, a) \notin R(G)$. Then, $(a, b) \notin R(G^{sk})$ implies $(a, b) \notin R(G)$. Since this is the case for any $a, b \in S$, $S \in cf(G)$ follows. The converse direction as well as showing that $F^{gk} = G^{gk}$ implies $cf(F) = cf(G)$ is by similar arguments. $\square$

We thus obtain that for any AFs F and G, $F \equiv_s^{\sigma} G$ implies $F \equiv_s^{naive} G$ (for $\sigma \in \{stable, stage, ground\}$). Together with our previous observation, a complete picture of implications in terms of strong equivalence wrt. to the different semantics can now be drawn, see Figure 3.

We also observe the following result in case of self-loop free AFs.

Corollary 2. *Strong equivalence between self-loop free AFs F and G wrt. admissible, preferred, complete, grounded, stable, semi-stable, ideal, stage, and cf2 semantics holds, if and only if $F = G$.*

For naive semantics, there are situations where $F \equiv_s^{naive} G$ holds although F and G are different self-loop free AFs. As a simple example consider $F = (\{a, b\}, \{(a, b)\})$ and $G = (\{a, b\}, \{(b, a)\})$. This is due to the fact that naive semantics do not take the orientation of attacks into account. This motivates to compare semantics wrt. strong equivalence for symmetric frameworks.

4.2 Strong Equivalence and Symmetric Frameworks

Symmetric frameworks have been studied in [7] and are defined as AFs (A, R) where R is symmetric, non-empty, and irreflexive. Let us start with a more relaxed such notion. We call an AF (A, R) *weakly symmetric* if R is symmetric (but not necessarily non-empty or irreflexive).

Strong equivalence between weakly symmetric AFs is defined analogously as in Definition 3, i.e. weakly symmetric AFs F and G are strongly equivalent wrt. a semantics σ iff $\sigma(F \cup H) = \sigma(G \cup H)$, for any AF H. Note that we do not restrict here that H is symmetric as well. We will come back to this issue later. When dealing with weakly symmetric AFs, we have two main observations.

First, one can show that for any weakly symmetric AF F, it holds that $F^{sk} = F^{ak}$. This leads to the following result.

Corollary 3. *Strong equivalence between weakly symmetric AFs F and G wrt. admissible, preferred, semi-stable, ideal, stable, and stage semantics coincides.*

Second, we can now give a suitable realization for the concept of a kernel also in terms of naive semantics.

Definition 5. *For an AF $F = (A, R)$, define $F^{nk} = (A, R^{nk})$ where*

$$R^{nk} = R \setminus \{(a, b) \mid a \neq b, (a, a) \in R \text{ or } (b, b) \in R\}.$$

Theorem 4. *For any weakly symmetric AFs F and G, $F \equiv_s^{naive} G$ iff $F^{nk} = G^{nk}$.*

This leads to four different kernels for strong equivalence between weakly symmetric AFs (below, we simplified the kernel F^{gk}, which is possible in this case).

- $F^{ck} = (A, R \setminus \{(a, b) \mid a \neq b, (a, a) \in R, (b, b) \in R\})$;
- $F^{sk} = (A, R \setminus \{(a, b) \mid a \neq b, (a, a) \in R\})$;
- $F^{gk} = (A, R \setminus \{(a, b) \mid a \neq b, (b, b) \in R\})$;
- $F^{nk} = (A, R \setminus \{(a, b) \mid a \neq b, (a, a) \in R \text{ or } (b, b) \in R\})$.

We note that for the *cf2* semantics, strong equivalence between weakly symmetric AFs still requires $F = G$ (basically, this follows from the fact that all steps in the proof of Theorem 3 can be restricted to such frameworks).

Finally, let us consider the case where the test for strong equivalence requires that also the augmented AF is symmetric.

Definition 6. *Two AFs F and G are **symmetric (strong) equivalent** to each other wrt. a semantics σ, iff for each symmetric AF H, $\sigma(F \cup H) = \sigma(G \cup H)$.*

Theorem 5. *Symmetric strong equivalence between symmetric AFs F and G wrt. admissible (resp., preferred, complete, grounded, stable, semi-stable, ideal, stage, naive, and cf2) semantics holds, if and only if $F^{nk} = G^{nk}$.*

4.3 Local Equivalence

In [12], the following relaxation of strong equivalence has also been investigated.

Definition 7. *AFs F and G are* **locally (strong) equivalent** *wrt. a semantics σ, in symbols* $F \equiv_l^\sigma G$, *if for each AF H with* $A(H) \subseteq A(F) \cup A(G)$, $\sigma(F \cup H) = \sigma(G \cup H)$.

In words, the considered augmentations of the compared frameworks must not introduce new arguments. Obviously, for any AFs F and G, we have that $F \equiv_s^\sigma G$ implies $F \equiv_l^\sigma G$ for all semantics σ. The other direction does not hold in general, but for naive semantics, it is clear by Theorem 1 that $F \equiv_s^{naive} G$ if and only if $F \equiv_l^{naive} G$ (similarly, Theorem 5 implies such a collapse for the other semantics in case of symmetric AFs). For stage semantics, strong and local equivalence are different concepts.

Example 4. Consider the frameworks F and G:

By Theorem 2, $F \not\equiv_s^{stage} G$ since adding $H = (\{a, c\}, \{(a, c), (c, a)\})$ yields $stage(F \cup H) = \{\{a\}\}$ and $stage(G \cup H) = \{\{a\}, \{c\}\}$. However, $F \equiv_l^{stage} G$ still holds, since no matter which AF H over arguments $\{a, b\}$ we add to F and G, $F \cup H$ and $G \cup H$ have the same stage extensions, viz. $\{a\}$ in case $(a, a) \notin R(H)$ or $\emptyset$ otherwise.   ◊

As the example shows, in order to get a counterexample for strong equivalence we require a new argument, in case all existing arguments except a are self-attacking.

Theorem 6. *Let an AF* $F = (A, R)$ *be called a-spoiled* $(a \in A)$ *if for each* $b \in A$ *different to a,* $(b, b) \in R$. *We have that for any AFs F and G,* $F \equiv_l^{stage} G$ *iff* $F \equiv_s^{stage} G$ *or both F and G are a-spoiled and* $A(F) = A(G)$.

Proof. If-direction: $F \equiv_s^{stage} G$ implies $F \equiv_l^{stage} G$. Thus, let F and G be a-spoiled AFs with $A(F) = A(G)$. Then, for any H with $A(H) \subseteq A$, $stage(F \cup H) = stage(G \cup H) = \{\{a\}\}$ in case $(a, a) \notin R(H)$; otherwise $stage(F \cup H) = stage(G \cup H) = \{\emptyset\}$.

Only-if direction: For $A(F) \neq A(G)$, $F \not\equiv_l^{stage} G$ by Lemma 2. So suppose $A = A(F) = A(G)$, $F \not\equiv_s^{stage} G$, and F and G are not both a-spoiled for some $a \in A$. Since $F \not\equiv_s^{stage} G$, $F^{sk} \neq G^{sk}$. Thus, let (a, b) be contained in either $R(F^{sk})$ or $R(G^{sk})$. In case $a = b$, we use Lemma 3 and obtain $F \not\equiv_l^{stage} G$. Thus in what follows, we assume $(e, e) \in R(F)$ iff $(e, e) \in R(G)$, for each argument e. Suppose now $a \neq b$ and wlog. let $(a, b) \in R(F^{sk}) \setminus R(G^{sk})$. By definition $(a, a) \notin R(F)$ and by above assumption $(a, a) \notin R(G)$. Thus $(a, b) \notin R(G)$, by definition of the kernel. Since F and G are not both a-spoiled there exists a $c \in A$ $(a \neq c)$ such that $(c, c) \notin R(F) \cap R(G)$. Since we assumed that F and G possess the same self loops, we even have $(c, c) \notin R(F) \cup R(G)$. Now, take $H = \{A, \{(b, b)\} \cup \{(c, d) \mid d \in A \setminus \{a\}\} \cup \{(a, d) \mid d \in A \setminus \{b\}\}\}$. This AF is similar as the one as used in the proof of Theorem 2, but now c is not a new argument. However, we again obtain $\{a\} \in stage(F \cup H) \setminus stage(G \cup H)$.   □

Interestingly, this characterization differs from the one given in [12] for local equivalence wrt. stable semantics (recall that for strong equivalence, stable and stage semantics yield the same characterization). AFs $F = (\{a, b\}, \{(b, b), (b, a)\})$ and $G = (\{b\}, \{(b, b)\})$ are such an example for $F \equiv_l^{stable} G$ and $F \not\equiv_l^{stage} G$.

Local equivalence wrt. *cf2* semantics is more cumbersome, and we leave a full characterization for further work.

5   Conclusion

In this work, we provided characterizations for strong equivalence wrt. stage, naive, and *cf2* semantics, completing the analyses initiated in [12]. Strong equivalence gives a handle to identify redundant attacks. For instance, our results show that an attack (a, b) can be removed from an AF, whenever (a, a) is present in that AF, without changing the stage extensions (no matter how the entire AF looks like). Such redundant attacks exist for all semantics (at least when self-loops are present), except for *cf2* semantics, which follows from our main result, that $F \equiv_s^{cf2} G$ holds, if and only if, $F = G$. In other words, each attack plays a role for the *cf2* semantics. This result also strengthens observations by Baroni *et al.* [4], who claim that *cf2* semantics treats self-loops in a more sensitive way than other semantics. Besides our results for strong equivalence, we also analyzed some variants, namely local and symmetric strong equivalence. Future work includes the investigation of other notions of strong equivalence, which are based, for instance on the set of credulously resp. skeptically accepted arguments, see [12].

Acknowledgments. The authors want to thank the anonymous referees for their valuable comments.

References

1. Amgoud, L., Dimopoulos, Y., Moraitis, P.: Making Decisions through Preference-Based Argumentation. In: Proc. KR 2008, pp. 113–123. AAAI Press, Menlo Park (2008)
2. Amgoud, L., Vesic, S.: Handling Inconsistency with Preference-Based Argumentation. In: Deshpande, A., Hunter, A. (eds.) SUM 2010. LNCS, vol. 6379, pp. 56–69. Springer, Heidelberg (2010)
3. Baroni, P., Giacomin, M.: On Principle-based Evaluation of Extension-based Argumentation semantics. Artif. Intell. 171(10-15), 675–700 (2007)
4. Baroni, P., Giacomin, M., Guida, G.: SCC-Recursiveness: A General Schema for Argumentation Semantics. Artif. Intell. 168(1-2), 162–210 (2005)
5. Caminada, M.: Semi-Stable Semantics. In: Proc. COMMA 2006. FAIA, vol. 144, pp. 121–130. IOS Press, Amsterdam (2006)
6. Caminada, M., Amgoud, L.: On the Evaluation of Argumentation Formalisms. Artif. Intell. 171(5-6), 286–310 (2007)
7. Coste-Marquis, S., Devred, C., Marquis, P.: Symmetric Argumentation Frameworks. In: Godo, L. (ed.) ECSQARU 2005. LNCS (LNAI), vol. 3571, pp. 317–328. Springer, Heidelberg (2005)
8. Dung, P.M.: On the Acceptability of Arguments and its Fundamental Role in Nonmonotonic Reasoning, Logic Programming and n-Person Games. Artif. Intell. 77(2), 321–358 (1995)
9. Dung, P.M., Mancarella, P., Toni, F.: Computing Ideal Sceptical Argumentation. Artif. Intell. 171(10-15), 642–674 (2007)
10. Gaggl, S.A., Woltran, S.: cf2 Semantics Revisited. In: Proc. COMMA 2010. FAIA, vol. 216, pp. 243–254. IOS Press, Amsterdam (2010)
11. Gaggl, S.A., Woltran, S.: Strong Equivalence for Argumentation Semantics based on Conflict-free Sets. Tech. Report DBAI-TR-2011-68, Technische Universität Wien (2011)
12. Oikarinen, E., Woltran, S.: Characterizing Strong Equivalence for Argumentation Frameworks. In: Proc. KR 2010, pp. 123–133. AAAI Press, Menlo Park (2010)
13. Verheij, B.: Two Approaches to Dialectical Argumentation: Admissible Sets and Argumentation Stages. In: Proc. NAIC 1996, pp. 357–368 (1996)

Backing and Undercutting in Defeasible Logic Programming*

Andrea Cohen, Alejandro J. García, and Guillermo R. Simari

Consejo Nacional de Investigaciones Científicas y Técnicas (CONICET)
Artificial Intelligence Research and Development Laboratory (LIDIA)
Department of Computer Science and Engineering (DCIC)
Universidad Nacional del Sur (UNS), Bahía Blanca, Argentina
{ac,ajg,grs}@cs.uns.edu.ar

Abstract. Two important notions within the field of classical argumentation are undercutting defeaters and backings. The former represent an attack to an inference step, and the latter intend to provide defense against this type of attack. Defeasible Logic Programming (DeLP) is a concrete argumentation system that allows to identify arguments whose conclusions or intermediate conclusions are in contradiction, capturing the notion of rebutting defeater. Nevertheless, in DeLP is not possible to represent neither undercutting defeaters nor backings. The aim of this work is to extend the formalism of DeLP to allow attack and support for defeasible rules. Thus, it will be possible to build arguments for representing undercutting defeaters and backings.

1 Introduction

Argumentation is a form of reasoning where a claim is accepted or rejected according to the analysis of the arguments for and against it. The way in which arguments and justifications for a claim are considered allows for an automatic reasoning mechanism where contradictory, incomplete and uncertain information may appear. In the last decade, argumentation has evolved as an attractive paradigm for conceptualizing commonsense reasoning [11]. As a consequence, several abstract argumentation frameworks and Rule-Based Argumentation Systems (RBAS) were formalized (*e. g.* [3,4,1,10,6]). Notwithstanding, a usual critique to some RBAS is that certain reasoning patterns studied in areas like legal reasoning and philosophy, which constitute important contributions to the argumentation community, were simplified or not considered in the systems formal definition. For instance, Pollock [9] stated that reasoning operates in terms of reasons that can be assembled to comprise arguments. He also established that *defeasible reasons* have defeaters, and that there are two kinds of defeaters: *rebutting defeaters* and *undercutting defeaters*. The former attack the conclusion of an inference by supporting the opposite one, while the latter attack the connection between the premises and the conclusion without attacking the conclusion directly. Another important contribution to the argumentation field was proposed by Toulmin [12]. He argued that arguments had to be analyzed using a richer format than the traditional one of formal logic. Whereas a formal logic analysis uses the dichotomy of premises and conclusions, Toulmin proposed

---

* Partially supported by UNS (PGI 24/ZN18) and CONICET (PIP 112-200801-02798).

W. Liu (Ed.): ECSQARU 2011, LNAI 6717, pp. 50–61, 2011.

a model for the layout of arguments that in addition to *data* and *claim* distinguishes four elements: *warrant, backing, rebuttal* and *qualifier*.

In this work, we aim to incorporate some of these elements into a concrete RBAS called Defeasible Logic Programming (DELP) [4]. Briefly, DELP is a formalism that combines argumentation and logic programming. It allows to identify arguments whose conclusions or intermediate conclusions are in contradiction, capturing Pollock's rebutting defeaters. However, as we will show, in DELP is not possible to represent neither Pollock's undercutting defeaters nor Toulmin's backings. Our proposal is partly based on [2], where a preliminary version of Extended Defeasible Logic Programing (E-DELP) was presented. The contribution of this work is to extend the formalism of DELP to capture undercutting defeaters and backings, allowing to build arguments that provide reasons for or against defeasible rules.

The rest of this paper is organized as follows. In Section 2 we present an overview of DELP and we introduce the motivation of this work. In Section 3 the extended representational language of E-DELP is proposed, and in Section 4 the notions of defeasible derivation, argument and defeater are introduced. Finally, in Section 5 some conclusions and related work are commented.

2   Background and Motivation

A short explanation of DELP is included below (see [4] for full details). As in Logic Programming, knowledge in DELP is represented using facts and rules. In addition, DELP has the declarative capability of representing weak information in the form of defeasible rules, and a defeasible argumentation inference mechanism for warranting the entailed conclusions.

A *defeasible logic program* (*de.l.p.*) is a set of facts, strict rules and defeasible rules, defined as follows. *Facts* are ground literals representing atomic information, or the negation of atomic information using *strong negation* "$\sim$" (*e. g.* $\sim electricity$ or day). *Strict Rules* represent non-defeasible information and are denoted $L_0 \leftarrow L_1, \ldots, L_n$, where L_0 is a ground literal and $\{L_i\}_{i>0}$ is a set of ground literals (*e. g.* $\sim night \leftarrow day$). *Defeasible Rules* represent tentative information that may be used if nothing could be posed against it and are denoted $L_0 \prec L_1, \ldots, L_n$, where L_0 is a ground literal and $\{L_i\}_{i>0}$ is a set of ground literals (*e. g.* $light\_on \prec switch\_on$). A defeasible rule "$Head \prec Body$" expresses that "*reasons to believe in the antecedent Body give reasons to believe in the consequent Head*". When required, a defeasible logic program $\mathcal{P}$ is denoted as (Π, Δ) distinguishing the subset Π of facts and strict rules, and the subset Δ of defeasible rules. From a program $\mathcal{P}$ contradictory literals could be derived, since strong negation is allowed in the head of rules.

For the treatment of contradictory knowledge DELP incorporates a defeasible argumentation formalism. This formalism allows the identification of the pieces of knowledge that are in contradiction, and a *dialectical process* is used for deciding which information prevails as warranted. The dialectical process involves the construction and evaluation of arguments that either support or interfere with the query under analysis. Briefly, an *argument* for a literal h, denoted $\langle \mathcal{A}, h \rangle$, is a minimal set $\mathcal{A}$ of defeasible rules such that $\mathcal{A} \cup \Pi$ is non-contradictory and there is a derivation for h from $\mathcal{A} \cup \Pi$.

A literal h is *warranted* if there exists a non-defeated argument $\mathcal{A}$ supporting h. To establish if $\langle \mathcal{A}, h \rangle$ is a non-defeated argument *defeaters* for $\langle \mathcal{A}, h \rangle$ are considered. A detailed explanation of DELP's dialectical process is not included here due to lack of space, but it can be found in [4].

As stated before, in DELP is not possible to represent neither Pollock's undercutting defeaters nor Toulmin's backings. To illustrate this let us consider that Toulmin's warrants are represented through defeasible rules. Since undercutting defeaters attack an inference, they can be thought as reasons against using defeasible rules. Similarly, given that Toulmin's backings provide support for warrants, they can be regarded as reasons for using defeasible rules.

There are different alternatives to express support or attack for a defeasible rule r : "$h \prec b$". One of them consists on placing the defeasible rule r in the head of another rule, whose body would express reasons for or against using the rule r respectively; however, DELP's language imposes the restriction that only literals can appear in the head of a rule. Therefore, to achieve this alternative, the representational language of DELP should be extended. Another possibility could be to associate a special literal (label) to each defeasible rule. In that way, we could identify a defeasible rule by a single literal, and express attack or support for the rule by attacking or supporting its label respectively. Nevertheless, since DELP's language has no consideration for labels, we should find another way to represent rule labels. An attempt to simulate a rule's label could be achieved by placing an additional literal in the rule's body. For instance, for de defeasible rule r introduce above, the resulting rule would be "$h \prec b, r$", where the literal "r" intends to simulate the rule's label. Suppose now that we want to express defeasible reasons against the use of this new rule, as well as defeasible reasons against the literal "b". This could be represented by two defeasible rules "$\sim r \prec f$" and "$\sim b \prec g$" respectively. However, following this representation some problems arise.

One one hand, in DELP there is no distinction between the literals in a rule's body. Hence, it is not possible to distinguish the "simulated label" literal. Furthermore, with that representation we could not distinguish an attack to an ordinary literal from an attack to a rule. For instance, given the defeasible rule "$h \prec b, r$" it would be not possible to distinguish the attacks "$\sim b \prec f$" and "$\sim r \prec g$". On the other hand, if labels were associated to rules in an univocal way (*i. e.* no pair of rules could have the same label) the inclusion of a simulated label in a rule's body might obstruct DELP's comparison process. In particular, it will be no longer possible to use *generalized specificity* [4] as the comparison criterion, since every defeasible rule would have a literal (its simulated label) that does not appear in the body of any other defeasible rule.

The above mentioned issues show clearly that the simulation of rule labels in DELP is not desirable. Consequently, if we wanted to provide attack and support for defeasible rules through any of the two proposed alternatives, we should extend DELP's representational language. In this work, we have chosen to apply the first alternative, incorporating two additional types of rules into the representational language: backing rules and undercutting rules. In that way, the proposed extension will provide the means for representing Pollock's undercutting defeaters and Toulmin's backings.

3   The Extended Representational Language

In this section we will introduce the syntax of Extended Defeasible Logic Programming (E-DELP), which is an extension of the language of DELP defined in [4]. This extended language will allow for the representation of Pollock's undercutting defeaters and Toulmin's backings.

The representational language of E-DELP is defined in terms of five disjoint sets: a set of *facts*, a set of *strict rules*, a set of *defeasible rules*, a set of *backing rules* and a set of *undercutting rules*. A literal "L" is considered to be a ground atom "A" or a negated ground atom "$\sim A$" (where "$\sim$" represents the *strong negation*), and can be used as a fact or as an element of a rule. Facts and strict rules express non-defeasible or indisputable information, whereas the remaining three types of rules express tentative information that may be used if nothing could be posed against it. The representation of facts, strict rules and defeasible rules in E-DELP is the same as in DELP. Hence, given that defeasible rules must have a non-empty body, a defeasible rule with an empty body will be called a *presumption* [7]. In our approach, a presumption "$P \prec$" would expresses that "*there are (defeasible) reasons to believe in P*".

The elements incorporated into the representational language of E-DELP are the backing and undercutting rules, which express support and attack for defeasible rules respectively. The addition of these new types of rules will allow to argue about the defeasible rules application, that is, to discuss whether they should be used or not.

Definition 1 (Backing Rule). *A Backing Rule is an ordered pair, denoted "$[Head] \leftarrow\oplus [Body]$", where $Head$ is a defeasible rule and $Body$ is a finite non-empty set of literals. A backing rule with head $R_{Head} \prec R_{Body}$ and body $\{L_1, \ldots, L_n\}$ can also be written as $[R_{Head} \prec R_{Body}] \leftarrow\oplus [L_1, \ldots, L_n]$ $(n \geq 1)$.*

Definition 2 (Undercutting Rule). *An Undercutting Rule is an ordered pair, denoted "$[Head] \leftarrow\otimes [Body]$", where $Head$ is a defeasible rule and $Body$ is a finite non-empty set of literals. An undercutting rule with head $R_{Head} \prec R_{Body}$ and body $\{L_1, \ldots, L_n\}$ can also be written as $[R_{Head} \prec R_{Body}] \leftarrow\otimes [L_1, \ldots, L_n]$ $(n \geq 1)$.*

Syntactically, the only difference between backing and undercutting rules is the use of $\oplus$ and $\otimes$ respectively; however, these two types of rules are semantically different. A backing rule "$[Head] \leftarrow\oplus [Body]$" would express that "*the antecedent $Body$ gives reasons for using the defeasible rule $Head$*". On the contrary, an undercutting rule "$[Head] \leftarrow\otimes [Body]$" would express that "*the antecedent $Body$ gives reasons against using the defeasible rule $Head$*".

Note that definitions 1 and 2 impose a restriction on the rules appearing in the head of backing and undercutting rules. Consequently, presumptions and strict rules are excluded from being supported or attacked. Strict rules should necessarily be excluded since they provide an unconditional connection between its antecedent and consequent. On the other hand, the reason to exclude presumptions is that backing and undercutting rules respectively support and attack the connection between the antecedent and consequent of a defeasible rule. If we consider a presumption as a defeasible rule with an empty body, the antecedent of the rule is missing and therefore, there is no connection between the antecedent and consequent of the rule.

Definition 3 (Extended Defeasible Logic Program). *An Extended Defeasible Logic Program (e-de.l.p.) $\mathcal{P}$ is a set of facts, strict rules, defeasible rules, backing rules and undercutting rules. When required, we will denote $\mathcal{P}$ as (Π, Δ, Σ) distinguishing the subset Π of facts and strict rules, the subset Δ of defeasible rules and presumptions, and the subset Σ of backing and undercutting rules.*

It is important to remark that the existence of backing and undercutting rules for a defeasible rule in an *e-de.l.p.* is not mandatory. Thus, a defeasible rule without backing rules can be regarded as applicable, since there are not explicit requirements for its use. To illustrate this, let us take into account the nature of Toulmin's warrants. According to Toulmin [12] there may be warrants of different kinds, which provide different degrees of force on the connection between data and claim. In E-DELP, warrants that authorize the acceptance of a claim unequivocally will be represented using strict rules. On the contrary, warrants allowing to draw a conclusion tentatively will be expressed through defeasible rules. For those warrants that could be challenged, backings may not always be explicitly shown. Therefore, when a warrant's backing is absent we will have a defeasible rule without backing rules. Finally, the presence or absence of undercutting rules for a defeasible rule R depends on the existence of conditions of exception for the application of the warrant expressed by R.

Next, we will introduce one of Toulmin's famous examples, which discusses whether Harry is a British subject or not. The claim that Harry is a British subject ("*british_subject*") is supported by the data that Harry was born in Bermuda ("*born_in_bermuda*"). The connection between data and claim is provided by the warrant that a man born in Bermuda will generally be a British subject. The warrant can be supported by the backing that there are certain statutes and other legal provisions to that effect ("*british_parliament_acts*"). Given that the warrant does not have total justifying force, the claim that Harry is a British subject must be qualified: it follows presumably. A possible rebuttal is that both Harry's parents were aliens ("*alien_parents*"). The program $\mathcal{P}_1 = (\Pi_1, \Delta_1, \Sigma_1)$ depicts a possible formulation of this scenario in E-DELP.

Example 1. *A possible formulation of Toulmin's example.*

$$\Pi_1 = \{born\_in\_bermuda,\ british\_parliament\_acts,\ alien\_parents\}$$
$$\Delta_1 = \{\ british\_subject \prec born\_in\_bermuda\ \}$$
$$\Sigma_1 = \left\{ \begin{array}{l} [british\_subject \prec born\_in\_bermuda] \leftarrow\!\oplus [british\_parliament\_acts] \\ [british\_subject \prec born\_in\_bermuda] \leftarrow\!\otimes [alien\_parents] \end{array} \right\}$$

The data "born_in_bermuda", the backing "british_parliament_acts" and the rebuttal "alien_parents" are represented as facts. The warrant is expressed by the defeasible rule "british_subject $\prec$ born_in_bermuda", since reasons to believe that Harry was born in Bermuda give reasons to believe that he is a British subject. The qualifier "presumably" is considered to be implicit in the defeasibility of the rule that represents the warrant. The backing rule "[british_subject $\prec$ born_in_bermuda] $\leftarrow\!\oplus$ [british_parliament_acts]" expresses that the backing "british_parliament_acts" provides support for the warrant. Finally, the undercutting rule "[british_subject $\prec$ born_in_bermuda] $\leftarrow\!\otimes$ [alien_parents]" expresses that the rebuttal "alien_parents" provides a condition of exception for the warrant.

Program rules in E-DELP are ground; however, the use of "schematic rules" with variables is allowed. Following the usual convention [5] schematic rules are instantiated by defining the set of all their ground instances. Given a schematic rule R we will consider $Ground(R)$ as the set of all ground instances of R. Thus, when computing over an e-de.l.p. $\mathcal{P}$, we will consider the set $Ground(\mathcal{P})$ which is the union of the sets $Ground(R)$ for every rule R in $\mathcal{P}$.

Allowing schematic rules into E-DELP provides for a better representation of situations that could be represented without using schematic rules, as well as the representation of new situations. To illustrate the former, recall Toulmin's definition of warrants as 'general, hypothetical statements, which can act as bridges, and authorise the sort of step to which our particular argument commits us' [12](page 98). Therefore, in the example about Harry, the warrant that a man born in Bermuda will generally be a British subject should be applicable not only for Harry, but for *any* man born in Bermuda. Then, the general nature of Toulmin's warrants can be captured in E-DELP by using schematic rules. The e-de.l.p. $\mathcal{P}_2=(\Pi_2, \Delta_2, \Sigma_2)$ provides a new representation for Toulmin's example about Harry, where schematic rules are used.

$$\Pi_2= \{born\_in\_bermuda(harry),\; british\_parliament\_acts,\; alien\_parents(harry)\}$$

$$\Delta_2= \{\; british\_subject(X) \prec born\_in\_bermuda(X) \;\}$$

$$\Sigma_2= \left\{ \begin{array}{l} [british\_subject(X) \prec born\_in\_bermuda(X)] \leftarrow\oplus [british\_parliament\_acts] \\ [british\_subject(X) \prec born\_in\_bermuda(X)] \leftarrow\otimes [alien\_parents(X)] \end{array} \right\}$$

4   Arguments and Defeaters

In this section we will define the notions of defeasible derivation, argument and defeater in E-DELP. First, the notion of defeasible derivation is extended to consider backing rules. Second, we present different types of arguments, distinguishing arguments for literals from arguments for and against using defeasible rules. Finally, a categorization of defeaters is provided, considering rebutting, undercutting and undermining defeaters.

Definition 4 (Defeasible Derivation). *Let* $\mathcal{P}=(\Pi,\Delta,\Sigma)$ *be an e-de.l.p. and L a literal. A defeasible derivation of L from* $\mathcal{S} \subseteq \mathcal{P}$, *denoted* $\mathcal{S}\vdash_{\mathcal{P}} L$, *consists on a finite sequence* $L_1, L_2, \ldots, L_n = L$ *of literals, where each literal* L_i *is in the sequence because:*

(a) *L_i is a fact in Π or a presumption in $\mathcal{S}$,*

(b) *there exists a strict rule in $\mathcal{S}$ with head L_i and body $B_1, \ldots, B_k$, and every B_t $(1 \leq t \leq k)$ is an element L_j of the sequence appearing before L_i $(j < i)$, or*

(c) *there exists a defeasible rule R in $\mathcal{S}$ with head L_i and body $B_1, \ldots, B_k$, where every B_t $(1 \leq t \leq k)$ is an element L_j of the sequence appearing before L_i $(j < i)$, and one of the following conditions holds:*

    i. *there is no backing rule in Σ with head R, or*

    ii. *there is a backing rule in Σ with head R and body $S_1, \ldots, S_m$, and every S_p $(1 \leq p \leq m)$ is an element L_v of the sequence appearing before L_i $(v < i)$.*

Condition (c) states that if there are explicit requirements for using a defeasible rule R they must be satisfied. Note that the set S contains all the elements available for obtaining the derivation; however, when looking for the existence of backing rules for R, the set $\mathcal{P}$ must be taken into account to consider all the constraints for using R. Thus, $\mathcal{P}$ is regarded as the context for the defeasible derivation, denoted as $\vdash_{\mathcal{P}}$.

A defeasible derivation for a literal L is called a *strict derivation* if either L is a fact or every rule used for obtaining the derivation sequence is a strict rule. In a valid E-DELP program $\mathcal{P}=(\Pi,\Delta,\Sigma)$ the subset Π of facts and strict rules must be *non-contradictory*. A set of rules S is contradictory if there exists a defeasible derivation for a pair of complementary literals (wrt. strong negation "$\sim$") from S.

Example 2. *Let $\mathcal{P}_3=(\Pi_3, \Delta_3, \Sigma_3)$ be the following e-de.l.p.:*

$$\Pi_3= \{switch\_on(l),\ night,\ lamp\_in\_room(l,r),\ electricity,\ broken\_lamp(l)\}$$

$$\Delta_3= \left\{ \begin{array}{l} light\_on(X) \prec switch\_on(X) \\ illuminated\_room(X) \prec day \\ \sim illuminated\_room(X) \prec night \\ illuminated\_room(X) \prec night,\ lamp\_in\_room(Y,X),\ light\_on(Y) \end{array} \right\}$$

$$\Sigma_3= \left\{ \begin{array}{l} [light\_on(X) \prec switch\_on(X)] \leftarrow\oplus [electricity] \\ [light\_on(X) \prec switch\_on(X)] \leftarrow\oplus [\sim electricity,\ emergency\_lamp(X)] \\ [light\_on(X) \prec switch\_on(X)] \leftarrow\otimes [\sim electricity] \\ [light\_on(X) \prec switch\_on(X)] \leftarrow\otimes [electricity,\ broken\_lamp(X)] \end{array} \right\}$$

The sequence "electricity, switch_on(l), light_on(l), lamp_in_room(l,r), night, illuminated_room(r)" is a defeasible derivation for the literal "illuminated_room(r)", using the following set of rules in $\mathcal{P}_3$: $\{([light\_on(l) \prec switch\_on(l)] \leftarrow\oplus [electricity]), (light\_on(l) \prec switch\_on(l)), (illuminated\_room(r) \prec night,\ lamp\_in\_room(l,r), light\_on(l))\}$.

The sequence "broken_lamp(l)" is a strict derivation for the literal "broken_lamp(l)", since the literal is a fact in $\mathcal{P}_3$.

Observe that undercutting rules are not used for obtaining defeasible derivations. As will be shown next, they will only be used to build arguments against using defeasible rules. The definition of argument is then extended to consider backing and undercutting rules, when required. In addition, we will distinguish three different types of arguments. The first type regards arguments for literals, while the other two deal with arguments for or against using defeasible rules respectively.

Definition 5 (Claim Argument). *Let $\mathcal{P}=(\Pi,\Delta,\Sigma)$ an e-de.l.p. and h a literal. $\langle \mathcal{A}, h \rangle$ is a claim argument for the literal h, obtained from $\mathcal{P}$, if the following conditions hold:*

(1) $\mathcal{A} \subseteq (\Delta \cup \Sigma)$,
(2) $\Pi \cup \mathcal{A} \vdash_{\mathcal{P}} h$,
(3) $\Pi \cup \mathcal{A}$ is non-contradictory, and
(4) $\mathcal{A}$ is minimal: there is no $\mathcal{B} \subset \mathcal{A}$ satisfying (2) and (3).

Definition 6 (Undercutting Argument). *Let $\mathcal{P}=(\Pi,\Delta,\Sigma)$ be an e-de.l.p. and r defeasible rule. $\langle \mathcal{A}, r \rangle_u$ is an undercutting argument for the defeasible rule r, obtained from $\mathcal{P}$, if $\mathcal{A} = \{[r] \leftarrow\otimes [L_1, \ldots, L_n]\} \cup \mathcal{A}'$ and the following conditions hold:*

(1) $\mathcal{A} \subseteq (\Delta \cup \Sigma)$,

(2) $\Pi \cup \mathcal{A}' \mathrel{\mid\!\sim}_p L_i$ $(1 \leq i \leq n)$,

(3) $\Pi \cup \mathcal{A}'$ *is non-contradictory, and*

(4) $\mathcal{A}'$ *is minimal: there is no* $\mathcal{B} \subset \mathcal{A}'$ *satisfying (2) and (3).*

Definition 7 (Backing Argument). *Let* $\mathcal{P} = (\Pi, \Delta, \Sigma)$ *be an e-de.l.p. and* r *a defeasible rule.* $\langle \mathcal{A}, r \rangle_b$ *is a backing argument for the defeasible rule* r, *obtained from* $\mathcal{P}$, *if* $\mathcal{A} = \{[r] \leftarrow\!\!\oplus [L_1, \dots, L_n]\} \cup \mathcal{A}'$ *and the following conditions hold:*

(1) $\mathcal{A} \subseteq (\Delta \cup \Sigma)$,

(2) $\Pi \cup \mathcal{A}' \mathrel{\mid\!\sim}_p L_i$ $(1 \leq i \leq n)$,

(3) $\Pi \cup \mathcal{A}'$ *is non-contradictory, and*

(4) $\mathcal{A}'$ *is minimal: there is no* $\mathcal{B} \subset \mathcal{A}'$ *satisfying (2) and (3).*

Example 3. *Let* $\mathcal{P}_3$ *be the e-de.l.p. of Example 2. Some arguments obtained from* $\mathcal{P}_3$ *follows.*

The claim argument $\langle \mathcal{A}_1, illuminated\_room(r) \rangle$ *for the literal "illuminated_room(r)",* *where* $\mathcal{A}_1 = \{(illuminated\_room(r) \prec night, \; lamp\_in\_room(l,r), \; light\_on(l)),$ $([light\_on(l) \prec switch\_on(l)] \leftarrow\!\!\oplus [electricity]), \; (light\_on(l) \prec switch\_on(l))\}.$

The undercutting argument $\langle \mathcal{A}_2, light\_on(l) \prec switch\_on(l) \rangle_u$ *for the defeasible rule* *"$light\_on(l) \prec switch\_on(l)$", where* $\mathcal{A}_2 = \{[light\_on(l) \prec switch\_on(l)] \leftarrow\!\!\otimes [electricity,$ $broken\_lamp(l)]\}.$

The backing argument $\langle \mathcal{A}_3, light\_on(l) \prec switch\_on(l) \rangle_b$ *for the defeasible rule* *"$light\_on(l) \prec switch\_on(l)$", where* $\mathcal{A}_3 = \{[light\_on(l) \prec switch\_on(l)] \leftarrow\!\!\oplus [electricity]\}.$

The claim argument $\langle \mathcal{A}_4, \sim illuminated\_room(r) \rangle$ *for the literal "$\sim illuminated\_room(r)$",* *where* $\mathcal{A}_4 = \{\sim illuminated\_room(r) \prec night\}.$

The three argument types are exclusive: an argument of one type is not an argument of any other type. When convenient, we will abstract from an argument's type, referring to it just as an argument (*i. e.* omitting its type). An argument $\langle \mathcal{B}, q \rangle$ is a *sub-argument* of another argument $\langle \mathcal{A}, h \rangle$ if $\mathcal{B} \subseteq \mathcal{A}$. In addition, given an e-de.l.p. $\mathcal{P} = (\Pi, \Delta, \Sigma)$ we will say that two literals h_1 and h_2 *disagree* if the set $\Pi \cup \{h_1, h_2\}$ is contradictory. Next, we will define the notions regarding attack and defeat among arguments.

Definition 8 (Rebutting Attack). *Let* $\langle \mathcal{A}_1, h_1 \rangle$ *be a claim argument and* $\langle \mathcal{A}_2, h_2 \rangle$ *any argument. We say that* $\langle \mathcal{A}_1, h_1 \rangle$ *rebuts* $\langle \mathcal{A}_2, h_2 \rangle$ *at the literal* h *if there exists a claim sub-argument* $\langle \mathcal{A}, h \rangle$ *of* $\langle \mathcal{A}_2, h_2 \rangle$ *such that the literals* h_1 *and* h *disagree.*

Another way of attack takes place when undercutting rules are involved. That is to say, when an argument uses a defeasible rule that another argument states it should not.

Definition 9 (Undercutting Attack). *Let* $\langle \mathcal{A}_1, r \rangle_u$ *be an undercutting argument and* $\langle \mathcal{A}_2, h \rangle$ *any argument. We say that* $\langle \mathcal{A}_1, r \rangle$ *undercuts* $\langle \mathcal{A}_2, h \rangle$ *at the rule* r *if* $r \in \mathcal{A}_2$.

Arguments are built on the basis of premises. These premises are the facts and presumptions that constitute the starting point of an argument. In particular, when attacking a premise, we will say that an *undermining attack* occurs. However, by condition (3) of definitions 5, 6 and 7, no arguments can be built against the strict knowledge. Thus, the only attackable premises of an argument are its presumptions.

Definition 10 (Undermining Attack). *Let* $\langle \mathcal{A}_1, h_1 \rangle$ *be a claim argument and* $\langle \mathcal{A}_2, h_2 \rangle$ *any argument. We say that* $\langle \mathcal{A}_1, h_1 \rangle$ *undermines* $\langle \mathcal{A}_2, h_2 \rangle$ *at the literal* h *if* $\langle \mathcal{A}_1, h_1 \rangle$ *rebuts* $\langle \mathcal{A}_2, h_2 \rangle$ *at the literal* h, *and* h *is a presumption.*

Whenever an argument $\langle \mathcal{A}_1, h_1 \rangle$ attacks another argument $\langle \mathcal{A}_2, h_2 \rangle$, these two arguments are compared to decide which one prevails. Briefly, if $\langle \mathcal{A}_2, h_2 \rangle$ is not better than $\langle \mathcal{A}_1, h_1 \rangle$ wrt. a comparison criterion, we will say that $\langle \mathcal{A}_1, h_1 \rangle$ *defeats* $\langle \mathcal{A}_2, h_2 \rangle$. Similarly to [4], the comparison criterion in E-DELP is modular and thus, it can be selected accordingly to the domain that is being represented. In the following definition we will abstract from the comparison criterion, and we will denote it using "$\succ$".

Definition 11 (Defeat). *Let* $\langle \mathcal{A}_1, h_1 \rangle$ *and* $\langle \mathcal{A}_2, h_2 \rangle$ *be a pair of arguments. We say that* $\langle \mathcal{A}_1, h_1 \rangle$ *defeats* $\langle \mathcal{A}_2, h_2 \rangle$ *if one of the following conditions hold:*

(a) $\langle \mathcal{A}_1, h_1 \rangle$ *rebuts or undermines* $\langle \mathcal{A}_2, h_2 \rangle$ *at the literal* h, *and the attacked sub-argument* $\langle \mathcal{A}, h \rangle$ *of* $\langle \mathcal{A}_2, h_2 \rangle$ *is such that* $\langle \mathcal{A}, h \rangle \nsucc \langle \mathcal{A}_1, h_1 \rangle$,

(b) $\langle \mathcal{A}_1, h_1 \rangle$ *undercuts* $\langle \mathcal{A}_2, h_2 \rangle$ *at the rule* h_1, *and there is no backing sub-argument of* $\langle \mathcal{A}_2, h_2 \rangle$ *for the rule* h_1, *or*

(c) $\langle \mathcal{A}_1, h_1 \rangle$ *undercuts* $\langle \mathcal{A}_2, h_2 \rangle$ *at the rule* h_1, *and the backing sub-argument* $\langle \mathcal{A}, h_1 \rangle$ *of* $\langle \mathcal{A}_2, h_2 \rangle$ *is such that* $\langle \mathcal{A}, h_1 \rangle \nsucc \langle \mathcal{A}_1, h_1 \rangle$.

In particular, we can distinguish among *rebutting defeat*, *undermining defeat* and *undercutting defeat* depending on the type of attack that results in defeat. Note that, unlike other approaches (*e. g.* [14,10]), undercutting attacks in E-DELP will not always succeed as defeats due to the existence of backing arguments.

Whereas an undercutting argument provides reasons against using a defeasible rule, a backing argument gives reasons for using a defeasible rule. Thus, in the case of an undercutting attack we compare the undercutting argument with the corresponding backing sub-argument of the attacked argument, when existing, to decide which one prevails. In that way, backing arguments are intended to defend their associated warrants to prevent an undercutting attack resulting in defeat.

In the following examples we will use *generalized specificity* [4], a comparison criterion that prefers more precise or more direct arguments. When comparing two arguments $\langle \mathcal{A}_1, h_1 \rangle$ and $\langle \mathcal{A}_2, h_2 \rangle$ an analysis of their activation is performed. Briefly, a set of literals S activates an argument $\langle \mathcal{A}, h \rangle$ if the argument can be obtained from the set $\Pi_r \cup S \cup \mathcal{A}$, where Π_r is the set of program strict rules. Then, $\langle \mathcal{A}_1, h_1 \rangle$ is strictly more specific than $\langle \mathcal{A}_2, h_2 \rangle$ (denoted $\langle \mathcal{A}_1, h_1 \rangle \succ \langle \mathcal{A}_2, h_2 \rangle$) if every set of literals H that non-trivially activates $\langle \mathcal{A}_1, h_1 \rangle$ also activates $\langle \mathcal{A}_2, h_2 \rangle$, and there exists a set of literals H' that non-trivially activates $\langle \mathcal{A}_2, h_2 \rangle$ but H' does not activate $\langle \mathcal{A}_1, h_1 \rangle$.

The notion of argument activation can also be applied in E-DELP since, according to the argument's construction, it would require a defeasible derivation for a single literal or a set of literals, depending on the argument's type. The activation of a claim argument $\langle \mathcal{A}, h \rangle$ requires a derivation for the literal h. The activation of a backing argument $\langle \mathcal{A}, r \rangle_b$ with a backing rule "$[r] \leftarrow\oplus [Body]$" requires a derivation for every literal $B_i \in Body$. Similarly, the activation of an undercutting argument $\langle \mathcal{A}, r \rangle_u$ with an undercutting rule "$[r] \leftarrow\otimes [Body]$" requires a derivation for every literal $B_i \in Body$. Taking into account the arguments activation in E-DELP, the *generalized specificity* criterion can be used to decide between conflicting arguments.

Example 4. *Given the arguments of Example 3 we have that* $\langle \mathcal{A}_1, illuminated\_room(r) \rangle$
rebuts $\langle \mathcal{A}_4, \sim illuminated\_room(r) \rangle$. *Moreover, since* $\langle \mathcal{A}_1, illuminated\_room(r) \rangle$ $\succ$
$\langle \mathcal{A}_4, \sim illuminated\_room(r) \rangle$, *the attack results in a rebutting defeat. In addition,*
$\langle \mathcal{A}_2, light\_on(l) \prec switch\_on(l) \rangle_u$ *undercuts* $\langle \mathcal{A}_1, illuminated\_room(r) \rangle$. *To resolve this*
attack we compare the argument $\langle \mathcal{A}_2, light\_on(l) \prec switch\_on(l) \rangle_u$ *and the backing sub-*
argument $\langle \mathcal{A}_3, light\_on(l) \prec switch\_on(l) \rangle_b$ *of* $\langle \mathcal{A}_1, illuminated\_room(r) \rangle$. *Therefore,*
since $\langle \mathcal{A}_2, light\_on(l) \prec switch\_on(l) \rangle_u \succ \langle \mathcal{A}_3, light\_on(l) \prec switch\_on(l) \rangle_b$, *the undercut-*
ting attack results in an undercutting defeat.

The following example illustrates a different scenario for the *e-de.l.p.* of Example 2,
where an undercutting attack fails.

Example 5. *Let* $\mathcal{P}_4 = (\Pi_4, \Delta_3, \Sigma_3)$ *be an e-de.l.p., where* $\Pi_4 = \{switch\_on(l)$, *night,*
lamp_in_room(l, r), $\sim electricity$, *emergency_lamp*$(l)\}$, *and the sets* Δ_3 *and* Σ_3 *corre-*
spond to the e-de.l.p. $\mathcal{P}_3$ *of Example 2. The following arguments can be obtained from* $\mathcal{P}_4$:

The claim argument $\langle \mathcal{A}_5, illuminated\_room(r) \rangle$ *for the literal "illuminated_room(r)",*
where $\mathcal{A}_5$ = $\{([light\_on(l) \prec switch\_on(l)] \leftarrow \oplus [\sim electricity, emergency\_lamp(l)])$,
$(light\_on(l) \prec switch\_on(l))$, $(illuminated\_room(r) \prec night, lamp\_in\_room(l, r)$,
$light\_on(l))\}$.

The undercutting argument $\langle \mathcal{A}_6, light\_on(l) \prec switch\_on(l) \rangle_u$ *for the defeasible rule*
"light_on(l) $\prec$ *switch_on(l)", where*

$$\mathcal{A}_6 = \{[light\_on(l) \prec switch\_on(l)] \leftarrow \otimes [\sim electricity]\}$$

The backing argument $\langle \mathcal{A}_7, light\_on(l) \prec switch\_on(l) \rangle_b$ *for the defeasible rule*
"light_on(l) $\prec$ *switch_on(l)", where*

$$\mathcal{A}_7 = \{[light\_on(l) \prec switch\_on(l)] \leftarrow \oplus [\sim electricity, emergency\_lamp(l)]\}$$

In this case, $\langle \mathcal{A}_6, light\_on(l) \prec switch\_on(l) \rangle_u$ *undercuts* $\langle \mathcal{A}_5, illuminated\_room(r) \rangle$ *at the*
rule "light_on(l) $\prec$ *switch_on(l)"; however, since* $\langle \mathcal{A}_7, light\_on(l) \prec switch\_on(l) \rangle_b$ $\succ$
$\langle \mathcal{A}_6, light\_on(l) \prec switch\_on(l) \rangle_u$, *the undercutting attack does not succeed as a defeat.*

Recall that DELP uses a dialectical process to decide which information prevails as
warranted. Briefly, the process involves the construction of a dialectical tree where every
node in the tree is a defeater for its parent. Once built, the tree is marked: (1) leave
nodes are marked as undefeated and (2) an inner node is marked as undefeated if all its
children are marked as defeated; otherwise it is marked as defeated. Then, a literal h is
warranted from a *de.l.p.* $\mathcal{P}$ if there exists an argument $\langle \mathcal{A}, h \rangle$ obtained from $\mathcal{P}$ such that
$\langle \mathcal{A}, h \rangle$ is the root of a marked dialectical tree and is marked as undefeated (see [4] for
full details). Since the notions of argument and defeat were introduced in E-DELP, we
can use the same dialectical process of DELP to compute the warranted literals from
a program in E-DELP. For instance, in Example 4 $\langle \mathcal{A}_4, \sim illuminated\_room(r) \rangle$ is
defeated by $\langle \mathcal{A}_1, illuminated\_room(r) \rangle$, but $\langle \mathcal{A}_1, illuminated\_room(r) \rangle$ is defeated
by $\langle \mathcal{A}_2, light\_on(l) \prec switch\_on(l) \rangle_u$. Therefore, $\langle \mathcal{A}_4, \sim illuminated\_room(r) \rangle$ is
reinstated and the literal "$\sim illuminated\_room(r)$" is warranted from $\mathcal{P}_3$.

Now that the formalism of E-DELP was introduced, we can show that an *e-de.l.p.*
without undercutting and backing rules is also a *de.l.p.*.

Proposition 1. *An extended defeasible logic program (e-de.l.p.)* $\mathcal{P} = (\Pi, \Delta, \emptyset)$ *is a*
defeasible logic program (de.l.p.) $\mathcal{P}' = (\Pi, \Delta)$.

5 Conclusions and Related Work

In this work an extension of DELP called Extended Defeasible Logic Programming (E-DELP) was proposed, inspired by the work of Pollock [9] and Toulmin [12]. This extension allows to express attack and support for defeasible rules by incorporating undercutting and backing rules respectively. In that way, the extended language of E-DELP enables the representation of Toulmin's backings and Pollock's undercutting defeaters, two notions were absent in the formalism of DELP described in [4]. In addition, DELP programs can also be represented in E-DELP by considering an empty set of backing and undercutting rules Finally, a categorization of attacks and defeats was provided, distinguishing rebutting, undercutting and undermining attack and defeat.

Nute's [8] *Logic for Defeasible Reasoning* (LDR) was the first formalism to provide defeasible reasoning with a simple representational language. In LDR there are three types of rules: strict rules, defeasible rules and defeater rules. The purpose of defeater rules is to account for the exceptions to defeasible rules. Hence, they could be used to simulate undercutting defeaters; however, in contrast to the other two types of rules, defeater rules cannot be used to derive literals. One main difference between Nute's formalism and E-DELP is that in LDR the notion of argument is absent. Thus, the decision between contradictory conclusions in Nute's LDR involves the comparison of pairs of rules with complementary consequents.

In [14] Verheij reconstructed Toulmin's ideas using a theory of dialectical argumentation called DEFLOG [13]. Briefly, its logical language has two connectives $\times$ and $\sim>$. The dialectical negation $\times S$ of a statement S expresses that the statement S is defeated. The primitive implication $\sim>$ is a binary connective used to express that one statement supports another, and only validates modus ponens. One difference between DEFLOG and E-DELP is that DEFLOG is sentence-based while E-DELP is based on logic programming. In addition, arguments in DEFLOG are sets of statements, whereas in E-DELP arguments are sets of specific rules. In DEFLOG is possible to combine and nest the connectives $\times$ and $\sim>$ to obtain more complex statements, allowing to represent both Toulmin's backings and Pollock's undercutting defeaters. Nevertheless, since dialectical negation indicates defeat, an argument for a statement $\times S$ will always be preferred to an argument for a statement S. Thus, in Verheij's approach it is not possible to express attack without defeat. On the contrary, attacks in E-DELP do not always succeed as defeats.

In [10] Prakken introduced ASPIC+, an abstract argumentation framework that instantiates Dung's approach [3], defining the structure of arguments and the nature of Dung's attack relation. Like in ASPIC+, three types of attack to arguments are distinguished in E-DELP (rebutting, undercutting and undermining attack), which lead to three corresponding types of defeat. In addition, ASPIC+ uses an external argument ordering to define preferences among conflicting arguments; however, in some cases the attacks succeed as defeats without considering the preferences defined by the argument ordering. On the contrary, the comparison criterion of E-DELP is used to resolve all attacks. This difference is manifested, for instance, when undercutting attacks occur. In E-DELP an undercutting argument for a defeasible rule is compared to a backing argument for the same rule, when existing, to decide whether this attack results in a defeat or not. On the other hand, since ASPIC+ has no account for backings, an undercutting attack in ASPIC+ will always succeed as a defeat. Prakken also shown that ASPIC+ satisfies the rationality postulates for Rule-Based Argumentation Systems proposed in [1]. The analysis of the properties satisfied by E-DELP, including these rationality postulates, was not included here due to lack of space.

Modgil [6] introduced *Extended Argumentation Frameworks* (EAFs), extending Dung's theory [3] to accommodate defeasible reasoning *about* as well as *with* preference information. In that work, he presented a new attack relation that originates from a preference argument and attacks an attack between the arguments that are the subject of the preference claim. Finally, Modgil defined the evaluation of the justified arguments of EAFs under Dung's semantics, extending the acceptability calculus so that both arguments and attacks need to be reinstated. As stated before, an external comparison criterion is used in E-DELP to define preferences among competing arguments. Notwithstanding, the incorporation of meta-level argumentation reasoning about preferences in the object level is an interesting aspect to take into account for further extensions.

References

1. Caminada, M., Amgoud, L.: On the evaluation of argumentation formalisms. Artificial Intelligence 171(5-6), 286–310 (2007)
2. Cohen, A., Garcia, A.J., Simari, G.R.: Extending DeLP with attack and support for defeasible rules. In: Kuri-Morales, A., Simari, G.R. (eds.) IBERAMIA 2010. LNCS, vol. 6433, pp. 90–99. Springer, Heidelberg (2010)
3. Dung, P.M.: On the acceptability of arguments and its fundamental role in nonmonotonic reasoning, logic programming and n-person games. Artif. Intell. 77(2), 321–358 (1995)
4. García, A.J., Simari, G.R.: Defeasible logic programming: An argumentative approach. Theory and Practice of Logic Programming 4(1-2), 95–138 (2004)
5. Lifschitz, V.: Foundations of logic programs. In: Brewka, G. (ed.) Principles of Knowledge Representation, pp. 69–128. CSLI Pub., Stanford (1996)
6. Modgil, S.: Reasoning about preferences in argumentation frameworks. Artificial Intelligence 173(9-10), 901–934 (2009)
7. Nute, D.: Defeasible reasoning: a philosophical analysis in PROLOG. In: Fetzer, J.H. (ed.) Aspects of Artificial Intelligence, pp. 251–288. Kluwer Academic Pub., Dordrecht (1988)
8. Nute, D.: Defeasible logic. In: Gabbay, D., Hogger, C., Robinson, J.A. (eds.) Handbook of Logic in Artificial Intelligence and Logic Programming, vol. 3, pp. 355–395. Oxford University Press, Oxford (1994)
9. Pollock, J.L.: Defeasible reasoning. Cognitive Science 11(4), 481–518 (1987)
10. Prakken, H.: An abstract framework for argumentation with structured arguments. Argument and Computation 1, 93–124 (2009)
11. Prakken, H., Vreeswijk, G.: Logics for defeasible argumentation. In: Gabbay, D., Guenthner, F. (eds.) Handbook of Philosophical Logic, vol. 4, pp. 218–319. Kluwer Academic Pub., Dordrecht (2002)
12. Toulmin, S.E.: The Uses of Argument. Cambridge University Press, Cambridge (1958)
13. Verheij, B.: Deflog: On the logical interpretation of prima facie justified assumptions. Journal of Logic and Computation 13(3), 319–346 (2003)
14. Verheij, B.: Evaluating arguments based on Toulmin's scheme. Argumentation 19(3), 347–371 (2005)

Arguing with Valued Preference Relations

Souhila Kaci[1] and Christophe Labreuche[2]

[1] Université Lille-Nord de France, Artois
CRIL, CNRS UMR 8188 - IUT de Lens
F-62307, France
kaci@cril.fr

[2] Thales Research & Technology
1 avenue Augustin Fresnel, F91767 Palaiseau Cedex, France
christophe.labreuche@thalesgroup.com

Abstract. Dung's argumentation is based on a Boolean binary defeat relation. Recently, this framework has been extended in order to consider the strength of the defeat relation, i.e., to quantify the degree to which an argument defeats another one. In the extended framework, the defeat relation with varied strength is abstract, i.e., its origin is not known. In this paper, we instantiate argumentation framework with varied-strength defeats by a preference-based argumentation framework with a certainty degree in the preference relation. A potential example of such valued preference relation is when a weight can be assigned to each argument. In this case, we give conditions on the construction of the valued preference relation from the weight. Moreover, we show that the set of conditions in which a defense holds with a valued preference relation is strictly included in the set of conditions in which a defense holds with a Boolean preference relation.

1 Introduction

Argumentation is a framework for reasoning about an inconsistent knowledge. It consists first in constructing the arguments, then identifying the acceptable ones and finally drawing conclusions. Argumentation can be used in many fields of Artificial Intelligence such as autonomous agents, decision making and non-monotonic reasoning. Dung has proposed an abstract argumentation framework that is composed of a set of arguments and a binary relation which is interpreted as a defeat between the arguments [7]. Two basic properties are necessary to define the acceptable arguments: the conflict freeness and the defense of an argument by a set of arguments. These two concepts define the output of an argumentation framework which is a set of sets of arguments that can be accepted together.

Preferences play an important role to solve conflicts between arguments. Preference-based argumentation frameworks are instantiation of Dung's framework in which the defeat relation is derived from an attack relation between arguments and a preference relation over the arguments [16,1,2,4,12,10]. An attack succeeds (thus called a defeat) if the attacked argument is not strictly preferred to the attacking one. However there are situations in which the defense obtained from a preference relation is not discriminative enough, so that some debatable extensions are obtained [6].

W. Liu (Ed.): ECSQARU 2011, LNAI 6717, pp. 62–73, 2011.

Dung's argumentation framework and its various instantiations consider a Boolean defeat relation over arguments. Recently, it has been argued that all defeats have not necessarily the same strength [3,13,14,8,5]. Consequently, Dung's argumentation framework has been extended to consider a defeat relation with varied strengths. Standard defeat (resp. preference) relations are particular cases of relations with varied strength that can take only two values, and will be thus called *Boolean* defeat (resp. preference) relations. One may compute this defeat relation in different ways. In the spirit of Dung's argumentation framework vs. preference-based argumentation framework, we investigate the way where the defeat relation with varied-strength is computed from an attack relation and a valued preference relation referring to the certainty/validity/intensity of preference between arguments. More precisely the larger the preference of an argument a over an argument b, the larger the defeat relation of a on b, if a attacks b. In this paper, we extend the framework proposed in [11] with a detailed analysis. An interesting particular case occurs when the valued preference relation is computed from weights associated with arguments.

An important result in this paper shows that the defense obtained from a valued preference relation is always more discriminative than that obtained from the corresponding Boolean preference relation. Moreover, when the valued preference relation is computed from weights, the discrimination gain is strict when the valued preference relation is not Boolean, under some mild conditions on the valued preference relation. In particular, the problem raised in [6] is solved by our framework. Finally, we give conditions on the construction of the valued preference relation from weights of the arguments. These conditions correspond to strengthening of the previous conditions.

The paper is organized as follows. The next section recalls Dung's argumentation framework, preference-based argumentation framework and argumentation framework with varied-strength defeats. In Section 3 we instantiate argumentation framework with varied-strength defeats by a preference-based argumentation framework where the preference relation is pervaded with intensity degrees. Section 4 compares the defense obtained with Boolean and valued preference relations. In Section 5 we study different ways to compute the intensity of a preference relation from weights associated to arguments. Section 6 surveys related works. Lastly we conclude.

2   Argumentation Theory

Argumentation is a reasoning process based on constructing arguments, determining potential conflicts between arguments and determining acceptable arguments.

2.1   Dung's Argumentation Framework

In Dung's framework [7], arguments are supposed to be given and conflicts between arguments are represented by a binary *defeat* relation (called attack by Dung).

Definition 1. *An argumentation framework (AF) is a tuple $\langle \mathcal{A}, \rightarrow \rangle$ where $\mathcal{A}$ is a finite set (of arguments) and $\rightarrow$ is a binary (defeat) relation defined over $\mathcal{A} \times \mathcal{A}$.*

The outcome of an argumentation framework is a set of sets of arguments, called *extensions*, that are robust against attacks. A set $A \subseteq \mathcal{A}$ *defends* a if $\forall b \in \mathcal{A}$ such that $b \rightarrow$

a, $\exists c \in A$ such that $c \rightarrow b$. A set $A \subseteq \mathcal{A}$ is *conflict-free* if there are no $a, b \in A$ such that $a \rightarrow b$. $A \subseteq \mathcal{A}$ is a *stable extension* if and only if it is conflict-free, it defends all elements in A, and it defeats any argument in $\mathcal{A} \setminus A$. Other semantics of extensions can be found in the literature [7].

2.2 Preference-Based Argumentation Framework

Preference-based argumentation framework [1] is an instantiation of Dung's framework which is based on a binary attack relation between arguments and a preference relation over the set of arguments.

Definition 2. *A preference-based argumentation framework (PAF) is a 3-tuple $\langle \mathcal{A}, \rightsquigarrow , \succ \rangle$ where $\mathcal{A}$ is a set of arguments, $\rightsquigarrow$ is a binary attack relation defined over $\mathcal{A} \times \mathcal{A}$ and $\succ$ is a complete or partial order over $\mathcal{A} \times \mathcal{A}$.*

$\succ$ is called a Boolean preference relation. A PAF $\langle \mathcal{A}, \rightsquigarrow, \succ \rangle$ is said to *represent* $\langle \mathcal{A}, \rightarrow \rangle$ ($\rightarrow$ is then called a *defeat*) iff

$$\forall a, b \in \mathcal{A} : \quad a \rightarrow b \text{ iff } (a \rightsquigarrow b \text{ and } \neg(b \succ a)). \tag{1}$$

The extensions of a PAF are simply the extensions of the AF it represents.

A possible way to construct a preference relation over the set of arguments in preference-based argumentation framework is to start from a set K of weighted propositional logic formulas [16]. An argument is a pair $\langle H, h \rangle$ where (1) h is a formula of the language, (2) H is a consistent subset of K, (3) H entails h and (4) H is minimal (i.e., no strict subset of H satisfies (1), (2) and (3)). One can then construct a function $w : \mathcal{A} \rightarrow [0, 1]$, where $w(\langle H, h \rangle)$ depends on the weights of formulas involved in the support H of the argument.

Definition 3. *A weighted preference-based argumentation framework (WPAF) is a 3-tuple $\langle \mathcal{A}, \rightsquigarrow, w \rangle$ where $\mathcal{A}$ is a set of arguments, $\rightsquigarrow$ is a binary attack relation defined over $\mathcal{A} \times \mathcal{A}$ and $w : \mathcal{A} \rightarrow [0, 1]$ is a weight function over the arguments.*

The WPAF $\langle \mathcal{A}, \rightsquigarrow, w \rangle$ is said to be *represented* by the PAF $\langle \mathcal{A}, \rightsquigarrow, \succ^w \rangle$, where $\succ^w$ is defined by

$$\forall a, b \in \mathcal{A} : \quad a \succ^w b \text{ iff } w(a) > w(b). \tag{2}$$

2.3 Argumentation Framework with Varied-Strength Defeats

Strengths of defeat relations have been incorporated in argumentation framework in two ways: a qualitative relative way by means of a partial preorder [13,14] and a quantitative way by means of a numerical function [8]. We follow the second modeling.

Definition 4. *[8] An argumentation framework with varied-strength defeats (AFV) is a 3-tuple $\langle \mathcal{A}, \rightarrow, VDef \rangle$ where $\langle \mathcal{A}, \rightarrow \rangle$ is a Dung's argumentation framework and VDef is a function defined from $\rightarrow$ to $[0, 1]$.*

For simplicity, we consider the interval $[0, 1]$ but any bipolar linearly ordered scale with top, bottom and neutral elements can be used as well. $VDef(a, b)$ is the degree of credibility of the statement "a defeats b". Values 0, $\frac{1}{2}$ and 1 for $VDef(a,b)$ mean that the validity of the previous statement is certainly false, unknown and certainly true respectively.

In [8] $VDef$ is a function defined on the interval $(0,1]$. In this paper we also need to consider the value 0 for $VDef(.)$ since $VDef(.)$ will be computed from a valued function in the next sections. We say that a *defeats* b w.r.t. $\langle \mathcal{A}, \rightarrowtail, VDef \rangle$ iff $a \rightarrowtail b$ and $VDef(a,b) > 0$. Therefore the two cases where, given $a, b \in \mathcal{A}$, $\neg(a \rightarrowtail b)$ and $(a \rightarrowtail b$ but $VDef(a,b) = 0$) will be considered as equivalent.

Extensions are also defined from the conflict freeness and the notion of defense. Intuitively, when $b \rightarrowtail a$ and $c \rightarrowtail b$, the strength of defeats should play a role in the definition of the defense since c is considered as a "serious" defender of a if the defeat of c on b is at least as strong as the defeat of b on a [13]. Formally, we say that c defends a w.r.t. $\langle \mathcal{A}, \rightarrowtail, VDef \rangle$ against the attack of b (i.e. $b \rightarrowtail a$), if

$$c \rightarrowtail b \text{ and } VDef(c,b) \geq VDef(b,a).$$

The defenses w.r.t. $\langle \mathcal{A}, \rightarrowtail, VDef \rangle$ and $\langle \mathcal{A}, \rightarrowtail \rangle$ are similar, if $VDef$ always equals 1. Regarding the notion of conflict-freeness, $A \subseteq \mathcal{A}$ is α-*conflict-free* w.r.t. $\langle \mathcal{A}, \rightarrowtail, VDef \rangle$ if [8]

$$\sum_{a,b \in A} VDef(a,b) \leq \alpha.$$

When $\alpha = 0$, this definition reduces to conflict-freeness of Dung's framework [13].

3 Valued Preference-Based Argumentation Framework

Consider the following example borrowed from [6].

Example 1. Let $\langle \mathcal{A}, \rightsquigarrow, \succ \rangle$ be a preference-based argumentation framework where $\mathcal{A} = \{a_1, a_2, a_3, a_4\}$, $a_1 \rightsquigarrow a_2$, $a_2 \rightsquigarrow a_1$, $a_1 \rightsquigarrow a_4$, $a_4 \rightsquigarrow a_1$, $a_2 \rightsquigarrow a_3$, $a_3 \rightsquigarrow a_2$, $a_3 \rightsquigarrow a_4$, $a_4 \rightsquigarrow a_3$, $a_2 \succ a_1$ and $a_4 \succ a_3$. $\langle \mathcal{A}, \rightsquigarrow, \succ \rangle$ represents Dung's AF $\langle \mathcal{A}, \rightarrow \rangle$ with $a_2 \rightarrow a_1$, $a_1 \rightarrow a_4$, $a_4 \rightarrow a_1$, $a_2 \rightarrow a_3$, $a_3 \rightarrow a_2$, $a_4 \rightarrow a_3$. There are two stable extensions $A = \{a_1, a_3\}$ and $B = \{a_2, a_4\}$. The authors of [6] have noticed that A should not be considered as a stable extension as each argument in A is less preferred to at least one argument in B (we have $a_2 \succ a_1$ and $a_4 \succ a_3$). Therefore B may be considered as the only stable extension.

One may consider in this example that the defense of A is not so strong. Indeed, considering the defense of $a_1 \in A$, the defeating argument a_2 is strictly preferred to a_1 while there is no evidence of relative strength between a_3 and a_2. On the contrary, the defense of B is stronger. Indeed, considering the defense of $a_2 \in B$, the defender a_4 of a_3 is strictly preferred to a_3 and there is no evidence of relative strength between a_3 and a_2. It is apparent that the defense in PAF is not discriminative enough.

The idea is thus to introduce varied levels of preference between arguments, and in particular to differentiate between strict preference and incomparability. To this end, the Boolean preference relation $\succ$ is refined as a valued preference relation (called fuzzy preference relation in preference modeling) [9]. A *valued preference relation* on $\mathcal{A}$ is a function $P : \mathcal{A} \times \mathcal{A} \rightarrow [0, 1]$. $P(a, b)$ is the degree of credibility of the statement "*a is strictly preferred to b*". $P(a, b) = 1$ means that the previous statement is certainly validated, $P(a, b) = 0$ means that the previous statement is certainly non-validated, and $P(a, b) = \frac{1}{2}$ means that it is unknown whether the previous statement is validated or not. The preference relation over arguments will serve to evaluate how strong a defeat relation is in preference-based argumentation framework. We instantiate AFV with a preference-based argumentation framework where preferences have varied intensity [11].

Definition 5. *A valued preference-based argumentation framework (VPAF) is a 3-tuple $\langle \mathcal{A}, \rightsquigarrow, P \rangle$ where $\mathcal{A}$ is the set of arguments, $\rightsquigarrow$ is a binary attack relation defined over $\mathcal{A} \times \mathcal{A}$ and P is a function defined from $\mathcal{A} \times \mathcal{A}$ to $[0, 1]$.*

The valued preference relation together with the attack relation will serve to compute a varied-strength defeat relation. Intuitively, the more an argument a is preferred to an argument b, the less the strength of the defeat of b on a is. A valued preference-based argumentation framework can represent an argumentation framework with varied-strength defeats. A valued preference-based argumentation framework $\langle \mathcal{A}, \rightsquigarrow, P \rangle$ represents an argumentation framework with varied-strength defeats $\langle \mathcal{A}, \rightarrow, VDef \rangle$ iff $\rightsquigarrow = \rightarrow$ and
$$VDef(a, b) = 1 - P(b, a).$$
Note that the Boolean condition $\neg (b \succ a)$ in Equation (1) is extended into the credibility value $1 - P(b, a)$. The extensions of a valued preference-based argumentation framework are the extensions of the argumentation framework with varied-strength defeats it represents.

Example 2. (Example 1 continued). From $\succ$, we define a valued preference relation $P_{\succ}$ as $P_{\succ}(a, b) = 1$ and $P_{\succ}(b, a) = 0$ if $a \succ b$, and $P_{\succ}(a, b) = \frac{1}{2}$ otherwise. Then we have $VDef(a_4, a_3) = 1$, $VDef(a_3, a_2) = \frac{1}{2}$, $VDef(a_2, a_3) = \frac{1}{2}$, $VDef(a_2, a_1) = 1$, $VDef(a_1, a_4) = \frac{1}{2}$, and $VDef(a_4, a_1) = \frac{1}{2}$. The other values of $VDef$ vanish. Now, $A = \{a_1, a_3\}$ is no more an admissible extension since the defeat of $a_2 \in B = \{a_2, a_4\}$ on $a_1 \in A$ is stronger than the defense that A can give. Hence there remains only one stable extension namely B. The problem raised by this example on the stable extension is thus solved by the introduction of the strength of defeat relations.

It is worth noticing that an argumentation framework with varied-strength defeats represented by a valued preference-based argumentation framework is general and can also capture Dung's argumentation framework represented by a PAF.

Proposition 1. *Let $\langle \mathcal{A}, \rightsquigarrow, \succ \rangle$ be a preference-based argumentation framework and $\langle \mathcal{A}, \rightarrow_1 \rangle$ be the Dung's argumentation framework it represents. Let $\langle \mathcal{A}, \rightsquigarrow, P_{\succ} \rangle$ be a valued preference-based argumentation framework where $P_{\succ}$ is constructed from $\succ$ in the following way: $P_{\succ}(a, b) = 1$ if $a \succ b$ and $P_{\succ}(a, b) = 0$ otherwise. Let $\langle \mathcal{A}, \rightarrow_2, VDef \rangle$ be the argumentation framework with varied-strength defeats represented by $\langle \mathcal{A}, \rightsquigarrow, P_{\succ} \rangle$. Let $\alpha = 0$. Then,*

- *$A \subseteq \mathcal{A}$ defends a w.r.t. $\langle \mathcal{A}, \rightarrow_2, VDef \rangle$ iff A defends a w.r.t. $\langle \mathcal{A}, \rightarrow_1 \rangle$.*
- *$A \subseteq \mathcal{A}$ is α-conflict-free w.r.t. $\langle \mathcal{A}, \rightarrow_2, VDef \rangle$ iff A is conflict-free w.r.t. $\langle \mathcal{A}, \rightarrow_1 \rangle$.*

The proofs are omitted due to the lack of space.

4 Link between the Defense for Boolean and Valued Preference Relations

In Example 1, there are two stable extensions obtained from a Boolean preference relation, and one of them is dominated by the other one and should not be a stable extension. This drawback of PAFs comes from the fact that the concept of a defense with Boolean preference relation is not discriminative enough. In Example 2, we also saw that the defense occurs less often with VPAF compared to PAF. We show that, under a very mild condition on the Boolean and valued preference relations, the defense is more discriminative with VPAF compared to PAF. Then we also prove that the defense occurs in the same situations for VPAF and PAF if and only if the valued preference relation P is somehow Boolean. In other words, whenever there are some real graduality in P, there are strictly less situations of defense in VPAF compared to PAF.

4.1 General Inclusion Result between the Defense for Boolean and Valued Preference Relations

Let $\langle \mathcal{A}, \rightsquigarrow, \succ \rangle$ and $\langle \mathcal{A}, \rightsquigarrow, P \rangle$. We introduce a very weak assumption on the relationship between P and $\succ$ to express that P is a refinement of $\succ$. It simply says that $P(a, b)$ is larger when a is strictly preferred to b than when it is not the case. Formally,

$$\forall a, b, c, d \in \mathcal{A} \ : \ \text{if} \ \ a \succ b \ \text{and} \ \neg(c \succ d) \ \text{then} \ P(a, b) > P(c, d). \tag{3}$$

Henceforth (3) is assumed to hold. Def. def:discri generalizes Ex. 2.

Definition 6. *The defense of the VPAF* $\langle \mathcal{A}, \rightsquigarrow, P \rangle$ *is said to be* more discriminative *than that of the PAF* $\langle \mathcal{A}, \rightsquigarrow, \succ \rangle$ *if*

$$\{(A, a) \mid A \subseteq \mathcal{A}, \ a \in A \ \text{and} \ A \ \text{defends} \ a \ \text{w.r.t.} \ \langle \mathcal{A}, \rightsquigarrow, P \rangle\}$$
$$\subseteq \{(A, a) \mid A \subseteq \mathcal{A}, \ a \in A \ \text{and} \ A \ \text{defends} \ a \ \text{w.r.t.} \ \langle \mathcal{A}, \rightsquigarrow, \succ \rangle\} \tag{4}$$

Proposition 2. *Under (3), the property (4) holds.*

4.2 Case When P Derives from a Valuation on the Arguments

We show that the property (4), where the inclusion is replaced with an equality, holds only when the valued preference relation is Boolean. We restrict ourselves in this section to the case when P derives from a valuation w on the arguments.

Let $\langle \mathcal{A}, \rightsquigarrow, w \rangle$ be a weighted preference-based argumentation framework and $\langle \mathcal{A}, \rightsquigarrow, \succ^w \rangle$ be its associated preference-based argumentation framework according to Equation (2). Let $\langle \mathcal{A}, \rightsquigarrow, P^w \rangle$ be a valued preference-based argumentation framework where P^w depends on w. The simplest expression of P^w is the one that is similar to $\succ^w$:

$$\forall a, b \in \mathcal{A}, P^w_{bool}(a, b) = \begin{cases} 1 & \text{if} \ w(a) > w(b) \\ 0 & \text{if} \ w(a) \leq w(b) \end{cases} \tag{5}$$

We will give other examples of functions P^w in Section 5.

Given w, we compare the defense in both frameworks $\langle \mathcal{A}, \rightsquigarrow, \succ^w \rangle$ and $\langle \mathcal{A}, \rightsquigarrow, P^w \rangle$.

We assume that the strict preference relation P^w can be written from w and a function $p : [0, 1]^2 \rightarrow [0, 1]$ [9]. It is denoted by P_p^w. Formally, we have

$$\forall a, b \in \mathcal{A} \qquad P_p^w(a, b) = p(w(a), w(b)). \tag{6}$$

We assume some monotonicity conditions on p: p is non-decreasing in the first argument and non-increasing in the second argument. Relation (3) corresponds to a reinforcement of the monotonicity conditions:

$$p(\alpha, \beta) > p(\delta, \gamma) \text{ whenever } \alpha > \beta \text{ and } \delta \leq \gamma. \tag{7}$$

Moreover, we have the boundary conditions:

$$p(0, 1) = 0 \text{ and } p(1, 0) = 1. \tag{8}$$

The function p shall be basically continuous in its two coordinates. However, in order to be able to encompass the case of the Boolean case P_{bool}^w, p is allowed to be discontinuous on the diagonal. This leads to the following assumption:

$$(t, v) \mapsto p(t, v) \text{ is continuous except at } t = v. \tag{9}$$

We obtain $VDef_p^w(a, b) = 1 - p(w(b), w(a))$. The situation $p(t, t)$ for $t \in [0, 1]$ corresponds to two arguments a and b having the same weight t. It is worth noticing that the degree of preference of a over b shall not depend on t. Hence, for symmetry reasons, we assume that

$$\forall t, v \in [0, 1] \ , \quad p(t, t) = p(v, v). \tag{10}$$

Due to the possible discontinuity on the diagonal, the previous assumption can be generalized in the following way:

$$\forall t, v \in (0, 1] \ , \quad p(t, t^-) = p(v, v^-), \tag{11}$$

with the notation $p(t, v^-) = \lim_{\varepsilon \to 0 \, , \, \varepsilon > 0} p(t, v - \varepsilon)$.

Among the previous properties, we assume in this section that (6), (8), (9) and (11) hold. The other properties (7) and (10) will be used in Section 5. Lastly, we also assume that the function p is fixed and does not depend on $\mathcal{A}$ nor on w.

Proposition 3. *Let $\langle \mathcal{A}, \rightsquigarrow, w \rangle$ be a weighted preference-based argumentation framework and $\langle \mathcal{A}, \rightsquigarrow, \succ^w \rangle$ be its associated preference-based argumentation framework according to Equation (2). Let $\langle \mathcal{A}, \rightsquigarrow, P_p^w \rangle$ be a valued preference-based argumentation framework where P_p^w is computed from w. Assume that p satisfies (8), (9) and (11). Then*

$$\{(A, a) \mid A \subseteq \mathcal{A}, \ a \in A \text{ and } A \text{ defends } a \text{ w.r.t. } \langle \mathcal{A}, \rightsquigarrow, \succ^w \rangle\} \tag{12}$$
$$= \{(A, a) \mid A \subseteq \mathcal{A}, \ a \in A \text{ and } A \text{ defends } a \text{ w.r.t. } \langle \mathcal{A}, \rightsquigarrow, P_p^w \rangle\}$$

is fulfilled iff $P_p^w = P_{bool}^w$ (see (5)).

5   From a Valuation of Arguments to a Valued Preference Relation

In this section, we study the case where the valued preference relation is computed from weights associated with arguments. We aim to provide some properties which should be satisfied by the valued preference relation.

Let $\langle \mathcal{A}, \rightsquigarrow, w \rangle$ be a WPAF and $\langle \mathcal{A}, \rightsquigarrow, \succ^w \rangle$ be its associated PAF. Let $\langle \mathcal{A}, \rightsquigarrow, P^w \rangle$ be a VPAF where P^w is computed from w. Let us give two examples.

$$\forall a, b \in \mathcal{A}, P_1^w(a, b) = \begin{cases} 1 & \text{if } w(a) > w(b) \\ w(a) - w(b) + 1 & \text{if } w(a) \leq w(b) \end{cases}$$

$$\forall a, b \in \mathcal{A}, P_2^w(a, b) = \begin{cases} 0 & \text{if } w(a) < w(b) \\ w(a) - w(b) & \text{if } w(a) \geq w(b) \end{cases}$$

Given w, we compare the defense in both frameworks $\langle \mathcal{A}, \rightsquigarrow, \succ^w \rangle$ and $\langle \mathcal{A}, \rightsquigarrow, P^w \rangle$ in order to derive the properties that P^w should satisfy.

5.1   Study of P_1^w

Following P_1^w, the strict preference between two arguments a and b is certain as soon as $w(a) > w(b)$. Hence we have $VDef_1^w(a, b) = 1 - P_1^w(b, a) = \max(w(a) - w(b), 0)$.

Let a, b and c be three arguments such that $c \rightsquigarrow b$ and $b \rightsquigarrow a$. We are interested in the defense provided by c in favor of a against b, in the two frameworks $\langle \mathcal{A}, \rightsquigarrow, \succ^w \rangle$ and $\langle \mathcal{A}, \rightsquigarrow, P_1^w \rangle$. Then we have the following five situations (see Table 1):

- *Situation α:* $w(c) < w(b) < w(a)$. There is no defeat of b on a nor that of c on b w.r.t. $\langle \mathcal{A}, \rightsquigarrow, \succ^w \rangle$ (since we have neither $b \rightarrow_w a$ nor $c \rightarrow_w b$) and $\langle \mathcal{A}, \rightsquigarrow, P_1^w \rangle$ (since $VDef_1^w(c, b) = VDef_1^w(b, a) = 0$).
- *Situation β:* $\{w(a), w(c)\} < w(b)$, which is a compact writing of $w(a) < w(b)$ and $w(c) < w(b)$. The defense of c fails w.r.t. both $\langle \mathcal{A}, \rightsquigarrow, \succ^w \rangle$ (since $b \rightarrow_w a$ but $not(c \rightarrow_w b)$) and $\langle \mathcal{A}, \rightsquigarrow, P_1^w \rangle$ (since $VDef_1^w(c, b) = 0$ and $VDef_1^w(b, a) > 0$).
- *Situation γ:* $w(b) < \{w(a), w(c)\}$. Hence c defeats b and b does not defeat a w.r.t. both $\langle \mathcal{A}, \rightsquigarrow, \succ^w \rangle$ (since $not(b \rightarrow_w a)$ but $c \rightarrow_w b$) and $\langle \mathcal{A}, \rightsquigarrow, P_1^w \rangle$ (since $VDef_1^w(c, b) > 0$ and $VDef_1^w(b, a) = 0$).
- *Situation $\delta 1$:* $w(a) < w(b) \ll w(c)$, which means that $w(b) - w(a) < w(c) - w(b)$. c defends a w.r.t. both $\langle \mathcal{A}, \rightsquigarrow, \succ^w \rangle$ (since $b \rightarrow_w a$ and $c \rightarrow_w b$) and $\langle \mathcal{A}, \rightsquigarrow, P_1^w \rangle$ (since $VDef_1^w(c, b) > VDef_1^w(b, a)$).
- *Situation $\delta 2$:* $w(a) \ll w(b) < w(c)$, i.e., $w(b) - w(a) > w(c) - w(b)$. We obtain different conclusions: c defends a w.r.t. $\langle \mathcal{A}, \rightsquigarrow, \succ^w \rangle$ (since $b \rightarrow_w a$ and $c \rightarrow_w b$) but not w.r.t. $\langle \mathcal{A}, \rightsquigarrow, P_1^w \rangle$ (since $VDef_1^w(c, b) < VDef_1^w(b, a)$).

In sum, we get the same conclusions w.r.t. $\langle \mathcal{A}, \rightsquigarrow, \succ^w \rangle$ and $\langle \mathcal{A}, \rightsquigarrow, P_1^w \rangle$, except in situation $\delta 2$. In the latter, the defeat of b on a is large whereas the defeat of c on b is weak. However, the intuition of the Boolean case ($\succ^w$) is valid: c is stronger than both b and a, and, because of that, c deserves to defend a against the attack of b (even if c is just slightly stronger than b). Consequently, we conclude that the expression P_1^w is not suitable.

Table 1. The Yes/No are the answers to the question "Does c defend a against the attack of b?", "−" means that b does not defeat a, the symbol "$\ll$" means that the gap between the compared values is large.

Situation	Condition on w	Defense w.r.t.	
		$\succ^w$	P_2^w
α	$w(c) < w(b) < w(a)$	−	−
β	$\{w(a), w(c)\} < w(b)$	No	No
γ	$w(b) < \{w(a), w(c)\}$	−	−
$\delta 1$	$w(a) < w(b) \ll w(c)$	Yes	Yes
$\delta 2$	$w(a) \ll w(b) < w(c)$	Yes	No

5.2   General Properties of P^w

As in Section 4.2, we assume that the valued preference depends on a function p, and is given by (6). It is denoted by P_p^w. We start from the assumptions (7), (8), (10) introduced in Section 4.2, and the monotonicity conditions on p. Moreover, condition (9) is strengthened. By virtue of Proposition 3, we consider a non-Boolean preference function P_p^w. Hence there shall be no discontinuity of p on the diagonal. Function p shall thus be continuous. We assume that p is fixed and does not depend on $\mathcal{A}$ and w. It is also supposed to satisfy all previous requirements.

The situation δ_2 raised in the study of P_1^w can be formalized in the following way.

> **Unrestricted positive defense (UPD):** Let $\mathcal{A}$ be a set of arguments, and w be a function from $\mathcal{A}$ to $[0, 1]$. Let $\langle \mathcal{A}, \rightsquigarrow, P_p^w \rangle$ be a valued preference-based argumentation framework, where P_p^w is given by (6), representing a VPAF $\langle \mathcal{A}, \rightarrow, VDef_p^w \rangle$. Let $a, b, c \in \mathcal{A}$. If $c \rightsquigarrow b$, $b \rightsquigarrow a$ and $w(c) \geq w(b) \geq w(a)$ then c defends a against b w.r.t. $\langle \mathcal{A}, \rightarrow, VDef_p^w \rangle$.

Consequently, we have the following result.

Proposition 4. *Under* **UPD***, $P_p^w(a, b) = 0$ whenever $w(a) \leq w(b)$.*

From Proposition 4, there is no way the statement "a is strictly preferred to b" (i.e., $P_p^w(a, b) > 0$) is validated when $w(a) \leq w(b)$. One is sure about the credibility of this assertion only when $w(a)$ is significantly larger than $w(b)$. Therefore P_1^w is ruled out and P_2^w is suitable.

Let us assume that $c \rightsquigarrow b$ and $b \rightsquigarrow a$. Considering P_2^w, $VDef_2^w(a, b) = \min(1 + w(a) - w(b), 1)$. We distinguish between five situations (see Table 2):

- *Situation $\alpha 1$:* $w(c) \ll w(b) < w(a)$, i.e., $w(b) - w(c) > w(a) - w(b)$. We obtain different conclusions: b does not defeat a w.r.t. $\langle \mathcal{A}, \rightsquigarrow, \succ^w \rangle$ (since $not(b \rightarrow_w a)$) but c does not defend a w.r.t. $\langle \mathcal{A}, \rightsquigarrow, P_2^w \rangle$ (since $VDef_2(c, b) < VDef_2(b, a)$).
- *Situation $\alpha 2$:* $w(c) < w(b) \ll w(a)$, i.e., $w(b) - w(c) < w(a) - w(b)$. In fact, b does not defeat a w.r.t. $\langle \mathcal{A}, \rightsquigarrow, \succ^w \rangle$ (since $not(b \rightarrow_w a)$) and c defends a w.r.t. $\langle \mathcal{A}, \rightsquigarrow, P_2^w \rangle$ (since $VDef_2(c, b) > VDef_2(b, a)$).
- *Situation β:* $\{w(a), w(c)\} < w(b)$. The defense of c fails w.r.t. both $\langle \mathcal{A}, \rightsquigarrow, \succ^w \rangle$ (since $b \rightarrow_w a$ but $not(c \rightarrow_w b)$) and $\langle \mathcal{A}, \rightsquigarrow, P_2^w \rangle$ (since $VDef_2(c, b) < 1$ and $VDef_2(b, a) = 1$).

Table 2. Case of P_2^w

Situation	Conditions on w	Defense	
		$\succ^w$	P_2^w
$\alpha 1$	$w(c) \ll w(b) < w(a)$	–	No
$\alpha 2$	$w(c) < w(b) \ll w(a)$	–	Yes
β	$\{w(a), w(c)\} < w(b)$	No	No
γ	$w(b) < \{w(a), w(c)\}$	–	Yes
δ	$w(a) < w(b) < w(c)$	Yes	Yes

- *Situation γ:* $w(b) < \{w(a), w(c)\}$. b does not defeat a w.r.t. $\langle \mathcal{A}, \rightsquigarrow, \succ^w \rangle$ (since $not(b \rightarrow_w a)$) and c defends a w.r.t. $\langle \mathcal{A}, \rightsquigarrow, P_2^w \rangle$ (since $VDef_2(c, b) = 1$ and $VDef_2(b, a) < 1$).
- *Situation δ:* $w(a) < w(b) < w(c)$. c defends a w.r.t. both $\langle \mathcal{A}, \rightsquigarrow, \succ^w \rangle$ (since $b \rightarrow_w a$ and $c \rightarrow_w b$) and $\langle \mathcal{A}, \rightsquigarrow, P_2^w \rangle$ (since $VDef_2(c, b) = 1$ and $VDef_2(b, a) = 1$).

Situation α in Table 1 (resp. δ in Table 2) is decomposed into two situations $\alpha 1$ and $\alpha 2$ in Table 2 (resp. $\delta 1$ and $\delta 2$ in Table 1). Having these correspondences in mind, we obtain different results in the two Tables. Situation δ actually follows from **UPD**. In situations $\alpha 1$ and $\alpha 2$, c is weaker than b, and b is weaker than a. Hence the defeats of c over b, and of b over a are weak. In situation $\alpha 1$, $w(c) \ll w(b) < w(a)$ means that c, that is supposed to defend a, is much weaker than a and b. It is thus reasonable that the defense of a by c fails in this case. In situation $\alpha 2$, condition $w(c) < w(b) \ll w(a)$ means that the weight of c is not too far from that of b compared to a. One then may admit that c is sufficiently strong to defend a against b. Hence the results of Table 2 are natural.

6   Related Work

The extension of Dung's argumentation framework with varied-strength defeat relations requires to define the basic notions namely admissibility (and thus defense) and conflict-freeness in the extended framework. We distinguish two main approaches in considering varied strengths of defeat relations. The authors of [8] model the strengths by a numerical function where each defeat relation is associated with a non-zero positive real number representing its strength. The idea is to use the strengths of defeat relations in order to define an inconsistency tolerance degree of a set of arguments. More precisely, a set of arguments is α-conflict-free if the strengths of the defeat relations between arguments of the set sum up to no more than α. Then the authors focus on the complexity of computing the grounded extension in the extended framework and do not explicitly study the incorporation of strengths in admissible extensions. Our framework resembles that framework in the way the strengths are modeled and the conflict-freeness notion is extended. Moreover we give a way to derive the strength of defeat relations from a valued preference relation over the set of arguments. The second approach to consider defeat relations with varied strengths has been proposed in [13,14]. Regarding the extension of the defense, our approach is conceptually similar to the one proposed in [13] but technically different leading to a different definition of admissibility. Our framework is different in the following four points:

1. in [13] the strength of defeat relations is modeled in a relative way by means of a partial/complete preorder on defeat relations. Our framework is more informative since strengths are modeled by a numerical function representing how strong a defeat relation is. The relative order between defeat relations is straightforwardly derived from the function. Note that incomparability between defeat relations can be modeled by a preorder but not by a numerical function; however this has no incidence on the framework as incomparability does not play any role in the definition of defense and admissibility,

2. in [13] four types of defenders have been defined. An argument a is a strong (resp. weak, normal, unqualified) defender of c against b if the defeat of a on b is stronger than (resp. equal to, incomparable to) the defeat of b on c. Then a set of arguments A defends c if each defender of c in A falls in one of the above types. Lastly a set A is admissible if it is conflict-free and defends all its elements. Then admissible extensions are compared w.r.t. to common arguments they contain. In our framework, the defense is more restrictive as we require each defender to be stronger than or equal to the defeater,

3. lastly, in [14] the strength of defeat relations is derived from a Boolean preference relation over arguments. An argument a is called a proper defeater of b if $a \succ b$, otherwise it is called blocking defeater of b. The concept of defense in this framework coincides with our definition of defense when $VDef$ is Boolean. In order to compute the strength of a defense, the authors of [14] computes a 3-valued preference relation over arguments, denoted $pref$, such that $pref(a, b) = 2$ if $a \succ b$, $pref(a, b) = 1$ if a and b have equal preference and $pref(a, b) = 0$ if a and b are incomparable. This function is then used to compute defenders. Let a be defeated by b, which is in turn defeated by c and d. Then c and d are equivalent in force defenders of a if $pref(c, b) = pref(d, b)$. c is a stronger defender than d if $pref(c, b) > pref(d, b)$. Here again sets of conflict-free arguments (a la Dung) are compared w.r.t. the strength of defense they provide to common arguments. In contrast, our framework is more general since we allow for different levels of strict preference between arguments. Moreover the strength of α-conflict-free sets of arguments is evaluated independently of other sets of arguments. Consequently the two frameworks do not lead to the same results. In Example 1, while the above framework returns both A and B as stable extensions, our framework returns B only.

7   Conclusion

Dung's argumentation framework has been extended to incorporate the strength of defeat relations [13,14,8]. While the notion of strengths remains abstract in these works, i.e., their origin is not known, we can imagine different ways to derive them. In this paper we investigated a way to capture the strength of a defeat relation from the validity of preferences over arguments: the larger the preference between two arguments, the larger the defeat. We have shown that the use of valued preference relations allows to (strictly) restrict the situations of defense. When the valued preference relation is constructed from a weight function w defined on the set $\mathcal{A}$ of arguments, a natural property, called **UPD**, comes up. It says that the defense of an argument a by an argument

b against the attack of c shall hold whenever $w(c) \geq w(b) \geq w(a)$. Then we showed that, for every a, b, a is clearly not strictly preferred to b w.r.t. the valued preference relation if $w(a) \leq w(b)$. The motivation for using valued preference relations instead of Boolean ones is that the defense is not discriminative enough in the latter case.

As a future work we intend to incorporate valued preference relations in other preference-based argumentation frameworks such as [4,15] and study their properties in that frameworks.

References

1. Amgoud, L., Cayrol, C.: Inferring from inconsistency in preference-based argumentation frameworks. International Journal of Approximate Reasoning 29(2), 125–169 (2002)
2. Amgoud, L., Cayrol, C., LeBerre, D.: Comparing arguments using preference orderings for argument-based reasoning. In: ICTAI 1996, pp. 400–403 (1996)
3. Barringer, H., Gabbay, D.M., Woods, J.: Temporal dynamics of support and attack networks: From argumentation to zoology. In: Hutter, D., Stephan, W. (eds.) Mechanizing Mathematical Reasoning. LNCS (LNAI), vol. 2605, pp. 59–98. Springer, Heidelberg (2005)
4. Bench-Capon, T.J.M.: Persuasion in practical argument using value-based argumentation frameworks. Journal of Logic and Computation 13(3), 429–448 (2003)
5. Cayrol, C., Devred, C., Lagasquie-Schiex, M.C.: Acceptability semantics accounting for strength of attacks in argumentation. In: ECAI, pp. 995–996 (2010)
6. Dimopoulos, Y., Moraitis, P., Amgoud, L.: Extending argumentation to make good decisions. In: Rossi, F., Tsoukias, A. (eds.) ADT 2009. LNCS, vol. 5783, pp. 225–236. Springer, Heidelberg (2009)
7. Dung, P.M.: On the acceptability of arguments and its fundamental role in non-monotonic reasoning, logic programming and n-person games. Artificial Intelligence 77, 321–357 (1995)
8. Dunne, P.E., Hunter, A., McBurney, P., Parsons, S., Wooldridge, M.: Inconsistency tolerance in weighted argument systems. In: AAMAS, pp. 851–858 (2009)
9. Fodor, J., Roubens, M.: Fuzzy preference modelling and multi-criteria decision aid. Kluwer Academic Publisher, Boston (1994)
10. Kaci, S.: Refined preference-based argumentation frameworks. In: COMMA, pp. 299–310 (2010)
11. Kaci, S., Labreuche, C.: Preference-based argumentation framework with varied-preference intensity. In: ECAI, pp. 1003–1004 (2010)
12. Kaci, S., van der Torre, L.: Preference-based argumentation: Arguments supporting multiple values. International Journal of Approximate Reasoning 48, 730–751 (2008)
13. Martínez, D.C., García, A.J., Simari, G.R.: An abstract argumentation framework with varied-strength attacks. In: KR, pp. 135–144 (2008)
14. Martínez, D.C., García, A.J., Simari, G.R.: Strong and weak forms of abstract argument defense. In: COMMA, pp. 216–227 (2008)
15. Modgil, S.: Reasoning about preferences in argumentation frameworks. Artificial Intelligence 173(9-10), 901–934 (2009)
16. Simari, G.R., Loui, R.P.: A mathematical treatment of defeasible reasoning and its implementation. Artificial Intelligence 53, 125–157 (1992)

Arguing about the Trustworthiness of the Information Sources

Serena Villata[1], Guido Boella[1], Dov M. Gabbay[2], and Leendert van der Torre[3]

[1] Dipartimento di Informatica, Universita di Torino
{villata,guido}@di.unito.it
[2] King's College, London
dov.gabbay@kcl.ac.uk
[3] CSC, University of Luxembourg
leendert@vandertorre.com

Abstract. Trust minimizes the uncertainty in the interactions among the information sources. To express the possibly conflicting motivations about trust and distrust, we reason about trust using argumentation theory. First, we show how to model the sources and how to attack untrustworthy sources. Second, we provide a focused representation of trust about the sources in which trust concerns not only the sources but also the information items and the relation with other information.

1 Introduction

Trust is a mechanism for managing uncertain information in decision making, considering the information sources. In their interactions, the information sources have to reason whether they should trust or not the other sources, and on the extent to which they trust those other sources. This is important, for example, in medical contexts, where doctors have to inform the patient of the pro and con evidence concerning some treatment, or in decision support systems where the user is not satisfied by an answer without explanations.

In this paper, a way to deal with the conflicts about trust using Dung's abstract argumentation framework is presented. A Dung argumentation framework [5] can be instantiated by the arguments and attacks defined by a knowledge base, and the knowledge base inferences are defined in terms of the claims of the justified arguments, e.g., the ASPIC+ framework instantiates Dung frameworks with accounts of the structure of arguments, the nature of attack and the use of preferences [14]. In such a kind of framework, arguments are instantiated by sentences of a single knowledge base, without reference to the information sources. The following example presents an informal dialogue illustrating conflicts about trust among the sources and the pieces of information they provide:

- *Witness1: I suspect that the man killed his boss in Rome. (a)*
- *Witness1: But his car was broken, thus he could not reach the crime scene. (b)*
- *Witness2: Witness1 is a compulsive liar. (c)*
- *Witness3: I repaired the suspect's car at 12pm of the crime day. (d)*
- *Witness4: I believe that Witness3 is not able to repair that kind of car. (e)*

W. Liu (Ed.): ECSQARU 2011, LNAI 6717, pp. 74–85, 2011.

- *Witness5: The suspect has another car. (f)*
- *Witness6: Witness5 saw that the suspect parked 2 cars in my underground parking garage 3 weeks ago. (g)*
- *Witness2: Witness5 was on holidays 3 weeks ago. (h)*

To deal with the dimension of conflict in handling trust, we propose to use argumentation theory, since it is a mechanism to reason about conflicting information. The problem is that it is difficult to formalize the example above with sentences from a single knowledge base only, e.g., to model it in ASPIC+ style instantiated argumentation. We address the following research question: *How to instantiate abstract argumentation with a finite number of knowledge bases instead of a single one, in which the pieces of information are thus indexed by the source?* This breaks down into the following subquestions:

1. How to represent the information sources and attack their trustworthiness?
2. How to represent pro and con evidence, as done in Carneades [7]?
3. How to attack the sources' trustworthiness about single information items?

To answer the research question we propose meta-argumentation [8,11,2]. Meta-argumentation provides a way to instantiate abstract arguments, i.e., abstract arguments are treated as meta-arguments. It allows us not only to reason about arguments such as sentences from a knowledge base indexed by the information source, but also to introduce in the framework other instances like arguments about the trustworthiness of sources. The advantage is that we do not extend Dung's framework in order to introduce trust but we instantiate his theory with meta-arguments. We do not claim that argumentation is the only way to model trust, but we underline that, when the sources argue, they are strongly influenced by the trustworthiness relationships with the other sources.

The paper follows the research questions. After a brief introduction on meta-argumentation, we describe our model for representing the information sources and the focused trust relationships involving them.

2   Meta-Argumentation

A Dung-style argumentation framework AF [5] is a tuple $\langle A, \rightarrow \rangle$ where A is a set of elements called *arguments* and $\rightarrow$ is a binary relation called *attack* defined on $A \times A$. A Dung's semantics consists of a set of arguments that does not contain an argument attacking another argument in the set. For more details, see [5].

Like Baroni and Giacomin [1] we use a function $\mathcal{E}$ mapping an argumentation framework $\langle A, \rightarrow \rangle$ to its set of extensions, i.e., to a set of sets of arguments. Since they do not give a name to the function $\mathcal{E}$, and it maps argumentation frameworks to the set of accepted arguments, we call $\mathcal{E}$ the *acceptance function*.

Definition 1. *Let $\mathcal{U}$ be the universe of arguments. An acceptance function $\mathcal{E}$:* $2^{\mathcal{U}} \times 2^{\mathcal{U} \times \mathcal{U}} \rightarrow 2^{2^{\mathcal{U}}}$ *is a partial function which is defined for each argumentation framework $\langle A, \rightarrow \rangle$ with finite $A \subseteq \mathcal{U}$ and $\rightarrow \subseteq A \times A$, and maps an argumentation framework $\langle A, \rightarrow \rangle$ to sets of subsets of A: $\mathcal{E}(\langle A, \rightarrow \rangle) \subseteq 2^{A}$.*

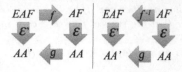

Fig. 1. The meta-argumentation methodology

Meta-argumentation instantiates Dung's theory with meta-arguments, such that *Dung's theory is used to reason about itself* [3]. Meta-argumentation is a particular way to define mappings from argumentation frameworks to extended argumentation frameworks: arguments are interpreted as meta-arguments, of which some are mapped to "argument a is accepted", $acc(a)$, where a is an abstract argument from the extended argumentation framework EAF. Moreover, auxiliary arguments are introduced to represent, for example, attacks, so that, by being arguments themselves, they can be attacked or attack other arguments. The meta-argumentation methodology is summarized in Figure 1.

The function f assigns to each argument a in the EAF, a meta-argument "argument a is accepted" in the basic argumentation framework. The function f^{-1} instantiates an AF with an EAF. We use Dung's acceptance functions $\mathcal{E}$ to find functions $\mathcal{E}'$ between EAFs and the acceptable arguments AA' they return. The accepted arguments of the meta-argumentation framework are a function of the EAF $AA' = \mathcal{E}'(EAF)$. The transformation function consists of two parts: the function f^{-1}, transforming an AF to an EAF, and a function g which transforms the acceptable arguments of the AF into acceptable arguments of the EAF. Summarizing $\mathcal{E}' = \{(f^{-1}(a), g(b)) \mid (a, b) \in \mathcal{E}\}$ and $AA' = \mathcal{E}'(EAF) = g(AA) = g(\mathcal{E}(AF)) = g(\mathcal{E}(f(EAF)))$.

The first step of the meta-argumentation approach is to define the set of EAFs. The second step consists of defining flattening algorithms as a function from this set of EAFs to the set of all basic AF: $f : EAF \to AF$. The inverse of the flattening is the instantiation of the AF. See [2,16] for further details. We define an EAF as a set of partial argumentation frameworks of the sources $\langle A, \langle A_1, \to_1 \rangle, \dots, \langle A_n, \to_n \rangle, \to \rangle$.

Definition 2. *An extended argumentation framework EAF is a tuple $\langle A, \langle A_1, \to_1 \rangle, \dots, \langle A_n, \to_n \rangle, \to \rangle$ where for each source $1 \leq i \leq n$, $A_i \subseteq A \subseteq \mathcal{U}$ is a set of arguments, $\to$ is a binary attack relation on $A \times A$, and $\to_i$ is a binary relation on $A_i \times A_i$. The universe of meta-arguments is $MU = \{acc(a) \mid a \in \mathcal{U}\} \cup \{X_{a,b}, Y_{a,b} \mid a, b \in \mathcal{U}\}$, where $X_{a,b}, Y_{a,b}$ are the meta-arguments corresponding to the attack $a \to b$. The flattening function f is given by $f(EAF) = \langle MA, \longmapsto \rangle$, where MA is the set of meta-arguments and $\longmapsto$ is the meta-attack relation. For a set of arguments $B \subseteq MU$, the unflattening function g is given by $g(B) = \{a \mid acc(a) \in B\}$, and for sets of subsets of arguments $AA \subseteq 2^{MU}$, it is given by $g(AA) = \{g(B) \mid B \in AA\}$.*

Given an acceptance function $\mathcal{E}$ for an AF, the extensions of accepted arguments of an EAF are given by $\mathcal{E}'(EAF) = g(\mathcal{E}(f(EAF)))$. The derived acceptance function $\mathcal{E}'$ of the EAF is thus $\mathcal{E}' = \{(f^{-1}(a), g(b)) \mid (a, b) \in \mathcal{E}\}$. We say *that the source i provides evidence in support of argument a when $a \in A_i$, and the source supports the attack $a \to b$ when $a \to b \in \to_i$.*

Note that the union of all the A_i does not produce A because A contains also those arguments which are not supported by the sources, and are just "put on the table". Definition 3 presents the instantiation of a basic AF as a set of partial argumentation frameworks of the sources using meta-argumentation.

Definition 3. *Given an $EAF = \langle A, \langle A_1, \to_1 \rangle, \ldots, \langle A_n, \to_n \rangle \rangle$ where for each source $1 \leq i \leq n$, $A_i \subseteq A \subseteq \mathcal{U}$ is a set of arguments, $\to \subseteq A \times A$, and $\to_i \subseteq A_i \times A_i$ is a binary relation over A_i. $MA \subseteq MU$ is $\{acc(a) \mid a \in A_1 \cup \ldots \cup A_n\}$, and $\longmapsto \subseteq MA \times MA$ is a binary relation on MA such that: $acc(a) \longmapsto X_{a,b}, X_{a,b} \longmapsto Y_{a,b}, Y_{a,b} \longmapsto acc(b)$ if and only if there is a source $1 \leq i \leq n$ such that $a, b \in A_i$ and $a \to b \in \to_i$.*

Intuitively, the $X_{a,b}$ auxiliary argument means that the attack $a \to b$ is "inactive", and the $Y_{a,b}$ auxiliary argument means that the attack is "active". An argument of an EAF is acceptable iff it is acceptable in the flattened AF.

3   Modelling Trust in Meta-Argumentation

A number of authors have highlighted that the definition of trust is difficult to pin down precisely, thus in the literature there are numerous distinct definitions. Castelfranchi and Falcone [4] define trust as "*a mental state, a complex attitude of an agent x towards another agent y about the behaviour/action a relevant for the goal g*" while Gambetta [6] states that "*trust is the subjective probability by which an individual A expects that another individual B performs a given action on which its welfare depends*". Common elements are a consistent degree of uncertainty and conflicting information associated with trust. In this paper, we do not refer to the actions of the sources, but we provide a model for representing the conflicts the sources have to deal with trust. We follow Liau [9] where the influence of trust on the assimilation of information into the source's mind is considered: "*if agent i believes that agent j has told him the truth on p and he trusts the judgement of j on p, then he will also believe p*". Extending the model by introducing goals to model the former two definitions is left for future work.

3.1   Information Sources

The reason why abstract argumentation is not suited to model trust is that an argument, if it is not attacked by another acceptable argument, is considered acceptable. This prevents us from modeling the situation where, for an argument to be acceptable, it must be related to some sources which provide the evidence for such an argument to be accepted. Without an explicit representation of the sources, it becomes impossible to talk about trust: the argument can only be attacked by conflicting information, but it cannot be made unacceptable due to the lack of trust in the source.

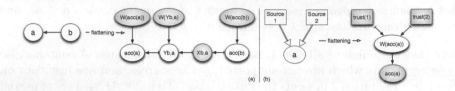

Fig. 2. (a) arguments and attack without evidence, (b) multiple evidence

Thus a challenge is how to model evidence, where sources are a particular type of evidence. Arguments needing evidence are well known in legal argumentation, where the notion of burden of proof has been introduced [7]. Meta-argumentation provides a means to model burden of proof in abstract argumentation without extending argumentation. The idea is to associate to each argument $a \in A$ put on the table, which is represented by means of meta-argument $acc(a)$, an auxiliary argument $W_{acc(a)}$ attacking it. Being auxiliary this argument is filtered out during the unflattening process. This means that without further information, just as being put on the table, argument a is not acceptable since it is attacked by the acceptable argument $W_{acc(a)}$ and there is no evidence defending it against this "default" attack, as visualized in Figure 2.a for arguments a and b. This evidence is modeled by arguments which attack auxiliary argument $W_{acc(a)}$, thus reinstating meta-argument $acc(a)$. Attacks are modeled as arguments as well. For each auxiliary argument $Y_{a,b}$, representing the activation of the attack, we associate an auxiliary argument $W_{Y_{a,b}}$.

Each argument a in the sources' mind is supported by means of an attack on $W_{acc(a)}$. Sources are introduced in the meta-argumentation framework under the form of meta-arguments "*source i is trustable*", $trust(i)$, for all the sources i. We represent the fact that one or more information sources support the same argument by letting them attack the same $W_{acc(a)}$ auxiliary argument. An example of multiple evidence is depicted in Figure 2.b. In the figures, we represent the information sources as boxes, and the arguments as circles where grey arguments are the acceptable ones. As for arguments, an attack to become active needs some trusted agent.

We have now to discuss which semantics we adopt for assessing the acceptability of the arguments and the sources. For example, suppose that two sources claim they are each untrustworthy. What is the extension? We adopt admissibility based semantics. We do not ask for completeness because if one wants to know whether a particular argument is acceptable, the whole model is not needed, just the part related to this particular argument is needed.

We extend the EAF proposed in Definition 2 by adding evidence provided by information sources and second-order attacks, such as attacks from an argument or attacks to another attack. For more details about second-order attacks in meta-argumentation, see [11,2]. The unflattening function g and the acceptance function $\mathcal{E}'$ are defined as above.

Definition 4. *An EAF with second-order attacks is a tuple* $\langle A, \langle A_1, \rightarrow_1, \rightarrow_1^2 \rangle$, $\ldots, \langle A_n, \rightarrow_n, \rightarrow_n^2 \rangle, \rightarrow \rangle$ *where for each source* $1 \leq i \leq n$, $A_i \subseteq A \subseteq \mathcal{U}$ *is a set* *of arguments, $\to \subseteq A \times A$, $\to_i$ is a binary relation on $A_i \times A_i$, $\to_i^2$ is a binary relation on $(A_i \cup \to_i) \times \to_i$.*

Definition 5 presents the instantiation of an EAF with second-order attacks as a set of partial frameworks of the sources using meta-argumentation.

Definition 5. *Given an $EAF = \langle A, \langle A_1, \to_1, \to_1^2 \rangle \ldots, \langle A_n, \to_n, \to_n^2 \rangle, \to \rangle$, the set of meta-arguments MA is $\{trust(i) \mid 1 \le i \le n\} \cup \{acc(a) \mid a \in A_1 \cup \ldots \cup A_n\} \cup \{X_{a,b}, Y_{a,b} \mid a,b \in A_1 \cup \ldots \cup A_n\} \cup \{W_{acc(a)} \mid a \in A_1 \cup \ldots \cup A_n\}$ and $\longmapsto \subseteq MA \times MA$ is a binary relation on MA such that:*

- *$acc(a) \longmapsto X_{a,b}$ iff $a,b \in A_i$ and $a \to_i b$, and $X_{a,b} \longmapsto Y_{a,b}$ iff $a,b \in A_i$ and $a \to_i b$, and $Y_{a,b} \longmapsto acc(b)$ iff $a,b \in A_i$ and $a \to_i b$, and*
- *$trust(i) \longmapsto W_{acc(a)}$ iff $a \in A_i$, and $W_{acc(a)} \longmapsto acc(a)$ iff $a \in A$, and*
- *$trust(i) \longmapsto W_{Y_{a,b}}$ iff $a,b \in A_i$ and $a \to_i b$, and $W_{Y_{a,b}} \longmapsto Y_{a,b}$ iff $a,b \in A_i$ and $a \to_i b$, and*
- *$acc(a) \longmapsto X_{a,b \to c}$ iff $a,b,c \in A_i$ and $a \to_i^2 (b \to_i c)$, and $X_{a,b \to c} \longmapsto Y_{a,b \to c}$ iff $a,b,c \in A_i$ and $a \to_i^2 (b \to_i c)$, and $Y_{a,b \to c} \longmapsto Y_{b,c}$ iff $a,b,c \in A_i$ and $a \to_i^2 (b \to_i c)$, and*
- *$Y_{a,b} \longmapsto Y_{c,d}$ iff $a,b,c \in A_i$ and $(a \to_i b) \to_i^2 (c \to_i d)$.*

We say that source i is trustworthy when meta-argument $trust(i)$ is acceptable, and we say that i provides evidence in support of argument a (or attack $a \to b$) when $a \in A_i$ (when $a \to b \in \to_i$), and $trust(i) \longmapsto W_{acc(a)}$ ($trust(i) \longmapsto W_{Y_{a,b}}$).

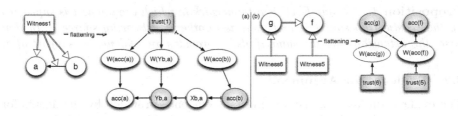

Fig. 3. Introducing (a) the sources, (b) evidence for the arguments

Example 1. Consider the informal dialogue in the introduction. We represent the sources in the argumentation framework, as shown in Figure 3.a. Witness1 proposes a and b and the attack $a \to b$. Using the flattening function of Definition 5, we add meta-argument $trust(1)$ for representing Witness1 in the framework and we add meta-arguments $acc(a)$ and $acc(b)$ for the arguments of Witness1. Witness1 provides evidence for these arguments, and the attack $b \to a$ by attacking the respective auxiliary arguments W. In the remainder of the paper, we model the other conflicts highlighted in the dialogue.

Let $trust(i)$ be the information source i and $acc(a)$ and $Y_{a,b}$ the argument a_i and the attack $a \to_i b$ respectively, as defined in Definitions 2 and 3. $trust(i)$ can provide evidence for $acc(a)$ and $Y_{a,b}$. Sources can attack other sources as well as their arguments and attacks. With a slight abuse of notation, we write

$a \in \mathcal{E}'(EAF)$, even if the latter is a set of extensions, with the intended meaning that a is in some of the extensions of $\mathcal{E}'$. We now provide some properties of our model. Some of the proofs are omitted due to the lack of space.

Proposition 1. *Assume admissibility based semantics, if an argument $a \in A$ is not supported by evidence, i.e., $a \notin A_i$ for all i, then a is not accepted, $a \notin \mathcal{E}'(EAF)$.*

Proof. We prove the contrapositive: if argument a is accepted, then argument a is supported. Assume argument a is accepted. Then auxiliary argument $W_{acc(a)}$ is rejected due to the conflict-free principle. Meta-argument $acc(a)$ is defended, so $W_{acc(a)}$ is attacked by an accepted argument using admissible semantics. Auxiliary argument $W_{acc(a)}$ can only be attacked by meta-argument $trust(i)$. We conclude that a is supported.

Proposition 1 is strengthened to Proposition 2.

Proposition 2. *If an argument a is not supported, $a \notin A_i$, then the extensions $\mathcal{E}'(EAF)$ are precisely the same as the extensions of the $AF = \langle A, \rightarrow \rangle$ in which $a \notin A$, and the attacks on a or from a do not exist, i.e., $b \rightarrow a \notin \rightarrow$ and $a \rightarrow c \notin \rightarrow$.*

Proposition 3. *If an attack $a \rightarrow b$ is not supported, i.e., $a \rightarrow b \notin \rightarrow_i$, then the extensions $\mathcal{E}'(EAF)$ are precisely the same as the extensions of the $AF = \langle A, \rightarrow \rangle$, in which the attack does not exist, $a \rightarrow b \notin \rightarrow$.*

Proposition 4. *Assume EAF is a framework in which argument a is supported by the trustworthy source i, and there is another trustworthy source j. In that case, the extensions are the same if also j provides an evidence in support of a.*

3.2 Evidence for Arguments

The evidence in favor of the arguments is evidence provided by the agents for the arguments/attacks they propose. At the meta-level, this is modeled as an attack from meta-argument $trust(i)$ to W auxiliary arguments. However, there are other cases in which more evidence is necessary to support the acceptability of an argument. Consider the case of Witness1. His trustworthiness is attacked by Witness2. What happens to the evidence provided by Witness1? Since the source is not trustworthy then it cannot provide evidence. Meta-argument $trust(1)$ becomes not acceptable and the same happens to all its arguments and attacks. What is needed to make them acceptable again is more evidence. This evidence can be provided under the form of another argument which reinstates the acceptability of these information items.

Definition 5 allows only the sources to directly provide evidence for the information items. As for Witness5 and Witness6 in the dialogue, sources can provide evidence also by means of other arguments. This cannot be represented using Definition 5, this is why we need to extend it with an evidence relation $\rightsquigarrow$ representing evidence provided under the form of arguments for the information items of the other sources.

Definition 6. *An EAF with evidence* $TEAF^2 = \langle A, \langle A_1, \rightarrow_1, \rightarrow_1^2, \looparrowright_1 \rangle, \ldots,$ $\langle A_n, \rightarrow_n, \rightarrow_n^2, \looparrowright_n \rangle, \rightarrow \rangle$ *where* $\looparrowright_i$ *is a binary relation on* $A_i \times A_j$ *and the set of meta-arguments* MA *is* $\{trust(i) \mid 1 \leq i \leq n\} \cup \{acc(a) \mid a \in A_1 \cup \ldots \cup A_n\} \cup \{X_{a,b}, Y_{a,b} \mid a, b \in A_1 \cup \ldots \cup A_n\} \cup \{W_{acc(a)} \mid a \in A_1 \cup \ldots \cup A_n\}$ *and* $\longmapsto \subseteq MA \times MA$ *is a binary relation on* MA *such that hold the conditions of Definition 5, and:* $acc(a) \longmapsto W_{acc(b)}$ *iff* $a, b \in A_i$ *and* $a \looparrowright_i b$, *and* $W_{acc(b)} \longmapsto acc(b)$ *iff* $b \in A$ *and* $a \looparrowright_i b$. *We say that a source* j *supports the evidence provided by other sources to argument* a *when* $a \notin A_j, b \in A_j$, *and* $acc(b) \longmapsto W_{acc(a)}$.

The following properties hold for Definition 6.

Proposition 5. *If there are multiple arguments* $a_1 \in A_1, \ldots, a_n \in A_n$ *providing evidence for an argument* $b \in A_k$ *(or an attack), and there are no attacks on the arguments,* $c_1 \rightarrow a_1 \not\rightarrow_1, \ldots, c_n \rightarrow a_n \not\rightarrow_n$, *then* b *(or the attack) is accepted,* $b \in \mathcal{E}'(EAF)$, *iff at least one of the sources is trustworthy, i.e.,* $trust(j) \in \mathcal{E}(f(EAF))$ *with* $j \in 1, \ldots, n$.

Proposition 6. *Suppose two sources* i *and* j *provide evidence for the same argument* a, *i.e.,* $a \in A_i$ *and* $a \in A_j$, *then it is the same whether a source* k *supports the evidence provided by* i *or* j, *i.e.,* $b \in A_k$ *and* $acc(b) \longmapsto W_{acc(a)}$.

Example 2. Consider the dialogue in the introduction. Argument g by Witness6 is an evidence for argument f by Witness5. This evidence is expressed in meta-argumentation in the same way as evidence provided by the sources, such as an attack to $W_{acc(f)}$ attacking $acc(f)$. In this case, it is meta-argument $acc(g)$ which attacks $W_{acc(f)}$, as visualized in Figure 3.b.

3.3   Focused Trust Relationships

In our model, trust is represented *by default* as the absence of an attack towards the sources or towards the information items and as the presence of evidence in favor of the pieces of information. On the contrary, the distrust relationship is modeled as a lack of evidence in support of the information items or as a direct attack towards the sources and their pieces of information.

In the informal dialogue, Witness2 attacks the trustworthiness of Witness1 as a credible witness. In this way, she is attacking each argument and attack proposed by Witness1. Witness4, instead, is not arguing against Witness3 but she is arguing against the attack $d \rightarrow b$ as it is proposed by Witness3. Finally, for Witness2 the untrustworthiness of Witness6 is related only to the argument g. We propose a focused view of trust in which the information sources may be attacked for being untrustworthy or for being untrustworthy only concerning a particular argument or attack. Definition 7 presents an EAF in which a new relation DT between sources is given to represent distrust.

Definition 7. *A trust-based extended argumentation framework* $TEAF$ *is a tuple* $\langle A, \langle A_1, \rightarrow_1, \rightarrow_1^2, \looparrowright_1, DT_1 \rangle, \ldots, \langle A_n, \rightarrow_n, \rightarrow_n^2, \looparrowright_n, DT_n \rangle, \rightarrow \rangle$ *where for each source* $1 \leq i \leq n$, $A_i \subseteq A \subseteq \mathcal{U}$ *is a set of arguments,* $\rightarrow \subseteq A \times A$, $\rightarrow_i \subseteq A_i \times A_i$

is a binary relation, $\rightarrow_i^2$ is a binary relation on $(A_i \cup \rightarrow_i) \times \rightarrow_i$, $\looparrowright_i$ is a binary relation on $A_i \times A_j$ and $DT \subseteq A_i \times \vartheta$ is a binary relation such that $\vartheta = j$ or $\vartheta \in A_j$ or $\vartheta \in \rightarrow_j$.

Definition 8 shows how to instantiate an *EAF* enriched with a distrust relation with meta-arguments. In particular, the last three points model, respectively, a distrust relationship towards an agent, towards an argument and towards an attack. The unflattening function g and the acceptance function $\mathcal{E}'$ are defined as above.

Definition 8. *Given a TEAF $= \langle A, \langle A_1, \rightarrow_1, \rightarrow_1^2, \looparrowright_1, DT_1 \rangle, \ldots, \langle A_n, \rightarrow_n, \rightarrow_n^2, \looparrowright_n, DT_n \rangle, \rightarrow \rangle$, see Definition 7, the set of meta-arguments MA is $\{trust(i) \mid 1 \le i \le n\} \cup \{acc(a) \mid a \in A_1 \cup \ldots \cup A_n\} \cup \{X_{a,b}, Y_{a,b} \mid a, b \in A_1 \cup \ldots \cup A_n\} \cup \{W_{acc(a)} \mid a \in A_1 \cup \ldots \cup A_n\}$ and $\longmapsto \subseteq MA \times MA$ is a binary relation on MA such that hold the conditions of Definitions 5 and 6, and:*

- *$acc(a) \longmapsto X_{a,b}$ iff $a, b \in A_i$ and $a \rightarrow_i b$, and $X_{a,b} \longmapsto Y_{a,b}$ iff $a, b \in A_i$ and $a \rightarrow_i b$, and $Y_{a,b} \longmapsto acc(b)$ iff $a, b \in A_i$ and $a \rightarrow_i b$, and*
- *$trust(i) \longmapsto X_{trust(i), W_{acc(a)}}$ iff $a \in A_i$, and $X_{trust(i), W_{acc(a)}} \longmapsto Y_{trust(i), W_{acc(a)}}$ iff $a \in A_i$, and $Y_{trust(i), W_{acc(a)}} \longmapsto W_{acc(a)}$ iff $a \in A_i$, and $W_{acc(a)} \longmapsto acc(a)$ iff $a \in A_i$, and*
- *$trust(i) \longmapsto X_{trust(i), W_{Y_{a,b}}}$ iff $a, b \in A_i$ and $a \rightarrow_i b$, and $X_{trust(i), W_{Y_{a,b}}} \longmapsto Y_{trust(i), W_{Y_{a,b}}}$ iff $a, b \in A_i$ and $a \rightarrow_i b$, and $Y_{trust(i), W_{Y_{a,b}}} \longmapsto W_{Y_{a,b}}$ iff $a, b \in A_i$ and $a \rightarrow_i b$, and $W_{Y_{a,b}} \longmapsto Y_{a,b}$ iff $a, b \in A_i$ and $a \rightarrow_i b$, and*
- *$trust(i) \longmapsto W_{acc(a)}$ iff $a \in A_i$ and $a DT_i trust(j)$, and $W_{acc(a)} \longmapsto acc(a)$ iff $a \in A$ and $a DT_i trust(j)$, and $acc(a) \longmapsto X_{acc(a), trust(j)}$ iff $a \in A_i$ and $a DT_i trust(j)$, and $X_{acc(a), trust(j)} \longmapsto Y_{acc(a), trust(j)}$ iff $a \in A_i$ and $a DT_i trust(j)$, and $Y_{acc(a), trust(j)} \longmapsto trust(j)$ iff $a \in A_i$ and $a DT_i trust(j)$, and*
- *$trust(i) \longmapsto W_{acc(a)}$ iff $a \in A_i, b \in A_j$ and $a DT_i b$, and $W_{acc(a)} \longmapsto acc(a)$ iff $a \in A, b \in A_j$ and $a DT_i b$, and $acc(a) \longmapsto X_{acc(a), Y_{trust(j)}, W_{acc(b)}}$ iff $a \in A_i, b \in A_j$ and $a DT_i b$, and $X_{acc(a), Y_{trust(j)}, W_{acc(b)}} \longmapsto Y_{acc(a), Y_{trust(j)}, W_{acc(b)}}$ iff $a \in A_i, b \in A_j$ and $a DT_i b$, and $Y_{acc(a), Y_{trust(j)}, W_{acc(b)}} \longmapsto Y_{trust(j), W_{acc(b)}}$ iff $a \in A_i, b \in A_j$ and $a DT_i b$, and*
- *$trust(i) \longmapsto W_{acc(a)}$ iff $a \in A_i, b, c \in A_j$ and $a DT_i(b \rightarrow_j c)$, and $W_{acc(a)} \longmapsto acc(a)$ iff $a \in A, b, c \in A_j$ and $a DT_i(b \rightarrow_j c)$, and $acc(a) \longmapsto X_{acc(a), Y_{trust(j)}, W_{Y_{b,c}}}$ iff $a \in A_i, b, c \in A_j$ and $a DT_i(b \rightarrow_j c)$, and $X_{acc(a), Y_{trust(j)}, W_{Y_{b,c}}} \longmapsto Y_{acc(a), Y_{trust(j)}, W_{Y_{b,c}}}$ iff $a \in A_i, b, c \in A_j$ and $a DT_i(b \rightarrow_j c)$, and $Y_{acc(a), Y_{trust(j)}, W_{Y_{b,c}}} \longmapsto Y_{trust(j), W_{Y_{b,c}}}$ iff $a \in A_i, b, c \in A_j$ and $a DT_i(b \rightarrow_j c)$.*

We say that a source i is untrustworthy when there is an attack from an argument $a_j \in A_j$ to i, $a_j DT_j i$. We say that an argument $a_i \in A_i$ or attack $a \rightarrow_i b \in \rightarrow_i$ is untrustworthy when there is an attack from an argument $a_j \in A_j$ to a_i or $a \rightarrow_i b$, $a_j DT_j a_i$ or $a_j DT_j(a \rightarrow_i b)$.

Proposition 7. *Assume that source i is the only source providing evidence for argument $a \in A_i$ and attack $c \rightarrow b \in \rightarrow_i$, and assume admissibility based semantics. If the information source i is considered to be untrustworthy, then a and $c \rightarrow b$ are not acceptable.*

Proof. We prove the contrapositive: if the arguments and attacks supported by an information source i are acceptable then the information source i is considered to be trustworthy. Assume the source supports argument a and the attack $c \rightarrow b$ and assume that this argument and this attack are acceptable. Then auxiliary arguments $W_{acc(a)}$ and $W_{Y_{c,b}}$ are rejected due to the conflict-free principle. Meta-arguments $acc(a)$ and $Y_{c,b}$ are defended, thus $W_{acc(a)}$ and $W_{Y_{c,b}}$ are attacked by an acceptable argument, using admissible semantics. We assumed that this argument and this attack have no other evidence, so auxiliary arguments $W_{acc(a)}$ and $W_{Y_{c,b}}$ can only be attacked by meta-argument $trust(i)$. Since they are attacked by an acceptable argument, we conclude that the source i is acceptable.

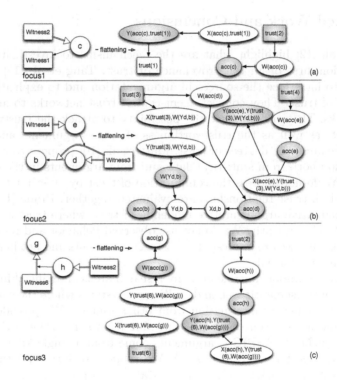

Fig. 4. Focused trust in argumentation

Example 3. Figure 4.a shows that Witness2 attacks the trustworthiness of Witness1 by means of argument c. In meta-argumentation, we have that $trust(2)$ provides evidence for $acc(c)$ by attacking meta-argument $W_{acc(c)}$ and, with meta-arguments X, Y, it attacks $trust(1)$. This means that if Witness1 is untrustworthy then each of his arguments and attacks cannot be acceptable either, if there is no more evidence. The set of acceptable arguments for the meta-argumentation framework is $\mathcal{E}(f(focus1)) = \{trust(2), acc(c), Y_{acc(c),trust(1)}\}$. In Figure 4.b-c, instead, the attack is directed against a precise information item provided by the source. In particular, Witness4 attacks the attack $d \rightarrow b$ of Witness3. This is achieved in meta-argumentation by means of an attack from meta-argument $acc(e)$, for which $trust(4)$ provides evidence, to the attack characterized by auxiliary argument $Y_{d,b}$. The set of acceptable arguments is $\mathcal{E}(f(focus2)) = \{trust(4), trust(3), acc(d), acc(e), acc(b), Y_{acc(e), Y_{trust(3)}, W_{Y_{b,d}}}, W_{Y_{d,b}}\}$. Witness3's attack $d \rightarrow b$ is evaluated as untrustworthy by Witness4 and thus it is not acceptable. Finally, Witness2 evaluates Witness6 as untrustworthy concerning argument g. In meta-argumentation, $trust(2)$, by means of meta-argument $acc(h)$, attacks meta-argument $acc(g)$ proposed by $trust(6)$. The set of acceptable arguments is $\mathcal{E}(f(focus3)) = \{trust(2), trust(6), acc(h), Y_{acc(h), Y_{trust(6)}, W_{acc(g)}}, W_{acc(g)}\}$.

4 Related Work and Conclusions

Parsons et al. [12] highlight what are the mechanisms to investigate through argumentation, first of all the provenance of trust. Tang et al. [15] present a framework to introduce the sources in argumentation and to explicitly express the degrees of trust. They connect agent-centric trust networks to argumentation networks. They do not have the possibility to attack the trustworthiness of the agents as well as the trustworthiness of single arguments and attacks. We do not express the degrees of trust. Matt et al. [10] propose to construct a belief function both from statistical data and from arguments in the context of contracts. We do not address the computation of trust by an evaluator in isolation, instead all trust relationships are evaluated together. Prade [13] presents a bipolar qualitative argumentative modeling of trust where trust and distrust are assessed independently. We do not use observed behavior and reputation to compute trust and we are interested in abstract arguments and not in arguments with an abductive format.

Trust plays an important role in many research areas of artificial intelligence, particularly in the semantic web and multiagent systems where the sources have to deal with conflicting information from other sources. We provide a model where the information sources can be introduced into the framework. In argumentation systems as ASPIC+, arguments come from a single knowledge base and they have the form $\langle\{p, p \rightarrow q\}, q\rangle$. We propose to introduce the sources, e.g., $\langle\{1 : p, 2 : p \rightarrow q\}, 2 : q\rangle$, by instantiating abstract argumentation with the different knowledge bases of the sources using meta-argumentation. In our model, arguments need to be supported in order to be accepted. Furthermore, the trustworthiness of the sources can be attacked directly, or the attack can be focused on single arguments or attacks.

We address several issues as future research. First, there is a bidirectional link between the source and its input: the provided data is more or less believable on the basis of the source's trustworthiness, but there is feedback such that the invalidation of the data feeds back on the sources' credibility [4]. Second, we will investigate two dimensions of trust that have to be independently evaluated such as the sincerity/credibility of a source and the competence of a source.

References

1. Baroni, P., Giacomin, M.: On principle-based evaluation of extension-based argumentation semantics. Artif. Intell. 171(10-15), 675–700 (2007)
2. Boella, G., Gabbay, D.M., van der Torre, L., Villata, S.: Meta-argumentation modelling I: Methodology and techniques. Studia Logica 93(2-3), 297–355 (2009)
3. Boella, G., van der Torre, L., Villata, S.: On the acceptability of meta-arguments. In: Procs. of IAT, pp. 259–262. IEEE, Los Alamitos (2009)
4. Castelfranchi, C., Falcone, R.: Trust Theory: A Socio-Cognitive and Computational Model. Wiley, Chichester (2010)
5. Dung, P.M.: On the acceptability of arguments and its fundamental role in non-monotonic reasoning, logic programming and n-person games. Artif. Intell. 77(2), 321–357 (1995)
6. Gambetta, D.: Can we trust them? Trust: Making and Breaking Cooperative Relations, 213–238 (1990)
7. Gordon, T.F., Prakken, H., Walton, D.: The Carneades model of argument and burden of proof. Artif. Intell. 171(10-15), 875–896 (2007)
8. Jakobovits, H., Vermeir, D.: Robust semantics for argumentation frameworks. J. Log. Comput. 9(2), 215–261 (1999)
9. Liau, C.-J.: Belief, information acquisition, and trust in multi-agent systems – A modal logic formulation. Artif. Intell. 149(1), 31–60 (2003)
10. Matt, P.-A., Morge, M., Toni, F.: Combining statistics and arguments to compute trust. In: Procs. of AAMAS, pp. 209–216 (2010)
11. Modgil, S., Bench-Capon, T.: Metalevel argumentation. Technical report (2009), www.csc.liv.ac.uk/research/techreports/techreports.html
12. Parsons, S., McBurney, P., Sklar, E.: Reasoning about trust using argumentation: A position paper. In: Procs. of ArgMAS (2010)
13. Prade, H.: A qualitative bipolar argumentative view of trust. In: Prade, H., Subrahmanian, V.S. (eds.) SUM 2007. LNCS (LNAI), vol. 4772, pp. 268–276. Springer, Heidelberg (2007)
14. Prakken, H.: An abstract framework for argumentation with structured arguments. Technical Report UU-CS-2009-019, Utrecht University (2009)
15. Tang, Y., Cai, K., Sklar, E., McBurney, P., Parsons, S.: A system of argumentation for reasoning about trust. In: Procs. of EUMAS (2010)
16. Villata, S.: Meta-Argumentation for Multiagent Systems: Coalition Formation, Merging Views, Subsumption Relation and Dependence Networks. PhD thesis, University of Turin (2010)

Two Roles of Preferences in Argumentation Frameworks

Leila Amgoud and Srdjan Vesic

Institut de Recherche en Informatique de Toulouse
118, route de Narbonne,
31062 Toulouse Cedex 9 France
{amgoud,vesic}@irit.fr

Abstract. In this paper, we show that preferences intervene twice in argumentation frameworks: i) to compute standard solutions (i.e. extensions), and ii) to refine those solutions (i.e. to return only the preferred extensions). The two roles are independent and obey to distinct postulates. After introducing and studying the postulates, we provide an example of a formal framework which models the two roles and verifies all the proposed postulates.

1 Introduction

An argumentation framework (AF) consists of a set of arguments and an attack relation among them. Arguments are evaluated using an acceptability semantics. This amounts to compute acceptable sets of arguments, called *extensions*. The attack relation is at the heart of all existing semantics. An attacker wins unless the attacked argument is defended by "good" arguments. Since [12], it has been argued that arguments may not have the same strength and some of them may be stronger or preferred to others. Consequently, several attempts were made in the literature for taking into account preferences in argumentation frameworks (e.g. [2,5]). Besides, preferences play a key role in non-monotonic reasoning [6]. They are used in order to narrow down the number of possible belief sets of a base theory. To say it differently, from a given base theory, a first set of *standard* solutions (belief sets) is computed, then a subset of those solutions (called *preferred* solutions) is chosen on the basis of available preferences. Thus, preferences refine the standard solutions.

In this paper, we show that preferences intervene twice in an argumentation framework. They are mandatory for: i) computing its standard solutions, and then ii) for narrowing the number of those solutions. The first role of preferences may not take into account *all* the available preferences. It focuses only on those which conflict with the attacks; such attacks are said *critical*. The idea is that an attack may fail if the attacked argument is stronger than its attacker. Ignoring this issue may lead to counter-intuitive standard solutions. This first role has largely been discussed in existing literature while the second role has only been pointed out recently in [7]. However, the difference between the two roles is still obscure. In this paper, we clarify the distinction between the two roles, and show that they are completely independent since none of them can be modeled by the other one. We propose postulates that should be satisfied by any

W. Liu (Ed.): ECSQARU 2011, LNAI 6717, pp. 86–97, 2011.
© Springer-Verlag Berlin Heidelberg 2011

preference-based argumentation framework. Some of them concern the first role while others concern the refinement role. Those postulates confirm again that the two roles are different. We propose a particular framework in which both roles are modeled. The properties of this framework are investigated.

The paper is structured as follows: We start by recalling Dung's AF, then we discuss informally the two roles of preferences. The two next sections propose postulates that guide the definition of 'approaches' for each role. Then, we propose a particular framework which considers both roles. Before concluding, we compare our contribution with existing works. Due to lack of space, the proofs are not included in the paper.

2 Basics of Argumentation

The abstract argumentation framework proposed in [8] consists of a set of arguments and an attack relation between them.

Definition 1. *An* argumentation framework *(AF) is a pair* $\mathcal{F} = (\mathcal{A}, \mathcal{R})$*, where* $\mathcal{A}$ *is a set of arguments and* $\mathcal{R} \subseteq \mathcal{A} \times \mathcal{A}$ *is an attack relation. For two arguments* a *and* b*, the notation* $a\mathcal{R}b$ *means that* a attacks b.

Different *acceptability semantics* for evaluating arguments were proposed in the same paper [8]. Each semantics amounts to define sets of acceptable arguments, called *extensions*. An extension represents a coherent position, thus it should be conflict-free and defends its elements. Formally:

Definition 2. *Let* $\mathcal{F} = (\mathcal{A}, \mathcal{R})$ *be an AF,* $\mathcal{E} \subseteq \mathcal{A}$ *and* $a \in \mathcal{A}$*.*

  – $\mathcal{E}$ *is* conflict-free *iff* $\nexists a, b \in \mathcal{E}$ *s.t.* $a\mathcal{R}b$*.*
  – $\mathcal{E}$ *defends* a *iff* $\forall b \in \mathcal{A}$ *s.t.* $b\mathcal{R}a$*,* $\exists c \in \mathcal{E}$ *s.t.* $c\mathcal{R}b$*.*

The following definition recalls the main semantics proposed in [8].

Definition 3. *Let* $\mathcal{F} = (\mathcal{A}, \mathcal{R})$ *be an AF and* $\mathcal{E} \subseteq \mathcal{A}$*.*

  – $\mathcal{E}$ *is an* admissible *set iff it is conflict-free and defends all its elements.*
  – $\mathcal{E}$ *is a* complete *extension iff it is admissible and contains all arguments it defends.*
  – $\mathcal{E}$ *is a* preferred *extension iff it is a maximal (for set inclusion) admissible set.*
  – $\mathcal{E}$ *is a* grounded *extension iff it is a minimal (for set inclusion) complete set.*
  – $\mathcal{E}$ *is a* stable *extension iff it is a preferred set that attacks any element in* $\mathcal{A} \setminus \mathcal{E}$*.*

Let $\mathrm{Ext}(\mathcal{F})$ *be the set of extensions of* $\mathcal{F}$ *under a given semantics.*

Example 1. *Let us consider the AF* $\mathcal{F}_1 = (\mathcal{A}_1, \mathcal{R}_1)$ *where* $\mathcal{A}_1 = \{a, b, c, d\}$*,* $a\mathcal{R}_1 b$*,* $b\mathcal{R}_1 c$*,* $c\mathcal{R}_1 d$ *and* $d\mathcal{R}_1 a$*.* $\mathcal{F}_1$ *has two stable extensions:* $\{a, c\}$ *and* $\{b, d\}$*.*

Extensions are used for defining the status of each argument as follows.

Definition 4. *Let* $\mathcal{F} = (\mathcal{A}, \mathcal{R})$ *be an AF and* $a \in \mathcal{A}$*.*

- *a is* skeptically accepted *iff* $\forall \mathcal{E} \in \text{Ext}(\mathcal{F})$, $a \in \mathcal{E}$.
- *a is* credulously accepted *iff* $\exists \mathcal{E} \in \text{Ext}(\mathcal{F})$ *s.t.* $a \in \mathcal{E}$.
- *a is* rejected *iff* $\forall \mathcal{E} \in \text{Ext}(\mathcal{F})$, $a \notin \mathcal{E}$.

Let $\text{Status}(a, \mathcal{F})$ *be a function that returns the status of an argument a in* $\mathcal{F}$.

Example 1 (Cont): The four arguments a, b, c, d are credulously accepted in $\mathcal{F}_1$.

3   Preferences in Argumentation: Informal Discussion

In what follows, we assume that $\mathcal{F} = (\mathcal{A}, \mathcal{R})$ is an arbitrary argumentation framework where $\mathcal{A}$ is *finite*. Let $\geq$ be a binary relation that expresses preferences between arguments of $\mathcal{A}$. For instance, an argument may be preferred to another if it is grounded on more certain information, or if it promotes a more important value. Throughout the paper, the relation $\geq \subseteq \mathcal{A} \times \mathcal{A}$ is assumed to be a *preorder* (i.e. *reflexive* and *transitive*). For arguments a and b, writing $a \geq b$ (or $(a, b) \in \geq$) means that a is at least as strong as b. The relation $>$ is the strict version of $\geq$ (i.e. $a > b$ iff $a \geq b$ and not $(b \geq a)$).

Let us now analyze the role that preferences between arguments can play in an argumentation framework. We will discuss different critical examples.

Example 1 (Cont): Assume that $a > b$ and $c > d$. According to 'Hoare' ordering, the stable extension $\{a, c\}$ is better than $\{b, d\}$ since each element of the latter is weaker than an element of the former. Thus, $\mathcal{F}_2$ would have only $\{a, c\}$ as extension.

Note that in Example 1, preferences *refine* the results obtained in the standard case. Indeed, the set of preferred solutions is a *subset of the set of the standard ones*. Preferences play here exactly the role described in nonmonotonic logic formalisms. Let us now consider a different example.

Example 2. *Let* $\mathcal{F}_2 = (\mathcal{A}_2, \mathcal{R}_2)$ *be s.t.* $\mathcal{A}_2 = \{a, b\}$ *and* $a\mathcal{R}_2 b$. $\mathcal{F}_2$ *has one stable extension: the set* $\{a\}$. *Now, if we assume that* $b > a$, *it is clear that the standard solution cannot be refined and* $\{a\}$ *is the preferred solution of the framework. What happened here is that the preferred argument is rejected when computing the standard solution. Thus, there is no way to apply the preference of b over a.*

However, is it intuitive to still consider $\{a\}$ *as an extension of* $\mathcal{F}_2$? *The answer is certainly no as illustrated next. Assume that* $\mathcal{F}_2$ *is is built over a knowledge base* $\mathcal{K} = \{x\}$ *and a set of defeasible rules* $\mathcal{D} = \{\Rightarrow y; y \Rightarrow \neg x\}$ *as in ASPIC system [1]. Let* $a :\Rightarrow y; y \Rightarrow \neg x$ *and* $b : x$. *If the attack relation is the one which allows to undermine a premise of another argument, then a undermines b in its premise x while b does not undermine a since it has no premise. If now we assume that x is more certain than both* $\Rightarrow y; y \Rightarrow \neg x$, *then it is natural to keep b and to reject a. To put it differently, the preferred solution of* $\mathcal{F}_2$ *would be the extension* $\{b\}$.

Contrarily to Example 1, the use of preferences in Example 2 completely modifies the original set of extensions. Consequently, the preferred solutions of a framework are not necessarily a subset of the standard ones. This is not surprising since preferences in this case are used in order to compute the standard solutions. Thus, $\{b\}$ is a standard solution. Preferred solutions refine the standard ones. In this example, $\{b\}$ is the only standard solution, thus it is also the unique preferred solution.

It is also worth mentioning that when preferences are used for computing the standard solutions of an argumentation framework, not all available preferences are exploited. Only those which conflict with the attacks, as in Example 2, are used. Consequently, the result which is returned may need to be refined as shown in the following example.

Example 3. *Let us consider the argumentation framework $\mathcal{F}_3 = (\mathcal{A}_3, \mathcal{R}_3)$ where $\mathcal{A}_3 = \{a, b, c, d, e\}$ and $\mathcal{R}_3 = \{(a, b), (b, c), (c, d), (d, a), (c, e), (e, b)\}$. This framework has one stable extension which is $\{a, c\}$. Assume now that $b > c$, $d > a$ and $b > e$. Note that only $b > e$ conflicts with the attack relation since e attacks b. Thus, only this preference is taken into account for computing the two standard solutions $\{a, c\}$ and $\{b, d\}$. Consequently, the two remaining preferences can be used in order to refine the standard result and to prefer the extension $\{b, d\}$.*

To summarize, two roles of preferences are distinguished:

1. To weaken the *critical* attacks (i.e. the attacks which conflict with the preferences) in an AF, and thus to compute intuitive standard solutions.
2. To refine the standard solutions computed after considering the first role.

Example 2 shows that a refinement does not solve the problem of critical attacks while Example 3 shows that the first role is not sufficient and its results may need to be refined as the first role does not exploit all the available preferences.

4   Handling Critical Attacks

The aim of this section is to propose the basic postulates that any preference-based argumentation framework (PAF) should satisfy. We focus here on the use of preferences for computing the standard solutions, thus for modeling the first role of preferences.

Definition 5 (PAF). *A preference-based argumentation framework (PAF) is a tuple $\mathcal{T} = (\mathcal{A}, \mathcal{R}, \geq)$ where $\mathcal{A}$ is a set of arguments, $\mathcal{R}$ is an attack relation and $\geq$ is partial or total preorder on $\mathcal{A}$.*

Note that we do not show how arguments are evaluated in such a PAF. In fact, we do not focus on a particular approach, we rather propose postulates that any approach should satisfy. Before presenting those postulates, let us first define critical attacks.

Definition 6 (Critical attack). *Let $\mathcal{T} = (\mathcal{A}, \mathcal{R}, \geq)$ be a PAF. An attack $(b, a) \in \mathcal{R}$ is critical iff $a > b$.*

The role of preferences which consists of handling critical attacks has already been identified in the literature, namely in [2,4,5,10]. While all these approaches agree that a strong argument may be accepted if it is attacked by a weaker argument, they disagree on whether the weak attacker should be rejected or not. Let us say it differently, in Example 2, the works [2,5,10] return one stable extension which contains both the attacker and the attacked argument, that is the set $\{a, b\}$. This extension violates one of the basic requirements of acceptability semantics, the *conflict-freeness* of extensions. In [4], the authors have argued that this is undesirable since the intuition behind an extension is that it encodes a 'coherent position'. This coherence is captured by the notion of conflict-freeness in acceptability semantics. That is why it is at the heart of all semantics. The authors have then proposed an alternative solution in which the argument a is rejected and the only stable extension of the framework $\mathcal{F}_2$ is $\{b\}$. In this paper, we argue that the extensions of an argumentation framework should be conflict-free, otherwise the whole theory of argumentation collapses. We propose four basic postulates that should be satisfied by any approach for preference-based argumentation that models the first role of preferences. The first postulate states that the extensions of a PAF should be conflict-free.

Postulate 1 (Conflict-freeness). *Let* $T = (\mathcal{A}, \mathcal{R}, \geq)$ *be a PAF and* $\text{Ext}(T)$ *it set of extensions. Each extension* $\mathcal{E} \in \text{Ext}(T)$ *should be conflict-free wrt* $\mathcal{R}$.

The second postulate says that when there are no critical attacks, then the output of the PAF should coincide with that of a system without preferences. The reason is that we suppose that a PAF is built over a well-founded basic system (i.e. the system constructed only from a pair $(\mathcal{A}, \mathcal{R})$).

Postulate 2 (Recovering existing semantics). *Let* $T = (\mathcal{A}, \mathcal{R}, \geq)$ *be a PAF and* $\mathcal{F} = (\mathcal{A}, \mathcal{R})$ *its basic version. If there are no critical attacks in* T, *then* $\text{Ext}(T) = \text{Ext}(\mathcal{F})$ *where* $\text{Ext}(\mathcal{F})$ *is the set of the extensions of* $\mathcal{F}$ *under a given semantics.*

The third postulate shows how to privilege a strong argument over a weak attacker.

Postulate 3 (Critical attacks). *Let* $T = (\mathcal{A}, \mathcal{R}, \geq)$ *be a PAF and* $a, b \in \mathcal{A}$. *Let* $\mathcal{E}_1, \mathcal{E}_2$ *be two conflict-free (wrt* $\mathcal{R}$) *subsets of* $\mathcal{A}$ *s.t.* $\mathcal{E}_1 = \mathcal{E} \cup \{a\}$ *and* $\mathcal{E}_2 = \mathcal{E} \cup \{b\}$. *If* $a\mathcal{R}b$ *and* $b > a$, *then* $\mathcal{E}_1 \notin \text{Ext}(T)$.

The last postulate states that attacks should win when they are not critical.

Postulate 4 (Normal attacks). *Let* $T = (\mathcal{A}, \mathcal{R}, \geq)$ *be a PAF and* $a, b \in \mathcal{A}$. *Let* $\mathcal{E}_1, \mathcal{E}_2$ *be two conflict-free (wrt* $\mathcal{R}$) *subsets of* $\mathcal{A}$ *s.t.* $\mathcal{E}_1 = \mathcal{E} \cup \{a\}$ *and* $\mathcal{E}_2 = \mathcal{E} \cup \{b\}$. *If* $a\mathcal{R}b$ *and* $not(b\mathcal{R}a)$ *and* $not(b > a)$, *then* $\mathcal{E}_2 \notin \text{Ext}(T)$.

Works in [2,5,10], proceed by removing critical attacks from an argumentation graph and applying Dung's semantics on the remaining sub-graph. It is easy to show that when there are no critical attacks, the two graphs coincide.

Property 1. Let $\mathcal{F} = (\mathcal{A}, \mathcal{R})$ be an AF, $\geq \subseteq \mathcal{A} \times \mathcal{A}$, and $\mathcal{F}' = (\mathcal{A}, \mathcal{R}_r)$ be such that $\mathcal{R}_r = \mathcal{R} \setminus \{a\mathcal{R}b \text{ s.t. } b > a\}$. If $\nexists a, b \in \mathcal{A}$ s.t. $a\mathcal{R}b$ and $b > a$, then $\mathcal{R} = \mathcal{R}_r$.

It can be shown that such an approach violates the conflict-freeness in some cases when the attack relation is not symmetric, and the third postulate (for example for admissible semantics), while it satisfies Postulates 2 and 4.

Proposition 1. *Let* $\mathcal{T} = (\mathcal{A}, \mathcal{R}, \geq)$ *be a PAF s.t.* $\text{Ext}(\mathcal{T}) = \text{Ext}((\mathcal{A}, \mathcal{R}_r))$ *where* $\mathcal{R}_r = \mathcal{R} \setminus \{a\mathcal{R}b \; s.t. \; b > a\}$. *Then,* $\mathcal{T}$ *verifies Postulates 2 and 4.*

When the attack relation is symmetric, Postulates 1 and 3 are verified.

Proposition 2. *Let* $\mathcal{T} = (\mathcal{A}, \mathcal{R}, \geq)$ *be a PAF s.t.* $\text{Ext}(\mathcal{T}) = \text{Ext}(\mathcal{F})$ *where* $\mathcal{F} = (\mathcal{A}, \mathcal{R}_r)$. *If* $\mathcal{R}$ *is symmetric, then* $\mathcal{T}$ *verifies Postulates 1 and 3.*

This means that when the attack relation is symmetric, all the postulates are verified. However, the following example shows that the result may still need to be refined.

Example 4. *Let* $\mathcal{A} = \{a, b, c, d\}$, $\mathcal{R} = \{(a, c), (c, a), (a, d), (d, a), (b, c), (c, b), (b, d), (d, b)\}$ *and* $a > c$, $b > d$. *The extensions of this PAF are* $\{a, b\}$ *and* $\{c, d\}$. *However,* $\{a, b\}$ *is clearly preferred to* $\{c, d\}$. *Thus, the frameworks developed in [2,5,10] do not take into account the second role of preferences even when the attack relation is symmetric.*

In the recent paper ([4]) an approach has been proposed which verifies all postulates.

Proposition 3. *The class of PAFs defined in [4] verifies Postulates 1 - 4.*

5 Refining AFs by Preferences

Until now, we have studied the first role of preferences. We have particularly shown that "some" preferences should be taken into account for computing the standard solutions of an argumentation framework. Examples 1 and 3 show that standard solutions may need to be narrowed down using the remaining preferences. What is worth noticing is that a refinement amounts to *compare* subsets of arguments. In Example 1, the so-called *democratic* relation, $\succeq_d$, is used for comparing the two sets $\{a, c\}$ and $\{b, d\}$:

$$\text{Let } \mathcal{E}, \mathcal{E}' \subseteq \mathcal{A}. \; \mathcal{E} \succeq_d \mathcal{E}' \text{ iff } \forall x' \in \mathcal{E}' \setminus \mathcal{E}, \exists x \in \mathcal{E} \setminus \mathcal{E}' \text{ s.t. } x > x'.$$

Relation $\succeq_d$ is not unique and different relations can be used as shown next.

Example 1 (Cont): Let us consider again $\mathcal{F}_1$ and assume that $a \approx b$ and $c > d$. According to relation $\succeq_d$, the two extensions $\{a, c\}$ and $\{b, d\}$ are incomparable. However, since $a \approx b$ and $c > d$, it is clear that one could prefer $\{a, c\}$ to $\{b, d\}$.

Let us now define the basic properties that such a relation should satisfy. The first property ensures that the refinement relation is a preorder, that is reflexive and transitive. Note that these are the basic properties of any preference relation.

Postulate 5 (Preorder). *Let* $\mathcal{A}$ *be a set of arguments. A refinement relation on* $\mathcal{P}(\mathcal{A})$ *is a preorder (reflexive and transitive).*

The second property ensures that the relation privileges sets that contain strong arguments (wrt the preference relation $\geq$).

Postulate 6 (Privileging strong arguments). *Let* $\mathcal{T} = (\mathcal{A}, \mathcal{R}, \geq)$ *be a PAF,* $a, b \in \mathcal{A}$ *and* $\mathcal{E}_1, \mathcal{E}_2 \in \mathcal{P}(\mathcal{A})$. *If* $\mathcal{E}_1 = \mathcal{E} \cup \{a\}$ *and* $\mathcal{E}_2 = \mathcal{E} \cup \{b\}$ *and* $a > b$, *then* $\mathcal{E}_1 \succeq \mathcal{E}_2$.

Property 2. The democratic relation verifies the two postulates 5 and 6.

6   A Particular Rich PAF

In this section, we propose a particular framework which models both roles of preferences and verifies all the postulates introduced in this paper. The framework follows
two steps: at the first step, it computes the standard solutions by handling correctly the
available critical attacks. These solutions are then refined using an appropriate refinement relation. In order to make the paper easy to read, we will call PAF the framework
which computes the standard solutions and rich PAF the one which refines the results
of the PAF.

Definition 7 (Rich PAFs). *A rich PAF is a tuple* $\mathcal{T} = (\mathcal{A}, \mathcal{R}, \geq, \succeq)$ *where* $\mathcal{A}$ *is a set
of arguments,* $\mathcal{R} \subseteq \mathcal{A} \times \mathcal{A}$ *is an attack relation,* $\geq \subseteq \mathcal{A} \times \mathcal{A}$ *is a (partial or total)
preorder and* $\succeq \subseteq \mathcal{P}(\mathcal{A}) \times \mathcal{P}(\mathcal{A})$ *is a relation which verifies Postulates 5 and 6. The
extensions of* $\mathcal{T}$ *(under a given semantics) are elements of* $\mathrm{Max}(\mathcal{S}, \succeq)$*, where* $\mathcal{S}$ *is the
set of extensions (under the same semantics) of the PAF* $(\mathcal{A}, \mathcal{R}, \geq)$*.*

In what follows, we propose a new approach that handles correctly critical attacks (i.e.
which satisfies the four postulates introduced in section 4). We exploit for that a simple result that is proved recently in [4]. In that paper, the authors have proposed a new
approach for taking into account preferences and which prevents the shortcomings of
existing ones, namely the problem of conflicting extensions. The basic idea is to integrate preferences in the definition of semantics. A refinement of stable semantics is
defined as a dominance relation which compares sets of arguments. The best sets wrt
that relation are the extensions of the PAF. In that paper, the authors have shown that
all their extensions are conflict-free and Postulates 2, 3 and 4 as satisfied as well. They
have also shown an important result for semantics that refine stable one with preferences. The result says that the extensions of their approach (i.e. the best sets wrt the
dominance relation) are exactly the stable extensions of the basic argumentation framework in which each critical attack is inverted. In what follows, we show that this idea
can be generalized to any acceptability semantics.

The idea of inverting the arrows of critical attacks in an argumentation graph allows
to take into account the preference (between the two arguments involved in a critical
attack) and in the same time the conflict between the two arguments of the attack is
represented. The intuition behind this is that an attack between two arguments represents two things: i) an incoherence between the two arguments (in logic-based systems,
it captures inconsistency between the supports of the two arguments), and ii) a kind of
preference determined by the direction of the attack. Thus, in our approach, the direction of the arrow represents a real preference between arguments. Moreover, the conflict
is kept between the two arguments. Dung's acceptability semantics are then applied on
the modified graph. In our approach, standard solutions are computed by the following
preference-based framework.

Definition 8 (Repaired PAF). *A repaired PAF is a tuple* $\mathcal{T} = (\mathcal{A}, \mathcal{R}, \geq)$ *where* $\mathcal{A}$ *is
a set of arguments,* $\mathcal{R} \subseteq \mathcal{A} \times \mathcal{A}$ *is an attack relation and* $\geq$ *is a preorder on* $\mathcal{A}$*.
The extensions of* $\mathcal{T}$ *under a given semantics are the extensions of the argumentation
framework* $(\mathcal{A}, \mathcal{R}_r)$*, called* repaired framework, *under the same semantics with:* $\mathcal{R}_r =
\{(a,b)|(a,b) \in \mathcal{R}$ *and not* $(b > a)\} \cup \{(b,a)|(a,b) \in \mathcal{R}$ *and* $b > a\}$*.*

From Definition 8, it is clear that if a PAF has no critical attacks, then the repaired framework coincides with the basic one.

Property 3. Let $\mathcal{T} = (\mathcal{A}, \mathcal{R}, \geq)$ be a PAF. If $\mathcal{T}$ has no critical attacks, then $\mathcal{R}_r = \mathcal{R}$.

This property shows also that when a PAF has no critical attacks, then preferences do not play any role in the evaluation process.

Our approach does not suffer from the drawback of existing ones. Indeed, it delivers conflict-free extensions of arguments. Thus, it satisfies Postulate 1.

Proposition 4. *Let* $\mathcal{T} = (\mathcal{A}, \mathcal{R}, \geq)$ *be a PAF and* $\mathcal{E}_1, \ldots, \mathcal{E}_n$ *its extensions under a given semantics. For all* $i = 1, \ldots, n$, $\mathcal{E}_i$ *is conflict-free wrt.* $\mathcal{R}$.

The next result confirms that our approach is *well-founded* in the sense that acceptable arguments are defended by "good" arguments. Moreover, it verifies the orderings between the attack relation and the preference relation, meaning that it verifies Postulates 3 and 4.

Proposition 5. *Let* $\mathcal{T} = (\mathcal{A}, \mathcal{R}, \geq)$ *be a PAF.*

- *For each admissible set* $\mathcal{E}$ *of* $\mathcal{T}$, *it holds that* $(\forall x \in \mathcal{E})$ $(\forall x' \notin \mathcal{E})$
  if $(x'\mathcal{R}x$ *and not* $(x > x'))$ *or* $(x\mathcal{R}x'$ *and* $x' > x)$ *then* $(\exists y \in \mathcal{E})$ *s.t.* $(y\mathcal{R}x'$ *and not* $(x' > y))$ *or* $(x'\mathcal{R}y$ *and* $y > x')$.
- *For each stable extension* $\mathcal{E}$ *of* $\mathcal{T}$, *it holds that* $(\forall x' \notin \mathcal{E})$ $(\exists x \in \mathcal{E})$ *s.t.* $(x\mathcal{R}x'$ *and not* $(x' > x))$ *or* $(x'\mathcal{R}x$ *and* $x > x')$.

The fact of inverting the arrows of critical attacks in an argumentation graph does not affect the status of arguments that are not related to the arguments of those attacks. This means that our approach has no side effects. Before presenting the formal result, let us first give a useful definition.

Definition 9. *Let* $\mathcal{F} = (\mathcal{A}, \mathcal{R})$ *be an AF and* $a, b \in \mathcal{A}$. *The arguments* a *and* b *are related in* $\mathcal{F}$ *iff there is exists a finite sequence* $a_1, \ldots, a_n$ *of arguments such that* $a_1 = a$, $a_n = b$ *and for all* $i = 1, \ldots, n - 1$, *either* $(a_i, a_{i+1}) \in \mathcal{R}$ *or* $(a_{i+1}, a_i) \in \mathcal{R}$.

Proposition 6. *Let* $\mathcal{T} = (\mathcal{A}, \mathcal{R}, \geq)$ *be a PAF. For all* $a \in \mathcal{A}$ *s.t.* $\nexists b, c \in \mathcal{A}$ *s.t.* $(b, c) \in \mathcal{R}$ *is a critical attack and* a *is related with* b, *it holds that:*

- Status$(a, (\mathcal{A}, \mathcal{R}))$ = Status$(a, (\mathcal{A}, \mathcal{R}_r))$ *(under preferred and grounded semantics).*
- *If* $(\mathcal{A}, \mathcal{R})$ *and* $(\mathcal{A}, \mathcal{R}_r)$ *both have at least one stable extension, then* Status $(a, (\mathcal{A}, \mathcal{R}))$ = Status$(a, (\mathcal{A}, \mathcal{R}_r))$ *(under this semantics).*

Our approach privileges the strongest arguments. Indeed, we show that these arguments are skeptically accepted when they are not conflicting. If such a strong argument is not skeptically accepted, then it is for sure attacked (wrt. $\mathcal{R}$) by another strongest argument. Before presenting the formal result, let us define the strongest arguments (or the top elements) wrt. a relation $\geq$.

Definition 10 (Maximal elements). *Let* $\mathcal{O}$ *be a set of objects and* $\geq \subseteq \mathcal{O} \times \mathcal{O}$ *is a (partial or total) preorder. The* maximal elements *of* $\mathcal{O}$ *wrt.* $\geq$ *are* Max$(\mathcal{O}, \geq)$ = $\{o \in \mathcal{O} \mid \nexists o' \in \mathcal{O}$ *s.t.* $o' > o\}$.

Property 4. Let $T = (\mathcal{A}, \mathcal{R}, \geq)$ be a PAF s.t $\geq$ is complete[1].

- If $\text{Max}(\mathcal{A}, \geq)$ is conflict-free (wrt. $\mathcal{R}$), then $\forall a \in \text{Max}(\mathcal{A}, \geq)$:
  - a is skeptically accepted in T wrt. preferred and grounded semantics.
  - if T has at least one stable extension, then a is skeptically accepted wrt. stable semantics.
- If a is not skeptically accepted (under preferred or grounded semantics), or there exists at least one stable extension and a is not skeptically accepted, then $\exists b \in \text{Max}(\mathcal{A}, \geq)$ s.t. $(b, a) \in \mathcal{R}$.

The following result shows that when the preference relation $\geq$ is a linear order (i.e. reflexive, antisymmetric, transitive and complete), then the corresponding PAF has a unique stable/preferred extension. Moreover, this extension is computed in $\mathcal{O}(n^2)$ time where $|\mathcal{A}| = n$. It is clear that in this case, there is no need to refine the result.

Proposition 7. *Let* $T = (\mathcal{A}, \mathcal{R}, \geq)$ *be a PAF s.t.* $\mathcal{R}$ *is irreflexive and* $\geq$ *is a linear order.*

- *T has exactly one stable extension.*
- *Stable, preferred and grounded extensions of T coincide.*
- *If $|\mathcal{A}| = n$, then this extension is computed in $\mathcal{O}(n^2)$ time.*

Let us now see what happens in case the attack relation is symmetric. The following result shows that our approach returns the same results as the approach developed in [2,5]. This means that inverting the arrows or removing them will lead to the same result.

Property 5. Let $T = (\mathcal{A}, \mathcal{R}, \geq)$ be a PAF where $\mathcal{R}$ is symmetric. Extensions of T coincide with extensions of $(\mathcal{A}, \mathcal{R}')$ (under the same semantics) where $\mathcal{R}' = \{(a, b) | (a, b) \in \mathcal{R} \text{ and} \neg (b > a)\}$.

We can also show that when the attack relation is symmetric, the extensions of a PAF are a subset of those of its basic framework. This means that preferences filter the extensions. However, the result is not optimal since it may need to be refined again as shown in Example 4.

Proposition 8. *Let* $T = (\mathcal{A}, \mathcal{R}, \geq)$ *be a PAF where* $\mathcal{R}$ *is symmetric. If* $\mathcal{E} \subseteq \mathcal{A}$ *is a preferred (stable) extension of system* T *then* $\mathcal{E}$ *is a preferred (stable) extension of* $(\mathcal{A}, \mathcal{R})$.

Recall that this result is not true in case the attack relation is not symmetric as shown in Example 2.

The following result characterizes the extensions of $(\mathcal{A}, \mathcal{R})$ that are discarded in a PAF when $\mathcal{R}$ is symmetric. The idea is that an extension is discarded iff some argument outside it is strictly preferred to any arguments of that extension with which it conflicts.

Property 6. Let $T = (\mathcal{A}, \mathcal{R}, \geq)$ be a PAF s.t. $\mathcal{R}$ is symmetric, and $\mathcal{E} \subseteq \mathcal{A}$. $\mathcal{E}$ is a stable extension of $(\mathcal{A}, \mathcal{R})$ but not of T iff $\exists x' \notin \mathcal{E}$ s.t. $\forall x \in \mathcal{E}$, if $x \mathcal{R} x'$, then $x' > x$.

---

[1] A relation $\geq$ on a set $\mathcal{A}$ is complete iff for all $a, b \in \mathcal{A}$, $a \geq b$ or $b \geq a$.

When the attack relation is symmetric and irreflexive, the corresponding PAF is *coherent* (i.e. its preferred and stable extensions coincide) and it has at least one stable extension.

Proposition 9. *Let* $T = (\mathcal{A}, \mathcal{R}, \geq)$ *be a PAF. If* $\mathcal{R}$ *is symmetric and irreflexive, then:*

- *T is coherent.*
- *T has at least one stable extension.*

Until now, we have proposed a particular framework for handling the first role of preferences. From now on, we will use the democratic relation for refining the results of this framework. Recall that this relation verifies the two postulates 5 and 6.

We will now show that when the preference relation $\geq$ is a linear order, then the democratic relation does not change the output of the underlying PAF.

Property 7. Let $T = (\mathcal{A}, \mathcal{R}, \geq, \succeq)$ be a rich PAF and $\mathcal{S}$ be the set of extensions (under a given semantics) of the repaired framework $(\mathcal{A}, \mathcal{R}_r)$. If $\mathcal{R}$ is irreflexive and $\geq$ is a linear order, then $\text{Max}(\mathcal{S}, \succeq) = \mathcal{S}$ holds for stable, preferred, grounded and complete semantics.

It is also easy to show that when a rich PAF has no critical attacks, then its extensions are a subset of the extensions of its basic version (i.e. without preferences).

Property 8. Let $T = (\mathcal{A}, \mathcal{R}, \geq, \succeq)$ be a rich PAF s.t. $\mathcal{R}$ has no critical attacks. Preferred (stable) extensions of T are exactly the elements of $\text{Max}(\mathcal{S}, \succeq)$ where $\mathcal{S}$ is the set of all preferred (stable) extensions of the AF $(\mathcal{A}, \mathcal{R})$.

Example 1 (Cont): Let us use the democratic relation $\succeq_d$. In $\mathcal{F}_1$, there is no critical attacks ($\mathcal{R}_r = \mathcal{R}$). The extensions of the rich PAF are $\text{Max}(\{\{a, c\}, \{b, d\}\}, \succeq_d) = \{\{a, c\}\}$. Thus, $\{a, c\}$ is the unique stable extension.

Example 2 (Cont): The repaired framework of $\mathcal{F}_2$ is $(\{a, b\}, \mathcal{R}_r)$ where $b\mathcal{R}a$. Thus, the PAF has one stable extension $\{b\}$ which is the only extension of the rich PAF: $\text{Max}(\{\{b\}\}, \succeq_d) = \{\{b\}\}$.

Example 3 (Cont): Recall that the repaired framework of $\mathcal{F}_3$ has two stable extensions: $\{a, c\}$ and $\{b, d\}$. Moreover, $\text{Max}(\{\{a, c\}, \{b, d\}\}, \succeq_d) = \{\{a, c\}\}$. Thus, $\{a, c\}$ is the unique stable extension of the rich PAF that uses the democratic relation.

7 Related Work

Introducing preferences in argumentation frameworks goes back to the paper by Simari and Loui in [12]. In that work, the authors have defined an AF in which arguments are built from a propositional knowledge base. The arguments grounded on specific information are considered as stronger than the ones built from more general information. This preference is used to solve dilemmas between any pair of conflicting arguments. Thus, it is used for handling critical attacks. The idea of this paper has been generalized in [2] then in [5] to any AF and to any preference relation. Unfortunately, the approach followed in [2,5] delivers correct results only when the attack relation is symmetric. When the attack relation is not symmetric, the approach suffers from two main drawbacks: the first is that it may return conflicting extensions as shown in Example 1 since it may put two conflicting arguments in the same extension. One of these arguments is clearly undesirable. The second drawback is a consequence of the first one. Indeed, since an undesirable argument may be accepted, then all the arguments that are defended by this argument are accepted as well to the detriment of good ones. Let us illustrate this issue on the following example.

Example 5. *Let us consider the argumentation framework* $\mathcal{F}_4 = (\mathcal{A}_4, \mathcal{R}_4)$ *where* $\mathcal{A}_4 = \{a, b, c, d\}$ *and* $\mathcal{R}_4 = \{(b, a), (b, c), (c, d)\}$. *Assume that* $a > b$. *The approach in [2,5] gets the framework* $\mathcal{F}_4' = (\mathcal{A}_4, \mathcal{R}_4')$ *where* $\mathcal{R}_4' = \{(b, c), (c, d)\}$. *Its grounded extension is the set* $\{a, b, d\}$. *This result is incorrect for two reasons: The first one is that the two arguments* a *and* b *cannot be both accepted. The second reason is that the argument* b *(which should be rejected) defends* d *against* c, *leading thus to an undesirable result. Indeed,* d *is defended by a "bad" argument! It is easy to check that our approach returns* $\{a, c\}$ *as the grounded extension and rejects the two other arguments: i.e.* b *and* c.

Our approach overcomes the limits of the one proposed in [2,5]. Moreover, it is more general since it models even the second role of preference (i.e. the refinement).

Recently, in [3], the authors have pointed out the first limit of the approach followed in [2,5], namely the violation of conflict-freeness. They have proposed a new approach for handling critical attacks where preferences are introduced at a semantics level. As shown in this paper, the approach developed in [3] satisfies the four rationality postulates. However, it completely neglects the second role of preferences, i.e. refinement. Another work which handles correctly the problem of critical attacks is that proposed in [11]. In that paper, Prakken has proposed a logic-based instantiation of Dung's framework in which three kinds of attacks are considered: rebuttal, assumption attack and undercut. For each relation, the author has found a way to avoid the problem of critical attack and ensured conflict-free extensions. We think that our work is more general since we solved the problem at an abstract level. This avoid the user who wants to use another attack relation to look for new ways to avoid conflicting extensions. Moreover, our approach is axiomatic, meaning that it is well founded. It is also worth mentioning that in [11], the second role of preferences is neglected. To the best of our knowledge, the only work on refinement is that appeared in [7]. The authors have proposed a particular refinement relation in case of stable semantics. In this sense, our work is more general since it accepts any refinement relation. Moreover, there is no restriction to particular semantics. Finally, we would like to mention the work done in [9]. In this paper, the author made a survey of the critics presented in [3,7] against existing approaches for PAFs. The author concluded that one should use a symmetric attack relation in order to avoid the problem of conflicting extensions and then to refine the result with the preference relation already mentioned in [7]. The first suggestion is certainly not realistic, especially in light of new results in the literature stating that symmetric relations should be avoided in logic-based argumentation systems.

8 Conclusion

This paper has studied deeply the difference between the two roles that preferences may play in an AF. We have shown that preferences intervene both for computing what is called standard solutions in nonmonotonic reasoning formalisms and for refining that result, and choosing a subset of those solutions. We have shown that the two roles are completely independent and should be taken into account in two steps. Main postulates that any approach modeling each role have been proposed. Finally, we have developed a particular framework that considers both roles. The framework satisfies the proposed postulates and its properties show that it is well-founded.

References

1. Amgoud, L., Caminada, M., Cayrol, C., Lagasquie, M., Prakken, H.: Towards a consensual formal model: inference part. Technical report, Deliverable D2.2: Draft Formal Semantics for Inference and Decision-Making. ASPIC project (2004)
2. Amgoud, L., Cayrol, C.: A reasoning model based on the production of acceptable arguments. Annals of Mathematics and Artificial Int. 34, 197–216 (2002)
3. Amgoud, L., Vesic, S.: Repairing preference-based argumentation systems. In: IJCAI 2009, pp. 665–670 (2009)
4. Amgoud, L., Vesic, S.: Generalizing stable semantics by preferences. In: Proceedings of COMMA 2010, pp. 39–50 (2010)
5. Bench-Capon, T.J.M.: Persuasion in practical argument using value-based argumentation frameworks. J. of Logic and Computation 13(3), 429–448 (2003)
6. Brewka, G., Niemela, I., Truszczynski, M.: Preferences and nonmonotonic reasoning. AI Magazine, 69–78 (2008)
7. Dimopoulos, Y., Moraitis, P., Amgoud, L.: Extending argumentation to make good decisions. In: Rossi, F., Tsoukias, A. (eds.) ADT 2009. LNCS, vol. 5783, pp. 225–236. Springer, Heidelberg (2009)
8. Dung, P.: On the acceptability of arguments and its fundamental role in nonmonotonic reasoning, logic programming and n-person games. AIJ 77, 321–357 (1995)
9. Kaci, S.: Refined preference-based argumentation framworks. In: Proceedings of COMMA 2010, pp. 299–310 (2010)
10. Modgil, S.: Reasoning about preferences in argumentation frameworks. AIJ 173(9-10), 901–934 (2009)
11. Prakken, H.: An abstract framework for argumentation with structured arguments. Journal of Argument and Computation (2010) (in press)
12. Simari, G., Loui, R.: A mathematical treatment of defeasible reasoning and its implementation. Artificial Intelligence Journal 53, 125–157 (1992)

A Re-definition of Mixtures of Polynomials for Inference in Hybrid Bayesian Networks

Prakash P. Shenoy

University of Kansas School of Business,
1300 Sunnyside Ave., Summerfield Hall, Lawrence, KS 66045-7601 USA
pshenoy@ku.edu

Abstract. We discuss some issues in using mixtures of polynomials (MOPs) for inference in hybrid Bayesian networks. MOPs were proposed by Shenoy and West for mitigating the problem of integration in inference in hybrid Bayesian networks. In defining MOP for multi-dimensional functions, one requirement is that the pieces where the polynomials are defined are hypercubes. In this paper, we discuss relaxing this condition so that each piece is defined on regions called hyper-rhombuses. This relaxation means that MOPs are closed under transformations required for multi-dimensional linear deterministic conditionals, such as $Z = X + Y$. Also, this relaxation allows us to construct MOP approximations of the probability density functions (PDFs) of the multi-dimensional conditional linear Gaussian distributions using a MOP approximation of the PDF of the univariate standard normal distribution. We illustrate our method using conditional linear Gaussian PDFs in two and three dimensions.

1 Introduction

An hybrid Bayesian network (BN) is a BN with a mix of discrete and continuous random variables. A random variable is said to be *discrete* if the cardinality of its state space is countable, and *continuous* otherwise. Each variable in a BN is associated with conditional distributions for the variable, one for each state of its parents. A conditional for a variable is said to be *deterministic* if the conditional variances of its conditional distributions are all zeroes.

Marginalizing a continuous variable involves integration of the product of all potentials that contain the variable in their domains. Often, these potentials are not integrable in closed form. This is a major problem in making inferences in hybrid BNs. We will call this problem the *integration* problem.

One solution to the integration problem is to approximate conditional PDFs by a family of functions called mixtures of truncated exponentials (MTEs) [4]. MTE functions are piecewise functions that are defined on regions called hyper-cubes, and the functions themselves are exponential functions of a linear function of the variables. Such functions are easy to integrate, and the family of MTE functions are closed under multiplication, addition, and integration, three operations that are used in finding marginals using the extended Shenoy-Shafer

W. Liu (Ed.): ECSQARU 2011, LNAI 6717, pp. 98–109, 2011.

architecture [7]. Cobb et al. [1] describe MTE approximations of several commonly used one-dimensional PDFs. Moral et al. [5] describe a mixed-tree method for representing an MTE approximation of a 2-dimensional CLG distribution.

Another method that is similar in principle to the mixture of truncated exponentials method is the mixture of polynomials (MOP) method proposed by Shenoy and West [8]. Instead of using piecewise exponential functions, the MOP method uses piecewise polynomials. Although a detailed comparison of MTE and MOP methods has yet to be done, an advantage of the MOP method is that one can easily find MOP approximations of differentiable PDFs using the Taylor series expansion of the PDF [8], or by using Lagrange interpolating polynomials [6].

In both the MTE and the MOP methods, the multi-dimensional piecewise functions are defined on regions called hypercubes. One advantage of this restriction is that such multi-dimensional piecewise functions are easy to integrate. However, the hypercube restriction poses two limitations. It is difficult to find an MTE or a MOP approximation of a multi-dimensional conditional PDF for dimensions greater than two. The mixed-tree method proposed by Moral et al. [5] and the Taylor series method proposed by Shenoy and West [8] do not scale up to higher dimensions in practice, i.e., the approximations using these methods have too many pieces or too many terms or have too high a degree for practical use.

Another problem is the presence of deterministic conditionals for continuous variables. For example, suppose X has PDF $f_X(x)$ and suppose Y has conditional PDF $f_{Y|x}(y)$, and suppose Z has a deterministic conditional given by the linear function $Z = X + Y$. To find the marginal distribution of Z, we need to combine $f_X(x)$ and $f_{Y|x}(z-x)$ and then integrate x out of the combination. The problem is that even if $f_{Y|x}(y)$ was defined on hypercubes, $f_{Y|x}(z-x)$ is no longer defined on hypercubes. This problem applies equally to the MTE and MOP methods.

In this paper, we suggest replacing the hypercube condition with a more general condition called hyper-rhombus. For one-dimensional functions, the two conditions coincide. However, for dimensions two or greater, the hyper-rhombus condition is a generalization of the hypercube condition. The hyper-rhombus condition has several important advantages. First, it allows us to define MOP approximations of high-dimensional CLG distributions using a MOP approximation of the one-dimensional standard normal PDF. Second, MOP functions defined on hyper-rhombuses are closed under operations required for multi-dimensional linear deterministic functions. This is not true for MTE functions, i.e., if the definition of MTE functions were generalized so that the hypercube condition was replaced by the hyper-rhombus condition, then MTE functions would not be closed under operations required for multi-dimensional linear deterministic functions. For example, the sum of two independent variables with exponential PDFs has a gamma PDF, which is not a MTE function. Third, MOP functions that are defined on hyper-rhombuses are closed under integration. Fourth, the computational penalty incurred by having hyper-rhombus condition for MOPs (compared to the hypercube condition) appears to be small.

An outline of the remainder of the paper is as follows. In Section 2, we provide a re-definition of high-dimensional MOP functions that are defined on regions called hyper-rhombuses. In Section 3, we describe how we can use the MOP approximation of the standard normal PDF to find MOP approximations of the PDFs of two- and three-dimensional CLG distributions. Finally in Section 4, we summarize our findings and discuss some issues for further research.

2   Mixture of Polynomials Functions

In this section, we define MOP functions. The definition we provide here is slightly more general than the definition provided in Shenoy and West [8] for the case of multi-dimensional functions.

2.1   MOP Functions

A one-dimensional function $f : \mathbb{R} \to \mathbb{R}$ is said to be a *mixture of polynomials* (MOP) function if it is a piecewise function of the form:

$$f(x) = \begin{cases} a_{0i} + a_{1i}x + \cdots + a_{ni}x^n & \text{for } x \in A_i, i = 1, \ldots, k, \\ 0 & \text{otherwise.} \end{cases} \tag{1}$$

where $A_1, \ldots, A_k$ are disjoint intervals in $\mathbb{R}$ that do not depend on x, and $a_{0i}, \ldots, a_{ni}$ are constants for all i. We will say that f is a k-piece (ignoring the 0 piece), and n-degree (assuming $a_{ni} \neq 0$ for some i) MOP function.

The definition given in Equation (1) is exactly the same as in Shenoy and West [8]. The main motivation for defining MOP functions is that such functions are easy to integrate in closed form, and that they are closed under multiplication, integration, and addition, the main operations in making inferences in hybrid Bayesian networks. The requirement that each piece is defined on an interval A_i is also designed to ease the burden of integrating MOP functions.

A multivariate polynomial is a polynomial in several variables. For example, a polynomial in two variables is as follows:

$$P(x_1, x_2) = a_{00} + a_{10}x_1 + a_{01}x_2 + a_{11}x_1x_2 + a_{20}x_1^2 + a_{02}x_2^2 \tag{2}$$
$$+ a_{21}x_1^2x_2 + a_{12}x_1x_2^2 + a_{22}x_1^2x_2^2$$

The degree of the polynomial in Equation (2) is 4 assuming a_{22} is a non-zero constant. In general, the degree of a multivariate polynomial is the largest sum of the exponents of the variables in the terms of the polynomial.

An m-dimensional function $f : \mathbb{R}^m \to \mathbb{R}$ is said to be a MOP function if

$$f(x_1, x_2, \ldots, x_m) =$$
$$\begin{cases} P_i(x_1, x_2, \ldots, x_m) & \text{for } (x_1, x_2, \ldots, x_m) \in A_i, i = 1, \ldots, k, \\ 0 & \text{otherwise} \end{cases} \tag{3}$$

where $P_i(x_1, x_2, \ldots, x_m)$ are multivariate polynomials in m variables for all i, and the regions A_i are as follows. Suppose π is a permutation of $\{1, ..., m\}$. Then each A_i is of the form:

$$l_{1i} \leq x_{\pi(1)} \leq u_{1i}, \tag{4}$$
$$l_{2i}(x_{\pi(1)}) \leq x_{\pi(2)} \leq u_{2i}(x_{\pi(1)}),$$

$$\vdots$$

$$l_{mi}(x_{\pi(1)}, \dots, x_{\pi(m-1)}) \leq x_{\pi(m)} \leq u_{mi}(x_{\pi(1)}, \dots, x_{\pi(m-1)})$$

where l_{1i} and u_{1i} are constants, and $l_{ji}(x_{\pi(1)}, \dots, x_{\pi(j-1)})$ and $u_{ji}(x_{\pi(1)}, \dots, x_{\pi(j-1)})$ are linear functions of $x_{\pi(1)}, x_{\pi(2)}, \dots, x_{\pi(j-1)}$ for $j = 2, \dots, m$, and $i = 1, \dots, k$. We will refer to the nature of the region described in Equation (4) as a *hyper-rhombus*. Although we have defined the hyper-rhombus as a closed region in Equation (4), each of the $2m$ inequalities can be either strictly $<$ or $\leq$.

The definition of a m-dimensional MOP function stated in Equation (3) is more general than the corresponding definition stated in Shenoy and West [8], which is as follows:

An m-dimensional function $f : \mathbb{R}^m \to \mathbb{R}$ is said to be a MOP function if:

$$f(x_1, \dots, x_m) = f_1(x_1) \cdot f_2(x_2) \cdots f_m(x_m) \tag{5}$$

where each $f_i(x_i)$ is a one-dimensional MOP function as defined in Equation (1).

It is easy to see that an m-dimensional function satisfying the condition in Equation (5) will also satisfy the condition in Equation (3), but the converse is not true. Thus, a function as follows:

$$f(x_1, x_2) = \begin{cases} x_1 x_2^2 + x_1^2 x_2 & \text{for } -3 \leq x_1 \leq 3 \text{ and } x_1 - 3 \leq x_2 \leq x_1 + 3 \\ 0 & \text{otherwise} \end{cases} \tag{6}$$

satisfies Equation (3) but not Equation (5) for two reasons. First, $x_1 x_2^2 + x_1^2 x_2$ cannot be obtained by a product of two one-dimensional polynomials. Second, the first piece is defined on the region $-3 \leq x_1 \leq 3$, $x_1 - 3 \leq x_2 \leq x_1 + 3$, which is not a hypercube, but is a hyper-rhombus.

Finally, high-dimensional MOP function defined on hyper-rhombuses remain MOP functions after integration. Thus, the family of MOP functions are closed under multiplication, addition, and integration. A disadvantage of the new definition is that it takes longer to integrate such functions compared to hypercubes. An advantage is that we can more easily construct high dimensional conditional PDFs such as the conditional linear Gaussian distributions. This is described in Section 3.

3   Fitting MOPs to Two- and Three-Dimensional CLG PDFs

In this section, we will find MOP approximations of the PDFs of 2- and 3-dimensional conditional linear Gaussian (CLG) distributions based on a MOP approximation of the 1-dimensional standard normal PDF. Our revised definition of multi-dimensional MOP functions in Equation (3) facilitates the task of finding MOP approximations of the PDFs of CLG conditional distributions.

3.1   Measuring Goodness of Fit of Approximations

There are several ways of measuring the goodness of fit of an approximation. First, we can use the Kullback-Liebler (KL) divergence [2] as a measure of the goodness of fit. If f is a PDF on the range (a, b), and g is a PDF that is an approximation of f such that $g(x) > 0$ for $x \in (a, b)$, then the KL divergence between f and g, denoted by $KL(f, g)$, is defined as

$$KL(f, g) = \int_a^b \ln\left(\frac{f(x)}{g(x)}\right) f(x) dx. \tag{7}$$

$KL(f, g) \geq 0$, and $KL(f, g) = 0$ if and only if $g(x) = f(x)$ for all $x \in (a, b)$. Typically, $KL(f, g) \leq .001$ is considered a good approximation.

Another measure of goodness of a fit is the maximum absolute deviation. Thus, if f is a PDF on the range (a, b), and g is a PDF that is an approximation of f, then the maximum absolute deviation between f and g, denoted by $MAD(f, g)$, is given by:

$$MAD(f, g) = sup\{|f(x) - g(x)| : a < x < b\} \tag{8}$$

Finally, other measures of goodness of fit are the absolute errors in the means and variances. Thus the absolute error of the mean, denoted by $AEM(f, g)$ and the absolute error of the variance, denoted by $AEV(f, g)$ are given by:

$$AEM(f, g) = |E(f) - E(g)| \tag{9}$$
$$AEV(f, g) = |V(f) - V(g)| \tag{10}$$

where $E(\cdot)$ and $V(\cdot)$ denote the expected value and the variance of a PDF, respectively.

3.2   One-Dimensional CLG Distributions

We start with a 4-piece, 3-degree MOP approximation g_1 of the truncated standard normal PDF φ described as follows:

$$g_1(z) = \begin{cases} 0.627801 + 0.503039z + 0.128574z^2 + 0.0100516z^3 & \text{if } -3 < z \leq -1, \\ 0.401108 - 0.00675769z - 0.240746z^2 - 0.0761647z^3 & \text{if } -1 < z \leq 0, \\ 0.401108 + 0.00675769z - 0.240746z^2 + 0.0761647z^3 & \text{if } 0 < z \leq 1, \\ 0.627801 - 0.503039z + 0.128574z^2 - 0.0100516z^3 & \text{if } 1 < z < 3 \\ 0 & \text{otherwise} \end{cases}$$

$$\tag{11}$$

This MOP approximation was found using Lagrange interpolating polynomial with Chebyshev points [6]. A graph of $g_1(z)$ overlaid on the graph of $\varphi(z)$ is shown in Figure 1. The goodness of fit measures are as follows:

$$KL(\varphi, g_1) \approx 0.00005, \qquad MAD(\varphi, g_1) \approx 0.0024,$$
$$AEM(\varphi, g_1) = 0, \qquad AEV(\varphi, g_1) \approx 0.0003.$$

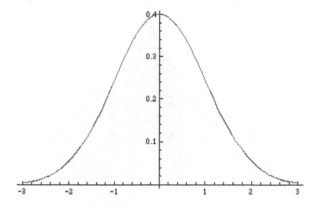

Fig. 1. A graph of $g_1(z)$ versus z (in red) overlaid on the graph of $\varphi(z)$ (in blue)

To find a MOP approximation of the PDF of the general $N(\mu, \sigma^2)$ distribution, where μ and σ are real constants such that $\sigma \neq 0$, we exploit the fact that MOP functions are closed under linear transformations. Thus, if $f(x)$ is a MOP function, then given any real constants a and b, $f(ax+b)$ is also a MOP function. If $Z \sim N(0,1)$, its PDF is approximated by a MOP function $g(z)$, and $X = \sigma Z + \mu$, then $X \sim N(\mu, \sigma^2)$, and a MOP approximation of the PDF of X is given by $(1/|\sigma|)g((x - \mu)/\sigma)$. Notice that $(1/|\sigma|)g((x - \mu)/\sigma)$ remains a MOP even if μ is a variable (and not a constant) as long as σ is a non-zero constant.

3.3 Two-Dimensional CLG Distributions

Consider the CLG conditional distribution $Y|z \sim N(z,1)$ (where $Z \sim N(0,1)$). We will find a MOP approximation of the conditional PDF of $Y|z$ on the two-dimensional region $z - 3 < y < z + 3$. In Shenoy and West [8], a 12-piece, 14-degree MOP approximation is found by covering the two-dimensional region $-3 < z < 3, z - 3 < y < z + 3$ by 12 squares (hypercubes in two dimensions), and then by using two-dimensional Taylor series approximation at the mid-point of each square. Here, we can use the one-dimensional 4-piece, 3-degree MOP approximation $g_1(z)$ of the standard normal distribution as follows. Let $h_1(z, y)$ denote a MOP approximation of the conditional PDF of $Y|z$. Then,

$$h_1(z, y) = g_1(y - z) \tag{12}$$

It follows from the remark at the end of Subsection 3.2, that $h_1(z, y)$ as defined in Equation (12) represents a MOP approximation of the PDF of $N(z, 1)$. Since $g_1(z)$ is a PDF, it follows that $h_1(z, y)$ is a PDF, i.e., $h_1(z, y) \geq 0$, and $\int h_1(z, y)dy = 1$ for all z. Notice that the four pieces of $h_1(z, y)$ are not defined on hypercubes, but rather on hyper-rhombuses (since we now have regions such as $-3 < y - z <= -1$, etc). A 3-dimensional plot of $h_1(z, y)$ is shown in Figure 2.

Since we are using the one-dimensional MOP approximation $g_1(z)$, the goodness of fit of $h_1(z, y)$ is same as that of $g_1(z)$. One question is how much of a

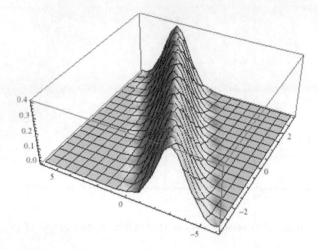

Fig. 2. A 3-dimensional plot of $h_1(z, y)$

penalty do we have to pay for using hyper-rhombuses instead of hypercubes. To answer this, we do two simple experiments.

First, we compute the marginal PDF of Y as follows. $g_1(z)h_1(z, y)$ represents a MOP approximation of the joint PDF of (Z, Y). To find the marginal PDF of Y, we integrate out Z. Thus, a MOP approximation of the marginal PDF of Y is given by:

$$h_2(y) = \int_{-\infty}^{\infty} g_1(z)h_1(z, y)dz \qquad (13)$$

It takes Mathematica© ≈ 14 seconds (on a laptop personal computer) to do the multiplication and integration in Equation (13), and $h_2(y)$ is computed as a 7-degree MOP function on the domain $(-6, 6)$. The exact joint distribution of (Z, Y) is bivariate normal with parameters $\mu_Z = \mu_Y = 0$, $\sigma_Z^2 = 1, \sigma_Y^2 = 2$, and $\sigma_{ZY} = 1$. Therefore, the exact marginal distribution of Y is $N(0, 2)$. Let $f_Y(y)$ denote the exact PDF of $N(0, 2)$ truncated to $(-6, 6)$. A plot of $h_2(y)$ overlaid on the plot of $f_Y(y)$ is shown in Figure 3. The goodness of fit between $f_Y(y)$ and $h_2(y)$ are as follows:

$$KL(f_Y, h_2) \approx 0.0005, \qquad MAD(f_Y, h_2) \approx 0.0015$$
$$AEM(f_Y, h_2) \approx 0.0000, \qquad AEV(f_Y, h_2) \approx 0.0532.$$

Second, consider the Bayesian network as shown in Figure 4 that includes W with a deterministic conditional, $W = Z + Y$. Suppose we use $g_1(z)$ as a MOP approximation of $N(0, 1)$, and $h_1(z, y)$ as a MOP approximation of $N(z, 1)$. The marginal distribution of W is then given by the convolution formula:

$$h_3(w) = \int_{-\infty}^{\infty} g_1(z)h_1(z, w - z)dz \qquad (14)$$

It takes Mathematica© ≈ 15 seconds to do the multiplication and integration in Equation (14). h_3 is computed as a 7-degree MOP function in the region $(-9, 9)$.

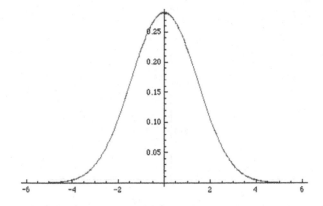

Fig. 3. A graph of $h_2(y)$ (in red) overlaid on the graph of $f_Y(y)$ (in blue)

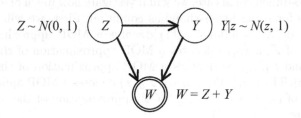

Fig. 4. A Bayesian network with a sum deterministic function

Since the exact joint distribution of (Z, Y) is bivariate normal with parameters $\mu_Z = \mu_Y = 0$, $\sigma_Z^2 = 1$, $\sigma_Y^2 = 2$, $\sigma_{ZY} = 1$, the exact marginal distribution of W is $N(0, 5)$. Let $f_W(w)$ denote the exact PDF of $N(0, 5)$ truncated to $(-9, 9)$. A plot of $h_3(w)$ overlaid on the the plot of $f_W(w)$ is shown in Figure 5. The goodness of fit between $f_W(w)$ and $h_3(w)$ are as follows:

$$KL(f_W, h_3) \approx 0.0009, \qquad MAD(f_W, h_3) \approx 0.0009$$
$$AEM(f_W, h_3) \approx 0.0000, \qquad AEV(f_W, h_3) \approx 0.1301.$$

3.4 Three-Dimensional CLG Distributions

Suppose $Z \sim N(0, 1)$, $Y|z \sim N(z, 1)$, and $X|(z, y) \sim N(z + y, 1)$. Notice that the conditional PDF of X is in three dimensions. As in the 2-dimensional case, we find a MOP approximation $h_4(z, y, x)$ of the PDF of $N(z + y, 1)$ in the 3-dimensional region $z + y - 3 < x < z + y + 3$ by using the 4-piece, 3-degree MOP approximation $g_1(z)$ for $N(0, 1)$ as follows:

$$h_4(z, y, x) = g_1(x - (z + y)) \tag{15}$$

Notice that the 4 pieces of h_4 are defined on regions $-3 < x - (z + y) \le -1$, etc. Therefore, h_4 is a MOP by our definition in Equation (3).

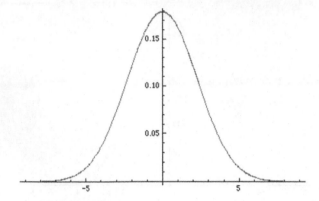

Fig. 5. A graph of $h_3(w)$ (in red) overlaid on the graph of $f_W(w)$ (in blue)

As in the two-dimensional case, we will investigate how much of a time penalty one has to pay for using hyper-rhombus condition. First, we will compute the marginal PDF of X as follows. $g_1(z)$ denotes a MOP approximation of the marginal PDF of Z, $h_1(z,y)$ denotes a MOP approximation of the conditional PDF of $Y|z$, and $h_4(z,y,x)$ denotes a MOP approximation of the conditional PDF of $X|(y,z)$. Thus, $g_1(z)h_1(z,y)h_4(z,y,x)$ denotes a MOP approximation of the joint PDF of (Z,Y,X). Thus, a MOP approximation of the marginal PDF of X is given by:

$$h_6(x) = \int_{-\infty}^{\infty}\int_{-\infty}^{\infty} g_1(z)h_1(z,y)h_4(z,y,x)dydz \qquad (16)$$

$$= \int_{-\infty}^{\infty} g_1(z)\left(\int_{-\infty}^{\infty} h_1(z,y)h_4(z,y,x)dy\right) dz$$

The integration in Equation (16) was done in two stages in Mathematica©. The inner integral (with respect to y) required approximately 79 seconds (≈ 1.3 minutes), and resulted in a 2-dimensional, 7-degree, MOP. The outer integral (with respect to z) required 118 seconds (≈ 2.0 minutes), and resulted in a 1-dimensional, 11-degree, MOP on the interval $(-12, 12)$. Thus, the two multiplications and the two integrations in Equation (16) require a total of approximately 197 seconds (or about 3.3 minutes) using Mathematica© on a laptop computer. The exact distribution of X can be shown to be $N(0,6)$. Let $f_X(x)$ denote the PDF of $N(0,6)$ truncated to the region $(-12,12)$. A graph of $h_6(x)$ overlaid on the graph of $f_X(x)$ is shown in Figure 6. The goodness of fit between $f_X(x)$ and $h_6(x)$ are as follows:

$$KL(f_X, h_6) \approx 0.0005 \qquad MAD(f_X, h_6) \approx 0.0010$$
$$AEM(f_X, h_6) \approx 0.0000 \qquad AEV(f_X, h_6) \approx 0.1618$$

Second, consider the Bayesian network as shown in Figure 7 that includes V with a deterministic conditional, $V = Z + Y + X$. Suppose we use $g_1(z)$ as a MOP approximation of $N(0,1)$, $h_1(z,y)$ as a MOP approximation of $N(z,1)$, and $h_4(z,y,x)$ as a MOP approximation of $N(z+y,1)$. The marginal distribution of V is then given by the convolution formula:

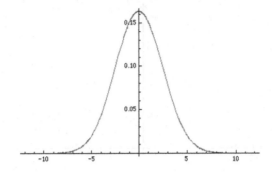

Fig. 6. A graph of $h_6(x)$ (in red) overlaid on the graph of $f_X(x)$ (in blue)

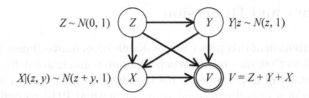

Fig. 7. A Bayesian network with a 3-dimensional conditional

$$h_8(v) = \int_{-\infty}^{\infty} \int_{-\infty}^{\infty} g_1(z)h_1(z,y)h_4(z,y,v-z-y)dydz \qquad (17)$$

$$= \int_{-\infty}^{\infty} g_1(z)\left(\int_{-\infty}^{\infty} h_1(z,y)h_4(z,y,v-z-y)dy\right)dz$$

The integration in Equation (17) was done in two stages in Mathematica©. The inner integral (with respect to y) required approximately 93 seconds (≈ 1.6 minutes), and resulted in a 2-dimensional, 7-degree, MOP. The outer integral (with respect to z) required 176 seconds (≈ 2.9 minutes), and resulted in a 1-dimensional, 11-degree, MOP on the interval $(-21, 21)$. Thus, the two multiplications and the two integrations in Equation (17) require a total of approximately 269 seconds (or ≈ 4.5 minutes) using Mathematica© on a laptop computer. The exact marginal distribution of V is $N(0, 21)$. Let $f_V(v)$ denote the exact PDF of $N(0, 21)$ truncated to $(-21, 21)$. A plot of $h_8(w)$ overlaid on the the plot of $f_V(v)$ is shown in Figure 8. The goodness of fit between $f_V(v)$ and $h_8(v)$ are as follows:

$$KL(f_V, h_8) \approx 0.0008, \qquad MAD(f_V, h_8) \approx 0.0005$$
$$AEM(f_V, h_8) \approx 0.0000, \qquad AEV(f_V, h_8) \approx 0.5648$$

In summary, the hyper-rhombus condition enables us to easily represent CLG conditionals in high dimensions. The computational cost of integrating a high-dimensional MOP function with a hyper-rhombus condition does not seem high for 2 or 3 dimensional CLG distributions, and there is no loss of precision compared to one-dimensional conditionals. Shenoy [6] discusses the tradeoffs between the hyper-rhombus and hypercube conditions in greater detail.

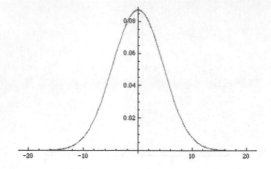

Fig. 8. A graph of $h_8(v)$ (in red) overlaid on the graph of $f_V(v)$ (in blue)

4   Summary and Discussion

A major contribution of this paper is a re-definition of multi-dimensional mixture of polynomials so that the regions where the polynomials are defined are hyper-rhombuses instead of hypercubes. This re-definition allows us to use the MOP approximation of a one-dimensional standard normal PDF to define MOP approximations of high-dimensional CLG PDFs. Also, the re-definition ensures that MOP functions are closed under transformations required for multi-dimensional linear deterministic functions, which was not true when MOP functions were defined on regions that are hypercubes.

Shenoy [6] compares the practical implications of the hyper-rhombus condition with the hypercube condition. He compares the time required for computation of marginals for a couple of simple Bayesian networks, and also the accuracy of the computed marginals.

The hyper-rhombus condition is of great use for constructing MOP approximations of multi-dimensional CLG distributions. However, it does not seem to be of much help in constructing MOP approximations of other multi-dimensional distributions such as the log-normal distribution. Constructing MOP approximations of the multi-dimensional log-normal distributions is of great interest in the finance literature where log-normal distributions are used to model stock price behavior [3]. This is a topic that needs further investigation.

Acknowledgements. The paper has benefitted from comments by three ECSQARU-11 reviewers.

References

1. Cobb, B.R., Shenoy, P.P., Rumí, R.: Approximating probability density functions in hybrid Bayesian networks with mixtures of truncated exponentials. Statistics & Computing 16(3), 293–308 (2006)
2. Kullback, S., Leibler, R.A.: On information and sufficiency. Annals of Mathematical Statistics 22, 76–86 (1951)

3. Li, Y., Shenoy, P.P.: Solving hybrid influence diagrams with deterministic variables. In: Grünwald, P., Spirtes, P. (eds.) Proceedings of the 26th Conference on Uncertainty in Artificial Intelligence, pp. 322–331. AUAI Press, Corvallis (2010)
4. Moral, S., Rumí, R., Salmerón, A.: Mixtures of truncated exponentials in hybrid bayesian networks. In: Benferhat, S., Besnard, P. (eds.) ECSQARU 2001. LNCS (LNAI), vol. 2143, pp. 156–167. Springer, Heidelberg (2001)
5. Moral, S., Rumí, R., Salmerón, A.: Approximating conditional MTE distributions by means of mixed trees. In: Nielsen, T.D., Zhang, N.L. (eds.) ECSQARU 2003. LNCS (LNAI), vol. 2711, pp. 173–183. Springer, Heidelberg (2003)
6. Shenoy, P.P.: Some issues in using mixtures of polynomials for inference in hybrid Bayesian networks. Working Paper 323, School of Business University of Kansas, Lawrence, KS (October 2010)
7. Shenoy, P.P., West, J.C.: Extended Shenoy-Shafer architecture for inference in hybrid Bayesian networks with deterministic conditionals. International Journal of Approximate Reasoning 52(6), 805–818 (2011)
8. Shenoy, P.P., West, J.C.: Inference in hybrid Bayesian networks using mixtures of polynomials. International Journal of Approximate Reasoning 52(5), 641–657 (2011)

Using Four Cost Measures
to Determine Arc Reversal Orderings

Cory J. Butz[1], Anders L. Madsen[2], and Kevin Williams[1]

[1] Department of Computer Science, University of Regina,
Regina, Saskatchewan, S4S 0A2 Canada
{butz,willikev}@cs.uregina.ca
[2] HUGIN EXPERT A/S, Gasværksvej 5, DK-9000 Aalborg, Denmark
Anders.L.Madsen@hugin.com

Abstract. Four cost measures s_1, s_2, s_3, s_4 were recently studied for sorting the operations in Lazy propagation with arc reversal (LPAR), a join tree propagation approach to Bayesian network inference. It has been suggested to use s_1 with LPAR, since there is an effectiveness ranking, say s_1, s_2, s_3, s_4, when applied in isolation. In this paper, we also suggest to use s_1 with LPAR, but to use s_2 to break s_1 ties, s_3 to break s_2 ties, and s_4 to break s_3 ties. Experimental results show that sometimes there is a noticeable gain to be made.

Keywords: Bayesian networks, arc reversal, join tree propagation.

1 Introduction

Bayesian networks [6,8,9,10,18] provide a rigorous foundation for uncertainty management by combining probability theory and graph theory. They have been applied in practice to a number of problem domains [19], including bioinformatics [16]. A Bayesian network consists of a *directed acyclic graph* (DAG) and a corresponding set of *conditional probability tables* (CPTs). The vertices in the DAG represent the random variables in the real-world problem, while the arcs in the graph represent probabilistic dependencies amongst the variables. More specifically, the probabilistic conditional independencies encoded in the DAG define the product of the given CPTs as a joint probability distribution.

While Cooper [5] has shown that the complexity of exact inference in discrete Bayesian networks is NP-hard, several approaches have been put forth that work quite well in practice. *Arc reversal* (AR) [17,20] removes a variable by reversing the arcs between the variable and its children and then building the CPTs corresponding to the modified DAG. Another approach, called *variable elimination* (VE) [1], eliminates a variable by multiplying together all of the distributions involving the variable and then summing the variable out of the obtained product. *Join tree propagation*, which Shafer [21] emphasizes is central to the theory and practice of probabilistic expert systems, first builds a secondary network, called a join tree, from the DAG of the Bayesian network and then performs inference by propagating probabilities in the join tree [2,3,4]. Madsen and

W. Liu (Ed.): ECSQARU 2011, LNAI 6717, pp. 110–121, 2011.
© Springer-Verlag Berlin Heidelberg 2011

Jensen [15] significantly advanced the field of join tree propagation with *Lazy Propagation* (LP), which maintains a factorization of distributions allowing for *barren* variables [20] and independencies induced by evidence to be exploited. Madsen [12,13] modified LP by replacing VE as the message construction algorithm with AR, giving LPAR, and conducted an empirical study of LP and LPAR. Very recently, Madsen [14] demonstrated that the order in which arcs are reversed in LPAR can affect the amount of computation needed. Experimental results suggest that *cpt-weight* (*cptw*) is the best of four measures [14].

Here we advocate using all four cost measures in ranked order starting with *cptw*. Our analysis in Section 4 shows that *cptw* seems to be the closest to optimizing the number of arithmetic operations as it is focused on reducing the size of the CPTs constructed. This is similar to reducing the weight of cliques when building join trees [10]. In the event of a *cptw* tie, reverse the best arc as determined by the second-best cost measure, *fill-in weight* (*fiw*). Similarly, proceed to the third-best cost measure *fill-in* (*fi*) to break *fiw* ties, and to *number-of-parents* (*nop*) to break *fi* ties. We illustrate in Section 4 how our approach can save computation, since [14] will reverse the first arc tied for the best *cptw* score. Our experiments in Section 5 show a small but observable computational improvement using five real-world BNs and three randomly-generated BNs.

The remainder is organized as follows. Section 2 contains definitions. We present our new approach in Section 3. Section 4 provides analysis. Experimental findings are given in Section 5. Conclusions are drawn in Section 6.

2   Definitions

Results from Bayesian networks, AR, and four AR cost measures, are reviewed.

2.1   Bayesian Networks

Consider a finite set of discrete random variables $U = \{v_1, v_2, \ldots, v_n\}$. Let $dom(v_i)$ denote the finite domain of values that each variable $v_i \in U$ can assume. For a subset $X \subseteq U$, the Cartesian product of the domains of the individual variables in X is $dom(X)$. An element $x \in dom(X)$ is a *configuration* or *row* of X. A *potential* [21] on $dom(X)$ is a function ϕ such that $\phi(x) \geq 0$, for each configuration $x \in dom(X)$, and at least one $\phi(x)$ is positive. For simplicity we speak of a potential as defined on X instead of on $dom(X)$, and we call X its domain rather than $dom(X)$ [21]. A *joint probability distribution* [21] on U, written $p(U)$, is a function p on U satisfying the following two conditions: (i) $0 \leq p(u) \leq 1$, for each configuration $u \in dom(U)$; (ii) $\sum_{u \in dom(U)} p(u) = 1$. Let X and Y be two disjoint subsets of U. A *conditional probability table* (CPT) [21] for Y given X, denoted $p(Y|X)$, is a nonnegative function on $X \cup Y$, satisfying the following condition: for each configuration $x \in dom(X)$, $\sum_{y \in dom(Y)} p(Y = y \mid X = x) = 1$.

A discrete *Bayesian network* [18] on $U = \{v_1, v_2, \ldots, v_n\}$ is a pair (D, C). D is a DAG with vertex set U. C is the set of CPTs $\{p(v_i|P_i) \mid i = 1, 2, \ldots, n\}$, where P_i denotes the parents of variable $v_i \in D$. For example, one Bayesian

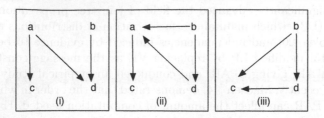

Fig. 1. Eliminating a in (i) by reversing arc (a, d) (ii) followed by arc (a, c) (iii)

network is the DAG in Figure 1 (i) together with CPTs $p(a)$, $p(b)$, $p(c|a)$ and $p(d|a, b)$. Here, the parents P_i of variable $v_i = d$ are $P_i = \{a, b\}$.

The *family* F_i of a variable v_i in a Bayesian network is the variable together with its parents, that is, $\{v_i\} \cup P_i$. By $p(X|Y)$, we always mean $p(X|Y - X)$. We use WZ to mean $W \cup Z$.

2.2   Arc Reversal

Arc reversal (AR) [17,20] eliminates a variable v_i by reversing the arcs (v_i, v_j) for each child v_j of v_i, where $j = 1, 2, \ldots, k$. With respect to multiplication, addition, and division, AR reverses one arc (v_i, v_j) as a three-step process:

$$p(v_i, v_j | P_i P_j) = p(v_i | P_i) \cdot p(v_j | P_j), \tag{1}$$

$$p(v_j | P_i P_j) = \sum_{v_i} p(v_i, v_j | P_i P_j), \tag{2}$$

$$p(v_i | P_i P_j v_j) = \frac{p(v_i, v_j | P_i P_j)}{p(v_j | P_i P_j)}. \tag{3}$$

Suppose the variable v_i to be removed has k children. The distributions defined in (1) - (3) are built for the first $k - 1$ children. For the last child v_k, however, only the distributions in (1) - (2) are built. When considering v_k, there is no need to build the final distribution for v_i in (3), since v_i will be removed as a barren variable. Therefore, AR removes a variable v_i with k children by building $3k - 1$ distributions. However, AR only outputs the k distributions built in (2).

2.3   Four Cost Measures for AR Child Orderings

The following is taken from Madsen [14]. The elimination of variable v_i by a sequence of AR operations produces an ordering of the v_i's children. We call this ordering a *child ordering* and denote it by ρ. The child ordering ρ determines the set of induced edges, which have an impact on the performance of belief update. Thereby, the child ordering p' leading to the best time and space performance should be chosen. Since it is not possible by local computations only to identify the sequence p' having the best time and space cost, the focus is on identifying the sequence ρ with minimum local cost.

Four different score functions for computing the cost of a child ordering ρ are considered: *cptw* (s_1), *fiw* (s_2), *fi* (s_3), and *nop* (s_4).

The cost of reversing arc (v_i, v_j) using the *cptw* score s_1 is:

$$s_1(v_i, v_j) = \prod_{v_k \in F_i F_j} |dom(v_k)|.$$

Thus, *cptw* is defined as the total state space size of v_i's CPT after reversal.

Using the *fiw* score s_2, the cost of reversing (v_i, v_j) is:

$$s_2(v_i, v_j) = \sum_{v_k \in F_j - F_i} w(v_k, v_i) + \sum_{v_l \in P_i - P_j} w(v_l, v_j),$$

where $w(v_a, v_b) = |dom(v_a)| \cdot |dom(v_b)|$. Then, *fiw* cost is equal to the sum of the edge weights of the new parents $F_j - F_i$ of v_i and $P_i - P_j$ of v_j.

The cost of reversing arc (v_i, v_j) using the *fi* score s_3 is:

$$s_3(v_i, v_j) = |F_j - F_i| + |P_i - P_j|,$$

namely, the *fi* cost is equal to the number of edges induced by the new parents $F_j - F_i$ of v_i and the new parents $P_i - P_j$ of v_j.

Using the *nop* score s_4, the cost of reversing (v_i, v_j) is:

$$s_4(v_i, v_j) = |P_i \cup F_j|,$$

i.e., the *nop* cost is the cardinality of v_i's parents after reversing (v_i, v_j).

Experimental results suggest an effectiveness ranking of s_1, s_2, s_3, s_4 [14].

Example 1. Consider eliminating variable a in Fig. 1 (i), where a, b, d are binary and c's domain has four values. Compute the *cptw* score of arcs (a, c) and (a, d) corresponding to the children c and d of a:

$$s_1(a, c) = \prod_{v_k \in \{a, c\}} |dom(v_k)| = 2 \cdot 4 = 8,$$

$$s_1(a, d) = \prod_{v_k \in \{a, b, d\}} |dom(v_k)| = 2 \cdot 2 \cdot 2 = 8.$$

Since $s_1(a, c)$ is equal to $s_1(a, d)$, *cptw* does not distinguish between arcs (a, c) and (a, d). Thus, one arc is randomly chosen, say (a, d), and reversed:

$$p(a, d|b) = p(a) \cdot p(d|a, b),$$

$$p(d|b) = \sum_a p(a, d|b),$$

$$p(a|b, d) = \frac{p(a, d|b)}{p(d|b)}.$$

The resulting DAG is shown in Fig. 1 (ii). The reversal of the other arc (a, c) gives Fig. 1 (iii) by computing:

$$p(a, c|b, d) = p(a|b, d) \cdot p(c|a),$$
$$p(c|b, d) = \sum_a p(a, c|b, d).$$

3   AR Child Orderings Using Four Cost Measures

While Madsen's [14] experimental results suggest that *cptw* may the best choice of the four cost measures, our extension, called *BreakTies* and given below, is to use *cptw* as our first cost measure but to rely on other cost measures to break ties. In other words, follow the fixed order s_1, s_2, s_3, s_4 to select the next arc to reverse, only progressing to the next cost measure to break ties.

> **Algorithm 1.** BreakTies (v_i, D)
> Input: v_i is the variable to be eliminated in DAG D
> Output: the arc (v_i, v_j) in D to be reversed next.
> **begin**
> **for** each remaining child v_j of v_i
>   compute $s_1(v_i, v_j)$
>   **if** unique lowest $s_1(v_i, v_j)$
>   reverse arc (v_i, v_j)
>   **else**
>   **for** each v_j tying for lowest $s_1(v_i, v_j)$
>   compute $s_2(v_i, v_j)$
>   **if** unique lowest $s_2(v_i, v_j)$
>   reverse arc (v_i, v_j)
>   **else**
>   **for** each v_j tying for lowest $s_2(v_i, v_j)$
>   compute $s_3(v_i, v_j)$
>   **if** unique lowest $s_3(v_i, v_j)$
>   reverse arc (v_i, v_j)
>   **else**
>   **for** each v_j tying for lowest $s_3(v_i, v_j)$
>   compute $s_4(v_i, v_j)$
>   **if** unique lowest $s_4(v_i, v_j)$
>   reverse arc (v_i, v_j)
>   **else**
>   randomly pick an arc (v_i, v_j)
> **return** (v_i, v_j)
> **end**

Example 2. With respect to Fig. 2 (i), let us revisit Example 1 using BreakTies. Variable a is to be eliminated and has two children c and d. As BreakTies always

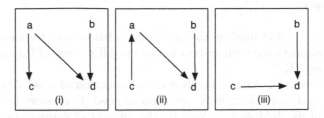

Fig. 2. Eliminating a in (i) by reversing arc (a, c) (ii) followed by arc (a, d) (iii)

starts with $cptw$, scores $s_1(a, c)$ and $s_1(a, d)$ are the same as before. In BreakTies, however, given a tie, we proceed to the second fiw score s_2 to decide which arc to reverse first:

$$s_2(a, c) = w(c, a) = 8,$$
$$s_2(a, d) = w(b, a) + w(d, a) = 4 + 4 = 8.$$

To break fiw ties, BreakTies proceeds to the fi cost measure s_3:

$$s_3(a, c) = 1,$$
$$s_3(a, d) = 2.$$

As $s_3(a, c)$ is the lowest, BreakTies reverses arc (a, c) first, as follows:

$$p(a, c) = p(a) \cdot p(c|a),$$
$$p(c) = \sum_a p(a, c),$$
$$p(a|c) = \frac{p(a, c)}{p(c)}.$$

The resulting DAG is shown in Figure 2 (ii). The reversal of (a, d) yields Figure 2 (iii) by computing

$$p(a, d|b, c) = p(a|c) \cdot p(d|a, b),$$
$$p(d|b, c) = \sum_a p(a, d|c, d).$$

Example 2 illustrates a couple of important points. Note that multiple cost measures were used. First, $cptw$ cost measures were computed and found to be tied. Second, fiw cost measures were computed and also found to be tied. Third, fi cost measures were computed and arc (a, c) was preferred as it had the lowest score. If fi scores had been tied, then nop cost measures would have been computed. Also notice how BreakTies starts with $cptw$, considered to be the best, and ends with nop, considered to be the weakest measure.

4   Analysis

In this section, we first analyze the *cptw* score with respect to one arc reversal. Next, we scrutinize *cptw* with respect to the overall process of Bayesian network inference using AR.

Bayesian network inference involves the elimination of a set X of variables. To eliminate each variable v_i in X, arc reversal needs to reverse the arc between v_i and each of its children v_j. Consider the amount of computation needed to reverse one arc (v_i, v_j). It can be seen that: (i) the number of multiplications in the first step is equal to $|dom(F_iF_j)|$; (ii) the number of additions in the second step is equal to $|dom(v_i) - 1| \cdot |dom(F_iF_j - v_i)|$; and, (iii) the number of divisions in the third step is equal to $|dom(F_iF_j)|$. This means that the amount of computation needed to reverse one arc is tied directly to *cptw*.

Now let us turn our attention away from reversing one arc to the larger problem of eliminating a set X of variables. The next example shows that randomly breaking *cptw* ties can cost more computation in the long run.

Example 3. Suppose we have to eliminate variable b after variable a has been eliminated in our running example.

If we only use *cptw* and randomly break ties as shown in Example 1, variable b needs to be eliminated from Figure 1 (iii). Since

$$s_1(b,c) = 2 \cdot 4 \cdot 2 = 16,$$
$$s_1(b,d) = 2 \cdot 2 = 4,$$

arc (b, d) is reversed as

$$p(b,d) = p(b) \cdot p(d|b),$$
$$p(d) = \sum_b p(b,d),$$
$$p(d|b) = \frac{p(b,d)}{p(d)}.$$

Arc (b, c) is then reversed as

$$p(b,c|d) = p(b|d) \cdot p(c|b),$$
$$p(c|d) = \sum_b p(b,c|d).$$

On the other hand, if we use multiple cost measures as done in Example 2, variable b needs to be eliminated from Figure 2 (iii). In this case, variable b only has one child d, which allows b to be eliminated more economically as

$$p(b,d|c) = p(b) \cdot p(d|b,c),$$
$$p(d|c) = \sum_b p(b,d|c).$$

Example 3 reveals that randomly breaking *cptw* ties can result in extra arcs being added. For instance, in our running example, the approach in [14] can add one more arc (b, c) in Fig. 1 (iii) than BreakTies did in Fig. 2 (iii). That is, b only has one child using BreakTies, whereas b has two children using *cptw* alone. Adding children to a variable to be subsequently removed means that the *cptw* cost measure in isolation can force more computation to be performed.

5 Experimental Results

The experiments use the LPAR method in [14], namely, AR is applied to build all messages and VE is applied to compute posterior marginals. The measure fiw is used to determine the elimination order and to compute posteriors. Experiments were conducted on 15 real-world networks and 30 randomly generated networks, but we report only on five real-world networks, called Barley [11], KK [11][1], Mildew[2], OOW [7], and ship-ship [7], and three randomly generated networks, called net100, net125, and net150 [14], which are all described in Table 1. For each size of evidence set, ten sets of evidence are generated, with the same evidence used in different runs. To reflect the potential time savings of breaking ties, the *best* and *worst* arcs are reversed based on the next cost measure in BreakTies. Figs. 3 - 6 show running times in seconds on our eight Bayesian networks.

Table 1. Description of test Bayesian networks and corresponding join tree nodes $\mathcal{N}$

BN	$|U|$	$|\mathcal{N}|$	max $|dom(\mathcal{N})|$	total size
Barley	48	36	7,257,600	17,140,796
KK	50	38	5,806,080	14,011,466
Mildew	35	29	1,249,280	3,400,464
OOW	40	29	1,644,300	4,651,788
ship-ship	50	35	4,032,000	24,258,572
net100	100	85	98,304	311,593
net125	125	109	165,888	408,889
net150	150	131	3,538,944	9,946,960

Let us look at a couple of cases. In Fig. 5 (left), for the case of six evidence variables, the average running time of breaking ties (best) is 1.6866 seconds, while the average running time for breaking ties (worst) is 2.0792 seconds. Hence, breaking ties (best) can result in a time savings of 18.9%. Now consider twenty evidence variables in Fig. 6 (right). The average running time of breaking ties (worst) is 1.5247, which can be bettered by 29.61% to 1.0739 when breaking ties (best). When considering thirty evidence variables in Fig. 6 (right), the results are even more promising. Here a time savings of 42.5% can be obtained when the running time is decreased from 1.9465 (worst) down to 1.1196 (best). While this demonstrates that there can be on average fewer multiplication and division

---

[1] KK is a preliminary version of Barley.
[2] A network developed by Finn V. Jensen, Jørgen Olesen and Uffe Kjærulff.

118   C.J. Butz, A.L. Madsen, and K. Williams

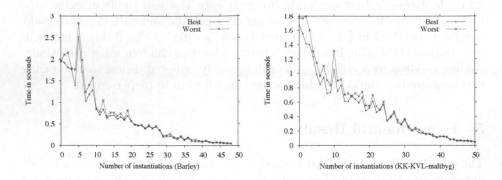

Fig. 3. Time savings of breaking ties by reversing the best and worst arcs as determined by the next cost measure in BreakTies on Barley (left) and KK (right)

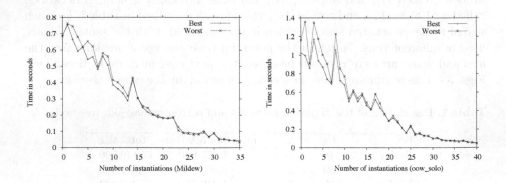

Fig. 4. Time savings of breaking ties by reversing the best and worst arcs as determined by the next cost measure in BreakTies on Mildew (left) and OOW (right)

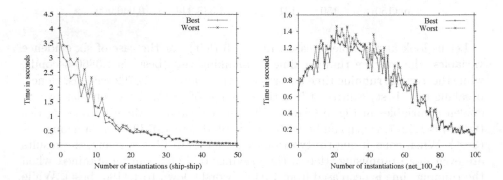

Fig. 5. Time savings of breaking ties by reversing the best and worst arcs as determined by the next cost measure in BreakTies on ship-ship (left) and net100 (right)

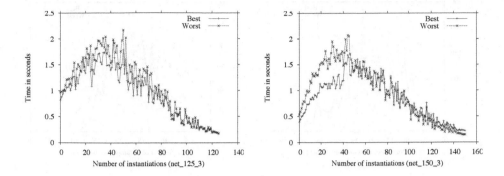

Fig. 6. Time savings of breaking ties by reversing the best and worst arcs as determined by the next cost measure in BreakTies on net125 (left) and net150 (right)

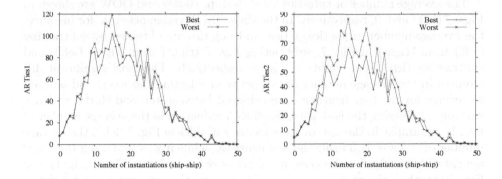

Fig. 7. Using BreakTies on ship-ship, the average number of *cptw* ties (left) and *cptw* and *fiw* ties (right)

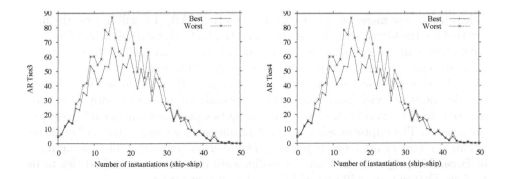

Fig. 8. Using BreakTies on ship-ship, the average number of *cptw, fiw,* and *fi* ties (left) and *cptw, fiw, fi,* and *nop* ties (right)

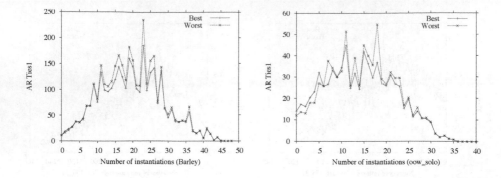

Fig. 9. The average number of *cptw* ties in BreakTies on Barley (left) and OOW (right)

operations when breaking ties, the average size of the largest CPT does not change noticeably.

The average number of *cptw* ties for ship-ship, Barley and OOW are shown in Figs. 7 (left) and 9, respectively. In the ship-ship Bayesian network, for instance, the average number of *fiw* ties, *fi* ties, and *nop* ties are obtained by subtracting (left) from (right) in Fig. 7, subtracting Fig. 7 (right) from Fig. 8 (left), and subtracting (left) from (right) in Fig. 8, respectively. The most significant differences in the average number of ties between selecting the *worst* and *best* arc to reverse for the four heuristics are achieved between ten and thirty evidence variables. Following the *best* heuristic offers a reduction in the average number of ties. For example, in the case of six evidence variables in Fig. 7 (left), the average number of ties was 41.3 using the *best* heuristic, while it was 46.3 using the *worst* heuristic. Similarly, for the case of six evidence variables in Fig. 7 (right) and Fig. 8 together, the average number of ties using the *best* and *worst* heuristics were 23.2 was 30.3, respectively.

6 Conclusions

When using cost measure *cptw* to reverse arcs in LPAR, [14] will reverse the first arc tied for the lowest score in the event of a tie. Instead, we suggest breaking ties with other cost measures *fiw*, *fi* and *nop*, in this order. Example 3 illustrates how random selection can result in more computation. The empirical experiments in Figs. 3 - 6 have produced two important findings. First, in most cases, breaking ties does not yield significant gains. Second, for both randomly generated and real-world networks, sometimes breaking ties produces a noticeable time improvement. The improvements are most significant for small subsets of evidence where the cost of inference is highest. The average number of ties encountered in BreakTies, reported in Figs. 7 - 9, illustrate that there are indeed ties to be broken. Future work will investigate combined cost measures.

Acknowledgments. This research is supported in part by NSERC Discovery Grant 238880.

References

1. Butz, C.J., Chen, J., Konkel, K., Lingras, P.: A Formal Comparison of Variable Elimination and Arc Reversal in Bayesian Network Inference. Intell. Dec. Analysis 3(3), 173–180 (2009)
2. Butz, C.J., Konkel, K., Lingras, P.: Join Tree Propagation Utilizing both Arc Reversal and Variable Elimination. Intl. J. Approx. Rea. (2010) (in press)
3. Butz, C.J., Hua, S., Konkel, K., Yao, H.: Join Tree Propagation with Prioritized Messages. Networks 55(4), 350–359 (2010)
4. Butz, C.J., Yao, H., Hua, S.: A Join Tree Probability Propagation Architecture for Semantic Modelling. J. Int. Info. Sys. 33(2), 145–178 (2009)
5. Cooper, G.F.: The Computational Complexity of Probabilistic Inference using Bayesian Belief Networks. Art. Intel. 42(2-3), 393–405 (1990)
6. Darwiche, A.: Modeling and Reasoning with Bayesian Networks. Cambridge University Press, New York (2009)
7. Hansen, P.F., Pedersen, P.T.: Risk Analysis of Conventional and Solo Watch Keeping. Research Report, Department of Naval Architecture and Offshore Engineering. Technical University of Denmark (1998)
8. Jensen, F.V., Nielsen, T.D.: Bayesian Networks and Decision Graphs. Springer, New York (2007)
9. Kjaerulff, U.B., Madsen, A.L.: Bayesian Networks and Influence Diagrams: a Guide to Construction and Analysis. Springer, New York (2008)
10. Koller, D., Friedman, N.: Probabilistic Graphical Models: Principles and Techniques. The MIT Press, Cambridge (2009)
11. Kristensen, K., Rasmussen, I.A.: The use of a Bayesian Network in the Design of a Decision Support System for Growing Malting Barley without use of Pesticides. Computers and Electronics in Agriculture 33, 192–217 (2002)
12. Madsen, A.L.: An Empirical Evaluation of Possible Variations of Lazy Propagation. In: 20th Conference in Uncertainty in Artificial Intelligence, pp. 366–373. AUAI Press, Arlington (2004)
13. Madsen, A.L.: Variations over the Message Computation Algorithm of Lazy Propagation. IEEE Trans. Sys. Man Cyb. B 36, 636–648 (2006)
14. Madsen, A.L.: Improvements to Message Computation in Lazy Propagation. Intl. J. Approx. Rea. 51(5), 499–514 (2010)
15. Madsen, A.L., Jensen, F.V.: A Junction Tree Inference Algorithm based on Lazy Evaluation. Art. Intel. 113(1-2), 203–245 (1999)
16. Neapolitan, R.E.: Probabilistic Methods for Bioinformatics with an Introduction to Bayesian Networks. Morgan Kaufmann, New York (2009)
17. Olmsted, S.: On Representing and Solving Decision Problems. Ph.D. Thesis, Department of Engineering Economic Systems. Stanford University, Stanford, California (1983)
18. Pearl, P.: Probabilistic Reasoning Intelligent Systems: Networks of Plausible Inference. Morgan Kaufmann, San Francisco (1988)
19. Pourret, O., Naim, P., Marcot, B. (eds.): Bayesian Networks: A Practical Guide to Applications. Wiley, New York (2008)
20. Shachter, R.: Evaluating Influence Diagrams. Oper. Research 34, 871–882 (1986)
21. Shafer, G.: Probabilistic Expert Systems. SIAM, Philadelphia (1996)

Using the Noisy-OR Model Can Be Harmful ...
But It Often Is Not

Steven P.D. Woudenberg and Linda C. van der Gaag

Department of Information and Computing Sciences, Utrecht University,
P.O. Box 80.089, 3508 TB Utrecht, The Netherlands
{stevenw,linda}@cs.uu.nl

Abstract. The noisy-OR model and its generalizations are frequently
used for alleviating the burden of probability elicitation upon building
Bayesian networks with the help of domain experts. The results from
empirical studies consistently suggest that, when compared with a fully
expert-quantified network, using the noisy-OR model will just have a
minor effect on the performance of a network. In this paper, we address
this apparent robustness and investigate its origin. Our results show that
ill-considered use of the noisy-OR model can substantially decrease a
network's performance, yet also that the model has broader applicability
than it was originally designed for.

1   Introduction

When building a Bayesian network with the help of domain experts, eliciting
all probabilities required for its quantification is generally considered the most
daunting among the engineering tasks involved: the elicitation task is quite time
consuming in itself [1,2], and is often further impeded by the experts feeling un-
comfortable with providing concrete numbers to describe their knowledge and
experience. In order to decrease the amount of time spent on probability elicitation and to alleviate the burden for the experts involved, probabilistic causal
interaction models can be used. The most popular among these models are the
noisy-OR model and its generalizations [3].

The noisy-OR model can be looked upon as a parameterized conditional probability table for the effect variable of a causal mechanism with multiple cause
variables. The model needs a restricted number of parameter probabilities, from
which the values for the other probabilities in the table are readily calculated.
The formulas provided for this purpose are derived from properties of probabilistic interaction which are assumed to hold among the variables of the mechanism.
Since only the parameter probabilities need to be provided, use of the noisy-OR
model implies a substantial reduction of the number of probabilities to be assessed explicitly by the experts: this number is reduced from exponential to
linear in the number of possible causes of the mechanism's effect.

Despite its clear advantages for Bayesian-network engineering, the noisy-OR
model cannot be applied just like that. Since the model's formulas build upon
specific properties of intercausal interaction, the calculated probability values

W. Liu (Ed.): ECSQARU 2011, LNAI 6717, pp. 122–133, 2011.

can only be considered approximates of the true probabilities if these properties actually do hold in the domain of application. In practice, however, Bayesian-network engineers are not all aware of the precise underlying properties, which makes the noisy-OR model subject to ill-considered use.

Various empirical studies have been conducted with the noisy-OR model to determine its effect in practical applications [4,5,6,7]. In most of these studies, noisy-OR calculated probability tables were substituted for the original expert-elicited probabilities of a network. The resulting networks were then compared with the original ones using various different performance indicators. The overall conclusion from these studies is that the networks with the noisy-OR calculated probability tables perform comparably to the original expert-quantified ones. In one of the studies, noisy-OR calculated probability tables were substituted for expert-provided ones without verifying any underlying properties, to mimic ill-considered use of the model. Even in this study did the noisy-OR quantified network show comparable performance to the original one [4]. The consistent results from these studies have led to the suggestion that Bayesian networks are quite robust against the changes that are induced in their conditional probability tables by using the noisy-OR model. The results even appear to suggest that the model can be applied for *any* causal mechanism, regardless of the precise probabilistic interaction among its variables.

In this paper, we demonstrate that ill-considered use of the noisy-OR model can result in poorly calibrated probability values. The propagation effects of such strongly deviating probabilities are largely unknown, yet are important for determining when use of the noisy-OR model can harm a network's performance. By means of sensitivity-analysis techniques, we will study these effects. Building upon the identified propagation effects, we then pose conditions under which use of the noisy-OR model will not be harmful, not even when the model's underlying assumptions are not met in practice. These conditions show that, while the noisy-OR model was designed originally to describe a particular type of probabilistic interaction, its use for mere pragmatic reasons is sometimes warranted.

The paper is organized as follows. In Sect. 2, we introduce our notational conventions and review the noisy-OR model; an overview of empirical studies with the model will also be provided. In Sect. 3, we study the conditions under which use of the noisy-OR model can be harmful to the performance of a Bayesian network; we address our results also in view of well-known generalizations and extensions of the noisy-OR model. The paper is concluded in Sect. 4.

2   Preliminaries

We introduce our notational conventions and review the noisy-OR model; upon doing so, we assume that the reader is acquainted with the basic concepts of Bayesian networks and probabilistic inference. We further review several empirical studies of Bayesian networks in which the noisy-OR model is being applied.

2.1   The Noisy-OR Model

We consider random variables V and assume these to be binary unless explicitly stated otherwise; each variable captures absence or presence of some concept, written $\bar{v}$ and v respectively. We further consider causal mechanisms, that is, network fragments including n random cause variables $C_1, \ldots, C_n$, $n \geq 2$, and a single effect variable E; a graphical representation of such a mechanism is shown in Fig. 1. For ease of exposition, we assume that the cause variables of the mechanism are mutually independent a priori; we will return to this assumption in Sect. 3. For the effect variable E, a conditional probability table is specified, containing the probability distributions $\Pr(E \mid C_1, \ldots, C_n)$ given all possible value combinations for the cause variables C_j; note that the number of distributions specified for E is exponential in the number of cause variables involved.

The noisy-OR model in essence specifies a parameterized conditional probability table for the effect variable E of a causal mechanism. The model takes for its parameters the conditional probabilities $\Pr(e \mid \bar{c}_1, \ldots, \bar{c}_{j-1}, c_j, \bar{c}_{j+1}, \ldots, \bar{c}_n)$ of the effect e to arise in the presence of just a single cause c_j and the absence of all other causes. The model further sets the conditional probability $\Pr(e \mid \bar{c}_1, \ldots, \bar{c}_n)$ to zero and defines the values of the remaining probabilities through

$$\Pr(e \mid \mathbf{c}) = 1 - \prod_{j \in J} (1 - \Pr(e \mid \bar{c}_1, \ldots, \bar{c}_{j-1}, c_j, \bar{c}_{j+1}, \ldots, \bar{c}_n))$$

where J is the set of indices of the cause variables C_j which are marked as being present in the combination of causes $\mathbf{c}$.

Underlying the noisy-OR model are the two properties of accountability and exception independence. The property of accountability states that the effect e cannot occur as long as none of its causes are present, that is $\Pr(e \mid \bar{c}_1, \ldots, \bar{c}_n) = 0$. The property of exception independence pertains to the exception mechanisms that may inhibit the effect to arise in the presence of a cause. We note that each arc $C_j \rightarrow E$ can be viewed as an essentially deterministic causal relation which has associated an inhibitor variable I_j to describe the uncertainty involved. Exception independence now states that these inhibitor variables I_j are mutually independent. For further details of the noisy-OR model, we refer to [3].

As a fictitious example, Fig. 2 shows a simple causal mechanism modeling the intake of alcohol (A) and of the GHB drug (G) as the possible causes of a stimulating effect (S). The figure further shows the conditional probability table which is established from applying the noisy-OR model for the effect variable S in the mechanism. The probabilities printed in bold are the two parameter

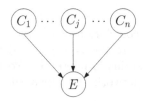

Fig. 1. Causal mechanism with n cause variables C_j and a single effect variable E

Alcohol (A)	GHB (G)	Stimulating (S)	
		yes	no
yes	yes	0.99	0.01
yes	no	**0.80**	0.20
no	yes	**0.95**	0.05
no	no	0.00	1.00

Fig. 2. Causal mechanism describing the stimulating effect (S) of the intake of alcohol (A) and GHB (G) (*left*), and the noisy-OR computed probability table for S (*right*)

probabilities for the model; in a real application, these probabilities would have to be assessed by experts. The probability $\Pr(s \mid \bar{a}\bar{g}) = 0$ in the table follows from the property of accountability, and the remaining probability $\Pr(s \mid ag) = 0.99$ is calculated from the two parameter probabilities. We note that for this specific mechanism the calculated probability value does not properly reflect the true probability $\Pr(s \mid ag)$. Simultaneous consumption of alcohol and GHB is known to have a depressing effect rather than a stimulating one; the probability $\Pr(s \mid ag)$ is not equal to 0.99 but will be closer to 0.05 instead.

2.2 Empirical Studies Involving the Noisy-OR Model

Several researchers investigated the effects on a network's performance of using the noisy-OR model for specifying its conditional probability tables. These empirical studies involved the standard noisy-OR model as reviewed above, and the more general leaky noisy-OR and noisy-MAX models. From these studies we summarize the results that are of direct relevance to the current paper.

Oniśko, Druzdzel and Wasyluk [5] conducted an empirical study of the use of the noisy-OR model in view of the medical HEPAR II network. For estimating the probabilities for their network, they had available a small collection of patient data. In this data set, many conditioning cases were represented by small numbers of records. Their experiments now focused on the use of the noisy-OR model for filling in parts of the network's probability tables. Experts were asked to select the causal mechanisms from the HEPAR II network for which the noisy-OR model could be used; they were further asked to provide assessments for the associated parameter probabilities. The authors subsequently compared the performance of their original network with that of the network which resulted from using the noisy-OR model with expert-provided parameters and with that of the network which resulted from using the noisy-OR model with data-provided parameter probabilities. The network which had resulted from using the noisy-OR model with expert-provided parameters was found to exhibit a poorer classification performance than the original network; with the network which had resulted from using the noisy-OR model with data-based parameters, better classification performance was found than with the two other networks.

Anand and Downs [8] conducted an empirical study with the noisy-OR model in view of a Bayesian network for asthma case finding. In their study, they compared the original network which was constructed from data, with a network that was obtained by substituting noisy-OR calculated probabilities wherever appropriate. Different performance indicators were used for the comparison, such as the area under the ROC (Receiver Operating Characteristic) curve. The authors found that neither of the two networks was significantly better than the other.

Bolt and Van der Gaag [4] also conducted an experiment in which original probability tables were substituted by noisy-OR calculated ones. Their study involved a Bayesian network for the early detection of Classical Swine Fever for which all probabilities had been assessed by domain experts. The authors substituted noisy-OR established probability tables for all variables for which this was technically possible, using the expert-assessed probabilities for the parameter probabilities of the model. These substitutions were performed regardless of whether or not the properties of accountability and exception independence were likely to hold in reality for the variables involved. Even with this ill-advised use of the noisy-OR model did the authors find hardly any effects on the sensitivity and specificity characteristics of their network.

The results from these and similar studies have led to the suggestion that Bayesian networks are quite robust against the changes that are induced in their conditional probability tables by the noisy-OR model. The consistency of results throughout the various studies even appears to suggest that the noisy-OR model can be applied in Bayesian networks for any causal mechanism, regardless of the precise interactions among the modeled variables.

3   The Propagation Effects of the Noisy-OR Model

Several researchers investigated the effects of substituting noisy-OR established probability tables for expert-provided ones. While the results from these studies showed that Bayesian networks are quite robust against such substitutions, our example from the previous section showed that probabilities calculated from the noisy-OR model can differ significantly from the true probabilities. The propagation effects of such deviating probabilities are largely unknown, yet are important for determining when using the noisy-OR model can harm a network's performance. In this section we study these propagation effects by means of sensitivity-analysis techniques; upon doing so, we distinguish between propagation in the causal direction, that is, in the direction of the arcs, and propagation in diagnostic direction, that is, against the arcs. We study the propagation effects in Sect. 3.1 and 3.2 for a basic causal mechanism; in Sect. 3.3, we will revisit our results in view of more involved mechanisms in larger networks.

3.1   Propagation in Causal Direction

We consider the conditional probability table $\Pr(C \mid AB)$ for the effect variable C of the causal mechanism from Fig. 3 and assume that it has been specified using the noisy-OR model: the probabilities $\Pr(c \mid \bar{a}b)$ and $\Pr(c \mid a\bar{b})$ have been provided by experts, $\Pr(c \mid ab)$ is calculated from the model's formulas, and $\Pr(c \mid \bar{a}\bar{b})$ is set to 0. By propagating information about the cause variables to the effect variable, we establish the (prior) probability of interest $\Pr(c)$ to be:

Fig. 3. Causal mechanism with the cause variables A and B and the effect variable C

$$\Pr(c) = \Pr(c \mid ab) \cdot \Pr(a) \cdot \Pr(b) + \Pr(c \mid \bar{a}b) \cdot \Pr(\bar{a}) \cdot \Pr(b) + \Pr(c \mid a\bar{b}) \cdot \Pr(a) \cdot \Pr(\bar{b})$$

for which we used the model's accountability property. We now assume that the noisy-OR calculated probability $\Pr(c \mid ab)$ from the conditional probability table deviates substantially from the true probability of the effect c to arise in the presence of the two causes a and b. The effect of this deviation on the probability of interest can be studied by writing $\Pr(c)$ as a function of $x = \Pr(c \mid ab)$. From well-established properties from sensitivity analysis of Bayesian networks [9], we have that the result is a linear function in x; more specifically, we find that

$$\Pr(c) = \alpha \cdot (\Pr(c \mid ab) + \beta') = \alpha \cdot (x + \beta')$$

where

$$\alpha = \Pr(a) \cdot \Pr(b)$$

$$\beta' = \left(\frac{\Pr(c \mid \bar{a}b)}{\Pr(a)} - \Pr(c \mid \bar{a}b) \right) + \left(\frac{\Pr(c \mid a\bar{b})}{\Pr(b)} - \Pr(c \mid a\bar{b}) \right)$$

The gradient α of the sensitivity function for $\Pr(c)$ determines the effect that deviations of a noisy-OR calculated value from the true probability $\Pr(c \mid ab)$ can have on the probability of interest. We observe that this gradient depends solely on the prior probabilities of the two causes a and b: large values for α are found only when both $\Pr(a)$ and $\Pr(b)$ have large values. The offset of the linear function equals $\alpha \cdot \beta'$, in which the constant β' also depends on the prior probabilities $\Pr(a)$ and $\Pr(b)$; β' is further dependent of the parameter probabilities $\Pr(c \mid \bar{a}b)$ and $\Pr(c \mid a\bar{b})$ of the noisy-OR model. We note that β' is undefined when at least one of the probabilities $\Pr(a)$ and $\Pr(b)$ equals 0. We further note that the constants α and β' in essence range over the intervals $(0, 1)$ and $(0, \infty)$, respectively; the offset $\alpha \cdot \beta'$, however, is restricted to the interval $(0, 1)$.

Fig. 4 depicts two example sensitivity functions expressing the probability of interest $\Pr(c)$ in terms of $x = \Pr(c \mid ab)$. For both functions, the two parameter probabilities $\Pr(c \mid \bar{a}b)$ and $\Pr(c \mid a\bar{b})$ were set to large values. For the graph on the left, the prior probabilities $\Pr(a)$ and $\Pr(b)$ were assigned small values; for the graph on the right, large values were chosen for these probabilities. The graph on the left shows that in view of small values for $\Pr(a)$ and $\Pr(b)$, even a substantial deviation of the noisy-OR calculated value from the true probability $\Pr(c \mid ab)$ can have only a minor effect on the probability of interest: the gradient α of the depicted function is 0.024. Given larger values for $\Pr(a)$ and $\Pr(b)$, the

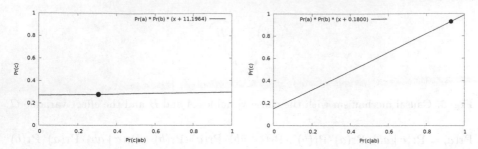

Fig. 4. Effects of varying $\Pr(c \mid ab)$ on $\Pr(c)$, given small values (*left*) and large values (*right*) for $\Pr(a)$ and $\Pr(b)$; effects of the noisy-OR calculated values for $\Pr(c \mid ab)$ are indicated by dots

effect on $\Pr(c)$ of such a deviation will increase, as is illustrated by the graph on the right; the gradient of this function equals 0.8372.

To summarize, the effect of a large deviation of a noisy-OR calculated value from a true probability depends to a large extent on the prior probabilities of the possible causes of the effect under study. The larger these prior probabilities, the larger the gradient of the sensitivity function describing the effect will be. And the larger this gradient, the more harm ill-considered use of the noisy-OR model can do to the network's performance.

3.2   Propagating in Diagnostic Direction

Having studied propagation in the causal direction, we now turn to propagation in the diagnostic direction, that is, we address the propagation of information between the two cause variables through the effect variable. We consider again the basic causal mechanism from Fig. 3, and express the probability of interest $\Pr(a \mid c)$ as a function of the probability $x = \Pr(c \mid ab)$. From Bayes' rule and the cause variables A and B being mutually independent, we find that

$$\Pr(a \mid c) = \frac{\Pr(c \mid ab) \cdot \Pr(a) \cdot \Pr(b) + \Pr(c \mid a\bar{b}) \cdot \Pr(a) \cdot \Pr(\bar{b})}{\Pr(c)}$$

$$= \frac{\Pr(c \mid ab) + \beta''}{\Pr(c \mid ab) + \beta'} = \frac{x + \beta''}{x + \beta'}$$

where

$$\alpha = \Pr(a) \cdot \Pr(b)$$

$$\beta' = \left(\frac{\Pr(c \mid \bar{a}b)}{\Pr(a)} - \Pr(c \mid \bar{a}b)\right) + \left(\frac{\Pr(c \mid a\bar{b})}{\Pr(b)} - \Pr(c \mid a\bar{b})\right)$$

$$\beta'' = \frac{\Pr(c \mid a\bar{b}) \cdot \Pr(\bar{b})}{\Pr(b)}$$

We note that the sensitivity function for the probability of interest $\Pr(a \mid c)$ is hyperbolic in the probability under study, consistent with earlier results from

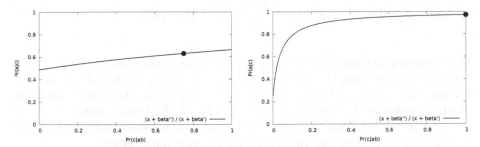

Fig. 5. Effects of varying $\Pr(c \mid ab)$ on $\Pr(a \mid c)$, given medium-sized values (*left*) and large values (*right*) for $\Pr(a)$ and $\Pr(b)$; effects of the noisy-OR calculated values for $\Pr(c \mid ab)$ are indicated by dots

sensitivity analysis. Fig. 5 shows two example functions expressing $\Pr(a \mid c)$ in $x = \Pr(c \mid ab)$. For both functions, the parameter probabilities $\Pr(c \mid \bar{a}b)$ and $\Pr(c \mid a\bar{b})$ were set to large values. For the graph on the left, the prior probabilities $\Pr(a)$ and $\Pr(b)$ were assigned medium-sized values; for the graph on the right, large values were chosen for these probabilities. The two graphs show that a large deviation of the noisy-OR computed value from the true probability $\Pr(c \mid ab)$ will often have a very small effect on the probability of interest; the graph on the right shows however, that the effect may also be quite large.

In order to gain further insight in the effect on the probability of interest of a large deviation of the noisy-OR calculated value from the true probability $\Pr(c \mid ab)$, we study various properties of our sensitivity function. For this purpose, we build upon concepts and properties from sensitivity analysis of Bayesian networks [9,10]. A (rectangular) hyperbola $f(x)$ has the general form

$$f(x) = \frac{w_1 \cdot x + w_2}{w_3 \cdot x + w_4} = \frac{r}{x - s} + t$$

where $w_1, \ldots, w_4$ are constants and

$$s = -\frac{w_4}{w_3}, \quad t = \frac{w_1}{w_3}, \text{ and } r = \frac{w_2 \cdot w_3 - w_1 \cdot w_4}{w_3^2}$$

The values of the constants s, t and r determine various properties of the hyperbola. The constant s indicates its vertical asymptote; the horizontal asymptote is defined by the constant t. These two constants determine the general shape of the hyperbola. The constant r further defines the location of the hyperbola's vertices. The vertex of a hyperbola branch is the point where the absolute value of the first derivative equals 1; it is located at one of the four points $(s \pm \sqrt{|r|}, t \pm \sqrt{|r|})$.

We now observe that the sensitivity function for our probability of interest $\Pr(a \mid c)$ is a part of a single hyperbola branch: since $\Pr(a \mid c)$ lies within the interval $[0, 1]$ and is defined for any $x = \Pr(c \mid ab) \in [0, 1]$, it is restricted to a unit window. Note that this observation is corroborated by the two graphs from Fig. 5. We further observe that our sensitivity function has a more restricted form than rectangular hyperbolas in general. More specifically, we have that

$$s = -\beta', \quad t = 1 \quad \text{and} \quad r = -\frac{\Pr(c \mid \bar{a}b)}{\Pr(a)} + \Pr(c \mid \bar{a}b)$$

The horizontal asymptote of our hyperbola branch thus equals 1. From $\beta' > 0$ it further follows that the vertical asymptote is found to the left of the unit window. We conclude that our hyperbola branch lies in the fourth quadrant, which is confirmed by the two graphs from Fig. 5. Its vertex then is found at $(s + \sqrt{|r|}, t - \sqrt{|r|})$. Note that the vertex may or may not be located within the unit window which delimits the sensitivity function under study.

The location of the vertex of our sensitivity function for the probability of interest $\Pr(a \mid c)$ is an important indicator for the effect of a deviation of the noisy-OR calculated value from the true probability $\Pr(c \mid ab)$. Informally speaking, when the vertical asymptote lies close to the unit window and the vertex in turn is close to this asymptote, even a small deviation in $\Pr(c \mid ab)$ can have a large effect on $\Pr(a \mid c)$. We recall that the vertical asymptote s can lie infinitesimally close to the unit window without reaching it. Small values $|s|$ are found with large values for the prior probability $\Pr(a)$. When the value of $\Pr(a)$ decreases, the asymptote will move to the left, further away from the unit window; the graph on the left of Fig. 6 depicts this relation between s and the prior probability $\Pr(a)$. We further recall that the x-coordinate of the vertex equals $s + \sqrt{|r|}$. The distance between the asymptote and the vertex thus equals $\sqrt{|r|} = \sqrt{|1 - \frac{\Pr(c|\bar{a}b)}{\Pr(a)} + \Pr(c \mid \bar{a}b)|}$. We now observe that for large values of $\Pr(a)$, the distance between the vertical asymptote and the vertex will be close to 0. For decreasing values of $\Pr(a)$, the vertex will first move slightly to the right but very soon the constant s becomes the dominant term in the x-coordinate of the vertex causing it to move to the left. The distance between the vertical asymptote and the vertex will then increase. The relation between the prior probability $\Pr(a)$ and the x-coordinate of the vertex is depicted in the graph on the left of Fig. 6.

The graph on the right of Fig. 6 shows the possible effects on the probability of interest $\Pr(a \mid c)$ of a deviation of a noisy-OR calculated value from the true probability $\Pr(c \mid ab)$. The effects are shown for different values of the prior probability $\Pr(a)$; for all depicted functions, the probabilities $\Pr(b)$, $\Pr(c \mid \bar{a}b)$ and $\Pr(c \mid a\bar{b})$ were fixed at large values. The graph shows that with a prior probability $\Pr(a)$ close to 1, in essence a large effect on $\Pr(a \mid c)$ can result from even a small deviation from the true probability $\Pr(c \mid ab)$. We note however, that the noisy-OR model will typically yield a large value for the probability $\Pr(c \mid ab)$. A large effect on the probability of interest can then only arise when the true probability is very small, that is, when the noisy-OR calculated probability value strongly deviates from reality. We recall that the alcohol-and-GHB example from Sect. 2 represented such a situation. When the value of the prior probability $\Pr(a)$ is somewhat smaller, the maximum effect on the probability of interest will also be smaller; an effect will arise over a somewhat larger range of values for the probability $\Pr(c \mid ab)$, however. The graph on the right of Fig. 6 further shows that, regardless of the value of the prior probability $\Pr(a)$, a small deviation of

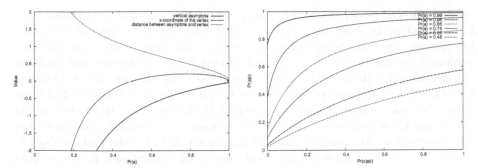

Fig. 6. The values of the vertical asymptote, the x-coordinate of the vertex and the distance between these values *(left)*; the effect of a decreasing probability $\Pr(a)$ *(right)*

the true probability $\Pr(c \mid ab)$ from a relatively large noisy-OR calculated value will always have just a little effect on the probability of interest.

To summarize, upon diagnostic propagation of information through a causal mechanism to a cause variable A, the effect of a large deviation of a noisy-OR calculated value from the true probability $\Pr(c \mid ab)$ is dependent to a large extent of the value of the prior probability $\Pr(a)$. The larger this value, the closer the vertical asymptote of the sensitivity function expressing $\Pr(a \mid c)$ lies to the unit window and the closer its vertex will be to the asymptote. A very small true probability $\Pr(c \mid ab)$ for which the noisy-OR model calculates a relatively large value can then substantially decrease the performance of the Bayesian network. We would like to note that, while in this section we focused on $\Pr(a \mid c)$, similar observations hold for the probability of interest $\Pr(b \mid c)$, with the prior probability $\Pr(b)$ as the most indicative factor.

3.3   Revisiting Our Results in View of Noisy-OR Generalizations

The results from our analysis above hold for application of the noisy-OR model for the basic causal mechanism from Fig. 3. In larger networks for real applications, however, the noisy-OR model will be applied to more involved causal mechanisms. The results from the empirical studies reviewed in Sect. 2 appear to support the conjecture that our results can be generalized to explain the apparent robustness of Bayesian networks in general to substitution of noisy-OR established probability tables. We underpin this conjecture informally.

For causal mechanisms involving more than two cause variables, the formulas of the noisy-OR model will lead to additional multiplications upon calculating the non-parameter probabilities for the probability table of the effect variable. These additional multiplications will result in increasingly larger noisy-OR calculated probabilities. Negative effects from ill-advised use of the model can then only be expected for large deviating true probabilities. The overall effect will be more limited than with two cause variables, however, as a result of a decreasing joint probability of the causes involved. When the property of accountability does not hold for the cause variables from a causal mechanism, the leaky variant of the noisy-OR model can be used [5,6,7]. In this model, a leak probability is defined, which is the probability that the effect will occur when none of the causes are present. The leaky noisy-OR model now in essence uses for its parameters the probabilities that the effect e is present when a cause c_i is present and all other causes, including the ones that are not modeled explicitly, are absent. Different views have been proposed of these parameter probabilities, yet with each of these views the leaky noisy-OR model can be mimicked by a noisy-OR model with an additional cause variable. From this observation, we cautiously conclude that our observations for multiple cause variables will hold for the leaky noisy-OR model as well. We further surmise that taking the context of a larger network into consideration will also not substantially affect our results. We note that the most important assumption made in our analysis is mutual independency of the cause variables. When the cause variables are dependent, the dependency can be either positive or negative, with a positive dependency stating that a large value for one of the causes will induce higher values for the other cause to become more likely. In the case of negative dependencies it becomes less likely that all causes are present simultaneously, thereby reducing the effect of propagation in the causal direction. We further expect that the effects of propagation in the diagnostic direction remain to be strongly dependent of the distribution of the marginal probabilities of the individual causes, since the general form of the sensitivity functions under study is not likely to change.

While several researchers have conducted studies with the noisy-OR model in real Bayesian networks, far less empirical evidence is available as to the effects of using the noisy-MAX model in practical networks. The noisy-MAX model was designed as an extension of the noisy-OR model to causal mechanisms involving non-binary variables [6,7], allowing different levels of presence of a cause. The noisy-MAX model is based upon two properties of the domains of the cause and effect variables: each cause variable must have a designated value which models absence, and the values of the effect variable must allow a total ordering. We note that the assumption of a value modeling absence of a cause is also implicit in the noisy-OR model. With the basic causal mechanism from Fig. 3, we performed some preliminary experiments assigning different numbers of values to the cause and effect variables involved. These experiments showed a consistently subdued effect on the probabilities of interest of large deviations of the true probabilities from the noisy-MAX computed ones. Further experimentation and an in-depth analysis are required, however, before any definite conclusions can be drawn.

4   Conclusions and Future Work

When building a Bayesian network with the help of domain experts, often the noisy-OR model is employed to ease probability elicitation. Since not all network engineers are fully aware of the properties upon which it is built, the model is subject to ill-considered use. The results from empirical studies moreover appear to advocate wide-spread use by showing that using the noisy-OR model does not harm the performance of a Bayesian network. We have demonstrated that caution is nonetheless advised. Especially when a modeled cause annihilates to some extent the effect of another cause, the probability values computed by the noisy-OR model will deviate substantially from the true probabilities. We have shown that large prior probabilities of the causes being present can then induce strong propagation effects which in turn can result in quite deviating posterior probabilities. Although the available empirical evidence suggests that similar results will hold for generalized variants of the noisy-OR model, further experimentation and analysis are required before we can establish the precise conditions under which these variants cannot harm a network's performance. Motivated by our results, we will also more closely investigate mechanisms embedding annihilation of causes, with the aim of designing parameterized conditional probability tables for this type of intercausal interaction.

Acknowledgment. With support from the Prevention of and Fight against Crime Programme of the EU European Commission - Directorate-General Home Affairs.

References

1. Druzdzel, M.J., van der Gaag, L.C.: Building probabilistic networks: "Where do the numbers come from?" Guest Editors Introduction. IEEE Transactions on Knowledge & Data Engineering 12, 481–486 (2000)
2. van der Gaag, L.C., Renooij, S., Witteman, C.L.M., Aleman, B.M.P., Taal, B.G.: Probabilities for a probabilistic network: a case study in oesophageal cancer. Artificial Intelligence in Medicine 25, 123–148 (2002)
3. Pearl, J.: Probabilistic Reasoning in Intelligent Systems: Networks of Plausible Inference. Morgan Kaufmann Publishers, San Francisco (1988)
4. Bolt, J., van der Gaag, L.C.: An Empirical Study of the Use of the Noisy-Or Model in a Real-Life Bayesian Network. In: Hüllermeier, E., Kruse, R., Hoffmann, F. (eds.) IPMU 2010. CCIS, vol. 80, pp. 11–20. Springer, Heidelberg (2010)
5. Oniśko, A., Druzdzel, M.J., Wasyluk, H.: Learning Bayesian network parameters from small data sets: Application of noisy-OR gates. International Journal of Approximate Reasoning 27, 165–182 (2001)
6. Henrion, M.: Some practical issues in constructing belief networks. In: Lemmer, J., Levitt, T., Kanal, L. (eds.) Proceedings of the Third Annual Conference on Uncertainty in Artificial Intelligence (UAI 1987), pp. 161–174. Elsevier, Amsterdam (1987)
7. Díez, F.J.: Parameter adjustment in Bayes networks. The generalized noisy-OR gate. In: Heckerman, D. (ed.) Proceedings of the 9th Conference on Uncertainty in Artificial Intelligence (UAI 2001), pp. 165–182. Morgan Kaufmann Publishers, San Francisco (2001)
8. Anand, V., Downs, S.M.: Probabilistic asthma case finding: a noisy-OR reformulation. In: Proceedings AMIA Symposium, pp. 6–10 (2008)
9. Coupé, V., van der Gaag, L.C.: Properties of sensitivity analysis of Bayesian belief networks. In: Proceedings of the Joint Session of the 6th Prague Symposium of Asymptotic Statistics and the 13th Prague Conference on Information Theory, Statistical Decision Functions and Random Processes, Prague, pp. 81–86 (1999)
10. Renooij, S., van der Gaag, L.C.: Exploiting evidence-dependent sensitivity bounds. In: Bacchus, F., Jaakkola, T. (eds.) Proceedings of the 21st Conference in Uncertainty in Artificial Intelligence, pp. 485–492. AUAI Press (2005)

Attaining Monotonicity for Bayesian Networks

Merel T. Rietbergen and Linda C. van der Gaag

Department of Information and Computing Sciences, Utrecht University
P.O. Box 80.089, 3508 TB Utrecht, The Netherlands
{merel,linda}@cs.uu.nl

Abstract. Many real-life Bayesian networks are expected to exhibit commonly known properties of monotonicity, in the sense that higher values for the observable variables should make higher values for the main variable of interest more likely. Yet, violations of these properties may be introduced into a network despite careful engineering efforts. In this paper, we present a method for resolving such violations of monotonicity by varying a single parameter probability. Our method constructs intervals of numerical values to which a parameter can be varied to attain monotonicity without introducing new violations. We argue that our method has a high runtime, yet can be of practical value for specific domains.

1 Introduction

Many real-life Bayesian networks are expected to exhibit commonly known properties of monotonicity, in the sense that higher values for the observable variables should make higher values for the main variable of interest more likely; if a network violates any such property, it will not be easily accepted by its users, not even if it shows high performance otherwise. Yet, during the construction of a Bayesian network, violations of monotonicity may inadvertently be introduced despite careful engineering efforts. To attain monotonicity for a network, all such violations must be identified and resolved. Experience has shown, however, that violations of monotonicity can hardly be detected by hand. Recently, moreover, it was established that automatically verifying monotonicity is of a high computational complexity; the problem was shown to be co-NP^{PP}-complete in general [1]. In view of this unfavorable complexity result, Van der Gaag et al. proposed a practical method for verifying monotonicity which proved to be feasible for studying at least parts of a real-life network in veterinary medicine [2].

Various methods may be considered for attaining monotonicity for a Bayesian network which does not yet exhibit the required property in its observable variables. In essence, these methods amount to changing the network's graphical structure, varying its parameter probabilities, or modifying both. In this paper we investigate the problem of resolving violations of monotonicity by varying a network's probabilities. We note that since the problem of verifying monotonicity in itself is already of a high computational complexity, we cannot expect to find an efficient, generally applicable method for resolving violations. We note moreover that the problem of attaining monotonicity by parameter variation is

W. Liu (Ed.): ECSQARU 2011, LNAI 6717, pp. 134–145, 2011.

closely related to the problem of tuning parameters to meet some constraints on the network's output [3], which was shown to be NP^{PP}-complete in general [4]. More specifically, for parameter tuning three general types of problem have been distinguished; these are to meet constraints on a single probability, on two probabilities given the same evidence, and on two probabilities of the same main variable of interest. For solving the first two types of problem, practical methods have been devised. To the best of our knowledge, no such method is available as yet for solving tuning problems on two probabilities of the same variable of interest given different evidence. Yet, it is this type of tuning problem, which is closest to our problem of attaining monotonicity.

Given the unfavorable complexity results of parameter tuning and verifying monotonicity, we focused our investigation of the problem of attaining monotonicity for Bayesian networks on the variation of single parameter probabilities. We present for this purpose a method, called the *intersection-of-intervals method*, which constructs a union of intervals of numerical values to which a parameter can be varied such that there are no more violations of monotonicity in the resulting modified network. Since resolving a single violation may cause new violations to arise, our method studies the effect of parameter variation for all possible combinations of evidence simultaneously rather than for only those combinations of evidence for which the property of monotonicity is violated. If the union of intervals constructed for a parameter probability is empty, then this parameter cannot, upon variation, resolve the identified violations without introducing new ones; otherwise, the parameter can be varied to any value from the union of intervals to attain monotonicity for the network at hand.

The paper is organized as follows. In Sect. 2, we introduce our notational conventions and review the concept of Bayesian network. In Sect. 3, we review the concept of monotonicity for Bayesian networks and study properties of its violations. In Sect. 4, we reduce the graphical structure of a network by eliminating variables for which parameter variation cannot serve to attain monotonicity. In Sect. 5, we detail our intersection-of-intervals method for resolving violations of monotonicity without introducing new ones; we also discuss the complexity of our method and its practical applicability. Finally, in Sect. 6, we outline our results and conclusions as well as some ideas for further study.

2   Bayesian Networks

A Bayesian network is a model of a joint probability distribution Pr over a set of random variables **V**. Before briefly reviewing the concept of Bayesian network, we introduce our notational conventions. We use (indexed) upper-case letters V_i to denote individual variables from the set **V** and bold-faced upper-case letters **S** to denote (sub)sets of variables. Each variable V_i has an associated domain of possible values, denoted $\Omega(V_i)$; the possible values for V_i are denoted v_i^k, $k = 1, \ldots, |\Omega(V_i)|$, and are ordered $v_i^k \leq v_i^{k+1}$. An assignment $V_i = v_i$ for some $v_i \in \Omega(V_i)$ will be referred to as an observation or as evidence for V_i, alternatively. The set of all joint value assignments to a set of variables **S** equals the Cartesian product of the domains of the variables involved, that is,

$\Omega(\mathbf{S}) = \times_{V_i \in \mathbf{S}} \Omega(V_i)$. Elements from $\Omega(\mathbf{S})$ are denoted by bold-faced lower-case letters $\mathbf{s}$ and are ordered by the partial ordering $\preceq$ induced by the total orderings $\leq$ of the domains of the individual variables. If ambiguity cannot occur, we will use v_i^k as a shorthand notation for $V_i = v_i^k$; similarly we will write $\mathbf{s}$ for $\mathbf{S} = \mathbf{s}$.

A Bayesian network $B = (G, P)$ includes a directed acyclic graph $G = (\mathbf{V}, A)$, in which the set of arcs A captures the probabilistic (in)dependencies between the random variables $\mathbf{V}$. We say that two variables V_i and V_j are d-separated by the available evidence if every chain between V_i and V_j contains either an observed variable with at least one emanating arc, or a variable V_k with two incoming arcs such that neither V_k itself nor any of its descendants in G have been observed; V_i and V_j are then considered mutually independent given the evidence. The strengths of the relationships between the variables are expressed by means of a set P of (conditional) probability distributions, which includes the distributions $p(V_i \mid \pi(V_i))$ for each variable V_i given all possible value assignments to its parents $\pi(V_i)$ in G. The separate probabilities in P are called the parameters of the network. The distributions specified for the variable V_i are said to constitute V_i's conditional probability table. The network's graphical structure and associated parameter probabilities represent the unique joint probability distribution $\Pr(\mathbf{V}) = \prod_{V_i \in \mathbf{V}} p(V_i \mid \pi(V_i))$ over the variables $\mathbf{V}$.

3 Monotonicity in Bayesian Networks

In most real-life applications of Bayesian networks, the represented variables have different roles. In many applications in fact, a set of observable input variables $\mathbf{E}$ and a single main variable of interest C are distinguished. The concept of monotonicity in Bayesian networks has been introduced to describe properties of the relationships between these variables [1]. The concept is defined as follows.

Definition 1. *A Bayesian network* $B = (G, P)$ *is* isotone in distribution *in its* observable variables $\mathbf{E}$ *if*

$$\mathbf{e} \preceq \mathbf{e}' \;\Rightarrow\; \Pr(C \leq c \mid \mathbf{e}') \leq \Pr(C \leq c \mid \mathbf{e})$$

for all $c \in \Omega(C)$ *and* $\mathbf{e}, \mathbf{e}' \in \Omega(\mathbf{E})$.

The results presented in the sequel hold also for the reverse property of antitonicity, which states that $\mathbf{e} \preceq \mathbf{e}'$ implies $\Pr(C \leq c \mid \mathbf{e}') \geq \Pr(C \leq c \mid \mathbf{e})$ for all $c \in \Omega(C)$ and $\mathbf{e}, \mathbf{e}' \in \Omega(\mathbf{E})$. Without loss of generality therefore, we will use the term monotonicity to refer to the property of isotonicity in distribution.

If a Bayesian network does not exhibit monotonicity in its observable variables, then there must be one or more pairs of joint value assignments $\mathbf{e}, \mathbf{e}' \in \Omega(\mathbf{E})$ with $\mathbf{e} \preceq \mathbf{e}'$ for which $\Pr(C \leq c \mid \mathbf{e}') > \Pr(C \leq c \mid \mathbf{e})$ for at least one value $c \in \Omega(C)$. In their work on identifying such violations of monotonicity [2], Van der Gaag et al. showed that it suffices to consider pairs of assignments $\mathbf{e}, \mathbf{e}' \in \Omega(\mathbf{E})$ that differ in the value for just a single observable variable $E_i \in \mathbf{E}$, that is, that share the joint value assignment to $\mathbf{E} \setminus \{E_i\} = \mathbf{E}_i^-$. In the sequel, we build upon this property and write $\mathbf{e}_{ij}^-$ to denote the jth assignment to $\mathbf{E}_i^-$ according to some ordering on $\Omega(\mathbf{E}_i^-)$. Studying monotonicity in a Bayesian network now amounts to establishing whether the property $\Pr\left(C \leq c \mid e_i^{k+1}, \mathbf{e}_{ij}^-\right) \leq \Pr\left(C \leq c \mid e_i^k, \mathbf{e}_{ij}^-\right)$ holds for all $E_i \in \mathbf{E}$ and all assignments $\mathbf{e}_{ij}^-$ to $\mathbf{E}_i^-$, for all consecutive values e_i^k, e_i^{k+1} for E_i, and all $c \in \Omega(C)$; we will use $viol(c, e_i^k, \mathbf{e}_{ij}^-)$ to denote the violation of this property for a particular observable variable $E_i \in \mathbf{E}$ and specific values $c \in \Omega(C)$, $e_i^k \in \Omega(E_i)$ and $\mathbf{e}_{ij}^- \in \Omega(\mathbf{E}_i^-)$.

If domain knowledge dictates that a Bayesian network should be monotone in its observable variables, all violations of this property must be identified and resolved. Various methods may be considered for attaining monotonicity for a network, based upon changing the graphical structure, varying the parameters or modifying both. In this paper we address the problem of resolving violations of monotonicity by varying a single parameter probability. Let $p(u \mid \boldsymbol{\pi})$ be a parameter probability for some variable U, where $u \in \Omega(U)$ and $\boldsymbol{\pi} \in \Omega(\pi(U))$ is a joint value assignment to the parents of U in the network's graph. Varying $p(u \mid \boldsymbol{\pi})$ is said to resolve the violation $viol(c, e_i^k, \mathbf{e}_{ij}^-)$ if there exists a numerical value $x \in [0, 1]$ for which

$$\Pr\left(C \leq c \mid e_i^{k+1}, \mathbf{e}_{ij}^-\right)\left(p(u \mid \boldsymbol{\pi}) = x\right) \leq \Pr\left(C \leq c \mid e_i^k, \mathbf{e}_{ij}^-\right)\left(p(u \mid \boldsymbol{\pi}) = x\right),$$

where $\Pr(\mathbf{V})\left(p(u \mid \boldsymbol{\pi}) = x\right)$ indicates the probability distribution over the variables $\mathbf{V}$ as established from the network after changing the numerical value of the parameter $p(u \mid \boldsymbol{\pi})$ to x; we thereby assume that the other parameter probabilities from the distribution $p(U \mid \boldsymbol{\pi})$ from the probability table of U are scaled proportionally, that is $p(u' \mid \boldsymbol{\pi}) := \frac{1-x}{1-p(u|\pi)} \cdot p(u' \mid \boldsymbol{\pi})$ for all $u' \in \Omega(U) \setminus \{u\}$. A parameter which serves to simultaneously resolve all violations of monotonicity for a network without introducing any new ones, will be termed a *resolvent parameter*. We note that a Bayesian network which includes one or more violations of monotonicity may or may not have such a resolvent parameter.

4   Reducing the Graphical Structure

Identifying the parameters that upon variation can resolve all violations of monotonicity in a Bayesian network carries a considerable computational burden. To reduce the number of computations involved, a network can be preprocessed by eliminating variables for which we know that their parameters cannot be resolvent since these are algebraically independent of the probability of interest.

By simple inspection of the graphical structure of a network, some variables with non-influential parameter probabilities can be feasibly identified without any reference to the parameters' numerical values. For this purpose, we exploit the concept of sensitivity set which was introduced before in sensitivity analysis of Bayesian networks [5]. The sensitivity set for a variable of interest C given observed variables $\mathbf{E}$ is the set of all variables for which the probability of interest is algebraically dependent of its parameter probabilities. This set is obtained as follows. From the graph G of the Bayesian network, we construct a new graph G^* by adding an auxiliary parent X_i to every vertex $V_i \in \mathbf{V}$; this parent X_i in essence represents the conditional probability table of V_i. The sensitivity set for C given $\mathbf{E}$, denoted $Sen(C, \mathbf{E})$, now is the set of all variables $V_i \in \mathbf{V}$ for which X_i and C are not d-separated by $\mathbf{E}$. We have that, if X_i and C are d-separated by $\mathbf{E}$, then the probability $\Pr(c \mid \mathbf{e})$ is algebraically independent of $p(V_i \mid \pi(V_i))$ for any $c \in \Omega(C)$ and $\mathbf{e} \in \Omega(\mathbf{E})$ [5]. For any variable $V_i \notin Sen(C, \mathbf{E})$, therefore, varying a parameter p from its conditional probability table cannot resolve any violation of monotonicity and thus cannot be used to attain monotonicity. For each variable from the sensitivity set, varying one of its parameter probabilities may serve to attain monotonicity for the network at hand, yet is not guaranteed to do so. These parameter probabilities thus need further investigation.

Building upon the concept of sensitivity set, we now preprocess a Bayesian network under consideration by restricting it to the part which is relevant for studying monotonicity. For this purpose we cannot simply remove all variables from the set $\mathbf{V} \setminus Sen(C, \mathbf{E})$, since some of these variables may still be needed to incorporate evidence into the network's computations. We therefore retain the variables from $Sen(C, \mathbf{E}) \cup \mathbf{E}$ and remove all other variables along with their incident arcs. If upon doing so the graphical structure of the network falls apart into multiple connected components, then the network is further restricted by removing all variables that are not included in the same component as the variable of interest C. In the remainder of the paper, we assume that a Bayesian network has been preprocessed as described above.

5   The Intersection-of-Intervals Method

In the previous section we showed that a Bayesian network can be restricted, based upon graphical considerations only, to the part that is relevant for studying monotonicity. For each of the remaining variables we must now determine whether varying a parameter from its conditional probability table can result in monotonicity for the network. For this purpose, we introduce a method which determines whether a specific parameter can be varied to a numerical value for which there are no more violations of monotonicity in the resulting modified network. Using this method we can then decide whether there exists a parameter that can be varied to attain monotonicity.

5.1   The Method

We consider a (restricted) Bayesian network $B = (G, P)$ with a variable of interest C and a set of observable variables $\mathbf{E}$. Suppose that B includes a single violation of monotonicity $viol(c, e_i^k, \mathbf{e}_{ij}^-)$. To resolve this violation by parameter variation, we must change the value of some parameter $p \in P$ to a numerical value x from the unit interval $[0, 1]$ such that $\Pr\left(C \le c \mid e_i^{k+1}, \mathbf{e}_{ij}^-\right)(p = x) \le \Pr\left(C \le c \mid e_i^k, \mathbf{e}_{ij}^-\right)(p = x)$. More generally however, a network may contain multiple violations of monotonicity. Also, resolving one such violation may cause other, possibly new violations to arise. To attain monotonicity for the network B, we must therefore vary some parameter $p \in P$ to a numerical value $x \in [0, 1]$ such that the entire system of inequalities

$$\Pr\left(C \le c \mid e_i^{k+1}, \mathbf{e}_{ij}^-\right)(p = x) \le \Pr\left(C \le c \mid e_i^k, \mathbf{e}_{ij}^-\right)(p = x)$$

holds for every $E_i \in \mathbf{E}$ and for all $c \in \Omega(C)$, $e_i^k \in \Omega(E_i)$ and $\mathbf{e}_{ij}^- \in \Omega(\mathbf{E}_i^-)$. This observation gives rise to the following method, called the intersection-of-intervals method. The method determines whether the value of a specific parameter $p \in P$ can be changed to a new value such that there are no more violations of monotonicity in the resulting network; it thus determines whether p is a resolvent parameter for B. More specifically, the intersection-of-intervals method determines for each combination of assignments $(c, e_i^k, \mathbf{e}_{ij}^-)$ separately, the union of intervals of values x for the parameter p for which the above inequality holds; we call this union of intervals the solution space of p for $(c, e_i^k, \mathbf{e}_{ij}^-)$. We can now only attain monotonicity by varying p to a value x which is included in the intersection of the solution spaces of p for all $(c, e_i^k, \mathbf{e}_{ij}^-)$ and every $E_i \in \mathbf{E}$.

Method 1 (Intersection-of-intervals method). Let C, $\mathbf{E}$ and p be as before, and for every $i \in \{1, 2 \ldots, |\mathbf{E}|\}$, let E_i and $\mathbf{E}_i^-$ be as defined above. Let $\mathbf{e}_{ij}$ be the jth element of an ordering of the domain $\Omega(\mathbf{E}_i^-)$ of $\mathbf{E}_i^-$. Now, let $I = [0, 1]$ and $i = 1$. While $i \le |\mathbf{E}|$ and $I \ne \varnothing$, repeat the following steps:

1a. Let $I_i = [0, 1]$ and $j = 1$. While $j \le |\Omega(\mathbf{E}_i^-)|$ and $I_i \ne \varnothing$, repeat the following steps:

2a. Let $I_{ij} = [0, 1]$ and $k = 1$. While $k < |\Omega(E_i)|$ and $I_{ij} \ne \varnothing$, repeat the following steps:

3a. Let $I_{ijk} = [0, 1]$ and $l = 1$. While $l < |\Omega(C)|$ and $I_{ijk} \ne \varnothing$, repeat the following steps:

4a. Compute solution space I_{ijkl}, which is the union of all intervals of values $x \in [0, 1]$ for p for which

$$\Pr\left(C \le c^l \mid e_i^{k+1}, \mathbf{e}_{ij}^-\right)(p = x) \le \Pr\left(C \le c^l \mid e_i^k, \mathbf{e}_{ij}^-\right)(p = x).$$

4b. Compute $I_{ijk} = I_{ijk} \cap I_{ijkl}$ and $l = l + 1$.
3b. Compute $I_{ij} = I_{ij} \cap I_{ijk}$ and $k = k + 1$.
2b. Compute $I_i = I_i \cap I_{ij}$ and $j = j + 1$.
1b. Compute $I = I \cap I_i$ and $i = i + 1$.

When applied for a specific parameter probability p, the intersection-of-intervals method results in a union of intervals I of values x for p for which there are no more violations of monotonicity in the resulting network B upon variation of p to x; we call this union of intervals I the solution space of p for all violations in B. More specifically, we have the following property for this solution space I.

Proposition 1. *Let B be a Bayesian network as before and let p be a parameter probability in B. Let I be the union of intervals of numerical values which results from applying the intersection-of-intervals method for p. Then, $I \ne \varnothing$ if and only if p is a resolvent parameter for B.*

Proof. We first assume that $I \neq \varnothing$. Then there must be some value $x \in I$ such that $x \in I_{ijkl}$ for all i, j, k, l with $1 \leq i \leq |\mathbf{E}|$, $1 \leq j \leq |\Omega(\mathbf{E}_i^-)|$, $1 \leq k < |\Omega(E_i)|$ and $1 \leq l < |\Omega(C)|$. It follows that x is included in the solution spaces of p for all combinations of assignments $(c^l, e_i^k, \mathbf{e}_{ij}^-)$ for all i, j, k, l. So, for every $E_i \in \mathbf{E}$ and each combination $(c^l, e_i^k, \mathbf{e}_{ij}^-)$, the property $\Pr\left(C \leq c^l \mid e_i^{k+1}, \mathbf{e}_{ij}^-\right)(p = x) \leq \Pr\left(C \leq c^l \mid e_i^k, \mathbf{e}_{ij}^-\right)(p = x)$ must hold. We conclude that varying the parameter p to x resolves all violations of monotonicity without introducing any new ones, which means that p is a resolvent parameter for B.

We now assume that p is a resolvent parameter for B. Then there must be some value $x \in [0, 1]$ for which for every $E_i \in \mathbf{E}$ and each combination $(c^l, e_i^k, \mathbf{e}_{ij}^-)$, the property $\Pr\left(C \leq c^l \mid e_i^{k+1}, \mathbf{e}_{ij}^-\right)(p = x) \leq \Pr\left(C \leq c^l \mid e_i^k, \mathbf{e}_{ij}^-\right)(p = x)$ holds. Then, $x \in I_{ijkl}$ for all i, j, k, l with $1 \leq i \leq |\mathbf{E}|$, $1 \leq j \leq |\Omega(\mathbf{E}_i^-)|$, $1 \leq k < |\Omega(E_i)|$ and $1 \leq l < |\Omega(C)|$. From the intersections performed, we have that the union of intervals I resulting from the method contains every value x' which is contained in all I_{ijkl} for all i, j, k, l. We conclude that $x \in I$, and hence $I \neq \varnothing$. □

5.2   Applying the Intersection-of-Intervals Method

From a computational point of view, the most complex step in each iteration within the intersection-of-intervals method is step 4a. This step serves to compute, for a given observable variable $E_i \in \mathbf{E}$, the solution space I_{ijkl} of p for the combination of value assignments $(c^l, e_i^k, \mathbf{e}_{ij}^-)$. This space consists of all intervals of numerical values x for the parameter p under study for which there is no violation $viol(c^l, e_i^k, \mathbf{e}_{ij}^-)$ in the network, that is, for which

$$\Pr\left(C \leq c^l \mid e_i^{k+1}, \mathbf{e}_{ij}^-\right)(p = x) \leq \Pr\left(C \leq c \mid e_i^k, \mathbf{e}_{ij}^-\right)(p = x).$$

To determine the solution space I_{ijkl} we compute the endpoints of its intervals, which amounts to computing the solutions that lie within the interval $[0, 1]$, of the following quadratic equation:

$$0 = (\alpha x + \beta)(\gamma' x + \delta') - (\alpha' x + \beta')(\gamma x + \delta),$$

where $\alpha, \alpha', \beta, \beta', \gamma, \gamma', \delta, \delta'$ are such that $\Pr\left(C \leq c^l \mid e_i^k, \mathbf{e}_{ij}^-\right)(p = x) = \frac{\alpha x + \beta}{\gamma x + \delta}$ and $\Pr\left(C \leq c^l \mid e_i^{k+1}, \mathbf{e}_{ij}^-\right)(p = x) = \frac{\alpha' x + \beta'}{\gamma' x + \delta'}$; note that from previous research on sensitivity analysis of Bayesian networks, we know that any probability of interest can be written as a function of a single parameter probability which has this hyperbolic form [5]. The intervals themselves are then found by determining on which side of the computed endpoints the above inequality holds. We note that for this purpose, we need to obtain the constants $\alpha, \alpha', \beta, \beta', \gamma, \gamma', \delta, \delta'$; an algorithm for computing these constants is readily available [8].

Example 1. We consider the small restricted Bayesian network B depicted in Fig. 1, which consists of a ternary variable of interest C, a binary observable variable E_1, a ternary observable variable E_2, and two binary intermediate variables V_1 and V_2. The conditional probability tables of these variables together are

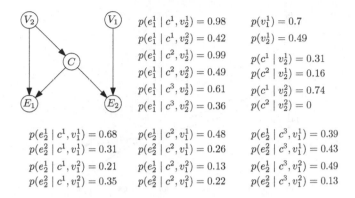

$$p(e_1^1 \mid c^1, v_2^1) = 0.98 \qquad p(v_1^1) = 0.7$$
$$p(e_1^1 \mid c^1, v_2^2) = 0.42 \qquad p(v_2^1) = 0.49$$
$$p(e_1^1 \mid c^2, v_2^1) = 0.99$$
$$p(e_1^1 \mid c^2, v_2^2) = 0.49 \qquad p(c^1 \mid v_1^1) = 0.31$$
$$\qquad\qquad\qquad\qquad\quad p(c^2 \mid v_1^1) = 0.16$$
$$p(e_1^1 \mid c^3, v_2^1) = 0.61$$
$$p(e_1^1 \mid c^3, v_2^2) = 0.36 \qquad p(c^1 \mid v_2^1) = 0.74$$
$$\qquad\qquad\qquad\qquad\quad p(c^2 \mid v_2^1) = 0$$

$$p(e_2^1 \mid c^1, v_1^1) = 0.68 \quad p(e_2^1 \mid c^2, v_1^1) = 0.48 \quad p(e_2^1 \mid c^3, v_1^1) = 0.39$$
$$p(e_2^2 \mid c^1, v_1^1) = 0.31 \quad p(e_2^2 \mid c^2, v_1^1) = 0.26 \quad p(e_2^2 \mid c^3, v_1^1) = 0.43$$
$$p(e_2^1 \mid c^1, v_1^2) = 0.21 \quad p(e_2^1 \mid c^2, v_1^2) = 0.13 \quad p(e_2^1 \mid c^3, v_1^2) = 0.49$$
$$p(e_2^2 \mid c^1, v_1^2) = 0.35 \quad p(e_2^2 \mid c^2, v_1^2) = 0.22 \quad p(e_2^2 \mid c^3, v_1^2) = 0.13$$

Fig. 1. A restricted Bayesian network including three violations

made up of forty parameter probabilities; for ease of presentation we have not included the complementary parameter probabilities in Fig. 1 as they can be readily computed from the twenty-four presented numbers.

Suppose that we wish the network B to show monotonicity in its observable variables. Upon computing the probabilities of interest $\Pr(c^1 \mid e_1^1, e_2^3) = 0.352$ and $\Pr(c^1 \mid e_1^2, e_2^3) = 0.407$ (rounded to three decimal places) however, we find that B does not exhibit this property. In addition to the violation $viol(c^1, e_1^1, e_2^3)$, the network includes the violations $viol(c^1, e_1^1, e_2^1)$ and $viol(c^1, e_1^1, e_2^2)$. To attain monotonicity, and thereby resolve these three violations without introducing any new ones, we apply the intersection-of-intervals method to B's parameter $p(v_2^1)$. For $\mathbf{E}_1^- = \{E_2\}$ and $\mathbf{E}_2^- = \{E_1\}$ we take the predefined ordering of the domains of E_2 and E_1, respectively. For E_1 the method now computes the following solution spaces of p in step 4a (Fig. 2 gives a graphical representation of the space I_{1311}):

$$I_{1111} = [0, 0.132] \cup [0.556, 1] \qquad I_{1112} = [0, 1]$$
$$I_{1211} = [0, 0.156] \cup [0.509, 1] \qquad I_{1212} = [0, 1]$$
$$I_{1311} = [0, 0.085] \cup [0.676, 1] \qquad I_{1312} = [0, 1]$$

Note that, although the variable of interest has three possible values, the method computes solution spaces only for the values c^1 and c^2; since $\Pr(C \leq c^3 \mid e) = 1$ for all $e \in \Omega(\mathbf{E})$, there can never be any violations $viol(c^3, e_i^k, \mathbf{e}_{ij}^-)$. The method subsequently intersects the above solution spaces in step 4b over two iterations of step 3a, which results in the following unions of intervals:

$$I_{111} = [0, 1] \cap I_{1111} \cap I_{1112} = [0, 0.132] \cup [0.556, 1]$$
$$I_{121} = [0, 1] \cap I_{1211} \cap I_{1212} = [0, 0.156] \cup [0.509, 1]$$
$$I_{131} = [0, 1] \cap I_{1311} \cap I_{1312} = [0, 0.085] \cup [0.676, 1]$$

Since E_1 has only two possible values in its domain, step 3b of the method easily computes the solution spaces I_{1j} for all j:

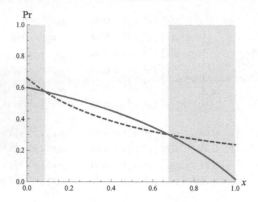

Fig. 2. Representation of the solution space I_{1311} of $p(v_2^1) = x$, in which $\Pr(c^1 \mid e_1^2, e_2^3)$ (——) is no greater than $\Pr(c^1 \mid e_1^1, e_2^3)$ (- - -)

$$I_{11} = [0, 1] \cap I_{111} = [0, 0.132] \cup [0.556, 1]$$
$$I_{12} = [0, 1] \cap I_{121} = [0, 0.156] \cup [0.509, 1]$$
$$I_{13} = [0, 1] \cap I_{131} = [0, 0.085] \cup [0.676, 1]$$

Step 2b then intersects these unions of intervals to find I_1:

$$I_1 = [0, 1] \cap I_{11} \cap I_{12} \cap I_{13} = [0, 0.085] \cup [0.676, 1]$$

For E_2, the intersection-of-intervals method essentially computes I_2 to be

$$I_2 = \bigcap_{j=1}^{|\Omega(\mathbf{E}_2^-)|} \left(\bigcap_{k=1}^{|\Omega(E_2)|-1} \left(\bigcap_{l=1}^{|\Omega(C)|-1} I_{2jkl} \right) \right) = [0, 0.842],$$

where $I_{2122} = [0, 0.842]$ and $I_{2jkl} = [0, 1]$ for all other j, k, l. Finally the method intersects I_1 and I_2 to find the solution space I of $p(v_2^1)$, which equals the union of intervals $[0, 0.085] \cup [0.676, 0.842]$. We conclude that we can attain monotonicity for the Bayesian network B by varying the network parameter $p(v_2^1)$ to any value from the solution space $I = [0, 0.085] \cup [0.676, 0.842]$. If we wish to make the smallest possible change to $p(v_2^1)$, we must vary the parameter to 0.676.

We would like to note that while monotonicity can be attained by varying the parameter probability $p(v_2^1)$, it is not the only resolvent parameter for the example network B. Applying the intersection-of-intervals method to all parameters of the network, serves to reveal fourteen resolvent parameters.   □

5.3   Complexity of the Intersection-of-Intervals Method

To address the computational complexity of the intersection-of-intervals method, we focus first on its most expensive step, which is step 4a. We observe that, given the quadratic equation from Sect. 5.2 for a single parameter p and a single combination $(c^l, e_i^k, \mathbf{e}_{ij}^-)$, the actual intervals of the solution space can be computed in constant time. For establishing the constants of this quadratic equation, an algorithm is available that has a runtime complexity of $O(\omega^q \cdot n^2)$, where $n = |\mathbf{V}|$, $\omega = \max_{V \in \mathbf{V}} \{|\Omega(V)|\}$ and q is the maximum clique size in the junction tree used for propagation [8]. Now, step 4a is performed exactly once for each iteration in step 3a, which is performed once for each iteration in step 2a, which in turn is performed once for each iteration in step 1a, which itself is performed once for each iteration in the method's main loop. Consequently, step 4a is performed at most $O(m \cdot \omega^{m+1})$ times, where $m = |\mathbf{E}|$. In the worst case, therefore, the total amount of time spent on step 4a is $O(m \cdot \omega^{q+m+1} \cdot n^2)$.

Steps 1b, 2b, 3b and 4b of the intersection-of-intervals method involve the computation of the intersection of one union of intervals with another. We observe that, in general, the intersection of a union of q_1 intervals with a union of q_2 intervals can be computed in $O(q_1 + q_2)$ time. At the lth iteration in step 3a, step 4b intersects at most l intervals with at most two intervals, which takes $O(l)$ time. As step 3a is performed at most $O(m \cdot \omega^m)$ times and itself performs at most $O(\omega)$ iterations, in the worst case, the total amount of time spent on step 4b is $O(m \cdot \omega^{m+2})$. At the kth iteration in step 2a, step 3b intersects at most $(k-1) \cdot \omega + 1$ intervals with at most $\omega + 1$ intervals, taking $O(k \cdot \omega)$ time. As step 2a is performed at most $O(m \cdot \omega^{m-1})$ times and itself performs at most $O(\omega)$ iterations, in the worst case the total amount of time spent on step 3b is also $O(m \cdot \omega^{m+2})$. Similarly, in the worst case, at most $O(m \cdot \omega^{2m})$ time is spent on step 2b, since it intersects, in $O(j \cdot \omega^2)$ time, at most $(j-1) \cdot \omega^2 + 1$ intervals with at most $\omega^2 + 1$ intervals at the jth iteration in step 1a, which is itself performed at most $O(m \cdot \omega^{m-1})$ times. Finally, in the worst case, at most $O(m^2 \cdot \omega^{m+1})$ time is spent on step 1b, as it intersects, in $O(i \cdot \omega^{m+1})$ time, at most $(i-1) \cdot \omega^{m+1} + 1$ intervals with at most $\omega^{m+1} + 1$ intervals in the ith iteration of the method's main loop, which is performed at most $O(m)$ times.

Combining the worst-case times spent on its various steps, we find that the intersection-of-intervals method has a runtime complexity of $O(m \cdot \omega^{q+m+1} \cdot n^2 + m \cdot \omega^{2m})$ for networks in general. Practical networks, however, tend to have a relatively small maximum clique size q and a limited maximum domain size ω. With small sets of observable variables whose size can be considered constant with respect to n, the algorithm can then run in $O(n^2)$ time; for sets of observable variables of size $O(n)$, the runtime complexity can increase to $O(n^2 \cdot \omega^{2n})$. Note that the overall runtime in general is further increased by the observation that the number of parameters to be investigated can be exponential in n with base ω. For practical networks, with small clique and domain sizes, however, a much more limited number of parameters needs to be investigated; this number can in fact be considered linear in the total number of variables involved.

The above considerations show that the intersection-of-intervals method has a very high runtime, as was to be expected given the already unfavorable computational complexity of the problem of verifying monotonicity of Bayesian networks. While upon practical application the runtime of the method depends to a large extent on the graphical structure of the network under study and on the domain sizes of its variables, it will inevitably become impractical for larger networks.

Observing that the problem of attaining monotonicity is not addressed upon daily problem solving but during the construction of a network only, an extensive overall runtime may be acceptable. If the runtime becomes too challenging altogether, it may be possible, as proposed by Van der Gaag et al. [7], to resolve the violations of monotonicity that arise in a fixed context of values for some of the observable variables. We note that doing so need not resolve all violations in the network and may in fact introduce new ones for other contexts. The practicability of this idea thus needs further investigation.

5.4 Some Practical Considerations

When applying the intersection-of-intervals method in practice, we must choose a single numerical value from the solution space I for a parameter p to actually attain monotonicity for the network under study. For this purpose, we suggest choosing the value from I which is closest to the original value of p to enforce the smallest possible change in p; note that this choice was used in Example 1. It is readily shown that, for a single resolvent parameter p, this choice will result in the smallest possible Kullback-Leibler distance between the joint probability distributions defined by the original and modified networks. When a network has multiple resolvent parameters, the Kullback-Leibler distance can be used as a heuristic for selecting the parameter to be varied to attain monotonicity; other examples of heuristics for parameter tuning are described in [6].

So far, we assumed that the domains of all observable variables of a Bayesian network allow a total ordering. In practice, however, this property may not always hold. Our intersection-of-intervals method is readily extended to accommodate observable variables with unordered domains. To this end, we observe that a difference in value assignment to such a variable only, cannot cause a violation of monotonicity. To attain monotonicity in the presence of observable variables without ordered domains, therefore, the intersection-of-intervals method is simply applied in the context of every joint value assignment to these variables.

6 Conclusions

When a Bayesian network is employed in a real-life application, its users expect it to exhibit commonly acknowledged properties of monotonicity. In this paper, we studied the problem of attaining monotonicity for networks in which these properties are violated. We restricted our investigations to the problem of finding a parameter such that changing its value will result in a network that does have the required properties. By building upon the previously known concept of sensitivity set, we efficiently restricted a network to a part which is relevant for studying monotonicity. We further presented the intersection-of-intervals method for computing, for a specific parameter of the restricted network, a union of intervals of numerical values to which this parameter can be varied in order to attain monotonicity. We showed that application of our method for every parameter in the restricted network can have a highly unfavorable runtime, yet argued that an efficient, generally applicable method could not be expected given the already high complexity of verifying monotonicity for a network. In view of these complexity considerations, we are currently investigating properties of Bayesian networks and their applications which may improve the feasibility of our method, such as restricted network topologies, patterns of evidence, and dependencies between violations. We are also studying the violations of monotonicity, and the possibilities of resolving them, in real-life networks.

Application of the intersection-of-intervals method to a Bayesian network can yield one or more parameters which each individually can be varied to attain monotonicity. Yet, the method may also uncover the impossibility of attaining monotonicity for a network by varying a single parameter. For such networks, it would be interesting to investigate attaining monotonicity by varying multiple parameters. We surmise that our method can be used to obtain a sequence of parameters which can be varied one after the other in order to attain monotonicity, although the result may not be optimal. Another option would be to vary several parameters simultaneously. We expect that for this option a fairly different method would be required, but that the results would be promising if such a method were to be found. Instead of attempting to attain monotonicity by varying one or more parameter probabilities from a Bayesian network, it may also be possible to do so by applying changes to its graphical structure. We hope to be able in the near future to report results from our further investigations.

References

1. van der Gaag, L.C., Bodlaender, H.L., Feelders, A.: Monotonicity in Bayesian networks. In: Chickering, M., Halpern, J. (eds.) Proceedings of the 20th Conference on Uncertainty in Artificial Intelligence, pp. 569–576. AUAI Press, Arlington (2004)
2. van der Gaag, L.C., Renooij, S., Geenen, P.L.: Lattices for studying monotonicity of Bayesian networks. In: Studený, M., Vomlel, J. (eds.) Proceedings of the Third European Workshop on Probabilistic Graphical Models, Prague, Czech Republic, pp. 99–106 (2006)
3. Chan, H., Darwiche, A.: When do numbers really matter? Journal of Artificial Intelligence Research 17, 265–287 (2002)
4. Kwisthout, J.H.P.: The Computational Complexity of Probabilistic Networks. Ph.D. thesis, Utrecht University (2009)
5. Coupé, V.M.H., van der Gaag, L.C.: Properties of sensitivity analysis of Bayesian belief networks. Annals of Mathematics and Artificial Intelligence 36, 323–356 (2002)
6. Chan, H., Darwiche, A.: A distance measure for bounding probabilistic belief change. International Journal of Approximate Reasoning 38, 149–174 (2005)
7. van der Gaag, L.C., Tabachneck-Schijf, H., Geenen, P.: Verifying monotonicity of Bayesian networks with domain experts. International Journal of Approximate Reasoning 50, 429–436 (2009)
8. van der Gaag, L.C., Kjærulff, U.: Making sensitivity analysis computationally efficient. In: Boutilier, G., Goldszmidt, M. (eds.) Proceedings of the 16th Conference on Uncertainty in Artificial Intelligence, pp. 317–325. Morgan Kaufmann Publishers, San Francisco (2000)

Importance Sampling on Bayesian Networks with Deterministic Causalities

Haohai Yu and Robert van Engelen

Department of Computer Science,
Florida State University,
Tallahassee, FL 32306

Abstract. Importance sampling is a powerful approximate inference technique for Bayesian networks. However, the performance tends to be poor when the network exhibits deterministic causalities. Deterministic causalities yield predictable influences between statistical variables. In other words, only a strict subset of the set of all variable states is permissible to sample. Samples inconsistent with the permissible state space do not contribute to the sum estimate and are effectively rejected during importance sampling. Detecting inconsistent samples is NP-hard, since it amounts to calculating the posterior probability of a sample given some evidence. Several methods have been proposed to cache inconsistent samples to improve sampling efficiency. However, cache-based methods do not effectively exploit overlap in the state patterns generated by determinism in a local network structure to compress state information. In this paper, we propose a new algorithm to reduce the overhead of caching by using an adaptive decision tree to efficiently store and detect inconsistent samples. Experimental results show that the proposed approach outperforms existing methods to sample Bayesian networks with deterministic causalities.

1 Introduction

The Bayesian Network (BN) [17] formalism provides a concise graphical representation of a joint probability distribution over a set of statistical variables and inference methods for reasoning with uncertainty [16] in many problem domains [21]. Approximate inference by importance sampling [20] is widely used because of the desirable real-time properties [12]. Examples are *self importance sampling* (SIS), *heuristic importance sampling* [23], *adaptive importance sampling* (AIS-BN) [4], *dynamic importance sampling* (DIS) [22, 15], and *evidence pre-propagation importance sampling* (EPIS-BN) [26, 27].

The performance of importance sampling on Bayesian networks that exhibit deterministic causalities tends to be poor [4, 25, 10], thereby limiting its use as a real-time inference method under certain conditions. Deterministic causalities form predictable influences between statistical variables in a network such that only a strict subset of the variable states is permissible. Samples inconsistent with the permissible state space have zero probability in the joint probability distribution. Inconsistent samples do not contribute to the sum estimate and are effectively "rejected" by the sampling algorithm.

Detecting inconsistent samples ahead of time to eliminate the cost of rejection is an NP-hard problem, since it requires the posterior probability of a sample given some

W. Liu (Ed.): ECSQARU 2011, LNAI 6717, pp. 146–157, 2011.

evidence, which is known to be an NP-hard problem [6]. The impact of sample rejection on performance of importance sampling has been studied extensively. Particularly in the work on adaptive sampling schemes [4], in the context of constraint propagation [9], and Boolean satisfiability problems [10]. Constraint propagation can be used to reduce the rejection rate [8], but cannot eliminate rejection. Systematically searching for a nonzero weight sample in constraint-based systems was proposed in [9] called *SampleSearch* and improved in [10]. SampleSearch algorithms generate *backtrack-free* distributions. SampleSearch is further generalized [11] as a sampling method for *Mixed Networks* [7, 14]. Sampling algorithms that use alternative formulations of Bayesian networks, such as conjunctive normal forms [10], also suffer from sample rejection because of the independent and identically distributed (i.i.d.) sampling requirement.

When the number of inconsistent samples is a small percentage and rejection rates are consequently relatively low, methods such as SampleSearch [11] are effective. SampleSearch uses constraint propagation as an "oracle" to resolve inconsistencies during sampling. In general, constraint propagation is an NP-complete problem. Thus, the computational demands for larger networks with high degrees of determinism is challenging. SampleSearch caches inconsistent samples as they are found during the sampling process, effectively eliminating the regeneration of previously-generated inconsistent samples. However, SampleSearch's tree-structured "cache" can grow exponentially in size as in the worst case the number of rejected samples is proportional to the state space of Bayesian network variable state configurations.

Typically, only the states of strict subsets of the variables yield impossible configurations. This is due to deterministic causalities between variables, i.e. the local dependence structures. For example, take a BN over a set of variables $\mathbf{V} = \{V_1, \ldots, V_n\}$ and suppose[1] $\Pr(v_i \mid v_j) = 0$. Then, all configurations of $\mathbf{V}$ with v_i, v_j are impossible, i.e. an exponential number of inconsistent samples with state patterns that overlap due to localized deterministic causalities. It is clear that efficient caching of samples suggests the exploitation of local network structure, especially for networks with high degrees of determinism, to mitigate exponentially-growing caching requirements.

In this paper, we propose a new algorithm to reduce the overhead of caching by using an adaptive decision tree to efficiently store and detect inconsistent samples. The tree stores the inconsistent sample configurations in compressed form, hence we refer to the method as *Compressed Vertex Tree (CVT) search*. Similar to SampleSearch, a CVT structure stores the vertices corresponding to statistical variables that have zero probability constraints in a tree. However, by contrast to SampleSearch, CVT is adaptive and maintained by a detecting and merging process that keeps the tree compressed, requiring only a small amount of overhead to perform the modifications. Hence, the CVT storage requirements are significantly lower and detecting inconsistent samples is more efficient compared to other methods as is demonstrated by the results in this paper.

The remainder of this paper is organized as follows. Section 2 presents the CVT approach to optimize importance sampling. Section 3 empirically verifies our proposed approach on two real-world Bayesian networks. Finally, Section 4 summarizes our conclusions.

---

[1] Throughout this paper we write $\Pr(v_i \mid v_j)$ for $\Pr(V_i = v_i \mid V_j = v_j)$ for brevity.

2   Importance Sampling with CVT

We introduce the CVT concept to store and detect zero probability constraints to optimize importance sampling on Bayesian networks with deterministic causalities.

2.1   Importance Sampling and Sample Rejection

Let $g(\mathbf{X})$ be a function over m variables $\mathbf{X} = \{X_1, \ldots, X_m\}$ over some domain $\Omega \subseteq \mathbb{R}^m$, such that computing $g(\mathbf{X})$ for any $\mathbf{X}$ is feasible. Let p be a probability density over $\mathbf{X}$. Consider the problem of estimating the integral: $\mathbf{E}[g(\mathbf{X})|p] = \int_\Omega g(\mathbf{X})p(\mathbf{X})\, d\mathbf{X}$. Assuming that p is a density that is easy to sample from, the integral can be approx-
imated by drawing a set of i.i.d. samples $\{\mathbf{x}_1, \ldots, \mathbf{x}_N\}$. Importance sampling uses
weights $w(\mathbf{x}_i) = \frac{p(\mathbf{x}_i)}{I(\mathbf{x}_i)}$ to estimate $\mathbf{E}[g(\mathbf{X})|p]$ by sampling (see [20]):

$$\hat{g}_N = \sum_{i=1}^{N} [g(\mathbf{x}_i)w(\mathbf{x}_i)] \ . \tag{1}$$

Importance sampling is a practical and efficient approximate inference method for
Bayesian networks and has become the basis for many sampling-based algorithms to es-
timate the prior $\Pr(\mathbf{X})$ and posterior $\Pr(\mathbf{X} \mid \mathbf{e})$ from a network. For example, SIS [23],
AIS-BN [4], and EPIS-BN [27] use importance sampling for Bayesian inference.

A sample $\mathbf{x}_i$ with $w(\mathbf{x}_i) = 0$ is called *inconsistent*, because $\mathbf{x}_i$ is an impossible
event $w(\mathbf{x}_i) = 0 \Rightarrow p(\mathbf{x}_i) = 0$. An inconsistent sample does not contribute to the sum
estimate (1) and is effectively "rejected". The phenomenon is caused by the presence
of a deterministic influences in the network. Consider Fig. 1 with deterministic causal
influences of B and C on D. Suppose D = 0 is observed, then any sample with C = 1
will be rejected in forward sampling (from the roots) which occurs at a rate of 1,000,000
to 1 since $\Pr(C = 1) = 0.999999$. Note that backward deterministic influences cannot
be inferred in sampling algorithms, which leads to the rejection problem. When D = 0
then C cannot be 1 and all such samples will be rejected. Hence, we refer to *deterministic causalities* (suggesting direction) as the root cause of the rejection problem.

Rejection also occurs in backward sampling, because forward sampling is part of all
backward sampling strategies. In backward sampling, a sampling ordering is selected.
Suppose B is sampled forward and C is sampled backward. Then B = 0 will be sampled
most frequently, because $\Pr(B = 0 \mid .) > 0.9999$. For C = 1 or C = 0 the sample is
always inconsistent, because $\Pr(D = 0 \mid B = 0, C = 0) = 0$ and $\Pr(D = 0 \mid B = 0, C = 1) = 0$. This problem also occurs when sampling C forward and B backward.

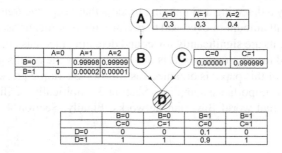

Fig. 1. A Bayesian Network with Deterministic Causalities through Zeros in the CPT of D

State-of-the-art importance sampling algorithms, e.g. AIS-BN [4], EPIS-BN [27], and RIS [24] mitigate this problem by learning methods that adjust the probabilities in the conditional probability tables of the network to reduce the sample rejection rate. None of these algorithms can completely eliminate sample rejection.

2.2   The CVT Approach

Configurations of variable states can be stored as patterns in a search tree to efficiently match zero probability constraints, e.g. those that originate from the example shown in Fig. 1. Assume that only configurations (B $= 1, $C $= 1$) and (A $= 0, $C $= 0$) that produce zero probability constraints are found at a certain stage of sampling example of Fig. 1. A search tree to store these patterns can be constructed. There are many ways to achieve this, resulting in considerable differences in tree sizes resulting from node orderings. Consider for example the three trees shown in Fig. 2. The left tree has the constraint (B $= 1, $C $= 1$) duplicated, due to the suboptimal top-down ordering A $\rightarrow$ B $\rightarrow$ C. The ordering C $\rightarrow$ B $\rightarrow$ A yields an optimal tree, as shown in Fig. 2(b).

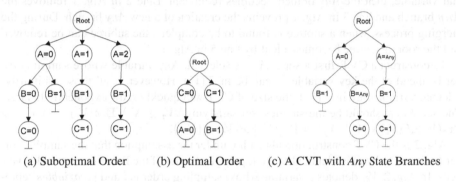

(a) Suboptimal Order   (b) Optimal Order   (c) A CVT with *Any* State Branches

Fig. 2. Possible Trees to Store Zero Probability Constraints

The problem is that the size of the resulting tree is very sensitive to the vertex ordering used in the top-down construction. Prior work on tree-based caching (such as SampleSearch) do not consider optimization of the tree structure. In the worst case this leads to a tree with redundant branches that represent identical states.

We propose two modifications of the tree-based sample search:

1. A branch can be marked "*Any*" to represent any state of a variable.
2. Adaptive refinement is used to dynamically optimize the tree structure by merging tree branches to reduce the tree size.

The suboptimal CVT with order A $\rightarrow$ B $\rightarrow$ C is shown in Fig. 2c. Because of the suboptimal order, the tree in Fig. 2c is not as efficient as the tree in Fig. 2(b). Clearly, the tree in Fig. 2(c) is optimal compared to Fig. 2(a). The key concept of our approach is to construct and reorder trees by way of combining parts to achieve optimized compressed trees, which is facilitated by wildcard "*Any*" states and a branch merging algorithm.

We first introduce some terminology. For a $BN = (G(\mathbf{V}, \mathbf{A}), \mathrm{Pr})$, evidence $\mathbf{e}$ and a sampling order δ, $\forall V_i \in \mathbf{V}$, $\mathcal{T}_{\mathbf{e}}^{\delta}(V_i)$ denotes the CVT of the variable V_i and V_i is called the *key variable* of $T_e^\delta(V_i)$. The family of all variables in $T_e^\delta(V_i)$ is denoted as[2] $F_e^\delta(V_i)$. Furthermore, $\forall V_j \in F_e^\delta(V_i)$, $\delta(V_j) \le \delta(V_i)$. In CVT $T_e^\delta(V_i)$ we refer to a path from the root node to a leaf node a *walk*. Furthermore, a *walk* is a *key walk* when the walk visits the key variable V_i.

To illustrate these definitions, consider Fig. 2(c). Sampling order is A → B → C and C is the key variable of $T(C)$. So $F(C) = \{A, B, C\}$. The walk $Root \to A = Any \to B = 1 \to C = 1$ is a key walk. The walk $Root \to A = 0 \to B = 1$ is a non-key walk.

2.3   CVT Construction and Sample Matching

CVT is an adaptive decision tree to match samples for rejection decisions. CVT allows for efficient adding, searching, and matching of zero probability constraints represented by tree walks. The process of constructing a CVT consists of repeatedly merging overlapping walks into a new CVT. Alg. 1 illustrates the method to add a zero constraint into a CVT. Lines 1 and 4 in Alg. 1 ensure that the subtree under the *Any* branch is also contained in any state-valued branch. When a node has a branch for each state for that variable, then the *Any* branch becomes redundant. Line 2 in Alg. 1 removes the *Any* branch and line 3 in Alg. 1 prevents the creation of a new *Any* branch. During the merging process, when a subtree is found to be complete, the subtree can be removed and the root of subtree becomes a leaf by line 5 in Alg. 1.

To construct a CVT, first a set $F(V_i)$ is selected. Any variable whose sampling order is ahead of the key variable V_i can be in $F(V_i)$. However, if all those arbitrarily-selected variables are in $F(V_i)$, the size of CVT will quickly grow exponentially large. The set $F(V_i)$ should be the smallest set satisfying $\forall V_j \in \mathbf{V} \setminus \mathbf{E}, \delta(V_j) < \delta(V_i) \Rightarrow \mathrm{Pre}(V_i \mid F(V_i) \setminus \{V_i\}, V_j) = \mathrm{Pre}(V_i \mid F(V_i) \setminus \{V_i\})$.

Alg. 2 is the CVT construction algorithm under the assumption that the sampling order (referred to by δ) is identical to the topological order of the Bayesian network's vertices. In Alg. 2, V_{δ_i} denotes a variable whose sampling order is i and t.*variables* represents all the variables that show up in the walk t and whose value in t is not *Any*.

When the sampling order is identical to the topological order of the network, the Refractoring algorithm (RIS) [24] or factorization algorithm of EPIS-BN [27] can be used to shrink $F(V_i)$ to the minimal set. If the sampling order is not identical to the topological order, techniques such as mini-bucket can be used to select $F(V_i)$.

Alg. 2 at line 1 uses the *refractoring algorithm* [24] to select $F(V_i)$. Since $\mathrm{Pre}(\cdot) = 0 \Leftrightarrow \mathrm{Pr}(\cdot, \mathbf{e}) = 0$, those zero entries in the *conditional probability table* (CPT) of the Bayesian network are critical for finding the zero constraints, thus function InitCVT will merge them. For an evidence variable, only the zero entry which is consistent with its observed value is merged and those entries are all non-key walks in CVT. Note that for a CVT $T(V_i)$, all its non-key walks are useless, because when sampling variable V_i, if the instantiation of previous sample variables contains one non-key walk, then no value of V_i can be sampled. Thus, non-key walks should be removed from the CVT and merged into the CVT of the variable that is ahead of V_i (in sampling order). The function BuildCVT is a process of backwards (in sampling order) moving non-key

---

[2] $T_e^\delta(V_i)$ and $F_e^\delta(V_i)$ will be written as $T(V_i)$ and $F(V_i)$ when the context of δ and $\mathbf{e}$ is clear.

```
Procedure MergeWalk (root, p)
Input: root node of tree,p a zero constraint
Result: merge walk p into tree rooted at root
cur ← root;
while cur ≠ null do
    if cur.var ∈ p then
        if cur[p[cur.var]] = null then
            if cur[Any] ≠ null then
1               cur[p[cur.var]] ← CopyTree(cur[Any]);
2               if ∀s ∈ Cfg(cur.var), cur[s] ≠ null then
                    delete cur[Any], cur[Any] ← null
                end
            else
                cur[p[cur.var]] ← new node(cur.var)
            end
        end
        cur ← cur[p[cur.var]];
    else
        if cur[Any] = null then
3           if ∃s ∈ Cfg(cur.var), cur[s] = null then
                cur[Any] ← new node(cur.var);
                cur ← cur[Any]
            else
                cur ← null
            end
        else
            cur ← cur[Any]
        end
        foreach s ∈ Cfg(cur.var) do
4           MergeWalk (cur[s], p)
    end
end
5 Cut complete sub-trees
```

Algorithm 1. Merging a Tree Walk into a CVT

walks from one CVT to another. If the sampling order is not consistent with topological order, then the function InitCVT should be modified according to the sampling order and importance functions. However, as long as InitCVT ensures that $\mathcal{F}(V_i)$ satisfies $\forall V_j \in \mathbf{V} \setminus \mathbf{E}, \delta(V_j) < \delta(V_i) \Rightarrow \mathrm{Pr_e}(V_i \mid \mathcal{F}(V_i) \setminus \{V_i\}, V_j) = \mathrm{Pr_e}(V_i \mid \mathcal{F}(V_i) \setminus \{V_i\})$ and all zero entries in CPTs are merged into a CVT, the CVT can be efficiently used to eliminate the rejection problem.

The sample matching algorithm Alg. 3 is used to match previously-recorded inconsistent samples for the purpose of filtering. The $cur.var$ represents the random variable that corresponds to the current tree node cur. In searching the CVT, if a branch corresponding to the query is found, the search will follow that branch. If not, it will follow through the Any branch.

When Alg. 3 returns MATCH, the probability of configuration $\mathbf{v}$ is 0. The importance function f_i of variable V_i can be redefined as $f_i(\mathcal{F}(V_i)) \times [\mathrm{SearchCVT}(\mathcal{F}(V_i))]$. Here, $[\mathrm{SearchCVT}(\mathcal{F}(V_i))] = 0$ if $\mathrm{SearchCVT}(\mathcal{F}(V_i))$ returns MATCH, otherwise $[\mathrm{SearchCVT}(\mathcal{F}(V_i))] = 1$. It is then straightforward to calculate the conditional probability from this new importance function. Since the branches of CVT represent zero constraints induced by evidences, the induced probability distribution is unbiased as long as the original importance function f_i is unbiased.

Procedure InitCVT $(BN, \mathbf{e}, \delta)$
Input: $BN : (G(\mathbf{V}, \mathbf{A}), \Pr)$, $\mathbf{e}$: observed values of $\mathbf{E}$, δ: the sampling order
Result: $\mathcal{T}$, $\forall V_i \in \mathbf{V}$, $\mathcal{T}(V_i)$ is initialized.
    foreach $V_i \in \mathbf{V} \setminus \mathbf{E}$ **do**
1   Use the refractoring algorithm to decide $\mathcal{F}(V_i)$
        foreach $\mathbf{c} \in Cfg(\pi(V_i))$, $v_i \in Cfg(V_i)$ **do**
            if $\Pr(v_i \mid \mathbf{c}) = 0$ **then** MergeWalk $(\mathcal{T}(V_i).root, (\mathbf{c}, v_i))$
        end
    end
    foreach $e_i \in \mathbf{e}$ *and* e_i *is* E_i*'s observed value* **do**
        $\mathcal{F}(E_i) \leftarrow \pi(E_i) \cup \{E_i\}$
        foreach $\mathbf{c} \in Cfg(\pi(E_i))$ **do**
            if $\Pr(e_i \mid \mathbf{c}) = 0$ **then** MergeWalk $(\mathcal{T}(E_i).root, \mathbf{c})$
        end
    end
    return $\mathcal{T}$

Procedure BuildCVT $(BN, \mathbf{e}, \delta)$
Input: Same as InitCVT
Result: $\mathcal{T}$
    $\mathcal{T} \leftarrow$ InitCVT$(BN, \mathbf{e}, \delta)$
    foreach $E_i \in \mathbf{E}$ **do**
        Add E_i to the end of δ and mark $\mathcal{T}(E_i)$
    end
    for $i = |\delta|$ *to 1* **do**
        if $\mathcal{T}(V_{\delta_i})$ *is marked* **then**
            foreach *non-key walk* $\mathbf{t}$ *in* $\mathcal{T}(V_{\delta_i})$ **do**
                if $\exists j, j < i \wedge \mathbf{t}.variables \subset \mathcal{F}(V_{\delta_j})$ **then**
                    MergeWalk $(\mathcal{T}(V_{\delta_j}), \mathbf{t})$
                    Mark $\mathcal{T}(V_{\delta_j})$ and remove $\mathbf{t}$ from $\mathcal{T}(V_{\delta_i})$
            end
        end
    end
    return $\mathcal{T}$

Algorithm 2. CVT Construction

Procedure SearchCVT $(root, \mathbf{v})$
Input: $root$ node of tree, $\mathbf{v}$: a configuration
    $cur \leftarrow root$;
    while cur *is not a leaf* **do**
        if $cur[\mathbf{v}[cur.var]] \neq null$ **then**
            $cur \leftarrow cur[\mathbf{v}[cur.var]]$
        else
            if $cur[Any] \neq null$ **then**
                $cur \leftarrow cur[Any]$
            else
                return NOMATCH
            end
        end
    end
    return MATCH

Algorithm 3. CVT Search to Match and Filter Inconsistent Samples

3 Results

This section presents the experimental validation and performance results of CVT for importance sampling on Pathfinder [13] and ANDES [5]. Tests were performed with an AMD Athlon 4200 1GHz 2GB memory and 512KB L1 cache. All programs are written in C++ and compiled with g++ 4.4.3 -O3 and run on Linux 2.6.32-27.

Pathfinder [13] and ANDES [5] exhibit determinism studied by several authors in this context. Both networks are reasonably large, with $|\mathbf{V}| = 109, |\mathbf{A}| = 195$ for Pathfinder and $|\mathbf{V}| = 223, |\mathbf{A}| = 338$ for ANDES. ANDES requires many more samples to converge closer to the exact solution as compared Pathfinder.

3.1 MSE Results

We measured the effect of rejection reduction on the quality of the estimate on ANDES and Pathfinder. That is, the samples that are filtered by CVT are not counted as a sample. To measure the deviation from the exact solution after a number of sampling iterations, we used the *MSE* (mean squared error) metric commonly used in comparative accuracy studies. We compared the MSE of the following methods:

- RIS-AIS [24],
- AIS-BN [4] with SampleSearch (AIS-BN+SampleSearch) [10],
- EPIS-BN [26, 27], and
- RIS-AIS with CVT (RIS-AIS+CVT) presented in this paper.

We randomly generated 50 test cases, each with 20 evidence vertices set in Pathfinder and 100 test cases, each with 25 evidence vertices that were set in ANDES to produce posterior distributions. For ANDES, we used 300,000 sampling iterations, and for Pathfinder, we used 12,000 sampling iterations. ANDES is more complex and requires more samples than Pathfinder. The MSE of RIS-AIS+CVT is the best and lowest of all sampling methods as is shown in Fig. 3.

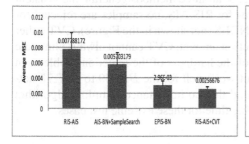 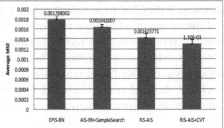

Fig. 3. Average MSE for Pathfinder (50 Test Cases and 12,000 Sampling Iterations) and ANDES (100 Test Cases and 300,000 Sampling Iterations)

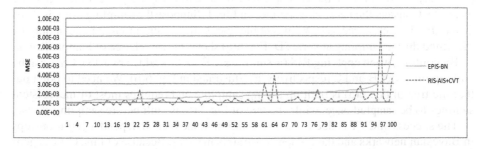

Fig. 4. MSE Results of 300,000 Sampling Iterations for 100 Test Cases (ANDES)

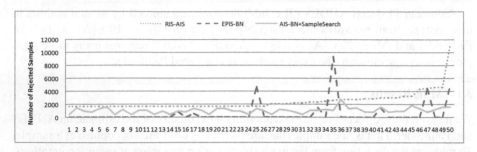

Fig. 5. Number of Rejected Inconsistent Samples in 12,000 Sampling Iterations for 50 Test Cases with RIS-AIS, AIS-BN+SampleSearch and EPIS-BN (Pathfinder)

The average MSE of EPIS-BN is close to that of RIS-AIS+CVT. To confirm the gains of RIS-AIS+CVT versus EPIS-BN, we compared the MSE for all the 100 test cases in Fig. 4. For all but 7 out of 100 test cases, RIS-AIS+CVT outperforms EPIS-BN, with a 4 times lower MSE in the best case.

3.2   Sample Rejection Reduction Results

To validate the sample rejection rate improvement, we evaluated the CVT algorithms for RIS-AIS [24]. Fig. 5 compares the number of inconsistent samples generated by importance sampling with three methods on Pathfinder for 50 random test cases (each with a different evidence configuration pattern). The results for ANDES were comparable (not shown). Without CVT, as shown in Fig. 5, all three methods generate inconsistent samples. With CVT to reduce rejection rates for RIS-AIS, no samples are rejected for Pathfinder and only 0.3% are rejected for ANDES (not shown in the Figure). CVT either eliminated or significantly reduced the rejection amount. CVT cannot always eliminate rejection, which is not surprising because of the hardness of the rejection problem. In our experiments we found that CVT did not work well for the BN_69 to BN_75 networks of the UAI competition [1]. We found that no importance sampling algorithm can generate consistent samples in reasonable time for these extreme test cases.

3.3   CVT Compared to Related Work

SampleSearch [11] caches zero constraints in a tree structure to detect inconsistent samples to reject. To compare the conceptual difference to CVT, we present the following example. Consider the network as defined in Fig. 1. Suppose the sampling order is A, B, C and that D is observed as 0. With SampleSearch the constraint violation can only be identified during sampling at vertex D. Fig. 6(a) shows the search tree of SampleSearch.

By contrast, when applying RIS (assuming arc B → C is added by RIS), CVT can be built up on vertex B and C respectively, as illustrated in Fig. 6(b). We need to point out that the tree in Fig. 6(a) is built up during sampling and requires most of inconsistent samples to be sampled once, while the tree of Fig. 6(b) is built before sampling starts.

The success of CVT is due to the exploitation of the local independent relationships in Bayesian networks and the hidden constraints in CPTs. Because of this, CVT is generally more effective to reduce inconsistent samples in Bayesian networks sampling but

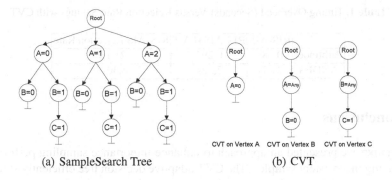

(a) SampleSearch Tree   (b) CVT

CVT on Vertex A   CVT on Vertex B   CVT on Vertex C

Fig. 6. SampleSearch Example Tree Compared to CVT

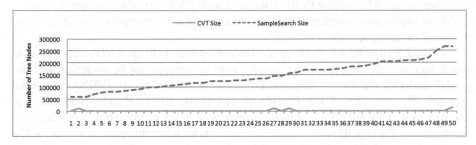

Fig. 7. Number of Tree Nodes in 12,000 Sampling Iterations for 50 Test Cases with CVT and SampleSearch (Pathfinder)

less effective in other frameworks such as CNF formulations. To verify this analysis, we compared the size of the trees (measured by number of nodes) for CVT and SampleSearch in Pathfinder's 50 test cases (Fig. 7). Fig. 7 shows that CVT uses far fewer tree nodes than SampleSearch.

In the worst case however, a CVT may still grow very large. The size of a CVT can be limited by a threshold to avoid excessive growth, but the difficulties are in how to choose zero constraints that are most likely to be encountered in the sampling process and keep those in the CVT.

3.4 Measuring the CVT Overhead

Filtering invalid samples before sampling should not be too costly and not much more costly then allowing invalid samples to be rejected. The initial construction of the CVT can be done offline. Searching the CVT incurs overhead. We measured the overhead of CVT on the sampling time of RIS-AIS using our testbed implementation.

The results are shown in Table 1. The timing overhead of CVT for Pathfinder is 3.6% while 21.1% of the total sampling time is saved by CVT filtering. The timing overhead of CVT for ANDES is 6.9% while 6.3% of the total sampling time is saved by CVT filtering. The results for Pathfinder show a significant gain in overall sampling efficiency. For ANDES the results are mixed. Our testbed implementation is not fully optimized for this study. We expect a better tradeoff with a memory layout of CVT nodes that increases spatial locality for caching to reduce memory traffic.

Table 1. Timing Overhead (Seconds) Versus Rejection Rate Savings with CVT

	RIS-AIS	RIS-AIS+CVT	RIS-AIS Rejection Rate
Pathfinder	0.28s	0.29s	21.1%
ANDES	21.7s	23.2s	6.30 %

4 Conclusions

In this paper we presented an approach to enhance importance sampling performance by reducing inconsistent samples. The CVT adaptive decision tree efficiently stores the zero constraints that must be filtered from the sampling process. It ensures efficient searching and matching of constraints. Empirical results show that Refractor Importance Sampling (RIS) with AIS-BN enhanced with CVT favorably compares to state-of-the-art importance sampling algorithms in terms of a lower approximation error and increased sampling speeds.

CVT and SampleSearch [11] are not the only methods to store zero constraints to match inconsistent samples. For example, zero constrains can be compiled as "no-goods" into *Ordered Binary Decision Diagrams* (OBDD) [3]. An OBDD is a global structure. By contrast to CVT, OBDDs do not utilize the local independencies represented by a wildcard "*Any*" branch. Furthermore, CVT construction identifies zero constraints, while OBDD relies on other algorithms to detect those zero constraints. On the other hand, CVT could utilize OBDD's *Directed Acyclic Graph* structure to save space. We believe this direction deserves further investigation.

Zero constraints can also be stored in CPTs or in importance function tables of the Bayesian networks. However, this is not deemed efficient. As was illustrated in Fig. 1, storing zero constraints in CPTs requires expanding each CPT exponentially to meet the in-degree requirements of additional variable influences. The positive values stored in CPTs give little information to expedite the rejection problem. Rule based [18, 19] storage is not a solution, because the search expense will be proportional to the number of rules. Another solution is to use Probability Tree [2]. Similar to CPTs, a complete probability tree also stores many positive values, which provide little information for the purpose of rejection decisions.

References

[1] Bilmes, J., Dechter, R.: Evaluation of Probabilistic Inference System (2006), http://ssli.ee.washington.edu/ bilmes/uai06InferenceEvaluation/
[2] Boutilier, C., Friedman, N., Goldszmidt, M., Koller, D.: Context-specific independence in Bayesian networks. In: Proc. Twelfth Conf. on Uncertainty in Artificial Intelligence (UAI 1996), pp. 115–123 (1996)
[3] Bryant, R.: Graph-based algorithms for boolean function manipulation. IEEE Transactions on Computers C-35(8), 677–691 (1986)
[4] Cheng, J., Druzdzel, M.J.: AIS-BN: An adaptive importance sampling algorithm for evidential reasoning in large Bayesian networks. Journal of Artificial Intelligence Research 13, 155–188 (2000)

[5] Conati, C., Gertner, A.S., VanLehn, K., Druzdzel, M.J.: On-line student modeling for coached problem solving using Bayesian networks. In: Proceedings of the Sixth International Conference on User Modeling (UM 1996), pp. 231–242. Springer, Vienna (1997)

[6] Cooper, G.F.: The computational complexity of probabilistic inference using Bayesian belief networks. Artificial Intelligence 42(2-3), 393–405 (1990)

[7] Dechter, R., Mateescu, R.: Mixtures of deterministic-probabilistic networks and their and/or search space. In: UAI 2004: Proceedings of the 20th Conference on Uncertainty in Artificial Intelligence, pp. 120–129. UAI Press, Arlington (2004)

[8] Gogate, V., Dechter, R.: Approximate inference algorithms for hybrid Bayesian networks with discrete constraints. In: Proceedings of Uncertainty in Artificial Intelligence, pp. 209–216 (2005)

[9] Gogate, V., Dechter, R.: A new algorithm for sampling CSP solutions uniformly at random. In: Benhamou, F. (ed.) CP 2006. LNCS, vol. 4204, pp. 711–715. Springer, Heidelberg (2006)

[10] Gogate, V., Dechter, R.: Approximate counting by sampling the backtrack-free search space. In: Conference on Artificial Intelligence (AAAI), pp. 198–203 (2007)

[11] Gogate, V., Dechter, R.: SampleSearch: Importance sampling in presence of determinism. Artificial Intelligence 175(2), 694–729 (2011)

[12] Guo, H., Hsu, W.: A survey on algorithms for real-time Bayesian network inference. In: The Joint AAAI 2002/KDD 2002/UAI 2002 Workshop on Real-Time Decision Support and Diagnosis Systems. Edmonton, Alberta (2002)

[13] Heckerman, D.E., Horvitz, E.J., Nathwani, B.N.: Toward normative expert systems: Part I the Pathfinder project. Methods of Information in Medicine 31, 90–105 (1992)

[14] Mateescu, R., Dechter, R.: Mixed deterministic and probabilistic networks. Annals of Mathematics and Artificial Intelligence 54(1-3), 3–51 (2008)

[15] Moral, S., Salmerón, A.: Dynamic importance sampling in Bayesian networks based on probability trees. International Journal of Approximate Reasoning 38, 245–261 (2005)

[16] Neapolitan, R.E.: Probabilistic Reasoning in Expert Systems. John Wiley and Sons, NY (1990)

[17] Pearl, J.: Probabilistic Reasoning in Intelligent Systems: Networks of Plausible Inference. Morgan Kaufmann Publishers, Inc., San Mateo (1988)

[18] Poole, D.: Exploiting contextual independence and approximation in belief network inference. Tech. rep., University of British Columbia (1997)

[19] Poole, D.: Probabilistic partial evaluation: Exploiting rule structure in probabilistic inference. In: Proc. 15th International Joint Conference on AI (IJCAI 1997), pp. 1284–1291 (1997)

[20] Rubinstein, R.Y.: Simulation and Monte Carlo Method. John Wiley and Sons, Hoboken (1981)

[21] Russell, S., Norvig, P.: Artificial intelligence: A modern approach. Prentice Hall Series in Artificial Intelligence. Prentice Hall, Englewood Cliffs (1995)

[22] Salmerón, A., Cano, A., Moral, S.: Importance sampling in Bayesian networks using probability trees. Comput. Stat. Data Anal. 34(4), 387–413 (2000)

[23] Shachter, R.D., Peot, M.A.: Simulation approaches to general probabilistic inference on belief networks. In: Proceedings of the 5th Conference on Uncertainty in Artificial Intelligence, vol. 5 (1990)

[24] Yu, H., van Engelen, R.: Refractor importance sampling. In: Proceedings of the 24th Conference on Uncertainty in Artificial Intelligence, pp. 603–611 (July 2008)

[25] Yuan, C., Druzdzel, M.J.: Importance sampling algorithms for Bayesian networks: Principles and performance. Mathematical and Computer Modelling 43, 1189–1207 (2006)

[26] Yuan, C., Druzdzel, M.J.: An importance sampling algorithm based on evidence pre-propagation. In: Proceedings of the 19th Conference on Uncertainty in Artificial Intelligence, pp. 624–631 (July 2003)

[27] Yuan, C., Druzdzel, M.J.: Importance sampling in Bayesian networks an influence-based approximation strategy for importance functions. In: Proceedings of the 21th Conference on Uncertainty in Artificial Intelligence, pp. 650–657 (July 2005)

Bayesian Networks and the Imprecise Dirichlet Model Applied to Recognition Problems

Cassio P. de Campos[1] and Qiang Ji[2]

[1] Dalle Molle Institute for Artificial Intelligence
Galleria 2, Manno-Lugano, Switzerland
[2] Rensselaer Polytechnic Institute
110 Eighth St., Troy, NY, USA
cassio@idsia.ch, jiq@rpi.edu

Abstract. This paper describes an Imprecise Dirichlet Model and the maximum entropy criterion to learn Bayesian network parameters under insufficient and incomplete data. The method is applied to two distinct recognition problems, namely, a facial action unit recognition and an activity recognition in video surveillance sequences. The model treats a wide range of constraints that can be specified by experts, and deals with incomplete data using an ad-hoc expectation-maximization procedure. It is also described how the same idea can be used to learn dynamic Bayesian networks. With synthetic data, we show that our proposal and widely used methods, such as the Bayesian maximum a posteriori, achieve similar accuracy. However, when real data come in place, our method performs better than the others, because it does not rely on a single prior distribution, which might be far from the *best* one.

1   Introduction

Bayesian Networks (BNs) encode joint probability distributions using a compact representation based on a directed acyclic graph where nodes are associated to random variables and conditional distributions are specified for variables given their parents in the graph. The adoption of BNs has increased in the past years. For instance, recent research in computer vision uses BNs for representing causal relationships in facial expression recognition, image segmentation, visual surveillance, activity understanding, among others [17,21].

Accuracy of results relies on the quality of model parameters. Ideally, with enough data, it is possible to learn parameters by standard statistical methods like maximum likelihood (ML) or maximum a posteriori (MAP) estimations. However, learning reliable parameters may require a large amount of training data. In spite of that, approximate domain knowledge through constraints on parameters is available in many real applications and can improve estimations. We propose a framework for parameter learning that combines training data and domain knowledge in the form of constraints, and where imprecise priors are considered. We use the Imprecise Dirichlet Model (IDM) [18] to work with prior distributions so that we have a set of Dirichlet distributions on which we

W. Liu (Ed.): ECSQARU 2011, LNAI 6717, pp. 158–169, 2011.

apply the maximum entropy principle to obtain a final estimation. The imprecise priors may be viewed as a conservative choice when data are scarce to avoid overfitting. Furthermore, the proposed idea requires less hyper-parameters to be specified by the user (for instance, we do not need to define the prior of a maximum a posteriori estimation), which makes it reliable and adaptive, as shown in the experiments with real data. In our formulation, convex programming can be used, which quickly finds the global optimum solution. For incomplete data sets, a variant of the Expectation–Maximization method is used, where the expectation step is done as usual and the maximization is replaced with the new formulation. The methods are general and deal with Dynamic Bayesian Networks as well. Experiments with synthetic and real data from a facial action unit recognition and a human activity recognition captured with surveillance cameras show better results than ML and Bayesian MAP results, which are among the most used methods to learn such networks.

Previous work has either explored constraints together with a precise criterion, such as isotonic regression [10], closed-form solutions for the constrained ML estimation with complete data [16], constrained EM method with penalties [11], or has used an imprecise model, such as the naive and the tree-augmented credal classifiers [6,7] or the imprecise decision trees [1]. Lukasiewicz [14] explores maximum entropy properties, but does not discuss a parameter learning procedure. de Campos and Cozman [4] work with constraints on priors and formulate the learning problem as a constrained optimization problem, but their formulation is restricted to complete data sets and uses a (somewhat slow) non-convex optimization procedure.

The paper is divided as follows. Section 2 introduces the notation and the problem of parameter learning. Maximum entropy and the Imprecise Dirichlet Model are presented, as well as constraints that can be used to guide the learning. Section 3 summaries the learning model and discusses the case of incomplete data. Section 4 presents experimental results and Section 5 concludes the paper.

2   BNs, Dynamic BNs and Parameter Learning

A BN can be defined as a triple $(\mathcal{G}, \mathcal{X}, \mathcal{P})$, where $\mathcal{G}$ is a directed acyclic graph with nodes associated to random variables $\mathcal{X} = \{X_1, \ldots, X_n\}$ (which we assume to be categorical), and $\mathcal{P}$ is a collection of parameters $p(x_{ik}|\pi_{ij})$, with $\sum_k p(x_{ik}|\pi_{ij}) = 1$, where $x_{ik} \in \Omega_{X_i}$ is a category or state of X_i and $\pi_{ij} \in \times_{Y \in \pi_i} \Omega_Y$ a complete instantiation of the parents π_i of X_i in $\mathcal{G}$ (j is viewed as an index for each parent configuration). In a BN every variable is conditionally independent of its non-descendants given its parents. The joint distribution is obtained by $p(x) = \prod_i p(x_{ik}|\pi_{ij})$, with $x \in \mathcal{X}$ and all x_{ik} and π_{ij} compatible with x.

We focus on parameter learning in a BN where the structure (i.e. the graph) is known. Given a data set D where each element is a sample of the BN variables, the goal is to find the most probable values for the whole parameter set $\mathcal{P}$. One way to quantify the result is by the log likelihood function $\log(p(D|\mathcal{P}))$. Assuming that samples are drawn independently from the underlying distribution, we maximize $\log \prod_{ijk} p(x_{ik}|\pi_{ij})^{n_{ijk}}$, where n_{ijk} indicates how many elements of D contain both x_{ik} and π_{ij}. ML estimation has its optimum at $p(x_{ik}|\pi_{ij}) = \frac{n_{ijk}}{\sum_k n_{ijk}}$.

Dynamic Bayesian Networks (DBNs) can be viewed as two-slice temporal BNs, where at time zero, we have a standard BN just as described, and for slices 1 to T a *transitional* BN is defined over the same variables but nodes have parents on time t and/or time $t - 1$. Conditional probability distributions for time $t > 0$ share the same parameters so that we can unroll the DBN to obtain the factorization $p(\mathcal{X}_{1:T}) = \prod_i p_0(X_i|\pi_i) \prod_{t=1}^{T} \prod_i p(X_i^t|\pi_i^t)$, where T is the number of slices, $p_0(\cdot)$ are conditional distributions of the initial BN and X_i^t, π_i^t represent the corresponding variables in time t. Learning parameters of DBNs is similar to the BN case, but we deal with counts n_{ijk} for both the initial BN and for the transitional BN. Thus counts are obtained from data sets with time sequences. In other words, we can reduce the learning problem in a DBN to the BN learning by carefully counting the frequencies on the data set. Therefore, all following discussion can be applied to both BNs and DBNs. We point out when additional care for DBNs is needed.

2.1   Constraints

When small amount of data is available, standard estimation methods may produce unreliable results. Constraints are available in many applications and may improve results. We describe here some constraints that may be accommodated in our learning procedure. In fact, such constraints can also be employed in the ML and the Bayesian MAP estimations, and we fully compare our method against these others (including their constrained versions). Constraints might be very effective, as we show for two computer vision problems (Section 4).

Let P be a sequence of parameters, α a corresponding sequence of constant numbers and β also a constant. A *linear relationship constraint* is defined as $\sum_{p(x_{ik}|\pi_{ij}) \in P} \alpha_{ijk} \cdot p(x_{ik}|\pi_{ij}) \leq \beta$, that is, any linear constraint over parameters can be expressed. Qualitative influences and synergies [19] are simple (but important) examples of linear constraints. Without quantitative statements, they allow us to encode that a given value for a variable makes more likely to observed another value in another variable, encoding an approximate domain knowledge. Other examples are sum of parameters, range, relationship, and ratio constraints [16], other types of influences and synergies, among many others. In fact, we have a very general assumption: constraints must define a convex parameter space, that is, any constraint in the form $h(P) \leq 0$, where h is convex, is allowed. Such flexibility helps us to properly describe our knowledge, while keeping the convexity assumption that guarantees a fast and global optimal algorithm. We have no restriction regarding the number of times a parameter appears in constraints or whether constraints involve distinct conditional distributions of the BN. They only need to be local to a node, otherwise they would violate the Markov condition of the BN. Although we do not use non-linear convex constraints in the experiments, they are also possible. To illustrate, suppose a *product relationship constraint* defined as $\prod_{p(x_{ik}|\pi_{ij}) \in P} p(x_{ik}|\pi_{ij}) \geq \beta$. Although non-convex, a simple log transformation makes it convex.

2.2 Imprecise Dirichlet Model

With the ML formulation, the idea is to fit parameters and data, even if the amount of data is very small. For example, with just a couple of samples, the estimation through ML will likely return undesired answers, as data are not representative of the actual distribution. Constraints applied to a ML formulation may help, but still the estimation will tend to the "incorrect" answer inside the space defined by the constraints. So only if the constraints are tight the performance will greatly improve. Another possible way not to obtain these unreliable estimations is to use a Bayesian approach, such as the MAP estimation, with a predefined prior. In this case the question is about the choice of the prior. If we can choose a good prior, such approach will lead to good estimations. However, in most cases the prior is hard to be selected and a *non-informative* prior is chosen, which may be far away from the correct distribution. The Imprecise Dirichlet Model (IDM) [18] alleviate such situations by introducing set-valued estimations instead of single point estimations. The idea is that parameters are more likely to be inside these sets, and so treating the whole set of estimations can lead to more reliable results.

In a Dirichlet model, the goal is to learn the parameters of multinomial distributions on $X_i|\pi_{ij}$ using training data and a Dirichlet prior as parametric model for $X_i|\pi_{ij}$, because of the conjugacy with the multinomial distribution [8]. A possible parametrization is $p(X_i|\pi_{ij}) \propto \prod_k p(x_{ik}|\pi_{ij})^{s\tau_{ijk}-1}$ for $s > 0$ and $\sum_k \tau_{ijk} = 1$, where the hyper-parameter s controls dispersion and hyper-parameters τ_{ijk} control location; s is interpreted as the *size* of a database encoding the same beliefs as the Dirichlet distribution. Using the IDM, s is fixed (usually between one and two [18]) but τ_{ijk} can freely vary between zero and one, so that our estimation lies in the interval

$$\frac{n_{ijk}}{s + \sum_k n_{ijk}} \leq p(x_{ik}|\pi_{ij}) \leq \frac{s + n_{ijk}}{s + \sum_k n_{ijk}}. \tag{1}$$

This roughly means that we are conservative with respect to the prior: instead of choosing a single prior, all possible priors (for a given s) are considered. We point out that we are using a local version of IDM, where the imprecision is (separately) considered for each local probability distribution that defines the Bayesian network. As mentioned, the advantage of this formulation is to avoid choosing the prior precisely as in the MAP estimation. Less hyper-parameters, more robust is the model and less sensitive to wrong user input choices. However, the outcome of IDM is a set of distributions. Next section describes and justifies maximum entropy as a way to select a single estimation from this set.

2.3 Maximum Entropy

The maximum entropy principle [12] can be used as a criterion to select a single conservative estimation from a set of distributions [1], in the sense that it avoids drastic conclusions. For example, a binomial distribution without constraints has the uniform distribution as the entropy maximizer. Furthermore, the distribution of maximum entropy from a set of distributions learned with IDM agrees (in the limit) with relative frequencies [18]. So, our goal is to have a learning model that achieves better solution for small amount of data, but which still tends to frequencies (as it should) when enough data are available. Note that the application of maximum entropy goes towards the opposite of ML, so it might seem at first contradictory, since we want to fit model and data. However, maximum entropy is employed only inside the learned IDM, which is responsible for the fitness (but considering all possible priors), while the idea of picking the distribution of maximum entropy (inside IDM) avoids overfitting by selecting the least fitting model among the IDM distributions. Thus, a possible objective is $\max_{\mathcal{P}} - \sum_{ijk} p(x_{ik}|\pi_{ij}) \log p(x_{ik}|\pi_{ij})$, which is put together with Equation (1), simplex constraints to ensure that answers are probability distributions and convex constraints defined in Section 2.1. The set of all such restrictions is denoted as $\mathcal{C}$. This formulation is based on the *local* maximum entropy criterion, that is, maximization is performed for each local conditional probability distribution in the network. Another approach is the Sequential Maximum Entropy [14]. However, such more sophisticated idea cannot (at least in a straightforward way) handle general constraints among parameters of distinct (yet local) distributions (even simple qualitative influences [19] relate parameters of distinct distributions). In Section 4 we present empirical results that support the choice of local maximum entropy.

3   The Learning Algorithm

In this section we summarize our formulation to solve the learning problem. For complete data, the idea is simple: all pieces described so far (constraints, IDM, and maximum entropy) lead to a convex optimization program. Just as likelihood, entropy is concave, so we have a maximization of a concave function subject to a collection $\mathcal{C}$ of convex constraints on parameters and the intervals of IDM of Equation (1). The important technical detail that is worth mentioning is that we use some auxiliary optimization variables to deal with the following situation: constraints of $\mathcal{C}$ defined by the expert can force parameters to lie outside the interval of Equation (1) imposed by the IDM, that is, in this case the problem would be unfeasible. However, we assume that expert's constraints are always correct and shall be included in the model only if the expert is completely sure about them (e.g. physical and physiological aspects, logical rules, domain scope, etc). Because of that, they receive more importance than Equation (1). To quantify this importance, we adopt an approach where the IDM interval must be satisfied as much as possible, while constraints of $\mathcal{C}$ must be always satisfied. The role of Equation (1) is to bring the estimation close to frequencies of parameters in the data set: (i) if Equation (1) and expert's constraints are not disjoint, then there are solutions (in the intersection if these sets) that satisfy all of them; one of them will be selected by entropy; (ii) if IDM intervals and expert's constraints are disjoint, we choose to first satisfy expert's constraints, but preferring estimations that are as close to the IDM intervals as possible. We leave for future analysis other ways to put together IDM and expert's constraints.

In this formulation, as the data set is smaller, as the result is more conservative, because of the entropy maximization and the wider intervals of Equation(1); as the data set is larger, as the result is closer to the ML estimation, because the interval shrinks: $\frac{s+n_{ijk}}{s+\sum_k n_{ijk}} - \frac{n_{ijk}}{s+\sum_k n_{ijk}} = \frac{s}{s+\sum_k n_{ijk}} \to 0$ as the values n_{ijk} increase (s is fixed). Hence, $p(x_{ik}|\pi_{ij})$ becomes closer to $\frac{n_{ijk}}{\sum_k n_{ijk}}$. Thus, the formulation is (automatically) more careful with scarce data and more aggressive towards the ML estimation with abundant data. We will see in the experiments with real data that this formulation provides a better trade-off than ML and than MAP. On the computational side, we have the challenge of solving the convex optimization. For example, we can use specialized interior point solvers or even some general optimization ideas, because convex programming has the attractive property that any local optimum is also a global optimum. Furthermore, such global optimum can be found in polynomial time in the size of input [3] (almost as fast as linear programming). Note that the input size here is small, as the problem can be solved for each node separately.

In the remaining of this section we discuss how to deal with incomplete data. Both the log-likelihood function and our formulation become non-convex, because the counts n_{ijk} from the data set are not precisely known. A common method to overcome this situation is the Expectation-Maximization (EM) algorithm [9], which starts from some initial guess, and then iteratively takes two types of steps (E-steps and M-steps) to get a local maximum. Particularly for discrete nodes, E-step computes the expected counts using the parametrization of the previous step, and M-step estimates new parameters by maximizing the likelihood function, given the counts from E-step, just like if a complete data set was in place. We can perform the same idea in our formulation. The E-step computes expected counts as usual, and the M-step is replaced by our formulation, with the constraints from $\mathcal{C}$ and from IDM. We stop when there is no possible improvement. Because of the convexity of the parameter space and the global optimizer, it suffices to include an extra linear constraint on $\mathcal{C}$ that forces the optimizer of the M-step to pick always an improving solution in case there is one, and thus the algorithm converges in the very same way as the EM. We cannot guarantee that it converges towards a local optimum, as the original EM also does not [20], but local optima are empirically verified in most situations. About time complexity, the time spent with the new idea is dominated by the E-step (which needs to perform queries in the network), and thus it is roughly as fast as the original EM version (which needs to run the same E-step).

This same Expectation–Maximization idea can be straightforward applied to DBNs. Note that the modified EM just described has a new M-step, but keeps the E-step unchanged. DBNs require the inference procedure that evaluates the expected counts to be adapted. As our formulation does not affect the E-step, we can directly apply any usual inference method of DBNs. We have used the Online Junction Tree Inference Algorithm [15] to obtain the expected counts, and then we treat the initial and transitional parts separately as if a complete data set was in place. This is employed in Section 4.2 for activity recognition.

4   Experiments

We apply the idea to both synthetic and real data of distinct computer vision problems with the aim of showing its generality and applicability to other problems. Figure 1 presents results for synthetic data of ML, Bayesian MAP with Dirichlet prior, local maximum entropy and IDM, and a formulation using sequential instead of local maximum entropy. The bars are average Kullback–Leibler (KL) divergences for 20 runs of constrained ML (first bar of each series), constrained MAP (second bar), constrained local maximum entropy and IDM (third bar), and constrained sequential maximum entropy and IDM (last bar of each series). The runs use random networks (random graphs with up to four states per variable), constraints and data. The size of the networks and data are presented in the figure's labels. Networks have 10, 20 and 40 nodes and data sets have 10, 100 and 500 samples. The same set of constraints and data were applied to each method in each iteration. We use randomly generated constraints in number equal to the number of local distributions in the network. We employ a constrained MAP formulation that uses a prior where τ is defined uniformly. MAP, local entropy with IDM and sequential entropy with IDM achieve similar results, and they are better than likelihood estimations with respect to KL divergences. For complete data, in some test cases MAP is slightly better than maximum entropy, while in others it is slightly worse. There is an advantage of the entropy with IDM against MAP, which relates to the amount of information the user must provide. For random networks, the choice of uniform τ as prior is reasonable and achieves good results. On the other hand, maximum entropy with IDM does not depend on a single prior but considers all possible priors, so achieving similar results as MAP (which has the correct prior) is a positive attribute, as maximum entropy with IDM requires less information as input and is clearly more adaptive (e.g. in real data domains).

4.1   Facial Action Unit Recognition

We now consider the problem of recognizing facial action units from real image data [13]. Based on the Facial Action Coding System, facial behaviors can be decomposed into a set of Action Units (denoted as AUs), which are related to contractions of specific sets of facial muscles. We work with recurrent 14 AUs.[1] Some AUs happen together to show a meaningful facial expression: AU_6 (cheek raiser) tends to occur together with AU_{12} (lip corner puller) when someone is smiling. On the other hand, some AUs may be mutually exclusive: AU_{25} (lips part) never happens simultaneously with AU_{24} (lip presser) since they are activated by the same muscles but with opposite motions.

A BN with 14 hidden nodes is employed, which has already demonstrated good performance in the literature [5,17]. Each node is associated to an AU with

---

[1] AU_1 (inner brow raiser), AU_2 (outer brow raiser), AU_4 (brow lowerer), AU_5 (upper lid raiser), AU_6 (cheek raiser and lid compressor), AU_7 (lid tightener), AU_9 (nose wrinkler), AU_{12} (lip corner puller), AU_{15} (lip corner depressor), AU_{17} (chin raiser), AU_{23} (lip tightener), AU_{24} (lip presser), AU_{25} (lips part), and AU_{27} (mouth stretch).

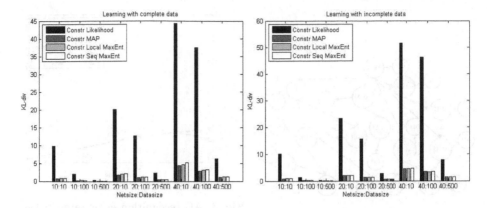

Fig. 1. Comparison between methods for synthetic random generated models using the KL divergence from the correct model. ML, even with constraints, is considerably less accurate than others. The right graph excludes constrained ML to clarify that differences are small among the other methods.

two states: activated and deactivated. Figure 2 depicts the structure of the BN. Note that every link between nodes has a sign, which is provided by a domain expert. Signs indicate whether there is positive or negative qualitative influence between AUs. For example, it is difficult to do AU_2 (outer brow raiser) alone without performing AU_1 (inner brow raiser), but we can do AU_1 without AU_2. The constraints are mainly based on physiological aspects, e.g. *mouth stretch* increases the chance of *lips apart*, and it decreases the chance of *cheek raiser and lid compressor* and *lip presser*. *Cheek raiser and lid compressor* increases the chance of *lip corner puller*. *Upper lid raiser* increases the chance of *inner brow raiser* and decreases the chance of *nose wrinkler*. *Nose wrinkler* increases the chance of *brow lowerer* and *lid tightener*. *Lip tightener* increases the chance of *lip presser*. We note that constraints are not tuned, but created by an expert.

Furthermore, 14 measurement nodes (unshaded in Figure 2, one for each AU) represent results derived from computer vision techniques. Links between AU and measurement nodes represent uncertainties in classifications. To obtain the measurement for each AU, first the face and eyes are detected in the images, and the face region is extracted and normalized based on the detected eye positions. Then each AU is detected individually by a two-class AdaBoost classifier with Gabor wavelet features [2]. The output is employed as the AU measurement in the BN model. For each measurement node, a domain expert provides ranges (usually tight) for $p(O_i|AU_i)$, which represent accuracy of classifiers.

We use 8000 images from Cohn and Kanade's DFAT-504 [13]: 20% are separated for testing and 80% for training (although just part of it is used at each time). We work with two data sets: one generated from computer vision measurements (used as evidence for testing) and one from human labeling (used for training), where uncertain labels are missing (data are incomplete). In Figure 3 we consider training data with 10, 100, 200 and 500 samples, randomly selected 20 times from the training set (results are averaged; standard deviation is below

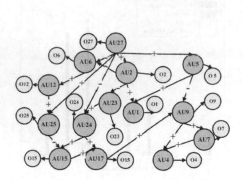

Fig. 2. Network for the AU recognition problem

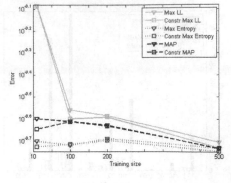

Fig. 3. AU recognition error rate (in log scale) on some BN parameter learning approaches

4 pp. in all cases, mostly below 2 pp.; the graph is in log-scale). We can see that the constrained maximum entropy is superior in all cases, and that such superiority begins to vanish as more data are used. Although our main goal is to compare the learning procedures against each other rather than surpassing the state-of-the-art methods, we obtain an overall recognition rate (percentage of correctly classified cases) of about 94% using just 1000 training samples, which is comparable to state-of-the-art results [17].

4.2 Activity Recognition

We also evaluate our approach using DBNs on a human activity recognition data set captured with a surveillance camera at a parking lot. The data set contains 110 sequences and we want to classify 7 possible activities: walking, running, leaving car, entering car, bending down, throwing and looking around. We first train DBNs for each activity and classify the activity according to the DBN with best fit for each test case. Their structure is shown in Figure 4.2, with three hidden nodes for position (Y), shape (S) and speed (V), and corresponding observation nodes. Each hidden node has two states. Temporal links exist from the time t to time $t + 1$ for each node. Furthermore, the temporal link between V^t and Y^{t+1} encodes the dynamic relationship between speed and position.

The measurements of the observation nodes are obtained from the motion detection results. We first perform background subtraction to detect the motion blob of the object. Position O_Y is measured as the distance to the car with 6 discrete values. Speed O_V is evaluated as the change of the blob center in pixels, which is discretized to 6 states. Shape measurements O_S are clustered in 4 features based on the aspect ratio of the bounding rectangle, filling ratio (the area of the blob with respect to the area of its bounding rectangle) and two first order moment features [21].

Given general constraints about smoothness, dynamics and physical attributes of the environment, we create a set of constraints on model parameters. Such

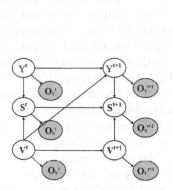

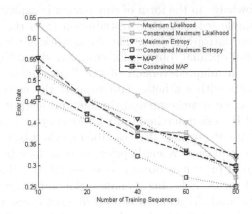

Fig. 4. DBN structure for human activity recognition

Fig. 5. Activity recognition results (error rate) using many DBN parameter learning approaches

constraints are applied to transitional probabilities of all activities, as they are general enough to be common to all activities. We note that constraints are acquired from experts and are not tuned to this specific data. We omit specific details about them because it would drive us far from the goal of this paper.

We randomly choose part of the activity sequences as training data and use the rest for testing. We compare ML, maximum a posteriori (MAP), and local maximum entropy, using both the unconstrained and constrained versions. We point out that other learning techniques do exist, such as regularized ML. Because we are discussing about a Dirichlet model and because ML with some regularization produces similar results as MAP, we have chosen to work with the latter instead. The training sets have 10, 20, 40, 60 and 80 sequences. For each size, we perform the test 10 times and the average recognition error is presented in Figure 4.2. It is worth noting that: (i) the use of constraints significantly decreases the error rate, as may be noted in Figure 4.2 by taking the curves two by two and analyzing constrained and respective unconstrained versions; (ii) when large amount of data is available, all methods tend to similar results. We can see that ML and MAP are already much closer when 80 training sequences are considered, and the same starts to happen with IDM; (iii) while results with synthetic data are not conclusive when comparing MAP and IDM with maximum entropy (the prior applied to MAP was enough there, and MAP was even slightly better), here constrained maximum entropy outperforms all others, for all test cases. This is probably because all priors are considered by the IDM, while MAP uses a single one. MAP might achieve better results, but that would strongly depend on the quality of the prior chosen by the expert.

5   Conclusion

This paper presents a framework for parameter learning using the Imprecise Dirichlet Model and its application to two recognition problems. Domain knowledge in the form of constraints is exploited to improve accuracy. To select a single (conservative) distribution from the Imprecise Dirichlet Model, maximum entropy is used. The framework is very fast and guarantees to find the global optimal solution for complete data. For incomplete data, we propose to use an adapted version of the Expectation–Maximization method. Empirical results with synthetic data support the method. Both with synthetic and real data, we have compared the method against widely used maximum likelihood and Bayesian maximum a posteriori estimations, with and without constraints. We point out that the described method has the advantage of not requiring the specification of a single prior, as it is done by the MAP estimation. MAP with a good prior may obtain good results, but that strongly relies on the quality of such prior. Selecting a single prior is not an easy task when dealing with real data, and the uniform is used in most cases, which may lead to inferior results. Using the data to select the prior might overfit the model, resulting in unreliable results that are only applicable to the specific contexts and data.

Empirical results with real data are treated for two computer vision problems: a facial action unit recognition problem and an activity recognition problem in video sequences. The constraints that are used in each problem are described, which translate the domain knowledge into a mathematical formulation. We note that the constraints were defined by an expert once and were not tuned. As expected, results with constraints are superior than those when constraints are not used. Furthermore, the Imprecise Dirichlet Model shows better accuracy in all scenarios with real data. Specifically, the single prior of MAP estimation employed while using real data does not achieve as good results as with synthetic data, and the IDM (which considers all possible priors) outperforms the other methods. In summary, we point out that (i) constraints are very helpful when scarce data are available, which is a common situation in computer vision problems; (ii) widely used methods such as maximum likelihood and Bayesian MAP estimators, which are the most common ideas to learn Bayesian network parameters, are defeated by the IDM plus maximum entropy when dealing with real data and constraints, even though they performed well for synthetic data.

Acknowledgments. This work is supported in part by the grant W911NF-06-1-0331 from the U.S. Army Research Office, and by the *Computational Life Sciences (CLS)* program phase II, canton Ticino, Switzerland.

References

1. Abellan, J., Moral, S.: Maximum of entropy for credal sets. Int. Journal Uncertain. Fuzziness Knowl.-Based Systems 11(5), 587–597 (2003)
2. Bartlett, M.S., Littlewort, G.C., Frank, M.G., Lainscsek, C., Fasel, I.R., Movellan, J.R.: Automatic recognition of facial actions in spontaneous expressions. Journal of Multimedia 1(6), 22–35 (2006)
3. Ben-Tal, A., Nemirovski, A.: Lectures on Modern Convex Optimization: Analysis, Algorithms, and Engineering Applications. MPSSeries on Optimization. SIAM, Philadelphia (2001)

4. de Campos, C.P., Cozman, F.G.: Belief updating and learning in semi-qualitative probabilistic networks. In: Conf. on Uncertainty in Artificial Intelligence, pp. 153–160 (2005)
5. de Campos, C.P., Tong, Y., Ji, Q.: Constrained maximum likelihood bayesian networks for facial expression recognition. In: Forsyth, D., Torr, P., Zisserman, A. (eds.) ECCV 2008, Part III. LNCS, vol. 5304, pp. 168–181. Springer, Heidelberg (2008)
6. Corani, G., de Campos, C.P.: A tree augmented classifier based on extreme imprecise dirichlet model. Int. Journal Approx. Reasoning 51, 1053–1068 (2010)
7. Corani, G., Zaffalon, M.: Learning reliable classifiers from small or incomplete data sets: the naive credal classifier 2. Journal of Machine Learning Research 9, 581–621 (2008)
8. DeGroot, M.: Optimal Statistical Decisions. McGraw-Hill, New York (1970)
9. Dempster, A., Laird, N., Rubin, D.: Maximum likelihood from incomplete data via the EM algorithm. Journal of the Royal Stat. Society B 39(1), 1–38 (1977)
10. Feelders, A., van der Gaag, L.C.: Learning Bayesian network parameters under order constraints. Int. Journal of Approximate Reasoning 42(1-2), 37–53 (2006)
11. Graca, J., Ganchev, K., Taskar, B.: Expectation maximization and posterior constraints. In: NIPS, pp. 569–576. MIT Press, Cambridge (2007)
12. Jaynes, E.T.: Information theory and statistical mechanics. Physical Review 106, 620–630 (1957)
13. Kanade, T., Cohn, J.F., Tian, Y.: Comprehensive database for facial expression analysis. In: Proceedings of the 4th IEEE Int. Conf. on Automatic Face and Gesture Recognition, pp. 46–53 (2000)
14. Lukasiewicz, T.: Credal networks under maximum entropy. In: Conf. on Uncertainty in Artificial Intelligence, pp. 363–370 (2000)
15. Murphy, K.P.: Dynamic Bayesian Networks: Representation, Inference and Learning. Ph.D. thesis, Univ. of California, Berkeley (2002)
16. Niculescu, R.S., Mitchell, T.M., Rao, R.B.: A theoretical framework for learning bayesian networks with parameter inequality constraints. In: Int. Joint Conf. on Artificial Intelligence, pp. 155–160 (2007)
17. Tong, Y., Liao, W., Ji, Q.: Facial action unit recognition by exploiting their dynamic and semantic relationships. IEEE Trans. on Pattern Analysis and Machine Intelligence, 1683–1699 (2007)
18. Walley, P.: Statistical Reasoning with Imprecise Probabilities. Chapman and Hall, London (1991)
19. Wellman, M.P.: Fundamental concepts of qualitative probabilistic networks. Artificial Intelligence 44(3), 257–303 (1990)
20. Wu, C.F.J.: On the convergence properties of the EM algorithm. The Annals of Statistics 11(1), 95–103 (1983)
21. Xiang, T., Gong, S.: Beyond tracking: Modelling activity and understanding behaviour. Int. Journal of Computer Vision 67(1), 21–51 (2006)

On Stopping Evidence Gathering
for Diagnostic Bayesian Networks

Linda C. van der Gaag and Hans L. Bodlaender

Department of Information and Computing Sciences,
Utrecht University, Utrecht, The Netherlands
{linda,hansb}@cs.uu.nl

Abstract. Sequential approaches to automated test selection for diagnostic Bayesian networks include a stopping criterion for deciding in each iteration whether or not gathering of further evidence is opportune. We study the computational complexity of the problem of deciding when to stop evidence gathering in general and show that it is complete for the complexity class NP^{PP}; we show that the problem remains NP-complete even when it is restricted to networks of bounded treewidth. We will argue however, that by reasonable further restrictions the problem can be feasibly solved for many realistic applications.

1 Introduction

Among the large variety of problems in their application domains, Bayesian networks are being designed for use in diagnostic problem-solving contexts. Well-known examples include the problem of troubleshooting of electrical equipment [1], of medical diagnosis [2,3], and of the detection of outbreaks of animal disease [4]. In many diagnostic contexts, not all relevant information for establishing a reliable diagnosis is available just like that. In order to decrease uncertainty, further information is then typically obtained through diagnostic testing. When the performance of tests is costly or otherwise undesirable, appropriate tests need to be carefully selected. Upon performing a full decision analysis to this end, all possible sequences of diagnostic tests, along with their costs and benefits, are modelled explicitly, from which the strategy that maximises expected utility is established. Performing such a full analysis can be computationally demanding, however, and in addition requires the elicitation of a multitude of scenario-dependent utilities. The analysis as a consequence is often approximated by a sequential approach in which a single diagnostic test is selected at a time.

A sequential approach to test selection includes an information measure, a test-selection loop, and a stopping criterion. Within the test-selection loop, diagnostic tests are selected from a collection of possible tests, based upon the information measure in use. The selection of tests is typically conducted in an iterated fashion, in which a single test is selected in each step [5]. After the information obtained from performing the selected test has been taken into consideration, a new test may be selected, or it may be decided that further gathering

W. Liu (Ed.): ECSQARU 2011, LNAI 6717, pp. 170–181, 2011.

of evidence is not opportune. The stopping criterion used with the test-selection loop now specifies the conditions under which information gathering is halted.

The design of the stopping criterion to be used with automated test selection is of major importance: on the one hand a good stopping criterion will lead to fewer tests being performed, and on the other hand it will prevent the test-selection loop to halt too early and thereby miss important information. Various different stopping criteria have been proposed for use with a test-selection strategy employing probabilistic information only. These criteria all build on the idea that further gathering of information can be safely stopped if the posterior probability of the most likely diagnosis is sufficiently stable. A well-known example criterion asks whether future test results can render another diagnosis to become highly likely, given the already available evidence. This criterion is commonly preferred over the simpler criterion of verifying whether or not the posterior probability of the most likely diagnosis exceeds a pre-defined threshold value, since the former criterion implements a notion of looking ahead; the example criterion is also preferred over a criterion which decides to halt further gathering of evidence based upon the expected effect of the remaining tests on the posterior probability of the most likely diagnosis, because the latter criterion can overlook test results with small probability incurring drastic changes.

In this paper, we focus on the stopping criterion outlined above for automated test selection for Bayesian networks. We formulate the criterion more generally and more formally as the STOP problem which asks whether there exists a joint value assignment $\mathbf{t}$ to all remaining test variables of a network such that the posterior probability $\Pr(\mathbf{c}\,|\,\mathbf{e}, \mathbf{t})$ of a particular joint value assignment $\mathbf{c}$ to the diagnostic variables exceeds a pre-specified probability p given the already available evidence $\mathbf{e}$. We will show that the STOP problem in general is complete for the complexity class $\mathsf{NP}^{\mathsf{PP}}$, and remains NP-complete when restricted to Bayesian networks of bounded treewidth. We will argue that, despite these unfavourable complexity results, reasonable further restrictions can render the STOP problem feasibly solvable for many realistic applications.

Although in this paper we introduce and discuss the STOP problem in the context of automated test selection for Bayesian networks, the problem is known to arise in other types of application as well. As an example, we would like to mention an application in which patients in an intensive care unit are monitored with the help of dynamic Bayesian networks [3]. In this application, patient information becomes available automatically and (almost) continuously. Based upon the posterior probabilities computed from the network over time, at regular intervals a stopping criterion needs to be evaluated which specifies the conditions under which the patient can be safely taken off intensive care.

The paper is organised as follows. In Sect. 2, we introduce our notational conventions and provide some preliminaries on complexity theory. In Sect. 3, we formally define the STOP problem. In Sect. 4, we formulate and prove various complexity results for the problem. In Sect. 5, we provide some considerations for feasibly solving the STOP problem in practical implementations. The paper ends with our concluding observations in Sect. 6.

2   Preliminaries

We introduce our notational conventions and provide some preliminaries from complexity theory.

2.1   Bayesian Networks

A Bayesian network $\mathcal{B} = (\mathbf{G}_\mathcal{B}, \Pr)$ is a model of a joint probability distribution $\Pr$ over a set of random variables. The network includes a directed acyclic graph $\mathbf{G}_\mathcal{B} = (\mathbf{V}, \mathbf{A})$, where $\mathbf{V}$ denotes its set of variables and $\mathbf{A}$ captures the probabilistic (in)dependencies among the variables. We use upper case letters X to denote individual variables from $\mathbf{V}$ and bold-faced upper case letters $\mathbf{X}$ to denote sets of variables; a lower case letter x is used to indicate a value of a variable X, and a bold-faced lower case letter $\mathbf{x}$ denotes a joint value assignment to a set of variables $\mathbf{X}$. In the sequel, we assume that the set of variables $\mathbf{V}$ of a network is partitioned into a set $\mathbf{C}$ of variables of interest, a set of information variables whose value can in essence be observed in practice, and a set of intermediate variables whose value cannot be observed. At any time during diagnostic reasoning, the set of information variables is partitioned into a set $\mathbf{E}$ of evidence variables whose values have actually been observed and a set $\mathbf{T}$ of test variables whose values are not known as yet.

To capture the strengths of the dependency relationships between the variables in its graphical structure, the Bayesian network further includes a set of (conditional) probability distributions $\Pr(X \mid \boldsymbol{\pi})$ for each variable X given all possible value assignments $\boldsymbol{\pi}$ to the set of parents $\boldsymbol{\pi}(X)$ of X in the graph. The network thereby models the joint probability distribution $\Pr(\mathbf{V}) = \prod_{X \in \mathbf{V}} \Pr(X \mid \boldsymbol{\pi}(X))$ over its variables [6]. Probabilistic inference with the network amounts to computing a posterior probability $\Pr(\mathbf{c} \mid \mathbf{e})$ for some combination of values $\mathbf{c}$ for the variables of interest, given a joint value $\mathbf{e}$ for the evidence variables. A commonly used decision variant of probabilistic inference asks whether $\Pr(\mathbf{c} \mid \mathbf{e}) > p$ for some pre-specified (rational) probability p. Inference with Bayesian networks of arbitrary topology is known to be PP-complete [7].

The concept of treewidth for a Bayesian network $\mathcal{B}$ pertains to the moralisation $\mathbf{G}_\mathcal{B}^M$ of its graph $\mathbf{G}_\mathcal{B}$. This moralisation is the undirected graph that is obtained from $\mathbf{G}_\mathcal{B}$ by adding arcs so as to connect all pairs of parents of a variable, and then dropping all directions. A triangulation of the moralised graph $\mathbf{G}_\mathcal{B}^M$ is any graph $\mathbf{G}_\mathbf{T}$ that embeds $\mathbf{G}_\mathcal{B}^M$ as a subgraph and in addition does not include loops of more than three variables without any pair being adjacent. A tree-decomposition of a triangulation $\mathbf{G}_\mathbf{T}$ now is a tree $\mathbf{T}_\mathbf{G}$ such that (*i*) each variable $\mathbf{X}_i$ in $\mathbf{T}_\mathbf{G}$ is a bag of variables constituting a clique in $\mathbf{G}_\mathbf{T}$; and (*ii*) for every i, j, k, if $\mathbf{X}_j$ lies on the path from $\mathbf{X}_i$ to $\mathbf{X}_k$ in $\mathbf{T}_\mathbf{G}$, then $\mathbf{X}_i \cap \mathbf{X}_k \subseteq \mathbf{X}_j$. The width of the tree-decomposition $\mathbf{T}_\mathbf{G}$ of a graph $\mathbf{G}_\mathbf{T}$ equals $\max_i(|\mathbf{X}_i|) - 1$, that is, it equals the size of the largest clique in $\mathbf{G}_\mathbf{T}$, minus 1. The treewidth of a Bayesian network $\mathcal{B}$ now is the minimum width over all possible tree-decompositions of triangulations of its moralised graph $\mathbf{G}_\mathcal{B}^M$.

The relevance of the concept of treewidth for the current paper lies in the computational complexity of establishing posterior probabilities $\Pr(c \mid \mathbf{e})$ from Bayesian networks of bounded treewidth: for such networks, a probability $\Pr(c \mid \mathbf{e})$ of the value c of a single variable C given evidence $\mathbf{e}$, can be computed in polynomial time, for example using the junction-tree propagation algorithm [6].

2.2 Complexity Theory

We now briefly review some basic constructs from computational complexity theory; for further details, we refer to for example [8,9].

We assume that for every computational problem P, there exists an encoding which translates arbitrary instances of P into strings such that the *yes*-instances of P constitute a language; the problem's *no*-instances are not included in the language. A complexity class now is a class of such languages. We say that a problem P is hard for a specific complexity class if every problem Q from the class can be reduced to P by a polynomial-time reduction: a problem Q is polynomial-time reducible to P if there exists a polynomial-time computable function f such that $x \in Q$ if and only if $f(x) \in P$. The problem P is complete for the class if it is hard for the class and in addition is a member of the class. The problem can then be regarded at least as hard as any other problem from the class: since any problem Q from the class can be reduced to P in polynomial time, a polynomial-time algorithm for P would imply a polynomial-time algorithm for every problem in the class.

The well-known complexity class NP is the class of languages that are decidable in polynomial time on a non-deterministic Turing machine. The class PP is the class of languages that are decidable in polynomial time on a probabilistic Turing machine with an error probability smaller than $\frac{1}{2}$. For these two classes, we have that NP $\subseteq$ PP. In addition to the classes NP and PP, we will use the complexity class NP^{PP} in this paper. This class is an example of an oracle class, in which a Turing machine can query an oracle. Such an oracle can be viewed as a black box that can answer membership queries in constant time. The complexity class NP^{PP} now is the class of languages for which inclusion can be verified in polynomial time given access to an oracle that decides languages from PP.

In this paper, we will construct reductions from the E-MAJSAT and PARTITION problems reviewed below.

E-MAJSAT

Instance: A Boolean formula $\phi(X_1, \ldots, X_n), n \geq 1$; a natural number $1 \leq k \leq n$ such that the set of variables $\mathbf{X} = \{X_1, \ldots, X_n\}$ is partitioned into the two sets $\mathbf{X_E} = \{X_1, \ldots, X_k\}$ and $\mathbf{X_M} = \{X_{k+1}, \ldots, X_n\}$.

Question: Is there a truth assignment $\mathbf{x_E}$ to $\mathbf{X_E}$ such that the majority of the truth assignments to $\mathbf{X_M}$, jointly with $\mathbf{x_E}$, satisfy ϕ ?

The E-MAJSAT problem is known to be complete for the complexity class NP^{PP} [10]. The PARTITION problem is NP-complete.

PARTITION

Instance: A set $X = \{x_1, \ldots, x_n\}$, $n \geq 1$, of positive integers x_i, $i = 1, \ldots, n$.

Question: Is there a partition $X = I \cup J$, $I \cap J = \varnothing$, of the set X such that

$$\sum_{x_i \in I} x_i = \sum_{x_j \in J} x_j \ ?$$

3   The STOP Problem

We formally define the STOP problem for diagnostic Bayesian networks.

STOP

Instance: A Bayesian network $\mathcal{B} = (\mathbf{G_B}, \mathrm{Pr})$, where the set of variables $\mathbf{V}$ of $\mathbf{G_B}$ is partitioned into a non-empty set $\mathbf{C}$ of variables of interest, a set $\mathbf{E}$ of observed variables, a non-empty set $\mathbf{T}$ of test variables, and a set of intermediate variables; a joint value assignment $\mathbf{c}$ of interest and a joint value assignment $\mathbf{e}$ of available evidence; a rational number $p \in [0, 1]$.

Question: Is there a joint value assignment $\mathbf{t}$ to $\mathbf{T}$ such that $\mathrm{Pr}(\mathbf{c} \,|\, \mathbf{e}, \mathbf{t}) \geq p$?

The STOP problem is closely related to the more widely known PARTIAL MAP problem, at least at first sight. In the PARTIAL MAP problem, a set $\mathbf{M}$ of MAP variables is discerned as well as a set of intermediate variables and a set $\mathbf{E}$ of observed variables with evidence $\mathbf{e}$. The question then is if there exists a joint value assignment $\mathbf{m}$ to the MAP variables such that $\mathrm{Pr}(\mathbf{m} \,|\, \mathbf{e})$ exceeds a given threshold probability p. The problem has been studied by several authors and has been shown to be $\mathsf{NP}^{\mathsf{PP}}$-complete in general [11]. The complexity of the problem is commonly studied not in terms of the conditional probability $\mathrm{Pr}(\mathbf{m} \,|\, \mathbf{e})$ but in terms of the marginal probability $\mathrm{Pr}(\mathbf{m}, \mathbf{e})$. The observation that the probability $\mathrm{Pr}(\mathbf{e})$ of the available evidence is a constant, renders the conditional and marginal probabilities equivalent from the problem's point of view [11,12]. We now observe that for the STOP problem, the conditional probability of interest cannot be studied in terms of just a marginal probability: since the sought-for joint value assignment $\mathbf{t}$ is included in the conditioning part of the posterior probability of interest, the term $\mathrm{Pr}(\mathbf{e}, \mathbf{t})$ in the expression $\mathrm{Pr}(\mathbf{c} \,|\, \mathbf{e}, \mathbf{t}) = \mathrm{Pr}(\mathbf{c}, \mathbf{e}, \mathbf{t}) / \mathrm{Pr}(\mathbf{e}, \mathbf{t})$ cannot be considered a constant.

4   Complexity Results

We study the computational complexity of the STOP problem as introduced in Sect. 3, and prove $\mathsf{NP}^{\mathsf{PP}}$-completeness for the problem in general. We further show that the problem remains NP-complete even when it is restricted to Bayesian networks of bounded treewidth.

To prove hardness of the problem in general for the class $\mathsf{NP}^{\mathsf{PP}}$, we will use a reduction from the E-MAJSAT problem. Our reduction follows to a large extent

the reduction used by Park and Darwiche to prove $\mathsf{NP^{PP}}$-hardness of the PAR-
TIAL MAP problem [11]. We begin by describing the construction of a Bayesian
network $\mathcal{B}_\phi$ that models the Boolean formula ϕ of an instance of the E-MAJSAT
problem. For each Boolean variable X_i in ϕ, we include a root variable X_i in the
network, with *true* and *false* for its possible values; for each such root variable,
we set a uniform prior probability distribution over its values. For each logical
operator in the formula ϕ, we create an additional variable in the network. The
parents of each such variable are the variables corresponding with the subformu-
las joined by the operator in ϕ; its conditional probability table is set to mimic
the operator's truth table. The variable associated with the top-level operator
of ϕ will be denoted by V_ϕ. From the above construction, it is now readily seen
that, given a joint value assignment $\mathbf{x}$ to the root variables X_i of the network,
we have that $\Pr(V_\phi = true \mid \mathbf{x}) = 1$ if and only if the truth assignment $\mathbf{x}$ to the
Boolean variables X_i satisfies the formula ϕ.

Theorem 1. STOP *is* $\mathsf{NP^{PP}}$-*complete.*

Proof. We prove membership of $\mathsf{NP^{PP}}$ for the STOP-problem as follows. Given
a non-deterministically chosen joint value assignment $\mathbf{t}$ to the test variables $\mathbf{T}$,
we can verify for any joint value assignments $\mathbf{c}$ and $\mathbf{e}$ whether $\Pr(\mathbf{c} \mid \mathbf{e}, \mathbf{t}) \geq p$ in
polynomial time given an oracle that decides INFERENCE. Since INFERENCE is
PP-complete, we conclude membership of $\mathsf{NP^{PP}}$ for STOP.

To prove hardness, we reduce the E-MAJSAT problem to STOP. Let (ϕ, k)
be an instance of E-MAJSAT. From the Boolean formula ϕ we construct the
Bayesian network $\mathcal{B}_\phi$ as described above. We now let V_ϕ be the variable of
interest for the STOP instance under construction, that is $\mathbf{C} = \{V_\phi\}$, and let $\mathbf{c}$
be the value assignment $V_\phi = true$. We further let the set of observed variables
$\mathbf{E}$ be empty, that is $\mathbf{E} = \varnothing$, and let $\mathbf{e} = \top$ denote universal truth. We set p to
$\frac{1}{2}$. The constructed instance of the STOP problem thus is $(\mathcal{B}_\phi, V_\phi = true, \top, \frac{1}{2})$;
note that the construction of this instance can be performed in polynomial time.

From the set of root variables $\mathbf{X}$ from $\mathcal{B}_\phi$, we now look upon $X_1, \ldots, X_k$ as
constituting the test variables of our instance; the variables $X_{k+1}, \ldots, X_n$ are
considered intermediate. From our previous observation that $\Pr(\mathbf{c} \mid \mathbf{x}) = 1$ for
any satisfying truth assignment $\mathbf{x}$ to ϕ, we find that

$$\Pr(\mathbf{c}, \mathbf{x}) = \begin{cases} \frac{1}{2^n} & \text{if } \mathbf{x} \text{ satisfies } \phi \\ 0 & \text{otherwise} \end{cases}$$

For any joint value assignment $\mathbf{t}$ to the test variables $X_1, \ldots, X_k$, we thus find

$$\Pr(\mathbf{c}, \mathbf{t}) = \sum_{X_{k+1}, \ldots, X_n} \Pr(\mathbf{t}, X_{k+1}, \ldots, X_n) = \frac{i}{2^n}$$

where i is the number of joint value assignments to the variables $X_{k+1}, \ldots, X_n$
which jointly with $\mathbf{t}$ satisfy the Boolean formula ϕ. Since there are 2^{n-k} joint

value assignments to the variables $X_{k+1}, \ldots, X_n$, we find that the majority of these assignments satisfies the formula ϕ jointly with $\mathbf{t}$ if and only if

$$\Pr(\mathbf{c}, \mathbf{t}) > \frac{1}{2^{k+1}}$$

We thus have that the E-MAJSAT instance (ϕ, k) is answered affirmatively if and only if $\Pr(\mathbf{c}, \mathbf{t}) > \frac{1}{2^{k+1}}$ in the constructed network $\mathcal{B}_\phi$.

To complete the reduction, we observe that any joint value assignment $\mathbf{t}$ to the test variables $\mathbf{T}$ has a prior probability of $\Pr(\mathbf{t}) = \frac{1}{2^k}$. From this observation, we find for each $\mathbf{t}$ that $\Pr(\mathbf{c}, \mathbf{t}) > \frac{1}{2^{k+1}}$ if and only if $\Pr(\mathbf{c} \mid \mathbf{t}) > \frac{1}{2}$. We conclude that (ϕ, k) is a *yes*-instance of E-MAJSAT if and only if $(\mathcal{B}_\phi, V_\phi = true, \top, \frac{1}{2})$ is a *yes*-instance of STOP.   □

In view of practical applications of Bayesian networks, we are interested not just in the computational complexity of the STOP problem in general. Since probabilistic inference is feasible only with Bayesian networks of bounded treewidth, its practical applications are restricted to networks of such limited topology. We therefore are interested also in the computational complexity of the STOP problem for this class of Bayesian networks. We will now show that even for this class the problem remains NP-complete.

To prove hardness for the complexity class NP of the STOP problem restricted to Bayesian networks of bounded treewidth, we will use a reduction from the PARTITION problem reviewed in Sect. 2.2. We begin again by describing the construction of a Bayesian network $\mathcal{B}$ that models the set of integers $\{x_1, \ldots, x_n\}$ of an instance of the PARTITION problem. For each integer x_i, we include a root variable X_i in the network, with *true* and *false* for its possible values; for each such root variable, we assume a uniform prior probability distribution over its values. To each variable X_i, we add two successors A_i and B_i, with arcs $X_i \to A_i$ and $X_i \to B_i$. We further connect the A_i variables by arcs $A_i \to A_{i+1}$; the B_i variables are similarly interconnected. For the A_i variables with $i > 1$, we set the following conditional probability distributions:

$$\Pr(a_i \mid A_{i-1}, X_i) = \begin{cases} 1 & \text{if } A_{i-1} = true \\ 0 & \text{if } A_{i-1} = false \text{ and } X_i = false \\ \frac{x_i}{s^3} & \text{otherwise} \end{cases}$$

where $s = \sum_{i=1,\ldots,n} x_i$. For the variable A_1, we set $\Pr(a_1 \mid X_1) = 0$ if $X_1 = false$, and $\Pr(a_1 \mid X_1) = \frac{x_1}{s^3}$ otherwise. For the B_i variables with $i > 1$, we set the conditional probability distributions

$$\Pr(b_i \mid B_{i-1}, X_i) = \begin{cases} 1 & \text{if } B_{i-1} = true \\ 0 & \text{if } B_{i-1} = false \text{ and } X_i = true \\ \frac{x_i}{s^3} & \text{otherwise} \end{cases}$$

For the variable B_1, we set $\Pr(b_1 \mid X_1) = 0$ if $X_1 = true$, and $\Pr(b_1 \mid X_1) = \frac{x_1}{s^3}$ otherwise. Note that the A_i variables on the one hand and the B_i variables on the other hand in essence represent a two-block partition of the set of integers

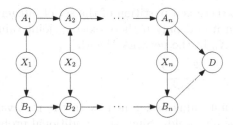

Fig. 1. The graphical structure of the Bayesian network constructed from an instance of the PARTITION problem

$\{x_1, \ldots, x_n\}$ of the original PARTITION instance. The Bayesian network $\mathcal{B}$ is now completed by the addition of a sink variable D with incoming arcs from the variables A_n and B_n. The conditional probability table for the variable D is set to mimic the logical *and*. The graphical structure of the thus configured network is depicted schematically in Fig. 1.

Theorem 2. STOP *restricted to Bayesian networks of bounded treewidth is* NP-*complete.*

Proof. We first prove membership of NP for the STOP problem for Bayesian networks of bounded treewidth. Given a non-deterministically chosen joint value assignment $\mathbf{t}$ to the test variables $\mathbf{T}$, we have to specify a polynomial-time certificate for verifying whether $\Pr(\mathbf{c} \mid \mathbf{e}, \mathbf{t}) \geq p$ for any joint value assignments $\mathbf{c}$ and $\mathbf{e}$. Let $\mathbf{C} = \{C_1, \ldots, C_m\}$ be the set of variables of interest. Let $\mathbf{c} = \bigwedge_{i=1,\ldots,m} c'_i$ be the joint value assignment of interest and let $\mathbf{c}_i^- = \bigwedge_{j=1,\ldots,i-1} c'_j$ be the joint assignment to the variables $C_1, \ldots, C_{i-1}$ compatible with $\mathbf{c}$. By applying the junction-tree propagation algorithm for computing each term in the expression

$$\Pr(\mathbf{c} \mid \mathbf{e}, \mathbf{t}) = \prod_{i=1,\ldots,m} \Pr(c_i \mid \mathbf{e}, \mathbf{t}, \mathbf{c}_i^-)$$

we can verify whether $\Pr(\mathbf{c} \mid \mathbf{e}, \mathbf{t}) \geq p$ in polynomial time, since the propagation algorithm takes polynomial time for the class of networks under study. We conclude membership of NP for the STOP problem.

To prove hardness, we reduce the PARTITION problem to the STOP problem for Bayesian networks of bounded treewidth. Let $\{x_1, \ldots, x_n\}$ be an instance of PARTITION, and let $s = \sum_{i=1,\ldots,n} x_i$. From the set to be partitioned, we construct a Bayesian network $\mathcal{B}$ as described above; it is not hard to show that the moralisation of $\mathcal{B}$ has a treewidth of three. We let the variable D be the variable of interest for the STOP instance under construction, that is $\mathbf{C} = \{D\}$, and let $\mathbf{c}$ be the assignment $D = true$. We further let the set of observed variables $\mathbf{E}$ be empty and let $\mathbf{e} = \top$ again denote universal truth. We set p to $\frac{s^2 - 2}{4\,s^6}$. The constructed instance of the STOP problem under study thus is $(\mathcal{B}, D = true, \top, \frac{s^2 - 2}{4\,s^6})$; note that the instance can be constructed in polynomial time.

We now show that there is a partition of the set of integers $\{x_1, \ldots, x_n\}$ into two sets of equal sum if and only if there exists a joint value assignment $\mathbf{x}$ to the variables $X_1, \ldots, X_n$ in the network $\mathcal{B}$ with

$$\Pr(D = true \,|\, \mathbf{x}) \;\geq\; \frac{s^2 - 2}{4\,s^6}$$

We first consider a joint value assignment $\mathbf{x}$ to the root variables $\mathbf{X}$ in $\mathcal{B}$ for which the above inequality holds. Since the conditional probability table of the variable D mimics the logical *and* of the variables A_n and B_n, we have that $\Pr(d \,|\, \mathbf{x}) = \Pr(a_n, b_n \,|\, \mathbf{x})$. We now define the set of indices $Q \subseteq \{1, \ldots, n\}$ by $i \in Q$ if and only if the variable X_i is set to *true* in $\mathbf{x}$; we use R to denote the complementary set $\{1, \ldots, n\} \setminus Q$. Note that the sets Q and R can be viewed as representing a two-block partition of the set of integers $\{x_1, \ldots, x_n\}$. By induction to i, it is readily shown that

$$\Pr(a_i \,|\, \mathbf{x}) \;\leq\; \sum_{j \in Q, j \leq i} \frac{x_j}{s^3} \qquad \text{and} \qquad \Pr(b_i \,|\, \mathbf{x}) \;\leq\; \sum_{j \in R, j \leq i} \frac{x_j}{s^3}$$

Since the variables A_n and B_n are mutually independent given $\mathbf{x}$, we find that

$$\Pr(d \,|\, \mathbf{x}) = \Pr(a_n \,|\, \mathbf{x}) \cdot \Pr(b_n \,|\, \mathbf{x}) \;\leq\; \left(\sum_{i \in Q} \frac{x_i}{s^3} \right) \cdot \left(\sum_{i \in R} \frac{x_i}{s^3} \right)$$

Now suppose that $\sum_{i \in Q} x_i \neq \frac{s}{2}$, that is, we suppose that the sets Q and R do not represent an equal-sum partition of the set of integers $\{x_1, \ldots, x_n\}$. Then,

$$\left(\sum_{i \in Q} x_i \right) \cdot \left(\sum_{i \in R} x_i \right) \;\leq\; \frac{s^2}{4} - 1$$

from which we have that $\Pr(d \,|\, \mathbf{x}) \leq \frac{s^2 - 4}{4\,s^6}$, which contradicts our assumption that $\Pr(d \,|\, \mathbf{x}) \geq \frac{s^2 - 2}{4\,s^6}$. We conclude that $\sum_{i \in Q} x_i = \frac{s}{2}$ and, hence, $\sum_{i \in R} x_i = \frac{s}{2}$, from which we have that there exists an equal-sum partition of $\{x_1, \ldots, x_n\}$.

We now assume that the set of integers $\{x_1, \ldots, x_n\}$ is partitioned into two sets of equal sum; we let Q and R be the sets of indices for the two blocks of the partition, that is, $\sum_{i \in Q} x_i = \sum_{i \in R} x_i = \frac{s}{2}$. Now let $\mathbf{x}^Q$ be the joint value assignment to the variables $X_1, \ldots, X_n$ of the constructed network $\mathcal{B}$ that sets each variable X_i, $i = 1, \ldots, n$, to *true* if and only if $i \in Q$. Using the observation that $\Pr(a_i \,|\, \mathbf{x}) \leq \frac{1}{s^2}$ and $\Pr(b_i \,|\, \mathbf{x}) \leq \frac{1}{s^2}$, we can show by induction that

$$\Pr(a_i \,|\, \mathbf{x}) \;\geq\; \left(1 - \frac{1}{s^2} \right) \cdot \left(\sum_{j \in Q, j \leq i} \frac{x_j}{s^3} \right)$$

and

$$\Pr(b_i \,|\, \mathbf{x}) \;\geq\; \left(1 - \frac{1}{s^2} \right) \cdot \left(\sum_{j \in R, j \leq i} \frac{x_j}{s^3} \right)$$

We now recall that $\sum_{i \in Q} x_i = \frac{s}{2}$ and $\sum_{i \in R} x_i = \frac{s}{2}$. Using mutual independence of the variables A_n and B_n given $\mathbf{x}$, we then find that

$$\Pr(d \,|\, \mathbf{x}) = \Pr(a_n \,|\, \mathbf{x}) \cdot \Pr(b_n \,|\, \mathbf{x}) \;\geq\; \left(1 - \frac{1}{s^2}\right)^2 \cdot \left(\frac{s}{2\,s^3}\right)^2 \;\geq\; \frac{s^2 - 2}{4\,s^6}$$

From a two-block equal-sum partition of the set of integers $\{x_1, \ldots, x_n\}$ it thus follows that there exists a joint value assignment $\mathbf{x}$ to the variables $X_1, \ldots, X_n$ of the network $\mathcal{B}$ with $\Pr(d \,|\, \mathbf{x}) \geq \frac{s^2 - 2}{4\,s^6}$, which concludes our proof. $\square$

5   Practical Considerations

Practical implementations of automated test selection for Bayesian networks typically take a sequential approach in which diagnostic tests are selected in an iterative fashion. Current implementations in fact take a myopic approach to evidence gathering, in which test variables are selected on a one-by-one basis [5]. With these implementations also a single diagnostic variable C of interest is assumed, rather than a set of such variables. In the basic test-selection loop, the expected effect on the posterior probability distribution $\Pr(C \,|\, \mathbf{e})$ given the already available evidence $\mathbf{e}$ is computed for each yet unobserved test variable T_i. Using some information measure, the test variable with the largest expected effect then is selected and the user is prompted for its value. For computing the expected effect of obtaining an observation for a test variable T_i on the posterior probability distribution $\Pr(C \,|\, \mathbf{e})$, the following property can be exploited:

$$\Pr(C \,|\, T_i, \mathbf{e}) = \frac{\Pr(T_i \,|\, C, \mathbf{e}) \cdot \Pr(C \,|\, \mathbf{e})}{\Pr(T_i \,|\, \mathbf{e})}$$

By retaining intermediate results from the computations involved, the number of propagations required from the junction-tree propagation algorithm in a single iteration of the test-selection loop is proportional with the number of values of the main diagnostic variable. Assuming that evaluation of the information measure used does not take exponential time, the computations involved in the selection of a single test variable thus require polynomial time.

From the complexity results from the previous section, we now know that, while the selection of a test variable takes polynomial time, the stopping criterion cannot be evaluated efficiently. We observe, however, that the computational burden of evaluating the stopping criterion under study lies in the look-ahead strategy employed, since any criterion which builds directly upon the posterior probability distribution $\Pr(C \,|\, \mathbf{e})$ computed in each step of the test-selection loop, can be evaluated in a time which is linear in the number of values of the diagnostic variable C. The property stated above now allows efficient evaluation of a stopping criterion employing a restricted look-ahead strategy. Such a stopping criterion asks whether there exists a value t_i of a yet unobserved test variable T_i such that $\Pr(c \,|\, t_i, \mathbf{e})$ exceeds some threshold probability p given the currently available evidence $\mathbf{e}$. Note that employing such a one-step look-ahead strategy with the stopping criterion is in line with the one-step look-ahead selection of test variables used in the main test-selection loop.

In many practical applications of Bayesian networks, a non-myopic approach in which test variables are selected groupwise might outperform any myopic method for selective evidence gathering. When developing a network for the staging of oesophageal cancer, for example, we found that the information-gathering strategy induced by a myopic approach to test selection would present a gross oversimplification of our experts' problem-solving practice [13]. We found that in their daily test-selection routines, our experts ordered diagnostic tests in packages so as to reduce the length in time of the diagnostic phase of a patient's management. Also, upon performing a single physical test, values would become available for various test variables in the network simultaneously.

From the complexity results presented in the previous section, we know that evaluating the stopping criterion in a non-myopic approach to test selection would just by itself already pose serious computational problems which cannot be overcome in general. In view of these results, we have designed for our medical diagnostic application a procedure for automated test selection which involves some degree of non-myopia [14,15]. The procedure is guided by a sequence of diagnostic subgoals, for which purpose it is provided with additional input. Each diagnostic subgoal is associated with a set of test variables which can provide information about that particular goal. For the selection of appropriate diagnostic tests, the procedure is further provided with a clustering of the test variables by the physical tests from which they get their values. The actual selection of tests now pertains to these clusters of test variables; the stopping criterion also considers clusters of variables, using a restricted look-ahead as described above. In general, this approach to automated test selection would rapidly become infeasible for larger clusters of variables. For our application in oncology, however, the clusters of test variables were found to be quite small. With these small clusters of test variables and through the use of subgoals for diagnostic reasoning, good results were obtained from initial experiments with our procedure [15].

6   Conclusions

In the context of sequential approaches to automated test selection for diagnostic Bayesian networks, we have studied the problem of deciding whether or not further gathering of evidence is opportune. More specifically, we have studied the computational complexity of the STOP problem and have shown that it is NP^{PP}-complete in general; we have also proven that the problem remains NP-complete even when it is restricted to networks of bounded treewidth. We have argued that the unfavourable computational complexity of the STOP problem can be attributed to its look-ahead strategy and provided some considerations by which automated test selection can be feasibly employed in practical implementations.

References

1. Skaanning, C., Jensen, F.V., Kjærulff, U.B.: Printer Troubleshooting Using Bayesian Networks. In: Loganantharaj, R., Palm, G., Ali, M. (eds.) IEA/AIE 2000. LNCS (LNAI), vol. 1821, pp. 367–380. Springer, Heidelberg (2000)
2. Oniśko, A.: Medical diagnosis. In: Naim, P., Pourret, O., Marcot, B. (eds.) Bayesian Networks: A Practical Guide to Applications, pp. 15–32. Wiley & Sons, Chichester (2008)
3. Charitos, T., van der Gaag, L.C., Visscher, S., Schurink, C.A.M., Lucas, P.J.F.: A dynamic Bayesian network for diagnosing ventilator-associated pneumonia in ICU patients. Expert Systems with Applications 36, 1249–1258 (2009)
4. van der Gaag, L.C., Bolt, J., Loeffen, W.L., Elbers, A.: Modelling patterns of evidence in Bayesian networks: a case-study in Classical Swine Fever. In: Hüllermeier, E., Kruse, R., Hoffmann, F. (eds.) IPMU 2010. LNCS, vol. 6178, pp. 675–684. Springer, Heidelberg (2010)
5. Madigan, D., Almond, R.G.: On test selection strategies for belief networks. In: Fisher, D.H., Lenz, H.-J. (eds.) CAAP 1981. LNCS, vol. 112, pp. 89–98. Springer, Heidelberg (1981)
6. Jensen, F.V., Nielsen, T.D.: Bayesian Networks and Decision Graphs, 2nd edn. Springer, New York (2007)
7. Littman, M.L., Majercik, S.M., Pitassi, T.: Stochastic Boolean statisfiability. Journal of Automated Reasoning 27, 251–296 (2001)
8. Garey, M.R., Johnson, D.S.: Computers and Intractability. A Guide to the Theory of NP-Completeness. W.H. Freeman and Co., San Francisco (1979)
9. Papadimitriou, C.H.: Computational Complexity. Addison-Wesley, Reading (1994)
10. Wagner, K.W.: The complexity of combinatorial problems with succint input representation. Acta Informatica 23, 325–356 (1986)
11. Park, J.D., Darwiche, A.: Complexity results and approximation strategies for MAP explanations. Journal of Artificial Intelligence Research 21, 101–133 (2004)
12. Bodlaender, H.L., van der Eijkhof, F., van der Gaag, L.C.: On the complexity of the MPA problem in probabilistic networks. In: van Harmelen, F. (ed.) Proceedings of the 15th European Conference on Artificial Intelligence, pp. 675–679. IOS Press, Amsterdam (2002)
13. Sent, D., van der Gaag, L.C., Witteman, C.L.M., Aleman, B.M.P., Taal, B.G.: Eliciting test-selection strategies for a decision-support system in oncology. Interdisciplinary Journal of Artificial Intelligence and the Simulation of Behaviour 1, 543–561 (2005)
14. Sent, D., van der Gaag, L.C.: Automated test selection in decision-support systems: a case study in oncology. In: Ubiquity: Technologies for Better Health in Aging Societies – Proceedings of MIE 2006. Studies in Health Technology and Informatics, vol. 124, pp. 491–496. IOS Press, Amsterdam (2006)
15. Sent, D., van der Gaag, L.C.: Enhancing automated test selection in probabilistic networks. In: Bellazzi, R., Abu-Hanna, A., Hunter, J. (eds.) AIME 2007. LNCS (LNAI), vol. 4594, pp. 331–335. Springer, Heidelberg (2007)

SemCaDo: A Serendipitous Strategy for Learning Causal Bayesian Networks Using Ontologies

Montassar Ben Messaoud[1,2], Philippe Leray[2], and Nahla Ben Amor[1]

[1] LARODEC, Institut Supérieur de Gestion Tunis
41, Avenue de la liberté, 2000 Le Bardo, Tunisie
benmessaoud.montassar@hotmail.fr, nahla.benamor@gmx.fr
[2] Knowledge and Decision Team
Laboratoire d'Informatique de Nantes Atlantique (LINA) UMR 6241
Ecole Polytechnique de l'Université de Nantes, France
philippe.leray@univ-nantes.fr

Abstract. Learning Causal Bayesian Networks (CBNs) is a new line of research in the machine learning field. Within the existing works in this direction [8,12,13], few of them have taken into account the gain that can be expected when integrating additional knowledge during the learning process. In this paper, we present a new serendipitous strategy for learning CBNs using prior knowledge extracted from ontologies. The integration of such domain's semantic information can be very useful to reveal new causal relations and provide the necessary knowledge to anticipate the optimal choice of experimentations. Our strategy also supports the evolving character of the semantic background by reusing the causal discoveries in order to enrich the domain ontologies.

1 Introduction

Bayesian networks (BNs), first introduced by Pearl [14], are compact graphical probabilistic models able to efficiently model uncertainty in real world problems.

One of the important properties relative to BNs is the *Markov equivalence property* which can be illustrated by the fact that the two networks $X \rightarrow Y$ and $X \leftarrow Y$ are equivalent (i.e. encode the same joint probability distribution). Nevertheless, only one of them is a correct from causal point of view. In fact, in the first network X causes Y, then, manipulating the value of X affects the value of Y contrary to the second one where Y is a cause of X meaning that manipulating X will not affect Y. Thus a BN cannot be considered as a proper causal network but the contrary is always true. This means that given a Causal Bayesian Network (CBN) one can use it even to determine how the observation of specific values (evidence) affects the probabilities of query variable(s) or to predict the effect of an intervention on the remaining variables [15].

Contrary to the non-Gaussian learning methods (also called LiNGAM) which use pure observational data (D_{obs}), the causal discovery in CBNs often requires

W. Liu (Ed.): ECSQARU 2011, LNAI 6717, pp. 182–193, 2011.

interventional data (D_{int}). In this work, we don't make use of LiNGAM methods since no suitable parametrization of the joint distribution can be established when working under the non-gaussianity assumption. This is the key reason for restricting our approach to only CBNs.

This paper provides a substantially extended version of our previous work [1] in which we introduce the preliminary findings for integrating a semantic distance calculus to choose the appropriate interventions. Further developments along this direction have been made in order to deploy more efficient strategies to integrate the semantic prior knowledge, improve the causal discovery process and reuse the new discovered information.

The remainder of this paper is arranged as follows: Section 2 gives the necessary background for both CBNs and ontologies and discusses some related works that combine the two formalisms. Section 3 sets out how to use the ontological knowledge to enhance the causal discovery and vice versa. In Section 4, we show simulation results to evaluate the performances of the proposed algorithm. Concluding remarks and future works are given in Section 5.

2 Basic Concepts and Background

2.1 Causal Bayesian Networks

A Causal Bayesian Network (CBN) is a Directed Acyclic Graph (DAG) where the set of nodes V represents discrete random variables X=$\{X_1, X_2,..., X_n\}$ and the set of edges E represents causal dependencies over V. We use D_i to denote the finite domain associated with each variable X_i and x_i to denote any instance of X_i. We denote by $Pa(X_i)$ the set of parents nodes for X_i and $Nei(X_i)$ the set of its neighboring variables.

In addition to the usual conditional independence interpretation, the CBN is also given a causal interpretation since each directed edge is traduced as that the source node is the direct cause of the target node. For this reason, CBNs are considered as proper bayesian networks (BNs) but the reverse is not necessarily true.

The main difference between the two formalisms lies in the nature of the data needed to learn the structure. In fact, contrary to BNs, when using only observational data, we may not have enough information to discover the true structure of the graph and the causal model will be restricted to the Completed Partially Directed Acyclic Graph (CPDAG). Thus we have to collect further information on causality via interventions (i.e. actions tentatively adopted without being sure of the outcome). Here, we should note that intervening on a system may be very expensive, time-consuming or even impossible to perform. For this reason, the choice of variables to experiment on can be vital when the number of interventions is restricted.

All those distinguishing features have motivated many researchers to develop a variety of techniques and algorithms to learn such models [8,12,13].

2.2 Ontologies

There are different definitions in the literature of what should be an ontology. The most notorious was given by Tom Gruber [7], stipulating that an ontology is an *explicit* specification of a *conceptualization*. The "conceptualization", here, refers to an abstract model of some phenomenon having real by identifying its relevant concepts. The word "explicit" means that all concepts used and the constraints on their use are explicitly defined.

In the simplest case, an ontology describes a hierarchy of concepts (i.e. classes) related by taxonomic relationships (is-a, part-of). In more sophisticated cases, an ontology describes domain classes, properties (or attributes) for each class, class instances (or individuals) and also the relationships that hold between class instances. It is also possible to add some logical axioms to constrain concept interpretation and express complex relationships between concepts.

Hence, more formally, an ontology can be defined as a set of labeled classes $C=\{C_1, ..., C_n\}$, hierarchically ordered by the subclass relations (i.e. is-a, part-of relations). For each concept C_i we identify k meaningful properties p_j, where $j \in [1, k]$. We use H_i to denote the finite domain of instance (i.e. concretizing the ontology concepts by setting their properties values) candidates with each concept C_i and c_i to denote any instance of C_i. We also use R to represent the set of semantical (i.e non-hierarchical) relations between concepts and R_c to represent the subset of causal ones. Finally, formal axioms or structural assertions $<c_i, c_j, s>$ can be included, where $s \in S$ is a constraint-relationship like "must, must not, should, should not, etc".

Practically speaking, the ontologies are often a very large and complex structure, requiring a great deal of effort and expertise to maintain and upgrade the existing knowledge. Such proposals can take several different forms such as a change in the domain, the diffusion of new discoveries or just an information received by some external source [6].

There are many ways to change the ontology in response to the fast-changing environment. One possible direction is the ontology evolution which consists in taking the ontology from one consistent state to another by updating (adding or modifying) the concepts, their properties and the associated relations [10].

The ontology evolution can be of two types [10]:

- Ontology population: When new concept instances are added, the ontology is said to be populated.
- Ontology enrichment: Which consists in updating (adding or modifying) concepts, properties and relations in a given ontology.

In order to establish the context in which the ontology evolution takes place, the principle of ontology continuity should be fulfilled [17]. It supposes that the ontology evolution should not make false an axiom that was previously true. When changes do not fulfill the requirement of ontological continuity, it is not any more an evolution, it is rather an ontology revolution.

2.3   Related Work

Recent studies have investigated some ways to combine both ontologies and BNs. The first line of research focused on how to integrate the power of BNs to enhance the potential of ontologies by supplementing it with the principle means of modeling uncertainty in ontologies. In this way, [18] have proposed the OntoBayes approach, an ontology-driven Bayesian model for uncertain knowledge representation, to extend ontologies to probability-annotated OWL in decision making systems. [5] also proposed an approach when they augment the OWL language to allow additional probabilistic markups so that probability values can be attached to individual concepts and properties. One of the main advantage of this probabilistic-extended ontology is that it can support common ontology-related reasoning tasks as probabilistic inferences.

On the other hand, other solutions were proposed in order to enhance the BN construction by integrating ontologies. For example, [9] developed a semi-automatic BN construction system based on e-health ontologies. Their framework enables probabilistic inferencing capability for various E-health applications and contributes to reduce the complexity of BN construction. A similar approach for BN construction using ontologies was proposed in [4]. Nevertheless, it presents an automatic solution, implemented in the context of an adaptive, self-configuring network management system in the telecommunication domain.

To our knowledge, we are the first to propose a real cooperation in both ways between ontologies and CBNs. Our previous work [1] focused on only one facet of the CBN-ontology combination by integrating the ontological knowledge to learn CBNs. Taking a further step in the same research direction, this work consists on designing a strategy that addresses issues to incorporate the second combination facet via reusing the causal discoveries to enrich the ontologies.

3   SemCaDo: A Serendipitous Causal Discovery Algorithm for Ontology Evolution

Generally, in the research area, scientific discoveries represent a payoff for years of well-planned works with clear objectives. This affirmation did not exclude the case of other important discoveries that are made while researchers were conducting their works in totally unrelated fields and the examples are abundant from Nobel's flash of inspiration while testing the effect of dynamite to Pasteur brainstorm when he accidentally discovered the role of attenuated microbes in immunization. In this way, we propose a new causal discovery algorithm which stimulates serendipitous discoveries when performing the experimentations using the following CBN-Ontology correspondences.

3.1   CBNs vs. Ontologies

One of the main motivations when realizing this work is the similarities between CBNs and ontologies. This is particularly true when comparing the structure of the two models as shown in the following correspondences:

1. Nodes (V_i) ↔ Concepts (C_i): The ontology concepts, which are relevant to the considered domain are traduced by the nodes of the CBN.
2. Random variables (X_i) ↔ Concept attributes $(C_i.p_j)$: All random variables in the CBN are represented as specific concept attributes in the ontology.
3. Causal dependencies (E) ↔ Semantic causal relations (R_c): The correspondence between the two models in term of causality will be as follows:
   - A causal relation between two concepts in the ontology will be traduced by a directed link between the corresponding CBN nodes. It is read as $c_Y.p_j$ is the direct consequence of $c_X.p_j$, where p_j is the concept attribute used to make the correspondence.
   - A causal dependency represented by a directed link in the CBN will be traduced by a specific causal relation between the appropriate concepts in the ontology.
4. Observational or experimental data $(D_{obs,int})$ ↔ Concept-attribute instances $(c_i.p_j)$: We make a correspondence between the observational (resp. interventional) data at our disposal and the instances of the domain ontology. Each observation (resp. intervention) can be viewed, in the ontological context, as a state instantiation of a given concept attribute.

3.2   SemCaDo Sketch

Our approach relies on extending the MyCaDo algorithm [12] in order to incorporate available knowledge from domain ontologies. The original character of the SemCaDo (Semantic Causal Discovery) algorithm is essentially its ability to make impressive discoveries and reuse the capitalized knowledge in CBNs.

The correspondences between CBNs and ontologies in SemCaDo must respect the following constraints:

- Only a single ontology should be specified for each causal discovery task.
- Each causal graph node must be modeled by a corresponding concept in the domain ontology. The concepts which are candidates to be a member of such correspondence have to share the same studied attribute p_j.
- The causal discoveries concern concepts sharing the same semantic type (e.g. direct transcriptional regulation between genes). This means that all concepts C_i modeled in the CBN must belong to the same super-concept SC and the causal relationship under study R_c should be defined for any element of SC to any other one.
- The ontology evolution should be realized without introducing inconsistencies or admitting axiom violations.

In this way, we will adopt the same basic scenario as in MyCaDo and describe the possible interactions with the domain ontology.

The general overview of the SemCaDo algorithm is given in Figure 1. As inputs, SemCaDo needs an observational dataset and a corresponding domain ontology. Then it will proceed through three main phases:

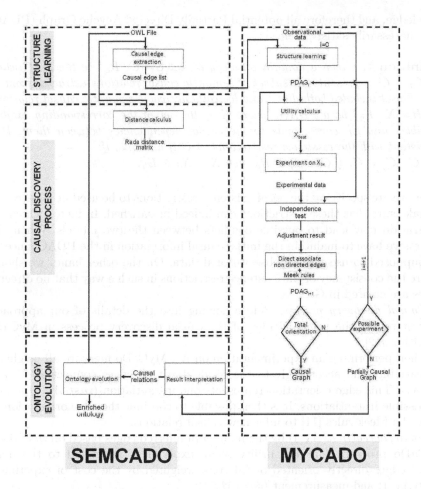

Fig. 1. SemCaDo: Extending MyCaDo to allow CBN-Ontology interactions

1) Learning the initial structure using causal prior knowledge: The ontology in input may contain some causal relations in addition to hierarchical and semantic relations. Those causal relations should be integrated from the beginning in the structure learning process in order to reduce the task complexity and better the final output. Therefore, such direct cause to effect relations will be incorporated as constraints when using structure learning algorithms. Our main objective is to narrow the corresponding search space by introducing some restrictions that all elements in this space must satisfy.

In our context, the only constraint that will be defined is edge existence. But we could also imagine in future work that some axioms in the ontology also give us some information about forbidden edges. All these edge constraints can easily be incorporated in usual BN structure learning algorithm [3]. Under some condition of consistency, these existence restrictions shall be fulfilled, in the sense that they are assumed to be true for the CBN representing the domain knowledge, and therefore all potential Partially Directed Acyclic Graph (PDAG) must necessarily satisfy them.

Definition 1. *Given a domain ontology $\mathcal{O}$, let $G=(C, R_c)$ be the DAG where $R_c\colon C_i \times C_j$ represents the subset of semantic causal relations extracted from $\mathcal{O}$. This subset included both direct and logically derivable semantic causal relations. Let $H=(X, E_h)$ be a PDAG, where X is the set of the corresponding random variables and E_h corresponds to the causal dependencies between them. H is consistent with the existence restrictions in G if and only if:*
$$\forall\ C_i,\ C_j\ \in C,\ if\ C_i{\rightarrow}C_j\ \in R_c\ then\ X_i{\rightarrow}X_j\ \in E_h.$$

When we are specifying the set of existence restrictions to be used, it is necessary to make sure that these restrictions can indeed be satisfied. In fact, such causal integration may lead to possible conflicts between the two models. When this occurs, we have to maintain the initial causal information in the PDAG since we are supposed to use perfect observational data. On the other hand, we should ensure the consistency of the existence restrictions in such a way that no directed cycles are created in G.

2) Causal discovery process: Before delving into the details of our approach, we first review the principal idea of the causal discovery process in MyCaDo algorithm [12].

When performing an experimentation on X_i, MyCaDo measure all neighboring variables and accordingly to the result direct all edges connecting X_i and $\text{Nei}(X_i)$. This edge orientation represents one instantiation $(inst(A_{X_i}))$ among all possible instantiations. It is then possible to continue the edge orientation by using the Meek rules [11] to infer new causal relations.

Let $inferred(inst(A_{X_i}))$ be the number of inferred edges based on $inst(A_{X_i})$. MyCaDo proposes that the utility of an experiment is related to the number of edges directly oriented or inferred, weighted by the cost of experiment $(cost(A_{X_i}))$ and measurement $(cost(M_{X_i}))$:

$$U(X_i) = \frac{Card(Nei(X_i)) + Card(inferred(inst(A_{X_i})))}{\alpha cost(A_{X_i}) + \beta cost(M_{X_i})} \tag{1}$$

where measures of importance α and $\beta \in [0,1]$ and Card(M) represents the cardinality of any set M.

It seems obvious that the gained information of such utility function is essentially the node connectivity (i.e. the number of undirected edges and those susceptible to be inferred) which serves to orient the maximal number of edges but not necessary the most informative ones.

To cope with this limitation, the strategy we propose in our approach makes use of a semantic distance calculus (e.g. Rada distance [16]) provided by the ontology structure. So, for each node in the graph, SemCaDo gives a generalization of the node connectivity by introducing the semantic inertia, denoted by $SemIn(X_i)$ and expressed as follows:

$$SemIn(X_i) = \frac{\displaystyle\sum_{X_j \in Nei(X_i) \cup X_i} dist_{Rada}(mscs(Nei(X_i) \cup X_i), X_j)}{Card(Nei(X_i) \cup X_i)} \quad (2)$$

where:

- $mscs(C_i, C_j)$: the most specific common subsumer of the two concepts C_i and C_j, where $i \neq j$.
- $dist_{Rada}(C_i, C_j)$: the shortest path between C_i and C_j, where $i \neq j$,

Moreover, the semantic inertia presents three major properties:

- When the experimented variable and all its neighbors lie at the same level in the concept hierarchy, the semantic inertia will be equal to the number of hierarchical levels needed to reach the mscs.
- If the corresponding concepts belong to the same super-class then SemIn will be proportional to Card(Nei(.)).
- It essentially depends on semantic distance between the studied concepts. This means that the more this distance is important, the more the SemIn will be maximized.

By this way, we will accentuate the serendipitous aspect of the proposed strategy and investigate new and unexpected causal relations on the graph.

Further to these, we also integrate a semantic cumulus relative to the inferred edges denoted by $Inferred\_Gain$ in our utility function. For this purpose, we use I(X_i) to denote the set of nodes attached by inferred edges after performing an experimentation on X_i. So, the $Inferred\_Gain$ formula is expressed as follows:

$$Inferred\_Gain(X_i) = \frac{\displaystyle\sum_{X_j \in I(X_i)} dist_{Rada}(mscs(I(X_i)), X_j)}{Card(I(X_i))} \quad (3)$$

$Inferred\_Gain$ also represents a generalization of Card(inferred(inst(.)) and depends on the semantic distance between the studied concepts. Note that we don't use here all the information provided by the ontology. We should also consider the axioms to check if any new relation could be inferred from the semantic point of view. Better interacting with the axioms is one of our perspectives for future work.

When using the two proposed terms, our utility function will be as follows:

$$U(X_i) = \frac{SemIn(X_i) + Inferred\_Gain(X_i)}{\alpha cost(A_{X_i}) + \beta cost(M_{X_i})} \quad (4)$$

where measures of importance α, $\beta \in [0,1]$.

This utility function will be of great importance to highlight the serendipitous character of SemCaDo algorithm by guiding the causal discovery process to investigate unexplored areas and conduct more informative experiments.

3) Edge orientation & ontology evolution: Once the specified intervention performed, we follow the same edge orientation strategy as in MyCaDo [12]. So if there are still some non-directed edges in the PDAG , we re-iterate over the second phase and so on, until no more causal discoveries can be made. Since certain experimentation can not be performed, either because of ethical reasons or simply because it is impossible to do it, the final causal graph can be either a CBN or a partially causal graph.

In both cases, the causal knowledge will be extracted and interpreted for an eventual ontology evolution. In this way, the causal relations will be traduced as semantic causal relations between the corresponding ontology concepts.

We note that, because of the priority given to the ontology axioms, only causal relations guaranteeing the consistency will be retained for the ontology evolution process.

3.3   Toy Example

In the following example, we briefly illustrate the various steps we followed to construct a CBN when using SemCaDo algorithm. As noted above, we assume that all random variables under study are modeled in the corresponding ontology (See Figure 2) as distinctly blue-colored concepts. We note that in order to simplify the semantic analysis, we restricted the ontology to only taxonomic relations and causal ones.

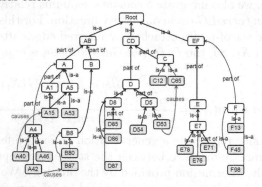

Fig. 2. An example of ontology: blue nodes denote the concepts under study, red relationships denote causal prior knowledge and black relationships are taxonomic relations

As first step, we use the graph in Figure 3 (a) to specify the existence restrictions to be satisfied. In our case, three causal relations (i.e. A42→B87, A40→A15 and D53→C65) extracted from the ontology in Figure 2 have to be modeled as directed arrows before learning the initial structure. Using this prior knowledge, Figure 3 (b) shows the resulting partially directed graph after performing a structure learning algorithm and applying the Meek rules [11] to infer edges.

When running the SemCaDo causal discovery process, the first best node to experiment on will be E71. This choice is strongly supported by the high semantic distance between E71 and its neighboring variables (i.e. E76 and A42)

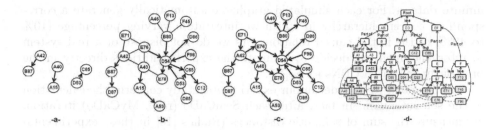

Fig. 3. (a) Existence restriction graph extracted from the ontology in Figure 2, (b) PDAG obtained after structure learning phase using previous restriction graph, (c) the CBN obtained after performing experiments on (E71, B80 and A42) and (d) the enriched ontology.

as well as the additional semantic cumulus relative to the edges susceptible to be inferred (i.e. E76-A40, A42-E76, A40-A42 and A40-E78). Thanks to this experimentation, we can investigate different causal relations between the more distant concepts in the ontology, in which we have not enough prior causal information (See Figure 2).

After finishing all the causal discovery step and learning the completed directed graph as shown in Figure 3 (c), the supplementary causal knowledge will be interpreted and reused in the corresponding ontology. The dashed lines in Figure 3 (d) indicate the ontology evolution (i.e. ontology enrichment) in response to SemCaDo discoveries.

4 Experimental Study

In the experimental evaluation, we will compare SemCaDo to MyCaDo algorithm [12] since both of them share the same assumptions and use the same input data.

For this purpose, we randomly create a set of syntectic 50 and 200 node graphs and apply a DAG-to-CPDAG algorithm [2] on those CBNs in order to simulate the result of a structure learning algorithm working with a perfect

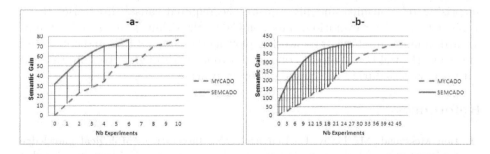

Fig. 4. The semantic gain given the number of experiments using MyCaDo and SemCaDo on relatively small graphs (a) and bigger ones (b)

infinite dataset. For each simulated graph, we automatically generate a corresponding concept hierarchy in which we integrate a varying percentage (10% to 40%) of the initial causal relations. As we do not dispose of a real system to intervene upon, we decide to simulate the experimentations directly in the previously generated CBNs as in [12].

Another point to consider in our experimental study concerns the calculation of the semantic gain. In fact, after each SemCaDo (resp. MyCaDo) iteration, we measure the sum of semantic distances (Rada's [16] in these experiments) relative to the new directed edges in the graph and update a semantic cumulus. In both strategies, the two corresponding curves are increasing in, meaning that the higher is the number of experimented variables, the higher is the value of the semantic gain. Nevertheless the more the curve is increasing faster, the more the approach is converging to the best and most impressive experiments.

Figure 4 shows that, during the experimentation process, our approach comfortably outperforms the MyCaDo algorithm in term of semantic gain. This is essentially due to the initial causal knowledge integration and the causal discovery strategy when performing the experimentations. But if the two curves reach the same maxima when obtaining a fully directed graph, where is the evolutionary contribution of SemCaDo? Let us remember that we are approaching a decision problem which is subject to the experimentation costs and the budget allocation. Taking into account this constraint, the domination of SemCaDo will be extremely beneficial when the number of experiments is limited.

All these experimental results show how the SemCaDo algorithm can adopt a serendipitous attitude with the minimum expected cost and effort. This is indeed a new avenue of causal investigation, moving far away from traditional techniques.

5   Conclusions and Future Works

In this paper, we outlined our serendipitous and cyclic approach which aims to i) integrate the causal prior knowledge contained in the corresponding ontology when learning the initial structure from observational data, ii) use a semantic distance calculus to guide the iterative causal discovery process to the more surprising relationships and iii) capture the required causal discoveries to be applied to ontology evolution. The SemCaDo algorithm is an initial attempt towards a more ambitious framework exploiting the power of BNs and ontologies. Future works will be devoted to ontology revolution through better interactions with the axioms during the causal discovery process.

References

1. Ben Messaoud, M., Leray, P., Ben Amor, N.: Integrating ontological knowledge for iterative causal discovery and visualization. In: Sossai, C., Chemello, G. (eds.) ECSQARU 2009. LNCS, vol. 5590, pp. 168–179. Springer, Heidelberg (2009)
2. Chickering, D.M.: Learning equivalence classes of bayesian-network structures. Journal of Machine Learning Research 2, 445–498 (2002)

3. de Campos, L.M., Castellano, J.G.: Bayesian network learning algorithms using structural restrictions. International Journal of Approximate Reasoning, 233–254 (2007)

4. Devitt, A., Danev, B., Matusikova, K.: Constructing bayesian networks automatically using ontologies. In: Second Workshop on Formal Ontologies Meet Industry, FOMI 2006, Trento, Italy (2006)

5. Ding, Z., Peng, Y.: A probabilistic extension to ontology language OWL. In: Proceedings of the 37th Hawaii International Conference on System Sciences, HICSS 2004 (2004)

6. Flouris, G., Manakanatas, D., Kondylakis, H., Plexousakis, D., Antoniou, G.: Ontology change: classification and survey. The Knowledge Engineering Review 23, 117–152 (2008)

7. Gruber, T.R.: Towards Principles for the Design of Ontologies Used for Knowledge Sharing. International Journal Human-Computer Studies 43(5-6), 907–928 (1995)

8. He, Y.B., Geng, Z.: Active learning of causal networks with intervention experiments and optimal designs. JMLR 9, 2523–2547 (2008)

9. Jeon, B.-J., Ko, I.-Y.: Ontology-based semi-automatic construction of bayesian network models for diagnosing diseases in e-health applications. In: FBIT, pp. 595–602. IEEE Computer Society, Los Alamitos (2007)

10. Khattak, A.M., Latif, K., Lee, S., Lee, Y.-K.: Ontology Evolution: A Survey and Future Challenges. In: Ślzak, D., Kim, T.-h., Ma, J., Fang, W.-C., Sandnes, F.E., Kang, B.-H., Gu, B. (eds.) U- and E-Service, Science and Technology, vol. 62, pp. 68–75. Springer, Heidelberg (2009)

11. Meek, C.: Causal inference and causal explanation with background knowledge. In: Proceedings of the Eleventh Conference Annual Conference on Uncertainty in Artificial Intelligence (UAI 1995), pp. 403–441. Morgan Kaufmann, San Francisco (1995)

12. Meganck, S., Leray, P., Manderick, B.: Learning causal bayesian networks from observations and experiments: A decision theoretic approach. In: Torra, V., Narukawa, Y., Valls, A., Domingo-Ferrer, J. (eds.) MDAI 2006. LNCS (LNAI), vol. 3885, pp. 58–69. Springer, Heidelberg (2006)

13. Murphy, K.P.: Active learning of causal bayes net structure. Technical report, University of California, Berkeley, USA (2001)

14. Pearl, J.: Probabilistic Reasoning in Intelligent Systems: Networks of Plausible Inference. Morgan Kaufmann Publishers Inc., San Francisco (1988)

15. Pearl, J.: Causality: models, reasoning, and inference. Cambridge University Press, Cambridge (2000)

16. Rada, R., Mili, H., Bicknell, E., Blettner, M.: Development and application of a metric on semantic nets. IEEE Transactions on Systems, Man and Cybernetics 19(1), 17–30 (1989)

17. Xuan, D.N., Bellatreche, L., Pierra, G.: A versioning management model for ontology-based data warehouses. In: Tjoa, A.M., Trujillo, J. (eds.) DaWaK 2006. LNCS, vol. 4081, pp. 195–206. Springer, Heidelberg (2006)

18. Yang, Y., Calmet, J.: Ontobayes: An ontology-driven uncertainty model. In: International Conference on Computational Intelligence for Modelling, Control and Automation (CIMCA), pp. 457–463 (2005)

Scaling Up the Greedy Equivalence Search Algorithm by Constraining the Search Space of Equivalence Classes*

Juan I. Alonso-Barba, Luis de la Ossa, Jose A. Gámez, and Jose M. Puerta

Department of Computing Systems
Intelligent Systems and Data Mining Lab,
Albacete Research Institute of Informatics,
University of Castilla-La Mancha, 02071 Albacete, Spain

Abstract. Greedy Equivalence Search (GES) is nowadays the state of the art algorithm for learning Bayesian networks (BNs) from complete data. However, from a practical point of view, this algorithm may not be fast enough to work in high dimensionality domains. This paper proposes some variants of GES aimed to increase its efficiency. Under faithfulness assumption, the modified algorithms preserve the same theoretical properties as the original one, that is, they recover a perfect map of the target distribution in the large sample limit. Moreover, experimental results confirm that, although they carry out much less computations, BNs learnt by those algorithms have the same quality as those learnt by GES.

1 Introduction

Bayesian network (BN) learning [8] has received a growing attention from researchers in the area of Data Mining. Although many approaches and methods have been proposed so far, there is still great interest on this topic. This is due to the fact that BN learning is a complex and highly time-consuming task, and existing algorithms usually do not scale well when dealing with many (hundreds of) variables. Thus, new algorithms, as well as improvements to existing ones, are being proposed in order to work with bigger datasets.

In the case of *score+search* methods defined over the space of Directed Acyclic Graphs (*D-space*), such improvements are usually based on the use of local search algorithms [10,5], since they allow avoiding a huge amount of computations. However, despite the fact that these methods speed up the learning process, they do not reach the results, in terms of score, of the networks obtained by more complex algorithms, as those defined over the space of Equivalence Classes (*E-space*) [7,3]. The most representative of these, GES (Greedy Equivalence Search) [3], is considered nowadays as the reference in BN learning since, under faithfulness conditions, it asymptotically obtains a perfect map of the target distribution.

As its name indicates, GES is also a local (greedy) algorithm. In a first stage, GES takes the equivalence class with no dependences as starting point, and adds

---

* Research Projects PCI08-0048-8577 and TIN2007-67418-C03-01.

W. Liu (Ed.): ECSQARU 2011, LNAI 6717, pp. 194–205, 2011.
© Springer-Verlag Berlin Heidelberg 2011

dependences until no edge can be added; then, it tries to progressively delete edges in a second stage. Despite considering only local changes in both phases, the algorithm has several drawbacks which limit its scalability. Thus, the cost of the algorithm is exponential in the size of the biggest clique in the network, since an exhaustive search must be carried out in order to find the best subset of head-to-head nodes with the tested edges in the constructive phase. Therefore, GES is very inefficient when dealing with structures where a node has a large number of adjacents. In order to alleviate this problem, it is common to restrict the number of parents. However, this decision is arbitrary, and an incorrect setting of that parameter may degrade the performance of the algorithm.

Since most computational effort of GES is carried out in the first stage, it would be of interest relaxing the search of these head-to-head subsets for each node in such a phase. In order to do that, we propose changing a exhaustive search, whose complexity is exponential in the number of adjacencies for a node, by a greedy one, which is linear.

Furthermore, it is possible to improve upon the scalability of GES by methods successfully used in the D-space [10,5,6], which basically consist in restricting the search space. Thus, computations carried out at each search step of the constructive phase of GES, allow detecting edges which should not be considered from then on. This way the search space is pruned progressively as the search advances.

As we show in this paper, the modifications of GES incorporating both changes exhibit the same theoretical properties as the original one. Moreover, experiments confirm that they are faster than the unconstrained/classical version, whereas they are able to learn BNs with the same score.

This paper is structured as follows. Section 2 shows an introduction to BN learning and a description of GES. Afterwards, our proposals to scale up GES are shown in 3, and an experimental analysis is carried out in Section 4. Lastly, Section 5 presents some conclusions.

2 Learning Bayesian Networks by Using Greedy Equivalence Search

Bayesian Networks (BNs) [9] efficiently represent n-dimensional probability distributions by means of a *directed acyclic graph* (DAG), $\mathcal{G} = (\boldsymbol{V}, \mathbf{E})$, and a set of numerical parameters ($\boldsymbol{\Theta}$), usually conditional probability distributions drawn from the graph structure.

Let $X_i \in \boldsymbol{V}$, and let $Pa_{\mathcal{G}}(X_i)$ be the parent set of X_i in $\mathcal{G}$. The joint probability distribution over $\boldsymbol{V}$ is obtained as:

$$P(X_1, X_2, \ldots, X_n) = \prod_{i=1}^{n} P(X_i | Pa_{\mathcal{G}}(X_i))$$

where $P(X_i | Pa_{\mathcal{G}}(X_i))$ is the conditional probability distribution of X_i given $Pa_{\mathcal{G}}(X_i)$.

We denote that variables in $\mathbf{X}$ are conditionally independent (through d-separation) of variables in $\mathbf{Y}$ given the set $\mathbf{Z}$, in a DAG $\mathcal{G}$ by $\langle \mathbf{X}, \mathbf{Y}|\mathbf{Z}\rangle_\mathcal{G}$. The same affirmation, but related to a probability distribution p, is denoted by $I_p(\mathbf{X}, \mathbf{Y}|\mathbf{Z})$. From these conditions, two definitions arise:

A DAG $\mathcal{G}$ is an *I-map* of a probability distribution p if $\langle \mathbf{X}, \mathbf{Y}|\mathbf{Z}\rangle_\mathcal{G} \Rightarrow I_p(\mathbf{X}, \mathbf{Y}|\mathbf{Z})$. And it is *minimal* if there is no arc such that, when removed, the resulting graph $\mathcal{G}'$ is still an *I-map*. $\mathcal{G}$ is a *D-map* of p if $\langle \mathbf{X}, \mathbf{Y}|\mathbf{Z}\rangle_\mathcal{G} \Longleftarrow I_p(\mathbf{X}, \mathbf{Y}|\mathbf{Z})$. When a DAG $\mathcal{G}$ is both an *I-map* and a *D-map* of p, it is said that $\mathcal{G}$ and p are *isomorphic* models (that is $\mathcal{G}$ is a *perfect-map* of p). Furthermore, a distribution p is faithful if there exists a graph, $\mathcal{G}$, to which it is faithful.

The problem of learning the structure of a Bayesian network can be stated as follows: Given a training dataset $D = \{\mathbf{v}^1, \ldots, \mathbf{v}^m\}$ of instances (configurations of values) of V, find a DAG $\mathcal{G}^*$ such that

$$\mathcal{G}^* = \arg \max_{\mathcal{G} \in \mathcal{G}^n} f(\mathcal{G} : D),$$

where $f(\mathcal{G} : D)$ is a scoring metric (or scoring criterion) which evaluates the merit of any candidate DAG $\mathcal{G}$ with respect to the dataset D, and $\mathcal{G}^n$ is the set containing all the DAGs with n nodes.

Although there are many methods to look for $\mathcal{G}^*$, the most used in practice are those based on local search algorithms [2]. Efficient evaluation of neighbors of DAGs in this local search algorithms is based on an important property of scoring metrics: *decomposability* in the presence of full data. In the case of BNs, decomposable metrics evaluate a given DAG as the sum of the scores of the sub-graphs formed by each node and its parents in $\mathcal{G}$. Formally, if f is decomposable, then:

$$f(\mathcal{G} : D) = \sum_{i=1}^{n} f_D(X_i, Pa_\mathcal{G}(X_i))$$

If a decomposable metric is used, graphs resulting of changing one arc can be efficiently evaluated. Thus, this kind of (local) methods reuse the computations carried out at previous stages, and only the statistics corresponding to the variables whose parents have been modified need to be recomputed.

Another important properties of scoring metrics are *global consistency* and *local consistency*. The first one indicates that the metrics prefer DAGs containing p (or closer to), and if there are two (or more) DAGs containing p, it prefers those with fewer parameters. Finally the second property can be stated as, let $\mathcal{G}$ be any DAG, and $\mathcal{G}'$ the DAG obtained by adding edge $X_i \rightarrow X_j$ to $\mathcal{G}$. A scoring metric is *locally consistent* if in the limit as data grows large the following conditions hold: 1) If $\neg I_p(X_i, X_j|Pa_\mathcal{G}(X_j))$, then $f(\mathcal{G} : D) < f(\mathcal{G}' : D)$; 2) If $I_p(X_i, X_j|Pa_\mathcal{G}(X_j))$, then $f(\mathcal{G} : D) > f(\mathcal{G}' : D)$. Commonly used metrics, such as BDE, MDL and BIC, are decomposable, locally and globally consistent [3].

2.1   The E-Space

A *partially DAG* (PDAG) (Fig. 1 (b)) is a graph that contains both directed and undirected edges. In a PDAG, a pair of nodes X and Y are neighbors if the are

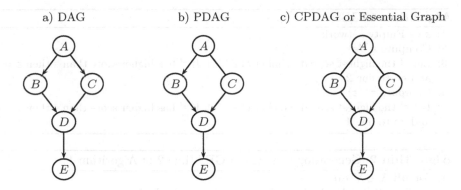

a) DAG   b) PDAG   c) CPDAG or Essential Graph

Fig. 1. DAG, PDAG and CPDAD or Essential Graph

connected by an undirected edge, and they are adjacent if they are connected by either an undirected edge or a directed edge.

A *v-structure* in a PDAG $\mathcal{P}$ is a subgraph of three nodes (X, Y, Z) where Z has two incoming edges ($X \rightarrow Z$ and $Y \rightarrow Z$) and X and Y are not adjacent, (In fig. 1 (a) the subgraph ($B \rightarrow D \leftarrow C$). The skeleton of a PDAG $\mathcal{P}$ is the graph resulting of converting the directed edges of $\mathcal{P}$ into undirected edges.

Let $\mathcal{P}$ denote an arbitrary PDAG. We define the equivalence class of DAGs $\varepsilon(\mathcal{P})$ corresponding to $\mathcal{P}$ as follows: $G \in \varepsilon(\mathcal{P})$ if and only if G and $\mathcal{P}$ have the same skeleton and the same set of v-structures.

Completed PDAGs (CPDAGs) or *Essential Graphs* are used to represent equivalence classes of DAGs, i.e. the set of DAGs that encode the same set of conditionals (in)dependences. In a CPDAG directed edges are call *compelled* and they represent an edge that has the same orientation for every member of the equivalence class. Undirected edges represent *reversible edges*, i.e. edges that are not compelled. Given an equivalence class of DAGs, the CPDAG representation is unique. Thus, CPDAGs are used to represent the space of equivalence classes (the E-space). Fig. 1 (c) shows a CPDAG representing an equivalence class ε and Fig. 1 (a) shows a DAG that belongs to ε.

2.2 Greedy Equivalent Search (GES)

GES algorithm [3] can be described as follows. It first initializes the state of the search to be the equivalence class ε corresponding to the (unique) DAG with no edges and then, it runs a local search that consists in two phases. In the first phase, a greedy search is performed over equivalence classes using a particular neighborhood. Once a local maximum is reached, a second phase proceeds from the previous local maximum using a second neighborhood. When the second phase reaches a local maximum, that equivalence class is returned as the solution.

The pseudocode of the algorithm is shown in Algorithm 1. $\varepsilon^{+}(\varepsilon)$ denotes the neighbors of state ε during the first phase of GES (lines 2-3). An equivalence class ε' is in $\varepsilon^{+}(\varepsilon)$ if and only if there is some DAG $\mathcal{G} \in \varepsilon$ to which we can add a single edge that results in a DAG $\mathcal{G}' \in \varepsilon'$. $\varepsilon^{-}(\varepsilon)$ denotes the neighbors of

---

Algorithm 1. GES

1: $\varepsilon \leftarrow$ Empty network
2: Compute $\varepsilon^+(\varepsilon)$
3: Let ε' the highest scored member of $\varepsilon^+(\varepsilon)$. If ε' has higher score than ε then $\varepsilon = \varepsilon'$
    and go to line 2.
4: Compute $\varepsilon^-(\varepsilon)$
5: Let ε' the highest scored member of $\varepsilon^-(\varepsilon)$. If ε' has higher score than ε then $\varepsilon = \varepsilon'$
    and go to line 4.

Algorithm 2. Generation of $\varepsilon^+(\varepsilon)$ in GES (line 2 of Algorithm 1)

1: **for all** $X \in \mathbf{V}$ **do**
2:     **for all** $Y \in \mathbf{V} \mid Y \neq X \wedge Y$ is not adjacent to X **do**
3:         **for all** $\mathbf{T} \subseteq \mathbf{T_0}$ **do**
4:             Test validity conditions and compute Insert$(X, Y, \mathbf{T})$
5:         **end for**
6:     **end for**
7: **end for**

---

state ε during the second phase of GES (lines 4-5). Its definition is completely analogous to that of $\varepsilon^+(\varepsilon)$, and contains the equivalence classes obtained by deleting a single edge from DAGs in ε.

Lemmas 9 and 10 in [3] show that the equivalence class that results at the end of the first phase of GES is, asymptotically, an I-map of p. And the equivalence class that results at the end of GES is, asymptotically, a perfect map of p.

Next, we focus on the first phase of GES. From a practical point of view, working directly with the definition of $\varepsilon^+(\varepsilon)$ over DAGs is not efficient. In [3] efficient operators to transverse the E-space are defined. In the ascendent phase, for a given state of the search (a CPDAG), we can move to other state by applying an operator Insert$(X, Y, \mathbf{T})$ and then transforming the obtained PDAG into a CPDAG.

Definition 1. *Insert(X, Y, **T**) ([3], Definition 12) For non-adjacent nodes* X *and* Y *in* $\mathcal{P}^C$, *and for any subset* $\mathbf{T} \subseteq \mathbf{T_0}$ *of the neighbors of* Y *that are not adjacent to* X, *the Insert(X, Y, **T**) operator modifies* $\mathcal{P}^C$ *by (1) inserting the directed edge* $X \to Y$, *and (2) for each* $T \in \mathbf{T}$, *directing the previously undirected edge between* T *and* Y *as* $T \to Y$.

Theorem 15 and Corollary 16 [3] show the conditions when the Insert operator can be applied in order to be valid and the way to score a new structure when one of this operator is applied.

Finally, when working with CPDAGs, the set $\varepsilon^+(\varepsilon)$ can be generated by running Algorithm 2, $\mathbf{V}$ being the set containing all variables and $\mathbf{T_0}$ the set of all neighbours of Y that are not adjacent to X.

From Algorithm 2, it follows that the number of operations is exponential in the size of the set $\mathbf{T_0}$. In a real domain, this number could be high. For example, Fig. 2a shows the structure of the HailFinder network [1] around variable

a) Partial HAILFINDER DAG   b) Step i of GES

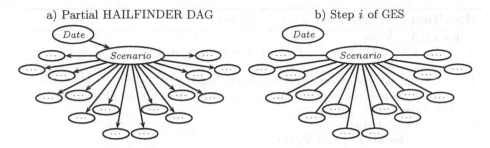

Fig. 2. a) Partial HAILFINDER DAG. The graph was obtained by removing from the complete network variables not in the Markov blanket of variable *Scenario*. b) Example of possible partial CPDAG obtained in the step i of GES.

Scenario. Fig. 2b shows the equivalence class ε of the network found in the step i of GES. Now, the algorithm has to compute the set $\varepsilon^{+}(\varepsilon)$. Thus, it has to compute the operation Insert(*Date*, *Scenario*, **T**) for each **T** in $\mathbf{T_0}$ being $\mathbf{T_0}$ the set of children of variable *Scenario* in the real network. As the set $\mathbf{T_0}$ has 16 variables, it has to compute 2^{16} different operations.

3   Scaling Up GES

In this section we propose some variants of the original GES algorithm. The idea behind these algorithms is to modify the first phase of GES in order to reduce the number of operations computed. The second phase is not modified.

3.1   GES$_G$

As shown above, GES tests the operation Insert($X, Y, \mathbf{T}$) for all $\mathbf{T} \subseteq \mathbf{T_0}$. For a set $\mathbf{T_0}$ of size k, it is needed to compute 2^k operations. In practice, to overcome this issue, a maximum number of parents (maximum size of **T**) is set a priori. However, this parameter is difficult to manage in general and its use may degrade the theoretical properties of the algorithm.

Our proposal is to reduce the candidate neighbors by, instead of performing an exhaustive search over all possible subsets of $\mathbf{T_0}$, performing a greedy search in order to find a reasonable good subset of $\mathbf{T_0}$. The algorithm, GES$_G$, uses a restricted subset of $\varepsilon^{+}(\varepsilon)$, denoted as $\varepsilon_G^{+}(\varepsilon)$, where the members are computed using a greedy procedure.

Algorithm 3 shows the procedure used to generate $\varepsilon_G^{+}(\varepsilon)$. For each pair of variables X and Y if first initializes $\mathbf{T_1} = \emptyset$ and it checks and computes the score of the operation Insert($X, Y, \mathbf{T_1}$). If this operation increases the score of the previous network, it checks and score the operations Insert($X, Y, \mathbf{T_2} = \mathbf{T_1} \cup \{T\}$) ($\forall T \in \mathbf{T_0} \setminus \mathbf{T_1}$). The algorithm iteratively replaces $\mathbf{T_1}$ with the best $\mathbf{T_2}$ and repeats this last step until no such replacement increases the score or when $\mathbf{T_1} = \mathbf{T_0}$.

Algorithm 3. Generation of $\varepsilon_G^+(\varepsilon)$ in GES_G

1: **for all** $X \in \mathbf{V}$ **do**
2:     **for all** $Y \in \mathbf{V} \mid Y \neq X \wedge Y$ is not adjacent to X **do**
3:         $\mathbf{T_1} \leftarrow \emptyset$.
4:         Test validity conditions and compute $\text{Insert}(X, Y, \mathbf{T_1})$
5:         If the network obtained in line 4 is better than ε then $ok \leftarrow$ **true**. Else, $ok \leftarrow$ **false**
6:         **while** ok **do**
7:             **for all** $T \in \mathbf{T_0} \setminus \mathbf{T_1}$ **do**
8:                 Test validity conditions and compute $\text{Insert}(X, Y, \mathbf{T_2} = \mathbf{T_1} \cup T)$
9:             **end for**
10:             Let $\mathbf{T_2^*}$ the best subset found in the previous bucle. If the network obtained by applying $\text{Insert}(X, Y, \mathbf{T_2^*})$ is better than the obtained by applying $\text{Insert}(X, Y, \mathbf{T_1})$ then $\mathbf{T_1} \leftarrow \mathbf{T_2^*}$ and $ok \leftarrow$ **true**. Else, $ok \leftarrow$ **false**
11:         **end while**
12:     **end for**
13: **end for**

Proposition 1. *Let ε denote the equivalence class that results at the end of the first phase of GES_G and p the generative probability distribution faithful to a DAG. Then, asymptotically ε contains p.*

Proof. Let us suppose the contrary, i.e., ε not contains p.. Then there is at least variables X_i and X_j such that $\langle X_i, X_j | \mathbf{Pa}_\varepsilon(X_i) \rangle_\varepsilon$ and $\neg I_p(X_i, X_j | \mathbf{Pa}_\varepsilon(X_i))$. Thus, ε cannot be a local optimum because the addition of the arc $X_j \to X_i$ has a positive difference.

3.2 GES_{iC}

In this second proposal, denoted as GES_C, we apply a similar approach to the progressive restriction of the neighborhood used in [6]. The idea behind the algorithm is to reduce the number of operations, by restricting the pair of variables X and Y for which the $\text{Insert}(X, Y, \mathbf{T})$ operations are tested.

The core idea is to have a set of forbidden parents for each variable X_i (denoted as $FP(X_i)$). The difference between this algorithm and the GES algorithm is that the definition of $\varepsilon^+(\varepsilon)$ is slightly modified to be $\varepsilon_C^+(\varepsilon)$ (see Algorithm 4). $\varepsilon_C^+(\varepsilon)$ is obtained from ε by computing for all variables X and all its non-adjacent variables Y such that $Y \notin FP(X)$, the operations $\text{Insert}(X, Y, \mathbf{T})$.

A variable X is added to the list of forbidden parents of another variable Y if the evaluation of every operation $\text{Insert}(X, Y, \mathbf{T})$ ($\forall \mathbf{T} \subseteq \mathbf{T_0}$) results in a network worse than the previous one. In this situation, according to the definition of local consistency, X and Y are independent.

Unfortunately, we cannot assure that the result of this first phase of this algorithm is an I-map. In order to solve that problem, we also propose an iterated version of this algorithm that we denote it as GES_{iC}. GES_{iC} can be described as follows. First, it runs GES_C. Then, it iteratively resets the sets of forbidden

---

Algorithm 4. Generation of $\varepsilon_C^+(\varepsilon)$ in GES$_C$

1: **for all** $X \in \mathbf{V}$ **do**
2:    **for all** $Y \in \mathbf{V} \mid Y \neq X \wedge Y \notin FP(X) \wedge Y$ is not adjacent to X **do**
3:        **for all** $\mathbf{T} \subseteq \mathbf{T_0}$ **do**
4:            Test validity conditions and compute Insert$(X, Y, \mathbf{T})$
5:        **end for**
6:        If all the neighbors generated in the previous bucle are worse scored than ε
    then $FP(Y) \to FP(Y) \cup X$.
7:    **end for**
8: **end for**

---

parents and runs GES$_C$ using as initial solution the final solution found by the previous iteration, until no improvement is achieved.

Proposition 2. *Let ε denote the equivalence class that results at the end of the first phase of GES$_{iC}$ and p the generative probability distribution faithful to a DAG. Then, asymptotically ε contains p.*

Proof. In the last iteration of the GES$_{iC}$ algorithm, all the sets of forbidden parents are empty. In this situation, the behavior of the algorithm would be the same as the behavior of GES.

3.3 GES$_{iCG}$

The two last algorithms proposed are denoted as GES$_{CG}$ and GES$_{iCG}$. The first one, GES$_{CG}$, uses both the greedy and the constrained approach, i.e. , it performs a greedy search over the space of candidate neighbors as GES$_C$ does, but it also uses a list of forbidden parents to constrain the search as GES$_C$ does. A variable X is added to the list of forbidden parents of another variable Y if the operation Insert$(X, Y, \emptyset)$ decreases the score of the network. Finally, GES$_{iCG}$ is the iterated version of GES$_{CG}$.

Proposition 3. *Let ε denote the equivalence class that results at the end of the first phase of GES$_{iCG}$ and p the generative probability distribution faithful to a DAG. Then, asymptotically ε contains p.*

Proof. In the last iteration of the GES$_{iCG}$ algorithm, all the sets of forbidden parents are empty. In this situation, the behavior of the algorithm would be the same as the behavior of GES$_G$.

Corollary 1. *Let p the generative probability distribution faithful to a DAG. The equivalence class that results at the end of GES$_G$, GES$_{iC}$ and GES$_{iCG}$ is asymptotically a perfect map of p.*

4   Experimental Evaluation

In this section we compare GES algorithm against the variants proposed in this paper.

Table 1. BNs used in the experiments

Name	# of vars	# of edges	max. parents	max. childrens	max. neigbors (CPDAG)
ALARM	37	46	4	5	1
BARLEY	48	84	4	5	3
CHILD	20	25	2	7	2
HAILFINDER	56	66	4	16	17
INSURANCE	27	52	3	7	8
MILDEW	35	46	3	3	0
PIGS	441	592	2	39	0

The algorithms are coded in Java and are based on the open implementation included in `Tetrad 4.3.9`[1]. The implementation of the algorithms includes the optimizations suggested in [3]. However, the maximum number of parents is not limited. The score metric used in the algorithms is the Bayesian Dirichlet equivalent in their uniform prior version BDeu [7]. The equivalent sample size (N') used in the experiments is 10 and the network priors are calculated as in [4] where the kappa parameter is $k = 1/(N' + 1)$.

We have selected a subset of the networks available in the Bayesian Network Repository[2]. The characteristics of these networks are shown in Table 1. For each one of the networks we obtained five datasets (each one with 5000 instances) by sampling from the networks.

4.1 Empirical Results

In order to compare the algorithms described in the previous section, we considered two kinds of factors as performance indicators: the quality of the network obtained by the algorithm, given by the value of the score metric (BDeu); and the complexity of each algorithm, given by the learning time and the number of computations of the score metric.

Table 2 shows the results regarding the performance of the algorithms. When the score of the resulting networks is equal than that obtained by GES, it is marked in bold. Otherwise, we also report the Structural Hamming Distance (SHD) of such network with respect to the one obtained by GES. The SHD is defined in CPDAGs and is computed as the number of the following operators required to make the CPDAGs match: add or delete an undirected edge, and add, remove, or reverse the orientation of an edge.

The reported results are the average of the results obtained using the five datasets sampled from each network. In our experiments, we have checked that when two algorithms had obtained the same result in one of the datasets, they also had obtained the same result in the other four datasets. For this reason, we can assume that the differences in the results depend on the structure of the networks.

---

[1] http://www.phil.cmu.edu/projects/tetrad/
[2] http://www.cs.huji.ac.il/labs/compbio/Repository/

Table 2. BDeu score of the networks obtained by the proposed algorithms

Network	GES	GES_G	GES_C	GES_{iC}	GES_{CG}	GES_{iCG}
ALARM	**-49535**	**-49535**	-49568 (1.6)	**-49535**	-49568 (1.6)	**-49535**
BARLEY	**-286062**	**-286062**	-287657 (1.0)	**-286062**	-287657 (1.0)	**-286062**
CHILD	**-69415**	**-69415**	**-69415**	**-69415**	**-69415**	**-69415**
HAILFINDER	-	**-253708**	-	-	-253711	**-253708**
INSURANCE	**-68580**	-68614 (2.4)	-68617 (1.0)	**-68580**	-68652 (3.4)	-68614 (2.4)
MILDEW	**-260536**	**-260536**	**-260536**	**-260536**	**-260536**	**-260536**
PIGS	**-1684625**	**-1684625**	**-1684625**	**-1684625**	**-1684625**	**-1684625**

Table 3. Learning time of the proposed algorithms

		Relative to GES				
Network	GES	GES_G	GES_C	GES_{iC}	GES_{CG}	GES_{iCG}
ALARM	10.60	0.72	0.48	0.61	0.45	0.53
BARLEY	276.82	0.64	0.53	0.84	0.51	0.73
CHILD	0.10	0.84	0.89	1.25	0.79	1.43
HAILFINDER	-	*43.2	-	-	*29.3	*38.4
INSURANCE	6.64	0.67	0.60	0.77	0.47	0.52
MILDEW	209.56	0.20	0.81	0.81	0.08	0.12
PIGS	16762.8	0.61	0.06	0.07	0.06	0.08
Mean	5924.5	0.52	0.48	0.62	0.34	0.49

* Absolute results since GES was not able to finish.

Another fact to take into account is that only the algorithms that made a greedy search over the space of candidate neighbors are able to recover the HAILFINDER network. This is due to the fact that, when transforming it into its corresponding CPDAG, one of the variables has 17 neighbors. Hence, the exhaustive search cannot be carried out, as explained at the end of Section 2.2.

We can reach some important conclusions by taking a simple look to the performance results. Apart from the issues regarding the HAILFINDER network, the differences between the GES algorithm and the proposed algorithms are, in general, minimal. For instance, GES_{iC} obtains the same results as GES and GES_G and GES_{iCG} obtain the same results as GES in 5 networks of a total of 6. From these results we can conclude that our algorithms GES_{iC}, GES_G and GES_{iCG} are comparable to GES in terms of accuracy.

With respect to the complexity of the algorithms, the results are shown in Table 3 and Table 4. We show the number of score computations obtained on average for the five datasets and the execution time. The results of our proposed algorithms are reported relative to the ones obtained by GES. From this last results, we can conclude that our algorithms perform less computations and are therefore faster than GES. Thus, GES_G only needs to carry out, on average, 52%

Table 4. Number of score computations performed by the proposed algorithms

Network	GES	Relative to GES				
		GES_G	GES_C	GES_{iC}	GES_{CG}	GES_{iCG}
ALARM	5562	0.57	0.56	0.67	0.41	0.52
BARLEY	8757	0.48	0.38	0.49	0.33	0.45
CHILD	407	0.98	0.98	0.98	0.98	0.98
HAILFINDER	-	*5943	-	-	*3889	*5718
INSURANCE	3287	0.55	0.52	0.63	0.42	0.53
MILDEW	3561	0.59	0.49	0.65	0.42	0.58
PIGS	549143	0.68	0.41	0.63	0.41	0.63
Mean	81531.2	0.64	0.56	0.68	0.50	0.61

* Absolute results since GES was not able to finish.

of the computations required by GES, whereas GES_{iC} needs 62% and GES_{iCG} only 49%. In terms of time, GES_G takes, on average, 64% of the time taken by GES to learn the networks, whereas GES_{iC} takes 68% of that time and GES_{iCG} takes only 61% , being the biggest improvements achieved in the most complex datasets. It is also worth pointing out that, although results obtained by GES_C and GES_{CG} are a bit worse than GES in terms of score, reductions obtained in terms of number of computations and execution time are very significant.

5   Conclusions

In this paper we have presented three main variants of the original GES algorithm. The first one, GES_G, performs a greedy search in the space of candidate neighbors avoiding the need of carrying out an exhaustive search. The second one, GES_C, and its iterative version, GES_{iC}, are able to reduce the search space by constraining it during its execution. Finally, GES_{CG} and GES_{iCG} algorithms take the advantages of both approaches.

Moreover, apart from the definition of the algorithms, we also have proved that, under the faithfulness assumption, GES_G, GES_{iC} and GES_{iCG} are asymptotically optimal.

The experimental evaluation of our algorithms has been carried out by measuring the accuracy and the efficiency of the algorithms. In terms of accuracy, GES_G, GES_{iC} and GES_{iCG} are comparable to the results obtained with GES. However, regarding efficiency, our algorithms are faster and perform less computations of the score metric than GES.

Finally, it is important to remark on the fact that algorithms performing a greedy search (GES_G, GES_{CG} and GES_{iCG}) are able to work with networks that the other algorithms are unable.

References

1. Abramson, B., Brown, J., Edwards, W., Murphy, A., Winkler, R.L.: Hailfinder: A Bayesian system for forecasting severe weather. Int. J. Forecasting 12(1), 57–71 (1996)
2. Buntine, W.: Theory refinement on Bayesian networks. In: UAI 1991, pp. 52–60. Morgan Kaufmann Publishers Inc., San Francisco (1991)
3. Chickering, D.: Optimal structure identification with greedy search. J. Mach. Learn. Res. 3, 507–554 (2002)
4. Chickering, D.M., Geiger, D., Heckerman, D.: Learning Bayesian networks: Search methods and experimental results. In: Proc. AISTATS 1995, pp. 112–128 (1995)
5. Friedman, N., Nachman, I., Pe'er, D.: Learning Bayesian network structure from massive datasets: The "Sparse Candidate" algorithm. In: UAI 1999, pp. 206–215 (1999)
6. Gámez, J.A., Mateo, J.L., Puerta, J.M.: Learning Bayesian networks by hill climbing: efficient methods based on progressive restriction of the neighborhood. Data Min. Knowl. Disc. (2010), doi:10.1007/s10618-010-0178-6 (to appear)
7. Heckerman, D., Geiger, D., Chickering, D.M.: Learning Bayesian networks: The combination of knowledge and statistical data. Mach. Learn. 20(3), 197–243 (1995)
8. Neapolitan, R.: Learning Bayesian Networks. Prentice-Hall, Englewood Cliffs (2003)
9. Pearl, J.: Probabilistic Reasoning in Intelligent Systems: Networks of plausible inference. Morgan Kaufmann, San Francisco (1988)
10. Tsamardinos, I., Brown, L.E., Aliferis, C.F.: The max-min hill-climbing Bayesian network structure learning algorithm. Mach. Learn. 65(1), 31–78 (2006)

Extensions of Decision-Theoretic Troubleshooting: Cost Clusters and Precedence Constraints

Václav Lín*

Institute of Information Theory and Automation of the ASCR,
Pod Vodárenskou věží 4, CZ-182 08, Prague, Czech Republic
lin@utia.cas.cz

Abstract. In decision-theoretic troubleshooting [5,2], we try to find a cost efficient repair strategy for a malfunctioning device described by a formal model. The need to schedule repair actions under uncertainty has required the researchers to use an appropriate knowledge representation formalism, often a probabilistic one.

The troubleshooting problem has received considerable attention over the past two decades. Efficient solution algorithms have been found for some variants of the problem, whereas other variants have been proven *NP*-hard [5,2,4,17,16].

We show that two troubleshooting scenarios — *Troubleshooting with Postponed System Test* [9] and *Troubleshooting with Cost Clusters without Inside Information* [7] — are *NP*-hard. Also, we define a troubleshooting scenario with precedence restrictions on the repair actions. We show that it is *NP*-hard in general, but polynomial under some restrictions placed on the structure of the precedence relation. In the proofs, we use results originally achieved in the field of Scheduling. Such a connection has not been made in the Troubleshooting literature so far.

Keywords: Computational Complexity, Dynamic Programming, Decision-Theoretic Troubleshooting, Scheduling.

1 Introduction

Suppose a man-made device failed to work – the exact cause of the failure is unknown, and the possible steps to fix it are costly and not 100% reliable. Any attempt to resolve the problem may fail, but the incurred cost has to be paid in any case. Solving problems such as this one has lead to development of the field of decision-theoretic troubleshooting [5,2]. The need to decide under uncertainty has necessitated the use of an appropriate formalism. Bayesian networks have been adopted for their clear semantics and computational tractability. The troubleshooting problem is known to be polynomial in few special cases and *NP*-hard

---

* This work was supported by the Ministry of Education of the Czech Republic through grant 1M0572 and by the Czech Science Foundation through grant ICC/08/E010.

W. Liu (Ed.): ECSQARU 2011, LNAI 6717, pp. 206–216, 2011.

in others [5,2,4,17,16]. Decision-theoretic troubleshooting has been successfully applied in the area of printer diagnosis and maintenance [2,13].

In this paper, we build on earlier work published in [4,7,9] and provide new results on computational complexity of the problems studied in the cited papers. In the first part – Section 2 – we give an overview of the troubleshooting scenarios studied in earlier literature. Specifically, Section 2.1 describes a very basic troubleshooting scenario taken from [5,2,4]. In the same Section, we define a novel scenario by adding a precedence relation on the troubleshooting actions. In Section 2.2, we review a generalization of basic troubleshooting — *Troubleshooting with Postponed System Test* – studied recently in [9], and describe a novel Dynamic Programming solution. In Section 2.3 we introduce a more general scenario of *Troubleshooting with Cost Clusters without Inside Information*, originally defined in paper [7].

The main results of the paper are found in Section 3. In Section 3.2, we show that troubleshooting with a postponed system test is *NP*-hard. As a corollary, troubleshooting with cost clusters without inside information is shown to be *NP*-hard in the same Section. In Section 3.3, we turn to troubleshooting with precedence constraints and show that it is *NP*-hard, but solvable in polynomial time when the precedence relation has a structure of series parallel directed graph [6,15]. In the *NP*-hardness proofs, we use results achieved originally in the field of Scheduling. We consider this to be one of the contributions of the paper, since such a connection has not been made in the Troubleshooting literature so far. In Section 4, we sum up the results and conclude the paper by suggesting directions for future research.

2 Troubleshooting Scenarios

Before proceeding with the formal definitions, we will illustrate the troubleshooting scenarios on a simple example inspired by [7,17].

Imagine you are printing a report but the colors come out very light. You have several options to choose from: restart the printer, change the print settings, reseat the toner cartridge or get a new cartridge altogether. These actions differ both in their difficulty and in the likelihood of fixing the print problem. You need to decide how to sequence the available repair actions so that the "expected difficulty level" of the repair is as low as possible. This kind of problem is solved in the basic troubleshooting scenario, described in Section 2.1.

Continuing with our print example, imagine that the printing itself is very expensive – you have to think twice before performing a test print to check that the repair actions have actually helped. Troubleshooting problems such as this one are defined in Section 2.2.

To make the example yet more complicated, assume that you are troubleshooting a complex industrial printer and some of the repair actions are only available after disassembling parts of the machine – and different actions may require different parts to be disassembled. To perform a test print, the machine has to be reassembled. Section 2.3 covers problems of this kind.

2.1 Basic Troubleshooting

The *Basic Troubleshooting* problem is given by

- a set $\mathcal{F} = \{F_1, \ldots, F_m\}$ of possible faults,
- a set $\mathcal{A} = \{A_1, \ldots, A_n\}$, $n \geq m$, of available repair steps,
- a probabilistic model $P(\mathcal{F} \cup \mathcal{A})$ describing interactions between the elements of $\mathcal{A}$ and $\mathcal{F}$.

Each action A_i bears a constant cost $c(A_i)$ and can either fail ($A_i = 0$) or fix the fault ($A_i = 1$). The following assumptions are made:

- There is exactly one fault present in the modeled system.
- Each action addresses exactly one fault.
- The model $P(\mathcal{F} \cup \mathcal{A})$ satisfies conditional independence assumptions encoded by the Bayesian network shown in Figure 1. Specifically, the actions are conditionally independent given the faults.

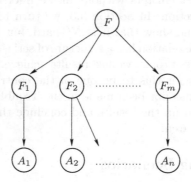

Fig. 1. Bayesian network encoding conditional independence of actions given faults. F is the fault variable with possible values $f_1, \ldots, f_m$. Variables $F_1, \ldots, F_m$ are Boolean indicators with $P(F_i = 1 | F = f_i) = 1$. Variables $A_1, \ldots, A_n$ are also Boolean. Each A_j has exactly one parent in the graph.

We assume that no new faults are introduced during the troubleshooting session, and the result of any action stays the same during a session. These two last assumptions are only implicit in most of the papers on troubleshooting. They are explicitly stated only in more recent papers, such as [9].

Let $\pi = \{\pi(1), \ldots, \pi(n)\}$ denote a permutation of indices $1, \ldots, n$; then the *troubleshooting strategy* is a sequence $A_{\pi(1)}, \ldots, A_{\pi(n)}$ of actions performed until the fault is fixed or all actions are exhausted. Thus, the action $A_{\pi(i)}$ will be performed only if all the preceding actions fail, that is, $A_j = 0$ for $j = \pi(1), \ldots, \pi(i-1)$. To solve the troubleshooting problem, we have to find a repair strategy with the lowest *Expected Cost of Repair*:

$$ECR(A_{\pi(1)}, \cdots, A_{\pi(n)}) = \sum_{i=1}^{n} c(A_{\pi(i)}) \cdot P\Big(\bigwedge_{j<i} \{A_{\pi(j)} = 0\}\Big)$$

The following proposition describes an easy method of finding the optimal troubleshooting sequence and computing its *ECR*.

Proposition 1 (Jensen et al., 2001 [4]). *Under the assumptions of*

- *single fault,*
- *each action addressing exactly one fault,*
- *conditional independence of actions given the faults,*

the optimal troubleshooting sequence is found in $O(n \cdot \log n)$ time by ordering the actions so that ratio values $P(A_j = 1)/c(A_j)$ are decreasing where

$$P(A_j = 1) = \sum_i P(A_j = 1 | F = f_i) \cdot P(F = f_i).$$

Further, the ECR can be computed as

$$ECR(A_{\pi(1)}, \cdots, A_{\pi(n)}) = \sum_{i=1}^{n} c(A_{\pi(i)}) \cdot \Big(1 - \sum_{j<i} P(A_{\pi(j)} = 1)\Big).$$

Proof. See Proposition 1, Proposition 2 and Theorem 1 in [4]. The $O(n \cdot \log n)$ time requirement is given by the complexity of sorting (see, e.g., [11]).   □

The assumptions of Proposition 1 are quite restrictive; however, weakening them often yields an *NP*-hard scenario as shown in papers [17,16].

The single fault assumption is relaxed in paper [14], where *multiple faults* are considered. However, it is assumed that the faults as well as actions are independent. The optimal sequence is found by ordering the actions so that the ratio values

$$\frac{P(A_j = 1)}{c(A_j) \cdot (1 - P(A_j = 1))}$$

are decreasing.

Troubleshooting with Precedence Constraints. In some applications, there may be restrictions imposed on the order of troubleshooting actions – some of the actions become available only after performing some other actions. A restriction on the order of actions does not typically correspond to the probabilistic dependence of actions. For an example of such an application, see Section 4.1 in paper [4].

Formally, we assume that there is a precedence relation described by an acyclic directed graph G with vertices labeled by the actions from $\mathcal{A}$. A troubleshooting sequence $A_{\pi(1)}, \cdots, A_{\pi(n)}$ is valid only if $A_{\pi(j)}$ is not a predecessor of $A_{\pi(i)}$ in G for all $i < j$. We will show in Section 3.3 that *Basic Troubleshooting with Precedence Constraints* is *NP*-hard for a general acyclic directed graph G, but is solvable in polynomial time for a wide class of *series parallel* graphs.

2.2 Troubleshooting with Postponed System Test

Following [9], we add the assumption that, after performing a troubleshooting action, we do not know whether the action has solved the problem. We have to perform a system test, requiring additional cost c_D, to find out whether the problem has been fixed. The need to schedule system tests complicates construction of the optimal sequence – when the system test is postponed too much, we risk performing needless repair actions; when we perform the test too early to check the system state, we risk missing a necessary repair action.

To solve the troubleshooting problem, we construct an *ordered partition* $\mathcal{A}_1$, $\ldots, \mathcal{A}_k$ of the set $\mathcal{A}$.[1] Actions of the sets $\mathcal{A}_1, \mathcal{A}_2, \ldots$ are performed sequentially. After performing all the actions of the set $\mathcal{A}_j$ $(j = 1, 2, \ldots)$, we perform the system test to check whether the actions contained in $\mathcal{A}_j$ have fixed the problem. The cost of $\mathcal{A}_j$ including the system test is

$$c(\mathcal{A}_j) = c_D + \sum_{A \in \mathcal{A}_j} c(A).$$

We seek an ordered partition minimimizing the *ECR*:

$$ECR(\mathcal{A}_1, \ldots, \mathcal{A}_k) = \sum_{i=1}^{k} c(\mathcal{A}_i) \cdot P\big(\bigwedge_{j<i, A \in \mathcal{A}_j} \{A = 0\}\big). \tag{1}$$

We shall write $P(\mathcal{A}_j = 1)$ as an abbreviation for $P\big(\bigvee_{A \in \mathcal{A}_j} \{A = 1\}\big)$. The following proposition simplifies computation of the *ECR*.

Proposition 2 (Ottosen and Jensen, 2010 [4]). *Under the assumptions of Proposition 1, the ECR can be computed as*

$$ECR(\mathcal{A}_1, \ldots, \mathcal{A}_k) = \sum_{i=1}^{k} c(\mathcal{A}_i) \cdot \big(1 - \sum_{j<i} P(\mathcal{A}_j = 1)\big),$$

where $P(\mathcal{A}_j = 1) = \sum_{A \in \mathcal{A}_j} P(A = 1)$.

Dynamic Programming. In [9], the authors give $\Theta(n^3)$ heuristics for *Troubleshooting with Postponed System Test* and an $\Theta(n^3 \cdot n!)$ exhaustive search algorithm. In this paragraph, we will show that by using Dynamic Programming, the time requirements of the exhaustive search can be traded for memory requirements.[2] We will use a recursive version of the definition of *ECR*, equivalent to the one given by Equation 1.

Definition 1 (Conditional ECR). *Let $\mathcal{A}$ be the set of available atomic actions and let $\mathcal{A}_1, \ldots, \mathcal{A}_k$ be an ordered partition of $\mathcal{A}$. For $1 \leq i \leq k$, denote*

$$\epsilon^i = \bigvee_{j \leq i, A \in \mathcal{A}_j} \{A = 0\},$$

---

[1] That is, $\mathcal{A} = \bigcup_{j=1}^{k} \mathcal{A}_j$, and $\forall_{i \neq j} \mathcal{A}_i \cap \mathcal{A}_i = \emptyset$.

[2] Dynamic Programming has already been used for troubleshooting in [17].

and put $\epsilon^0 = \emptyset$. For $1 \leq i \leq k$, define Conditional Expected Cost of Repair *as*

$$ECR(\mathcal{A}_i, ..., \mathcal{A}_k | \epsilon^{i-1}) = c(\mathcal{A}_i) + P(\mathcal{A}_i = 0 | \epsilon^{i-1}) \cdot ECR(\mathcal{A}_{i+1}, ..., \mathcal{A}_k | \epsilon^i).$$

and put $ECR(\emptyset | \epsilon^k) = 0$.

Proposition 3 (Bellman Principle). *Ordered partition $\mathcal{A}_1, \ldots, \mathcal{A}_k$ is optimal if and only if each subsequence $\mathcal{A}_i, \ldots, \mathcal{A}_k$, $1 \leq i \leq k$, is optimal with respect to ϵ^{i-1}, i.e., there is no other ordered partition $\mathbf{s}$ defined on $\cup_{j=i}^k \mathcal{A}_j$ such that*

$$ECR(\mathbf{s} | \epsilon^{i-1}) < ECR(\mathcal{A}_i, \ldots, \mathcal{A}_k | \epsilon^{i-1}).$$

However trivial, we include proof of the "if" direction.

Proof. Assume that $\mathcal{A}_1, \ldots, \mathcal{A}_k$ has a subsequence $\mathcal{A}_i, \ldots, \mathcal{A}_k$ which is not optimal with respect to ϵ^{i-1}. In that case there exists another sequence $\mathbf{s}$, defined on $\cup_{j=i}^k \mathcal{A}_j$, optimal with respect to ϵ^{i-1}. Concatenated sequence $\mathcal{A}_1, \ldots, \mathcal{A}_{i-1}, \mathbf{s}$ has lower ECR than the original ordered partition. □

The Dynamic Programming algorithm works in a bottom-up fashion, constructing candidate ordered partitions from the last subset. In each round, candidate subsequences that are not conditionally optimal are pruned. Correctness of the Dynamic Programming algorithm follows from Proposition 3. At the i-th round of the algorithm, 2^{n-i+1} candidates are generated, the time requirements are therefore $\Theta(2^n + 2^{n-1} + 2^{n-2} + \ldots) = \Theta(2^{n+1})$. The space requirements are dominated by the requirements of the first round, that is $\Theta(2^n)$.

2.3   Troubleshooting with Cost Clusters without Inside Information

The problem of *Troubleshooting with Postponed System Test* is a special case of *Troubleshooting with Cost Clusters without Inside Information* [7]. In the latter scenario, we assume the set $\mathcal{A}$ of atomic actions is partitioned into a family of 'cost clusters' $\{\mathcal{C}_l\}$. To access an action within the cost cluster, additional cost has to be paid for 'opening' the cluster. After opening the cluster, say $\mathcal{C}_1$, all the actions $A \in \mathcal{C}_1$ are available and actions from other clusters are not available. To access an action in a different cluster, $\mathcal{C}_1$ has to be closed and its actions are not available anymore. Furthermore, it is assumed that when any cluster is open, information about the system state is not available – the cluster has to be closed to see whether the actions taken have fixed the fault.

Solving the troubleshooting problem requires construction of an ordered partition $\mathcal{A}_1, \ldots, \mathcal{A}_k$ of $\mathcal{A}$, where each $\mathcal{A}_j$ is a subset of some $\mathcal{C} \in \{\mathcal{C}_l\}$. For $\mathcal{A}_j \subseteq \mathcal{C}_l$, denote by $c_{\mathcal{C}(\mathcal{A}_j)}$ the cost of opening the cluster $\mathcal{C}_l$. The cost of $\mathcal{A}_j$ including the cluster cost is

$$c(\mathcal{A}_j) = c_{\mathcal{C}(\mathcal{A}_j)} + \sum_{A \in \mathcal{A}_j} c(A).$$

The ECR of troubleshooting sequence is computed as in Proposition 2.

The authors of [7] provide a heuristic algorithm for finding a suboptimal troubleshooting sequence. A related scenario, solvable in polynomial time, is studied in [8].

3   Complexity Results

We shall prove *NP*-hardness of the troubleshooting scenarios introduced in Section 2 by reducing suitable scheduling problems[3]. Moreover, we will see that the scheduling problems are equivalent to the troubleshooting scenarios in the sense that the polynomial-time reductions work both ways. Therefore, algorithms developed for the scheduling problems can be used for the troubleshooting problems without a loss of efficiency.

3.1   Reduction

We will use variants of *Single Machine Scheduling with Weighted Completion Time*. The problem is formulated as follows. There are n jobs J_i to be processed on a single machine. Each job is given with a processing time $p_i > 0$ and weight $w_i \geq 0$. We assume that processing starts at time 0 and there is no idle time between consecutive jobs. Since the processing times p_i are known and fixed, the completion time C_i of each job J_i is well determined for any given job sequence. The objective is to find a feasible sequence minimizing the *weighted completion time* $\sum_i w_i \cdot C_i$.

Single Machine Scheduling with Weighted Completion Time can easily be reduced to *Basic Troubleshooting*. Identify jobs J_i with actions A_i and put

- $p_i \longrightarrow c(A_i)$,
- $w_i / \sum_i w_i \longrightarrow P(A_i = 1)$.

The scheduling objective function can be written

$$\sum_{i=1}^{n} w_i \cdot C_i = \sum_{i=1}^{n} w_i \cdot \sum_{j \leq i} p_i$$

$$= \sum_{i=1}^{n} p_i \cdot \sum_{j \geq i} w_j. \tag{2}$$

Consider the troubleshooting problem. Assuming $P(\bigvee_{A \in \mathcal{A}} \{A = 1\}) = 1$ under the conditions of Proposition 1, we use Proposition 1 and rewrite the definition of *ECR*:

$$ECR(A_1, \ldots, A_n) = \sum_{i=1}^{n} c(A_i) \cdot \left(1 - \sum_{j < i} P(A_j = 1)\right)$$

$$= \sum_{i=1}^{n} c(A_i) \cdot \sum_{j \geq i} P(A_j = 1). \tag{3}$$

It is clear that Equation 3 is minimized whenever Equation 2 is minimized.   □

In analogy to Proposition 1, the *Single Machine Scheduling with Weighted Completion Time* problem can be solved by sequencing the jobs in non-increasing order of the ratios w_i/p_i. This result can be traced back to a 1950's paper by Smith [12].

---

[3] See [3] for an overview of the field.

3.2 Troubleshooting with Cost Clusters without Inside Information

We reduce *Single machine s-batching with weighted completion time* [1,3]. As above, there are n jobs given with processing time p_i and weight w_i. The jobs are scheduled in *batches* on a single machine. A batch is a set of jobs which are processed jointly. Processing time of a batch equals the sum of processing times of its jobs plus a *batch setup time s*. *Completion time C_i* of a job coincides with the completion time of the last scheduled job in its batch (completion times of all jobs in a batch are therefore equal). The task is to find a sequence of jobs and partition it into batches such that we minimize $\sum_{i=1}^{n} w_i \cdot C_i$. We sum up properties of the batching problem in a proposition.

Proposition 4 (Albers and Brucker, 1993 [1]). *Single machine s-batching with weighted completion time is NP-hard. Given a fixed sequence of jobs, the split into batches can be done in $O(n)$ time. When $w_i = 1$ or $p_i = p$ for all i, the problem becomes solvable in $O(n \log n)$ time.*

Proposition 5. *Troubleshooting with Postponed System Test is NP-hard, even under the assumptions of Proposition 1.*

Proof. We will use a description of solutions of the batching problem taken from [3]. Consider a fixed but arbitrary job sequence $J_1, \ldots, J_n$. Denote the batch setups by S. Then the solution takes on the form

$$S, J_{\lambda(1)}, \ldots J_{\lambda(2)-1}, S, J_{\lambda(2)}, \ldots, J_{\lambda(k)-1}, S, J_{\lambda(k)}, \ldots, J_n$$

where k is the number of batches, $\lambda(j)$ is the starting index of the j-th batch, and

$$1 = \lambda(1) < \lambda(2) < \ldots < \lambda(k) \leq n$$

The processing time of the j-th batch is

$$P_j = s + \sum_{\ell = \lambda(j)}^{\lambda(j+1)-1} p_\ell.$$

The objective function can now be written as

$$\sum_{i=1}^{n} w_i \cdot C_i = \sum_{j=1}^{k} P_j \cdot \sum_{\ell = \lambda(j)}^{n} w_\ell \tag{4}$$

We proceed with the reduction as in the beginning of Section 3.1. Using Proposition 2 and assuming $P(\bigvee_{A \in \mathcal{A}} \{A = 1\}) = 1$, we rewrite

$$ECR(\mathcal{A}_1, \ldots, \mathcal{A}_k) = \sum_{j=1}^{k} c(\mathcal{A}_i) \cdot \sum_{\ell \geq i} P(\mathcal{A}_\ell = 1). \tag{5}$$

The correspondence of Equations 5 and 4 is obvious.   □

We can also easily perform the reduction in the opposite direction. Therefore, Proposition 4 applies to *Troubleshooting with Postponed System Test* (under the assumptions of single fault, and actions conditionally independent given faults). In particular, the $O(n)$ bound on partitioning a fixed sequence of actions is an improvement over $\Theta(n^3)$ given in [9].

Corollary 1 (of Proposition 5). *Troubleshooting with Cost Clusters without Inside Information is* NP-*hard, even under the assumptions of Proposition 1.*

Proof. Consider a troubleshooting problem where all the actions belong to a single cost cluster C_1 with the cost of opening C_1 being c_D. This problem is equivalent to *Troubleshooting with Postponed System Test.*   □

Remark 1. The *decision variants* of all the troubleshooting scenarios studied in this paper clearly belong to *NP* – a nondeterministic procedure can guess a troubleshooting sequence and then check in polynomial time whether the *ECR* is lower than a predefined constant. Therefore, by Proposition 5 and Corollaries 1 and 2, the decision variants of the respective troubleshooting scenarios are *NP*-complete.

3.3   Troubleshooting with Precedence Constraints

We now introduce *Single Machine Scheduling with Weighted Completion Time and Precedence Constraints* [6]. The problem is the same as *Single Machine Scheduling with Weighted Completion Time*, with an additional requirement that the sequencing of the jobs has to be consistent with precedence constraints imposed by a given acyclic directed graph $G = (V, E)$. Each vertex $i \in V$ is identified with a job. Job J_i is to precede job J_j if there is a directed path from i to j in G.

Proposition 6 (Lawler, 1978 [6]). *Single Machine Scheduling with Weighted Completion Time and Precedence Constraints is* NP-*complete, even if all* $w_i = 1$ *or all* $p_i = 1$.

Corollary 2. *Basic Troubleshooting with Precedence Constraints is* NP-*hard, even under the assumptions of Proposition 1.*

Proof. Use the reduction from Section 3.1.   □

Next, we define a class of series parallel directed graphs for which *Single Machine Scheduling with Weighted Completion Time and Precedence Constraints* is known to be polynomial. This class subsumes chains and rooted trees. As such, it is quite useful for applications.

Definition 2 (*MSP – Minimal Series Parallel Graph*, [15]). *The graph consisting of a single vertex and no edges is MSP.*
If directed graphs $G_1 = (V_1, E_1)$ *and* $G_2 = (V_2, E_2)$ *are MSPs, so is either of the directed graphs constructed by the following operations:*

- Parallel composition: $G = (V_1 \cup V_2, E_1 \cup E_2)$.
- Series composition: $G = (V_1 \cup V_2, E_1 \cup E_2 \cup N_1 \times R_2)$. Here N_1 is the set of sinks of G_1 (i.e., vertices without successors), and R_2 is the set of sources of G_2 (i.e., vertices without predecessors).

Recall the concept of *transitive closure* – given a directed graph $G = (V, E)$, its transitive closure $G_T = (V, E_T)$ is obtained by adding a directed edge (u, v) for all u and v such that there is a path from u to v in G and $(u, v) \notin E$. A *transitive reduction* of $G = (V, E)$ is a minimal graph G_R defined on V such that the transitive closures of G and G_R are the same.

Definition 3 (*GSP – General Series Parallel Graph*, [15]). *A directed graph is GSP if its transitive reduction is an MSP.*

Proposition 7 (Lawler, 1978 [6]). *Single Machine Scheduling with Weighted Completion Time and Precedence Constraints is solvable in $O(n \cdot \log n)$ time when the precedence graph G is a GSP.*

Reversing the reduction, we get the following easy consequence.

Corollary 3. *Basic Troubleshooting with Precedence Constraints is solvable in $O(n \cdot \log n)$ time under the following conditions:*

- *all the assumptions of Proposition 1 are satisfied,*
- $P\left(\vee_{A \in \mathcal{A}} \{A = 1\} \right) = 1$,
- *the precedence graph is a GSP.*

4   Conclusions and Future Research

We have established a link to the well developed field of Scheduling, opening the possibility of applying results of decades of research in Scheduling to Troubleshooting. We have reduced scheduling problems to derive proofs of *NP*-hardness for three troubleshooting scenarios. The scenario of *Basic Troubleshooting with Precedence Constraints* is novel. We believe this scenario is useful in practice. Moreover, it is polynomial for a wide class of graphs encoding the precedence relation.

An interesting problem for future research is that of *approximability* [10] of troubleshooting problems: for some special cases there might exist approximation algorithms with performance guarantees, whereas for others, finding such an approximation would amount to proving $P = NP$.

Since most realistic troubleshooting scenarios are *NP*-hard, it is worthwhile to study heuristic solution algorithms [17,7,9] and identify worst-case conditions, under which they perform badly. To benchmark the heuristic algorithms, we can use Dynamic Programming introduced in Section 2.2.

Acknowledgments. I would like to thank Thorsten J. Ottosen and Jiří Vomlel for valuable discussions over the subject matter of the paper. I also thank the anonymous reviewers for their comments.

References

1. Albers, S., Brucker, P.: The Complexity of One-Machine Batching Problems. Discrete Applied Mathematics 47, 87–107 (1993)
2. Breese, J.S., Heckerman, D.: Decision-Theoretic Troubleshooting: A Framework for Repair and Experiment. In: Proceedings of Twelfth Conference on Uncertainty in Artificial Intelligence, pp. 124–132. Morgan Kaufmann, San Francisco (1996)
3. Brucker, P.: Scheduling Algorithms, 3rd edn. Springer, Heidelberg (2001)
4. Jensen, F.V., Kjærulff, U., Kristiansen, B., Langseth, H., Skaanning, C., Vomlel, J., Vomlelová, M.: The SACSO Methodology for Troubleshooting Complex Systems. Artificial Intelligence for Engineering Design, Analysis and Manufacturing 15, 321–333 (2001)
5. Kalagnanam, J., Henrion, M.: A Comparison of Decision Analysis and Expert Rules for Sequential Diagnosis. In: Proceedings of the Fourth Annual Conference on Uncertainty in Artificial Intelligence (UAI 1988), pp. 271–282. North-Holland, Amsterdam (1990)
6. Lawler, E.L.: Sequencing Jobs to Minimize Total Weighted Completion Time Subject to Precedence Constraints. Annals of Discrete Mathematics 2, 75–90 (1978)
7. Langseth, H., Jensen, F.V.: Heuristics for Two Extensions of Basic Troubleshooting. In: Proceedings of Seventh Scandinavian Conference on Artificial Intelligence, SCAI 2001, pp. 80–89. IOS Press, Amsterdam (2001)
8. Ottosen, T.J., Jensen, F.V.: The Cost of Troubleshooting Cost Clusters with Inside Information. In: Proceedings of 26th Conference on Uncertainty in Artificial Intelligence (UAI 2010), pp. 409–416. AUAI Press (2010)
9. Ottosen, T.J., Jensen, F.V.: When to Test? Troubleshooting with Postponed System Test. Technical Report 10-001, Department of Computer Science, Aalborg University, Denmark (2010)
10. Papadimitriou, C.H.: Computational complexity. Addison-Wesley Publishing Company, Reading (1994)
11. Sedgewick, R.: Algorithms in C. Addison-Wesley Publishing Company, Reading (1998)
12. Smith, W.E.: Various Optimizers for Single-Stage Production. Naval Research Logistics Quarterly 3, 59–66 (1956)
13. Skaanning, C., Jensen, F.W., Kjærulff, U.: Printer Troubleshooting Using Bayesian Networks. In: IEA/AIE 2000 Proceedings of the 13th International Conference on Industrial and Engineering Applications of Artificial Intelligence and Expert Systems, pp. 367–379. Springer, Heidelberg (2000)
14. Srinivas, S.: A Polynomial Algorithm for Computing the Optimal Repair Strategy in a System with Independent Component failures. In: Proceedings of Eleventh Conference on Uncertainty in Artificial Intelligence, pp. 515–552. Morgan Kaufmann, San Francisco (1995)
15. Valdes, J., Tarjan, R.E., Lawler, E.L.: The Recognition of Series Parallel Digraphs. In: STOC 1979 Proceedings of the Eleventh Annual ACM Symposium on Theory of Computing, pp. 1–12. ACM, New York (1979)
16. Vomlelová, M.: Complexity of Decision-Theoretic Troubleshooting. International Journal of Intelligent Systems 18, 267–277 (2003)
17. Vomlelová, M., Vomlel, J.: Troubleshooting: NP-hardness and Solution Methods. Soft Computing Journal 7(5), 357–368 (2003)

Locally Averaged Bayesian Dirichlet Metrics

Andrés Cano, Manuel Gómez-Olmedo, Andrés R. Masegosa, and Serafín Moral

Department of Computer Science and Artificial Intelligence,
University of Granada, Spain
{acu,mgomez,andrew,smc}@decsai.ugr.es

Abstract. The marginal likelihood of the data computed using Bayesian score metrics is at the core of *score+search* methods when learning Bayesian networks from data. However, common formulations of those Bayesian score metrics depend of free parameters which are hard to asses. Recent theoretical and experimental works have also shown as the commonly employed BDeu score metric is strongly biased by the particular assignments of its free parameter known as *the equivalent sample size* and, also, as an optimal selection of this parameter depends of the underlying distribution. This sensibility causes that wrong choices of this parameter lead to inferred models which do not properly represent the distribution generating the data even with large sample sizes. To overcome this issue we introduce here an approach which tries to marginalize this free parameter with a simple averaging method. As experimentally shown, this approach robustly performs as well as an optimum selection of this parameter while it prevents from the choice of wrong settings for this widely applied Bayesian score metric.

1 Introduction

The so-called Bayesian scoring metrics are based on the computation of the marginal likelihood of the data given the graph structure of a Bayesian network (BN) [6]. They are one of the most used scoring functions when learning BNs from data [2,4]. To compute this marginal likelihood for multinomial data, it is assumed a Dirichlet prior over the parameters of the BN. In the case of the widely applied BDeu metric [4], these Dirichlet priors depends of a meta-parameter known as the *equivalent sample size* (ESS). Roughly speaking, this meta-parameter captures the strength of our prior belief in the uniformity of the distribution of the parameters of the network.

In an empirical evaluation on 20 UCI data sets, a recent work [8] has shown that the chosen ESS value of the BDeu score strongly affects the selection of the *maximum a posteriori* (MAP) model . They found as high (low) ESS values used to retrieve very dense(sparse) BN models (in some data sets, the number of edges monotonically increased from an empty network to a fully connected BN model). This same sensitivity was also found in simple independence assessments between two binary variables [5,1]. These works showed as Type I and Type II errors of the hypothesis tests made by Bayesian metrics are affected when changing the value of the ESS.

W. Liu (Ed.): ECSQARU 2011, LNAI 6717, pp. 217–228, 2011.

This sensitivity of the BDeu metric to the ESS has been theoretically analyzed for very large or very small values of this parameter in several works [10,9,11]. They found that BDeu score has an intrinsic tendency to favor either the presence or the absence of an edge between two variables depending of the particular ESS value. Even more, for large ESS values, this tendency was found to be independent of the particular probabilistic dependency between the variables. Specifically, Steck [9] showed as BDeu can predict dependency among two independent random variables if they have very skewed marginals. A major consequence of this sensitivity of Bayesian scores is that if they are employed in knowledge discovery tasks, they can provide very little reliable inferences. Let us imagine which is the confident in the inferred knowledge if we find that the different conditional independencies which are discovered in the data strongly depends of a free parameter which, although it is supposed to represent our prior beliefs, is extremely complex to assess in practical settings.

A possible solution, firstly suggested in [8], for the sensitivity of BDeu metric to this parameter is to use a Bayesian approach: assume a prior distribution on the ESS parameter and to marginalize it out in the score value. As no closed form solution is known to compute the integral required to perform the marginalization, a uniform over the ESS parameter was assumed and the integral was approximated by a simple averaging operation. However, in that work, there was not given any evidence about if this integrating approach retrieve an optimal approximation either in terms of prediction capacity of unseen data or in terms of correct inference of the underlying structure generating the data. The only showed as this integration approach retrieves the same BN model than the one inferred using some single ESS values.

This paper is devoted to analyze the performance of these score metrics in which the ESS parameter is marginalized. We justify that the averaging approach pursed in [8] is not an optimal strategy to eliminate the effect of this parameter in Bayesian metrics. In that way, we introduce a novel approach to marginalize this free parameter which is more powerful and, in consequence, able to make better inferences when the parameter space of the model generating the data is quite complex. In a experimental evaluation, we show as this strategy is quite robust and able to remove the sensitivity of this Bayesian metric to this free parameter. In that way, this approach prevents the elicitation of spurious conditional independencies relationships due to wrong assessments of the ESS and can help to make the *score+search* methods for learning BN from data more robust and usable approaches for knowledge discovery tasks.

The paper is organized as follows. In Section 2 we introduce the formulation of a Bayesian score metric to learn the graph structure from a data set. In Section 3 it is motivated and detailed our new proposal of locally averaged Bayesian metrics. The experimental evaluation of these proposals is depicted in Section 4. And finally, Section 5 contains the main conclusions and future works.

2   Bayesian Score Metrics

Let us assume we are given a vector of n random variables $\mathbf{X} = (X_1, ..., X_n)$ each of which taking values in some finite domain $Val(X_i)$. A BN is defined by a directed acyclic graph, denote as G, which represents the dependency structure among the variables in the BN. More precisely, this graph G is specified by means of a vector with the parents sets, $\Pi_i \subset \mathbf{X}$ (those variables with an edge pointing to X_i), of each variable: $G = (\Pi_1, ..., \Pi_n)$. The definition of a BN model is complete with a numerical vector, denoted as Φ, which contains the parameters of the conditional probability distributions encoded in this graph G: ϕ_{ij} is a vector of length $|Val(X_i)|$ ($|\cdot|$ is the cardinality operator) associated to the conditional multinomial distribution of $P(X_i|\Pi_i = j)$, where $\Pi_i = j$ denotes the jth value combination of the variables in Π_i. We also denote as $|Val(\Pi_i)|$ to the number of all these possible combinations.

Let us also assume we are given a fully observed multinomial data set D. To compute the marginal likelihood of the data given the graph structure, $P(D|G) = \int P(D|G, \Phi)P(\Phi|G)d\Phi$, the most common settings [4] defines a prior Dirichlet distribution for each parameter ϕ_{ij} with parameter vector α, $\phi_{ij} \sim Dir(\alpha)$. They also assume a set of parameter independence assumptions in order to factorize the joint probabilities and make feasible the computation of the multidimensional integral.

In that way, the marginal likelihood of data given a graph structure and a vector of Dirichlet parameters, α, has the following well-known close-form equation:

$$P(D|G) = \prod_i^n \prod_{j=1}^{|Val(\Pi_i)|} \frac{\Gamma(\alpha_{ij})}{\Gamma(\alpha_{ij} + N_{ij})} \prod_{k=1}^{|Val(X_i)|} \frac{\Gamma(\alpha_{ijk} + N_{ijk})}{\Gamma(\alpha_{ijk})} \qquad (1)$$

where N_{ijk} are the number of data instances in D consistent with j-th assignment of Π_i and $X_i = k$, while $N_{ij} = \sum_k N_{ijk}$ and $\alpha_{ij} = \sum_k \alpha_{ijk}$. In the case of the Bayesian Dirichlet equivalent metric or BDeu metric these α_{ijk} are set to $\alpha_{ijk} = \frac{S}{|Val(\Pi_i)||Val(X_i)|}$, where S is the aforementioned *equivalent sample size*. The relevancy of these settings relies on the following property of this Bayesian metric known as *likelihood equivalence*: if two different BN models encode the same conditional independencies, the score metric assigns them the same score value.

Finally, with the definition of a modular prior distribution for the graph structures, $P(G) = \prod_i P(\Pi_i)$, we fully specify the *Bayesian score metric* of a graph as a product of local score functions as follows:

$$P(G|D) \propto \prod_i score(X_i, \Pi_i|D) \qquad (2)$$

where $score(X_i, \Pi_i|D)$ accounts for the product of the prior $P(G)$ and the marginal likelihood, Equation (1), corresponding to the variable X_i (usually the logarithm of this value is computed). This formulation satisfies the *local decomposition property* which is very useful in the *score+search* learning methods

[4] because local changes (i.e. adding/removing an edge) can be evaluated just recomputing the local score, $score(X_i, \Pi_i | D)$, of the involved variables.

In order to account for the problem of "multiplicity correction" [7] (i.e. if the number of candidate parents for a variable X_i grows, the probability of edge inclusion should be decreased in order to control the number of false positive edges) we employ the following prior distribution $P(\Pi_i) \propto \binom{i}{|\Pi_i|}^{-1}$.

3   Averaged Bayesian Dirichlet Metrics

3.1   Motivation

As previously detailed, BDeu metric assumes a Dirichlet priors where the α_{ijk} values are made exponentially small either with the size of the parent set or with the cardinality of the involved variables. When small α_{ijk} values are used, it is assumed that ϕ_{ij} will be located in the borders of the $|Val(X_i)|$-simplex. That is to say, the vector ϕ_{ij} will contain very asymmetrical or extreme probabilities. The problem is that the smaller the α_{ijk} values, the stronger this prior belief. Then, if S is not very high and we are dealing with random variables with a high number of values or a high number of parents, it will be implicitly assumed that the conditional probability distributions for this variable are very skewed. But if this is not the case, the BDeu metric will not support these probabilistic relationships and will over-regularize the model leaving many edges unrecovered, as it has been theoretically and experimentally shown [10,9].

In those cases it could be worth to choose higher S values in order to avoid that problem, but we also have to be very careful because high S values can make BDeu metric to recover spurious edges between unconditionally independent variables if they have very skewed marginal distributions, as pointed out in [9]. The following example illustrates this trade-off and shows as the selection of an optimal S is unpractical in many learning situations.

Example 1. Let us assume we have a BN model with three multinomial variables: X (ternary); Y (binary) and Z (binary); only one edge, $Z \to X$; and the following (un)conditional probabilities: $P(Z = 0) = 0.95$, $P(Y = 0) = 0.95$, $P(X|Z = 0) = (0.4, 0.4, 0.2)$ and $P(X|Z = 1) = (0.2, 0.4, 0.4)$. As can be seen, the marginal distributions of Z and Y are very skewed while the conditional $P(X|Z)$ are close to the uniform distribution. We then generate by means of logic sampling one thousands data samples from this BN model and we evaluate what the BDeu metric *says* about the presence/absence of the edges $Z \to X$ and $Z \to Y$ using different S values. For that purpose, we just compare the scores of the models with and without any of these two edges and we select the model with the highest score. The results are shown in Table 1.

As can be seen, only for three S values (7, 8 and 9) BDeu metric induces the correct BN. If lower S values are chosen, then the edge $Z \to X$ is not selected: the prior belief implied by a Dirichlet distribution with small alpha values is contradictory with the empirical conditional distributions which are close to the uniform. Only when S is higher and, then, the α values are close to

Table 1.

S	$Z \to X$	$Z \to Y$
...		
1.0	non-selected	non-selected
2.0	non-selected	non-selected
3.0	non-selected	non-selected
...		
7.0	selected	non-selected
8.0	selected	non-selected
9.0	selected	non-selected
10.0	selected	selected
...		

1 ($\alpha_{ijk} = \frac{7}{2\cdot 3}$) and matches with the empirical conditional distribution, the BDeu metric recovers the edge $Z \to X$. However if the S value is *too high* ($S \geq 10$), BDeu metric incorrectly infers the edge $Z \to Y$, as theoretically analyzed in [9].

3.2   Locally and Globally Averaged Bayesian Dirichlet Metrics

As commented in the introduction, the marginalization of the *equivalent sample size* parameter was firstly studied in [8] as a Bayesian solution to alleviate the sensibility of the BDeu metric to this parameter and to prevent from wrong assignments which leads to erroneous inferences of conditional independencies relationships. In that way, we will not be forced to choose a particular prior distribution saying if the parameters are uniform ($\alpha_{ijk} > 1$), strongly uniform ($\alpha_{ijk} >> 1$), skewed ($\alpha_{ijk} < 1$) or strongly skewed ($\alpha_{ijk} << 1$). More precisely, they pursued what we call here a *global marginalization* approach, as the operation is carried on the whole graph: $P(D|G) = \int P(D|G, s)P(s|G)ds$. Although it maintains the *likelihood equivalence property*, one of problems of this approach is the loss of the *local decomposability property* (it can not be computed as a product of independent terms as in Equation (2)) which makes its employment in *score+search* methods much more involved. For example, in the BN model of Example 1 the evaluation of the addition of the edge $Z \to X$ (i.e. an increment in the score of the model) may be affected by the presence/absence of the edge $Z \to Y$ (in opposite with locally decomposable scores).

But, under our point of view, the main problem of this approach is the particular assumptions we make about the distributions of the parameters of the model. In this case we are assuming that all the parameter vectors, ϕ_{ij}, are drawn from a common Dirichlet distribution with the same parameter S. This implies that if S is chosen to be very high (low), we will be assuming that all the parameters are strongly uniform (skewed). We found that this assumption do not properly represents the wide variety of parameter configurations that can be found at the same time in a real model (BN models where some of the parameters are very close to the uniform distribution and others very skewed).

In order to alleviate the previous problems of the assumption of a global distribution which generates the different parameter vectors, we introduce a local marginalization method which assumes that each parameter vector ϕ_{ij} is drawn from a different Dirichlet distribution with a different parameter S which is independent of the others. The immediate consequence of this assumption is that the marginalized score of a graph can be expressed as a product of local scores where the marginalization of parameter S is locally carried out: $P(D|G) = \prod_i \prod_j \int score(X, \Pi_i = j|D, s)P(s|\Pi_i = j)ds$.

The main advantage of this local approach is that we do not need to assume the same prior for all the parameters of the BN as in the global counterpart. This will allow us to model much more complex parameters distributions which are often present in many real models. As we will see in the experimental section, this means that with this much more flexible assumptions we can recover more complex models than with the global approach. In addition to this, these assumptions generate a Bayesian metric which is *locally decomposable* although it loses the *likelihood equivalence property*. However, under out point of view, although this is a very well established and desirable property, it is accompanied by very hard assumptions about the distribution of the parameters of the model that, in many real problems, are far from reality and generates unstable inferences as shown in Example 1.

In any case, to implement any of the marginalization approaches we need to compute the respective integrals. Firstly, as pointed out in [8], it is not clear which kind of prior depending of the graph structures could be chosen in both cases, $P(S|G)$ and $P(S|\Pi_i = j)$; and, secondly, even choosing a uniform prior for S, no closed-form solution is known to compute the integration and the application of a numerical integration technique could be too costly to be used by *score+search* methods. Similarly to [8], we took an straightforward approach: to assume a simple prior and to approximate the integration by an averaging on a finite set of S values, denoted as $\mathcal{S}_L$. As we will see in the experimental section, this simple approach is quite robust and retrieves results which are always as good, and sometimes better, as an optimally chosen S value and it only adds a constant term (i.e., $|\mathcal{S}_L|$) to the time complexity of the scores (the sufficient statistics N_{ijk} only have to be computed once).

To select a finite set of S values to perform this averaging, we decided to choose values higher and lower than 1, because in that ways we average using a wide range of different priors: uniform ($S > 1$), strongly uniform ($S >> 1$), skewed ($S < 1$) or strongly skewed ($S << 1$). More precisely, we chose different power of two values: $\mathcal{S}_L = \{2^{-L}, 2^{-L+1}, ..., 2^{L-1}, 2^L\}$. So, the locally averaged Bayesian metric is computed as follows:

$$score(X_i, \Pi_i|D) = \prod_{j=1}^{|Val(\Pi_i)|} \sum_{s \in \mathcal{S}_L} \frac{\Gamma(\alpha_{ij})}{\Gamma(\alpha_{ij}^s + N_{ij})} \prod_{k=1}^{|Val(X_i)|} \frac{\Gamma(\alpha_{ijk}^s + N_{ijk})}{\Gamma(\alpha_{ijk}^s)} \quad (3)$$

The next example tries to shed light on the differences between the local and the global approach.

Example 2. If we take the data set generated in Example 1 and we employ the locally and the globally averaged Bayesian metrics using different sets $\mathcal{S}_L$

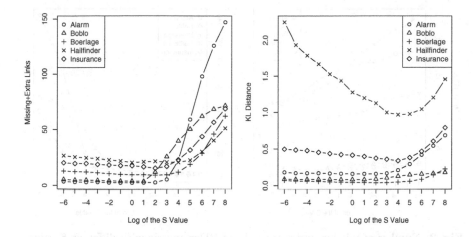

Fig. 1. Number of errors and KL distance of BDeu metric with different S values

$(L = 1, ..., 10)$ in order to select the BN model with the highest score, we will find the following results: the global approach always selects the empty network; while the local method selects the right model when $L > 5$.

As we saw in Example 1, when the prior is far from the real parameters, the BDeu metric fails to recover the right model. The local averaging avoids this problem because it evaluates the presence/absence of the edges averaging over very different priors: from strongly skewed to strongly uniform distributions. But when this averaging is not made locally but globally it does not work in this case. The reason is that in the global approach we jointly evaluate two very different parameter sets: one very uniform, $P(X|Z)$, and other very skewed, $P(Z)$ and $P(Y)$, with the same prior (either assuming uniformity or assuming skewness). As can be seen, the locally averaged metric is able to adapt to more complex situations than the globally averaged version.

4   Experiments

4.1   Experimental Settings

We evaluate the locally and globally averaged Bayesian metrics in artificially generated data sets from 5 standard BNs (*Alarm, boblo, boerlage92, hailfinder* and *insurance*). We do not employ other kind of data sets, as in [8], because, in that way, we know the true model generating the data and we can measure how well the different metrics are able to recover the true model. More precisely, we assume that we are given the topological order of the variables in the BN which generates the data set and we employ the different Bayesian metrics to learn the set of parents of each variable by means of a simple greedy search procedure: it starts with an empty set of parents; at each step, given a set of parents Π_i, it computes all the scores $\{score(X_i, \Pi_i \cup \{Y\}|D) \mid Y \in Pred(X_i) - \Pi_i\}$ (scores adding links) and $\{score(X_i, \Pi_i - \{Y\}|D) \mid Y \in \Pi_i\}$ (scores of deleting links)

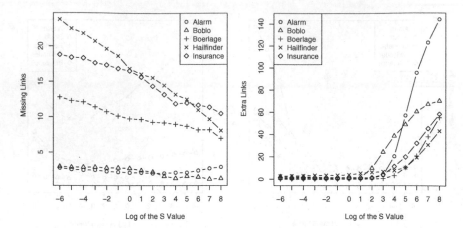

Fig. 2. Number of missing and extra links of BDeu metric with different S values

where $Pred(X_i)$ is the set of variables preceding X_i in the given topological order; and, finally, it updates the set of parents to the one with highest score between these two sets of scores and repeats the process until no improvement is found. In the case of the locally averaged metric, the computation of these scores is straightforward as it is a locally decomposable metric. For the globally averaged metric, we also applied the same search procedure. But now the independence among the parent sets of the variables does not held because the metric is not locally decomposable. To deal with this problem we keep in memory all the scores that are being averaged, which are each of them decomposable. So, in each step we make a local computation of these scores averaging the results. However, another problem remains: the set of parents of a node can depend of the computed set of parents of the other nodes in the graph. To solve this problem we followed a simple procedure: we computed the set of parents following the topological ordering of the nodes; when considering a node X_i, the parents of the preceding nodes where taking into account to compute the global scores of the graph; and it was assumed that the set of parents of the subsequent nodes is empty.

As the composition property [6] is verified in this problem, this greedy algorithm is able to find the correct set of parents if the decision of the Bayesian scores are correct: $score(G \cup \{Y \rightarrow X_i\}|D) - score(G|D) \leq 0$ if and only if X_i is conditionally independent of Y given Π_i for any $Y \in Pred(X_i)$. So, under these settings, the number of errors (missing+extra links) of the inferred model will only depend of the ability of the different Bayesian metrics to rightly detect the different conditional independencies.

For these experiments, we randomly generate data samples by means of logic sampling from each one of the 5 BNs with different sample sizes: 100, 500 and 1000 cases. All the experiments were conducted with each of these data samples and were repeated 10 times. In order to simplify the exposition of the results we only show results with 1000 cases because quite similar conclusions can be thrown from the other sample sizes.

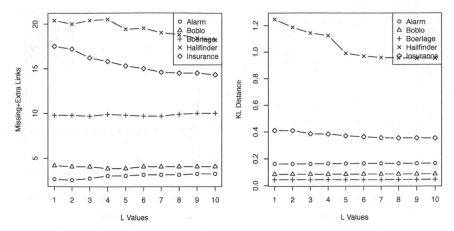

Fig. 3. Number of errors and KL distance of locally averaged Bayesian Dirichlet metric with different L values

BDeu Metric

In Figure 1, we depict the number of errors (missing plus extra links wrt the true BN model), plotted in the Y-axis, of the inferred models using the BDeu metric with different S values (the logarithm of the S values are plotted in the X-axis). As can be seen, in the 5 BNs the number of errors is slowly improved as the S parameter changes for very small values to higher values but it reaches the minimum at different S values depending of the particular BN model. Following a similar trend, but also at different S values, the number of errors suddenly increases and quickly move away from this minimum in the five BN models. The same can be said about the behavior of Kullback-Leibler (KL) distance wrt the true BN.

This highlight the sensitivity of the BDeu metric to the particular S value as previously shown in [8] with other different experimental settings. If we independently look at the evolution of the number of missing and extra links, depicted in Figure 2, we can observe the previously commented trend of the BDeu metric to over-regularized with lower S values and to recover a higher number of spurious links with high S values. The problem is that these anomalous behavior happens at different intervals of the parameter S and with a different intensity depending of the particular model which generates the data. Let us look, for example, how the number of extra links is suddenly soared when S increases in the *Alarm* and the *Boblo* models.

That shows how the selection of an optimal S value is quite hard not to say that it is impossible because, in practical settings, we do not know which is the true model. We will only observe as increasing (decreasing) S new edges are recovered (removed). Only if we are able to elicit expert/domain knowledge about the distribution of the different parameters we can be sure of avoiding the wrong assessment of a S value, but this is not a common situation at all.

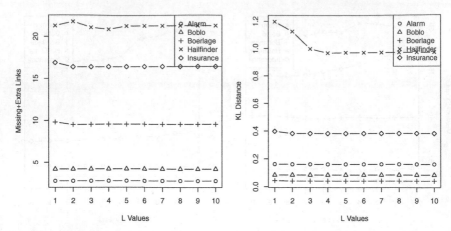

Fig. 4. Number of errors and KL distance of globally averaged Bayesian Dirichlet metric with different L values

Averaged Bayesian Dirichlet Metrics

We now look to the quality of the retrieved models using the locally averaged Bayesian Dirichlet metric. In Figure 3, we display the number of missing+extra links and KL distance wrt true BN using different set S_L of S values (see Section 3.2). As can be seen, the higher the set of averaged S values, the better the inferred model, specially for *Hailfinder* and *Insurance* model. But the main point is to see how the averaging over higher set of S values produce stable results, in opposite to the employment of single S values.

The behavior of globally averaged Bayesian Dirichlet metric, as shown in Figure 4, is not exactly the same than its local counterpart. On the one hand, it is even more stable and since $L > 5$ there is any change in the number of missing+extra links and the KL distance. But, on the other hand, it does not get further improvements when increasing the set of averaged S values when applied to the *Hailfinder* and *Insurance* models.

A direct comparison between the global and local approach is given in Figure 5 (a). In this figure, we plot the difference between the number of missing+extra links of the globally and locally averaged Bayesian metrics. So, positive differences implies that the local method finds better models than the global approach. As can be seen, for the *Alarm*, *Boblo* and *Boerlage* models the difference between the local and global versions are negligible (a 0.5 difference in the worst case). However, for the *Hailfinder* and *Insurance* model the locally averaged metric gets better results. This positive difference follows from the ability of the locally averaged metric to fit more complex parameter sets as shown in Example 2.

The main question is finally answered in Figure 5 (b). There, we plot the difference between the number of missing+extra links of the locally averaged Bayesian Dirichlet metric and the BDeu metric with the best possible single S value across different S_L values. That is to say, for each L we take the best inferred model using the BDeu metric with any S value in the set $\{2^{-L}, 2^{-L+1}, \ldots, 2^L\}$. Again,

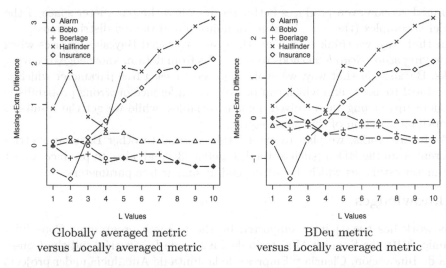

Globally averaged metric
versus Locally averaged metric

BDeu metric
versus Locally averaged metric

Fig. 5. Difference in the number of errors of Global, Local and BDeu metric

positive differences imply that the local method finds better models than the BDeu metric with any S value. As can be seen, when the number of averaged S values is bigger, for some of models (*Alarm, Boblo* and *Boerlage*) the differences remains stable: in the worst case, using the best possible S value we have a negative difference of 0.5 links. And for the other two BN (*Hailfinder* and *Insurance*), the locally averaged metric infers even better models when averaging over a big set of S values.

In that way, we can see as the averaged Bayesian metrics prevent from the need to assess a particular S value, which as shown in the above analysis can lead to wrong and unstable model inferences. In fact, this simple averaging approach is able to retrieve models which are as good as an optimal selection of S value. In addition to this, when using the locally averaged we are able to fit more complex parameter spaces than the BDeu metric using a single S value and infer more accurate BNs.

5 Conclusions and Future Works

In this paper we have introduced a novel strategy based on a simple local averaging approach to overcome the problem of assessing the free parameters of one of the most widely employed Bayesian score metrics. This new formulation is efficient (only adds a constant factor to the time complexity) and satisfies the *local decomposition property*, so it perfectly works with *score+search* methods to learn BN from data.

In the experimental evaluation it has been shown as this averaged Bayesian metric robustly infers models with the same number of structural errors than the BDeu metric with an optimal ESS. This result is remarkable as the S_L is not selected with any procedure based on the data, while the ESS was selected as the one given best results, once the experiments were carried out. The locally averaged version even produces better results when the parameter space of the model is complex (there is a mixture of uniform and skewed distributions).

In that way, we think that it worth to use averaged Bayesian metrics when employing *score+search* methods to learn BNs from data in knowledge discovery tasks. Because, in that way, we avoid the need to set a free parameter which is quite hard to assess and which can provoke the inference of wrong probabilistic relationships among the involved domain variables, while we get the results of an optimal selection of this parameter.

As future works, we plan to extend this method to other Bayesian metrics different from the BDeu (such as the K2 metric [3]) and, also, to produce robust parameter estimates which do not depend of similar free parameters.

Acknowledges

This work has been jointly supported by the research programme Consolider Ingenio 2010, the Spanish Ministerio de Ciencia de Innovación and the Consejería de Innovación, Ciencia y Empresa de la Junta de Andalucía under projects CSD2007-00018, TIN2010-20900-C04-01 and TIC-6016, respectively.

References

1. Abellán, J., Moral, S.: A new score for independence based on the imprecise dirichlet model. In: International Symposium on Imprecise Probabilities and their Applications, pp. 1–10 (2005)
2. Buntine, W.: Theory refinement on Bayesian networks. In: Proceedings of the Seventh Conference on Uncertainty in Artificial Intelligence, San Francisco, CA, USA, pp. 52–60 (1991)
3. Cooper, G., Herskovits, E.: A Bayesian method for the induction of probabilistic networks from data. Machine Learning 9, 309–347 (1992)
4. Heckerman, D., Geiger, D., Chickering, D.: Learning Bayesian networks: The combination of knowledge and statistical data. Machine Learning 20(3), 197–243 (1995)
5. Moral, S.: An empirical comparison of score measures for independence. In: Information Processing and Management of Uncertainty in Knowledge-Based Systems, IPMU 2004, pp. 1307–1314 (2004)
6. Pearl, J.: Probabilistic Reasoning with Intelligent Systems. Morgan-Kaufman, San Francisco (1988)
7. Scott, J.G., Berger, J.O.: An exploration of aspects of Bayesian multiple testing. Journal of Statistical Planning and Inference 136(7), 2144–2162 (2006)
8. Silander, T., Kontkanen, P., Myllymaki, P.: On sensitivity of the MAP Bayesian network structure to the equivalent sample size parameter. In: Proceedings of the Twenty-Third Annual Conference on Uncertainty in Artificial Intelligence (UAI 2007), pp. 360–367. AUAI Press, Corvallis (2007)
9. Steck, H.: Learning the Bayesian network structure: Dirichlet prior vs data. In: McAllester, D.A., Myllymäki, P. (eds.) UAI, pp. 511–518. AUAI Press (2008)
10. Steck, H., Jaakkola, T.: On the Dirichlet prior and Bayesian regularization. In: Becker, S., Thrun, S., Obermayer, K. (eds.) NIPS, pp. 697–704. MIT Press, Cambridge (2002)
11. Ueno, M.: Learning networks determined by the ratio of prior and data. In: Grnwald, P., Spirtes, P. (eds.) Proceedings of the 26th Conference on Uncertainty in Artificial Intelligence (UAI 2010). AUAI Press (2010)

Mixture of Markov Trees for Bayesian Network Structure Learning with Small Datasets in High Dimensional Space

Sourour Ammar and Philippe Leray

Knowledge and Decision Team
Laboratoire d'Informatique de Nantes Atlantique (LINA) UMR 6241
Ecole Polytechnique de l'Université de Nantes, France
{sourour.ammar,philippe.leray}@univ-nantes.fr

Abstract. The recent explosion of high dimensionality in datasets for several domains has posed a serious challenge to existing Bayesian network structure learning algorithms. Local search methods represent a solution in such spaces but suffer with small datasets. MMHC (Max-Min Hill-Climbing) is one of these local search algorithms where a first phase aims at identifying a possible skeleton by using some statistical association measurements and a second phase performs a greedy search restricted by this skeleton. We propose to replace the first phase, imprecise when the number of data remains relatively very small, by an application of "Perturb and Combine" framework we have already studied in density estimation by using mixtures of bagged trees.

Keywords: Bayesian networks, mixture of trees, bootstrap, structure learning.

1 Introduction

Bayesian networks are probabilistic graphical models that encode a joint distribution over a set of variables by a product of conditional probability distributions, one for each variable conditionally to its parents in the directed graph. These models may be learned from data and used to perform probabilistic inferences over the encoded distribution [15]. However, learning the graphical structure of such models from data is NP-hard [7]. In general, there are two main approaches for learning Bayesian network structure from data. The search-and-score approach, with algorithms such as K2 [10] or GS [8], attempts to identify the network that maximizes a given scoring function used to indicate how well the network fits the data. The second approach, constraint-based, with algorithms such as IC [16] or PC [18], attempts to estimate conditional independences between variables using statistical independence tests.

The recent explosion of high dimensionality in datasets for several domains such as the biomedical domain with hundreds or thousands of variables, has posed a serious challenge to existing Bayesian network structure learning algorithms. These algorithms are not scalable to high dimensional spaces because

W. Liu (Ed.): ECSQARU 2011, LNAI 6717, pp. 229–238, 2011.

of their excessive computational complexity [5]. The local search methods, hybrid between constraint-based and score-based ones, are the most appropriate solution in such spaces.

Moreover, in the context of high dimensional space, the datasets are generally very small comparatively to the space dimension. Structure learning algorithms are known to be unstable in such context : small changes in training data can cause large changes in the learned structures. So, learning a single model from small dataset will not produce a good estimation. Several works demonstrated that in such conditions, the use of the "Perturb and Combine" principle such as bagging (model averaging and bootstrap replicas) improves considerably the results. In this direction, [6] applied the bagging principle to the greedy hill-climbing algorithm with randomized restarts.

In this paper, we propose to apply the "Perturb and Combine" idea to develop a new methodology for bayesian network structure learning in the context of high dimensional space and small datasets. We propose to first learn a mixture of trees on a set of bootstrap replicas of the original dataset, and then use this mixture to guide a local search algorithm.

The rest of this paper is organized as follows. Section 2 recalls Bayesian network structure learning framework in high dimension. Section 3 presents how can we apply the Bagging principle to learn a mixture of trees from data and Section 4 describes our proposition. Section 5 presents our experimental protocol and collects our simulation results. Section 6 concludes and highlights some directions for further research.

2   Bayesian Network Structure Learning in High Dimension

2.1   Introduction

Bayesian network structure learning is NP-hard and existing algorithms are not scalable to very high dimensional spaces. Some approaches have been proposed to provide scalable algorithms, such as the Sparse Candidate algorithm [11] that constrains the search of a score-based algorithm by limiting the set of possible parents of each variable to contain at most k candidate parents. The other scalable structure learning approaches, *local search methods*, can be seen as a generalization of the sparse candidate principle. This kind of methods consists in, first, applying statistical tests to identify local structures around a target variable (e.g. a Markov Blanket (MB) or a set of candidate parents and children (CPC)), and then in using another heuristic to learn the full structure by considering the previous local results. Many heuristics have been proposed for local structure identification, IAMB [19] and MBOR [13] for Markov blanket and MMPC (Max-Min Parent Children) [20] for set of Parents and Children.

2.2   MMHC Algorithm

The Max-Min Hill-Climbing (MMHC) algorithm [21] briefly described in Algorithm 1 is one of these local search structure learning algorithm. Its first phase

Algorithm 1. MMHC algorithm

Require: data D
Ensure: a DAG structure

 % Restrict
 for every variable $X \in V$ **do**
  $PC(X) = MMPC(X, D)$
 end for
 % Search
 Starting from an empty graph perform Greedy Hill-Climbing with operators *add-edge, delete-edge, reverse-edge*. Only try operator *add-edge*$(Y \rightarrow X)$ if $Y \in PC(X)$

 return the highest scoring DAG found

---

consists in identifying the set of CPC for each variable by using the MMPC algorithm. The second phase consists in using a score-based algorithm (Hill-climbing) by constraining the classical *AddEdge* operator to edges discovered by MMPC in the first phase.

MMHC is scalable to high dimensional spaces with hundreds of variables and can identify a structure with higher score in less time than the Sparse Candidate algorithm.

MMPC is used in order to reconstruct a possible skeleton of the Bayesian network. This phase relies on statistical tests on training data to detect conditionally independence between variables. In the context of high dimensional space (thousands of variables) and small data sets (few hundreds samples), detecting conditionally independence between variables from data can both require an excessive computational complexity and, more damaging, return very imprecise results.

3 Mixture of Bayesian Networks Structured Trees

Let $X = \{X_1, \ldots, X_n\}$ be a finite set of discrete random variables, and $D = (x^1, \cdots, x^N)$ be a sample (dataset) of joint observations $x^i = \{x_1^i, \cdots, x_n^i\}$ independently drawn from some data-generating density $\mathbb{P}_G(X_1, \ldots, X_n)$.

A mixture distribution $\mathbb{P}_{\hat{T}}(X_1, \ldots, X_n)$ induced by a multiset $\hat{T} = \{T_1, \ldots, T_m\}$ of m Markov trees is defined as a convex combination of elementary Markov tree densities, i.e.

$$\mathbb{P}_{\hat{T}}(X) = \sum_{i=1}^{m} \mu_i \mathbb{P}_{T_i}(X),$$

where $\mu_i \in [0, 1]$, $\sum_{i=1}^{m} \mu_i = 1$, and $\mathbb{P}_{T_i}(X)$ is the probability density over X encoded by the graphical model composed of the Markov tree structure S_i and its parameter set $\tilde{\theta}_i$:

$$\mathbb{P}_{T_i}(X) = \mathbb{P}_{S_i, \tilde{\theta}_i}(X) = \prod_{p=1}^{n} P_{\tilde{\theta}_i}(X_p | Pa_{S_i}(X_p)),$$

Algorithm 2. Markov tree Mixture learning algorithm (MtM)

Require: dataset D, mixture size m

  for $i = 1, \cdots, m$ **do**
    $D_i = BootstrapReplica(D)$
    $T_i = BuildMarkovTreeStructure(D_i)$
    $\tilde{\theta}_i = LearnPars(T_i, D)$
  end for
  $(\mu)_{i=1}^{m} = CompWeights((T_i, \tilde{\theta}_i)_{i=1}^{m}, D)$

  return $\left(\mu_i, T_i, \tilde{\theta}_i \right)_{i=1}^{m}$

---

where $Pa_{S_i}(X_p)$ is the parent variable of X_p in the tree structure S_i.

Several versions of Markov tree mixture learning algorithm described in Algorithm 2 were proposed in [2,4] as an alternative to classical methods for density estimation in the context of high-dimensional space and small datasets : mixtures of tree structures generated in a totally randomized fashion and ensembles of optimal trees derived from bootstrap replicas of the dataset by the Chow and Liu algorithm [9] (i.e. bagging of Markov trees). In [4,3], we also proposed three sub-quadratic heuristics to approximate the optimal tree and then to construct mixture of trees in a sub-quadratic way. Our best heuristic (Inertial search heuristic) complexity is $n \log(n) \log(n \log(n))$. These works have fruitful results for density estimation in terms of scalability and efficiency. But result of these methods, described by a mixture of several models, cannot directly identify a single model that can be graphically visualized and interpreted.

4 MtMHC Algorithm

4.1 MtMHC Principle

On the one hand, scalable structure learning algorithms like MMHC can give very unstable results with small datasets. On the other hand, scalability and robustness of Markov tree mixtures for density estimation in the context of high dimensional space and small datasets make this approach attractive in such context.

For these reasons, we propose in this work to exploit the advantages of both methods with the MtMHC algorithm described in Algorithm 3. This algorithm is very similar to MMHC algorithm, but our idea is using mixtures of Markov trees in order to identify a set of candidate parents and children instead of MMPC algorithm. This new CPC identification algorithm, named MtMPC, is described in the next section.

4.2 MtMPC Algorithm

Algorithm 4 describes the use of mixtures of Markov trees in order to identify a set of candidate parents and children. Given a dataset D, we first use our MTM

Algorithm 3. MtMHC algorithm

Require: dataset D, mixture size m
Ensure: a DAG structure

    % Restrict
    $\{PC(X)\}_{X \in V} = MtMPC(D, m)$
    % Search
    Starting from an empty graph perform Greedy Hill-Climbing with operators *add-edge*, *delete-edge*, *reverse-edge*. Only try operator *add-edge*$(Y \to X)$ if $Y \in PC(X)$

    return the highest scoring DAG found

Algorithm 4. MtMPC algorithm

Require: dataset D, mixture size m
    $\{T_i\} = MtM(D, m)$
    for every variable X in V **do**
        MtMPC(X) = $\emptyset$
        for $i = 1...m$ **do**
            MtMPC(X) = MtMPC(X) $\cup\ Ne_{T_i}(X)$
        end for
    end for

    return MtMPC(X)$_{X \in V}$

---

algorithm described in Algorithm 2 to construct a set of m Markov models. We make here the hypothesis that the union of the Markov tree models can be a good approximation of the CPC set. We then define the CPC set of a given variable A as the union of the neighbors of this variable in each tree of the mixture $Ne_{T_i}(A)$.

Using bootstrap replicas in our mixture allows to deal with small datasets. Another related solution would have been to consider more robust conditional independence tests in MMPC algorithm such as permutation tests as proposed in [17,22].

Note that we are only working with the Markov tree skeletons without taking into account their corresponding weights μ_i. We have demonstrated in our previous work that using uniform weights in the mixture provides the best results with small datasets, so these weights are non informative for our MtMPC algorithm.

Figure 1 illustrates an example of this algorithm. An undirected skeleton G summarizing the set of all CPC is built from the ten trees of the mixture. As an illustration, the set of $CPC(A)$ appears in blue.

4.3   MtMHC Optimization

Because of the variability induced by boostraping data during the mixture learning, some edges only appear in a few models in the mixture. Moreover, the

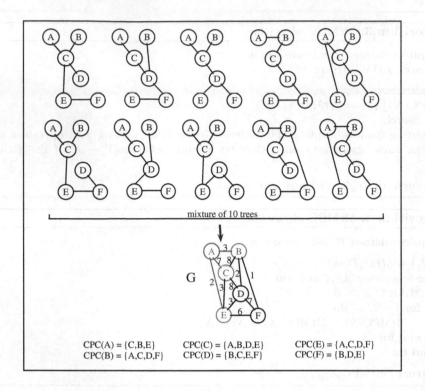

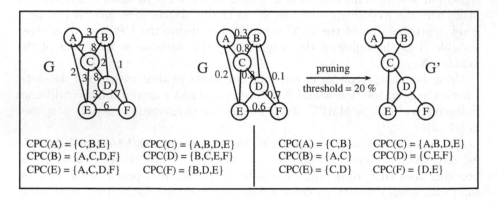

Fig. 1. Example of execution of the MtMPC algorithm

Fig. 2. Example of execution of the MtMPC algorithm with pruning phase

complexity of the second step of MtMHC algorithm (hill climbing) is directly related to the size of the PC set returned by MtMPC.

We propose one possible optimization of our MtMHC algorithm by pruning the edges non frequent in the set of Markov tree. This pruning phase is usual when we want to describe a set of graphs, as proposed in [14].

Figure 2 describes an example of CPC refinement when using this pruning optimization. When we construct the graph G from the different mixture trees, we use for each connexion in G a weight given by the number of occurence of the corresponding edge in the mixture. Then, after constructing the graph G, these weights are divised by the mixture size. So, connexions with low weight (under a given percentage) will be deleted. Figure 2 shows that connexions in G with a weight under 0.2 (threshold = 20%) ($A - E$ and $B - F$) are pruned.

5   Empirical Simulations and Results

5.1   Experimental Protocol

In order to evaluate the results of our proposition, we carried out repetitive experiments for different structures, by proceeding in the following way. All our experiments were carried out with models for a set of $n = 100$ binary random variables. To choose a target density, we first decide whether it will factorize according to a general directed acyclic graph structure. Then we use the appropriate random structure [12] and parameter generation algorithm (described in [1]) to draw a structure and their parameters.

For each target density and dataset size, we generated 10 different datasets by sampling values of the random variables using the Monte-Carlo method with the target structure and parameter values. We carried out simulations with dataset sizes of $N = 50$ and 200 elements. Given the total number of 2^n possible data configurations of our n random variables, we thus look at rather small datasets in such context.

For the tree mixture learning, we tested different sizes : $m = 50$, 100, 150 and 300 trees in order to observe the potential influence of the mixture size on the quality of the result.

For this preliminary work, we concentrate our study to MtMPC results with or without pruning. Pruning threshold is set to 10% in order to illustrate the interest of the pruning optimisation.

We measure the quality of the obtained CPC sets by estimating the percentage of true positive (TP) edges with respect to the number of correct edges in the true model (edges present in the target structure and truly discovered by the algorithm) and false positive (FP) edges with respect to the number of edges absent in the true model (edges absent in the target structure and falsely discovered).

We also provide results obtained in the same conditions by MMPC algorithm using an usual statistical test (the χ^2 test with a parameter $\alpha = 5\%$), even if we know that these tests are not well appropriate for small datasets. Using more sophisticated test is part of our future work.

5.2   Results

Table 1 contains MtMPC and MMPC results for a very small dataset ($N = 50$ samples) without and with pruning. Tables 2 contains similar results for small dataset ($N = 200$).

Table 1. Results obtained with MtMPC algorithm ($n = 100$, $N = 50$)

	TP	FP	TP	FP
	no pruning phase		with pruning phase	
MtMPC (m=50)	35.29 %	12.78 %	29.11 %	0.31 %
MtMPC (m=100)	39.21 %	18.58 %	28.92 %	0.27 %
MtMPC (m=150)	40.19 %	21.52 %	28.92 %	0.25 %
MtMPC (m=300)	45.09 %	23.95 %	28.82 %	0.24 %
MMPC	1.96 %	0.69 %		

Table 2. Results obtained with MtMPC algorithm ($n = 100$, $N = 200$)

	TP	FP	TP	FP
	no pruning phase		with pruning phase	
BTM-PC (m=50)	43.13 %	11.84 %	30.39 %	0.38 %
BTM-PC (m=100)	43.17 %	17.46 %	30.30 %	0.35 %
BTM-PC (m=150)	43.13 %	19.87 %	30.29 %	0.33 %
MMPC	5.88 %	1.63 %		

Previous work demonstrates that increasing the mixture size gives us a better estimation of the target joint distribution. This property is illustrated by the fact that the percentage of good edges (TP) discovered by our algorithm also increases in the left part of table 1 and table 2. We can also observe that it also increases the variability of the obtained trees and the number of false positives (FP).

In both tables, we can discover about 45% of the right edges in very extrem context (small datasets, $N = 50$ and 200).

The right parts of tables 1 and 2 illustrate the influence of the pruning phase. FP highly decreases to less than 0.4%, to the detriment of FP which also decreases from 45% to 30%.

As we want to plug our MtMPC results into a constraint Hill Climbing algorithm, the behavior of this pruning optimization is no so interesting. Even if we want to control the complexity of the greedy search by decreasing the number of edges of the CPC generated by MtMPC, we would like that the pruning procedure mainly affect the FP. Pruning interesting edges is dangerous because the Hill Climbing procedure will not be able to add them again.

6   Summary and Future Works

We proposed in this work to apply the "Perturb and Combine" idea to develop a new methodology for bayesian network structure learning in the context of high dimensional space and small datasets. We proposed a new approach MtMHC, based on mixture of trees that have fruitful results for density estimation in such space, to guide a local search structure learning.

Our proposed algorithm for estimating the set of candidate parents and children, MtMPC, quasi-linear with respect to the number of variables, provides interesting results with very small datasets. We also proposed a potential optimization for our algorithm, but first results indicate that this optimization could be counterproductive.

As further work, we have to develop the experimentation part in several directions, by working in higher spaces, by examining the final results of MtMHC instead of the intermediate one given by MtMPC, by comparing our algorithm to specific algorithm designed for handling small datasets inspired from [17,22].

References

1. Ammar, S., Leray, P., Defourny, B., Wehenkel, L.: High-dimensional probability density estimation with randomized ensembles of tree structured bayesian networks. In: Proceedings of the Fourth European Workshop on Probabilistic Graphical Models (PGM 2008), pp. 9–16 (2008)
2. Ammar, S., Leray, P., Defourny, B., Wehenkel, L.: Probability density estimation by perturbing and combining tree structured markov networks. In: Sossai, C., Chemello, G. (eds.) ECSQARU 2009. LNCS, vol. 5590, pp. 156–167. Springer, Heidelberg (2009)
3. Ammar, S., Leray, P., Schnitzler, F., Wehenkel, L.: Sub-quadratic markov tree mixture learning based on randomizations of the chow-liu algorithm. In: The Fifth European Workshop on Probabilistic Graphical Models (PGM 2010), Helsinki, Finland, pp. 17–25 (2010)
4. Ammar, S., Leray, P., Wehenkel, L.: Sub-quadratic markov tree mixture models for probability density estimation. In: 19th International Conference on Computational Statistics (COMPSTAT 2010), Paris, France, pp. 673–680 (2010)
5. Auvray, V., Wehenkel, L.: On the construction of the inclusion boundary neighbourhood for markov equivalence classes of bayesian network structures. In: Darwiche, A., Friedman, N. (eds.) Proceedings of the 18th Conference on Uncertainty in Artificial Intelligence (UAI 2002), pp. 26–35. Morgan Kaufmann Publishers, S.F (2002)
6. Broom, B., Do, K., Subramanian, D.: Model averaging for structure learning in bayesian networks: an experimental study. Tech. rep., Computer Science Department, Rice University (2008)
7. Chickering, D., Geiger, D., Heckerman, D.: Learning bayesian networks is NP-hard. Tech. Rep. MSR-TR-94-17, Microsoft Research Technical Report (1994), http://citeseer.nj.nec.com/140425.html
8. Chickering, D.: Optimal structure identification with greedy search. Journal of Machine Learning Research 3, 507–554 (2003)
9. Chow, C., Liu, C.N.: Approximating discrete probability distributions with dependence trees. IEEE Transactions on Information Theory 14(3), 462–467 (1968)
10. Cooper, G., Herskovits, E.: A bayesian method for the induction of probabilistic networks from data. Machine Learning 9, 309–347 (1992)
11. Friedman, N., Nachman, I., Per, D.: Learning bayesian network structure from massive datasets: The "sparse candidate" algorithm. In: Fifteenth Conference on Uncertainty in Artificial Intelligence (UAI), pp. 206–215 (1999)
12. Ide, J., Cozman, F., Ramos, F.: Generating random bayesian networks with constraints on induced width. In: ECAI, pp. 323–327 (2004)

13. de Morais, S.R., Aussem, A.: A novel markov boundary based feature subset selection algorithm. Neurocomputing 73(4-6), 578–584 (2010)
14. Nguyen, H.T., Leray, P., Ramstein, G.: Summarizing and visualizing a set of bayesian networks with quasi essential graphs. Tech. rep., University of Nantes (2011)
15. Pearl, J.: Fusion, propagation, and structuring in belief networks. Artificial Intelligence 29, 241–288 (1986)
16. Pearl, J., Verma, T.S.: A theory of inferred causation. In: Allen, J.F., Fikes, R., Sandewall, E. (eds.) Principles of Knowledge Representation and Reasoning, KR 1991, pp. 441–452. Morgan Kaufmann, San Mateo (1991), http://citeseer.nj.nec.com/pearl91theory.html
17. Scutari, M.: Measures of Variability for Graphical Models. Ph.D. thesis, University of Padova (2011)
18. Spirtes, P., Glymour, C., Scheines, R.: Causation, prediction, and search. Springer, Heidelberg (1993)
19. Tsamardinos, I., Aliferis, C., Statnikov, A.: Algorithms for large scale markov blanket discovery. In: The 16th International FLAIRS Conference, pp. 376–380 (2003)
20. Tsamardinos, I., Aliferis, C., Statnikov, A.: Time and sample efficient discovery of markov blankets and direct causal relations. In: Proceedings of the 9th CAN SIGKDD International Conference on Knowledge Discovery and Data Mining, pp. 673–678 (2003)
21. Tsamardinos, I., Brown, L., Aliferis, C.: The max-min hill-climbing bayesian network structure learning algorithm. Machine Learning 65, 31–78 (2006)
22. Tsamardinos, I., Borboudakis, G.: Permutation testing improves bayesian network learning. In: Balcázar, J., Bonchi, F., Gionis, A., Sebag, M. (eds.) ECML PKDD 2010. LNCS, vol. 6323, pp. 322–337. Springer, Heidelberg (2010)

Finding P–Maps and I–Maps to Represent Conditional Independencies

Marco Baioletti[1], Giuseppe Busanello[2], and Barbara Vantaggi[2]

[1] Dipartimento di Matematica ed Informatica
Università degli Studi di Perugia, Italy
baioletti@dmi.unipg.it
[2] Dipartimento Scienze di Base e Applicate per l'Ingegneria
Università La Sapienza Roma, Italy
{busanello,vantaggi}@dmmm.uniroma1.it

Abstract. The representation problem of independence models is studied by focusing on acyclic directed graph (DAG). We present the algorithm PC$_*$ in order to look for a perfect map. However, when a perfect map does not exist, so that PC$_*$ fails, it is interesting to find a minimal I–map, which represents as many triples as possible in J_*. Therefore we describe an algorithm which finds such a map by means of a backtracking procedure.

Keywords: Independence models, DAG, Perfect map, Independence map.

1 Introduction

Graphical models [7,10,13,17] play a fundamental role in order to represent conditional independence models. Given an independence model J, a relevant problem is to find all the independence statements θ which are implied by J, i.e. which hold under every probability distribution agreeing with J. This problem, known as implication problem, has not been solved yet and perhaps is undecidable. However, it is possible to study its syntactical counterpart, i.e. to find whether θ can be derived from J by using some axiomatic system. For this aim, the closure $\bar{J}$ of a given set J of independencies, with respect to (semi)graphoid properties, would be useful. Since it can be exponentially larger than $\bar{J}$, a suitable subset J_* ("fast closure") of $\bar{J}$, gathering the same information as $\bar{J}$, has been introduced [16,2].

Another relevant problem is to represent a set J of conditional independence relations by means of an acyclic directed graph (DAG), called perfect map (P–map). A graphical representation of conditional independencies is important because a graph provides a human readable form of encoding these information. Graphs are simple to understand and d–separation gives a fast way of finding new conditional independencies.

However it is known that there are independence models, which admit no perfect map. This problem has been faced by providing necessary conditions

W. Liu (Ed.): ECSQARU 2011, LNAI 6717, pp. 239–250, 2011.
© Springer-Verlag Berlin Heidelberg 2011

[12] or a complete solution [14], however these methods require to solve a large number of implication/deduction problems.

In [5] we consider graphoid structures (related to independence models induced by strictly positive probability) and we give a necessary and sufficient condition for the existence of a P–map. This condition characterizes the orderings on the random variables which generate a perfect map by means of the fast closure set J_*. Starting from this result, we introduced an algorithm based on a backtracking procedure, that is able to check whether a set J of independencies is representable through a P–map.

In this paper we deal with the same problem and we provide a new algorithm (called PC_*), which adapt the technique of Pearl and Verma's algorithm [14] to the fast closure. This algorithm looks for a perfect map whether it exists; otherwise PC_* fails and in this case it is important to find a minimal I–map G, which represents as many triples as possible in the fast closure J_*. Such a graph G can be considered as one of the "best possible I–map" for J_* and so it can be seen as a sort of "lower approximation" of a P–map, for those sets of independencies which do not have a P–map. For this aim, a simple algorithm which finds the graph which represents the maximum number of triples in J_* is described.

2   Graphoids and Fast Closure

Let $\tilde{S} = \{Y_1, \ldots, Y_n\}$ be a finite not empty set of variables and $S = \{1, \ldots, n\}$ the set of indices associated to $\tilde{S}$. Given a probability P on $\tilde{S}$, a conditional independence statement $Y_A \perp\!\!\!\perp Y_B | Y_C$, compatible with P, is simply denoted by the ordered triple (A, B, C), where A, B, C are disjoint subsets of S. Then, in the following we do not distinguish $\tilde{S}$ from S.

Let $S^{(3)}$ denote the set of all (ordered) triples (A, B, C) of disjoint subsets of S, such that A and B are not empty. A conditional independence model $\mathcal{I}$ is therefore a subset of $S^{(3)}$. In particular, we refer to a graphoid structure, which is a couple $(S, \mathcal{I})$, where $\mathcal{I}$ is a ternary relation on S satisfying the following properties :

G1 if $(A, B, C) \in \mathcal{I}$, then $(B, A, C) \in \mathcal{I}$ (Symmetry);
G2 if $(A, B \cup C, D) \in \mathcal{I}$, then $(A, B, D) \in \mathcal{I}$ (Decomposition);
G3 if $(A, B \cup C, D) \in \mathcal{I}$, then $(A, B, C \cup D) \in \mathcal{I}$ (Weak Union);
G4 if $(A, B, C \cup D) \in \mathcal{I}$ and $(A, C, D) \in \mathcal{I}$, then $(A, B \cup C, D) \in \mathcal{I}$ (Contraction);
G5 if $(A, B, C \cup D) \in \mathcal{I}$ and $(A, C, B \cup D) \in \mathcal{I}$, then $(A, B \cup C, D) \in \mathcal{I}$ (Intersection);

where A, B, C, D are pairwise disjoint subsets of S.

Given a set J of conditional independence statements, compatible with a probability, a relevant problem is to find the closure of J with respect to graphoid rules G1–G5

$$\bar{J} = \{\theta \in S^{(3)} : \theta \text{ is obtained from } J \text{ by G1–G5}\}.$$

A related problem, called deduction, concerns to establish whether a triple $\theta \in S^{(3)}$ can be derived from J, see [6,19]. It is clear that the deduction problem can be easily solved once the closure has been computed. But, the computation of $\bar{J}$ is infeasible because its size can be exponentially larger than the size of J.

In order to deal with this problem, we need to recall some definitions. Given $\theta = (A, B, C)$, we denote by θ^T the triple (B, A, C) obtained from θ through G1. Given a pair of triples $\theta_1, \theta_2 \in S^{(3)}$, we say that θ_1 is *generalized–included* in θ_2 (briefly g–included and in symbol $\theta_1 \sqsubseteq \theta_2$) if θ_1 can be obtained from θ_2 by a finite number of applications of the unary rules G1, G2 and G3.

A triple $\theta \in J$ is said to be maximal in J if there exists no triple $\theta' \in J$, different from θ and θ^T, such that $\theta \sqsubseteq \theta'$.

The $\sqsubseteq$ relation can be easily extended to sets. Indeed given two sets $J, K \subseteq S^{(3)}$, $J \sqsubseteq K$ if for each $\theta \in J$, there exists a triple $\tau \in K$ such that $\theta \sqsubseteq \tau$.

By using the relation $\sqsubseteq$, it is possible to define a set J_* which is in general much smaller than $\bar{J}$, but having the same information as $\bar{J}$. This set is called *fast closure* of J and is defined as

$$J_* = \{\tau \in \bar{J} : \tau \text{ is maximal in } \bar{J}\}.$$

In [2] we show that J_* can be computed by a fast procedure (FC2), based on two inference rules G4* and G5*, which generalize G4 and G5. Another method for computing J_*, introduced in the same paper, is the procedure FC1 based on a unique inference rule U. FC1 has been shown to be an effective way for computing the fast closure through an extensive empirical evaluations, given in [1,3,2], and outperforms FC2 in computation time.

In the rest of the paper, we use m for $|J_*|$, i.e. the cardinality of the fast closure for a generic set J.

3   Graph Representation

In this section we recall some notions about graphs and the representation of an independence model by an acyclic directed graph (DAG) [12]. We denote by $G = (\mathcal{U}, \mathcal{E})$ a graph with a set $\mathcal{U}$ of nodes and a set $\mathcal{E}$ of directed arcs. For any $u \in \mathcal{U}$, as usual, we denote with $pa(u)$ the parents of u, $ch(u)$ the children of u, $ds(u)$ the sets of descendants and $an(u)$ the set of ancestors.

Definition 1. *If A, B and C are three disjoint subsets of nodes of $\mathcal{U}$ given DAG $G = (\mathcal{U}, \mathcal{E})$, then C is said to d–separate A from B (in symbol $(A, B, C)_G$) if for each non–directed path between a node in A and a node in B, there exists a node x in the path which satisfies one of these two conditions*

1. *x is a collider (i.e. both edges point to x), $x \notin C$ and $ds(x) \cap C = \emptyset$;*
2. *x is not a collider and $x \in C$.*

In order to study the representation of an independence model, we need to distinguish between dependence maps and independence maps, since there are models that cannot be completely represented by a DAG (see e.g. [10,12,17]).

Definition 2. *Let J be a set of conditional independence relations on S. A DAG $G = (S, \mathcal{E})$ is a* dependence map *(briefly a D–map) for $\bar{J}$ if for each triple $(A, B, C) \in S^{(3)}$*

$$(A, B, C) \in \bar{J} \Rightarrow (A, B, C)_G.$$

Moreover, $G = (S, \mathcal{E})$ is an independence map *(briefly an I–map) for $\bar{J}$ if for each triple $(A, B, C) \in S^{(3)}$*

$$(A, B, C)_G \Rightarrow (A, B, C) \in \bar{J}.$$

G is a minimal I–map *for $\bar{J}$ if deleting any arc, G is no more an I–map.*

Finally, G is said to be a perfect map *(briefly a P–map) for $\bar{J}$ if it is both a I–map and a D–map.*

A P–map for $\bar{J}$ needs not be unique. The *skeleton* of a DAG G is an undirected graph which is obtained from G by removing direction in each edge. A triple (i, j, k) of vertices in a DAG G is called a *v–structure* ([14,11]) if the edge (i, j) and (k, j) appears in G, but there is no edge between i and k.

Definition 3. *Two DAGs $G_1 = (S, \mathcal{E}_1)$ and $G_2 = (S, \mathcal{E}_2)$ with the same vertices are equivalent if they have the same skeleton and the same set of v–structures.*

Then, it is known from [12] that

Proposition 1. *If $G_1 = (S, \mathcal{E}_1)$ and $G_2 = (S, \mathcal{E}_2)$ are both P–map, then they are equivalent. On the other hand, if G_1 is a P–map for $\bar{J}$ and G_2 is equivalent to G_1, then G_2 is also a P–map for $\bar{J}$.*

3.1   The BN–Draw Procedure

Given an ordering π on S, it is possible to find a minimal I–map G_π for $\bar{J}$, starting from J_*, as shown in [5].

The function which accomplishes this task is called BN–DRAW and uses the following operation: for each $\theta = (A, B, C) \in S^{(3)}$, for any $x \in S$ and $T \subseteq S$, define

$$\Pi(\theta, T, x) = \begin{cases} T \cap (A \cup C) & \text{if } C \subseteq T \subseteq A \cup B \cup C \text{ and } x \in A; \\ T \cap (B \cup C) & \text{if } C \subseteq T \subseteq A \cup B \cup C \text{ and } x \in B; \\ T & \text{otherwise.} \end{cases}$$

For a given $x \in S$, we denote by $S_{(x)}$ the set of all the elements of S which precede x with respect to π. Thus, among all the sets $\Pi(\theta, S_{(x)}, x)$, for each $\theta \in J_*$, there exists a minimal one with respect to inclusion (see [5,12]). Such a minimal set is computed by the function PARENTS.

Hence, BN–DRAW simply calls PARENTS for each node (following the ordering π) and draws the graph.

function BN–DRAW(n, π, J_*)
   $T \leftarrow \emptyset$
   $G \leftarrow$ a graph with S as vertex set and no edges
   for $i \leftarrow 2$ **to** n
      $T \leftarrow T \cup \{\pi_{i-1}\}$
      $pa \leftarrow$ PARENTS(π_i, T, J_*)
      draw an arc in G from each index in pa to π_i
   end for
   return G
end function

The overall cost of BN–DRAW is $O(mn)$, since the function PARENTS is called n times and each call uses $O(m)$ steps.

3.2 The DAG–Representability Theorem

In [5] we have given a necessary and sufficient condition for the existence of a P–map for a given set J of conditional independencies. This result is based on the fast closure of J, so it allows to identify all the possible orderings for which BN–DRAW returns a P–map.

We have also described an algorithm to check whether $\bar{J}$ admits a P–map and, in the affirmative case, to find one of them.

Unfortunately, the worst case complexity of the related procedure is exponential with respect to the number n of variables, while it is linear with respect to the cardinality m of J_*. Anyway, some empirical evaluations presented in [4,5] show that it is possible to handle sets of some hundreds of conditional independencies and tens of variables in a reasonable amount of time.

4 The Algorithm PC$_*$

In this section we describe a new algorithm which finds, if any, a perfect map for a set of conditional independencies J which uses the fast closure J_*. The algorithm, divided in 6 phases, takes inspiration from PC algorithm [14] and its variants [9], thus it is called PC$_*$. The input is J_* and the output is a P–map for J_* or a failure when J_* is not representable with a P–map.

Preprocessing phase
For each unordered couple $i, j \in S$, with $i \neq j$, compute the sets

$$\mathcal{C}_{ij} = \{A \cup B \cup C \setminus \{i,j\} \,:\, (A,B,C) \in J_* \text{ s.t. } (i \in A \text{ and } j \in B) \text{ or } (i \in B \text{ and } j \in A)\}$$

and $W_{ij} = \bigcup_{K \in \mathcal{C}_{ij}} K$.

This phase requires $O(m)$ step, in which at most n sets among $\mathcal{C}_{ij}$ and W_{ij} are updated. The sets W_{ij} are called "witnesses" in other works (see for instance [11]).

Computing the skeleton
Create the undirected graph $G_u = (S, E_u)$ by taking

$$E_u = \{\{i,j\} : i,j \in S, i \neq j, W_{ij} = \emptyset\}.$$

The graph G_u contains the skeleton of every potential P–map for $\bar{J}$, but without a direction.

Proposition 2. *If G is a P–map for $\bar{J}$, then there is no edge between i and j in G if and only if the triple (i,j,C) is g–included in J_*, for some $C \subseteq S$.*

Proof. In [4] we prove that $\bar{J} \sqsubseteq J_*$ and $J_* \subseteq \bar{J}$, that is for any triple $\theta \in \bar{J}$ there is a triple $\theta' \in J_*$ such that $\theta \sqsubseteq \theta'$ and any $\theta' \in J_*$ belongs to $\bar{J}$.

Therefore, if a DAG G is a P–map for $\bar{J}$ and $\{i,j\}$ is a pair of nodes such that between them there is no edge in G, then there exists a set C of nodes (possibly empty), with $i,j \notin C$, such that by d–separation $(\{i\}, \{j\}, C)_G$. Now, by Definition 2 it follows that $(\{i\}, \{j\}, C)_G \Leftrightarrow (\{i\}, \{j\}, C) \in \bar{J}$ and so if and only if there is triple $\theta' \in J_*$ which g-includes $(\{i\}, \{j\}, C)$. □

It is simple to see that this phase requires at most $O(n^2)$ steps. Let SKELETON be the function which accomplishes these two first phases.

Directing the v–structures
The third phase defines the direction of some edges, by creating the v–structure, taking into account of the witnesses. Let i, j, k be three nodes such that there is an undirected edge between i and j and an undirected edge between k and j, but there is no edge between i and k (this configuration is called *immorality*), we make a v–structure $i \to j \leftarrow k$ if and only if $j \notin W_{ik}$.

Hence, this step computes

$$E'_d = \{(i,j),(k,j) : \text{ for } i,j,k \in S, \{i,j\} \in E_u, \{k,j\} \in E_u, \{i,k\} \notin E_u, j \notin W_{ik}\}$$

and E'_u, which is composed by all the other edges in E_u.

At the end of this phase, which needs $O(n^3)$ steps to be executed, we obtain a partially directed graph $G_p = (S, E'_d \cup E'_u)$. The main property of G_p is that

Proposition 3. *If G is a P–map for $\bar{J}$, then there is a v-structure $i \to j \leftarrow k$ in G if and only if no triple (i,k,C), for any set C containing j, is g–included in J_*.*

Proof. Since $\bar{J} \sqsubseteq J_*$ and $J_* \subseteq \bar{J}$ (see [4]) the proof trivially follows from Definition 1 and Proposition 2. □

Therefore, if $\bar{J}$ is representable with a P–map, then G_p contains all the edges (even if some edges in G_p can be still undirected) and all the v–structures of any P–map for $\bar{J}$.

This phase, one through the function V–STRUCTURES, requires at most $O(n^3)$ steps, because it must check all the possible triples of vertices and eventually select the directions of two edges per step.

Creating the DAG
Now, let us choose the direction to all the remaining undirected edges, by avoiding to create loops or new v–structures. The step, called PROPAGATE, consists in forming a (partial) directed acyclic graph G_d, where E_d'' are the directed edges and E_u'' the undirected edges. Initially G_d is equal to G_u. PROPAGATE repeatedly selects directions for edges by means of the following propagation rules

R1 if $(i,j) \in E_d''$, $\{j,k\} \in E_u''$, and $\{i,k\} \notin E_u''$ then add (j,k) to E_d'' and remove $\{j,k\}$ from E_u'';

R2 if $(i,k) \in E_d''$, $(k,j) \in E_d''$, and $\{i,j\} \in E_u''$ then add (i,j) to E_d'' and remove $\{i,j\}$ from E_u'';

R3 if $(i,k) \in E_d''$, $(k,j) \in E_d''$, $(i,l) \in E_d''$, $(l,j) \in E_d''$, and $\{i,j\} \in E_u''$ then add (i,j) to E_d'' and remove $\{i,j\}$ from E_u''.

If this phase is compelled to create loops or new v–structures, then the entire procedure fails, because it can be proved that no P–map exists.

On the other hand, if G_d still contains undirected edges, the procedure PROPAGATE should be executed again, after having selected an undirected edge and chosen any direction for it, until all the edges are directed.

This phase ends either with a failure or with a DAG G_d extending G_p.

Since R1–R3 do not introduce loops or new v–structure, it follows that

Proposition 4. *The set J_* is representable with a P–map if and only if G_d is a P–map for J_*.*

Proof. If G is a P–map for $\bar{J}$ (and also for J_*), then it is equivalent to G_d. In fact, G has the same skeleton of G_d by Proposition 2 and the same v-structure by Proposition 3. Therefore, by Proposition 1 G_d is a P–map.

Vice versa, if G_d is not a P–map for J_*, then from Proposition 1, Proposition 2 and Proposition 3 it follows that J_* is not representable.

The cost of this phase is polynomial with respect to n, indeed each edge can receive one direction and there are $O(n^2)$ edges and to check R1–R3, $O(n^3)$ elementary steps are necessary.

Check if G_d is a I–map
First, G_d is tested to be an I–map. This can be done by first finding a topological order $\prec$ on S, such that there is an edge from (i,j) only if $i \prec j$. Then, for each $i \in S$, we must check if $(i, S_{(i)} \setminus pa(i), pa(i))$ is g–included in J_*, where, as in the previous section, $S_{(i)}$ is the set of all variables j such that $j \prec i$.

This phase, realized by the function CHECK–I–MAP, requires $O(mn)$ steps, because each triple $(i, S_{(i)} \setminus pa(i), pa(i))$ must be searched in J_*.

Obviously, the failure of this phase leads to the failure of the entire procedure PC$_*$.

Check if G_d is a D–map
The last phase is to check whether G_d is a D–map. In the affirmative case, $\bar{J}$ is representable with G_d. Moreover, it is possible to find the maximal partial DAG

which represents $\bar{J}$, i.e. the partial DAG which "contains" all the P–map for $\bar{J}$, by storing the result of the first call of PROPAGATE.

To perform this step, it is necessary to check whether A is d–separated from B by C, for each $(A, B, C) \in J$ and this is done by means of function CHECK–D–MAP. One of the best method is the algorithm 3.1 of [9] which has a linear time complexity with respect to the graph size.

The overall procedure
The algorithm is then summarized in the function PC_*, whose computation time is linear in m and polynomial in n.

function $\mathrm{PC}_*(J_*)$
    if SKELETON(J_*) fails **then return** FAILURE
    if V–STRUCTURES(J_*) fails **then return** FAILURE
    let G the graph produced so far
    while G has an undirected edge
        select an undirected edge and choose a direction
        if PROPAGATE(G) fails **then return** FAILURE
    end while
    if not CHECK–I–MAP(G) **then return** FAILURE
    if not CHECK–D–MAP(G) **then return** FAILURE
    return G
end function

5 Finding an I–Map

When a perfect map for an independence model does not exist, it is however possible to find several I–maps and to determine for each of them the number of relations which are representable. Therefore, an interesting problem is to find a **minimal I–map which represents the largest possible number of relations**. In this context, we focus only on maximal triples (those in J_*) and the corresponding map is denoted by $G(J_*)$.

Theorem 1. *Let J be a set of independence relations, consider its closure $\bar{J}$ and its fast closure J_*. Then, there is an I–map representing $J_1 \subseteq \bar{J}$ if there exists an ordering π on the variables such that for each $\tau \in J_1$ there exists a triple $\theta = (A, B, C) \in J^*$ such that $\tau \sqsubseteq \theta$ and satisfying the following conditions*

C1 for each $c \in C$ such that $S_{(c)} \cap A \neq \emptyset$ and $S_{(c)} \cap B \neq \emptyset$, there exists a triple $\theta_c \in J_*$ such that $\Pi(\theta_c, S_{(c)}, c) \cap A = \emptyset$ or $\Pi(\theta_c, S_{(c)}, c) \cap B = \emptyset$;

C2 for each $a \in A$ such that $S_{(a)} \cap B \neq \emptyset$ or $S_{(a)} \cap (S \setminus \mathcal{X}) \neq \emptyset$ there exists a triple $\theta_a \in J_*$ such that $\Pi(\theta_a, S_{(a)}, a) \cap [B \cup (S \setminus \mathcal{X})] = \emptyset$;

C3 for each $b \in B$ such that $S_{(b)} \cap A \neq \emptyset$ or $S_{(b)} \cap (S \setminus \mathcal{X}) \neq \emptyset$ there exists a triple $\theta_b \in J_*$ such that $\Pi(\theta_b, S_{(b)}, b) \cap [A \cup (S \setminus \mathcal{X})] = \emptyset$;

C4 for each $c \in C$ such that $S_{(c)} \cap (S \setminus \mathcal{X}) \neq \emptyset$, there exists a triple $\theta_c' \in J_*$ such that $\Pi(\theta_c', S_{(c)}, c) \cap (S \setminus \mathcal{X}) = \emptyset$.

Proof. The proof goes along the same line of the proof of Theorem related to condition C1–C4 given in [5].

Note that Theorem 1 assures that the triples in J_1 are representable, but no conclusion can be drawn on those belonging to $J_2 = \bar{J} \setminus J_1$. In fact there could be some non maximal triple in J_2 which is representable, even if it is not g–included on some not representable maximal triple.

Example 1. *Let*

$$J = \{(\{3\}, \{2\}, \{1\}), (\{4\}, \{1\}, \{2,3\}), (\{5\}, \{1,2,4\}, \{3\})\}$$

be a set of triples, then the related fast closure is

$$J_* = \{(\{5\}, \{1,2,4\}, \{3\}), (\{2\}, \{3,5\}, \{1\}), (\{4\}, \{1,5\}, \{2,3\}), (\{1\}, \{4,5\}, \{2,3\})\}.$$

Given the ordering $\pi = <2,3,4,1,5>$ the associated DAG G_π represents the set

$$J_1 = \{(\{5\}, \{1,2,4\}, \{3\}), (\{4\}, \{1,5\}, \{2,3\}), (\{1\}, \{4,5\}, \{2,3\})\}$$

but not $J_2 = \{(\{2\}, \{3,5\}, \{1\})\}$.
Moreover, G_π represents $(\{2\}, \{5\}, \{1,3\}) \sqsubseteq (\{2\}, \{3,5\}, \{1\})$.

Note that there exists a P–map representing the set J_* of the previous example: it is enough to consider the ordering $\pi' = <1,2,3,4,5>$.

Then, we propose to compute the number of the maximal represented triples and to compare the I–maps according to this criterion. This comparison allows to have a computational cost that is less than usual one based on the number of the represented triples in $\bar{J}$.

5.1   An Algorithm to Find $G(J_*)$

In this section we describe an algorithm to find $G(J_*)$ starting from the fast closure J_* of a set of conditional independencies.

The algorithm is based on a backtracking search process, which is executed by function SEARCH described below. The search space is the set of all the sequences π of indices in S without duplicates. A sequence represents a partial ordering on S: $\pi_i = x$ means that x is the i–th variable in the ordering. The sequence π is filled starting from the left, i.e. from the first variable in the ordering, and adding a variable at a time in the leftmost empty position in π. A total ordering corresponds to a complete sequence of indices, i.e. a permutation of S.

In the following, given a set K of conditional independencies, we refer to a partition of K composed by the three subsets K_+, K_- and $K_?$, which contain, respectively, the triples represented, the non representable triples and the triples whose state is unknown. When the ordering is complete, $K_? = \emptyset$.

When SEARCH chooses x as i–th element of π, the partition K must be updated by finding

- all the triples in $\theta \in K_?$ which cannot be represented, this happens when x appears in θ and some of conditions $C1$–$C4$ is violated;
- all the triples in $\theta \in K_?$ which are fully represented, this happens when all the conditions $C1$–$C4$ are satisfied and all the variables appearing in θ are placed in π.

The function UPDATE performs this task is then

```
function UPDATE (π, i, K)
    T ← π[1, ..., i − 1]
    Q ← PARENTS(πᵢ, T, K)
    for each θ = (A, B, C) ∈ K?
        if [(πᵢ ∈ A) ∧ (A ∩ Q ≠ ∅)]∨
           [(πᵢ ∈ B) ∧ (B ∩ Q ≠ ∅)]∨
           [(πᵢ ∈ C) ∧ (A ∩ Q ≠ ∅) ∧ (B ∩ Q ≠ ∅)] then
                K₋ ← K₋ ∪ {θ}
                K? ← K? \ {θ}
        else if A ∪ B ∪ C ⊆ T ∪ {x} then
                K₊ ← K₊ ∪ {θ}
                K? ← K? \ {θ}
    end for
    return K
end function
```

The function SEARCH performs a backtracking search in which, at i-th step, it tries all the possible variables to be placed at the i-th place in π. The variables π^{best} and K^{best}, which contain the best found ordering and its corresponding partition, are global variables. The search process is pruned when $|K_+ \cup K_?| \leq |K_+^{best}|$, i.e. when the number of representable triples cannot be greater than the number of triples represented in the best ordering found so far. In this way, it is not necessary to find all the completions of π, thus avoiding useless computational efforts, because each of these completions would provide an I–map which cannot be better than that induced by π^{best}.

```
function SEARCH (π, i, V, K)
    if V = ∅ then
        if |K₊| > |K₊ᵇᵉˢᵗ| then (πᵇᵉˢᵗ, Kᵇᵉˢᵗ) ← (π, K)
        return
    end if
    if |K₊ ∪ K?| ≤ |K₊ᵇᵉˢᵗ| then return
    for each x ∈ V
        πᵢ ← x
        K' ← UPDATE(π, i, K)
        SEARCH(π, i + 1, V \ {x}, K')
    end for
end function
```

Finally, the main function is MAX–I–MAP, which calls SEARCH with an initial empty sequence.

function MAX–I–MAP(J_*)
    $K^{best} \leftarrow\ < \emptyset, \emptyset, J_* >$
    SEARCH($\emptyset, 1, S, < \emptyset, \emptyset, J_* >$)
    return BN–DRAW(π^{best}, K^{best})
end function

6   Conclusions

We show how to apply the technique used in the well known PC algorithm [14,15] in the context of fast closure, by defining an algorithm which finds, if any, a P–map for a set J in a time which is polynomial in both n and m (the size of the fast closure). This is an enhancement with respect to Verma and Pearl's algorithm [14,13] and successive versions [11,15], in which it is necessary to perform a huge number of queries to the independence model, since it is impossible to have an explicit representation in memory of the complete closure $\bar{J}$. This is an improvement also with respect to the procedure in [4,5], which uses a backtracking search method through the space of orderings and which is, in the worst case, exponential with respect to n.

Another relevant result is related to find a "best possible graph" for $\bar{J}$ when no P–map does exist. This concept is important because it allows to have a graphical *incomplete* representation for any set of conditional independencies. A major point of future works is to find a different mathematical characterization of $G(J_*)$ which allows to define faster algorithms.

It would be worth to investigate the application of the PC$_*$ approach to the problem of learning the structure of a Bayesian networks from data (as done e.g. in [18]). Hence, an interesting point is to establish whether there exists a way of testing only "maximal" conditional independencies, thus reducing the number of tests to be performed. Moreover, it would be interesting to study how to extract $G(J_*)$ from data and to compare it with the DAGs found by the usual algorithms, mainly when data are generated from a non decomposable distribution.

References

1. Baioletti, M., Busanello, G., Vantaggi, B.: Algorithms for the closure of graphoid structures. In: Proc. of 12th Inter. Conf. IPMU 2008, Malaga, pp. 930–937 (2008)
2. Baioletti, M., Busanello, G., Vantaggi, B.: Conditional independence structure and its closure: Inferential rules and algorithms. Int. J. Approx. Reasoning 50, 1097–1114 (2009)
3. Baioletti, M., Busanello, G., Vantaggi, B.: Acyclic directed graphs to represent conditional independence models. In: Sossai, C., Chemello, G. (eds.) ECSQARU 2009. LNCS, vol. 5590, pp. 530–541. Springer, Heidelberg (2009)

4. Baioletti, M., Busanello, G., Vantaggi, B.: An algorithm to find a perfect map for graphoid structures Proc. of 13th Inter. In: Hüllermeier, E., Kruse, R., Hoffmann, F. (eds.) IPMU 2010. Communications in Computer and Information Science, vol. 80, pp. 1–10. Springer, Heidelberg (2010)
5. Baioletti, M., Busanello, G., Vantaggi, B.: Acyclic directed graphs representing independence models. Int. J. Approx. Reasoning 52, 2–18 (2011)
6. Bouckaert, R.R., Studený, M.: Racing algorithms for conditional independence inference. Int. J. Approx. Reasoning 45, 386–401 (2007)
7. Cowell, R.G., Dawid, A.P., Lauritzen, S.L., Spiegelhalter, D.J.: Probabilistic Networks and Expert Systems. Springer, New York (1999)
8. Jensen, F.V., Lauritzen, S.L.: Probabilistic networks Handbook of Defeasible Reasoning and Uncertainty Management Systems. Kluwer Academic Publishers, Netherlands (2000)
9. Koller, D., Friedman, N.: Probabilistic Graphical Models: Principles and Techniques. MIT Press, Cambridge (2009)
10. Lauritzen, S.L.: Graphical models. Clarendon Press, Oxford (1996)
11. Meek, C.: Causal inference and causal exploration with background knowledge. In: 11th Conf. in Uncertainty in Artificial Intelligence, UAI 1995, pp. 403–410 (1995)
12. Pearl, J.: Probabilistic reasoning in intelligent systems: networks of plausible inference. Morgan Kaufmann, Los Altos (1988)
13. Pearl, J.: Causality. Cambridge University Press, Cambridge (2000)
14. Pearl, J., Verma, T.: An Algorithm for Deciding if a Set of Observed Independencies Has a Causal Explanation. In: 8th Conf. in Uncertainty in Artificial Intelligence, UAI 1992, pp. 323–330 (1992)
15. Spirtes, P., Glymour, C., Scheines, R.: Causation, Prediction, and Search. MIT Press, Cambridge (2001)
16. Studený, M.: Semigraphoids and structures of probabilistic conditional independence. Ann. Math. Artif. Intell. 21, 71–98 (1997)
17. Studený, M.: Probabilistic Conditional Independence Structures. Springer, London (2005)
18. Tsamardinos, I., Brown, L.E., Aliferis, C.F.: The max–min hill–climbing Bayesian network structure learning algorithm. Machine Learning 65, 31–78 (2006)
19. Wong, S.K.M., Butz, C.J., Wu, D.: On the Implication Problem for Probabilistic Conditional Independency. IEEE Transactions on Systems, Man, and Cybernetics, Part A: Systems and Humans 30(6), 785–805 (2000)

Marginalization without Summation
Exploiting Determinism in Factor Algebra

Sander Evers and Peter J.F. Lucas

Institute for Computer and Information Sciences
Radboud University Nijmegen
{s.evers,peterl}@cs.ru.nl

Abstract. It is known that solving an exact inference problem on a discrete Bayesian network with many deterministic nodes can be far cheaper than what would be expected based on its treewidth. In this article, we introduce a novel technique for this: to the operations of factor multiplication and factor summation that form the basis of many inference algorithms, we add *factor indexing*. We integrate this operation into variable elimination, and extend the minweight heuristic accordingly. A preliminary empirical evaluation gives promising results.

Keywords: Bayesian networks, exact inference, factor algebra, deterministic variables.

1 Introduction

In general, exact inference on a Bayesian network with discrete variables is known to take $O(d^w)$ time, where d is the domain size (assuming it is the same for each variable) and w is the treewidth of the network's moral graph[4]. In the canonical technique for exact inference, *variable elimination*[11], this constraint manifests itself as the minimal size of the largest factor that is created during the execution of the algorithm; implemented as a multidimensional array, it has w dimensions and d entries per dimension.

When a network contains deterministic nodes, inference can be much faster. One example where this can be seen is the approach of Chavira and Darwiche[1], in which a Bayesian network is transformed into a logical theory, and inference is performed by counting the models of this theory. These models should be consistent with the constraints imposed by the deterministic nodes. A good model counting algorithm can use these constraints effectively to prune the model search space. This approach, however, is quite remote from other inference algorithms in that it does not compute per-variable probabilities 'in bulk' by multiplication and summation of factors.

An approach by Larkin and Dechter[8] does use these factor operations. Here, a factor is implemented not as an array (with an entry for each possible variable assignment), but as a list of variable assignments that are nonzero (sometimes called a *sparse array*). The length of this list can be much smaller than the size of the array, but the overhead for multiplying and marginalizing factors is larger,

W. Liu (Ed.): ECSQARU 2011, LNAI 6717, pp. 251–262, 2011.

because the list has to be searched for values (possibly using a hash table). With this alternative implementation of factors, ordinary variable elimination can be performed.

The inference approach presented in this article is also based on the familiar factor operations. Firstly, we use a cheap representation of factors for deterministic variables. More importantly, we introduce a new marginalization method for these variables, which requires no summation and can therefore be much faster. We apply this method in a variable elimination algorithm, and propose an extended minweight heuristic informed by this method. However, because the marginalization method is formulated as a rewrite rule for factor expressions, its potential use is not limited to variable elimination, but can be extended to all inference algorithms that use factor operations.

The remainder of the article has the following outline. Sect. 2 summarizes the formal preliminaries for inference on Bayesian networks. In Sect. 3, we review variable elimination, with an emphasis on the use of factor algebra. Our main contribution, *factor indexing*, is presented in Sect. 4, followed by an empirical evaluation in Sect. 5. In Sect. 6, we conclude and propose future work.

2   Formal Preliminaries

We consider Bayesian networks over a set $\mathbf{V} = \{V_1, \ldots, V_n\}$ of n discrete variables; each V_i has a finite domain $\mathrm{dom}(V_i)$. Formally, an *instantiation* $\mathbf{v} = \{V_1 = v_1, \ldots, V_n = v_n\}$ of these variables is a function that maps each V_i to a value $v_i \in \mathrm{dom}(V_i)$, often also called a *state*. With a little abuse of notation, we write $\mathbf{v} \in \mathbf{V}$ to let a variable $\mathbf{v}$ range over the possible instantiations of $\mathbf{V}$, e.g. in a summation. We follow the convention of using upper case for variables, lower case for instantiations/values and boldface for sets.

A *factor* f over variables $\mathbf{V}$ is a function that maps every instantiation $\mathbf{v} \in \mathbf{V}$ to a number $f(\mathbf{v})$ (often a probability). It is similar to an ordinary mathematical function with multiple arguments, only it refers to them by name instead of position. For example, where for ordinary functions in general $f(x, y) \neq f(y, x)$, for factors it is the case that $f(X = x, Y = y) = f(Y = y, X = x)$; formally, the factor f is applied to the set $\{X = x, Y = y\}$, but we omit the braces to reduce clutter.

In inference implementations, factors are stored as multidimensional arrays. Where for ordinary functions these dimensions would be *numbered* conforming to the function arguments, for factors they are *named* after variables, hence it seems natural to define f's dimensionality as the whole set: $\dim(f) \stackrel{\mathrm{def}}{=} \mathbf{V}$. The *weight* of a factor equals the size of the array needed to store all its values: $\mathsf{weight}(f) \stackrel{\mathrm{def}}{=} \prod_{V_j \in \dim(f)} |\mathrm{dom}(V_j)|$.

Factor algebra provides the tools for manipulating factors:

- *Application* $f(\mathbf{v})$: Applying a factor f to an instantiation $\mathbf{v}$ with $\mathbf{v} \in \dim(f)$ is simply function application, and results in a single value. However, a factor can also be partially applied, i.e. to an instantiation $\mathbf{w} \in \mathbf{W} \subset \dim(f)$. The result of this operation is a factor $f' = f(\mathbf{w})$ with $\dim(f') = \dim(f) \setminus \mathbf{W}$. Superfluous variables ($\notin \dim(f)$) are simply ignored: $f(\mathbf{v}, V_{n+1} = x) = f(\mathbf{v})$.

$$(f(\mathbf{w}))(\mathbf{u}) \overset{\text{def}}{=} f(\mathbf{u}, \mathbf{w}) \qquad\qquad\qquad f \otimes 1 = f \qquad\qquad (1)$$

$$(f \otimes g)(\mathbf{v}) \overset{\text{def}}{=} f(\mathbf{v}) \cdot g(\mathbf{v}) \qquad\qquad f \otimes g = g \otimes f \qquad\qquad (2)$$

$$(\Sigma_{\mathbf{W}} f)(\mathbf{u}) \overset{\text{def}}{=} \sum_{\mathbf{w} \in \mathbf{W}} f(\mathbf{u}, \mathbf{w}) \qquad f \otimes (g \otimes h) = (f \otimes g) \otimes h = \bigotimes\{f, g, h\} \qquad (3)$$

$$\Sigma_V \Sigma_W f = \Sigma_W \Sigma_V f = \Sigma_{V,W} f \qquad\qquad (4)$$

$$\Sigma_V (f \otimes g) = \Sigma_V f \otimes g \quad \text{if } V \in \dim(f), \qquad (5)$$
$$V \notin \dim(g)$$

$$f[V{=}d](\mathbf{u}) \overset{\text{def}}{=} f(\mathbf{u}, V{=}d(\mathbf{u}))$$

$$\mathbb{1}_{V=d}(V{=}v, \mathbf{u}) \overset{\text{def}}{=} \begin{cases} 1 & \text{if } v = d(\mathbf{u}) \\ 0 & \text{if } v \neq d(\mathbf{u}) \end{cases} \qquad \Sigma_V (f \otimes g) = f \otimes \Sigma_V g \quad \text{if } V \notin \dim(f), \qquad (6)$$
$$V \in \dim(g)$$

$$(f \otimes g)(\mathbf{e}) = f(\mathbf{e}) \otimes g(\mathbf{e}) \qquad\qquad (7)$$

Fig. 1. Factor algebra. First, the commonly found operations *application, multiplication* and *summation*; next, our new operations *indexing* and *concretization*.

$$(\Sigma_V f)(\mathbf{e}) = \Sigma_V f(\mathbf{e}) \quad \text{if } \mathbf{e} \text{ does not} \qquad (8)$$
$$\text{instantiate } V$$

Fig. 2. Laws of factor algebra

- *Multiplication $f \otimes g$*: Multiplication of factors is lifted value multiplication. The result of this operation is a factor $h = f \otimes g$ with $\dim(h) = \dim(f) \cup \dim(g)$. Multiplication is associative and commutative; we write $\bigotimes_{1 \leq j \leq n} f_j = f_1 \otimes f_2 \otimes \ldots \otimes f_n$ for n-way multiplication, and $\mathbb{1}$ for its unit element.
- *Summation $\Sigma_{\mathbf{W}} f$*: Summation over variables $\mathbf{W}$ removes the $\mathbf{W}$ variables from the dimensionality of a factor by summing up all the values of instantiations that differ only at $\mathbf{W}$ variables.

Formal definitions of these operations are listed in Fig. 1 (top). They obey several equality laws (Fig. 2) which we will use to prove correctness of inference.

As our work is expressed in factor algebra, we go as far as to *define* Bayesian networks in terms of factor algebra, in order to keep notation as coherent as possible. A *Bayesian network* is a triple $(\mathbf{V}, \mathsf{par}, \mathbf{cpd})$, where $\mathbf{V}$ consists of n discrete variables as above; the function par maps each variable V_j to a set of *parents* $\mathbf{V}_{\mathsf{par}(j)} \subset \mathbf{V}$ in such a way that there are no cycles; the set $\mathbf{cpd} = \{cpd_1, \ldots, cpd_n\}$ contains, for each V_j, a factor cpd_j over $\{V_j\} \cup \mathbf{V}_{\mathsf{par}(j)}$ with $(\Sigma_{V_j} cpd_j)(\mathbf{v}_{\mathsf{par}(j)}) = 1$ for each $\mathbf{v}_{\mathsf{par}(j)} \in \mathbf{V}_{\mathsf{par}(j)}$. Each Bayesian network defines a factor jpd known as its *joint probability distribution*: $jpd \overset{\text{def}}{=} \bigotimes_{1 \leq j \leq n} cpd_j$. It can be proven that $\Sigma_{\mathbf{V}} jpd = 1$. An example (fragment) of a Bayesian network with $\mathbf{V} = \{X, Y, Z, A, M, \ldots\}$ is shown in Fig. 3, and applying the $\otimes$ and Σ operations to its $\mathbf{cpd}$ factors is demonstrated in Fig. 4.

An *inference query* is defined as the joint distribution over a set of query variables $\mathbf{Q} \subseteq \mathbf{V}$ and an instantiation $\mathbf{e}$ of evidence variables $\mathbf{E} \subseteq \mathbf{V}$:

$$inf_{\mathbf{Q},\mathbf{e}} \overset{\text{def}}{=} (\Sigma_{\mathbf{R}} jpd)(\mathbf{e}) \qquad \text{where } \mathbf{R} = \mathbf{V} \setminus (\mathbf{Q} \cup \mathbf{E})$$

An *inference procedure* is an algorithm that, given an arbitrary Bayesian network, query variables $\mathbf{Q}$ and evidence $\mathbf{e}$, calculates the value of $inf_{\mathbf{Q},\mathbf{e}}$.

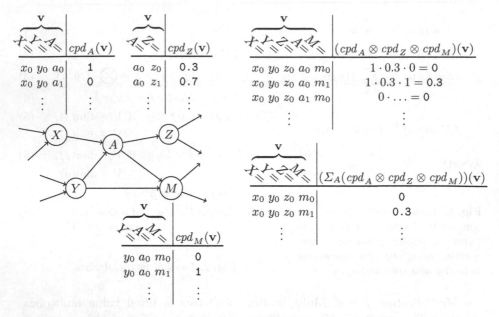

Fig. 3. Example fragment of a Bayesian network, in which the *cpd* factors for variables A, Z and M are partially given. An array implementation of the factors would store the values in `typewriter` font.

Fig. 4. Examples of applying the factor algebra operators $\otimes$ and Σ_A to the factors from the Bayesian network. Note: as $X=x_0$ and $Y=y_0$ together determine that $A=a_0$, the first two values in the bottom factor equal those in the top factor.

Relation to the conventional definition. The *jpd* factor corresponds to the joint probability distribution in the conventional definition: $P(\mathbf{v}) = jpd(\mathbf{v})$, and it is easily shown that the conditional probability distributions $P(v_j | \mathbf{v}_{\mathsf{par}(j)})$ derived from this joint distribution equal the cpd_j factors. The reason that we avoid the P notation is that it often clashes with factor application. For example, for $\mathbf{W} \subset \mathbf{V}$, $P(\mathbf{W})$ denotes a distribution over $\mathbf{W}$ while $jpd(\mathbf{w})$ is a factor over the complement $\mathbf{V} \setminus \mathbf{W}$. The two notations are related as follows: for a marginal distribution, $P(\mathbf{W}) = \Sigma_{\mathbf{V} \setminus \mathbf{W}} jpd$, and for partial evidence, $P(\mathbf{e}) = (\Sigma_{\mathbf{V} \setminus \mathbf{E}} jpd)(\mathbf{e})$.

3   Variable Elimination as Factor Rewriting

In this section, we review the inference procedure of variable elimination[11]. More precisely, variable elimination is a family of inference procedures parameterized by a *variable elimination order* which mostly determines its efficiency. The order we use is the *minweight* heuristic, known in practice to outperform other heuristics when variables have different domain sizes[7].

The algorithm, its correctness proof and the rationale for the heuristic presented here serve as a basis for our extended version, which will be introduced in Sec. 4 and exploits deterministic variables.

Algorithm 1. Minweight variable elimination.

Input: – Bayesian network $(\mathbf{V}, \mathrm{par}, \{cpd_1, \ldots, cpd_n\})$
           – query variables $\mathbf{Q} \subseteq \mathbf{V}$; evidence $\mathbf{e}$ (instantiation of $\mathbf{E} \subseteq \mathbf{V}$)
Output: *result*, a factor over $\mathbf{Q}$ equal to $\mathit{inf}_{\mathbf{Q},\mathbf{e}}$

$\mathbf{W} := \mathbf{V} \setminus (\mathbf{Q} \cup \mathbf{E})$
foreach cpd_j **do** $f_j := cpd_j(\mathbf{e})$

while $\mathbf{W}$ is not empty **do**
   | choose $V_i \in \mathbf{W}$ for which the cost of $eliminate(V_i)$ is smallest
   | $eliminate(V_i)$
   | $\mathbf{W} := \mathbf{W} \setminus \{V_i\}$

$result := \bigotimes\{\text{all remaining } f_j\}$

procedure $eliminate(V_i)$
   | $p := \mathbb{1}$
   | **foreach** f_j s.t. $V_i \in \dim(f_j)$ **do**
   | | $p := p \otimes f_j$
   | | delete f_j
   | $f_i := \varSigma_{V_i} p$

Variable elimination (Alg. 1) roughly proceeds as follows: it starts out from the collection of cpd_j factors and directly applies the evidence $\mathbf{e}$; then it repeatedly selects a variable V_i from $\mathbf{R}$, removes the factors containing V_i from the collection and replaces them by their product, with V_i summed out. These steps are repeated until all variables from $\mathbf{R}$ have been eliminated. Note that at any time, the remaining factors are stored in the f_j variables (where the j indices are in general not contiguous, as these variables are progressively deleted); this scheme is chosen for the sake of extension into Alg. 2.

Postponing the question of the variable elimination order (i.e. selecting the smallest cost) for a while, we first set out to prove that Alg. 1 produces the correct result: a factor algebra expression that is equal to $\mathit{inf}_{\mathbf{Q},\mathbf{e}}$.

Proof. Specifically, the invariant $\mathit{inf}_{\mathbf{Q},\mathbf{e}} = \varSigma_{\mathbf{W}} \bigotimes\{\text{all remaining } f_j\}$ holds at the start of each loop iteration. At the first iteration,

$$\varSigma_{\mathbf{W}} \bigotimes\{\text{all remaining } f_j\} = \varSigma_{\mathbf{R}} \bigotimes_{1 \le i \le n} cpd_i(\mathbf{e}) = \left(\varSigma_{\mathbf{R}} \bigotimes_{1 \le i \le n} cpd_i \right)(\mathbf{e})$$

with the last equality due to laws (7) and (8). This equals $\mathit{inf}_{\mathbf{Q},\mathbf{e}}$ by definition. Next, by law (6):

$$\varSigma_{\mathbf{W}} \left(\bigotimes_{V_i \notin \dim(f_j)} f_j \otimes \bigotimes_{V_i \in \dim(f_j)} f_j \right) = \varSigma_{\mathbf{W} \setminus V_i} \left(\bigotimes_{V_i \notin \dim(f_j)} f_j \otimes \varSigma_{V_i} \bigotimes_{V_i \in \dim(f_j)} f_j \right)$$

Assume that the invariant holds at the start of the loop, so $\mathit{inf}_{\mathbf{Q},\mathbf{e}}$ equals the left expression (in which we have divided up 'all remaining f_j' for convenience into those that do and do not contain V_i). Now, at the end of the loop, $\mathbf{W}$ will be set to $\mathbf{W} \setminus \{V_i\}$, and the f_j factors with $V_i \in \dim(f_j)$ will be replaced with $f_i := \Sigma_{V_i} \bigotimes_{V_i \in \dim(f_j)} f_j$. Thus, the expression at the right is equal to $\Sigma_{\mathbf{W}} \bigotimes \{\text{all remaining } f_j\}$ for the values of $\mathbf{W}$ and f_j at the start of the next loop, and the invariant holds again. After the last loop, $\mathbf{W}$ is empty, so $\inf_{\mathbf{Q},\mathbf{e}} = \bigotimes \{\text{all remaining } f_j\} = result$. $\qquad\square$

Having established that the algorithm produces a correct result, let us examine what this result actually consists of. Although Alg. 1 can certainly be read to perform array operations at factor assignments such as $p := p \otimes f_j$ and $f_i := \Sigma_{V_i} p$, and return an array with the correct values at the end, it does not have to perform any array operations *at all*. Instead, we prefer the reading where it performs a *symbolic construction* of a new factor algebra expression at these points. In that case, the result of the algorithm is not an array, but a large symbolic expression which, as we have just proven, is a rewriting of $\inf_{\mathbf{Q},\mathbf{e}}$. It can be evaluated at a later stage to produce said array. Thus, the inference procedure is divided into a *rewrite* phase and an *evaluation* phase.

The purpose of rewriting $\inf_{\mathbf{Q},\mathbf{e}}$ is that the resulting expression is somehow 'more efficient', i.e. needs less time or space to execute. For this statement to make any sense, we need to ascribe an *operational semantics* to factor algebra expressions (as opposed to the denotational semantics of Fig. 1, in which both expressions are equivalent, as they have the same value). This is easily done (e.g. to perform $f \otimes g$, first perform f and store its resulting array somewhere, then do the same for g, and finally construct the result array by multiplying the stored values); we do not elaborate any further on this. With an operational semantics in place, one can define a cost function in terms of space or time needed.

The order in which Alg. 1 picks variables can now be explained in terms of this cost function: at each iteration, it greedily picks the one which is cheapest to eliminate (paying no attention to the effect that this might have on eliminating other variables later on). To model the cost of an elimination step, we use the size of the largest array constructed in that step, i.e. weight(p) for the final value of p in $eliminate(V_i)$. We define the cost like this in order to simulate the existing minweight heuristic; it might pay off to consider other cost functions. Note that, as weight(p) can be determined from the symbolic expression p, the cost of $eliminate(V_i)$ can be calculated without actually executing p.

This evokes an interesting parallel to query optimization in database management systems, in which it is common practice to construct and optimize a query plan before executing it. Drawing on this parallel, it has already been shown that variable elimination plans can be further optimized using database techniques[2].

4   Factor Indexing

This section presents the main contribution of this article: *factor indexing*, and its integration in variable elimination. We propose a rewrite rule for marginalization without summation, and express it in factor algebra by introducing a new indexing operation. Then, we extend Alg. 1 into Alg. 2, which uses this rule to eliminate deterministic variables.

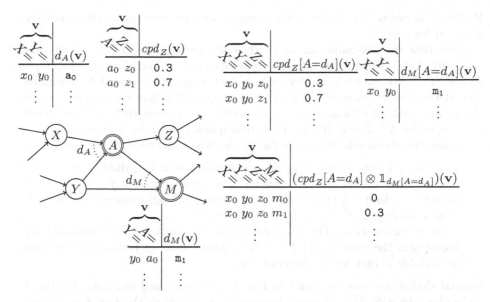

Fig. 5. Same fragment as Fig. 3, with explicit deterministic variables A,M. Their *deterministic factors* store states of A,M instead of probabilities.

Fig. 6. Applying the factor indexing operation to the cpd_Z and d_M factors from the Bayesian network. Their product equals the summed factor in Fig. 4.

A variable $Y \in \mathbf{V}$ is called *deterministic* if its value is functionally determined by the value of its parents (here $\mathbf{X} \subset \mathbf{V}$). This means that its conditional probability distribution has the following form:

$$cpd_Y(Y{=}y, \mathbf{x}) = \begin{cases} 1 & \text{if } y = d_Y(\mathbf{x}) \\ 0 & \text{if } y \neq d_Y(\mathbf{x}) \end{cases}$$

where d_Y is a factor over $\mathbf{X}$ with values in $\mathrm{dom}(Y)$, which we call Y's *deterministic factor*. To make deterministic variables explicit, we now extend the definition of a Bayesian network to $(\mathbf{V}, \mathsf{par}, \mathbf{cpd}, \mathbf{d})$: the set $\mathbf{cpd}$ still contains the factors for non-deterministic variables $V_1, \ldots, V_m$, and the new set $\mathbf{d}$ contains the deterministic factors for deterministic variables $V_{m+1}, \ldots, V_n$. So, factor d_j must be a factor over $\mathsf{par}(V_j)$ with values in $\mathrm{dom}(V_j)$ (unlike a cpd_j factor, $V_j \notin \mathrm{dim}(d_j)$). An example is shown in Fig. 5; it is the same Bayesian network fragment as in Fig. 3, but now with explicit deterministic variables.

To emphasize the simplicity and generality of our rewrite rule, we first present it in conventional notation for our running example. We show the *marginalization without summation* of deterministic variable A:

$$\sum_{a \in A} \mathsf{P}(a|x,y)\mathsf{P}(z|a)\mathsf{P}(m|a,y) = \mathsf{P}(z|A{=}d_A(x,y))\mathsf{P}(m|A{=}d_A(x,y),y)$$

It relies on the following observation: given a certain x and y, the summation contains only one nonzero term, because there is only one value for a that makes

$P(a|x,y)$ nonzero. So, instead of summing, we can just substitute this value $d_A(x,y)$ for every a.

Note that the left-hand side of the formula corresponds to the calculations made by Alg. 1 when eliminating A: first the product $cpd_A \otimes cpd_Z \otimes cpd_M$ is created (a factor over 5 variables), which is subsequently reduced by summing. The deterministic variable elimination that we will define corresponds to the right-hand side; to eliminate A, all we need to do is construct the two factors over variables XYZ and MXY. Their multiplication can be postponed.

To use the above substitution in factor algebra, we introduce new operations:

- *Indexing* $f[V{=}d]$: Factor f is indexed in dimension $V \in \dim(f)$ by another factor d, which has values in $\mathrm{dom}(V)$. The resulting factor $f' = f[V{=}d]$ has $\dim(f') = (\dim(f) \setminus \{V\}) \cup \dim(d)$. Contrary to conventional indexing, the dimensionality of f' can be larger than that of f.
- *Concretization* $\mathbb{1}_{V=d}$: Deterministic factor d is turned into a 'probabilistic' factor over the variables $\{V\} \cup \dim(d)$, whose value is 1 wherever the value of variable V matches d's function value.

Formal definitions can be found in Fig. 1 (bottom), and examples in Fig. 6. Note that the definition of concretization corresponds to the factor containing the conditional probability distribution of a deterministic variable. So, translating a network with explicit deterministic variables into a conventional one is done by setting $cpd_j = \mathbb{1}_{V_j=d_j}$ for all $m < j \leq n$. We include the concretization operation because, in general, not every deterministic variable is eliminated by factor indexing in our algorithm: sometimes it is necessary to treat its deterministic factor as a conventional one.

With these definitions in place, we can express the above (example) rewrite rule in factor algebra:

$$\Sigma_A(\mathbb{1}_{A=d_A} \otimes \mathbb{1}_{M=d_M} \otimes cpd_Z) = \mathbb{1}_{M=d_M}[A{=}d_A] \otimes cpd_Z[A{=}d_A]$$

This formulation merits some clarification. As we cannot directly multiply deterministic and probabilistic factors with each other, the equality is stated at a 'probabilistic' level, i.e. with all deterministic factors concretized. An additional complication is that A is not the only deterministic variable involved: M is deterministic as well. We can choose to ignore this fact, i.e. treat M as probabilistic and just index its concretization, which results in the factor $\mathbb{1}_{M=d_M}[A{=}d_A]$. However, this turns out to equal $\mathbb{1}_{M=d_M[A=d_A]}$, in which the deterministic factor d_M is indexed by another deterministic factor d_A. Unlike with multiplication, this is no problem; see also Fig. 6. Consequently, we do not have to concretize the d_M factor when eliminating A in our elimination algorithm.

As we mentioned, the above rewrite rule can be generalized to any deterministic variable. The elimination of deterministic variable V_i from a product of factors f_j and deterministic factors d_j can be rewritten without Σ_{V_i} summation:

$$\Sigma_{V_i}\left(\mathbb{1}_{V_i=d_i} \otimes \bigotimes_{V_j \in \dim(f_j)} f_j \otimes \bigotimes_{V_j \in \dim(d_j)} \mathbb{1}_{V_j=d_j}\right) = \bigotimes_{V_j \in \dim(f_j)} f_j[V_i{=}d_i] \otimes \bigotimes_{V_j \in \dim(d_j)} \mathbb{1}_{V_j=d_j[V_i=d_i]}$$

This rewrite rule can be seen as an addition to the laws in Fig. 2. It provides more possibilities for rewriting an inference query, and can as such be used in any inference procedure that makes use of factor operations. Here, we apply it in a variable elimination algorithm with factor indexing (Alg. 2). It has the same structure as Alg. 1, but is extended as follows:

- For a deterministic variable V_i, we store d_i instead of $\mathbb{1}_{V_i=d_i}$.
- To eliminate a deterministic variable V_i, we use the rewrite rule: we index all currently existing f_j and d_j factors over V_i by $V_i=d_i$, and delete d_i itself.
- Not all deterministic variables are eliminated like this: during the elimination of a non-deterministic variable V_i, all deterministic factors over V_i have to be concretized. Also, for a deterministic *evidence* variable, its factor is concretized during initialization.

The proposed elimination heuristic is again the *cost* of the next elimination step. However, we update the definition of this cost to reflect the size of the factors produced in this step. If V_i has *no* deterministic factor d_j associated with it, the cost is still $\mathsf{weight}(p)$. If it *does*, we define the cost to be

$$\sum_{V_i \in \dim(f_j)} \mathsf{weight}(f_j[V_i=d_i]) + \sum_{V_i \in \dim(d_j)} \mathsf{weight}(d_j[V_i=d_i])$$

For Alg. 2, a correctness proof is similar to the one above can be given. Its invariant is:

$$inf_{\mathbf{Q,e}} = \Sigma_{\mathbf{W}} \left(\left(\bigotimes \{\text{all remaining } f_j\} \right) \otimes \bigotimes \{ \mathbb{1}_{V_j=d_j} \mid \text{all remaining } d_j \} \right)$$

5   Empirical Evaluation

We have implemented the factor algebra described above in Python, using the package NumPy which provides an n-dimensional array and executes array operations using fast C loops (not unlike MATLAB). The $\otimes$ operator directly translates to NumPy's array multiplication, which can handle the situation where the operands have different dimensions. Indexing an array with another array is supported in NumPy as well.

We perform inference on 4 networks with deterministic nodes known from the Bayesian network literature (the students network is from the UAI'08 evaluation track). We also investigated 6 generated networks of 100 nodes, with 30 root nodes and 70 nodes with 2 parents (randomly chosen from earlier generated nodes). Each node has randomly generated probabilities; each of the 70 non-root nodes has a chance of being deterministic, in which case we randomly generate a deterministic function. Each variable has the same domain; between networks, we vary the domain size (2 or 4). Also, we vary the fraction of deterministic nodes (30%, 60%, 90% of the non-root nodes).

Algorithm 2. Minweight variable elimination with factor indexing.

Input: – Bayesian network w/det. vars $(\mathbf{V}, \mathsf{par}, \{cpd_1, \ldots, cpd_m\}, \{d_{m+1}, \ldots, d_n\})$
              – query variables $\mathbf{Q} \subseteq \mathbf{V}$; evidence $\mathbf{e}$ (instantiation of $\mathbf{E} \subseteq \mathbf{V}$)
Output: *result*, a factor over $\mathbf{Q}$ equal to $inf_{\mathbf{Q},\mathbf{e}}$

$\mathbf{W} := \mathbf{V} \setminus (\mathbf{Q} \cup \mathbf{E})$
foreach cpd_j **do** $f_j := cpd_j(\mathbf{e})$
foreach d_j **do**
  if $V_j \in \mathbf{E}$ **then**
  | $f_j := \mathbb{1}_{V_j = d_j}(\mathbf{e})$
  else
  | $d_j := d_j(\mathbf{e})$

while $\mathbf{W}$ is not empty **do**
  | choose $V_i \in \mathbf{W}$ for which the cost of *eliminate*(V_i) is smallest
  | *eliminate*(V_i)
  | $\mathbf{W} := \mathbf{W} \setminus \{V_i\}$

result $:= (\bigotimes \{$all remaining $f_j\}) \otimes \bigotimes \{ \mathbb{1}_{V_j = d_j} \mid$ all remaining $d_j \}$
procedure *eliminate*(V_i)
  if d_i exists **then**
    | **foreach** d_j s.t. $V_i \in \dim(d_j)$ **do** $d_j := d_j[V_i = d_i]$
    | **foreach** f_j s.t. $V_i \in \dim(f_j)$ **do** $f_j := f_j[V_i = d_i]$
    | delete d_i
  else
    | $p := \mathbb{1}$
    | **foreach** d_j s.t. $V_i \in \dim(d_j)$ **do**
    | | $p := p \otimes \mathbb{1}_{V_j = d_j}$
    | | delete d_j
    | **foreach** f_j s.t. $V_i \in \dim(f_j)$ **do**
    | | $p := p \otimes f_j$
    | | delete f_j
    | $f_i := \Sigma_{V_i} p$

For each network, we take medians over 10 runs; in each run, we instantiate 10 randomly chosen[1] evidence variables $\mathbf{e}$ and choose one random query variable Q. Then we use algorithms Alg. 1 and Alg. 2 to generate a symbolic expression (a *plan*) for $inf_{\mathbf{Q},\mathbf{e}}$, i.e. we execute them as a *rewrite phase* as discussed in Sect. 3. As it is completely implemented in Python (without regard for speed), we do not time this phase; its performance would severely distort the overall timing results.

We record the cost of the generated plans, i.e. the summed weight of all the intermediate factors. In the second phase, we evaluate the plans and record the (wall clock) duration. The experiments were performed on a machine with a 3GHz Intel Core2Duo processor and 2GB RAM.

Results are shown in Table 1: the factor indexing technique provides speedups ranging up to 16×. Expectations are confirmed that it works best with a high

---

[1] However, for students, we took the 9 easiest evidence files from the UAI'08 evaluation.

Table 1. Experimental results. Numbers are median values over 10 random queries.

network	# vars (det.)	plan cost Alg. 1	plan cost Alg. 2	cost impr. Alg. 1/Alg. 2	eval. time (s) Alg. 1	eval. time (s) Alg. 2	speedup Alg. 1/Alg. 2
munin-1	189 (65)	278M	260M	1.00	6.94	7.91	0.935
munin-4	1041 (411)	23.3M	19.2M	1.22	0.481	0.382	1.25
diabetes	413 (24)	13.2M	13.1M	1.00	0.148	0.151	0.994
students	376 (304)	4.32M	14.7K	293	0.205	0.053	4.13
random-2-30	100 ($\pm$21)	16.3K	3.85K	2.91	0.0120	0.0106	1.15
random-2-60	100 ($\pm$42)	19.6K	2.47K	5.82	0.0121	0.0088	1.35
random-2-90	100 ($\pm$63)	14.6K	0.711K	15.0	0.0117	0.0064	1.90
random-4-30	100 ($\pm$21)	6.28M	2.38M	9.23	0.122	0.0536	5.38
random-4-60	100 ($\pm$42)	2.27M	49.0K	55.1	0.0504	0.0098	5.39
random-4-90	100 ($\pm$63)	4.41M	14.7K	257	0.0908	0.0065	16.3

fraction of deterministic nodes and/or larger domain sizes. However, we noticed that the variance in performance between runs can be high: we suspect that the current heuristic can easily guide the algorithm in the wrong way, and will investigate more robust heuristics in the future.

6   Conclusions and Future Work

We propose a new variable elimination technique for exact inference on Bayesian networks, in which deterministic variables are eliminated not by summation but by a factor indexing operation. We emphasize the role of factor algebra, which enables (a) a concise definition of the algorithm, (b) a straightforward correctness proof, and (c) a model for defining an elimination order heuristic in terms of the *cost* of array operations. Indeed, our updated minweight heuristic has little to do with the network's graph structure anymore; this is in line with common knowledge that treewidth is not so important for highly deterministic networks.

A preliminary empirical evaluation shows that the technique performs decently on real-world networks (small speedups) and good on randomly generated networks (speedups of 1–16). We expect much room for improvement here: first, by developing heuristics that take into account the *actual* cost of performing the different array operations instead of the size of the resulting array; second, by exploiting low-level machine knowledge to decrease these actual costs (building on the connection between inference optimization and database research which we have pointed out). For example, current CPUs and GPUs often feature vectorized processing modes, which we expect can be exploited for the bulk array operations of probabilistic inference. When used properly, this might outperform inference techniques for determinism that cannot be expressed as array operations, e.g. [1,8].

Furthermore, we argue that our technique has much potential for combination with other inference algorithms that use factor operations, e.g. junction tree propagation[9], recursive conditioning[3] and factor decomposition techniques [5,6,10].

Acknowledgements

The authors have been supported by the OCTOPUS project under the responsibility of the Embedded Systems Institute. The OCTOPUS project is partially supported by the Netherlands Ministery of Economic Affairs under the Embedded Systems Institute program.

References

1. Chavira, M., Darwiche, A.: On probabilistic inference by weighted model counting. Artif. Intell. 172(6-7), 772–799 (2008)
2. Corrada Bravo, H., Ramakrishnan, R.: Optimizing MPF queries: decision support and probabilistic inference. In: SIGMOD Conference, pp. 701–712 (2007)
3. Darwiche, A.: Recursive conditioning. Artif. Intell. 126(1-2), 5–41 (2001)
4. Dechter, R.: Bucket elimination: A unifying framework for reasoning. Artif. Intell. 113(1-2), 41–85 (1999)
5. Díez, F.J., Galán, S.F.: Efficient computation for the Noisy MAX. Int. J. Intell. Syst. 18(2), 165–177 (2003)
6. Heckerman, D., Breese, J.S.: Causal independence for probability assessment and inference using Bayesian networks. IEEE Transactions on Systems, Man and Cybernetics, Part A 26(6), 826–831 (1996)
7. Kjærulff, U.: Triangulation of graphs — algorithms giving small total state space. Tech. Rep. R-90-09, Dept. of Mathematics and Computer Science, Aalborg University (1990), http://www.cs.aau.dk/~uk/papers/R90-09.ps.gz
8. Larkin, D., Dechter, R.: Bayesian inference in the presence of determinism. In: Bishop, C.M., Frey, B.J. (eds.) Proceedings of Ninth International Workshop on Artificial Intelligence and Statistics, Key West, USA (2003)
9. Lauritzen, S.L., Spiegelhalter, D.J.: Local computations with probabilities on graphical structures and their application to expert systems. Journal of the Royal Statistical Society. Series B 50(2), 157–224 (1988)
10. Vomlel, J.: Exploiting functional dependence in Bayesian network inference. In: Darwiche, A., Friedman, N. (eds.) UAI 2002, Proceedings of the 18th Conference in Uncertainty in Artificial Intelligence, University of Alberta, Edmonton, Alberta, Canada, pp. 528–535. Morgan Kaufmann, San Francisco (2002)
11. Zhang, N.L., Poole, D.: Exploiting causal independence in bayesian network inference. J. Artif. Intell. Res. (JAIR) 5, 301–328 (1996)

Independence and 2-Monotonicity: Nice to Have, Hard to Keep

Sebastien Destercke

INRA/CIRAD, UMR1208, 2 place P. Viala, F-34060 Montpellier cedex 1, France
sdestercke@gmail.com

Abstract. When using lower probabilities to model uncertainty about the value assumed by a variable, 2-monotonicity is an interesting property to satisfy, as it greatly facilitates further treatments (such as the computation of lower/upper expectation bounds). In this paper, we show that multivariate joint models induced from marginal ones by strong independence, epistemic independence or epistemic irrelevance do not usually preserve such a property, even if it is satisfied by all marginal models. We then propose a joint model outer-approximating those induced by strong and epistemic independence and study some of its properties.

Keywords: factorisation properties, credal sets, propagation, lower previsions.

1 Introduction

In imprecise probability theories where uncertainty is represented by so-called *credal sets* (i.e., convex sets of probabilities), or equivalently by lower expectation bounds (called coherent lower previsions by Walley), independence modeling and tractability are two important issues.

Indeed, the notion of independence plays an essential role in uncertainty theories when dealing with multivariate spaces, its associated factorization properties allowing to decompose a complex problem into simpler ones, or to easily build joint models from marginal ones. When probabilities or expectations are made imprecise, the notion of stochastic independence used in probability theory can be extended in several ways, and such extensions have been proposed and compared by many authors (see, for example, Walley [1] and Couso *et al.* [2]).

On the other hand, tractability is essential in many applications, and although using general uncertainty models is certainly attractive from a theoretical point of view, their complexity often makes them difficult to handle computationally. In practice, tractability can be improved by restricting oneself to classes of uncertainty models that presents a good trade-off between generality and computational convenience. 2-monotone lower probabilities, that encompass many useful uncertainty models (e.g., p-boxes [3], possibility distributions [4], belief functions [5], probability intervals [6]), correspond to such a class, as satisfying the property of 2-monotonicity greatly facilitates the handling of uncertainty in information treatments (e.g., to compute lower and upper expectation bounds). This is why researchers have devoted a lot of attention to such models [7,8].

In this paper, we consider the problem of whether the property of 2-monotonicity is preserved when building a joint representation induced from marginal representations

W. Liu (Ed.): ECSQARU 2011, LNAI 6717, pp. 263–274, 2011.

and a strong independence, an epistemic irrelevance or an epistemic independence assumption. After introducing notations and required preliminaries in Section 2, we show in Section 3 that 2-monotonicity is not preserved under none of the assumptions of strong independence, epistemic independence or epistemic irrelevance. In order to solve this issue, we propose in Section 4 an outer approximation by extending the notion of random set independence to 2-monotone lower probabilities. We also study some properties of this approximation, concluding that, while this approximation may be useful in some cases, its usefulness within Walley's theory of imprecise probabilities may be limited. In order to simplify our exposure, we will limit ourselves to the case of two variables, however most presented results readily extend to any number of dimensions.

2   Preliminaries

This section recalls basic notions and introduces main notations used in the rest of the paper. Although we deal with marginal uncertainty models defined by 2-monotone lower probabilities, we will start from lower expectations, as they are needed to express the joint models resulting from different independence assumptions.

2.1   Lower Expectations and Credal Sets

Consider a variable X whose value lies in a finite space $\mathscr{X}$. We assume here that the uncertainty on X is described by a lower expectation (or coherent lower prevision in Walley's terms) $\underline{P} : \mathscr{L}(\mathscr{X}) \to \mathbb{R}$ defined over the set $\mathscr{L}(\mathscr{X})$ of all real-valued functions over $\mathscr{X}$. The lower probability of an event $A \subseteq \mathscr{X}$ corresponds to the value $\underline{P}(\mathbf{1}_A)$, where $\mathbf{1}_A$ is the indicator function of A. Here, it will be denoted by $\underline{P}(A)$ when no confusion is possible. From a lower expectation, one can consider the dual notion of upper expectation $\overline{P}$, linked to lower expectation by the relation $\underline{P}(f) = -\overline{P}(-f)$. In the specific case of lower probabilities, the dual notion of upper probability is such that $\underline{P}(A) = 1 - \overline{P}(\overline{A})$, with $\overline{A}$ the complement of A. A classical expectation operator will be denoted $P : \mathscr{L}(\mathscr{X}) \to \mathbb{R}$, the corresponding mass function p being defined as $p(x) := P(\mathbf{1}_x), x \in \mathscr{X}$ with $P(f) = \sum_{x \in \mathscr{X}} p(x) f(x)$.

A lower expectation $\underline{P}$ induces a corresponding closed convex set $\mathscr{M}(\underline{P})$ of dominating probability distributions, here called *credal set*, such that

$$\mathscr{M}(\underline{P}) = \{p \in \mathbb{P}_{\mathscr{X}} | P(f) \geq \underline{P}(f) \ \forall f \in \mathscr{L}(\mathscr{X})\},$$

where $\mathbb{P}_{\mathscr{X}}$ is the set of all probability masses over $\mathscr{X}$. One can show that there is a one-to-one correspondence between lower expectations and credal sets (that is, each credal set correspond to one and only one lower expectation, and vice-versa).

In practice, the information contained in $\underline{P}$ can often be restricted to, or is given for, a finite subset $\mathscr{K}$ of $\mathscr{L}(\mathscr{X})$, and the induced credal set is then

$$\mathscr{M}(\underline{P}) = \{p \in \mathbb{P}_{\mathscr{X}} | P(f) \geq \underline{P}(f) \ \forall f \in \mathscr{K}\}.$$

In such a case, the lower expectation, or *natural extension*[1] induced by $\underline{P}$ on any function $g \in \mathscr{L}(\mathscr{X})$ is given by $\underline{P}(g) = \min\{P(g) | p \in \mathscr{M}(\underline{P})\}$. This natural extension

---

[1] Note that here, we use the same notation for $\underline{P}$ and its natural extension, as we only deal with so-called coherent lower previsions.

represents the most conservative inference one can make when all the information we have about X is represented by the initial lower prevision.

The evaluation of this natural extension, which plays an essential role in further inferences, may represent a heavy computational burden, especially when the space $\mathscr{X}$ is large (as happens in the multivariate case). An important case where this computational burden can be reduced is when $\underline{P}$ can be restricted to events (i.e., is a lower probability) and satisfy the property of 2-monotonicity. This property is satisfied if, for any pair $A, B \subseteq \mathscr{X}$ of events, the following inequality holds:

$$\underline{P}(A) + \underline{P}(B) \leq \underline{P}(A \cup B) + \underline{P}(A \cap B).$$

Such a property ensures, for instance, that extreme points of $\mathscr{M}(\underline{P})$ can be easily determined [9], or that natural extension over any function can be computed thanks to a Choquet integral. Also, 2-monotonicity is a sufficient condition for $\underline{P}$ to be coherent.

2.2 2-Monotone Lower Probability and Möbius Inverse

Let $\underline{P}$ be a lower probability on $\mathscr{X}$. Its Möbius inverse $m : \wp(\mathscr{X}) \to \mathbb{R}$ is defined as a mapping from the power set of $\mathscr{X}$ to the real space such that, for every subset $E \subseteq \mathscr{X}$,

$$m(E) = \sum_{A \subseteq E} (-1)^{|E \backslash A|} \underline{P}(A), \qquad (1)$$

with $|E \backslash A|$ the cardinality of $E \backslash A$. Note that for any lower probability, $\sum_{E \subseteq \mathscr{X}} m(E) = 1$, $m(\emptyset) = 0$ and $m(\{x\}) \geq 0$ for any $x \in \mathscr{X}$. From the Möbius inverse m, the lower probability $\underline{P}(A)$ of an event A can be found back through the formula

$$\underline{P}(A) = \sum_{E \subseteq A} m(E). \qquad (2)$$

Chateauneuf and Jaffray [9] (among other things) have proved the following relation between 2-monotone lower probabilities and their Möbius inverse:

Proposition 1. $\underline{P}$ is a 2-monotone lower probability if and only if its Möbius inverse m is such that, for any $A \subseteq \mathscr{X}$ and all $\{x_1, x_2\} \in A$, $x_1 \neq x_2$,

$$\sum_{\{x_1, x_2\} \subseteq B \subseteq A} m(B) \geq 0$$

This proposition have the following corollary.

Corollary 1. If $\underline{P}$ is a 2-monotone lower probability, then $m(E) \geq 0$ for all E such that $|E| \leq 2$.

However, the inverse is not true, i.e., any mapping m with $\sum_{E \subseteq \mathscr{X}} m(E) = 1$ and $m(E) \geq 0$ for all E such that $|E| \leq 2$ will not induce a 2-monotone lower probability, as shows the next example:

Example 1. Consider a 3 element space $\mathscr{X} = \{x_1, x_2, x_3\}$ with the mass function m such that

$$m(\{x_1\}) = 0.1, \quad m(\{x_2\}) = 0.2, \quad m(\{x_3\}) = 0.5, \quad m(\{x_1, x_2\}) = 0,$$
$$m(\{x_1, x_3\}) = 0.2, \quad m(\{x_2, x_3\}) = 0.3, \quad m(\mathscr{X}) = -0.3.$$

Using Eq (2), we get $\underline{P}(\{x_1\}) = 0.1$ and $\underline{P}(\{x_2, x_3\}) = 1$, a non-coherent lower probability which therefore cannot be 2-monotone (another means to see it is to consider the pair of events $A = \{x_1, x_3\}$ and $B = \{x_2, x_3\}$).

Chateauneuf and Jaffray have also shown that, in the case of 2-monotone lower probabilities, natural extension can be computed using the Möbius inverse.

Proposition 2. *Let $\underline{P}$ be a 2-monotone lower probability and m its Möbius inverse. Then, its natural extension to any function $f \in \mathcal{L}(\mathcal{X})$ is given by*

$$\underline{P}(f) = \sum_{E \subseteq \mathcal{X}} m(E) \inf_{x \in E} f(x). \tag{3}$$

These results will be instrumental in the rest of the paper.

3   2-Monotonicity Preservation Under Independence Assumptions

We now assume that the uncertainty about two variables X and Y taking their values on finite spaces $\mathcal{X}$ and $\mathcal{Y}$, respectively, are modeled by the 2-monotone lower probabilities $\underline{P}_X$ and $\underline{P}_Y$, respectively. In order to make inferences on the whole space $\mathcal{X} \times \mathcal{Y}$, one needs to build a joint uncertainty model $\underline{P} : \mathcal{L}(\mathcal{X} \times \mathcal{Y}) \to \mathbb{R}$ over it that respects the marginal information given by $\underline{P}_X$ and $\underline{P}_Y$.

As recalled in the introduction, independence assumptions allow one to easily build such a joint uncertainty model from marginal ones. In probability theory, this is done by using the notion of stochastic independence. When considering lower expectations as a model of uncertainty, there exist many ways in which stochastic independence can be extended [2]. Also, one may require, when building the joint uncertainty model, that this joint model remains 2-monotone, if only for computational convenience.

We will show in this section, by the means of simple counter-examples, that the joint models obtained from the marginals $\underline{P}_X$, $\underline{P}_Y$ and the various assumptions of strong independence, epistemic irrelevance or epistemic independence (each of them briefly recalled in the corresponding subsection) are not, in general, 2-monotone lower probabilities.

3.1   Strong Independence

The concept of strong independence directly extends the concept of stochastic independence to sets of probabilities, in the sense that it corresponds to take the stochastic product of every probability mass function inside $\mathcal{M}(\underline{P}_X)$ and $\mathcal{M}(\underline{P}_Y)$. The joint lower expectation obtained by such an assumption, denoted by $\underline{P}_{SI}$, is then such that for any $f \in \mathcal{L}(\mathcal{X} \times \mathcal{Y})$,

$$\underline{P}_{SI}(f) = \inf\{P_{12}(f) | P_{12} = P_1 \otimes P_2, P_1 \in \mathcal{M}(\underline{P}_X), P_2 \in \mathcal{M}(\underline{P}_Y)\},$$

where $\otimes$ is the classical stochastic product. Let us now show that 2-monotonicity is, in general, not preserved by an assumption of strong independence.

Example 2. Consider two binary spaces $\mathscr{X} = \{x_1, x_2\}$ and $\mathscr{Y} = \{y_1, y_2\}$. Recall that any lower expectation on such spaces can be restricted to their values on singletons. Hence they are lower probabilities, which happens to always be 2-monotone. Consider then the following marginal lower probabilities:

$$\underline{P}_X(\{x_1\}) = 0.3, \underline{P}_X(\{x_2\}) = 0.5 \quad \text{and} \quad \underline{P}_Y(\{y_1\}) = 0.4, \underline{P}_Y(\{y_2\}) = 0.4$$

Now, consider the two events $A = \{\mathscr{X} \times y_1\}$ and $B = \{(x_1 \times y_2) \cup (x_2 \times y_1)\}$ on $\mathscr{X} \times \mathscr{Y}$. Under an assumption of strong independence, we have

$$\underline{P}_{SI}(A) = \underline{P}_Y(\{y_1\}) = 0.4,$$
$$\underline{P}_{SI}(B) > 0.4,$$

where the second inequality follows from the fact that all probability masses p which dominate $\underline{P}_{SI}$ must satisfy $p(y_1|x_2) \geq \underline{P}_Y(\{y_1\}) = 0.4$ and $p(y_2|x_1) \geq \underline{P}_Y(\{y_2\}) = 0.4$, whence

$$P(B) = p(y_1|x_2)p(x_2) + p(y_2|x_1)p(x_1) \geq 0.4(p(x_2) + p(x_1)) = 0.4$$

for all probabilities P which dominate $\underline{P}_{SI}$. The actual value is 0.46, obtained by choosing probability masses $p(x_1) = 0.3$ and $p(y_1) = 0.4$. Then, using the factorization properties of $\underline{P}_{SI}$ over events, we have

$$\underline{P}_{SI}(A \cap B) = \underline{P}(x_2 \times y_1) = \underline{P}(x_2)\underline{P}(y_2) = 0.2,$$
$$\underline{P}_{SI}(A \cup B) = \underline{P}(\overline{x_2 \times y_2}) = 1 - \overline{P}(x_2)\overline{P}(y_2) = 0.58,$$

hence, $\underline{P}_{SI}$ violates 2-monotonicity, as

$$\underline{P}_{SI}(A) + \underline{P}_{SI}(B) \geq 0.8 \geq \underline{P}_{SI}(A \cup B) + \underline{P}_{SI}(A \cap B) = 0.78.$$

3.2 Epistemic Irrelevance

The concept of epistemic irrelevance [10] corresponds to an asymmetric concept, expressing the idea that learning the value of a variable does not modify the uncertainty (or the knowledge) about the value of another variable (not excluding the possibility that learning the value of the latter may modify our uncertainty about the former). Here, we consider the statement that X is epistemically irrelevant to Y and denote it by $X \not\rightarrow Y$. The corresponding joint lower expectation, denoted by $\underline{P}_{X \not\rightarrow Y}$, is such that, for any $f \in \mathscr{L}(\mathscr{X} \times \mathscr{Y})$,

$$\underline{P}_{X \not\rightarrow Y}(f) = \underline{P}_X(\underline{P}_Y(f(\mathscr{X}, \cdot))), \tag{4}$$

where $\underline{P}_Y(f(\mathscr{X}, \cdot))$ is a function on $\mathscr{X}$ assuming the value $\underline{P}_Y(f(x, \cdot))$ for every $x \in \mathscr{X}$. Note that, when X is epistemically irrelevant to Y, we have that the sets

$$\{P(\cdot|x)|P \in \mathscr{M}(\underline{P}_{X \not\rightarrow Y})\} = \mathscr{M}(\underline{P}_Y)$$

coincide for every $x \in \mathscr{X}$, with $P(\cdot|x)$ the conditional expectation of P. Recall that, given a joint probability mass p over $\mathscr{X} \times \mathscr{Y}$, the conditional expectation $P(f|x)$ of a function $f : \mathscr{Y} \rightarrow \mathbb{R}$ is the expectation of f w.r.t. the conditional probability mass $p(\cdot|x)$. This links epistemic irrelevance with credal sets.

Example 3. Consider the same model as in Example 2. The same arguments than for strong independence (factorization and bounds on conditional dominated probabilities) still hold, hence epistemic independence still violates 2-monotonicity. Note that, in this case, the value $\underline{P}_{X \nrightarrow Y}(B) = 0.4$ is exact and can be computed by linear programming.

3.3 Epistemic Independence

The concept of epistemic independence [11] is the symmetric counterpart of epistemic irrelevance. It corresponds to the statements that X and Y are epistemically irrelevant of each others, denoted by $X \nleftrightarrow Y$. The corresponding joint lower expectation, denoted by $\underline{P}_{X \nleftrightarrow Y}$, is such that, for any $f \in \mathscr{L}(\mathscr{X} \times \mathscr{Y})$,

$$\underline{P}_{X \nleftrightarrow Y}(f) = \inf\{P(f)|P \in \left(\mathscr{M}(\underline{P}_{X \nrightarrow Y}) \cap \mathscr{M}(\underline{P}_{Y \nrightarrow X})\right)\}.$$

Similarly to epistemic irrelevance, we have that the sets

$$\{P(\cdot|x)|P \in \mathscr{M}(\underline{P}_{X \nleftrightarrow Y})\} = \mathscr{M}(\underline{P}_Y) \text{ and } \{P(\cdot|y)|P \in \mathscr{M}(\underline{P}_{X \nleftrightarrow Y})\} = \mathscr{M}(\underline{P}_X)$$

coincide for every $x \in \mathscr{X}$ and $y \in \mathscr{Y}$.

Example 4. Consider the same model as in Example 2. The same arguments than for strong independence (factorization and bounds on conditional dominated probabilities) still hold, hence epistemic independence still violates 2-monotonicity. Note that, in this case, the value $\underline{P}_{X \nleftrightarrow Y}(B) = 0.4$ is again exact and can be computed by linear programming.

4   A 2-Monotone Outer-Approximation

In this section, we propose and study a notion that allows one to easily build, from marginals, a joint lower probability that is still 2-monotone and outer-approximates the joint uncertainty models obtained by independence assumptions of Section 3.

4.1   Definition and Basic Properties

We start by defining how the uncertainty joint model is built, and call the associated notion *Möbius inverse independence* (MI).

Definition 1 (Möbius inverse independence). *Consider two lower probabilities $\underline{P}_X$, $\underline{P}_Y$ defined on finite spaces $\mathscr{X}, \mathscr{Y}$ and their respective Möbius inverse m_X, m_Y. The Möbius inverse m_{MI} obtained under an assumption of Möbius inverse independence is defined as the mapping $m_{MI} : \mathscr{X} \times \mathscr{Y} \to \mathbb{R}$ such that, for every $A \times B \subseteq \mathscr{X} \times \mathscr{Y}$,*

$$m_{MI}(A \times B) = m_X(A)m_Y(B) \tag{5}$$

This notion of independence is symmetrical. The joint lower probability $\underline{P}_{MI}$ induced by m_{MI} over $\mathscr{X} \times \mathscr{Y}$ is then defined for every event $E \subseteq \mathscr{X} \times \mathscr{Y}$ as

$$\underline{P}_{MI}(E) = \sum_{(A \times B) \subseteq E} m_{MI}(A \times B).$$

The MI notion can simply be seen as an extension of the notion of random set independence [2]. Random set independence notion applies to specific kinds of 2-monotone lower probabilities, i.e., belief functions. Recall that a belief function $\underline{P}_{bel} : \mathscr{X} \to [0,1]$ is a lower probability such that, for any collection of events $\{A_1, \ldots, A_n\} \subseteq \mathscr{X}$, the following inequality

$$\underline{P}_{bel}(\bigcup_{i=1^n} A_i) \geq \sum_{\mathscr{I} \subseteq \{1,\ldots,n\}} (-1)^{|\mathscr{I}|+1} \underline{P}(\bigcap_{i \in \mathscr{I}} A_i)$$

holds. Belief functions are also characterised by the fact that their Möbius inverse are non-negative. Given this similarity, we can expect the resulting joint uncertainty model $\underline{P}_{MI}$ to share some properties fo the joint model obtained under an assumption of random set independence (i.e. preservation of n-monotonicity and outer-approximating other joint models studied in Section 3). It should be noted that the Möbius inverse and the corresponding independence notion are here used as a mathematically and computationally convenient tool, and that no semantic is associated to it. Indeed, how to interpret non-positive weights on subsets is still an open problem.

Proposition 3. *Let $\underline{P}_X, \underline{P}_Y$ be 2-monotone lower probabilities, then $\underline{P}_{MI}$ is a 2-monotone lower probability.*

Proof. In order to show that $\underline{P}_{MI}$ is 2-monotone, we have to show that m_{MI} has the following properties:

1. $m_{MI}(\emptyset) = 0$
2. $\sum_{A \times B \subseteq \mathscr{X} \times \mathscr{Y}} m_{MI}(A \times B) = 1$
3. For any $A \times B \subseteq \mathscr{X}$ and all $\{x_1 \times y_1, x_2 \times y_2\} \in A \times B$, $\sum_{\{x_1 \times y_1, x_2 \times y_2\} \subseteq C \subseteq A \times B} m(C) \geq 0$ holds (using Prop. 1).

The first property is easily shown, as $m_X(\emptyset) = m_Y(\emptyset) = 0$. The second property follows from

$$\sum_{A \times B \subseteq \mathscr{X} \times \mathscr{Y}} m_{MI}(A \times B) = \sum_{A \subseteq \mathscr{X}} \sum_{B \subseteq \mathscr{Y}} m_X(A) m_Y(B) = \sum_{A \subseteq \mathscr{X}} m_X(A) \sum_{B \subseteq \mathscr{Y}} m_Y(B) = 1.$$

Now, let us show the third property. We have

$$\sum_{\{x_1 \times y_1, x_2 \times y_2\} \subseteq C \subseteq A \times B} m(C) = \sum_{\{x_1 \times y_1, x_2 \times y_2\} \subseteq A' \times B' \subseteq A \times B} m(A') m(B')$$

$$= \sum_{\{x_1, x_2\} \subseteq A' \subseteq A} m(A') \sum_{\{y_1, y_2\} \subseteq B' \subseteq A} m(B') \geq 0,$$

where the last inequality comes from the fact that the two sums are positive (according to Prop. 1). $\qquad\square$

Let us now show that the joint lower probability $\underline{P}_{MI}$ outer-approximates the joint uncertainty models obtained by other independence notions.

Proposition 4. *Let $\underline{P}_X$, $\underline{P}_Y$ be 2-monotone lower probabilities, then the joint uncertainty model $\underline{P}_{MI}$ outer-approximates the joint uncertainty models $\underline{P}_{X \not\rightarrow Y}, \underline{P}_{Y \not\rightarrow X}, \underline{P}_{X \not\leftrightarrow Y}$, $\underline{P}_{SI}$, in the sense that for any $f \in \mathscr{L}(\mathscr{X} \times \mathscr{Y})$,*

$$\underline{P}_{MI}(f) \leq \min\{\underline{P}_{X \not\rightarrow Y}(f), \underline{P}_{Y \not\rightarrow X}(f), \underline{P}_{X \not\leftrightarrow Y}(f), \underline{P}_{SI}(f)\}.$$

Proof. First, recall that joint models obtained by independence assumptions are related in the following way:

$$\max\{\underline{P}_{X \not\rightarrow Y}, \underline{P}_{Y \not\rightarrow X}\} \leq \underline{P}_{X \not\leftrightarrow Y} \leq \underline{P}_{SI}$$

where the joint uncertainty models are obtained from the same marginals $\underline{P}_X, \underline{P}_Y$. Hence, it is sufficient to show that $\underline{P}_{MI} \leq \underline{P}_{X \not\rightarrow Y}$ to prove that $\underline{P}_{MI}$ outer-approximates the other joint uncertainty models.

Consider a function $f \in \mathscr{L}(\mathscr{X} \times \mathscr{Y})$. Using the fact that $\underline{P}_X, \underline{P}_Y$ are 2-monotone lower probabilities and combining Eq. (3) with Eq. (4), we obtain that $\underline{P}_{X \not\rightarrow Y}(f)$ can be reformulated as follows:

$$\underline{P}_{X \not\rightarrow Y}(f) = \sum_{A \subseteq \mathscr{X}} m_X(A) \inf_{x \in A} \left(\sum_{B \subseteq \mathscr{Y}} m_Y(B) \inf_{y \in B} f(x,y) \right).$$

Similarly, since we have shown that $\underline{P}_{MI}$ is 2-monotone, we can use Eq. (3) and obtain

$$\begin{aligned}
\underline{P}_{MI}(f) &= \sum_{A \times B \subseteq \mathscr{X} \times \mathscr{Y}} m_{MI}(A \times B) \inf_{x,y \in A \times B} f(x,y) \\
&= \sum_{A \subseteq \mathscr{X}} \sum_{B \subseteq \mathscr{Y}} m_X(A) m_Y(B) \inf_{x \in A} \inf_{y \in B} f(x,y) \\
&= \sum_{A \subseteq \mathscr{X}} m_X(A) \sum_{B \subseteq \mathscr{Y}} m_Y(B) \inf_{x \in A} \inf_{y \in B} f(x,y).
\end{aligned}$$

This shows that $\underline{P}_{MI}(f) \leq \underline{P}_{X \not\rightarrow Y}(f)$, since

$$\sum_{B \subseteq \mathscr{Y}} m_Y(B) \inf_{x \in A} \inf_{y \in B} f(x,y) \leq \inf_{x \in A} \left(\sum_{B \subseteq \mathscr{Y}} m_Y(B) \inf_{y \in B} f(x,y) \right). \qquad \square$$

Next section discusses the interest of the proposed approximation for various applications.

4.2   Discussion about Practical Interest

To simplify notations, we identify in this section a function g defined on space $\mathscr{X}$ with its cylindrical extension to the cartesian product $\mathscr{X} \times \mathscr{Y}$ (defined, for every $x \in \mathscr{X}$ and all $y \in \mathscr{Y}$, as $g(x,y) = g(x)$), and we identify similarly functions defined on space $\mathscr{Y}$. Within the theory of lower prevision, recent works [12,13] have focused at characterising interesting factorisation properties of joint models. One of the weakest properties developed in these works is the one of productivity, defined as follows in the case of two variables:

Definition 2 (Productivity). *Consider a joint lower expectation* $\underline{P}$ *on* $\mathscr{L}(\mathscr{X} \times \mathscr{Y})$. *This lower expectation is called* productive *if for all* $g \in \mathscr{L}(\mathscr{X})$ *(resp. all* $g \in \mathscr{L}(\mathscr{Y})$*) and all non-negative* $f \in \mathscr{L}(\mathscr{Y})$ *(resp. all* $f \in \mathscr{L}(\mathscr{X})$*),* $\underline{P}(f[g - \underline{P}(g)]) \geq 0$.

Unfortunately, the next example shows that the joint uncertainty model $\underline{P}_{MI}$ obtained under an MI assumption does not satisfy this property.

Example 5. Let $\mathscr{X} = \{x_1, x_2\}$ and $\mathscr{Y} = \{y_1, y_2\}$ be two binary spaces. Consider two 2-monotone lower probabilities $\underline{P}_Y$ and $\underline{P}_X$ defined on this space and their Möbius inverses m_X and m_Y (note that they are positive), such that

$$m_X(\{x_1\}) = \alpha_1, m_X(\{x_2\}) = \alpha_2 \text{ and } m_X(\mathscr{X}) = 1 - \alpha_1 - \alpha_2;$$

$$m_Y(\{y_1\}) = \beta_1, m_Y(\{y_2\}) = \beta_2 \text{ and } m_Y(\mathscr{Y}) = 1 - \beta_1 - \beta_2;$$

Now consider two functions $g \in \mathscr{L}(\mathscr{X})$ and $f \in \mathscr{L}(\mathscr{Y})$ such that $g(x_1) = a < g(x_2) = b$ and $0 < f(y_1) = c < f(y_2) = d$. Consider now $\underline{P}_{MI}$ as a joint uncertainty model, and let us calculate $\underline{P}_{MI}(f[g - \underline{P}_{MI}(g)])$. Let us first consider $\underline{P}_{MI}(g)$. As $g \in \mathscr{L}(\mathscr{X})$, we have that

$$\underline{P}_{MI}(g) = \alpha_2 b + (1 - \alpha_2)a,$$

and the function $h = f[g - \underline{P}(g)]$ on $\mathscr{X} \times \mathscr{Y}$ is summarised in Table 1 below.

Table 1. Function $f[g - \underline{P}(g)]$ of Example 5

$h = f[g - \underline{P}_{MI}(g)]$	x_1		x_2
y_1	$c\alpha_2(a-b)$	$<$	$c(1-\alpha_2)(b-a)$
	$\vee$		$\wedge$
y_2	$d\alpha_2(a-b)$	$<$	$d(1-\alpha_2)(b-a)$

The inequalities in Table 1 are due to the two inequalities $a \leq b$ and $0 \leq c \leq d$ and to the fact that $(a - b) \leq 0$, $(1 - \alpha_2) \geq 0$. Note that the four values are totally ordered. Using Eq. (3) and Definition 1, we have that

$$\underline{P}_{MI}(h) = (1 - \alpha_2)(1 - \beta_1)h(x_1, y_2) + \beta_1(1 - \alpha_2)h(x_1, y_1) + \alpha_2(1 - \beta_2)h(x_2, y_1) + \alpha_2\beta_2 h(x_2, y_2)$$
$$= (1 - \alpha_2)((1 - \beta_1)h(x_1, y_2) + \beta_1 h(x_1, y_1)) + \alpha_2((1 - \beta_2)h(x_2, y_1) + \beta_2 h(x_2, y_2))$$
$$= ((1 - \alpha_2)\alpha_2(a - b)(d - \beta_1 d + \beta_1 c)) + (\alpha_2(1 - \alpha_2)(b - a)(c - \beta_2 c + \beta_2 d))$$
$$= (1 - \alpha_2)\alpha_2(b - a)(c - d)(1 - \beta_2 - \beta_1) = (1 - \alpha_2)\alpha_2(b - a)(c - d)\beta_3$$

If we assume that $0 < \alpha_2 < 1$, then this value is negative (as $b - a > 0$ and $c - d < 0$), unless $\beta_3 = 0$, that is unless $\underline{P}_Y$ is a precise probability. If we extend these conclusions to all possible f and g satisfying Def. 2, this means that $\underline{P}_{MI}(f[g - \underline{P}_{MI}(g)]) \geq 0$ only in degenerated cases (that is, when $\underline{P}_X$ and $\underline{P}_Y$ are either both precise probabilities or vacuous models).

This example shows that we cannot expect the notion of Möbius inverse independence (and also of random set independence) to satisfy productivity as well as other stronger factorization properties that imply productivity. In the framework of lower previsions, such factorisation properties allows to easily derive laws of large numbers, or are instrumental in the construction of generalisation of Bayesian networks. However, it should be noted that random set independence (of which Möbius inverse independence is a direct extension) has been used in graphical models [14], hence not satisfying productivity does not mean that this independence gathered notion cannot be useful in such models.

Also, the computational convenience of this approximation may be useful in some practical applications involving the computation of natural extension. One such application, illustrated by the following (simple) example, may be multi-criteria decision-making under uncertainty.

Example 6. Assume that some decision maker (DM) wants to build a new airport in a region, and has retained some sites to do so. After selecting sites whose building costs are roughly equivalent, the DM decides to base his/her decision on some additional criteria: the easiness of access to main roads (variable X defined on $\mathscr{X}$), the generated pollution impact on nearby lands (variable Y defined on $\mathscr{Y}$) and the public opinion (variable Z defined on $\mathscr{Z}$). Each criterion is evaluated on a utility scale ranging from 1 to 4, 1 being the worst case, 4 the best. Criteria values are then aggregated according to a weighted average $f = w_X X + w_Y Y + w_Z Z$ to obtain the global utility of a given alternative, where $w_X = 0.2, w_Y = 0.4, w_Z = 0.4$ are the importance weights given to each criterion.

Now, consider an alternative where the utility of each criterion is uncertainly known. The uncertainty concerning variable X is given by the following probability intervals (i.e. upper and lower probabilities over singletons):

$$\overline{P}(\{1\}) = 0.1, \ \overline{P}(\{2\}) = 0.2, \ \overline{P}(\{3\}) = 0.6, \ \overline{P}(\{4\}) = 0.7$$

$$\underline{P}(\{1\}) = 0, \ \underline{P}(\{2\}) = 0, \ \underline{P}(\{3\}) = 0.3, \ \underline{P}(\{4\}) = 0.3$$

This uncertainty can correspond to the fact that a major road is likely to be built in the future in the region, but that this fact is not fully certain. Uncertainty can come, for example, from an expert. These probability intervals are 2-monotone (we refer to [6] for details on probability intervals) and their Möbius inverse is such that

$$m_X(\{3\}) = m_X(\{4\}) = 0.3, \ m_X(\{3,4\}) = m_X(\{1,2,4\}) = m_X(\{1,3,4\}) = 0.1,$$

$$m_X(\{2,3,4\}) = 0.2, \ m_X(\mathscr{X}) = -0.1.$$

Concerning variable Y, risk analysis shows that pollution impact may be high, and the related uncertainty is modeled by the possibility distribution (recall that possibility distributions have Möbius inverses which are positive and are such that non-null masses are given to nested sets)

$$m_Y(\{1\}) = 0.3, \ m_Y(\{1,2\}) = 0.7.$$

Finally, public opinion has been gathered by a survey where answers could be imprecise (hence, frequencies are given to set of values). The results are such that

$$m_Z(\{2\}) = 0.3, \ m_Z(\{4\}) = 0.2, \ m_Z(\{1,2\}) = 0.2, \ m_Z(\mathscr{Z}) = 0.3.$$

The weighted average (or any other aggregation functions) is a mapping $f : \mathcal{X} \times \mathcal{Y} \times \mathcal{Z} \to \mathbb{R}$, and as it seems reasonable to assume that each criterion is independent of the other, we can use m_{MI} as a joint model over $\mathcal{X} \times \mathcal{Y} \times \mathcal{Z}$ to compute lower and upper expectations outer approximating results given by other (more complex) joint models. Using m_X, m_Y, m_Z as uncertainty models, the results are (for lower and upper expectations)

$$\underline{P}_{MI}(f) = 1.936 \quad ; \quad \overline{P}_{MI}(f) = -\underline{P}_{MI}(-f) = 2.62.$$

Note that, in the above example, f can be replaced by any mapping or by any indicator function on the resulting output of f, thus allowing one to perform uncertainty propagation through f.

Finally, let us make two remarks concerning complexity related issues:

- storing information in terms of the Möbius inverse means storing at most $2^{|\mathcal{X}|}$ values, as for lower probabilities on every events. This can be compared to the maximum number of extreme points of a credal set induced by a 2-monotone lower probability [9], which is $|\mathcal{X}|!$ (i.e., the number of permutations among elements of $\mathcal{X}$);
- when working in a multivariate space, computing the lower expectation $\underline{P}_{MI}(f)$ has a complexity that increases exponentially with the number of variables. This is comparable to the complexity associated to the computations under an assumption of forward irrelevance [10]. Also, if an important number of Möbius inverses are positive (i.e., if marginal probabilities often correspond to belief functions), then exact computations could be combined with efficient simulation techniques [15].

5   Conclusions

Independence notions play a central role in many applications of uncertainty reasoning. We have shown that the joint models obtained by independence notions proposed in the theory of imprecise probabilities, in which uncertainty is modeled by the means of credal sets or lower previsions, do not preserve the 2-monotonicity property of marginal uncertainty models (when these latter models satisfy it).

This is a practical downside of these independence notions, as satisfying 2-monotonicity increases the computational tractability of imprecise probabilistic models. To solve this issue, we have proposed a 2-monotone outer-approximation by simply extending the notion of random set independence to 2-monotone lower probabilities.

This approximation does not satisfy the weak property of productivity, which is implied by many other factorization properties of joint models. This means that this approximation cannot benefit from results associated to such properties. Still, there remains applications where this approximation may be useful, such as the one involving uncertainty propagation or expectation bound computations. Especially, since this approximation is an extension of the random set independence, it may benefits from algorithms and methods originating from random set and evidence theory.

Acknowledgements

Examples of Section 3 are the results of discussion with M. Troffaes and E. Miranda.

References

1. Walley, P.: Statistical reasoning with imprecise Probabilities. Chapman and Hall, New York (1991)
2. Couso, I., Moral, S., Walley, P.: A survey of concepts of independence for imprecise probabilities. Risk Decision and Policy 5, 165–181 (2000)
3. Ferson, S., Ginzburg, L., Kreinovich, V., Myers, D., Sentz, K.: Constructing probability boxes and dempster-shafer structures. Technical report, Sandia National Laboratories (2003)
4. Dubois, D., Prade, H.: Possibility Theory: An Approach to Computerized Processing of Uncertainty. Plenum Press, New York (1988)
5. Shafer, G.: A mathematical Theory of Evidence. Princeton University Press, New Jersey (1976)
6. de Campos, L., Huete, J., Moral, S.: Probability intervals: a tool for uncertain reasoning. I. J. of Uncertainty, Fuzziness and Knowledge-Based Systems 2, 167–196 (1994)
7. Bronevich, A., Augustin, T.: Approximation of coherent lower probabilities by 2-monotone measures. In: ISIPTA 2009: Proc. of the Sixth Int. Symp. on Imprecise Probability: Theories and Applications, SIPTA, pp. 61–70 (2009)
8. Miranda, E., Couso, I., Gil, P.: Extreme points of credal sets generated by 2-alternating capacities. I. J. of Approximate Reasoning 33, 95–115 (2003)
9. Chateauneuf, A., Jaffray, J.Y.: Some characterizations of lower probabilities and other monotone capacities through the use of Mobius inversion. Mathematical Social Sciences 17(3), 263–283 (1989)
10. de Cooman, G., Miranda, E.: Forward irrelevance. Journal of Statistical Planning and Inference 139, 256–276 (2009)
11. Vicig, P.: Epistemic independence for imprecise probabilities. Int. J. of Approximate Reasoning 24, 235–250 (2000)
12. de Cooman, G., Miranda, E., Zaffalon, M.: Independent natural extension. In: Hüllermeier, E., Kruse, R., Hoffmann, F. (eds.) IPMU 2010. LNCS, vol. 6178, pp. 737–746. Springer, Heidelberg (2010)
13. de Cooman, G., Miranda, E., Zaffalon, M.: Factorisation properties of the strong product. In: Proceedings of the Fifth International Conference on Soft Methods in Probability and Statistics, SMPS 2010 (2010)
14. Xu, H., Smets, P.: Reasoning in evidential networks with conditional belief functions. Int. J. Approx. Reasoning 14(2-3), 155–185 (1996)
15. Wilson, N.: Algorithms for Dempster-Shafer Theory. In: Handbook of Defeasible Reasoning and Uncertainty Management. Algorithms, vol. 5, pp. 421–475. Kluwer Academic, Dordrecht (2000)

Constructing Dynamic Frames of Discernment in Cases of Large Number of Classes

Yousri Kessentini[1], Thomas Burger[2], and Thierry Paquet[1]

[1] Université de Rouen, Laboratoire LITIS EA 4108, site du Madrillet, St Etienne du Rouvray, France
{yousri.kessentini,thierry.paquet}@univ-rouen.fr
[2] Université Européenne de Bretagne, Université de Bretagne-Sud, CNRS, Lab-STICC, F-56017 Vannes cedex, France
thomas.burger@univ-ubs.fr

Abstract. The Dempster-Shafer theory (DST) is particularly interesting to deal with imprecise information. However, it is known for its high computational cost, as dealing with a frame of discernment Ω involves the manipulation of up to $2^{|\Omega|}$ elements. Hence, classification problems where the number of classes is too large cannot be considered. In this paper, we propose to take advantage of a context of ensemble classification to construct a frame of discernment where only a subset of classes is considered. We apply this method to script recognition problems, which by nature involve a tremendous number of classes.

Keywords: Dempster-Shafer theory, Dynamic frames of discernment, Data fusion.

1 Introduction

The Dempster-Shafer theory (DST) [1,2] is a particularly interesting theory to deal with imprecise, conflictive or partial sources of information. The counterpart of this efficiency is its high computational complexity. One of the main reasons for this complexity is related to the state-space (or frame of discernment): When the actual value ω_0 taken by a variable W is only known to belong to a set $\Omega = \{\omega_1, \ldots, \omega_{|\Omega|}\}$ of possible values, the distributions encoding some knowledge on W are defined over $2^{|\Omega|}$ focal elements (the element of the power set of Ω, noted $\mathcal{P}(\Omega)$), leading to an exponential number of elements to deal with. To balance that, several methods exist. The most natural idea is to try to reduce the number of such focal elements, by forcing some mass assignments to 0, so that the remaining ones display a particular structure which is supposed to be relevant with respect to the knowledge encoded (for instance, Bayesian [3], consonant [4], and k-additive mass functions [5]). Another natural idea is to reduce the size of Ω with various low-cost processings, so that the refined modeling of DST is left only to the most interesting possible values for W. In [6], mass functions are defined directly on Ω rather than $\mathcal{P}(\Omega)$, but it is only possible if Ω is fitted with a partially ordered structure. Finally, in [7],

W. Liu (Ed.): ECSQARU 2011, LNAI 6717, pp. 275–286, 2011.

the authors propose to consider coarsened frames, to reduce the computational cost of the following Dempster's rule. On the contrary, many works consider a problem dual of ours, i.e. constructing an exhaustive frame thanks to multiple evidences based on partial frames, such as in [8] or [9].

In this paper, we consider classification problems (i.e. the variable W is a class variable) where the number of classes involved (i.e. $|\Omega|$) is very large, such as in handwriting word recognition, where a dictionary may contain up to $100,000$ words. To face the corresponding computational issue, we propose to reduce the size of Ω. To do so, we propose to take advantage of a context of ensemble classification to construct a frame of discernment where only a subset of classes is considered. These classes are dynamically selected according to the diversity of the classifiers involved. We propose and compare different strategies to build such a dynamic frame. We show that the proposed strategies considerably reduce the complexity of a DST approach to ensemble classification, while providing a statistically significant improvement of the classification performances with respect to classical probabilistic combination methods.

The paper is structured as follows: In Section 2, we recall the basis of handwriting recognition, and we recall some results on ensemble classification in the context of DST. In Section 3, we present four different strategies to define dynamic frames of discernment. Finally, we compare them in Section 4 on Latin and Arabic handwriting datasets, and we discuss the results.

2   Handwriting Word Recognition

2.1   Background

One of the most popular technique for automatic handwriting recognition is to use generative classifiers based on Hidden Markov Models (or HMM) [10]. For each word ω_i of a lexicon $\Omega_{lex} = \{\omega_1, ..., \omega_V\}$ of V words, a HMM λ_i, $i \leq V$ is defined, so that λ_i best fits a *training set* made of several different instances of words (these instances are called *example words*). Practically, this training phase is conducted by using the Viterbi EM or the Baum-Welch algorithm [10].

Then, when a new unknown word ω is considered (a *test word* from a *testing set*), the likelihoods $\mathbb{P}(\omega|\lambda_i)$, $\forall i \leq V$ are approximated by the likelihoods provided by the Viterbi decoding algorithm (noted $L(\omega_i)$, $\forall i$), and ω is recognized as ω_j for which $L(\omega_j) \geq L(\omega_i), \forall i \leq V$. Generally, in the evaluation step, the classifier does not provide only the "best" class, but an ordered list of the TOP N best classes. Then, for each value of $n \leq N$, a recognition rate can be computed as the percentage of words for which the ground truth class is proposed in the first n elements of the TOP N list.

This complete set-up is called an HMM classifier. In order to improve recognition accuracy, it is classical to define several HMM classifiers, each working on different features (then, the likelihood of the q-th classifier for ω_i is noted $L_q(\omega_i)$), and to combine them [11,12,13,14]. It has been established in [15], that using a set of three classifiers working respectively on the upper contour of the pen mark, the lower contour, and the ink density, provides accurate results both on Latin and Arabic datasets.

There are several ways to combine these classifiers. The most classical way is to consider the product of the Q likelihoods for each class. It corresponds to the assumptions that the features used by the classifiers are independent, and that the product of the likelihoods[1] is the likelihood of the resulting ensemble classification. In the sequel, we refer to this method as the *reference probabilistic method* (RPM). On the other hand, we have demonstrated in [16,17] the superiority of several evidential combination methods to several classical probabilistic combination strategies, including the RPM (which appears to be the best non evidential method).

2.2   DST Combination of HMM Classifiers

We assume that the reader is familiar with the basic elements of the Dempster-Shafer theory. Unfamiliar readers should refer to [1,2], where the following notions are presented: power set, mass function, focal element, vacuous/categoric/consonant/Bayesian mass functions, conjunctive (or Dempster's rule of-) combination, pignistic transform and discounting. The combination of several probabilistic classifiers in the DST is a widely studied topic [11,18,19,20,21,22,23,24,25], that we have already reviewed in previous works of ours [17,26].

Here, to combine the results of several HMM classifiers, we use the following procedure inspired from previous works of ours [17]: First, for each of the Q classifiers, we normalize the likelihoods so that they sum up to one over the whole set of classes. Second, a mass function is derived from each of the Q classifiers. Third, the accuracy rates of the classifiers (derived from a cross-validation procedure) are used to weight each mass function according to the reliability of each classifier. Fourth, the Q mass functions are combined together. Finally, a probabilistic transform is applied, and the so-derived probability values are sorted decreasingly to provide the TOP N list.

Concerning the first and second steps, several methods may be used. We have compared several of them in [16,17], and finally, we consider the use of a sigmoid function for the normalization, and the use of the inverse pignistic transform [4] for the conversion onto a mass function. The inverse pignistic transform converts an initial probability distribution p into a consonant mass assignment. The resulting consonant mass assignment, denoted by $\widehat{p}$, is built as follows: The elements of Ω are ranked by decreasing probabilities such that $p(\omega_1) \geq \ldots \geq p(\omega_{|\Omega|})$, and we have

$$\widehat{p}\left(\{\omega_1, \omega_2, \ldots, \omega_{|\Omega|}\}\right) = \widehat{p}(\Omega) = |\Omega| \times p(\omega_{|\Omega|}) \qquad (1)$$
$$\widehat{p}(\{\omega_1, \omega_2, \ldots, \omega_i\}) = i \times [p(\omega_i) - p(\omega_{i+1})] \ \forall \ i < |\Omega|$$
$$\widehat{p}(.) = 0 \qquad \text{otherwise.}$$

---

[1] These likelihoods are possibly weighted by the TOP 1 accuracy rate of each classifier, if the information is available after a cross-validation procedure.

The reason for this choice is manifold: First, it corresponds to the best trade-off between computational complexity and performances. Second, it has no parameter to tune. Third, it provides a consonant mass function, which is interesting for computational as well as epistemological reasons. As a matter of fact, the result of a classifier is an ordered list, the natural representation of which in the DST is a consonant mass function [26]. Then, the probability distribution provided by each classifier can be seen as the pignistic transform of a particular consonant mass function, that is recovered via the inverse pignistic transform.

Concerning the third step, it is either possible to use all the TOP N accuracy rates $\forall N \leq |\Omega_{lex}|$, in a manner similar to that of [17] (which generalizes the method of [11]), or to simply use the TOP 1 accuracy rates, by the application of a classical discounting. In spite of involving less information, we have chosen the second option. The reason is that exactly the same information (only the TOP 1 accuracy rates) can be used to weight the classifiers in the RPM (by multiplying each probability value given by a classifier, by its TOP 1 accuracy rate). On the other hand, the method described in [17] (involving all the TOP N accuracy rates) has no counterpart in the RPM. Hence, by choosing the second option, we guarantee that the probabilistic and DST-based methods remain comparable.

In the fourth step, we consider by default a conjunctive combination. The reasons for such a default choice are those which are detailed in [27]. It is also possible to perform differently, as detailed in [28], where different combination are considered depending on the pairwise conflict among the classifiers. Despite its real interest from a performance point of view, the conditions required to make a choice among the different combinations are not adapted to handwriting recognition problems, and the framework proposed in [27] better corresponds to our situation.

Finally, the probability transform we use is the pignistic transform, which sounds natural, to remain coherent with respect to the processings of step 2. Hence, if $\div$ is is the pignistic transform, and if p_q is the probability provided by the qth classifier, then, we consider the following classification procedure:

$$\omega_* = \arg\max_i \overline{m(\omega_i)} \qquad \text{where} \quad m = \bigcirc_{q=1}^{Q} [\widehat{p_q}]$$

2.3   Computational Issues

In handwritten word recognition, the set of classes is of a very high size with respect to the cardinality of the state space in classical DST problems (up to $100,000$ words). When dealing with a lexicon set of V words, the mass functions involved are defined on 2^V values. Moreover, the conjunctive combination of two mass functions involves up to 2^{2^V} multiplications and 2^V additions. Thus, the computational cost is exponential with respect to the size of the lexicon, and $100,000$ worlds are not directly tractable.

To remain efficient, even for large vocabularies, it is mandatory either to reduce the complexity, or to reduce the size of the lexicon involved. To do so, as noted in the previous section, consonant mass functions (with only V focal elements) may be considered. In addition, it is also possible to reduce the size of the lexicon by eliminating all the word classes which are obviously not adapted to the test word under consideration. Hence, we consider only the few word classes among which a mistake is possible because of the difficulty of discrimination. Consequently, instead of working on $\Omega_{lex} = \{\omega_1, ..., \omega_V\}$, we use another frame Ω_W, defined according to each particular test word W we aim at classifying. That is why we say that such a frame is dynamically defined.

This strategy is rather intuitive and simple. On the other hand, to our knowledge, no work has been published on a comparison of the different strategies which can be used to define such frames. This is achieved in this paper. The next section presents several strategies that will be compared in the sequel.

3 Dynamic Frames of Discernment

In this section, we describe several strategies to derive a frame Ω_W of reduced size from Ω_{lex}, the latter being too large. Note that, depending on the test word W, the number of classes among which the discrimination remains difficult may vary. Hence, naturally, the size of Ω_W may vary accordingly. On the other hand, it is possible to force the frames to be of the same cardinality whatever the test word (by truncating or extending it with useless classes). Hence, there are two options: A fix or a variable cardinality of the frames $\Omega_W, \forall W$. In this paper, we have chosen the second option. It does not improve the results, but it helps to have a more standard basis for the comparison of the different strategies, as a poor strategy to select the classes to built Ω_W will not be balanced by looser constraints on the acceptance/rejection of the classes.

Let us consider Q classifiers. Each classifier q provides an ordered list $l^q = \{\omega_1^q, ..., \omega_N^q\}$ of the TOP N best classes and their corresponding likelihoods noted $L(\omega_i^q)$, $\forall i < N$. The different strategies described below take as input the lists l^q $\forall q \le Q$ and construct a dynamic frame with a controlled size $M \le N \le |\Omega_{lex}|$.

3.1 Strategy 1: Intersection

Here, the frame Ω_W is made of all the words which are common to the output lists l^q, $\forall q < Q$. Obviously, $|\Omega_W|$ depends on the lists: If the Q classifiers globally concur, their respective lists are similar and an important proportion of their N words are likely to be found in their intersection. On the contrary, if the Q classifiers mostly disagree, very few words belong to the intersection of the lists.

Here, we expect $|\Omega_W|$ to remain constant. Hence, the lists of all the Q classifiers are considered for increasing values of N, until the intersection of the lists is made of exactly M words (draws are randomly sorted). As the algorithm on which the classifiers are based requires having all the probability values of each of the Ω_{lex} words, the lists with $N = |\Omega_{lex}|$ are directly available and this iterative strategy has no influence from a computational point of view.

Intuitively, the motivation for this strategy is to use the intersection scheme to reduce the number of potential classes for the test word. The idea behind it is that the conjunctive combination is also based on intersections of sets, and that, by discarding all the empty intersections before its computation, unnecessary computations are suppressed while keeping the important ones.

3.2   Strategy 2: Union

This strategy is exactly similar to the previous one, but the frame of discernment is made of the union of lists rather than on the intersection. Contrary to previous strategie, if the Q classifiers globally concur, their respective lists are similar and very few words belong to the union of the lists. On the contrary, if the Q classifiers mostly disagree, an important proportion of their N words are likely to be found in their union. Hence, we adjust the value of N to control the size of the powerset, in practice a powerset size between 15 and 20 is used. The idea motivating this strategy is the following: If a single classifier fails and provides too bad a rank to the real class, the other classifiers will not balance the mistake when considering the intersection strategy. Then, the union may be preferable.

3.3   Strategy 3: Borda Count

A major problem with the two previous strategies, is that, the rank in each list is not involved in the creation of $\Omega_{\mathcal{W}}$. Hence, we propose to use a Borda Count procedure: Each class receives a number of votes corresponding to the sum of its ranks in the Q lists. Then, the M word classes with the smallest number of votes are selected to compose $\Omega_{\mathcal{W}}$. From a computational cost point of view, this preprocessing is rather light, as it involves $Q \times |\Omega_{lex}|$ additions and a call to a sorting function. In practice a powerset size of 15 classes is used.

3.4   Strategy 4: Probabilistic Pre-processing

In spite of its lack of accuracy, the RPM is interesting: First, it is rather cheap from a computational point of view. Second, whatever the value δ, it is possible to achieve an accuracy of $100 - \delta\%$ at TOP N if N is great enough. Trivially, if $N = |\Omega_{lex}|$, then, the TOP N accuracy rates is 100%, but most of the time, an accuracy rate of 100% is achieved for smaller values of N.

Then, the idea is simply to select for $\Omega_{\mathcal{W}}$ the M best classes according to the RPM, (among which the real class is likely to belong to), i.e. the M classes for which the product of the likelihood is the greatest, and to use the DST ensemble classification as a tool to refine the decision. Thus, the RPM is used to discard all the classes but M (even if it corresponds to a great number of classes, this is the simple step involving less computation), and afterward, the DST based method is used to discard the remaining $M - 1$ classes (this discrimination being more complex, more computational resources are allowed to it), so that a single class (hopefully, the right one) remains. In practice a powerset size of 15 classes is used.

The four proposed strategies built a dynamic powerset with a fixed size in order to reduce the computational cost. In practice, a powerset size of maximum 20 classes is used. This represents a good compromise between complexity and performance. Note that it is practically impossible to deal with powerset size of 100 due to the high the computational cost.

4   Experiments and Results

4.1   Datasets and HMM Classifiers

Experiments have been conducted on two publicly available databases: IFN/ENIT benchmark database of arabic words and RIMES database for latin words. The IFN/ENIT [29] contains a total of 32,492 handwritten words (Arabic script) of 946 Tunisian town/village names written by 411 different writers. Four different sets (a, b, c, d) are predefined in the database for training and one set (e) for testing. The RIMES database [30] is composed of isolated handwritten word snippets extracted from handwritten letters (Latin script). In our experiments, 36,000 snippets of words are used to train the different HMM classifiers and 3,000 words are used in the test. The dictionary is composed of 1,612 words. Even if the number of words is rather small with respect to a real size lexicon (up to $100,000$), they are far too numerous, as a frame of discernment of more than 20 classes is not tractable from a computational point of view.

Three classifiers are defined, each working on different feature sets: upper contour, lower contour and density, such as described in [15] (see Fig. 1). The TOP 1 and TOP 2 accuracy rates of each of these classifiers is derived from a 10-fold cross-validation on the training sets, which are given in Table 1. This table clearly shows that the two data sets are of heterogeneous difficulty. Moreover, the lower contour is always the less informative feature. Practically, in these experiments, we only use the TOP 1 accuracy rate to weight the different classifiers during their combination, either in the RPM or in DST-based methods. More precisely, the DST-based method is derived according to the four strategies described above: Intersection (S1), Union (S2), Borda Count (S3) and Probabilistic Pre-Processing, or PPP for short (S4). Practically, we consider for each word, a dynamic frame made of 15 words, in order to have a great enough set, while keeping a reasonable computational complexity.

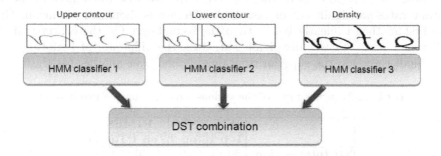

Fig. 1. DST combination of HMM classifiers

Table 1. Individual performances of the HMM classifiers

	IFN/ENIT		RIMES	
	Top 1	Top 2	Top 1	Top 2
HMM 1: Upper contour	73.60	79.77	54.10	66.40
HMM 2: Lower contour	65.90	74.03	38.93	51.57
HMM 3: Density	72.97	79.73	53.23	65.83

4.2   Results and Discussion

Table 2 displays the results provided by the four strategies including the RPM. First of all, it appears that the worst results are given by the RPM, and that, the DST-based methods are always more efficient. Second, S1 provides the poorest results among the DST-based methods, and the results are rather similar to that of the RPM, whereas all the other strategies provide similar results which are far better to that of the RPM. To us, the most appealing aspect of DST-based methods with respect to probabilistic ones, lies in the possibility that the various sources of information remain imprecise. In other words, with them, it is possible that the first choice of the classifier is not the good one. Hence, the intersection strategy, by preventing any mistake of a classifier to be balanced by the output of the other classifiers, prevents the combination of the sources to behave as with DST principles. Thus, to us, it seems understandable that S1 has a behavior similar to that of the RPM, rather than to that of the other DST-based strategies. Thus, the various methods/strategies can be divided into two groups: Group 1 is made S2, S3, S4 and group 2 is made of S1 and RPM. More precisely, among group 1, it can be seen that (1) on RIMES, S4 is the best one and S3 is slightly better than S2, (2) on IFN/ENIT, S2 is slightly better than S4, which is in turn better than S3. This would lead us to promote the fourth strategy, based on a probabilistic pre-processing. Nonetheless, this assertion should be motivated.

Thus, the next point is to check whether the pairwise differences in the accuracy rates are significant or not. If a difference is significant, it means that the first method is clearly better than the second one. On the contrary, if the difference is not statistically significant, then, the difference of performance is too small to decide the superiority of one method over another (as the results

Table 2. Accuracy rates of the various strategies on the two datasets

	IFN/ENIT		RIMES	
	Top 1	Top 2	Top 1	Top 2
S1: Intersection	80.30	83.90	65.50	74.90
S2: Union	82.00	86.53	68.30	79.80
S3: Borda Count	81.17	85.73	68.67	80.13
S4: PPP	81.83	86.53	69.47	80.23
RPM	80.07	83.23	64.80	73.10

Table 3. The p-values of MacNemar's test for all the pairwise comparisons on the IFN/ENIT dataset

	S1	S2	S3	S4	RPM
S1: Intersection		6.6×10^{-7}	0.0124	4.0×10^{-5}	0.5050
S2: Union	.		5.6×10^{-3}	0.6400	7.2×10^{-8}
S3: Borda Count	.	.		0.0336	2.8×10^{-3}
S4: PPP	.	.	.		6.5×10^{-6}
RPM	.	.	.	.	

Table 4. The p-values of MacNemar's test for all the pairwise comparisons on the RIMES dataset

	S1	S2	S3	S4	RPM
S1: Intersection		6.0×10^{-10}	8.8×10^{-2}	7.1×10^{-14}	0.2175
S2: Union	.		0.4363	1.3×10^{-2}	7.6×10^{-10}
S3: Borda Count	.	.		9.1×10^{-2}	6.6×10^{-13}
S4: PPP	.	.	.		4.8×10^{-16}
RPM	.	.	.	.	

would be slightly different with other training/testing sets). Test of significance is a particular type of statistical hypothesis testing. In our case, the null hypothesis is the equivalence of the methods. Practically, we use MacNemar's test [31], which is a χ^2 test adapted to the comparison of proportions. In Tables 3 and 4, we consider all the pairwise comparisons between two methods, and for each, we compute the p-value, i.e. the probability that the null hypothesis is true. The smaller the p-value, the more the difference of accuracy is likely to be significant.

First off all, the p-values confirm our qualitative interpretations of the accuracy rates: On the two datasets S1 and RPM behave similarly, as the probabilities that the differences between the proportions is not significant are rather high (50.50% on IFN/ENIT, and 21.75% on RIMES).

Moreover, let us put the methods in decreasing order of performance (S2, S4, S3, S1, RPM for IFN/ENIT and S4, S3, S2, S1, RPM for RIMES), and let us consider the p-values associated to the comparisons of two consecutive methods according to the previous orders (0.6400, 0.0336, 0.0124, 0.5050 for IFN/ENIT and 9.1×10^{-2}, 0.4663, 6.0×10^{-10}, 0.2175 for RIMES). In this setting, we compare each strategy to the 1 or 2 closest other strategies. It can be noted that whatever the dataset, the smallest p-value (i.e. the most significant difference) corresponds to the comparison of the worst strategy of group 1 (S2, S3 and S4) and the best strategy of group 2 (S1 and RPM), which stresses the relevance of these two groups.

Amongst group 1, on the two datasets, the strategies are not sorted in the same order with respect to the accuracy rates, and the p-values are rather high, indicating that these methods are roughly equivalent. Nonetheless, S4 appears to be slightly more efficient, and, from our experiments, the latter strategy (Probabilistic Pre-Processing) should be preferred, even if this choice relies on rather weak assumptions, as the similarity of the different methods involved requires further experiments for a strong statistical discrimination.

Finally, let us point out that the p-value associated to the comparison of S4 and the RPM is so small, that it is almost immaterial. Hence, it proves that, regarding the kind of data involved, the choice of the combination method is no longer questionable, as the DST-based method is definitely more efficient.

5   Conclusion

In this article, we have considered a problem of classifier combinations in the framework of the Dempster-Shafer theory. More precisely, we have considered problems where the set of classes is too large to be considered as a frame of discernment, such as in handwriting word recognition, where a lexicon may contain up to 100,000 words. Thus, we propose to select for each test word, a reduced number of words (those among which the discrimination is the most difficult according to the test word) in the lexicon to build the frame. This frame is dedicated to a particular test word, which led us to call it *dynamic*. Then, we propose several procedures to select the words of the lexicon to build the dynamic frame. We compare them on 2 different datasets corresponding to Latin and Arabic words, containing respectively 1,612 and 946 word classes each. From our results, the DST provides significantly more accurate results than the reference probabilistic method, in spite of the approximation due to the use of a dynamic frame which does not contain all the words. Thus, our method provides more accurate results while keeping the computational complexity under control. Moreover, among the various strategies to build this dynamic frame, the most efficient one corresponds to the selection of the M words which are ranked the best according to the probabilistic reference method. As a conclusion, probabilistic ensemble classification seems to be an interesting pre-processing to a DST-based ensemble classification on a dynamic frame, when the number of classes in the problem is too great. Further works will include an exhaustive comparison of the various means to take into account information from cross-validation (using various types of discounting, or the method from [17]), and the use of multiple hypothesis testing to make a choice amongst the various strategies described in this article.

References

1. Shafer, G.: A Mathematical Theory of Evidence, Princeton, edn. Princeton University Press, Princeton (1976)
2. Smets, P., Kennes, R.: The transferable belief model. Artificial Intelligence 66(2), 191–234 (1994)
3. Voorbraak, F.: A computationally efficient approximation of Dempster-Shafer theory. International Journal on Man-Machine Studies 30, 525–536 (1989)
4. Dubois, D., Prade, H., Smets, P.: New semantics for quantitative possibility theory. In: Benferhat, S., Besnard, P. (eds.) ECSQARU 2001. LNCS (LNAI), vol. 2143, pp. 410–421. Springer, Heidelberg (2001)

5. Grabisch, M.: K-order additive discrete fuzzy measures and their representation. Fuzzy Sets and Systems 92, 167–189 (1997)
6. Masson, M.-H., Denoeux, T.: Belief functions and cluster ensembles. In: Sossai, C., Chemello, G. (eds.) ECSQARU 2009. LNCS, vol. 5590, pp. 323–334. Springer, Heidelberg (2009)
7. Denoeux, T., Yaghlane, A.B.: Approximating the combination of belief functions using the fast moebius transform in a coarsened frame. International Journal of Approximate Reasoning 31(1-2), 77–101 (2002)
8. Janez, F., Appriou, A.: Theory of evidence and non-exhaustive frames of discernment: Plausibilities correction methods. International Journal of Approximate Reasoning 18(1-2), 1–19 (1998)
9. Schubert, J.: Constructing and Reasoning about Alternative Frames of Discernment. In: Proceedings of the Workshop on the Theory of Belief Functions (2010)
10. Rabiner, L.R.: A tutorial on hidden markov models and selected applications in speech recognition. Proceedings of the IEEE, 257–286 (1989)
11. Xu, L., Krzyzak, A., Suen, C.: Methods of combining multiple classifiers and their applications to handwriting recognition. IEEE Trans. Syst., Man, Cybern. (3) (1992)
12. Kim, J.H., Kim, K.K., Nadal, C.P., Suen, C.Y.: A methodology of combining hmm and mlp classifiers for cursive word recognition. In: International Conference on Pattern Recognition, vol. 2, pp. 319–322 (2000)
13. Prevost, L., Michel-Sendis, C., Moises, A., Oudot, L., Milgram, M.: Combining model-based and discriminative classifiers: application to handwritten character recognition. In: International Conference on Document Analysis and Recognition, vol. 1, pp. 31–35 (2003)
14. Arica, N., Yarman-Vural, F.T.: An overview of character recognition focused on off-line handwriting. IEEE Trans. Systems, Man and Cybernetics, Part C: Applications and Reviews (2), 216–232 (2001)
15. Kessentini, Y., Paquet, T., Hamadou, A.B.: Off-line handwritten word recognition using multi-stream hidden markov models. Pattern Recognition Letters 30(1), 60–70 (2010)
16. Kessentini, Y., Paquet, T., Burger, T.: Comparaison des méthodes probabilistes et évidentielles de fusion de classifieurs pour la reconnaissance de mots manuscrits. In: CIFED (2010)
17. Kessentini, Y., Burger, T., Paquet, T.: Evidential ensemble hmm classifier for handwriting recognition. In: Proceedings of IPMU, vol. 6178, pp. 445–454 (2010)
18. Al-Ani, A., Deriche, M.: A new technique for combining multiple classifiers using the Dempster-Shafer theory of evidence. Journal of Artificial Intelligence Research 17(1), 333–361 (2002)
19. Altınçay, H.: A dempster-shafer theoretic framework for boosting based ensemble design. Pattern Analysis & Applications 8(3), 287–302 (2005)
20. Burger, T., Aran, O., Caplier, A.: Modeling hesitation and conflict: A belief-based approach for multi-class problems. In: Fourth International Conference on Machine Learning and Applications, pp. 95–100 (2006)
21. Mercier, D., Cron, G., Denoeux, T., Masson, M.-H.: Fusion de décisions postales dans le cadre du modéle des croyances transférables. Traitement du Signal 24(2), 133–151 (2007)
22. Valente, F., Hermansky, H.: Combination of acoustic classifiers based on dempster-shafer theory of evidence. In: IEEE International Conference on Acoustics, Speech and Signal Processing, ICASSP, vol. 4, pp. 1129–1132 (April 2007)

23. Burger, T., Aran, O., Urankar, A., Akarun, L., Caplier, A.: A dempster-shafer theory based combination of classifiers for hand gesture recognition. In: Computer Vision and Computer Graphics - Theory and Applications. CCIS (2008)
24. Bi, Y., Guan, J., Bell, D.A.: The combination of multiple classifiers using an evidential reasoning approach. Artif. Intell. 172(15), 1731–1751 (2008)
25. Aran, O., Burger, T., Caplier, A., Akarun, L.: A belief-based sequential fusion approach for fusing manual and non-manual signs. Pattern Recognition 42(5), 812–822 (2009)
26. Burger, T., Kessentini, Y., Paquet, T.: A tutorial on using dempster-shafer theory to combine probabilistic classifiers - application to hand gesture and handwriting recognition. Submitted to Journal of Zhejiang University, Elsevier (2011)
27. Haenni, R.: Are alternatives to Dempster's rule of combination alternatives. Int. J. Information Fusion 3, 237–241 (2002)
28. Quost, B., Masson, M., Denoeux, T.: Classifier fusion in the Dempster-Shafer framework using optimized t-norm based combination rules. International Journal of Approximate Reasoning (2010)
29. Pechwitz, M., Maddouri, S., Maergner, V., Ellouze, N., Amiri, H.: Ifn/enit - database of handwritten arabic words. Colloque International Francophone sur l'Ecrit et le Doucement, 129–136 (2002)
30. Grosicki, E., Carre, M., Brodin, J., Geoffrois, E.: Results of the rimes evaluation campaign for handwritten mail processing. In: International Conference on Document Analysis and Recognition, pp. 941–945 (2009)
31. McNemar, Q.: Note on the sampling error of the difference between correlated proportions or percentages. Psychometrika 12(2), 153–157 (1947)

On Consistent Approximations of Belief
Functions in the Mass Space

Fabio Cuzzolin

Oxford Brookes University, Oxford, UK
fabio.cuzzolin@brookes.ac.uk

Abstract. In this paper we study the class of consistent belief functions, as counterparts of consistent knowledge bases in classical logic. We prove that such class can be defined univocally no matter our definition of proposition implied by a belief function. As consistency can be desirable in decision making, the problem of mapping an arbitrary belief function to a consistent one arises, and can be posed in a geometric setup. We analyze here all the consistent transformations induced by minimizing L_p distances between belief functions, represented by the vectors of their basic probabilities.

1 Introduction

Belief functions (b.f.s) [1,2] are complex objects, in which different and sometimes contradictory bodies of evidence may coexist, as they mathematically describe the fusion of possibly conflicting expert opinions and/or imprecise/ corrupted measurements, et caetera. Indeed, conflict and combinability play a central role in the theory of evidence [3,4,5], and have been recently subject to novel analyses [6,7,8]. As a consequence, making decisions based on such objects can be misleading. This is a well known problem in classical logics, where the application of inference rules to inconsistent sets of assumptions or "knowledge bases" may lead to incompatible conclusions, depending on the set of assumptions we start reasoning from [9]. A set of formulas Φ is said consistent iff there does not exist another formula ϕ such that Φ implies both ϕ and $\neg\phi$.

As each formula ϕ can be put in correspondence with the set $A(\phi)$ of interpretations under which it holds, a straightforward extension of classical logic consists on assigning a probability value to such sets of interpretations, i.e, to each formula. If all possible interpretations are collected in a frame of discernment, we can easily define a belief function on such a frame, and attribute to each formula ϕ a belief value $b(\phi) = b(A(\phi))$ through the associated set of interpretations $A(\phi)$. A belief function can therefore be seen, in this context, as the generalization of a knowledge base [10].

A variety of approaches have been proposed in the context of classical logics to solve the problem of inconsistent knowledge bases, such as fragmenting the latter into maximally consistent subsets, limiting the power of the formalism, or adopting non-classical semantics [11,12]. Even when a knowledge base is formally

W. Liu (Ed.): ECSQARU 2011, LNAI 6717, pp. 287–298, 2011.

inconsistent, though, it may contain potentially useful information. Paris [9], for instance, tackles the problem by not assuming each proposition in the knowledge base as a fact, but by attributing to it a certain degree of belief in a probabilistic logic approach. This leads to something similar to a belief function.

To identify the counterparts of consistent knowledge bases in the theory of evidence we need to specify the notion of a belief function "implying" a certain proposition $A(\phi)$. As we show in this paper, under two different sensible definitions of such implication, the class of belief functions which generalize consistent knowledge bases is uniquely determined as the set of BFs whose non-zero mass "focal elements" have non-empty intersection. We are therefore allowed to call them *consistent* belief functions (cs.b.f.s).

Analogously to consistent knowledge bases, consistent b.f.s are characterized by null internal conflict. It may therefore be desirable to transform a generic belief function into a consistent one prior to making a decision, or picking a course of action. A similar transformation problem has been widely studied in both the probabilistic [13,14] and possibilistic [15] case. A sensible approach, in particular, consists on studying the geometry [16,17] of the class of b.f.s of interest and project the original belief function onto the corresponding geometric locus.

In [18] the author has indeed investigated the consistent transformation problem in the space of belief functions, represented by the vectors of their belief values. This paper further extends this line of research. Its goals are two-fold: 1. to formalize the notion of consistent belief functions as counterparts of consistent knowledge bases in belief calculus, and 2. to study the consistent transformation problem in the mass space of the basis probability vectors. We therefore introduce in Section 2 the notion of consistent belief function and prove that they generalize consistent knowledge bases under two distinct definitions of implication. Section 3 illustrates the consistent transformation problem in geometric terms. Finally, in Section 4 we solve the approximation problem in the mass space, using the classical L_1 (4.1), L_∞ (4.2) and L_2 (4.3) norms to measure distances between mass vectors. The results are interpreted and compared with those obtained in the belief space.

2 Semantics of Consistent Belief Functions

A *basic probability assignment* on a finite set *(frame of discernment [1])* Θ is a function $m_b : 2^\Theta \to [0,1]$ on $2^\Theta \doteq \{A \subseteq \Theta\}$ s.t. $m_b(\emptyset) = 0$, $\sum_{A \subseteq \Theta} m_b(A) = 1$, $m_b(A) \geq 0$ for all $A \subseteq \Theta$. Subsets of Θ associated with non-zero values of m_b are called *focal elements*, and their intersection *core*: $C_b \doteq \bigcap_{A \subseteq \Theta : m_b(A) \neq 0} A$.

The *belief function* $b : 2^\Theta \to [0,1]$ associated with a basic probability assignment m_b on Θ is defined as: $b(A) = \sum_{B \subseteq A} m_b(B)$. A dual mathematical representation of the evidence encoded by a belief function b is the *plausibility function* (pl.f.) $pl_b : 2^\Theta \to [0,1]$, $A \mapsto pl_b(A)$ where the plausibility value $pl_b(A)$ of an event A is given by $pl_b(A) \doteq 1 - b(A^c) = 1 - \sum_{B \subseteq A^c} m_b(B) = \sum_{B \cap A \neq \emptyset} m_b(B) \geq b(A)$ and expresses the amount of evidence *not against* A.

Belief logic interpretation. Generalizations of classical logic in which propositions are assigned probability, rather than truth, values have been proposed in the past. As belief functions naturally generalize probability measures, it is quite natural to define non-classical logic frameworks in which propositions are assigned *belief values* instead. This approach has been brought forward in particular by Saffiotti [19], Haenni [10], and others.

In propositional logic, propositions or formulas are either true or false, i.e., their truth value is either 0 or 1 [20]. Formally, an *interpretation* or *model* of a formula ϕ is a valuation function mapping ϕ to the truth value "true" (1). Each formula can therefore be associated with the set of interpretations or models under which its truth value is 1. If we define the frame of discernment of all the possible interpretations, each formula ϕ is associated with the subset $A(\phi)$ of this frame which collects all its interpretations. If the available evidence allows to define a belief function on this frame of possible interpretations, to each formula $A(\phi) \subseteq \Theta$ it is then naturally assigned a degree of belief $b(A(\phi))$ between 0 and 1 [19,10], measuring the total amount of evidence supporting the proposition "ϕ is true".

Consistent belief functions generalize consistent knowledge bases. In classical logic, a set Φ of formulas or "knowledge base" is said *consistent* if and only if there does not exist another formula ϕ such that the knowledge base implies both such formula and its negation: $\Phi \vdash \phi$, $\Phi \vdash \neg\phi$. In other words, it is impossible to derive incompatible conclusions from the set of propositions that form a consistent knowledge base. This is obviously crucial if we want to derive univocal, non-contradictory conclusions from a given body of evidence.

A knowledge base in propositional logic $\Phi = \{\phi : T(\phi) = 1\}$ corresponds in a belief logic framework [19] to a belief function, i.e., a set of propositions together with their non-zero belief values: $b = \{A \subseteq \Theta : b(A) \neq 0\}$. Therefore, to determine what consistency amounts to in such a framework, we need to formalize the notion of proposition implied by a belief function. One option is to decide that $b \vdash B \subseteq \Theta$ if B is implied by all the propositions supported by b:

$$b \vdash B \Leftrightarrow A \subseteq B \quad \forall A : b(A) \neq 0. \tag{1}$$

Alternatively, we could require the proposition B itself to receive non-zero support by the belief function b:

$$b \vdash B \Leftrightarrow b(B) \neq 0. \tag{2}$$

In both cases we can define the class of consistent belief functions as the set of b.f.s which cannot imply contradictory propositions.

Definition 1. *A belief function b is consistent if there exists no proposition A such that both A and its negation A^c are implied by b.*

When adopting the implication relation (1), it is easy to see that $A \subseteq B \ \forall A : b(A) \neq 0$ is equivalent to $\bigcap_{b(A) \neq 0} A \subseteq B$. Furthermore, as each proposition with non-zero belief value must by definition contain a focal element C s.t. $m_b(C) \neq 0$, the intersection of all non-zero belief propositions reduces to that of all focal elements of b, i.e., the core of b: $\bigcap_{b(A) \neq 0} A = \bigcap_{\exists C \subseteq A : m_b(C) \neq 0} A = \bigcap_{m_b(C) \neq 0} C = \mathcal{C}_b.$

Indeed, regardless the chosen definition of implication, the class of consistent belief functions corresponds to the set of b.f.s whose core is not empty.

Definition 2. *A belief function is said to be* consistent *if its core is non-empty.*

We can prove that, under either definition (1) or definition (2) of the implication $b \vdash B$, Definitions 1 and 2 are equivalent.

Theorem 1. *A belief function* $b : 2^{\Theta} \rightarrow [0, 1]$ *has non-empty core if and only if there do not exist two complementary propositions* $A, A^c \subseteq \Theta$ *which are both implied by* b *in the sense (1).*

Proof. We have seen above that a proposition A is implied (1) by b iff $\mathcal{C}_b \subseteq A$. Accordingly, in order for both A and A^c to be implied by b we would need $\mathcal{C}_b = \emptyset$.

Theorem 2. *A b.f.* $b : 2^{\Theta} \rightarrow [0, 1]$ *has non-empty core if and only if there do not exist two complementary propositions* $A, A^c \subseteq \Theta$ *which both enjoy non-zero support from* b, $b(A) \neq 0$, $b(A^c) \neq 0$ *(i.e., they are implied by* b *in the sense (2)).*

Proof. By Definition 1, in order for a subset (or proposition, in a propositional logic interpretation) $A \subseteq \Theta$ to have non-zero belief value it has to contain the core of b: $A \supseteq \mathcal{C}_b$. In order to have both $b(A) \neq 0$, $b(A^c) \neq 0$ we need both to contain the core, but in that case $A \cap A^c \supseteq \mathcal{C}_b \neq \emptyset$ which is absurd as $A \cap A^c = \emptyset$.

It is worth noticing, however, that other authors have introduced a slightly different notion of consistency, by requiring simply that the mass of the empty set be null $m_b(\emptyset) = 0$, or equivalently that the core of probabilities dominating b be non-empty [21,22].

3   The L_p Consistent Approximation Problem

The amount of *internal conflict* of a b.f. is typically defined as $c(b) \doteq 1 - \max_{x \in \Theta} pl_b(x)$ or, alternatively, $c(b) \doteq \sum_{A,B \subseteq \Theta : A \cap B = \emptyset} m_b(A) m_b(B)$. In both cases a belief function b is consistent if and only if its internal conflict is zero, $c(b) = 0$. As cs.b.f.s are the belief logic equivalent of consistent knowledge bases, it can be considered desirable to transform a generic belief function to a consistent one prior to drawing conclusions on the phenomenon at hand.

   Consistent transformation. Consistent transformations can be built by solving a minimization problem of the form

$$cs[b] = \arg \min_{cs \in CS} dist(b, cs). \tag{3}$$

where $dist$ is some distance measure between belief functions, and CS denotes the collection of all consistent b.f.s. We call (3) the *consistent approximation problem*. Plugging in different distance functions in (3) we get different consistent transformations. In [18] we have studied transformations induced by norms of vectors of belief values $\boldsymbol{b}$ in the belief space $\mathcal{B}$. Similarly, we can measure distances between b.f.s via geometric norms between vectors of *mass values*. Here we focus in particular on what happens when using L_p norms in the space of basic probability assignments. This is supported by the fact that the contour function $pl_b(x)$ of a consistent belief function is a possibility distribution, which is in turn related to the L_p norm via $Pos(A) = \max_{x \in A} Pos(x)$. Note, however, that the plausibility measure of a b.f. is a necessity measure iff b is consonant, i.e., its focal elements are nested.

Mass space representation. To solve the consistent approximation problem (3) we need to understand the structure of the space in which consistent belief functions live. Each belief function is uniquely associated with the related set of mass values $\{m(A), \emptyset \subsetneq A \subseteq \Theta\}$ and can therefore be seen as a point of $\mathbb{R}^{N-2}$, $N = |2^\Theta|$, the vector $\boldsymbol{m}$ of its $N - 1$ mass components minus the mass of Θ which is univocally determined by the normalization constraint:

$$\boldsymbol{m} = \sum_{\emptyset \subsetneq B \subseteq \Theta} m_b(B) \boldsymbol{m}_B, \tag{4}$$

where $\boldsymbol{m}_B$ is the vector of mass values associated with the ("categorical") mass function $\boldsymbol{m}_A$ assigning all the mass to a single event A: $\boldsymbol{m}_A(A) = 1$, $\boldsymbol{m}_A(B) = 0$ $\forall B \neq A$. The collection $\mathcal{M}$ of points of $\mathbb{R}^{N-2}$ which are valid basic probability

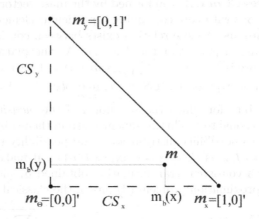

Fig. 1. The mass space $\mathcal{M}$ for a binary frame is a triangle of $\mathbb{R}^2$ whose vertices are the mass vectors associated with the categorical b.f.s focused on $\{x\}$, $\{y\}$ and Θ. Consistent b.f.s live in the union of the two segments $\mathcal{CS}_x = Cl(\boldsymbol{m}_\Theta, \boldsymbol{m}_x)$ and $\mathcal{CS}_y = Cl(\boldsymbol{m}_\Theta, \boldsymbol{m}_y)$.

assignments is a "simplex" (in rough words a higher-dimensional triangle), which we call *mass space*. $\mathcal{M}$ is the convex closure[1] $\mathcal{M} = Cl(\boldsymbol{m}_A, \emptyset \subsetneq A \subseteq \Theta)$.

Binary case. As an example let us consider a frame of discernment formed by just two elements, $\Theta_2 = \{x, y\}$. In this very simple case each belief function $b : 2^{\Theta_2} \to [0, 1]$ is completely determined by its mass values $m_b(x)$, $m_b(y)$ as $m_b(\Theta) = 1 - m_b(x) - m_b(y)$, $m_b(\emptyset) = 0$ $\forall b$. We can then represent each b.f. b as the vector of its basic probabilities (masses) $\boldsymbol{m} = [m_b(x), m_b(y)]'$ of $\mathbb{R}^{N-2} = \mathbb{R}^2$ (since $N = 2^2 = 4$). Since $m_b(x) \geq 0$, $m_b(y) \geq 0$, $m_b(x) + m_b(y) \leq 1$ the set

---

[1] Here Cl denotes the convex closure operator: $Cl(\boldsymbol{m}_1, ..., \boldsymbol{m}_k) = \{\boldsymbol{m} \in \mathcal{M} : \boldsymbol{m} = \alpha_1 \boldsymbol{m}_1 + \cdots + \alpha_k \boldsymbol{m}_k, \sum_i \alpha_i = 1, \alpha_i \geq 0 \; \forall i\}$.

$\mathcal{M}_2$ of all the possible belief functions on Θ_2 is the triangle of Figure 1, whose vertices are the points $\boldsymbol{m}_\Theta = [0,0]'$, $\boldsymbol{m}_x = [1,0]'$, $\boldsymbol{m}_y = [0,1]'$ which correspond respectively to the vacuous belief function b_Θ $(m_{b_\Theta}(\Theta) = 1)$, the Bayesian b.f. b_x with $m_{b_x}(x) = 1$, and the Bayesian b.f. b_y such that $m_{b_y}(y) = 1$.

In the binary case consistent belief functions can have as list of focal elements either $\{\{x\}, \Theta_2\}$ or $\{\{y\}, \Theta_2\}$. Therefore the space of cs.b.f.s $\mathcal{CS}_2$ is the union of two line segments: $\mathcal{CS}_2 = \mathcal{CS}_x \cup \mathcal{CS}_y = Cl(\boldsymbol{m}_\Theta, \boldsymbol{m}_x) \cup Cl(\boldsymbol{m}_\Theta, \boldsymbol{m}_y)$.

The consistent complex. In the general case the geometry of consistent belief functions can be described by resorting to the notion of *simplicial complex* [23]. A simplicial complex is a collection Σ of simplices of arbitrary dimensions possessing the following properties: 1. if a simplex belongs to Σ, then all its faces of any dimension belong to Σ; 2. the intersection of any two simplices is a face of both the intersecting simplices. It has been proven that [24,18] the region $\mathcal{CS}$ of consistent belief functions in the belief space is a simplicial complex, the union $\mathcal{CS}_B = \bigcup_{x \in \Theta} Cl(\boldsymbol{b}_A, A \ni x)$. It is not difficult to see that the same holds in the mass space, where the consistent complex is the union $\mathcal{CS} = \bigcup_{x \in \Theta} Cl(\boldsymbol{m}_A, A \ni x)$ of maximal simplices $Cl(\boldsymbol{m}_A, A \ni x)$ formed by the mass vectors associated with all the belief functions with core containing a particular element x of Θ.

Why use L_p norms. A close relation exists between consistent belief functions and L_p norms, in particular the L_∞ one. As the plausibility of all the elements in their core is 1 $(pl_b(x) = \sum_{A \supseteq \{x\}} m_b(A) = 1 \; \forall x \in C_b)$, the region of consistent b.f.s can be expressed as $\mathcal{CS} = \{b : \max_{x \in \Theta} pl_b(x) = 1\} = \{b : \|\vec{pl}_b\|_{L_\infty} = 1\}$, i.e., the set of b.f.s for which the L_∞ norm of the *plausibility distribution* $\vec{pl}_b(x) = pl_b(\{x\})$ is equal to 1. This argument is strengthened by the observation that cs.b.f.s relate to possibility distributions, and possibility measures Pos are inherently related to L_∞ as $Pos(A) = \max_{x \in A} Pos(x)$. It makes therefore sense to conjecture that a consistent transformation obtained by picking as distance function in the approximation problem (3) one of the classical L_p norms

$$\|\boldsymbol{m} - \boldsymbol{m}'\|_{L_1} = \sum_{A \subseteq \Theta} |m_b(A) - m_b'(A)|, \; \|\boldsymbol{m} - \boldsymbol{m}'\|_{L_2} = \sqrt{\sum_{A \subseteq \Theta} (m_b(A) - m_b'(A))^2},$$
$$\|\boldsymbol{m} - \boldsymbol{m}'\|_{L_\infty} = \max_{A \subseteq \Theta} \{|m_b(A) - m_b'(A)|\}$$
$$(5)$$

would be meaningful. In the probabilistic case, $p[b] = \arg\min_{p \in \mathcal{P}} dist(b,p)$, the use of L_p norms leads indeed to quite interesting results. On one side, the L_2 approximation induces the so-called "orthogonal projection" of b onto $\mathcal{P}$ [14]. On the other, the set of L_1/L_∞ probabilistic approximations of b (in the belief space) coincides with the set of probabilities dominating b: $\{p : p(A) \geq b(A)\}$ (at least in the binary case).

Distance of a point from a simplicial complex. As the consistent complex $\mathcal{CS}$ is a collection of linear spaces (better, simplices which generate a linear space) solving the problem (3) involves finding a number of partial solutions: $cs_{L_p}^x[b] = \arg\min_{cs \in \mathcal{CS}_x} \|\boldsymbol{m} - \boldsymbol{cs}\|_{L_p}$ (see Figure 2). Afterwards, the distance of b from all such partial solutions has to be assessed in order to select a global

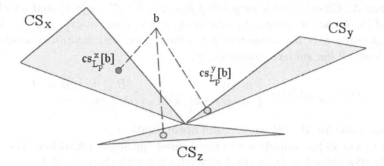

Fig. 2. To minimize the distance of a point from a simplicial complex, we need to find all the partial solutions on all the maximal simplices in the complex (empty circles), and compare these partial solutions to select a global optimum (black circle).

optimal approximation. We will apply here this scheme to the approximation problems associated with the L_1, L_2, and L_∞ norms in the mass space.

4   Consistent Approximation in $\mathcal{M}$

Using the notation $\boldsymbol{cs} = \sum_{B \supseteq \{x\}, B \neq \Theta} m_{cs}(B) \boldsymbol{m}_B$, $\boldsymbol{m} = \sum_{B \subsetneq \Theta} m_b(B) \boldsymbol{m}_B$ (as in $\mathbb{R}^{N-2}$ $m_b(\Theta)$ is not included by normalization) the difference vector is

$$\boldsymbol{m} - \boldsymbol{cs} = \sum_{B \supseteq \{x\}, B \neq \Theta} (m_b(B) - m_{cs}(B)) \boldsymbol{m}_B + \sum_{B \not\supseteq \{x\}} m_b(B) \boldsymbol{m}_B \qquad (6)$$

so that its classical L_p norms read as

$$\|\boldsymbol{m} - \boldsymbol{cs}\|_1^{\mathcal{M}} = \sum_{B \supseteq \{x\}, B \neq \Theta} |m_b(B) - m_{cs}(B)| + \sum_{B \not\supseteq \{x\}} |m_b(B)|,$$

$$\|\boldsymbol{m} - \boldsymbol{cs}\|_2^{\mathcal{M}} = \sqrt{\sum_{B \supseteq \{x\}, B \neq \Theta} |m_b(B) - m_{cs}(B)|^2 + \sum_{B \not\supseteq \{x\}} |m_b(B)|^2}, \qquad (7)$$

$$\|\boldsymbol{m} - \boldsymbol{cs}\|_\infty^{\mathcal{M}} = \max \left\{ \max_{B \supseteq \{x\}, B \neq \Theta} |m_b(B) - m_{cs}(B)|, \max_{B \not\supseteq \{x\}} |m_b(B)| \right\}.$$

4.1 L_1 Approximation

Let us tackle first the L_1 case. After introducing the auxiliary variables $\beta(B) \doteq m_b(B) - m_{cs}(B)$ we can write the L_1 norm of the difference vector as

$$\|\boldsymbol{m} - \boldsymbol{cs}\|_1^{\mathcal{M}} = \sum_{B \supseteq \{x\}, B \neq \Theta} |\beta(B)| + \sum_{B \not\supseteq \{x\}} |m_b(B)|, \qquad (8)$$

which is obviously minimized by $\beta(B) = 0$, for all $B \supseteq \{x\}$, $B \neq \Theta$. Therefore:

Theorem 3. *Given an arbitrary belief function* $b : 2^{\Theta} \to [0,1]$ *and an element* $x \in \Theta$ *of the frame, its unique* L_1 *consistent approximation* $cs^x_{L_1,\mathcal{M}}[b]$ *in* $\mathcal{M}$ *with core containing* x *is the consistent b.f. whose mass distribution coincides with that of* b *on all the subsets containing* x:

$$m_{cs^x_{L_1,\mathcal{M}}[b]}(B) = \begin{cases} m_b(B) & \forall B \supseteq \{x\}, B \neq \Theta \\ m_b(\Theta) + b(\{x\}^c) & B = \Theta. \end{cases} \qquad (9)$$

The mass value for $B = \Theta$ comes from normalization.

The mass of all the subsets not in the desired "principal ultrafilter" $\{B \supseteq \{x\}\}$ is simply re-assigned to Θ. A similarity emerges with the case of L_1 conditional belief functions [25], when we recall that the set of L_1 conditional belief functions $b_{L_1,\mathcal{M}}(.|A)$ with respect to A in $\mathcal{M}$ is the simplex whose vertices are each associated with a subset $\emptyset \subsetneq B \subseteq A$ of the conditional event A, and have b.p.a.:

$$m'(B) = m_b(B) + 1 - b(A), \quad m'(X) = m_b(X) \quad \forall \emptyset \subsetneq X \subsetneq A, X \neq B.$$

In the L_1 conditional case, each vertex of the set of solutions is obtained by re-assigning the mass *not in the conditional event* A to a single subset of A, just as in L_1 consistent approximation all the mass *not in the principal ultrafilter* $\{B \supseteq \{x\}\}$ is re-assigned to the top of the ultrafilter, Θ.

Global approximation. The global L_1 consistent approximation in $\mathcal{M}$ is the partial approximation (9) at minimal distance from the original b.p.a. $\boldsymbol{m}$. By (8) the partial approximation focussed on x has distance $b(\{x\}^c) = \sum_{B \not\supseteq \{x\}} m_b(B)$ from $\boldsymbol{m}$. The global L_1 approximation $m_{cs_{L_1,\mathcal{M}}[b]}$ is therefore the partial approximation associated with the maximal plausibility singleton: $\hat{x} = \arg\min_x b(x^c) = \arg\max_x pl_b(x)$.

4.2 L_∞ Approximation

In the L_∞ case $\|\boldsymbol{m} - \boldsymbol{cs}\|^{\mathcal{M}}_\infty = \max\Big\{ \max_{B \supseteq \{x\}, B \neq \Theta} |\beta(B)|, \max_{B \not\supseteq \{x\}} m_b(B) \Big\}$. The L_∞ norm of the difference vector is obviously minimized by $\{\beta(B)\}$ such that: $|\beta(B)| \leq \max_{B \not\supseteq \{x\}} m_b(B)$ for all $B \supseteq \{x\}, B \neq \Theta$, i.e., $- \max_{B \not\supseteq \{x\}} m_b(B) \leq m_b(B) - m_c(B) \leq \max_{B \not\supseteq \{x\}} m_b(B) \quad \forall B \supseteq \{x\}, B \neq \Theta$.

Theorem 4. *Given an arbitrary belief function* $b : 2^{\Theta} \to [0,1]$ *and an element* $x \in \Theta$ *of the frame, its* L_∞ *consistent approximations* $cs^x_{L_\infty,\mathcal{M}}[b]$ *with core containing* x *in* $\mathcal{M}$ *are those whose mass values on all the subsets containing* x *differ from the original ones by the maximum mass of the subsets not in the ultrafilter: for all* $B \supset \{x\}, B \neq \Theta$

$$m_b(B) - \max_{C \not\supseteq \{x\}} m_b(C) \leq m_{cs^x_{L_\infty,\mathcal{M}}[b]}(B) \leq m_b(B) + \max_{C \not\supseteq \{x\}} m_b(C). \qquad (10)$$

Clearly this set of solutions can include pseudo belief functions, i.e., b.f.s whose mass function is not necessarily non-negative.

Global approximation. Once again, the global L_∞ consistent approximation in $\mathcal{M}$ coincides with the partial approximation (10) at minimal distance from the original b.p.a. $\boldsymbol{m}$. The partial approximation focussed on x has distance $\max_{B \not\supseteq \{x\}} m_b(B)$ from $\boldsymbol{m}$. The global L_∞ approximation $m_{cs_{L_\infty,\mathcal{M}}}[b]$ is therefore the partial approximation associated with the singleton such that:
$$\hat{x} = \arg\min_x \max_{B \not\supseteq \{x\}} m_b(B).$$

4.3 L_2 Approximation

To find the L_2 consistent approximation in $\mathcal{M}$ we need to minimize the L_2 norm of the difference vector $\|\boldsymbol{m} - \boldsymbol{cs}\|_2^{\mathcal{M}}$, or, equivalently, impose a condition of orthogonality between the difference vector itself $\boldsymbol{m} - \boldsymbol{cs}$ and the vector space associated with consistent mass functions focused on $\{x\}$. Clearly the generators of such linear space are the vectors in $\mathcal{M}$: $\boldsymbol{m}_B - \boldsymbol{m}_{\{x\}}$, for all $B \supseteq \{x\}$. The desired orthogonality condition reads therefore as $\langle \boldsymbol{m} - \boldsymbol{cs}, \boldsymbol{m}_B - \boldsymbol{m}_{\{x\}}\rangle = 0$ where $\boldsymbol{m} - \boldsymbol{cs}$ is given by Equation (6), while $\boldsymbol{m}_B - \boldsymbol{m}_{\{x\}}(C) = 1$ if $C = B$, $= -1$ if $C = \{x\}$, 0 elsewhere. Therefore, using once again the variables $\{\beta(B)\}$, the condition simplifies as follows:

$$\langle \boldsymbol{m} - \boldsymbol{cs}, \boldsymbol{m}_B - \boldsymbol{m}_{\{x\}}\rangle = \begin{cases} \beta(B) - \beta(\{x\}) = 0 & \forall B \supsetneq \{x\}, B \neq \Theta; \\ -\beta(x) = 0 & B = \Theta. \end{cases} \quad (11)$$

Notice that, when using vectors $\boldsymbol{m}$ of $\mathbb{R}^{N-1}$ (including $B = \Theta$) to represent b.f.s, the orthogonality condition reads instead as:

$$\langle \boldsymbol{m} - \boldsymbol{cs}, \boldsymbol{m}_B - \boldsymbol{m}_{\{x\}}\rangle = \beta(B) - \beta(\{x\}) = 0 \quad \forall B \supsetneq \{x\}. \quad (12)$$

Theorem 5. *Given an arbitrary belief function $b : 2^\Theta \to [0,1]$ and an element $x \in \Theta$ of the frame, its unique L_2 partial consistent approximation $cs_{L_2,\mathcal{M}}^x[b]$ with core containing x in $\mathcal{M}$ coincides with its partial L_1 approximation $cs_{L_1,\mathcal{M}}^x[b]$. However, when using the mass representation in $\mathbb{R}^{N-1}$, the partial L_2 approximation is obtained by equally redistributing to each element of the ultrafilter $\{B \supseteq \{x\}\}$ an equal fraction of the mass of focal elements not in it:*

$$m_{cs_{L_2,\mathcal{M}}^x[m_b]}(B) = m_b(B) + \frac{b(\{x\}^c)}{2^{|\Theta|-1}} \quad \forall B \supseteq \{x\}. \quad (13)$$

Proof. In the $N-2$ representation, by (11) we have that $\beta(B) = 0$, i.e., $m_{cs}(B) = m_b(B)$ $\forall B \supseteq \{x\}$, $B \neq \Theta$. By normalization we get $m_{cs}(\Theta) = m_b(\Theta) + m_b(x^c)$: but this is exactly the L_1 approximation (9).

In the $N-1$ representation, by (12) we have that $m_{cs}(B) = m_{cs}(x) + m_b(B) - m_b(x)$ for all $B \supsetneq \{x\}$. By normalizing we get $\sum_{\{x\} \subseteq B \subseteq \Theta} m_{cs}(B) = m_{cs}(x) + \sum_{\{x\} \subsetneq B \subseteq \Theta} m_{cs}(B) = 2^{|\Theta|-1} m_{cs}(x) + pl_b(x) - 2^{|\Theta|-1} m_b(x) = 1$, i.e., $m_{cs}(x) = m_b(x) + (1 - pl_b(x))/2^{|\Theta|-1}$, as there are $2^{|\Theta|-1}$ subsets in the ultrafilter containing x. By replacing the value of $m_{cs}(x)$ into the first equation we get (13). The partial L_2 approximation in $\mathbb{R}^{N-1}$ redistributes the mass equally to all the elements of the ultrafilter.

Global approximation. The global L_2 consistent approximation in $\mathcal{M}$ is again given by the partial approximation (13) at minimal L_2 distance from m_b. In the $N - 2$ representation, by definition of L_2 norm in $\mathcal{M}$ (7), the partial approximation focussed on x has distance from m_b: $(b(x^c))^2 + \sum_{B \not\supseteq \{x\}} (m_b(B))^2 =$ $\left(\sum_{B \not\supseteq \{x\}} m_b(B) \right)^2 + \sum_{B \not\supseteq \{x\}} (m_b(B))^2$. The latter is minimized by the element(s) $\hat{x} \in \Theta$ such that $\hat{x} = \arg\min_x \sum_{B \not\supseteq \{x\}} (m_b(B))^2$, which in turn determines the global L_2 approximation(s). In the $N - 1$-dimensional case, instead, we get

$$\sum_{B \supseteq \{x\}, B \neq \Theta} \left[m_b(B) - \left(m_b(B) + \frac{b(x^c)}{2^{|\Theta|-1}} \right) \right]^2 + \sum_{B \not\supseteq \{x\}} (m_b(B))^2 =$$

$$\sum_{B \supseteq \{x\}, B \neq \Theta} \left(\frac{b(x^c)}{2^{|\Theta|-1}} \right)^2 + \sum_{B \not\supseteq \{x\}} (m_b(B))^2 = \frac{\left(\sum_{B \not\supseteq \{x\}} m_b(B) \right)^2}{2^{|\Theta|-1}} + \sum_{B \not\supseteq \{x\}} (m_b(B))^2$$

which is minimized by the same singleton(s). In any case, even though (in the $N - 2$ representation) the partial L_1 and L_2 approximations coincide, the global approximations in general may fall on different components of the complex.

5 Comparison with Approximation in the Belief Space

It is interesting to compare the above results with those obtained in the belief space [18]. The partial L_1/L_2 consistent approximations of b (in the belief space $\mathcal{B}$) focused on a given element x coincide, and have b.p.a.:

$$m_{cs^x_{L_1}}(A) = m_{cs^x_{L_2}}(A) = m_b(A) + m_b(A \setminus \{x\}) \tag{14}$$

for all events A such that $\{x\} \subseteq A \subsetneq \Theta$. To get a consistent b.f. focused on a singleton x, the mass contribution of all the events B such that $B \cup \{x\} = A$ coincide is assigned indeed to A. They coincide with Dubois and Prade's "focused consistent transformations" [15].

It can be useful to illustrate the different approximations in the toy case of a ternary frame, $\Theta = \{x, y, z\}$. Assuming we want the consistent approximation to focus on x, by (14) the partial L_1/L_2 approximations in $\mathcal{B}$ are given by (using the simplified notation $m'(A)$): $m'(x) = m_b(x)$, $m'(x, y) = m_b(y) + m_b(x, y)$, $m'(x, z) = m_b(z) + m_b(x, z)$ $m'(\Theta) = 1 - b(x, y)$. The partial approximations induced by L_p norms in $\mathcal{M}$ can be computed via (9), (13) and (10). Figure 3 illustrates the different partial consistent approximations in the simplex $Cl(\boldsymbol{m}_x, \boldsymbol{m}_{x,y}, \boldsymbol{m}_{x,z}, \boldsymbol{m}_\Theta)$ of consistent belief functions focussed on x in a ternary frame, for the belief function with masses $m_b(x) = 0.2, m_b(y) = 0.1, m_b(z) = 0, m_b(x, y) = 0.4, m_b(x, z) = 0, m_b(y, z) = 0.3$. This is a tetrahedron with four vertices, delimited by dark solid edges.

The set of partial L_∞ approximations in $\mathcal{M}$ is depicted in Figure 3 as a green cube. As expected, it does not entirely fall inside the tetrahedron of admissible consistent belief functions. Its barycenter (the green star) coincides with the

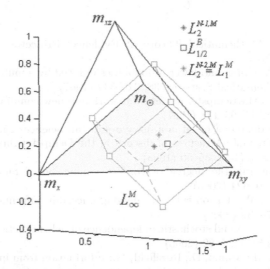

Fig. 3. The simplex (solid black tetrahedron) $Cl(\boldsymbol{m}_x, \boldsymbol{m}_{x,y}, \boldsymbol{m}_{x,z}, \boldsymbol{m}_\Theta)$ of consistent belief functions focussed on x in $\Theta = \{x, y, z\}$, and the related L_p partial consistent approximations of the b.f. with mass assignment (14).

L_1 partial consistent approximation in $\mathcal{M}$. The L_2^{N-2} approximation does also coincide, as expected, with the L_1 approximation. It remains to be seen if this holds for general frames of discernment as well. Regardless, there seems to exist a strong case for the latter transformation, which possesses a natural interpretation in terms of mass assignment: all the mass outside the ultrafilter is reassigned to Θ, increasing the overall uncertainty of the belief state.

The L_2 partial approximation in the $N - 1$ representation (blue star) is distinct from the previous ones, but still falls inside the polytope of L_∞ partial approximations and is admissible, as it falls in the interior of the simplicial component $Cl(\boldsymbol{m}_x, \boldsymbol{m}_{x,y}, \boldsymbol{m}_{x,z}, \boldsymbol{m}_\Theta)$. Its interpretation is rather compelling, as it splits the mass not in the ultrafilter focused on x equally among all the subsets in the ultrafilter. Finally, the unique L_1/L_2 partial approximation in $\mathcal{B}$ is shown (red square). It has something in common with the $L_2^{N-2,M} = L_1^M = \overline{L_\infty}^M$ approximation (green star), as they both fall exactly on the border of admissible consistent b.f.s (the face highlighted in yellow): they assign zero mass to $\{x, z\}$, which fails to be supported by any focal element of the original belief function.

6   Conclusions

In this paper we proved that consistent belief functions are the counterparts of consistent knowledge bases in belief calculus, analyzed consistent transformations induced by L_p norms in the mass space, and compared them with analogous transformations obtained in the belief space. The open-world scenario in which the current frame of discernment does not necessarily cover all possible alternatives, represented by the assumption $m_b(\emptyset)$ was not covered in this paper, but will be explored in the near future.

References

1. Shafer, G.: A Mathematical Theory of Evidence. Princeton University Press, Princeton (1976)
2. Dempster, A.P.: Upper and lower probabilities induced by a multivariate mapping. Annals of Mathematical Statistics 38, 325–339 (1967)
3. Yager, R.R.: On the dempster-shafer framework and new combination rules. Information Sciences 41, 93–138 (1987)
4. Smets, P.: The degree of belief in a fuzzy event. Inf. Sciences 25, 1–19 (1981)
5. Ramer, A., Klir, G.J.: Measures of discord in the Dempster-Shafer theory. Information Sciences 67(1-2), 35–50 (1993)
6. Liu, W.: Analyzing the degree of conflict among belief functions. Artif. Intell. 170(11), 909–924 (2006)
7. Hunter, A., Liu, W.: Fusion rules for merging uncertain information. Information Fusion 7(1), 97–134 (2006)
8. Lo, K.C.: Agreement and stochastic independence of belief functions. Mathematical Social Sciences 51(1), 1–22 (2006)
9. Paris, J.B., Picado-Muino, D., Rosefield, M.: Information from inconsistent knowledge: A probability logic approach. In: Advances in Soft Computing, vol. 46, pp. 291–307. Springer, Heidelberg (2008)
10. Haenni, R.: Towards a unifying theory of logical and probabilistic reasoning. In: Proceedings of ISIPTA 2005, pp. 193–202 (2005)
11. Priest, G., Routley, R., Norman, J.: Paraconsistent logic: Essays on the inconsistent. Philosophia Verlag (1989)
12. Batens, D., Mortensen, C., Priest, G.: Frontiers of paraconsistent logic. In: Studies in Logic and Computation, vol. 8. Research Studies Press (2000)
13. Daniel, M.: On transformations of belief functions to probabilities. International Journal of Intelligent Systems 21(6), 261–282 (2006)
14. Cuzzolin, F.: Two new Bayesian approximations of belief functions based on convex geometry. IEEE Tr. SMC-B 37(4), 993–1008 (2007)
15. Dubois, D., Prade, H.: Consonant approximations of belief functions. International Journal of Approximate Reasoning 4, 419–449 (1990)
16. Black, P.: An examination of belief functions and other monotone capacities. PhD dissertation, Department of Statistics, Carnegie Mellon University (1996)
17. Cuzzolin, F.: A geometric approach to the theory of evidence. IEEE Transactions on Systems, Man and Cybernetics Part C 38(4), 522–534 (2008)
18. Cuzzolin, F.: Consistent approximations of belief functions. In: Proceedings of ISIPTA 2009, pp. 139–148 (2009)
19. Saffiotti, A.: A belief-function logic. In: Universit Libre de Bruxelles, pp. 642–647. MIT Press, Cambridge
20. Mates, B.: Elementary Logic. Oxford University Press, Oxford (1972)
21. Cattaneo, M.E.G.V.: Combining belief functions issued from dependent sources. In: ISIPTA, pp. 133–147 (2003)
22. de Cooman, G.: Belief models: An order-theoretic investigation. Annals of Mathematics and Artificial Intelligence 45(1-2), 5–34 (2005)
23. Dubrovin, B.A., Novikov, S.P., Fomenko, A.T.: Sovremennaja geometrija. Metody i prilozenija, Nauka, Moscow (1986)
24. Cuzzolin, F.: An interpretation of consistent belief functions in terms of simplicial complexes. In: Proc. of ISAIM 2008 (2008)
25. Cuzzolin, F.: Geometric conditioning of belief functions. In: Proceedings of BELIEF 2010, Brest, France (2010)

Generalized Information Theory Based on the Theory of Hints

Marc Pouly

Interdisciplinary Centre for Security, Reliability and Trust,
University of Luxembourg

Abstract. The *aggregate uncertainty* is the only known functional for
Dempster-Shafer theory that generalizes the Shannon and Hartley measures and satisfies all classical requirements for uncertainty measures,
including subadditivity. Although being posed several times in the literature, it is still an open problem whether the aggregate uncertainty is
unique under these properties. This paper derives an uncertainty measure
based on the theory of hints and shows its equivalence to the *pignistic
entropy*. It does not satisfy subadditivity, but the viewpoint of hints uncovers a weaker version of subadditivity. On the other hand, the pignistic
entropy has some crucial advantages over the aggregate uncertainty. i.e.
explicitness of the formula and sensitivity to changes in evidence. We
observe that neither of the two measures captures the full uncertainty of
hints and propose an extension of the pignistic entropy called *hints entropy* that satisfies all axiomatic requirements, including subadditivity,
while preserving the above advantages over the aggregate uncertainty.

Keywords: Generalized Information Theory, Theory of Hints, Dempster-
Shafer Theory, Pignistic Entropy, Hints Entropy.

1 Introduction

Generalizing the Shannon entropy from probability theory to the various notions of imprecise probabilities, in particular to the Dempster-Shafer theory of
evidence [2,19], has been a long discussed issue in the literature. The challenge
is to come up with a functional that satisfies all properties one would expect
from an uncertainty measure and also reduces to the well-established Shannon
and Hartley measures on special cases. Since the early 1980s, various functionals
have been proposed for this task, but they were all shown under closer inspection
to violate some of the essential properties of uncertainty. In most cases, this was
the property of *subadditivity*. We refer to [10] for a historical survey of these
unsuccessful attempts. Ultimately, several groups of researchers independently
proposed a functional called *aggregate uncertainty* [6,1,15] that satisfies all basic
properties and also generalizes the Shannon and Hartley measures. To this day
and to the best knowledge of the author, no other functional with the same properties was found. It is further a well-known fact in information theory that the
Hartley and Shannon measures are both unique under specific sets of properties.

W. Liu (Ed.): ECSQARU 2011, LNAI 6717, pp. 299–313, 2011.

This naturally raises the question whether the aggregate uncertainty is also fully characterized. Although being posed several times in the literature, for example in [5,10], uniqueness of the aggregate uncertainty remains an open problem. Instead, it was only shown that the aggregate uncertainty satisfies an additional property called *monotone dispensability* [4], from which it follows that the measure is smallest among all functionals that satisfy the classical requirements and monotone dispensability, provided that such functionals exist of course.

A promising candidate for disproving uniqueness of the aggregate uncertainty was the *pignistic entropy* proposed in [9]. This functional operates on mass functions and was claimed to satisfy all classical properties, but a technical mistake in the proof of subadditivity was later found by [11]. Nonetheless, the pignistic entropy has some advantages over the aggregate uncertainty. The practical utility of the latter has often been criticised, because it is defined in terms of the solution to a nonlinear optimisation problem. Although an algorithm for this problem exists [7], it nevertheless prevents us from calculating even very simple examples by hand. The pignistic entropy is expressed by an explicit formula and therefore does not suffer from such a defect. Also, it was observed that the aggregate uncertainty is highly insensitive to changes in evidence [10], which lead to the study of composed functionals to overcome this practical shortcoming [21]. Again, there is no indication for a similar weakness of the pignistic entropy.

This paper analyses the pignistic entropy from the perspective of the *theory of hints* [13,16,14,17], which is a particular approach to Dempster-Shafer theory. Hints are defined as multi-valued mappings between a probability space and the usual frame of discernment. The relationship to mass functions is then established by an equivalence relation between hints that only considers the information with respect to the frame of discernment. Compared to mass functions, hints therefore express more fine-grained information. It will be shown in this paper that the pignistic entropy derives very naturally from this basic model of a hint. Moreover, the additional structure of hints enables a more differentiated view on the lack of subadditivity of the pignistic entropy, and it turns out that the defective argument in [9] can be corrected to prove a weaker version of subadditivity for hints. Also, we show that the pignistic entropy does not satisfy monotone dispensability, but it will be argued that from the viewpoint of hints it has little justification as an axiomatic requirement for uncertainty measures. If we consider the aggregate uncertainty and the pignistic entropy as uncertainty measures in the theory of hints, we notice that both functionals quantify uncertainty with respect to the frame of discernment, ignoring the information on the probability space. We therefore extend the pignistic entropy to take the complete uncertainty of hints into consideration. This leads to a new uncertainty measure called *hints entropy* that also generalizes the Shannon and Hartley measures and further satisfies all classical requirements, including the strong version of subadditivity, while preserving the advantages of the pignistic entropy over the aggregate uncertainty.

The outline of this paper is as follows: Section 2 introduces the theory of hints and establishes the connection to mass functions. Section 3 derives the pignistic entropy, whose properties are analysed in Section 4. Based on the observation that the pignistic entropy does not capture the full uncertainty, this measure is extended to the hints entropy in Section 5. We verify all classical properties for the hints entropy and contrast it with the aggregate uncertainty in Section 6.

2   The Theory of Hints

Let r be a countable set of variables. Each variable $X \in r$ has a finite set Θ_X of possible values. A configuration θ over a finite set of variables $s \subseteq r$ associates a value from Θ_X with each variable $X \in s$. We write Θ_s for the set of all possible configurations over s. A hint $\mathcal{H}$ with domain s refers to a question whose true but unknown answer is contained in the set Θ_s called *frame of discernment*. We further assume a finite set Ω of possible *interpretations*. Each interpretation restricts the possible answers within Θ_s. If $\omega \in \Omega$ is the correct interpretation, then the correct answer must belong to some non-empty subset $\Gamma(\omega) \subseteq \Theta_s$, where Γ is a multi-valued mapping from interpretations Ω to the powerset $\mathcal{P}(\Theta_s)$. The set $\Gamma(\omega)$ is called the *focal set* of the interpretation $\omega \in \Omega$. However, not all interpretations are equally likely. We therefore assume a probability distribution p that assigns a probability $p(\omega) > 0$ to each interpretation $\omega \in \Omega$. A hint $\mathcal{H}$ with domain $d(\mathcal{H}) = s$ is thus defined as a quadruple $\mathcal{H} = (\Theta_s, \Omega, p, \Gamma)$. Subsequently, we simply write Θ for the frame of discernment of a hint, if the domain of the latter is not significant. Also, we refer to (Ω, p) as the probability space with σ-algebra $\mathcal{P}(\Omega)$, over which the hint $\mathcal{H}$ is defined.

From a hint $\mathcal{H} = (\Theta, \Omega, p, \Gamma)$ we derive a mapping $m : \mathcal{P}(\Theta) \to [0,1]$ by

$$m(A) = \sum_{\omega \in \Omega : \Gamma(\omega) = A} p(\omega) \tag{1}$$

for all $A \subseteq \Theta$. Since $m(\emptyset) = 0$ and $\sum_{A \subseteq \Theta_s} m(A) = 1$ this mapping defines a *mass function* or *basic probability assignment* [19]. The *support* of m is defined as $supp(m) = \{A \subseteq \Theta : m(A) > 0\}$. Observe that several hints can produce the same mass function due to the sum in (1). Given two hints $\mathcal{H}_1$ and $\mathcal{H}_2$, we write $\mathcal{H}_1 \equiv \mathcal{H}_2$ if, and only if, they induce the same mass function. This defines an equivalence relation on the universe of hints Φ with equivalence classes $[\mathcal{H}] = \{\tilde{\mathcal{H}} \in \Phi : \mathcal{H} \equiv \tilde{\mathcal{H}}\}$. Note also that equivalent hints have the same domain. Given a mass function $m : \mathcal{P}(\Theta) \to [0,1]$, we can always find a canonical hint $\mathcal{H}_c$ in the equivalence class of all hints that induce m. If $supp(m) = \{A_1, \dots, A_n\}$ the canonical hint associated with m is $\mathcal{H}_c = (\Theta, \Omega, p, \Gamma)$ with $\Omega = \{\omega_1, \dots, \omega_n\}$, $\Gamma(\omega_i) = A_i$ and $p(\omega_i) = m(A_i)$.

We distinguish some important classes of hints. A hint $\mathcal{H} = (\Theta, \Omega, p, \Gamma)$ expresses vacuous information about Θ, if for all $\omega \in \Omega$ we have $\Gamma(\omega) = \Theta$. This represents total ignorance with respect to the question that is represented by the possible answers in Θ. The induced mass function is $m(\Theta) = 1$ and $m(A) = 0$ for all $A \subset \Theta$. If all focal sets are singletons, then the hint is called *precise*. In this case Γ represents a random variable and there is full contradiction between interpretations pointing to different singletons. Hence, all discrete random variables can be seen as precise hints. If the focal sets of a hint are disjoint, i.e. if $\omega_1 \neq \omega_2$ implies $\Gamma(\omega_1) \cap \Gamma(\omega_2) = \emptyset$ for all $\omega_1, \omega_2 \in \Omega$, the hint is called *Bayesian*.

Consider two hints $\mathcal{H}_1 = (\Theta, \Omega_1, p_1, \Gamma_1)$ and $\mathcal{H}_2 = (\Theta, \Omega_2, p_2, \Gamma_2)$ on the same frame of discernment Θ. The combined hint $\mathcal{H} = \mathcal{H}_1 \otimes \mathcal{H}_2$ is defined for interpretations (ω_1, ω_2) with $\omega_1 \in \Omega_1$ and $\omega_2 \in \Omega_2$. Then, $\Gamma(\omega_1, \omega_2) = \Gamma_1(\omega_1) \cap \Gamma_2(\omega_2)$ is the set of possible answers from Θ, if both interpretations ω_1 and ω_2 hold. However, certain interpretations (ω_1, ω_2) may be contradictory, i.e. $\Gamma_1(\omega_1) \cap \Gamma_2(\omega_2) = \emptyset$. We therefore define the combined interpretation set Ω as the set of all contradiction-free pairs of interpretations, $\Omega = \{(\omega_1, \omega_2) : \omega_1 \in \Omega_1, \omega_2 \in \Omega_2 \text{ and } \Gamma_1(\omega_1) \cap \Gamma_2(\omega_2) \neq \emptyset\}$. A general rule for computing the probabilities of interpretations in Ω can be given, if the probability distributions p_1 and p_2 of the two hints are independent. We then also say that the two hints are *independent*. The probability that two interpretations from independent hints are contradictory is

$$K = \sum_{(\omega_1, \omega_2) \in \Omega_1 \times \Omega_2 : \Gamma(\omega_1, \omega_2) = \emptyset} p(\omega_1) \cdot p(\omega_2).$$

We condition the probability on contradiction-free interpretations and obtain

$$p(\omega_1, \omega_2) = \frac{p_1(\omega_1) \cdot p_2(\omega_2)}{1 - K}$$

for $(\omega_1, \omega_2) \in \Omega$. If the two hints are fully contradictory, i.e. if all intersections of focal sets are empty, then $K = 1$ and the combination is undefined, see [13]. The hint $\mathcal{H} = \mathcal{H}_1 \otimes \mathcal{H}_2$, obtained from combining two independent hints $\mathcal{H}_1$ and $\mathcal{H}_2$, is given by $\mathcal{H} = (\Theta, \Omega, p, \Gamma)$. This procedure is called *Dempster's rule of combination* [2]. Further, the combination rule is generalized to dependent hints by replacing the product probability on Ω by a probability measure that reflects the stochastic dependencies between the interpretations of the two hints. As an important special case of dependent hints, we assume two non-contradictory hints $\mathcal{H}_1 = (\Theta, \Omega, p, \Gamma_1)$ and $\mathcal{H}_2 = (\Theta, \Omega, p, \Gamma_2)$ over the same probability space. Their combination simply yields $\mathcal{H}_1 \otimes \mathcal{H}_2 = (\Theta, \Omega, p, \Gamma_1 \cap \Gamma_2)$. Finally, it is shown in [13] that hints $\mathcal{H}_1$ and $\mathcal{H}_2$ on different domains $d(\mathcal{H}_1) \neq d(\mathcal{H}_2)$ can always be brought to the common domain $d(\mathcal{H}_1) \cup d(\mathcal{H}_2)$ by an operation called *vacuous extension*. This enables the application of the above procedure for combination.

Suppose that $\mathcal{H}_1$ and $\mathcal{H}_2$ are two independent hints with domains $d(\mathcal{H}_1) = s$ and $d(\mathcal{H}_2) = t$ inducing the mass functions m_1 and m_2, respectively. We can obtain the mass function of the combined hint $\mathcal{H}_1 \otimes \mathcal{H}_2$ by combining the two mass functions m_1 and m_2. Following [13] and using the notation of natural join, this combination rule is defined as $m_1 \otimes m_2(\emptyset) = 0$ and

$$m_1 \otimes m_2(A) = \frac{1}{1 - K} \sum_{B \subseteq \Theta_s, C \subseteq \Theta_t : B \bowtie C = A} m_1(B) \cdot m_2(C) \qquad (2)$$

for all other sets $\emptyset \subset A \subseteq \Theta_{s \cup t}$ with

$$K = \sum_{B \subseteq \Theta_s, C \subseteq \Theta_t : B \bowtie C = \emptyset} m_1(B) \cdot m_2(C).$$

Moreover, the combination rule (2) for mass functions becomes particularly simple, if the mass functions are derived from independent hints with disjoint domains $s \cap t = \emptyset$. Such hints and their associated mass functions are subsequently called *non-interactive*. The proof of the following lemma is given in [10].

Lemma 1. *It holds that*

$$m_1 \otimes m_2(A) = \begin{cases} m_1(B) \cdot m_2(C) & \text{if } B \times C = A \\ 0 & \text{otherwise,} \end{cases}$$

if, and only if, m_1 and m_2 are non-interactive mass functions.

3   The Pignistic Entropy

We now derive an entropy notion for hints based on Shannon's entropy. Given a hint $\mathcal{H} = (\Theta, \Omega, p, \Gamma)$, we know that under the interpretation $\omega \in \Omega$, the true answer belongs to the set $\Gamma(\omega) \subseteq \Theta$, but there is no more precise information about which element in $\Gamma(\omega)$. Hence, under the interpretation $\omega \in \Omega$ the remaining uncertainty about the true answer is most naturally expressed by Hartley's measure, i.e. $H(\mathcal{H}|\omega) = \log |\Gamma(\omega)|$[1]. Likewise, we can see Hartley's measure as a special case of the Shannon entropy applied to a uniform probability distribution. The above claim is therefore equivalent to assuming $p(\theta|\omega) = 1/|\Gamma(\omega)|$ for all $\theta \in \Gamma(\omega)$ and evaluating Shannon's entropy. Hence, the joint probability $p(\theta, \omega)$ for all $\omega \in \Omega$ and $\theta \in \Theta$ is $p(\theta, \omega) = p(\omega)/|\Gamma(\omega)|$ if $\theta \in \Gamma(\omega)$ and $p(\theta, \omega) = 0$ otherwise. From this we derive the marginal distribution

$$p(\theta) = \sum_{\omega \in \Omega : \theta \in \Gamma(\omega)} p(\theta, \omega) = \sum_{\omega \in \Omega : \theta \in \Gamma(\omega)} \frac{p(\omega)}{|\Gamma(\omega)|}, \tag{3}$$

which is called the *pignistic probability distribution* [3,20] associated with $\mathcal{H}$. Hence, we define the entropy of a hint $\mathcal{H}$ with respect to the elements of its frame of discernment Θ as Shannon's entropy applied to the pignistic distribution.

Definition 1. *Let $\mathcal{H}$ be a hint with pignistic probabilities $p(\theta)$ for all $\theta \in \Theta$ as defined in (3). The pignistic entropy $H_{\mathcal{H}}(\Theta)$ of $\mathcal{H}$ is defined as*

$$H_{\mathcal{H}}(\Theta) = - \sum_{\theta \in \Theta} p(\theta) \log p(\theta). \tag{4}$$

The next lemma expresses pignistic distributions in terms of mass functions.

---

[1] We always take logarithms to the base 2.

Lemma 2. *If the hints $\mathcal{H}$ induces the mass function m, we have for all $\theta \in \Theta$*

$$p(\theta) = \sum_{A \subseteq \Theta : \theta \in A} \frac{m(A)}{|A|}. \tag{5}$$

Proof. It follows from equation (1) that

$$\sum_{A \subseteq \Theta : \theta \in A} \frac{m(A)}{|A|} = \sum_{A \subseteq \Theta : \theta \in A} \sum_{\omega \in \Omega : \Gamma(\omega) = A} \frac{p(\omega)}{|A|} = \sum_{\omega \in \Omega : \theta \in \Gamma(\omega)} \frac{p(\omega)}{|\Gamma(\omega)|} = p(\theta).$$

$\square$

In the previous section we called two hints equivalent if they induce the same mass function. It follows from Lemma 2 that equivalent hints share the same pignistic probability distribution and therefore have the same pignistic entropy, i.e. $\mathcal{H}_1 \equiv \mathcal{H}_2$ implies $H_{\mathcal{H}_1}(\Theta) = H_{\mathcal{H}_2}(\Theta)$. This property allows us to apply the pignistic entropy to mass function. We define $H_m(\Theta)$ of a mass function m by the pignistic entropy $H_{\mathcal{H}_c}(\Theta)$ of its canonical hint $\mathcal{H}_c$. It follows that the pignistic entropy coincides with the *ambiguity measure* given in [9].

A meaningful measure for uncertainty in Dempster-Shafer theory must satisfy some basic properties. Such a set of requirements is given in [4,10]. We will next discuss these properties for the pignistic entropy of Definition 1. Since this functional corresponds to the Shannon measure applied to a particular probability distribution, we may directly transfer some properties of the Shannon measure to the pignistic entropy. First, we observe that the pignistic distribution of a mass function $m : \mathcal{P}(\Theta) \to [0, 1]$ has exactly $|\Theta|$ values. From the corresponding *range* property of the Shannon measure follows that $0 \le H_m(\Theta) \le \log |\Theta|$. Likewise, we know that the Shannon measure is *continuous* in its arguments. According to Lemma 2, each value of the pignistic distribution is given as a finite sum of values from the mass function. Since the limit distributes over finite sums we conclude that the pignistic entropy is also continuous in the values of the mass function. Next, the pignistic entropy must reproduce the Shannon measure on probabilistic evidence. Indeed, a mass function m defines a probability distribution if all focal sets are singletons. The pignistic probability distribution then satisfies $p(\theta) = m(\{\theta\})$ for all $\theta \in \Theta$ which proves the following lemma.

Lemma 3 (Probability Consistency). *If a mass function m defines a probability distribution, then the pignistic entropy is equal to Shannon's entropy*

$$H_m(\Theta) = -\sum_{\theta \in \Theta} m(\{\theta\}) \log m(\{\theta\}).$$

This has been observed in [9]. Moreover, it is shown there that the pignistic entropy reproduces Hartley's measure if all mass is given to a single focal set.

Lemma 4 (Set Consistency). *If a mass function m has a single focal set $A \subseteq \Theta$, the pignistic entropy is equal to Hartley's measure $H_m(\Theta) = \log |A|$.*

Proof. If m has a single focal set $A \subseteq \Theta$, we obtain the canonical hint $\Omega = \{\omega\}$, $\Gamma(\omega) = A$ and $p(\omega) = 1$. This induces the pignistic distribution $p(\theta) = 1/|A|$, if $\theta \in A$, and $p(\theta) = 0$ otherwise. Then the statement follows immediately.   □

If a mass function m has a single focal set with exactly two elements, then $H_m(\Theta) = 1$ due to Lemma 4. This shows that the functional is *normalized*. Also, the pignistic entropy is *extensible*, i.e. if a new element θ is added to the frame of discernment and no mass is given to this element, its pignistic probability is $p(\theta) = 0$ and the pignistic entropy does not change. It is further proved in [9] that the pignistic entropy is additive only for non-interactive mass functions.

Lemma 5 (Additivity). *Assume two hints $\mathcal{H}_1$ and $\mathcal{H}_2$ with domain $d(\mathcal{H}_1) = s$ and $d(\mathcal{H}_2) = t$. It holds that $H_{\mathcal{H}_1 \otimes \mathcal{H}_2}(\Theta_{s \cup t}) = H_{\mathcal{H}_1}(\Theta_s) + H_{\mathcal{H}_2}(\Theta_t)$ if, and only if, the two hints are non-interactive.*

The last and most profound property for an uncertainty measure in Dempster-Shafer theory is subadditivity. We start the discussion by first proving a weaker version of the definition given in [4]. The proof is based on Gibbs' theorem: If $(p_1, \ldots, p_n)$ and $(q_1, \ldots, q_n)$ are two probability distributions, then

$$-\sum_{i=1}^{n} p_i \log p_i \leq -\sum_{i=1}^{n} p_i \log q_i. \tag{6}$$

Theorem 1 (Weak Subadditivity). *If $\mathcal{H}_1$ and $\mathcal{H}_2$ are hints with disjoint domains $d(\mathcal{H}_1) \cap d(\mathcal{H}_2) = \emptyset$ it holds that $H_{\mathcal{H}_1 \otimes \mathcal{H}_2}(\Theta_{s \cup t}) \leq H_{\mathcal{H}_1}(\Theta_s) + H_{\mathcal{H}_2}(\Theta_t)$.*

Proof. Let $\mathcal{H}_1 = (\Theta_s, \Omega_1, p_1, \Gamma_1)$ and $\mathcal{H}_2 = (\Theta_t, \Omega_2, p_2, \Gamma_2)$ be two hints with disjoint domains $s \cap t = \emptyset$ and $\mathcal{H}_1 \otimes \mathcal{H}_2 = (\Theta_{s \cup t}, \Omega, p, \Gamma)$ with $\Omega = \Omega_1 \times \Omega_2$ their combination as defined in Section 2. Since the domains are disjoint we have $\Gamma(\omega_1, \omega_2) = \Gamma_1(\omega_1) \times \Gamma_2(\omega_2)$ for all $(\omega_1, \omega_2) \in \Omega_1 \times \Omega_2$. We further write $\tilde{p}_1$ and $\tilde{p}_2$ for the pignistic distributions of $\mathcal{H}_1$ and $\mathcal{H}_2$ and $\tilde{p}$ for the pignistic distribution of $\mathcal{H}_1 \otimes \mathcal{H}_2$. Since p is the joint probability distribution over $\Omega_1 \times \Omega_2$, it has p_1 and p_2 as marginal distributions. The pignistic probability $\tilde{p}_1$ of $\mathcal{H}_1$ can thus be written for all $\theta_1 \in \Theta_s$ as

$$\tilde{p}_1(\theta_1) = \sum_{\omega_1 \in \Omega_1 : \theta_1 \in \Gamma_1(\omega_1)} \frac{p_1(\omega_1)}{|\Gamma_1(\omega_1)|} = \sum_{\substack{\omega_1 \in \Omega_1 : \\ \theta_1 \in \Gamma_1(\omega_1)}} \sum_{\omega_2 \in \Omega_2} \frac{p(\omega_1, \omega_2)}{|\Gamma_1(\omega_1)|}$$

$$= \sum_{\substack{(\omega_1, \omega_2) \in \Omega : \\ \theta_1 \in \Gamma_1(\omega_1)}} \frac{p(\omega_1, \omega_2)}{|\Gamma_1(\omega_1)|} = \sum_{\substack{(\omega_1, \omega_2) \in \Omega : \\ \theta_1 \in \Gamma_1(\omega_1)}} \frac{p(\omega_1, \omega_2)}{|\Gamma_1(\omega_1)|} \sum_{\substack{\theta_2 \in \Theta_t : \\ \theta_2 \in \Gamma_2(\omega_2)}} \frac{1}{|\Gamma_2(\omega_2)|}$$

$$= \sum_{\theta_2 \in \Theta_t} \sum_{\substack{\omega_1 \in \Omega_1 : \\ \theta_1 \in \Gamma_1(\omega_1)}} \sum_{\substack{\omega_2 \in \Omega_2 : \\ \theta_2 \in \Gamma_2(\omega_2)}} \frac{p(\omega_1, \omega_2)}{|\Gamma_1(\omega_1)||\Gamma_2(\omega_2)|}$$

$$= \sum_{\theta_2 \in \Theta_t} \sum_{\substack{(\omega_1, \omega_2) \in \Omega : \\ (\theta_1, \theta_2) \in \Gamma(\omega_1, \omega_2)}} \frac{p(\omega_1, \omega_2)}{|\Gamma(\omega_1, \omega_2)|} = \sum_{\theta_2 \in \Theta_t} \tilde{p}(\theta_1, \theta_2).$$

A similar argument shows that $\tilde{p}_2$ is the marginal distribution of $\tilde{p}$ for t. It then follows from Gibbs' theorem (6) that

$$
\begin{aligned}
H_{\mathcal{H}_1 \otimes \mathcal{H}_2}(\Theta_{s \cup t}) &= - \sum_{(\theta_1, \theta_2) \in \Theta_{s \cup t}} \tilde{p}(\theta_1, \theta_2) \log \tilde{p}(\theta_1, \theta_2) \\
&\leq - \sum_{(\theta_1, \theta_2) \in \Theta_{s \cup t}} \tilde{p}(\theta_1, \theta_2) \log \left[\tilde{p}_1(\theta_1) \tilde{p}_2(\theta_2) \right] \\
&= - \sum_{(\theta_1, \theta_2) \in \Theta_{s \cup t}} \tilde{p}(\theta_1, \theta_2) \log \tilde{p}_1(\theta_1) - \sum_{(\theta_1, \theta_2) \in \Theta_{s \cup t}} \tilde{p}(\theta_1, \theta_2) \log \tilde{p}_2(\theta_2) \\
&= - \sum_{\theta_2 \in \Theta_t} \sum_{\theta_1 \in \Theta_s} \tilde{p}(\theta_1, \theta_2) \log \tilde{p}_1(\theta_1) - \sum_{\theta_1 \in \Theta_s} \sum_{\theta_2 \in \Theta_t} \tilde{p}(\theta_1, \theta_2) \log \tilde{p}_2(\theta_2) \\
&= - \sum_{\theta_1 \in \Theta_s} \tilde{p}_1(\theta_1) \log \tilde{p}_1(\theta_1) - \sum_{\theta_2 \in \Theta_t} \tilde{p}_2(\theta_2) \log \tilde{p}_2(\theta_2) \\
&= H_{\mathcal{H}_1}(\Theta_s) + H_{\mathcal{H}_2}(\Theta_t).
\end{aligned}
$$

This proof simplifies considerably if both hints are on the same probability space.   □

The stronger version of subadditivity [4] is based on the projection operator for hints. Given a hint $\mathcal{H} = (\Theta_s, \Omega, p, \Gamma)$ with domain $d(\mathcal{H}) = s$, the projection of $\mathcal{H}$ to $t \subseteq s$ is defined as $\mathcal{H}^{\downarrow t} = (\Theta_t, \Omega, p, \Gamma^{\downarrow t})$ with $\Gamma^{\downarrow t}(\omega) = \{\theta^{\downarrow t} : \theta \in \Gamma(\omega)\}$.

Definition 2 (Strong Subadditivity). *An uncertainty measure $H : \Phi \to \mathbb{R}_{\geq 0}$ for hints satisfies strong subadditivity, if for all $\mathcal{H} \in \Phi$ and $d(\mathcal{H}) = s \cup t$ with $s \cap t = \emptyset$ we have $H(\mathcal{H}) \leq H(\mathcal{H}^{\downarrow s}) + H(\mathcal{H}^{\downarrow t})$.*

Weak subadditivity states that the uncertainty of a combined hint is not larger than the sum of the uncertainties of the two individual hints. This setting corresponds to additivity in Lemma 5 without the additional assumption of independence. In contrast, strong subadditivity assumes a single hint and requires that its uncertainty is not larger than the sum of the uncertainties of its projections to disjoint subdomains. Indeed, from weak subadditivity only follows

$$
H_{\mathcal{H}^{\downarrow s} \otimes \mathcal{H}^{\downarrow t}}(\Theta_{s \cup t}) \leq H_{\mathcal{H}^{\downarrow s}}(\Theta_s) + H_{\mathcal{H}^{\downarrow t}}(\Theta_t), \tag{7}
$$

but not that $H_{\mathcal{H}}(\Theta_{s \cup t}) \leq H_{\mathcal{H}^{\downarrow s} \otimes \mathcal{H}^{\downarrow t}}(\Theta_{s \cup t})$. Moreover, [11] gave a simple counterexample for strong subadditivity of the pignistic entropy.

Lemma 6. *The pignistic entropy does not satisfy strong subadditivity.*

The proof of weak subadditivity for the pignistic entropy exploits that the marginals of the pignistic distribution of $\mathcal{H}_1 \otimes \mathcal{H}_2$ correspond to the pignistic distributions of $\mathcal{H}_1$ and $\mathcal{H}_2$. According to (7) this holds also between $\mathcal{H}^{\downarrow s} \otimes \mathcal{H}^{\downarrow t}$ and its factors, but generally not between $\mathcal{H}$ and its projections $\mathcal{H}^{\downarrow s}$ and $\mathcal{H}^{\downarrow t}$ as shown by the counter-example in [11]. This crucial observation lead to the wrong proof of strong subadditivity for the pignistic entropy in [9].

4   Pignistic Entropy and Aggregate Uncertainty

It is well-known in Dempster-Shafer theory that to every mass function we can associate a belief function via the so-called Moebius transform. This mapping from mass functions to belief functions is bijective [19,12]. The *aggregate uncertainty AU* measures the uncertainty of a mass function m in terms of its associated belief function bel,

$$AU(bel) = \max_{P_{bel}} \left[-\sum_{\theta \in \Theta} p(\theta) \log p(\theta) \right]. \tag{8}$$

Here, the maximum is taken over all probability distributions that dominate the belief function bel. It is shown in [6,10] that the aggregate uncertainty satisfies the properties of probability and set consistency, range, subadditivity and additivity. The question, whether the aggregate uncertainty is the only mapping from mass functions to real numbers that satisfies these properties, is posed as an open problem in [5,10]. Since equivalent hints induce the same mass function, the aggregate uncertainty can as well be considered as an uncertainty measure for hints with respect to the elements in Θ. It was shown in Section 3 how the viewpoint of hints gives rise to another uncertainty measure in a very natural way. But this measure, called pignistic entropy, suffers from the clear defect that it does not satisfy strong subadditivity. On the other hand, it has been observed in [10] that the aggregate uncertainty is sometimes too insensitive with respect to changes in evidence, which is a severe practical shortcoming.

Example 1. Let $\Theta = \{\theta_1, \theta_2\}$ and assume a mass function m defined as $m(\{\theta_1\}) = \alpha$, $m(\{\theta_2\}) = \beta$ and $m(\Theta) = 1 - \alpha - \beta$ with $\alpha, \beta \geq 0$ and $\alpha + \beta \leq 1$. Example 6.14 in [10] gives the associated belief function $bel(\{\theta_1\}) = \alpha$, $bel(\{\theta_2\}) = \beta$ and $bel(\Theta) = 1$ and finally obtains $AU(bel) = 1$ for $0 \leq \alpha, \beta \leq 0.5$. The aggregate uncertainty is therefore insensitive to changes of α and β in the interval $[0, 0.5]$.

There is no indication that the pignistic entropy suffers from a similar lack of insensitivity [9,11]. Indeed, the following example shows that we obtain a different pignistic distribution for different values of α and β in Example 1.

Example 2. The canonical hint $\mathcal{H}_c = (\Theta, \Omega, p, \Gamma)$ for the mass function of Example 1 has $\Omega = \{\omega_1, \omega_2, \omega_3\}$, $\Gamma(\omega_1) = \{\theta_1\}$, $\Gamma(\omega_2) = \{\theta_2\}$ and $\Gamma(\omega_3) = \Theta$ with $p(\omega_1) = \alpha$, $p(\omega_2) = \beta$ and $p(\omega_3) = 1 - \alpha - \beta$. We then obtain for the pignistic probability distribution $p(\theta_1) = \alpha + 0.5(1 - \alpha - \beta)$ and $p(\theta_2) = \beta + 0.5(1 - \alpha - \beta)$. This gives a pignistic entropy of $H(m) = H(\mathcal{H}_c) = 1$ if, and only if, $\alpha = \beta$.

To overcome the insensitivity problem of the aggregate uncertainty, another measure GS is proposed in [21,10], defined as the difference between the aggregate uncertainty and the *generalized Hartley measure* [8] GH

$$GS(bel) = AU(bel) - GH(m), \quad \text{where} \quad GH(m) = \sum_{A \subseteq \Omega} m(A) \log |A|. \tag{9}$$

It is shown in [10] that for Bayesian mass functions m we have

$$GS(bel) = -\sum_{A \subseteq \Theta} m(A) \log m(A), \tag{10}$$

and it then follows from equation (9) that

$$AU(bel) = -\sum_{A \subseteq \Theta} m(A) \log \left[\frac{m(A)}{|A|} \right]. \tag{11}$$

The pignistic entropy and the aggregate uncertainty are clearly different, since they disagree on strong subadditivity. On the other hand, both measures satisfy set and probability consistency and therefore give equal results for mass functions with a single focal set and hints that define a probability distribution. Moreover, the following lemma shows that the same holds for Bayesian hints.

Lemma 7. *If $\mathcal{H}$ denotes a Bayesian hint, m its induced mass function and bel the associated belief function, we have $H_{\mathcal{H}}(\Theta) = AU(bel)$.*

Proof. Since focal sets are disjoint we have $p(\omega) = m(A)$ if $\Gamma(\omega) = A$. Every $\theta \in \Theta$ is contained in exactly one focal set, which implies that $p(\theta) = p(\omega)/|\Gamma(\omega)|$ for $\omega \in \Omega$ with $\theta \in \Gamma(\omega)$. Moreover, if θ_1 and θ_2 are contained in the same focal set $\Gamma(\omega)$ for some $\omega \in \Omega$ then $p(\theta_1) = p(\theta_2)$ and therefore

$$H_{\mathcal{H}}(\Theta) = -\sum_{\theta \in \Theta} p(\theta) \log p(\theta) = -\sum_{\omega \in \Omega} |\Gamma(\omega)| \cdot \frac{p(\omega)}{|\Gamma(\omega)|} \log \frac{p(\omega)}{|\Gamma(\omega)|}$$

$$= -\sum_{\omega \in \Omega} p(\omega) \log \frac{p(\omega)}{|\Gamma(\omega)|} = -\sum_{A \subseteq \Theta} m(A) \log \left[\frac{m(A)}{|A|} \right] = AU(bel).$$

$\square$

Another disadvantage of the aggregate uncertainty is that its evaluation requires the solution to a nonlinear optimization problem, see (8). Although an algorithm exists for this task, the lack of a closed form is nonetheless inconvenient. In contrast, the pignistic entropy only requires to compute the pignistic probability distribution, which essentially corresponds to the evaluation of a probability tree.

If we compare the aggregate uncertainty and the pignistic entropy, we observe that both functionals apply the Shannon entropy to a particular probability distribution, i.e. the dominating distribution in case of the aggregate uncertainty and the pignistic distribution in case of the pignistic entropy. Let us consider this commonality in more detail. If Θ denotes a frame of discernment, we write P for the set of all probability distributions over Θ and Ψ for the set of all mass functions over Θ. Next, assume a functional $h : \Psi \to [0, \log |\Theta|]$ that satisfies the property of (range and) probability consistency. Since P is a convex set and the Shannon entropy $S : P \to [0, \log |\Theta|]$ is continuous, it follows from the generalized intermediate value theorem that for every mass function $m \in \Psi$ there exists a probability distribution $p \in P$ such that $h(m) = S(p)$. On the other hand, a probability distribution $p \in P$ can always be considered as a precise mass function m_p and probability consistency ensures that $h(m_p) = S(p)$. Hence, it follows that for every mass function $m \in \Psi$ there exists a precise mass function m_p such that $h(m) = h(m_p) = S(p)$. This proves that the observed property does not only hold for the aggregate uncertainty and the pignistic entropy but for all functionals $h : \Psi \to [0, \log |\Theta|]$ that satisfy probability consistency.

Lemma 8. *If $h : \Psi \to [0, \log |\Theta|]$ satisfies probability consistency, it holds for all $m \in \Psi$ that $h(m) = S(\pi(m))$ for some mapping $\pi : \Psi \to P$.*

Finally, [4] proves that the aggregate uncertainty satisfies a property called *monotone dispensability*, which says that the uncertainty should not decrease after transferring part of a focal set's mass to a superset.

Lemma 9. *Let $m : \mathcal{P}(\Theta) \to [0, 1]$ be a mass function and $A \subseteq \Theta$ a focal set. For a superset $B \supseteq A$ and $0 \leq \alpha \leq 1$ we derive a mass function m' by $m'(A) = \alpha m(A)$, $m'(B) = m(B) + (1 - \alpha)m(A)$ and $m'(C) = m(C)$ for all $C \subseteq \Theta$ with $C \neq A$ and $C \neq B$. If bel and bel' denote the associated belief functions, we have $AU(bel) \leq AU(bel')$.*

This property is not satisfied by the pignistic entropy:

Example 3. Let $\Theta = \{\theta_1, \theta_2\}$ and assume a mass function m defined as $m(\{\theta_1\}) = m(\{\theta_2\}) = 0.5$. We obtain for the pignistic distribution $p(\theta_1) = p(\theta_2) = 0.5$. Next, choose $A = \{\theta_1\}$, $B = \{\theta_1, \theta_2\}$ and $\alpha = 0.5$. We obtain $m'(\{\theta_1\}) = 0.25$, $m'(\{\theta_2\}) = 0.5$ and $m'(\{\theta_1, \theta_2\}) = 0.25$. This gives a pignistic distribution of $p(\theta_1) = 3/8$, $p(\theta_2) = 5/8$ and therefore $H_m(\Theta) > H_{m'}(\Theta)$.

The Shannon entropy is maximal only for uniform distributions. Lemma 2 shows that the pignistic probability distribution strongly depends on the values of the mass function such that every modification of the latter in Example 3 will lead to a different pignistic distribution and therefore to a smaller pignistic entropy. This contradicts the statement of monotone dispensability. Likewise, it is equally simple to come up with an example for $H_m(\Theta) < H_{m'}(\Theta)$. Take for instance $m(\{\theta_1\}) = 0.1$ and $m(\{\theta_2\}) = 0.9$ in Example 3. This non-monotonic behaviour is semantically well-justified. If mass is moved from the focal set $A = \{\theta_1\}$ to a superset $B = \Theta$, it decreases the value for $p(\theta_1)$ and increases the value for $p(\theta_2)$. But the difference $|p(\theta_1) - p(\theta_2)|$ can either increase or decrease, which must affect uncertainty in different ways. Accordingly, the Shannon entropy is small if the difference is large and large if the difference is small. In other words, the absence of this property in case of the pignistic entropy again alludes to the sensitivity of this functional with respect to changes in evidence. For particular applications monotone dispensability may be a desirable property but we refrain from considering it as an axiomatic requirement for uncertainty measures.

5   The Hints Entropy

The foregoing section showed that the pignistic entropy satisfies all required properties for an uncertainty measure in Dempster-Shafer theory except strong subadditivity. However, given a hint $\mathcal{H} = (\Theta, \Omega, p, \Gamma)$ the pignistic entropy measures uncertainty with respect to Θ, but the hint $\mathcal{H}$ clearly contains information on both sets Ω and Θ. We therefore consider the join entropy of $\mathcal{H}$ given as

$$
H_{\mathcal{H}}(\Omega, \Theta) = -\sum_{\omega \in \Omega} \sum_{\theta \in \Theta} p(\omega, \theta) \log p(\omega, \theta) = -\sum_{\omega \in \Omega} \sum_{\theta \in \Gamma(\omega)} \frac{p(\omega)}{|\Gamma(\omega)|} \log \frac{p(\omega)}{|\Gamma(\omega)|}
$$

$$
= -\sum_{\omega \in \Omega} p(\omega) \log p(\omega) + \sum_{\omega \in \Omega} p(\omega) \log |\Gamma(\omega)|.
$$

Observe that the second summand, which is also the conditional Shannon entropy of Θ given Ω, corresponds the generalized Hartley measure of equation (9). Indeed, it follows from equation (1) that

$$
GH(\mathcal{H}) = \sum_{\omega \in \Omega} p(\omega) \log |\Gamma(\omega)| = \sum_{A \subseteq \Omega} m(A) \log |A|. \tag{12}
$$

Definition 3. *The* hints entropy *of $\mathcal{H} = (\Theta, \Omega, p, \Gamma)$ is defined as*

$$
H_{\mathcal{H}}(\Omega, \Theta) = H_{\mathcal{H}}(\Omega) + GH(\mathcal{H}). \tag{13}
$$

Due to equation (12) the generalized Hartley measure is completely determined by the mass function. The value of the generalized Hartley measure is therefore the same for equivalent hints, i.e. $\mathcal{H}_1 \equiv \mathcal{H}_2$ implies $GH(\mathcal{H}_1) = GH(\mathcal{H}_2)$. However, equivalent hints may differ in the probabilities assigned to interpretations, which thus leads to different values of $H_{\mathcal{H}_1}(\Omega_1)$ and $H_{\mathcal{H}_2}(\Omega_2)$. It thus follows from (13) that equivalent hints do not necessarily share the same hints entropy, naturally because the equivalence relations was defined with respect to the frame of discernment only. This again confirms that hints contain more information than their associated mass functions. We next investigate uncertainty related properties of the hints entropy. First, we observe that the generalized Hartley measure is zero if all focal sets are singletons. This proves the following statement.

Lemma 10 (Probability Consistency). *If a hint defines a probability distribution, then the hints entropy is equal to Shannon's entropy $H_{\mathcal{H}}(\Omega, \Theta) = H_{\mathcal{H}}(\Omega)$.*

Conversely, if Ω is a singleton, we have $H_{\mathcal{H}}(\Omega) = 0$ and $GH(\mathcal{H}) = \log |\Gamma(\omega)|$. This proves the following more restrictive version of set consistency.

Lemma 11 (Set Consistency). *If a hint has a single interpretation $\Omega = \{\omega\}$ the hints entropy is equal to Hartley's measure $H_{\mathcal{H}}(\Omega, \Theta) = \log |\Gamma(\omega)|$.*

Lemma 12 (Additivity). *Given two hints $\mathcal{H}_1 = (\Theta_s, \Omega_1, p_1, \Gamma_1)$ and $\mathcal{H}_2 = (\Theta_t, \Omega_2, p_2, \Gamma_2)$ it holds that $H_{\mathcal{H}_1 \otimes \mathcal{H}_2}(\Omega, \Theta_s \times \Theta_t) = H_{\mathcal{H}_1}(\Omega_1, \Theta_s) + H_{\mathcal{H}_2}(\Omega_2, \Theta_t)$ if, and only if, the two hints are non-interactive.*

Proof. According to [10] the generalized Hartley measure is additive only for non-interactive hints. Likewise, the Shannon entropy is additive only for independent distributions. This proves additivity of the hints entropy.   □

Theorem 2 (Strong Subadditivity). *For* $\mathcal{H} = (\Theta_{s\cup t}, \Omega, p, \Gamma)$ *with* $s \cap t = \emptyset$
we have $H_{\mathcal{H}}(\Omega, \Theta_{s\cup t}) \leq H_{\mathcal{H}^{\downarrow s}}(\Omega, \Theta_s) + H_{\mathcal{H}^{\downarrow t}}(\Omega, \Theta_t)$.

Proof. According to [10] the generalized Hartley measure is subadditive, hence

$$H_{\mathcal{H}}(\Omega, \Theta_{s\cup t}) \leq 2H_{\mathcal{H}}(\Omega) + GH(\mathcal{H}) \leq 2H_{\mathcal{H}}(\Omega) + H_{\mathcal{H}^{\downarrow s}}(\Omega, \Theta_s) + H_{\mathcal{H}^{\downarrow t}}(\Omega, \Theta_t)$$
$$= H_{\mathcal{H}^{\downarrow s}}(\Omega, \Theta_s) + H_{\mathcal{H}^{\downarrow t}}(\Omega, \Theta_t).$$

It then follows from the theory of valuation algebras [12] and strong subadditivity that the hints entropy satisfies weak subadditivity as well.

6 Hints Entropy and Aggregate Uncertainty

If we compare the aggregate uncertainty, as an uncertainty measure for hints, and the hints entropy of Definition 3, we observe that both measures satisfy the properties of probability and set consistency, additivity and strong subadditivity. However, we refrain from saying that the hints entropy completely disproves the uniqueness claim for the aggregate uncertainty, because the two measures differ in their range property, i.e. the hints entropy measures uncertainty with respect to Ω and Θ, whereas the aggregate uncertainty only focusses on Θ. This observation leads to a very interesting insight. The pignistic probability distribution was derived in equation (3) as the marginal distribution of the joint probability over Ω and Θ. It therefore holds that

$$H_{\mathcal{H}}(\Omega, \Theta) = H_{\mathcal{H}}(\Theta) + H_{\mathcal{H}}(\Omega|\Theta), \tag{14}$$

where $H_{\mathcal{H}}(\Omega|\Theta)$ denotes the conditional entropy of Ω given Θ. In the hint model, interpretations $\omega \in \Omega$ give information with respect to the elements in Θ by restricting the set of possible answers to a subset $\Gamma(\omega) \subseteq \Theta$. Conversely, also the elements $\theta \in \Theta$ give information about the correct interpretation in Ω via the inverse mapping. Given $\theta \in \Theta$, the remaining uncertainty about the elements in Ω is measured by the conditional entropy $H_{\mathcal{H}}(\Omega|\theta)$ with $H_{\mathcal{H}}(\Omega|\Theta)$ as expected value. The transformation from hints to mass functions looses this information, see equation (1), which also prevents the uncertainty measures for mass functions to take this information into account. This is confirmed by equation (14), showing that the hints and pignistic entropy differ in exactly $H_{\mathcal{H}}(\Omega|\Theta)$. Moreover, we observed that strong subadditivity only holds for the hints entropy $H_{\mathcal{H}}(\Omega, \Theta)$ but not for the pignistic entropy $H_{\mathcal{H}}(\Theta)$. We may therefore conclude that ignoring the additional information brought by the inverse mapping destroys the property of strong subadditivity. Bayesian hints have disjoint focal sets, which intuitively means that the same information is contained in Γ and its inverse. Indeed, this is confirmed by the following theorem extending Lemma 7.

Theorem 3. *If* $\mathcal{H}$ *denotes a Bayesian hint and bel the associated belief function we have* $H_{\mathcal{H}}(\Omega, \Theta) = H_{\mathcal{H}}(\Theta) = AU(bel)$.

Proof. It remains to show that $H_{\mathcal{H}}(\Omega,\Theta) = AU(bel)$ for Bayesian hints. Since focal sets are disjoint we have $p(\omega) = m(A)$ if $\Gamma(\omega) = A$. Using (11) we obtain

$$H_{\mathcal{H}}(\Omega,\Theta) = H_{\mathcal{H}}(\Omega)+GH(\mathcal{H}) = - \sum_{A\subseteq\Theta} m(A) \log\left[\frac{m(A)}{|A|}\right] = AU(bel). \qquad \square$$

Finally, an equally simple counter-example as in Example 3 shows that the hints entropy does not satisfy monotone dispensability.

7 Conclusion

This paper derives the pignistic entropy for Dempster-Shafer theory based on the theory of hints and proves its equivalence to the known measure for ambiguity. The functional agrees with the Shannon and Hartley measure on corresponding cases and satisfies all classical requirements, which are generally imposed on an uncertainty measure, except subadditivity. But the viewpoint of hints allows us to prove a weaker form of subadditivity. In contrast, the aggregate uncertainty is the only known functional that satisfies all properties including subadditivity, and uniqueness of this measure under the classical properties is stated as an open problem in the literature. Despite the lack of strong subadditivity, the pignistic entropy has some crucial advantages over the aggregate uncertainty, most notably explicitness of the formula and sensitivity with respect to changes in evidence. However, we observed that both uncertainty measures do not capture all information contained in the hint model and therefore extend the pignistic entropy to the hints entropy that takes the total information of a hint into account. This new measure still generalizes the Shannon and Hartley measures and further satisfies all classical requirements, including strong subadditivity, while preserving the advantages of the pignistic entropy over the aggregate uncertainty.

Acknowledgement

The author would like to thank Juerg Kohlas and Peter Y. A. Ryan for the fruitful discussions on the pignistic and hints entropy and the relevance of monotone dispensability. Early considerations about uncertainty of hints were also made in [18]. Also, I thank Wojtek Jamroga for his valuable comments on subadditivity and the anonymous reviewers for their important suggestions.

References

1. Chau, C., Lingras, P., Wong, S.: Upper and lower entropies of belief functions using compatible probability functions. In: Komorowski, J., Raś, Z.W. (eds.) ISMIS 1993. LNCS, vol. 689, pp. 306–315. Springer, Heidelberg (1993)
2. Dempster, A.P.: A generalization of bayesian inference. J. Royal Stat. Soc. B 30, 205–247 (1968)

3. Dubois, D., Prade, H.: A note on measures of specificity for fuzzy sets. Int. J. Gen. Systems 10(4), 279–283 (1985)
4. Harmanec, D.: Toward a characterization of uncertainty measure for the dempster-shafer theory. In: UAI 1995: Proc. of the 11th Conference Annual Conference on Uncertainty in Artificial Intelligence, pp. 255–261 (1995)
5. Harmanec, D.: Measure of uncertainty and information. In: Imprecise Probability Project (1999)
6. Harmanec, D., Klir, G.: Measuring total uncertainty in dempster-shafer theory: a novel approach. Int. J. Gen. Systems 22(4), 405–419 (1994)
7. Harmanec, D., Resconi, G., Klir, G.J., Pan, Y.: On the computation of uncertainty measure in the dempster-shafer theory. Int. J. Gen. Systems 25(2), 153 (1996)
8. Higashi, M., Klir, G.J.: Measures of uncertainty and information based on possibility distributions. Int. J. Gen. Systems 9(1), 43–58 (1982)
9. Jousselme, A.-L., Liu, C., Grenier, D., Bossé, E.: Measuring ambiguity in the evidence theory. IEEE Trans. on Systems, Man, and Cybernetics, Part A 36(5), 890–903 (2006)
10. Klir, G.J.: Uncertainty and Information: Foundations of Generalized Information Theory. John Wiley & Sons, Inc., Binghamton University (2005)
11. Klir, G.J., Lewis, H.W.: Remarks on "measuring ambiguity in the evidence theory". IEEE Trans. on Systems, Man, and Cybernetics, Part A 38(4), 995–999 (2008)
12. Kohlas, J.: Information Algebras: Generic Structures for Inference. Springer, Heidelberg (2003)
13. Kohlas, J., Monney, P.-A.: A Mathematical Theory of Hints. An Approach to the Dempster-Shafer Theory of Evidence. LNEMS. Springer, Heidelberg (1995)
14. Kohlas, J., Monney, P.-A.: Statistical Information. Assumption-Based Statistical Inference. Sigma Series in Stochastics, vol. 3. Heldermann (2008)
15. Maeda, Y., Ichihashi, H.: An uncertainty with monotonicity under the random set inclusion. Int. J. Gen. Systems 21(4), 379 (1993)
16. Monney, P.-A.: A Mathematical Theory of Arguments for Statistical Evidence. Contributions to Statistics. Physica-Verlag, Heidelberg (2003)
17. Pouly, M., Kohlas, J.: Generic Inference - A Unifying Theory for Automated Reasoning. John Wiley & Sons, Inc., Chichester (2011)
18. Schneuwly, C.: Information - eine diskussion. Term Paper, University of Fribourg (1999)
19. Shafer, G.: A Mathematical Theory of Evidence. Princeton University Press, Princeton (1976)
20. Smets, P., Kennes, R.: The transferable belief model. Artif. Intell. 66(2), 191–234 (1994)
21. Smith, R.: Generalized Information Theory: Resolving some old Questions and opening some new ones. PhD thesis, University of Binghamton (2000)

Towards an Alarm for Opposition Conflict in a Conjunctive Combination of Belief Functions

Éric Lefèvre[1], Zied Elouedi[2], and David Mercier[1]

[1] Univ. Lille Nord of France,
UArtois EA 3926 LGI2A, France
`firstname.name@univ-artois.fr`
[2] University of Tunis, Institut Supérieur de Gestion de Tunis,
LARODEC, Tunisie
`zied.elouedi@gmx.fr`

Abstract. In the framework of belief functions, information fusion is based on the construction of a unique belief function resulting from the combination of available belief functions induced from several information sources. When sources are reliable and distinct, Smets' conjunctive rule, which is equivalent to Dempster's rule of combination without the normalization process, can be considered. This rule offers interesting properties, but in return the empty set is an absorbing element: a series of conjunctive combinations tends to bring a mass equal to 1 to the empty set, making impossible the distinction between a real problem and an effect due to this absorbing effect of the empty set. Then a formalism allowing the preservation of the conflict which reflects the opposition between sources, is introduced in this paper. Based on the normalization process and on distance measures between belief functions, it is tested and compared with classic conjunctive operators on synthetic belief functions.

1 Introduction

Since more than about twenty years, the scientific community has been showing an increasing interest in information fusion [5,16,39]. Generally based on confidence measures including probability measure, fuzzy sets, possibility and belief measures, information fusion allows the consideration of the redundancy and the complementarity of different available pieces of information to improve the global quality of these inputs, and consequently reach a better decision-making. In the framework of belief functions [33], information fusion has been used in several fields such as multi-sensor fusion [1,4], classification [17,27], diagnosis [6,31] or multi-object tracking [2,29]. It is based on the application of an operator allowing the combination of belief functions representing different propositions or hypotheses relative to a given problem.

One classical rule is the conjunctive rule of combination. Introduced by Smets [34,37], it is equivalent to Dempster's rule of combination [12,33] without the

W. Liu (Ed.): ECSQARU 2011, LNAI 6717, pp. 314–325, 2011.

normalization process. Its properties are well established as well as the hypotheses the sources must verify to be combined by the use of this rule [36, Section 3.2.2].

In a nutshell, sources must be distinct, reliable and must refer to the same object. As a consequence, this rule provides an orthogonal behaviour which is very valuable when a rapid and clear convergence on a solution is required, but in return the empty set is an absorbing element.

Smets [36, Section 6.1] supports the existence of this mass on the empty set to play an alarm role. Indeed, this conflict should not be hidden as it expresses important pieces of information which can be gathered together into two main categories:

– prerequisites for the application of the conjunctive rule are not fulfilled: two sources may not be distinct, one of the sources at least is not reliable (maybe a sensor is broken or ineffective in some unknown condition, etc), or the sources do not deal with the same object.
– the model itself suffers from a bad adequacy to the reality: the frame of discernment is not exhaustive (it is not composed of all the possible values the variable of interest can take), the choice of the frame(s) is not appropriate, etc.

On account of its absorbing effect, a series of conjunctive combinations tends then to bring a mass equal to 1 to the empty set, making impossible the distinction between a real problem and an effect due to the absorbing power of the empty set [24][36, Section 7].

Let us note that other works have been undertaken to complete this definition of the conflict. In [24], a definition of the conflict between belief functions is proposed. It is based on quantitative measures of both the mass on the empty set after a conjunctive combination of these belief functions and the distance between betting commitments of these same belief functions, the mass on the empty set being then no more sufficient to define the conflict. This behaviour is also described by Osswald et al. [25,30] who defined the *auto-conflict* as the amount of intrinsic conflict of a belief function.

In this paper, the opposition between belief functions is quantified by a dissimilarity measure between these functions. This approach, called Combination With Adapted Conflict (CWAC), allows the mass on the empty set to keep its initial role of alarm signal.

This paper is organized as follows. A rapid overview of the basic concepts needed on belief functions is exposed in Section 2, details can be found in [33,37]. In Section 3, the classical combinations of information in the belief function framework are detailed. The postulates and principles of our contribution are explained in Section 4. Then, tests on synthetic belief functions are presented in Section 5 showing the efficiency of the introduced formalism. Finally, Section 6 sums up our contributions and advances possible future work.

2 Belief Function Theory: Basic Concepts

2.1 Representing Information

Let $\Omega = \{\omega_1, \ldots, \omega_K\}$, named the frame of discernment, be a finite non empty set including all the elementary hypotheses related to a given problem. These hypotheses are assumed to be exhaustive and mutually exclusive.

To represent the impact of a piece of evidence on the subsets of hypotheses of the frame of discernment Ω, the so-called basic belief assignment (bba) is defined as a function $m : 2^\Omega \to [0,1]$ satisfying:

$$\sum_{A \subseteq \Omega} m(A) = 1. \tag{1}$$

The quantity $m(A)$, called a basic belief mass (bbm) or a mass for short, represents the part of belief which is exactly committed to the subset A of Ω.

Shafer [33] has initially proposed a normality condition expressed by: $m(\emptyset) = 0$. As previously exposed in the introduction of this paper, Smets proposes to keep the value $m(\emptyset)$ and to consider it as the amount of conflict between the pieces of evidence, which is also considered in this paper.

All the subsets A of Ω such that $m(A)$ is strictly positive, are called the focal elements of m.

2.2 Discounting Information

A doubt on the reliability of a bba m is sometimes possible. The discounting operation [33] of m by $\alpha \in [0,1]$, named *discount rate*, allows one to take into account this *meta knowledge* on the information m. This correction operation of m is defined by:

$$\begin{cases} m^\alpha(A) = (1-\alpha)m(A), & \forall A \subset \Omega, \\ m^\alpha(\Omega) = (1-\alpha)m(\Omega) + \alpha. \end{cases} \tag{2}$$

The coefficient $\beta = (1 - \alpha)$ represents the reliability degree of the source. If the source is not reliable, this degree β is equal to 0, the discount rate α is equal to 1, and m^α is equal to the vacuous bba m_Ω. On the contrary, if the source is reliable, the discounting rate α is null, and m will not be discounted.

2.3 Pignistic Transformation

To make a decision, Smets proposes to transform beliefs to a probability measure. This latter, denoted $BetP$ [37], is called pignistic probability and is defined by:

$$BetP(\omega) = \sum_{A \subseteq \Omega, \omega \in A} \frac{1}{|A|} \frac{m(A)}{1 - m(\emptyset)}, \tag{3}$$

where $|A|$ is the cardinality of subset A. $BetP$ can be extended as a function on 2^Ω as $BetP(A) = \sum_{\omega \in A} BetP(\omega)$. Beyond the pignistic, lots of probability transforms of belief functions have been proposed [7,8,10].

2.4   Distance between Two Belief Functions

Many distance measures between two bbas have been developed (e.g. [21,22,38]).

Tessem's distance is among those based on the pignistic transformation [3,18,38], it is used in several applications [3,24]. Let m_1 and m_2 be two bbas and, respectively $BetP_{m_1}$ and $BetP_{m_2}$ their pignistic transformations. Tessem's distance is then defined as follows:

$$d_T(m_1, m_2) = \max_{A \subseteq \Omega}(|BetP_{m_1}(A) - BetP_{m_2}(A)|) \qquad (4)$$

In [24], this measure is called the *distance between betting commitments* of m_1 and m_2.

Jousselme et al.'s distance is one of the most used in the framework of belief functions and satisfies useful properties such as non-negativity, non-degeneracy and symmetry. It is defined as follows:

$$d_J(m_1, m_2) = \sqrt{\frac{1}{2}(m_1 - m_2)^t \mathcal{D}(m_1 - m_2)} \qquad (5)$$

where $\mathcal{D}$ is the Jaccard index defined by:

$$\mathcal{D}(A, B) = \begin{cases} 0 & \text{if } A = B = \emptyset \\ \frac{|A \cap B|}{|A \cup B|} & \forall A, B \in 2^\Omega. \end{cases} \qquad (6)$$

3   Combining Different Pieces of Information

The objective of the combination is to synthesize a set of belief functions into a unique belief function. Two main approaches may be distinguished: conjunctive and disjunctive rules.

3.1   Conjunctive Rules of Combination

When sources are considered as distinct and reliable (note that they can have been adjusted according to their reliability, this adjustment being possibly realized through a discounting operation (see equation (2)) from additional information [18,28] or by comparing the belief functions to combine with each others [23,25,32] by means of a distance), the combination of Demspter [12] can be classically used. This combination is noted $\oplus$ and defined, m_1 and m_2 being two bbas, by:

$$m_\oplus(A) = \frac{1}{1 - m_{\bigcirc}(\emptyset)} m_{\bigcirc}(A) \quad \forall A \neq \emptyset \quad \text{and} \quad m_\oplus(\emptyset) = 0 \qquad (7)$$

with:

$$m_{\bigcirc}(A) = \sum_{B \cap C = A} m_1(B)m_2(C) \quad \forall A \subseteq \Omega. \qquad (8)$$

Combination $m_{\bigcirc}$ is called the conjunctive rule of combination [37]. The value $m(\emptyset)$ is called conflict because it represents the disagreement between sources involved in the fusion. Let us note that the cautious conjunctive rule of combination developed by Denœux [13] has also a conjunctive behaviour, and it can be applied when sources are not distinct.

3.2 Disjunctive Rule of Combination

When one source is not reliable, and we do not know which one and an adjustment is not possible, the conjunctive combination cannot be used directly. Several combinations were then proposed like the disjunctive rule of combination [14] defined by:

$$m_{\bigcirc}(A) = \sum_{B \cup C = A} m_1(B)m_2(C) \qquad \forall A \subseteq \Omega. \tag{9}$$

This rule represents the dual rule of the conjunctive combination. It is discussed within the framework of the Generalized Bayes Theorem by Smets [35]. The universe Ω is the absorbing element of this rule. In the same spirit as the cautious rule, Denoeux [13] has proposed the bold disjunctive rule of combination, when belief functions to combine are provided by sources which are neither distinct nor reliable.

Other combination rules having intermediate behaviour between the conjunctive and the disjunctive combination have been proposed. For instance, the following rules may be mentionned: the combination of Dubois and Prade [15], the one of Delmotte et al. [11], Martin et al.'s mixed rules [26] or more recently the robust rule of combination of Florea et al. [20]. For other combination rules, it is a question of distributing the partial conflict [19,26]. Objectives of all these rules is to distribute the conflict which arises during the fusion. This redistribution may be seen as a loss of information about a possible dysfunction.

4   Combination with Adapted Conflict (CWAC)

In this paper, sources are assumed to be distinct and reliable. In this context, the conflict $m(\emptyset)$ obtained during a conjunctive combination allows the decision maker to turn his attention to a possible problem related to a bad modelling, an unreliable source, etc.

However, when applying the conjunctive combination on a large number of belief functions, the conflict can take important proportions without reflecting a problem. This phenomenon is due to the absorbing effect of the empty set. On the other hand, most of the combination propositions found in the literature (see Section 3) try to redistribute this conflict and not to use it as an indicator.

Based on this analysis, we wish to develop a method which allows us to transform the value of the conflict and to adapt it in order to be a real indicator of problems, even if the number of sources to combine is important. This rule is called Combination With Adapted Conflict (CWAC). Considering that there is a serious problem when sources produce strongly different belief functions, the conflict should be kept during the fusion. On the contrary, in the case of the combination of information sources for which the bbas are equivalent, the conflict does not have to exist. To define the CWAC, a measure allowing one to distinguish similarities between bbas is necessary.

4.1   With Two Belief Functions

First, the case of only two bbas m_1 and m_2 is studied. The notion of dissimilarity is obtained through a distance measure. This distance can be obtained by one of both measures presented in Section 2.4 and is noted $d(m_1, m_2)$[1]. The borders of d are:

- $d(m_1, m_2) = 0$: m_1 and m_2 are similar (and are thus in agreement) and their combination should not generate a conflict. In this case, the conflict will be redistributed in the same way as Dempster's rule of combination.
- $d(m_1, m_2) = 1$: m_1 and m_2 are antinomic (i.e. $m_1(\{\omega_j\}) = 1$ and $m_2(\{\omega_i\}) = 1$ with $\omega_i \neq \omega_j$). Their combination will produce a conflictual mass expressing this opposition. The conflict will be kept in the same manner as the conjunctive rule.

The CWAC is defined by an adaptive weighting between the conjunctive and Dempster's rules, making the rule acting like a conjunctive rule when the belief functions are antinomic and like Dempster's rule when belief functions are similar. Between these two extremes, a gradual evolution can be considered. The following combination rule noted $\ominus$ is then proposed, it is defined by:

$$m_{\ominus}(A) = \gamma_1 m_{\odot}(A) + \gamma_2 m_{\oplus}(A) \qquad \forall A \subseteq \Omega \tag{10}$$

with:

$$m_{\oplus}(A) = (m_1 \oplus m_2)(A) \qquad \forall A \subseteq \Omega \tag{11}$$
$$m_{\odot}(A) = (m_1 \odot m_2)(A) \qquad \forall A \subseteq \Omega \tag{12}$$

and with γ_1 and γ_2 are functions of the distance $d(m_1, m_2)$. These functions should satisfy the following constraints:

$$\gamma_1 = f_1(d(m_1, m_2)) \quad \text{with} \quad f_1(0) = 0 \quad \text{and} \quad f_1(1) = 1 \tag{13}$$
$$\gamma_2 = f_2(d(m_1, m_2)) \quad \text{with} \quad f_2(0) = 1 \quad \text{and} \quad f_2(1) = 0 \tag{14}$$

with $\gamma_1 + \gamma_2 = 1$. Although other functions are possible, we can take, at first, linear functions such that:

$$\gamma_1 = d(m_1, m_2) \tag{15}$$
$$\gamma_2 = 1 - d(m_1, m_2). \tag{16}$$

---

[1] However, other measures of dissimilarity could be used [7,9]. Details on distance measure can be found in [22]. The aim of this article is not to compare these measures but to quantify the opposition between belief functions.

Hence, the combination can be written $\forall A \subseteq \Omega$ and $m_{\bigcirc\!\!\!\wedge}(\emptyset) \neq 1$:

$$m_{\bigcirc\!\!\!\vee}(A) = m_1 \;\bigcirc\!\!\!\vee\; m_2(A) = d(m_1, m_2)m_{\bigcirc\!\!\!\wedge}(A) + (1 - d(m_1, m_2))\, m_{\oplus}(A). \quad (17)$$

When $m_{\bigcirc\!\!\!\wedge}(\emptyset) = 1$, then we get $m_{\bigcirc\!\!\!\vee}(\emptyset) = 1$.

4.2 General Case

The question of the generalization of this approach is natural when we have more than two information sources to fuse. Indeed, the problem settles because the distance measure used here, is defined between only two bbas. Let $m_1, \ldots, m_i \ldots, m_N$ be N bbas which have to be combined. The measure of dissimilarity between these functions, which is necessary for our proposed combination rule, may be a synthesis of the distances between these bbas. The objective is to identify if at least one of the sources is in disagreement with the others. This synthesis can be obtained by taking, for example, the maximal value of all the distances. So, the value of D can be defined as $D = \max\limits_{i,j}\,[d(m_i, m_j)]$ with $i \in [1, N]$ and $j \in [1, N]$. The combination rule becomes then $\forall A \subseteq \Omega$ and $m_{\bigcirc\!\!\!\wedge}(\emptyset) \neq 1$:

$$m_{\bigcirc\!\!\!\vee}(A) = \left(\bigcirc\!\!\!\vee_i m_i\right)(A) = Dm_{\bigcirc\!\!\!\wedge}(A) + (1 - D)m_{\oplus}(A) \quad (18)$$

and

$$m_{\bigcirc\!\!\!\vee}(\emptyset) = 1 \quad when \quad m_{\bigcirc\!\!\!\wedge}(\emptyset) = 1 \quad (19)$$

with:

$$m_{\bigcirc\!\!\!\wedge}(A) = \left(\bigcirc\!\!\!\wedge_i m_i\right)(A) \quad and \quad m_{\oplus}(A) = \left(\bigoplus_i m_i\right)(A) \quad \forall i \in [1, N]. \quad (20)$$

4.3 Properties

- **Commutativity:** The combination of two mass functions m_1 and m_2 using the CWAC is commutative. Since the two basic rules composing the CWAC (the conjunctive rule and Dempster's rule) are commutative and since the CWAC is a weighted sum of these rules based on distance which is also commutative, the CWAC is commutative.
- **Associativity:** The CWAC operator is not associative. It is however possible to find operators that produce associative rules or quasi-associative.
- **Neutral element:** The neutral element of the CWAC is Ω. When combining a piece of evidence m_1 with $m(\Omega) = 1$, we have $m_1 \oplus m = m_1$ and $m_1 \bigcirc\!\!\!\wedge m = m_1$. The CWAC can be written: $m_{\bigcirc\!\!\!\vee}(A) = d(m_1, m)m_1(A) + (1 - d(m_1, m))m_1(A) = m_1(A)$. Thus, the CWAC preserves the neutral impact of the $m(\Omega) = 1$.
- **Absorbing element:** From equation (19), the absorbing element of the CWAC is $\emptyset$.
- **Idempotent:** As both Dempster's rule and the conjunctive rule of combination, the CWAC operator is not idempotent.

5   Results

In this Section, the CWAC operator is compared on synthetic data with the conjunctive rule. The CWAC operator is used with two dissimilarity measures: Tessem's distance and Jousselme et al.'s distance presented in Section 2.4.

5.1   Example 1

In this first example, two sources are considered as being in agreement: they have a similar distribution of masses. These distributions and the combinations results by the operators $\oplus$, $\odot$ and $\ominus$ are given in Table 1. Bba $m_{\ominus}^{J}$ is obtained by the CWAC operator with Jousselme et al.'s distance and $m_{\ominus}^{T}$ is obtained by the CWAC operator with Tessem's distance. The conflict induced by the conjunctive combination is relatively important which is not the case for the proposed combination (0.363 against 0.004). Now these two bbas are considered

Table 1. Results of the fusion between two sources in agreement

	m_1	m_2	$m_\oplus$	$m_\odot$	$m_{\ominus}^{J}$	$m_{\ominus}^{T}$
$\{\omega_1\}$	0.60	0.59	0.742	0.473	0.74	0.74
$\{\omega_2\}$	0.30	0.31	0.242	0.154	0.24	0.24
Ω	0.10	0.10	0.016	0.01	0.016	0.016
$\emptyset$	0	0	0	**0.363**	**0.004**	**0.004**

Table 2. Results of the fusion between two sources in disagreement

	m_1	m_2	$m_\oplus$	$m_\odot$	$m_{\ominus}^{J}$	$m_{\ominus}^{T}$
$\{\omega_1\}$	0.60	0.31	0.501	0.277	0.436	0.436
$\{\omega_2\}$	0.30	0.59	0.481	0.266	0.419	0.419
Ω	0.1	0.1	0.018	0.01	0.015	0.015
$\emptyset$	0	0	0	**0.447**	**0.13**	**0.13**

in disagreement (Table 2). If we compare these results to those obtained in the previous test, we observe that there is only 23 % of increase of the conflict for the conjunctive combination (while the distribution of masses are radically different). Regarding our rule, the increase of the conflict is of the order of 3150% which reflects well the difference between the first test and the second one.

5.2   Example 2

In this second example, a number N of sources is considered with N varying from 2 to 25. All the bbas are firstly chosen in agreement and are defined, with $\Omega = \{\omega_1, \omega_2, \omega_3\}$, as follows with ϵ a random value between $[-0.1; 0.1]$:

$$m(\{\omega_1\}) = 0.6 + \epsilon \quad m(\{\omega_1, \omega_2\}) = 0.15 - \epsilon \quad m(\{\omega_3\}) = 0.15 \quad m(\Omega) = 0.1.$$

Conflict evolution for operators $\odot$ and $\ominus$ according to the number of sources N to combine is presented in Figure 1. The absorbing effect of the empty set can be observed: even if the bbas are in agreement the value of the conflict increases with the number of combinations. In a second time, one bba is now chosen as being in contradiction with the others. It is defined in the following way:

$$m(\{\omega_1\}) = 0.15 + \epsilon \quad m(\{\omega_1, \omega_2\}) = 0.15 - \epsilon \quad m(\{\omega_3\}) = 0.6 \quad m(\Omega) = 0.1$$

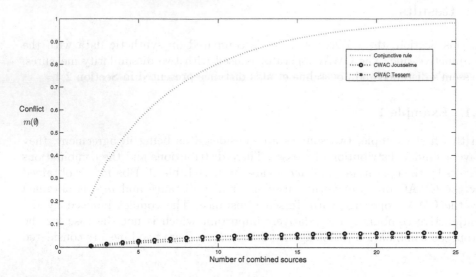

Fig. 1. Conflict evolution of the combination of N not contradictory bbas

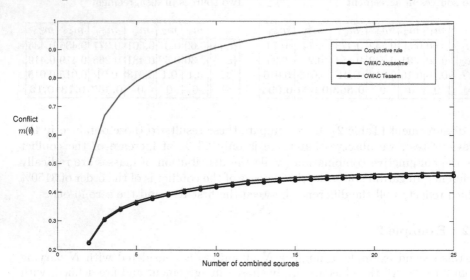

Fig. 2. Conflict evolution of the combination of $N - 1$ not contradictory bbas and one in conflict

Figure 2 illustrates the evolution of the conflict in this configuration, the latter being compared with the previous in Figure 3.

In this last figure 3, it can be observed that after more that 20 belief functions to combine, the value of the conflict obtained by the conjunctive combination does not allow any more the identification of a possible contradiction between bbas while it is not the case for the CWAC operator. The behaviour of the CWAC operator is equivalent with both dissimilarity measures. However,

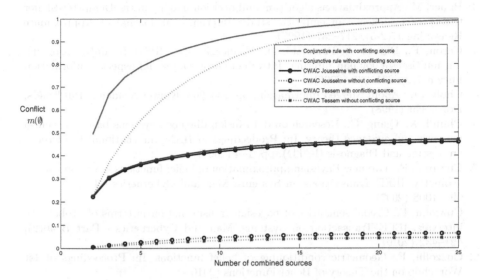

Fig. 3. Comparison between the combination of N similar functions and the combination of $N-1$ similar functions and of a contradictory function

Tessem's distance allows one to have a difference between the two simulations more important. So, Tessem's distance is a better measure than Jousselme et al.'s distance for judging how contradict the two beliefs are [24].

6   Conclusion and Future Work

In this paper, we have proposed a combination rule with adapted conflict having the objective to better handle the conflict induced from the fusion of several bbas. Our proposed CWAC rule makes an adaptive weighting between conjunctive and Dempster's rules using Tessem's and Jousseleme et al.'s distances in order to reduce the absorbing power of the conflict and to more strengthen its initial role of alarm signal. As future work, more attention will be given to obtain the similarity measure between all belief functions involved in the combination. For each similarity measure, different properties of CWAC will be defined. Moreover, it will be interesting to study the behaviour of this operator when Jousselme et al.'s distance (or others) is approximately equal to 0.5.

References

1. Appriou, A.: Multisensor signal processing in the framework of the theory of evience. In: Application of Mathematical Signal Processing Techniques to Mission Systems, pp. (5–1)–(5–31). Research and Technology Organization, Lecture Series (1999)
2. Bar-Shalom, Y., Li, X.: Multitarget-Multisensor Tracking: Principles and Techniques. YBS Publishing, Storrs (1995)

3. Bauer, M.: Approximations algorithm and decision making in the Dempster-Shafer theory of evidence - an empirical study. International Journal of Approximate Reasoning 17(2-3), 217–237 (1997)
4. Caron, F., Duflos, E., Pomorski, D., Vanheeghe, P.: GPS/IMU data fusion using multisensor kalman filtering: Introduction of contextual aspects. Information Fusion 7(2), 221–230 (2006)
5. Cholvy, L.: About Merged Information, pp. 233–263. Kluwer Academic Publishers, Dordrecht (1998)
6. Chunli, X., Qiang, G.: Research on data fusion diagnosis systems based on neural network and evidence theory. In: Prodeedings of IEEE International Conference on Testing and Diagnosis (ICTD), pp. 1–4 (2009)
7. Cuzzolin, F.: Two new Bayesian approximation of belief functions based on convex geometry. IEEE Transactions on Systems, Man and Cybernetics - Part B 37(4), 993–1008 (2007)
8. Cuzzolin, F.: Credal semantics of bayesian transformation in terms of probability intervals. IEEE Transaction on Systems, Man and Cybernetics - Part B 40(2), 421–432 (2010)
9. Cuzzolin, F.: Geometric conditioning of belief functions. In: Proceedings of 1st Workshop on the Theory of Belief Functions (2010)
10. Daniel, M.: On transformation of belief functions to probabilites. International Journal of Intelligent Systems, Special Issue on Uncertainty Processing 21(3), 261–282 (2006)
11. Delmotte, F., Dubois, L., Desodt, A., Borne, P.: Using trust in uncertainty theories. Information and Systems Engineering 1, 303–314 (1995)
12. Dempster, A.: Upper and lower probabilities induced by a multivalued mapping. Annals of Mathematical Statistics 38, 325–339 (1967)
13. Denoeux, T.: Conjunctive and disjunctive combination of belief functions induced by non distinct bodies of evidence. Artificial Intelligence 172(23), 234–264 (2008)
14. Dubois, D., Prade, H.: A set theoric view of belief functions: Logical operation and approximations by sets. International Journal of General Systems 12(3), 193–226 (1986)
15. Dubois, D., Prade, H.: Representation and combination of uncertainty with belief functions and possibility measures. Computational Intelligence 4, 244–264 (1988)
16. Dubois, D., Prade, H.: Possibility theory and data fusion in poorly informed environments. Control Engineering Practice 2(5), 811–823 (1994)
17. Elouedi, Z., Mellouli, K., Smets, P.: Belief decision trees: Theorical foundations. International Journal of Approximate Reasoning 28(2-3), 91–124 (2001)
18. Elouedi, Z., Mellouli, K., Smets, P.: Assessing sensor reliability for multisensor data fusion with the Transferable Belief Model. IEEE Transaction on Systems, Man and Cybernetics, Part B 34, 782–787 (2004)
19. Florea, M., Dezert, J., Valin, P., Smarandache, F., Jousselme, A.L.: Adaptative combination rule and proportional conflict redisribution rule for information fusion. In: Proceedings of COGnitive Systems with Interactive Sensors, COGIS 2006 (2006)
20. Florea, M., Jousselme, A.L., Boisé, E., Grenier, D.: Robust combination rules for evidence theory. Information Fusion 10(2), 183–197 (2009)
21. Jousselme, A.L., Grenier, D., Boissé, E.: A new distance between two bodies of evidence. Information Fusion 2, 91–101 (2001)
22. Jousselme, A.L., Maupin, P.: On some properties of distance in evidence theory. In: Proceedings of 1st Workshop on the Theory of Belief Functions (2010)

23. Klein, J., Colot, O.: Automatic discounting rate computation using a dissent criterion. In: Proceedings of 1st Workshop on the Theory of the Belief Functions (2010)
24. Liu, W.: Analyzing the degree of conflict among belief functions. Artificial Intelligence 170(11), 909–924 (2006)
25. Martin, A., Jousselme, A., Osswald, C.: Conflict measure for the discountng operation on belief functions. In: Proceedings of Int. Conf. Information Fusion (FUSION 2008), pp. 1003–1010 (2008)
26. Martin, A., Osswald, C.: Toward a combination rule to deal with partial conflict and specificity in belief functions theory. In: Proceedings of Int. Conf. On Information Fusion, Fusion 2007 (2007)
27. Mercier, D., Cron, G., Denoeux, T., Masson, M.H.: Decision fusion for postal address recognition using belief functions. Experts Systems with Applications 36(issue 3, part1), 5643–5653 (2009)
28. Mercier, D., Lefevre, E., Delmotte, F.: Belief functions contextual discounting and cononical decomposition. International Journal of Approximate Reasoning (2011) (accepted for publication)
29. Mercier, D., Lefevre, E., Jolly, D.: Object association in the TBM framework, application to vehicle driving aid. In: Proceedings of 6th International Symposium on Imprecise Probability: Theories and Applications (ISIPTA), Durham, United Kingdom, pp. 317–326 (2009)
30. Osswald, C., Martin, A.: Understanding the large family of Dempster-Shafer theory's fusion operators - a decsion-based measure. In: Proceedings of Int. Conf. On Information Fusion, FUSION 2006 (2006)
31. Périsse, F., Mercier, D., Lefevre, E., Roger, D.: Robust diagnostics of stator insulation based on high frequency measurements. IEEE Transactions on Dielectrics and Electrical Insulation 16(5), 1496–1502 (2009)
32. Schubert, J.: Conflict management in Dempster-Shafer theory using the degree of falsity. International Journal of Approximate Reasoning 52(3), 449–460 (2011)
33. Shafer, G.: A Mathematical Theory of Evidence. Princeton University Press, Princeton (1976)
34. Smets, P.: The combination of evidence in the transferable belief model. IEEE Trans. on Pattern Analysis and Machine Intelligence 12(5), 447–458 (1990)
35. Smets, P.: Belief functions: The disjunctive rule of combination and the generalized Bayesian theorem. International Journal of Approximate Reasoning 9, 1–35 (1993)
36. Smets, P.: Analyzing the combination of conflicting belief functions. Information Fusion 8(4), 387–412 (2007)
37. Smets, P., Kennes, R.: The Transferable Belief Model. Artificial Intelligence 66, 191–234 (1994)
38. Tessem, B.: Approximations for efficient computation in the theory of evidence. Artificial Intelligence 61(2), 315–329 (1993)
39. Yager, R.: A framework for multi-source data fusion. Information Sciences 163(1-3), 175–200 (2004)

E2GK: Evidential Evolving Gustafsson-Kessel Algorithm for Data Streams Partitioning Using Belief Functions

Lisa Serir, Emmanuel Ramasso, and Noureddine Zerhouni

FEMTO-ST Institute, UMR CNRS 6174 - UFC / ENSMM / UTBM,
Automatic Control and Micro-Mechatronic Systems Dep., 25000, Besançon, France
{lisa.serir,emmanuel.ramasso,noureddine.zerhouni}@femto-st.fr

Abstract. A new online clustering method, called E2GK (Evidential Evolving Gustafson-Kessel) is introduced in the theoretical framework of belief functions. The algorithm enables an online partitioning of data streams based on two existing and efficient algorithms: Evidantial c-Means (ECM) and Evolving Gustafson-Kessel (EGK). E2GK uses the concept of credal partition of ECM and adapts EGK, offering a better interpretation of the data structure. Experiments with synthetic data sets show good performances of the proposed algorithm compared to the original online procedure.

1 Introduction

Given a set of N data points, clustering refers to a wide variety of algorithms that aim at discovering c groups (clusters) $\omega_1, ..., \omega_c$ whose members are similar in some way. The purpose is to summarize the data or to verify an existing structure of the data. In most cases, a cluster is defined as a subset of data for which the similarity between data within this subset is larger than the similarity with the data in other subsets. In many cases, the Euclidean distance between data is used as a dissimilarity measure.

A wide variety of clustering methods has been developed. The most commonly used methods are divided into two main categories: hierarchical and non-hierarchical methods. Among the latter, the K-means algorithm [4] is the most commonly used. The idea of K-means algorithm is to randomly create K clusters and to assign each data point to the closest one in an iterative way, reallocating points until a convergence criterion is satisfied.

Using hard partitioning methods, data are grouped in an exclusive way, i.e., data can't belong to two (or more) different clusters. In fuzzy partitioning, each data can belong to more than one cluster with different membership degrees. The most popular fuzzy partitioning method is Bezdek's Fuzzy C-means (FCM) algorithm [3]. One can also mention the Gustafson-Kessel fuzzy clustering algorithm [10] that is capable of detecting hyper-ellipsoidal clusters of different sizes and orientations by adjusting the covariance matrix of data.

Another concept of partition, introduced in [7], is the *credal* partition based on belief functions theory. A credal partition extends the existing concepts of

W. Liu (Ed.): ECSQARU 2011, LNAI 6717, pp. 326–337, 2011.

hard, fuzzy (probabilistic) and possibilistic partition by allocating, for each data, a *mass of belief*, not only to single clusters, but also to any subset of $\Omega = \{\omega_1, ..., \omega_c\}$. This particular representation allows coding all the situations, from certainty to total ignorance of membership to clusters. In the Evidential c-Means (ECM) algorithm [13], the credal partition is in particular exploited for outliers detection.

Online clustering is an important problem that frequently arises in many fields, such as pattern recognition and machine learning [8]. Numerous techniques have been developed for clustering data in a static environment [4]. However, in many real-life applications, non-stationary data (i.e., with time-varying parameters) are commonly encountered. The task of online clustering is to group incoming data into clusters in a temporal sequence. Also called *incremental clustering* in machine learning [11], online clustering, is generally unsupervised and has to manage recursive training in order to incorporate new information gradually and to take into account model evolutions over time.

In this paper, we propose the Evidential Evolving Gustafson Kessel algorithm (E2GK) which permits to adapt a credal partition matrix as data gradually arrive. This clustering algorithm is introduced in the theoretical framework of belief functions, and more precisely of Smets' Transferable Belief Model (TBM, [14]). E2GK is composed of two main steps, both performed online:

1. Determination of clusters' prototypes (also called centers), either by moving existing prototypes or by creating new ones. To do so, we use some results from the Evolving Gustafson-Kessel algorithm (EGK) proposed in [9].
2. Allocation of the belief masses to the different subsets of classes. This step is based on some results of the Evidential c-means algorithm (ECM) [13].

E2GK benefits from two efficient algorithms: EGK and ECM, by dealing with - in an online manner - doubt between clusters and outliers. Doubt is generally encountered in data transition and can be useful to limit the number of clusters in the final partition. Moreover, outliers are well managed using the conflict degree explicitly emphasized in the TBM framework.

In Section 2, we present GK and ECM algorithms as well as some tools of the theory of belief functions giving the necessary background for Section 3 in which we introduce E2GK. Some results are finally presented in Section 4.

2   Background

Let the data be in the form of a collection $\{x_1, \ldots, x_k, \ldots, x_N\}$ of feature vectors $x_k \in \Re^q$, and c the number of clusters, each of them characterized by a prototype (or a center) $v_i \in \Re^q$.

2.1   Gustafson-Kessel Algorithm

Clustering algorithms based on an optimization process aim at minimizing a suitable fuction J that represents the fitting error of the clusters regarding the data:

$$J(V,U) = \sum_{i=1}^{c} \sum_{k=1}^{N} (u_{ik})^{\beta} d_{ik}^{2} \ , \tag{1}$$

where

- u_{ik} is the membership degree of point k to the i-th prototype (cluster center),
- $U = [u_{ij}]$ is the resulting partition matrix with dimension $c \times N$,
- $V = [v_i]$ is the $c \times q$ matrix of prototypes,
- d_{ik} is the distance between the k-th data point x_k and the i-th prototype,
- Paramater $\beta > 1$ is a weighting exponent that controls the fuzziness of the partition (it determines how much clusters may overlap).

The distance d_{ik} used in the GK algorithm is a squared inner-product distance norm (Mahalanobis) that depends on a positive definite symmetric matrix A_i defined by:

$$d_{ik}^{2} = \|x_k - v_i\|_{A_i}^{2} = (x_k - v_i) A_i (x_k - v_i)^{T} \ . \tag{2}$$

This adaptive distance norm is unique for each cluster as the norm inducing matrix A_i, $i = 1...c$, is calculated by estimates of the data covariance

$$A_i = [\rho_i det(F_i)]^{1/q} \, F_i^{-1} \ , \tag{3}$$

where ρ_i is the cluster volume of the i-th cluster and F_i is the fuzzy covariance matrix calculated as follows:

$$F_i = \frac{\sum_{k=1}^{N} (u_{ik})^{\beta} (x_k - v_i)^{T} (x_k - v_i)}{\sum_{k=1}^{N} (u_{ik})^{\beta}} \ . \tag{4}$$

The objective function is minimized using an iterative algorithm, which alternatively optimizes the cluster centers and the membership degrees:

$$v_i = \frac{\sum_{k=1}^{N} (u_{ik})^{\beta} x_k}{\sum_{k=1}^{N} (u_{ik})^{\beta}}, \ i = 1 \cdots c, \ k = 1 \cdots N \ , \tag{5}$$

and

$$u_{ik} = \frac{1}{\sum_{j=1}^{c} (d_{ik}/d_{jk})^{2/\beta-1}}, \ i = 1 \cdots c, \ k = 1 \cdots N \ . \tag{6}$$

The GK algorithm has the great advantage to adapt the clusters according to their real shape.

2.2   Belief Functions and Credal Partition

Dempster-Shafer theory of evidence, also called belief functions theory, is a theoretical framework for reasoning with partial and unreliable information. It was first introduced by A. P. Dempster (1968), then developed by G. Shafer (1976). Later, Ph. Smets proposed a general framework, the *Transferable Belief Model* (TBM) [14], for uncertainty representation and combination of various pieces of information without additional priors.

Considering a variable ω taking values in a finite set called the *frame of discernment* Ω, the *belief* of an agent in subsets of Ω can be represented by a *basic belief assignment* (BBA), also called *belief mass assignment*:

$$
\begin{aligned}
m : 2^{\Omega} &\to [0, 1] \\
A &\mapsto m(A) \ ,
\end{aligned}
\tag{7}
$$

with $\sum_{A \subseteq \Omega} m(A) = 1$. A belief mass can not only be assigned to a singleton ($|A| = 1$), but also to a *subset* ($|A| > 1$) of variables *without any assumption concerning additivity*. This property permits the explicit modeling of doubt and conflict, and constitutes a fundamental difference with probability theory. The subsets A of Ω such that $m(A) > 0$, are called the *focal elements* of m. Each focal element A is a set of possible values of ω. The quantity $m(A)$ represents a fraction of a unit mass of belief allocated to A. Complete ignorance corresponds to $m(\Omega) = 1$, whereas perfect knowledge of the value of ω is represented by the allocation of the whole mass of belief to a unique singleton of Ω, and m is then said to be *certain*. In the case of all focal elements being singletons, m boils down to a probability function and is said to be *bayesian*.

A positive value of $m(\emptyset)$ is considered if one accepts the *open-world assumption* stating that the set Ω might not be complete, and thus ω might take its values outside Ω. This value represents the *degree of conflict* and is then interpreted as a mass of belief given to the hypothesis that ω might not lie in Ω. This interpretation is useful in clustering for outliers detection [13].

Belief functions theory is largely used in clustering and classification problems [6,12]. Recently (2003) was proposed the use of belief functions for cluster analysis. Similar to the concept of fuzzy partition but more general, the concept of *Credal Partition* was introduced. It particularly permits a better interpretation of the data structure. A credal partition is constructed by assigning a BBA to each possible subset of clusters. Partial knowledge regarding the membership of a datum i to a class j is represented by a BBA m_{ij} on the set $\Omega = \{\omega_1, \ldots, \omega_c\}$. This particular representation makes it possible to code all situations, from certainty to total ignorance.

Example 1. Considering $N = 4$ data and $c = 3$ classes, Tab. 1 gives an example of a credal partition. BBAs for each datum in Tab. 1 illustrate various situations: datum 1 certainly belongs to class 1, whereas the class of datum 2 is completely unknown. Partial knowledge is represented for datum 3. As $m_4(\emptyset) = 1$, datum 4 is considered as an outlier, i.e., its class does not lie in Ω.

Table 1. Example of a credal partition

A	$\emptyset$	ω_1	ω_2	$\{\omega_1, \omega_2\}$	ω_3	$\{\omega_1, \omega_3\}$	$\{\omega_2, \omega_3\}$	$\{\omega_1, \omega_2, \omega_3\}$
$m_1(A)$	0	1	0	0	0	0	0	0
$m_2(A)$	0	0	0	0	0	0	0	1
$m_3(A)$	0	0	0	0	0.2	0.5	0	0.3
$m_4(A)$	1	0	0	0	0	0	0	0

2.3   ECM: Evidential C-Means Algorithm

Our approach for developing E2GK (Evidential Evolving GK algorithm) is based on the concept of credal partition as described in ECM [13] where the objective function was defined as:

$$J_{ECM}(M,V) = \sum_{k=1}^{N} \sum_{\{i/A_i \neq \emptyset, A_i \subseteq \Omega\}} |A_i|^{\alpha} m_{ki}^{\beta} d_{ki}^{2} + \sum_{k=1}^{N} \delta^2 m_k(\emptyset)^{\beta} \,, \qquad (8)$$

subject to

$$\sum_{\{i/A_i \neq \emptyset, A_i \subseteq \Omega\}} m_{ki} + m_k(\emptyset) = 1 \quad \forall k = 1, \ldots, N \,, \qquad (9)$$

where:

- α is used to penalize the subsets of Ω with high cardinality,
- $\beta > 1$ is a weighting exponent that controls the fuzziness of the partition,
- d_{ki} denotes the Euclidean distance between datum k and prototype v_i,
- δ controls the amount of data considered as outliers.

The $N \times 2^c$ partition matrix M is derived by determining, for each datum k, the BBAs $m_{ki} = m_k(A_i)$, $A_i \subseteq \Omega$ such that m_{ki} is low (resp. high) when the distance d_{ki} between datum k and focal element A_i is high (resp. low). The matrix M is computed by the minimization of criterion (8) and was shown to be [13], $\forall k = 1 \ldots N$, $\forall i/A_i \subseteq \Omega$, $A_i \neq \emptyset$:

$$m_{ki} = \frac{|A_i|^{-\alpha/(\beta-1)} d_{ki}^{-2/(\beta-1)}}{\sum_{A_l \neq \emptyset} |A_l|^{-\alpha/(\beta-1)} d_{kl}^{-2/(\beta-1)} + \delta^{-2/(\beta-1)}} \,, \qquad (10)$$

and $m_k(\emptyset) = 1 - \sum_{A_i \neq \emptyset} m_{ki}$. The distance between a datum and any non empty subset $A_i \subseteq \Omega$ is then defined by computing the center of each subset A_i. The latter is the barycenter $\overline{v_i}$ of the clusters' centers (obtained by minimizing criterion (8)) composing A_i.

3   Deriving E2GK

GK algorithm [10] has the great advantage to adapt the clusters according to their real shape. The resulting clusters are hyper-ellipsoids with arbitrary orientation and are well suited for a variety of practical problems. However, GK is not able to deal with streams of data (relies on an iterative optimization scheme). Moreover, it assumes that the number of clusters is known in advance.

In [9], an online version of GK clustering algorithm (EGK) was developed to enable online partitioning of data streams based on a similar principle to the one used in the initial GK algorithm [10]. In particular, online updating of the fuzzy partition matrix relies on the same formula (6). Rules were then proposed to decide whether a new cluster has to be created or existing prototypes should evolve.

3.1   E2GK: Evidential Evolving Gustafsson-Kessel Algorithm

The adaptation of the EGK algorithm to belief functions is introduced in this section. The E2GK algorithm is presented in Tab. 2. It relies on some parts developed in [9] and the proposed adaptations are emphasized in bold characters.

Step 1 – Initialization: At least one cluster's center should be provided. Otherwise, the first point is chosen as the first prototype. If more than one prototype is assumed in the initial data, GK or ECM algorithm can be applied to identify an initial partition matrix. The result of the initialization phase is a set of c prototypes v_i and a covariance matrix[1] F_i.

Step 2 – Decision making: The boundary of each cluster is defined by the cluster radius r_i, defined as the *medium* distance between the cluster center v_i and the points belonging to this cluster with membership degrees larger or equal to a given threshold u_h:

$$r_i = \underset{\forall x_j \in \; i\text{-}th \; cluster \; and \; P_{ji} > u_h}{\text{median}} \|v_i - x_j\|_{A_i} . \tag{11}$$

where P_{ij} is the confidence degree that point j belongs to $\omega_i \in \Omega$ and can be obtained by three main processes: either by using the belief mass $m_j(\omega_i)$, or the pignistic transformation [14] that converts a BBA into a probability distribution, or by using the plausibility transform [5]. We propose here to choose the pignistic transformation. The *median* value is used (instead of the *maximum* rule in EGK) to reduce the sensitivity to extreme values. Moreover, the minimum membership degree u_h - initially introduced in [9] and requiring to decide whether a data point belongs or not to a cluster - can be difficult to assess. It may depend on the density of the data as well as on the level of cluster overlapping. We rather set u_h automatically to $1/c$ in order to reduce the number of parameters while ensuring a natural choice for its value.

Step 3 – Computing the partition matrix: Starting from the resulting set of clusters at a given iteration, we build the partition matrix M (10) using the Mahalanobis distance (2)(3). We assumed that each cluster volume $\rho_i = 1$ as in standard GK algorithm.

Step 4 – Adapting the structure: Given a new data point x_k, two cases are considered:

Case 1: x_k belongs to an existing cluster, thus a clusters' update has to be performed. Data point x_k is assigned to the closest cluster p if $d_{pk} \leq r_p$. Then, the p-th cluster is updated:

$$v_{p,new} = v_{p,old} + \theta \cdot (x_k - v_{p,old}) , \tag{12}$$

and

$$F_{p,new} = F_{p,old} + \theta \cdot \left((x_k - v_{p,old})^T (x_k - v_{p,old}) - F_{p,old} \right) , \tag{13}$$

---

[1] To obtain a covariance matrix from ECM, one can also use the Mahalanobis distance as proposed in [1].

where θ is a learning rate, $v_{p,new}$ and $v_{p,old}$ denote respectively the new and old values of the center, and $F_{p,new}$ and $F_{p,old}$ denote respectively the new and old values of the covariance matrix.

Case 2: x_k is not within the boundary of any existing cluster (i.e. $d_{pk} > r_p$), thus a new cluster may be defined and a clusters' update has to be performed. The number of clusters is thus incremented: $c = c + 1$. Then, the incoming data x_k is accepted as the center v_{new} of the new cluster and its covariance matrix F_{new} is initialized with the covariance matrix of the closest cluster $F_{p,old}$.

In the initial EGK algorithm [9], a parameter P_i was introduced to assess the number of points belonging to the i-th cluster. The authors suggested a threshold parameter P_{tol} to guarantee the validity of the covariance matrices and to improve the robustness. This (context-determined) parameter corresponds to the desired minimal amount of points falling within the boundary of each cluster. The new created cluster is then rejected if it contains less than P_{tol} data points.

After creating a new cluster, the data structure evolves. However, the new cluster may contain data points previously assigned to another cluster. Thus, the number of data points in previous clusters could change. We propose an additional step to verify, after the creation of a new cluster, that all clusters have at least the required minimum amount of data points (P_{tol} or more). If not, the cluster with the lowest number of points is deleted. Therefore, compared to the initial EGK algorithm, in which the number of clusters only increases, E2GK is more flexible because the structure can change either by increasing or decreasing the number of clusters.

The overall algorithm is presented in Tab. 2 where the proposed adaptation appears in bold.

4   Application of E2GK

To illustrate the ability of the proposed algorithm, let consider the following synthetic data randomly generated from five different bivariate gaussian distributions with parameters as given in Tab. 3.

Initial clusters (Fig. 1) of $N = 15$ data points each, of type G_1 and G_2, were identified by batch GK procedure with $u_h = 0.5$, $P_{tol} = 20$ and $\theta = 0.1$. To test the updating procedure, we gradually (one point at a time) added the following data points (in this given order): 1) 15 data points of type G_1, 2) 15 data points of type G_2, 3) 15 data points of type G_3, 4) 30 data points of type G_4, 5) 15 data points of type G_3, 6) 90 data points of type "noise", 7) 6 data points at the following positions: [10.1 3.2], [10.1 −3.2], [−4.1 −3.1], [−2.3 8.3], [8.6 −3.1] and [6.2 9.2]. E2GK parameters were set to: $P_{tol} = 20$, $\theta = 0.1$, $\delta = 10$, $\alpha = 1$ and $\beta = 2$.

Each new incoming data point leads to a new credal partition. Figure 2 shows the final resulting partition. The center of gravity of each cluster is marked by a big star (the notation ω_{ij} stands for $\{\omega_i, \omega_j\}$). A data point falling in a subset ω_{ij} means that this point could either belong to ω_1 or ω_2. The points represented in circles are those with the highest mass given to the empty set and considered as

Table 2. E2GK algorithm

Initialization	1. Take the first point as a center or apply the off-line GK or ECM algorithm to get the initial number of clusters c and the corresponding centers V and covariances F_i, $i = 1 \cdots c$ **2. Calculate $\overline{v_j}$, the barycenter of the clusters' centers** composing $A_j \subseteq \Omega$ **3. Calculate the credal partition M, using (10)**

Updating	*Repeat* for each new data point x_k
	4. Find the closest cluster p
	5. Decision-making: Calculate the radius r_p of the closest cluster using (11) with the **median value**
	If $d_{pk} \leq r_p$
	  6. Update the center v_p (12)
	  7. Update the covariance matrix F_p (13)
	else
	  8. Create a new cluster: $v_{c+1} := x_k$; $F_{c+1} := F_p$
	end
	9. Recalculate the credal partition M using (10)
	10. Check the new structure: remove the cluster with the minimum number of data points if less than P_{tol}

Table 3. Parameters of the synthetic data

type	μ	σ
G_1	[0 5]	0.3
G_2	[0 0]	0.3
G_3	[6 6]	0.6
G_4	[6 0]	0.6
noise	[2.5 2.5]	2

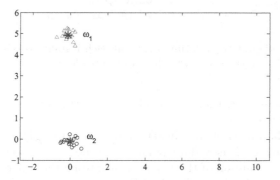

Fig. 1. Initialization of E2GK algorithm using some data from two clusters. Centers are represented by stars.

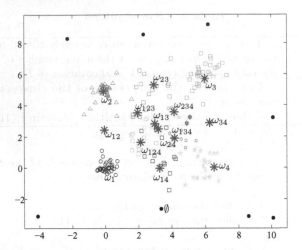

Fig. 2. Credal partition with $\delta = 10$, $\alpha = 1$, $\beta = 2$, $\theta = 0.1$, $P_{tol} = 20$. Big stars represent centers. We also displayed the centers corresponding to subsets, e.g. ω_{123}, and atypical data (dots) are well detected.

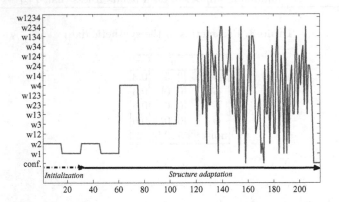

Fig. 3. Structure adaptation: a datum arrives at each instant (x-axis) and is assigned to one of all possible subsets (y-axis). The set of possible subsets also evolves with the number of clusters.

outliers. It can be seen that a meaningful partition is recovered and that outliers are correctly detected.

The online adaptation of the clusters is illustrated in Figure 3. One can see how E2GK assigns each new data point to the desired cluster or subset. The figure depicts the evolution of the partition regarding the order of arrival of the data (like mentionned before). The first 30 points are used to initialize clusters ω_1 and ω_2. Then, from $t = 31$ to 45 points are assigned by E2GK to cluster ω_2. The next 15 points are assigned to ω_1 then to ω_4, ω_3 (30 points) and to ω_4. The next points correspond to noise and are mainly assigned to subsets, for example point 160 to ω_{134}.

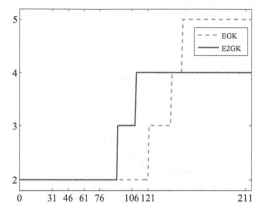

Fig. 4. Structure evolution: the number of clusters at each instant varies as data arrive

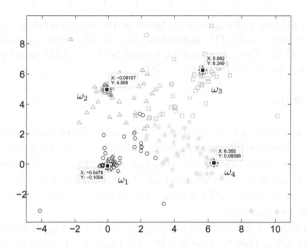

Fig. 5. Decision on clusters for each point based on the pignistic probabilities obtained from the credal partition (Fig. 2) using E2GK algorithm. Also are displayed the coordinates of the centers found by E2GK.

Figure 4 also depicts the structure evolution, that is the number of clusters at each instant. The scenario given at the begining of this section is recovered: at $t = 76$ data from group G_3 arrive but still, not enough data are available to create clustrs while a cluster is created at $t = 93$ and $t = 110$ for group G_4 and G_3 respectively. "Noise" and atypical points arriving from $t = 181$ to $t = 211$ do not affect the structure. This figure does not illustrate clusters' removing because this operation is made within the algorithm.

Figure 5 describes the dataset partitioning after decision making by applying the pignistic transformation [14] on the final credal partition matrix. Datatips provide the center coordinates, which are close to the real parameters (Tab 3). In comparison, we also provide in Figure 6 the centers obtained by EGK algorithm with parameters $P_{tol} = 20$, $u_h=1/c$ and $\theta = 0.1$ (the same as in E2GK).

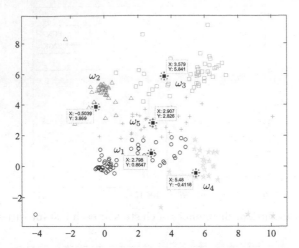

Fig. 6. Decision on clusters for each point based on the maximum degree of membership from the fuzzy partition using GK algorithm. Also are displayed the coordinates of the centers found by EGK. The parameter u_h was set to $1/c$ and the other parameters are the same as in E2GK ($\theta = 0.1$ and $P_{tol} = 20$).

5   Conclusion

To our knowledge, only one *incremental* approach to clustering using belief functions has been proposed [2]. However, in this approach the number of clusters is known in advance so this is not adapted for online applications. Moreover, data are described by a given number of attributes, each labeled by a mass of belief provided by an expert. This prior information is generally not available in pattern recognition problems.

E2GK algorithm, described in this paper, is an evolving clustering algorithm using belief functions theory, which relies on the credal partition concept. This type of partition allows a finer representation of datasets by emphasizing doubt between clusters as well as outliers. Doubt is important for data streams analysis from real systems because it offers a suitable representation of gradual changes in the stream. E2GK relies on some parts of EGK algorithm [9], initially based on a fuzzy partition, to which we bring some modifications:

- using the median operator to calculate cluster radius (vs. max. for EGK),
- using the credal partitioning (vs. fuzzy for EGK),
- changing the partitionning structure by adding or removing clusters (vs. adding only in EGK).

Simulation results show that E2GK discovers relatively well the changes in the data structure. A thorough analysis of parameters' sensitivity (P_{tol} and θ) is now required to properly and automatically set them.

References

1. Antoine, V., Quost, B., Masson, M.H., Denoeux, T.: Cecm - adding pairwise constraints to evidential clustering. In: IEEE World Congress on Computational Intelligence (July 2010)
2. Ben-Hariz, S., Elouedi, Z.: IK-BKM: An incremental clustering approach based on intra-cluster distance. In: Eighth ACS/IEEE International Conference on Computer Systems and Applications (2010)
3. Bezdek, J.C.: Pattern Recognition with fuzzy objective function algorithms. Plenum Press, New York (1981)
4. Bishop, C.M.: Neural networks for pattern recognition. Oxford University Press, Oxford (1995)
5. Cobb, B., Shenoy, P.: On the plausibility transformation method for translating belief function models to probability models. International Journal of Approximate Reasoning 41(3), 314–330 (2006)
6. Denoeux, T.: A k-nearest neighbor classification rule based on dempster-shafer theory. IEEE Trans. on Systems, Man and Cybernetics 25(5), 804–813 (1995)
7. Denoeux, T., Masson, M.H.: Evclus: Evidential clustering of proximity data. IEEE Transactions on Systems, Man and Cybernetics Part B 34(1), 95–109 (2004)
8. Duda, R., Hart, P., Stork, D.: Pattern Classification. Wiley, New york (2001)
9. Georgieva, O., Filev, D.: Gustafson-kessel algorithm for evolving data stream clustering. In: International Conference on Computer Systems and Technologies (2009)
10. Gustafson, E., Kessel, W.: Fuzzy clustering with a fuzzy covariance matrix. In: IEEE Conference on Decision and Control (1978)
11. Jänichen, S., Perner, P.: Acquisition of concept descriptions by conceptual clustering. In: Perner, P., Imiya, A. (eds.) MLDM 2005. LNCS (LNAI), vol. 3587, pp. 153–162. Springer, Heidelberg (2005)
12. Kim, H., Swain., P.H.: Evidential reasoning approach to multisource-data classification in remote sensing. IEEE Transactions on Systems, Man and Cybernetics 25(8), 1257–1265 (1995)
13. Masson, M.H., Denoeux, T.: ECM: An evidential version of the fuzzy c-means algorithm. Pattern Recognition 41(4), 1384–1397 (2008)
14. Smets, P., Kennes, R.: The transferable belief model. Artificial Intelligence 66, 191–234 (1994)

Evidential Markov Decision Processes

Hélène Soubaras, Christophe Labreuche, and Pierre Savéant

Thales Research & Technology France, Laboratoire LMTD,
Campus Polytechnique, 1 av. Angustin Fresnel, F-91767 Palaiseau Cédex
helene.soubaras@thalesgroup.com

Abstract. This paper proposes a new model, the EMDP (Evidential Markov Decision Process). It is a MDP (Markov Decision Process) for belief functions in which rewards are defined for each state transition, like in a classical MDP, whereas the transitions are modeled as in an EMC (Evidential Markov Chain), i.e. they are sets transitions instead of states transitions. The EMDP can fit to more applications than a MDPST (MDP with Set-valued Transitions). Generalizing to belief functions allows us to cope with applications with high uncertainty (imprecise or lacking data) where probabilistic approaches fail. Implementation results are shown on a search-and-rescue unmanned rotorcraft benchmark.

1 Introduction

The problem we address in this paper is decision-making when there is high uncertainty (incomplete, imprecise or unreliable data) and however it is necessary to make a decision rapidly. This is the case for example in crisis management applications. The ongoing situation is one state of a system, and there are several possible actions to move to another state. When the effects of the actions are probabilistic, determining which one must be chosen for each system state is the problem of *planning under uncertainty* [4]. The Markov Decision Process (MDP) is one classical model to solve this problem. But in our context one must take into account additional uncertainties at two levels: the current system state, and the probabilities of the possible effects of the actions. In crisis management-type applications there is no time to learn the model, and the available data are poor, so the probabilities are unknown; this is why probabilistic methods are no longer sufficient to identify the system; we need to involve theories that are more general than the probability theory. There exist several candidate theories generalizing probabilities, such as Imprecise Probabilities [25]. In this work, we focus on the theory of belief functions (also called Dempster-Shafer theory of Evidence) [16], because it offers a powerful mathematical framework, it can perform combination and aggregation of belief masses, and it allows us to compute decision criteria with algorithms of low complexity.

In this paper, we shall remind some existing generalizations of MDPs, then we will introduce our proposed EMDP (Evidential Markov Decision Process). A solving method will be given, and finally we will give some results on a search-and-rescue unmanned rotorcraft benchmark of the IPC-6 (International Planning Competition[1]).

---

[1] http://ipc.icaps-conference.org

W. Liu (Ed.): ECSQARU 2011, LNAI 6717, pp. 338–349, 2011.

2 Existing Extensions of the MDP Model

After a reminder about the classical MDP model, this section offers an overview of generalizations that have been proposed in the field of uncertainty theories. Let us consider a system. Ω will denote the space of all the possible states s in which this system can be. In all this work, Ω is supposed to be finite. Remind that a *Markov chain* is the triple (Ω, Q, P_0) where Q is a state transition matrix whose elements are $q_{ij} = Pr(s' = x_i | s = x_j)$ (i.e. the probabilty of transition from state s to state s'), and P_0 is the initial probability vector.

2.1 The Classical MDP Model

As we will propose a generalization of MDPs to belief functions, it is necessary to describe the classical (or probabilistic, or *exact*) MDP model. A *Markov Decision Process* (MDP) [11] is a planning problem where actions do not always have necessarily one unique deterministic effect. There may be several effects, with given probabilities which depend on the previous state, the action, and the following state. It is a sequential decision-making process, i.e. a system where an action must be performed at each time step t. Each action has two effects: it influences the following system state, and it provides a gain called *reward*. The MDP is modeled by a tuple (Ω, A, Q, R, P_0) where A is the space of all possible actions a. The applications Q and R:

$$Q : \Omega \times A \times \Omega \rightarrow [0, 1] \text{ with } Q(s, a, s') = Pr(s'|a, s)$$
$$R : \Omega \times A \times \Omega \rightarrow \mathbb{R}$$

are respectively the transition probability and the reward obtained when moving from state s at time t to state s' at the following time $t + 1$ on action a. P_0 is the vector of the initial probabilities for each possible state.

Let (Ω, A, Q, R, P_0) be a MDP. A *policy* is a function: $\pi : \Omega \rightarrow A$ defining which action $a = \pi(s)$ is to be done for each state s of the system. Solving a MDP is finding out the optimal policy, i.e. which action is optimal for each state. Note that a MDP in which a given policy is applied behaves as a Markov chain. The criterion to be optimized is the *value function* V which is the total expected cumulated future reward. For each state s, with a given policy, the value $V(s)$ satisfies the Bellman equation [11]. We will consider the infinite-horizon Bellman equation:

$$V(s) = \sum_{s' \in \Omega} Q(s, \pi(s), s')\left(R(s, \pi(s), s') + \gamma V(s') \right) \tag{1}$$

where the s' are the possible following states, $Q(s, \pi(s), s')$ and $R(s, \pi(s), s')$ are respectively the probability and the reward obtained in transition from state s to state s' on action $\pi(s)$, and γ is a discounting factor. This expression can be written with matrix products:

$$V = \mathcal{V} + \gamma Q^T V$$

where $\mathcal{V}$ is the vector of expected immediate reward for each state. Its coordinates are $\mathcal{V}_s = \sum_{s' \in \Omega} Q(s, \pi(s), s')R(s, \pi(s), s')$.

When there are several possible actions a to do, the optimal policy $\pi(s)$ provides for each state s an action a to do such that $\pi(s) = Argmax_{a \in A} V(s)$. One classical dynamic programming algorithm to solve the infinite-horizon Bellman equation is the policy iteration method. It consists in initializing π_0 (arbitrarily) and setting $\pi_{n+1}(s)$ is the action a which maximizes

$$V(s,a) = \sum_{s'} Q(s,a,s')\left(R(s,a,s') + \gamma V_n(s')\right).$$

and this maximal value $V_{\pi_{n+1}(s)}(s)$ is denoted as $V_{n+1}(s)$. It has been shown that this algorithm converges [11].

2.2 The EMC Model

Introduced by Pieczynski [3,7,10], the *Evidential Markov Chain* (EMC) is not a MDP but a genralization of the Markov chain model to belief functions. It will be the basis for the new EMDP we will propose in this paper. Before introducing it, we shall remind some basic concepts of the theory of belief functions [16].

Ω will be considered as a so-called *frame of discernment* (space of all hypotheses). A *mass function* is a mapping $m : 2^{\Omega} \to [0; 1]$ such that $\sum_{A \subseteq \Omega} m(A) = 1$. A subset of Ω which mass is non zero is called a *focal set*.

The random variable representing the possible states of a Markov chain-modeled system is replaced by a random (focal) set in the EMC model. It is a 4-uple $(\Omega, \mathcal{F}, Q, M_0)$ where $\mathcal{F}$ is a set of focal sets of Ω and $(\mathcal{F}, Q, M_0)$ is a Markov chain. (Thus, M_0 is the vector of the initial masses of the focal sets). (Note that if $\mathcal{F}$ is the set of the singletons of Ω, the EMC coincides with a classical Markov chain.)

2.3 Existing Generalizations of the MDP

The purpose of this paper is to generalize MDPs to belief functions. But some works already exist for more general theories like imprecise probabilities and capacity theory [6,24]. In summary, these are the MDPIP (MDP with Imprecise transition Probabilities) [14] and the BMDP (Bounded-parameter MDP) [5], in which the transition probabilities and the rewards are replaced by intervals; the AMDP (Algebraic MDP) [8], which is concerned with extensions of probabilities that can be written in an algebraic form (this is not the case of the belief functions); a possibilistic model has been proposed for qualitative MDPs [13], in which the observations and the preferences of the decision-maker are both modeled with the possibility theory; but the only generalization for belief functions is the MDPST (MDP with Set-valued Transitions) [23], which manipulates random sets (thus belief functions):

A MDPST is modeled by a tuple (Ω, A, F, R, P_0) where the parameters are defined as for a MDP except that the transition function F is set-valued, as follows:

$$F : \Omega \times A \to 2^{\Omega} \text{ with } F(s,a) = S' \subseteq \Omega$$

with a probability $m(S'|s,a)$ defined on $(\Omega \times A \times 2^{\Omega})$. One has for any (s,a): $\sum_{S' \in 2^{\Omega}} m(S'|s,a) = 1$ and the reward $R : \Omega \times A \to \mathbb{R}$.

In conclusion, the MDPST is the only existing model devoted to belief functions. But its reward is restricted because it depends only on two parameters (s, a) and not on the three parameters (s, a, s'). This simplifies the solving method (no need to do an average to know the immediate reward term in the Bellman equation) but it does not fit to all the practical problems. This is why we shall propose hereafter a more general model.

3 The Proposed Approach

In this section we introduce our new EMDP model, which is based on the EMC. A solving method will be proposed.

3.1 The New EMDP Model

The proposed *Evidential Markov Decision Process* (EMDP) model consists in replacing the probabilities of transitions of a MDP by transitions between focal sets as in an EMC. But the rewards are still defined as in a MDP. The model is the following:

An EMDP is a tuple $(\Omega, \mathcal{F}, A, Q, R, M_0)$ where Ω, A and R are the set of states, the set of actions and the reward matrix defined on $\Omega \times A \times \Omega$ (as for a MDP); $\mathcal{F} \subseteq 2^{\Omega}$ is a set of (focal) sets; and for each action $a \in A$, Q is the transition matrix defined on $\mathcal{F} \times A \times \mathcal{F}$ (as for an EMC for a given a). M_0 is the initial mass vector. (Note that the reward matrix is defined more precisely than the transition matrix. This is because in the physical system the reward has a value for each state transition.)

3.2 Link with the MDPST Model

The transition function of a MDPST assigns a focal (random) set so a state, whereas in the EMDP tre transitions are characterized from one focal set to another. Thus, the MDPST is defined when the state of the system itself is observed, but in the EMDP what is observed is a set. This is why the resulting policy is defined on the states for the MDPST, and on the focal sets for the EMDP.

The other minor difference between the two models is that the reward does not depend on the following state in the MDPST. In fact the reward models can become equivalent with a redefinition of the state space.

3.3 Solving Method for EMDPs

In an EMDP the current state of the system is not known completely. The observed measure at each time t is a random (focal) set. It is possible to provide a policy as a function of the observed focal set. For that, we will propose a generalization of this Bellman equation (1) and a method to solve it.

Bellman equation expression for an EMDP. The Bellman equation is a sum of terms which are immediate expected rewards. At each time step t, for each current state s and for each possible action a, the immediate reward $R(s, a, s')$ is a function of the next state s'. We need to compute its expectation on all s', but it is not possible since in an EMDP we do not know the exact probability of s'. Anyway we know its mass function.

It is known [18,2,15,17] that for any real variable R with a mass $m(S')$ given for each focal set S', the expectation is bounded by the Choquet integrals of the cumulated belief function and the cumulated plausibility function, which have the following expressions:

$$\sum_{S'\in\mathcal{F}} m(S')min(S') \le \mathbb{E}[R] \le \sum_{S'\in\mathcal{F}} m(S')max(S')$$

Now, we are in an EMDP, so we have a current focal set S (instead of a single state s' as in a classical MDP). So the above $min(S')$ and $max(S')$ are replaced by:

$$\underline{R}(S,a,S') = min_{s,s'}(R(s,a,s')|s \in S, s' \in S')$$

and

$$\overline{R}(S,a,S') = max_{s,s'}(R(s,a,s')|s \in S, s' \in S')$$

In the Bellman equation, then, the value $\mathcal{V}$ (expected immediate reward) will be replaced by an interval whose bounds are calculated as follows:

$$\underline{\mathcal{V}}(S) = \sum_{S'\in\mathcal{F}} Q(S,a,S')\underline{R}(S,a,S') \text{ and } \overline{\mathcal{V}}(S) = \sum_{S'\in\mathcal{F}} Q(S,a,S')\overline{R}(S,a,S')$$

We obtain the following bounds for V, extending the infinite-horizon Bellman equation:

$$\underline{V}(S) = \underline{\mathcal{V}}(S)+\gamma \sum_{S'\in\mathcal{F}} Q(S,a,S')\underline{V}(S') \text{ and } \overline{V}(S) = \overline{\mathcal{V}}(S)+\gamma \sum_{S'\in\mathcal{F}} Q(S,a,S')\overline{V}(S') \quad (2)$$

V is the so-called *value function* that is to be maximized in all Bellman equations (it is in fact the total expected cumulated reward). V is updated by the expected immediate reward $\mathcal{V}$ with the discounting factor γ. Note that the value function is characterized for each focal set $S \in \mathcal{F}$; thus the policy that will be determined from it is also a function of S.

The proposed solving method. For determining an optimal policy, one can choose between maximizing the lower bound of the value function or maximizing its upper bound. The corresponding algorithms will be named the *maxmin* and the *maxmax*, as for the MDPIP [14]). To do that, we propose to use the policy iteration method. It was described in Section 2.1 for a MDP. To generalize it to an EMDP, here is the proposed method:

- at step 0, the initial policy π_0 can be initialized arbitrarily such that $\pi_0(S) \in A$, and the value $\underline{V}(S)$ (or $\overline{V}(S)$) is initialized as zero, for all $S \in \mathcal{F}$;
- at step n, we have the policy π_n and the value function is $\underline{V}_n(S)$ (for the maxmin) or $\overline{V}_n(S)$ (for the maxmax) for each $S \in \mathcal{F}$;
- for the maxmin algorithm, $\pi_{n+1}(S)$ will be the action a which maximizes

$$\underline{V}_a(S) = \sum_{S'\in\mathcal{F}} Q(S,a,S')\left(\underline{R}(S,a,S') + \gamma\underline{V}_n(S')\right).$$

- for the maxmax algorithm, $\pi_{n+1}(S)$ will be the action a which maximizes

$$\overline{V}_a(S) = \sum_{S' \in \mathcal{F}} Q(S, a, S') \left(\overline{R}(S, a, S') + \gamma \overline{V}_n(S') \right).$$

- for the maxmin (resp. maxmax), this maximal value $\underline{V}_{\underline{\pi}_{n+1}(S)}(S)$ (resp. $\overline{V}_{\overline{\pi}_{n+1}(S)}(S)$) is denoted as $\underline{V}_{n+1}(S)$ (resp. $\overline{V}_{n+1}(S)$).
- more generally, one can choose a linear combination between the minimum and the maximum value; $\pi_{n+1}(S)$ will be the action a which maximizes $\alpha \underline{V}_a(S) + \beta \overline{V}_a(S)$.

The algorithm is described in Table 1.

Table 1. Policy iteration algorithm so solve an EMDP. For example, $\alpha = 1$ and $\beta = 0$ is the maximin; $\alpha = 0$ and $\beta = 1$ is the maximax.

Policy iteration algorithm for solving an EMDP

---

for all $(S, a, S') \in \mathcal{F} \times A \times \mathcal{F}$ do
$\quad R(S, a, S') = \alpha \underline{R}(S, a, S') + \beta \overline{R}(S, a, S')$
$n \leftarrow 0$
initialize π_0 (arbitrarily)
initialize $V_0(S) = 0$ foa all $S \in \mathcal{F}$
repeat
$\quad$ for all $S \in \mathcal{F}$ do
$\qquad v(S, a) = \sum_{S' \in \mathcal{F}} Q(S, a, S')(R(S, a, S') + \gamma V_n(S))$
$\qquad \pi_{n+1}(S) \in argmax_{a \in A} v(S, a)$
$\qquad V_{n+1}(S) = v(S, \pi_{n+1}(S))$
$\quad n \leftarrow n + 1$
until $\| V_{n+1} - V_n \| \leq \varepsilon$

Proposition 1. *The policy iteration algorithm proposed in Table 1 for solving EMDPs converges towards an optimal policy.*

Proof. This is true because we constructed a new reward $R(S, a, S') = \alpha \underline{R}(S, a, S') + \beta \overline{R}(S, a, S')$ wich is defined on $\mathcal{F} \times A \times \mathcal{F}$. So we defined a classical MDP on the new space $\mathcal{F}$ instead of the initial state space Ω. Solving the EMDP is thus equivalent to solving this new classical MDP. It is known [11] that the policy iteration algorithm converges towards an optimal policy in classical MDPs. ∎

Note that there are two other classical methods to solve classical MDPs: first, the value iteration method, which is another dynamic programming algorithm (and which must converge in the case of the EMDP for the same reason as the policy iteration). And there is also the linear programming method; its generalization can raise problems of convergence because of dynamical inconsistency [9].

4   Illustrative Example

This section provides an example of a planning problem, the search-and-rescue (SAR) benchmark. It was proposed at The Sixth International Planning Competition organized by the International Conference on Automated Planning and Scheduling in 2008. It consists of an unmanned rotorcraft which has to land near somebody to be rescued, as described by Teichteil [21], who has proposed algorithms to solve this type of problem [19,20,12,22]. It is a purely probabilistic MDP problem that we will modify to build an EMDP. This is why we did not do the competition.

4.1   Context of the Application Example

A search-and-rescue unmanned rotorcraft has to check a wounded person and to bring him back to its base. At the beginning of the mission, one knows that there is a survivor in a given area. The rotorcraft performs a first flight at high altitude on the overall area in order to locate, thanks to its imaging sensors, the zones where it could possibly try to land [21].

Then, the rotorcraft will perform its mission: it starts from its base, it flies towards one zone, and it explores it in order to know whether it is landable or not. Then it can fly towards another zone or land (if it is landable). When it is on ground, the survivor has to climb into the rotorcraft by himself, but he will not succeed systematically. If he fails, the rotorcraft can try another zone. At each stage, the survivor has a probability to die. If the survivor is on-board, or if he is dead, the mission ends and the rotorcraft goes back to its base. Figure 1 shows the overview of the area, the rotorcraft, the base and the zones.

Fig. 1. Overview of the area for a search-and-rescue unmanned rotorcraft which must check a survivor. Three zones where it could possibly land are displayed.

As any PDDL[2] benchmark, the model is split in two parts: on one hand the application domain description which includes all possible generic actions (state transitions functions) and on the other hand a problem scenario which specify an init state and a

---

[2] Planning Domain Description Language.

set of goals to reach. For the competition, the domain came with 20 instance scenarios with a varying number of zones. This number multiplies the combinations, the objective being to test the scaling up of the candidate planner.

Description of the model. We describe here the model obtained after a preprocessing of the IPC benchmark. It consist in some simplifications, which consist of merging states, lead to a reduced number of states and combined actions; for example, we merged the states corresponding to the action land and the action take off because after landing there is no other possible action.

The exhaustive list of all the possible resulting states is described in Table 2. We choose $N_z = 2$ zones, so there are 23 states. We denote as (i, x_1, x_2) the state where the rotorcraft is located at zone $i \in \{1, 2\}$ and the status of each zone $j \in \{1, 2\}$ is x_j.

The initial model is a classical MDP. We have modified it to obtain an EMDP. So, the system behavior will be slightly different. Here the focal sets have been defined as a function of the answer to the questions: "is the rotorcraft located to a landable place? Or to an unexplored place?". We obtain the following $N_a = 8$ actions:

- take off, goto unexplored
- explore
- land, take off
- goto unexplored
- goto landable
- goto unlandable
- goto base, land
- end-mission

With this reasoning, we obtain $N_f = 14$ focal sets. They are listed with the resulting policy in Table 3. It is important to notice that their interpretation can be independent from the number of zones. The focal sets transition matrix Q appears also in this Table. The reward matrix is extracted directly from the benchmark data.

Table 2. The system states in the SAR domain

STATE	DESCRIPTION
A_0	At base, on ground human alive, but not on-board
(i, x_1, x_2) with cases: $x_j = 0$ $x_j = 1$ $x_j = 2$	at zone i with: zone j not explored zone j nlandable zone j nnot landable human alive but not on board
B	not at base, human alive and on-board
C	not at base, human dead
S	at base, success (human rescued)
F	at base, failure (human dead)

Table 3. Policy obtained with the maxmin algorithm on the EMDP derived from the SAR model

Current	Action	Next	Probability
(A0)	take off, goto unexplored	((1, 0, 0) (2, 0, 0))	1.00
((1, 0, 0) (2, 0, 0))	explore	((1, 1, 0) (2, 0, 1))	0.70
		((1, 2, 0) (2, 0, 2))	0.30
((1, 1, 0) (2, 0, 1))	land, take off	((1, 2, 0) (2, 0, 2))	0.16
		(B)	0.64
		(C)	0.20
((1, 2, 0) (2, 0, 2))	explore	((1, 1, 0) (2, 0, 1))	0.70
		((1, 2, 0) (2, 0, 2))	0.30
(B)	goto base, land	(S)	0.76
		(F)	0.24
(C)	goto base, land	(F)	1.00
(S)	end-mission	(S)	1.00
(F)	end-mission	(F)	1.00

4.2   Obtained Results

With the maxmin algorithm we obtained the policy in Table 3. There are some focal sets that are never reached. They correspond to the case where the rotorcraft is at one zone and the other one is not unexplored (so it has already been to it).

Note that in this policy, the rotorcraft never goes to the other zone (except at the beginning). The action "goto" is not used between the zones.

With the maxmax algorithm we obtained a policy which is different from the policy provided by the maxmin algorithm. But after removing all the focal sets that are never reached, the final result becomes identical (in this example; but this was not always true for other examples we tested).

Conclusion about the results.   The number of states N_x increases exponentially with the number of zones N_z since it is:

$$N_x = 5 + N_z \times 3^{N_z}$$

The policy we obtained shows that it is more interesting to explore again the place where we are than to move to another place. One could guess this result since moving to another place and exploring, are actions which provide no reward but they are time consuming, so they decrease the value of the Bellman equation because of the γ factor.

Extension to a large number of zones.   As it was explained above, the focal sets of the proposed EMDP models have an interpretation which is mostly independent of the number of zones. So, for any number of zones N_z, one can propose the following focal sets:

- the 5 singletons containing A0, B, C, S an F, as listed in Table 3;
- all the sets defined by 3 parameters: a status with 3 possibilities: (0) the rotorcraft is at an unexplored zone, or (1) it is at a landable zone, or (2) at an unlandable zone; the number N_u of unexplored zones; the number N_l of landable zones.

One has the condition $N_u + N_l \leq N_z$. The number of unlandable zones is $N_z - N_u - N_l$. So, the total number of sets is

$$5 + 3 \times \frac{N_z(N_z + 1)}{2} - 3$$

This is proportional to the complexity of the corresponding EMDP. It grows with N_z in a polynomial way. So, even if the implementation results have been tested only for $N_z = 2$ in this work, we know that it is theoretically possible to reach a large number of zones without excessive complexity. We can even guess that the conclusion of the obtained policy is that, in this particular SAR example, the rotorcraft will still have better interest in exploring again the zone where it is rather than going to another zone.

In these results, the algorithm was usually implemented with the discounting factor $\gamma = 0.8$. Trials with a smaller value for γ showed that the solution never converges towards the goal (e.g. the search-and-rescue rotorcraft turns and turns but never tries to rescue the survivor). This is because the memory depth is not sufficient in this case. Generally, when γ is too small, the rewards provided by the possible future states are penalized by their delay since they receive a coefficient γ^n where n is the number of time steps of delay.

5 Conclusion

We proposed the EMDP model which generalizes the MDP to the belief functions, in a more general sense than MDPSTs. In the EMDP model the rewards are defined for the states themselves but the transition matrix is defined for sets of states. With this new model we introduced, we proposed an algorithm and a formalism to solve it. It uses the policy iteration method in which we adapted the infinite-horizon Bellman equation by calculating two bounds. The solving method has been tested. The obtained results on an EMDP model constructed from a search-and-rescue problem correspond to the common sense, so they show the feasibility of the EMDP model. A complementary work have been proposed [1] for the search-and-rescue application to translate the inaccuracies about the survivor location into belief functions. This approach can be associated to an EMDP.

We showed that our EMDP solving method converges since it corresponds to an equivalent MDP in the space of the focal sets; anyway the EMDP brings an operational interest, in comparison to the classical MDP, which is to get the benefits of the belief functions: it allows us to cope with imprecise data, particularly if they are extracted from textual observations. The EMDP model is more inaccurate than a MDP, so it should be more robust and also the learning of the model should be faster. In fact when we construct an EMDP model by modifying a MDP we obtain a different behavioi (e.g. actions may become possible, or impossible, for some states); one could study in further work how to find good criteria for the comparison between the MDP and EMDP model. One other interesting property is that it allows us to handle large subsets of states that have similar properties; this allows us to reduce considerably the complexity in some planning problems. For example, in the search-and-rescue application, the number of handled focal sets is independent of the actual number of possible landing zones.

For further work, one could study the finite-horizon case. And of course, there remains also an interesting topic of research this paper did not tackle with: how to perform the learning of an EMDP model. Since reinforcement learning techniques are probabilistic, it will be interesting to study their generalization to belief functions.

References

1. Doré, P.-E., Martin, A., Abi-Zeid, I., Jousselme, A.-L., Maupin, P.: Belief functions induced by multimodal probability density functions, an application to search and rescue pronlem. RAIRO Operations Research 44 (October-December 2010)
2. Ferson, S., Kreinovich, V., Ginzburg, L., Myers, D.S., Sentz, K.: Constructing probability boxes and Dempster-Shafer structures. Sand report no sand2002-4015, Sandia National Laboratories, Albuquerque, New Mexico and Livermore, California (January 2003)
3. Fouque, L., Appriou, A., Pieczynski, W.: An evidential Markovian model for data fusion and unsupervised image classification. In: Proc. of 3rd Int. Conf. on Information Fusion (FUSION), Paris, France, pp. YuB4-25–TuB4-31, July 10-13 (2000)
4. Geffner, H.: Planning under uncertainty: a survey. In: Ghallab, M., Hertzberg, J., Traverso, P. (eds.) Proc. of 6th Int. Conf. on Artificial Intelligence Planning Syst (AIPS), Toulouse, France, April 23-27 (2002)
5. Givan, R., Leach, S., Dean, T.: Bounded-parameter Markov decision processes. In: Steel, S. (ed.) ECP 1997. LNCS, vol. 1348, pp. 234–246. Springer, Heidelberg (1997)
6. Harmanec, D.: Generalizing Markov decision processes to imprecise probabilities. J. Stat. Planning and Inference 105, 199–213 (2002)
7. Lanchantin, P., Pieczynski, W.: Unsupervised restoration of hidden nonstationary Markov chains using evidential priors. IEEE Trans. on Signal Processing 53, 3091–3098 (2005)
8. Perny, P., Spanjaard, O., Weng, P.: Algebraic Markov decision processes. In: Proc. of the 19th IJCAI, Edinburgh, Scotland, July 30-August 5, pp. 1372–1377 (2005)
9. Perny, P., Weng, P.: On finding compromise solutions in multiobjective Markov decision processes. In: Porc. of 5th Multidisciplinary M-PREF Workshop on Advances in Preference Handling (ECAI 2010), Lisbon, Portugal, August 2010, pp. 55–60 (2010)
10. Pieczynski, W.: Multisensor triplet Markov chain and theory of evidence. Int. J. Approximate Reasoning 45, 1–16 (2007)
11. Puterman, M.L.: Markov Decision Processes. Wiley, New York (1994)
12. Rachelson, E., Teichteil, F., Garcia, F.: XMDP: un modèle de planification temporelle dans l'incertain á actions paramétriques. Journées Françaises Planification Décision Apprentissage (2007)
13. Sabbadin, R.: Une Approche Ordinale de la Decision dans l'Incertain: Axiomatisation, Representation Logique et Application à la Décision Séquentielle. Ph.d. thesis, Université Paul Sabatier, Toulouse, France (December 1998)
14. Satia, J.K., Lave, R.E.: MDPs with uncertain transition probabilities. Operations Research 21, 728–740 (1970)
15. Schmeidler, D.: Subjective probability and expected utility without additivity. Econometrica 57, 571–587 (1989)

16. Shafer, G.: A Mathematical Theory of Evidence. Princeton Univ. Press, Princeton (1976)
17. Soubaras, H.: An Evidential Measure of Risk in Evidential Markov Chains. In: Sossai, C., Chemello, G. (eds.) ECSQARU 2009. LNCS, vol. 5590, pp. 863–874. Springer, Heidelberg (2009)
18. Soubaras, H.: Probabilistic and non-probabilistic measures of risk in Markov-type systems for Planning under Uncertainty. Ph.d. thesis, Télécom ParisTech, France, January 21 (2011)
19. Teichteil-Konigsbuch, F., Fabiani, P.: An hybrid probabilistic model for autonomous exploration. In: Proc. of 20th RFIA (2004)
20. Teichteil-Konigsbuch, F., Fabiani, P.: Symbolic heuristic policy iteration algorithms for structured decision-theoretic exploration problems. In: Proc. of Workshop WS6 of ICAPS 2005, Monterye, CA, June 6-10 (2005)
21. Teichteil-Konigsbuch, F., Fabiani, P.: A multi-thread decisional architecture for real-time planning under uncertaint. In: Proc. of 3rd Workshop on Planning and Plan Execution for Real-World Syst., September 22 (2007)
22. Teichteil-Konigsbuch, F., Infantes, G.: MDP hybrides sans intégration analytique en utilisant régression, échantillonnage et mises-à-jour locales. In: Proc. of JFPDA (April 2009)
23. Trevizan, F.W., Cozman, F.G., de Barros, L.N.: Planning under risk and Knightian uncertainty. In: Proc. of 20th IJCAI, Hyderabad, India, January 6-12, pp. 2023–2028 (2007)
24. Trevizan, F.W., Cozman, F.G., de Barros, L.N.: Mixed probabilistic and nondeterministic factored planning through Markov decision processes with set-valued transitions. In: Proc. of 18th Int. Conf. on Automated Planning and Scheduling (ICAPS), Sydney, Australia, September 14-18 (2008)
25. Walley, P.: Statistical Reasoning With Imprecise Probabilities. Chapman & Hall, New York (1991)

Continuous Belief Functions to Qualify Sensors Performances

Pierre-Emmanuel Doré[1], Christophe Osswald[1], Arnaud Martin[2],
Anne-Laure Jousselme[3], and Patrick Maupin[3]

[1] E^3I^2, ENSTA Bretagne, 2 rue François Verny 29806 Brest Cedex 9, France
{pierre-emmanuel.dore,christophe.osswald}@ensta-bretagne.fr
[2] IRISA, Université de Rennes 1, Lannion, France
arnaud.martin@univ-rennes1.fr
[3] R & D Defence Canada - Valcartier, Decision Support Systems for Command and
Control (DSS-C2) section, 2459 Pie XI North, Quebec, QC, G3J 1X5, Canada
{Anne-Laure.Jousselme,Patrick.Maupin}@drdc-rddc.gc.ca

Abstract. In this paper, we deal with the problem of sensor performance estimation. As we assume that the sensor is described with only
few data, we decide to use the theory of belief functions to represent the
inherent uncertainty of our information. Hence, we introduce the belief
functions framework, especially in the continuous approach. We describe
the model of sensor adopted in our study. Knowing the experimental
setting, we suggest an approach to model the sources of information describing our sensor. Finally, we combine these sources in order to estimate
sensor performances.

Keywords: Sensor performances, Continuous belief function, Parametric model, Inference, Fusion.

1 Introduction

The theory of belief functions has been introduced by the famous works of
A. Dempster about upper and lower probabilities [3,4] and those of G. Shafer [13]
on the theory of evidence. The work of Ph. Smets [14] contributed to spread it in
the scientific community. Recently, thanks to new breakthroughs [18,12,15,16,2],
the application of belief functions on continuous framework has gained some
interest. Hence, we apply these results to describe sensor performances.

Wireless sensors networks are more and more used in monitoring applications
[11,9]. One crucial issue in this domain is the sensors placement. Indeed, the aim
is to place the sensors in order to maximize the chance to detect an intrusion.
To fulfil this objective, we have to characterize the performances of a sensor
as a detector. To estimate the performance of a sensor, we adopt a parametric
approach. As we only have a small amount of measures to define it, we decide to
use the belief function framework to take into account the lack of information.

In a first part (section 2), we present the theory of belief function within
a continuous frame of discernment. Then, we introduce a parametric model

W. Liu (Ed.): ECSQARU 2011, LNAI 6717, pp. 350–361, 2011.

describing sensor performances (section 3). As we have few data, we present some results obtained by A. Dempster and we suggest an approach funded on the maximum necessity and likelihood principles to the estimate the parameters describing the sensor performances (section 4). Hence, considering that the experimental settings provide us three cognitive independant sources of informations (we take measures in three different places), we merge their respective beliefs about the value of the sensor parameters (section 5). Finally, we analyse our results in section 6. Thanks to these operations, we are able to characterize more accurately the sensor performances.

2   Belief Function Framework

The theory of belief functions is a tool used to represent the imperfection of a source of information. There are many kinds of imperfection a belief function can describe such as ignorant, vagueness, uncertainty, ... The purpose of this section is to recall some useful parts of this theory.

2.1   Belief on Real Numbers

In [15], Ph. Smets describes an approach of belief functions on real number. He suggests to assign mass on the intervals of $\overline{\mathbb{R}} = \mathbb{R} \cup \{-\infty, \infty\}$. There is a lot of advantage to procede in this way. Indeed, we can easily associate a basic belief density on $\overline{\mathbb{R}}$ to a probability density function on $\overline{\mathbb{R}}^2$. However, this framework is quite restrictive and we cannot use it to describe belief function with basic belief assignement on unconnected sets. In a previous work [6], we suggest to scan the set of focal elements (the subset of $\overline{\mathbb{R}}$ whose the basic belief assignement is not null), $\mathcal{F}$, using an index function f and a specific index space I.

$$f^I : I \longrightarrow \mathcal{F}$$
$$y \longmapsto f^I(y) \tag{1}$$

With this index function, we consider a positive measure[1] μ^Ω such as $\int_I d\mu^\Omega(y) \leqslant 1$.

Hence, to define a belief function, we have to consider the pair (f^I, μ^Ω). In order to compute belief functions, we need to define for all A in $\mathcal{P}(\Omega)$ (a family of subset of Ω):

$$F_{\subseteq A} = \{y \in I | f^I(y) \subseteq A\} \tag{2}$$

$$F_{\cap A} = \{y \in I | (f^I(y) \cap A) \neq \varnothing\} \tag{3}$$

$$F_{\supseteq A} = \{y \in I | A \subseteq f^I(y)\} \tag{4}$$

Once these subsets are defined, we can compute the following belief functions:

- The belief function:

$$bel^\Omega(A) = \int_{F_{\subseteq A}} d\mu^\Omega(y) \tag{5}$$

---

[1] For the sake of simplicity, it happens we considers that $d\mu^\Omega(y) = m^\Omega(f^I(y))$.

− The plausibility function:

$$pl^\Omega(A) = \int_{F \cap A} d\mu^\Omega(y) \tag{6}$$

− The communality function:

$$q^\Omega(A) = \int_{F \supseteq A} d\mu^\Omega(y) \tag{7}$$

In this framework, we define some basic tools. One of them is the conjunctive rule of combination which allow us to merge sources of information. Let (f_1^I, μ_1^Ω) and (f_2^I, μ_2^Ω) two belief functions. The conjunctive rule of combination [17] brings the belief function $\left(f_{1 \bigcirc 2}^I, \mu_{1 \bigcirc 2}^\Omega \right)$ [6] such that:

$$q_{1 \bigcirc 2}^\Omega(A) = q_1^\Omega(A) \cdot q_2^\Omega(A) \tag{8}$$

Within this framework, we will study a particular type of belief functions, the consonant ones.

A consonant belief function is a belief function whose the focal sets are nested. This allows us to create a total ordering on $\mathcal{F}$ linked to the $\subseteq$ relation. Hence, we can define an index function f from $\mathbb{R}^+$, to $\mathcal{F}$ such as $(y \geqslant x) \Longrightarrow (f(y) \subseteq f(x))$ [15]. To generate consonant sets, we can use g, a continuous function from $\mathbb{R}^n$ to $I = [0, \alpha_{max}] \subset \mathbb{R}^+$. The α-cuts of g are the set such as:

$$f_{cs}^I(\alpha) = \{ x \in \mathbb{R}^n | g(x) \geqslant \alpha \} \tag{9}$$

We have the property that $F_{\subseteq A}^{cs}$ is an element of Borel algebra. Indeed:

$$F_{\subseteq A}^{cs} \neq \varnothing \Rightarrow \exists \alpha_{\inf} = \inf \{ \alpha \in I | f_{cs}^I(\alpha) \cap A \neq \varnothing \} \\ \Rightarrow F_{\subseteq A}^{cs} = |\alpha_{\inf}, \alpha_{\max}] \tag{10}$$

Using a similar argument, we can prove that $F_{\supseteq A}^{cs}$ and $F_{\cap A}^{cs}$ are elements of Borel algebra. Hence, we can define the index function:

$$\begin{aligned} f_{cs}^I : I = [0, \alpha_{\max}] &\longrightarrow \{ f_{cs}^I(\alpha) | \alpha \in I \} \\ \alpha &\longmapsto f_{cs}^I(\alpha) \end{aligned} \tag{11}$$

If we consider a probability measure $\mu^{\mathbb{R}^n}$ on $\mathcal{I}$, the brace $\left(f_{cs}^I, \mu^{\mathbb{R}^n} \right)$ refers to a belief function.

2.2 Maximum of Necessity

When we work with an "objective" source of information, we can apply the principle of maximum of necessity. This principle comes from the theory of possibility [7,8,10]. The theory of possibility is a particular case of the theory of belief functions (focal elements are always nested). In this situation, the plausibility corresponds to possibility distribution and we consider the necessity which

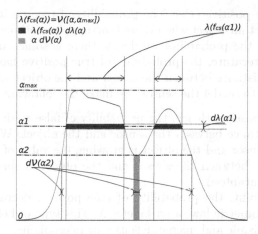

Fig. 1. How to build belief functions from a probability density function $Betf$

corresponds to the belief function. The idea is to work with the most informative distribution of possibility (for the necessity ordering) which fulfils the following assumptions. The first one is that the possibility dominates the probability, *i.e.* for all A measurable $\Pi(A) \geqslant P(A)$. The second one is that the ordering must be kept, *i.e.* $P(A) \geqslant P(A') \Leftrightarrow \Pi(A) \geqslant \Pi(A')$.

These conditions can be transposed in the framework of belief functions [10]. Finding a belief function which verifies these properties is equivalent to find a nested focal sets family such as for all A belonging to this family, A is the smallest set (for the inclusion ordering) such as $P(A) = \beta$. This sets family corresponds to the confidence sets in theory of probability. If we have as input a continuous probability density function $Betf$, the focal set $\left(f_{cs}^I(\alpha)\right)$ is the α-cuts of $Betf$. We obtain a belief function defined by $\left(f_{cs}^I, \mu^{\mathcal{B}}(\mathbb{R})\right)$ such as if we adapt the result of [10], we obtain [6] (*cf.* figure 1):

$$pl^{\mathcal{B}}(\mathbb{R})(x) = 1 - BetP\left(f_{cs}^I(Betf(x))\right) \tag{12}$$

i.e.[2]:

$$d\mu^{\mathbb{R}}(\alpha) = \alpha dV(\alpha) \text{ with } V([\alpha, \alpha_{\max}]) = \lambda\left(f_{cs}^I(\alpha)\right) \tag{13}$$

Within this framework, we can build belief functions on real number with complex focal sets. In most of the cases, the information given by a sensor is represented with a probability distribution. However, it happens we do not have enough information to precizely define a distribution of probability. A belief function can be useful to take this phenomenom into account.

3   Model of Sensor

We consider in this paper that a sensor is a detector. Each detector is defined using two caracteristic measures, the probability of true positive (P_t) and the

---

[2] λ refers to the Lebegue's measure.

probability of false positive (P_f). The probability of true positive is the probability that we detect an object when there is actually something. The probability of false positive is the probability we decide there is something when there is nothing. In the litterature, the probability of true positive has been defined as a function of the distance between the sensor and the object we want to detect. In our study case, to model the sensor, we make the following assumptions:

1. The sensor is passive. Hence, the probability of false positive is not a function of the distance between the sensor and the object. When the distance between the sensor and the object is growing, the value of P_t tends to P_f.
2. If the distance between the sensor and the object is smaller than α, the detection is guaranteed.
3. Beyond this point, the probability of true positive decreases such as the inverse of a geometric law of parameter λ. This type of behaviour has been observed on seismic and magnetic sensor or microphone.

Hence, the following equation describes the probability of detection according a distance d between the sensor and the target, the parameters α, λ and P_f:

$$P_t(d) = \begin{cases} 1 & \text{if } d \leqslant \alpha \\ \alpha^\lambda \cdot \dfrac{1 - P_f}{d^\lambda} + P_f & \text{otherwise} \end{cases} \qquad (14)$$

This is a trade off between the Elfe's model [9] and the geometric model of sensors [11]. The shape of the sensor coverage (the probability of true positive according the distance) described in equation (14) is represented in figure 2.

We will estimate the coverage of a sensor, using our parametric model, when we dispose of only a small amount of measures.

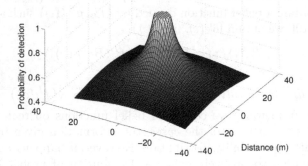

Fig. 2. Probability of detection on a grid. The sensor position defines the origin of our coordinates ($\alpha = 4$, $\lambda = 0.5$, $P_f = 0.15$).

4   Belief Functions Induced by Sampling

The size of the sample set is not large enough to define precizely a distribution of probability. As measure prospecting is an expensive process, we have to find a way to describe imprecise knowlegde on true and false positive probabilities using a small sample set. We will apply our work to the estimation of the sensor performances.

4.1 Experimental Settings

In order to illustrate our work, we assume we monitor vehicles moving on three roads at different distances of the sensor (*cf.* figure 3). In each case, we have

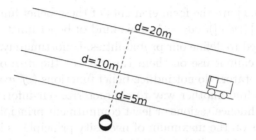

Fig. 3. The experimental setting

obtained a different empirical value of the probability of detection according the distance. The generic values used in our work are described in table 1.

Table 1. Generic values

Distance sensor/vehicule d	number of test n	number of detection k
5 m	20	18
10 m	20	14
20 m	20	10

As we work on a small amount of data, the estimates of probabilities of true positive are imprecise. In fact, a family of probability distibutions can fit with the data we obtain. The theory of belief functions is an efficient framework to represent a family of probability distributions. Hence, we present some methods to model information induced by a small learning set in the belief functions framework.

4.2 The Dempster's Approach

The first motive of Dempster [5] when he developed the theory of upper and lower probabilities was to propose a mathematical framework to model statistical inference. One of his main results in this domain concerns the binomial sampling. When we have a small amount of samples following a binomial law, it is impossible to precizely define the parameter p of this law. Hence we define a set of distributions of probability using belief functions theory. Let $\mathcal{P}$ be the interval $[0, 1]$ which describes the parameter p of a binomial law. Let n be the size of the sample set and k be the number of samples belonging to one of the two classes of the binomial sampling. We obtain a conditional belief function $m^{\mathcal{P}}$ on the value of p over $\mathcal{P}$ knowing n and k [5] :

$$
\begin{aligned}
m^{\mathcal{P}}[n, k]([u, v]) &= \frac{n!}{(k-1)!(n-k-1)!} u^{k-1}(1-v)^{n-k-1} & 0 < k < n \\
m^{\mathcal{P}}[n, k]([0, v]) &= n(1-v)^{n-1} & k = 0 \\
m^{\mathcal{P}}[n, k]([u, 1]) &= nu^{n-1} & k = n
\end{aligned}
\tag{15}
$$

where $[u, v] \subseteq \mathcal{P}[0, 1]$ are the focal elements of these belief functions. We notice that $\int_{[0,1]} m^{\mathcal{P}}[n, k]([u, v]) du dv = 1$. This kind of belief function can model our problem and be used to define our probabilities. Unfortunately, they are difficult to handle and we cannot use on them the max or the min operators. Indeed, generally, these operators do not induce belief functions (*cf.* example in table 2). Hence, we have to find another way to characterize our information. There are methods using confidence regions or least commitment principle [1]. However, in this paper we focus on the maximum of necessity principle as it will sum up the information contained by all the confidence regions in an unique function.

Table 2. The max operator does not induce a belief function

focal elements	$\varnothing$	a	b	c	ab	ac	bc	abc
$m1$	0	0.25	0.11	0.03	0.06	0.10	0.15	0.3
$m2$	0	0.22	0.07	0.04	0.09	0.10	0.13	0.35
$pl1$	0	0.68	0.59	0.94	0.61	0.89	0.75	1
$pl2$	0	0.71	0.59	0.91	0.67	0.93	0.78	1
$pl_{max} = \max(pl1, pl2)$	0	0.71	0.59	0.94	0.67	0.93	0.78	1
m_{max}	0	0.415	0.1723	0.0040	0.1446	0.0923	0.2003	−0.0285

4.3 Likelihood and Maximum of Necessity Principles

As we cannot apply max operator on the belief function defined in equation (15), we decide to use the maximum likelihood principle [14] to define a belief function associated to a binomial sampling. This principle can be resumed as following:

Assuming a likelihood function l, the likelihood of a parameter θ knowing that x is true is equal to the likelihood of x knowing that θ is true.

$$
l[x](\theta) = l[\theta](x)
\tag{16}
$$

The likelihood function l must satisfy several properties. One of them is that the likelihood of a set of hypothesis is higher than the likelihood of its subsets:

$$l\left(\Theta\right) \geqslant l\left(\theta\right), \theta \subseteq \Theta \tag{17}$$

Another one is that the likelihood function must be a sub-additive function:

$$l\left(\theta_A \cup \theta_B\right) \leqslant l\left(\theta_A\right) + l\left(\theta_B\right) \tag{18}$$

Indeed, two disjoint sets of hypothesis can have a likehood equals to 1. Hence, we can use the plausibility as a likehood function. In our study, according the likelihood principle, we obtain for π subset of $\mathcal{P}$ and k in $[\![0,n]\!]$ an equation similar to equation (16):

$$pl\left[n,k\right]\left(\pi\right) = pl\left[n,\pi\right]\left(k\right) \tag{19}$$

Hence we have to define $pl\left[n,\pi\right]\left(k\right)$. The distribution of probability P describing a binomial law of parameter p is equal to :

$$P\left[n,p\right]\left(k\right) = \binom{n}{k} p^k \left(1-p\right)^{n-k}, 0 \leqslant k \leqslant n \tag{20}$$

Applying the maximum of necessity principle to this distribution of probability [8], we define a consonant continuous belief function $pl\left[n,p\right]$. This one is entirely described by his contour function computed using algorithm 1. In parametric models, data are highly dependant, hence we prefer not to use a conjunctive rule to merge source of information but a disjunctive one:

$$pl\left[n,k\right]\left(\pi\right) = pl\left[n,\pi\right]\left(k\right) = \max_{p\in\pi}\left(pl\left[n,p\right]\left(k\right)\right) \tag{21}$$

Result: Plausibility of p for a given pair (n,k).
$tmp = 0$;
$M = \binom{n}{k} p^k \left(1-p\right)^{n-k}$;
for $i \in [0,n]$ **do**
$\quad$ $P\left[n,p\right]\left(i\right) = \binom{n}{i} p^i \left(1-p\right)^{n-i}$;
$\quad$ **if** $P\left[n,p\right]\left(i\right) \leqslant M$ **then**
$\quad\quad$ | $tmp = tmp + P\left[n,p\right]\left(i\right)$;
$\quad$ **end**
end
$pl\left[n,p\right]\left(k\right) = tmp$; // maximum of necessity principle.
$pl\left[n,k\right]\left(p\right) = pl\left[n,p\right]\left(k\right)$; // likelihood principle.

Algorithm 1. How to compute plausibility of p knowing (n,k)

5 Combination of Information

We have previously defined belief functions to describe the plausibility of P_t and P_f for given values of d. As we want to define these probabilities on the whole space, we have, using the model of sensor described by equation (14), to infer the plausibility of the 3-tuplet (α, k, P_f).

5.1 Independant Sources of Information

Using table 1 and algorithm 1, we can define $pl_d^P(P_t)$. Thanks to the sensor model (*cf.* equation (14)), we can associate for each distance d of measure a 3-tuplet (α, k, P_f) to a given probability of true positive P_t. Let $\mathcal{T}$ be the parameter framework. If we assume that the plausibility of the 3-tuplet is equal to the one of P_t, we can do the following operation which corresponds to a mass transfert:

$$pl_d^{\mathcal{T}}(\alpha, \lambda, P_f) = pl_d^P(P_t) \tag{22}$$

The experiments which lead us to define P_t for given distances d are cognitively independent. Hence we can merge these different sources of information using the conjective rule of combination[17]. As we use consonant belief functions, this operation can be written:

$$pl^{\mathcal{T}}(\alpha, \lambda, P_f) = \prod_{d \in \{5,10,20\}} pl_d^{\mathcal{T}}(\alpha, \lambda, P_f) \tag{23}$$

Hence, we assume that all the sources of information are relevant and reliable.

5.2 Inference Using the Max

For a given distance d and probability of true positive (P_t), there is, according the sensor model described in equation (14), a set $\mathcal{D}$ of 3-tuples (α, λ, P_f) matching. As we know the plausibility of each 3-tuples in $\mathcal{D}$, we should be able to compute the plausibility of P_t. However, if we use the likelihood principle and set:

$$pl_d^P(P_t) = pl^{\mathcal{T}}(\mathcal{D}) \tag{24}$$

we obtain an inextricable equation. Indeed, after combination, the plausibility function described in equation (23) is not consonant anymore. Then, we cannot derive the plausibility function from the contour function. Hence, we decide to define a consonant plausibility function such that its contour function fulfil this condition:

$$pl_d^P(P_t) = \max_{(\alpha, \lambda, P_f) \in \mathcal{D}} pl^{\mathcal{T}}(\alpha, \lambda, P_f) \tag{25}$$

In this case, this belief function is more specific than the one we would obtain using equation (24). However, as the plausibility of each 3-tuple is built using a singleton P_t of $\mathcal{P}$, it can be considered like a good trade-off.

The algorithm 2 sums up all the results obtained in section 5 and helps us to compute the plausibity to detect an object at a given distance of the sensor.

Data: *cf.* table 1
Result: Plausibility function of P_t for a given distance d
initialization;
for $C_i = (\alpha, \lambda, Pf) \in [0 : h : 1] \times [0 : h : 1] \times [0 : h : 1]$ **do**
    for $d_j \in \{5, 10, 20\}$ **do**
        $P_{t(i,dj)} = function(C_i, d_j);$ // cf. equation (14)
        $pl^{\mathcal{P}}_{dj}\left(P_{t(i,dj)}\right) = function(n_{dj}, k_{dj}, P_{t(i,dj)});$ // cf. algorithm 1
        $pl^{\mathcal{T}}_{dj}(C_i) = pl^{\mathcal{P}}_{dj}\left(P_{t(i,dj)}\right);$
    end
    $pl^{\mathcal{T}}(C_i) = \prod\limits_{j} pl^{\mathcal{T}}_{dj}(C_i);$
    $P_{t(i,d)} = function(C_i, d);$
end
$\mathcal{D} = \left\{C_i | abs\left(P_{t(i,d)} - P_t\right) \leqslant h\right\};$
$pl^{\mathcal{P}}_d\left(P_t\right) = \max\limits_{C_i in \mathcal{D}} pl^{\mathcal{T}}(C_i)$

Algorithm 2. How to compute plausibility

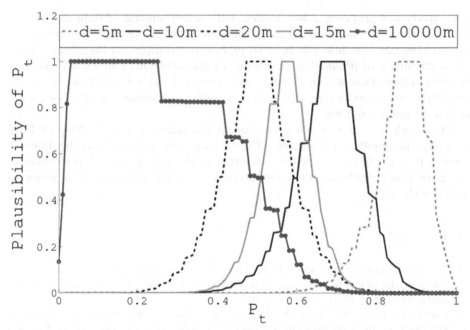

Fig. 4. Plausibilities of P_t for different distances

6   Results

The results of this work appear in figure 4. The curve $d = 5m$ (respectively $d = 10m$ and $d = 20m$), represents the plausibility that the probability of true positive of the sensor is equal to P_f at the distance $d = 5m$ (respectively $d = 10m$ and $d = 20m$). To build this curve, we have only used data given by the table 1 and the reasoning described in the section 4. To plot the other curves, we have used the sensor model described in the section 3 and the combination and inference process suggest in section 5.

We remark three things. Firstly, the plausibility function of P_t when $d = 10000$ could be linked to the one of P_f as P_t tends to P_f when d increases. Indeed, we have assumed that we use a passive sensor. Secondly, the closer the sensor is of our points of measure, the smaller is the peak of the plausibility function of P_t. Hence in this case the estimate of the probability of detection is more accurate. Thirdly, the plausibility functions look like step-wise functions. It is normal as we found the construction of a plausibility function on the binomial law ($\mathcal{B}(n, k)$) which is discrete.

7   Conclusion

This study has proposed a way to deal with small amount of data in order to estimate the performance of a sensor. Continuous belief fonctions have been used in two contexts, the first has been to represent an uncertain knowledge about the distribution of probability describing an phenomenon. The second has been to infer information within a parametric model. In this kind of situation, we are often faced inextricable situation and we have to make our approach more simple to find a solution.

This work is a step to define the coverage a sensor networks. Now we have to study the question a the fusion of the information coming from the different sensors in order to have a better estimation of the global network performance. We have also to include some consideration about the reliability of a sensor to improve the study.

References

1. Aregui, A., Denœux, T.: Constructing consonant belief functions from sample data using confidence sets of pignistic probabilities. International Journal of Approximate Reasoning 49(3), 575–594 (2008)
2. Caron, F., Ristic, B., Duflos, E., Vanheeghe, P.: Least committed basic belief density induced by a multivariate Gaussian: formulation with applications. International Journal of Approximate Reasoning 48(2), 419–436 (2008)
3. Dempster, A.: Upper and lower probabilities induced by a multi-valued mapping. The Annals of Mathematical Statistics 38(2), 325–339 (1967)
4. Dempster, A.: Upper and lower probabilities generated by a random closed interval. The Annals of Mathematical Statistics 39(3), 957–966 (1968)

5. Dempster, A.: A Generalization of Bayesian Inference. Journal of the Royal Statistical Society 2(30), 205–247 (1968)
6. Doré, P.-E., Martin, A.: About using beliefs induced by probabilities. In: Workshop on the Theory of Belief Functions, Brest France (2010)
7. Dubois, D., Prade, H.: The principle of minimum specificity as a basis for evidential reasoning. In: Bouchon, B., Yager, R.R. (eds.) Uncertainty in Knowledge-based Systems, pp. 75–84. Springer, Berlin (1987)
8. Dubois, D., Prade, H., Sandri, S.: On possibility/probability transformations. In: Proceedings of 4th IFSA Conference. Citeseer, pp. 103–112 (1993)
9. Elfes, A.: Occupancy Grids: A Stochastic Spatial Representation for Active Robot Perception. In: Autonomous Mobile Robots: Perception, Mapping, and Navigation, vol. 1, pp. 60–70. IEEE Computer Society Press, Los Alamitos (1991)
10. Mauris, G.: Transformation of bimodal probability distributions into possibility distributions. IEEE Transactions on Instrumentation and Measurement 59(1), 39–47 (2010)
11. Meguerdichian, S., Koushanfar, F., Qu, G., Potkonjak, M.: Exposure in wireless ad-hoc sensor networks. In: Proceedings of the 7th Annual International Conference on Mobile Computing and Networking, pp. 139–150 (2001)
12. Ristic, B., Smets, P.: Belief function theory on the continuous space with an application to model based classification. In: Proceedings of Information Processing and Management of Uncertainty in Knowledge-Based Systems, IPMU, pp. 4–9 (2004)
13. Shafer, G.: A mathematical theory of evidence. Princeton University Press, Princeton (1976)
14. Smets, P.: Belief functions: the disjunctive rule of combination and the generalized Bayesian theorem. International Journal of Approximate Reasoning 9, 1–1 (1993)
15. Smets, P.: Belief functions on real numbers. International Journal of Approximate Reasoning 40(3), 181–223 (2005)
16. Smets, P., Ristic, B.: Kalman filter and joint tracking and classification based on belief functions in the TBM framework. Information Fusion 8(1), 16–27 (2007)
17. Smets, P., Ristic, B.: The combination of evidence in the transferable belief model. IEEE Transactions on Pattern Analysis and Machine Intelligence 12(5), 447–458 (1990)
18. Strat, T.: Continuous belief functions for evidential reasoning. In: Proceedings of the 4th National Conference on Artificial Intelligence, University of Texas at Austin (1984)

Measuring Consistency Gain and Information Loss in Stepwise Inconsistency Resolution

John Grant[1] and Anthony Hunter[2]

[1] Department of Mathematics, Towson University, Towson, MD 21252, USA
and Department of Computer Science, University of Maryland,
College Park, MD 20742, USA
grant@cs.umd.edu
[2] Department of Computer Science, University College London,
Gower Street, London WC1E 6BT, UK
a.hunter@cs.ucl.ac.uk

Abstract. Inconsistency is a usually undesirable feature of many kinds of data and knowledge. But altering the information in order to make it less inconsistent may result in the loss of information. In this paper we analyze this trade-off. We review some existing proposals and make new proposals for measures of inconsistency and information. We prove that in both cases the various measures are all pairwise incompatible. Then we introduce the concept of stepwise inconsistency resolution and show what happens in case an inconsistency resolution step applies a deletion, a weakening, or a splitting operation.

1 Introduction

Inconsistency, and deciding how to deal with it, is a well-recognized problem in many areas of computer science including data and knowledge engineering, software engineering, robotics, and natural language. Often it is not possible to determine with high confidence which items of data or knowledge are incorrect. It might be that to find this out would cost more than the information is actually worth. Or it might be that it is just not possible to acquire this information. In these situations, it may however be useful to delete or update items of information that are involved in inconsistencies based on the nature of those inconsistencies. But since it is often unclear which items of information should be changed, the process of inconsistency resolution can result in a gain in the degree of consistency, but at the price of a loss of information.

In this paper, we propose the use of inconsistency and information measures to take account of this trade-off. We start by investigating what are essential properties of inconsistency and information measures. We propose three requirements in both cases and consider various definitions, mostly ones previously proposed. Each proposal has some rationale, so it is worthwhile to investigate their compatibility with one another. We will show that in a well-defined sense each measure is incompatible with every other measure, and this goes both for inconsistency measures and information measures. These results suggest that there does not exist a single inconsistency measure or information measure that coincides with intuition in general. Nonetheless, the framework

W. Liu (Ed.): ECSQARU 2011, LNAI 6717, pp. 362–373, 2011.

for inconsistency and information measures is potentially useful for choosing measures according to specific applications.

To illustrate some of the key issues in stepwise inconsistency resolution, we consider the following example. Let $K = \{a, \neg a \wedge \neg b \wedge \neg c, b, d\}$. K has two minimal inconsistent subsets: $M_1 = \{a, \neg a \wedge \neg b \wedge \neg c\}$ and $M_2 = \{\neg a \wedge \neg b \wedge \neg c, b\}$; and two maximal consistent subsets $N_1 = \{a, b, d\}$ and $N_2 = \{\neg a \wedge \neg b \wedge \neg c, d\}$. As we want to show how to reduce the inconsistency of K in a stepwise fashion, one formula at a time, we will apply three inconsistency resolution functions: delete a formula, weaken a formula, and split a formula.

- **Deletion.** We delete a formula that is in a minimal inconsistent subset. Thus we can delete either $\neg a \wedge \neg b \wedge \neg c$ or a or b. In the first case, since $\neg a \wedge \neg b \wedge \neg c$ is in both minimal inconsistent subsets, the result is consistent. This is the most drastic of the three options because this operation loses the most information.
- **Weakening.** We change a formula to another formula logically implied by it. Typically, we add a disjunct or change a conjunction to a disjunction. For instance, we can weaken $\neg a \wedge \neg b \wedge \neg c$ to $(\neg a \vee \neg b) \wedge \neg c$ or $\neg a \vee \neg b \vee \neg c$. We can weaken a to $a \vee b$ or even $a \vee \neg a$, and so on. While this operation may reduce the number of minimal inconsistent subsets, the size of the minimal inconsistent subsets may rise, as seen here, where the first weakening results in one minimal inconsistent subset $\{a, (\neg a \vee \neg b) \wedge \neg c, b\}$.
- **Splitting.** We split a formula into its conjuncts. This may isolate the really problematic conjuncts. For instance, we can split $\neg a \wedge \neg b \wedge \neg c$ into $\neg a$, $\neg b$, and $\neg c$. In this case, we get a new knowledgebase $\{a, \neg a, b, \neg b, \neg c, d\}$ that is still inconsistent, though by some inconsistency measures it is less inconsistent. Also, this allows us at a later step to delete just the portion of the conjunction involved in the inconsistency.

In an inconsistent knowledgebase, any formula involved in an inconsistency can be selected for one of the resolution operations (of deletion, weakening or splitting). So there is a question of how to choose a formula and which operation to apply. In general, inconsistency and information measures offer possible answers to this question. Our guiding principle is to minimize information loss while reducing inconsistency as we resolve an inconsistent knowledgebase by stepwise resolution.

2   Preliminary Definitions

We assume a propositional language $\mathcal{L}$ of formulae composed from a set of atoms $\mathcal{A}$ and the logical connectives $\wedge$, $\vee$, $\neg$. We use ϕ and ψ for arbitrary formulae and α and β for atoms. All formulae are assumed to be in conjunctive normal form. Hence every formula ϕ has the form $\psi_1 \wedge \ldots \wedge \psi_n$, where each ψ_i, $1 \leq i \leq n$, has the form $\beta_{i1} \vee \ldots \vee \beta_{im}$, where each β_{ik}, $1 \leq k \leq m$ is a literal (an atom or negated atom). A knowledgebase K is a finite set of formulae. We let $\vdash$ denote the classical consequence relation, and write $K \vdash \perp$ to denote that K is inconsistent. Logical equivalence is defined in the usual way: $K \equiv K'$ iff $K \vdash K'$ and $K' \vdash K$. We find it useful to define also a stronger notion of equivalence we call b(ijection)-equivalence as follows.

α	T	T	T	B	B	B	F	F	F
β	T	B	F	T	B	F	T	B	F
$\alpha \vee \beta$	T	T	T	T	B	B	T	B	F
$\alpha \wedge \beta$	T	B	F	B	B	F	F	F	F
$\neg \alpha$	F	F	F	B	B	B	T	T	T

Fig. 1. Truth table for three valued logic (3VL). This semantics extends the classical semantics with a third truth value, B, denoting "contradictory". Columns 1, 3, 7, and 9, give the classical semantics, and the other columns give the extended semantics.

Knowledgebase K is b(ijection)-equivalent to knowledgebase K', denoted $K \equiv_b K'$ iff there is a bijection $f : K \rightarrow K'$ such that for all $\phi \in K$, ϕ is logically equivalent to $f(\phi)$. For example, $\{a, b\}$ is logically equivalent but not b(ijection)-equivalent to $\{a \wedge b\}$. We write $\mathcal{R}^{\geq 0}$ for the set of nonnegative real numbers and $\mathcal{K}$ for the set of all knowledgebases (in some presumed language $\mathcal{L}$).

For a knowledgebase K, $\text{MI}(K)$ is the set of minimal inconsistent subsets of K, and $\text{MC}(K)$ is the set of maximal consistent subsets of K. Also, if $\text{MI}(K) = \{M_1, ..., M_n\}$ then $\text{Problematic}(K) = M_1 \cup ... \cup M_n$, and $\text{Free}(K) = K \setminus \text{Problematic}(K)$. So $\text{Free}(K)$ contains the formulae in K that are not involved in any inconsistency and $\text{Problematic}(K)$ contains the formulae in K that are involved in at least one inconsistency. The set of formulae in K that are individually inconsistent is given by the function $\text{Selfcontradictions}(K) = \{\phi \in K \mid \{\phi\} \vdash \bot\})$. In the next section we will use these functions in definitions for syntactic measures of inconsistency.

The corresponding semantics uses Priest's three valued logic (3VL) [11] with the classical two valued semantics augmented by a third truth value denoting inconsistency. The truth values for the connectives are defined in Figure 1. An interpretation i is a function that assigns to each atom that appears in K one of three truth values: $i :$ $\text{Atoms}(K) \rightarrow \{F, B, T\}$. For an interpretation i it is convenient to separate the atoms into two groups, namely the ones that are assigned a classical truth value and the ones that are assigned B.

$$\text{Binarybase}(i) = \{\alpha \mid i(\alpha) = T \text{ or } i(\alpha) = F\}$$

$$\text{Conflictbase}(i) = \{\alpha \mid i(\alpha) = B\}$$

For a knowledgebase K we define the models as the set of interpretations where no formula in K is assigned the truth value F: $\text{Models}(K) = \{i \mid \text{ for all } \phi \in K, i(\phi) = T \text{ or } i(\phi) = B\}$ Then, as a measure of inconsistency for K we define

$$\text{Contension}(K) = \text{Min}\{|\text{Conflictbase}(i)| \mid i \in \text{Models}(K)\}$$

So the contension gives the minimal number of atoms that need to be assigned B in order to get a 3VL model of K.

Example 1. For $K = \{a, \neg a, a \vee b, \neg b\}$, there are two models of K, i_1 and i_2, where $i_1(a) = B$, $i_1(b) = B$, $i_2(a) = B$, and $i_2(b) = F$. Therefore, $\text{Conflictbase}(i_1) = 2$ and $\text{Conflictbase}(i_2) = 1$. Hence, $\text{Contension}(K) = 1$.

Finally, we consider some useful definitions based on the notion of implicants. A consistent set of literals X is an **implicant** for a knowledgebase K iff for each $\phi \in K$, $X \vdash \phi$. A minimal implicant is called a **prime implicant**. For example, for $K = \{a, \neg b \lor c\}$, the prime implicants are $X_1 = \{a, \neg b\}$ and $X_2 = \{a, c\}$. A **proxy** for K is a set of literals X such that X is a prime implicant of a maximal consistent subset of K. Let the set of proxies for K (denoted $\mathsf{Proxies}(K)$) be defined as follows.

$$\mathsf{Proxies}(K) = \{X \mid X \text{ is a prime implicant of } K' \in \mathsf{MC}(K)\}$$

For example, for $K = \{a, \neg a, b \lor c\}$, $\mathsf{Proxies}(K) = \{\{a, b\}, \{\neg a, b\}, \{a, c\}, \{\neg a, c\}\}$.

We see that each proxy represents an "interpretation" of the possible literals that hold, and so the number of proxies rises by increasing the number of disjuncts in any formula, and by increasing the number of conflicting formulae. The cardinality of each proxy rises with the amount of information in each alternative, and so adding conjuncts to a formula will increase the size of one or more proxies (as long as the conjunction is consistent).

3   Inconsistency and Information Measures

In this section, we study inconsistency and information measures. We consider both existing and new proposals. Our main result is that for both inconsistency measures and information measures, the various measures are incompatible with one another. This result strongly implies that unlike some other intuitive concepts, such as the concept of effective computability, where different definitions using recursion, λ-calculus, and Turing machines are equivalent, both inconsistency measure and information measure are too elusive to be captured by a single definition. Additionally, for information measures we also consider various plausible constraints and investigate which measures satisfy them.

3.1   Inconsistency Measures for Knowledgebases

An inconsistency measure assigns a nonnegative real value to every knowledgebase. We make three requirements for inconsistency measures. The constraints ensure that all and only consistent knowledgebases get measure 0, the measure is monotonic for subsets, and the removal of a formula that does not participate in an inconsistency leaves the measure unchanged.

Definition 1. *An inconsistency measure* $I : \mathcal{K} \to \mathcal{R}^{\geq 0}$ *is a function such that the following three conditions hold:*

1. *$I(K) = 0$ iff K is consistent.*
2. *If $K \subseteq K'$, then $I(K) \leq I(K')$.*
3. *For all $\alpha \in \mathsf{Free}(K), (I(K) = I(K \backslash \{\alpha\})$.*

The above requirements are taken from [3] where (1) is called *consistency*, (2) is called *monotony*, and (3) is called *free formula independence*.

Next we introduce five inconsistency measures: the rationale for each is given below.

Definition 2. *For a knowledgebase K, the inconsistency measures I_C, I_P, I_B, I_S, and I_R are s.t.*

- $I_C(K) = |\text{MI}(K)|$
- $I_M(K) = (|\text{MC}(K)| + |\text{Selfcontradictions}(K)|) - 1$
- $I_P(K) = |\text{Problematic}(K)|$
- $I_B(K) = \text{Contension}(K)$
- $I_Q(K) = \begin{cases} 0 & \text{if } K \text{ is consistent} \\ \sum_{X \in \text{MI}(K)} \frac{1}{|X|} & \text{otherwise} \end{cases}$

We explain the measures as follows: $I_C(K)$ counts the number of minimal inconsistent subsets of K; $I_M(K)$ counts the sum of the number of maximal consistent subsets together with the number of contradictory formulae but 1 must be subtracted to make $I(K) = 0$ when K is consistent; $I_P(K)$ counts the number of formulae in minimal inconsistent subsets of K; $I_B(K)$ counts the minimum number of atoms that need to be assigned B amongst the 3VL models of K; and I_Q computes the weighted sum of the minimal inconsistent subsets of K, where the weight is the inverse of the size of the minimal inconsistent subset (and hence smaller minimal inconsistent subsets are regarded as more inconsistent than larger ones). Each of these measures satisfies the definition of being an inconsistency measure (i.e. Definition 1).

There is a rationale for each inconsistency measure. We cannot require these differently defined measures to give identical numerical values but it would be reasonable to assume that at least some of them place the knowledgebases in the same order with respect to inconsistency. Define I_x and I_y to be *order-compatible* if for all knowledgebases K_1 and K_2, $I_x(K_1) < I_x(K_2)$ iff $I_y(K_1) < I_y(K_2)$ and *order-incompatible* otherwise. The next theorem shows that order-compatibility doesn't hold for any pair of the inconsistency measures we have defined, leading us to think that inconsistency is too elusive a concept to be captured in a single measure.

Theorem 1. [1] *I_C, I_M, I_P, I_B, and I_Q are pairwise order-incompatible.*

Although the five inconsistency measures are quite different, four of them give identical results on bijection-equivalent knowledge bases.

Proposition 1. *If $K \equiv_b K'$ then $I_Z(K) = I_Z(K')$ for $Z \in \{C, M, P, Q\}$.*

Interestingly, b-equivalence does not guarantee equality for I_B. The problem is with self-contradictions. For instance, if $K = \{a \wedge \neg a\}$ and $K' = \{a \wedge \neg a \wedge b \wedge \neg b\}$, then $K \equiv_b K'$, but $I_B(K) = 1 \neq I_B(K') = 2$.

The use of minimal inconsistent subsets, such as I_C, I_P, and I_Q, and the use of maximal consistent subsets such as I_M, have been proposed previously for measures of inconsistency [2,4]. The idea of a measure that is sensitive to the number of formulae to produce an inconsistency eminates from Knight [8] in which the more formulae needed to produce the inconsistency, the less inconsistent the set. As explored in [4], this sensitivity is obtained with I_Q. Another approach involves looking at the proportion

---

[1] All proofs and additional references are given in a technical report available at
www.cs.ucl.ac.uk/staff/a.hunter/papers/stepwise.pdf

of the language that is touched by the inconsistency such as I_B. Whilst model-based techniques have been proposed before for measures of inconsistency, I_B is a novel proposal since it is based on three-valued logic, and as such, is simpler than the ones based on four-valued logic (e.g. [5]).

3.2 Information Measures for Knowledgebases

Another dimension to analysing inconsistency is to ascertain the amount of information in a knowledgebase. The following novel proposal for an information measure assigns a nonnegative real number to every knowledgebase. The constraints ensure that the empty set has measure 0, the measure is subset monotonic for consistent knowledgebases, and a consistent knowledgebase that does not contain only tautologies has nonzero measure.

Definition 3. *An* **information measure** $J : \mathcal{K} \rightarrow \mathcal{R}^{\geq 0}$ *is a function such that the following three conditions hold:*

1. *If* $K = \emptyset$ *then* $J(K) = 0$.
2. *If* $K' \subseteq K$, *and* K *is consistent, then* $J(K') \leq J(K)$.
3. *If* K *is consistent and* $\exists \phi \in K$ *such that* ϕ *is not a tautology, then* $J(K) > 0$.

The above definition is a general definition that allows for a range of possible measures to be defined. Next we introduce seven information measures; the rationale for each is given below. We note here that in the definition of J_B we will use the concept of Models as previously defined for 3VL. However, in the case of J_L we will need a model concept using classical 2-valued interpretations. We write $\text{2VModels}(K) = \{i|$ is a 2-valued interpretation and for all $\phi \in K, i(\phi) = T\}$.

Definition 4. *For a knowledgebase K, the information measures J_A, J_S, J_F, J_C, J_B, J_P, and J_L are such that*

- $J_A(K) = |\text{Atoms}(K)|$
- $J_S(K) = |K|$
- $J_F(K) = |\text{Free}(K)|$
- $J_C(K) = \text{Max}\{ |M| \mid M \in \text{MC}(K)\}$
- $J_B(K) = \text{Max}\{ |\text{Binarybase}(i)| \mid i \in \text{Models}(K)\}$
- $J_P(K) = \text{Max}\{ |X| \mid X \in \text{Proxies}(K)\}$
- $J_L(K) = \log_2 \frac{2^n}{|\bigcup\{\text{2VModels}(K')|K' \in \text{MC}(K)\}|}$ *where* $n = |\text{Atoms}(K)|$ *if* $n \geq 1$, *else* $J_L(K) = 0$.

The first two measures do not actually deal with inconsistency at all: J_A counts the number of atoms and J_S counts the number of formulae. For the other four measures: J_F counts the number of free formulae; J_C finds the size of the largest maximal consistent subset; J_B finds the maximum number of atoms that need not be assigned B in the 3VL models; J_P finds the size of the largest proxy; and J_L uses an information-theoretic approach that is discussed further at the end of this section. All seven measures are information measures according to Definition 3.

In analogy to inconsistency measures, we can define order-compatibility and order-incompatibility for information measures. Similarly, we find that order-compatibility does not hold for any pair of information measures, leading us to think that information is also too elusive a concept to be captured in a single measure.

Theorem 2. $J_A, J_S, J_F, J_C, J_B, J_P,$ and J_L are pairwise order-incompatible.

Next we prove some results concerning information measures followed by some that relate information measures with inconsistency measures.

Proposition 2. If K is consistent, then $J_S(K) = J_F(K) = J_C(K)$.

Proposition 3. If K is a set of literals, then $J_A(K) = J_C(K) = J_P(K)$.

Proposition 4. For any knowledgebase K, $J_S(K) - J_F(K) = I_P(K)$.

Proposition 5. For any knowledgebase K, $J_A(K) - J_B(K) = I_B(K)$.

Proposition 6. No information measure is also an inconsistency measure.

Since our definition of information measure (i.e. Definition 3) is rather weak we consider additional constraints that can be useful for comparing information measures. For an information measure J, and for any knowledgebases $K, K' \subseteq \mathcal{L}$, we call J:

- (Monotonic) If $K \subseteq K'$, then $J(K) \leq J(K')$.
- (Clarity) For all $\phi \in K$, $J(K) \geq J(K \cup \{\psi\})$, where ψ is the cnf of $\neg\phi$.
- (Equivalence) If K is consistent and $K \equiv K'$, then $J(K) = J(K')$.
- (Bijection-Equivalence) If $K \equiv_b K'$, then $J(K) = J(K')$.
- (Closed) If K is consistent, and $K \vdash \phi$, then $J(K) = J(K \cup \{\phi\})$.
- (Cumulative) If $K \cup \{\phi\}$ is consistent, and $K \nvdash \phi$, then $J(K) < J(K \cup \{\phi\})$.

A monotonic measure is monotonic even for inconsistent knowledgebases. A clarity measure does not increase when the negation of a formula in the knowledgebase is added. An equivalence measure assigns the same value to logically equivalent consistent knowledgebases. A bijection-equivalence measure (which was first proposed in [8]) has the same value for a pair of knowledgebases when the formulae are pairwise equivalent. A closed measure (which was first proposed in [9]) does not have increased information for a consistent knowledgebase when entailed formulae are added. A cumulative measure (which was first proposed in [9]) has increased information for a consistent knowledgebase when a non-entailed formula is added that is consistent with it. We note that if an information measure has the equivalence property then it is closed because if $K \vdash \phi$ then $K \equiv K \cup \{\phi\}$.

Theorem 3. Figure 2 indicates the constraints that hold for each of the information measures $J_A, J_S, J_F, J_C, J_B, J_P,$ and J_L.

Depending on which constraints one considers important, one may choose from those measures that satisfy them. In particular, J_P satisfies all seven constraints.

The $J_A, J_S, J_F,$ and J_C measures are simple syntactic measures that have been considered in some form before (see for example [2] for a discussion)). However, the J_B and J_P are novel proposals for information measures. There have also been proposals for measures of information for propositional logic based on Shannon's information theory (see for example [6]). Essentially, these measures consider the number of models of the set of formulae (the less models, the more informative the set), and in case the set of formulae is consistent, the result is intuitive. However, when the set is inconsistent, the set is regarded as having null information content. To address the need to consider inconsistent information, Lozinskii proposed a generalization of the information-theoretic approach to measuring information [9] that we called J_L earlier.

	J_A	J_S	J_F	J_C	J_B	J_P	J_L
Monotonic	×	×		×		×	
Clarity	×		×		×	×	×
Equivalence						×	×
B-Equivalence		×	×	×		×	×
Closed						×	×
Cumulative		×	×	×		×	×

Fig. 2. Summary of constraints that hold (indicated by ×) for particular information measures

4 Stepwise Inconsistency Resolution

Generally, when a knowledgebase is inconsistent, we would like to reduce its inconsistency value, preferably to 0. The problem is that a reduction in inconsistency may lead to a corresponding reduction in information. Consider, for instance, J_S. This measure counts the number of formulae in the knowledgebase. Hence any deletion reduces it. Our goal is to reduce inconsistency with as little information loss as possible, a task that depends on the choice of both the inconsistency measure and the information measure.

We start by formally defining the three functions that we allow in the process of inconsistency resolution. They appear to be representative of all options. These operations will be applied to inconsistent knowledgebases.

Definition 5. *An inconsistency resolution function* irf, *is one of the following three functions* $d(\phi)$ *or* $w(\phi, \psi)$ *or* $s(\phi)$ *where* $\phi \in K$:

- *(Deletion)* $d(\phi) = K \setminus \{\phi\}$.
- *(Weakening)* $w(\phi, \psi) = (K \setminus \{\phi\}) \cup \{\psi\}$ *where* $\phi \vdash \psi$.
- *(Splitting)* $s(\phi) = (K \setminus \{\phi\}) \cup \{\phi_1, \ldots, \phi_n\}$ *where* $\phi_1, \ldots, \phi_n$ *are the conjuncts in* ϕ.

Then irf(K) *is the knowledgebase obtained by applying* irf *to* K. *Also* irf$(K) = K$ *in case* $\phi \notin K$.

In the stepwise inconsistency resolution process we will usually have multiple applications of such functions. A stepwise resolution function sequence (abbr. *function sequence*) $\mathcal{F} = \langle \text{irf}_1, \ldots, \text{irf}_n \rangle$ is a sequence of such functions. A stepwise inconsistency resolution knowledgebase sequence (abbr. *knowledgebase sequence*) $\mathcal{K}_{\mathcal{F}} = \langle K_0, \ldots, K_n \rangle$ is a sequence of knowledgebases obtained by using $\mathcal{F}$ such that K_0 is the initial knowledgebase and irf$_i(K_{i-1}) = K_i$ for $1 \leq i \leq n$. We also write $\mathcal{F}(K_0) = K_n$ and observe that $K_n = \text{irf}_n(\ldots \text{irf}_1(K_0) \ldots)$.

The goal of stepwise inconsistency resolution is to reduce the inconsistency of the knowledgebase. Next we define a simple way to measure the reduction . We will be interested in applying this definition to the case where $\mathcal{F}(K) = K'$ for some function sequence $\mathcal{F}$.

	α					
	a	$\neg a \wedge b$	$\neg b \vee c$	$\neg c$	$c \vee d$	$\neg d$
$R_{I_C}(K, K \setminus \{\alpha\})$	1	2	1	2	1	1
$R_{I_M}(K, K \setminus \{\alpha\})$	1	3	0	4	3	3
$R_{I_P}(K, K \setminus \{\alpha\})$	1	3	1	4	2	2
$R_{I_B}(K, K \setminus \{\alpha\})$	1	1	0	1	0	0
$R_{I_Q}(K, K \setminus \{\alpha\})$	3/6	5/6	2/6	4/6	2/6	2/6

Fig. 3. Illustration of resolution measures applied to knowledgebases obtained by deleting a formula from the knowledgebase $K = \{a, \neg a \wedge b, \neg b \vee c, \neg c, c \vee d, \neg d\}$. Here we see that according to I_P, $\neg c$ is the optimal choice for deletion, while for I_Q, it is $\neg a \wedge b$.

Definition 6. *Given an inconsistency measure I, an inconsistency resolution measure $R_I : \mathcal{K} \times \mathcal{K} \to \mathcal{R}$ is defined as follows:*

$$R_I(K, K') = I(K) - I(K')$$

For illustration we give two examples. The example given in Figure 3 corresponds to deletion, and Example 2 corresponds to splitting a formula.

Example 2. Let $K = \{a, \neg a \wedge \neg b, b\}$. Splitting K by applying $s(\neg a \wedge \neg b)$ we obtain $K' = \{a, \neg a, b, \neg b\}$. Here we see that splitting does not reduce inconsistency according to any of the five inconsistency measures. Indeed, for several measures it causes an increase in inconsistency .

$$R_{I_C}(K, (K \setminus \{\neg a \wedge \neg b\}) \cup \{\neg a, \neg b\}) = 0$$
$$R_{I_M}(K, (K \setminus \{\neg a \wedge \neg b\}) \cup \{\neg a, \neg b\}) = -2$$
$$R_{I_P}(K, (K \setminus \{\neg a \wedge \neg b\}) \cup \{\neg a, \neg b\}) = -1$$
$$R_{I_B}(K, (K \setminus \{\neg a \wedge \neg b\}) \cup \{\neg a, \neg b\}) = 0$$
$$R_{I_Q}(K, (K \setminus \{\neg a \wedge \neg b\}) \cup \{\neg a, \neg b\}) = 0$$

Some simple observations concerning the R_I measure are the following: (1) If $\phi \notin K$, then $R_I(K, K \setminus \{\phi\}) = 0$ and (2) If $\phi \in \text{Free}(K)$ then $R_I(K, K \setminus \{\phi\}) = 0$.

In the stepwise resolution process we try to minimize the loss of information as well. For this reason we now define a way to measure the loss of information.

Definition 7. *Given an information measure J, an information loss measure $R_J : \mathcal{K} \times \mathcal{K} \to \mathcal{R}$ is defined as follows.*

$$R_J(K, K') = J(K) - J(K')$$

Our general goal is to simultaneously maximize R_I and minimize R_J. In the following subsections we consider some of the issues for each of the options we have (i.e. for deletion, for weakening, and for splitting).

4.1   Inconsistency Resolution by Deletion

Deletion is the simplest, and yet most drastic, of the options we have for dealing with inconsistency. In terms of deciding of how to proceed, if deletion is the only function used, it is just a matter of choosing a formula to delete at each step. The following result describes the possibilities for both R_I and R_J when K' is obtained from K by a single deletion.

Theorem 4. *Let K' be obtained from an inconsistent K by deleting a single formula. (a) For all 5 inconsistency measures $R_I(K, K') \geq 0$. (b) For the information measures J_F, J_B and J_L, $R_J(K, K')$ may be negative; in the other cases $R_J(K, K')$ is a nonnegative integer.*

The following result follows immediately from the second constraint of an information measure and will be useful in narrowing the knowledgebases that need to be considered for minimal information loss when inconsistency resolution is done by deletions.

Proposition 7. *If K is consistent then $R_J(K, K \setminus \{\phi\}) \geq 0$.*

This result shows that once we delete enough formulae from an inconsistent knowledgebase to make it consistent (and thereby make any inconsistency measure 0), we might as well stop because additional deletions may only cause information loss. This gives the following result.

Corollary 1. *Suppose that stepwise inconsistency resolution is done by deletions only. To find a consistent knowledgebase with minimal information loss (i. e. where $R_J(K, K')$ is minimal) it suffices to consider only those function sequences $\mathcal{F}$ where $\mathcal{F}(K) \in MC(K)$.*

4.2 Inconsistency Resolution by Weakening

In this subsection we investigate the case where the inconsistency of a knowledgebase is resolved by using weakenings only. Thus we start with an inconsistent knowledgebase K and by applying one or more weakenings we obtain a consistent K'. Our concern here is what happens to the information measure during this process. In order to analyze this situation we will exclude the case where a formula is weakened by using an atom not in K such as by applying a disjunction with such an atom. We do this because it does not seem reasonable to change the language of the knowledgebase when our purpose is to weaken it for consistency. Also, by excluding this case we make sure that the information measure cannot become arbitrarily large by simply taking bigger and bigger disjuncts with new atoms.

Our result is summarized in the following theorem.

Theorem 5. *Let K be an inconsistent knowledgebase that is transformed to a consistent knowledgebase K' by one or more weakenings without introducing any atom not already in K. Then*

1. $J_A(K') \leq J_A(K)$.
2. $J_S(K') \leq J_S(K)$.
3. $J_F(K') \geq J_F(K)$.
4. $J_C(K') \geq J_C(K)$.
5. *No inequality holds between $J_B(K')$ and $J_B(K)$.*
6. $J_P(K') \leq J_P(K)$.
7. $J_L(K') \geq J_L(K)$.

4.3 Inconsistency Resolution Using Splitting

Here we consider what happens when splitting is applied. First we note that unlike deletion and weakening, splitting by itself cannot resolve inconsistencies. Hence splitting must be used in conjunction with deletion or weakening. We start by considering what happens when just splitting is applied. Just as in the case of deletions and weakenings, we split only formulae in Problematic(K).

Theorem 6. *Let K' be obtained from an inconsistent knowledgebase K by splitting a single formula in* Problematic(K). *Then*

(a) *1. $I_C(K') \geq I_C(K)$,*
     2. $I_M(K') \geq I_M(K)$,
     3. $I_P(K') \geq I_P(K)$,
     4. $I_B(K') = I_B(K)$,
     5. No inequality holds between $I_Q(K')$ and $I_Q(K)$.
(b) *1. $J_A(K') = J_A(K)$,*
     2. $J_S(K') > J_S(K)$,
     3. $J_F(K') \geq J_F(K)$,
     4. $J_C(K') \geq J_C(K)$,
     5. $J_B(K') = J_B(K)$,
     6. $J_P(K') = J_P(K)$
     7. No inequality holds between $J_L(K')$ and $J_L(K)$.

This theorem shows that splitting decreases neither inconsistency nor information (except possibly for I_Q and J_L), and for some measures it increases both. Anyway, as pointed out earlier, splitting must be combined with another operation to eliminate inconsistency.

5 Discussion

In general, inconsistency resolution should be guided by the aim of decreasing inconsistency without excessive loss of information. However, there is a trade-off between the amount to which inconsistency is decreased and the amount of information loss that can be accepted. Futhermore, there can be numerous choices over what resolution steps to take at any state of the knowledgebase.

A common criterion is that some or all operations are not permitted on some formulae. Alternatively, there may be a preference ordering over the formulae such that the less preferred formulae should be considered for being subject to a resolution operation before the more preferred formulae. However, in situations, where two or more formulae can be subjected to a resolution operation, the use of inconsistency and information measures may help in making a choice.

Turning to the question of which measures to use, this depends on the application and the users involved. If they all agree to use specific measures in advance, then that could be their prerogative. However, in general, when agents discuss specific options for stepwise resolution, they may also need to discuss on a stepwise basis which measures to take into account and why.

In this paper, we have clarified the space of inconsistency and information measures and then shown how a wide variety of proposals conform to these general definitions. It is surprising that all different measures are incompatible with one another. We have also shown how inconsistency and information measures can be used to direct stepwise resolution of inconsistency so that inconsistency can be decreased whilst minimising information loss.

References

1. Grant, J.: Classifications for inconsistent theories. Notre Dame Journal of Formal Logic 19, 435–444 (1978)
2. Hunter, A., Konieczny, S.: Approaches to measuring inconsistent information. In: Bertossi, L., Hunter, A., Schaub, T. (eds.) Inconsistency Tolerance. LNCS, vol. 3300, pp. 189–234. Springer, Heidelberg (2005)
3. Hunter, A., Konieczny, S.: Shapley inconsistency values. In: Proceedings of KR 2006, pp. 249–259. AAAI Press, Menlo Park (2006)
4. Hunter, A., Konieczny, S.: Measuring inconsistency through minimal inconsistent sets. In: Proceedings of KR 2008, pp. 358–366. AAAI Press, Menlo Park (2008)
5. Hunter, A.: Measuring inconsistency in knowledge via quasi-classical models. In: Proc of AAAI 2002, pp. 68–73. MIT Press, Cambridge (2002)
6. Kemeny, J.: A logical measure function. J. of Symbolic Logic 18, 289–308 (1953)
7. Konieczny, S., Lang, J., Marquis, P.: Quantifying information and contradiction in propositional logic through epistemic actions. In: Proceedings of the 18th International Joint Conference on Artificial Intelligence (IJCAI 2003), pp. 106–111 (2003)
8. Knight, K.: Measuring inconsistency. J. of Philosophical Logic 31, 77–98 (2001)
9. Lozinskii, E.: Resolving contradictions: A plausible semantics for inconsistent systems. Journal of Automated Reasoning 12, 1–31 (1994)
10. Mu, K., Jin, Z., Lu, R., Liu, W.: Measuring inconsistency in requirements engineering. In: Godo, L. (ed.) ECSQARU 2005. LNCS (LNAI), vol. 3571, pp. 440–451. Springer, Heidelberg (2005)
11. Priest, G.: Logic of paradox. Journal of Philosophical Logic 8, 219–241 (1979)

Relating Truth, Knowledge and Belief in Epistemic States

Costas D. Koutras[1] and Yorgos Zikos[2,*]

[1] Department of Computer Science and Technology,
University of Peloponnese,
end of Karaiskaki Street, 22 100 Tripolis, Greece
ckoutras@uop.gr

[2] Graduate Programme in Logic, Algorithms and Computation (MPLA),
Department of Mathematics, University of Athens,
Panepistimioupolis, 157 84 Ilissia, Greece
zikos@sch.gr

Abstract. We define and investigate a structure incorporating *what is true*, *what is known* and *what is believed* by a rational agent in models of the **S4.2** logic of knowledge. The notion of KB_R-structures introduced, provides a fine-grained modal analysis of an agent's epistemic state, actually one that differentiates knowledge from belief and accounts for an agent without full introspective power (concerning her knowledge sets). Many epistemic properties of this structure are proved and it is shown that belief collapses in the form of a Stalnaker stable set (while knowledge does not). Finally, a representation theorem is proved, which exactly matches KB_R-structures to **S4.2** models of the world.

Keywords: Knowledge Representation, modal epistemic logic, epistemic states.

1 Introduction

Epistemic Logic [10,15] has been concerned with the rigorous analysis of the *propositional attitudes* 'A knows φ' and 'A believes that φ'. It has grown as an area of Philosophical Logic but it has been given a fresh, new perspective in Computer Science; examples of applications abound: distributed systems [5], multi-agent systems [19] and many others. In its current form, Epistemic Logic has been greatly benefited by the development of Modal Logic and, in particular, by the advent of '*possible-world*' (or Kripke) *semantics*. Nowadays, many rich epistemic languages have been introduced and applied in various fields of computing; see [1] for a short presentation and many pointers to the literature, and also [4] for a compilation of various concrete paradigms on the *logics of knowledge and change*.

Artificial Intelligence has provided a new, '*introspective*' perspective on modal epistemic reasoning. In Knowledge Representation, the issue of a '*good*' representation of a rational agent's (typically acting in a domain of interest and holding partial, incomplete information about the world) epistemic state is very important. A simple, yet very

---

* The second author gratefully acknowledges financial support by the Greek Ministry of Education, Lifelong Learning and Religious Affairs under the scheme of educational leave.

W. Liu (Ed.): ECSQARU 2011, LNAI 6717, pp. 374–385, 2011.

successful and influential notion is Stalnaker's definition of a *stable belief set* ([18], [16]), which has played a significant role in the development of modal Non-Monotonic Reasoning (NMR). Succint and expressive logical definitions of an agent's epistemic state are of interest to other branches of Knowledge Representation too, such as *belief revision* and *reasoning about actions*.

In this paper we proceed to work on a detailed analysis of the epistemic and doxastic theories held by a rational agent, operating in a complex possible-worlds environment, under the realistic condition that the information acquired by the agent allows him to distinguish (at least) some of the possible worlds in the picture. This is definitely different from the S5 picture of the Stalnaker stable sets, worked around the universal model paradigm, where no possible world is distinguishable from the others. Here, we actually place the (important for KR) question of the formal representation of an agent's knowledge and belief, under the lens of classical modal epistemic reasoning and revisit the notion of epistemic state(s) under a new, semantic perspective. **Our objective is to describe the *epistemic* and *doxastic* status of a rational agent *without* full introspection** (which has been strongly criticized in epistemic logic [15, p.35][7, p.117]), **taking a modal approach, which differentiates knowledge from belief.** We introduce a notion of KB_R-structures, intending to capture the interplay between *truth*, *knowledge* and *belief* held by an agent operating in a domain modelled as a set of possible-worlds. We examine several proof-theoretic properties of KB_R-structures and provide a representation theorem for these structures, which proves an exact correspondence to the models of **S4.2**, the logic advocated by W. Lenzen as the '*correct*' logic of knowledge [15]. It is hardly surprising that the initial motivation of this research has been the ambition to define simple variants of Stalnaker's stable sets inspired from interesting, existing models, such as the models of **S4.2**. Due to space limitations, this Conference version contains no proofs; however, all technical details and proofs are readily accessible over the web, in the full technical report [13].

2 Notation and Terminology

In this section we gather the necessary background material and results: for the basics of *Modal Logic* and *modal Non-Monotonic Reasoning* the reader is referred to the books [2,3,11,16]. We assume a modal propositional language $\mathcal{L}_\square$, endowed with an epistemic operator $\square\varphi$, read as '*it is known that φ holds*'. Sentence symbols include $\top$ (for *truth*) and $\bot$ (for *falsity*). Some of the important axioms in epistemic/doxastic logic are: **K.** $(\square\varphi \wedge \square(\varphi \supset \psi)) \supset \square\psi$, **T.** $\square\varphi \supset \varphi$ (the axiom of *true, justified knowledge*), **4.** $\square\varphi \supset \square\square\varphi$ (the axiom of *positive introspection*), **5.** $\neg\square\varphi \supset \square\neg\square\varphi$ (the axiom of *negative introspection*), **G.** $\neg\square\neg\square\varphi \supset \square\neg\square\neg\varphi$.

The epistemic interpretation of **G** will be made clear below. *Modal* logics are sets of modal formulas containing classical propositional logic (i.e. containing all tautologies in the augmented language $\mathcal{L}_\square$) and closed under rule $\textbf{MP}\frac{\varphi,\varphi\supset\psi}{\psi}$. The smallest modal logic is denoted as **PC** (propositional calculus in the augmented language). Those modal logics, which contain all instances of axiom **K** and are closed under rule $\textbf{RN}\frac{\varphi}{\square\varphi}$, are called *normal*. By $\textbf{KA}_1 \ldots \textbf{A}_n$ we denote the smallest normal modal logic containing the axiom schemata $\textbf{A}_1$ to $\textbf{A}_n$. Among others, some well-known epistemic logics are **KT45 (S5)** (a *strong logic of knowledge*) and **S4.2**, which is an entrenched name for **KT4G**. We assume that the reader of this extended abstract is acquainted with the notion of *strong provability from premises* in modal logic (as in [16]) and the related notions of *consistency* and *maximal consistent sets*. We will not provide definitions here, as there are no proofs of the results; the reader is referred to the full technical report [13] for details. Just two remarks on notation: given a logic Λ and a consistent with Λ theory I, $mIc\Lambda$ denotes a *maximal I-consistent with Λ* set, and $Cn_\Lambda(I)$ denotes the set of all formulas proved from I in Λ.

Normal modal logics are interpreted over Kripke models: a *Kripke model* $\mathfrak{M} = \langle W, R, V \rangle$ consists of a set of *possible worlds (states, situations)* W and a binary accessibility relation between them $R \subseteq W \times W$: whenever wRv, we say that world w '*sees*' world v, or that v is an alternative to w. The valuation V determines which propositional variables are true inside each possible world. Within a world w, the propositional connectives ($\neg, \supset, \wedge, \vee$) are interpreted classically, while $\Box\varphi$ is true at w iff it is true in every world '*seen*' by w (notation: $\mathfrak{M}, w \Vdash \Box\varphi$). The pair $\mathfrak{F} = \langle W, R \rangle$ is called the *frame* underlying $\mathfrak{M}$. A logic Λ is *determined* by a class of frames iff it is *sound* and *complete* with respect to this class; it is known that **S5** is determined by the class of frames with a *universal* accessibility relation, while **S4.2** is determined by the class of frames with a reflexive, transitive and directed[1] accessibility relation [8].

Regarding epistemic logic, our perspective is very much influenced by W. Lenzen's work in [15], where many interesting formulations of knowledge and belief are discussed. The language assumed is monomodal with an epistemic operator $\Box$; a belief operator is defined by $\neg\Box\neg\Box\varphi$. Given this, the interpretation of **G** becomes: '*if someone believes that ϕ, then she does not disbelieve it*'. It is a *principle of consistent belief*. We subsequently refer to some of the properties mentioned in [15], namely $\neg\Box\neg\Box\varphi \supset \neg\Box\neg\Box\Box\varphi$ (property B2.1) and $\neg\Box\neg\Box\varphi \supset \Box\neg\Box\neg\Box\varphi$ (properties B2.3 and B2.4). In order to work with models of transitive logics, a cluster-based analysis is usually employed [8, Chap.8][17]. We provide the necessary definitions and results below, with a bit of personal flavour in terminology.

Some useful facts. We will restrict ourselves to possible-worlds frames with a reflexive, transitive and directed relation (henceforth called *rtd-relation*), keeping in mind that in the class of reflexive and transitive frames, directedness is equivalent to weak directedness[2] [8, p. 30]. The following definition for these relations, captures the notion of a cluster, as a maximal subset of states, inside which the (restriction of the) accessibility relation is universal. **The frames we consider need not be finite; it suffices that they 'collapse' to a finite number of clusters.** Following this definition, we gather some properties of clusters inside rtd-relations.

Definition 1. *Let $R \subseteq W \times W$ be any (binary) rtd-relation on W, and $\varnothing \neq C \subseteq W$. C is a* cluster *of R iff $(\forall s, t \in C)sRt$ and $(\forall u \in W \setminus C)(\exists v \in C)(\neg uRv$ or $\neg vRu)$. It is called a* final *cluster   iff   in addition $(\forall u \in W \setminus C)(\exists v \in C)\, uRv$.*

Fact 1. *(i) $(\forall s \in W)(\exists C : cluster)\, s \in C$, (ii) $(\forall\ clusters\ C, C' \subseteq W)\, C \cap C' = \varnothing$, (iii) $(\forall\ clusters\ C, C' \subseteq W)(\forall s \in C, s' \in C')(sRs' \implies (\forall t \in C, t' \in C')\, tRt')$,*

---

[1] i.e. $(\forall w, v \in W)(\exists u \in W)(wRu\ \&\ vRu)$.
[2] i.e. $(\forall w, v, u \in W)((wRv\ \&\ wRu) \Rightarrow (\exists t \in W)(vRt\ \&\ uRt))$

(iv) $(\forall \text{ clusters } C, C' \subseteq W)(\forall s \in C, s' \in C')\big((C \neq C' \ \& \ sRs') \implies (\forall t \in C, t' \in C') \neg t'Rt\big)$, *(v) There exists a final cluster, which is unique.*

As we will prove, there is no loss of generality in further 'collapsing' the clusters by defining a relation on the clusters' indices (the indices will be members of $D = \{0, \ldots, n\}$). The lemma following the definition makes clear that the relation constructed inherits properties from its 'generator' R.

Definition 2. *Let R be an rtd-relation on W. Then, a* pattern-relation $R_p \subseteq D \times D$ *of R is any relation on D s.t.* $(\forall i, j \in D)$

$$iR_p j \iff (\exists s \in C_i, t \in C_j) \ sRt$$

where $C_0, \ldots, C_n \subseteq W$ is an enumeration of the clusters of R.

Lemma 1. *Let R be an rtd-relation on W and R_p a pattern-relation of R (for clusters $C_0, \ldots, C_n \subseteq W$). Then,*

(i) $(\forall i, j \in D)(iR_p j \iff (\forall s \in C_i, t \in C_j) \ sRt)$
(ii)   *R_p is also an rtd-relation.*
(iii) *All clusters of R_p are singletons.*

The property (iii) entails another one (property (Gd) in lemma 2), which is important for our next results, so we will focus on rtd-relations endowed with (iii). These relations deserve a name. Lemma 2 and Corollary 1 follow immediately.

Definition 3. *Every binary relation which is reflexive, transitive, directed and has only singleton clusters is called a* simple rtd-relation (s-rtd).

Lemma 2. *Let R be an s-rtd-relation on W. Then, there is an $f \in W$ s.t.*

$$(Gd) \qquad (\forall i \in W)\ \big(iRf \ \& \ (i \neq f \Rightarrow \neg fRi)\big)$$

Corollary 1. *Let R be an rtd-relation on W and R_p a pattern relation of R (for clusters $C_0, \ldots, C_n \subseteq W$). Then, R_p is an s-rtd-relation and satisfies (Gd), where $W = D$.*

3 KB_R-Structures

3.1   Motivation

Suppose we have an agent inside a possible-worlds model. Obviously, in every world (or *situation*) of this model, some propositional variables are true, some others are not. According to the information available to the agent, she might not know exactly which variables are true in a situation i and which are true in another situation j. So, in her eyes, i and j could be two *alternatives* of the true state of the world, i.e. i and j could be *indistinguishable* for her. In this case, and supposed that she is in i, we relate i with j using the relation R of the model. In such an interpretation of R, it is natural to think that the agent knows φ iff in all alternative situations (i.e. indistinguishable situations from there) φ holds. In the standard concept of an epistemic model, the relation R is considered to be symmetric, i.e. that all R-arrows are bidirectional. This is a consequence of the standard approach's assumption, that information is uniformly distributed, and hence, if an agent being in i can not distinguish situation j from there, then, since she would have exactly the same information in j, she wouldn't be able to distinguish i from j either. But this assumption is not always true in real situations (see the full report for examples [13, p.6,20]). Furthermore, the standard assumption about the symmetry of the epistemic models, has another drawback: it acknowledges that the agent has *negative introspection* capabilities. Let us see why. Since (as we will explain later) all epistemic models must be considered reflexive and transitive, symmetry equips R with following property: if situation i is related to j and k, then k is related to j. Now, suppose that an agent, being in a situation i, does not know φ. Then, there must be an indistinguishable from i situation j, where $\neg\varphi$ holds. Since every other indistinguishable from i situation k sees j, it will also in k be true that our agent does not know φ (a witness for that is j). Hence, our agent does know in i that she doesn't know φ. So, within every situation, it does hold that, if the agent does not know something, then she is aware of her ignorance about that.

In our approach, trying to find a remedy for these drawbacks, we will assume that *information is not uniformly distributed* all over the situations. We intend to establish a formal representation of knowledge sets, which will not necessarily be the same globally, but different for each situation (in fact, we will describe the properties of those sets, not necessarily for each situation, but for 'blocks' of indistinguishable situations). So, assuming that there are n different situations, we denote for any situation $i \in \{0, \ldots, n\}$ the agent's knowledge set as Γ_i (the exact role and content of each Γ_i will be made clear below). **To be able to define those sets, we have to consider sets T_i, which will contain all true formulas in situation i.** Our agent does not necessarily know every formula in T_i; and anything believed by her, might not be true. Furthermore, being in a situation i the agent might distinguish between her current situation and another, because she has some information, which allows her to do so. But she also might not distinguish between her current situation i and another j. As explained previously, if j is an alternative situation for i, then it is not necessarily true that i is an alternative situation for j, since being in j, our agent might be provided with extra information, which might allow her to distinguish between j and i.

A very fundamental idea in epistemic reasoning with possible-worlds semantics, is that the agent does not know in which situation she is located. If we know that the agent is in situation i and that, say, j, k and l are alternative situations for i (i.e. indistinguishable from i), she might not know that she is in i. She rather knows that i, j, k and l are all indistinguishable situations. Speaking about indistinguishable situations *from i* means that we do know that if our agent were in i, she would consider these situations (including i) as alternative variations of her present, unknown to her! Furthermore, we could know – since **we enjoy the "eagle's view"** – that if our agent were in situation j, she would have the information to distinguish between her situation and, say, k, but this is something that she does not know. Only if she actually were in j she would know that. Now, assume that in the previous example our agent is aware of the fact that in all alternative situations (included the unknown to her, current situation i) a formula φ is true (i.e. $\varphi \in T_i \cap T_j \cap T_k \cap T_l$). Then, it is natural to say that she is sure about φ, that she *knows* φ. Therefore, given a relation $R \subseteq \{0, \ldots, n\}$, representing all couples of indistinguishable situations (i.e. iRj means that j is an alternative situation for i), we will define in the next section, Γ_i as $\bigcap_{iRj} T_j$.

As mentioned previously, in our modal language $\mathcal{L}_\square$ **the modality denotes knowledge**. Hence, we have two ways of denoting knowledge of φ: using formula $\square\varphi$, and saying that $\varphi \in \Gamma_i$. To be consistent with our intuitions, we have to demand that

$$\text{if } \varphi \in \Gamma_i, \text{ then } \square\varphi \in T_i \qquad (1)$$

(i.e. if our agent knows φ, then, obviously, it is true that she does know it!), and

$$\text{if } \varphi \notin \Gamma_i, \text{ then } \neg\square\varphi \in T_i \qquad (2)$$

One might wonder why don't we simply demand $\varphi \in \Gamma_i$ iff $\square\varphi \in T_i$. Then, $\varphi \notin \Gamma_i$ would simply entail $\square\varphi \notin T_i$, which seams to be natural, since *"it is not true that I know φ"* looks equivalent to *"it is true that I do not know φ"*! This equivalence is obviously true, if we see each situation i as a unique state of affairs, as we did hitherto. But in a more general case, we could consider bunches of situations (possibly, infinite many situations in a bunch), where all situations of the same bunch are indistinguishable to each other, i.e. for every situation s of a bunch, any other of the same bunch, is an alternative one for s. From now on we will call those bunches, *clusters* and we will denote them as i, j, k etc. The situations itself will be denoted as s, t, u etc. We intend to define those clusters in a such way, that if some situation s of a cluster i considers situation t of any other cluster as an alternative one, then every other situation of i will consider t as an alternative one. And if we say that φ is true in cluster i, obviously, we would like to mean that φ is true in every situation of i, i.e. that T_i contains all formulas valid in i. Hence, $\square\varphi \notin T_i$ does not necessarily entail that $\neg\square\varphi \in T_i$. But the inverse is true. That's why we chose the stronger property: $\varphi \notin \Gamma_i \Rightarrow \neg\square\varphi \in T_i$. Note also that now, R does not anymore relate situations, rather than clusters, in the sense that iRj means that our agent, being in any situation s of i considers as indistinguishable from s any situation of j.

We will also adopt the option of defining belief through knowledge. To do so, we will follow the idea introduced by W. Lenzen [15], who argued that the following definition of belief is acceptable even by the *'most scrupulous epistemologist'*: **an agent believes that φ iff she does not know that she doesn't know** φ (i.e. $\neg\square\neg\square\varphi$ defines *'believing in φ'*). Now, our agent knows that she doesn't know φ iff $\varphi \notin \Gamma_j$ for every alternative situation j for i, hence, she would believe that φ iff $\varphi \in \Gamma_j$ for some alternative situation j for i. Therefore – assuming that the belief sets, containing everything believed by our agent in any situation of i, will be denoted as Δ_i – it is consistent with Lenzen's definition to identify Δ_i as $\bigcup_{iRj} \Gamma_j$. As noted above, there exists a direct way to speak about *"believing"* in φ: $\neg\square\neg\square\varphi$. So, to be consistent with our intuitions, we have to define the theories T_i and Δ_i in such a way, that they will satisfy the following conditions:

$$\text{if } \varphi \in \Delta_i, \text{ then } \neg\square\neg\square\varphi \in T_i \qquad (3)$$

(i.e. if our agent believes that φ, then, it is true that she does not know that she doesn't know it), and

$$\text{if } \varphi \notin \Delta_i, \text{ then } \square\neg\square\varphi \in T_i \qquad (4)$$

3.2   Definition of KB_R-Structures

Let us have in mind that $D = \{0,\ldots,n\}$ contains the (indices of the) clusters of the epistemic situations considered, and that $T_0,\ldots,T_n$ are the corresponding theories, containing exactly all formulas, valid there. Firstly, we describe all those properties, which these theories should satisfy, and we give the overall structure a name.

Definition 4. *Let $R \subseteq D \times D$ be an s-rtd-relation on D and $T_0,\ldots,T_n \subseteq \mathcal{L}_\square$ be consistent theories s.t. $(\forall i \in D)$*

(PC_i) $\mathbf{PC}_{\mathcal{L}_\square} \subseteq T_i$ *and T_i is closed under* **MP**

(P_i) $(\forall \varphi \in \mathcal{L}_\square)(\varphi \in \bigcap_{iRj} T_j \Rightarrow \square\varphi \in T_i)$

(N_i) $(\forall \varphi \in \mathcal{L}_\square)(\varphi \notin T_i \Rightarrow \neg\square\varphi \in \bigcap_{jRi} T_j)$

Furthermore, for any $i \in D$, we define Γ_i and Δ_i as

$$\Gamma_i = \bigcap_{iRj} T_j \quad and \quad \Delta_i = \bigcup_{iRj} \Gamma_j$$

Then, the ordered triple $\langle (T_i), (\Gamma_i), (\Delta_i) \rangle_{i \in D}^R$ is called a **KB_R-structure**. *In fact, it is a triple consisting of three $(n+1)$-tuples of theories.*

The following simple example demonstrates that Stalnaker stable sets correspond to a trivial case of our setting, i.e. one that originates from a simple cluster.

Example 1. Consider $D = \{0\}$, a consistent theory $T_0 \subseteq \mathcal{L}_\square$, and the corresponding $KB_{\{(0,0)\}}$-structure $\langle T_0, \Gamma_0, \Delta_0 \rangle^{\{(0,0)\}}$ (for the trivial s-rtd-relation over D, $\{(0,0)\}$). Then, by Def.4, T_0 satisfies: $(\forall \varphi \in \mathcal{L}_\square)$

(PC_0) $\mathbf{PC}_{\mathcal{L}_\square} \subseteq T_0$ and T_0 is closed under **MP**

(P_0) $\varphi \in T_0 \Rightarrow \square\varphi \in T_0$

(N_0) $\varphi \notin T_0 \Rightarrow \neg\square\varphi \in T_0$

T_0 is a stable set according to Stalnaker's definition. Furthermore, $\Gamma_0 = \Delta_0 = T_0$.

Example 2. Let us consider now the s-rtd-relation $R = \{(0,0),(1,1),(1,0)\}$ and the corresponding KB_R-structure $\langle (T_i),(\Gamma_i),(\Delta_i) \rangle_{i \in D}^R$. Then, Def.4 says that T_0 and T_1 are meant to be consistent and to satisfy all conditions listed below: $(\forall \varphi \in \mathcal{L}_\square)$, $(PC_{0,1})$: $\mathbf{PC}_{\mathcal{L}_\square} \subseteq T_0, T_1$ and T_0, T_1 are closed under **MP**, (P_0): $\varphi \in T_0 \Rightarrow \square\varphi \in T_0$, (N_0): $\varphi \notin T_0 \Rightarrow \neg\square\varphi \in T_0$ & $\neg\square\varphi \in T_1$, (P_1): $\varphi \in T_0$ & $\varphi \in T_1 \Rightarrow \square\varphi \in T_1$, (N_1): $\varphi \notin T_1 \Rightarrow \neg\square\varphi \in T_1$. Furthermore, $\Gamma_0 = T_0$, $\Gamma_1 = T_0 \cap T_1$, $\Delta_0 = T_0$ and $\Delta_1 = T_0 \cup (T_0 \cap T_1) = T_0$. The fact that $\Delta_0 = \Delta_1 = T_0$ is not a coincidence, but a result of some properties, which are satisfied by R, and which will be proved below (Fact 3). The next Fact shows that everything in Def.4 is consistent with what we said in section 3.1.

Fact 2. $(\forall i \in D)((P_i) \iff (1)$ & $(N_i) \iff (2))$. *Definition 4 entails properties (3), (4) and $(\forall i \in D)(\forall \varphi \in \mathcal{L}_\square)$*

$$\varphi \in \Gamma_i \iff \square\varphi \in T_i \quad and \quad \varphi \in \Delta_i \iff \neg\square\neg\square\varphi \in T_i \qquad (5)$$

3.3   Epistemic Properties of KB_R-Structures

Even without any restrictions to R, Definition 4 would endow all theories appearing there with axiom **K**, as the first lemma verifies. Further on our discussion in the motivation section, it would be desirable that the properties of R would lead to the incorporation of some intuitively acceptable properties of knowledge and belief in Γ_i and Δ_i. The lemmata which follow, state that **reflexivity** leads to two desirable properties: the *entailment thesis* (**knowledge implies belief**) and the property requiring that **knowledge implies certainty**.

Lemma 3. *Let* $\langle (T_i), (\Gamma_i), (\Delta_i) \rangle_{i \in D}^R$ *be any* KB_R-*structure. Then,*

$$(\forall i \in D)(\forall \varphi, \psi \in \mathcal{L}_\square) \; \mathbf{K} \in T_i$$

Lemma 4. *Let* $\langle (T_i), (\Gamma_i), (\Delta_i) \rangle_{i \in D}^R$ *be any* KB_R-*structure. Then,* $(\forall i \in D)$ $\Gamma_i \subseteq T_i \cap \Delta_i$ *(i.e. everything our agent knows is true, and she believes it).*

Lemma 5. *Let* $\langle (T_i), (\Gamma_i), (\Delta_i) \rangle_{i \in D}^R$ *be any* KB_R-*structure. Then,*

$$(\forall i \in D)(\forall \varphi \in \mathcal{L}_\square) \; \mathbf{T} \in T_i$$

Not really surprisingly, **transitivity** entails **positive introspection concerning knowledge**. Next, Lemma 6 along with the definition of Δ_i entail Lemma 7.

Lemma 6. *Let* $\langle (T_i), (\Gamma_i), (\Delta_i) \rangle_{i \in D}^R$ *be any* KB_R-*structure. Then,* $(\forall i \in D)$

$$(PI_i) \qquad (\forall \varphi \in \mathcal{L}_\square)(\varphi \in \Gamma_i \Rightarrow \square \varphi \in \Gamma_i)$$

Lemma 7. *Let* $\langle (T_i), (\Gamma_i), (\Delta_i) \rangle_{i \in D}^R$ *be any* KB_R-*structure. Then,*

$$(\forall i \in D)(\forall \varphi \in \mathcal{L}_\square)(\varphi \in \Delta_i \Rightarrow \square \varphi \in \Delta_i)$$

Note that Lemma 7, in light of (5) (see section 3.1), shows that *if our agent believes something, then she believes that she knows it* (which is similar to Lenzen's property (B2.1) [15]). Transitivity of R is embedded in every theory of Def.4 through axiom 4. Finally, Lemma 9 is technically useful in the next section.

Lemma 8. *Let* $\langle (T_i), (\Gamma_i), (\Delta_i) \rangle_{i \in D}^R$ *be any* KB_R-*structure. Then,*

$$(\forall i \in D)(\forall \varphi \in \mathcal{L}_\square) \; 4 \in T_i$$

Lemma 9. *Let* $\langle (T_i), (\Gamma_i), (\Delta_i) \rangle_{i \in D}^R$ *be any* KB_R-*structure. Then,* $(\forall i, j \in D)$

$$iRj \Rightarrow \Gamma_i \subseteq \Gamma_j$$

Finally, **directedness** of R leads to properties, similar to Lenzen's (B2.3) and (B2.4) [15, p.43-44]. The *former* one, which should be acceptable by a *"realistic epistemologist"*, says that **if an agent believes something, then she can not believe that she doesn't know it**. The *latter* property, which should be acceptable – according to Lenzen – by a *"simplifier"*, states that **if an agent believes something, then she knows that she believes it**.

Lemma 10. *Let* $\langle (T_i), (\Gamma_i), (\Delta_i) \rangle_{i \in D}^{R}$ *be any* KB_R-*structure. Then,*
$(\forall i \in D)(\forall \varphi \in \mathcal{L}_\square)$

   (B2.3) $\varphi \in \Delta_i \Rightarrow \neg\square\varphi \notin \Delta_i$ *and*   *(B2.4)* $\varphi \in \Delta_i \Rightarrow \neg\square\neg\square\varphi \in \Gamma_i$

Now, let us focus on the last presumption for R: being a **simple** rtd-relation. Then, by Lemma 2, property (Gd) is true for R. Without loss of generality, we will tacitly assume that the '*final*' element of R is 0, i.e. that (Gd) appears in the following form:

$$(Gd) \qquad (\forall i \in D)\ (iR0\ \&\ (i > 0 \Rightarrow \neg 0Ri))$$

This property endows every theory of Def.4 with axiom **G** and leads to the next two results.

Lemma 11. *Let* $\langle (T_i), (\Gamma_i), (\Delta_i) \rangle_{i \in D}^{R}$ *be any* KB_R-*structure. Then,*

$$(\forall i \in D)(\forall \varphi \in \mathcal{L}_\square)\ \mathbf{G} \in T_i$$

Fact 3. *Let* $\langle (T_i), (\Gamma_i), (\Delta_i) \rangle_{i \in D}^{R}$ *be any* KB_R-*structure. Then,* $(\forall i \in D)$
(i) $\Delta_i = \Gamma_0 = T_0$
(ii) Δ_i *is a stable theory according to Stalnaker's definition*

Now, it is immediate that our belief sets follow the **principle of consistency of belief**, i.e. that **if an agent believes that** φ**, she can not believe that** $\neg\varphi$.

Lemma 12. *Let* $\langle (T_i), (\Gamma_i), (\Delta_i) \rangle_{i \in D}^{R}$ *be any* KB_R-*structure. Then,* $(\forall i \in D)(\forall \varphi \in \mathcal{L}_\square)$

$$\varphi \in \Delta_i \Rightarrow \neg\varphi \notin \Delta_i$$

All previous lemmata seem to justify the choice of the KB_R notion in Def.4: KB_R-structures contain K(nowledge) theories (the Γ_i's), and B(elief) theories (the Δ_i's). According to Fact 3, one of the Γ_i's coincides with everything believed in any situation. Without loss of generality, it is assumed that this one is Γ_0. In following section we will present a model-theoretic characterization of KB_R-structures. To do so, we need the next important result, in which we employ a notion of strong provability.

Lemma 13. *If* $\langle (T_i), (\Gamma_i), (\Delta_i) \rangle_{i \in D}^{R}$ *is any* KB_R-*structure, then,* $(\forall i \in D)$
(i) Γ_i *is closed under strong* **S4.2** *provability, i.e.* $Cn_{\mathbf{S4.2}}(\Gamma_i) = \Gamma_i$.
(ii) Γ_i *is a consistent with* **S4.2** *theory (c***S4.2***-theory).*

4   S4.2 Representation of KB_R-Structures

Definition 5. *Assume any Kripke model* $\mathfrak{M} = \langle W, R, V \rangle$ *and any* $C \subseteq W$. *Then,* $Th_{\mathfrak{M}}(C) =_{def} \{\varphi \in \mathcal{L}_\square \mid (\forall w \in C)\ \mathfrak{M}, w \Vdash \varphi\}$, $K_{\mathfrak{M}}(C) =_{def} \{\varphi \in \mathcal{L}_\square \mid (\forall w \in C)\ \mathfrak{M}, w \Vdash \square\varphi\}$, $B_{\mathfrak{M}}(C) =_{def} \{\varphi \in \mathcal{L}_\square \mid (\forall w \in C)\ \mathfrak{M}, w \Vdash \neg\square\neg\square\varphi\}$.

Intuitively, $Th_{\mathfrak{M}}(C)$ is the theory containing formulas, which are true in every situation of C, $K_{\mathfrak{M}}(C)$ is *everything our agent knows in every situation of* C, and $B_{\mathfrak{M}}(C)$ is *everything she believes*, in every situation of C. Our first result states that **in the case of an epistemic S4.2-model, everything she knows and everything she believes, can be captured syntactically by the notion of** KB_R**-structures. Furthermore, everything she believes, is the same in all clusters, and coincides with everything she knows in the final cluster.**

Theorem 4. *Let* $\mathfrak{M} = \langle W, R, V \rangle$ *be any* **S4.2**-*model with clusters* $C_i \subseteq W$ $(i \in D)$, *where* C_0 *is the final cluster. Then, there is a relation* $P \subseteq D \times D$ *such that* $\langle (Th_{\mathfrak{M}}(C_i)), (K_{\mathfrak{M}}(C_i)), (B_{\mathfrak{M}}(C_i)) \rangle_{i \in D}^{P}$ *is a* KB_P-*structure and* $B_{\mathfrak{M}}(C_i) = K_{\mathfrak{M}}(C_0)$.

Similarly to parts (a), (b) and (c) of the proof of Theorem 4 (see [13]) one can prove that, having fixed modal-free, consistent and closed under propositional consequence theories $S_0, \ldots, S_n$ and an s-rtd-relation P, we can find a KB_P-structure $\langle (T_i), (\Gamma_i), (\Delta_i) \rangle_{i \in D}^{P}$ such that the non-modal part of the theories $T_0, \ldots, T_n$, is exactly $S_0, \ldots, S_n$ respectively.

Proposition 1. *Let* $S_0, \ldots, S_n \subseteq \mathcal{L}$ *be modal-free, consistent and closed under propositional consequence theories, and* $P \subseteq D \times D$ *an s-rtd-relation. Then, there exists a* KB_P-*structure* $\langle (T_i), (\Gamma_i), (\Delta_i) \rangle_{i \in D}^{P}$ *s.t.* $T_i \cap \mathcal{L} = S_i$ $(i \in D)$.

As an application of Proposition 1, let us consider again s-rtd-relation R of Example 2. Furthermore, consider $p \in \Phi$, $S_0 = Cn_{\mathbf{PC}_{\mathcal{L}}}(\{p\})$ and $S_1 = Cn_{\mathbf{PC}_{\mathcal{L}}}(\varnothing)$. It is easy to see that $S_0 = Cn_{\mathbf{PC}_{\mathcal{L}}}(S_0)$ and $S_1 = Cn_{\mathbf{PC}_{\mathcal{L}}}(S_1)$. Clearly, both are satisfiable, hence, by the soundness theorem for propositional logic, they are consistent. So, by Proposition 1, there is a KB_R-structure $\langle (T_0, T_1), (\Gamma_0, \Gamma_1), (\Delta_0, \Delta_1) \rangle^{R}$ s.t. $T_0 \cap \mathcal{L} = S_0$ and $T_1 \cap \mathcal{L} = S_1$. Hence, $p \in T_0$ and $p \notin T_1$ (for otherwise, $p \in S_1$, so $\vdash_{\mathbf{PC}_{\mathcal{L}}} p$, hence p would be a tautology, which is absurd). Then, since $p \notin T_1$, by definition of Γ_1, $p \notin \Gamma_1$. But, $p \in T_0$, hence, by (P_0), $\Box p \in T_0$, and since T_0 is consistent, $\neg\Box p \notin T_0$, so, $\neg\Box p \notin \Gamma_1$. Therefore, $p \notin \Gamma_1 \nRightarrow \neg\Box p \in \Gamma_1$. This counterexample verifies the next lemma, which is most welcomed.

Lemma 14. *There are* KB_R-*structures, whose knowledge-part (some* Γ_i's) *does not satisfy the negative introspection property concerning knowledge.*

Our next goal is to prove the converse of Theorem 4, i.e. for a given KB_R-structure, there is an epistemic **S4.2**-model, in which everything an agent knows and believes, is described by the KB_R-structure given, and furthermore, everything she believes, is described by one of the knowledge-theories in structure KB_R. The model, which we are searching for, will be a construction similar to the well known canonical model for a modal logic, and it will be based on the normal modal logic **S4.2**, which we will denote as Λ. The proof employs standard techniques related to the canonical model construction, every technical detail appears in [13].

Definition 6. *Let* $\langle (T_i), (\Gamma_i), (\Delta_i) \rangle_{i \in D}^{R}$ *be any* KB_R-*structure. The* canonical model *for it, is Kripke model* $\mathfrak{M}^c = \langle W^c, R^c, V^c \rangle$, *where*

(i) $W^c = \bigcup_{i \in D} W_i^c$, *where* $W_i^c = \{(i, \Theta) \in D \times \mathcal{P}(\mathcal{L}_{\Box}) \mid \Theta : m\Gamma_i c\Lambda\}$ $(i \in D)$

(ii) $(\forall (i, \Theta), (j, z) \in W^c)((i, \Theta) R^c(j, z) \iff$
$$(iRj \ \ \& \ \ (\forall \varphi \in \mathcal{L}_{\Box})(\Box\varphi \in \Theta \Rightarrow \varphi \in z)))$$

(iii) $(\forall p \in \Phi)(V^c(p) = \{(i, \Theta) \in W^c \mid p \in \Theta\})$

Remark 1.   Firstly, notice that W^c is the disjoint union of all $m\Gamma_i c\Lambda$ theories with indexes in D. Furthermore, by Lemma 13(ii), every Γ_i $(i \in D)$ is $c\Lambda$, hence, to refer to $m\Gamma_i c\Lambda$-theories is meaningful, and $\Gamma_i \nvdash_\Lambda \bot$, so, $\{\top\}$ is $\Gamma_i c\Lambda$, and by Lindenbaum's Lemma, there exists a $m\Gamma_i c\Lambda$-theory (which, by the way, contains $\{\top\}$), therefore, every $W_i^c \neq \varnothing$ $(i \in D)$.

Lemma 15 (Truth Lemma). $(\forall \varphi \in \mathcal{L}_\square)(\forall (i, \ominus) \in W^c)(\mathfrak{M}^c, (i, \ominus) \Vdash \varphi \Leftrightarrow \varphi \in \ominus)$.

Lemma 16. *Let* $\langle (T_i), (\Gamma_i), (\Delta_i) \rangle^R_{i \in D}$ *be any* KB_R-*structure, and* $\mathfrak{M}^c$ *its canonical model. Then,* $(\forall i \in D)(\forall \varphi \in \mathcal{L}_\square)$

$$\Gamma_i \vdash_\Lambda \varphi \iff (\forall (i, \ominus) \in W_i^c) \; \mathfrak{M}^c, (i, \ominus) \Vdash \square \varphi$$

Now, we are ready to prove a representation theorem for KB_R-structures.

Theorem 5. *Let* $\langle (T_i), (\Gamma_i), (\Delta_i) \rangle^R_{i \in D}$ *be any* KB_R-*structure. Then, there exists an* **S4.2**-*model* $\mathfrak{M} = \langle W, R, V \rangle$ *and* $C_i \subseteq W$ *s.t.* $(\forall i \in D)$

$$\Gamma_i = K_{\mathfrak{M}}(C_i) \qquad \Delta_i = B_{\mathfrak{M}}(C_i) = \Gamma_0$$

5   Related Work - Further Research

The identification of logical theories, which capture the epistemic content of a rational agent's view of the world, is a very important topic in Knowledge Representation. A very important notion has been the notion of a stable belief set, introduced by R.Stalnaker [18] and further investigated in modal non-monotonic reasoning [16]. The original motivation of this paper (rather distinctly far from the final result) has been the idea to derive logically interesting notions of stable epistemic states out of a model-theoretic starting point, and prove that they possess intuitive syntactic characterizations. This seems natural to do: stable belief sets can be *represented* as **S5** *theories* or *sets of beliefs held inside a* **KD45** *situation* [9,16]. In a previous paper [14] we obtained interesting syntactic variations of epistemic states and proved representation theorems, in terms of possible-world models for non-normal modal logics. It (still) seems natural to investigate the other way around: *to define epistemic theories in terms of possible-worlds models for interesting epistemic logics* (such as **S4.2, S4.4**), *and then syntactically characterize these theories with simple context-rules,* such as the ones encountered in Stalnaker's stable belief sets. On the way, it became clear to us that, from a purely epistemological viewpoint that takes into account the information available to the agent inside each situation, the **S5**-like analysis of epistemic reasoning is too simple to furnish a realistic view (although there exists a compensation, in terms of various handy technical properties). Thus, we took a step back to start from the very beginning: the notion of accessibility between possible worlds, its epistemic content and its logical interpretations. This led us to the semantic analysis discussed in section 3.1 and to the origination of KB_R-structures.

The KB_R-structures introduced here represent a somewhat complex, yet interesting, description of the epistemic status of a *rational* (but *not fully introspective*) agent, allowing a differentiation of knowledge from belief. It would be interesting to embed them in core KR techniques, such as default reasoning or belief revision; actually it is a very challenging (albeit complex) task to define reasoning procedures that will take into account the subtle differences between knowledge and belief. Such a task is bound to be complex but it will be necessarily useful to deviate from the currently dominating model of a logically omniscient, fully introspective agent. As a more short-term goal, it is definitely interesting to identify the computational cost of reasoning with KB_R-structures.

Acknowledgements. We wish to thank the anonymous referees for many valuable comments which led to a simplification of definitions and improvement of the presentation (both in this, as well as in the full version of this paper).

References

1. van Benthem, J.: Modal Logic for Open Minds. CSLI Publications, Stanford (2010)
2. Blackburn, P., de Rijke, M., Venema, Y.: Modal Logic. Cambridge Tracts in Theoretical Computer Science, vol. 53. Cambridge University Press, Cambridge (2001)
3. Chellas, B.F.: Modal Logic, an Introduction. Cambridge University Press, Cambridge (1980)
4. van Ditmarsch, H., van der Hoek, W., Kooi, B.: Dynamic Epistemic Logic. Springer, Heidelberg (2007)
5. Fagin, R., Halpern, J., Moses, Y., Vardi, M.: Reasoning about Knowledge. MIT Press, Cambridge (2003)
6. Gabbay, D.M., Woods, J. (eds.): Logic and the Modalities in the Twentieth Century. Handbook of the History of Logic, vol. 7. North-Holland, Amsterdam (2006)
7. Gochet, P., Gribomont, P.: Epistemic logic. In: Gabbay, Woods (eds.) [6], vol. 7, pp. 99–195 (2006)
8. Goldblatt, R.: Logics of Time and Computation, 2nd edn. CSLI Lecture Notes, vol. 7. Center for the Study of Language and Information, Stanford University (1992)
9. Halpern, J.: A theory of knowledge and ignorance for many agents. Journal of Logic and Computation 7(1), 79–108 (1997)
10. Hintikka, J.: Knowledge and Belief: an Introduction to the Logic of the two notions. Cornell University Press, Ithaca (1962)
11. Hughes, G.E., Cresswell, M.J.: A New Introduction to Modal Logic. Routledge, New York (1996)
12. Janhunen, T., Niemelä, I. (eds.): JELIA 2010. LNCS, vol. 6341. Springer, Heidelberg (2010)
13. Koutras, C., Zikos, Y.: Relating Truth, Knowledge and Belief in epistemic states. Technical Report, draft version, available through the authors' web pages, in particular (January 2011), http://users.att.sch.gr/zikos/index/logic/KZ-KBr-full.pdf
14. Koutras, C.D., Zikos, Y.: Stable belief sets revisited. In: Janhunen, Niemelä (eds.) [12], pp. 221–233
15. Lenzen, W.: Epistemologische Betrachtungen zu [S4,S5]. Erkenntnis 14, 33–56 (1979)
16. Marek, V.W., Truszczyński, M.: Non-Monotonic Logic: Context-dependent Reasoning. Springer, Heidelberg (1993)
17. Segerberg, K.: An essay in Clasical Modal Logic. Filosofiska Studies, Uppsala (1971)
18. Stalnaker, R.: A note on non-monotonic modal logic. Artificial Intelligence 64, 183–196 (1993); Revised version of the unpublished note originally circulated in 1980
19. Wooldridge, M.: An Introduction to Multi Agent Systems. John Wiley & Sons, Chichester (2009)

How Strong Can an Agent Believe Reported Information ?

Laurence Cholvy

ONERA Centre de Toulouse
2 avenue Edouard Belin
31055 Toulouse, France
cholvy@onera.fr

Abstract. This paper[1] aims at studying how an agent can believe a new piece of information when it is reported through different sources, each of them citing another one. Two models are presented, the first one in modal logic and the other one in the Theory of Evidence. They both consider important two properties of the information sources: their validity i.e their ability of reporting true information and their invalidity, i.e their ability of reporting false information.

Keywords: Beliefs, Validity, Invalidity, Logic, Theory of Evidence.

1 Motivation

Before making a decision, a rational agent has to update or revise [1], [10], [8] its own belief base with new information it considers sufficiently supported. Thus one important question for the agent is to estimate how a new piece of information is supported i.e, how strong it can believe it.

Obviously, the agent may believe a new piece of information if it trusts the information source for delivering true information or equivalently, if it trusts the information source for not delivering false information. Thus, knowing if the source is truthful or if it lies will help the agent to have an epistemic position towards the new information.

For instance, assume that in order to know if it will rain this afternoon, I look at Météo-France web site and read that indeed it will rain. If I trust Météo-France for delivering correct forecast, then I can believe what Météo-France is reporting i.e I can believe it will rain. At the opposite, assume that I open my newspaper and read that it will rain. If I know that the forecast provided in this newspaper is always false, then I can believe that what my newspaper is reporting is false i.e I can believe that it will not rain.

One work which influenced our study is Demolombe's work, mainly [6] which, in particular, studies the relations which exist between a piece of information, its truth and the mental attitudes of the agent which produces this piece of

---

[1] This work has been granted by ANR (Agence Nationale de Recherche) under project CAHORS.

W. Liu (Ed.): ECSQARU 2011, LNAI 6717, pp. 386–397, 2011.
© Springer-Verlag Berlin Heidelberg 2011

information. The operators of the modal logic used in this paper are : B_i (B_ip means "agent i believes that p"), I_i^j ($I_i^j p$ means "agent i informs agent j that p"). Operator B_i obeys KD system which is quite usual for beliefs and operator I_i^j only obeys rule of equivalence substitutivity [2] . The author first defines several properties agents can have, called epistemic properties, among which the following are worth noting.

Sincerity: Agent i is sincere with regard to agent j for information p iff, if i informs j that p, then i believes p. I.e. a sincere agent believes what it says. Thus $sincere(i,j,p) \equiv I_i^j p \rightarrow B_i p$.

Competence: Agent i is competent about p iff, if i believes p then p is true. I.e. the beliefs of a competent agent are true. Thus $competent(i,p) \equiv B_i p \rightarrow p$.

Validity: Agent i is valid with regard to j for p iff, if i informs j about p, then p is true. I.e. a valid agent tells the truth. Thus $valid(i,j,p) \equiv I_i^j p \rightarrow p$.

Notice that in Demolombe's model, for any i,j and p, it is the case that $sincere(i,j,p) \wedge competent(i,p) \rightarrow valid(i,j,p)$.

These notions can then be used to derive the beliefs of an agent who receives a piece of information. For instance, $B_i I_j^i p \wedge B_i valid(j,i,p) \rightarrow B_i p$ is a theorem or equivalently $B_i I_j^i p \rightarrow (B_i valid(j,i,p) \rightarrow B_i p)$ is a theorem. It shows that an agent's belief about the validity of the agent who emits the new information influences its own belief about this information. An instance of this theorem is: $B_i I_{MF}^i rain \rightarrow (B_i valid(MF,i,rain) \rightarrow B_i rain)$ which means that if I am aware that Météo-France is reporting that it will rain then, if I believe that Météo-France is valid with regard to the forecast then I believe that it will rain.

This work is interesting because it shows that our belief in the validity of an agent positively influences our own belief in what it reports. However, we think that we could consider another kind of beliefs. More precisely, we think that our belief in the fact that an agent is a lier also influences, but negatively, our belief in what it reports.

Recently, [7] addresses very close questions by using Dempster-Shafer's Theory [9]. This work proposes a mechanism for computing the plausibility of a piece of information which is emitted by an agent i given our uncertain belief about i's reliability. For the authors, the reliability of an agent is defined by its relevance and its truthfulness so that (1) information provided by a non-relevant information source is ignored i.e a non-relevant source brings no information; (2) we can believe the piece of information provided by a relevant and truthful source; (3) we can believe the negation of the piece of information provided by a relevant but non-truthful source. Notice that "being relevant and truthful" is very close to "being valid" as introduced by Demolombe; "being relevant and non truthful" is close to "being invalid" as we introduced it [5]. Notice however that the notion of relevance and the impact of non relevant information is rather new.

In this present work, our aim is to adress a more general case and study how to estimate our belief in a new piece of information when it is *reported information* i.e when a source reports that another source has reported that very information (this process can even be longer). This is the case for instance when I am informed by my neighbour that, according to Météo-France web site, it will rain. Here, my neighbour does not tell me that it will rain but he reports that Météo-France reported it will rain. Consequently, trusting my neighbour for delivering true forecast is not useful here. However, trusting my neighbour for telling me the truth regarding what it read on Météo-France web site (i.e, it is indeed true that Météo-France reports that it will rain) and trusting Météo-France for delivering true forecast, will allow me to believe that it will rain.

Acquiring reported information can even be more complex when, for instance, my meighbour tells me that his newspaper writes that Météo-France reports that it will rain. Here, the very information which interests me is reported through three different agents, each of them citing the previous one: my neighbour, the newspaper, Météo-France.

The question of estimating how strong an agent can believe a reported piece of information is the object of our current research. In this paper, we present two models. The first one is defined in modal logic and can be considered as an extension of [6]. It emphasizes the importance of validity i.e the ability of reporting true facts and introduces a dual property called invalidity as the ability of reporting false facts. This model is presented in section 2. In order to be more general and to deal with uncertainty, we propose to use Dempster-Shafer's Theory to define the second model. It is presented in section 3. We show that it generalizes some results obtained in the first model regarding to what can believe an agent when it gets reported information. Finally, section 4 is devoted to a discussion.

2   A Model of Reported Information in Modal Logic

The modal logic we consider is inspired from [6]. It is based on a family of modal operators R_i, where i are agents. $R_i\phi$ means that agent i reports ϕ. These operators satify the following axiom:

$$R_i(\alpha \wedge \beta) \leftrightarrow R_i\alpha \wedge R_i\beta$$

and obey the following inference rule:

$$\frac{A \leftrightarrow B}{R_i A \leftrightarrow R_i B}$$

Besides, there are operators B_i ($B_i A$ means "agent i believes that A") which obey KD axioms:

$$B_i \neg A \rightarrow \neg B_i A$$

$$B_i A \wedge B_i(A \rightarrow B) \rightarrow B_i B$$

and necessitation as well:

$$\frac{A}{B_i A}$$

We successively examine the case of a single level of nesting, then the case of two levels then finally the general case.

2.1   First Case: One Level of Nesting

In this case, an agent i thinks that another agent j reports a piece of information ϕ. I.e, we have: $B_i R_j \phi$. The question we ask is: how can i believe ϕ ? In order to answer this question, we come back to the notion of validity introduced in [6], we simplify it and we add a dual notion we call invalidity.

Definition 1. *Agent i is valid for information ϕ as soon as we can deduce that ϕ is true when i reports ϕ. It is denoted:*

$$valid(i, \phi) \equiv R_i \phi \rightarrow \phi$$

Definition 2. *Agent i is invalid towards for information ϕ as soon as we can deduce that ϕ is false when i reports ϕ. It is denoted:*

$$invalid(i, \phi) \equiv R_i \phi \rightarrow \neg\phi$$

Notice that $invalid(i, \phi) \leftrightarrow \neg valid(i, \phi)$ is not a theorem.
But $R_i \phi \rightarrow (invalid(i, \phi) \leftrightarrow \neg valid(i, \phi))$ is.

Proposition 1. *For any agents i, j :*

$$B_i R_j \phi \wedge B_i valid(j, \phi) \rightarrow B_i \phi$$

$$B_i R_j \phi \wedge B_i invalid(j, \phi) \rightarrow B_i \neg\phi$$

Thus if agent i believes that j is valid (resp invalid) for information ϕ and if it believes that j reported ϕ, then it believes that ϕ is true (resp, false).

2.2   Second Case: Two Levels of Nesting

In this case, a first agent i thinks that a second agent j reported that a third agent k reports a piece of information ϕ. I.e, we have: $B_i R_j R_k \phi$. The question is now: how can i believe ϕ ?

Proposition 2. *For any agents i, j, k:*

$$B_i R_j R_k \phi \wedge B_i valid(j, R_k \phi) \wedge B_i valid(k, \phi) \rightarrow B_i \phi$$

$$B_i R_j R_k \phi \wedge B_i valid(j, R_k \phi) \wedge B_i invalid(k, \phi) \rightarrow B_i \neg\phi$$

$$B_i R_j R_k \phi \wedge B_i invalid(j, R_k \phi) \nrightarrow B_i \phi$$

$$B_i R_j R_k \phi \wedge B_i invalid(j, R_k \phi) \nrightarrow B_i \neg\phi$$

Thus in this model, if agent i believes that j is valid in its reporting $R_k\phi$ and if i believes that k is valid (resp invalid) in its reporting ϕ, then we can conclude that i believes ϕ (resp $\neg\phi$). However, if i believes that j is invalid in its reporting $R_k\phi$, then we cannot infer that i believes ϕ nor believes $\neg\phi$. More precisely, the only belief we can infer that i believes that k did not report ϕ.

Example 1. Let us illustrate this on the example given in introduction. Consider that my neighbour tells me that his newpaper wrote it will rain. Notice that here, agents i, j and k are respectively myself, my neighbour and his newpaper.

- If I consider that my neighbour is valid (his newspaper really wrote it will rain) and if I consider his newspaper valid (the forecast is always true in this newspaper) l then, I can conclude that indeed, it will rain.
- If I consider that my neighbour is valid and if I consider his newspaper invalid (the forecast is always false in this newspaper) then I can conclude that it will not rain
- But If I consider that my neighbour is invalid (i.e, his newspaper did not write that it will rain because for instance the newspaper were not distributed today) then I cannot conclude it will rain nor conclude it will not rain.

2.3 General Case

The previous result can easily been extended. Here we assume that $B_i R_{j_1}...R_{j_n}\phi$.

Proposition 3

$$B_i R_{j_1}...R_{j_n}\phi \wedge B_i(\bigwedge_{m=1...(n-1)} valid(j_m, R_{j_{m+1}}...R_{j_n}\phi)) \wedge B_i valid(j_n, \phi) \rightarrow B_i\phi$$

$$B_i R_{j_1}...R_{j_n}\phi \wedge B_i(\bigwedge_{m=1...(n-1)} valid(j_m, R_{j_{m+1}}...R_{j_n}\phi)) \wedge B_i invalid(j_n, \phi) \rightarrow B_i\neg\phi$$

$$B_i R_{j_1}...R_{j_n}\phi \wedge B_i(\bigwedge_{m=1...(m_0-1)} valid(j_m, R_{j_{m+1}}..R_{j_n}\phi)) \wedge B_i invalid(j_{m_0}, R_{j_{m_0}+1}...R_{j_n}\phi) \not\rightarrow$$

$$B_i\phi$$

$$B_i R_{j_1}...R_{j_n}\phi \wedge B_i(\bigwedge_{m=1...(m_0-1)} valid(j_m, R_{j_{m+1}}..R_{j_n}\phi)) \wedge B_i invalid(j_{m_0}, R_{j_{m_0}+1}...R_{j_n}\phi) \not\rightarrow$$

$$B_i\neg\phi$$

Example 2. For instance, assume that my neighbour tells me that his colleague told him that the newspaper wrote that it will rain.

If I consider that my neighbour is valid (it is true that his colleague told him that the newspaper wrote that it will rain) but if consider that his colleague is invalid then I can have no idea about the weather. The only conclusion I can draw is that the newspaper did not write it will rain.

3 A Model of Reported Information in the Theory of Evidence

The previous model allows an agent to reason with its beliefs about the validity or invality of the entwined sources in a binary way. No uncertainty can be managed and the reason is the use of a modal logic. This is why, we looked at another kind of formalism dedicated to uncertainty management, the Theory of Evidence or Dempster-Shafer's Theory. Two models have been already presented [4] [5]. Here, we improve the last one by emphasing the Belief Function instead of the Plausibility Function. We also show that, regarding to what can believe an agent when it gets reported information, it is more general than the logical model presented in section 2.

3.1 First Case: One Agent

We suppose agent j reports a piece of information ϕ to agent i. The question we ask is still: how can i believe ϕ ?

In order to answer this question in an uncertainty setting, we take into account the degrees at which i thinks that the source j is valid and the degree at which i thinks that j is invalid. These degrees intend to model the uncertainty of i as regard to the validity and invalidity of j.

We consider a classical propositional language the two letters of which are: ϕ and $R_j\phi$, representing respectively the facts "information ϕ is true" and "agent j reported information ϕ". The four interpretations of this language[2] are $\{w_1, w_2, w_3, w_4\}$ so that: w_1, denoted $w_1 = \{R_j\phi, \phi\}$, represents the situation in which j has reported information ϕ and ϕ is true; $w_2 = \{R_j\phi, \neg\phi\}$ represents the situation in which j has reported information ϕ and ϕ is false; $w_3 = \{\neg R_j\phi, \phi\}$ represents the situation in which j did not report information ϕ and ϕ is true; $w_4 = \{\neg R_j\phi, \neg\phi\}$ represents the situation in which j did not report information ϕ and ϕ is false.

We consider the discernment $\Theta = \{w_1, w_2, w_3, w_4\}$.

Definition 3. *Consider two agents i and j and a piece of information ϕ. Let $d_j \in [0,1]$ and $d'_j \in [0,1]$ two real numbers[3] such that $0 \leq d_j + d'_j \leq 1$. d_j is the degree at which i thinks that j is valid for ϕ and d'_j is the degree at which i thinks that j is invalid for ϕ (written $VI(i, j, \phi, d_j, d'_j)$) iff i's beliefs can be modelled by the mass assignment $m^{(i,j,\phi,d_j,d'_j)}$ defined by:*

$$m^{(i,j,\phi,d_j,d'_j)}(w_1 \vee w_3 \vee w_4) = d_j$$
$$m^{(i,j,\phi,d_j,d'_j)}(w_2 \vee w_3 \vee w_4) = d'_j$$
$$m^{(i,j,\phi,d_j,d'_j)}(w_1 \vee w_2 \vee w_3 \vee w_4) = 1 - (d_j + d'_j)$$

---

[2] Notice that this language is not a modal language. In particular, here, ϕ is a letter and not a formula and $R_j\phi$ is a propositional letter and not a modal formula. This implies that the language of the model we are defining here is less expressive than the language of the logic introduced before, and we some deduction power. For instance, the same letter will denote any equivalent formula.

[3] These degrees should be indexed by i but index i is omitted for readibility.

Let us recall that assigning a mass on a disjunction of w_k is equivalent to assigning this mass on any propositional formula satisfied by all the w_k in the disjunction ([3]). Consequently, the mass assignment defined in the previous definition can be reformulated by:

$$m^{(i,j,\phi,d_j,d'_j)}(R_j\phi \to \phi) = d_j$$
$$m^{(i,j,\phi,d_j,d'_j)}(R_j\phi \to \neg\phi) = d'_j$$
$$m^{(i,j,\phi,d_j,d'_j)}(True) = 1 - (d_j + d'_j)$$

Thus, according to this definition, if i believes at degree d_j that j is valid for ϕ and believes at degree d'_j that j is invalid then its belief degree in the fact "if j reports ϕ then ϕ is true" is d_j; its belief degree in the fact "if j reports ϕ then ϕ is false" is d'_j; and its total ignorance degree is $1 - (d_j + d'_j)$.

The following particular cases are worth detailing:

- $(d_j = 1)$ and $(d'_j = 0)$ i.e, $VI(i, j, \phi, 1, 0)$. In this case, $m^{(i,j,\phi,1,0)}(R_j\phi \to \phi) = 1$. I.e, i is certain that if j reports ϕ then ϕ is true, i.e, i is certain that j is *valid* for ϕ.
- $(d_j = 0)$ and $(d'_j = 1)$ i.e, $VI(i, j, \phi, 0, 1)$. In this case, $m^{(i,j,\phi,0,1)}(R_j\phi \to \neg\phi) = 1$. I.e. i is certain that if j reports ϕ then ϕ is false, i.e, i is certain that j is *invalid* for ϕ.

Definition 4. $m^{i,R_j\phi}$ *is the mass assignment defined by:* $m^{i,R_j\phi}(R_j\phi) = 1$ *or equivalently,* $m^{i,R_j\phi}(w_1 \vee w_2) = 1$.

$m^{i,R_j\phi}$ represents the fact that, agent i is certain that j has reported information ϕ.

Definition 5. *Consider two agents i and j such that $VI(i, j, \phi, d_j, d'_j)$. If i is certain that j reports ϕ, then i's beliefs can be modelled by the mass assignment m obtained by Dempster's combination of $m^{(i,j,\phi,d_j,d'_j)}$ and $m^{i,R_j\phi}$. I.e.,*

$$m = m^{(i,j,\phi,d_j,d'_j)} \oplus m^{i,R_j\phi}$$

This assigment represents i's beliefs when i is certain that j has reported ϕ given that d_j is the degree at which i thinks that j is valid for ϕ and d'_j is the degree at which i thinks that j is invalid for ϕ,

Proposition 4

$$m(R_j\phi \wedge \phi) = d_j$$
$$m(R_j\phi \wedge \neg\phi) = d'_j$$
$$m(R_j\phi) = 1 - (d_j + d'_j)$$

Proposition 5. *Let Bel be the belief function associated with assignment m.*

$$Bel(\phi) = d_j$$
$$Bel(\neg\phi) = d'_j$$

Consequently, when i thinks that $R_i\phi$ and when $VI(i,j,\phi,d_j,d'_j)$ then i believes ϕ more than $\neg\phi$ if and only if $d_j > d'_j$ i.e, its belief degree in j's validity is greater that its belief degree in j's invalidity. This is quite obvious.

The following proposition details two interesting cases.

Proposition 6

If $VI(i,j,\phi,1,0)$, then $Bel(\phi) = 1$ and $Bel(\neg\phi) = 0$ i.e, i believes ϕ and does not believe $\neg\phi$;

If $VI(i,j,\phi,0,1)$, then $Bel(\phi) = 0$ and $Bel(\neg\phi) = 1$ i.e, i does not believe $\neg\phi$ and believes ϕ.

This comes to proposition 1.

3.2   Second Case: Two Agents

Here, agent i thinks that agent j reports that agent k has reported ϕ. The question is still: how can i believe ϕ is ?

We consider a propositional language the letters of which are: ϕ, $R_k\phi$, and $R_j R_k \phi$. This language has got 8 interpretations $w_1 = \{R_j R_k \phi, R_k \phi, \phi\}$; $w_2 = \{R_j R_k \phi, R_k \phi, \neg\phi\}$; $w_3 = \{R_j R_k \phi, \neg R_k \phi, \phi\}$; $w_4 = \{R_j R_k \phi, \neg R_k \phi, \neg\phi\}$; $w_5 = \{\neg R_j R_k \phi, R_k \phi, \phi\}$; $w_6 = \{\neg R_j R_k \phi, R_k \phi, \neg\phi\}$; $w_7 = \{\neg R_j R_k \phi, \neg R_k \phi, \phi\}$; $w_8 = \{\neg R_j R_k \phi, \neg R_k \phi, \neg\phi\}$; The of discernment is the set $\Theta = \{w_1, ... w_8\}$.

As before, we will assign mass on formulas and not on disjunctions of w_i.

Definition 6. *Assume that i thinks that $R_j R_k \phi$ and that $VI(i,k,\phi,d_k,d'_k)$ and $VI(i,j,R_k\phi,d_j,d'_j)$. Then, i's beliefs are defined by the mass assignment denoted m defined by[4]:*

$$m = m^{(i,k,\phi,d_k,d'_k)} \oplus m^{(i,j,R_k\phi,d_j,d'_j)} \oplus m^{R_j R_k \phi}$$

This assigment represents i's beliefs when i is certain that $R_j R_i \phi$, given that d_k (resp d'_k) is the degree at which i thinks that k is valid (resp, invalid) for ϕ and d_j (resp d'_j) is the degree at which i thinks that j is valid (resp invalid) for $R_k\phi$.

Proposition 7.

$$m(R_j R_k \phi \wedge R_k \phi \wedge \phi) = d_k.d_j$$
$$m(R_j R_k \phi \wedge R_k \phi \wedge \neg\phi) = d'_k d_j$$
$$m(R_j R_k \phi \wedge R_k \phi) = (1 - (d_k + d'_k)).d_j$$
$$m(R_j R_k \phi \wedge \neg R_k \phi \wedge (R_k \phi \rightarrow \phi)) = d_k.d'_j$$
$$m(R_j R_k \phi \wedge \neg R_k \phi \wedge (R_k \phi \rightarrow \neg\phi)) = d'_k.d'_j$$
$$m(R_j R_k \phi \wedge \neg R_k \phi) = (1 - (d_k + d'_k)).d'_j$$
$$m(R_j R_k \phi \wedge (R_k \phi \rightarrow \phi)) = d_k.(1 - (d_j + d_j))$$
$$m(R_j R_k \phi \wedge (R_k \phi \rightarrow \neg\phi)) = d'_k.(1 - (d_j + d'_j))$$
$$m(R_j R_k \phi) = (1 - (d_k + d'_k)).(1 - (d_j + d'_j))$$

---

[4] Again, index i is omitted.

Proposition 8. *Let Bel be the belief function associated with m. Then*

$$Bel(\phi) = d_k.d_j$$

$$Bel(\neg\phi) = d'_k.d_j$$

Proposition 9.

$$Bel(\phi) > bel(\neg\phi) \iff d_j \neq 0 \text{ and } d_k > d'_k$$

I.e. i believes ϕ more than $\neg\phi$ iff according to i j can be valid and the degree at which i thinks that k is valid is greater than the degree at which i thinks that k is invalid.

The following proposition shows that even in this two-agent case, this model provides the same result than the logical model presented in section 2.

Proposition 10.

If $VI(i, j, R_k\phi, 1, 0)$ and $VI(i, k, \phi, 1, 0)$ then $Bel(\phi) = 1$ and $Bel(\neg\phi) = 0$, *i.e, i believes ϕ and does not believe $\neg\phi$;*

If $VI(i, j, R_k\phi, 1, 0)$ and $VI(i, k, \phi, 0, 1)$ then $Bel(\phi) = 0$ and $Bel(\neg\phi) = 1$, *i.e, i believes $\neg\phi$ more than ϕ;*

If $VI(i, j, R_k\phi, 0, 1)$ then $Bel(\phi) = 0$ and $Bel(\neg\phi) = 0$, *i.e, i does not believe ϕ nor $\neg\phi$.*

This comes to proposition 2.

3.3   General Case

The previous result can easily been extended. Assume that agent i believes that $R_{j_1}...R_{j_n}\phi$. How can i believe ϕ ?

We consider a propositional language the $n+1$ letters of which are ϕ, $R_{j_n}\phi$, $R_{j_{n-1}}R_{j_n}\phi$, ..., $R_{j_1}...R_{j_n}\phi$. This language has got 2^{n+1} interpretations which form the discernment frame we consider but we do not detail them. As before, we assign masses to formulas.

Definition 7. *Consider that i thinks that $R_{j_1}...R_{j_n}\phi$ so that $VI(i, j_n, \phi, d_{j_n}, d'_{j_n})$ ..., $VI(i, j_1, R_{j_2}...R_{j_n}\phi, d_{j_1}, d'_{j_1})$. Then, i's beliefs are defined by the following mass assignment*[5]*:*

$$m = m^{(i,j_n,\phi,d_{j_n},d'_{j_n})} \oplus ... \oplus m^{(i,j_1,R_{j_2}...R_{j_n}\phi,d_{j_1},d'_{j_1})} \oplus m^{R_{j_1}...R_{j_n}\phi}$$

This assigment represents i's beliefs when i is certain that $R_{j_1}...R_{j_n}\phi$, given that d_{j_m} (resp d'_{j_m}) is the degree at which i thinks that j_m is valid (resp, invalid) for $R_{j_dm+1}...R_{j_n}\phi$ and d_{j_n} (resp d'_{j_n}) is the degree at which i thinks that j_n is valid (resp, invalid) for ϕ.

---

[5] Again, index i is omitted.

Proposition 11. *Let Bel be the belief function associated with m. Then*

$$Bel(\phi) = d_{j_1}...d_{j_{n-1}}.d_{j_n}$$
$$Bel(\neg\phi) = d_{j_1}...d_{j_{n-1}}.d'_{j_n}$$

Proposition 12

$$Bel(\phi) > Bel(\neg\phi) \Longleftrightarrow \forall k = j_1...j_{n-1} \quad d_k \neq 0 \text{ and } d_{j_n} > d'_{j_n}$$

Thus, i believes ϕ more than $\neg\phi$ iff according to i, $j_1...j_{n-1}$ can be valid and the degree at which i thinks that j_n is valid is stricty greater that the degree at which it thinks that j_n is invalid.

Proposition 13

If $\forall k = j_1...j_n \quad d_k = 1$ then $Bel(\phi) = 1$ and $Bel(\neg\phi) = 0$ i.e i believes ϕ and does not believe $\neg\phi$;

If $\forall k = j_1...j_{n-1} \quad d_k = 1$ and $d_{j_n} = 0$ then $Bel(\phi) = 0$ and $Bel(\neg\phi) = 1$ i.e i believes $\neg\phi$ and does not believe ϕ;

If $\forall k = j_1...j_{m_0-1} \quad d_k = 1$ and $d_{j_{m_0}} = 0$ then $Bel(\phi) = 0$ and $Bel(\neg\phi) = 0$ i.e i does not believe ϕ nor $\neg\phi$.

This comes to proposition 3 and shows that in the general case, this model in the Theory of Evidence provides the same result than the logical model described in section 2 as for the conclusion agent i can draw concerning information ϕ.

4   Discussion

The question of estimating how an agent can belief information when it is reported by several entwined sources each one citing the previous one, is a question which has received few attention. The reason is maybe because this question can be confused with the question of estimating how an agent can believe a piece of information when it is passed from a source to another one so that each source can pass it correctly or can lie. As the example given in the introduction showed, these two questions must not be confused. Indeed, when my neigbour tells me that according to Météo-France it will rain, the information my neighbour reports is not that it will rain.

We have shown that the agent's beliefs depend on its beliefs in the abilities of the sources for reporting true information (what is called validity) and abilities of reporting false information (called invalidity). A logical model has been defined which helps to clarify the notions. But it cannot manage uncertainty.

This is why we have studied another model, in the Theory of Evidence, and showed that it extends the logical one regarding to the conclusion that the agent who receives reported information can draw. This model requires that this agent has degrees of beliefs in the validity and invalidity of sources concerning what they report.

It assumes that for any sources and any information these degrees are unique. i.e here, it is assumed that the degrees do not depend on the current environment in which the validity and the invalidity of the source are evaluated. This is questionnable and obviously simplistic. However, it is complex enough because a hard question is to evaluate these degrees. Under this simple hypothesis we can imagine to estimate theses degrees with some knowledge on the sources obtained by past experience.

Another question which can be discussed is the choice of the combination rule for defining the mass assigment which characterizes the beliefs of an agent given its beliefs degrees in the validity and invalidity. We have naturally used the classical Demspter's combination rule but studying the impact of choosing another rule should be done.

Furthermore, let us notice that here, for estimating how the agent trust the new piece of information, it does not take into account its current belief base. It estimates it only from its own beliefs about the validity and invalidity of the sources.

Also, the potential revision of the agent's current belief base has not been studied here but the present work offers a prerequisite to do it.

Finally, let us note that the logic defined in section 2, even if it does not manage uncertainty, offers the possibility to make not only deductive reasoning but also abductive reasoning with epistemic properties of the agents. For instance given that $B_i R_j R_k \phi$ and $B_i valid(j, R_k \phi)$ we can abductively find the epistemic properties of the agents that are required to explain $B_i \phi$. Here, one of this plausible assumption is $B_i valid(k, \phi)$. This is one of the greatest interest of logic to offer these kinds of reasoning. And studying this abductive reasoning in a graph of communicating agents constitutes an interesting extension of this present work.

Acknowledgements

I thank the reviewers whose comments and remarks helped me to improve the paper.

References

1. Alchourron, C.E., Gardenfors, P., Makinson, D.: On the logic of theory change: Partial meet contraction and revision functions. Journal of Symbolic Logic 50, 510–530 (1985)
2. Chellas, B.F.: Modal logic: An introduction. Cambridge University Press, Cambridge (1980)
3. Cholvy, L.: Using Logic to Understand Relations between DSmT and Dempster-Shafer Theory. In: Sossai, C., Chemello, G. (eds.) ECSQARU 2009. LNCS, vol. 5590, pp. 264–274. Springer, Heidelberg (2009)
4. Cholvy, L.: Evaluation of Information Reported: A Model in the Theory of Evidence. In: Hüllermeier, E., Kruse, R., Hoffmann, F. (eds.) IPMU 2010. Communications in Computer and Information Science, vol. 80, pp. 258–267. Springer, Heidelberg (2010)

5. Cholvy, L.: Plausibility of information reported by successive sources. In: Deshpande, A., Hunter, A. (eds.) SUM 2010. LNCS, vol. 6379, pp. 126–136. Springer, Heidelberg (2010)

6. Demolombe, R.: Reasonig about trust: a formal logical work. In: Proc. 2d International Conference iTrust, Oxford (2004)

7. Dubois, D., Denoeux, T.: Relevance and Truthfulness in Information Correction and Fusion. International Journal of Approximate Reasoning (accepted for publication, 2011)

8. Katsuno, H., Mendelzon, A.: On the Difference between Updating a Knowledge Base and Revising it. In: Proce of Principles of Knowledge Representation and Reasoning, KR (1991)

9. Shafer, G.: A mathematical Theory of Evidence. Princeton University Press, Princeton (1976)

10. Winslett, M.: Updating Logical Databases. Cambridge University Press, Cambridge (1990)

Logic-Based Fusion of Complex Epistemic States

Amílcar Mata Díaz and Ramón Pino Pérez

Departamento de Matemáticas
Facultad de ciencias
Universidad de Los Andes
Mérida, Venezuela
{amilcarmata,pino}@ula.ve

Abstract. In this work we extend the framework of logic-based fusion by Konieczny and Pino Pérez [8,9,10,11] to complex epistemic states. We present some postulates given in terms of the finite propositional logic which define merging operators of complex epistemic states. We state some representation theorems for these operators. When we consider concrete spaces, namely those where the epistemic states are total preorders over valuations, we obtain strong representation theorems. This new framework allows us to generalize, in a natural way, the revision operators presented by Benferhat et ál. [2]. As an application of our representation theorems, we define some merging operators over complex epistemic states and show some examples of these operators at work.

Introduction

Knowledge fusion studies the methods leading to extract a coherent piece of information from many sources, which may be mutually contradictory. The applications in this domain go from decision making, passing by medical diagnosis, policy planning, to automatic integration of data. Understanding the theoretical models is important to develop future applications. We work in this direction.

In this work we extend the framework of logic-based fusion of epistemic states presented by Konieczny and Pino Pérez (KP) [8,9,10,11]. In those works the epistemic states considered are defined by sets of propositional sentences. It is important to notice that the KP framework generalizes the seminal belief revision operators presented by Alchourrón, Gardenfors and Makinson [1,6,7]. Actually the KP framework generalizes the Katsuno-Mendelzon finite presentation of AGM in which an epistemic state is represented by a a set of propositional sentences or equivalently a formula.

However, the necessity of considering more complex representations of epistemic states has been stated in the work of Darwiche and Pearl [3,4]. Thus, Meyer [13,14] gave a merging model of more complex epistemic states. In Meyer's work the epistemic states were defined by ranking functions over valuations. However, in this context, Meyer did not establish semantic representation theorems for his operators even if he gives a list of postulates and examines which of them are satisfied by some of his concrete operators.

W. Liu (Ed.): ECSQARU 2011, LNAI 6717, pp. 398–409, 2011.

In the current work, we present some postulates given in terms of the finite propositional logic which define merging operators of complex epistemic states. We state some representation theorems for these operators. When we consider concrete spaces, namely those where the epistemic states are total pre-orders over valuations, we obtain strong representation theorems. This new framework allows us to generalize, in a natural way, the revision operators presented by Benferhat et ál. [2].

As an application of our representation theorems, we define some merging operators over complex epistemic states and show some examples of these operators at work.

We omit the proofs of our results for space reasons. All the proofs can be find in [12]. The reader who knows the technique of proof of the representation theorems of Darwiche and Pearl [3,4] and the representation theorems of Konieczny and Pino Pérez [10] should be able to reconstruct most of the proofs.

This work is organized as follows: Section 1 is devoted to define the concepts used throughout the paper. Section 2 is devoted to give the syntactical postulates and the semantical counterparts. In Section 3 we study a concrete class of epistemic states and give a strong representation theorem. In section 4 we build an operator using the results of previous sections. Finally we make some concluding remarks in Section 5.

1   Preliminaries

Let $\mathcal{L}$ be the set of propositional formulas built over a finite set $\mathcal{P}$ of atomic propositions. $\mathcal{L}^*$ will denote the set of non contradictory formulas. Let $\mathcal{W}$ be the set of valuations. If φ is a formula, we denote by $[\![\varphi]\!]$ the set of models of φ, *i.e.* $[\![\varphi]\!] = \{w \in \mathcal{W} : w \models \varphi\}$. If I is a nonempty set of valuations, we denote by φ_I a formula such that $[\![\varphi_I]\!] = I$.

In this work a *belief base* will be represented[1] by a formula in $\mathcal{L}$. It encodes the set of propositions believed by an agent. Most of the time we refer to a belief base as *the beliefs* (of an agent). The intuitive meaning of a (complex) *epistemic state* is to have in addition to a belief base, other information, possibly null. Many concrete representations of epistemic states have been proposed. The first one is, of course, that of the AGM framework [1,6], where an Epistemic State is a logical theory. Darwiche and Pearl [3,4] represent Epistemic States by total preorders over $\mathcal{W}$. Spohn [16] uses Ordinal Conditional Functions. Probability and possibility measures have been used to represent epistemic states [5]. An abstract model to represent Epistemic States was presented by Benferhat et ál. [2]. We will adopt this through this paper except when we study the concrete representation of total preorders over valuations.

---

[1] Usually a belief base is a set of propositional formulas. Here, by simplicity and due to the fact we work in the finite case, we identify this set with a formula having the same models.

Definition 1 (Epistemic space). *A triple* $(\mathcal{E}, B, \mathcal{L})$ *is called an epistemic space if* $\mathcal{E}$ *is a nonempty set,* $\mathcal{L}$ *is the set of formulas and* B *is a function from* $\mathcal{E}$ *into* $\mathcal{L}$, *such that the image of* B *is all the set* $\mathcal{L}^*$.

The elements of $\mathcal{E}$ are called *Epistemic States*; B is called *belief function*; for any E, $B(E)$ is called the *belief base* of E (it represents the most entrenchment beliefs of E). Notice that if I is a nonempty set of valuations, there exists E, such that $B(E) = \varphi_I$.

A profile Φ is a finite multiset of Epistemic States. Thus, if $E_1, E_2, \ldots, E_n$ are Epistemic States, not necessarily different, $\Phi = \{E_1, E_2, \ldots, E_n\}$ is a profile.

The set of profiles will be denoted $\mathcal{M}(\mathcal{E})$. The profile $\Phi = \{E\}$, most of the time, will be denoted simply E.

Let A be a set. A binary relation $\preceq$ over A is a total preorder if it is total[2] (therefore reflexive) and transitive. Let $\preceq$ be a total preorder over A. We define the strict relation $\prec$ and the indifference $\simeq$ associated to $\preceq$ as follows: $a \prec b$ if and only if $a \preceq b$ and $b \not\preceq a$; $a \simeq b$ if and only if $a \preceq b$ and $b \preceq a$.

It is clear that any linear order is a total preorder. For instance, the lexicographical order $\preceq^{l_n}$ over vectors of real numbers of length n is a linear order and then a total preorder. Another important example is the lexicographical combination of two total preorders defined below. Let A be a nonempty set and let $\preceq_1$ and $\preceq_2$ be two total preorders over A. We define $lex(\preceq_1, \preceq_2)$ over A, denoted $\preceq^{lex}$, by putting:

$$a \preceq^{lex} b \Leftrightarrow \begin{cases} a \prec_1 b, \text{ or} \\ a \simeq_1 b \ \& \ a \preceq_2 b \end{cases}$$

It is not hard to see that $\preceq^{lex}$ is a total preorder over A.

Let $\preceq$ be a total preorder over A. Let C be a subset of A. We say that c is a minimal element of C with respect to $\preceq$ if $c \in C$ and for all $x \in C$, $x \not\prec c$. The set of minimal elements of C will be denoted $min(C, \preceq)$. The minimal elements of the whole set A in which the total preorder is defined will be denoted $min(\preceq)$.

2   Epistemic States Fusion Operators

2.1   Rationality Postulates

We fix an Epistemic space $(\mathcal{E}, B, \mathcal{L})$. A function of the form $\nabla : \mathcal{M}(\mathcal{E}) \times \mathcal{E} \longrightarrow \mathcal{E}$ will be called an epistemic state combination operator, for short, an ES combination operator. $\nabla(\Phi, E)$ represents the result of combining the epistemic states in Φ under the *integrity constraint* E. The idea to have a full epistemic state as an integrity constraint is to force the result of the combination to *satisfy* as much as possible the integrity constraint. This is stated in postulate **(ESF1)** only at level of beliefs. However, in specific representations, we could establish more precisely this *satisfaction* or adequation.

---

[2] That is, $\forall x, y \in A, x \preceq y \lor y \preceq x$. Some authors say *connected* instead of total.

Now we establish the rationality postulates of fusion in the setting of Epistemic States. Most of them are adapted from IC merging postulates proposed by Konieczny and Pino Pérez [9,10,11]. Some of the postulates are new.

Notice that the only known part of Epistemic States, with a well known logical structure, are the beliefs. Thus, it is a very natural issue to express the rationality postulates for our operators in logical terms at level of beliefs.

(ESF0) *If $B(E)$ is consistent, then $B(\nabla(\Phi, E))$ is consistent.*

(ESF1) $B(\nabla(\Phi, E)) \vdash B(E)$.

(ESF2) *If $B(E_1) \equiv B(E_2)$ then $B(\nabla(\Phi, E_1)) \equiv B(\nabla(\Phi, E_2))$*

(ESF3) *If $B(E) \equiv B(E_1) \wedge B(E_2)$ then $B(\nabla(\Phi, E_1)) \wedge B(E_2) \vdash B(\nabla(\Phi, E))$.*

(ESF4) *If $B(E) \equiv B(E_1) \wedge B(E_2)$ and $B(\nabla(\Phi, E_1)) \wedge B(E_2) \nvdash \bot$,   then* $B(\nabla(\Phi, E)) \vdash B(\nabla(\Phi, E_1)) \wedge B(E_2)$.

(ESF5) *If $E_1 \neq E_2$, then there exists E such that $B(\nabla(E_1, E)) \not\equiv B(\nabla(E_2, E))$.*

(ESF6) *If $\bigwedge_{E' \in \Phi} B(E') \wedge B(E) \nvdash \bot$, then $B(\nabla(\Phi, E)) \equiv \bigwedge_{E' \in \Phi} B(E') \wedge B(E)$.*

(ESF7) $B(\nabla(\Phi_1, E)) \wedge B(\nabla(\Phi_2, E)) \vdash B(\nabla(\Phi_1 \sqcup \Phi_2, E))$

(ESF8) $B(\nabla(\Phi_1 \sqcup \Phi_2, E)) \vdash B(\nabla(\Phi_1, E)) \wedge B(\nabla(\Phi_2, E))$ *if $B(\nabla(\Phi_1, E)) \wedge B(\nabla(\Phi_2, E)) \nvdash \bot$.*

(ESF0) says that the beliefs of the resulting Epistemic State have to be consistent whenever the beliefs of the constraint are consistent. Because of the definition of epistemic space, for every Epistemic State E', $B(E')$ is consistent and, therefore, the postulate is trivially satisfied for the ES combination operators.

(ESF1) says that the belief of the result has to be logically at least as strong as the belief of the constraint.

(ESF2) is the syntax irrelevance property at the level of beliefs for the integrity constraints.

(ESF3) and **(ESF4)** together determine one important property in which the beliefs are chosen. They correspond to postulates IC7 and IC8 of IC merging.

(ESF5) is a new postulate. It says that given two different Epistemic States there is a constraint E that leads to different results at level of belief, *i.e.* the beliefs of the result of the operator applied to each Epistemic State with the constraint E, will not be equivalent. This is a minimal rational requirement in order to avoid trivial operators like constant operators.

(ESF6) expresses that if all the agents of the profile agree at the level of belief with the constraint, this agreement will coincide with the belief resulting after application of the operator.

(ESF7) tells us that for any partition of a group into two subgroups, the conjunction of belief of the result of applying the operator to each subgroup will be logically stronger than the beliefs resulting of the application of the operator to the whole group.

(ESF8) expresses that if we can divide a group into two subgroups such that the application of the operator to each subgroup leads to beliefs which are mutually consistent, then the conjunction of these beliefs will be the beliefs resulting from applying the operator to the whole group.

A weaker property than **(ESF8)** is the following one:

(ESF8W) *If* $B\big(\nabla(\Phi_1, E)\big) \wedge B\big(\nabla(\Phi_2, E)\big) \nvdash \bot$, *then*
$$B\big(\nabla(\Phi_1 \sqcup \Phi_2, E)\big) \vdash B\big(\nabla(\Phi_1, E)\big) \vee B\big(\nabla(\Phi_2, E)\big).$$

This property tells us that if a group is divided into two subgroups and after application of the operator the beliefs of the subgroups are consistent, then the beliefs of the whole group after application of the operator have to entail the disjunction of the beliefs of each subgroup.

There is another interesting property, called *iteration postulate*, which concerns the behavior under iteration of integrity constraints: the beliefs, after two iterations, are the beliefs obtained as the result when the integrity constraint is the epistemic state resulting of the combination of the two integrity constraints. More precisely:

(ESF-It) $B\Big(\nabla\big(\Phi, \nabla(E_1, E_2)\big)\Big) \equiv B\Big(\nabla\big(\nabla(\Phi, E_1), E_2\big)\Big)$

The rationale behind this postulate, is that at level of beliefs, iterating the operator with respect a sequence of integrity constraints is the same that performing one application of the operator respect to an integrity constraint obtained by application of the operator to the sequence of integrity constraints. This sort of associativity of the operator, at level of integrity constraints, is very natural.

Assuming very few postulates, the last postulate entails (ESF3) and (ESF4). More precisely:

Proposition 1. *Let* ∇ *be an ES combination operator satisfying* **(ESF1)**, **(ESF2)** *and* **(ESF6)**. *Then, if* ∇ *satisfies* **(ESF-it)**, ∇ *satisfies* **(ESF3)** *and* **(ESF4)**.

In general, the converse of this result is not true. However, in some particular situations the postulates **(ESF3)** and **(ESF4)**entail **(ESF-it)**. More precisely:

Proposition 2. *Let* ∇ *be an ES combination operator satisfying* **(ESF1)**,**(ESF2)** *and* **(ESF6)**. *Suppose* ∇ *satisfies* **(ESF3)** *and* **(ESF4)**. *Then, for all profiles* Φ *and all Epistemic States* E_1 *and* E_2 *such that* $B\big(\nabla(\Phi, E_1)\big)$ *is consistent with* $B(E_2)$, *we havee*

$$B\Big(\nabla\big(\Phi, \nabla(E_1, E_2)\big)\Big) \equiv B\Big(\nabla\big(\nabla(\Phi, E_1), E_2\big)\Big).$$

Now we proceed to make a classification of ES combination operators according to which postulates are satisfied.

Definition 2 (Epistemic state basic fusion operators). *Let* ∇ *be an ES combination operator.* ∇ *is said to be an epistemic state basic fusion operator (ES basic fusion operator for short) if it satisfies the postulates* **(ESF1)**–**(ESF4)**.

Definition 3 (Epistemic state fusion operators). *Let* ∇ *be an ES combination operator.* ∇ *is said to be an epistemic state fusion operator (ES fusion operator for short) if it satisfies the postulates* **(ESF1)**–**(ESF8)**.

Definition 4 (Epistemic state quasi-fusion operators). *Let ∇ be an ES combination operator. ∇ is said to be an epistemic state quasi-fusion operator (ES quasi-fusion operator for short) if it satisfies the postulates* **(ESF1)**–**(ESF7)** *and* **(ESF8W)**.

Definition 5 (Iterable epistemic state fusion operators). *Let ∇ be an ES combination operator. ∇ is said to be an iterable epistemic state fusion operator (iterable ES fusion operator for short) if it satisfies the postulates* **(ESF1)**, **(ESF2)**, **(ESF5)**–**(ESF8)** *and* **(ESF-it)**.

Definition 6 (Iterable epistemic state quasi-fusion operators). *Let ∇ be an ES combination operator. ∇ is said to be an iterable epistemic state quasi-fusion operator (iterable ES quasi-fusion operator for short) if it satisfies the postulates* **(ESF1)**, **(ESF2)**, **(ESF5)**–**(ESF7)**, **(ESF8W)** *and* **(ESF-it)**.

Notice that, by virtue of Proposition 1, every iterable ES (quasi) fusion operator, is an ES (quasi) fusion operator.

2.2   Faithful Assignments

Definition 7 (Assignment). *An assignment is a map $\Phi \mapsto \preceq_\Phi$ mapping every profile Φ into a total preorder over valuations.*

We consider the following properties for assignments:

1. If $E_1 \neq E_2$, then $\preceq_{E_1} \neq \preceq_{E_2}$
2. If $\Phi = \{E_1, \ldots, E_n\}$ and $\forall i \leq n$, $w, w' \models B(E_i)$, then $w \simeq_\Phi w'$
3. If $\Phi = \{E_1, \ldots, E_n\}$, for all $i < n$, $w \models B(F_i)$ and there exists $j \leq n$ such that $w' \not\models B(E_j)$, then $w \prec_\Phi w'$
4. If $w \preceq_{\Phi_1} w'$ and $w \preceq_{\Phi_2} w'$ then $w \preceq_{\Phi_1 \sqcup \Phi_2} w'$
5. If $w \preceq_{\Phi_1} w'$ and $w \prec_{\Phi_2} w'$ then $w \prec_{\Phi_1 \sqcup \Phi_2} w'$

Property **1** imposes that different Epistemic States lead to different total preorders (injectivity of the assignment restricted to profiles of size one).

Properties **2** and **3** together tells that, if there are models of the conjunction of the beliefs of the Epistemic States of the profile, they are exactly the minimal models of the total preorder associated to the profile.

Property **4** expresses that if one model w_1 is preferred to w_2 for one group, and the same occurs for a second group, then for the group resulting of the union of these groups, w_1 will be preferred to w_2.

Property **5** is similar to the previous one, except that if there is one strict preference for one of subgroups, this will be the case for the whole group.

We say that the belief function B satisfies the *minimality condition* with respect to the assignment $\Phi \mapsto \preceq_\Phi$ if, for every Epistemic State E, $\llbracket B(E) \rrbracket = min(\preceq_E)$.

It is easy to see that if an assignment satisfies Properties **2** and **3**, then B satisfies the minimality condition.

Despite the apparent independence of properties **2**, **3**, **4** and **5**, in some situations they are very related. Actually we have the following result:

Proposition 3. *Let $\Phi \mapsto \preceq_\Phi$ be an assignment. Suppose B satisfies the minimality condition. Then the following statements hold:*

(i) Property 4 entails Property 2.
(ii) Property 4 plus Property 5 entail Property 3.

The following property is a weakenig of Property **5**: if for two groups w is strictly preferred over w', the same occurs for the group resulting from joining the two groups. More precisely:

5'. *If $w \prec_{\Phi_1} w'$ and $w \prec_{\Phi_2} w'$ then $w \prec_{\Phi_1 \sqcup \Phi_2} w'$*

It is clear that Property **5** entails **5'**. But the converse is not true.

Now we introduce a property which depends upon an ES combination operator ∇:

6. $\preceq_{\nabla(\Phi,E)} = lex(\preceq_E, \preceq_\Phi)$

This strong property determines the way in which the assignment acts over the results of an ES combination operator. However, it is important to notice that this property operator does not define the operator unless epistemic states are total preorders and we have the property of structuring preserving (see Section 3), that is $E = \preceq_E$ for all epistemic state E.

In case of revision operators, that is when the profile is a singleton (a total preorder in some concrete representations) and the integrity constraint is a preorder of two levels (a formula) the previous property determines the lexicographical revision operators studied by Nayak et al. [15].

Now we classify the assignments according to the properties they satisfy.

Definition 8 (Faithful assignment). *An assignment $\Phi \mapsto \preceq_\Phi$ is said to be a faithful assignment if it satisfies Properties 1–5.*

Definition 9 (quasi-faithful assignment). *An assignment $\Phi \mapsto \preceq_\Phi$ is said to be a quasi-faithful assignment if it satisfies Properties 1–4 and 5'.*

Definition 10 (Lexi-faithful assignment). *Let ∇ be an ES combination operator. An assignment $\Phi \mapsto \preceq_\Phi$ is said to be a lexi-faithful assignment if it satisfies Properties 1–6.*

The assignment is said to be a lexi-quasi-faithful assignment if it is a quasi-faithful assignment satisfying 6.

2.3 Representation Theorems

We present some results which help to understand the behavior of the operators defined previously. This allows us to describe the operators, at least partially, in a semantical form. Thus, we call these results weak representation by opposition to some true results of representation in concrete structures that we will see below.

Theorem 1 (Weak representation for ES basic fusion operators). *An ES combination operator* ∇ *is an ES basic fusion operator if and only if there exists a unique assignment* $\Phi \mapsto \preceq_\Phi$ *such that:*

$$[\![B(\nabla(\Phi, E))]\!] = min([\![B(E)]\!], \preceq_\Phi) \qquad \text{(B-Rep)}$$

This result allows us to obtain very tight relations between the (syntactical) postulates for fusion and the properties of the assignments. More precisely, we have the following result:

Proposition 4. *Let* ∇ *be an ES basic fusion operator. Let* $\Phi \mapsto \preceq_\Phi$ *the assignment given by Theorem 1. Then the following conditions hold:*

  (i) ∇ *satisfies* **(ESF5)** $\Leftrightarrow$ *the assignment satisfies* **1**.
 (ii) ∇ *satisfies* **(ESF6)** $\Leftrightarrow$ *the assignment satisfies Properties* **2** *and* **3**.
(iii) ∇ *satisfies* **(ESF7)** $\Leftrightarrow$ *the assignment satisfies* **4**.
 (iv) ∇ *satisfies* **(ESF8)** $\Leftrightarrow$ *the assignment satisfies* **5**.
  (v) ∇ *satisfies* **(ESF8W)** $\Leftrightarrow$ *the assignment satisfies* **5'**.
 (vi) ∇ *satisfies* **(ESF-it)** $\Leftrightarrow$ *the assignment satisfies* **6**.

The following results are corollaries of Proposition 4.

Theorem 2 (Weak representation for ES fusion operators). *An ES combination operator* ∇ *is an ES fusion operator if and only if there exists a unique faithful assignment* $\Phi \mapsto \preceq_\Phi$ *satisfying* **(B-Rep)**.

Theorem 3 (Weak representation for ES quasi-fusion operators). *An ES combination operator* ∇ *is an ES quasi-fusion operator if and only if there exists a unique quasi-faithful assignment* $\Phi \mapsto \preceq_\Phi$ *satisfying* **(B-Rep)**.

Theorem 4 (Weak representation for iterable ES quasi-fusion operators). *An ES combination operator* ∇ *is an iterable ES (quasi) fusion operator if and only if there exists a unique lexi-faithful (lexi-quasi-faithful) assignment* $\Phi \mapsto \preceq_\Phi$ *satisfying* **(B-Rep)**.

Unlike the representation theorem for IC merging operators, the previous theorems don't allow us to construct ∇ from the assignment. However, they allow us to represent the beliefs of the result via the total preorders of the assignment.

3   Fusion in a Concrete Representation of Epistemic States

The weak representations obtained so far describe only the beliefs of the epistemic state resulting after application of the operator, but we lose the general structure of the Epistemic State. We show in this section that in the case of the epistemic state which are total preorders over the valuations, the representation is complete.

From now on $\mathcal{E}$ will be the set of total preorders over the valuations $\mathcal{W}$. We consider the following properties for assignments:

(PI) *If* $\Phi = \{\preceq_1, \ldots, \preceq_n\}$ *and* $\forall i \leq n$, $w \simeq_i w'$, *then* $w \simeq_\Phi w'$.

(PF) *If* $\Phi = \{\preceq_1, \ldots, \preceq_n\}$, $\forall i \leq n$, $w \preceq_i w'$ *and* $\exists j \leq n$ *such that* $w \prec_j w'$, *then* $w \prec_\Phi w'$.

(PU) *If* $\Phi = \{\preceq_1, \ldots, \preceq_n\}$ *and* $\forall i \leq n$, $w \prec_i w'$, *then* $w \prec_\Phi w'$.

These properties are very natural in aggregation of preferences in Social Choice Theory. They correspond to Pareto indifference **(PI)**, Strong Pareto **(PF)** and Pareto unanimity **(PU)**. They express rational behavior at the moment of merging the preferences of a group of agents.

Property **(PI)** establishes that if two options are equally plausible for all the members of a group, they are equally plausible with respect to the plausibility of the group.

Property **(PF)** tells us that if all the members of a group prefer an alternative w over w' and there is a member of the group preferring strictly w over w', then w will be strictly preferred over w' for the group.

Property **(PU)** expresses the fact that if all the members of a group prefer strictly an alternative w over w', this will be the case for the group. Notice that every assignation satisfying Property **(PF)**, will satisfy property **(PU)**.

A very natural property for the assignments, in this setting, is the preservation of the structure of Epistemic States. More precisely, we have the following definition:

Definition 11. *We say that an assignment* $\Phi \mapsto \prec_\Phi$ *is* structure preserving *if and only if for every Epistemic State E, $\preceq_E = E$.*

We have to notice that one can construct without major difficulty assignments which are not structure preserving and in despite of this having good properties [12].

This property, together with other properties already mentioned, allows us to prove the properties (PI),(PF) and (PU). More precisely we have the following proposition:

Proposition 5. *Let* $\Phi \mapsto \preceq_\Phi$ *be a structure preserving assignment, then:*

(*i*) *If the assignment satisfies* **4** *then it satisfies* **(PI)**.
(*ii*) *If the assignment satisfies* **4** *and* **5** *then it satisfies* **(PF)**.
(*iii*) *If the assignment satisfies* **5'** *then it satisfies* **(PU)**.

The properties **(PI)**, **(PF)** and **(PU)** entail the structure preserving property. More precisely, we have the following result:

Proposition 6. *Let* $\Phi \mapsto \preceq_\Phi$ *be an assignment. Then the following conditions hold*

(*i*) *If the assignment satisfies* **(PI)** *and* **(PU)**, *then it is structure preserving.*
(*ii*) *If the assignment satisfies* **(PI)** *and* **(PU)**, *then it satisfies Property* **1**.
(*iii*) *If the assignment satisfies* **(PI)** *and* **(PF)**, *and the minimality condition is satisfied, then the assignment satisfies Properties* **2** *and* **3**.

Now we consider more syntactical postulates about ES combination operators:
Let $\Phi = \{E_1, E_2, \ldots, E_n\}$ be a profile and let E be an Epistemic State.

(ESF-PI) $\forall i \leq n,\ B(\nabla(E_i, E)) \equiv B(E) \Rightarrow B(\nabla(\Phi, E)) \equiv B(E)$.

(ESF-PF) $\bigwedge_{i=1}^{n} B(\nabla(E_i, E)) \not\vdash \bot \Rightarrow B(\nabla(\Phi, E)) \vdash \bigwedge_{i=1}^{n} B(\nabla(E_i, E))$.

(ESF-PU) $\forall i, j \leq n,\ B(\nabla(E_i, E)) \equiv B(\nabla(E_j, E)) \Rightarrow \forall i \leq n,\ B(\nabla(\Phi, E)) \vdash B(\nabla(E_i, E))$

Postulate **(ESF-PI)** says that if the beliefs of each agent coincides with the beliefs of the constraint, the belief of the group will be the belief of the constraint.

Postulate **(ESF-PF)** expresses that if when we revise each agent by the constraint there is a global agreement, then the belief of the group has to satisfy this agreement.

Postulate **(ESF-PU)** expresses the fact that if each agent obtains the same beliefs after revision by the constraint, the global belief has to entail these common beliefs. Notice that the Postulate **(ESF-PU)** is weaker than the Postulate **(ESF-PF)**.

Proposition 7. *Let ∇ be an ES basic fusion operator. If the assignment associated to the operator is structure preserving, the following conditions hold:*

*(i) ∇ satisfies **(ESF-PI)** if and only if the assignment satisfies **(PI)**.*
*(ii) ∇ satisfies **(ESF-PF)** if and only if the assignment satisfies **(PF)**.*
*(iii) ∇ satisfies **(ESF-PU)** if and only if the assignment satisfies **(PU)**.*

Theorem 5 (Representation theorem). *Let ∇ an ES basic fusion operator. Suppose that the assignment $\Phi \mapsto \preceq_\Phi$, representing ∇ is structure preserving. Then, ∇ satisfies **(ESF7)**, **(ESF8)** and **(ESF-it)** if and only if the assignment $\Phi \mapsto \preceq_\Phi$, representing ∇, satisfies Properties **4**, **5**, **6**, and the following equation is satisfied:*

$$\nabla(\Phi, E) = lex(E, \preceq_\Phi). \tag{Rep}$$

Moreover, if B satisfies the minimality condition, then ∇ is an iterable ES fusion operator.

4 A Concrete Example

It is easy to see that every total preorder over $\mathcal{W}$ can be represented by a function $r : \mathcal{W} \longrightarrow \mathbb{N}$ such that the image is an initial segment of the natural numbers, *i.e.* the set is of the form $\{0, 1, 2, \ldots, n\}$, and $w \preceq w'$ iff $r(w) \leq r(w')$. We call $r(w)$ the rank (or level) of w in the total preorder $\preceq$. A natural way for aggregating total preorders is using the sum of the ranks. If $\Phi = \{\preceq_1, \ldots, \preceq_k\}$ we define $\preceq_\Phi$ in the following way:

$$w \preceq_\Phi w' \quad \Leftrightarrow \quad \sum_{i=1}^{k} r_i(w) \leq \sum_{i=1}^{k} r_i(w')$$

It is easy to check that the assignment defined in this manner is a faithful assignment. Thus, if the beliefs are given by the minimal models of the preorders representing the Epistemic State, we have the minimality condition. Then we can define ∇ like in Theorem 5, that is to say $\nabla(\Phi, E) = lex(E, \preceq_\Phi)$. In this way we have an iterable ES fusion operator. The reader can verify that if $\Phi = \{E_1, E_2\}$ and E are given graphically by the three total preorders below

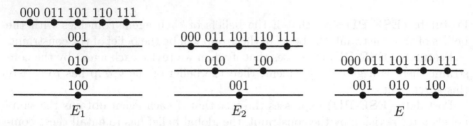

we get as a result the following total preorder:

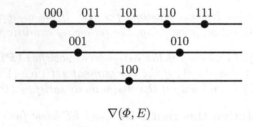

$$\nabla(\Phi, E)$$

This kind of construction can be generalized to other aggregation functions different from the addition. For instance, if we take the max aggregation function instead of the addition we obtain an iterable ES quasi-fusion operator.

5   Conclusion

Adapting the postulates of Konieczny and Pino Pérez [9,10,11], we have succeded in giving syntactical postulates for the fusion operators of complex epistemic states. All the language we need is finite propositional logic. Our operators generalize the revision operators introduced by Benferhat et ál. [2] and the IC merging operators defined by Konieczny and Pino Pérez.

Under these postulates, we obtain a weak representation in semantical form. However, we obtain a strong representation when we consider concrete epistemic states, namely the structure of total preorders over valuations.

The main contribution of this work lies in the fact of having found the right axioms, both the syntactical ones and the semantical ones, and the relations between them.

We have to notice the strong utilization in our central result (Theorem 5) of the structure preserving property. We don't know for the moment about a syntactical counterpart for this property. In spite of the fact that this property is quite natural and rational, to find its syntactical counterpart seems a difficult task. We continue making efforts for finding the syntactical counterpart of the structure preserving property.

Acknowledgements

The second author was partially supported by the research project CDCHT-ULA N° C-1451-07-05-A.

References

1. Alchourrón, C.E., Gärdenfors, P., Makinson, D.: On the logic of theory change: Partial meet contraction and revision functions. J. Symb. Log. 50(2), 510–530 (1985)
2. Benferhat, S., Konieczny, S., Papini, O., Pino Pérez, R.: Iterated revision by epistemic states: Axioms, semantics and syntax. In: Horn, W. (ed.) ECAI, pp. 13–17. IOS Press, Amsterdam (2000)
3. Darwiche, A., Pearl, J.: On the logic of iterated belief revision. In: Fagin, R. (ed.) TARK, pp. 5–23. Morgan Kaufmann, San Francisco (1994)
4. Darwiche, A., Pearl, J.: On the logic of iterated belief revision. Artificial Intelligence 89, 1–29 (1997)
5. Dubois, D., Prade, H.: Belief revision and possibility theory. In: Gärdenfors, P. (ed.) Belief Revision. Cambridge University Press, Cambridge (1992)
6. Gärdenfors, P.: Knowledge in Flux: Modeling the Dynamics of Epistemic States. MIT Press, Cambridge (1988)
7. Katsuno, H., Mendelzon, A.O.: Propositional knowledge base revision and minimal change. Artif. Intell. 52(3), 263–294 (1992)
8. Konieczny, S., Pino Pérez, R.: On the logic of merging. In: Cohn, A.G., Schubert, L.K., Shapiro, S.C. (eds.) KR, pp. 488–498. Morgan Kaufmann, San Francisco (1998)
9. Konieczny, S., Pino Pérez, R.: Merging with integrity constraints. In: Hunter, A., Parsons, S. (eds.) ECSQARU 1999. LNCS (LNAI), vol. 1638, pp. 233–244. Springer, Heidelberg (1999)
10. Konieczny, S., Pino Pérez, R.: Merging information under constraints: A logical framework. J. Log. Comput. 12(5), 773–808 (2002)
11. Konieczny, S., Pino Pérez, R.: Propositional belief base merging or how to merge beliefs/goals coming from several sources and some links with social choice theory. European Journal of Operational Research 160(3), 785–802 (2005)
12. Mata, A.: Sobre la fusión de estados epistémicos. Tesis de Maestría, Mérida (Junio 2010)
13. Meyer, T.: Merging epistemic states. In: Mizoguchi, R., Slaney, J.K. (eds.) PRICAI 2000. LNCS, vol. 1886, pp. 286–296. Springer, Heidelberg (2000)
14. Meyer, T.: On the semantics of combination operations. Journal of Applied Non-Classical Logics 11(1-2), 59–84 (2001)
15. Nayak, A.C., Pagnucco, M., Peppas, P.: Dynamic belief revision operators. Artificial Intelligence 142(2), 193–228 (2003)
16. Spohn, W.: Ordinal conditional functions: A dynamic theory of epistemic states. In: Harper, W.L., Skyrms, B. (eds.) Causation in Decision: Belief Change and Statistics, pp. 105–134. Kluwer, Dordrecht (1988)

Latent Tree Classifier

Yi Wang[1], Nevin L. Zhang[2], Tao Chen[3], and Leonard K. M. Poon[2]

[1] Department of Computer Science
National University of Singapore
Singapore 117417, Singapore
wangy@comp.nus.edu.sg
[2] Department of Computer Science & Engineering
The Hong Kong University of Science & Technology
Clear Water Bay, Kowloon, Hong Kong
{lzhang,lkmpoon}@cse.ust.hk
[3] Shenzhen Institute of Advanced Technology
Chinese Academy of Sciences
Shenzhen, China
tao.chen@siat.ac.cn

Abstract. We propose a novel generative model for classification called latent tree classifier (LTC). An LTC represents each class-conditional distribution of attributes using a latent tree model, and uses Bayes rule to make prediction. Latent tree models can capture complex relationship among attributes. Therefore, LTC can approximate the true distribution behind data well and thus achieve good classification accuracy. We present an algorithm for learning LTC and empirically evaluate it on 37 UCI data sets. The results show that LTC compares favorably to the state-of-the-art. We also demonstrate that LTC can reveal underlying concepts and discover interesting subgroups within each class.

Keywords: Bayesian network classifier, latent variable model.

1 Introduction

Classification is one of the most active areas in machine learning research. The task is to predict the class label of an instance based on a set of attributes that describe the instance. Approaches to this problem divide into two categories: Generative and discriminative [19]. Let C be the class variable and $\mathbf{X}$ be the set of attributes. Generative approaches build models for the joint distribution $P(C, \mathbf{X})$, compute the posterior distribution $P(C|\mathbf{X})$ using Bayes rule, and assign an instance to the most likely class. In contrast, discriminative approaches directly model $P(C|\mathbf{X})$. In this paper, we focus on generative approaches and assume categorical attributes.

The simplest generative model is the naive Bayes (NB) classifier [8]. It assumes that attributes are mutually independent given the class label. All dependencies among attributes are ignored. Despite its simplicity, NB has been shown to be surprisingly effective in a number of domains [7].

W. Liu (Ed.): ECSQARU 2011, LNAI 6717, pp. 410–421, 2011.

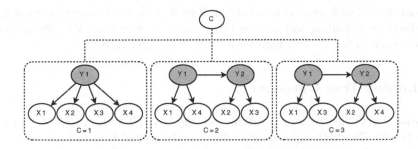

Fig. 1. An example latent tree classifier. C is the class variable with 3 classes, X_1–X_4 are four attributes. Each rectangle contains a latent tree model for a specific class, in which Y_1 and Y_2 are latent variables.

The conditional independence assumption underlying NB is rarely true in practice. Violating this assumption could lead to poor prediction. The past decade has seen a large body of work on relaxing this unrealistic assumption. To mention two successful instances, tree augmented naive Bayes (TAN) [10] builds a Chow-Liu tree [5] to model the attribute dependencies, while averaged one-dependence estimators (AODE) [21] constructs a set of tree models over the attributes and averages them to make prediction.

In this paper, we propose a novel approach to model the relationship among attributes. Our approach is based on latent tree models. A *latent tree model* (LTM) [23] is a tree-structured Bayesian network in which variables at leaf nodes are observed and called *manifest variables*, whereas variables at internal nodes are hidden and called *latent variables*. The model represents a set of complex relationship among the manifest variables in a compact way. To see this point, consider eliminating all the latent variables from the model. This will result in a fully connected Bayesian network over all the manifest variables.

In our approach, we treat attributes as manifest variables and build LTMs to model the relationship among them. The relationship could be different across classes. Therefore, we build an LTM for each class. We refer to the collection of LTMs plus the prior class distribution as a latent tree classifier (LTC). An example is shown in Fig. 1. Each rectangle in the figure contains the LTM for a class. Since the LTMs can model complex relationship among attributes, we expect LTC to approximate the true distribution behind data well and thus to achieve good classification accuracy. We empirically verify this hypothesis in the experiments.

In addition to good classification performance, building LTCs on the basis of LTMs also makes it possible to discover latent structures behind data. In particular, we will demonstrate that the latent variables introduced during the learning process can reveal concepts embedded in data as well as interesting subgroups within each class. This merit can boost user confidence in LTCs.

The rest of this paper is structured as follows. We formally define LTC in Sect. 2 and present an algorithm for learning LTC in Sect. 3. In Sect. 4, we empirically evaluate LTC on 37 UCI data sets, and compare it with a spectrum of generative classifiers as well as C4.5 [18]. In Sect. 5, we demonstrate that LTC can discover appealing latent structures using an example. We discuss some related work in Sect. 6 and finally conclude this paper in Sect. 7.

2 Latent Tree Classifier

We start by briefly reviewing latent tree models (LTMs). An LTM is a pair $\mathcal{M} = (m, \boldsymbol{\theta})$. The first component m denotes the rooted tree and the set of cardinalities of the latent variables. The second component $\boldsymbol{\theta}$ denotes the collection of parameters in $\mathcal{M}$. It contains a conditional probability table (CPT) for each node given its parent.

Let $\mathbf{X}$ and $\mathbf{Y}$ be the set of manifest variables and the set of latent variables in $\mathcal{M}$, respectively. We use $P(\mathbf{X}, \mathbf{Y}|\mathcal{M})$ to denote the joint distribution represented by $\mathcal{M}$. Two LTMs $\mathcal{M}$ and $\mathcal{M}'$ are *marginally equivalent* if they share the same set of manifest variables $\mathbf{X}$ and $P(\mathbf{X}|\mathcal{M}) = P(\mathbf{X}|\mathcal{M}')$.

Let $|Z|$ denote the cardinality of variable Z. For a node Z in $\mathcal{M}$, we denote the set of its neighbors by $\mathbf{nb}(Z)$. An LTM is *regular* if for any latent node Y, $|Y| \leq \frac{\prod_{Z \in \mathbf{nb}(Y)} |Z|}{\max_{Z \in \mathbf{nb}(Y)} |Z|}$, and the inequality strictly holds when Y has only two neighbors. As shown by [23], an irregular model $\mathcal{M}$ is over-complicated and can be reduced to a regular model $\mathcal{M}'$ which is marginally equivalent but contains fewer parameters than $\mathcal{M}$. Henceforth, we consider only regular models.

We consider the classification problem where each instance is described using n attributes $\mathbf{X} = \{X_1, X_2, \ldots, X_n\}$, and belongs to one of the r classes $C = 1, 2, \ldots, r$. A *latent tree classifier* (LTC) consists of a prior distribution $P(C)$ on C and a collection of r LTMs over the attributes $\mathbf{X}$. We denote the c-th LTM by $\mathcal{M}_c = (m_c, \boldsymbol{\theta}_c)$ and the set of latent variables in $\mathcal{M}_c$ by $\mathbf{Y}_c$. The LTC represents a joint distribution over C and $\mathbf{X}$, $\forall c = 1, 2, \ldots, r$,

$$P(C = c, \mathbf{X}) = P(C = c) P(\mathbf{X}|\mathcal{M}_c)$$
$$= P(C = c) \sum_{\mathbf{Y}_c} P(\mathbf{X}, \mathbf{Y}_c|\mathcal{M}_c) . \tag{1}$$

Given an LTC, we classify an instance $\mathbf{X} = \mathbf{x}$ to the class c^*, where

$$c^* = \arg\max_C P(C|\mathbf{X} = \mathbf{x})$$
$$= \arg\max_C P(C, \mathbf{X} = \mathbf{x}) . \tag{2}$$

Note that, according to (1), this requires us to sum out all the latent variables $\mathbf{Y}_c$ for each class c. Thanks to the tree structures of LTMs, the summation could be done in linear time in the number of attributes, as formalized below.

Proposition 1. *The time complexity of classifying an unlabeled instance with an LTC is $O(rnv^2)$, where r is the number of classes, n is the number of attributes, and v is the maximum cardinality of variables in the LTC.*

Proof. The time complexity of summing out all the latent variables $\mathbf{Y}_c$ from the c-th LTM $\mathcal{M}_c$ is $O\big((|\mathbf{Y}_c|+n)v_c^2\big)$ [17], where v_c denotes the maximum cardinality of the variables in $\mathcal{M}_c$. It is know that a regular LTM contains less than n latent variables [23]. Therefore, the overall time complexity for classifying an instance is $O(rnv^2)$.   □

3   A Learning Algorithm

Given a labeled training set $\mathcal{D}$, we consider how to learn a good LTC from $\mathcal{D}$. This amounts to learning the prior distribution $P(C)$ and a good LTM $\mathcal{M}_c$ for each class $c = 1, 2, \ldots, r$.

The prior $P(C)$ can be easily estimated from $\mathcal{D}$ by counting the number of instances belonging to each class. In the following, we focus on the more challenging task of learning the LTMs.

3.1   Model Selection

We first partition $\mathcal{D}$ by class label and obtain r data sets $\{\mathcal{D}_c | c = 1, 2, \ldots, r\}$. Each $\mathcal{D}_c$ contains only the attributes $\mathbf{X}$. We then learn an LTM $\mathcal{M}_c$ from each $\mathcal{D}_c$ independently.

The LTM is of high quality if it is close to the true distribution underlying $\mathcal{D}_c$. Nonetheless, the true distribution is unknown. Therefore, we use AIC score [1] for model selection,

$$AIC(m_c|\mathcal{D}_c) = -2\log P(\mathcal{D}_c|m_c, \boldsymbol{\theta}_c^\star) + 2d(m_c) \ , \tag{3}$$

where $\boldsymbol{\theta}_c^\star$ is the maximum likelihood estimate to the parameters $\boldsymbol{\theta}_c$, and $d(m_c)$ is the number of free parameters in model m_c. The AIC score is an approximation to the expected KL divergence of $\mathcal{M}_c$ from the true distribution. The lower the score, the smaller the difference between $\mathcal{M}_c$ and the true distribution, and the better the LTM.

In literatures, BIC score is used more often for learning Bayesian network classifiers [10]. However, BIC score over-penalizes complex models and can lead to poor approximation to the true distribution. In a preliminary study [20], we empirically compared AIC with BIC for learning LTCs. We observed that AIC produces LTMs that better fit unseen data. The LTCs learned using AIC also achieve better classification accuracy than those learned using BIC.

3.2   Model Search

We adopt a recently developed hill-climbing algorithm called EAST [3] to search for high scoring LTMs. EAST explores the model space using five search operators. They are *node introduction* (NI), *node deletion* (ND), *node relocation* (NR), *state introduction* (SI), and *state deletion* (SD). Given an LTM, NI applies to a latent variable and two of its neighbors. It adds a new latent variable to mediate the latent variable and the two neighbors, and sets its cardinality to the same

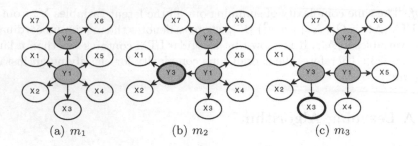

Fig. 2. Illustration of NI, ND, and NR operators

as the existing latent variable. Figure 2 shows such an example. The model m_2 is obtained from m_1 by introducing a new latent variable Y_3. ND is the reverse of NI. It applies to two neighboring latent variables, removes one of them and links its neighbors to the other. In Fig. 2, by deleting Y_3 one goes from m_2 back to m_1. NR operator adjusts the connections in an LTM. It considers two latent variables, disconnects a neighbor from the first latent variable, and links it to the second latent variable. In Fig. 2, one relocates X_3 in m_2 from Y_1 to Y_3 and obtains m_3. The last two operators modify domains of latent variables. SI adds a new state to a latent variable. SD does the reverse.

Given a data set, EAST starts with the simplest LTM, i.e., the LTM that contains only one latent variable whose cardinality equals to 1, and greedily improves the model. In each search step, it applies some operators to the current model, obtains a collection of candidate models, evaluates them using the AIC score, and picks the best one to seed the next search step. The process repeats itself until the model score ceases to increase. Note that, if EAST never improves the initial model, the final LTC reduces to NB.

In each search step, one could apply all the five operators to the current model. This could, however, produce a large number of candidate models. Evaluating them could take a long time. Therefore, the search procedure in EAST is structured into three phases: Expansion, simplification, and adjustment. In each phase, we consider only one or two operators and thus obtain much fewer candidate models. In the expansion phase, we only apply NI and SI. Both operators make the current model more expressive and thus improve the first term in AIC score. In the simplification phase, we consider only ND and SD. Both operators simplify the current model and thus improve the second term in AIC score. In the adjustment phase, we apply NR to adjust the structure of the current model. It helps avoid local maxima. EAST iteratively goes through these three phases and alternatively improves the two terms in AIC score.

To evaluate a candidate model, one needs to run the EM algorithm [6] to compute the MLE $\theta^\star$. EM is known to be expensive. To speed up the evaluation process, we run local EM instead. The key observations are that (1) the parameters of the current model have already been optimized, and (2) a candidate model only differs from the current model in a small part. Therefore, in local EM, we fix the parameters of the unaltered part, and optimize only the parameters that are foreign to the current model. Consider the model m_2 in Fig. 2 that is obtained from m_1 using NI. In local EM, we only optimize the CPTs of Y_3, X_1, and X_2. In our implementation, we run local EM for a predetermined number of iterations. It might not converge, but the obtained estimation is accurate enough for ranking candidate models. After we obtain the best candidate model, we optimize its parameters using full EM before comparing it with the current model.

4   Empirical Evaluation

In this section, we empirically compare LTC with a spectrum of generative classifiers, ranging from the simplest NB, to more advanced TAN and AODE, and to the most general *Bayesian network augmented naive Bayes* (BAN) [10]. We also include C4.5 decision tree [18] in the comparison as a reference.

4.1   Experimental Settings

We used the 37 UCI data sets [2] that are recommended by WEKA [22] in our experiments. The learning algorithms of TAN and AODE proposed by [10] and [21] do not handle missing values. Thus, we removed incomplete instances from the data sets. TAN, AODE, BAN, and LTC require discrete attributes. Therefore, we discretized the data sets using the supervised discretization method proposed by [9]. Table 1 summarizes the characteristics of the data sets obtained after preprocessing.

We implemented LTC in Java. The detailed settings are as follows. We ran 40 iterations of local EM to evaluate each candidate model. For the best candidate model, we ran full EM to optimize its parameters. The EM was terminated if the improvement in loglikelihoods is smaller than 0.01, or the number of iterations reaches 500. For both local and full EM, we adopted the pyramid strategy proposed by [4] to avoid local maxima. The number of starting points was set at 16 and 64, respectively.

We used the WEKA implementations of the other classification algorithms in our experiments. Some details are given below:

- **AODE:** We set the frequency limit on super parents at 30 as suggested by [21].
- **BAN:** We set the initial models to be naive Bayes and used hill-climbing to search for good BANs with high AIC scores. The Markov blanket correction built in WEKA was conducted on the final models to ensure every attribute is in the Markov blanket of the class variable.

Following the common practice in machine learning, we smoothed the parameters for all the trained generative classifiers using Laplace correction. We set the smoothing factor $\alpha = 1$. Preliminary experimental results show that the parameter smoothing leads to significant improvement in classification accuracy [20].

Table 1. The 37 data sets used in the experiments, their characteristics (columns 2-4), and the classification accuracy of various algorithms (columns 5-10). For each data set, the best accuracy is highlighted in boldface.

Domain	Attr.	Class	Size	LTC	NB	TAN	AODE	BAN	C4.5
anneal	38	6	898	97.78±1.96	96.10±2.54	98.66±1.15	98.33±1.59	97.99±1.47	**98.77±0.98**
australian	14	2	690	85.36±4.29	85.51±2.65	85.22±5.33	**86.09±3.50**	85.51±4.10	85.65±4.07
autos	25	7	159	**85.50±8.44**	72.88±10.12	79.25±8.84	81.08±7.39	77.29±6.40	78.58±8.54
balance-scale	4	3	625	70.24±3.10	70.71±4.08	**71.03±3.51**	69.59±4.01	70.24±4.44	69.59±4.27
breast-cancer	9	2	277	72.87±9.31	75.41±6.44	71.11±5.14	**76.49±7.96**	71.42±6.54	74.39±7.34
breast-w	9	2	683	**97.51±1.54**	97.51±2.19	96.63±2.08	97.36±2.04	97.07±1.95	95.76±2.61
corral	6	2	128	**100.00±0.00**	85.96±7.05	99.23±2.43	89.10±8.98	97.69±3.72	94.62±8.92
credit-a	15	2	653	86.38±4.38	87.29±3.53	86.84±3.02	**87.59±3.51**	85.31±3.44	86.99±4.48
credit-g	20	2	1000	73.20±3.97	75.80±4.32	74.00±4.40	**77.10±4.38**	74.90±3.54	72.10±4.46
diabetes	8	2	768	76.44±2.44	77.87±3.50	78.77±3.32	78.52±4.11	**78.91±3.62**	78.26±3.97
flare	10	2	1066	**83.21±2.77**	80.30±3.42	82.84±2.27	82.46±2.31	82.93±2.33	82.09±1.80
glass	9	7	214	76.19±7.41	74.37±8.97	**76.19±9.88**	76.19±7.41	74.46±11.28	73.94±9.76
glass2	9	2	163	**85.18±9.44**	83.97±8.99	85.18±9.89	83.97±9.91	85.18±9.89	84.01±7.32
heart-c	13	5	296	82.46±4.66	**84.11±7.85**	82.80±5.74	83.10±7.17	83.10±6.99	74.66±6.49
heart-statlog	13	2	270	81.85±9.63	**83.33±6.36**	82.22±6.94	81.85±6.86	80.00±7.65	81.85±5.91
hepatitis	19	2	80	88.75±12.43	85.00±15.37	88.75±13.76	85.00±12.91	87.50±11.79	**90.00±14.19**
ionosphere	34	2	351	**94.31±2.99**	90.60±3.83	93.17±3.60	92.31±2.34	93.17±4.07	89.17±5.35
iris	4	3	150	94.00±5.84	94.00±5.84	94.00±5.84	93.33±5.44	94.00±5.84	94.00±4.92
kr-vs-kp	36	2	3196	96.62±1.19	87.89±1.81	92.21±2.30	91.18±0.83	97.06±0.92	**99.44±0.48**
letter	16	26	20000	**92.71±0.47**	74.04±1.04	85.61±0.63	88.91±0.50	85.01±0.84	78.63±0.62
lymph	18	4	148	**89.14±6.65**	83.67±6.91	85.10±7.01	85.62±8.66	87.05±9.99	78.33±10.44
mofn-3-7-10	10	2	1324	94.48±2.48	85.35±1.53	91.16±1.79	89.05±2.53	**100.00±0.00**	**100.00±0.00**
mushroom	22	2	5644	**100.00±0.00**	97.41±0.72	99.81±0.26	**100.00±0.00**	99.95±0.09	**100.00±0.00**
pima	8	2	768	77.35±3.92	78.13±4.24	78.65±4.62	**78.65±3.81**	77.87±4.53	78.38±2.90
primary-tumor	17	22	132	45.60±11.04	**47.14±11.59**	41.04±12.56	46.37±10.12	45.60±8.64	43.24±10.55
satimage	36	6	6435	**89.57±1.24**	82.42±1.51	88.50±0.89	89.26±0.59	87.91±1.01	84.37±1.34
segment	19	7	2310	**95.67±1.47**	91.52±1.60	95.32±1.74	95.63±1.23	95.06±1.80	95.32±1.63
shuttle-small	9	7	5800	99.88±0.14	99.34±0.27	99.81±0.15	99.84±0.13	99.86±0.11	99.59±0.19
sonar	60	2	208	82.31±9.19	85.62±5.41	86.60±7.72	**87.07±6.31**	80.29±8.85	79.81±8.14
soybean	35	19	562	**93.78±2.52**	91.64±4.44	93.41±3.38	91.99±4.22	92.17±4.70	91.82±3.75
splice	61	3	3190	94.51±2.07	95.36±1.00	95.30±1.41	**96.21±1.07**	94.48±1.40	94.36±1.58
vehicle	18	4	846	**74.94±4.29**	62.65±4.15	73.99±4.44	73.06±4.65	72.94±5.00	71.99±3.45
vote	16	2	232	**95.86±3.38**	89.91±4.45	94.03±4.72	94.03±4.07	93.81±4.93	95.18±4.48
vowel	13	11	990	80.30±3.02	67.07±6.14	**87.37±2.94**	81.92±4.11	82.22±3.96	80.91±2.31
waveform-21	21	3	5000	86.02±1.99	81.76±1.49	83.10±1.46	**86.60±1.26**	83.10±1.25	75.44±2.10
waveform-5000	40	3	5000	86.06±1.39	80.74±1.38	82.02±1.26	**86.36±1.65**	82.44±1.21	76.48±1.47
zoo	17	7	101	94.18±6.60	93.18±7.93	95.18±8.15	95.09±5.18	**96.09±5.05**	92.18±8.94
Mean				**86.49±4.26**	83.12±4.72	85.80±4.43	85.85±4.40	85.66±4.41	84.32±4.59
# Wins				15	3	4	11	3	5

4.2 Classification Accuracy

We estimated the classification accuracy of an algorithm using stratified 10-fold cross validation [12]. All the algorithms were run on the same training/test splits. The mean and the standard deviation of accuracy are shown in Table 1. For each data set, the best accuracy is highlighted in boldface. For each algorithm, Table 1 also reports its average accuracy over all the data sets and the number of wins, i.e., the number of data sets on which it achieves the best accuracy.

From Table 1, we can see that LTC achieves the best overall accuracy, followed by AODE, TAN, BAN, C4.5, and NB, in that order. In terms of the number of wins, LTC is also the best (15 wins), with AODE (11 wins) and C4.5 (5 wins) being the two runners-up.

Table 2. The number of times that LTC significantly wins, ties with, and loses to the other algorithms

	NB	TAN	AODE	BAN	C4.5
# Wins	17	8	5	5	11
# Ties	19	27	29	29	24
# Loses	1	2	3	3	2

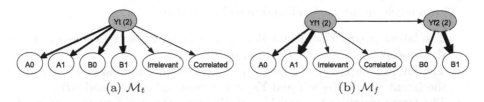

(a) $\mathcal{M}_t$ (b) $\mathcal{M}_f$

Fig. 3. The structures of the LTMs for corral data. The numbers in the parentheses denote the cardinalities of the latent variables. The width of an edge denote the mutual information between the incident nodes.

To compare LTC with the other algorithms, we also conducted two-tailed paired t-test with $p = 0.05$. The number of significant wins, ties, and loses is given in Table 2. It shows that LTC significantly outperforms NB (17 wins/1 loses) and C4.5 (11/2). LTC is also better than TAN (8/2), AODE (5/3), and BAN (5/3).

5 Discovery of Latent Structures

One advantage of LTC is that it can capture concepts underlying domains and automatically discover interesting subgroups within each class. In this section, the readers will see one such example. More examples will be given in an extended version of this paper.

The example is involved with the corral data [11]. It contains two classes *true* and *false*, and six boolean attributes A_0, A_1, B_0, B_1, *Irrelevant*, and *Correlated*. The target concept is $(A_0 \wedge A_1) \vee (B_0 \wedge B_1)$. *Irrelevant* is an irrelevant random attribute, and *Correlated* matches the class label 75% of the time.

We learned an LTC from the corral data and obtained two LTMs, one for each class. We denote the LTMs by $\mathcal{M}_t$ and $\mathcal{M}_f$, respectively. Their structures are shown in Fig. 3. $\mathcal{M}_t$ contains one latent variable Y_t, and $\mathcal{M}_f$ contains two latent variables Y_{f1} and Y_{f2}. All the latent variables are binary.

5.1 Main Findings

We first observe that in both models, the four attributes A_0, A_1, B_0, and B_1 are closely correlated to their latent parents. In contrast, *Irrelevant* and *Correlated* are almost independent of their parents (notice the difference in edge widths in Fig. 3). This is interesting as both models correctly pick the four relevant attributes to the target concept.

We further studied the meanings of the latent variables and obtained more appealing findings. The latent variable Y_t in $\mathcal{M}_t$ takes two values. Therefore, Y_t represents a soft partition over the samples in the *true* class into two groups, each group corresponding to one value of Y_t. We refer to those groups as *latent groups*, and denote them by the corresponding values of Y_t. The latent variables Y_{f1} and Y_{f2} in $\mathcal{M}_f$ also take two values. Similarly, each latent variable represents a peculiar soft partition over the samples in the *false* class into two latent groups.

Our analysis in the next subsection will show that:

1. The latent groups $Y_t = 1$ and $Y_t = 2$ correspond to the two components of the concept, $A_0 \wedge A_1$ and $B_0 \wedge B_1$, respectively;
2. The latent groups $Y_{f1} = 1$ and $Y_{f1} = 2$ correspond to $\neg A_0$ and $\neg A_1$, while the latent groups $Y_{f2} = 1$ and $Y_{f2} = 2$ correspond to $\neg B_0$ and $\neg B_1$;
3. The latent variables Y_{f1} and Y_{f2} jointly enumerate the four cases when the target concept $(A_0 \wedge A_1) \vee (B_0 \wedge B_1)$ does not satisfy.

Before diving into the details, we would like to point out that LTC successfully discovering the underlying concept and intra-class subgroups gives rise to its perfect classification result on the corral data (see Table 1). We argue that the capability of discovering such latent patterns is one reason why LTC achieves good classification accuracy.

5.2   Detailed Analysis

To understand the characteristics of each latent group, we examine the conditional distribution of each attribute, i.e., $P(X|Y = 1)$ and $P(X|Y = 2)$ for all $X \in \{A_0, A_1, B_0, B_1\}$ and $Y \in \{Y_t, Y_{f1}, Y_{f2}\}$. Those distributions are plotted in Fig. 4. The height of a bar indicates the corresponding probability value.

We start by the latent groups associated with Y_t. In latent group $Y_t = 1$, A_0 and A_1 always take value *true*, while B_0 and B_1 emerge at random. Clearly, this group of instances belong to class *true* because they satisfy $A_0 \wedge A_1$. In contrast, in latent group $Y_t = 2$, B_0 and B_1 always take value *true*, while A_0 and A_1 emerge at random. Clearly, this group corresponds to the concept $B_0 \wedge B_1$.

We next examine the two latent variables in $\mathcal{M}_f$. It is clear that A_0 never occurs in latent group $Y_{f1} = 1$, while A_1 never occurs in latent group $Y_{f1} = 2$. Therefore, the two latent groups correspond to $\neg A_0$ and $\neg A_1$, respectively. Y_{f1} thus reveals the two cases when $A_0 \wedge A_1$ does not satisfy. Similarly, we find that B_0 never occurs in latent group $Y_{f2} = 1$, while B_1 never occurs in latent group $Y_{f2} = 2$. Therefore, the two latent groups correspond to $\neg B_0$ and $\neg B_1$, respectively. Y_{f2} thus reveals the two cases when $B_0 \wedge B_1$ does not satisfy. Consequently, Y_{f1} and Y_{f2} jointly represent the four cases when the target concept $(A_0 \wedge A_1) \vee (B_0 \wedge B_1)$ does not satisfy.

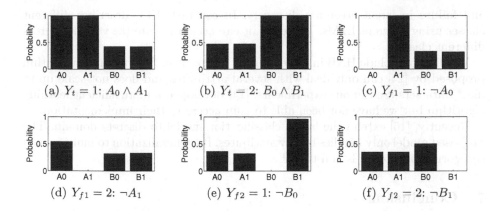

Fig. 4. The attribute distributions in each latent group and the corresponding concept

6   Related Work

There are a large body of literatures that attempt to improve classification accuracy by exploiting attribute dependencies. They mainly divide into two categories: Those that directly model relationship among attributes, and those that capture such relationship using latent variables. TAN, AODE, and BAN fall into the first category. Another representative from this category is Bayesian multi-net [10]. It learns a Bayesian network for each class and uses them jointly to make prediction. Our method is based on the similar idea, but we learn an LTM to represent the joint distribution of each class.

Our method falls into the second category. In this category, various latent variable models have been tested for continuous data. To give two examples, [16] combine finite mixture model with naive Bayes classifier. [13] propose latent classification model. It uses a mixture of factor analyzers to represent attribute dependencies.

In contrast, we are aware of much less work on categorical data. The one that is the most closely related to ours is the hierarchical naive Bayes model (HNB) [24,14]. HNB also exploits LTM to model the relationship among attributes. However, it differs from LTC in two aspects. First, attributes in HNB are usually partitioned into disjoint subsets, while each subset is modeled using a separate LTM. The root (latent) nodes of those LTMs can be treated as features extracted from different subsets of attributes, and are put together with the class variable to form a naive Bayes model for classification. In contrast, LTC builds one single LTM to connect all attributes for each class. The LTM as a whole gives a generative model for that class, which is used in the prediction phase to compute the likelihood of new data points.

Second, HNB assumes homogeneous latent structure, i.e., the LTMs in HNB are identical throughout all classes. This assumption could be unrealistic in real world applications. See, for example, the corral data presented in Sect. 5. Violating this assumption could lead to degenerated classification performance and failure in latent structure discovery. In contrast, LTC describes different classes using different LTMs. Therefore, it can accommodate the variance across different classes.

We did not include HNB in our empirical comparison. The learning algorithm proposed by [24] can only deal with several attributes and does not scale up to most data sets used in our experiments. [14] developed a more efficient learning algorithm but we have not been able to gain access to their implementation.

Recently, [15] extend the latent classification model to discrete domain. The proposed model only handles binary attributes. Its generalization to multi-valued categorical attributes is non-trivial.

7   Conclusions

We propose a novel generative classifier, namely, latent tree classifier. It builds upon the powerful yet compact representation of latent tree models, and respects the inter-class heterogeneity of the relationships among attributes. We empirically show that LTC compares favorably to NB, TAN, AODE, BAN, and C4.5 in classification accuracy. We also demonstrate that the learned LTC can reveal underlying concepts and discover interesting subgroups within each class. As far as we know, the second feature is unique to our method. We argue that the capability of discovering such latent patterns is one reason why LTC achieves good classification performance.

We used a hill-climbing algorithm, EAST, to learn LTC. For most of the data sets used in the experiments, the training finished within a few seconds to a few hours. For the 5 large data sets, kr-vs-kp, letter, mushroom, satimage, and splice, the training took up to a few days. Thus, LTC is currently most suitable for applications which allow a long offline training phase but demand good online classification performance. On the other hand, we believe that the promising results presented in this paper warrant future research on fast learning algorithms for LTCs.

Acknowledgments. We are grateful to Gang Wang for his inspiring discussions. Research on this work was supported by Hong Kong Research Grants Council GRF Grant #622408, MDA GAMBIT Grant R-252-000-398-490, the National Basic Research Program of China (aka the 973 Program) under project 2011CB505101, and the Shenzhen New Industry Development Fund #CXB201005250021A.

References

1. Akaike, H.: A new look at the statistical model identification. IEEE T. Automat. Contr. 19(6), 716–723 (1974)
2. Asuncion, A., Newman, D.J.: UCI machine learning repository (2007)
3. Chen, T., Zhang, N.L., Wang, Y.: Efficient model evaluation in the search-based approach to latent structure discovery. In: 4th European Workshop on Probabilistic Graphical Models, pp. 57–64 (2008)

4. Chickering, D.M., Heckerman, D.: Efficient approximations for the marginal likelihood of Bayesian networks with hidden variables. Mach. Learn. 29, 181–212 (1997)
5. Chow, C.K., Liu, C.N.: Approximating discrete probability distributions with dependence trees. IEEE T. Inform. Theory 14(3), 462–467 (1968)
6. Dempster, A.P., Laird, N.M., Rubin, D.R.: Maximum likelihood from incomplete data via the EM algorithm. J. Roy. Stat. Soc. B Met. 39(1), 1–38 (1977)
7. Domingos, P., Pazzani, M.: On the optimality of the simple Bayesian classifier under zero-one loss. Mach. Learn. 29, 103–130 (1997)
8. Duda, R.O., Hart, P.E.: Pattern Classification and Scene Analysis. Wiley, Chichester (1973)
9. Fayyad, U.M., Irani, K.B.: Multi-interval discretization of continuous-valued attributes for classification learning. In: 13th International Joint Conference on Artificial Intelligence, pp. 1022–1027 (1993)
10. Friedman, N., Geiger, D., Goldszmidt, M.: Bayesian network classifiers. Mach. Learn. 29(2-3), 131–163 (1997)
11. John, G.H., Kohavi, R., Pfleger, K.: Irrelevant features and the subset selection problem. In: 11th International Conference on Machine Learning, pp. 121–129 (1994)
12. Kohavi, R.: A study of cross-validation and bootstrap for accuracy estimation and model selection. In: 14th International Joint Conference on Artificial Intelligence, pp. 1137–1145 (1995)
13. Langseth, H., Nielsen, T.D.: Latent classification models. Mach. Learn. 59(3), 237–265 (2005)
14. Langseth, H., Nielsen, T.D.: Classification using hierarchical naive Bayes models. Mach. Learn. 63(2), 135–159 (2006)
15. Langseth, H., Nielsen, T.D.: Latent classification models for binary data. Pattern Recogn. 42, 2724–2736 (2009)
16. Monti, S., Cooper, G.F.: A Bayesian network classifier that combines a finite mixture model and a naive Bayes model. In: 11th Annual Conference on Uncertainty in Artificial Intelligence, pp. 447–456 (1995)
17. Pearl, J.: Probabilistic Reasoning in Intelligent Systems: Networks of Plausible Inference. Morgan Kaufmann, San Francisco (1988)
18. Quinlan, J.R.: C4.5: Programs for Machine Learning. Morgan Kaufmann, San Francisco (1993)
19. Rubinstein, Y.D., Hastie, T.: Discriminative vs informative learning. In: 3rd International Conference on Knowledge Discovery and Data Mining, pp. 49–53 (1997)
20. Wang, Y.: Latent Tree Models for Multivariate Density Estimation: Algorithms and Applications. Ph.D. thesis, Hong Kong University of Science & Technology (2009)
21. Webb, G.I., Boughton, J.R., Wang, Z.: Not so naive Bayes: Aggregating one-dependence estimators. Mach. Learn. 58, 5–24 (2005)
22. Witten, I.H., Frank, E.: Data Mining: Practical machine learning tools and techniques. Morgan Kaufmann, San Francisco (2005)
23. Zhang, N.L.: Hierarchical latent class models for cluster analysis. Journal of Mach. Learn. Research 5(6), 697–723 (2004)
24. Zhang, N.L., Nielsen, T.D., Jensen, F.V.: Latent variable discovery in classification models. Artif. Intell. Med. 30(3), 283–299 (2004)

When Learning Naive Bayesian Classifiers Preserves Monotonicity

Barbara F.I. Pieters, Linda C. van der Gaag, and Ad Feelders

Department of Information and Computing Sciences, Utrecht University
P.O. Box 80.089, 3508 TB Utrecht, The Netherlands
{bpieters,linda,ad}@cs.uu.nl

Abstract. Naive Bayesian classifiers are used in a large range of application domains. These models generally show good performance despite their strong underlying assumptions. In this paper, we demonstrate however, by means of an example probability distribution, that a data set of instances can give rise to a classifier with counterintuitive behaviour. We will argue that such behaviour can be attributed to the learning algorithm having constructed incorrect directions of monotonicity for some of the feature variables involved. We will further show that conditions can be derived for the learning algorithm to retrieve the correct directions.

1 Introduction

Nowadays a multitude of methods, algorithms and associated software are available for learning stochastic models from a collection of gathered data. Among these are methods for constructing Bayesian network classifiers [1]. These models include a designated variable of interest, called the class variable, and multiple feature variables, each of which is related directly to the class variable. Of the Bayesian network classifiers, especially naive Bayesian classifiers have become quite popular for classification purposes. These classifiers build upon the assumption that all feature variables are mutually independent whenever a value for the class variable is known. Naive Bayesian classifiers are quite easy to construct from a collection of data and, despite their strong underlying assumptions of independency, show a tendency to outperform more complex models [2].

In general, a data set of instances from which a naive Bayesian classifier is to be constructed, may not exhibit the independency properties assumed by the classifier's learning algorithm, that is, the data set may embed dependencies among the recorded feature variables in view of a particular value of the class variable. Yet, good classification performance is generally observed also for such data sets, even in the presence of quite strong conditional dependencies among the feature variables. In view of this finding, researchers have investigated the effects of the presence of particular types of dependency on a classifier's performance. Several researchers have studied, for example, the effects of dependencies that originate from redundancy among the feature variables. Insights from these studies have resulted in methods for feature selection [3,4,5], which aim at removing redundancies from the classifier and thereby enhancing its classification

W. Liu (Ed.): ECSQARU 2011, LNAI 6717, pp. 422–433, 2011.

performance. In general however, the dependencies among the feature variables embedded in a data set may not all be attributable to information redundancy. The effects of the removal of non-redundant dependencies on the classification performance of a naive Bayesian classifier are largely unexplored as yet.

From previous research, it is well known that dependencies which are embedded in a true probability distribution among the feature variables, can affect the strengths of the direct influences that are included in a naive Bayesian classifier. In this paper, we will demonstrate that such embedded dependencies do not affect just the strengths of the influences of the feature variables on the class variable, but can also change the monotonicity directions of these influences. We say that a conditional probability distribution over the class variable is monotonically increasing (decreasing) in a designated feature variable if a higher value for this feature variable makes a higher value for the class variable more (less) likely, regardless of the joint value assignment to the other feature variables. Learning a naive Bayesian classifier from a data set of instances now does not necessarily preserve the directions of the embedded monotonicities. We will address the conditions under which the learning algorithm will retrieve the correct monotonicity directions. We will further show, by means of an example distribution, that an incorrect monotonicity direction in a classifier can result in quite unexpected behaviour. As argued before by Van der Gaag *et al.* [6], counterintuitive reasoning behaviour is likely to result in reduced acceptance of the model in daily practice, even if it shows good performance otherwise.

The paper is structured as follows. In Sect. 2, we introduce our notational conventions and review the concepts used in our analyses. In Sect. 3, we introduce an example probability distribution and demonstrate counterintuitive behaviour of the naive Bayesian classifier constructed from the distribution. In Sect. 4, we analyse the example in depth and attribute the classifier's counterintuitive behaviour to an incorrect direction of monotonicity for one of the feature variables involved. We compare our result with those from earlier research on retrieving monotonicity directions in Sect. 5. The paper ends in Sect. 6 with our concluding remarks and suggestions for further research.

2   Preliminaries

We briefly review Bayesian networks and naive Bayesian classifiers to introduce our notational conventions. We further present the qualitative concepts of probability which will be used for the analyses in the remainder of the paper, and discuss the notion of monotonicity for Bayesian networks in general.

2.1   Bayesian Networks and Classifiers

We consider a set of random variables $\mathbf{V}$. We assume all variables from $\mathbf{V}$ to be binary, that is, each variable $V_i \in \mathbf{V}$ adopts one of the values *true* and *false*; the value assignment $V_i = true$ will be denoted as v_i, and $V_i = false$ will be written as $\bar{v}_i$. Joint value assignments to a subset of variables $\mathbf{U} \subseteq \mathbf{V}$ will be denoted by bold-faced letters **u**. A Bayesian network now is a model of a joint probability distribution over the set of variables **V**. It includes a directed acyclic graph in which each node captures a random variable and where the set of arcs models the probabilistic (in)dependencies between the variables through the well-known d-separation criterion. The strengths of the dependency relationships between the variables are expressed by means of (conditional) probability distributions. For each variable V_i, the distributions $\Pr(V_i \mid \pi(V_i))$ are specified, where $\pi(V_i)$ is the set of parents of V_i in the network's graph; together these distributions constitute the conditional probability table for the variable V_i. The network now represents the joint probability distribution Pr over the variables **V**, with

$$\Pr(\mathbf{V}) = \prod_{V_i \in \mathbf{V}} \Pr(V_i \mid \pi(V_i))$$

In essence, a Bayesian network allows the computation of any probability of interest over its variables. Efficient algorithms are available, more specifically, for computing (conditional) marginal distributions over single variables [7].

Naive Bayesian classifiers are Bayesian networks of restricted topological structure. A naive Bayesian classifier partitions its set of random variables into a designated class variable C and a set **F** of feature variables F_i, $i = 1, \ldots, n$, $n \geq 1$. A joint value assignment to all feature variables is termed a case; a joint value assignment to all variables involved is called an instance. The graphical structure of the classifier is a directed tree in which the class variable C is the unique root and each feature variable F_i has C for its only parent; it thereby captures dependency of the class variable on each feature variable separately and independency of any two feature variables given this class variable. The classifier specifies a prior probability distribution $\Pr(C)$ over its class variable and conditional probability distributions $\Pr(F_i \mid C)$ for each feature variable separately. The classifier represents the joint probability distribution $\Pr(\mathbf{F}, C)$ over its variables factorised according to:

$$\Pr(\mathbf{F}, C) = \Pr(C) \cdot \prod_{i=1}^{n} \Pr(F_i \mid C)$$

A naive Bayesian classifier is commonly used for establishing the posterior probability distribution $\Pr(C \mid \mathbf{f})$ over the class variable for a case **f**. Associated with the classifier is a decision rule which serves to assign the presented case to a single class based upon the computed posterior distribution [1,2]. Since the exact rule used is not relevant for this paper, we refrain from further discussion.

Learning a naive Bayesian classifier from a data set of instances amounts to first configuring the variables involved in the simple graphical structure outlined above. Subsequently, maximum-likelihood estimates for all required probabilities are extracted from the available data as proportions over (sub)sets of instances.

2.2   Qualitative Concepts of Probability

A Bayesian network models the (in)dependencies among its variables by means of arcs in its graphical structure. An arc $A \rightarrow B$ expresses that the variable A exerts

Table 1. The $\otimes$- and $\oplus$-operators for combining signs

$\otimes$	+	−	0	?		$\oplus$	+	−	0	?
+	+	−	0	?		+	+	?	+	?
−	−	+	0	?		−	?	−	−	?
0	0	0	0	0		0	+	−	0	?
?	?	?	0	?		?	?	?	?	?

a direct probabilistic influence on the variable B, in the sense that observing a value for A occasions a shift in the probability distribution for B. The direction of this shift can be positive, negative or ambiguous. More formally, a positive influence of the variable A on the variable B along the arc $A \rightarrow B$ expresses that observing the value *true* for A makes the value *true* for B more likely, regardless of any other direct influences on B, that is, $\Pr(b \mid a, \mathbf{x}) - \Pr(b \mid \bar{a}, \mathbf{x}) \geq 0$ for any combination of values $\mathbf{x}$ for the set $\mathbf{X} = \pi(B) \setminus \{A\}$ of parents of B other than A; the influence is denoted $S^+(A, B)$, where '+' is termed the sign of the influence. A negative influence, denoted by S^-, and a zero influence, denoted by S^0, are defined analogously, replacing $\geq$ in the above formula by $\leq$ and $=$, respectively. For a positive, negative or zero influence of A on B, the difference $\Pr(b \mid a, \mathbf{x}) - \Pr(b \mid \bar{a}, \mathbf{x})$ has the same sign for *all* combinations of values $\mathbf{x}$ for the set $\mathbf{X}$. These influences thus describe a monotone effect of a shift in A's probability distribution on the distribution for B. If the influence of A on B is positive given one particular combination of values for $\mathbf{X}$ and negative given another combination, the influence of A and B is non-monotone, and is associated with the sign '?' to indicate that its effect is unknown apriori.

The signs of all influences of a Bayesian network exhibit various important composition properties that can be used for establishing the sign of a compound influence between any two variables [8]. The property of symmetry, for example, states that if a network includes the direct influence $S^\delta(A, B)$ for some $\delta \in \{+, -, 0, ?\}$, then also the influence $S^\delta(B, A)$ holds, for the same value of δ. The transitivity property asserts that the influences along a chain that specifies at most one incoming arc for each variable, combine into a net influence whose sign is defined by the $\otimes$-operator from Table 1. The property of composition asserts that multiple influences between two variables along parallel chains combine into a net influence whose sign is defined by the $\oplus$-operator. From the definition of the $\oplus$-operator in Table 1, we observe that the composition of two influences with opposite signs along parallel chains will give rise to an unknown result, which is captured by the sign '?'.

2.3 Monotonicity of Bayesian Networks

For addressing the conditions under which correct monotonicity directions are learned for a naive Bayesian classifier, we review the notion of monotonicity for probability distributions is general. We say that a conditional probability distribution $\Pr(C \mid \mathbf{F})$ over a class variable C is monotonically increasing in the feature variable F_i if $\Pr(c \mid f_i, \mathbf{f}_i^-) \geq \Pr(c \mid \bar{f}_i, \mathbf{f}_i^-)$ for all joint value assignments $\mathbf{f}_i^-$ to the feature variables other than F_i; decreasing monotonicity is defined analogously. The direction of the monotonicity of the relation between the feature variable F_i and the class variable C will be denoted by a sign d_i, where $d_i = +$ is used to indicate an increasing monotonicity and $d_i = -$ a decreasing one. Note that for probability distributions which are defined by a Bayesian network of general topology, a monotonicity direction d_i may or may not coincide with the qualitative sign of a specific arc.

Learning a naive Bayesian classifier will result in a graphical structure in which the arcs model dependencies of the separate feature variables on the class variable. Each arc $C \rightarrow F_i$ then captures a direct probabilistic influence, as reviewed above, and has associated a qualitative sign δ_{CF_i}. From the mutual independency of any two feature variables given the class variable, we have that if the qualitative sign δ_{CF_i} of the probabilistic influence of C on F_i is $+$, then the conditional probability distribution $\Pr(C \mid \mathbf{F})$ modelled by the classifier will be monotonically increasing in F_i, and vice versa; a similar observation holds for a negative influence. For the probability distribution defined by a naive Bayesian classifier therefore, we have that a monotonicity direction d_i does coincide with the qualitative sign δ_{CF_i} of a specific arc for all feature variables F_i.

3   An Example of Counterintuitive Behaviour

Upon learning a naive Bayesian classifier from a data set of instances, the learning algorithm will identify and model the dependencies of each feature variable on the class variable involved. We will show by means of an example that upon doing so the algorithm will not always be able to recover the monotonicity properties embedded in the data. Our example will demonstrate in fact, that a resulting classifier can show quite counterintuitive classification behaviour.

Our example pertains to the weather in the Netherlands and to how it is perceived by the Dutch. The Netherlands have a moderate maritime climate with cool summers and mild winters. The Dutch like to talk about their weather, and to complain about it. Our fictitious network, depicted on the left in Fig. 1,

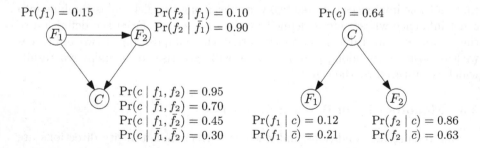

Fig. 1. The example Bayesian network (*left*) and the constructed classifier (*right*), together with their (conditional) probability tables

includes some weather aspects about which the Dutch tend to mope. The variable C captures whether or not the weather feels damp; the value *true* denotes a sense of humidity. The variable F_1 models temperature; the value *true* denotes a temperature of 18°C or more, which is relatively warm by Dutch standards. The variable F_2 captures cloudiness, with the value *true* indicating an overcast sky. The graphical structure of the network reflects the dependencies among the three variables. The network's conditional probability tables express for example, that the Dutch have a warm day with a probability of 0.15; such days are not very likely to be cloudy. The probability table for the variable C further shows that the Dutch are likely to perceive the weather as moist whenever the sky is overcast, and especially so on a warm day; on bright days the weather is less likely to give rise to dampness. Now suppose that we are interested in predicting the Dutch' sense of humidity of their weather. From the network, the prior probability of a sense of humidity is computed to be $\Pr(c) = 0.64$. For a warm day with an overcast sky, the probability of the weather being perceived as damp is found to increase from 0.64 to $\Pr(c \mid f_1, f_2) = 0.95$. Note that an increase of this probability would indeed be expected from the available domain knowledge.

We constructed a naive Bayesian classifier for the same prediction problem. To supplement the classifier's graphical structure, we computed all required probabilities directly from the probability distribution represented by the original model, and not from artificially generated data; by doing so we are guaranteed that any observed effect cannot have originated from chance properties of a necessarily finite data set. We computed from the original model the prior probability distribution over the class variable C and the conditional probability distributions for the feature variables F_1 and F_2, respectively, given C. The thus constructed classifier is shown on the right in Fig. 1. From the classifier, we now compute the same probabilities of interest as from the original model. The prior probability of a sense of dampness again is found to be $\Pr(c) = 0.64$. For a warm day with an overcast sky, we find a posterior probability of $\Pr(c \mid f_1, f_2) = 0.58$. So, while according to the true distribution we should find an increased probability of a sense of dampness, the constructed classifier actually returns a decrease ! Dependent upon the decision rule used with the classifier, the weather condition could in fact even be assigned to a different class.

4   Incorrect Monotonicity Directions

The example from the previous section served to show that learning a naive Bayesian classifier from a data set of instances from a joint probability distribution can result in quite unexpected classification behaviour. In this section, we investigate the exhibited behaviour and attribute its counterintuitive character to an incorrect monotonicity direction for one of the feature variables in the classifier. We further identify the conditions under which the learning algorithm will extract the correct directions of monotonicity from the true distribution.

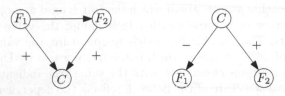

Fig. 2. The signs of the direct influences in the true network (*left*) and in the constructed classifier (*right*)

4.1   Investigating the Example

We study the behaviour of the example Bayesian network and of the constructed classifier from Sect. 3 respectively, in terms of the signs of their direct influences. From the probability distributions specified for the class variable C in the true model, we find that the direct influence of the variable F_1 on C is positive:

$$\Pr(c \mid f_1, f_2) - \Pr(c \mid \bar{f}_1, f_2) = 0.95 - 0.7 = 0.25 \;\geq\; 0, \quad \text{and}$$
$$\Pr(c \mid f_1, \bar{f}_2) - \Pr(c \mid \bar{f}_1, \bar{f}_2) = 0.45 - 0.3 = 0.15 \;\geq\; 0$$

Using the notation t to indicate influences in the true model, we thus have that $\delta^t_{F_1 C} = +$. Similarly, we find that $\delta^t_{F_2 C} = +$. The true model in addition includes a direct qualitative influence of F_1 on F_2, which is found to be negative:

$$\Pr(f_2 \mid f_1) - \Pr(f_2 \mid \bar{f}_1) = 0.10 - 0.90 = -0.80 \;\leq\; 0$$

that is, $\delta^t_{F_1 F_2} = -$. The monotonicity directions d^t_i for the two feature variables are now found by investigating the true probability distributions $\Pr(C \mid F_1, F_2)$. Since the probability table of the class variable C specifies these distributions, it is readily established that $\Pr(C \mid F_1, F_2)$ is monotonically increasing in both F_1 and F_2, that is, we find that $d^t_1 = +$ and $d^t_2 = +$. Note that these monotonicity directions match the signs of the direct influences of F_1 and F_2 on C, respectively.

From the probability distributions specified for the feature variable F_2 in the constructed classifier, we find the qualitative influence of C on F_2 to be positive:

$$\Pr(f_2 \mid c) - \Pr(f_2 \mid \bar{c}) = 0.86 - 0.63 = 0.23 \;\geq\; 0$$

Using the notation c to indicate influences in the classifier, we thus have that $\delta^c_{C F_2} = +$. Similarly, we find the probabilistic influence of C on F_1 to be negative:

$$\Pr(f_1 \mid c) - \Pr(f_1 \mid \bar{c}) = 0.12 - 0.21 = -0.09 \;\leq\; 0$$

that is, $\delta^c_{C F_1} = -$. From our observations in Sect. 2.3, we conclude that $d^c_1 = \delta^c_{C F_1} = -$ and $d^c_2 = \delta^c_{C F_2} = +$. Fig. 2 again depicts the true model and its corresponding naive Bayesian classifier respectively, now supplemented with the signs of their direct qualitative influences.

From our investigation of the monotonicity directions in the true distribution and in the corresponding classifier, it is readily seen that $d^t_1 \neq d^c_1$. The observed discrepancy originates from how the learning algorithm computes the direct influences for the naive Bayesian classifier from the true probability distribution. For the direct influence of C on F_1 for the classifier, the learning algorithm establishes from the true distribution the *compound* influence composed of the direct influence of F_1 on C and the indirect influence of F_1 on C via F_2. The sign of this compound influence is computed to be $\delta_{F_1C}^t \oplus (\delta_{F_2C}^t \otimes \delta_{F_1F_2}^t) = \,?$, that is, the sign cannot be determined by qualitative considerations only and is dependent on the strengths of the direct and indirect influences in the true model. With the specified probability distributions, the compound influence is computed to be negative, which gives rise to an incorrect sign for the influence of C on F_1 in the classifier, and hence to an incorrect monotonicity direction for the feature variable F_1. It is this incorrect monotonicity direction from which the classifier's counterintuitive behaviour originates.

4.2 Deriving Correct Monotonicity Directions

Having studied the behaviour of our concrete example Bayesian network and classifier, we now abstract from the precise numbers involved and address the conditions under which the learning algorithm will find the correct monotonicity directions for the probability distribution represented by the naive Bayesian classifier. Upon doing so, we will use the sign notations for the various direct influences involved as shown in Fig. 3.

We have argued above that for establishing the direct influence of the class variable C on the feature variable F_1 for the naive Bayesian classifier, the learning algorithm combines the direct and indirect influences of C on F_1 from the true distribution; a similar observation holds for the direct influence of C on the feature variable F_2. More specifically, the learning algorithm establishes the following signs for the direct influences in the constructed classifier:

$$\delta_{CF_i}^c = \delta_{CF_i}^t \oplus (\delta_{F_iF_j}^t \otimes \delta_{CF_j}^t)$$

where $i, j = 1, 2, i \neq j$. The learning algorithm thus computes the sign $\delta_{CF_i}^c$ to be

$$\delta_{CF_i}^c = \begin{cases} \delta_{CF_i}^t & \text{if } \delta_{CF_i}^t = + \text{ and } \delta_{F_iF_j}^t = \delta_{CF_j}^t \\ \delta_{CF_i}^t & \text{if } \delta_{CF_i}^t = - \text{ and } \delta_{F_iF_j}^t \neq \delta_{CF_j}^t \\ ? & \text{otherwise} \end{cases}$$

Note that in the last case the sign of the computed influence is dependent on the concrete probabilities in the true distribution.

The correct monotonicity directions for the two feature variables are established from the true model by investigating the conditional probability distributions $\Pr(C \mid F_1, F_2)$. We find that the monotonicity direction for the feature variable F_1 equals $d_1 = \delta_{CF_1}^t$; for the variable F_2, the correct direction of monotonicity is $d_2 = \delta_{CF2}^t$. We conclude that the learning algorithm finds the correct monotonicity directions for the classifier whenever $\delta_{CF_i}^t = \delta_{CF_i}^c$, that is, whenever the true model includes three positive direct influences or when it includes two negative influences and a single positive one. Note that these conditions indeed are not met by the true network from our running example.

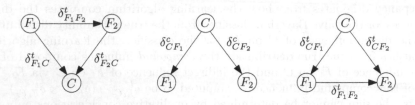

Fig. 3. Notations for the direct influences in the true network (*left*), the constructed classifier (*middle*) and in a network equivalent to the true network (*right*)

We would like to note that similar analyses apply to all equivalent true networks with different arc orientations. From the network shown in Fig. 3 on the right, for example, the direct influence of C on F_1 is computed for the classifier to have the sign $\delta^c_{CF_1} = \delta^t_{CF_1}$; the sign for the direct influence of C on F_2 for the classifier is computed as $\delta^c_{CF_2} = \delta^t_{CF_2} \oplus (\delta^t_{CF_1} \otimes \delta^t_{F_1F_2})$. The correct monotonicity directions now are $d_1 = \delta^t_{CF_1} \oplus \delta^t_{CF_1|F_2}$ and $d_2 = \delta^t_{CF_2}$, where $\delta^t_{CF_1|F_2}$ denotes the qualitative sign of the intercausal influence induced by the observation for F_2; for further information on induced intercausal influences, we refer to [9].

4.3   Classification Behaviour

We return to the original example network and associated classifier from Fig. 1, and address the counterintuitive behaviour of the classifier in view of the incorrectly identified monotonicity direction for the feature variable F_1.

The true Bayesian network specifies a prior probability $\Pr^t(c)$ for the class variable C. From the monotonicity directions $d_1 = +$ and $d_2 = +$ represented by the network, we know that entering the evidence f_1, f_2 will result in a posterior probability $\Pr^t(c \mid f_1, f_2)$ larger than the prior probability $\Pr^t(c)$. Similarly, upon entering $\bar{f}_1, \bar{f}_2$, we will find a probability $\Pr^t(c \mid \bar{f}_1, \bar{f}_2)$ smaller than $\Pr^t(c)$. We thus see the following relation between these prior and posterior probabilities:

$$\Pr^t(c \mid f_1, f_2) \;\geq\; \Pr^t(c) \;\geq\; \Pr^t(c \mid \bar{f}_1, \bar{f}_2)$$

We have not included the posterior probabilities $\Pr^t(c \mid \bar{f}_1, f_2)$ and $\Pr^t(c \mid f_1, \bar{f}_2)$ in this relation, since we have no strong expectation about the relation between the prior and posterior probabilities when one feature variable is observed to be *true* and the other has adopted the value *false*.

Especially if the monotonicity directions exhibited by the true model are common knowledge, a user will expect the same behaviour from the constructed naive Bayesian classifier, that is, he expects to find that

$$\Pr^c(c \mid f_1, f_2) \;\geq\; \Pr^c(c) \;\geq\; \Pr^c(c \mid \bar{f}_1, \bar{f}_2)$$

When computing the probabilities involved from the classifier, however, the following unexpected result is found:

$$\Pr^c(c \mid f_1, f_2) = 0.58 \;<\; \Pr^c(c) = 0.64$$

Note that as a result of the incorrect sign $\delta^c_{CF_1} = -$ of the qualitative influence of the feature variable F_1 on the class variable C, we cannot establish, apriori, an ordering of the posterior probabilities $\Pr^c(c \mid f_1, f_2)$ and $\Pr^c(c \mid \bar{f}_1, \bar{f}_2)$ with respect to the prior probability $\Pr^c(c)$ from the classifier.

Incorrect monotonicity directions in a naive Bayesian classifier will not always result in such obvious counterintuitive behaviour. We consider again the true network from Fig. 1. When we alter the probability distribution for the variable F_1 from $\Pr(f_1) = 0.15$ to $\Pr(f_1) = 0.45$, for example, we still find that $\delta^c_{CF_1} = -$ and $\delta^c_{CF_2} = +$. The relation between the prior and posterior probabilities computed from the learnt classifier now has become as expected by the user:

$$\Pr^c(c \mid f_1, f_2) = 0.64 \;>\; \Pr^c(c) = 0.59 \;>\; \Pr^c(c \mid \bar{f}_1, \bar{f}_2) = 0.51$$

We note that this does not mean that the classifier establishes the correct ordering relation between the posterior probabilities $\Pr(c \mid F_1, F_2)$ for all value assignments to the feature variables F_1 and F_2, however. For example, while we have $\Pr^t(c \mid f_1, f_2) \geq \Pr^t(c \mid \bar{f}_1, f_2)$ from the true network, we find that $\Pr^c(c \mid \bar{f}_1, f_2) \geq \Pr^c(c \mid f_1, f_2)$ from the constructed classifier. Although this finding also is counterintuitive in itself, we feel that it is less likely to be noticed by a user in a more involved real-life application than a violation of an expected relation between a posterior probability and the prior probability $\Pr(c)$.

5   Related Work

Several researchers have investigated the problem of enforcing given monotonicity constraints in learning algorithms for Bayesian networks [10,11]. Little research however, has focused on the problem of learning correct monotonicity directions from data. A notable exception is the work of Magdon-Ismail and Sill [12]. They have investigated whether a linear model approximating the monotone function g will produce the correct monotonicity directions, given that the linear model minimizes expected squared error

$$E(w_0, \mathbf{w}) = \int (w_0 + \mathbf{w}^\mathrm{T}\mathbf{f} - g(\mathbf{f}))^2 \Pr(\mathbf{f})d\mathbf{f}$$

Here, $\mathbf{w}$ denotes the set of weights $(w_1, \ldots, w_n)^\mathrm{T}$. They prove that the following conditions are both sufficient for producing the correct monotonicity directions:

1. The feature variables F_i are independent, that is,

$$\Pr(\mathbf{F}) = \prod_{i=1}^{n} \Pr(F_i)$$

2. The probability distribution $\Pr(\mathbf{F})$ belongs to the class of Mahalanobis densities, which includes normal densities as an important subclass.

If we take $g(\mathbf{f}) = \Pr(c \mid \mathbf{f})$, then the relation with the problem considered in the current paper is clear. The assumption that $\Pr(c \mid \mathbf{f})$ is a linear function of

$\mathbf{f}$ is quite unusual in view of binary classification, however, because a linear fit could result in values outside the interval $[0,1]$. The log-odds function $\ln\{\Pr(c \mid \mathbf{f})/\Pr(\bar{c} \mid \mathbf{f})\}$ is monotone given that the function $\Pr(c \mid \mathbf{f})$ is monotone. The assumption that the log-odds

$$\ln\left\{\frac{\Pr(c \mid \mathbf{f})}{\Pr(\bar{c} \mid \mathbf{f})}\right\} = w_0 + \mathbf{w}^{\mathrm{T}}\mathbf{f}$$

is a linear function of $\mathbf{f}$ is quite common; it is the central assumption of logistic regression, for example. It is also well known that for naive Bayesian classifiers, the log-odds is a linear function of the features, where weights $\mathbf{w}$ for a naive Bayesian classifier with binary variables are determined by

$$w_i = \ln\mathrm{cpr}(C, F_i) = \ln\left\{\frac{\Pr(c, f_i)\Pr(\bar{c}, \bar{f}_i)}{\Pr(c, \bar{f}_i)\Pr(\bar{c}, f_i)}\right\}$$

where $\mathrm{cpr}(C, F_i)$ is the so-called cross-product ratio between C and F_i, which is a well-known measure of association between two binary random variables. If the cross-product ratio is larger than one, there is a positive association between C and F_i, that is, $\delta^c_{CF_i} = +$. Similarly, if $\mathrm{cpr}(C, F_i) < 1$, then $\delta^c_{CF_i} = -$. Unfortunately, since we are considering binary random variables, they evidently do not follow a normal (or other Mahalanobis) distribution. Hence, we cannot invoke the second sufficient condition of Magdon-Ismail and Sill. In addition, we do not minimise expected squared error, but the Kullback-Leibler divergence

$$\sum_{c,\mathbf{f}}\Pr^t(\mathbf{c}, \mathbf{f})\ln\left\{\frac{\Pr^t(\mathbf{c}, \mathbf{f})}{\Pr^c(\mathbf{c}, \mathbf{f})}\right\}$$

instead. These observations lead to the conclusion that, given our true probability distribution and the accompanying naive Bayesian classifier, we cannot assume that a linear model approximating the true distribution will retrieve the correct monotonicity directions.

6   Conclusions and Further Research

Naive Bayesian classifiers are quite popular stochastic classification models, especially since they are easy to construct from a collection of data and are known to perform well, even when compared to more complex models. Naive Bayesian classifiers build however, on the rather strong assumption of mutual independence of their feature variables given the class variable. This observation has induced researchers to investigate the effects of several different types of dependency between the feature variables on the performance of a constructed naive Bayesian classifier. In this paper, we have contributed to this line of research by showing that dependencies embedded in a true probability distribution can cause incorrect monotonicity directions to be learned for the influences of the feature variables on the class variable in a classifier. We have further demonstrated that incorrect monotonicity directions in a classifier have the potential of giving rise to unexpected classification behaviour. For a limited type of probability distribution, we have established the conditions under which the learning algorithm will retrieve the correct monotonicity directions. Although our distribution under study is quite simple, it is evident that similar effects can arise from more realistic distributions as well. Our future investigations will be directed to a study of the conditions under which correct monotonicity directions will be learned from more involved probability distributions.

Acknowledgement. This research was funded by the Netherlands Organisation for Scientific Research (NWO).

References

1. Friedman, N., Geiger, D., Goldszmidt, M.: Bayesian network classifiers. Machine Learning 29, 131–163 (1997)
2. Domingos, P., Pazzani, M.: On the optimality of the simple Bayesian classifier under zero-one loss. Machine Learning 29, 103–130 (1997)
3. Kohavi, R., John, G.H.: Wrappers for feature subset selection. Artificial Intelligence 97, 273–324 (1997)
4. Langley, P.: Selection of relevant features in machine learning. In: Proceedings of the AAAI Fall Symposium on Relevance, pp. 140–144. AAAI Press, Menlo Park (1994)
5. Geenen, P.L., van der Gaag, L.C., Loeffen, W.L.A., Elbers, A.R.W.: On the robustness of feature selection with absent and non-observed features. In: Barreiro, J.M., Martin-Sanchez, F., Maojo, V., Sanz, F. (eds.) Proceedings of the Fifth International Symposium on Biological and Medical Data Analysis, pp. 148–159. Springer, Heidelberg (2004)
6. van der Gaag, L.C., Tabachneck-Schijf, H.J.M., Geenen, P.L.: Verifying monotonicity of Bayesian networks with domain experts. International Journal of Approximate Reasoning 50, 429–436 (2009)
7. Jensen, F.V., Nielsen, T.D.: Bayesian Networks and Decision Graphs. Springer, New York (2007)
8. Wellman, M.P.: Fundamental concepts of qualitative probabilistic networks. Artificial Intelligence 44, 257–303 (1990)
9. Druzdzel, M.J., Henrion, M.: Efficient reasoning in qualitative probabilistic networks. In: Proceedings of the Eleventh National Conference on Artificial Intelligence, pp. 548–553. AAAI Press, Menlo Park (1993)
10. Altendorf, E.A., Restificar, A.C., Dietterich, T.G.: Learning from sparse data by exploiting monotonicity constraints. In: Bacchus, F., Jaakkola, T. (eds.) Proceedings of the 21st Conference on Uncertainty in Artificial Intelligence, pp. 18–25. AUAI Press (2005)
11. Feelders, A., van der Gaag, L.C.: Learning Bayesian network parameters under order constraints. International Journal of Approximate Reasoning 42, 37–53 (2006)
12. Magdon-Ismail, M., Sill, J.: A linear fit gets the correct monotonicity directions. Machine Learning 70, 21–43 (2008)

Possibilistic Classifiers for Uncertain Numerical Data

Myriam Bounhas[1], Henri Prade[2], Mathieu Serrurier[2], and Khaled Mellouli[1]

[1] LARODEC Laboratory, ISG de Tunis, 41 rue de la Liberté, 2000 Le Bardo, Tunisie
[2] IRIT, UPS-CNRS, 118 route de Narbonne, 31062 Toulouse Cedex-France
Myriam_Bounhas@yahoo.fr, {prade,serrurie}@irit.fr,
Khaled.Mellouli@topnet.tn

Abstract. In many real-world problems, input data may be pervaded with uncertainty. Naive possibilistic classifiers have been proposed as a counterpart to Bayesian classifiers to deal with classification tasks in presence of uncertainty. Following this line here, we extend possibilistic classifiers, which have been recently adapted to numerical data, in order to cope with uncertainty in data representation. We consider two types of uncertainty: i) the uncertainty associated with the class in the training set, which is modeled by a possibility distribution over class labels, and ii) the imprecision pervading attribute values in the testing set represented under the form of intervals for continuous data. We first adapt the possibilistic classification model, previously proposed for the certain case, in order to accommodate the uncertainty about class labels. Then, we propose an extension principle-based algorithm to deal with imprecise attribute values. The experiments reported show the interest of possibilistic classifiers for handling uncertainty in data. In particular, the probability-to-possibility transform-based classifier shows a robust behavior when dealing with imperfect data.

Keywords: Possibility Theory, Classification, Numerical Data, Uncertainty.

1 Introduction

Possibility theory [7] [6] has been recently proposed as a counterpart of probability theory to deal with classification tasks in presence of uncertainty. There are only few works that treat possibilistic classification and most of existing naïve possibilistic classifiers deal only with categorical attributes. In this paper, we study possibilistic classifiers applied to *imperfect* numerical data. Given a new piece of data to classify, these classifiers seeks to estimate the plausibility of each class with respect to its description (built from the training set of examples), and assigns the class having the highest plausibility value. The objective of this work is to extend the possibilistic classifiers proposed in [17] in order to cope with uncertainty in data sets (in the training and testing sets).

The paper is structured as follows. Section 2 reviews some related works. Section 3 briefly restates the basis of possibilistic classification. In Section 4, we

W. Liu (Ed.): ECSQARU 2011, LNAI 6717, pp. 434–446, 2011.
© Springer-Verlag Berlin Heidelberg 2011

consider two forms of uncertainty, and in Section 5 we extend possibilistic classifiers to the handling of imperfect data: the first type concerns the processing of *uncertain* classes in the training set, whereas the second one deals with uncertain attribute values in the testing set. Uncertainty on attribute values is modeled by intervals. The experimentation results are given in Section 6. The experiments reported show the interest of possibilistic classifiers to deal with imperfect data. Finally, Section 7 concludes and suggests some directions for future research.

2   Related Works

Some approaches have already proposed the use of a possibilistic data representation in classification methods based on decision trees, or on Bayesian-like or case-based approaches. A discussion about the appropriateness of fuzzy set methods in machine learning has been proposed in [10].

Ben Amor et al. [19] developed a qualitative approach based on the decision tree technique and used it to classify examples having possibilistic uncertain attribute values. This work aims at searching the most plausible class labeling a vector, knowing its possibility distribution on attribute values given by an expert. In [13], possibilistic decision trees are induced from instances associated with categorical attributes and vaguely specified classes. Uncertainty, modeled through possibility theory, concerns only class attribute whereas other predictive attributes are supposed to be certain. A Naive Bayes Style Possibilistic Classifier (NBSPC) is proposed by Borgelt et al. [4] to deal with imprecise training sets. For this classifier, imprecision concerns only attribute values of instances (the class attribute and the testing set are supposed to be perfect). Given the class attribute, possibility distributions for attributes are estimated from the computation of the maximum-based projection [5] over the set S of precise instances (S is included in the extended dataset) which contains both the target value of the considered attribute with the class.

A naive possibilistic network classifier, proposed by Haouari et al. [1], presents a building procedure that deals with imperfect dataset attributes and classes, and a classification procedure used to classify unseen examples which may have imperfect attribute values. This imperfection is modeled through a possibility distribution given by an expert who expresses his partial ignorance, due to a lack of a priori knowledge. Benferhat and Tabia [21] propose an efficient algorithm for revising, using Jeffrey's rule, possibilistic knowledge encoded by a naive product-based possibilistic network classifier on the basis of uncertain inputs. The main advantage of the proposed algorithm is its capability to process the classification task in polynomial time with respected to the number of attributes.

Most of previously cited works [19,1,13,4,21] deal only with discrete attribute values and are not appropriate for continuous attribute values. These approaches require a preliminary discretization phase for the continuous attribute values. In [20], the authors propose a new Bayesian classifier for uncertain categorical or continuous data by integrating uncertainty in the Bayesian theorem and propose a new parameter estimation method. An attempt to treat uncertainty in

continuous data is proposed in [2], where authors developed a classification algorithm able to generate rules from uncertain continuous data. For the two works
[2] [20], uncertainty over continuous attribute values is represented by intervals.
This imprecision is handled by a regular probabilistic process.

Some case-based classification techniques, which make use of possibility theory
and fuzzy sets, are also proposed in the literature. In [11], the authors propose
a possibilistic version of the classical instance-based learning paradigm using a
similarity measure and model uncertainty in order to support incomplete information. In a more recent work [3], the authors develop a bipolar possibilistic
method for case-based learning and prediction.

3   Possibilistic Classification

As in the case of Bayesian classification, possibilistic classification is based on the
possibilistic version of the Bayes theorem. Given a vector $X = \{x_1, x_2, ..., x_M\}$
of n observed variables and the set of classes $C = \{c_1, c_2, ..., c_C\}$, the classification problem consists in estimating a possibility distribution on classes and in
choosing the class with the highest possibility for the vector X, i.e.:

$$\pi(c_j|x_1, x_2, ..., x_M) = \frac{\pi(c_j) * \pi(x_1, x_2, ..., x_M|c_j)}{\pi(x_1, x_2, ..., x_M)} \tag{1}$$

where * stands for product in quantitative possibility settings. Assuming the
independence between variables x_i in the context of classes [18], this possibility
distribution can easily be specified by the *product* (or the *minimum*) of the
conditional possibilities $\pi(x_i|c_j)$ for all variables x_i. Each conditional possibility
represents the possibility of x_i knowing c_j. Note that the term $\pi(x_1, x_2, ..., x_M)$
is a normalization factor and it is the same over all class labels.

In this paper, considering an unknown test instance I_{ts} with attribute values
$(a_1, ..., a_M)$, the classification task amounts to calculating values of possibilities
for each class: $\Pi(c_j|I_{ts})$. Assuming attribute independence, the plausibility of
each class for a given instance is computed as:

$$\Pi(c_j|I_{ts}) = \pi(c_j) * \prod_{i=1}^{M} \Pi(a_i|c_j) \tag{2}$$

where conditional possibilities $\Pi(a_i|c_j)$ in formula (2) represent to what extent
a_i is a possible value for the attribute A_i in the presence of the class c_j. $\Pi(c_j)$
is the possibility of the class c_j. In a product-based setting, a given instance is
assigned to the most plausible class c*:

$$c^* = arg \max_{c_j}(\pi(c_j) * \prod_{i=1}^{M} \Pi(a_i|c_j)) \tag{3}$$

Using the min-based setting, the classification is based on selecting the class
having the highest minimum:

$$c^* = arg \max_{c_j}(\pi(c_j) * \min_{i=1}^{M} \Pi(a_i|c_j)) \tag{4}$$

4 Possibilistic Distributions for Imperfect Numerical Data

In this paper, we extend the possibilistic classifiers proposed in [17] in order to handle uncertainty in the data representation. Uncertainty pervades attribute valuess in the testing instances and classes in the training instances. All uncertain possibilistic classifiers, proposed in this paper, are based on the following hypotheses:

   - All training instances are assumed to have perfect (certain and precise) attribute values as in "classical" possibilistic classifiers [17].

   - All testing instances have imprecise attribute values modeled by intervals.

   - The class of any training instances is represented through a possibility distribution over the class values thus reflecting uncertainty on the classification.

4.1 Processing of Uncertain Classes in the Training Set

Let Tr be a training set composed of N instances involving M numerical attributes. Instead of an exact class label, for each instance we assign a possibility distribution on the different possible labels. Our problem is to estimate a possibility distribution for each attribute a_i given the class c_j which can be the most specific representation for *uncertain* numerical data:

$$\pi(a_i|c_j) = \frac{\pi(a_i, c_j)}{\pi(c_j)} \tag{5}$$

To combine possibility distributions over the training instances belonging to a specific class, one can exploit the mean operator (equation 6) as in the perfect case. It is proved in [1] and then in [17] that the arithmetic mean is consistent in this estimation problem and it provides a faithful representation of the data.

$$\pi(a_i, c_j) = \frac{1}{N} \sum_{k=1}^{N} \pi(a_i, c_{jk}) = \frac{1}{N} \sum_{k=1}^{N} \pi(a_i|c_{jk}) * \pi(c_{jk}) \tag{6}$$

The max operator may also be used in this case:

$$\pi(a_i, c_j) = \max_{k=1}^{N} \pi(a_i, c_{jk}) = \max_{k=1}^{N} \pi(a_i|c_{jk}) * \pi(c_{jk}) \tag{7}$$

$\pi(c_{jk})$ represents the individual possibility of the class c_j for each training instance k. To compute $\pi(c_j)$, in equation 5, we may also use the mean or the maximum operator applied to $\pi(c_{jk})$. We note that the proposed model, supporting uncertainty in the class labels, also includes the certain case where $\pi(c_{jk})$ is 1 for the the true label and 0 otherwise.

4.2   Processing of Imprecise Attributes in the Testing Set

Each testing instance may include perfect or imperfect attribute values. Since we are only interested in continuous data in this framework, the proposed model allows an expert to express his/her uncertain knowledge (imperfect attributes) through an interval restricting the attribute value. For each imprecise attribute, the observed value is in the form of $I_i = [L_i, U_i]$ where L_i and U_i are respectively the lower and the upper bounds for the the true attribute value a_i such that $L_i < a_i < U_i$.

In the following we propose an algorithm for handling imprecision in attribute values in the testing set. Let us consider a function F which estimates conditional possibilities for attribute values in the perfect case. For each *observed* attribute value x_i, this function estimates $\pi_{(a_i|c_j)}(x_i)$. Knowing that the observed value of an attribute is no longer a fixed value in the domain of the attribute but rather an interval, the problem returns the estimate $\pi_{(a_i|c_j)}(I_i)$.

In order to handle the evaluation of interval possibilities, we use the extension principle [22]. Let F be a real function such that $F : X \to R, R$ being the set of real numbers. Let $F(x) = u$ and let $\pi_F(u)$ be the possibility for u. Using the extension principle, the possibility distribution for u is:

$$\pi_F(u) = sup\{\pi(x)|F(x) = u\}. \tag{8}$$

Assume $I_1, ..., I_n$ are uncertain observations for attributes $a_1, ..., a_n$. To estimate the possibility distribution for an interval I_i, the equation (8) becomes:

$$\pi(I_i|c_j) = sup\{\pi(a_i|c_j), a_i \in I_i\} \tag{9}$$

To define conditional possibilities for each uncertain observation I_i of the testing instance, we consider the following algorithm:

1) Search for all attribute values a_i in the training set such that $a_i \in I_i$,
2) Compute the possibility of attribute values a_i given the class c_j by eq. 5
3) Consider the highest possibility to estimate the possibility of I_i

5   Individual Possibility Distribution

In this section, we describe individual possibility distributions for attributes over training instances. As in the classical certain possibilistic classifiers, we investigate two kinds of approaches, either based on probability-possibility transformation [9,12], or on a direct interpretation of data taking advantage of the idea of proximity. We give here only the general principle of these two classification methods (see [17] for more details and for a comparative study).

5.1   Probability to Possibility Transformation-Based Classifiers

We apply the probability to possibility transformation method proposed by [9,12] to the case of Naive Bayesian classifiers (NBC), where the distribution is assumed to be normal, and then to its flexible extension FNPC (using a combination of normal distributions).

Let us consider a Gaussian distribution $g_{ij} = g(a_i, \mu_{ij}, \sigma_{ij})$ that corresponds to the conditional probability of a_i knowing c_j, where μ_{ij} is the mean of the attribute a_i for the class c_j and σ_{ij} is its standard deviation for the same class. If I_{a_i} is the confidence interval centered at μ_{ij}, its probability $P(I_{a_i}|c_j)$ can be estimated by: $2*G(a_i, \mu_{ij}, \sigma_{ij}) - 1$, where G is a Gaussian cumulative distribution easily evaluated using the table of the Standard Normal Distribution. $\pi(a_i|c_j)$ is estimated by $1 - P(I_{a_i}|c_j)$ using the following formula:

$$\pi(a_i|c_j) = 1 - (2*G(a_i, \mu_{ij}, \sigma_{ij}) - 1) = 2*(1 - G(a_i, \mu_{ij}, \sigma_{ij})). \tag{10}$$

The FNPC is exactly the same as the NPC in all respects, the only difference between the two classifiers is the method used for density estimation on continuous attributes. Although using a single Gaussian to estimate each continuous attribute, we choose to investigate kernel density estimation as in the FNBC. Kernel estimation with Gaussian kernels looks much the same except that the estimated density is averaged over a large set of kernels. For the FNPC we adapt the equation (10) as follows:

$$\pi(a_i|c_{jk}) = 2*(1 - G(a_i, \mu_{ik}, \sigma)). \tag{11}$$

where k ranges over the N_j instances of the training set in class c_j and $\mu_{ik} = a_{ik}$. For all distributions, the standard deviation is estimated by: $\sigma = \frac{1}{\sqrt{N}}$.

In this approach and for all the rest of this work, all attribute values a_i's are normalized using: $a_{i_n} = \frac{a_i - min(a_i)}{max(a_i) - min(a_i)}$.

5.2   Proximity Based Classifiers

In [17] we also proposed two other methods for building a possibility distribution without computing a Gaussian probability distribution first. These approaches take into account the similarity between attribute values and observed values of the same attribute in the training set. The two suggested classification methods use an *approximate equality relation* between numerical values. Let d be the distance between the two values, this fuzzy relation, namely $\mu_E(d(a_i, a_{ik}))$ estimates to what extent the attribute value a_i is close to other attributes a_{ik} in each training instance k as follows:

$$\pi(a_i|c_{jk}) = \mu_E(d(a_i, a_{ik})) = max(0, min(1, \frac{\alpha + \beta - d(a_i, a_{ik})}{\beta})), \alpha \geq 0; \beta > 0. \tag{12}$$

This relation is parameterized by α and β. In the first algorithm named Fuzzy Histogram Classifier (FuHC), we use the approximate equality function to build a fuzzy histogram for attribute a_i given a class c_j using equation (6). In the second algorithm, named Nearest Neighbor-based Possibilistic Classifier (NNPC), we apply the maximum operator as in equation (7) to the approximate equality relation to estimate proximities between the attribute values a_{ik} belonging to each instance k labeled with class c_j without counting them.

6 Experiments and Discussion

This section provides experimental results of the proposed uncertain possibilitic classifiers. The experimental study is based on several datasets taken from the U.C.I. repository of machine learning databases [16]. A brief description of these datasets is given in Table 1. Since we have chosen to deal only with numerical attributes in this study, all these datasets have numerical attribute values. For each dataset, we used a ten-fold cross validation to evaluate the generalization accuracy of classifiers.

Table 1. Description of datasets

Database	Data	Attributes	Classes
Iris	150	4	3
W. B. Cancer	699	8	2
Wine	178	13	3
Diabetes	768	7	2
Magic gamma telescope	1074	10	2
Transfusion	748	4	2
Satellite Image	1090	37	6
Segment	1500	20	7
Yeast	1484	9	10
Ecoli	336	8	8
Glass	214	10	7

6.1 Generation of Imperfect Data

Data sets described in Table 1 are initially perfect with certain and precise attributes and classes. In order to evaluate possibilistic classifiers in the imperfect case, we have artificially introduced imperfection in these data sets by transforming the original precise and certain instances into imperfect ones.

Uncertainty on the training set is created by replacing the certain class label of each instance by a possibility distribution over class labels. To generate a possibility distribution, we suppose that we have two independent experts and that they are, to some extent, unable to classify each training instance in a certain manner. So we ask each expert to give a possibility distribution over class labels reflecting his/her knowledge about this uncertain situation. Then we apply an information fusion procedure [8] to produce the final possibility distribution for each instance. Each expert may simply be a possibilistic classifier trained on the perfect (certain and precise) data set. In this experiment we have used the certain FNPC and the FuHC classifiers, as presented in Section 5, to simulate experts. For information fusion, we apply a *disjunctive operator* [8] to create the final possibility distribution $\pi_{I_{tr}}: \forall \omega \in \Omega, \pi_\vee(\omega) = \oplus_{i=1..n}\pi_i(\omega) = \max_{i=1}^n \pi_i(\omega)$. We prefer the disjunctive operator to the conjunctive one since the two classifiers may disagree and we cannot be sure which one is more reliable. Moreover, possibilistic distributions generated with this operator cover the imprecise case where more than one class may have a possibility degree equal to 1. We create uncertain training set by the following:

1- Train the FNPC and the FuHC using the original crisp training set.

2- Use the obtained possibilistic classifiers to predict the class labels.

3- For each training instance I_{tr}, fuse the two possibility distributions obtained from each classifier using a *disjunctive operator*.

4- Keep the attribute values of each instance in the training set unchanged and replace the crisp class label by $\pi_{I_{tr}}$.

Attributes in the testing set are made uncertain in the following way. In each testing instance, we convert each attribute value into an uncertain interval. For each attribute, we scan all of its value in the database and get its minimum value X_{min} and its maximum value X_{max}. Then we replace each attribute value by a generated interval I = [L, U] in order to create imprecision on this attribute. If x is the perfect value of the current attribute, its lower bound L(Resp. upper bound U) is calculated as follows: $L = x - (x - X_{min}) * rand1$ (resp. $U = x + (X_{max} - x) * rand2$), where $rand1$ and $rand2$ denote two random numbers reflecting the uncertainty level $AttrL$ on this attribute. $AttrL$ is a level which describes the larger of the interval and takes values in $\{0.25, 0.5, 0.75$ or $1)\}$. For each level $AttrL$, we generate an uncertain dataset U_{AttrL} where $rand1$ and $rand2$ range between 0 and $AttrL$. Hence, for each perfect testing set, we create four uncertain datasets $U_{0.25}, U_{0.5}, U_{0.75}$ and U_1.

6.2 Classification Results

To measure the accuracy of possibilistic classifiers, we use two evaluation criteria:

- The percentage of Most Plausible Correct Classification (MPcc) which counts the percentage of instances whose all most plausible classes, predicted by the possibilistic classifier, are *exactly the same* as their initial most plausible classes given by the possibility distribution labeling each testing instance.

$$MPcc = \frac{Number\_of\_exactly\_well\_classified\_instances}{Total\_nbr\_classified\_instances} * 100 \quad (13)$$

- The Information Affinity-based Criterion [14] is a degree of affinity between the predicted and the real possibility distribution labeling the testing instances

$$InfoAffC = \frac{\sum_{i=1}^{n} Aff(\pi_i^{real}, \pi_i^{pred})}{Total\_nbr\_classified\_instances} \quad (14)$$

$$Aff(\pi_1, \pi_2) = 1 - \frac{d(\pi_1, \pi_2) + Inc(\pi_1, \pi_2)}{2} \quad (15)$$

where $d(\pi_1, \pi_2)$ is the Manhattan distance between π_1 and π_2 and $Inc(\pi_1, \pi_2) = Inc(\pi_1 \wedge \pi_2)$ is the degree of inconsistency between π_1 and π_2 calculated as follows: $Inc(\pi) = 1 - \max_{\omega \in \Omega}\{\pi(\omega)\}$. $InfoAffC$ ranges in [0,1].

The experimental study is divided in two parts. First, we evaluate the uncertain possibilistic classifiers to handle uncertainty only in class attribute and we keep attributes in the testing set perfect. Second, we test the accuracy of the proposed classifiers when attributes in the testing set are uncertain whereas

Table 2. Experimental results for uncertain classes given as the mean and the standard deviation of 10 cross-validations

	FNPC		FuHC		NNPC	
	MPcc	AffC	MPcc	AffC	MPcc	AffC
Iris	94.0±7.0	0.94±0.01	93.33±6.7	0.95±0.0	88.67±7.3	0.88±0.01
Cancer	96.19±2.0	0.99±0.0	95.31±2.0	0.99±0.01	42.05±13.4	0.79±0.01
Wine	91.6±5.7	0.94±0.01	92.08±5.2	0.95±0.0	87.08±8.6	0.8±0.01
Diabetes	77.08±3.9	0.96±0.01	54.41±6.7	0.95±0.0	58.6±5.7	0.95±0.0
Magic	74.11±5.6	0.93±0.0	61.27±10.0	0.94±0.01	66.2±4.7	0.92±0.01
Transfusion	83.99±5.7	0.98±0.0	62.46±6.4	0.98±0.0	51.89±5.3	0.98±0.0
SatImage	90.18±3.5	0.97±0.01	90.37±3.3	0.98±0.01	89.18±3.3	0.7±0.01
Segment	70.93±4.1	0.92±0.01	63.13±4.4	0.95±0.0	79.6±3.3	0.8±0.01
Yeast	58.36±3.9	0.96±0.0	20.15±3.8	0.93±0.01	22.1±2.8	0.9±0.0
Ecoli	80.35±2.9	0.93±0.01	65.1±13.8	0.91±0.01	78.0±6.4	0.88±0.01
Glass	51.43±15.8	0.92±0.01	35.99±13.0	0.9±0.08	44.46±14.6	0.83±0.02

training set is kept perfect. We choose to test each uncertainty type independently in order to check the efficiency of possibilistic classifiers to deal with each situation. Note that we have only consider normalized attribute values in this paper. For the FuHC and NNPC, in order to guarantee in (12) a significant value of the approximate equality function $(0 < \mu_E(d(x,y)) < 1)$, α and β are respectively fixed to 0 and 1, once d is normalized in $[0, 1]$, for all attributes.

Table 2 shows the classification performance (MPcc and InfoAffC criterion) obtained with the FNPC, FuHC and NNPC for the eleven uncertain data sets.

In this study, we have used a rigid MPcc criteria which considers an instance as incorrectly classified if the difference between predicted and real full plausible classes is at least equal to 1. Although this rigid criteria and even for 100% uncertainty level (all training instances are uncertain), the FNPC and FuHC classifiers shows a high ability to deal with imperfect instances almost as good as with perfect ones (See [17]).

If we analyze results in Table 2, we note that:

• For the FNPC, 3 of the 11 report an increase in accuracy if compared to the perfect case, 7 of the 11 data sets report a decrease in accuracy but in 6 of the 7 the decrease is less than 5% and the highest decrease is for the segment which is about 20% but the MPcc remains > 70%. For the FuHC and NNPC the decrease in accuracy is more considerable and the highest one is reported for the Yeast and Cancer which is respectively about 30% (FuHc) and 50% (NNPC).

• To compare the three classifiers in terms of MPcc, we use the Wilcoxon Matched-Pairs Signed-Ranks Test as proposed by Demsar [15]. It is a non-parametric alternative to the paired t-test that enables us to compare two classifiers over multiple data sets. Comparison results given in Table 3 show that the FNPC is always significantly better $(p - value < 0.05)$ than the two other classifiers for all data sets whereas the two proximity based classifiers have competitive performance. This result is not surprising since, as reported in the perfect case, the FNPC shows a high ability to detect the most plausible classes.

Table 3. Results for the Wilcoxon Matched-Pairs Signed-Ranks Test

FNPC Vs FuHC	FNPC Vs NNPC	FuHC Vs NNPC
$p \leq 0,005859$	$p \leq 0.01855$	$p \leq 0.8311$

• By analyzing the InfoAffC criteria we can see that the values are high for the different classifiers and for almost all data sets. For all data sets, the InfoAffC is > 0.9 for the FNPC, the FuHc and > 0.7 for the NNPC. From these results, we can conclude that the possibilistic classifiers are able to predict possibility distributions *highly* consistent with the initial uncertain distributions.

• For the majority of data sets, the InfoAffC criteria confirms the results reported by the MPcc. However we can see a significant divergence between the values of InfoAffC and MPcc for some data sets and mainly for the NNPC (for example, for the Yeast the MPcc value is 22.1% and the AffC is 0.9). This divergence means that for many testing instances, the possibilistic classifier provides possibility degrees *too close* to the initial possibility distribution (high InfoAffC) but the predicted and real full plausible classes are *not exactly* the same (weak MPcc). So we can say that the bad results for the NNPC for the Cancer (42.05%) and Yeast (22.01%) data s ets (if compared to the perfect case respectively 93.4% and 43.06%) can be explained by the following: Indeed the NNPC, by using the maximum operator in formula (7), looks only for *one nearest neighbor* which makes conditionals possibilities on classes to tend to 1 for more than one particular class. That's why the NNPC confuses much between near classes. Furthermore, the rigid nature of the MPcc criteria causes a 0 classification percentage for many instances in the data set where the classifier provides more than one fully plausible class whereas in the real distribution only one class is fully plausible.

• The results of the NNPC could be improved if we consider a more relaxed MPcc criterion for which we allow to an instance to be classified with a particular percentage $p \in [0, 1]$, for example $p = 1/2$ if only one full plausible class is in the initial distribution among two full plausible classes detected by the classifier. By applying this relaxed criterion, the MPcc for the Cancer in the case of NNPC becomes 69.34% (instead of 42.05%).

Table 4 shows the MPcc and the InfoAffC results obtained with the three classifiers for each imprecision level on attributes and for the eleven mentioned data sets. C1, C2 and C3 in Table 4 are respectively the FNPC, the FuHC and the NNPC. By comparing the classification performance we see that the accuracies of the three algorithms decrease when the imprecision level of attributes increases (when intervals are broader). Despite this decrease we note that:

• The FNPC and FuHC have reported relatively high performance if compared to the perfect case. We can also note that the decrease in accuracy for the FNPC is relatively stable and not acute.

• Despite the decrease in accuracy, we note that the ratio remains high in average mainly for the FNPC and FuHc. For instance, if we analyze the results relative to the FNPC, we remark that the MPcc remains higher than 60% for the highest uncertainty level (U_1)(the worst case) and this for all data sets except the Yeast and Glass where the value is respectively about 32% and 43%. The low results

Table 4. Experimental results for uncertain attributes given as the mean and the standard deviation of 10 cross-validations

		$U_{0.25}$		$U_{0.5}$		$U_{0.75}$		U_1	
		MPcc	AffC	MPcc	AffC	MPcc	AffC	MPcc	AffC
Iris	C1	94.67±5.0	0.96±0.04	93.33±8.9	0.94±0.05	88.66±9.0	0.92±0.05	80.67±8.7	0.88±0.04
	C2	92.0±8.8	0.87±0.03	86.67±9.9	0.85±0.04	79.33±17.0	0.83±0.05	66.0±17.8	0.77±0.08
	C3	88.0±5.8	0.77±0.01	82.0±10.3	0.77±0.01	77.33±11.6	0.76±0.01	62.67±10.4	0.73±0.03
Cancer	C1	97.36±1.3	0.97±0.02	95.9±1.3	0.96±0.01	94.73±1.6	0.95±0.01	94.15±2.3	0.94±0.02
	C2	96.05±2.1	0.97±0.02	95.9±1.8	0.97±0.01	94.73±3.3	0.95±0.02	92.84±3.6	0.93±0.02
	C3	31.19±4.7	0.78±0.01	29.43±5.8	0.77±0.0	25.63±5.1	0.76±0.0	23.14±5.4	0.76±0.0
Wine	C1	96.04±3.6	0.97±0.02	95.42±4.4	0.96±0.03	92.15±5.6	0.95±0.03	90.0±6.5	0.92±0.04
	C2	93.05±8.0	0.9±0.02	90.9±6.9	0.88±0.02	86.18±11.0	0.84±0.05	71.74±24.0	0.77±0.11
	C3	91.67±6.2	0.74±0.01	75.42±9.2	0.72±0.01	62.43±7.9	0.7±0.01	47.71±9.7	0.68±0.03
Diabetes	C1	73.82±3.2	0.76±0.02	69.66±3.9	0.75±0.02	67.07±4.2	0.74±0.03	64.45±2.8	0.72±0.02
	C2	72.39±5.6	0.76±0.01	71.35±5.4	0.76±0.01	66.92±6.0	0.75±0.01	59.13±5.6	0.73±0.01
	C3	39.47±6.4	0.75±0.0	39.88±9.1	0.75±0.0	37.68±8.9	0.75±0.0	35.86±8.1	0.75±0.0
Magic	C1	71.78±6.3	0.77±0.04	71.41±4.7	0.78±0.03	72.99±3.8	0.78±0.02	71.41±3.8	0.76±0.02
	C2	67.14±6.2	0.75±0.02	66.3±5.7	0.74±0.02	65.2±7.5	0.73±0.03	60.91±6.2	0.71±0.02
	C2	64.81±7.2	0.75±0.0	60.81±7.7	0.75±0.0	59.69±7.8	0.75±0.0	58.21±7.2	0.75±0.0
Transf.	C1	63.27±7.9	0.72±0.04	64.47±7.1	0.73±0.04	63.13±6.8	0.72±0.04	58.45±5.0	0.72±0.02
	C2	61.94±7.5	0.75±0.01	57.78±7.2	0.74±0.01	53.49±5.1	0.74±0.01	46.11±5.9	0.73±0.01
	C3	6.86±5.5	0.75±0.0	9.26±5.1	0.75±0.0	6.72±5.1	0.75±0.0	6.32±5.8	0.75±0.0
S.Image	C1	89.54±1.6	0.93±0.01	86.88±2.3	0.91±0.02	85.41±3.9	0.91±0.02	84.5±2.1	0.91±0.01
	C2	87.25±2.9	0.93±0.02	83.21±5.4	0.9±0.03	75.78±8.6	0.85±0.06	60.28±10.0	0.75±0.07
	C3	91.1±2.0	0.68±0.0	87.25±3.1	0.67±0.01	80.55±2.4	0.66±0.01	75.23±3.1	0.66±0.0
Segment	C1	87.0±2.2	0.93±0.01	82.33±2.6	0.9±0.01	77.33±3.1	0.88±0.02	75.2±3.7	0.87±0.02
	C2	77.33±2.6	0.88±0.01	73.0±3.9	0.86±0.01	65.4±5.0	0.83±0.02	51.2±2.9	0.75±0.02
	C3	79.67±2.8	0.72±0.01	68.67±4.2	0.7±0.0	59.73±4.2	0.69±0.01	38.2±2.8	0.64±0.0
Yeast	C1	54.52±3.7	0.79±0.01	47.7±3.9	0.76±0.01	39.76±2.7	0.73±0.01	32.68±2.6	0.7±0.01
	C2	49.94±3.3	0.69±0.01	41.23±4.3	0.68±0.01	37.93±3.8	0.67±0.01	35.98±5.4	0.67±0.01
	C3	8.49±2.5	0.63±0.0	6.74±1.7	0.62±0.01	4.92±1.4	0.62±0.0	3.78±1.6	0.62±0.0
Ecoli	C1	80.94±7.3	0.91±0.03	79.81±6.7	0.89±0.03	69.31±8.0	0.86±0.04	60.92±8.7	0.84±0.04
	C2	77.45±8.2	0.82±0.02	69.14±7.3	0.79±0.01	61.0±7.9	0.77±0.01	53.82±7.2	0.75±0.02
	C3	71.63±6.8	0.73±0.01	64.78±8.1	0.72±0.01	61.68±10.5	0.72±0.01	55.98±9.6	0.71±0.01
Glass	C1	48.66±11.0	0.77±0.05	46.24±4.9	0.77±0.04	38.33±10.2	0.76±0.04	43.51±11.4	0.75±0.06
	C2	34.2±9.5	0.71±0.02	31.84±13.2	0.7±0.02	29.96±10.6	0.68±0.02	27.12±13.7	0.67±0.03
	C3	52.81±11.6	0.64±0.02	50.43±7.5	0.64±0.01	45.26±9.0	0.64±0.02	47.62±13.5	0.63±0.02

reported for the these data sets are not related to the FNPC since the MPcc reported for the original certain version of these data sets is about 52% for the Yeast and 58% for the Glass for the certain FNPC.

• However the NNPC seems to find difficulties when classifying instances with imprecise attributes mainly for data sets "Cancer", "Transfusion", "Diabetes" and "Yeast". As reported in the uncertain case (Tab.2), low accuracies are related to the max operator, used in NNPC, combined with the rigid MPcc criterion.

• As in the uncertain case (Table 2), the accuracy of the FNPC is always (even slightly) better than other classifiers for all uncertainty levels expect the case of "Glass" database, in which this classifier performs worse than the NNPC.

• The values of the InfoAffC criterion reported for the different classifiers and for the different data sets are relatively high. For 8 of the 11 data sets, this value remains higher than 0.7, for all uncertainty levels and for the three classifiers and it is higher than 0.6 for the remaining data sets. So, we can say that the predicted and initial possibility distributions are relatively consistent.

From results given in Tables 2 and 4, we can see that FNPC is more accurate that the two others and can be considered as a good classifier which is suitable for dealing with perfect or imperfect continuous data and all types of databases. However results of the proximity based classifiers could be improved if i)we use a more appropriate MPcc criterion and ii) we refine theses approaches by using a Nearest-Neighbor heuristic to separate indistinguishable classes.

7 Conclusion

In this paper, we extend the possibilistic classifiers previously proposed in [17] to handle uncertainty and imprecision in input data sets. Two types of uncertainty are considered: i) uncertainty related to class attribute in the training set and ii) uncertainty related to attribute values in the testing set. To test possibilistic classifiers in the uncertain case, we have artificially introduced imperfection in data sets from the UCI machine learning repository [16]. While the FNPC shows a high ability to detect the full plausible class labels with possibility distributions very consistent with initial distributions, possibilistic classifiers exploiting proximity are competitive with the FNPC. Besides, the NNPC has some difficulties to distinguish between near classes, which decreases its performance although predicted possibilities distributions are valuable. However, the way possibility distributions are obtained and the choice of the aggregation operator essentially rely on an empirical basis. In the future, the promising results reported have to be confirmed on a more theoretical basis.

References

1. Haouari, B., Ben Amor, N., Elouadi, Z., Mellouli, K.: Naïve possibilistic network classifiers. Fuzzy Set and Systems 160(22), 3224–3238 (2009)
2. Qin, B., Xia, Y., Prabhakar, S., Tu, Y.: A rule-based classification algorithm for uncertain data. In: IEEE International Conference on Data Engineering (2009)
3. Hüllermeier, E., Beringer, J.: Case-based learning in a bipolar possibilistic framework. Inter. J. of Intelligent Systems, 1119–1134 (2008)
4. Borgelt, C., Gebhardt, J.: A naïve Bayes style possibilistic classifier. In: Proc. 7th Europ. Cong. on Intelligent Techniques and Soft Computing, pp. 556–565 (1999)
5. Borgelt, C., Kruse, R.: Efficient maximum projection of database-induced multivariate possibility distributions. In: Proc. 7th Fuzz-IEEE Conf., pp. 663–668 (1998)
6. Dubois, D., Prade, H.: Possibility theory. Plenum Press, New York (1988)
7. Dubois, D., Prade, H.: Possibility theory: Qualitative and quantitative aspects. Handbook on Defeasible Reasoning and Uncertainty Manag. Syst. 1, 169–226 (1998)
8. Dubois, D., Prade, H.: Possibility theory in information fusion. In: Proceeding of the 3rd International Conference on Information Fusion, pp. 6–19 (2000)
9. Dubois, D., Prade, H., Sandri, S.: On possibility/probability transformations. In: Lowen, R. (ed.) Fuzzy Logic, pp. 103–112. D. Reidel, Dordrechtz (1993)
10. Hüllermeier, E.: Fuzzy methods in machine learning and data mining:status and prospects. Fuzzy Sets and Systems, 387–406 (2005)
11. Hüllermeier, E.: Possibilistic instance-based learning. Art. Intell., 335–383 (2003)

12. Dubois, D., Foulloy, L., Mauris, G., Prade, H.: Probability-possibility transformations, triangular fuzzy sets, and probabilistic inequalities. Relia. Comp. 10, 273–297 (2004)
13. Jenhani, I., Ben Amor, N., Elouedi, Z.: Decision trees as possibilistic classifiers. Inter. J. of Approximate Reasoning 48(3), 784–807 (2008)
14. Jenhani, I., Benferhat, S., Elouedi, Z.: Learning and evaluating possibilistic decision trees using informat. affinity. Int. J. Comp. Sys. Sci. Eng. 4, 206–212 (2010)
15. Demsar, J.: Statistical comparisons of classifiers over multiple data sets. Journal of Machine Learning Research, 1–30 (2006)
16. Mertz, J., Murphy, P.M.: Uci repository of machine learning databases, ftp://ftp.ics.uci.edu/pub/machine-learning-databases
17. Bounhas, M., Mellouli, K., Prade, H., Serrurier, M.: From bayesian classifiers to possibilistic classifiers for numerical data. In: Deshpande, A., Hunter, A. (eds.) SUM 2010. LNCS, vol. 6379, pp. 112–125. Springer, Heidelberg (2010)
18. Ben Amor, N., Mellouli, K., Benferhat, S., Dubois, D., Prade, H.: A theoretical framework for possibilistic independence in a weakly ordered setting. Int. J.of Uncertainty, Fuzziness and Knowledge-Based Systems 10, 117–155 (2002)
19. Ben Amor, N., Benferhat, S., Elouedi, Z.: Qualitative classification and evaluation in possibilistic decision trees. In: In FUZZ-IEEE 2004, vol. 1, pp. 653–657 (2004)
20. Xia, Y., Qin, B., Li, F.: A Bayesian classifier for uncertain data. In: The 25th ACM Symposium on Applied Computing, SAC (2010)
21. Benferhat, S., Tabia, K.: An Efficient Algorithm for Naive Possibilistic Classifiers with Uncertain Inputs. In: Greco, S., Lukasiewicz, T. (eds.) SUM 2008. LNCS (LNAI), vol. 5291, pp. 63–77. Springer, Heidelberg (2008)
22. Zadeh, L.A.: Fuzzy sets. Inform. and Control 8 8, 338–353 (1965)

Relational Probabilistic Conditional Reasoning at Maximum Entropy

Matthias Thimm[1], Gabriele Kern-Isberner[1], and Jens Fisseler[2]

[1] Department of Computer Science, Technische Universität Dortmund, Germany
[2] Faculty of Mathematics and Computer Science, FernUniversität in Hagen, Germany

Abstract. This paper presents and compares approaches for reasoning with relational probabilistic conditionals, i. e. probabilistic conditionals in a restricted first-order environment. It is well-known that conditionals play a crucial role for default reasoning, however, most formalisms are based on propositional conditionals, which restricts their expressivity. The formalisms discussed in this paper are relational extensions of a propositional conditional logic based on the principle of maximum entropy. We show how this powerful principle can be used in different ways to realize model-based inference relations for first-order probabilistic knowledge bases. We illustrate and compare the different approaches by applying them to several benchmark examples, and we evaluate each approach with respect to properties adopted from default reasoning. We also compare our approach to Bayesian logic programs (BLPs) from the field of statistical relational learning which focuses on the combination of probabilistic reasoning and relational knowledge representation as well.

1 Introduction

Conditional logic [9] is a popular choice for the representation of common sense knowledge and rules. A conditional $(B \mid A)$ expresses the relation "If A then usually (mostly, likely, probably) B" between two formulas A and B of some underlying logic. In contrast to classical implication $A \Rightarrow B$ a conditional models *defeasible* belief and as such models of conditionals do not have to strictly obey these relations. Conditionals can be quantified yielding a probabilistic conditional logic. A quantified conditional $(B \mid A)[\alpha]$ can be interpreted as a constraint for probability distributions via $P \models (B \mid A)[\alpha]$ iff $P(B \mid A) = \alpha$. Usually, the underlying logic for representing A and B is propositional and as such the expressive power of probabilistic conditional logic is limited. In the past ten years the area of *statistical relational learning* (or *probabilistic inductive logic programming*) developed many approaches to extend traditional probabilistic models for reasoning like Bayes and Markov Networks [10] to relational (first-order) representations of knowledge. Among these are Bayesian Logic Programs [7], and Markov Logic Networks [11], to name only a few. Most of these approaches employ a grounding of relational probabilistic problems to propositional ones in order to benefit from reasoning techniques developed for propositional probabilistic reasoning. In this paper, we discuss relational extensions of probabilistic conditional logic.

Example 1 (Common Cold). Assume we want to model uncertain knowledge pertaining to the possible causes resp. the probability of catching a common cold. A simple representation using uncertain *if-then*-rules can be given via

W. Liu (Ed.): ECSQARU 2011, LNAI 6717, pp. 447–458, 2011.

$$
\begin{array}{llll}
R1: & cold(U) & & [0.01] \\
R2: & \textbf{if } susceptible(U) & \textbf{then } cold(U) & [0.1] \\
R3: & \textbf{if } contact(U,V) \quad \textbf{and} \quad cold(V) & \textbf{then } cold(U) & [0.6]
\end{array}
\tag{1}
$$

The uncertain rule R1 states that one normally does not have a common cold, i. e. only with a diminutive probability of 0.01. Rule R2 denotes that a person catches a common cold with probability 0.1 if this person is susceptible to it, and rule R3 represents the knowledge that person U, which is in contact with another person V which has the common cold, also gets a common cold with probability 0.6.

In contrast to the weights of formulas in Markov Logic Networks [11] the values of probabilistic conditionals have a probabilistic interpretation and as such exhibit a more intuitive way of representing uncertain knowledge. However, assigning probabilities to conditionals that contain variables may be ambiguous and their interpretation may be subjective or statistical [1]. This paper aims at investigating formal semantics and reasoning techniques for relational probabilistic logic. We built on approaches of previous works [6,2] that rely on the principle of maximum entropy, a popular choice for model-based reasoning in propositional probabilistic conditional logic [3,4]. By selecting the unique model of a set of probabilistic conditionals that maximizes entropy and as such represents the given knowledge in the most unbiased way, we obtain inference mechanisms that are optimal from an information-theoretical point of view, cf. [4]. In this paper, we investigate the performance of these approaches with respect to the system P properties for default reasoning [8]. Furthermore, we compare the behavior of our inference mechanims and illustrate that approaches for statistical relational learning are not apt for relational probabilistic default reasoning.

The rest of this paper is organized as follows. We continue by giving the syntax for our relational extension of probabilistic conditional logic and providing a brief introduction to Bayesian Logic Programs in Sec. 2. Afterwards in Sec. 3 we discuss common sense properties that should be fulfilled by reasonable inference relations. In Sec. 4 we propose and discuss three different approaches for defining semantics to relational probabilistic conditional logic and apply these for probabilistic reasoning in Sec. 5. Finally, we review related work in Sec. 6 and conclude in Sec. 7.

2   Relational Probabilistic Knowledge Representation

Let $\mathcal{L}$ be a propositional relational language, i. e. the fragment of a first-order language over a signature Σ containing only predicates and constants. An *atom* is a predicate together with a list of terms, which may be constants or variables or a mixture of these. Formulas are built with atoms using the usual connectives disjunction, conjunction, and negation but without any quantifiers. If appropriate we abbreviate conjunctions $A \wedge B$ by AB. We denote variables with a beginning uppercase, constants with a beginning lowercase letter, and vectors of these with $\boldsymbol{X}$ resp. $\boldsymbol{a}$. A ground formula, i. e. a formula that does not contain any variables, is called a *sentence*. A possible world semantics is provided by Herbrand interpretations over the Herbrand universe $\mathcal{H}$ that contains all constants in Σ. Herbrand interpretations correspond to complete conjunctions of ground literals from the Herbrand base. Let Ω be the set of all such possible worlds

ω. A possible world ω *satisfies* a ground atom A, denoted by $\omega \models A$, iff $A \in \omega$. Satisfaction of arbitrary sentences is defined in the usual way.

The conditional relational language $(\mathcal{L}|\mathcal{L})$ consists of all (qualitative) conditionals of the form $(B(c_B, X)|A(c_A, X))$ with $A(c_A, X), B(c_B, X)$ being formulas from $\mathcal{L}^{rel}$. In this a bit sloppy notation, the vectors c_A, c_B contain all constants occurring in A and B, and without loss of generality, we assume X to cover exactly all variables occurring both in A and in B. For any $\phi = (B(c_B, X)|A(c_A, X)) \in (\mathcal{L}|\mathcal{L})$, let $\mathcal{H}^\phi$ be the set of all constant vectors a used for the proper groundings of the variables X occurring in ϕ from the Herbrand universe $\mathcal{H}$. The language $(\mathcal{L}|\mathcal{L})^p$ consists of all probabilistic conditionals of the form $\phi[\mu]$ with $\phi \in (\mathcal{L}|\mathcal{L})$ and $\mu \in [0, 1]$. Conditionals can not be nested, but $\mathcal{L}$ should be considered as a fragment of $(\mathcal{L}|\mathcal{L})$ by identifying relational propositional formulas $A(c_A, X)$ with conditionals $(A(c_A, X)|\top)$ with tautological antecedent. Conditionals that contain variables are called *open* conditionals while conditionals that contain no variables are called *ground* conditionals.

Example 2. We represent Ex. 1 using $(\mathcal{L}|\mathcal{L})^p$. Let $\mathcal{R}_{cold} = \{r_1, r_2, r_3, r_4, r_5\}$ be defined as

$$r_1 = (cold(X))[0.01] \qquad\qquad r_2 = (cold(X) \mid susc(X))[0.1]$$
$$r_3 = (cold(X) \mid contact(X, Y), cold(Y))[0.6] \quad r_4 = (contact(X, X))[0]$$
$$r_5 = (contact(X, Y) \mid contact(Y, X))[1]$$

Conditionals r_4 resp. r_5 ensure that the relation induced by literals of the predicate *contact* are irreflexive resp. symmetric.

Let $Int_{prob}(\Sigma)$ consist of all probability functions P on Ω, which assign to each possible world a (subjective) probability of it being the real world. Let $\models^\#$ be a semantic entailment relation between probability functions and probabilistic relational conditionals, specifying when $P \in Int_{prob}(\Sigma)$ is a *#-model* of $\phi[\mu] \in (\mathcal{L}|\mathcal{L})^p$: $P \in Mod^\#(\phi[\mu])$ iff $P \models^\# \phi[\mu]$. We will present several ways of instantiating the parametrical superscript $\#$ below. As usual, $\models^\#$ can be lifted to a classical (monotonic) entailment relation between formulas: $\mathcal{R} \models^\# \phi[\mu]$ iff $Mod^\#(\mathcal{R}) \subseteq Mod^\#(\phi[\mu])$ for $\mathcal{R} \subseteq (\mathcal{L}|\mathcal{L})^p$ and $\phi[\mu] \in (\mathcal{L}|\mathcal{L})^p$. If $\mathcal{S} \subseteq (\mathcal{L}|\mathcal{L})^p$ is another set of probabilistic relational conditionals, then $\mathcal{R} \models^\# \mathcal{S}$ iff $\mathcal{R} \models^\# \phi[\mu]$ for all $\phi[\mu] \in \mathcal{S}$, and $\mathcal{R} \equiv^\# \mathcal{S}$ iff $Mod^\#(\mathcal{R}) = Mod^\#(\mathcal{S})$.

We will compare our formalisms with a specific approach for statistical relational learning. Although these approaches were not developed for default reasoning current research on combining probability theory and relational knowledge representation focuses on this area. For example, Bayesian logic programming combines logic programming and Bayesian networks [7]. Due to space restriction and matters of presentation we only give a simplified definition for BLPs in the following. The basic structure for knowledge representation in Bayesian logic programs are *Bayesian clauses* which model probabilistic dependencies between atoms. Let $\mathbb{B}$ denote the set Boolean truth values $\mathbb{B} = \{\text{true}, \text{false}\}$. A *Bayesian clause* c is an expression $(H \mid B_1, \ldots, B_n)$ with atoms $H, B_1, \ldots, B_n$. To each such clause, a *conditional probability distribution* $\text{cpd}_c : \mathbb{B}^{n+1} \to [0, 1]$ is associated such that

$$\text{cpd}_c(\text{true}, x_1, \ldots, x_n) + \text{cpd}_c(\text{false}, x_1, \ldots, x_n) = 1 \quad \text{for all } (x_1, \ldots, x_n) \in \mathbb{B}^n \quad .$$

A function cpd_c for a Bayesian clause c expresses the conditional probability distribution $P(\text{head}(c) \mid \text{body}(c))$ and thus partially describes an underlying probability distribution P.

In order to aggregate probabilities that arise from applications of different Bayesian clauses with the same head BLPs make use of *combining rules*. A combining rule cr_p for a predicate p/n is a function cr_p that assigns to the conditional probability distributions of a set of Bayesian clauses a new conditional probability distribution that represents the *joint* probability distribution obtained from aggregating the given clauses. For example, given clauses $c_1 = (b(X) \mid a_1(X))$ and $c_2 = (b(X) \mid a_2(X))$ the result $f = \text{cr}_b(\{\text{cpd}_{c_1}, \text{cpd}_{c_2}\})$ of the combining rule cr_b is a function $f : \mathbb{B}^3 \to [0,1]$ for the combined clause $(b(X) \mid a_1(X), a_2(X))$. Appropriate choices for such functions are *average* or *noisy-or*, cf. [7]. For example, noisy-or is defined as $no(p_1, p_2) = 1 - (1 - p_1)(1 - p_2)$.

A *Bayesian logic program B* is a tuple $B = (C, D, R)$ with a (finite) set of Bayesian clauses $C = \{c_1, \ldots, c_n\}$, a set of conditional probability distributions (one for each clause in C) $D = \{\text{cpd}_{c_1}, \ldots, \text{cpd}_{c_n}\}$, and a set of combining functions (one for each Bayesian predicate appearing in C) $R = \{\text{cr}_{p_1}, \ldots, \text{cr}_{p_m}\}$. Semantics are given to Bayesian logic programs via transformation into propositional forms, i. e. into Bayesian networks [10]. Given a specific (finite) universe U a Bayesian network BN can be constructed by introducing a node for every ground Bayesian atom in B and computing the corresponding (joint) conditional probability distributions. For a more detailed description of Bayesian Logic Programs we refer to [7].

3   Default Reasoning Properties – System P^{prob}

The classical probabilistic entailment relation $\models^{\#}$ specified in Sec. 2 will usually be quite weak, as is the case for propositional probabilistic logic. In this paper, we will focus on investigating non-monotonic inference relations $\hspace{0.1em}\sim\hspace{-0.8em}\mid\hspace{0.1em}^{\#}$ by which relational probabilistic conditionals can be inferred plausibly from knowledge bases.

So, let $\hspace{0.1em}\sim\hspace{-0.8em}\mid\hspace{0.1em}^{\#}$ describe a relation $\mathcal{R} \hspace{0.1em}\sim\hspace{-0.8em}\mid\hspace{0.1em}^{\#} \phi[\mu]$ with $\mathcal{R} \subseteq (\mathcal{L}|\mathcal{L})^p$ and $\phi[\mu] \in (\mathcal{L}|\mathcal{L})^p$. We will present three different approaches for realizing $\hspace{0.1em}\sim\hspace{-0.8em}\mid\hspace{0.1em}^{\#}$ in the following section, being based on different probabilistic entailment relations $\models^{\#}$ and the principle of maximum entropy, respectively. In order to be able to evaluate and compare these approaches, we will first set up a set of postulates applicable to such inference relations which are inspired by the system P properties from default reasoning ([8], see also [1]). Let $\mathcal{R}, \mathcal{R}_1, \mathcal{R}_2 \subseteq (\mathcal{L}|\mathcal{L})^p$ and $\phi[\mu], \psi[\nu] \in (\mathcal{L}|\mathcal{L})^p$.

(Reflexivity) For all $\phi[\mu] \in \mathcal{R}$, it holds that $\mathcal{R} \hspace{0.1em}\sim\hspace{-0.8em}\mid\hspace{0.1em}^{\#} \phi[\mu]$.
(Left Logical Equivalence) If $\mathcal{R}_1 \equiv^{\#} \mathcal{R}_2$, then $\mathcal{R}_1 \hspace{0.1em}\sim\hspace{-0.8em}\mid\hspace{0.1em}^{\#} \phi[\mu]$ iff $\mathcal{R}_2 \hspace{0.1em}\sim\hspace{-0.8em}\mid\hspace{0.1em}^{\#} \phi[\mu]$.
(Right Weakening) If $\mathcal{R} \hspace{0.1em}\sim\hspace{-0.8em}\mid\hspace{0.1em}^{\#} \phi[\mu]$ and $\phi[\mu] \models^{\#} \psi[\nu]$, then $\mathcal{R} \hspace{0.1em}\sim\hspace{-0.8em}\mid\hspace{0.1em}^{\#} \psi[\nu]$.
(Cumulativity) If $\mathcal{R} \hspace{0.1em}\sim\hspace{-0.8em}\mid\hspace{0.1em}^{\#} \phi[\mu]$, then $\mathcal{R} \hspace{0.1em}\sim\hspace{-0.8em}\mid\hspace{0.1em}^{\#} \psi[\nu]$ iff $\mathcal{R} \cup \{\phi[\mu]\} \hspace{0.1em}\sim\hspace{-0.8em}\mid\hspace{0.1em}^{\#} \psi[\nu]$.

Note that *cumulativity* subsumes both *cautious monotony* and *cut* [8].

Besides the common cold example (Ex. 2), we will illustrate the properties of our different semantical approaches using another benchmark example taken from [1].

Example 3 (From [1]). Consider the knowledge base $\mathcal{R}_{chirps} = \{r_1, r_2, r_3, r_4\}$ with

$$r_1 = (chirps(X) \mid bird(X))[0.9] \quad r_2 = (chirps(X) \mid magpie(X), moody(X))[0.2]$$
$$r_3 = (bird(X) \mid magpie(X))[1] \quad r_4 = (magpie(tweety))[1]$$

The knowledge represented in $\mathcal{R}_{chirps}$ concerns the default probabilities that a bird chirps (r_1) and that a moody magpie chirps (r_2). Knowing that every magpie is a bird (r_3) and given an actual magpie Tweety (r_4) the question at hand is to which probability Tweety chirps. As we have no knowledge whether Tweety is moody or not we cannot commit to any specific "reference class".

4 Semantics for Relational Probabilistic Conditional Logic

In this section we investigate different possibilities to define the semantic entailment relation $\models^\#$ and the nonmonotonic inference relation $\mid\sim^\#$. In difference to the propositional case, assigning semantics to relational probabilistic conditionals is not straightforward. Nonetheless, we want to get some compatibility to the propositional case. Let $(B|A)[\mu]$ be a *ground* conditional, i.e. $(B|A)[\mu]$ contains no variables and therefore is of the form $(B(c_B, X)|A(c_A, X))[\mu]$ with X being the empty vector. Then a probability distribution $P \in Int_{prob}(\Sigma)$ should be a #-model of $(B|A)[\mu]$ iff it is a probabilistic model in the classical propositional sense: $P \in Mod^\#((B|A)[\mu])$ iff $P \models^\# (B|A)[\mu]$. As P is defined on Herbrand interpretations the above is well-defined given that $P(A) = \sum_{\omega \in \Omega, \omega \models A} P(\omega)$ and $P(B|A) = P(AB)/P(A)$ for any sentences A and B. But if a conditional $(B(c_B, X)|A(c_A, X))[\mu]$ contains variables, the expression $\omega \models A(c_A, X)$ for a possible world $\omega \in \Omega$ is not well-defined given our underlying Herbrand semantics and so is the relation $\models^\#$. In order to extend the semantical satisfaction of conditionals (see above) to conditionals that may contain variables, we investigate different strategies in the following subsections. Moreover, in order to obtain a non-monotonic inference relation $\mid\sim^\#$ from $\models^\#$ we employ for each of the approaches the principle of maximum entropy [3,4] to the corresponding set of #-models. The entropy $H(P)$ of a probability distribution P is defined as $H(P) = -\sum_{\omega \in \Omega} P(\omega) \log P(\omega)$. Given a set of conditionals $\mathcal{R}$ and a concrete semantical entailment relation $\models^\#$ we define the (usually, unique) probability distribution $ME^\#(\mathcal{R})$ with maximum entropy as follows

$$ME^\#(\mathcal{R}) = \underset{P \models^\# \mathcal{R}}{\operatorname{argmax}} H(P). \tag{2}$$

Using $ME^\#(\mathcal{R})$ we define an inference relation $\mid\sim^\#_{ME}$ as

$$\mathcal{R} \mid\sim^\#_{ME} \phi[\mu] \quad \text{iff} \quad ME^\#(\mathcal{R}) \models^\# \phi[\mu], \tag{3}$$

for any conditional $\phi[\mu] \in (\mathcal{L}|\mathcal{L})^p$.

4.1 Grounding Semantics with Constraints

The first formalism uses a *grounding semantics* for relational probabilistic conditionals [2], similar to formalisms for statistical relational learning, see e.g. Markov Logic

Networks [11]. Within this formalism, any relational probabilistic conditional $\phi[\mu] = (B(c_B, X)|A(c_A, X))[\mu] \in (\mathcal{L}|\mathcal{L})^p$ induces a set $gnd(\phi[\mu])$ of *ground instances*, which are obtained by substituting the free variables X by all combinations of constants in Σ. However, straightforward substitution easily yields inconsistent ground conditionals. Assume we are given the probabilistic relational conditional $(p(U, V)|p(V, U))[\mu]$. If both variables are substituted with the same constant, e. g. c, there exists no probability distribution P satisfying $P(p(c, c)|p(c, c)) = \mu$, except if $\mu = 1.0$. To avoid such inconsistencies, the grounding semantics approach supplements conditionals with *constraint formulas*, which restrict the set of admissible combinations of constants when grounding. An *atomic constraint formula* is a *term equation* $t_1 = t_2$, with terms t_1, t_2, and predicate symbol $=$, denoting equality. A negated term equation is called a *term disequation* and is written as $t_1 \neq t_2$. Complex equational formulas are built using the usual logical connectives conjunction, disjunction and negation, but without quantifiers. Constraint formulas are interpreted by ground substitutions. A ground substitution σ satisfies an equality constraint $t_1 = t_2$ iff $\sigma(t_1)$ and $\sigma(t_2)$ evaluate to the same constant. This satisfaction relation is canonically extended to complex constraint formulas.

For any $\langle\phi[\mu], C\rangle = \langle(B(c_B, X)|A(c_A, X))[\mu], C\rangle$, i. e. a probabilistic relational conditional $\langle\phi[\mu], C\rangle$ with an associated constraint formula C, we assume that the variables occurring in C are a subset of X. Interpreting the (possible) elements of $\mathcal{H}^\phi$ as ground substitutions, C restricts the set of ground instances of $\phi[\mu]$ by requiring that $a \in \mathcal{H}^\phi$ satisfies C:

$$gnd(\langle(B(c_B, X)|A(c_A, X))[\mu], C\rangle)$$
$$:= \left\{ (B(c_B, a)|A(c_A, a))[\mu] \,\middle|\, \begin{matrix} a \in \mathcal{H}^{\langle(B(c_B, X)|A(c_A, X)), C\rangle}, \\ a \text{ satisfies } C \end{matrix} \right\}.$$

We can now define the semantic entailment relation $\models^{gnd}$ between a probability distribution $P \in Int_{prob}(\Sigma)$ and a probabilistic relational conditional $\langle\phi[\mu], C\rangle$:

$$P \models^{gnd} \langle\phi[\mu], C\rangle \quad \text{iff} \quad \forall \phi_{gnd}[\mu] \in gnd(\langle\phi[\mu], C\rangle) : P(\phi_{gnd}) = \mu.$$

That is, P is a model of the probabilistic relational conditional $\langle\phi[\mu], C\rangle$ iff it is a model of all admissible ground instances of $\langle\phi[\mu], C\rangle$. As an additional condition, we require that all Herbrand interpretations which contain a ground atom that is not part of any ground instance of $\langle\phi[\mu], C\rangle$ have probability 0.0. This is because the grounding semantics actually restricts the Herbrand universe to only contain ground atoms which are part of at least one ground instance of $\langle\phi[\mu], C\rangle$. Hence possible worlds containing ground atoms which are not part of any ground instance are considered impossible.

4.2 Averaging Semantics

While the previous approach relies on expressing relational conditionals in propositional terms and thus interprets open relational conditionals in a classical sense, in this and the next subsection we develop semantics using a non-classical interpretation. Both semantics have been previously introduced in [6]. Our first approach gives semantics to probabilistic conditionals by averaging conditional probabilities. The motivation for this semantics stems from the intuition that probabilistic rules such as

$(B(c_B, X)|A(c_A, X))[\alpha]$, given an adequately large universe, should describe an expected value on the probability of $(B(c_B, d_B)|A(c_A, d_A))[\alpha]$ for some randomly chosen d_B, d_A. Thus, given the actual probabilities of $(B(c_B, d_B)|A(c_A, d_A))$ for each possible instantiation we expect the *average* of these probabilities should match α. Hence, let $\models^\varnothing$ be the semantic entailment relation on probabilistic conditionals defined as $P \models^\varnothing (B(c_B, X)|A(c_A, X))[\alpha]$ iff

$$\frac{\sum_{a \in \mathcal{H}^{(B(c_B, X)|A(c_A, X))}} P((B(c_B, a)|A(c_A, a))[\alpha])}{|\mathcal{H}^{(B(c_B, X)|A(c_A, X))}|} = \alpha \qquad (4)$$

Intuitively spoken, a probability distribution P $\varnothing$-satisfies a conditional $\phi[\mu]$ if the average of the individual instantiations of $\phi[\mu]$ is α. As one can see, for a ground conditional $(B|A)[\alpha]$ the relation $\models^\varnothing$ coincides with the propositional case.

4.3 Aggregating Semantics

Our third semantical approach is inspired by statistical approaches. However, instead of counting objects, or tuples of objects, respectively, that make a formula true, we sum up the probabilities of the correspondingly instantiated formulas. In this way, both population-based and subjective belief aspects of probabilities can be combined. More precisely, we propose a mean value of subjective probabilities to interpret probabilistic rules.

To make the key idea of the approach clear, consider the relational probabilistic conditional $(B(c_B, X)|A(c_A, X))[\alpha]$. If some first-order interpretation ω with a fixed domain is given, its statistical interpretation is provided by the relative frequency

$$\frac{|\{a \mid \omega \models A(c_A, a)B(c_B, a)\}|}{|\{a \mid \omega \models A(c_A, a)\}|} = \alpha,$$

i. e. the number of tuples of individuals a is counted that satisfy the premise and the antecedent, in relation to the number of tuples that satisfy only the premise. Aggregating the information coming from all models of $A(c_A, a)B(c_B, a)$, resp. $A(c_A, a)$, for each a, gives rise to a subjective, population-based probability:

$$\frac{\sum_a P(A(c_A, a)B(c_B, a))}{\sum_a P(A(c_A, a))} = \alpha,$$

If we allow P to represent (subjective) beliefs, then the above equation expresses the average subjective belief that in any situation in which we observe individuals a satisfying $A(c_A, a)$, we expect them to satisfy $B(c_B, a)$ as well with probability α. This switches the view from a frequentistic perspective to a possible worlds semantics.

So, the entailment relation $\models^\odot$ between functions from $Int_{prob}(\Sigma)$ and relational probabilistic conditionals is defined by $P \models^\odot (B(c_B, X) \mid A(c_A, X))[\alpha]$ iff

$$\frac{\sum\limits_{a \in \mathcal{H}^{(B(c_B, X)|A(c_A, X))}} P(A(c_A, a)B(c_B, a))}{\sum\limits_{a \in \mathcal{H}^{(B(c_B, X)|A(c_A, X))}} P(A(c_A, a))} = \alpha. \qquad (5)$$

As for $\models^\varnothing$, for a ground conditional, the operator $\models^\odot$ coincides with the usual propositional interpretation using conditional probabilities.

5   Relational Probabilistic Conditional Reasoning

In the following, we discuss the inference operators $\vdash^{gnd}_{ME}$, $\vdash^{\varnothing}_{ME}$, and $\vdash^{\odot}_{ME}$ that derive from the application of the different semantics $\models^{gnd}$, $\models^{\varnothing}$, and $\models^{\odot}$, respectively. All three formalisms implement a model-based probabilistic inference, using the maximum entropy model of a knowledge base as its most appropriate model. This ensures that all inference relations defined in the previous sections comply with all basic demands for relational probabilistic reasoning, as the next proposition shows.

Proposition 1. *Let $\models^{\#}$ be any of the semantical entailment relations defined above. Then the inference relation $\vdash^{\#}_{ME}$ satisfies (Reflexivity), (Left Logical Equivalence), (Right Weakening), and (Cumulativity).*

Proof.   We only show satisfaction of (Cumulativity). The proofs of the other properties are similar.

(Cumulativity). *It holds $Mod^{\#}(\mathcal{R} \cup \{\phi[\mu]\}) \subseteq Mod^{\#}(\mathcal{R})$ and $ME(\mathcal{R}) \in Mod^{\#}(\mathcal{R} \cup \{\phi[\mu]\})$ as $\mathcal{R} \vdash^{\#}_{ME} \phi[\mu]$. Suppose $ME(\mathcal{R} \cup \{\phi[\mu]\}) \neq ME(\mathcal{R})$, then $H(ME(\mathcal{R} \cup \{\phi[\mu]\})) > H(ME(\mathcal{R}))$ and $ME(\mathcal{R} \cup \{\phi[\mu]\})$ should be the ME-model of $\mathcal{R}$ as well because $ME(\mathcal{R} \cup \{\phi[\mu]\}) \in Mod^{\#}(\mathcal{R})$. Hence, $ME(\mathcal{R} \cup \{\phi[\mu]\}) = ME(\mathcal{R})$ and therefore $\mathcal{R} \vdash^{\#}_{ME} \psi[\nu]$ iff $\mathcal{R} \cup \{\phi[\mu]\} \vdash^{\#}_{ME} \psi[\nu]$ for any $\psi[\nu]$.* □

It is obvious that the satisfaction of the common sense properties discussed in Sec. 3 is mainly due to the principle of maximum entropy and independent of the actual used semantical entailment relation. This is not surprising as *ME*-inference is an optimal, model-based inference operation, and the semantical entailment relation is used in defining the properties themselves.

As for BLPs (dis-)satisfaction of these default reasoning properties is not so easy to see as the formalism of BLPs is much less based on classical logic. Consider again the postulate.

(Cumulativity). If $\mathcal{R} \vdash^{\#} \phi[\mu]$, then $\mathcal{R} \vdash^{\#} \psi[\nu]$ iff $\mathcal{R} \cup \{\phi[\mu]\} \vdash^{\#} \psi[\nu]$.

Let B be a Bayesian Logic Program, c a Bayesian clause, and cpd_c a conditional probability distribution for c. BLPs allow only to determine probabilities for some ground atom given some set of ground atoms as evidence. So the expression $B \vdash (c, \mathrm{cpd}_c)$ is not well-defined for a clause c that contains variables, cf. [13]. However, if c contains no variables the probability of the head of c for every truth assignment of the body atoms can be computed. But even for ground clauses (Cumulativity) is not satisfied for BLPs. Consider the following example.

Example 4. Let B be a BLP consisting of the single clause $c = (B(X) \mid A(X))$ with $\mathrm{cpd}_c(\mathrm{true}, \mathrm{true}) = \mathrm{cpd}_c(\mathrm{true}, \mathrm{false}) = \mathrm{cpd}_c(\mathrm{false}, \mathrm{true}) = \mathrm{cpd}_c(\mathrm{false}, \mathrm{false}) = 0.5$. Let *noisy-or* be the combining rule for B. For some constant a it follows clearly that for $c' = (B(a) \mid A(a))$ with $\mathrm{cpd}_{c'} = \mathrm{cpd}_c$ is holds that $B \vdash (c', \mathrm{cpd}_{c'})$. However, when determining the probability of c' in $B \cup \{(c', \mathrm{cpd}_{c'})\}$ different results arise due to aggregating via noisy-or, e. g. the probability of $B(a)$ given that $A(a)$ holds computes to $1 - (1 - 0.5)(1 - 0.5) = 0.75$.

Similar problems arise when translating the other default reasoning postulates to the BLP framework. For example, (Reflexivity) is trivially dissatisfied if a BLP contains at least one clause with variables. These categorical problems are not surprising as BLPs were not developed for default reasoning per se. Further discussions on this topic can be found in [13].

In order to comprehend the differences between the individual approaches we go on by investigating their behavior in the benchmark examples introduced above.

Example 5. We investigate Ex. 2 that has also been discussed in the introduction. In order to investigate this example for the grounding semantics, we have to modify the rules slightly. This is because rule $r_3 : (cold(X) \mid contact(X, Y), cold(Y))[0.6]$ yields inconsistencies if the variables X and Y are substituted with the same constant, even if rule r_4 is part of the knowledge base. Hence we must complement this conditional with the constraint formula $X \neq Y$, thereby forbidding these substitutions:

$$r_3' : \langle (cold(X) \mid contact(X, Y), cold(Y))[0.6], X \neq Y \rangle.$$

One thing to notice in the formalization of the knowledge base in Ex. 2 is that we have not represented any specific knowledge on particular individuals. Due to this representation the inferences drawn from $\mathcal{R}_{cold}$ using any of the proposed semantics $\mathord{\vdash}^{gnd}_{ME}$, $\mathord{\vdash}^{\varnothing}_{ME}$, and $\mathord{\vdash}^{\odot}_{ME}$ are identical and as follows (assuming that the given signature contains three constants $\{a, b, c\}$):

$$\mathcal{R}_{cold} \mathrel{\vdash^{\#}} (cold(a))[0.01]$$
$$\mathcal{R}_{cold} \mathrel{\vdash^{\#}} (cold(b) \mid susc(b))[0.1]$$
$$\mathcal{R}_{cold} \mathrel{\vdash^{\#}} (cold(c) \mid contact(c, a) \wedge cold(a))[0.6]$$
$$\mathcal{R}_{cold} \mathrel{\vdash^{\#}} (cold(c) \mid contact(c, a) \wedge cold(a) \wedge cold(b))[0.9]$$

where $\mathord{\vdash^{\#}}$ is one of $\{\mathord{\vdash}^{gnd}_{ME}, \mathord{\vdash}^{\varnothing}_{ME}, \mathord{\vdash}^{\odot}_{ME}\}$. In order to understand why the inferences are identical consider the conditional $(cold(X) \mid susc(X))[0.1]$. For grounding semantics this conditional yields the ground instance $(cold(a) \mid susc(a))[0.1]$ (among others). Now consider the averaging semantics which basically demands that the average probability of $(cold(F) \mid susc(F))$ for $F \in \{a, b, c\}$ is 0.1. As $\mathcal{R}_{cold}$ does not say anything about different conditions for $\{a, b, c\}$ the most rational thing to do is to treat all instantiations equally. This is also pursued by the maximum entropy inference procedure because any deviation from this uniform assignment would yield a higher entropy. Hence, in order to have an average probability of 0.1 for all three instances the inference procedure exactly assigns a probability of 0.1 to all three instances. A similar explanation applies to aggregating semantics.

If we add probabilistic facts like $(contact(a, b))[1]$ or $(cold(c))[1]$ to $\mathcal{R}_{cold}$ the situation changes and now different inferences can be drawn from the different semantics.

The scenario above cannot easily be modeled with BLPs. As BLPs rely on Bayesian networks one important requirement is *acyclicity* of the represented knowledge. In the above example, the probability of some a catching a cold may depend on the probability of b catching a cold which itself may depend again on the probability of a catching a cold. In order to represent the example properly with a BLP these cycles have to be broken, e. g. by assuming some order on the individuals and by inhibiting *contact* to be symmetric. However, these changes would alter the modeled knowledge drastically.

Note that our approach does not forbid cyclic dependencies as the status of conditionals is validated in a global way, taking every dependency into account.

Example 6. We now come to Ex. 3 and assume that our given signature contains three constants $\{tweety, huey, dewey\}$ which are also all assumed to be birds. We obtain the following inferences[1]:

$$\mathcal{R}_{chirps} \hspace{0.3em}\vert\!\!\!\sim_{ME}^{gnd} (chirps(tweety))[0.90] \qquad \mathcal{R}_{chirps} \hspace{0.3em}\vert\!\!\!\sim_{ME}^{gnd} (chirps(huey))[0.90]$$

$$\mathcal{R}_{chirps} \hspace{0.3em}\vert\!\!\!\sim_{ME}^{\varnothing} (chirps(tweety))[0.86] \qquad \mathcal{R}_{chirps} \hspace{0.3em}\vert\!\!\!\sim_{ME}^{\varnothing} (chirps(huey))[0.92]$$

$$\mathcal{R}_{chirps} \hspace{0.3em}\vert\!\!\!\sim_{ME}^{\odot} (chirps(tweety))[0.86] \qquad \mathcal{R}_{chirps} \hspace{0.3em}\vert\!\!\!\sim_{ME}^{\odot} (chirps(huey))[0.92]$$

Here, the grounding semantics yields the same probabilities for *Tweety* and *Huey* regarding *chirps*. As there is no knowledge on whether *Tweety* is moody conditional r_1 is responsible for yielding a probability of 0.9 for *chirps(tweety)*. As for both the averaging and aggregating semantics we obtain identical results in this example. For both averaging and aggregating semantics *Tweety* is assumed to chirp, with a slightly lower probability than *Huey*. This complies with our intuition, as *Tweety* is known to be a magpie, and in case it is moody, its probability to chirp would decrease considerably. For *Huey*'s probability of chirping, we observe some compensating effect caused by the situation of *Tweety* being moody which is rarely the case (0.12 for both averaging and aggregating semantics).

Example 3 can be represented as a BLP B as it contains no cyclic dependencies. For example, conditional r_1 can be represented as a Bayesian clause $c_1 = (chirps(X) \mid bird(X))$ with $\mathrm{cpd}_c(\mathrm{true}, \mathrm{true}) = 0.9$, $\mathrm{cpd}_c(\mathrm{false}, \mathrm{true}) = 0.9$, $\mathrm{cpd}_c(\mathrm{true}, \mathrm{false}) = 0.5$, and $\mathrm{cpd}_c(\mathrm{false}, \mathrm{false}) = 0.5$, the latter two probabilities being some default assumptions for the case when X is no bird. However, inference in B depends crucially on the combining rule chosen for *chirps*. If Tweety is moody both clauses deriving from the conditionals r_1 and r_2 are applicable and the resulting probabilities 0.9 and 0.2 have to be combined. In this scenario, the combining rule *noisy-and* defined via $na(p_1, p_2) = p_1 p_2$ would be an appropriate choice yielding a combined probability of 0.18. If noisy-or would be chosen this results in a probability of 0.92 which shows that combining rule have to be chosen very carefully. Another problem with the BLP representation is that B is not able to compute any probability for *chirps(huey)* as there is no evidence on whether *huey* is a magpie or even a bird.

6   Related Work

There are several other approaches to defining a probabilistic semantics for a fragment of first-order logic, some of which also make use of the principle of maximum entropy. The research presented in [1,3] aims at combining subjective and statistical probabilistic knowledge by deriving subjective probabilistic beliefs about a specific individual from statistical knowledge about sets of individuals, considering approximative probabilities and limits. Although this approach gives the same results as the principle of maximum entropy, the authors argue that the principle of maximum entropy cannot be

---

[1] All probabilities are rounded off to two decimal places.

applied on knowledge bases containing n-ary predicates, $n > 1$. Approaches allowing the representation of statistical probabilities suffer from these problems arising from the fact that the size of the universe constraints the representable probabilities. This is not the case for the semantics presented in this work, as they have no underlying frequentistic interpretation. Moreover, the application of the principle of maximum entropy to knowledge bases with arbitrary predicates seems to be unproblematic, but this has to be investigated more thoroughly in further work.

The grounding semantics in particular is similar to the probabilistic logic program semantics with entailment under maximum-entropy and the closed-world assumption as introduced in [5]. However, the maximum entropy inference relation $\vdash_{ME}^{gnd}$, which is defined for $\models^{gnd}$ via Equations (2) and (3), is independent of the query. That is, the maximum entropy model defined for a given set $\mathcal{R}$ via the grounding semantics is independent of the query, whereas the maximum entropy model defined via entailment under maximum-entropy and the closed-world assumption depends on the given query.

7 Conclusions and Discussion

We have introduced and evaluated three different semantics for relational probabilistic conditionals that differ with respect to their approaches to dealing with the conflicts and inconsistencies arising from the quantification of conditionals with precise probabilities. The aggregating as well as the averaging semantics try to deal with these conflicts by allowing some "exceptional" individuals to deviate from the overall behavior of a given population, while the grounding semantics utilizes constraints to restrict the set of individuals which may be used for generating the ground instances of the probabilistic conditionals.

We have shown that all semantics satisfy common sense properties inspired by similar properties for default reasoning and we have compared them on several example knowledge bases. We have also shown that approaches to statistical relational learning are inadequate for probabilistic default reasoning in relational settings. It turned out that all proposed semantics coincide on knowledge bases that do not model knowledge on exceptional individuals. In the presence of specific knowledge on individuals, however, the inferences drawn from the different approaches may vary significantly. While the grounding semantics seems to yield the most robust and predictable inferences it suffers from the additional demand to specify constraint formulas to inhibit an inconsistent grounding of the knowledge base. Nonetheless, inference based on grounding semantics benefits from research on propositional inference using maximum entropy and thus can be solved quite efficiently [12]. Both the averaging and aggregating semantics do not need constraint formulas but require a universe of sufficient size in order to compensate for exceptions explicitly represented. Furthermore, they allow for a smoother interpretation of conditionals and consider the interactions between the represented knowledge more deeply. While the averaging and aggregating semantics may differ only slightly, from a computational point of view, inference based on aggregating semantics is easier as Equation (5) describes a linear constraint whereas Equation (4) describes a non-linear constraint. From the point of view of modeling, the grounding semantics is most adequate for a population with well-defined homogeneous subpopulations whereas the average semantics provides probabilities that are means of the corresponding subjective probabilities, expressing that on the average, e.g., individuals show a certain behavior with the respective probability. Hence, they compute a statistics of subjective (conditional) probabilities. Finally, the aggregating semantics mimics the form of statistical probabilities but replaces frequencies by subjective estimations and allows for even more compensation effects. In particular, by assigning low probabilities to formulas involving abnormal individuals, the influence of such individuals on probabilities of general statements can be weakened.

Further work will comprise a more thorough evaluation of the formalisms presented here, as well as the development of appropriate (with respect to the underlying semantics) methods for learning probabilistic relational conditionals from data and efficient methods for inference.

Acknowledgements. The research reported here was partially supported by the Deutsche Forschungsgemeinschaft (grants KE 1413/2-1 and BE 1700/7-1).

References

1. Bacchus, F., Grove, A.J., Halpern, J.Y., Koller, D.: From Statistical Knowledge Bases to Degrees of Belief. Artificial Intelligence 87(1-2), 75–143 (1996)
2. Fisseler, J.: Learning and Modeling with Probabilistic Conditional Logic. Dissertations in Artificial Intelligence, vol. 328. IOS Press, Amsterdam (2010)
3. Grove, A.J., Halpern, J.Y., Koller, D.: Random Worlds and Maximum Entropy. Journal of Artificial Intelligence Research (JAIR) 2, 33–88 (1994)
4. Kern-Isberner, G.: Conditionals in Nonmonotonic Reasoning and Belief Revision. LNCS (LNAI), vol. 2087. Springer, Heidelberg (2001)
5. Kern-Isberner, G., Lukasiewicz, T.: Combining probabilistic logic programming with the power of maximum entropy. Artificial Intelligence 157, 139–202 (2004)
6. Kern-Isberner, G., Thimm, M.: Novel semantical approaches to relational probabilistic conditionals. In: Proceedings of the 12th Int. Conf. on Knowledge Representation, KR (2010)
7. Kersting, K., De Raedt, L.: Bayesian logic programming: Theory and tool. In: Getoor, L., Taskar, B. (eds.) An Introduction to Statistical Relational Learning, MIT Press, Cambridge (2005)
8. Makinson, D.: General theory of cumulative inference. In: Non-monotonic Reasoning, vol. 346, pp. 1–18. Springer, Berlin (1989)
9. Nute, D., Cross, C.: Conditional logic. In: Handbook of Philosophical Logic, vol. 4, pp. 1–98. Kluwer, Dordrecht (2002)
10. Pearl, J.: Probabilistic Reasoning in intelligent Systems: Networks of plausible inference. Morgan Kaufmann, San Francisco (1998)
11. Richardson, M., Domingos, P.: Markov logic networks. Machine Learning 62(1-2), 107–136 (2006)
12. Rödder, W., Meyer, C.H.: Coherent Knowledge Processing at Maximum Entropy by SPIRIT. In: Proc. of the Twelfth Conf. on Uncertainty in Artificial Intelligence, pp. 470–476 (1996)
13. Thimm, M., Finthammer, M., Kern-Isberner, G., Beierle, C.: Comparing Approaches to Relational Probabilistic Reasoning: Theory and Implementation (submitted)

Probabilistic Approach to Nonmonotonic Consequence Relations

Dragan Doder[1], Aleksandar Perović[2], and Zoran Ognjanović[3]

[1] University of Belgrade, Faculty of Mechanical Engineering, Kraljice Marije 16,
11000 Belgrade, Serbia
ddoder@mas.bg.ac.rs
[2] University of Belgrade, Faculty of Transportation and Traffic Engineering,
Vojvode Stepe 305, 11000 Belgrade, Serbia
pera@sf.bg.ac.rs
[3] Mathematical Institute of Serbian Academy of Sciences and Arts,
Kneza Mihaila 36, 11000 Belgrade, Serbia
zorano@mi.sanu.ac.rs

Abstract. The paper offers a probabilistic characterizations of determinacy preservation, fragmented disjunction and conditional excluding middle for preferential relations. The paper also presents a preferential relation that is above Disjunctive rationality and strictly below Rational monotonicity. This so called ε, μ-relation is constructed using a positive infinitesimal ε and a finitely additive hyperreal valued probability measure μ on the set of propositional formulas.

1 Introduction

The notion of default rule is one of the main notions of non-monotonic reasoning. Roughly speaking, defaults are rules with exceptions, which allow inferring defeasible conclusions from available, but incomplete information. In [10], Gabbay suggested that the study of default reasoning should be focused on the corresponding consequence relations. Soon after, Kraus, Lehmann and Magidor proposed in [11] a set of properties, named System P (P stands for preferential), that every non-monotonic consequence relation should satisfy. Those properties are widely accepted as the core of non-monotonic reasoning (see, for example, [9]).

It is shown in [11] that each preferential relation is generated by some preferential structure. In the paper [12] of Lehmann and Magidor, the additional rule of Rational monotonicity is considered and both preferential and nonstandard probabilistic semantics are given.

After the work of Kraus, Lehmann and Magidor, many researchers studied the subclasses of preferential relations obtained by adding a number of rules to System P, see [3,4,7,8,16,21]. The preferential semantics for some preferential consequence relations that are obtained by adding certain rules stronger than Rational monotonicity is presented in [4]. Similarly, the addition of rules weaker than Rational monotonicity had led to new subclasses of preferential relations; the corresponding preferential semantics is developed in [20,21]. On the other

W. Liu (Ed.): ECSQARU 2011, LNAI 6717, pp. 459–471, 2011.
© Springer-Verlag Berlin Heidelberg 2011

hand, to the best of our knowledge, there are no probabilistic characterizations of those relations.

Our aim is to provide probabilistic representations for various preferential relations. In the case of determinacy preservation, fragmented disjunction and conditional excluding middle, we have identified the corresponding subclasses of hyperreal valued finitely additive probability measures that induces them, and proved the corresponding representation theorems. It is not difficult to see that probabilistic semantics proposed by Lehmann and Magidor could not be used for preferential relations that are not rational. For each infinitesimal $\varepsilon > 0$ and each finitely additive hyperreal probability measure μ on formulas, we have introduced a new consequence relation $\hspace{-0.5em}\sim_{\varepsilon,\mu}$ (ε, μ-relation) and proved that it is a preferential relation that is strictly below Rational monotonicity and above Disjunctive rationality.

The rest of the paper is organized as follows: Section 2 contains necessary definitions and facts; in Section 3 we provide probabilistic representation of conditional excluding middle, determinacy preservation and fragmented disjunction; in Section 4 we introduce $\hspace{-0.5em}\sim_{\varepsilon,\mu}$ relation, prove that $\hspace{-0.5em}\sim_{\varepsilon,\mu}$ satisfies P+DR for all ε and μ, and construct counterexamples for WD and WRM; concluding remarks are in the final section.

2 Preliminaries

2.1 Hyperreal Numbers

A hyperreal number is an element of some fixed ω_1-saturated elementary extension $\mathbb{R}^*$ of the ordered field of reals $\mathbb{R}$. By $[0, 1]^*$ we will denote the unit hyperreal interval, i.e. the set of all $a \in \mathbb{R}^*$ such that $0 \leqslant a \leqslant 1$. An infinitesimal is any element of $\mathbb{R}^*$ that is strictly lesser than every positive real number, and strictly greater than every negative real number.

The expression $a \approx b$ means that $a - b$ is an infinitesimal. A hyperreal number $a \in \mathbb{R}^*$ is a proper infinitesimal if $a \approx 0$ and $a \neq 0$ (ω_1-saturatedness provides existence of proper infinitesimals); $a \in \mathbb{R}^*$ is finite if there is $b \in \mathbb{R}$ such that $a \approx b$. The standard part of the finite $a \in \mathbb{R}^*$ is the unique $b \in \mathbb{R}$ such that $a \approx b$. The standard part of a will be denoted as usual by $st(a)$. For more information about nonstandard analysis we refer the reader to [17].

Let $a, b \in \mathbb{R}^*$, $a \geqslant 0$, $b > 0$. We say that a is of strictly lesser order than b (denoted $a \ll b$), if a/b is an infinitesimal. The important properties of the relation $\ll$ are:

$a \not\ll b$ and $a \not\ll c$ imply $a \not\ll b + c$; $a \ll c$ and $b \ll c$ imply $a + b \ll c$.

2.2 Nonstandard Probability Measures

Let $\mathcal{P}$ be an at most countable set of propositional letters and let $For_{\mathcal{P}}$ be the corresponding set of propositional formulas. A nonstandard (finitely additive) probability measure on $For_{\mathcal{P}}$ is a function $\mu : For_{\mathcal{P}} \longrightarrow [0, 1]^*$ which satisfies

1. $\mu(\alpha) = 1$, whenever α is a tautology,
2. $\mu(\alpha \vee \beta) = \mu(\alpha) + \mu(\beta)$, whenever $\alpha \wedge \beta$ is a contradiction.

It is easy to show that any probability measure μ satisfies the following:

- $\mu(\neg\alpha) = 1 - \mu(\alpha)$,
- $\mu(\alpha \vee \beta) = \mu(\alpha) + \mu(\beta) - \mu(\alpha \wedge \beta)$,
- $\mu(\alpha) = \mu(\beta)$, whenever $\alpha \leftrightarrow \beta$ is a tautology.

A probability measure μ is neat if $\mu(\alpha) = 0$ implies that α is a contradiction. Conditional probabilities are defined as usual: for $\mu(\alpha) \neq 0$, $\mu(\beta|\alpha) = \frac{\mu(\alpha \wedge \beta)}{\mu(\alpha)}$.

2.3   Preferential Relations

A preferential relation [11] is a binary relation $\vdash\sim$ on $For_{\mathcal{P}}$ which satisfies the following properties of so called System P (*REF*–Reflexivity, *LLE*–Left logical equivalence, *RW*–Right weakening, *CM*–Cautious monotonicity):

$$REF : \frac{}{\alpha \vdash\sim \alpha}; \qquad LLE : \frac{\vdash \alpha \leftrightarrow \beta, \ \alpha \vdash\sim \gamma}{\beta \vdash\sim \gamma};$$

$$RW : \frac{\vdash \alpha \to \beta, \ \gamma \vdash\sim \alpha}{\gamma \vdash\sim \beta}; \qquad AND : \frac{\alpha \vdash\sim \beta, \ \alpha \vdash\sim \gamma}{\alpha \vdash\sim \beta \wedge \gamma};$$

$$OR : \frac{\alpha \vdash\sim \gamma, \ \beta \vdash\sim \gamma}{\alpha \vee \beta \vdash\sim \gamma}; \qquad CM : \frac{\alpha \vdash\sim \beta, \ \alpha \vdash\sim \gamma}{\alpha \wedge \beta \vdash\sim \gamma}.$$

A relation is non-monotonic in the sense that it doesn't satisfy Monotonicity rule:

$$M : \frac{\alpha \vdash\sim \gamma}{\alpha \wedge \beta \vdash\sim \gamma}.$$

A preferential relation $\vdash\sim$ is said to be rational if it satisfies a restricted form of Monotonicity, so called Rational monotonicity:

$$RM : \frac{\alpha \vdash\sim \gamma, \ \alpha \not\vdash\sim \neg\beta}{\alpha \wedge \beta \vdash\sim \gamma}.$$

Let μ be a finitely additive nonstandard probability measure on $For_{\mathcal{P}}$. A binary relation $\vdash\sim_\mu$ on $\mathcal{B}$ defined by

$$\alpha \vdash\sim_\mu \beta \ \text{ iff } \ \mu(\beta|\alpha) \approx 1 \text{ or } \mu(\alpha) = 0$$

is a rational relation, [12].

Lehmann and Magidor have proved in [12] that each rational relation is generated by some neat finitely additive probability measure, i.e. for each rational relation $\vdash\sim$ there is a neat finitely additive hyeprreal valued probability measure μ on $For_{\mathcal{P}}$ such that $\vdash\sim = \vdash\sim_\mu$.

2.4   Hierarchy of Preferential Relations

[7,8] introduced Negation rationality and Disjunction rationality-rules:

$$NR : \frac{\alpha \vdash\sim \beta, \ \alpha \wedge \gamma \not\vdash\sim \beta}{\alpha \wedge \neg\gamma \vdash\sim \beta} \qquad DR : \frac{\alpha \vee \beta \vdash\sim \gamma, \ \alpha \not\vdash\sim \gamma}{\beta \vdash\sim \gamma}.$$

It is known that NR is strictly weaker than DR and that DR is strictly weaker than RM (we assume, as in the rest of this section, the presence of System P). Another inference rule, so called Weak rational monotonicity, that is strictly weaker than RM and incomparable with both NR and DR, is introduced in [21] as follows:

$$WRM : \frac{\alpha \hspace{1pt}\vdash\hspace{-3pt}\sim \gamma, \ \alpha \wedge \beta \hspace{1pt}\not\vdash\hspace{-3pt}\sim \gamma, \ \alpha \hspace{1pt}\not\vdash\hspace{-3pt}\sim \neg\beta}{\top \hspace{1pt}\vdash\hspace{-3pt}\sim \neg\alpha}$$

The Determinacy preservation rule

$$DP : \frac{\alpha \hspace{1pt}\vdash\hspace{-3pt}\sim \beta, \ \alpha \wedge \gamma \hspace{1pt}\not\vdash\hspace{-3pt}\sim \neg\beta}{\alpha \wedge \gamma \hspace{1pt}\vdash\hspace{-3pt}\sim \beta},$$

introduced by Makinson in [13], lies between RM and M.

Rational contraposition and Weak determinacy

$$RC : \frac{\alpha \hspace{1pt}\vdash\hspace{-3pt}\sim \beta, \ \neg\beta \hspace{1pt}\not\vdash\hspace{-3pt}\sim \alpha}{\neg\beta \hspace{1pt}\vdash\hspace{-3pt}\sim \neg\alpha}; \qquad WD : \frac{\top \hspace{1pt}\vdash\hspace{-3pt}\sim \neg\alpha, \ \alpha \hspace{1pt}\not\vdash\hspace{-3pt}\sim \beta}{\alpha \hspace{1pt}\vdash\hspace{-3pt}\sim \neg\beta}.$$

are weaker that DP and incomparable with RM, see [4,3]. It is known that RC implies WD and that DP=WD+RM.

Fragmented disjunction and conditional excluding middle

$$FD : \frac{\alpha \hspace{1pt}\vdash\hspace{-3pt}\sim \beta \vee \gamma, \ \alpha \hspace{1pt}\not\vdash\hspace{-3pt}\sim \beta, \ \alpha \hspace{1pt}\not\vdash\hspace{-3pt}\sim \gamma}{\neg\beta \hspace{1pt}\vdash\hspace{-3pt}\sim \gamma}; \qquad CEM : \frac{\alpha \hspace{1pt}\not\vdash\hspace{-3pt}\sim \beta}{\alpha \hspace{1pt}\vdash\hspace{-3pt}\sim \neg\beta}.$$

are incomparable with M and strictly above DP, see [4,16]. Furthermore, CEM is strictly above FD.

From now on, we will call a preferential relation which satisfy some of the additional rules by that rule (for example, a DP-relation is a preferential relation which satisfy the rule Determinacy preservation). The following diagram summarizes the relationships between the mentioned rules, explained above:

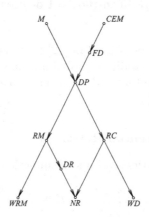

3   Probabilistic Representations of Inference Relations

As we have announced in the introduction, this rather technical section contains a probabilistic representation of Conditional excluding middle, Determinacy preservation and Fragmented disjunction. The structure of presentation is same for all three classes of preferential relations: first we define a class of nonstandard probability measures that is a probabilistic counterpart of the underlying class, then we prove the corresponding equivalence theorem, and conclude with the proof of the representation theorem. We say that a neat nonstandard probability measure μ induces a rational relation $\vdash\!\!\!\sim$ iff

$$\alpha \vdash\!\!\!\sim \beta \ \text{ iff } \ \mu(\beta|\alpha) \approx 1 \text{ or } \mu(\alpha) = 0.$$

3.1   Conditional Excluding Middle

Definition 1. *A finitely additive probability measure $\mu : For_{\mathcal{P}} \longrightarrow [0,1]^*$ is a CEM-measure iff*

$$\frac{\mu(\alpha)}{\mu(\beta)} \approx 0 \quad \text{or} \quad \frac{\mu(\beta)}{\mu(\alpha)} \approx 0$$

for all $\alpha, \beta \in For_{\mathcal{P}}$ such that $\vdash \neg(\alpha \wedge \beta)$, and $\mu(\alpha) \neq 0$ or $\mu(\beta) \neq 0$.

Theorem 1. Let $\vdash\!\!\!\sim$ be a rational relation. Then the following are equivalent:

1. $\vdash\!\!\!\sim$ is a CEM-relation;
2. Every measure μ that induces $\vdash\!\!\!\sim$ is a CEM-measure.

Proof. $2 \Rightarrow 1$: Suppose that $\vdash\!\!\!\sim$ is a rational relation which does not satisfy CEM, i.e. there are α and β so that $\alpha \not\vdash\!\!\!\sim \beta$ and $\alpha \not\vdash\!\!\!\sim \neg\beta$. Let μ be any measure that induces $\vdash\!\!\!\sim$. Then,

$$\frac{\mu(\alpha \wedge \beta)}{\mu(\alpha)} \not\approx 1 \quad \text{and} \quad \frac{\mu(\alpha \wedge \neg\beta)}{\mu(\alpha)} \not\approx 1. \tag{1}$$

Since $\frac{\mu(\alpha \wedge \beta)}{\mu(\alpha)} + \frac{\mu(\alpha \wedge \neg\beta)}{\mu(\alpha)} = 1$, it follows from (1) that

$$\frac{\mu(\alpha \wedge \beta)}{\mu(\alpha)} \not\approx 0 \quad \text{and} \quad \frac{\mu(\alpha \wedge \neg\beta)}{\mu(\alpha)} \not\approx 0.$$

Consequently,

$$\frac{\mu(\alpha \wedge \beta)}{\mu(\alpha \wedge \neg\beta)} \not\approx 0 \quad \text{and} \quad \frac{\mu(\alpha \wedge \neg\beta)}{\mu(\alpha \wedge \beta)} \not\approx 0.$$

In addition, $\alpha \wedge \beta$ and $\alpha \wedge \neg\beta$ are disjoint formulas, so μ is not a CEM-measure.

$1 \Rightarrow 2$: Suppose that μ induces $\vdash\!\!\!\sim$ and that there are disjoint formulas β and γ so that $\frac{\mu(\beta)}{\mu(\gamma)} \not\approx 0$ and $\frac{\mu(\gamma)}{\mu(\beta)} = k \not\approx 0$. Then, $st(k) > 0$. If α is the formula $\beta \vee \gamma$, then

$$\mu(\beta|\alpha) = \frac{\mu(\beta)}{\mu(\beta) + \mu(\gamma)} = \frac{1}{k+1} \not\approx 1.$$

Similarly, $\mu(\neg\beta|\alpha) = \frac{k}{k+1} \not\approx 1$. In other words, $\alpha \not\vdash\!\!\!\sim \beta$ and $\alpha \not\vdash\!\!\!\sim \neg\beta$, so $\vdash\!\!\!\sim$ is not a CEM-relation. $\qquad\square$

Theorem 2 (Representation of CEM). A preferential relation $\mathrel{|\!\sim}$ satisfies CEM if and only if there is a CEM-measure μ that induces $\mathrel{|\!\sim}$.

Proof. $\Rightarrow$: Suppose that a preferential relation $\mathrel{|\!\sim}$ satisfies CEM. In the presence of the system P, CEM implies RM. By the representation theorem of Lehmann and Magidor for rational relations, there is a neat nonstandard finitely additive probability measure μ on formulas such that

$$\alpha \mathrel{|\!\sim} \beta \quad \text{iff} \quad \mu(\beta|\alpha) \approx 1 \text{ or } \alpha = \bot$$

for all $\alpha, \beta \in For_\mathcal{P}$. By Theorem 1, μ is a CEM-measure.

$\Leftarrow$: Suppose that μ is a CEM-measure that induces $\mathrel{|\!\sim}$. Again by Theorem 1, $\mathrel{|\!\sim}$ satisfies CEM. $\qquad\square$

3.2   Determinacy Preservation

Definition 2. *A finitely additive probability measure* $\mu : For_\mathcal{P} \longrightarrow [0,1]^*$ *is a DP-measure iff*

$$\frac{\mu(\alpha)}{\mu(\beta)} \approx 0 \quad \text{or} \quad \frac{\mu(\beta)}{\mu(\alpha)} \approx 0$$

for all $\alpha, \beta \in For_\mathcal{P}$ *such that* $\vdash \neg(\alpha \wedge \beta)$, $\mu(\alpha) \neq 0$ *or* $\mu(\beta) \neq 0$, *and* $\mu(\alpha) \approx 0$ *and* $\mu(\beta) \approx 0$.

Theorem 3. Let $\mathrel{|\!\sim}$ be a rational relation. Then the following are equivalent:

1. $\mathrel{|\!\sim}$ is a DP-relation;
2. Every measure μ that induces $\mathrel{|\!\sim}$ is a DP-measure.

Proof. In the proof we will use the fact that a preferential relation is DP-relation iff it satisfies RM and WD.

$2 \Rightarrow 1$: Suppose that rational relation $\mathrel{|\!\sim}$ does not satisfy DP and let μ be any measure that induces $\mathrel{|\!\sim}$. Then there are α and β so that

$$\mu(\alpha) \approx 0, \quad \frac{\mu(\alpha \wedge \beta)}{\mu(\alpha)} \not\approx 1 \quad \text{and} \quad \frac{\mu(\alpha \wedge \neg\beta)}{\mu(\alpha)} \not\approx 1. \tag{2}$$

We can prove, as in the proof of Theorem 1, that

$$\frac{\mu(\alpha \wedge \beta)}{\mu(\alpha \wedge \neg\beta)} \not\approx 0 \quad \text{and} \quad \frac{\mu(\alpha \wedge \neg\beta)}{\mu(\alpha \wedge \beta)} \not\approx 0.$$

Since $\mu(\alpha \wedge \beta), \mu(\alpha \wedge \neg\beta) \leqslant \mu(\alpha) \approx 0$, μ is not a DP-measure.

$1 \Rightarrow 2$: Similarly as in the proof of $1 \Rightarrow 2$ in Theorem 1, provided additional condition $\mu(\beta) \approx 0$ and $\mu(\gamma) \approx 0$. $\qquad\square$

Theorem 4 (Representation of DP). A preferential relation $\mathrel{|\!\sim}$ satisfies DP if and only if there is a DP-measure μ that induces $\mathrel{|\!\sim}$.

Proof. Similar as the proof of Theorem 2. $\qquad\square$

3.3 Fragmented Disjunction

Definition 3. *A finitely additive probability measure* $\mu : For_P \longrightarrow [0,1]^*$ *is an FD-measure iff* μ *is a DP-measure such that* $\mu(\alpha) \approx 0$ *or* $\mu(\beta) \approx 0$ *or* $\mu(\gamma) \approx 0$ *whenever* α, β *and* γ *are pairwise disjoint.*

Theorem 5. Let $\mathrel{|\!\sim}$ be a rational relation. Then the following are equivalent:

1. $\mathrel{|\!\sim}$ is a FD-relation;
2. Every measure μ that induces $\mathrel{|\!\sim}$ is an FD-measure.

Proof. $2 \Rightarrow 1$: Suppose that μ is an FD-measure that induces $\mathrel{|\!\sim}$. Let $\alpha \mathrel{|\!\sim} \beta \vee \gamma$, $\alpha \mathrel{|\!\!\!/\sim} \beta$ and $\alpha \mathrel{|\!\!\!/\sim} \gamma$. Furthermore, let

$$a = \mu(\alpha \wedge \neg\beta \wedge \neg\gamma), \qquad b = \mu(\alpha \wedge \beta \wedge \neg\gamma),$$
$$c = \mu(\alpha \wedge \neg\beta \wedge \gamma), \qquad d = \mu(\alpha \wedge \beta \wedge \gamma).$$

Then,

(1) $\mu(\beta|\alpha) = \frac{b+d}{a+b+c+d} \not\approx 1$

(2) $\mu(\gamma|\alpha) = \frac{c+d}{a+b+c+d} \not\approx 1$

(3) $\mu(\beta \vee \gamma|\alpha) = \frac{b+c+d}{a+b+c+d} \approx 1$.

From (3) directly follows that $a \approx 0$. Note that $\mu(\alpha) = a + b + c + d$.

Claim 1. $\mu(\alpha) \not\approx 0$.

Indeed, if the alternative $\mu(\alpha) \approx 0$ is true, then $\ll$ is a total order on $\{a, b, c, d\}$ since μ is a DP-measure as well. From (1) follows that neither b nor d are maximal elements of $\langle\{a, b, c, d\}, \ll\rangle$; similarly, c is not maximal by (2), so a is the maximum. On the other hand, maximality of a with respect to $\ll$ implies that $\mu(\beta \vee \gamma|\alpha) \approx 0$, which contradicts (3).

Claim 2. $b \not\approx 0$ and $c \not\approx 0$.

Indeed, if $b \approx 0$, then $\frac{c+d}{a+b+c+d} \approx \frac{c+d}{c+d} = 1$ (a is an infinitesimal) which contradicts (2). Notice that $b + c + d \not\approx 0$ by Claim 1. Similarly, the assumption $c \approx 0$ contradicts (1).

Claim 3. $\mu(\neg\alpha) \approx 0$.

This is an immediate consequence of the previous claim and the facts that $\neg\alpha$, $\alpha \wedge \beta \wedge \neg\gamma$ and $\alpha \wedge \beta \wedge \neg\gamma$ are pairwise disjoint formulas and that μ is an FD-measure.

Finally, using previous claims, we obtain

$$\mu(\neg\gamma|\neg\beta) = \frac{\mu(\neg(\beta \vee \gamma))}{\mu(\neg\beta)} \leqslant \frac{\mu(\neg\alpha) + \mu(\alpha \wedge \neg\beta \wedge \neg\gamma)}{\mu(\alpha \wedge \neg\beta \wedge \gamma)}$$

$$= \frac{\mu(\neg\alpha) + a}{c} \approx 0,$$

or, in other words, $\neg\beta \mathrel{|\!\sim} \gamma$.

$1 \Rightarrow 2$: We will use the counter-position argument. On the one hand, suppose that μ induces $\hspace{-2pt}\sim$ and that μ is not a DP-measure. By Theorem 3, $\hspace{-2pt}\sim$ is not a *DP*-relation, so it cannot be an FD-relation. On the other hand, suppose that μ induces $\hspace{-2pt}\sim$, μ is a DP-measure and that there are pairwise disjoint formulas β, γ and δ so that $\mu(\beta) \not\approx 0$, $\mu(\gamma) \not\approx 0$ and $\mu(\delta) \not\approx 0$. Let α be the formula $\beta \vee \gamma$. It is easy to see that $\alpha \hspace{-2pt}\sim \beta \vee \gamma$, $\alpha \not\hspace{-2pt}\sim \beta$ and $\alpha \not\hspace{-2pt}\sim \gamma$, but

$$\mu(\neg\gamma | \neg\beta) = \frac{\mu(\neg(\beta \vee \gamma))}{\mu(\neg\beta)} \geqslant \frac{\mu(\delta)}{\mu(\neg\beta)} \not\approx 0,$$

so $\neg\beta \not\hspace{-2pt}\sim \gamma$. Consequently, $\hspace{-2pt}\sim$ is not an FD-relation. □

Theorem 6 (Representation of FD). A preferential relation $\hspace{-2pt}\sim$ satisfies FD if and only if there is an FD-measure μ that induces $\hspace{-2pt}\sim$.

Proof. Similar as the proof of Theorem 2. □

4   The ε, μ Preferential Relation

We believe that any natural probabilistic representation of consequence relations should involve conditional probabilities. As we have mentioned in the introduction, $\mu(\alpha|\beta) \approx 1$ could not be used for the representation of relations weaker than RM. The $\hspace{-2pt}\sim_{\varepsilon,\mu}$ relation, which is the topic of this section, is connected with our study of inconsistent set of formulas presented in [5], where we have showed that various relations of the form

$$\alpha \hspace{-2pt}\sim \beta \quad \text{iff} \quad \mu(\beta|\alpha) \geqslant 1 - a,$$

where $a \in (0,1)^*$, fail to be a preferential relation. The current definition of $\hspace{-2pt}\sim_{\varepsilon,\mu}$ is actually a modification of the condition $\mu(\beta|\alpha) \geqslant 1 - \varepsilon$ ($\varepsilon > 0$ is an infinitesimal).

Through this section ε will be a fixed positive infinitesimal and $\mu : For_\mathcal{P} \longrightarrow [0,1]^*$ a fixed finitely additive probability measure. The ε, μ relation $\hspace{-2pt}\sim_{\varepsilon,\mu}$ on $For_\mathcal{P}$ is defined by

$$\alpha \hspace{-2pt}\sim_{\varepsilon,\mu} \beta \text{ iff } \varepsilon \not\ll \mu(\neg\beta|\alpha) \text{ or } \mu(\alpha) = 0.$$

For the sake of simplicity, we will also assume that μ is a neat measure. Notice that $\perp \hspace{-2pt}\sim_{\varepsilon,\mu} \alpha$ for all α.

Theorem 7. $\hspace{-2pt}\sim_{\varepsilon,\mu}$ is a preferential relation.

Proof. In the verification of REF–CM we will only consider nontrivial cases, i.e. cases in which neither $\perp$ nor $\top$ have no occurrence.

Since $\mu(\alpha|\alpha) = 1$ and μ is a finitely additive probability measure, we have that $\mu(\neg\alpha|\alpha) = 0$, so $\varepsilon \not\ll \mu(\neg\alpha|\alpha)$, i.e. $\alpha \hspace{-2pt}\sim_{\varepsilon,\mu} \alpha$. Hence, Reflexivity is verified.

Right weakening. Suppose that $\gamma \mathrel{|\!\sim_{\varepsilon,\mu}} \alpha$ and that α implies β. Then, $\neg\beta$ implies $\neg\alpha$, so $\neg\beta \wedge \gamma$ implies $\neg\alpha \wedge \gamma$. Now we have that

$$\mu(\neg\beta|\gamma) = \frac{\mu(\neg\beta \wedge \gamma)}{\mu(\gamma)} \leqslant \frac{\mu(\neg\alpha \wedge \gamma)}{\mu(\gamma)} = \mu(\neg\alpha|\gamma),$$

so $\varepsilon \not\ll \mu(\neg\beta|\gamma)$, i.e. $\gamma \mathrel{|\!\sim_{\varepsilon,\mu}} \beta$.

Left logical equivalence. Suppose that α and α' are equivalent and $\alpha \mathrel{|\!\sim_{\varepsilon,\mu}} \beta$. Then, $\alpha \wedge \beta$ and $\alpha' \wedge \beta$ are equivalent as well; consequently, $\mu(\alpha) = \mu(\alpha')$ and $\mu(\alpha \wedge \beta) = \mu(\alpha' \wedge \beta)$, so $\mu(\beta|\alpha) = \mu(\beta|\alpha')$. Furthermore, using

$$\mu(\neg\gamma_1|\gamma_2) + \mu(\gamma_1|\gamma_2) = 1,$$

it is easy to see that $\mu(\neg\beta|\alpha) = \mu(\neg\beta|\alpha')$. By definition of $\mathrel{|\!\sim_{\varepsilon,\mu}}$, from the above we can derive that $\alpha' \mathrel{|\!\sim_{\varepsilon,\mu}} \beta$, which concludes the verification of LLE.

And. Suppose that $\alpha \mathrel{|\!\sim_{\varepsilon,\mu}} \beta$ and $\alpha \mathrel{|\!\sim_{\varepsilon,\mu}} \gamma$. Then, $\varepsilon \not\ll \mu(\neg\beta|\alpha)$ and $\varepsilon \not\ll \mu(\neg\gamma|\alpha)$, so

$$\varepsilon \not\ll \mu(\neg\beta|\alpha) + \mu(\neg\gamma|\alpha).$$

In addition,

$$\mu(\neg(\beta \wedge \gamma)|\alpha) = \mu(\neg\beta \vee \neg\gamma|\alpha) \leqslant \mu(\neg\beta|\alpha) + \mu(\neg\gamma|\alpha),$$

so $\varepsilon \not\ll \mu(\neg(\beta \wedge \gamma)|\alpha)$, i.e. $\alpha \mathrel{|\!\sim_{\varepsilon,\mu}} \beta \wedge \gamma$.

Or. Suppose that $\alpha \mathrel{|\!\sim_{\varepsilon,\mu}} \gamma$ and $\beta \mathrel{|\!\sim_{\varepsilon,\mu}} \gamma$. Then, by the definition of $\mathrel{|\!\sim_{\varepsilon,\mu}}$, there are positive $r, s \in \mathbb{R}^*$ such that $r \not\approx 0$, $s \not\approx 0$, $\varepsilon/\mu(\neg\gamma|\alpha) = r$ and $\varepsilon/\mu(\neg\gamma|\beta) = s$. From this we can derive

$$\mu(\neg\gamma \wedge \alpha) = \frac{\varepsilon}{r}\mu(\alpha) \text{ and } \mu(\neg\gamma \wedge \beta) = \frac{\varepsilon}{s}\mu(\beta).$$

Since

$$\frac{1}{2}\left(\mu(\alpha_1) + \mu(\alpha_2)\right) \leqslant \mu(\alpha_1 \vee \alpha_2) \leqslant \mu(\alpha_1) + \mu(\alpha_2) \tag{3}$$

for any $\alpha_1, \alpha_2 \in For_\mathcal{P}$, we have that

$$\begin{aligned}
\mu(\neg\gamma|\alpha \vee \beta) &= \frac{\mu((\neg\gamma \wedge \alpha) \vee (\neg\gamma \wedge \beta))}{\mu(\alpha \vee \beta)} \\
&\leqslant \frac{\mu(\neg\gamma \wedge \alpha) + \mu(\neg\gamma \wedge \beta)}{\frac{1}{2}(\mu(\alpha) + \mu(\beta))} \\
&= \frac{\frac{2\varepsilon}{r}\mu(\alpha) + \frac{2\varepsilon}{s}\mu(\beta)}{\mu(\alpha) + \mu(\beta)} \\
&\leqslant \frac{2\varepsilon}{\min(r,s)},
\end{aligned}$$

which implies that

$$\frac{\varepsilon}{\mu(\neg\gamma|\alpha \vee \beta)} \geqslant \frac{\min(r,s)}{2},$$

i.e. $\varepsilon \nll \mu(\neg\gamma|\alpha\vee\beta)$, which is by the definition of $\vdash_{\varepsilon,\mu}$ equivalent to $\alpha\vee\beta \vdash_{\varepsilon,\mu} \gamma$.

Cautious monotonicity. Suppose that $\alpha \vdash_{\varepsilon,\mu} \beta$ and $\alpha \vdash_{\varepsilon,\mu} \gamma$. From $\varepsilon \nll \mu(\neg\beta|\alpha)$ follows that $\mu(\neg\beta|\alpha) \approx 0$, so $\mu(\beta|\alpha) \approx 1$. Furthermore,

$$\mu(\neg\gamma|\alpha\wedge\beta) = \frac{\mu(\alpha\wedge\beta\wedge\neg\gamma)}{\mu(\alpha\wedge\beta)} = \frac{\mu(\alpha\wedge\beta\wedge\neg\gamma)/\mu(\alpha)}{\mu(\alpha\wedge\beta)/\mu(\alpha)} = \frac{\mu(\beta\wedge\neg\gamma|\alpha)}{\mu(\beta|\alpha)},$$

so

$$\frac{\varepsilon}{\mu(\neg\gamma|\alpha\wedge\beta)} = \frac{\varepsilon\cdot\mu(\beta|\alpha)}{\mu(\beta\wedge\neg\gamma|\alpha)} \geqslant \frac{\varepsilon\cdot\mu(\beta|\alpha)}{\mu(\neg\gamma|\alpha)} \nll 0,$$

since $\frac{\varepsilon}{\mu(\neg\gamma|\alpha)} \nll 0$ and $\mu(\beta|\alpha) \approx 1$. Finally, by definition of $\vdash_{\varepsilon,\mu}$, $\alpha\wedge\beta \vdash_{\varepsilon,\mu} \gamma$. $\square$

Theorem 8. $\vdash_{\varepsilon,\mu}$ satisfies DR and NR.

Proof. Suppose that $\varepsilon \ll \mu(\neg\gamma|\alpha)$ and $\varepsilon \ll \mu(\neg\gamma|\beta)$. Then, there are positive infinitesimals δ and η such that $\frac{\varepsilon}{\mu(\neg\gamma|\alpha)} = \delta$ and $\frac{\varepsilon}{\mu(\neg\gamma|\beta)} = \eta$, which is equivalent to $\mu(\neg\gamma\wedge\alpha) = \frac{\varepsilon}{\delta}\mu(\alpha)$ and $\mu(\neg\gamma\wedge\beta) = \frac{\varepsilon}{\eta}\mu(\beta)$. Furthermore, by (3),

$$\begin{aligned}
\frac{\varepsilon}{\mu(\neg\gamma|\alpha\vee\beta)} &= \frac{\varepsilon\mu(\alpha\vee\beta)}{\mu((\neg\gamma\wedge\alpha)\vee(\neg\gamma\wedge\beta))} \\
&\leqslant \frac{2\varepsilon(\mu(\alpha)+\mu(\beta))}{\mu(\neg\gamma\wedge\alpha)+\mu(\neg\gamma\wedge\beta)} \\
&= \frac{2\varepsilon(\mu(\alpha)+\mu(\beta))}{\frac{\varepsilon}{\delta}\mu(\alpha)+\frac{\varepsilon}{\eta}\mu(\beta)} \\
&\leqslant \frac{2\varepsilon(\mu(\alpha)+\mu(\beta))}{\frac{\varepsilon}{\max(\delta,\eta)}(\mu(\alpha)+\mu(\beta))} \\
&= 2\max(\delta,\eta) \\
&\approx 0,
\end{aligned}$$

thus $\alpha\vee\beta \nvdash_{\varepsilon,\mu} \gamma$. Since DR implies NR, we have our claim. $\square$

Theorem 9. Weak determinacy, Rational contraposition, Determinacy preservation, Fragmented disjunction, Conditional excluding middle, Monotonicity, Rational monotonicity and Weak rational monotonicity need not to be satisfied by $\vdash_{\varepsilon,\mu}$.

Proof. According to the diagram in Subsection 2.4, it is sufficient to show that Weak determinacy and Weak rational monotonicity fail for $\vdash_{\varepsilon,\mu}$. For the proof of the existence of the measures constructed bellow, we refer the reader to [14].

Let us construct a counterexample for WD. Suppose that μ is any neat measure such that $\mu(p_0) = 2\mu(p_0\wedge p_1) = 1-\varepsilon$. Then:

$$\frac{\varepsilon}{\mu(\neg p_0|\top)} = \frac{\varepsilon}{1-\mu(p_0)} = \frac{\varepsilon}{1-(1-\varepsilon)} = 1;$$

$$\frac{\varepsilon}{\mu(\neg p_1|p_0)} = \frac{\varepsilon}{1 - \mu(p_1|p_0)} = \frac{\varepsilon\mu(p_0)}{\mu(p_0) - \mu(p_0 \wedge p_1)} = \frac{\varepsilon(1 - \varepsilon)}{\frac{1}{2}(1 - \varepsilon)} = 2\varepsilon;$$

$$\frac{\varepsilon}{\mu(p_1|p_0)} = \frac{\varepsilon\mu(p_0)}{\mu(p_0 \wedge p_1)} = \frac{\varepsilon(1 - \varepsilon)}{\frac{1}{2}(1 - \varepsilon)} = 2\varepsilon.$$

Therefore, $\top \mathrel{|\!\sim}_{\varepsilon,\mu} \neg p_0$, $p_0 \mathrel{|\!\not\sim}_{\varepsilon,\mu} p_1$ and $p_0 \mathrel{|\!\not\sim}_{\varepsilon,\mu} \neg p_1$, so WD fails.

Let us construct a counterexample for WRM. Let κ and λ be infinitesimals so that $\varepsilon \ll \kappa$ and $\varepsilon \ll \lambda$. Furthermore, let α, β and γ be any formulas so that $\alpha \wedge \neg\gamma$ implies $\alpha \wedge \beta$ (consequently, $\alpha \wedge \neg\gamma \wedge \beta$ is equivalent with $\alpha \wedge \neg\gamma$), $\mu(\alpha) = \kappa$, $\mu(\alpha \wedge \neg\gamma) = \varepsilon\kappa$ and $\mu(\alpha \wedge \beta) = \lambda\kappa$. Since $\alpha \wedge \neg\gamma \wedge \beta$ is equivalent with $\alpha \wedge \neg\gamma$, we have that $\mu(\alpha \wedge \neg\gamma \wedge \beta) = \mu(\alpha \wedge \neg\gamma) = \varepsilon\kappa$.

$-\ \alpha \mathrel{|\!\sim}_{\varepsilon,\mu} \gamma$: $\dfrac{\varepsilon}{\mu(\alpha|\top)} = \dfrac{\varepsilon}{\kappa} \approx 0;$

$-\ \alpha \wedge \beta \mathrel{|\!\not\sim}_{\varepsilon,\mu} \gamma$: $\dfrac{\varepsilon}{\mu(\neg\gamma|\alpha \wedge \beta)} = \dfrac{\varepsilon\mu(\alpha \wedge \beta)}{\mu(\alpha \wedge \neg\gamma \wedge \beta)} = \dfrac{\varepsilon\mu(\alpha \wedge \beta)}{\mu(\alpha \wedge \neg\gamma \wedge \beta)} = \dfrac{\varepsilon\lambda\kappa}{\varepsilon\kappa} = \lambda \approx 0;$

$-\ \alpha \mathrel{|\!\not\sim}_{\varepsilon,\mu} \neg\beta$: $\dfrac{\varepsilon}{\mu(\beta|\alpha)} = \dfrac{\varepsilon\mu(\alpha)}{\mu(\alpha \wedge \beta)} = \dfrac{\varepsilon\kappa}{\lambda\kappa} = \dfrac{\varepsilon}{\lambda} \approx 0;$

$-\ \top \mathrel{|\!\not\sim}_{\varepsilon,\mu} \neg\alpha$: $\dfrac{\varepsilon}{\mu(\alpha|\top)} = \dfrac{\varepsilon}{\kappa} \approx 0.$

Hence, WRM fails.   □

5 Concluding Remarks

The main novelty of this work is the development of probabilistic semantics for some nonmonotonic consequence relations, which may be seen as a natural extension of the research of Lehmann and Magidor presented in [12]. Although characterizations of nonmonotonic inference relations in terms of probability measures have been already studied [1,2,6,5,12,15,18,19], we are not aware of any probabilistic representation of the relations considered in this paper.

Probabilistic semantics for rational relations is a nice bridge between the general study of consequence relations and probability logics. For instance, in [15], a Hilbert style probability logic Ax_{LPP^S} was introduced to axiomatize reasoning about conditional probabilities whose range is the unit interval of the Hardy field $\mathbb{Q}(\varepsilon)$. Due to the representation theorem of Lehmann and Magidor, any rational relation $\mathrel{|\!\sim}$ can be formally represented by an Ax_{LPP^S}-theory. We leave for further research to develop probability logics expressible enough to represent CEM, DP, FD and $\mathrel{|\!\sim}_{\varepsilon,\mu}$ relations.

The immediate consequence of results presented in Section 4 is the fact that $\mathrel{|\!\sim}_{\varepsilon,\mu}$ is above disjunctive rationality and strictly below rational monotonicity. The exact relation between DR and $\mathrel{|\!\sim}_{\varepsilon,\mu}$ (i.e., whether DR can be represented by $\mathrel{|\!\sim}_{\varepsilon,\mu}$, or some new rules should be added in order to obtain the corresponding representation theorem) is an open question.

Acknowledgements

The work presented here was partially supported by the Serbian Ministry of Education and Science (projects ON174026, III44006 and III41013).

References

1. Beierle, C., Kern-Isberner, G.: The Relationship of the Logic of Big-Stepped Probabilities to Standard Probabilistic Logics. In: Link, S., Prade, H. (eds.) FoIKS 2010. LNCS, vol. 5956, pp. 191–210. Springer, Heidelberg (2010)
2. Benferhat, S., Duboas, D., Prade, H.: Possibilistic and standard probabilistic semantics of conditional knowledge bases. Journal of Logic and Computation 9(6), 873–895 (1999)
3. Bezzazi, H., Pino Pérez, R.: Rational Transitivity and its models. In: Proceedings of the 26th International Symposium on Multiple-Valued Logic, pp. 160–165. IEEE Computer Society Press, Los Alamitos (1996)
4. Bezzazi, H., Makinson, D., Pino Pérez, R.: Beyond rational monotony: some strong non-Horn rules for nonmonotonic inference relations. Journal of Logic and Computation 7(5), 605–631 (1997)
5. Doder, D., Rašković, M., Marković, Z., Ognjanović, Z.: Measures of inconsistency and defaults. International Journal of Approximate Reasoning 51, 832–845 (2010)
6. Dubois, D., Fargier, H., Prade, H.: Ordinal and Probabilistic Representations of Acceptance. J. Artificial Intelligence Research 22, 23–56 (2004)
7. Freund, M.: Injective models and disjunctive relations. Journal of Logic and Computation 3(3), 231–247 (1993)
8. Freund, M., Lehmann, D.: On negation rationality. Journal of Logic and Computation 6(2), 263–269 (1996)
9. Friedman, N., Halpern, J.Y.: Plausibility measures and default reasoning. Journal of the ACM 48, 648–685 (2001)
10. Gabbay, D.: Theoretical foundations for non-monotonic reasoning in expert systems. In: Logics and Models of Concurrent Systems, pp. 439–457. Springer, Heidelberg (1985)
11. Kraus, S., Lehmann, D., Magidor, M.: Nonmonotonic reasoning, preferential models and cumulative logics. Artificial Intelligence 44(1-2), 167–207 (1990)
12. Lehmann, D., Magidor, M.: What does a conditional knowledge base entail? Artificial Intelligence 55, 1–60 (1992)
13. Makinson, D.: General patterns in nonmonotonic reasoning. In: Handbook of Logic in Artificial Intelligence and Logic Programming. Non Monotonic Reasoning and Uncertain Reasoning, vol. 3, pp. 35–110. Clarendon Press, Oxford (1994)
14. Bhaskara Rao, K.P.S., Bhaskara Rao, M.: Theory of charges. Academic Press, London (1983)
15. Rašković, M., Ognjanović, Z., Marković, Z.: A logic with approximate conditional probabilities that can model default reasoning. International Journal of Approximate Reasoning 49(1), 52–66 (2008)
16. Stalnaker, R.C.: A theory of conditionals. In: Rescher, N. (ed.) Studies in Logical Theory. American Philosophical Quarterly Monograph Series, vol. 2. Blackwell, Oxford (1968)

17. Stroyan, K.D., Luxemburg, W.A.J.: Introduction to the theory of infinitesimals. Academic Press, London (1976)
18. Weydert, E.: Doxastic Normality Logic: A Qualitative Probabilistic Modal Framework for Defaults and Belief. In: Logic, Action and Information, pp. 152–172. Walter de Gruyter, Berlin (1996)
19. Weydert, E.: Defaults, Logic and Probability – A Theoretical Perspective. KI 15(4), 44–49 (2001)
20. Zhu, Z., Xiao, W.: Two Representation Theorems for Non-monotonic Inference Relations. Journal of Logic and Computation 17(4), 727–747 (2007)
21. Zhu, Z., Zhang, D., Chen, S., Zhu, W.: Some contributions to nonmonotonic consequence. Journal of Computer Science and Technology 16(4), 297–314 (2001)

Bridging the Gap between Reinforcement Learning and Knowledge Representation: A Logical Off- and On-Policy Framework

Emad Saad

Department of Computer Science,
Gulf University for Science and Technology,
Mishref, Kuwait
saad.e@gust.edu.kw

Abstract. Knowledge Representation is an important issue in reinforcement learning. In this paper, we bridge the gap between reinforcement learning and knowledge representation, by providing a rich knowledge representation framework, based on normal logic programs with answer set semantics, that is capable of solving model-free reinforcement learning problems for more complex domains and exploits the domain-specific knowledge. We prove the correctness of our approach. We show that the complexity of finding an offline and online policy for a model-free reinforcement learning problem in our approach is NP-complete. Moreover, we show that any model-free reinforcement learning problem in an MDP environment can be encoded as a SAT problem. The importance of that is model-free reinforcement learning problems can be now solved as SAT problems.

1 Introduction

Reinforcement learning is the problem of learning to act by trial and error interaction in dynamic environments. Under the assumption that a complete model of the environment is known, a reinforcement learning problem is modeled as a Markov Decision Process (MDP), in which an optimal policy can be learned. Operation research methods, in particular dynamic programming by value iteration, have been extensively used to learn the optimal policy for a reinforcement learning problem in MDP environment. However, an agent may not know the model of the environment. In addition, an agent may not be able to consider all possibilities and use its knowledge to plan ahead, because of the agent's limited computational abilities to consider all states systematically [30]. Therefore, Q-learning [30] and SARSA [20] are proposed as model-free reinforcement learning algorithms that learn optimal policies without the need for the agent to know the model of the environment.

Q-learning and SARSA are incremental dynamic programming algorithms, that learns optimal policy from actual experience from interaction with the environment, where to guarantee convergence the following assumptions must hold; the action-value function is represented as a look-up table; the environment is a deterministic MDP; for each starting state and action, there are an infinite number of episodes; and the learning rate is decreased appropriately over time. However, these assumptions imply that all actions are tried in every possible state and every state must be visited infinitely many times, which leads to a slow convergence, although, it is sufficient for the agent to try all possible actions in every possible state only once to learn about the reinforcements resulting from executing actions in states and finding optimal policies. In addition, in some situations it is not possible for the agent to visit a state more than once. Consider a deer that eats in an area where a cheetah appears and the deer flees and survived. If the deer revisits this area again it will be eaten and does not learn anymore. This is unavoidable in Q-learning and SARSA because of the iterative dynamic programming approach they adopt and their convergence assumptions. Moreover, dynamic programming methods use primitive representation of states and actions and do not exploit domain-specific knowledge of the problem domain, in addition they solve MDP with relatively small domain sizes [19]. However, using richer knowledge representation frameworks for MDP allow to efficiently find optimal policies in more complex and larger domains.

A logical framework to model-based reinforcement learning has been proposed in [25] that overcomes the representational limitations of dynamic programming methods and capable of representing domain specific knowledge. The framework in [25] is based on the integration of model-based reinforcement learning in MDP environment with normal hybrid probabilistic logic programs with probabilistic answer set semantics [22] that allows representing and reasoning about a variety of fundamental probabilistic reasoning problems including probabilistic planning [23], contingent probabilistic planning [24], the most probable explanation in belief networks, and the most likely trajectory [26].

In this paper we integrate model-free reinforcement learning with normal logic programs with answer set semantics and SAT, providing a logical framework to model-free reinforcement learning using Q-learning and SARSA update rules to learn the optimal off- and on-policy respectively. This framework is considered a model-free extension to the model-based reinforcement learning framework of [25]. The importance of the proposed framework is twofold. First, the proposed framework overcomes the representational limitations of dynamic programming methods to model-free reinforcement learning and capable of representing domain-specific knowledge, and hence bridges the gap between reinforcement learning and knowledge representation. Second, it eliminates the requirement of visiting every state infinitely many times which is required for the convergence of the Q-learning and SARSA.

This is achieved by encoding the representation of a model-free reinforcement learning problem in a new high level action language we develop called, $\mathcal{B}_{\mathcal{Q}}$, into normal logic program with answer set semantics, where all actions are tried in every state only once. We show the correctness of the translation. We prove that the complexity of finding an off- and on-policy in our approach is NP-complete. In addition, we show that any model-free reinforcement learning problem in MDP environment can be encoded as SAT problem.

2   Preliminaries

As in the underlying assumptions of the original Q-learning and SARSA, the subsequent results in the rest of this paper assume that the considered MDPs are deterministic. Normal logic programs [7] and Q-learning [30] and SARSA [20] are reviewed in this section.

2.1   Normal Logic Programs

Let $\mathcal{L}$ be a first-order language with finitely many predicate symbols, function symbols, constants, and infinitely many variables. The Herbrand base of $\mathcal{L}$ is denoted by $\mathcal{B}$. A Herbrand interpretation is a subset of the Herbrand base $\mathcal{B}$. A normal logic program is a finite set of rules of the form

$$a \leftarrow a_1, \ldots, a_n, not\ b_1, \ldots, not\ b_m$$

where $a, a_1, \ldots, a_n, b_1, \ldots, b_m$ are atoms and not is the negation-as-failure. A normal logic program is ground if no variables appear in any of its rules. Let Π be a ground normal logic program and S be a Herbrand interpretation, then, we say that the above rule is satisfied by S iff $a \in S$, whenever $\{a_1, \ldots, a_n\} \subseteq S$ and $\{b_1, \ldots, b_m\} \cap S = \emptyset$, or for some $i \in \{1, \ldots, n\}$, $j \in \{1, \ldots, m\}$, $a_i \notin S$ or $b_j \in S$.

A Herbrand model of Π is a Herbrand interpretation that satisfies every rule in Π. A Herbrand interpretation S of a normal logic program Π is an answer set of Π if S is the minimal Herbrand model (with respect to the set inclusion) of the reduct, denoted by Π^S, of Π w.r.t. S, where $\{b_1, \ldots, b_m\} \cap S = \emptyset$ and

$$a \leftarrow a_1, \ldots, a_n \in \Pi^S \text{ iff}$$
$$a \leftarrow a_1, \ldots, a_n, not\ b_1, \ldots, not\ b_m \in \Pi$$

2.2   Q-Learning and SARSA

Q-learning learns the optimal Q-function, Q^*, from the agent's experience (set of episodes) by repeatedly estimating the optimal Q-value for every state-action pair $Q^*(s, a)$. The Q-value, $Q(s, a)$, given a policy (a mapping from states to actions), is defined as the expected sum of discounted rewards resulting from executing the action a in a state s and then following the policy thereafter. Given Q^*, an optimal policy, π^*, can be determined by identifying the optimal action in every state, where a is optimal in a state s, i.e., $\pi^*(s) = a$, if $\pi^*(s) = \arg\max_{a'} Q^*(s, a') = a$ and a' is executable in s. An episode is an exploration of the environment which is a sequence of state-action-reward-state of the form $e \equiv s_0, a_0, r_1, s_1, a_1, r_2, \ldots, s_{n-1}, a_{n-1}, r_n, s_n$, where for each $(0 \leq t \leq n - 1)$, $s_t, a_t, r_{t+1}, s_{t+1}$ means that an agent executed action a_t in state s_t and rests in state s_{t+1} where it received reward r_{t+1}. s_0 denotes an initial state and s_n is a terminal (goal) state. Given that the agent sufficiently explored the environment, the optimal Q-values are repeatedly estimated by the following algorithm:

$\forall (s, a)$ initialize $Q(s, a)$ arbitrary
Repeat forever for each episode
    Select the initial state s_t of an episode
    Repeat
        Choose an action a_t for the current state s_t
        Execute the action a_t in s_t
        Observe the subsequent state s_{t+1}
        Receive an immediate reward $\mathcal{R}(s_t, a_t, s_{t+1})$
        $Q(s_t, a_t) \leftarrow (1 - \alpha)Q(s_t, a_t) + \alpha[\mathcal{R}(s_t, a_t, s_{t+1}) + \gamma \max_a Q(s_{t+1}, a)]$
        Set $s_t \leftarrow s_{t+1}$
    Until s_t is the end of an episode

where α is the learning rate, γ is the discount factor, and $\mathcal{R}(s_t, a_t, s_{t+1})$ is the reward received in s_{t+1} from executing a_t in s_t. Q-learning is an offline algorithm that learns the optimal Q-function while executing another policy. Under the same convergence assumptions as in Q-learning, SARSA [20] has been developed as an online model-free reinforcement learning algorithm, that learns optimal Q-function while exploring the environment. Similar to Q-learning, SARSA is an iterative dynamic programming algorithm whose update rule is given by:

$$Q(s_t, a_t) \leftarrow (1 - \alpha)Q(s_t, a_t) + \alpha[\mathcal{R}(s_t, a_t, s_{t+1}) + Q(s_{t+1}, a_{t+1})]$$

In addition, SARSA converges slowly to Q^*, since it requires every state to be visited infinitely many times with all actions are tried, although, it is sufficient for an agent to try all possible actions in every possible state only once to learn about the reinforcements resulting from executing every possible action in every possible state. This assumption could not be eliminated in Q-learning and SARSA, since both are iterative dynamic programming algorithms. However, under the assumption that the environment is finite-horizon Markov decision process with finite length episodes, estimating the optimal Q-function, Q^*, for Q-learning, can be simply computed recursively as:

$$Q^*(s_t, a_t) = \mathcal{R}(s_t, a_t, s_{t+1}) + \gamma \max_a Q^*(s_{t+1}, a)$$

$$= \max_a (\mathcal{R}(s_t, a_t, s_{t+1}) + \gamma \, Q^*(s_{t+1}, a)) = \max_{e \in \mathbf{E}} \left[\sum_{i=t}^{n-1} \gamma^i \mathcal{R}(s_i, a_i, s_{i+1}) \right] \quad (1)$$

Similarly, the estimate of the optimal Q-function for SARSA can be described as:

$$Q^*(s_t, a_t) = \mathcal{R}(s_t, a_t, s_{t+1}) + \gamma Q^*(s_{t+1}, a_{t+1}) = \sum_{i=t}^{n-1} \gamma^i \mathcal{R}(s_i, a_i, s_{i+1}) \quad (2)$$

where $\mathbf{E}$ is the set of all episodes, $\mathcal{R}(s_i, a_i, s_{i+1}) = r_{i+1}$ for $(t \leq i \leq n - 1)$, and $e \equiv s_t, a_t, r_{t+1}, s_{t+1}, a_{t+1}, \dots, s_{n-1}, a_{n-1}, r_n, s_n \in \mathbf{E}$. Equations (1) and (2) show that it is sufficient to consider the rewards collected from the set of all episodes, $\mathbf{E}$, only once to calculate estimate of the optimal Q-function, Q^*, which eliminates the need to visit every possible state infinitely many times.

Unlike Q-learning, our estimate of Q^*, can be computed online as well as offline. It can be computed online by accumulating estimate of Q^* during the exploration of the environment. On the other hand, it can be computed offline by first exploring the environment and collecting the set of all possible episodes, then computing estimate of Q^*.

3   Action Language $\mathcal{B_Q}$

This section develops the action language, $\mathcal{B_Q}$, that represents model-free reinforcement learning problems and extends the action language $\mathcal{B}$ [8].

3.1   Language Syntax

A fluent is a predicate, which may contain variables, that describes a property of the environment. Let $\mathcal{F}$ be a set of fluents and $\mathcal{A}$ be a set of action names that can contain variables. A fluent literal is either a fluent $f \in \mathcal{F}$ or $\neg f$, the negation of f. Conjunctive fluent formula is a conjunction of fluent literals of the form $l_1 \wedge \ldots \wedge l_n$, where $l_1, \ldots, l_n$ are fluent literals. Sometimes we abuse the notation and refer to a conjunctive fluent formula as a set of fluent literals ($\emptyset$ denotes $true$). An action theory, $\mathbf{T}$, in $\mathcal{B_Q}$ is a tuple of the form $\mathbf{T} = \langle S_0, \mathcal{D}, \gamma \rangle$, where S_0 is a proposition of the form (3), $\mathcal{D}$ is a set of propositions from (4-6), and $0 \leq \gamma < 1$ is a discount factor as follows:

$$\mathbf{initially}\{\psi_i | 1 \leq i \leq n\} \tag{3}$$

$$\mathbf{executable} \ a \ \mathbf{if} \ \psi \tag{4}$$

$$l \ \mathbf{if} \ \psi \tag{5}$$

$$a \ \mathbf{causes} \ \phi \ : \ r \ \mathbf{if} \ \psi \tag{6}$$

where l is a fluent literal, $\phi, \psi, \psi_1, \ldots, \psi_n$ are conjunctive fluent formulas, $a \in \mathcal{A}$ is an action, and r is a real number in $\mathbb{R}$. Proposition (3) represents the set of possible initial states. Proposition (4) states that an action a is executable in any state in which ψ holds, where each variable that appears in a also appears in ψ. *Indirect effect of action* is described by proposition (5), which says that l holds in every state in which ψ also holds. A proposition of the form (6) represents the conditional effects of an action a along with the rewards received in a state resulting from executing a. All variables that appear in ϕ also appear in a and ψ. Proposition (6) says that a causes ϕ to hold with reward r is received in a successor state to a state in which a is executed and ψ holds. An action theory is ground if it does not contain any variables.

Example 1. Consider an elevator of n-story building domain adapted from [4] that is represented by an action theory, $\mathbf{T} = \langle S_0, \mathcal{D}, \gamma \rangle$, in $\mathcal{B_Q}$, where S_0 is described by (7) (j is a particular value in $\{1, \ldots, n\}$ and $1 \leq i \leq k$ for $k \leq n$) and $\mathcal{D}$ is represented by (8)-(14).

$$\mathbf{initially} \{\{on(i), \neg opened, current(j)\}\} \quad (7)$$

$$up(N) \ \mathbf{causes} \ current(N), \neg on(N), opened \ : \ r \ \mathbf{if} \ on(N), \neg opened \quad (8)$$

$$down(N) \ \mathbf{causes} \ current(N), \neg on(N), opened \ : \ r \ \mathbf{if} \ on(N), \neg opened \quad (9)$$

$$close \ \mathbf{causes} \ \neg opened \ : \ r' \ \mathbf{if} \ opened \quad (10)$$

$$current(N) \ \mathbf{if} \ \neg current(M), N \neq M \quad (11)$$

$$\mathbf{executable} \ up(N) \ \mathbf{if} \ current(M), M < N \quad (12)$$

$$\mathbf{executable} \ down(N) \ \mathbf{if} \ current(M), M > N \quad (13)$$

$$\mathbf{executable} \ close \ \mathbf{if} \ \{\} \quad (14)$$

The actions in the elevator domain are $up(N)$ for move up to floor N, $down(N)$ for move down to floor N, and $close$ for closing the elevator door. In addition, r and r' are any suitable rewards. The predicates $current(N)$, $on(N)$, and $opened$ are fluents represent respectively that the elevator current floor is N, light of floor N is on, and elevator door is opened. The target is to get all floors serviced and $\neg on(N)$ is true for all N.

3.2   Semantics

We say a set of ground literals ϕ is consistent if it does not contain a pair of complementary literals. If a literal $l \in \phi$, then we say l holds in ϕ, and l does not hold in ϕ if $\neg l \in \phi$. A set of literals σ holds in ϕ if σ is contained in ϕ, otherwise, σ does not hold in ϕ. We say that a set of literals ϕ satisfies an indirect effect of action of the form (5), if l belongs to ϕ whenever ψ is contained in ϕ or ψ is not contained in ϕ. Let $\mathbf{T}$ be an action theory in $\mathcal{B}_{\mathcal{Q}}$ and ϕ be a set of literals. Then $\mathcal{C}_{\mathbf{T}}(\phi)$ is the smallest set of literals that contains ϕ and satisfies all indirect effects of actions propositions in $\mathbf{T}$. A state s is a complete and consistent set of literals that satisfies all the indirect effects of actions propositions in $\mathbf{T}$.

Definition 1. *Let* $\mathbf{T} = \langle S_0, \mathcal{D}, \gamma \rangle$ *be a ground action theory in* $\mathcal{B}_{\mathcal{Q}}$, *s be a state, a* **causes** ϕ : *r* **if** ψ *be a proposition in* $\mathcal{D}$. *Then,* $s' = \mathcal{C}_{\mathbf{T}}(\Phi(a, s))$ *is the state resulting from executing a in s, given that a is executable in s, where* $\Phi(a, s)$ *is defined as:*

- $l \in \Phi(a, s)$ *and* $\neg l \notin \Phi(a, s)$ *if* $l \in \phi$ *and* $\psi \subseteq s$.
- $\neg l \in \Phi(a, s)$ *and* $l \notin \Phi(a, s)$ *if* $\neg l \in \phi$ *and* $\psi \subseteq s$.
- *Otherwise,* $l \in \Phi(a, s)$ *iff* $l \in s$ *and* $\neg l \in \Phi(a, s)$ *iff* $\neg l \in s$.

where the reward received in s' is $\mathcal{R}(s, a, s') = r$.

An episode in $\mathbf{T} = \langle S_0, \mathcal{D}, \gamma \rangle$ is an expression of the form $e \equiv s_0, a_0, r_1, s_1, a_1, \dots,$ $s_{n-1}, a_{n-1}, r_n, s_n$, where for each $(0 \leq t \leq n - 1)$, $s_{t+1} = \mathcal{C}_{\mathbf{T}}(\Phi(a_t, s_t))$ and $\mathcal{R}(s_t, a_t, s_{t+1}) = r_{t+1}$.

Definition 2. *Let* $\mathbf{T} = \langle S_0, \mathcal{D}, \gamma \rangle$ *be a ground action theory and* $\mathbf{E}$ *be the set of all episodes in* $\mathbf{T}$. *Then, for* $(0 \leq t \leq n - 1)$, *where* $Q^*(s_n, a_n) = 0$, *the optimal Q-function,* Q^*, *for Q-learning and SARSA are respectively estimated by*

$$Q^*(s_t, a_t) = \max_{e \in \mathbf{E}} \sum_{i=t}^{n-1} \gamma^i \mathcal{R}(s_i, a_i, s_{i+1})$$
$$Q^*(s_t, a_t) = \sum_{i=t}^{n-1} \gamma^i \mathcal{R}(s_i, a_i, s_{i+1})$$

Considering SARSA, the optimal Q-function can be computed incrementally as follows. For any episode in $\mathbf{E}$, the optimal Q-value for the initial state-action pair is estimated by $Q^*(s_0, a_0) = \sum_{t=0}^{n-1} \gamma^t \mathcal{R}(s_t, a_t, s_{t+1})$ that is calculated online during the exploration of the environment. Then, for any state-action pair, (s_t, a_t), in the episode, $Q^*(s_t, a_t)$, is calculated from $Q^*(s_0, a_0)$ by

$$Q^*(s_t, a_t) = \frac{Q^*(s_0, a_0) - \sum_{i=1}^{t} \gamma^{i-1} \mathcal{R}(s_{i-1}, a_{i-1}, s_i)}{\gamma^t} \tag{15}$$

However, for Q-learning, Q^* can be computed incrementally as well by first computing Q^* incrementally using (15), then (16) is used as an update rule only once, where for $0 \le t \le n-1$,

$$Q^*(s_t, a_t) = \mathcal{R}(s_t, a_t, s_{t+1}) + \gamma \max_a Q^*(s_{t+1}, a) \tag{16}$$

Notice that, unlike [30], by using (15) and (16), Q-learning can be computed online during the exploration of the environment as well as offline.

4   Off- and On-Policy Model-Free Reinforcement Learning Using Answer Set Programming

We provide a translation from any action theory $\mathbf{T} = \langle S_0, \mathcal{D}, \gamma \rangle$, a representation of a model-free reinforcement learning problem into a normal logic program with answer set semantics $\Pi_{\mathbf{T}}$, where the rules in $\Pi_{\mathbf{T}}$ encode (1) the set of possible initial states S_0, (2) the transition function Φ, (3) the set of propositions in $\mathcal{D}$, (4) and the discount factor γ. The answer sets of $\Pi_{\mathbf{T}}$ correspond to episodes in $\mathbf{T}$, with associated estimated optimal Q-values. This translation follows some related translations described in [29,23,25].

We assume the environment is a finite-horizon Markov decision process, where the length of each episode is known and finite. We use the predicates; $holds(L, T)$ to represent a literal L holds at time moment T; $occ(A, T)$ for action A executes at time T; $reward(r, a, T)$ for reward received at time T after executing a is r; $Q(V, A, T)$ says the estimate of the optimal Q-value of the initial state-action pair, in a given episode, T steps from the initial state is V; and $factor(\gamma)$ for the discount factor. We use lower case letters to represent constants and upper case letters to represent variables.

Let $\Pi_{\mathbf{T}}$ be the normal logic program translation of $\mathbf{T} = \langle S_0, \mathcal{D}, \gamma \rangle$ that contains a set of rules described as follows. To simplify the presentation, given p is a predicate and $\psi = \{l_1, \ldots, l_n\}$ be a set of literals, we use $p(\psi)$ to denote $p(l_1), \ldots, p(l_n)$.

– For each action $a \in \mathcal{A}$, $\Pi_{\mathbf{T}}$ includes the set of facts

$$action(a) \leftarrow \tag{17}$$

– Literals describe states of the world are encoded by

$$literal(A) \leftarrow atom(A) \tag{18}$$
$$literal(\neg A) \leftarrow atom(A) \tag{19}$$

where $atom(A)$ is a set of facts that describe the properties of the world. To specify that A and $\neg A$ are contrary literals the following rules are added to $\Pi_{\mathbf{T}}$.

$$contrary(A, \neg A) \leftarrow atom(A) \tag{20}$$
$$contrary(\neg A, A) \leftarrow atom(A) \tag{21}$$

– The set of initial states, **initially**$\{\psi_i, 1 \leq i \leq n\}$, is encoded as follows. Let $s_1, s_2, \ldots, s_n$ be the set of initial states, where for $1 \leq i \leq n$, $s_i = \{l_1^i, \ldots, l_m^i\}$. Moreover, let $s = s_1 \cup s_2 \cup \ldots \cup s_n$, $s' = s_1 \cap s_2 \cap \ldots \cap s_n$, $\widehat{s} = s - s'$, and $s'' = \{l \mid l \in \widehat{s} \vee \neg l \in \widehat{s}\}$. Intuitively, for any literal l in $\widehat{s}$, if l or $\neg l$ belongs to $\widehat{s}$, then s'' contains only l. For each literal $l \in s'$, $\Pi_{\mathbf{T}}$ includes

$$holds(l, 0) \leftarrow \tag{22}$$

which says l holds at time 0. Literals in s' belong to every initial state. For each $l \in s''$, $\Pi_{\mathbf{T}}$ includes

$$holds(l, 0) \leftarrow not\ holds(\neg l, 0) \tag{23}$$
$$holds(\neg l, 0) \leftarrow not\ holds(l, 0) \tag{24}$$

which says that l (similarly $\neg l$) holds at time 0, if $\neg l$ (similarly l) does not hold at the time 0.

– Each proposition of the form (4) is encoded in $\Pi_{\mathbf{T}}$ as

$$exec(a, T) \leftarrow holds(\psi, T) \tag{25}$$

– Each a **causes** ϕ : r **if** ψ in $\mathcal{D}$ is encoded as

$$holds(l_i, T + 1) \leftarrow occ(a, T), exec(a, T), holds(\psi, T) \tag{26}$$

$\forall\, l_i \in \phi$ and $\phi = \{l_1, \ldots, l_m\}$, which says that if a occurs at time T and ψ holds at the same time moment, then l_i holds at time $T + 1$.

– The reward r received at time $T + 1$ after executing a at time T given that a is executable is encoded by

$$reward(r, a, T + 1) \leftarrow occ(a, T), exec(a, T) \tag{27}$$

– Estimate of the optimal Q-value of an initial state-action pair, in a given episode, $T + 1$ steps away from the initial state, is equal to the estimate of the optimal Q-value of the same initial state-action pair, in the same episode, T steps away from the initial state added to the discounted reward (by γ^T) received at time $T + 1$, where $V \in \mathbb{R}$ and $0 \leq \gamma < 1$.

$$Q(V + r * \gamma^T, a, T + 1) \leftarrow Q(V, a', T), factor(\gamma), reward(r, a, T + 1),$$
$$occ(a, T), exec(a, T), holds(\psi, T), holds(\phi, T + 1) \tag{28}$$

- The following rule says that L holds at the time moment $T+1$ if it holds at the time moment T and its contrary does not hold at the time moment $T+1$.

$$holds(L, T+1) \leftarrow holds(L, T), not\ holds(L', T+1), contrary(L, L') \quad (29)$$

- A literal L and its negation $\neg L$ cannot hold at the same time is encoded in Π_T by

$$\leftarrow holds(L, T), holds(\neg L, T) \quad (30)$$

- Rules that generate actions occurrences once at a time are encoded by

$$occ(AC^i, T) \leftarrow action(AC^i), not\ abocc(AC^i, T) \quad (31)$$
$$abocc(AC^i, T) \leftarrow action(AC^i), action(AC^j), occ(AC^j, T), AC^i \neq AC^j \quad (32)$$

Let $\mathcal{G} = g_1 \wedge \ldots \wedge g_m$ be a goal expression, then $\mathcal{G}$ is encoded in Π_T as

$$goal \leftarrow holds(g_1, T), \ldots, holds(g_m, T) \quad (33)$$

Estimates of the optimal Q-value of initial state-action pair, $Q^*(s_0, a_0)$, is represented in Π_T by $Q(V, A, T)$, for $0 \leq T \leq n$, where $Q(V, A, n)$ represents the estimate of $Q^*(s_0, a_0)$ at the end of episode of length n. These Q-values, $Q(V, A, T)$, can be computed online during the exploration of the environment as well as offline after the exploration of the environment. Moreover, the action generation rules (31) and (32) in our translation, choose actions greedily at random. However, other action selection strategies can be encoded instead.

Example 2. The normal logic program encoding, Π_T, of the elevator domain described in Example 1 is given as follows, where Π_T consists of the following rules, along with the rules (18), (19), (20), (21), (29), (30), (31), (32):

$$action(open(N)) \leftarrow \qquad action(down(N)) \leftarrow \qquad action(close) \leftarrow$$

for $1 \leq N \leq n$. The atoms $on(.)$, $current(.)$, and $opened$ describe properties of the world that for $1 \leq N \leq n$ are encoded as:

$$atom(on(N)) \leftarrow \qquad atom(current(N)) \leftarrow \qquad atom(opened) \leftarrow$$

The initial state is encoded as follows, where $1 \leq X \leq k$, for $k \leq n$ and for some j in $\{1, \ldots, n\}$.

$$holds(on(X), 0) \leftarrow \qquad holds(current(j), 0) \leftarrow \qquad holds(\neg opened, 0) \leftarrow$$

The executability conditions of actions, for $1 \leq N, M \leq n$, are encoded as

$$\begin{aligned} exec(up(N), T) &\leftarrow holds(current(M), T), M < N \\ exec(down(N), T) &\leftarrow holds(current(M), T), M > N \\ exec(close, T) &\leftarrow \end{aligned}$$

Effects, rewards, and the Q-value of the initial state-action pair resulting after executing the actions $up(N)$ and $down(N)$, for $1 \leq N \leq n$, are given by

$$holds(current(N), T + 1) \leftarrow occ(AC, T), exec(AC, T), holds(on(N), T),$$
$$holds(\neg opened, T)$$
$$holds(\neg on(N), T + 1) \leftarrow occ(AC, T), exec(AC, T), holds(on(N), T),$$
$$holds(\neg opened, T)$$
$$holds(opened, T + 1) \leftarrow occ(AC, T), exec(AC, T), holds(on(N), T),$$
$$holds(\neg opened, T)$$
$$reward(r, AC, T + 1) \leftarrow occ(AC, T), exec(AC, T)$$
$$Q(V + r * \gamma^T, AC, T + 1) \leftarrow Q(V, A, T), factor(\gamma), reward(r, AC, T + 1),$$
$$occ(AC, T), exec(AC, T), holds(\psi, T), holds(\phi, T + 1)$$

where $AC = \{up(N), down(N)\}$, $Q(0, AC, 0)$ is a fact, $\psi = \{on(N), \neg opened\}$, and $\phi = \{current(N), \neg on(N), opened\}$. Effects of the *close* action is given by

$$holds(\neg opened, T + 1) \leftarrow occ(close, T), exec(close, T),$$
$$holds(opened, T)$$

The reward received after executing *close* is given by

$$reward(r', close, T + 1) \leftarrow occ(close, T), exec(close, T)$$

Q-value of the initial state-action pair is given by the following rule, where $Q(0, close, 0)$ is a fact.

$$Q(V + r' * \gamma^T, close, T + 1) \leftarrow Q(V, A, T), factor(\gamma), reward(r', close, T + 1),$$
$$occ(close, T), exec(close, T), holds(opened, T), holds(\neg opened, T + 1)$$

The goal is encoded by the following rule for some $k \leq n$

$$goal \leftarrow holds(\neg on(1), T), \ldots, holds(\neg on(k), T)$$

5   Correctness

This section shows the correctness of our translation. We prove that the answer sets of the normal logic program translation of an action theory, $\mathbf{T}$ in $\mathcal{B}_Q$, correspond to episodes in $\mathbf{T} = \langle S_0, \mathcal{D}, \gamma \rangle$, associated with estimates of the optimal Q-values. Moreover, we show that the complexity of finding a policy for $\mathbf{T}$ in our approach is NP-complete. Let the domain of T be $\{0, \ldots, n\}$. Let Φ be a transition function associated with $\mathbf{T}$, s_0 is an initial state, and $a_0, \ldots, a_{n-1}$ be a set of actions in $\mathcal{A}$. An episode in $\mathbf{T}$ is state-action-reward-state sequence of the form $e \equiv s_0, a_0, r_1, s_1, a_1, r_2, \ldots, s_{n-1}, a_{n-1}, r_n, s_n$, such that $\forall (0 \leq i \leq n-1)$, s_i, s_{i+1} are states, a_i is an action, $s_{i+1} = \mathcal{C}_\mathbf{T}(\Phi(a_i, s_i))$, and $\mathcal{R}(s_i, a_i, s_{i+1}) = r_{i+1}$.

Theorem 1. *Let $\mathbf{T}$ be an action theory representing a model-free reinforcement learning problem in $\mathcal{B}_Q$. Then, $s_0, a_0, r_1, s_1, a_1, r_2, \ldots, s_{n-1}, a_{n-1}, r_n, s_n$ is an episode in T iff $occ(a_0, 0), reward(r_1, a_0, 1), \ldots, occ(a_{n-1}, n - 1), reward(r_n, a_{n-1}, n)$ is true in an answer set of $\Pi_\mathbf{T}$.*

482   E. Saad

Theorem 1 says that an action theory, **T**, in $\mathcal{B}_Q$, can be translated into a normal logic program, $\Pi_\mathbf{T}$, such that an answer set of $\Pi_\mathbf{T}$ is equivalent to an episode in **T**.

Theorem 2. *Let* **T** *be an action theory in* $\mathcal{B}_Q$, S *be an answer set of* $\Pi_\mathbf{T}$, *and* **E** *be the set of all episodes in* **T**. *Let* $\mathcal{OCC}$ *be a set such that* $s_0, a_0, r_1, s_1, a_1, r_2, \ldots,$ $s_{n-1}, a_{n-1}, r_n, s_n \in \mathbf{E}$ *iff* $occ(a_0, 0), reward(r_1, a_0, 1), \ldots, occ(a_{n-1}, n-1)$, *reward* $(r_n, a_{n-1}, n) \equiv o \in \mathcal{OCC}$. *Then, the estimate of* $Q^*(s_0, a_0)$ *is given for Q-learning and SARSA respectively by*

$$Q^*(s_0, a_0) = \max_{S \models Q(v, a_{n-1}, n) \wedge S \models o \in \mathcal{OCC}} v$$

$$Q^*(s_0, a_0) = v, \text{ for some } S \models Q(v, a_{n-1}, n) \wedge S \models o \in \mathcal{OCC}$$

Theorem 2 asserts that, given an action theory **T** and by considering Q-learning update rule, the expected sum of discounted rewards resulting after executing an action a_0 in a state s_0 and following the optimal policy thereafter, $Q^*(s_0, a_0)$, is equal to the maximum over v, appearing in $Q(v, a_{n-1}, n)$ which is satisfied by every answer set S of $\Pi_\mathbf{T}$ for which $o \equiv occ(a_0, 0), reward(r_1, a_0, 1), \ldots, occ(a_{n-1}, n-1), reward(r_n, a_{n-1}, n)$ is also satisfied. However, by considering the update rule of SARSA, $Q^*(s_0, a_0)$ is equal to v in $Q(v, a_{n-1}, n)$ that is satisfied by some answer set of $\Pi_\mathbf{T}$ for which o is also satisfied. For any a_t and s_t in SARSA, $Q^*(s_t, a_t)$ is calculated from $Q^*(s_0, a_0)$ by (15), where $Q^*(s_n, a_n) = 0$ and $\mathcal{R}(s_{i-1}, a_{i-1}, s_i) = r_i$. But, for Q-learning, for any a_t and s_t, $Q^*(s_t, a_t)$ is calculated from $Q^*(s_0, a_0)$ by (15), then (16) is used as an update rule only once.

In addition, we show that any model-free reinforcement learning problem in MDP environment can be encoded as SAT problem. Hence, state-of-the-art SAT solvers can be used to solve model-free reinforcement learning problems. Any normal logic program, Π, can be translated into a SAT problem, $\mathcal{S}$, where the models of $\mathcal{S}$ are equivalent to the answer sets of Π [16]. Hence, the normal logic program encoding of a model-free reinforcement learning problem **T** can be translated into an equivalent SAT problem, where the models of $\mathcal{S}$ correspond to episodes in **T**.

Theorem 3. *Let* **T** *be an action theory in* $\mathcal{B}_Q$ *and* $\Pi_\mathbf{T}$ *be the normal logic program encoding of* **T**. *Then, the models of the SAT encoding of* $\Pi_\mathbf{T}$ *are equivalent to valid episodes in* **T**.

Normal logic programs with answer set semantics find optimal policies for model-free reinforcement learning in finite horizon MDP environments using the flat representation of the problem domains. Hence, Theorem 5 follows directly from Theorem 4 [17].

Theorem 4. *The stationary policy existence problem for finite-horizon MDP in the flat representation is NP-complete.*

Theorem 5. *The policy existence problem for a model-free reinforcement learning problem in MDP environment using normal logic programs with answer set semantics and SAT is NP-complete.*

6   Conclusions and Related Work

The translation from an action theory in $\mathcal{B}_Q$ into a normal logic program builds on similar translations described in [29,23,25]. The literature is rich with action languages that are capable of representing and reasoning about MDPs and actions with probabilistic effects, which include [1,2,5,11,15]. The main difference between these languages and $\mathcal{B}_Q$ is that $\mathcal{B}_Q$ allows the factored characterization of MDP for model-free reinforcement learning.

A logic based approach for solving MDP, for probabilistic planning, has been presented in [18]. The approach of [18] converts MDP specification of a probabilistic planing problem into a stochastic satisfiability problem and solving the stochastic satisfiability problem instead. First-order logic representation of MDP for model-based reinforcement learning has been described in [14] based on first-order logic programs without nonmonotonic negations. Similar to the first-order representation of MDP in [14], $\mathcal{B}_Q$ allows objects and relations. However, unlike $\mathcal{B}_Q$, [14] finds policies in the abstract level. A more expressive first-order representation of MDP than [14] has been presented in [3,28] that is a probabilistic extension to Reiter's situation calculus. Although more expressive, it is more complex than [14]. Unlike the logical model-based reinforcement learning framework of [25] that uses normal hybrid probabilistic logic programs to encode model-based reinforcement learning problems, normal logic program with answer set semantics is used to encode model-free reinforcement learning problems.

References

1. Baral, C., Tran, N., Tuan, L.C.: Reasoning about actions in a probabilistic setting. In: AAAI (2002)
2. Boutilier, C., Dean, T., Hanks, S.: Decision-theoretic planning: structural assumptions and computational leverage. Journal of AI Research 11, 1–94 (1999)
3. Boutilier, C., Reiter, R., Price, B.: Symbolic dynamic programming for first-order MDPs. In: 17th IJCAI (2001)
4. Crites, R., Barto, A.: Improving elevator performance using reinforcement learning. In: Advances in Neural Information Processing (1996)
5. Eiter, T., Lukasiewicz, T.: Probabilistic reasoning about actions in nonmonotonic causal theories. In: 19th UAI (2003)
6. Ernst, M., Millstein, T., Weld, D.: Automatic SAT-compilation of planning problems. In: IJCAI (1997)
7. Gelfond, M., Lifschitz, V.: The stable model semantics for logic programming. In: ICSLP. MIT Press, Cambridge (1988)
8. Gelfond, M., Lifschitz, V.: Action languages. Electronic Transactions on AI 3(16), 193–210 (1998)
9. Giunchiglia, E., Lierler, Y., Maratea, M.: Answer set programming based on propositional satisfiability. Journal of Automated Reasoning 36(4), 345–377 (2006)
10. Castellini, C., Giunchiglia, E., Tacchella, A.: SAT-based planning in complex domains: Concurrency, constraints and nondeterminism. AIJ 147(1-2), 85–117 (2003)
11. Iocchi, L., Lukasiewicz, T., Nardi, D., Rosati, R.: Reasoning about actions with sensing under qualitative and probabilistic uncertainty. In: 16th ECAI (2004)

484   E. Saad

12. Kaelbling, L., Littman, M., Moore, A.: Reinforcement learning: A survey. JAIR 4, 237–285 (1996)
13. Kautz, H., Selman, B.: Pushing the envelope: planning, propositional logic, and stochastic search. In: 13th AAAI (1996)
14. Kersting, K., De Raedt, L.: Logical Markov decision programs and the convergence of logical TD(λ). In: 14th ILP (2004)
15. Kushmerick, N., Hanks, S., Weld, D.: An algorithm for probabilistic planning. Artificial Intelligence 76(1-2), 239–286 (1995)
16. Lin, F., Zhao, Y.: ASSAT: Computing answer sets of a logic program by SAT solvers. Artificial Intelligence 157(1-2), 115–137 (2004)
17. Littman, M., Goldsmith, J., Mundhenk, M.: The computational complexity of probabilistic planning. Journal of Artificial Intelligence Research 9, 1–36 (1998)
18. Majercik, S., Littman, M.: MAXPLAN: A new approach to probabilistic planning. In: 4th ICAPS, pp. 86–93 (1998)
19. Majercik, S., Littman, M.: Contingent planning under uncertainty via stochastic satisfiability. Artificial Intelligence 147(1-2), 119–162 (2003)
20. Rummery, G., Niranjan, M.: Online Q-learning using connectionist systems. Technical report, CUED/F-INFENG/TR166, Cambridge University (1994)
21. Saad, E., Pontelli, E.: Towards a more practical hybrid probabilistic logic programming framework. In: Hermenegildo, M.V., Cabeza, D. (eds.) PADL 2004. LNCS, vol. 3350, pp. 67–82. Springer, Heidelberg (2005)
22. Saad, E., Pontelli, E.: A new approach to hybrid probabilistic logic programs. Annals of Mathematics and Artificial Intelligence Journal 48(3-4), 187–243 (2006)
23. Saad, E.: Probabilistic planning in hybrid probabilistic logic programs. In: 1st Scalable Uncertainty Management (2007)
24. Saad, E.: Probabilistic planning with imperfect sensing actions using hybrid probabilistic logic programs. In: 3rd Scalable Uncertainty Management (2009)
25. Saad, E.: A logical framework to reinforcement learning using hybrid probabilistic logic programs. In: Greco, S., Lukasiewicz, T. (eds.) SUM 2008. LNCS (LNAI), vol. 5291, pp. 341–355. Springer, Heidelberg (2008)
26. Saad, E.: On the relationship between hybrid probabilistic logic programs and stochastic satisfiability. In: Greco, S., Lukasiewicz, T. (eds.) SUM 2008. LNCS (LNAI), vol. 5291, pp. 356–371. Springer, Heidelberg (2008)
27. Saad, E.: Probabilistic reasoning by SAT solvers. In: Sossai, C., Chemello, G. (eds.) ECSQARU 2009. LNCS, vol. 5590, pp. 663–675. Springer, Heidelberg (2009)
28. Sanner, S., Boutilier, G.: Pratical solution techniques for first-order MDPs. AI 173(5-6), 748–788 (2009)
29. Son, T., Baral, C., Nam, T., McIlraith, S.: Domain-dependent knowledge in answer set planning. ACM Transactions on Computational Logic 7(4), 613–657 (2006)
30. Watkins, C.: Learning from delayed rewards. Ph.D. dissertation, University of Cambridge (1989)

Answer Set Programming for Computing Decisions Under Uncertainty

Roberto Confalonieri[1] and Henri Prade[2]

[1] Universitat Politècnica de Catalunya
Dept. Llenguatges i Sistemes Informàtics
C/ Jordi Girona Salgado 1-3
E - 08034 Barcelona
confalonieri@lsi.upc.edu
[2] Institut de Recherche en Informatique Toulouse (IRIT)
Universitè Paul Sabatier
118 Route de Narbonne
31062 Toulouse Cedex 9, France
prade@irit.fr

Abstract. Possibility theory offers a qualitative framework for modeling decision under uncertainty. In this setting, pessimistic and optimistic decision criteria have been formally justified. The computation by means of possibilistic logic inference of optimal decisions according to such criteria has been proposed. This paper presents an Answer Set Programming (ASP)-based methodology for modeling decision problems and computing optimal decisions in the sense of the possibilistic criteria. This is achieved by applying both a classic and a possibilistic ASP-based methodology in order to handle both a knowledge base pervaded with uncertainty and a prioritized preference base.

1 Introduction

Existing Answer Set Programming (ASP)-based methodologies for handling decision making problems [2,14] amount to compile a decision problem as a logic program able to generate the space of possible decision solutions and to specify an order between them by means of an ordered disjunction connective [4]. Although such approaches are enough to cover decisions in completely certain environment, they become less effective when the knowledge is pervaded with uncertainty. Moreover the existing methods consider empirical decision rules.

The decision under uncertainty problem with qualitative preferences and uncertainty has been studied in the setting of possibility theory assuming a commensurateness hypothesis between the level of certainty and the preferences priority. As in classical utility theory, pessimistic and optimistic criteria have been proposed and justified on the basis of postulates [12]. This approach has been adapted in the setting of possibilistic propositional logic where the available knowledge is described by formulas which are more or less certainly true, and the goals are described in a separate prioritized propositional base.

W. Liu (Ed.): ECSQARU 2011, LNAI 6717, pp. 485–496, 2011.

This paper intends to propose a counterpart of the possibilistic logic-based decision setting within two ASP-based frameworks: Logic Programs with Ordered Disjunction (LPODs) [4] and its possibilistic extension, Logic Programs with Possibilistic Ordered Disjunction (LPPODs) [6]. The motivation behind this work is twofold. First, it is interesting to bridge ASP with qualitative decision making under uncertainty, since to the best of our knowledge any proposal has been made in this respect. Secondly, the use of ASP allows to compute optimal decision in a practical way. Hence, although we do not address implementation issues here, our approach can be implemented on top of two existing ASP-based solvers, *psmodels*[1] and *posPsmodels*[2] which provide a computation of the LPODs and LPPODs semantics.

The paper is structured as follows. After presenting some background concepts about qualitative decision in the possibilistic setting (Section 2), we address the decision problem in ASP by means of LPODs when there is no uncertainty and no priority between the goals (Section 3). Then, we extend this result to the general case with uncertainty and prioritized preferences using LPPODs (Section 4). We compare the proposed approach to previous works in Section 5. Finally, Section 6 concludes the paper.

2   Qualitative Decision in Stratified Propositional Bases

The logical view of a decision problem can be stated in the following way. Let K be the knowledge base describing what is known about the world, D be the set of decision literals, and P another base describing goals delimiting preferred states of the world. Then, a decision, defined as a conjunction d of decision literals such that $K \wedge d \vdash P$ (with $K \wedge d$ consistent) is for sure a good decision (if it exists) since it makes certain that all the goals are satisfied. Looking only for such a decision corresponds to a cautious, pessimistic, attitude. A much more optimistic attitude would correspond to consider also potential decisions d such that $K \wedge d \wedge P \neq \perp$ (which expresses that the possibility of satisfying all the goals remains open).

These two points of view can be extended to the case where K and P are possibilistic logic bases [8], *i.e.* when uncertainty and preferences are matters of degrees. Then K is a set of more or less certain pieces of knowledge and P is a set of goals with associated levels of priority. The certainty and priority levels are supposed to belong to the same linearly ordered scale S made of $n + 1$ levels $\alpha_1 = 1 > \alpha_2 > \ldots > \alpha_n > \alpha_{n+1} = 0$. Two sets of postulates for qualitative decision have been proposed that turn to be respectively equivalent to the maximization of a pessimistic criterion and of an optimistic one [12,11]. These two criteria are respectively estimating the necessity and the possibility that a sufficiently satisfactory state is reached (in the sense of qualitative possibility theory). The exact counterpart of these two criteria, when the knowledge and the preferences are expressed under the form of two possibilistic knowledge bases,

---

[1] http://www.tcs.hut.fi/Software/smodels/priority/

[2] https://github.com/rconfalonieri/posPsmodels

have been defined in [13,10]. Given n as an order reversing map of scale $\mathcal{S}$ such that $n(\alpha_i) = \alpha_{n+2-i}$ $(1 \leq i \leq n+1)$, K_α as the set of formulas in K having certainty at least equal to α without their certainty levels, and P_β as the set of goals having a priority strictly greater than β without their priority levels, the following criteria are defined [13,10]:

Definition 1. *The pessimistic utility $u_*(d)$ of a decision d is the maximal value of $\alpha \in [0,1]$ such that $K_\alpha \wedge d \vdash P_{n(\alpha)}$.*

The optimistic utility $u^*(d)$ of a decision d is the maximal value of $n(\alpha) \in [0,1]$ such that $K_{\underline{\alpha}} \wedge d \wedge P_{\underline{\alpha}} \neq \bot$.

with the convention $\max \emptyset = \mathbf{0}$. The intuition below $u_*(d)$ is that we are interested in finding a decision d (if it exists) such that $K_\alpha \wedge d \vdash P_\beta$ with α high and β low, *i.e.* such that the decision d together with the most certain part of K entails the satisfaction of the goals, even those with low priority. Taking $\beta = n(\alpha)$ requires that the certainty and priority scales be commensurate. The optimistic utility can be understood in a similar way.

The computation of pessimistic and optimistic decisions has been explored in [13], in the context of possibilistic logic, and later on in [10] by proposing an Assumption Truth Maintenance System (ATMS)-based computation procedure.

An alternative way to compute the pessimistic criteria is to apply possibilistic logic resolution rule. In fact, it has been proved that:

Lemma 1. *[8] Let $K = \{(\phi_i, \alpha_i) \mid 1 \leq i \leq n\}$ be a possibilistic knowledge base, $K_\alpha = \{\phi_i \in K \mid \alpha_i \geq \alpha\}$, (p, β) be a possibilistic formula, and d a literal. Then $K_\alpha \wedge d \vdash_c p$ if and only if $\exists \alpha$ s.t. $K \wedge (d,1) \vdash_p (p,\alpha)$ and $\alpha \geq \beta$, where $\vdash_c$ and $\vdash_p$ are the classical and possibilistic logic inference respectively.*

The aim of this paper is to characterize the qualitative decision making problem under uncertainty in the setting of ASP. Along the paper we will use a running example taking from [13] to exemplify our approach.

Example 1. An agent is supposed i) to know that *if I have an umbrella then I will be not wet*; *if it rains and I do not have an umbrella, then I will be wet*; and *typically if it is cloudy it will rain* (this rule is uncertain) ii) it is known that the sky is cloudy, and iii) being not wet is more important than not carrying an umbrella. The problem then is to decide whether or not to take an umbrella.

3   Making Decision in ASP

In this section we translate a decision problem into a problem tractable by an ASP-based computation. Since the similarity between decision making and abduction is striking [16], it is natural to encode a decision problem by means of LPODs [4] which have been used by Brewka to model abduction [3].

3.1 LPODs and Abduction

In this section we recall the basic notions underlying LPODs [4], and its use in modeling an abduction problem [3]. In the following we assume that the reader has some knowledge about *answer set semantics* (for details see [1]).

Let us consider a propositional language $\mathcal{L}$, with atomic symbols called atoms. A literal is an atom or a negated atom (by classical negation $\neg$). LPODs are sets of rules using ordered disjunction $\times$ in the head of rules to express preferences among literals in the head. An LPOD P is a finite set of ordered disjunction rules of the form $c_1 \times \ldots \times c_k \leftarrow \mathcal{B}^+ \wedge not\ \mathcal{B}^-$, where $\mathcal{B}^+ = \{b_1, \ldots, b_m\}$ and $\mathcal{B}^- = \{b_{m+1}, \ldots, b_{m+n}\}$, and the c_i's $(1 \leq i \leq k)$ and b_j's $(1 \leq j \leq m+n)$ are literals. An ordered disjunction rule (rule for short) r says that if body is satisfied then some c_i must be in the answer set, most preferably c_1, or c_2 if c_1 is impossible, *etc.* If $\forall r \in P$, $k = 1$, then P is an *extended normal program* (*i.e.* $\times$-free); if $k = 1$ and $n = 0$, then P is an *extended definite logic program* (*i.e.* $\times$- and *not*-free). Rules with empty bodies are also known as *facts* (as usual we omit $\leftarrow$) and rules with empty heads are special rules also called *constraints*.

An answer set of an LPOD P is defined as any consistent set of literals M (a and $\neg a$ do not belong to the same set) such that M is a minimal model of the reduced program $P_\times^M$ and that satisfies each rule of P (with $P_\times^M = \bigcup_{r \in P} r_\times^M$ where $r_\times^M = \{c_i \leftarrow \mathcal{B}^+ \mid c_i \in M \wedge M \cap (\{c_1, \ldots, c_{i-1}\} \cup \mathcal{B}^-) = \emptyset\}$). An answer set M can satisfy rules like r to different degrees, where smaller degrees are better. Intuitively, if the body of r is satisfied, then the satisfaction degree is the smallest index i such that $c_i \in M$ (where c_i is in the head of r). Otherwise, the rule is irrelevant and it does not count. Thus, based on the satisfaction degrees of single rules a global preference ordering on answer sets is defined. The comparison criterion between two answer sets M_1 and M_2 is Pareto-based: M_1 is preferred to M_2 ($M_1 \succ M_2$) if and only if there is a rule satisfied better in M_1 than in M_2, and no rule is satisfied better in M_2 than in M_1.

Example 2. Let an LPOD P consist of rules $\{r_1 = a \times b \leftarrow not\ c, r_2 = b \times c \leftarrow not\ d\}$. Then P has three answer sets $M_1 = \{a, b\}$, $M_2 = \{c\}$, $M_3 = \{b\}$ with $M_1 \succ M_2$, $M_1 \succ M_3$, while $M_2 \not\succ M_3$ and $M_3 \not\succ M_2$.

Abduction is the process of generating explanations for a set of observations. An abduction problem usually consists of a set of formulas H of possible explanations, a set of formulas K representing background knowledge, and a set of formulas O describing the observations to be explained. Then, an explanation is a minimal subset H' of H such that $H' \cup K$ is consistent and $H' \cup K \models O$. Brewka [3] has proposed an encoding for the abduction based on LPODs and the credulous inference relation $\models_c$ under answer set semantics.

Definition 2. *Given an LPOD P and a set of literals S, $P \models_c S$ holds, if $\exists M \in SEM_{LPOD}(P)$ such that $S \subseteq M$, where $SEM_{LPOD}(P)$ is the mapping which assigns to P the set of all answer sets of P.*

Example 3. Let P be the LPOD in Example 2. Therefore the following consequences are valid $P \models_c \{a\}$, $P \models_c \{b\}$, $P \models_c \{a, b\}$, $P \models_c \{c\}$.

3.2   Fully Certain Knowledge and All-or-Nothing Preferences

We propose to translate a decision problem into a problem encoded by an LPOD. In the following we restrict preferences to literals for space reason, even if $\models_c$ could be extended to any propositional formula [5].

Definition 3. *A decision making problem DM is represented as a tuple $\langle K, D, Pref \rangle$ where K is an extended definite logic program[3], $D = \{d_1, \ldots, d_m\}$ is a set of decision literals, and $Pref = \{p_1, \ldots, p_n\}$ is a set of preference literals.*

Example 4. Let us consider the decision problem in Example 1 without any uncertainty and keeping all the goals as equally important. Then, $K = \{r_1 = \neg w \leftarrow u, r_2 = w \leftarrow r \wedge \neg u, r_3 = r \leftarrow c, r_4 = c\}$, $D = \{u, \neg u\}$, and $Pref = \{\neg w, \neg u\}$.[4]

As in the case of the logical view of the decision problem, we can define optimal decisions according to the pessimistic criteria (the optimistic case could be handled in a similar way). When K expresses completely certain knowledge and *Pref* are all-or-nothing, optimal decisions, according to a pessimistic point of view, are decisions that, in conjunction with the knowledge, lead to the satisfaction of all the preferences:

Definition 4. *Given a $DM = \langle K, D, Pref \rangle$, an optimal pessimistic decision is a minimal set of decision literals $\Delta \subseteq D$ such that $K \cup \Delta \models_c Pref$. This set is called the label of Pref and it is denoted by $label_K(Pref)$.*

3.3   Computation of Optimal Pessimistic Decisions

The computation of an optimal pessimistic decision is shown in Algorithm 1. The basic *DM* translation is performed according to Definition 5 where the main construction is borrowed from [3].

Definition 5. *Given a $DM = \langle K, D, Pref \rangle$, a decision Δ for DM is computed by an LPOD $P_{dm}(\langle K, D, Pref \rangle) = P_K \cup \{\leftarrow not\ p \mid p \in Pref\} \cup \{\neg ass(d) \times ass(d) \mid d \in D\} \cup \{d \leftarrow ass(d) \mid d \in D\}$, where $ass(d)$ reads d is assumed.*

The generated LPOD P_{dm} can be explained as follows: the use of ordered disjunction rules generates all the possible combinations of decisions, while the use of constraints eliminates the answer sets where preferences are not satisfied. As such, once the answer sets of P_{dm} are computed ($SEM_{LPOD}(P_{dm})$), the optimal set of decisions (`getDecisionLiterals(D,M)`) which are minimal ($label_K(Pref)$) belongs to the most preferred answer set only (`maxPreferredAS` $(SEM_{LPOD}(P_{dm}))$).

---

[3] In the following we assume that rules in K are strict rules. In the case of default rules, rules' exceptions have to be properly handled. For this purpose the rewriting procedure proposed in [7] can be employed.

[4] We leave $\neg$ negated atoms explicit, although in ASP it is common to replace them with new atoms symbols not belonging to the signature of the program [1].

Algorithm 1. computePessimisticDecisions(DM) : $\langle label_K(Pref), u_* \rangle$

Input: $\Big\{ A\ DM = \langle K, D, Pref \rangle$

Output: $\begin{cases} label_K(Pref) : \text{optimal decisions} \\ u_* : \text{pessimistic utility} \end{cases}$

$label_K(Pref) \leftarrow \emptyset;\ u_* \leftarrow \mathbf{0};$

$P_{dm} \leftarrow decisionMakingToLPOD(DM)$

if $(SEM_{LPOD}(P_{dm}) \neq \emptyset)$ **then**

$\quad M \leftarrow maxPreferredAS(SEM_{LPOD}(P_{dm}))$

$\quad label_K(Pref) \leftarrow getDecisionLiterals(D, M)$

$\quad u_* \leftarrow 1$

end if

return $\langle label_K(Pref), u_* \rangle$

Proposition 1. *Let* $DM = \langle K, D, Pref \rangle$ *be a decision making problem and let* P_{dm} *be the LPOD generated by Algorithm 1. Then,* $\Delta \in label_K(Pref)$ *is an optimal pessimistic decision iff there is a consistent maximally preferred answer set* M *of* P_{dm} *such that* $\Delta = \{d \in D \mid ass(d) \in M\}$.

Example 5. Let us consider the DM in Example 4 and its computation with Algorithm 1. LPOD $P_{dm} = \{r_1 = \neg w \leftarrow u, r_2 = w \leftarrow r \wedge \neg u, r_3 = r \leftarrow c, r_4 = c, r_5 = \neg ass(u) \times ass(u), r_6 = \neg ass(\neg u) \times ass(\neg u), r_7 = u \leftarrow ass(u), r_8 = \neg u \leftarrow ass(\neg u), r_9 = \leftarrow not\ \neg w, r_{10} = \leftarrow not\ \neg u\}$. By LPOD semantics, in this case, there is not any answer set which can satisfy all the preferences. As such, the set of best decisions is empty and $u_* = \mathbf{0}$.

Similarly to what happens in possibilistic logic, this criterion can be extended to the case where K is a possibilistic logic program and $Pref$ is a set of possibilistic literals, *i.e.* when uncertainty and preferences are matters of degrees.

4   Making Decision Under Uncertainty in ASP

To be able to capture uncertain knowledge and graded preferences we first introduce LPPODs [6], the possibilistic extension of LPODs.

4.1   Basic Definitions of LPPODs

LPPODs are a recently defined logic programming framework based on LPODs and possibilistic logic [6]. An LPPOD is a finite set of possibilistic ordered disjunction rules of the form $r = \alpha : c_1 \times \ldots \times c_k \leftarrow \mathcal{B}^+ \wedge\ not\ \mathcal{B}^-$, where $\alpha \in \mathcal{S}$ and $c_1 \times \ldots \times c_k \leftarrow \mathcal{B}^+ \wedge\ not\ \mathcal{B}^-$ is an ordered disjunction rule as defined in Section 3.1. $N(r) = \alpha$ is the necessity degree representing the certainty level of the information described by r. A *possibilistic definite program* is defined in a similar way as in Section 3.1. Rules with empty bodies are known as *possibilistic facts* and rules with empty heads are called *possibilistic constraints*.

A *possibilistic literal* is a pair $p = (l, \beta) \in \mathcal{L} \times \mathcal{S}$ where $\mathcal{L}$ is a set of literals and $\mathcal{S}$ a linearly ordered scale. $N(p) = \beta$, while the projection $*$ for a possibilistic literal p is defined as $p^* = l$. Given a set of possibilistic literals M, the projection of $*$ over M is defined as $M^* = \{p^* \mid p \in M\}$. The projection $*$ for a possibilistic ordered disjunction rule r, is $r^* = c_1 \times \ldots \times c_k \leftarrow \mathcal{B}^+ \wedge \ not\ \mathcal{B}^-$ and the projection of $*$ over P is defined as $P^* = \{r^* \mid r \in P\}$. Notice that P^* is an LPOD.

The LPPODs semantics is defined in terms of a possibilistic counterpart of the program reduction $P_\times^{M^*}$ (which reduces an LPPOD to a possibilistic definite program, see [6]) and of a possibilistic consequence operator ΠT_P (which characterizes the possibilistic stable semantics for possibilistic definite programs in terms of a possibilistic minimal model ΠCn, see [15]). Due to lack of space, the complete definitions of $P_\times^{M^*}$ and ΠT_P are omitted and we refer to [6,15]. However, it is worthy to point out that the ΠT_P captures the possibilistic *modus ponens* of possibilistic logic [8]. In [6] it is also shown how LPPODs are a proper generalization of LPODs, thus rule satisfaction degrees and the Pareto-based comparison criterion between possibilistic answer sets are properly generalized as well. As such, this criterion can be used to compare possibilistic answer sets.

Definition 6. [6] *Let P be an LPPOD, M be a set of possibilistic literals such that M^* is an answer set of P^*. M is a possibilistic answer set of P if and only if $M = \Pi Cn(P_\times^{M^*})$. $SEM_{LPPOD}(P)$ is the mapping which assigns to P the set of all possibilistic answer sets of P.*

Example 6. Let an LPPOD P consist of rules $\{r_1 = \mathbf{1} : a \times b \leftarrow c, r_2 = \alpha : c\}$, where $\mathbf{0} < \alpha < \mathbf{1}$. P has two possibilistic answer sets $M_1 = \{(a, \alpha), (c, \alpha)\}$, $M_2 = \{(b, \alpha), (c, \alpha)\}$ with $M_1 \succ M_2$.

Based on the above definitions we generalize the notion of $\models_c$ to deal with sets of possibilistic literals as:

Definition 7. *Given an LPPOD P and a set of possibilistic literals S, $P \models_p S$ holds, if $\exists M \in SEM_{LPPOD}(P)$ such that $S \sqsubseteq M$ where the relation between sets of possibilistic literals $\sqsubseteq$ is defined as:*
$$S \sqsubseteq M \iff S^* \subseteq M^* \wedge \forall \varphi, \alpha, \beta, (\varphi, \alpha) \in S \wedge (\varphi, \beta) \in M \text{ then } \alpha \leq \beta.$$

4.2   Uncertain Knowledge and Prioritized Preferences

Definitions in Section 3.2 are extended in the following way.

Definition 8. *A decision making problem under uncertainty DMU is represented as a tuple $\langle K, D, Pref \rangle$ where, K is a possibilistic definite logic program, D is a set of decision literals, and $Pref = \{((p_1, \beta_1) \ldots, (p_n, \beta_n)\}$ is a set of possibilistic literals, where $\beta_i \in \mathcal{S}$ is the priority of preference p_i.*

Let K_α denote the α-cut of K as $K_\alpha = \{r^* \in K \mid N(r) \geq \alpha\}$, and let $Pref_\beta$ be the β-cut of $Pref$ as $Pref_\beta = \{(p_i, \beta_i)^* \in Pref \mid \beta_i \geq \beta\}$. We also use the notations $K_{\underline{\alpha}}$ and $Pref_{\underline{\beta}}$ (with $\alpha < \mathbf{1}$ and $\beta < \mathbf{1}$, $\mathbf{1}$ being the top element of the scale) for denoting the set of rules and the set of preferences with certainty and priority strictly greater than α and β respectively. In particular $K_{\underline{0}} = K^*$ and $P_{\underline{0}} = Pref^*$ (**0** being the bottom element of the scale) where K^* and $Pref^*$ denote the set of rules K and the set of preferences $Pref$ without their certainty and priority levels respectively.

Example 7. Let us consider the decision problem in Example 1 with uncertainty levels and prioritized goals. Then, $K = \{r_1 = 1 : \neg w \leftarrow u, r_2 = 1 : w \leftarrow r \wedge \neg u, r_3 = \lambda : r \leftarrow c, r_4 = 1 : c\}$, $D = \{u, \neg u\}$, and $Pref = \{(\neg w, 1), (\neg u, \delta)\}$, where $0 < \lambda < 1$ and $0 < \delta < 1$.

Definition 9. *Given a DMU $= \langle K, D, Pref \rangle$, an optimal pessimistic decision is a set of decision literals $\Delta \subseteq D$ that maximizes α such that $K_\alpha \cup \Delta \models_c Pref_{\underline{n(\alpha)}}$. This set is called the label of $Pref_{\underline{n(\alpha)}}$ and it is denoted by $label_{K_\alpha}(Pref_{\underline{n(\alpha)}})$.*

The above definition expresses the fact that an optimal pessimistic decision belongs to an answer set computed with the most certain part of K and that selected preferences, even those with low priority, are satisfied.

4.3   Classical ASP-Based Computation

We are now able to describe an algorithm for the pessimistic case. The algorithm is based on successive computations of labels of formulas of $Pref$ which can be computed on the basis of Algorithm 1.

The behavior of Algorithm 2 can be described as follows. First, only the entire knowledge base and highest labelled preferences are considered. If such label is not empty, then we increase our expectations trying to prove less preferred preferences by means of less knowledge. The procedure stops when a set of preferences cannot be proved.

Example 8. As seen in Example 7, K and $Pref$ contain two layers (both scales are commensurate). First of all, according to function $Inc(\alpha)$, α is incremented to the lowest non-nul value, *i.e.* $\alpha = \min\{\lambda, n(\delta)\}$. Whatever the relative positions of λ and δ, $K_\alpha = K^*$. However, we have the following cases: (i) if $\lambda > n(\delta)$ then $\alpha = n(\delta)$ and we have to compute $label_{K^*}(Pref_{\underline{\delta}})$. This means that $Pref_{\underline{\delta}} = \{\neg w\}$, and Algorithm 1 will return the decision $\{u\}$ as label for this preference. As a next step, $\alpha = \lambda$, but the computation of $label_{K^*}(Pref^*)$ is found to be empty. Therefore the set of best pessimistic decisions is in this case $\mathcal{D} = \{u\}$ with utility $u_* = n(\delta)$. (ii) If $\lambda < n(\delta)$ then $\alpha = \lambda$ and we have to compute $label_{K^*}(Pref_{\underline{n(\lambda)}})$. As $n(\lambda) > \delta$, $Pref_{\underline{n(\lambda)}} = \{\neg w\}$, and $label_{K^*}(\neg w) = \{u\}$. A next step is performed where $\alpha = n(\delta)$ and $label_{K_{n(\delta)}}(Pref_{\underline{\delta}}) = \{u\}$. We then have to perform a last step, where $\alpha = 1$, but the computation of $label_{K_1}(Pref^*)$ is equal to $\emptyset$. Therefore, the set of optimal decisions is in this case $\mathcal{D} = \{u\}$ with utility $u_* = n(\delta)$. (iii) If $\lambda = n(\delta)$ then $\alpha = \lambda = n(\delta)$ and we have to compute $label_{K^*}(Pref_{\underline{\delta}})$ which is equal to the computation of $label_{K^*}(\neg w)$ which returns $\{u\}$. Then a next step is performed where $\alpha = 1$ but $label_{K_1}(Pref^*) = \emptyset$.

Algorithm 2. computePessimisticDecisionsUU(DMU) : $\langle \mathcal{D}, u_* \rangle$

Input: $\Big\{ A\ DMU = \langle K, D, Pref \rangle$

Output: $\begin{cases} \mathcal{D} : \text{the set of best pessimistic decisions} \\ u_* : \text{the utility of the best pessimistic decisions} \end{cases}$

$\alpha, u_* \leftarrow \mathbf{0};\ \mathcal{D} \leftarrow \emptyset;\ finish \leftarrow false;$
while $(not\ finish)$ **do**
    $\alpha \leftarrow Inc(\alpha)$ // $Inc(\alpha)$ increases value of α into the immediately above value
    if $(\alpha = 1)$ **then**
        $finish \leftarrow true$
    end if
    $label_{K_\alpha}(Pref_{\underline{n(\alpha)}}) \leftarrow computePessimisticDecisions(\langle K_\alpha, D, Pref_{\underline{n(\alpha)}} \rangle)$
    if $(label_{K_\alpha}(\overline{Pref_{n(\alpha)}}) = \emptyset)$ **then**
        $finish \leftarrow true$
    else
        $u_* \leftarrow \alpha$
        $\mathcal{D} \leftarrow label_{K_\alpha}(Pref_{\underline{n(\alpha)}})$
    end if
end while
return $\langle \mathcal{D}, u_* \rangle$

Thus the best pessimistic solution of the running example is always to take an umbrella with utility $n(\delta)$. Notice that here optimal pessimistic decisions does not depend on the exact value of λ and δ, and even not on their relative positions. However, in the general case, only the positions of the priority and certainty levels matter.

Proposition 2. *Let $DMU = \langle K, D, Pref \rangle$ be a decision making problem under uncertainty and let P_{dm} be the LPOD generated by Algorithm 1. Then, $\Delta \in label_{K_\alpha}(Pref_{\underline{n(\alpha)}})$ such that $\Delta \subseteq D$ is an optimal pessimistic decision maximizing α iff there is a consistent maximally preferred answer set M of P_{dm} such that $\Delta = \{d \in D \mid ass(d) \in M\}$.*

4.4   Possibilistic ASP-Based Computation

In the previous section we have provided a method for computing pessimistic decisions reducing the problem to a successive computation of preference labels. In general, the computation of pessimistic decisions (and pessimistic utility) can also be realized by means of an approach closer to possibilistic logic inference, based on the LPPODs semantics. This view is motivated by the possibilistic logic property expressed in Lemma 1.

Algorithm 3 describes an LPPOD-based procedure to compute the set of pessimistic decisions. P_{dm} is constructed by a method `decisionMakingToLPPOD` (DMU) which generalizes Definition 5. To each rule of P_{dm} it associates the corresponding necessity values. However, preference constraints are not added, since the preference satisfaction is checked by means of $\models_p$.

Algorithm 3. computePessimisticDecisionsUU(DMU) : $\langle \mathcal{D}, u_* \rangle$

Input: $\Big\{ A\ DMU = \langle P_k, D, Pref \rangle$

Output: $\begin{cases} \mathcal{D} : \text{the set of best pessimistic decisions} \\ u_* : \text{the utility of the best pessimistic decisions} \end{cases}$

$\mathcal{D} \leftarrow \emptyset;\ finish \leftarrow false$

$u_* \leftarrow 0;\ \gamma^* \leftarrow 1;\ \beta \leftarrow 1$

$P_{dm} \leftarrow decisionMakingToLPPOD(DMU)$

while $(\gamma^* \geq n(\beta))$ and $(not\ finish)$ **do**

   if $(P_{dm} \models_p (p_\beta, \beta_\beta))$ **then**

      $\mathcal{D} \leftarrow getDecisionLiterals(SEM_{LPPOD}(P_{dm}), p_\beta)$

      $\gamma^* \leftarrow getNecessityValuesMin(SEM_{LPPOD}(P_{dm}), p_\beta)$

      $Dec(\beta)$

   else

      $finish \leftarrow true$

   end if

end while

$u_* \leftarrow \min\{\gamma^*, n(\beta)\}$

return $\langle \mathcal{D}, u_* \rangle$

Example 9. Given the DMU in Example 7, the corresponding LPPOD P_{dm} is $\{r_1 = 1 : \neg w \leftarrow u, r_2 = 1 : w \leftarrow r, \neg u, r_3 = \lambda : r \leftarrow c, r_4 = 1 : c, r_5 = 1 : \neg ass(u) \times ass(u), r_6 = 1 : \neg ass(\neg u) \times ass(\neg u), r_7 = 1 : u \leftarrow ass(u), r_8 = 1 : \neg u \leftarrow ass(\neg u)\}$.

Returning to the description of the algorithm, γ^* is the certainty value according to which preferences belonging to a stratum $n(\beta)$ of the preference base have been satisfied. In fact, according to Definition 7 a preference literal is satisfied if and only if its certainty value in a maximally preferred possibilistic answer set of P_{dm} is greater than its priority. While this condition is satisfied, we keep on iterating on the preferences in order to minimize β as much as possible. getDecisionLiterals returns the sets of decision literals on the basis of the maximally preferred possibilistic answer sets of P_{dm} which satisfy p_β. In case there is more than one possibilistic answer set satisfying p_β, the smallest certainty value by which p_β has been proved is retrieved by getNecessityValuesMin.

Example 10. At the beginning $\gamma^* = 1$ and $\beta = 1$, *i.e.* we try to satisfy higher prioritized preferences with the most certain part of P_k. By applying the LPPOD semantics to P_{dm} in Example 9 two maximally preferred possibilistic answer sets are obtained: $M_1 = \{(\neg u, 1), (ass(\neg u), 1), (c, 1), (r, \lambda), (w, \lambda), (\neg ass(u), 1)\}$ and $M_2 = \{(u, 1), (ass(u), 1), (c, 1), (r, \lambda), (\neg w, 1), (\neg ass(\neg u), 1)\}$. $P_{dm} \models_p (\neg w, 1)$ since $(\neg w, 1) \sqsubseteq M_2$. Thus, $\mathcal{D} = M_2^* \cap D = \{u\}$ and $\gamma^* = N(\neg w) = 1$. The next level of β to be considered is δ. Since $\gamma^* \geq \delta$ whatever δ value is, we try to satisfy $(\neg u, \delta)$. It is easy to see how $(\neg u, \delta) \not\sqsubseteq M_1$ and $(\neg u, \delta) \not\sqsubseteq M_2$. Thus, we are finished. Then the set of best pessimistic decisions is $\mathcal{D} = \{u\}$ with an utility $u_* = \min\{1, n(\delta)\}$, *i.e.* $u_* = n(\delta)$. This agrees, as expected, with the label-based computation presented in the previous section.

Proposition 3. *Let $DMU = \langle K, D, Pref \rangle$ be a decision making problem under uncertainty, let P_{dm} be the LPPOD built using Algorithm 3. Then, $\Delta \in label_{K_\alpha}(Pref_{\underline{n(\alpha)}})$ s.t. $\Delta \subseteq D$ is an optimal pessimistic decision maximizing α iff there exists a consistent possibilistic answer set M of $P_{dm_\alpha} = \{r \in P_{dm} \mid N(r) \geq \alpha\}$ s.t. $\{(p_i, \beta_i) \in Pref \mid \beta_i > n(\alpha)\} \sqsubseteq M$ and $\Delta = \{d \in D \mid ass(d) \in M^*\}$.*

5   Related Work

To the best of our knowledge there are only few works in the literature about modeling qualitative decision problems in ASP [2,14]. These two approaches use the ordered disjunction connective $\times$ introduced in [4] to represent preferences to rank-order different possible states of the world represented as different answer sets. However, they differ on the way uncertainty is handled. In [2] uncertainty is not explicitly represented, since the method is based on the assumption that states of the world which are not normal are disregarded, while taken-into-account states are considered plausible. As such, states can be either negligible or plausible. But, in the latter case, no distinction between the degrees of plausibility of the states can be made, and no further distinctions between the generated answer sets are possible. Grabos in [14] proposed to use $\times$ not only for modeling preferences but also for modeling the plausibility degrees of states. Depending whether a commensurability assumption between the two degrees of plausibility and of preferences is made (or not), decision rules give more importance (or not) to one of the degree in order to select the best answer set according to the attitude of the decision maker w.r.t. the risk. Although this method offers a way to represent uncertainty, decision rules are empirical and are not based on postulates like the possibilistic criteria. Moreover, although our commensurability assumption is a strong assumption, it has been noticed in [9] that working without it leads to an ineffective decision method.

6   Concluding Remarks

In this paper we have presented an ASP-based methodology to compute decision making problems under uncertainty by considering two knowledge bases whose degrees of certainty and priority are commensurate. We have first shown how to encode fully certain knowledge and all-or-nothing preferences, and then, on top of that, how to compute optimal pessimistic decisions.

The reader may be concerned why we have chosen not to take into account ASP optimization techniques (via objective functions) and to compute preferences at meta-level rather than inside LPODs and LPPODs. Our design choice can be motivated by the need of handling two separate knowledge bases and of having a formal handling of uncertainty (in terms of possibilistic logic). In this way we have been able to provide a possibilistic ASP-based methodology which computes the same decisions of the label-based computation. This result agrees both with the classical and the possibilistic resolution views for computing optimal decisions in possibilistic logic.

As general improvements, the decision method used is not able to identify decisions that may satisfy all the goals from the highest level to the lowest one, except one goal at some level β. In fact the algorithm stops at the first unsatisfied preference and does not proceed with preferences at lower strata. The algorithm can be modified accordingly to deal with this case. We also plan to extend the definition of $\models_c$ and $\models_p$ to handle more complex preferences expressions.

References

1. Baral, C.: Knowledge Representation, Reasoning and Declarative Problem Solving. Cambridge University Press, Cambridge (2003)
2. Brewka, G.: Answer Sets and Qualitative Decision Making. Synthese 146(1-2), 171–187 (2005)
3. Brewka, G.: Answer Sets and Qualitative Optimization. Logic Journal of the IGPL 14(3), 413–433 (2006)
4. Brewka, G., Niemelä, I., Syrjänen, T.: Logic Programs with Ordered Disjunction. Computational Intelligence 20(2), 333–357 (2004)
5. Brewka, G., Niemelä, I., Truszczynski, M.: Answer Set Optimization. In: Gottlob, G., Walsh, T. (eds.) 18th Int. Joint Conf. on Artificial Intelligence (IJCAI 2003), pp. 867–872. Morgan Kaufmann, San Francisco (2003)
6. Confalonieri, R., Nieves, J.C., Osorio, M., Vázquez-Salceda, J.: Possibilistic Semantics for Logic Programs with Ordered Disjunction. In: Link, S., Prade, H. (eds.) FoIKS 2010. LNCS, vol. 5956, pp. 133–152. Springer, Heidelberg (2010)
7. Confalonieri, R., Prade, H., Nieves, J.C.: Handling Exceptions in Logic Programming without Negation as Failure. Accepted in the 11th European Conference on Symbolic and Quantitative Approaches to Reasoning with Uncertainty (2011)
8. Dubois, D., Lang, J., Prade, H.: Possibilistic Logic. In: Handbook of Logic in Artificial Intelligence and Logic Programming, pp. 439–513. Oxford Univ. Press, Oxford (1994)
9. Dubois, D., Fargier, H., Prade, H., Perny, P.: Qualitative decision theory: from Savage's axioms to nonmonotonic reasoning. J. ACM 49(4), 455–495 (2002)
10. Dubois, D., Le Berre, D., Prade, H., Sabbadin, R.: Using Possibilistic Logic for Modeling Qualitative Decision: ATMS-based Algorithms. Fundamenta Informaticae 37(1-2), 1–30 (1999)
11. Dubois, D., Prade, H.: Possibility theory as a basis for qualitative decision theory. In: 14th Int. Joint Conf. on Artificial Intelligence (IJCAI 1995), pp. 1924–1930. Morgan Kaufmann, San Francisco (1995)
12. Dubois, D., Prade, H., Sabbadin, R.: Decision-theoretic foundations of qualitative possibility theory. Europ. Journal of Operational Research 128(3), 459–478 (2001)
13. Dubois, D., Prade, H., Sabbadin, R.: A Possibilistic Logic Machinery for Qualitative Decision. In: AAAI Spring Symposium on Qualitative Preferences in Deliberation and Practical Reasoning, pp. 47–54. AAAI Press, Menlo Park (1997)
14. Grabos, R.: Qualitative model of decision making. In: Bussler, C.J., Fensel, D. (eds.) AIMSA 2004. LNCS (LNAI), vol. 3192, pp. 480–489. Springer, Heidelberg (2004)
15. Nicolas, P., Garcia, L., Stéphan, I., Lefèvre, C.: Possibilistic uncertainty handling for answer set programming. Annals of Mathematics and Artificial Intelligence 47(1-2), 139–181 (2006)
16. Sabbadin, R.: Decision As Abduction? In: Prade, H. (ed.) Proceedings of 13th European Conference on Artificial Intelligence, pp. 600–604. Wiley, Chichester (1998)

Quasi Conjunction and Inclusion Relation in Probabilistic Default Reasoning

Angelo Gilio[1] and Giuseppe Sanfilippo[2]

[1] Dipartimento di Scienze di Base e Applicate per l'Ingegneria,
University of Rome "La Sapienza", Italy
angelo.gilio@uniroma1.it
[2] Dipartimento di Scienze Statistiche e Matematiche "S. Vianelli",
University of Palermo, Italy
sanfilippo@unipa.it

Abstract. We study in the setting of probabilistic default reasoning under coherence the quasi conjunction, which is a basic notion for defining consistency of conditional knowledge bases, and the Goodman & Nguyen inclusion relation for conditional events. We deepen two results given in a previous paper: the first result concerns p-entailment from a finite family $\mathcal{F}$ of conditional events to the quasi conjunction $\mathcal{C}(\mathcal{S})$, for each nonempty subset $\mathcal{S}$ of $\mathcal{F}$; the second result analyzes the equivalence between p-entailment from $\mathcal{F}$ and p-entailment from $\mathcal{C}(\mathcal{S})$, where $\mathcal{S}$ is some nonempty subset of $\mathcal{F}$. We also characterize p-entailment by some alternative theorems. Finally, we deepen the connections between p-entailment and inclusion relation, by introducing for a pair $(\mathcal{F}, E|H)$ the class of the subsets $\mathcal{S}$ of $\mathcal{F}$ such that $\mathcal{C}(\mathcal{S})$ implies $E|H$. This class is additive and has a greatest element which can be determined by applying a suitable algorithm.

Keywords: Coherence, probabilistic default reasoning, quasi conjunction, Goodman & Nguyen inclusion relation, QAND rule, p-entailment.

1 Introduction

Nonmonotonic reasoning typically concerns situations of partial knowledge where conclusions, which are reached from a set of premises, may be retracted when some premises are added. This topic is especially important in the field of artificial intelligence and has been studied by many authors, by using symbolic and/or numerical formalisms (see, e.g. [2,3,4,9]). Among the numerical formalisms connected with nonmonotonic reasoning, a remarkable theory is represented by the Adams probabilistic logic of conditionals ([1]). The approach of Adams can be developed with full generality by exploiting a coherence-based probabilistic reasoning; as is well known, in the setting of coherence, conditional probabilities can be directly assigned to conditional assertions, without assuming that conditioning events have a positive probability ([5]). In Adams work a basic notion is the quasi conjunction of conditionals, which has a strict relationship with the

W. Liu (Ed.): ECSQARU 2011, LNAI 6717, pp. 497–508, 2011.

property of consistency of conditional knowledge bases. Quasi conjunction also plays a relevant role in the work of Dubois and Prade on conditional objects ([4]), where a suitable QAND rule is introduced to characterize entailment from a conditional knowledge base. Recently ([7]), we have studied some probabilistic aspects related with the QAND rule and with the conditional probabilistic logic of Adams. In this paper, among other things, we continue the study of the quasi conjunction and the Goodman & Nguyen inclusion relation, by examining aspects especially related with results obtained in [2].

The paper is organized as follows: In Section 2 we first recall some notions and results on coherence; then, we recall basic notions in probabilistic default reasoning; finally, we recall the operation of quasi conjunction and the inclusion relation for conditional events. In Section 3 we first define, for two finite families of conditional events $\mathcal{F}$ and Γ, the p-entailment of Γ from $\mathcal{F}$; then, we deepen two results, given in [7], connected with the probabilistic semantics of $QAND$ rule; the first result concerns p-entailment from a family of conditional events $\mathcal{F}$ to the quasi conjunction $\mathcal{C}(\mathcal{F})$; the second result analyzes many aspects connected with the equivalence between p-entailment from $\mathcal{F}$ and p-entailment from $\mathcal{C}(\mathcal{S})$, where $\mathcal{S}$ is some nonempty subset of $\mathcal{F}$; then, we characterize p-entailment by some alternative theorems. In Section 4, among other things, we introduce for a pair $(\mathcal{F}, E|H)$ the class $\mathcal{K}$ of the subsets $\mathcal{S}$ of $\mathcal{F}$ such that $\mathcal{C}(\mathcal{S})$ implies $E|H$, by showing that $\mathcal{K}$ is additive and has a greatest element (if any) which can be determined by a suitable algorithm. In Section 5 we give some conclusions.

2   Some Preliminary Notions

In this section we recall some basic notions and results.

Basic notions on coherence. Given any events A and B, we simply write $A \subseteq B$ to denote that A logically implies B. Moreover, we denote by AB (resp., $A \vee B$) the logical intersection, or conjunction (resp., logical union, or disjunction). The conditional event $B|A$, with $A \neq \emptyset$, is looked at as a three-valued logical entity which is true, or false, or indeterminate, according to whether AB is true, or AB^c is true, or A^c is true. We use the same symbols for events and their indicators. Given a real function $P : \mathcal{F} \to \mathcal{R}$, where $\mathcal{F}$ is an arbitrary family of conditional events, let us consider a subfamily $\mathcal{F}_n = \{E_1|H_1, \ldots, E_n|H_n\} \subseteq \mathcal{F}$, and the vector $\mathcal{P}_n = (p_1, \ldots, p_n)$, where $p_i = P(E_i|H_i)$, $i = 1, \ldots, n$. We denote by $\mathcal{H}_n$ the disjunction $H_1 \vee \cdots \vee H_n$. Notice that, as $E_i H_i \vee E_i^c H_i \vee H_i^c = \Omega$, $i = 1, \ldots, n$, where Ω is the sure event, by expanding the expression $\bigwedge_{i=1}^{n}(E_i H_i \vee E_i^c H_i \vee H_i^c)$, we can represent Ω as the disjunction of 3^n logical conjunctions, some of which may be impossible. The remaining ones are the constituents generated by the family $\mathcal{F}_n$. We denote by $C_1, \ldots, C_m$ the constituents contained in $\mathcal{H}_n$ and (if $\mathcal{H}_n \neq \Omega$) by C_0 the further constituent $\mathcal{H}_n^c = H_1^c \cdots H_n^c$, so that

$$\mathcal{H}_n = C_1 \vee \cdots \vee C_m, \quad \Omega = \mathcal{H}_n^c \vee \mathcal{H}_n = C_0 \vee C_1 \vee \cdots \vee C_m, \quad m+1 \leq 3^n.$$

With the pair $(\mathcal{F}_n, \mathcal{P}_n)$ we associate the random gain $\mathcal{G} = \sum_{i=1}^{n} s_i H_i(E_i - p_i)$, where $s_1, \ldots, s_n$ are n arbitrary real numbers. Let g_h be the value of $\mathcal{G}$ when

C_h is true; of course $g_0 = 0$. Denoting by $\mathcal{G}|\mathcal{H}_n$ the restriction of $\mathcal{G}$ to $\mathcal{H}_n$, it is $\mathcal{G}|\mathcal{H}_n \in \{g_1, \ldots, g_m\}$. Then, we have

Definition 1. The function P defined on $\mathcal{F}$ is said *coherent* if and only if, for every integer n, for every finite sub-family $\mathcal{F}_n \subseteq \mathcal{F}$ and for every $s_1, \ldots, s_n$, one has: $\min \mathcal{G}|\mathcal{H}_n \leq 0 \leq \max \mathcal{G}|\mathcal{H}_n$.

With each C_h contained in $\mathcal{H}_n$ we associate a point $Q_h = (q_{h1}, \ldots, q_{hn})$, where $q_{hj} = 1$, or 0, or p_j, according to whether $C_h \subseteq E_j H_j$, or $C_h \subseteq E_j^c H_j$, or $C_h \subseteq H_j^c$. Denoting by $\mathcal{I}$ the convex hull of the points $Q_1, \ldots, Q_m$, based on the penalty criterion, the following result can be proved

Theorem 1. The function P is coherent if and only if, for every finite subfamily $\mathcal{F}_n \subseteq \mathcal{F}$, one has $\mathcal{P}_n \in \mathcal{I}$.

The condition $\mathcal{P}_n \in \mathcal{I}$ amounts to solvability of the following system Σ in the unknowns $\lambda_1, \ldots, \lambda_m$

$$(\Sigma) \qquad \begin{cases} \sum_{h=1}^m q_{hj}\lambda_h = p_j \, , \quad j = 1, \ldots, n \, ; \\ \sum_{h=1}^m \lambda_h = 1 \, , \quad \lambda_h \geq 0, \ h = 1, \ldots, m. \end{cases}$$

Checking coherence of the assessment $\mathcal{P}_n$ on $\mathcal{F}_n$. Let S be the set of solutions $\Lambda = (\lambda_1, \ldots, \lambda_m)$ of the system Σ. Then, define

$$\Phi_j(\Lambda) = \Phi_j(\lambda_1, \ldots, \lambda_m) = \sum_{r:C_r \subseteq H_j} \lambda_r \, , \quad j = 1, \ldots, n \, ;$$
$$M_j = \max_{\Lambda \in S} \Phi_j(\Lambda) \, , \quad j = 1, \ldots, n \, ; \quad I_0 = \{j : M_j = 0\} \, .$$

Notice that $I_0 \subset \{1, \ldots, n\}$. We denote by $(\mathcal{F}_0, \mathcal{P}_0)$ the pair associated with I_0. Given the pair $(\mathcal{F}_n, \mathcal{P}_n)$ and a subset $J \subset \{1, \ldots, n\}$, we denote by $(\mathcal{F}_J, \mathcal{P}_J)$ the pair associated with J and by Σ_J the corresponding system. We observe that Σ_J is solvable if and only if $\mathcal{P}_J \in \mathcal{I}_J$, where $\mathcal{I}_J$ is the convex hull associated with the pair $(\mathcal{F}_J, \mathcal{P}_J)$. Then, we have

Theorem 2. Given a probability assessment $\mathcal{P}_n$ on the family $\mathcal{F}_n$, if the system Σ associated with $(\mathcal{F}_n, \mathcal{P}_n)$ is solvable, then for every $J \subset \{1, \ldots, n\}$, such that $J \setminus I_0 \neq \emptyset$, the system Σ_J associated with $(\mathcal{F}_J, \mathcal{P}_J)$ is solvable too.

By the previous results, we obtain

Theorem 3. The assessment $\mathcal{P}_n$ on $\mathcal{F}_n$ is coherent if and only if the following conditions are satisfied: (i) $\mathcal{P}_n \in \mathcal{I}$; (ii) if $I_0 \neq \emptyset$, then $\mathcal{P}_0$ is coherent.

Then, we can check coherence by the following procedure:

Algorithm 1. Let the pair $(\mathcal{F}_n, \mathcal{P}_n)$ be given.

1. Construct the system Σ and check its solvability.
2. If the system Σ is not solvable then $\mathcal{P}_n$ is not coherent and the procedure stops, otherwise compute the set I_0.
3. If $I_0 = \emptyset$ then $\mathcal{P}_n$ is coherent and the procedure stops; otherwise set $(\mathcal{F}_n, \mathcal{P}_n) = (\mathcal{F}_0, \mathcal{P}_0)$ and repeat steps 1-3.

Basic notions on probabilistic default reasoning. We now give the notions of p-consistency and p-entailment of Adams ([1]), as defined in the setting of coherence in ([5,6]). Given a conditional knowledge base $\mathcal{KB}_n = \{H_i \sim E_i, \ i = 1, \ldots, n\}$, we denote by $\mathcal{F}_n = \{E_i|H_i, \ i = 1, \ldots, n\}$ the associated family of conditional events.

Definition 2. The knowledge base $\mathcal{KB}_n = \{H_i|\sim E_i, \ i = 1, \ldots, n\}$ is *p-consistent* if and only if, for every set of lower bounds $\{\alpha_i, i = 1, \ldots, n\}$, with $\alpha_i \in [0, 1)$, there exists a coherent probability assessment $\{p_i, i = 1, \ldots, n\}$ on $\mathcal{F}_n$, with $p_i = P(E_i|H_i)$, such that $p_i \geq \alpha_i, i = 1, \ldots, n$.

We say that $\mathcal{F}_n$ is p-consistent when the associated knowledge base $\mathcal{KB}_n$ is p-consistent.

Remark 1. We point out that p-consistency of $\mathcal{F}_n$ is equivalent to coherence of the assessment $(p_1, p_2, \ldots, p_n) = (1, 1, \ldots, 1)$ on $\mathcal{F}_n$ (strict p-consistency, [5]).

Definition 3. A p-consistent knowledge base $\mathcal{KB}_n = \{H_i|\sim E_i, \ i = 1, \ldots, n\}$ *p-entails* the conditional $A|\sim B$, denoted $\mathcal{KB}_n \Rightarrow_p A|\sim B$, if and only if there exists a nonempty subset $\Gamma \subseteq \{1, \ldots, n\}$ such that, for every $\alpha \in [0, 1)$, there exists a set of lower bounds $\{\alpha_i, i \in \Gamma\}$, with $\alpha_i \in [0, 1)$, such that for all coherent probability assessments $\{z, p_i, i \in \Gamma\}$ defined on $\{B|A, E_i|H_i, \ i \in \Gamma\}$, with $z = P(B|A)$ and $p_i = P(E_i|H_i)$, if $p_i \geq \alpha_i$ for every $i \in \Gamma$, then $z \geq \alpha$.

Remark 2. We say that a family of conditional events $\mathcal{F}_n$ p-entails a conditional event $B|A$ when the associated knowledge base $\mathcal{KB}_n$ p-entails the conditional $A|\sim B$. Therefore, p-entailment of $B|A$ from $\mathcal{F}_n$ amounts to the existence of a nonempty subset $\mathcal{S} = \{E_i|H_i, \ i \in \Gamma\}$ of $\mathcal{F}_n$ such that, defining $P(E_i|H_i) = p_i, P(B|A) = z$, for every $\alpha \in [0, 1)$, there exist lower bounds $\alpha_i, i \in \Gamma$, with $\alpha_i \in [0, 1)$, such that $p_i \geq \alpha_i, \ i \in \Gamma$, implies $z \geq \alpha$.

Quasi conjunction and inclusion relation. We recall below the notion of quasi conjunction of conditional events.

Definition 4. Given any events A, H, B, K, with $H \neq \emptyset, K \neq \emptyset$, the quasi conjunction of the conditional events $A|H$ and $B|K$, as defined in [1], is the conditional event $\mathcal{C}(A|H, B|K) = (AH \vee H^c) \wedge (BK \vee K^c)|(H \vee K)$. More in general, given a family of n conditional events $\mathcal{F}_n = \{E_i|H_i, i = 1, \ldots, n\}$, it is $\mathcal{C}(\mathcal{F}_n) = \mathcal{C}(E_1|H_1, \ldots, E_n|H_n) = \bigwedge_{i=1}^{n}(E_i H_i \vee H_i^c)|(\bigvee_{i=1}^{n} H_i)$.

Quasi conjunction is associative; that is, for every subset $J \subset \{1, \ldots, n\}$, defining $\Gamma = \{1, \ldots, n\} \setminus J$, it holds that $\mathcal{C}(\mathcal{F}_n) = \mathcal{C}(\mathcal{F}_J \cup \mathcal{F}_\Gamma) = \mathcal{C}[\mathcal{C}(\mathcal{F}_J), \mathcal{C}(\mathcal{F}_\Gamma)]$.

Assuming A, H, B, K logically independent, we have ([6]): (i) the probability assessment (x, y) on $\{A|H, B|K\}$ is coherent for every $(x, y) \in [0, 1]^2$; (ii) given a coherent assessment (x, y) on $\{A|H, B|K\}$, the probability assessment $\mathcal{P} = (x, y, z)$ on $\mathcal{F} = \{A|H, B|K, \mathcal{C}(A|H, B|K)\}$, with $z = P[\mathcal{C}(A|H, B|K)]$, is a coherent extension of (x, y) if and only if

$$\max(x + y - 1, 0) = l \leq z \leq u = \begin{cases} \frac{x+y-2xy}{1-xy}, & (x, y) \neq (1, 1), \\ 1, & (x, y) = (1, 1). \end{cases}$$

A more general analysis for quasi conjunction, concerning the lower and upper bounds and some related aspects, has been given in [7].

The notion of logical inclusion among events has been generalized to conditional events by Goodman & Nguyen in [8]. We recall below this generalized notion.

Definition 5. Given two conditional events $A|H$ and $B|K$, we say that $A|H$ implies $B|K$, denoted by $A|H \subseteq B|K$, if and only if AH *true* implies BK *true* and B^cK *true* implies A^cH *true*; i.e., if and only if $AH \subseteq BK$ and $B^cK \subseteq A^cH$.

3   Probabilistic Entailment and Quasi Conjunction

We recall that in [4], based on a three-valued calculus of conditional objects, a logic for nonmonotonic reasoning has been proposed. Conditional objects can be seen as the counterpart of the conditional assertions and, for what concerns logical operations, we can look at them as conditional events. Given a set of conditional objects $\mathcal{KB}$, we denote by $\mathcal{C}(\mathcal{KB})$ the quasi conjunction of the conditional objects in $\mathcal{KB}$. The inclusion relation $\subseteq$ among conditional events corresponds to the logical entailment $\models$ among conditional objects in [4], where the following definition has been given.

Definition 6. $\mathcal{KB}$ entails a conditional object $q|p$ if and only if there exists a nonempty subset $\mathcal{S}$ of $\mathcal{KB}$ such that $\mathcal{C}(\mathcal{S}) \models q|p$, or $p \models q$.

Moreover, in [4] the following inference rule has been introduced:

(QAND) $\mathcal{KB} \Rightarrow \mathcal{C}(\mathcal{KB})$.

Definition 3 can be generalized to p-entailment of a family (of conditional events) Γ from another family $\mathcal{F}$ in the following way.

Definition 7. Given two p-consistent finite families of conditional events $\mathcal{F}$ and Γ, we say that $\mathcal{F}$ p-entails Γ if $\mathcal{F}$ p-entails $E|H$, for every $E|H \in \Gamma$.

We remark that, from Definition 3, we trivially have that $\mathcal{F}$ p-entails $E|H$, for every $E|H \in \mathcal{F}$; then, by Definition 7, it immediately follows

$$\mathcal{F} \Rightarrow_p \mathcal{S}, \ \forall \mathcal{S} \subseteq \mathcal{F}. \tag{1}$$

The next result, related to Adams work, generalizes Theorem 6 given in [7] and deepens in the framework of coherence the probabilistic semantics of the QAND rule introduced by Dubois and Prade in their paper on conditional objects ([4]).

Theorem 4. Given a p-consistent family of conditional events $\mathcal{F}_n$, for every nonempty subfamily $\mathcal{S} = \{E_i|H_i, i = 1, \dots, s\} \subseteq \mathcal{F}_n$, we have

$$\mathcal{F}_n \Rightarrow_p \mathcal{C}(\mathcal{S}). \tag{2}$$

Proof. Based on Definition 7 and formula (1), in order to prove (2) it is enough to show that $\mathcal{S}$ p-entails $\mathcal{C}(\mathcal{S})$. This amounts to show that, for every $\varepsilon \in (0, 1]$

there exist $\delta_1 \in (0,1], \ldots, \delta_s \in (0,1]$ such that, for every coherent assessment $(p_1, \ldots, p_s, z)$ on $\mathcal{S} \cup \{\mathcal{C}(\mathcal{S})\}$, where $p_i = P(E_i|H_i)$, $z = P(\mathcal{C}(\mathcal{S}))$, if $p_1 \geq 1 - \delta_1, \ldots, p_s \geq 1 - \delta_s$, then $z \geq 1 - \varepsilon$.

We distinguish two cases: (i) the events $E_i, H_i, i = 1, \ldots, s$, are logically independent; (ii) the events $E_i, H_i, i = 1, \ldots, s$, are logically dependent.

(i) The case $s = 2$, with $\mathcal{F} = \{A|H, B|K\}$, has been already examined in [6], by observing that, given any coherent assessment (x, y, z) on the family $\{A|H, B|K, \mathcal{C}(A|H, B|K)\}$ and any number $\gamma \in [0,1)$, for every $\alpha_1 \in [\gamma, 1)$, $\alpha_2 \in [\gamma, 1)$, with $\alpha_1 + \alpha_2 \geq \gamma + 1$, one has

$$(x, y) \in [\alpha_1, 1] \times [\alpha_2, 1] \implies z \geq \alpha_1 + \alpha_2 - 1 \geq \gamma. \tag{3}$$

We observe that, for $\gamma = 1 - \varepsilon$, $\alpha_1 = 1 - \delta_1$, $\alpha_2 = 1 - \delta_2$, with $\alpha_1 + \alpha_2 \geq \gamma + 1$, i.e. $\delta_1 + \delta_2 \leq \varepsilon$, formula (3) becomes

$$x \geq 1 - \delta_1, \ y \geq 1 - \delta_2 \implies z \geq 1 - \delta_1 + 1 - \delta_2 - 1 \geq 1 - \varepsilon.$$

More in general, denoting by $\mathcal{L}_\gamma$ the set of the coherent assessments $(p_1, \ldots, p_s)$ on $\mathcal{S}$ such that, for each $(p_1, \ldots, p_s) \in \mathcal{L}_\gamma$, one has $P[\mathcal{C}(\mathcal{S})] \geq \gamma$, it can be proved (see [7], Theorem 4) that

$$\mathcal{L}_\gamma = \{(p_1, \ldots, p_s) \in [0,1]^s : p_1 + \cdots + p_s \geq \gamma + s - 1\}.$$

In particular, given any $\varepsilon > 0$, it is

$$\mathcal{L}_{1-\varepsilon} = \{(p_1, \ldots, p_s) \in [0,1]^s : p_1 + \cdots + p_s \geq s - \varepsilon\}.$$

Then, given any positive vector $(\delta_1, \ldots, \delta_s)$ in the set

$$\Delta_\varepsilon = \{(\delta_1, \ldots, \delta_s) : \delta_1 + \cdots + \delta_s \leq \varepsilon\},$$

if $(p_1, \ldots, p_s, z)$ is a coherent assessment on $\mathcal{S} \cup \{\mathcal{C}(\mathcal{S})\}$ such that $p_1 \geq 1 - \delta_1, \ldots,$ $p_s \geq 1 - \delta_s$, it follows $p_1 + \cdots + p_s \geq s - \varepsilon$, so that $(p_1, \ldots, p_s) \in \mathcal{L}_{1-\varepsilon}$, and hence $z = P[\mathcal{C}(\mathcal{S})] \geq 1 - \varepsilon$. Therefore $\mathcal{S} \Rightarrow_p \mathcal{C}(\mathcal{S})$ and hence $\mathcal{F}_n \Rightarrow_p \mathcal{C}(\mathcal{S})$, $\forall \mathcal{S} \subseteq \mathcal{F}_n$.

(ii) Since the events $E_i, H_i, i = 1, \ldots, s$ are logically dependent, it is

$$\mathcal{L}_{1-\varepsilon} \subseteq \{(p_1, \ldots, p_s) \in [0,1]^s : p_1 + \cdots + p_s \geq s - \varepsilon\},$$

with $\mathcal{L}_{1-\varepsilon} \neq \emptyset$ by p-consistency of $\mathcal{F}_s$. Then, by the same reasoning as in case (i), we still obtain $\mathcal{S} \Rightarrow_p \mathcal{C}(\mathcal{S})$, and hence $\mathcal{F}_n \Rightarrow_p \mathcal{C}(\mathcal{S})$, for every $\mathcal{S} \subseteq \mathcal{F}_n$.

The next result characterizes in the setting of coherence Adams' notion of p-entailment of a conditional event $E|H$ from a family $\mathcal{F}_n$. It generalizes Theorem 7 given in [7] and provides a probabilistic semantics to the notion of entailment given in Definition 6 for conditional objects.

Theorem 5. Let be given a p-consistent family $\mathcal{F}_n = \{E_1|H_1, \ldots, E_n|H_n\}$ and a conditional event $E|H$. The following assertions are equivalent:

1. $\mathcal{F}_n$ p-entails $E|H$;
2. The assessment $\mathcal{P} = (1,\dots,1,z)$ on $\mathcal{F} = \mathcal{F}_n \cup \{E|H\}$, where $P(E_i|H_i) = 1$, $i = 1,\dots,n$, $P(E|H) = z$, is coherent if and only if $z = 1$;
3. The assessment $\mathcal{P} = (1,\dots,1,0)$ on $\mathcal{F} = \mathcal{F}_n \cup \{E|H\}$, where $P(E_i|H_i) = 1$, $i = 1,\dots,n$, $P(E|H) = z$, is not coherent;
4. Either there exists a nonempty $\mathcal{S} \subseteq \mathcal{F}_n$ such that $\mathcal{C}(\mathcal{S})$ implies $E|H$, or $H \subseteq E$.
5. There exists a nonempty $\mathcal{S} \subseteq \mathcal{F}_n$ such that $\mathcal{C}(\mathcal{S})$ p-entails $E|H$.

Proof. We will prove that 1. $\Rightarrow$ 2. $\Rightarrow$ 3. $\Rightarrow$ 4. $\Rightarrow$ 5. $\Rightarrow$ 1.
(1. $\Rightarrow$ 2.) Assuming that $\mathcal{F}_n$ p-entails $E|H$, then $EH \neq \emptyset$, so that the assessment $z = 1$ on $E|H$ is coherent; moreover, the assessment $(1,\dots,1,z)$ on $\mathcal{F}_n \cup \{E|H\}$, where $z = P(E|H)$, is coherent if and only if $z = 1$. In fact, if by absurd the assessment $(1,\dots,1,z)$ were coherent for some $z < 1$, then given any ε, such that $1 - \varepsilon > z$, the condition

$$P(E_i|H_i) = 1, \; i = 1,\dots,n \implies P(E|H) > 1 - \varepsilon,$$

which is necessary for p-entailment of $E|H$ from $\mathcal{F}_n$, would be not satisfied.
(2. $\Rightarrow$ 3.) It immediately follows by the previous point, when $z = 0$.
(3. $\Rightarrow$ 4.) As the assessment $\mathcal{P} = (1,\dots,1,0)$ on $\mathcal{F} = \mathcal{F}_n \cup \{E|H\}$ is not coherent, by applying Algorithm 1 to the pair $(\mathcal{F}, \mathcal{P})$, at a certain iteration, say the k-th one, the initial system Σ_k will be not solvable and the algorithm will stop. The system Σ_k will be associated with a pair, say $(\mathcal{F}_k, \mathcal{P}_k)$, where $\mathcal{F}_k = \mathcal{S}_k \cup \{E|H\}$, with $\mathcal{S}_k \subseteq \mathcal{F}_n$, and where $\mathcal{P}_k = (1,\dots,1,0)$ is the sub-vector of $\mathcal{P}$ associated with $\mathcal{F}_k$. We distinguish two cases: (i) $\mathcal{S}_k \neq \emptyset$; (ii) $\mathcal{S}_k = \emptyset$.

(i) For the sake of simplicity, we set $\mathcal{S}_k = \{E_1|H_1,\dots,E_s|H_s\}$, with $s \leq n$; then, we denote by $C_1,\dots,C_m$ the constituents generated by the family $\mathcal{S}_k \cup \{E|H\}$ and contained in $H_1 \vee \cdots \vee H_s \vee H$. Now, we will prove that $\mathcal{C}(\mathcal{S}_k) \subseteq E|H$.

We have $\mathcal{C}(\mathcal{S}_k) = (E_1 H_1 \vee H_1^c) \wedge \cdots \wedge (E_s H_s \vee H_s^c) \,|\, (H_1 \vee \cdots \vee H_s)$ and, if it were $\mathcal{C}(\mathcal{S}_k) \not\subseteq E|H$, then there would exist at least a constituent, say C_1, of the following kind:
(a) $C_1 = B_1 A_1 \cdots B_r A_r A_{r+1}^c \cdots A_s^c E^c H$, $1 \leq r \leq s$, or
(b) $C_1 = H_1^c H_2^c \cdots H_s^c E^c H$, or
(c) $C_1 = B_1 A_1 \cdots B_r A_r A_{r+1}^c \cdots A_s^c H^c$, $1 \leq r \leq s$,
where $B_i|A_i = E_{j_i}|H_{j_i}$, $i = 1,\dots,s$, for a suitable permutation $(j_1,\dots,j_s)$ of $(1,\dots,s)$.
For each one of the three cases, (a), (b), (c), the vector $(\lambda_1, \lambda_2, \dots, \lambda_m) = (1, 0, \dots, 0)$, associated with the constituents $C_1, C_2, \dots, C_m$, would be a solution of the system Σ_k; then, Σ_k would be solvable, which would be a contradiction; hence, it cannot exist any constituent of kind (a), or (b), or (c); therefore, $\mathcal{C}(\mathcal{S}_k) \subseteq E|H$. Hence the assertion 4 is true for $\mathcal{S} = \mathcal{S}_k$.

(ii) If $\mathcal{S}_k = \emptyset$, then $\mathcal{F}_k = \{E|H\}$ and the algorithm stops as the assessment $P(E|H) = 0$ is not coherent; hence $E^c H = \emptyset$ which amounts to $H \subseteq E$.
(4. $\Rightarrow$ 5.) If $\mathcal{C}(\mathcal{S}) \subseteq E|H$ for some nonempty $\mathcal{S} \subseteq \mathcal{F}_n$, then, observing that by p-consistency of $\mathcal{F}_n$ the assessment $P[\mathcal{C}(\mathcal{S})] = 1$ is coherent, $\mathcal{C}(\mathcal{S})$ p-entails $E|H$. Otherwise, if $H \subseteq E$, then the unique coherent assessment on $E|H$ is $P(E|H) = 1$ and trivially $\mathcal{C}(\mathcal{S})$ p-entails $E|H$ for every nonempty $\mathcal{S} \subseteq \mathcal{F}_n$.

$(5. \Rightarrow 1.)$ Assuming that $\mathcal{C}(\mathcal{S})$ p-entails $E|H$ for some nonempty $\mathcal{S} \subseteq \mathcal{F}_n$, by Theorem 4 we have $\mathcal{F}_n \Rightarrow_p \mathcal{S} \Rightarrow_p \mathcal{C}(\mathcal{S}) \Rightarrow_p E|H$. Therefore $\mathcal{F}_n \Rightarrow_p E|H$.

The result below, which immediately follows by Theorem 5, illustrates the relation between p-entailment and the inclusion relation among conditional events.

Corollary 1. Given two conditional events $A|B, E|H$, with $AB \neq \emptyset$, we have

$$A|B \Rightarrow_p E|H \iff A|B \subseteq E|H \text{ or } H \subseteq E.$$

Proof. Since $AB \neq \emptyset$, the family $\{A|B\}$ is p-consistent. Then, the proof immediately follows by applying Theorem 5 with $n = 1$, $\mathcal{F}_1 = \{A|B\}$.

We observe that p-consistency of $\mathcal{F}_n \cup \{E|H\}$ is not sufficient for the p-entailment of $E|H$ from $\mathcal{F}_n$. More precisely, we have

Theorem 6. Given a family of n conditional events $\mathcal{F}_n = \{E_1|H_1, \ldots, E_n|H_n\}$ and a conditional event $E|H$, assume that $\mathcal{F}_n \cup \{E|H\}$ is p-consistent. Then, exactly one of the following alternatives holds:
(i) $\mathcal{F}_n$ p-entails $E|H$;
(ii) the assessment $\mathcal{P} = (1, \ldots, 1, z)$ on $\mathcal{F}_n \cup \{E|H\}$, where $P(E_i|H_i) = 1, i = 1, \ldots, n$, $P(E|H) = z$, is coherent for every $z \in [0, 1]$.

Proof. If statement (i) holds, by Theorem 5 the assessment $\mathcal{P}_0 = (1, \ldots, 1, 0)$ on $\mathcal{F} = \mathcal{F}_n \cup \{E|H\}$ is not coherent; hence, statement (ii) does not hold.
Conversely, if (i) doesn't hold, by Theorem 5 the assessment $\mathcal{P}_0 = (1, \ldots, 1, 0)$ on $\mathcal{F}_n \cup \{E|H\}$ is coherent. Moreover, by p-consistency of $\mathcal{F}_n \cup \{E|H\}$ the assessment $\mathcal{P}_1 = (1, \ldots, 1, 1)$ on $\mathcal{F}_n \cup \{E|H\}$ is coherent. Hence, the assessment $\mathcal{P} = (1, \ldots, 1, z)$ on $\mathcal{F}_n \cup \{E|H\}$ is coherent for every $z \in [0, 1]$; in other words, statement (ii) holds.

When $\mathcal{F}_n \cup \{E|H\}$ is not p-consistent, both statements (i) and (ii), in Theorem 6, do not hold. Concerning this aspect, we have

Theorem 7. Given a p-consistent family of n conditional events $\mathcal{F}_n$ and a further conditional event $E|H$, let $\mathcal{P} = (1, \ldots, 1, z)$ be a probability assessment on $\mathcal{F}_n \cup \{E|H\}$, where $P(E_i|H_i) = 1, i = 1, \ldots, n$, $P(E|H) = z$. Then, exactly one of the following statements is true:
(a) $\mathcal{P}$ is coherent if and only if $z = 1$;
(b) $\mathcal{P}$ is coherent for every $z \in [0, 1]$;
(c) $\mathcal{P}$ is coherent if and only if $z = 0$.

Proof. We distinguish two cases: 1) $\mathcal{F}_n \cup \{E|H\}$ p-consistent; 2) $\mathcal{F}_n \cup \{E|H\}$ not p-consistent. In case 1 statements (a) and (b) coincide with statements (i) and (ii) in Theorem 6; then, exactly one of them holds.

In case 2 the assessment $(1, \ldots, 1, 1)$ on $\mathcal{F}_n \cup \{E|H\}$ is not coherent; that is, the assessment $(1, \ldots, 1, 0)$ on $\mathcal{F}_n \cup \{E^c|H\}$ is not coherent and, by Theorem 5, $\mathcal{F}_n$ p-entails $E^c|H$. Then, the assessment $(1, \ldots, 1, p)$ on $\mathcal{F}_n \cup \{E^c|H\}$ is coherent if and only if $p = 1$, which amounts to say that the assessment $(1, \ldots, 1, z)$ on $\mathcal{F}_n \cup \{E|H\}$ is coherent if and only if $z = 0$; hence, statement (c) holds.

4   Further Results on Quasi Conjunction and Inclusion Relation

In this section we deepen the analysis of the quasi conjunction and the Goodman & Nguyen inclusion relation, by examining aspects which are especially related with results obtained in [2]. Given a family of n conditional events $\mathcal{F}_n$ and a further conditional event $E|H$, we give some results on the subsets $\mathcal{S}$ of $\mathcal{F}_n$ such that $\mathcal{C}(\mathcal{S}) \subseteq E|H$. We start by showing that the relation $\mathcal{C}(\mathcal{S}) \subseteq E|H$ amounts to unsolvability of a suitable system Σ.

Theorem 8. Given a p-consistent family of s conditional events $\mathcal{S} = \{E_1|H_1,$ $\ldots, E_s|H_s\}$, with $s \geq 1$, and a further conditional event $E|H$, let $\mathcal{P} = (1, \ldots, 1, 0)$ be a probability assessment on $\mathcal{F} = \mathcal{S} \cup \{E|H\}$. Moreover, let Σ be the starting system associated with the pair $(\mathcal{F}, \mathcal{P})$ when applying Algorithm 1. We have

$$\Sigma \text{ unsolvable} \iff \mathcal{C}(\mathcal{S}) \subseteq E|H. \tag{4}$$

Proof. ($\Rightarrow$) If Σ is unsolvable, then $\mathcal{P} = (1, \ldots, 1, 0)$ is not coherent and, by applying the part ($3 \Rightarrow 4$) of Theorem 5 with $\mathcal{F}_n = \mathcal{S}$, Algorithm 1 stops at $\Sigma_k = \Sigma, \mathcal{S}_k = \mathcal{S}$. Then, we have $\mathcal{C}(\mathcal{S}_k) = \mathcal{C}(\mathcal{S}) \subseteq E|H$.

($\Leftarrow$) Assume that $\mathcal{C}(\mathcal{S}) \subseteq E|H$ and, by absurd, that Σ is solvable. This means that the point $\mathcal{P}$ belongs to the convex hull $\mathcal{I}$ of the points Q_h associated with the pair $(\mathcal{F}, \mathcal{P})$; that is, $\mathcal{P}$ is a linear convex combination of the points Q_h. Then, as $\mathcal{P}$ is a vertex of the unitary hypercube $[0, 1]^{s+1}$, which contains $\mathcal{I}$, the condition $\mathcal{P} \in \mathcal{I}$ is satisfied if and only if there exists a point Q_h, say Q_1, which coincides with $\mathcal{P}$. Then, there exists at least a constituent C_1 of the kind (a), or (b), or (c), as defined in the proof of Theorem 5, and this implies that $\mathcal{C}(\mathcal{S}) \not\subseteq E|H$, which contradicts the hypothesis.

Given a family $\mathcal{F}_n$ and a further conditional event $E|H$, let $\mathcal{K}(\mathcal{F}_n, E|H)$ be the class of all nonempty subsets $\mathcal{S}$ of $\mathcal{F}_n$ such that $\mathcal{C}(\mathcal{S}) \subseteq E|H$. As the family $\mathcal{F}_n$ is finite, the class $\mathcal{K}(\mathcal{F}_n, E|H)$ is finite too. For the sake of simplicity, we simply denote $\mathcal{K}(\mathcal{F}_n, E|H)$ by $\mathcal{K}$. In the next result we show that $\mathcal{K}$ is additive.

Theorem 9. Given two nonempty subsets $\mathcal{S}'$ and $\mathcal{S}''$ of $\mathcal{F}_n$ and a conditional event $E|H$, assume that $\mathcal{S}' \in \mathcal{K}$, $\mathcal{S}'' \in \mathcal{K}$. Then, $\mathcal{S}' \cup \mathcal{S}'' \in \mathcal{K}$.

Proof. By the associative property, it is $\mathcal{C}(\mathcal{S}' \cup \mathcal{S}'') = \mathcal{C}(\mathcal{C}(\mathcal{S}'), \mathcal{C}(\mathcal{S}''))$; then:
(i) $\mathcal{C}(\mathcal{S}' \cup \mathcal{S}'')$ *true* implies $\mathcal{C}(\mathcal{S}')$ *true*, or $\mathcal{C}(\mathcal{S}'')$ *true*; hence, $E|H$ is *true*;
(ii) $E|H$ *false* implies that $\mathcal{C}(\mathcal{S}')$ and $\mathcal{C}(\mathcal{S}'')$ are both *false*; hence, $\mathcal{C}(\mathcal{S}' \cup \mathcal{S}'')$ is *false*. Therefore: $\mathcal{C}(\mathcal{S}' \cup \mathcal{S}'') \subseteq E|H$. Hence $\mathcal{S}' \cup \mathcal{S}'' \in \mathcal{K}$; that is $\mathcal{K}$ is additive.

It immediately follows

Corollary 2. Given two subsets $\mathcal{S}$ and $\mathcal{U}$ of $\mathcal{F}_n$, assume that $\mathcal{S} \subset \mathcal{U}$, with $\mathcal{C}(\mathcal{S}) \subseteq E|H$, $\mathcal{C}(\mathcal{U}) \not\subseteq E|H$. Then: $\mathcal{C}(\mathcal{U} \setminus \mathcal{S}) \not\subseteq E|H$.

Proof. The proof immediately follows by Theorem 9 by observing that, if $\mathcal{C}(\mathcal{U} \setminus \mathcal{S}) \subseteq E|H$, then $\mathcal{C}[\mathcal{S} \cup (\mathcal{U} \setminus \mathcal{S})] = \mathcal{C}(\mathcal{U}) \subseteq E|H$, which contradicts the hypothesis.

We observe that $A|H \subseteq B|K$ amounts to $H^c B^c K = AHB^c K = AHK^c = \emptyset$; then $\mathcal{C}(A|H, B|K) = (AH \vee H^c BK)|(H \vee K)$ and, as we can verify, it is

$$A|H \subseteq \mathcal{C}(A|H, B|K) \subseteq B|K. \tag{5}$$

Theorem 10. Let $\mathcal{F}_n$ be a family of n conditional events, with $n \geq 2$, and $E|H$ be a further conditional event. Moreover, let $\mathcal{S}$ and Γ be two nonempty subfamilies of $\mathcal{F}_n$ such that $\mathcal{C}(\mathcal{S}) \subseteq \mathcal{C}(\Gamma)$ and $\mathcal{C}(\mathcal{S} \cup \Gamma) \subseteq E|H$. Then, we have $\mathcal{C}(\mathcal{S}) \subseteq E|H$.

Proof. By the associative property of quasi conjunction we have $\mathcal{C}(\mathcal{C}(\mathcal{S}), \mathcal{C}(\Gamma)) = \mathcal{C}(\mathcal{S} \cup \Gamma)$; then, by applying (5), with $A|H = \mathcal{C}(\mathcal{S})$ and $B|K = \mathcal{C}(\Gamma)$, we obtain $\mathcal{C}(\mathcal{S}) \subseteq \mathcal{C}(\mathcal{S} \cup \Gamma) \subseteq \mathcal{C}(\Gamma)$. As $\mathcal{C}(\mathcal{S} \cup \Gamma) \subseteq E|H$, it follows $\mathcal{C}(\mathcal{S}) \subseteq E|H$.

We observe that, in case $H \subseteq E$, trivially $\mathcal{F}_n$ p-entails $E|H$ and at the same time the class $\mathcal{K}$ could be empty. We have

Theorem 11. Given a family of n conditional events $\mathcal{F}_n$ and a further conditional event $E|H$, with $H \not\subseteq E$, assume that $\mathcal{F}_n$ p-entails $E|H$. Then, the class $\mathcal{K}$ is not empty and has a greatest element $\mathcal{S}^*$. Moreover, for every nonempty subset $\mathcal{S}$ of $\mathcal{F}_n$, it holds that $\mathcal{S}$ p-entails $E|H$ if and only if $\mathcal{S} \in \mathcal{K}$.

Proof. Since $\mathcal{F}_n$ p-entails $E|H$, by assertion 4 in Theorem 5, $\mathcal{K}$ is not empty; moreover, by recalling Theorem 9, $\mathcal{K}$ is additive. Then, denoting by $\mathcal{S}^*$ the union of all elements of $\mathcal{K}$, it holds that $\mathcal{S}^* \in \mathcal{K}$. Of course, $\mathcal{S}^*$ is the greatest element of $\mathcal{K}$; that is, $\mathcal{S} \subseteq \mathcal{S}^*$, for every $\mathcal{S} \in \mathcal{K}$.

We observe that, assuming $H \not\subseteq E$, by Theorem 5 we have that $\mathcal{F}_n$ p-entails $E|H$ if and only if there exists a nonempty subset $\mathcal{S}_k$ of $\mathcal{F}_n$ such that, when applying Algorithm 1 to the assessment $\mathcal{P} = (1, \ldots, 1, 0)$ on $\mathcal{F} = \mathcal{F}_n \cup \{E|H\}$, the system Σ_k, associated with the family $\mathcal{S}_k \cup \{E|H\}$, is not solvable and the algorithm will stop. We have

Theorem 12. Let $\mathcal{P} = (1, \ldots, 1, 0)$ be a probability assessment on the family $\mathcal{F} = \mathcal{F}_n \cup \{E|H\}$, where $\mathcal{F}_n$ p-entails $E|H$, with $H \not\subseteq E$. Then, by applying Algorithm 1 to the pair $(\mathcal{F}, \mathcal{P})$, the nonempty subset $\mathcal{S}_k$, associated with the iteration where Algorithm 1 stops, coincides with the greatest element $\mathcal{S}^*$ of $\mathcal{K}$.

Proof. By Theorem 5 it is $\mathcal{C}(\mathcal{S}_k) \subseteq E|H$, so that $\mathcal{S}_k \in \mathcal{K}$ and hence $\mathcal{S}_k \subseteq \mathcal{S}^*$. In order to prove that $\mathcal{S}_k = \mathcal{S}^*$, we will show that $\mathcal{S}_k \subset \mathcal{S}^*$ gives a contradiction. If $\mathcal{S}_k = \mathcal{F}_n$, then $\mathcal{S}_k = \mathcal{S}^*$. Assume that $\mathcal{S}_k \subset \mathcal{F}_n$ and, by absurd, that $\mathcal{S}_k \subset \mathcal{S}^*$. By applying Algorithm 1 to the pair $(\mathcal{F}, \mathcal{P})$ we obtain a partition $\Gamma^{(1)}, \Gamma^{(2)}, \ldots, \Gamma^{(k)}$, with $k > 1$, such that is

$$\mathcal{F}_n \cup \{E|H\} = \Gamma^{(1)} \cup \Gamma^{(2)} \cup \cdots \cup \Gamma^{(k)}; \quad \Gamma^{(i)} \cap \Gamma^{(j)} = \emptyset, \text{ if } i \neq j,$$

where $\Gamma^{(k)} = \mathcal{F}_k = \mathcal{S}_k \cup \{E|H\}$. Then $\mathcal{S}^* \cap \Gamma^{(k)} = \mathcal{S}_k$. Now, by the hypothesis $\mathcal{S}_k \subset \mathcal{S}^*$ it follows $\mathcal{S}^* \cap \Gamma^{(j)} \neq \emptyset$ for at least an index $j < k$. Let r be the minimum index such that $\mathcal{S}^* \cap \Gamma^{(r)} \neq \emptyset$ and set $\mathcal{F}^{(j)} = \Gamma^{(j)} \cup \cdots \cup \Gamma^{(k)}$, $j = r, r+1$. Hence

$\mathcal{S}^* \subseteq \mathcal{F}^{(r)}$, $\mathcal{S}^* \setminus \mathcal{F}^{(r+1)} \neq \emptyset$; moreover, the system $\Sigma^{(r)}$ associated with the pair $(\mathcal{F}^{(r)}, \mathcal{P}^{(r)})$ is solvable. We set $J = \{j : E_j|H_j \in \mathcal{S}^*\}$, $\mathcal{F}_J = \mathcal{S}^* \cup \{E|H\}$; moreover, we denote by $\mathcal{P}_J$ the sub-vector of $\mathcal{P}$ associated with $\mathcal{F}_J$. Then, by Theorem 2 it follows that the system Σ_J associated with the pair $(\mathcal{F}_J, \mathcal{P}_J)$ is solvable and by Theorem 8 we have $\mathcal{C}(\mathcal{S}^*) \not\subseteq E|H$, which is absurd as $\mathcal{S}^* \in \mathcal{K}$. Therefore $\mathcal{S}_k = \mathcal{S}^*$.

Based on Remark 1 and Theorem 12, we give below a suitably modified version of Algorithm 1, which allows to examine the following aspects: (i) checking for p-consistency of $\mathcal{F}_n$; (ii) checking for p-entailment of $E|H$ from $\mathcal{F}_n$; (iii) computation of the greatest element $\mathcal{S}^*$.

Algorithm 2. Let be given the pair $(\mathcal{F}_n, E|H)$, with $\mathcal{F}_n = \{E_1|H_1, \ldots, E_n|H_n\}$ and $H \not\subseteq E$.

1. Set $\mathcal{P}_n = (1, 1, \ldots, 1)$, where $P(E_i|H_i) = 1$, $i = 1, \ldots, n$. Check the coherence of $\mathcal{P}_n$ on $\mathcal{F}_n$ by Algorithm 1. If $\mathcal{P}_n$ on $\mathcal{F}_n$ is coherent then $\mathcal{F}_n$ is p-consistent, set $\mathcal{F} = \mathcal{F}_n \cup \{E|H\}$, $\mathcal{P} = (\mathcal{P}_n, 0)$ and go to step 2; otherwise $\mathcal{F}_n$ is not p-consistent and procedure stops.
2. Construct the system Σ associated with $(\mathcal{F}, \mathcal{P})$ and check its solvability.
3. If the system Σ is not solvable then $\mathcal{F}_n$ p-entails $E|H$, $\mathcal{S}^* = \mathcal{F} \setminus \{E|H\}$ and the procedure stops; otherwise compute the set I_0.
4. If $I_0 = \emptyset$ then $\mathcal{F}_n$ does not p-entail $E|H$ and the procedure stops; otherwise set $(\mathcal{F}, \mathcal{P}) = (\mathcal{F}_0, \mathcal{P}_0)$ and repeat steps 2-4.

We didn't make any comparison with other algorithms existing in literature for checking p-consistency and p-entailment; we just note, as a further aspect, that Algorithm 2 determines the greatest element (if any), $\mathcal{S}^*$.
The example below illustrates Theorems 5 and 10.

Example 1. Given four logically independent events A, B, C, D, consider the family $\mathcal{F}_5 = \{C|B, B|A, A|(A \vee B), B|(A \vee B), D|A^c\}$ and the further conditional event $C|A$. It can be proved that the assessment $\mathcal{P}_5 = (1, 1, 1, 1, 1)$ on $\mathcal{F}_5$ is coherent; hence $\mathcal{F}_5$ is p-consistent. We have $\mathcal{C}(\mathcal{F}_5) = (ABC \vee A^c B^c D)|\Omega \not\subseteq C|A$. Moreover, defining

$$\mathcal{S}_1 = \mathcal{F}_5 \setminus \{D|A^c\} = \{C|B, B|A, A|(A \vee B), B|(A \vee B)\},$$

we have $\mathcal{C}(\mathcal{S}_1) = ABC|(A \vee B) \subset C|A$; hence, by Theorem 5, $\mathcal{F}_5$ p-entails $C|A$ and then it is $\mathcal{S}^* = \mathcal{S}_1$. We observe that, defining

$$\mathcal{S}_2 = \mathcal{S}_1 \setminus \{B|(A \vee B)\} = \{C|B, B|A, A|(A \vee B)\},$$

it is: $\mathcal{C}(\mathcal{S}_2) = ABC|(A \vee B) \subset B|(A \vee B)$; hence, by Theorem 10, $\mathcal{C}(\mathcal{S}_2) \subset C|A$, that is $\mathcal{S}_2 \in \mathcal{K}$. We also observe that, defining

$$\mathcal{S}_3 = \mathcal{S}_1 \setminus \{B|A\} = \{C|B, A|(A \vee B), B|(A \vee B)\},$$

it is: $\mathcal{C}(\mathcal{S}_3) = ABC|(A \vee B) \subset B|A$; hence, by Theorem 10, $\mathcal{C}(\mathcal{S}_3) \subset C|A$, that is $\mathcal{S}_3 \in \mathcal{K}$. Finally, it can be proved that $\mathcal{K} = \{\mathcal{S}_1, \mathcal{S}_2, \mathcal{S}_3\}$.

5   Conclusions

We obtained some results on quasi conjunction and Goodman & Nguyen inclusion relation for conditional events, in the setting of probabilistic default reasoning under coherence. We deepened two results given in a recent paper ([7]); the first one concerns the probabilistic semantics of $QAND$ rule; the second one concerns the equivalence between p-entailment from $\mathcal{F}_n$ and p-entailment from $\mathcal{C}(\mathcal{S})$, for some nonempty subset $\mathcal{S}$ of $\mathcal{F}_n$. We also characterized p-entailment by some alternative theorems. Finally, we introduced for a pair $(\mathcal{F}_n, E|H)$ the class $\mathcal{K}$ of the subsets $\mathcal{S}$ of $\mathcal{F}_n$ such that $\mathcal{C}(\mathcal{S})$ implies $E|H$, by showing that $\mathcal{K}$ is additive and its greatest element $\mathcal{S}^*$ can be determined by Algorithm 2.

Acknowledgments. The authors thank the Referees for their very useful comments and suggestions.

References

1. Adams, E.W.: The Logic of Conditionals. D. Reidel, Dordrecht (1975)
2. Biazzo, V., Gilio, A., Lukasiewicz, T., Sanfilippo, G.: Probabilistic Logic under Coherence, Model-Theoretic Probabilistic Logic, and Default Reasoning in System P. Journal of Applied Non-Classical Logics 12(2), 189–213 (2002)
3. Coletti, G., Scozzafava, R.: Probabilistic Logic in a Coherent Setting, Trends in Logics, vol. 15. Kluwer Academic Publishers, Dordrecht (2002)
4. Dubois, D., Prade, H.: Conditional Objects as Nonmonotonic Consequence Relationships. IEEE Trans. Syst. Man Cybern. 24, 1724–1740 (1994)
5. Gilio, A.: Probabilistic Reasoning under Coherence in System P. Ann. Math. Artif. Intell. 34(1-3), 5–34 (2002)
6. Gilio, A.: On Császár's Condition in Nonmonotonic Reasoning. In: 10th International Workshop on Non-Monotonic Reasoning. Special Session: Uncertainty Frameworks in Non-Monotonic Reasoning, Whistler BC, Canada, June 6-8 (2004), http://events.pims.math.ca/science/2004/NMR/uf.html
7. Gilio, A., Sanfilippo, G.: Quasi Conjunction and p-entailment in Nonmonotonic Reasoning. In: Borgelt, C., et al. (eds.) Combining Soft Computing and Statistical Methods in Data Analysis. Advances in Intelligent and Soft Computing, vol. 77, pp. 321–328. Springer, Heidelberg (2010)
8. Goodman, I.R., Nguyen, H.T.: Conditional Objects and the Modeling of Uncertainties. In: Gupta, M.M., Yamakawa, T. (eds.) Fuzzy Computing: Theory, Hardware, and Applications, pp. 119–138. North-Holland, Amsterdam (1988)
9. Kraus, S., Lehmann, D.J., Magidor, M.: Nonmonotonic Reasoning, Preferential Models and Cumulative Logics. Artif. Intell. 44(1-2), 167–207 (1990)

Handling Exceptions in Logic Programming without Negation as Failure

Roberto Confalonieri[1], Henri Prade[2], and Juan Carlos Nieves[1]

[1] Universitat Politècnica de Catalunya
Dept. Llenguatges i Sistemes Informàtics
C/ Jordi Girona Salgado 1-3
E - 08034 Barcelona
{confalonieri,jcnieves}@lsi.upc.edu
[2] Institut de Recherche en Informatique Toulouse (IRIT)
Universitè Paul Sabatier
118 Route de Narbonne
31062 Toulouse Cedex 9, France
prade@irit.fr

Abstract. Default rules, i.e. statements of the form *normally a's are b's*, are usually handled in Answer Set Programming by means of negation as failure which provides a way to capture exceptions to normal situations. In this paper we propose another approach which offers an operational counterpart to negation as failure, and which may be thought as a corresponding dual attitude. The approach amounts to an explicit rewriting of exceptions in default rules, together with the addition of completion rules that are consistent with current knowledge. It is shown that the approach can be applied to restore the consistency of inconsistent programs that implicitly involve specificity ordering between the rules. The approach is compared to previous works aiming at providing support to the rewriting of default rules. It is also shown how the proposed approach agrees with the results obtained in the classical way.

1 Introduction

Nonmonotonic reasoning is one of the distinctive features of Answer Set Programming (ASP) when addressing knowledge representation problems with inheritance hierarchies [1]. Default rules, *i.e.* normative statements of the form *normally p's are q's*, are usually modeled by normal rules $q \leftarrow p, not\ ab$, or by extended normal rules $q \leftarrow p, not\ ab, not\neg q$ (when factual knowledge with strong negation is allowed) which contain abnormality atoms (ab) preceded by negation as failure (not). Modeling exceptions by means of negated-as-failure atoms amounts, from a semantics point of view, to check whether a strong exception, *i.e. ab*, or a weak exception, *i.e.* $\neg q$ can be proved. In such case, more specific information is preferred to that which is more general, in accordance to the *inheritance reasoning principle* [16].

According to this classical ASP approach, exceptions have to be made explicit for capturing abnormal situations and blocking the applicability of conflicting

W. Liu (Ed.): ECSQARU 2011, LNAI 6717, pp. 509–520, 2011.
© Springer-Verlag Berlin Heidelberg 2011

default rules in the reasoning process [1]. Writing exceptions explicitly is not always the easiest way to go. For instance, when different nodes of knowledge encoded by default rules are integrated, the knowledge produced can be inconsistent and can contain different levels of specificity. In such a case, an automatic handling of rules exceptions based on specificity can prevent the knowledge engineer from a manual and time-consuming exceptions specification.

Specificity is a well-known notion in nonmonotonic reasoning [14,11]. For instance, System Z [14] provides a good example of a system that implicitly prefers more specific information. But what about if we want to rewrite exceptions to default rules in an automatic way? Approaches such as [3,6] have shown that generating exceptions based on the notion of specificity is appealing in nonmonotonic logics such as default logic.

More recently, some approaches to exception rewriting based on specificity have been proposed in the context of ASP [8,9]. Garcia *et al.* in [9] have recently adapted the work in [6] to propose a methodology for representing default rules with exceptions by automatically generating negated-by-failure exceptions from a compact representation of the information. However, sometimes it can be interesting to model exceptions in a way closer to classical logic. For instance, in a recently proposed methodology for modeling qualitative decision making in ASP [4], knowledge about the world is encoded by means of extended definite logic programs, *i.e.* negation-as-failure free. When such knowledge contains default rules, exceptions must be properly handled.

In this paper we propose a novel approach which offers an operational counterpart to negation as failure. Our approach amounts to an explicit rewriting of exceptions in terms of strong negated atoms in extended definite rules, together with the addition of completion rules that are consistent with current knowledge. Thus, it may be viewed as a dual attitude w.r.t. classical methods that rely on negation as failure. In fact, in ASP, rules with negation as failure remain intrinsically default rules, while in our approach the default rules become strict rules after a proper rewriting, as suggested in the following example.

Example 1. Let us consider a set of default rules Δ representing the typical birds and penguins knowledge representation problem: *birds normally fly, birds normally have legs, penguins normally are birds,* and *penguins normally do not fly.* From $\Delta = \{r_1 = f \leftarrow b, r_2 = l \leftarrow b, r_3 = b \leftarrow p, r_4 = f' \leftarrow p\}$ we want to obtain a set of strict rules $S = \{r_1 = f \leftarrow b \wedge p', r_2 = l \leftarrow b, r_3 = b \leftarrow p, r_4 = f' \leftarrow p\}$ and the set of completion rules $CR = \{cr_1 = p' \leftarrow b\}$.[1]

The proposed method, described in this paper, turns to be simple to process and to have several noticeable features: it defines a rewriting of default rules into strict ones and it is able to restore the consistency of inconsistent programs that implicitly involve specificity ordering between the rules. It allows to face the blocking inheritance problem (a weakness of the Z-ordering) and to infer floating information (as in the Nixon diamond example). It takes its inspiration from a proposal made in the setting of possibilistic logic [15].

---

[1] Atoms with the prime denote strong negated atoms as we will discuss in Section 2.

The article is organized as follows. After introducing some background and the notation we use throughout the paper (Section 2), in Section 3 we describe the algorithm which allows to handle default knowledge without negation as failure. Section 4 relates our approach to the classical handling of exceptions in ASP. Finally, Section 5 points out some future work and concludes the paper.

2   Background and Notation

In this paper we will consider logic programs which contain only one type of negation, in particular the so called *strong negation* in ASP community denoted by $\neg$. Following Gelfond and Lifschitz' notation [10], a *literal* is a formula of the form a or $\neg a$, where a is an atom. Hence, *an extended definite rule r* is of the form $r = l_0 \leftarrow l_1 \wedge \ldots \wedge l_m$, where l_i's $(0 \leq i \leq m)$ are literals. In a slight abuse of notation we sometimes write a rule r as $l \leftarrow \mathcal{B}$ where $head(r) = l$ is a literal called the *head* and $\mathcal{B} = \{l_1, \ldots, l_m\}$ is a literal set called the body (also denoted by $body(r)$). If $body(r) = \emptyset$ then $r = l \leftarrow \top$ is known as a fact and we write it as l. Then, an *extended definite logic program P* is a finite set of extended definite rules. By $\mathcal{L}_P$, we denote the set of atoms in the language of P.

In our logic programs we will manage strong negation ($\neg$) as it is done in ASP [1]. Basically, each extended atom $\neg a$ is replaced by a new atom symbol a' which does not appear in the language of the program $\mathcal{L}_P$. Then the new language of the program is $\mathcal{L}'_P$. More precisely we define:

Definition 1. *Let φ be a mapping function s.t.* $\varphi(x) = \begin{cases} x' : & \text{if } x \in \mathcal{L}_P \\ x : & \text{if } x \in \mathcal{L}'_P \setminus \mathcal{L}_P \end{cases}$

Please notice that an extended definite rule r with the $\neg$ replacement above is a definite rule. As a consequence, we are basically dealing with *definite logic programs* in this paper. Given a rule r and an atom set A, we say that r is applicable in A if $body(r) \subseteq A$. An atom set A is closed under a program P if and only if for each rule r in P, if $body(r) \subseteq A$ then $head(r) \in A$. Given a set of rules R, we define a consequence operator T_R which maps a set of atoms to another one as $T_R(A) = Head(App(R, A))$, where $App(R, A)$ is a set $R' \subseteq R$ such that R' is applicable w.r.t. A and $Head(R') = \{head(r) \mid r \in R'\}$. $T_R(A)$ computes the set of atoms deducible from A by means of R. $T_R(A)$ allows to define the sequence $T_R^0 = T_R(\emptyset)$, $T_R^{k+1} = T_R(T_R^k)$, $\forall k \geq 0$. The operator is monotonic and it always reaches a fix-point which contains all the atoms which can be produced by a set of rules. The consequence operator provides an operational way to characterize the minimal model of a definite logic program P. Indeed, $Cn(P) = \bigcup_{k \geq 0} T_P^k$ contains all the consequences of P and denotes its unique minimal model (that always exists, see [13]).

We say that a set of atoms A is inconsistent if there exists a such that $\{a, a'\} \subset A$, otherwise it is consistent. By **cons**(A) (resp., **incons**(A)), we denote two Boolean functions which return true (resp., false) if the set of atoms A is consistent (resp., inconsistent). A definite logic program P is inconsistent when its minimal model is inconsistent, and consistent otherwise.

In this paper we will assume that a program P consists with different sets of definite rules. In particular, we define:

Definition 2. *A definite logic program* $P_{\langle \Delta, S, FC, CR \rangle}$ *is a tuple* $\langle \Delta, S, FC, CR \rangle$, *such that* Δ *is a finite set of definite rules we call default rules, S is a finite set of definite rules we call strict rules, FC is a finite set of facts we call factual context, and CR is a finite set of definite rules we call completion rules.*

Intuitively, Δ is the set of rules which can admit exceptions, S is the set of rewritten rules from Δ where exceptions have been made explicit, FC is the set of contextual knowledge, and CR is the set of additional rules needed to cope with incomplete information. By convention we omit the subindex in the writing of $P_{\langle \Delta, S, FC, CR \rangle}$ whenever the corresponding set of rules is empty, *e.g.* $P_{\langle S, FC, CR \rangle}$ when $\Delta = \emptyset$, $P_{\langle S, FC \rangle}$ when $\Delta = \emptyset$ and $CR = \emptyset$. For representation issues throughout the paper we denote rules belonging to Δ by $r_\Delta = l_\Delta \leftarrow \mathcal{B}_\Delta$ and rules belonging to S by $r_s = l_s \leftarrow \mathcal{B}_s$.

Example 2. Let us consider the set of default rules Δ in Example 1. It can be checked that the program $P_{\langle \Delta, FC \rangle}$ where $FC = \{p\}$ is the factual context about a penguin p, is inconsistent since $Cn(P) = \{p, b, l, f, f'\}$ is inconsistent.

3   Handling Default Reasoning

In [15] Dupin de Saint-Cyr and Prade have made a proposal for handling uncertain default rules in the possibilistic logic setting. Indeed possibility theory provides a framework both for modeling qualitative uncertainty and for modeling default rules of the form *if p then generally q* by means of constraints stating that having $p \wedge q$ true is strictly more possible than having $p \wedge \neg q$ true. The exploitation of such constraints induces a priority ordering between defaults according to their specificity [2]. This ordering has been proved to be the same as the one given by System Z [14]. Since uncertain default rules are associated with both an uncertainty level and a priority level, there was a need for rewriting defaults as ordinary possibilistic logic formulas associated only with an uncertainty level. It is this kind of rewriting idea that we introduce in the ASP setting.

The algorithm we are proposing allows to mirror nonmonotonic reasoning in logic programming without negation as failure by making exceptions explicit in rules while adding completion rules for coping with incomplete information. The method consists in four general steps (Algorithm 1) we briefly summarize before discussing them in details in the next subsections.

First, program rules which have not the same specificity have to be localized; this is done by using the notion of tolerance of a rule of system Z [14] adapted to ASP programs (line 3). Secondly, default rules which are exceptional w.r.t. other more specific rules are rewritten in order to make the condition part more explicit. At the same time, completion rules aiming at completing the encountered exceptional situations are added; this is done by the rewriting algorithm (line 4). When factual context is added to the rewritten program, a consistency check

---

Algorithm 1. General Algorithm

Input: $\begin{cases} \Delta : \text{a set of default rules} \\ FC : \text{factual context} \end{cases}$

Output: $\big\{ M : \text{the minimal model of } P_{\langle S,FC,CR \rangle} \big\}$
1: $S = \emptyset;$ // the set of strict rules
2: $CR = \emptyset;$ // the set of completion rules
3: $\langle \Delta_0, \ldots, \Delta_n \rangle \leftarrow Z - ordering(\Delta)$
4: $\langle S, CR \rangle \leftarrow writeExceptions(\langle \Delta_0, \ldots, \Delta_n \rangle)$
5: $P_{\langle S,FC,CR \rangle} \leftarrow testConsistency(S, FC, CR)$
6: $M \leftarrow Cn(P_{\langle S,FC,CR \rangle})$
7: **return** $\langle M \rangle$

---

is made between the context, the completion rules, and the relevant rewritten rules (line 5). Finally, factual context and consistent completion rules are added to the rewritten program, and the minimal model is computed (line 6).

3.1 Ordering Rules by Specificity

Pearl [14] provides an algorithm which gives a stratification of a set of default rules in a way that reflects the *specificity* of the rules. Roughly speaking, the first stratum contains the most specific rules, *i.e.* which do not admit exceptions (at least, expressed in the considered default base), the second stratum has exceptions only in the first stratum and so on. Thus, in System Z, a set of rules R is stratified into subsets $R_0, \ldots, R_n$ where the resulting partitioning is called a Z-ordering. Although there can be several orderings compatible with a set of default rules, the *minimal specificity ordering* is unique [14]. We assume this unique ordering for the sake of this paper.

As we are dealing with set of atoms rather than interpretations, we have to adapt the notion of tolerance of a rule to ASP. For this reason we have reused the definition of *rule tolerance* introduced in [9].

Definition 3. *A rule* r_Δ *is said to be* tolerated *by a set of default rules* Δ *iff there is an atom set* A, *closed under* Δ *and consistent, which verifies* r_Δ. *A verifies* r_Δ *if* $\mathcal{B}_\Delta \subseteq A \wedge l_\Delta \in A$.

The tolerance of the rule characterizes the fact that its application does not generate any contradiction. From this notion of tolerance, it is possible to obtain a stratification of the program which allows us to stratify Δ into $(\Delta_0, \Delta_1, \ldots, \Delta_n)$ such that: Δ_0 contains the set of rules of Δ tolerated by Δ; Δ_1 contains the set of rules of $\Delta \backslash \Delta_0$ tolerated by $\Delta \backslash \Delta_0$; Δ_2 contains the set of rules of $\Delta \backslash (\Delta_0 \cup \Delta_1)$ tolerated by $\Delta \backslash (\Delta_0 \cup \Delta_1)$ *etc.*

Example 3. Let us consider the set of rules in Example 1 $\Delta = \{ r_1 = f \leftarrow b,$ $r_2 = l \leftarrow b$, $r_3 = b \leftarrow p$, $r_4 = f' \leftarrow p \}$. $A = \{b, f, l\}$ verifies r_1, is closed under Δ and it is consistent. So r_1 is tolerated in Δ, and $r_1 \in \Delta_0$. Similarly r_2 belongs to Δ_0. The only set which verifies r_3 and is closed w.r.t. r_1, r_2, and r_4

is $A' = \{b, p, l, f, f'\}$, but it is inconsistent. So $r_3 \in \Delta_1$. In the same way, we obtain $r_4 \in \Delta_1$. Thus, the Z-ordering associated to Δ is $\Delta_0 = \{r_1 = f \leftarrow b, r_2 = l \leftarrow b\}$, $\Delta_1 = \{r_3 = b \leftarrow p, r_4 = f' \leftarrow p\}$.

3.2   Rules Rewriting

The general idea of the rewriting is to generate automatically from Δ a set of rules in which the condition parts explicitly state that we are not in an exceptional context to which other default rules refer. In practice, this amounts to transform the set of default rules Δ into a set of strict rules S with explicit exceptions and a set of completion rules CR.

In order to make exceptions explicit, the proposed rewriting considers rules specificity. At the beginning rules in the last stratum of the Z-ordering are accepted as strict rules (since they are the most specific ones). Then, lower strata are processed in order to identify the set of exceptions of less specific default rules (if any) w.r.t. the strict rules. Default rules are rewritten into strict ones where exceptions are made explicit. In case of exceptions, completion rules aiming at completing contextual knowledge are added. The procedure keeps on fixing lower strata based on the computed strict rules until all strata have been considered. In order to define the algorithm in a more precise way we need several definitions.

Definition 4 (Exceptional Set). *Let* $S = \{r_{s_i} = l_{s_i} \leftarrow \mathcal{B}_{s_i} \mid 1 \leq i \leq n\}$ *be a set of strict rules. For any given default rule* $r_\Delta = l_\Delta \leftarrow \mathcal{B}_\Delta$ *we define the exceptional set in* r_{s_i} *to the rule* r_Δ *as* $E_i(r_\Delta, r_{s_i}) = \mathcal{B}_{s_i}$ *s.t.* $l_{s_i} \leftarrow \mathcal{B}_{s_i} \in S \wedge \mathbf{cons}(\mathcal{B}_\Delta \cup \mathcal{B}_{s_i}) \wedge \mathbf{incons}(\{l_\Delta\} \cup \{l_{s_i}\})$. *Then, the set of exceptional sets in* S *to a rule* r_Δ *is defined as* $\mathcal{E}(r_\Delta, S) = \{E_i(r_\Delta, r_{s_i}) \mid r_{s_i} \in S\}$.

The above definition collects all the exceptional sets in all strict rules to a given default rule r_Δ. For instance for a default rule $r'_\Delta = f \leftarrow b$ and strict rules $S = \{r_{s_1} = f' \leftarrow a \wedge c, r_{s_2} = f' \leftarrow p\}$, then $\mathcal{E}(r_\Delta, S) = \{\{a, c\}, \{p\}\}$. This distinction is crucial for handling the case where the body of a strict rule is not a singleton. Once all the exception of a default rule w.r.t. a set of strict rules have been identified, the default rule can be rewritten in the following way.

Definition 5 (Default Rule Rewriting). *Let* $r_\Delta = l_\Delta \leftarrow \mathcal{B}_\Delta$ *be a default rule,* $S = \{r_{s_i} = l_{s_i} \leftarrow \mathcal{B}_{s_i} \mid 1 \leq i \leq n\}$ *be a set of strict rules, and* $\mathcal{E}(r_\Delta, S)$ *be the set of exceptional sets in* S *to the rule* r_Δ. *Then, for each* $E_i(r_\Delta, r_{s_i})$, r_Δ *is rewritten into a new strict rule* r_s *by setting:* $r_s = l_\Delta \leftarrow \mathcal{B}_\Delta \cup \{\varphi(x) \mid x \in E_i(r_\Delta, r_{s_i})\}$.

The rewritten rule is added to the set S. Please notice that when the exceptional set is not a singleton, then a default rule is rewritten into more than one strict rule. For instance, following with the above remark, r'_Δ is rewritten into $f \leftarrow b \wedge a'$, $f \leftarrow b \wedge c'$, $f \leftarrow b \wedge p'$ and counterintuitive rewritings are avoided.

Special (strict) rules called *completion rules* stating that we are not in an exceptional situation are added to a new set denoted by CR. The use of these

---

Algorithm 2. writeExceptions($(\langle \Delta_0, \ldots, \Delta_n \rangle)$): $\langle S, CR \rangle$

Input: $\left\{ \langle \Delta_0, \ldots, \Delta_n \rangle : \text{the stratification given by the Z-ordering} \right.$

Output: $\begin{cases} S : \text{the set of strict rules obtained by rewriting default rules} \\ CR : \text{the set of completion rules} \end{cases}$

$\quad k \leftarrow n - 1; CR \leftarrow \emptyset; S = \{r_{s_i} = l_{s_i} \leftarrow B_{s_i} \mid r_{\Delta_{n_i}} \in \Delta_n\}$ //initialization
$\quad$**while** $k \geqslant 0$ **do**
$\quad\quad S_k \leftarrow \emptyset$
$\quad\quad$**for all** $r_{\Delta_k} = l_{\Delta_k} \leftarrow B_{\Delta_k}$ s.t. $r_{\Delta_k} \in \Delta_k$ **do**
$\quad\quad\quad \mathcal{E}(r_\Delta, S) \leftarrow \emptyset$ //Set of exceptional sets of a default rule r_Δ w.r.t. S
$\quad\quad\quad$**for all** $r_{s_i} \in S$ s.t. $\mathbf{cons}(B_{\Delta_k} \cup B_s) \wedge \mathbf{incons}(\{l_{\Delta_k}\} \cup \{l_s\})$ **do**
$\quad\quad\quad\quad CR \leftarrow CR \cup \{\varphi(x) \leftarrow B_{\Delta_k} \mid x \in B_{s_i}\}$
$\quad\quad\quad\quad E_i(r_{\Delta_k}, r_{s_i}) \leftarrow B_{s_i}$ //Exceptional set of a default rule r_{Δ_k} w.r.t. r_{s_i}
$\quad\quad\quad\quad \mathcal{E}(r_\Delta, S) \leftarrow \mathcal{E}(r_\Delta, S) \cup E_i(r_{\Delta_k}, r_{s_i})$
$\quad\quad\quad$**end for**
$\quad\quad\quad$**if** $\mathcal{E}(r_\Delta, S) \neq \emptyset$ **then**
$\quad\quad\quad\quad$**for all** $E_i(r_{\Delta_k}, r_{s_i}) \in \mathcal{E}(r_\Delta, S)$ **do**
$\quad\quad\quad\quad\quad S_k \leftarrow S_k \cup \{l_{\Delta_k} \leftarrow B_{\Delta_k} \cup \{\varphi(x) \mid x \in E_i(r_\Delta, r_{s_i})\}\}$
$\quad\quad\quad\quad$**end for**
$\quad\quad\quad$**else**
$\quad\quad\quad\quad S_k \leftarrow S_k \cup \{l_{\Delta_k} \leftarrow B_{\Delta_k}\}$
$\quad\quad\quad$**end if**
$\quad\quad$**end for**
$\quad\quad S \leftarrow S \cup S_k$
$\quad\quad k \leftarrow k - 1$
$\quad$**end while**
$\quad$**return** $\langle S, CR \rangle$

---

completion rules is motivated by the need of reasoning in presence of incomplete information. In fact completion rules allow to apply strict rules which now have a more precise condition part.

Definition 6 (Completion Rule). *Let $r_\Delta = l_\Delta \leftarrow B_\Delta$ be a default rule, and $r_s = l_s \leftarrow B_s$ be a strict rule such that $E(r_\Delta, r_s) = B_s$. Then, a completion rule related with r_Δ is defined as $\varphi(x) \leftarrow B_\Delta$ where $x \in E(r_\Delta, r_s)$.*

Based on the above definitions we can proceed with the description of Algorithm 2. Note that the rules of the last stratum Δ_n do not admit exceptions w.r.t. Δ since they are the most specific ones and they are directly copied into S. Thus, the algorithm begins with the rules of the stratum $n-1$. The stratum $n-1$ contains rules that admit exceptions only because of rules in the last stratum. More generally, a stratum k contains rules that admit exceptions only because of rules in strata with rank greater or equal to $k + 1$. More precisely for each rule in a given stratum, all its exceptions (coming from strata with a greater rank) are computed in order to rewrite this rule by explicitly stating that the exceptional situations are excluded in its condition part. Moreover, completion rules are added for each exceptional case found. A completion rule is used only if it is consistent with the current context and the relevant rewritten rules.

Algorithm 3. testConsistency(S,FC,CR): $P_{\langle S,FC,CR\rangle}$

Input: $\begin{cases} S : \text{the set of strict rules} \\ FC : \text{factual context} \\ CR : \text{the set of completion rules} \end{cases}$

Output: $\left\{ P_{\langle S,FC,CR\rangle} : \text{the definite program} \right.$

$App_{CR} = Apl(CR, FC, S)$
$Rel_{CR} = Rel(App_{CR}, S)$
if incons$(Cn(FC \cup App_{CR} \cup Rel_{CR}))$ **then**
    $App_{CR} \leftarrow \emptyset$
end if
$P_{\langle S,FC,CR\rangle} \leftarrow S \cup FC \cup App_{CR}$
return $P_{\langle S,FC,CR\rangle}$

Example 4. Let us apply the algorithm to rewrite the rules in Example 3 by describing explicitly their exceptions starting from the last stratum of the Z-ordering. It can be checked that the algorithm gives the following set of strict rules $S = \{r_1 = f \leftarrow b \wedge p', r_2 = l \leftarrow b, r_3 = b \leftarrow p, r_4 = f' \leftarrow p\}$ and one completion rule $CR = \{cr_1 = p' \leftarrow b\}$.

3.3 Consistency Test

As said before, completion rules in CR are useful to state in what respect the current context is not exceptional and they are used to apply the rewritten rules which now have a more precise condition part. However, completion rules can only be used if they are consistent with the context described by FC and the set of rewritten rules S. Hence, a consistency test is required (Algorithm 3). To retrieve all the applicable completion rules w.r.t. the factual context and the set of strict rules we provide the following definitions.

Definition 7. *Let S be a set of strict rules obtained by Δ. Let CR be the set of completion rules and FC the factual context to be added to S. Then we define:*

- $Apl(CR, FC, S) = \{cr \in CR \mid body(cr) \subseteq Cn(S \cup FC)\}$
- $Rel(Apl(CR, FC, S), S) = \{r_s \in S \mid r_s \text{ is associated with } Apl(CR, FC, S)\}$[2]

The consistency test amounts to check whether the set of atoms produced by the operator T_R^k applied to the set of rules obtained by merging the factual context FC, the set of the completion rules which are applicable w.r.t. the current context (App_{CR}), and the set of strict rules associated to the completion rules (Rel_{CR}), is consistent. Depending on this consistency check, a new program $P_{\langle S,FC,CR\rangle}$ is returned which contains the applicable completion rules (if any). It is worthy to point out that, once the default rules have been rewritten, this consistency test is performed only when the context FC is changed.

---

[2] Informally, *associated* is a mapping between a rewritten rule r_s and its completion rules produced in the rewriting.

Example 5. Let us consider the set of strict rules S, the set of completion rules CR in Example 4 and the following contexts: $FC_1 = \{b\}$, $FC_2 = \{p\}$, and $FC_3 = \{b, f'\}$. The completion rule $\{cr_1 = p' \leftarrow b\}$ is consistent w.r.t. the context $FC_1 = \{b\}$ and the strict rule r_1. Thus the program $P_{\langle S, FC_1, CR \rangle}$ is built. In $FC_2 = \{p\}$, CR is not consistent w.r.t. the factual knowledge and hence it cannot be taken into account. Finally, $FC_3 = \{b, f'\}$ illustrates the case in which CR is consistent w.r.t. the context, but it is not consistent with the rewritten rule r_1. Also in this case, the completion rule cannot be considered.

3.4   Minimal Model Computation

Since the program obtained by the consistency test is a definite logic program, we can apply directly the minimal model computation $(Cn(P))$.

Example 6. Let us continue with Example 5. Different minimal models are retrieved for each of the programs obtained after the consistency test. Hence, $Cn(P_{\langle S, FC_1, CR \rangle}) = \{b, l, f, p'\}$, $Cn(P_{\langle S, FC_2 \rangle}) = \{b, p, l, f'\}$, and $Cn(P_{\langle S, FC_3 \rangle}) = \{b, f', l\}$.

All these results agree with the intuition behind the birds and penguins knowledge representation problem. In particular the proposed method refines the Z-ordering since it can deal with the blocking inheritance problem. Our method also handles floating information as shown in the next example.

Example 7. Let Δ be a set of default rules representing the Nixon Diamond example: *Quakers normally are pacifists, Quakers normally are Americans, Americans normally like base-ball, Quakers generally do not like base-ball* and *Republicans are generally not pacifists*. Thus $\Delta = \{r_1 = p \leftarrow q, r_2 = a \leftarrow q, r_3 = b \leftarrow a, r_4 = b' \leftarrow q, r_5 = p' \leftarrow r\}$. The rewriting produces $S = \{r_1 = p \leftarrow q, r_2 = a \leftarrow q, r_3 = b \leftarrow a \wedge q', r_4 = b' \leftarrow q, r_5 = p' \leftarrow r \wedge q'\}$ and $CR = \{cr_1 = q' \leftarrow a, cr_2 = q' \leftarrow r\}$. In context $FC = \{q, r\}$, CR is inconsistent w.r.t. FC and $Cn(P_{\langle S, FC \rangle}) = \{p, a, b'\}$. An intuitive interpretation of the fact that pacifist is obtained is that the context Quaker is more specific than Republican in Δ, since Republican is compatible with all the rules which is not the case for Quaker.

We can observe that there are some interesting properties of our algorithm.

Proposition 1. *Algorithm 1 terminates.*

Moreover, our approach offers a straightforward methodology to restore the consistency of inconsistent definite programs which implicitly involve some specificity order between the rules.

Proposition 2. *The program $P_{\langle S, FC, CR \rangle}$ returned by Algorithm 1 is consistent.*

It is natural now to wonder how our method behaves w.r.t. the classical handling of nonmonotonic reasoning in ASP.

4   Related Work

Although several proposals have been made for handling exceptions and specificity in logic programming [12,5,8,7], the closest work to ours is the recent work of Garcia *et al.* in [9] where a rewriting procedure for exceptions is proposed.

Although the automatic generation of exceptions in [9] may look similar to ours at first glance, it is intrinsically different in spirit since exceptions are captured by means of negation as failure. Thus, it is interesting to compare our approach to nonmonotonicity, based on rules rewriting and completion rules, to the standard nonmonotonic reasoning characterized in terms of *not*. For doing this, let us consider the following example taken from [9].

Example 8. From the set of default rules Δ in Example 1 using the algorithm in [9] the following extended normal logic program is obtained $P'_s = \{r_1 = f \leftarrow b \wedge not\ f' \wedge not\ p,\ r_2 = l \leftarrow b,\ r_3 = b \leftarrow p,\ r_4 = f' \leftarrow p \wedge not\ f\}$. Let us consider the contexts $FC_1 = \{b\}$, $FC_2 = \{p\}$, and $FC_3 = \{p, f\}$. The answer sets of P'_s are $M'_1 = \{l, b, f\}$, $M'_2 = \{l, p, b, f'\}$, and $M'_3 = \{p, f, b, l\}$ respectively.

Comparing our generated program (Example 4) with P'_s above, it can be noticed that a model in our approach generally contains more knowledge than the corresponding model of P'_s (*e.g.* $Cn(P_{\langle S, FC_1, CR\rangle}) = \{l, b, f, p'\}$ is also telling that a bird that flies is not a penguin). This extra knowledge can be justified by the corresponding dual attitude w.r.t. negation as failure played by the completion rules. In fact, the intuitive meaning of a rule with default negation like $f \leftarrow b \wedge not\ p$ is that *if it can be proved that we are in the bird context b and nothing proves that we are in a penguin context p, then we can conclude f.* In order to use the default rule about birds, we should not derive p. Alternatively, in our approach, the role of the completion rule ($p' \leftarrow b$) is to complete the factual knowledge triggering the applicability of the rule $f \leftarrow b \wedge p'$ whose condition part now is more specific. In a way the completion rule is playing the dual part of strong exception rules used in the classical handling of exceptional situations in ASP. On a closer inspection, when the completion rule is inconsistent w.r.t. the rewritten rule and it is not added to the program (see Example 5), it also serves as weak exception rule, preventing the rewritten rule to be used.

Since our approach only rewrites exceptions which are implicit inherited by the specificity order among the set of default rules, any (weak) exception related to the rules in the last stratum of the Z-ordering is ignored (*e.g.* the exception captured in $f' \leftarrow p, not\ f$ in P'_s). In this case the two approaches can lead to different solutions (*e.g.* in context $\{p, f\}$). To recover the same results we add a pair of *additional rules* to define an *abstract specificity level* in order to introduce an exceptional situation w.r.t. the class of the last stratum.

Definition 8 (Abstract Specificity Level). *Let $\{c_1, \ldots, c_k\}$ be a set of atoms representing classes with a hierarchy relation ($c_1 \supset c_2 \supset \ldots \supset c_k$), encoded by rules $c_i \leftarrow c_{i+1}$ (with $1 \leq i \leq k - 1$). Let $\{p_1, \ldots, p_{k'}\}$ be a set of atoms representing class properties, encoded by rules $p_j \leftarrow c_i$ (with $1 \leq j \leq k'$ and $1 \leq i \leq k$). Then, an abstract specificity level c_{k+1} with property $p_{k'+1}$ is captured by two additional rules $c_k \leftarrow c_{k+1}$ and $p_{k'+1} \leftarrow c_{k+1}$ s.t. $p_{k'+1} = \varphi(p_{k'})$.*

Thanks to the additional rules our approach can agree with the results obtained in [9]. Moreover, in some cases it leads to larger models due to effect of completion rules which can contribute to add more factual knowledge. We illustrate this idea by means of the following example.

Example 9. Let us consider Δ in Example 1 with an abstract specificity level introduced by adding the rules *super-penguins are penguins* (r_5) and *super-penguins normally fly* (r_6). Then $\Delta = \{r_1 = f \leftarrow b, r_2 = l \leftarrow b, r_3 = b \leftarrow p, r_4 = f' \leftarrow p, r_5 = p \leftarrow sp, r_6 = f \leftarrow sp\}$. The Z-ordering induced by rules specificity is $\Delta_0 = \{r_1 = f \leftarrow b, r_2 = l \leftarrow b\}, \Delta_1 = \{r_3 = b \leftarrow p, r_4 = f' \leftarrow p\}, \Delta_2 = \{r_5 = p \leftarrow sp, r_6 = f \leftarrow sp\}$. Intuitively, r_6 belongs to a higher stratum w.r.t. r_4 as it encodes more specific information. Applying Algorithm 1 (in context $FC = \{p, f\}$), Δ is rewritten into $S = \{r_1 = f \leftarrow b \wedge p', r_2 = f \leftarrow b \wedge sp, r_3 = l \leftarrow b, r_4 = b \leftarrow p, r_5 = f' \leftarrow p \wedge sp', r_6 = p \leftarrow sp, r_7 = f \leftarrow sp\}$ and $CR = \{cr_1 = p' \leftarrow b, cr_2 = sp \leftarrow b, cr_3 = sp' \leftarrow p\}$. Then, $Cn(P_{\langle S,FC,CR_2 \rangle}) = \{p, f, b, sp, l\}$.

Since the initial set of default rules contains an implicit inheritance relation, the generated normal program in [9] is a stratified logic program. Stratified logic programs have an important property: they have a unique answer set [1]. Based on this observation, we can establish the following relation.

Proposition 3. *Let Δ be a set of default rules with an implicit inheritance relation, FC be a factual context, and AR be a pair of rules according to Definition 8. Let P' be the extended normal logic program obtained by the algorithm in [9]. Let $\Delta' = \Delta \cup AR$, and $P_{\langle S,FC,CR \rangle}$ be the program obtained by Algorithm 1. If M is answer set of $P' \cup FC$ and $M' = Cn(P_{\langle S,FC,CR \rangle})$ then $M \subseteq M'$.*

Therefore, our approach can offer an operational counterpart to negation-as-failure in knowledge representation problems which consist of default rules with an implicit specificity order between them.

5   Concluding Remarks

In this paper we have proposed a new algorithm that rewrites default rules into strict rules where exceptions are made explicit and completion rules are added for coping with incomplete information. We have shown how the method can be used to restore the consistency of logic programs encoding knowledge representation problems with inheritance hierarchies. The methods refines the Z-ordering and it faces the blocking inheritance problem. We have also discussed the non-monotonicity in our approach w.r.t. the classical ASP nonmonotonicity. We have established that, under certain conditions, we can recover the results obtained by the method proposed in [9]. This result is significative since it suggests how negation as failure can be captured by an operational approach which provides a dual view to nonmonotonic reasoning in logic programs.

The described method can be applied in a recent proposed methodology for qualitative decision making in ASP [4] in which the knowledge base can consist of a set of default rules. In such a case, the rewriting algorithm presented in this paper can be used to rewrite default rules into strict ones, before proceeding to the computation of an optimal decision.

As future work we aim to identify the main features characterizing the logic programs obtained by the rewriting algorithm and to discuss its complexity which can intuitively be bound to the complexity of the Z-ordering computation.

References

1. Baral, C.: Knowledge Representation, Reasoning and Declarative Problem Solving. Cambridge University Press, Cambridge (2003)
2. Benferhat, S., Dubois, D., Prade, H.: Practical Handling of Exception-Tainted Rules and Independence Information in Possibilistic Logic. Applied Intelligence 9, 101–127 (1998)
3. Brewka, G.: Adding Priorities and Specificity to Default Logic. In: Proc. of the European Workshop on Logics in Artificial Intelligence, pp. 247–260. Springer, Heidelberg (1994)
4. Confalonieri, R., Prade, H.: Answer Set Programming for Computing Decisions Under Uncertainty. Accepted in the 11th European Conference on Symbolic and Quantitative Approaches to Reasoning with Uncertainty (2011)
5. Delgrande, J., Schaub, T., Tompits, H., Wang, K.: A Classification and Survey of Preference Handling Approaches in Nonmonotonic Reasoning. Computational Intelligence 20(2), 308–334 (2004)
6. Delgrande, J.P., Schaub, T.H.: Compiling specificity into approaches to nonmonotonic reasoning. Artif. Intell. 90, 301–348 (1997)
7. García, A.J., Simari, G.R.: Defeasible logic programming: an argumentative approach. Theory Pract. Log. Program 4, 95–138 (2004)
8. Garcia, B.B., Lopes, J.G.P., Varejão, F.: Compiling default theory into extended logic programming. In: Proc. of the 7th Ibero-American Conference on Artificial Intelligence, pp. 207–216. Springer, Heidelberg (2000)
9. Garcia, L., Ngoma, S., Nicolas, P.: Dealing Automatically with Exceptions by Introducing Specificity in ASP. In: Proc. of the 10th European Conference on Symbolic and Quantitative Approaches to Reasoning with Uncertainty, pp. 614–625. Springer, Heidelberg (2009)
10. Gelfond, M., Lifschitz, V.: Classical Negation in Logic Programs and Disjunctive Databases. New Generation Computing 9(3/4), 365–386 (1991)
11. Goldzsmidt, M., Morris, P., Pearl, J.: A Maximum Entropy Approach to Nonmonotonic Reasoning. IEEE Trans. Pattern Anal. Mach. Intell. 15, 220–232 (1993)
12. Kowalski, R., Sadri, F.: Logic Programs with Exceptions. New Generation Computing 9, 387–400 (1991)
13. Lloyd, J.W.: Foundations of logic programming, 2nd edn. Springer, Heidelberg (1987)
14. Pearl, J.: System z: a natural ordering of defaults with tractable applications to nonmonotonic reasoning. In: Proc. of the 3rd Conference on Theoretical Aspects of Reasoning about Knowledge, pp. 121–135. Morgan Kaufmann, San Francisco (1990)
15. Dupin de Saint-Cyr, F., Prade, H.: Handling uncertainty and defeasibility in a possibilistic logic setting. Int. J. Approx. Reasoning 49, 67–82 (2008)
16. Touretzky, D.S., Horty, J.F., Thomason, R.H.: A clash of intuitions: the current state of nonmonotonic multiple inheritance systems. In: Proc. of Int. Joint Conf. on Artificial Intelligence, pp. 476–482. Morgan Kaufmann, San Francisco (1987)

Probabilistic Stit Logic

Jan M. Broersen

Department of Information and Computing Sciences,
Utrecht University,
The Netherlands

Abstract. We define an extension of stit logic that encompasses subjective probabilities representing beliefs about simultaneous choice exertion of other agents.
This semantics enables us to express that an agent sees to it that a condition obtains under a minimal chance of success. We first define the fragment of XSTIT
where choice exertion is not collective. Then we add effect probability lower
bounds to the stit syntax, and define the semantics in terms of subjective probabilities concerning choice exertion of other agents. We show how the resulting
probabilistic stit logic faithfully generalizes the non-probabilistic XSTIT
fragment.

1 Introduction

A predominant formal theory of agency in philosophy is *stit* theory [2]. *Stit* theory
gives an elegant and thoroughly elaborated view on the question of how agents exercise
control over the courses of events that constitute our dynamic world. Also *stit* theory
provides a view on the fundamentals of cooperation and the limits and possibilities of
acting together and / or in interaction. Recently, *stit* theory attracted the attention of
computer scientist who are interested in deontic logic and logic for the specification of
multi-agent systems [4,5,1].

One shortcoming of *stit* theory is that its central notion of choice exertion is one that
assumes that a choice is always successful. But it is highly unrealistic for formalisms
aimed at modeling (group) choice of intelligent agents to assume that action can never
fail. This problem cannot be solved by making the connection with dynamic logic or
the situation calculus, since these formalisms also lack a theory about how actions can
be unsuccessful.

This paper assumes we measure success of action against an agent's beliefs about
the outcome of its choice. So, the perspective is an internal, subjective one, and the
criterion of success is formed by an agent's beliefs about its action. To represent these
beliefs we choose here to use probabilities. In particular, we will represent beliefs about
simultaneous choice exertion of other agents in a system as subjective probabilities.
Several choices have to be made. We will pose that an agent can never be mistaken
about its own choice, but that it can be mistaken about choices of others. The actual
action performed results from a simultaneous choice exertion of all agents in the system.
Then, if an agent can be mistaken about the choices of other agents (including possibly
an agent with special properties called 'nature'), the action can be unsuccessful. As a
very basic example, consider the opening of a door. An agent exercises its choice to

W. Liu (Ed.): ECSQARU 2011, LNAI 6717, pp. 521–531, 2011.

open the door. It cannot be mistaken about that: it knows what it chooses to do. It does this under the belief that there is no other agent on the other side exercising its choice to keep the door closed. So it assigns a low probability to such a choice of any other agent. However, here the agent can be mistaken. And here comes in the notion of unsuccessful action modeled in this paper: as it turns out, in the situation described there actually is an agent at the other side of the door choosing to keep it closed and the agent's opening effort is unsuccessful.

To model this, we endow *stit* theory with probabilities in the object language, enabling us to say that an agent exercises a choice for which it believes to have a chance higher than c to see to it that φ results in the next state.

As far as we know, our proposal is the first combining *stit* logic and probability. Possibly unsuccessful actions have been considered in the context of Markov Decision Processes, temporal logic and ATL [8]. Two differences with the present work are that here we start from the richer *stit* theory and that we focus on fundamental properties of the resulting logic in stead of on issues related to planning, policy generation or model checking. An independent motivation for considering action with a chance of success comes from the relation between *stit* theory and game theory. Kooi and Tamminga [9] investigate how to characterize pure strategy equilibria as *stit* formulas. An extension of *stit* logic with probabilistic effects would enable us to also characterize mixed strategy equilibria.

2   The Base Logic: XSTIT^p

In this section we define the base logic, which is a variant of the logic XSTIT that we call XSTIT^p. The difference with XSTIT is embodied by an axiom schema concerning modality-free propositions p, which explains the name. Another difference with XSTIT is that we do not define the semantics in terms of *relations*, but in terms of functions. We introduce h-relative effectivity functions, which specialize the notion of effectivity function from Coalition Logic [10] by defining choices relative to histories. The function-based semantics explains the formalism better than XSTIT's earlier semantics in terms of relations.

Definition 1. *Given a countable set of propositions P and $p \in P$, and given a finite set Ags of agent names, and $ag \in Ags$, the formal language $\mathcal{L}_{XSTIT^p}$ is:*

$$\varphi := p \mid \neg\varphi \mid \varphi \wedge \varphi \mid \Box\varphi \mid [\{ag\}\ \textbf{\textit{xstit}}]\varphi \mid X\varphi$$

Besides the usual propositional connectives, the syntax of XSTIT^p comprises three modal operators. The operator $\Box\varphi$ expresses 'historical necessity', and plays the same role as the well-known path quantifiers in logics such as CTL and CTL* [7]. Another way of talking about this operator is to say that it expresses that φ is 'settled'. We abbreviate $\neg\Box\neg\varphi$ by $\Diamond\varphi$. The operator $[A\ \textsf{xstit}]\varphi$ stands for 'agents A jointly see to it that φ in the next state'. We abbreviate $\neg[A\ \textsf{xstit}]\neg\varphi$ by $\langle A\ \textsf{xstit}\rangle\varphi$. The third modality is the next operator $X\varphi$. It has a standard interpretation as the transition to a next state.

Definition 2. *A function-based XSTIT^p-frame is a tuple* $\langle S, H, E \rangle$ *such that*[1]:

1. S *is a non-empty set of static states. Elements of S are denoted s, s', etc.*
2. H *is a non-empty set of possible system histories of the form* $\ldots s_{-2}, s_{-1}, s_0, s_1,$ $s_2, \ldots$ *with* $s_x \in S$ *for* $x \in \mathbb{Z}$. *Elements of H are denoted h, h', etc. We denote that s' succeeds s on the history h by $s' = succ(s, h)$ and by $s = prec(s', h)$. Furthermore:*

   a. *if* $s \in h$ *and* $s \in h'$ *then* $prec(s, h) = prec(s, h')$
3. $E : S \times H \times Ags \mapsto 2^S$ *is an h-effectivity function yielding for an agent ag the set of next static states allowed by the actions taken by the agent relative to a history*

   a. *if* $s \notin h$ *then* $E(s, h, ag) = \emptyset$
   b. $succ(s, h) \in E(s, h, ag)$
   c. *if* $s' \in E(s, h, ag)$ *then* $\exists h' : s' = succ(s, h')$
   d. *if* $s' = succ(s, h)$ *and* $s' \in h'$ *then* $s' \in E(s, h', ag)$
   e. $E(s, h, ag_1) \cap E(s, h', ag_2) \neq \emptyset$ *for* $ag_1 \neq ag_2$

In definition 2 above, we refer to the states s as 'static states'. This is to distinguish them from 'dynamic states', which are combinations $\langle s, h \rangle$ of static states and histories. Dynamic states function as the elementary units of evaluation of the logic. This means that the basic notion of 'truth' in the semantics of this logic is about dynamic conditions concerning choice exertions. This distinguishes *stit* from logics like Dynamic Logic and Coalition Logic whose central notion of truth concerns static conditions holding for static states.

The name 'h-effectivity functions' for the functions defined in item **3** above is short for 'h-relative effectivity functions'. This name is inspired by similar terminology in Coalition Logic whose semantics is in terms of 'effectivity functions'. Condition **3.a** above states that h-effectivity is empty for history-state combinations that do not form a dynamic state. Condition **3.b** states that the static state next of some other static state on a history is always in the effectivity set relative to that history state pair for any group of agents. Condition **3.c** ensures that next state effectivity as seen from a current state s does not contain states s' that are not reachable from the current state through some history. Condition **3.d** expresses the well-known *stit* condition of 'no choice between undivided histories'. Condition **3.e** above states that simultaneous choices of different agents never have an empty intersection. This is the central condition of 'independence of agency'. It reflects that a choice exertion of one agent can never have as a consequence that some other agent is limited in the choices it can exercise simultaneously.

The conditions on the frames are not as tight as the conditions in the classical *stit* formalisms of Belnap, Perloff and Horty [2]. Appart from the crucial difference concerning the effect of actions (in XSTIT^p actions take effect in next states), the classical *stit* formalisms assumes a condition that in our meta-language can be represented as:

   h. $E(s, h, ag) \neq E(s, h', ag)$ *implies* $E(s, h, ag) \cap E(s, h', ag) = \emptyset$

---

[1] In the meta-language we use the same symbols both as constant names and as variable names, and we assume universal quantification of unbound meta-variables.

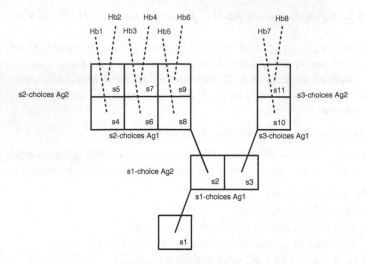

Fig. 1. visualization of a partial two agent XSTIT^p frame

Condition **h.** says that the choices of an agent ag are mutually disjoint. Since they result in much tidier pictures, in the example visualization of a frames we consider below, we assume this condition. However, we do not include it in the formal definition of the frames, because it is not modally expressible (e.g., in modal logic we can give axioms characterizing that an intersection is non-empty, but we cannot characterize that an intersection is empty). This means that they will not have an effect on our modal logic of agency whose semantics we will define in terms of the above frames.

Figure 1 visualizes a frame of the type defined by definition 2. The columns in the games forms linked to each state are the choices of agent ag_1 and the rows are the choices of agent ag_2. Independence of choices is reflected by the fact that the game forms contain no 'holes' in them. Choice exertion in this 'bundled' semantics is thought of as the separation of two bundles of histories: one bundle ensured by the choice exercised and one bundle excluded by that choice.

We now define models by adding a valuation of propositional atoms to the frames of definition 2. We impose that all dynamic state relative to a static state evaluate atomic propositions to the same value. This reflects the intuition that atoms, and modality-free formulas in general do not represent dynamic information. Their truth value should thus not depend on a history but only on the static state. This choice does however make the situation non-standard. It is a constraint on the models, and not on the frames.

Definition 3. *A frame $\mathcal{F} = \langle S, H, E \rangle$ is extended to a model $\mathcal{M} = \langle S, H, E, \pi \rangle$ by adding a valuation π of atomic propositions:*

- *π is a valuation function $\pi : P \longrightarrow 2^S$ assigning to each atomic proposition the set of static states relative to which they are true.*

We evaluate truth with respect to dynamic states built from a dimension of histories and a dimension of static states.

Definition 4. *Relative to a model* $\mathcal{M} = \langle S, H, E, \pi \rangle$, *truth* $\langle s, h \rangle \models \varphi$ *of a formula* φ *in a dynamic state* $\langle s, h \rangle$, *with* $s \in h$, *is defined as:*

$$\langle s, h \rangle \models p \qquad\qquad \Leftrightarrow s \in \pi(p)$$
$$\langle s, h \rangle \models \neg\varphi \qquad\qquad \Leftrightarrow not \ \langle s, h \rangle \models \varphi$$
$$\langle s, h \rangle \models \varphi \wedge \psi \qquad\quad \Leftrightarrow \langle s, h \rangle \models \varphi \ and \ \langle s, h \rangle \models \psi$$
$$\langle s, h \rangle \models \Box\varphi \qquad\qquad \Leftrightarrow \forall h' : if \ s \in h' \ then \ \langle s, h' \rangle \models \varphi$$
$$\langle s, h \rangle \models X\varphi \qquad\qquad \Leftrightarrow if \ s' = succ(s, h) \ then \ \langle s', h \rangle \models \varphi$$
$$\langle s, h \rangle \models [\{ag\} \ \textbf{\textit{xstit}}]\varphi \Leftrightarrow \forall s', h' : if \ s' \in E(s, h, \{ag\}) \ and$$
$$s' \in h' \ then \ \langle s', h' \rangle \models \varphi$$

Satisfiability, validity on a frame and general validity are defined as usual.

Note that the historical necessity operator quantifies over one dimension, and the next operator over the other. The *stit* modality combines both dimensions. Now we proceed with the axiomatization of the base logic.

Definition 5. *The following axiom schemas, in combination with a standard axiomatization for propositional logic, and the standard rules (like necessitation) for the normal modal operators, define a Hilbert system for* **XSTIT**^{p}:

(p) $p \to \Box p$ *for* p *modality free*
         S5 for $\Box$
(D) $\neg[\{ag\} \ \textbf{\textit{xstit}}]\bot$
(Lin) $\neg X \neg \varphi \leftrightarrow X\varphi$
(Sett) $\Box X\varphi \to [\{ag\} \ \textbf{\textit{xstit}}]\varphi$
(XSett) $[\{ag\} \ \textbf{\textit{xstit}}]\varphi \to X\Box\varphi$
(Agg) $[\{ag\} \ \textbf{\textit{xstit}}]\varphi \wedge [\{ag\} \ \textbf{\textit{xstit}}]\psi \to [\{ag\} \ \textbf{\textit{xstit}}](\varphi \wedge \psi)$
(Mon) $[\{ag\} \ \textbf{\textit{xstit}}](\varphi \wedge \psi) \to [\{ag\} \ \textbf{\textit{xstit}}]\varphi$
(Ind) $\Diamond[\{ag_1\} \ \textbf{\textit{xstit}}]\varphi \wedge \Diamond[\{ag_2\} \ \textbf{\textit{xstit}}]\psi \to \Diamond([\{ag_1\} \ \textbf{\textit{xstit}}]\varphi \wedge [\{ag_2\} \ \textbf{\textit{xstit}}]\psi)$

Theorem 1. *The Hilbert system of definition 5 is complete with respect to the semantics of definition 4.*

The proof strategy is as follows. First we establish completeness of the system *without* the axiom $p \to \Box p$, relative to the frames of definition 2. All remaining axioms are in the Sahlqvist class. This means that all the axioms are expressible as first-order conditions on frames and that together they are complete with respect to the frame classes thus defined, cf. [3]. It is easy to find the first-order conditions corresponding to the axioms, for instance, by using the on-line SQEMA system [6]. So, now we know that every formula consistent in the slightly reduced Hilbert system has a model based on an abstract frame. Left to show is that we can associate such an abstract model to a concrete model based on an XSTIT^p frame as given in definition 2. This takes some effort, since we have to associate worlds in the abstract model to dynamic states in the frames of definition 2 and check all the conditions of definition 2 against the conditions in the abstract model (**3.b** corresponds with the D axiom, **3.c** corresponds to (Sett), **3.d** to (XSett), **3.e** to (Ind)). Once we have done this, we have established completeness of the axioms relative to the conditions on the frames. Now the second step is to add the axiom

$p \rightarrow \Box p$. This axiom does not have a corresponding frame condition. Indeed, the axiom expresses a condition on the models. But then, to show completeness, we only have to show that we can always find a model obtained by the construction just described that satisfies the axiom $p \rightarrow \Box p$. But this is straightforward. From all the possible models resulting from the first step, we select the ones where propositional atoms in dynamic states based on the same static state have identical valuations. Since consistent formulas also have to be consistent with the axiom $p \rightarrow \Box p$ for any non-modal formula p, we can always do that. This means that a satisfying model for a consistent formula is always obtainable in this way and that completeness is preserved.

The independence axiom given here is simpler than Xu's independence axiom in his axiomatization for instantaneous deliberative *stit* (see the chapter in [2]). In Xu's axiomatization, a set of independence axioms of the form $\Diamond[\{ag_1\} \text{ dstit}]\varphi \wedge \ldots \wedge \Diamond[\{ag_n\} \text{ dstit}]\psi \rightarrow \Diamond([\{ag_1\} \text{ dstit}]\varphi \wedge \ldots \wedge [\{ag_n\} \text{ dstit}]\psi)$ is given. A set of axioms of this form is not needed here, because $[\{ag\} \text{ xstit}]\varphi$ is a normal modality, while $[\{ag\} \text{ dstit}]\varphi$ is not normal (it is a weak, monotonic modal operator). This will be different however if we add probability to the *stit* operator, as we will see in the next section.

3   Choice with a Bounded Chance of Success

We introduce operators $[\{ag\} \text{ xstit}^{\geq c}]\varphi$ with the intended meaning that agent ag exercises a choice for which it believes to have a chance of at least c of bringing about φ. Roughly, the semantics for this new operator is as follows. We start with the multi-agent *stit*-setting of the previous section. Now to the semantic structures we add functions such that in the little game-forms, as visualized by figure 1, for each choice of an agent ag we have available the subjective probabilities applying to the choices of the other agents in the system. For agent ag the sum of these probabilities over the choices of each particular other agent in the system add up to one. So, the probabilities represent agent ag's beliefs concerning what choices are exerted simultaneously by other agents. In terms of the subjective probability function we define for each choice the sum of the probabilities for each of the choices of all other agents in the system leading to a situation obeying φ.

For the definition of the probabilistic frames, we first define an augmentation function returning the choices a group of agent has in a given state.

Definition 6. *The range function* $Range : S \times Ags \mapsto 2^{2^S \setminus \emptyset} \setminus \emptyset$ *yielding for a state s and an agent ag, the choices this agent has in s is defined as:*
$Range(s, ag) = \{Ch \mid \exists h : s \in h \text{ and } Ch = E(s, h, ag)\}$

A range function is similar to what in Coalition Logic is called an 'effectivity function'. Now we are ready to define the probabilistic *stit* frames.

Definition 7. *A probabilistic XSTIT^p-frame is a tuple $\langle S, H, E, B \rangle$ such that:*

1. $\langle S, H, E \rangle$ *is a function based* **XSTIT**^{p}*-frame*
2. $B : S \times Ags \times Ags \times 2^S \mapsto [0,1]$ *is a subjective probability function such that* $B(s, ag_1, ag_2, Ch)$ *expresses agent 1's believe that in static state s agent 2 performs a choice resulting in one of the static states in Ch. We apply the following constraints.*

   a. $B(s, ag, ag', Ch) = 0$ *if* $ag \neq ag'$ *and* $Ch \notin Range(s, ag')$
   b. $B(s, ag, ag', Ch) > 0$ *if* $ag \neq ag'$ *and* $Ch \in Range(s, ag')$
   c. $\displaystyle\sum_{Ch \in Range(s, ag')} B(s, ag, ag', Ch) = 1$ *if* $ag \neq ag'$
   d. $B(s, ag, ag, Ch) = 1$

Condition **2.a** says that agents only assign non-zero subjective probabilities to choices other agents objectively have. Condition **2.b** says these probabilities are strictly larger than zero. Condition **2.c** says that the sum of the subjective probabilities over the possible choices of other agents add up to 1. Condition **2.d** says that agents always know what choice they exercise themselves. Note that this is not the same as claiming that agents always know what action they perform (which is not the case in our conceptualization). We already explained this difference between choice and action in section 2.

In the sequel we will need an augmentation function yielding for an agent and an arbitrary next static state the chance an agent ascribes to the occurrence of this state (given its belief, i.e., subjective probabilities about simultaneous choice exertion of other agents). For this, we first need the following proposition. To guarantee that the proposition is true, we need the condition **h.** as one of the conditions posed on the frames in definition 2. As we argued, assuming this condition **h.** does not change the logic.

Proposition 1. *For any pair of static states s and s' for which there is an h such that $s' = succ(s, h)$ there is a unique 'choice profile' determining for each agent ag in the system a unique choice $Ch = E(s, h, ag)$ relative to s and s'.*

Now we can define the subjective probabilities agents assign to possible system outcomes. Because of the idea of independence of agency, we can multiply the chances for the choices of the individual agents relative to the system outcome (the resulting static state). Note that this gives a new and extra dimension to the notion of independence that is not available in standard *stit* theories.

Definition 8. $BX : S \times Ags \times S \mapsto [0,1]$ *is a subjective probability function concerning possible next static states, defined by*
$$BX(s, ag, s') = \prod_{ag' \in Ags} B(s, ag, ag', E(s, h, ag')) \quad \text{for some } h \text{ such that } s' = succ(s, h)$$

Note that $BX(s, ag, s')$ expresses agent ag's belief in state s that its choice ends up in s' modulo the assumption that ag actually chooses such as to make s' a possible outcome; if ag chooses such that s' is excluded by its choice, the chance for s' is of course 0.

Now before we can define the notion of 'seeing to it under a minimal probability of success' formally as a truth condition on the frames of definition 7 we need to do more preparations. First we assume that the intersection of the h-effectivity functions of all agents together yields a unique static state. We can safely assume this, because, again, this condition is not modally expressible. In general we can express uniqueness of next states in terms of a D axiom. But note that here the units of evaluation are dynamic states. With a unique next static state corresponds a set of next dynamic states: all the dynamic states that can be built with the static state. We can not characterize uniqueness of this set using a D axiom. This justifies definition 10 below, that establishes a function characterizing the static states next of a given state that satisfy a formula φ relative to the current choice of an agent.

But, first we define an additional range function for choices resulting from several agents choosing simultaneously (which is not the same as choosing together or in a coalition). Due to independence of agency for any combination of choices (that is, for any choice profile), there is a non-empty set of static static states in the intersection of the choices in the profile.

Definition 9. *The range function* $RangeG : S \times 2^{Ags} \mapsto 2^{2^S}$ *yielding for a state s and a group of agents A, the sets of possible next static states resulting from the simultaneous choices in the group is defined as:*
$RangeG(s, A) = \{Ch \mid \bigcap_{ag \in A} E(s, h, ag) \text{ for some } h \text{ such that } s \in h\}$

Definition 10. *The 'possible next static φ-states' function* $PosX : S \times H \times Ags \times \mathcal{L} \mapsto 2^S$ *which for a state s, a history h, an agent ag and a formula φ gives the possible next static states obeying φ given the agent's current choice determined by h, is defined by:* $PosX(s, h, ag, \varphi) = \{s' \mid E(s, h, ag) \cap Ch = \{s'\} \text{ for } Ch \in RangeG(s, Ags \setminus \{ag\}) \text{ and } \langle s', h' \rangle \models \varphi \text{ for all } h' \text{ with } s' \in h'\}.$

Now we can formulate the central 'chance of success' (CoS) function that will be used in the truth condition for the new operator. The chance of success relative to a formula φ is the sum of the chances the agent assigns to possible next static states validating φ.

Definition 11. *The chance of success function* $CoS : S \times H \times Ags \times \mathcal{L} \mapsto [0, 1]$ *which for a state s and a history h an agent ag and a formula φ gives the chance the agent's choice relative to h is an action resulting in φ is defined by:* $CoS(s, h, ag, \varphi) = 0$ *if* $PosX(s, h, ag, \varphi) = \emptyset$ *or else* $CoS(s, h, ag, \varphi) = \sum_{s' \in PosX(s,h,ag,\varphi)} BX(s, ag, s').$

Extending the probabilistic frames of definition 7 to models in the usual way, the truth condition of the new operator is defined as follows.

Definition 12. *Relative to a model* $\mathcal{M} = \langle S, H, E, B, \pi \rangle$, *truth* $\langle s, h \rangle \models [\{ag\} \text{ xstit}^{\geq c}]\varphi$ *of a formula* $[\{ag\} \text{ xstit}^{\geq c}]\varphi$ *in a dynamic state* $\langle s, h \rangle$, *with* $s \in h$, *is defined as:*

$$\langle s, h \rangle \models [\{ag\} \text{ xstit}^{\geq c}]\varphi \Leftrightarrow CoS(s, h, ag, \varphi) \geq c$$

We now formulate the result that the logic following from definitions 4 and 12 naturally extends the base *stit* logic.

Theorem 2. *Consider a trivial translation T of probabilistic stit formulas to xstit formulas determined by the mapping: $[\{ag\}\ \textsf{xstit}]\varphi = [\{ag\}\ \textsf{xstit}^{\geq 1}]\varphi$. Other formulas are mapped to their identical twin. Now, a formula φ is satisfiable in an xstit model according to semantics of definition 4 if and only if $T(\varphi)$ is satisfiable in a probabilistic stit model according to the semantics of definition 12.*

The proof of this theorem follows by careful examination of the the probabilistic semantics. If the chance of success must be one, than an agent's beliefs about choice exertion by other agents is irrelevant. The only way in which the agent can be sure is be ensuring φ holds irrespective of what other agents chose. This condition brings the standard xstit semantics back in the probabilistic setting. If we would combine both modalities in one language, we would get the axiom $[\{ag\}\ \textsf{xstit}]\varphi \leftrightarrow [\{ag\}\ \textsf{xstit}^{\geq 1}]\varphi$. This shows that the probabilistic *stit* operator we gave in definition 12 faithfully generalizes the *stit* operator of our base $\textsf{XSTIT}^p$ system: the objective *stit* operator $[\{ag\}\ \textsf{xstit}]\varphi$ discussed in section 2 comes out as the probabilistic *stit* operator assigning a probability 1 to establishing the effect φ. This is very natural. Where in the standard *stit* setting we can talk about 'ensuring' a condition, in the probabilistic setting we can only talk about establishing an effect with a certain lower bound on the probability of succeeding.

We now define a Hilbert system for the probabilistic stit logic. The system is parametric is probabilistic variables c and k. This means that the system encodes infinitely many axioms, since there can be infinitely many values for c and k. To obtain a standard Hilbert system we can pose a prior limit to the possible values of probabilities.

Definition 13. *Relative to the semantics following from definitions 4 and 12 we define the following Hilbert system. We assume all the standard derivation rules for the normal modalities X and $\square$. Furthermore, we assume the standard derivation rules for the weak modality $[\{ag\}\ \textsf{xstit}^{\geq c}]\varphi$, like closure under logical equivalence.*

(p) $p \rightarrow \square p$ *for p modality free*
  $S5$ *for* $\square$
(D) $\neg[\{ag\}\ \textsf{xstit}^{\geq c}]\bot$ *for* $c > 0$
(Triv) $[\{ag\}\ \textsf{xstit}^{\geq 0}]\varphi$
(Lin) $\neg X \neg \varphi \leftrightarrow X\varphi$
(Sett) $\square X \varphi \rightarrow [\{ag\}\ \textsf{xstit}^{\geq c}]\varphi$
(XSett) $[\{ag\}\ \textsf{xstit}^{\geq 1}]\varphi \rightarrow X\square\varphi$
(Min) $[\{ag\}\ \textsf{xstit}^{\geq c}]\varphi \rightarrow [\{ag\}\ \textsf{xstit}^{\geq k}]\varphi$ *for* $c \geq k$
(Add) $[\{ag\}\ \textsf{xstit}^{\geq c}]\varphi \wedge [\{ag\}\ \textsf{xstit}^{\geq k}]\psi \rightarrow [\{ag\}\ \textsf{xstit}^{\geq c+k-1}](\varphi \wedge \psi)$ *for* $c + k > 1$
(Mon) $[\{ag\}\ \textsf{xstit}^{\geq c}](\varphi \wedge \psi) \rightarrow [\{ag\}\ \textsf{xstit}^{\geq c}]\varphi$
(Ind) $\Diamond[\{ag_1\}\ \textsf{xstit}^{\geq c}]\varphi \wedge \ldots \wedge \Diamond[\{ag_n\}\ \textsf{xstit}^{\geq k}]\psi \rightarrow$
  $\Diamond([\{ag_1\}\ \textsf{xstit}^{\geq c}]\varphi \wedge \ldots \wedge [\{ag_n\}\ \textsf{xstit}^{\geq k}]\psi)$ *for* $Ags = \{\{ag_1\}, \ldots, \{ag_n\}\}$

Proposition 2. *The Hilbert system is sound relative to the semantics.*

This proposition follows by careful inspection of the semantics.

Proposition 3. *The Hilbert system reduces to the complete Hilbert system for xstit after substitution of 1 for the parameter c.*

Note that the set of independence axioms given here generalized the single independence axiom given for xstit. This is because the operator $[\{ag\}\ \mathsf{xstit}^{\geq c}]\varphi$ is not a normal modal operator (for $c < 1$), but a monotonic modal operator, which prevents us from agglomerating the conjunction within the scope of the diamond. Also note that all axioms for xstit have a natural generalization in the above Hilbert system. The most interesting one is agglomeration that generalizes from the standard normal modal logic axiom (Agg) to the set of weak modal scheme's (Add).

Conjecture 1. The Hilbert system is complete relative to the semantics.

To prove the conjecture we might consider a standard neighborhood semantics for the modality $[\{ag\}\ \mathsf{xstit}^{\geq c}]\varphi$. The completeness of the logic relative to a neighborhood semantics can be obtained using standard techniques for this type of semantics. The second step would than be to show the relation between the probabilistic models given here and the neighborhood semantics.

From the system we can derive several intuitive properties.

Proposition 4. *Derivable properties are the following.*

    a. $[\{ag\}\ \mathsf{xstit}^{\geq c}]\varphi \rightarrow [\{ag\}\ \mathsf{xstit}^{\geq c}](\varphi \vee \psi)$
    b. $[\{ag\}\ \mathsf{xstit}^{\geq c}](\varphi \vee \psi) \wedge [\{ag\}\ \mathsf{xstit}^{\geq 1}]\neg\varphi \rightarrow [\{ag\}\ \mathsf{xstit}^{\geq c}]\psi$
    c. $[\{ag\}\ \mathsf{xstit}^{\geq c}]\varphi \wedge [\{ag\}\ \mathsf{xstit}^{\geq 1}]\psi \rightarrow [\{ag\}\ \mathsf{xstit}^{\geq c}](\varphi \wedge \psi)$
    d. $\neg([\{ag\}\ \mathsf{xstit}^{\geq c}]\varphi \wedge [\{ag\}\ \mathsf{xstit}^{\geq k}]\neg\varphi)$ for $c + k > 1$
    e. $[\{ag\}\ \mathsf{xstit}^{\geq c}]\varphi \rightarrow \langle\{ag\}\ \mathsf{xstit}^{\geq c}\rangle\varphi$

For instance, property **d.** tells us that it is not possible, by means of one choice, to have at the same time a chance of c for φ and a chance of k for $\neg\varphi$ if $c + k > 1$.

4   Conclusion and Discussion

This paper starts out by defining a base *stit* logic, which is a variant on XSTIT. However, we define the semantics in terms of h-effectivity functions, which does more justice to the nature of the structures interpreting the language. We show completeness relative to this semantics. Then we proceed by generalizing the central *stit* operator of the base language to a probabilistic variant. The original operator comes out as the probabilistic operator assigning a chance 1 to success of a choice.

There are several opportunities for future work. The first objective is to prove completeness of the axiomatization for the probabilistic *stit* operator. We already briefly sketched the proof direction we have in mind.

An interesting route for investigation is the generalization of the theory in this paper to group choices of agents. If a group makes a choice, we may assume all kinds of conditions on the pooling of information within the group. This means that the chances that agents assign to choices made by agents within the group are generally different than the chances they assign to choices by agents outside the group. How this pooling of information takes form in a setting where beliefs are modeled as subjective probabilities is still an open question to us.

References

1. Balbiani, P., Herzig, A., Troquard, N.: Alternative axiomatics and complexity of deliberative stit theories. Journal of Philosophical Logic (2007)
2. Belnap, N., Perloff, M., Xu, M.: Facing the future: agents and choices in our indeterminist world. Oxford (2001)
3. Blackburn, P., de Rijke, M., Venema, Y.: Modal Logic. Cambridge Tracts in Theoretical Computer Science, vol. 53. Cambridge University Press, Cambridge (2001)
4. Broersen, J.M., Herzig, A., Troquard, N.: Embedding Alternating-time Temporal Logic in strategic STIT logic of agency. Journal of Logic and Computation 16(5), 559–578 (2006)
5. Broersen, J.M., Herzig, A., Troquard, N.: A normal simulation of coalition logic and an epistemic extension. In: Samet, D. (ed.) Proceedings Theoretical Aspects Rationality and Knowledge (TARK XI), Brussels, pp. 92–101. ACM Digital Library (2007)
6. Conradie, W., Goranko, V., Vakarelov, D.: Algorithmic correspondence and completeness in modal logic I: The core algorithm SQEMA. Logical Methods in Computer Science 2(1), 1–26 (2006)
7. Emerson, E.A.: Temporal and modal logic. In: van Leeuwen, J. (ed.) Handbook of Theoretical Computer Science. Formal Models and Semantics, vol. B, ch. 14, pp. 996–1072. Elsevier Science, Amsterdam (1990)
8. Jamroga, W.: A temporal logic for markov chains. In: AAMAS 2008: Proceedings of the 7th International Joint Conference on Autonomous Agents and Multiagent Systems, Richland, SC, pp. 697–704 (2008); International Foundation for Autonomous Agents and Multiagent Systems
9. Kooi, B.P., Tamminga, A.M.: Conflicting obligations in multi-agent deontic logic. In: Goble, L., Meyer, J.-J.C. (eds.) DEON 2006. LNCS (LNAI), vol. 4048, pp. 175–186. Springer, Heidelberg (2006)
10. Pauly, M.: A modal logic for coalitional power in games. Journal of Logic and Computation 12(1), 149–166 (2002)

Overriding Subsuming Rules

Philippe Besnard[1], Éric Grégoire[2], and Sébastien Ramon[2]

[1] IRIT, F-31062 Toulouse
CNRS UMR 5505, F-31062
118 route de Narbonne, F-31062 Toulouse France
besnard@irit.fr
[2] Université Lille - Nord de France, Artois, F-62307 Lens
CRIL, F-62307 Lens
CNRS UMR 8188, F-62307
rue Jean Souvraz SP18, F-62307 Lens France
{gregoire,ramon}@cril.univ-artois.fr

Abstract. This paper is concerned with intelligent agents that are able to perform nonmonotonic reasoning, not only *with*, but also *about* general rules with exceptions. More precisely, the focus is on enriching a knowledge base Γ with a general rule that is subsumed by another rule already there. Such a problem is important because evolving knowledge needs not follow logic as it is well-known from e.g. the belief revision paradigm. However, belief revision is mainly concerned with the case that the extra information logically conflicts with Γ. Otherwise, the extra knowledge is simply doomed to extend Γ with no change altogether. The problem here is different and may require a change in Γ even though no inconsistency arises. The idea is that when a rule is to be added, it might need to override any rule that subsumes it: preemption must take place. A formalism dedicated to reasoning with and about rules with exceptions is introduced. An approach to dealing with preemption over such rules is then developed.

Keywords: Dynamics of knowledge, Logic, Default reasoning.

1 Introduction

Assume a knowledge base Γ contains the rule *If the switch is on then the light is on*. When *If the switch is on and the lamp bulb is ok then the light is on* needs to be introduced inside Γ, it seems natural to require this new rule to preempt the older rule: it is no longer enough to know that the switch is on to be able to conclude that the light is on, it must additionally be the case that Γ yields the information that the lamp bulb is ok. First, let us observe that a monotonic logic cannot capture such dynamics of reasoning by simply adding the new rule. According to monotonicity, any conclusion drawn from a given set of premises can still be inferred whatever additional premises happen to supplement this set. In such a logic, the statement *the light is on* (concluded from the former rule and the statement *the switch is on*) is still concluded even though the second rule is added, and, worse yet, regardless of any information stating that the lamp bulb is broken. Also, the usual approaches to belief revision [AGM85] fail to address this issue because they make the new information to be set-theoretically unioned with Γ in case no inconsistency arises. Let us stress that moving to a nonmonotonic formalism where

W. Liu (Ed.): ECSQARU 2011, LNAI 6717, pp. 532–544, 2011.
© Springer-Verlag Berlin Heidelberg 2011

exception to rules depends on consistency checks like adding *If the switch is on and if it can be consistently assumed that the lamp bulb is ok, then the light is on* does not change the problem.

Technically, the problem can be described as follows. Given a set Γ of formulas and a rule R, what changes should Γ undergo so as to infer R but not to infer any R' subsuming R? In symbols, where Γ^* stands for Γ after these changes have taken place,

$$\Gamma^* \mathrel{\vert\!\sim} R \qquad \text{and} \qquad \Gamma^* \mathrel{\vert\!\not\sim} R'$$

Clearly, the problem first requires several matters to be settled. First, the syntax for rules (in which $R, R', \ldots$ are expressed) is to be defined. Second, an inference relation (denoted $\vert\!\sim$) allowing rules to be handled needs to be settled. Third, a concept of implicant for rules expressing what does R' subsuming R mean needs to be proposed, before an approach to solve the above preemption issue can be defined.

Accordingly, the paper is organized as follows. In the next Section, a general formalism for representing rules with exceptions is introduced with the aim of encompassing various logic-based approaches allowing such rules, including default reasoning. Section 3 introduces useful inference tools to reason about such rules, while Section 4 connects the tools with default logic. In Section 5, a useful X-derivation concept is proposed, allowing both plain formulas and rules to be inferred under the possible assumption of additional formulas or other rules with exceptions. Section 6 investigates a concept of implicant for rules with exceptions. The approach to the preemption issue is then developed in Section 7, based on the X-derivation and the latter implicant concepts. Finally, some avenues for future research are provided in the conclusion.

Throughout the paper, the following notations are used: $\neg$, $\vee$, $\wedge$ and $\supset$ denote the classical negation, disjunction, conjunction and material implication connectives, respectively. When Ω is a set of formulas, $Cn(\Omega)$ denotes the deductive closure of Ω under a given logic, of which $\Vdash$ denotes the consequence relationship, $\perp$ denotes absurdity, and $\top$ denotes any tautology.

2 Rules with Exceptions

2.1 Defaults

In the Artificial Intelligence research community, some of the most popular tools to handle forms of defeasible reasoning remain rules with exceptions, e.g., in the form of defaults [Rei80]. They permit an inference system to jump to default conclusions and to withdraw them when new information shows that these conclusions now lead to inconsistency. Usually, such a rule is based on logical formulas, that is, expressions of a formal language upon which an inference system (no matter how poor or rich) models some kind of reasoning.

For instance, in default logic [Rei80], a *default* is of the form:

$$\frac{\alpha : \beta}{\gamma}$$

where α, β, γ are formulas of classical logic.

Intuitively, such a default is intended to allow the reasoning *"Provided that α is inferred and provided that β is consistent w.r.t. what is inferred, infer γ".*

Importantly, the inference notion alluded to is based on a logic (Reiter made it to be classical logic but it is possible to have another logic instead: see paraconsistent default logic [PB91] for example).

2.2   PEC Rules

Let us first concentrate on rules with exceptions under consistency tests. Our leading example is then expressed as *If the switch is on and if it can be consistently assumed that the lamp bulb is ok, then the light is on* and consists of three parts: its premises, its exceptions, and its conclusions. E.g., it could be represented by the default

$$\frac{switch\_on : lamp\_bulb\_ok}{light\_on}$$

We aim at representing such rules in a uniform way within a unified setting that is, among other things, meant to be general enough as to encompass default logic while allowing us to instantiate it to other logical formalisms. It should also allow the representation of both monotonic knowledge and rules involving consistency checks.

Given a logical language, a PEC rule (for Premises-Exceptions-Conclusions) is a triple consisting of three sets of formulas. First, the premises, which are the necessary conditions for *this* rule to apply. Then, the exceptions, which are based on consistency tests. Finally, the conclusions, which list the claims that can be made whenever the rule applies.

Definition 1. *A PEC rule is a triple $\mathcal{R} = (\mathcal{P}, \mathcal{E}, \mathcal{C})$ where $\mathcal{P} = \{\rho_1, \ldots, \rho_k\}$ and $\mathcal{C} = \{\varsigma_1, \ldots, \varsigma_n\}$ are consistent sets of formulas and $\mathcal{E} = \{\epsilon_1, \ldots, \epsilon_m\}$ is a set of non-tautological formulas.*

Importantly, we impose no constraint on the language: there may, or may not, be connectives such as negation, conjunction, disjunction and the like. There may even be no connective at all. However, an underlying inference relation $\Vdash$ must be available. Of course, this means that the logical formalism used must have a form of tautology (please note the subtlety here: this does not mean that the logical formalism used must have tautologies!).

A PEC rule can be interpreted in different ways, depending on how its set of premises and its set of conclusions are captured logically (presumably, conjunctively or disjunctively). In the sequel, we consider only unary PEC rules, that is, PEC rules whose sets of premises and sets of conclusions are singletons. Abusing the notation in order to improve readability, we often omit curly brackets for these singletons.

Definition 2. *A PEC rule $\mathcal{R} = (\mathcal{P}, \mathcal{E}, \mathcal{C})$ is unary iff $\mathcal{P}$ and $\mathcal{C}$ are singleton sets.*

Example 1. The PEC rule $(switch\_on, \{\neg lamp\_bulb\_ok\}, light\_on)$ is an encoding of the rule with exception *If the switch is on and, consistently assuming that the lamp bulb is ok, then the light is on.*

Example 2. The PEC rule $(\{switch\_on, lamp\_bulb\_ok\}, \emptyset, light\_on)$ is an encoding of a similar rule where the impossibility to derive e.g. $lamp\_bulb\_ok$ can block the inference of $light\_on$. In this respect, $\neg lamp\_bulb\_ok$ would be an exception to the rule, which is however not to be included in the set of exceptions of the PEC rule, since it is not a consistency-based exception.

Example 3. The PEC rule $(\top, \emptyset, light\_on)$ is an encoding of the fact *the light is on.*

Example 4. The PEC rules $(switch\_on, \emptyset, light\_on)$, $(switch\_on \supset light\_on, \emptyset, \emptyset)$ and $(\emptyset, \emptyset, switch\_on \supset light\_on)$ are various encodings of the exception-free rule *If the switch is on then the light is on.*

As can be seen in the examples, exceptions to a rule that are supposed to be derived in the monotonic fragment of the logic (vs. consistency checks) are not included in the set of exceptions in the PEC rule, which is devoted to exceptions based on consistency checks. As regards exception-free statements, we represent them as PEC rules whose sets of exceptions are empty; regarding the premises, various choices are possible (e.g., the set of premises being a tautological singleton). In this respect, it follows that $\Vdash$ is assumed to admit $\top$ to represent effectively some formula. The various possible encodings of knowledge between premises and conclusions is similar to the well-known difference in default logic between defaults with prerequisites and the corresponding prerequisite-free defaults (cf [Bra93]).

3   Reasoning with and about PEC Rules

Let us define a concept of a derivation for the very general language of PEC rules. Interestingly, it will not only allow us to handle both monotonic and defeasible rules in the same setting, but it will also allow us to derive both of them.

A word of warning: In the following, $\vdash$ does not represent an inference relation. $\vdash \alpha$ (resp. $\nvdash \alpha$) means that α has (resp. does not) the status "inferred" *within the derivation.* Also, "not inferred within the derivation" does not mean "whose negated form cannot be inferred using the inferred formulas occurring in the derivation" (which is a weaker and less interesting notion). *A word of terminology:* $\vdash \alpha$ and $\nvdash \alpha$ are said to be *signed formulas.* Most naturally, $\vdash \gamma$ (resp. $\nvdash \gamma$) is said to be positive (resp. negative).

Definition 3. *Let Γ be a set of unary PEC rules and $\aleph$ be a PEC rule $(\rho, \{\epsilon_1, \ldots, \epsilon_n\}, \varsigma)$. A derivation of $\aleph$ from Γ is a tree T whose nodes are signed formulas such that*

1. *for each leaf of the form $\vdash \alpha$, either $(\alpha_1, \emptyset, \alpha_2) \in \Gamma$ and $\alpha = \alpha_1 \supset \alpha_2$, or $\alpha = \rho$,*
2. *for each leaf of the form $\nvdash \beta$,*
   $\beta \notin Cn(\{\gamma_1 \supset \gamma_2 \mid (\gamma_1, \emptyset, \gamma_2) \in \Gamma\} \cup \{\alpha \mid \vdash \alpha \text{ is a node of } T\})$,
3. *if $\nvdash \beta$ is a node then it is a leaf,*
4. *each node, if not a leaf, has a tuple $(\vdash \alpha_1, \ldots, \vdash \alpha_k, \nvdash \beta_1, \ldots, \nvdash \beta_m)$ as its parents $(k > 1$ only if $m = 0)$,[1]*

---

[1] This restriction is due to considering only unary rules in our presentation, it is lifted in the general case.

5. *if $\vdash \alpha$ is a node whose parents are a tuple $(\vdash \alpha_1, \ldots, \vdash \alpha_k)$ then $\alpha \in Cn(\{\alpha_1, \ldots, \alpha_k\})$,*
6. *if $\vdash \alpha$ is a node whose parents are a tuple $(\vdash \alpha_1, \nvdash \beta_1, \ldots, \nvdash \beta_m)$ then $(\alpha_1, \{\beta_1, \ldots, \beta_m\}, \alpha) \in \Gamma$,*
7. *$\rho \in \{\alpha \mid \vdash \alpha$ is a leaf of $T\} \cup \{\top\}$, and $\{\epsilon_1, \ldots, \epsilon_n\} = \{\beta \mid \nvdash \beta$ is a node of $T\}$, and $\vdash \varsigma$ is the root of T.*

We write $\Gamma \mathrel{\vert\!\sim}^{\{\epsilon_1, \ldots, \epsilon_n\}} \aleph$ and, whenever $\{\epsilon_1, \ldots, \epsilon_n\}$ is empty, $\Gamma \mathrel{\vert\!\sim} \aleph$.

Let us provide some intuitions and examples. Let us start with the simple case of classical logic: items 2, 3, and 6 are ineffective because there are no negative nodes, while items 4 and 7 gets simpler for the same reason. In fact, the derivation then is a classical proof: it contains only positive nodes and merely displays classical deductive steps. Thus, the conclusion is a PEC rule $\aleph = (\rho, \emptyset, \varsigma)$ where ς is the root of the derivation tree and ρ either is $\top$ or is a formula from a rule of Γ representing a fact (cf $\top \supset a$ in Example 5) or is an extra formula that plays the rôle of an additional hypothesis (cf. a in Example 6, $a \supset b$ in Example 7, $\neg a$ in Example 8). Still in the case that no exception is mentioned, classical trivialization from inconsistency threatens (cf Example 8).

Example 5. Let $\Gamma = \{(a, \emptyset, b), (\top, \emptyset, a), (b, \emptyset, c)\}$. The tree 3.1 is a derivation of $(\top \supset a, \emptyset, c)$ and $(a \supset b, \emptyset, c)$ from Γ. The tree 3.1 is also a derivation of $(\top, \emptyset, c)$ from Γ (please note that the first part of item 7 is satisfied by $\rho \in \{\top\}$).

Example 6. Let $\Gamma = \{(a, \emptyset, b), (b, \emptyset, c)\}$. The tree 3.2 is a derivation of $(a, \emptyset, c)$ from Γ (please note that a plays the rôle of an additional hypothesis). The tree 3.2 is also a derivation of $(a, \emptyset, c)$ from $\Gamma \cup \{(\top, \emptyset, a)\}$. Please compare with the tree 3.1 being a derivation of $(\top \supset a, \emptyset, c)$ from $\Gamma \cup \{(\top, \emptyset, a)\}$.

Example 7. Let $\Gamma = \{(\top, \emptyset, a), (b, \emptyset, c)\}$. The tree 3.1 is a derivation of $(a \supset b, \emptyset, c)$ from Γ.

Example 8. Let $\Gamma = \{(\top, \emptyset, a)\}$. The tree 3.3 is a derivation of $(\neg a, \emptyset, c)$ from Γ.

$$\frac{\dfrac{\vdash \top \supset a}{\vdash a} \quad \vdash a \supset b}{\dfrac{\vdash b \qquad \vdash b \supset c}{\vdash c}}$$

$$(3.1)$$

$$\frac{\dfrac{\vdash a \quad \vdash a \supset b}{\vdash b} \quad \vdash b \supset c}{\vdash c}$$

$$(3.2)$$

$$\frac{\vdash \neg a \quad \dfrac{\vdash \top \supset a}{\vdash a}}{\vdash c}$$

$$(3.3)$$

If some PEC rules in Γ have a non-empty set of exceptions, derivation trees may capture reasoning under some proviso(s) (meaning that there are possible exceptions) as can be seen in Example 9. Item 2 guarantees reasoning to be consistent in the sense that exception-free information from Γ (that may, or may not, occur as positive nodes) does not yield exceptions whose absence is required for the reasoning developed to be acceptable (cf Example 10 with Cn being classical logic and Example 11 with Cn being an arbitrary logic). This needs not prevent trivialization (in which case only derivations with no negative node may exist). Item 3 indicates that consistency statements occur as hypotheses, they are not inferred. Item 4 makes sure that each node, if not a leaf, is inferred from exception-free information and/or consistency hypotheses. As to items 5 and 6, they state that only inference steps from Cn and rules (with exceptions) in Γ may apply. Lastly, item 7 specifies what components the PEC rule derived consists of:

- Its conclusion is the root of the derivation tree.
- Its exceptions exhaust all consistency hypotheses occurring in the derivation tree (cf Example 9).
- Its premise, if not $\top$, either amounts to some exception-free statement represented by a rule from Γ, or it is an extra formula that plays the rôle of an additional hypothesis in the reasoning (cf Example 9).

Example 9. Let $\Gamma = \{(a \wedge b, \{d, e\}, f), (f, \emptyset, c)\}$. The tree 3.4 is a derivation of $(a \wedge b, \{d, e\}, c)$ from Γ (please note that ρ is $a \wedge b$ that plays the rôle of an additional hypothesis and that $\{d, e\}$ exhausts all negative nodes of the derivation tree). The tree 3.4 is not a derivation of $(a \wedge b, \{d, e, g\}, c)$ from Γ (item 7 in the definition of a derivation fails because g is listed as an exception of the PEC rule derived but $\nvdash g$ is not a node of the derivation tree). The tree 3.4 is not a derivation of $(a, \{d, e\}, c)$ from Γ (here, item 7 is failed for a different reason: the purported ρ is a but $\vdash a$ is not a leaf of the derivation tree).

Example 10. Let $\Gamma = \{(a \wedge b, \{d, e\}, f), (f, \emptyset, c), (\top, \emptyset, \neg f)\}$.

If Cn is taken to be classical logic, the tree 3.4 is not a derivation of $(a \wedge b, \{d, e\}, c)$ from Γ. The reason is that item 2 in the definition of a derivation fails as follows. First, $\vdash f$ is a node of the derivation tree hence $f \in \{\alpha \mid \vdash \alpha$ is a node of $T\}$. Second, $(\top, \emptyset, \neg f)$ belongs to Γ hence $\top \supset \neg f \in \{\gamma_1 \supset \gamma_2 \mid (\top, \emptyset, \gamma_1 \supset \gamma_2) \in \Gamma\}$. Third, item 2 then becomes $\beta \notin Cn(\{f, \ldots, \top \supset \neg f\})$ that must be checked for β being d and e. However, as Cn is classical logic, $Cn(\{f, \ldots, \top \supset \neg f\})$ contains all formulas of the language, among them are d and e.

Example 11. Let $\Gamma = \{(a \wedge b, \{d, e\}, f), (f, \emptyset, d), (d, \{\neg c\}, c)\}$. The tree 3.5 is not a derivation of $(a \wedge b, \{d, e, \neg c\}, c)$ from Γ because item 2 is failed. First, $\vdash d$ is a node of the derivation tree hence $d \in \{\alpha \mid \vdash \alpha$ is a node of $T\}$. As $\nvdash d$ is a leaf, $\beta \notin Cn(\{\alpha \mid \vdash \alpha$ is a node of $T\})$ must be checked for β being d and failure is clear.

$$\frac{\dfrac{\vdash a \wedge b \quad \nvdash d \quad \nvdash e}{\vdash f} \qquad \vdash f \supset c}{\vdash c}$$

$$(3.4)$$

$$\frac{\dfrac{\dfrac{\vdash a \wedge b \quad \nvdash d \quad \nvdash e}{\vdash f} \qquad \vdash f \supset d}{\vdash d} \qquad \nvdash \neg c}{\vdash c}$$

$$(3.5)$$

4   A Versatile Approach

It must be clear that the present work is *not* the definition of a new nonmonotonic logic and its proof theory. Instead, it is the definition of a framework expressive enough to capture an approach to the problem of overriding subsumed rules, and general enough to be instantiated by a number of logical formalisms. Importantly, the concept of a derivation is only a tool towards this aim which can be tailored to the proof theory of various logics.

For instance, and importantly, the above concept of a derivation does *not* match inference in default logic. To start with, there is no notion of an extension. Moreover, there is no counterpart to the requirement that a default *must* apply whenever it can. Also, it happens that derivations exist although there is no extension (cf Example 12).

Example 12. Let $\Gamma = (\Delta, \Sigma)$ be a default theory with $\Delta = \{\frac{\top:a}{\neg a}, \frac{b:d,e}{c}\}$ and $\Sigma = \{b\}$. Let us represent Γ by the PEC rules $\Gamma' = \{(\top, \{\neg a\}, \neg a), (b, \{\neg d, \neg e\}, c), (\top, \emptyset, b)\}$. Γ has no extension because Δ contains the default $\frac{\top:a}{\neg a}$, yet there exists a derivation of the PEC rule $(\top, \{\neg d, \neg e\}, c)$ from Γ', as can be seen from the tree 4.1.

Similarly, Example 13 shows that it may happen that a formula is in no extension although there exists a derivation for it.

Example 13. Let $\Gamma = (\Delta, \Sigma)$ be a default theory with $\Delta = \{\frac{\top:a}{b}, \frac{a:\neg b}{c}\}$ and $\Sigma = \{a\}$. Let us represent Γ by the set of PEC rules $\Gamma' = \{(\top, \{\neg a\}, b), (a, \{b\}, c), (\top, \emptyset, a)\}$. Γ has a single extension, i.e., $E = Cn(\{a, b\})$. Although the formula c is not in E, there exists a derivation of the PEC rule $(\top, \{b\}, c)$ from Γ' as shown by the tree 4.2.

$$
\frac{\top \supset b}{\vdash b} \quad \not\vdash \neg d \quad \not\vdash \neg e \qquad\qquad \frac{\vdash \top \supset a}{\vdash a} \quad \not\vdash b
$$
$$
\frac{}{\vdash c} \qquad\qquad\qquad\qquad\qquad \frac{}{\vdash c}
$$
$$
(4.1) \qquad\qquad\qquad\qquad\qquad (4.2)
$$

Still, the concept of a derivation is powerful enough to capture credulous reasoning as modeled by default logic. More precisely, if φ is a formula that belongs to an extension of a default theory Γ then there exists a derivation of $\vdash \varphi$ from the set of PEC rules encoding Γ, which amounts to $\Gamma \vdash^{\{\epsilon_1, \ldots, \epsilon_n\}} (\top, \{\epsilon_1, \ldots, \epsilon_n\}, \varphi)$.

5   X-Derivations

We are now to extend the concept of a derivation by taking into account an additional hypothesis, which, in full generality, can be a PEC rule (with or without exceptions). This full-fledged account is called an X-derivation, the details of which are explained and more generally discussed after the formal definition below.

Definition 4. *Let Γ be a set of PEC rules. Let X be a PEC rule. An X-derivation of $\aleph = (\rho, \{\epsilon_1, \ldots, \epsilon_n\}, \varsigma)$ from Γ is a tree T whose nodes are signed formulas such that*

1. *for each leaf of the form $\vdash \alpha$, either $(\alpha_1, \emptyset, \alpha_2) \in \Gamma \cup \{X\}$ and $\alpha = \alpha_1 \supset \alpha_2$, or $\alpha = \rho$,*
2. *for each leaf of the form $\not\vdash \beta$,*
   $\beta \notin Cn(\{\gamma_1 \supset \gamma_2 \mid (\gamma_1, \emptyset, \gamma_2) \in \Gamma\} \cup \{\alpha \mid \vdash \alpha \text{ is a node of } T\})$,
3. *if $\not\vdash \beta$ is a node then it is a leaf,*
4. *each node, if not a leaf, has a tuple $(\vdash \alpha_1, \ldots, \vdash \alpha_k, \not\vdash \beta_1, \ldots, \not\vdash \beta_m)$ as its parents $(k > 1$ only if $m = 0)$,*

5. *if* $\vdash \alpha$ *is a node whose parents are a tuple* $(\vdash \alpha_1, \ldots, \vdash \alpha_k)$ *then* $\alpha \in Cn(\{\alpha_1,$
$\ldots, \alpha_k\})$,

6. *if* $\vdash \alpha$ *is a node whose parents are a tuple* $(\vdash \alpha_1, \nvdash \beta_1, \ldots, \nvdash \beta_m)$ *then*
$(\alpha_1, \{\beta_1, \ldots, \beta_m\}, \alpha) \in \Gamma \cup \{X\}$,

7. $\rho \in \{\alpha \mid \vdash \alpha \text{ is a leaf of } T\} \cup \{\top\}$, *and* $\{\epsilon_1, \ldots, \epsilon_n\} = \{\beta \mid \nvdash \beta \text{ is a node of } T\}$,
and $\vdash \varsigma$ *is the root of* T.

We write $\Gamma \mathrel{\vdash}_{X}^{\{\epsilon_1, \ldots, \epsilon_n\}} \aleph$ *and, should* $\{\epsilon_1, \ldots, \epsilon_n\}$ *be empty,* $\Gamma \mathrel{\vdash}_X \aleph$.

The extra hypothesis X mainly comes into play through items 1 and 6. This means
that the PEC rule X is actually regarded as supplementing the set of PEC rules Γ.
Accordingly, if $X = (\top, \emptyset, \top)$, then an X-derivation of $\aleph$ from Γ happens to be a
derivation of $\aleph$ from Γ (cf Example 14). The rôle of each of the three components of
the derived rule $\aleph$ is detailed by item 7. Importantly, item 1 expresses that if a positive
leaf (tautologies aside) is not some exception-free information encoded as a PEC rule
from Γ then it is the premise of $\aleph$. Similarly to Definition 3, conditional reasoning
can be conducted using exception-free information as an extra hypothesis, turning it
into a positive leaf. However, the conditional piece can now be the X rule itself (more
exactly, an equivalent form) when X represents a formula of classical logic for instance
(cf Example 16). When X is a PEC rule $(\varrho, \{\xi_1, \ldots, \xi_h\}, \nu)$ that does have exceptions,
if its premise ϱ stands as a positive leaf (i.e., $\vdash \varrho$) not issued from a rule in Γ (that is,
there exists no $(\kappa, \emptyset, \zeta)$ in Γ such that $\kappa \supset \zeta$ be ϱ), then ϱ turns out to be the premise
of $\aleph$ (cf Example 18).

When X is used in the derivation and that the premise ϱ of X is not a leaf, then ϱ
comes from a subproof in the tree (cf Example 19).

In all cases, when X is used in the derivation, its premise occurs (as an hypothesis
or an intermediate conclusion) higher in the tree. Therefore, not only is X introduced
as an extra hypothesis, but when it is mentioned in the tree, if its premise ϱ does not
come from a subproof then $\vdash \varrho$ occurs as a leaf (and is regarded as established); hence
ϱ enters the set of premises of $\aleph$ (where $\aleph$ is the PEC rule which is the conclusion of
the derivation).

More generally, an X-derivation encompasses conditional reasoning in various forms
because it involves consistency hypotheses, it can include an extra rule X, and assumes
the premise of $\aleph$ (the PEC rule to be inferred).

Example 14. Let us return to Example 9, i.e., $\Gamma = \{(a \wedge b, \{d, e\}, f), (f, \emptyset, c)\}$.

The tree below, reproduced from Example 9, is both a derivation and a $(\top, \emptyset, \top)$-
derivation of $(a \wedge b, \{d, e\}, c)$ from Γ.

$$\dfrac{\dfrac{\vdash a \wedge b \quad \nvdash d \quad \nvdash e}{\vdash f} \qquad \vdash f \supset c}{\vdash c} \qquad (3.4)$$

Example 15. Again, $\Gamma = \{(a \wedge b, \{d, e\}, f), (f, \emptyset, c)\}$ as in Example 9.

The tree (3.4) above, reproduced from Example 9, is a $(\top, \emptyset, a \wedge b)$-derivation of
$(a \wedge b, \{d, e\}, c)$ from Γ, although in a rather vacuous way because the extra hypothesis
$X = (\top, \emptyset, a \wedge b)$ is left unused.

The tree (3.4) is not a $(\top, \emptyset, a \wedge b)$-derivation of $(\top, \{d, e\}, c)$ from Γ. The reason is that item 1 in the definition of an X-derivation is not satisfied because $a \wedge b$ is not of the form $\alpha_1 \supset \alpha_2$ while $\rho = \top$.

In contrast, the tree in the next example is a $(\top, \emptyset, a \wedge b)$-derivation of $(\top, \{d, e\}, c)$ from Γ.

Example 16. Let us still consider $\Gamma = \{(a \wedge b, \{d, e\}, f), (f, \emptyset, c)\}$. The following tree is a $(\top, \emptyset, a \wedge b)$-derivation of $(\top, \{d, e\}, c)$ from Γ (informally meaning that assuming $a \wedge b$ allows us to conclude c, unless d or e be the case).

$$\frac{\dfrac{\vdash \top \supset a \wedge b}{\vdash a \wedge b} \quad \nvdash d \quad \nvdash e}{\dfrac{\vdash f}{\vdash c}} \qquad \vdash f \supset c \qquad (5.1)$$

Example 17. Once more, $\Gamma = \{(a \wedge b, \{d, e\}, f), (f, \emptyset, c)\}$.

The tree (3.4) reproduced above in Example 14 is a $(a \wedge b, \{d, e\}, f)$-derivation of $(a \wedge b, \{d, e\}, c)$ from Γ although in a rather vacuous way because $X = (a \wedge b, \{d, e\}, f)$ is in Γ.

Indeed, the tree (3.4) is also a $(a \wedge b, \{d, e\}, f)$-derivation of $(a \wedge b, \{d, e\}, c)$ from Γ' where Γ' is taken to be $\Gamma \setminus \{(a \wedge b, \{d, e\}, f)\}$.

Example 18. Let $\Gamma = \{(f, \{e\}, c)\}$. The following tree is a $(a \wedge b, \{d\}, f)$-derivation of $(a \wedge b, \{d, e\}, c)$ from Γ.

$$\frac{\dfrac{\vdash a \wedge b \quad \nvdash d}{\vdash f} \quad \nvdash e}{\vdash c} \qquad (5.2)$$

Please observe that the premise of X, namely $a \wedge b$, is not issued from Γ hence is also the premise of $\aleph$ (here, X is $(a \wedge b, \{d\}, f)$ and $\aleph$ is $(a \wedge b, \{d, e\}, c)$).

Example 19. Let $\Gamma = \{(a \wedge b, \{d, e\}, f)\}$. The following tree is a $(f, \{g\}, c)$-derivation of $(a \wedge b, \{d, e, g\}, c)$ from Γ.

$$\frac{\dfrac{\vdash a \wedge b \quad \nvdash d \quad \nvdash e}{\vdash f} \quad \nvdash g}{\vdash c} \qquad (5.3)$$

Importantly, X-derivations are not meant to be optimal proofs: There is no endeavour as to avoid detours or to impose shortcuts.

Lastly, a concept of consistency can be introduced into the PEC framework.

Definition 5. *Γ is consistent iff $\Gamma \nvdash \bot$.*

As usual, a notion of consistency opens up a choice of negations. Whatever such a choice of a negation $\sim$ for PEC rules, it is likely to be such that both $\Gamma \vdash R$ and $\Gamma \vdash \sim R$ while $\Gamma \nvdash R \,\&\, \sim R$ (where $\&$ stands for some conjunction of PEC rules, again whatever choice is made there) is possible. Purposedly, we have left out any notion of inferential closure and similarly any subgrouping of consequences, e.g. in forms of extensions *à la* default logic.

6   PEC-Implicants

Definition 6. *Let Γ be a set of unary PEC rules and $R = (\rho, \{\epsilon_1, \ldots, \epsilon_m\}, \varsigma)$ be a unary PEC rule. A unary PEC rule R' is a PEC-implicant of R modulo Γ iff there exists an R'-derivation $\mathcal{D}$ of (ρ, E^*, ς) from Γ such that*

1. $\forall e' \in E^*, \exists e \in \{\epsilon_1, \ldots, \epsilon_m\}$ *s.t.* $e \in Cn(\{e'\})$,
2. $\forall e'' \in \{\epsilon_1, \ldots, \epsilon_m\} \setminus E^*, e'' \notin Cn\{\alpha \mid \vdash \alpha$ *is a node of* $\mathcal{D}\}$.

Definition 7. *Let Γ be a set of unary PEC rules. Let R and R' be two unary PEC rules. R' is a strict PEC-implicant of R modulo Γ iff R' is a PEC-implicant of R and R is not a PEC-implicant of R'.*

To simplify matters, Cn stands for classical logic in all of the following examples.

Example 20. Let Γ be empty. Let $R = (a \wedge b, \{\neg d, \neg e\}, c)$ and $R' = (a, \{\neg d\}, c)$.
    R' is a PEC-implicant of R modulo Γ. Indeed, the tree 6.1 below is an R'-derivation of $(a \wedge b, \{\neg d\}, c)$ from Γ, $\neg d$ is in the set of exceptions of $\mathcal{R}$ (taking care of item 1), and $\neg e$ does not follow from $\{a, a \wedge b, c\}$ (taking care of item 2).

Example 21. Let $\Gamma = \{(\top, \emptyset, a \supset \neg e), (\top, \emptyset, \neg e \supset f)\}$. Let $R = (a \wedge b, \{\neg d, \neg e\}, c)$ and let $R' = (f, \{\neg d\}, c)$.
    Considering the following tree 6.2, R' is not a PEC-implicant of R modulo Γ. Although this tree is an R'-derivation of $(a \wedge b, \{\neg d\}, c)$ from Γ, item 2 from the definition of a PEC-implicant is not satisfied: $\vdash \neg e$ is a node of the tree although $\neg e$ is an exception of R. Informally, R' then fails to subsume R because the way R' is applied when attempting to infer this "neighbouring" version of R involves a case that happens to be an exception to R.

$$\frac{\dfrac{\dfrac{\vdash a \wedge b}{\vdash a}}{\vdash c} \quad \not\vdash \neg d}{\vdash c}$$
(6.1)

$$\frac{\dfrac{\dfrac{\dfrac{\vdash a \wedge b}{\vdash a} \quad \vdash a \supset \neg e}{\vdash \neg e} \quad \vdash \neg e \supset f}{\vdash f}}{\vdash c} \quad \not\vdash \neg d}{\vdash c}$$
(6.2)

$$\frac{\dfrac{\dfrac{\dfrac{\vdash a \wedge b}{\vdash a} \quad \not\vdash h}{\vdash g} \quad \not\vdash \neg d}{\vdash c}}{\vdash c}$$
(6.3)

$$\frac{\dfrac{\top \supset (a \supset b)}{\vdash a \supset b} \quad \vdash a}{\vdash b}$$
(6.4)

$$\frac{\vdash a \quad \not\vdash \neg d \wedge \neg f}{\vdash c}$$
(6.5)

Example 22. Let $\Gamma = \{(a, \{h\}, g)\}$. Let $R = (a \wedge b, \{\neg d, \neg h\}, c)$ and let $R' = (g, \{\neg d\}, c)$.
    Considering the tree 6.3., R' is not a PEC-implicant of R modulo Γ. Although the tree 6.3 is an R'-derivation of $(a \wedge b, \{\neg d, h\}, c)$ from Γ, item 1 in the definition of a PEC-implicant is failed because h is a formula in E^* from which no formula in $\{\neg d, \neg h\}$ (i.e., $\{\epsilon_1, \ldots, \epsilon_m\}$) can be inferred. Informally, R' then fails to subsume R because the way R' is applied when attempting to infer this "neighbouring" version of R introduces a new exception.

Example 23. Let Γ be empty. Let $R = (a, \{\neg b\}, b)$ and let $R' = (\top, \emptyset, a \supset b)$.

R' is a PEC-implicant of R modulo Γ. Witness, the tree 6.4 is an R'-derivation of $(a, \emptyset, b)$ from Γ, item 1 is trivially satisfied as E^* is empty, and, as regards item 2, $\neg b$ cannot be deduced from $\{a, b, \top \supset (a \supset b)\}$ (i.e., the formulas in the positive nodes of the tree). This example shows that the context is taken into when it comes to assessing whether a rule subsumes another one, in the sense of being a PEC-implicant. Indeed, the implicant and the implicate need not have the same premise.

Example 24. Let Γ be empty. Let $R = (a, \{\neg d, \neg e\}, c)$ and let $R' = (a, \{\neg d \wedge \neg f\}, c)$.

R' is a PEC-implicant of R modulo Γ. Firstly, the tree 6.5 is an R'-derivation of $(a, \{\neg d \wedge \neg f\}, c)$ from Γ. As to item 1, $\neg d \wedge \neg f$ (namely, the only member of E^*) entails $\neg d$ (a member of $\{\epsilon_1, \dots, \epsilon_m\}$). As to item 2, neither $\neg d$ nor $\neg e$ (the members of $\{\epsilon_1, \dots, \epsilon_m\}$) are entailed by $\{a, c\}$ (the formulas in the positive nodes of the tree).

Fairly weak requirements about Cn are enough to show that being a PEC-implicant defines a pre-order. Of special interest then is the case that two PEC rules are PEC-implicants of each other: They surely are equivalent in a strong sense closely related to Cn-equivalence of exceptions. It is possible to obtain such a result, as follows.

Given two unary PEC rules $R = (\rho, \{\epsilon_1, \dots, \epsilon_m\}, \varsigma)$ and $R' = (\rho', \{\epsilon'_1, \dots, \epsilon'_n\}, \varsigma')$, if R is a PEC-implicant of R' modulo Γ, and R' is a PEC-implicant of R modulo Γ where $\Gamma = \emptyset$ then:

1. $\rho \Vdash \rho'$ and $\rho' \Vdash \rho$,
2. $\forall \epsilon_i \in \{\epsilon_1, \dots, \epsilon_m\}, \exists \epsilon_j, \epsilon'_k$ where $\epsilon_j \in \{\epsilon_1, .., \epsilon_m\}$ and $\epsilon'_k \in \{\epsilon'_1, .., \epsilon'_n\}$, s.t. $\epsilon_j \Vdash \epsilon_i$ et $\epsilon_j \Vdash \epsilon'_k$ and $\epsilon'_k \Vdash \epsilon_j$.

In particular, item 2 means that exceptions in R and R' are the same, up to logical equivalence (by subsumption, there can be more exceptions in R or in R', though).

7   Overriding Subsuming Rules

We are now ready to introduce our approach to override subsuming rules.

To override the subsuming rules of a PEC rule R and make R preempt, it is presumably not sufficient to "withdraw" all strict PEC-implicants of R and insert R (or "revise" by R in case of inconsistency). Indeed, there may remain in the resulting Γ some information of a self-conflicting change, e.g. so that whenever R is derivable, one of its strict PEC-implicants is also derivable. Accordingly, the process will be a little more elaborate.

In the sequel, we assume two operators $\oplus$ and $\setminus$ to be available in the PEC framework with the following features. Intuitively, $\setminus$ is a kind of contraction operator which applies to a set of PEC rules and to a pair of PEC rules: $\Gamma \setminus (R, R')$ is intended to contract Γ of R' in the presence of R. Intuitively, $\oplus$ is some revision operator in the PEC framework that restores consistency while enforcing means to derive a given PEC rule. More formally, the following properties are required upon these two operators:

- $\Gamma \setminus (R, R') \not\Vdash^\varepsilon_R R'$
- $\Gamma \setminus (R, R') \Vdash^\varepsilon R'' \quad \Rightarrow \quad \Gamma \Vdash^\varepsilon R''$

- $\Gamma \setminus (R, R') = Cn(\Gamma \setminus (R, R'))$
- $\Gamma \oplus R$ is consistent
- $\Gamma \oplus R \mid\!\sim^\varepsilon R$

whenever R, R', R'' are PEC rules and Γ is a set of PEC rules that does not need to be consistent.

Definition 8. *Let R' be a strict PEC-implicant of R modulo Γ.*
$\Gamma \oplus_{\rangle R' \langle} R =_{def} \Gamma \setminus (R, R') \cup \{R\}$.

Theorem 1. *Let R' be a strict PEC-implicant of R modulo Γ.*

$$\Gamma \oplus_{\rangle R' \langle} R \not\mid\!\sim^\varepsilon R'.$$

$$\Gamma \oplus_{\rangle R' \langle} R \mid\!\sim^\varepsilon R.$$

The next step consists in iterating the above process on all strict implicants of X. Assuming that the $\setminus$ operator is extended so that it applies to all the elements of its second argument which is now a set of PEC rules, we only need one more definition.

Let $\mathcal{Y}$ be the finite set of strict PEC-implicants of R modulo Γ.

Definition 9. $\Gamma \oplus_{\rangle \mathcal{Y} \langle} R =_{def} \Gamma \setminus (R, \mathcal{Y}) \cup \{R\}$.

Theorem 2. $\Gamma \oplus_{\rangle \mathcal{Y} \langle} R \not\mid\!\sim R'$ *for all R' that is a strict PEC-implicant of R modulo Γ.*
Also, $\Gamma \oplus_{\rangle \mathcal{Y} \langle} R \mid\!\sim R$.

8   Conclusions and Future Work

The contribution of this paper is at least twofold. First, a unified framework has been presented that allows both monotonic knowledge and defeasible rules to be represented and reasoned about in a uniform way. Derivation tools have been defined allowing to reason and infer both kinds of knowledge indifferently. The next step will be to address algorithmic aspects of X-derivations and associated inference, within the propositional setting. Also, the X-derivation concept implements the possibility to state defeasible rules as extra assumptions, which are coming in addition to the defeasible character of rules with exceptions. We believe that this two-levels form of hypothetical reasoning could be further explored and refined. Also, a whole family of forms of implicants could be devised for defeasible rules, depending on the actual form of reasoning that is modelled and on the intended actual epistemological rôles of the involved exceptions, premises and conclusion. Second, this framework has been exploited to solve a specific problem in knowledge representation and reasoning that has not received much attention so far. Namely, how could new information override the relevant subsuming available one? We claim that such an issue should not be taken for granted. Indeed, in real life we do often get information that is logically weaker but that appears *more precise* than the previously recorded one, and should therefore be preferred.

544   P. Besnard, É. Grégoire, and S. Ramon

References

[AGM85] Alchourrón, C.E., Gärdenfors, P., Makinson, D.: On the logic of theory change: Partial meet contraction and revision functions. J. Symb. Log. 50(2), 510–530 (1985)

[Bra93] Brass, S.: On the semantics of supernormal defaults. In: Thirteenth International Joint Conference on Artificial Intelligence (IJCAI 1993), pp. 578–583 (1993)

[PB91] Pequeno, T., Buchsbaum, A.: The logic of epistemic inconsistency. In: Second International Conference on Principles of Knowledge Representation and Reasoning (KR 1991), pp. 453–460 (1991)

[Rei80] Reiter, R.: A logic for default reasoning. Artificial Intelligence 13, 81–132 (1980)

Pseudo-polynomial Functions over Finite Distributive Lattices

Miguel Couceiro[1] and Tamás Waldhauser[1,2]

[1] University of Luxembourg
6, rue Richard Coudenhove-Kalergi, L-1359 Luxembourg
`miguel.couceiro@uni.lu`
[2] Bolyai Institute, University of Szeged
Aradi vértanúk tere 1, H-6720 Szeged, Hungary
`twaldha@math.u-szeged.hu`

Abstract. In this paper we extend the authors' previous works [6,7] by considering an aggregation model $f \colon X_1 \times \cdots \times X_n \to Y$ for arbitrary sets $X_1, \ldots, X_n$ and a finite distributive lattice Y, factorizable as

$$f(x_1, \ldots, x_n) = p(\varphi_1(x_1), \ldots, \varphi_n(x_n)),$$

where p is an n-variable lattice polynomial function over Y, and each φ_k is a map from X_k to Y. Following the terminology of [6,7], these are referred to as pseudo-polynomial functions.

We present an axiomatization for this class of pseudo-polynomial functions which differs from the previous ones both in flavour and nature, and develop general tools which are then used to obtain all possible such factorizations of a given pseudo-polynomial function.

Keywords: Sugeno integral, Sugeno utility function, pseudo-polynomial function, factorization, distributive lattice.

1 Introduction and Motivation

The Sugeno integral (introduced by Sugeno [14,15]) remains as one of the most noteworthy aggregation functions, and this is partially due to the fact that it provides a meaningful way to fuse or merge values within universes where essentially no structure, other than an order, is assumed. Even though primarily defined over real intervals, this concept of Sugeno integral can be extended to wider domains, namely, distributive lattices, via the notion of lattice polynomial function (i.e., a combination of variables and constants using the lattice operations $\wedge$ and $\vee$). As it turned out (see e.g. [5,13]), idempotent lattice polynomial functions coincide with (discrete) Sugeno integrals.

Recently, the Sugeno integral has been generalized via the notion of quasi-polynomial function (see [3]) originally defined as a mapping $f \colon X^n \to X$ on a bounded chain X and which can be factorized as

$$f(x_1, \ldots, x_n) = p(\varphi(x_1), \ldots, \varphi(x_n)), \tag{1}$$

W. Liu (Ed.): ECSQARU 2011, LNAI 6717, pp. 545–556, 2011.

where $p\colon X^n \to X$ is a polynomial function and $\varphi\colon X \to X$ is an order-preserving map. This notion was later extended in two ways.

In [4], the input and output universes were allowed to be arbitrary, possibly different, bounded distributive lattices X and Y so that $f\colon X^n \to Y$ is factorizable as in (1), where now $p\colon Y^n \to Y$ and $\varphi\colon X \to Y$. These functions appear naturally within the scope of decision making under uncertainty since they subsume overall preference functionals associated with Sugeno integrals whose variables are transformed by the utility function φ. Several axiomatizations for this function class were proposed, as well as all possible factorizations described.

In [6] and [7] a different extension was considered, now appearing within the realm of multicriteria decision making. Essentially, the aggregation model was based on functions $f\colon X_1 \times \cdots \times X_n \to Y$ for bounded chains $X_1,\ldots,X_n$ and Y, which can be factorized as compositions

$$f(x_1,\ldots,x_n) = p(\varphi_1(x_1),\ldots,\varphi_n(x_n)), \tag{2}$$

where $p\colon Y^n \to Y$ is a Sugeno integral, and each $\varphi_k\colon X_k \to Y$ is an order-preserving map. Such functions were referred to as Sugeno utility functions in [6]. Pseudo-polynomial functions were defined as functions of the form (2), where p is an arbitrary (possibly non-idempotent) lattice polynomial function, and each φ_k satisfies a certain boundary condition (which is weaker than order-preservation). Note that every quasi-polynomial function (1) can be regarded as a pseudo-polynomial function, where $X_1 = \cdots = X_n = X$ and $\varphi_1 = \cdots \varphi_n = \varphi$. Moreover, pseudo-polynomial functions naturally subsume Sugeno utility functions, and several axiomatizations were established for this function class in [6]. The question of factorizing a given Sugeno utility function into a composition (2) was addressed in [7], where a method for producing such a factorization was presented.

In the current paper we extend the previous results by letting $X_1,\ldots,X_n$ to be arbitrary sets and Y to be an arbitrary finite distributive lattice, thus subsuming the frameworks in [4,6,7]. Moreover, we develop general tools which allow us to produce all possible factorizations of a given pseudo-polynomial function into compositions (2) of a lattice polynomial function $p\colon Y^n \to Y$ with maps $\varphi_k\colon X_k \to Y$.

The structure of the paper is as follows. In Sect. 2 we introduce the basic notions and terminology needed throughout the paper, and recall some preliminary results. For further background on aggregation functions and their use in decision making, we refer the reader to [2,11]; for basics in the theory of lattices, see [9,12]. In Sect. 3 we develop a general framework used to derive an axiomatization of pseudo-polynomial functions of somewhat different nature than those proposed in [4,6,7], and which will provide tools for determining all possible factorizations of given pseudo-polynomial functions. These results are then illustrated in Sect. 4 by means of a concrete example, and in Sect. 5 we show how our new procedure can be applied to derive the algorithm provided in [7,8].

2 Preliminaries

Throughout this paper, Y is assumed to be a finite distributive lattice with meet and join operations denoted by $\wedge$ and $\vee$, respectively. Being finite, Y has a least element and a greatest element, denoted by 0 and 1, respectively. By Birkhoff's Representation Theorem [1], Y can be embedded into $\mathcal{P}(U)$, the power set of a set U. Identifying Y with its image under this embedding, we will consider Y as being a sublattice of $\mathcal{P}(U)$ with $0 = \emptyset, 1 = U$. The complement of a set $S \in \mathcal{P}(U)$ will be denoted by $\overline{S}$. Since Y is closed under intersections, it induces a closure operator cl on U, and since Y is closed under unions, it also induces a dual closure operator int (also known as interior operator):

$$\mathrm{cl}\,(S) := \bigwedge_{\substack{y \in Y \\ y \geq S}} y, \quad \mathrm{int}\,(S) := \bigvee_{\substack{y \in Y \\ y \leq S}} y.$$

It is easy to verify that these two operators satisfy the following identities for any $S_i \in \mathcal{P}(U)\,(i \in I)$:

$$\mathrm{cl}\Big(\bigvee_{i \in I} S_i\Big) = \bigvee_{i \in I} \mathrm{cl}\,(S_i), \quad \mathrm{int}\Big(\bigwedge_{i \in I} S_i\Big) = \bigwedge_{i \in I} \mathrm{int}\,(S_i).$$

A function $p \colon Y^n \to Y$ is a *polynomial function* if it can be obtained as a composition of the lattice operations $\wedge$ and $\vee$ with variables and constants. As observed in [13], *Sugeno integrals* coincide exactly with those lattice polynomial functions p which are idempotent, i.e., satisfy the identity $p\,(y, \ldots, y) = y$. An important lattice polynomial function (in fact, a Sugeno integral) is the *median* function med$\colon Y^3 \to Y$ defined by

$$\mathrm{med}\,(y_1, y_2, y_3) = (y_1 \wedge y_2) \vee (y_2 \wedge y_3) \vee (y_3 \wedge y_1)$$
$$= (y_1 \vee y_2) \wedge (y_2 \vee y_3) \wedge (y_3 \vee y_1).$$

Polynomial functions over bounded distributive lattices have very neat representations, for instance, in disjunctive normal form [10]. To describe this disjunctive normal form, let us define $\mathbf{1}_I$ to be the *characteristic vector* of $I \subseteq [n] := \{1, \ldots, n\}$, i.e., the n-tuple in Y^n whose i-th component is 1 if $i \in I$, and 0 otherwise.

Theorem 1 (Goodstein [10]). *A function $p \colon Y^n \to Y$ is a polynomial function if and only if*

$$p(y_1, \ldots, y_n) = \bigvee_{I \subseteq [n]} \Big(p(\mathbf{1}_I) \wedge \bigwedge_{i \in I} y_i\Big). \tag{3}$$

Furthermore, the function given by (3) is a Sugeno integral if and only if $p(\mathbf{0}) = 0$ and $p(\mathbf{1}) = 1$.

Let $X_1, \ldots, X_n$ be arbitrary sets with at least two elements, and for each $k \in [n]$ let us fix two distinct elements $0_{X_k}, 1_{X_k}$ of X_k . With no danger of ambiguity, we simply write 0 and 1 instead of 0_{X_k} and 1_{X_k}. We shall say that a mapping $\varphi_k \colon X_k \to Y$ satisfies the *boundary condition* if for every $x_k \in X_k$,

$$\varphi_k(0) \leq \varphi_k(x_k) \leq \varphi_k(1). \tag{4}$$

Observe that if X_k is a partially ordered set with least element 0 and greatest element 1, and if φ_k is order-preserving, then it satisfies the boundary condition.

A function $f \colon \prod_{i \in [n]} X_i \to Y$ is said to be a *pseudo-polynomial function*, if there is a polynomial function $p \colon Y^n \to Y$ and there are unary functions $\varphi_k \colon X_k \to Y$ ($k \in [n]$), satisfying the boundary conditions, such that

$$f(\mathbf{x}) = p(\boldsymbol{\varphi}(\mathbf{x})) = p(\varphi_1(x_1), \ldots, \varphi_n(x_n)) \tag{5}$$

holds for all $\mathbf{x} = (x_1, \ldots, x_n) \in \prod_{i \in [n]} X_i$. If p is a Sugeno integral, then we say that f is a *pseudo-Sugeno integral*. As it turns out, the notions of pseudo-polynomial function and pseudo-Sugeno integral are equivalent.

Proposition 2. *A function* $f \colon \prod_{i \in [n]} X_i \to Y$ *is a pseudo-polynomial function if and only if it is a pseudo-Sugeno integral.*

Clearly, if f is a pseudo-polynomial function, then it satisfies the following n-variable analogue of the boundary condition (4):

$$f(\mathbf{x}_k^0) \leq f(\mathbf{x}) \leq f(\mathbf{x}_k^1) \text{ for all } k \in [n], \mathbf{x} \in \prod_{i \in [n]} X_i, \tag{6}$$

where $\mathbf{x}_k^a \in \prod_{i \in [n]} X_i$ denotes the n-tuple which coincides with $\mathbf{x}$ in all but the k-th component, whose value is a.

Next we define a property that can be used to characterize pseudo-polynomial functions. We say that $f \colon \prod_{i \in [n]} X_i \to Y$ is *pseudo-median decomposable*, if for each $k \in [n]$ there is a unary function $\varphi_k \colon X_k \to Y$ satisfying (4), such that

$$f(\mathbf{x}) = \mathrm{med}\left(f(\mathbf{x}_k^0), \varphi_k(x_k), f(\mathbf{x}_k^1)\right) \tag{7}$$

for every $\mathbf{x} \in \prod_{i \in [n]} X_i$. Note that if f is pseudo-median decomposable w.r.t. unary functions $\varphi_k \colon X_k \to Y$ ($k \in [n]$) satisfying (4), then (6) holds.

Theorem 3. *Let* $f \colon \prod_{i \in [n]} X_i \to Y$ *be a function. Then f is a pseudo-polynomial function if and only if f is pseudo-median decomposable.*

The following theorem provides a disjunctive normal form of a polynomial function p_0 which can be used to factorize a given pseudo-median decomposable function f. Here $\widehat{\mathbf{1}}_I$ denotes the characteristic vector of $I \subseteq [n]$ in $\prod_{i \in [n]} X_i$, i.e., the n-tuple in $\prod_{i \in [n]} X_i$ whose i-th component is 1_{X_i} if $i \in I$, and 0_{X_i} otherwise.

Theorem 4. *If* $f \colon \prod_{i \in [n]} X_i \to Y$ *is pseudo-median decomposable w.r.t. unary functions* $\varphi_k \colon X_k \to Y$ ($k \in [n]$), *then* $f(\mathbf{x}) = p_0(\boldsymbol{\varphi}(\mathbf{x}))$, *where p_0 is given by*

$$p_0(y_1, \ldots, y_n) = \bigvee_{I \subseteq [n]} \left(f(\widehat{\mathbf{1}}_I) \wedge \bigwedge_{i \in I} y_i\right). \tag{8}$$

Remark 5. Proposition 2 and Theorems 3 and 4 were proved in [6,7,8] for complete chains, but the proofs presented there do not make use of the fact that the underlying sets are totally ordered (only that they are distributive lattices), and thus the proofs apply verbatim to finite distributive lattices.

3 Characterization and Factorization of Pseudo-polynomial Functions

Let $f\colon \prod_{i\in[n]} X_i \to Y$ be function satisfying (6), and for each $k \in [n]$ let us define two auxiliary functions $\Phi_k^-, \Phi_k^+\colon X_k \to Y$ as follows:

$$\Phi_k^-(a_k) := \bigvee_{x_k=a_k} \mathrm{cl}\big(f(\mathbf{x}) \wedge \overline{f(\mathbf{x}_k^0)}\big) \quad \text{and} \quad \Phi_k^+(a_k) := \bigwedge_{x_k=a_k} \mathrm{int}\big(f(\mathbf{x}) \vee \overline{f(\mathbf{x}_k^1)}\big).$$

Note that from (6) it follows that Φ_k^- and Φ_k^+ satisfy the boundary condition (4). With the help of these functions, we will give a necessary and sufficient condition for f to be a pseudo-polynomial function. The following lemma formulates a simple observation that allows us to solve equation (7) for $\varphi_k(x_k)$.

Lemma 6. *For any $u \le m \le w, v \in Y$ the following two conditions are equivalent:*

1. $\mathrm{med}\,(u, v, w) = m$;
2. $m \wedge \overline{u} \le v \le m \vee \overline{w}$.

Let us suppose that $f(\mathbf{x}) = p(\boldsymbol{\varphi}(\mathbf{x}))$ is a pseudo-polynomial function. Then (7) holds by Theorem 3, and applying Lemma 6 with $u = f(\mathbf{x}_k^0), m = f(\mathbf{x}), w = f(\mathbf{x}_k^1)$ and $v = \varphi_k(x_k)$, we see that $f(\mathbf{x}) \wedge \overline{f(\mathbf{x}_k^0)} \le \varphi_k(x_k) \le f(\mathbf{x}) \vee \overline{f(\mathbf{x}_k^1)}$. Moreover, since $\varphi_k(x_k) \in Y$, we have

$$\mathrm{cl}\big(f(\mathbf{x}) \wedge \overline{f(\mathbf{x}_k^0)}\big) \le \varphi_k(x_k) \le \mathrm{int}\big(f(\mathbf{x}) \vee \overline{f(\mathbf{x}_k^1)}\big).$$

Considering these inequalities for all $\mathbf{x} \in \prod_{i\in[n]} X_i$ with a fixed k-th component $x_k = a_k$, it follows that $\Phi_k^-(a_k) \le \varphi_k(a_k) \le \Phi_k^+(a_k)$ for all $k \in [n], a_k \in X_k$. Thus we obtain the following necessary condition for f to be a pseudo-polynomial function.

Proposition 7. *If $f\colon \prod_{i\in[n]} X_i \to Y$ is a pseudo-polynomial function, then it satisfies (6) and*

$$\Phi_k^- \le \Phi_k^+, \quad \text{for all } k \in [n]. \tag{9}$$

In order to prove that the necessary condition presented in the above proposition is also sufficient, we verify that (6) and (9) imply that f is pseudo-median decomposable with respect to $\Phi_1^-, \ldots, \Phi_n^-$ and also with respect to $\Phi_1^+, \ldots, \Phi_n^+$.

Proposition 8. *Suppose that $f\colon \prod_{i\in[n]} X_i \to Y$ satisfies (6) and (9). Then for all $\mathbf{x} \in \prod_{i\in[n]} X_i$ and $k \in [n]$, we have*

$$f(\mathbf{x}) = \mathrm{med}\,\big(f(\mathbf{x}_k^0), \Phi_k^-(x_k), f(\mathbf{x}_k^1)\big) = \mathrm{med}\,\big(f(\mathbf{x}_k^0), \Phi_k^+(x_k), f(\mathbf{x}_k^1)\big).$$

Propositions 7 and 8 together with Theorem 3 yield the following characterization of pseudo-polynomial functions.

Theorem 9. *A function* $f\colon \prod_{i\in[n]} X_i \to Y$ *is a pseudo-polynomial function if and only if it satisfies conditions* (6) *and* (9).

Let us suppose that $f\colon \prod_{i\in[n]} X_i \to Y$ satisfies (6) and (9). According to the above theorem, f is a pseudo-polynomial function, i.e., it has a factorization of the form $f(\mathbf{x}) = p(\boldsymbol{\varphi}(\mathbf{x}))$, where $p\colon Y^n \to Y$ is a polynomial function and each $\varphi_k\colon X_k \to Y$ $(k \in [n])$ is a unary map satisfying (4). We now show how to construct such a factorization; in fact, we will find all possible factorizations. If $\Phi_k^- \le \varphi_k \le \Phi_k^+$ holds for all $k \in [n]$, then

$$
\begin{aligned}
f(\mathbf{x}) &= \operatorname{med}\left(f(\mathbf{x}_k^0), \Phi_k^-(x_k), f(\mathbf{x}_k^1)\right) \\
&\le \operatorname{med}\left(f(\mathbf{x}_k^0), \varphi_k(x_k), f(\mathbf{x}_k^1)\right) \\
&\le \operatorname{med}\left(f(\mathbf{x}_k^0), \Phi_k^+(x_k), f(\mathbf{x}_k^1)\right) = f(\mathbf{x})
\end{aligned}
$$

by Proposition 8, therefore f is pseudo-median decomposable with respect to $\varphi_1, \ldots, \varphi_n$. Hence, by Theorem 4 we have $f(\mathbf{x}) = p_0(\boldsymbol{\varphi}(\mathbf{x}))$. This observation together with Theorem 9 yields the following result.

Theorem 10. *For any function* $f\colon \prod_{i\in[n]} X_i \to Y$ *satisfying* (6) *and unary maps* $\varphi_k\colon X_k \to Y$ $(k \in [n])$ *satisfying* (4), *the following three conditions are equivalent:*

(i) $\Phi_k^- \le \varphi_k \le \Phi_k^+$ *holds for all* $k \in [n]$;
(ii) *there exists a polynomial function* $p\colon Y^n \to Y$ *such that* $f(\mathbf{x}) = p(\boldsymbol{\varphi}(\mathbf{x}))$;
(iii) $f(\mathbf{x}) = p_0(\boldsymbol{\varphi}(\mathbf{x}))$.

Theorem 10 describes all those unary maps $\varphi_1, \ldots, \varphi_n$ that can occur in a factorization of f, but it does not provide all possible polynomial functions p. (We know that p_0 can be used in any factorization, but there may be others as well.) To find all factorizations (5) of f, let us fix unary functions $\varphi_k\colon X_k \to Y$ $(k \in [n])$ satisfying (4), such that $\Phi_k^- \le \varphi_k \le \Phi_k^+$ for each $k \in [n]$. To simplify notation, let $a_k = \varphi_k(0_{X_k})$, $b_k = \varphi_k(1_{X_k})$, and for each $I \subseteq [n]$ let $\mathbf{e}_I \in Y^n$ be the n-tuple whose i-th component is a_i if $i \notin I$ and b_i if $i \in I$. Clearly, if $p\colon Y^n \to Y$ is a polynomial function such that $f(\mathbf{x}) = p(\boldsymbol{\varphi}(\mathbf{x}))$, then

$$
p(\mathbf{e}_I) = f(\widehat{\mathbf{1}}_I) \quad \text{for all } I \subseteq [n]. \tag{10}
$$

In fact, one can verify that (10) is actually equivalent to $f(\mathbf{x}) = p(\boldsymbol{\varphi}(\mathbf{x}))$. For a given f and given $a_k, b_k \in Y$, (10) gives rise to a polynomial interpolation problem over Y: the values of the unknown polynomial function p are prescribed at certain (2^n many) points in Y^n. It can be shown that the least solution of this interpolation problem is

$$
p^-(\mathbf{y}) = \bigvee_{I \subseteq [n]} \left(c_I^- \wedge \bigwedge_{i \in I} y_i \right), \quad \text{where } c_I^- = \operatorname{cl}\!\left(f(\widehat{\mathbf{1}}_I) \wedge \bigwedge_{i \notin I} \overline{a_i} \right),
$$

whereas the greatest solution is

$$p^+\left(\mathbf{y}\right) = \bigvee_{I \subseteq [n]} \left(c_I^+ \wedge \bigwedge_{i \in I} y_i\right), \quad \text{where } c_I^+ = \mathrm{int}\big(f\big(\widehat{\mathbf{1}}_I\big) \vee \bigvee_{i \in I} \overline{b}_i\big).$$

In other words, a polynomial function p is a solution of (10) if and only if $p^- \le p \le p^+$. Since, by Theorem 1, p is uniquely determined by its values on the tuples $\mathbf{1}_I$ $(I \subseteq [n])$, this is equivalent to

$$c_I^- = p^-\left(\mathbf{1}_I\right) \le p\left(\mathbf{1}_I\right) \le p^+\left(\mathbf{1}_I\right) = c_I^+ \quad \text{for all } I \subseteq [n].$$

Thus we obtain the following description of all possible factorizations of a given pseudo-polynomial function f.

Theorem 11. *Let* $f \colon \prod_{i \in [n]} X_i \to Y$ *be a function satisfying* (6), *for each* $k \in [n]$ *let* $\varphi_k \colon X_k \to Y$ *be a given function satisfying* (4), *and let* $p \colon Y^n \to Y$ *be a polynomial function. Then* $f\left(\mathbf{x}\right) = p\left(\varphi\left(\mathbf{x}\right)\right)$ *if and only if* $\Phi_k^- \le \varphi_k \le \Phi_k^+$ *for each* $k \in [n]$, *and we have* $p^- \le p \le p^+$.

Remark 12. Clearly, $c_I^- \le f\big(\widehat{\mathbf{1}}_I\big) \le c_I^+$ holds independently of a_k, b_k, hence the polynomial function p_0 can be used in any factorization of f, as it was already shown in Theorem 4.

Remark 13. If X_k is a partially ordered set for each $k \in [n]$ and f is order-preserving, then Φ_k^- and Φ_k^+ are also order-preserving. This shows that every order-preserving pseudo-polynomial function has a factorization where each φ_k is order-preserving. Consequently, order-preserving pseudo-Sugeno integrals coincide with Sugeno utility functions (cf. Corollary 4.2 in [8]).

4   An Example

We illustrate the results of the previous section with a simple example. A university plans to hire a professor to teach in its bachelor's, master's and/or doctoral program in mathematics. The candidates are evaluated with respect to their academic qualifications and language skills. Let $x_1 = $ EF, E, F or N if the candidate speaks both English and French, only English, only French, or none of these two languages, respectively. Let $x_2 = $ C or M corresponding to whether the candidate's area of expertise is computer science or mathematics. Finally, let $x_3 = $ MSc or PhD corresponding to the degree that the candidate holds in his/her area of expertise. Thus the scales X_1, X_2, X_3 are the following:

$$X_1 := \{\mathrm{N}, \mathrm{E}, \mathrm{F}, \mathrm{EF}\} \text{ with } 0_{X_1} = \mathrm{N}, 1_{X_1} = \mathrm{EF},$$
$$X_2 := \{\mathrm{C}, \mathrm{M}\} \text{ with } 0_{X_2} = \mathrm{C}, 1_{X_2} = \mathrm{M},$$
$$X_3 := \{\mathrm{MSc}, \mathrm{PhD}\} \text{ with } 0_{X_3} = \mathrm{MSc}, 1_{X_3} = \mathrm{PhD}.$$

Let $f\left(x_1, x_2, x_3\right)$ describe which mathematics courses a candidate with profile (x_1, x_2, x_3) is qualified to teach, according to the university's policies: B (only

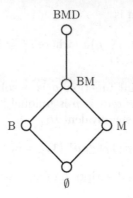

Fig. 1. The lattice Y

bachelor's), M (only master's), BM (bachelor's and master's), BMD (bachelor's, master's and doctoral), $\emptyset$ (none). This yields a function $f \colon X_1 \times X_2 \times X_3 \to Y$ (see Table 1(a)), where Y is the lattice shown on Fig. 1.

Hereinafter, we write a subset of $U = \{B, M, D\}$ as the juxtaposition of its elements, e.g., BM stands for $\{B, M\}$, etc. It is easy to verify that Y is a sublattice of $\mathcal{P}(U)$. Clearly, for $y \in Y$ we have $\mathrm{cl}(y) = \mathrm{int}(y) = y$. For the three sets D, BD and MD that belong to $\mathcal{P}(U)$ but not to Y, the closures and interiors are the following :

$$\mathrm{cl\,(D)} = \mathrm{BMD}, \quad \mathrm{cl\,(BD)} = \mathrm{BMD}, \quad \mathrm{cl\,(MD)} = \mathrm{BMD},$$
$$\mathrm{int\,(D)} = \emptyset, \qquad \mathrm{int\,(BD)} = \mathrm{B}, \qquad \mathrm{int\,(MD)} = \mathrm{M}.$$

Table 1(b) shows the auxiliary functions Φ_k^-, Φ_k^+ corresponding to the function f. We give the details of the computation of $\Phi_1^+(E)$, the other values can be calculated similarly:

$$\Phi_1^+(E) = \bigwedge_{\substack{x_2 \in X_2 \\ x_3 \in X_3}} \mathrm{int}\big(f(E, x_2, x_3) \vee \overline{f(EF, x_2, x_3)}\big)$$

$$= \mathrm{int}\big(f(E, C, MSc) \vee \overline{f(EF, C, MSc)}\big) \wedge \mathrm{int}\big(f(E, C, PhD) \vee \overline{f(EF, C, PhD)}\big)$$

$$\wedge \, \mathrm{int}\big(f(E, M, MSc) \vee \overline{f(EF, M, MSc)}\big) \wedge \mathrm{int}\big(f(E, M, PhD) \vee \overline{f(EF, M, PhD)}\big)$$

$$= \mathrm{int}\big(\emptyset \vee \overline{B}\big) \wedge \mathrm{int}\big(M \vee \overline{BM}\big) \wedge \mathrm{int}\big(\emptyset \vee \overline{B}\big) \wedge \mathrm{int}\big(M \vee \overline{BMD}\big)$$

$$= \mathrm{int\,(MD)} \wedge \mathrm{int\,(MD)} \wedge \mathrm{int\,(MD)} \wedge \mathrm{int\,(M)}$$

$$= M \wedge M \wedge M \wedge M = M.$$

We can see that $\Phi_k^- \le \Phi_k^+$ for $k = 1, 2, 3$, therefore f is a pseudo-polynomial function by Theorem 9. From Theorem 10 we can infer that in any factorization $f(x_1, x_2, x_3) = p(\varphi_1(x_1), \varphi_2(x_2), \varphi_3(x_3))$ of f, we must have $\varphi_1 = \Phi_1^- = \Phi_1^+$, while we have 4 possibilities for φ_2 (as $\varphi_2(C)$ can be chosen to be $\emptyset$, B, M or BM, and $\varphi_2(M)$ must be BMD), and we have 2 possibilities for φ_3 (as $\varphi_3(MSc)$

Table 1. The university example

(a) The function f

x_1	x_2	x_3	$f(x_1,x_2,x_3)$
N	C	MSc	$\emptyset$
N	C	PhD	$\emptyset$
N	M	MSc	$\emptyset$
N	M	PhD	$\emptyset$
E	C	MSc	$\emptyset$
E	C	PhD	M
E	M	MSc	$\emptyset$
E	M	PhD	M
F	C	MSc	B
F	C	PhD	B
F	M	MSc	B
F	M	PhD	B
EF	C	MSc	B
EF	C	PhD	BM
EF	M	MSc	B
EF	M	PhD	BMD

(b) The functions Φ_k^-, Φ_k^+

x_1	$\Phi_1^-(x_1)$	$\Phi_1^+(x_1)$
N	$\emptyset$	$\emptyset$
E	M	M
F	B	B
EF	BMD	BMD

x_2	$\Phi_2^-(x_2)$	$\Phi_2^+(x_2)$
C	$\emptyset$	BM
M	BMD	BMD

x_3	$\Phi_3^-(x_3)$	$\Phi_3^+(x_3)$
MSc	$\emptyset$	B
PhD	BMD	BMD

can be chosen to be $\emptyset$ or B, and φ_3 (PhD) must be BMD). Thus there are 8 triples of functions $(\varphi_1,\varphi_2,\varphi_3)$ that allow us to factorize f. Theorem 10 also shows that in all of these 8 cases one can use the polynomial function

$$p_0(y_1,y_2,y_3) = (B \wedge y_1) \vee (B \wedge y_1 \wedge y_2) \vee (BM \wedge y_1 \wedge y_3) \vee (BMD \wedge y_1 \wedge y_2 \wedge y_3)$$
$$= (B \wedge y_1) \vee (BM \wedge y_1 \wedge y_3) \vee (y_1 \wedge y_2 \wedge y_3).$$

Computing the coefficients c_I^-, c_I^+ for $(\Phi_1^-,\Phi_2^-,\Phi_3^-)$, one can see that in this case $p^- = p_0 = p^+$, i.e., $p = p_0$ is the only polynomial function such that $f(x_1,x_2,x_3) = p(\Phi_1^-(x_1),\Phi_2^-(x_2),\Phi_3^-(x_3))$. On the other hand, choosing $(\varphi_1,\varphi_2,\varphi_3) = (\Phi_1^+,\Phi_2^+,\Phi_3^+)$, we obtain $p^- = y_1 \wedge y_2 \wedge y_3$ and $p^+ = p_0$, thus in this case there are 11 polynomial functions p such that $f(x_1,x_2,x_3) = p(\Phi_1^+(x_1),\Phi_2^+(x_2),\Phi_3^+(x_3))$. Probably the most natural choice is $p = p^-$, which gives the following very simple factorization:

$$f(x_1,x_2,x_3) = \Phi_1^+(x_1) \wedge \Phi_2^+(x_2) \wedge \Phi_3^+(x_3).$$

From this latter factorization we can draw the following conclusions. The bachelor's courses are taught in French, while the master's courses are taught in English.[1] In order to teach in the bachelor's program, the professor must have

---

[1] As it is the case, e.g., at the University of Luxembourg.

at least an MSc, and in order to teach in the master's program, the professor must have a PhD (in either computer science or mathematics). Moreover, a member of the doctoral program must have a PhD in mathematics, and must speak both English and French.

5   Pseudo-polynomial Functions over Chains

In this section we consider the case when Y is a finite chain. As we will see, in this case the results of Sect. 3 lead to a generalization of Algorithm SUFF presented in [8]. As before, we will suppose that Y is a sublattice of $\mathcal{P}(U)$ for some set U, with least element $\emptyset$ and greatest element U. We may assume without loss of generality that $U = [m] = \{1, 2, \ldots, m\}$, and $Y = \{[0], [1], \ldots, [m]\}$, where $[0] = \emptyset$. The closure of a set $S \subseteq U$ is the smallest set of the form $[k]$ that contains S, while the interior of S is the largest set of the form $[k]$ that is contained in S (see Fig. 2). Formally, we have

$$\mathrm{cl}\,(S) = [\max S], \quad \mathrm{int}\,(S) = \left[\min \overline{S} - 1\right].$$

Let us assume that $f \colon \prod_{i \in [n]} X_i \to Y$ satisfies (6). Then $f\left(\mathbf{x}_k^0\right) = [u]$, $f(\mathbf{x}) = [v]$, $f\left(\mathbf{x}_k^1\right) = [w]$ with $u \leq v \leq w$, hence we have

$$f\,(\mathbf{x}) \wedge \overline{f\,(\mathbf{x}_k^0)} = \{u+1, \ldots, v\},$$
$$f\,(\mathbf{x}) \vee \overline{f\,(\mathbf{x}_k^1)} = \{1, \ldots, v, w+1, \ldots, m\}.$$

Therefore the terms in the definition of Φ_k^- and Φ_k^+ can be determined as follows:

$$\mathrm{cl}\bigl(f\,(\mathbf{x}) \wedge \overline{f\,(\mathbf{x}_k^0)}\bigr) = \begin{cases} f\,(\mathbf{x}), & \text{if } f\left(\mathbf{x}_k^0\right) < f\,(\mathbf{x}); \\ \emptyset, & \text{if } f\left(\mathbf{x}_k^0\right) = f\,(\mathbf{x}); \end{cases} \tag{11}$$

$$\mathrm{int}\bigl(f\,(\mathbf{x}) \vee \overline{f\,(\mathbf{x}_k^1)}\bigr) = \begin{cases} f\,(\mathbf{x}), & \text{if } f\left(\mathbf{x}_k^1\right) > f\,(\mathbf{x}); \\ U, & \text{if } f\left(\mathbf{x}_k^1\right) = f\,(\mathbf{x}). \end{cases} \tag{12}$$

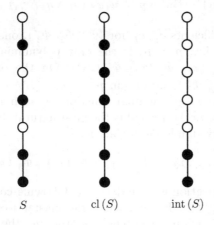

$$S \qquad\qquad \mathrm{cl}\,(S) \qquad\qquad \mathrm{int}\,(S)$$

Fig. 2. The closure and interior of a subset of a chain

Let us now define the following three sets for any $k \in [n], a_k \in X_k$, as in [8]:

$$\mathcal{W}_{a_k}^f = \{f(\mathbf{x}) : x_k = a_k \text{ and } f(\mathbf{x}_k^0) < f(\mathbf{x}) < f(\mathbf{x}_k^1)\},$$
$$\mathcal{L}_{a_k}^f = \{f(\mathbf{x}) : x_k = a_k \text{ and } f(\mathbf{x}_k^0) < f(\mathbf{x}) = f(\mathbf{x}_k^1)\},$$
$$\mathcal{U}_{a_k}^f = \{f(\mathbf{x}) : x_k = a_k \text{ and } f(\mathbf{x}_k^0) = f(\mathbf{x}) < f(\mathbf{x}_k^1)\}.$$

From (11) and (12) it follows that $\Phi_k^-(a_k) = \bigvee \mathcal{L}_{a_k}^f \vee \bigvee \mathcal{W}_{a_k}^f$ and $\Phi_k^+(a_k) = \bigwedge \mathcal{U}_{a_k}^f \wedge \bigwedge \mathcal{W}_{a_k}^f$, hence the condition $\Phi_k^- \le \varphi_k \le \Phi_k^+$ in Theorem 10 can be reformulated as follows:

(a) either $\mathcal{W}_{a_k}^f = \{\varphi_k(a_k)\}$ or $\mathcal{W}_{a_k}^f = \emptyset$;
(b) $\varphi_k(a_k) \ge \bigvee \mathcal{L}_{a_k}^f$;
(c) $\varphi_k(a_k) \le \bigwedge \mathcal{U}_{a_k}^f$.

Thus by Theorem 10, f is a pseudo-polynomial function if and only if there are functions φ_k satisfying the above three conditions. If each X_k is a bounded chain and f is an order-preserving function depending on all of its variables, then Algorithm SUFF of [8] does not return the value **false** if and only if (a),(b),(c) hold (cf. equation (4.5) in [8]). Therefore, in the finite case, Theorem 4.1 of [8] follows as a special case of Theorem 10. Moreover, the results of Sect. 3 not only generalize Algorithm SUFF to arbitrary finite distributive lattices (instead of finite chains) and to pseudo-polynomial functions (instead of Sugeno utility functions), but they provide all possible factorizations of a given pseudo-polynomial function f (whereas Algorithm SUFF constructs only one factorization).

Acknowledgments. The second named author acknowledges that the present project is supported by the National Research Fund, Luxembourg, and cofunded under the Marie Curie Actions of the European Commission (FP7-COFUND), and supported by the Hungarian National Foundation for Scientific Research under grants no. K77409 and K83219.

References

1. Birkhoff, G.: On the combination of subalgebras. Proc. Camb. Phil. Soc. 29, 441–464 (1933)
2. Bouyssou, D., Dubois, D., Prade, H., Pirlot, M. (eds.): Decision-Making Process – Concepts and Methods. ISTE/John Wiley (2009)
3. Couceiro, M., Marichal, J.-L.: Axiomatizations of quasi-polynomial functions on bounded chains. Aequationes Mathematicae 396(1), 195–213 (2009)
4. Couceiro, M., Marichal, J.-L.: Axiomatizations of quasi-polynomial functions over bounded distributive lattices. Aequationes Mathematicae 80(3), 319–334 (2010)
5. Couceiro, M., Marichal, J.-L.: Characterizations of discrete Sugeno integrals as polynomial functions over distributive lattices. Fuzzy Sets and Systems 161(5), 694–707 (2010)
6. Couceiro, M., Waldhauser, T.: Sugeno utility functions I: Axiomatizations. In: Torra, V., Narukawa, Y., Daumas, M. (eds.) MDAI 2010. LNCS (LNAI), vol. 6408, pp. 79–90. Springer, Heidelberg (2010)

7. Couceiro, M., Waldhauser, T.: Sugeno utility functions II: Factorizations. In: Torra, V., Narukawa, Y., Daumas, M. (eds.) MDAI 2010. LNCS (LNAI), vol. 6408, pp. 91–103. Springer, Heidelberg (2010)
8. Couceiro, M., Waldhauser, T.: Axiomatizations and factorizations of Sugeno utility functions. Submitted to International Journal of Uncertainty, Fuzziness and Knowledge-Based Systems, http://arxiv.org/abs/1101.4962
9. Davey, B.A., Priestley, H.A.: Introduction to Lattices and Order. Cambridge University Press, New York (2002)
10. Goodstein, R.L.: The solution of equations in a lattice. Proc. Roy. Soc. Edinburgh Section A 67, 231–242 (1967)
11. Grabisch, M., Marichal, J.-L., Mesiar, R., Pap, E.: Aggregation Functions. In: Encyclopedia of Mathematics and its Applications. Cambridge University Press, Cambridge (2009)
12. Grätzer, G.: General Lattice Theory. Birkhäuser, Basel (2003)
13. Marichal, J.-L.: Weighted lattice polynomials. Discrete Mathematics 309(4), 814–820 (2009)
14. Sugeno, M.: Theory of Fuzzy Integrals and its Applications. PhD thesis, Tokyo Institute of Technology, Tokyo (1974)
15. Sugeno, M.: Fuzzy measures and fuzzy integrals – a survey. In: Gupta, M.M., Saridis, G.N., Gaines, B.R. (eds.) Fuzzy Automata and Decision Processes, pp. 89–102. North-Holland, New York (1977)

A Bridge between Probability and Possibility in a Comparative Framework

Giulianella Coletti[1], Romano Scozzafava[2], and Barbara Vantaggi[2]

[1] University of Perugia, Italy
coletti@dmi.unipg.it
[2] University "La Sapienza", Rome, Italy
{romscozz,vantaggi}@dmmm.uniroma1.it

Abstract. The paper studies the connection between comparative probability and comparative plausibility, with a particular emphasis on comparative possibility. We consider a comparative probability on an algebra and extend it to a different algebra. We prove that, in general, the upper extension of the given comparative probability is a comparative plausibility. By considering a suitable condition of weak logical independence between the two partitions related to the atoms of the two algebras, we prove that the upper ordinal relation is a comparative possibility. These results hold for comparative probability not necessarily representable by a numerical probability.

Keywords: Ordinal relations, Probability, Possibility, Comparative probability.

1 Introduction

A decision maker or a field expert may have on hand only information concerning events different from those of interest. So it is necessary to make inference, i.e. to gather information on the latter. More precisely, given an assessment consisting of a suitable degree of belief in a specific framework (singled out by an uncertainty measure), making inference means extending the given assessment to new events. To deal with the inferential problem, we start from a probability assessment by following the lines of de Finetti approach. Then, the inferential process with respect to each new event is ruled by coherence and it does not necessarily lead to a unique value.

In the extension processes, for purely syntactical reasons the lower and upper envelopes of the enlargements can lead to uncertainty measures which are different from the initial ones. For instance (see e.g. [13], [20], [6]), if we start from a probability P on an algebra, and consider any other algebra $\mathcal{B}$, then the lower [upper] envelope of the class of probabilities extending P to $\mathcal{B}$ is a belief [plausibility] function.

In [7] we proved that under suitable logical conditions (weak logical independence) between the two algebras, the upper envelope (i.e. plausibility) is a possibility and the lower envelope is a necessity. Nevertheless the decision maker

W. Liu (Ed.): ECSQARU 2011, LNAI 6717, pp. 557–568, 2011.
© Springer-Verlag Berlin Heidelberg 2011

may have at hand (or is able to give) only a binary relation expressing degrees of belief on a family of events different from that of interest. So he needs to make inference starting from this information.

The aim of this paper is in fact to deal with the above inferential problem in a comparative setting.

Clearly, we could obtain an ordinal relation representable by a plausibility (comparative plausibility) starting from an ordinal relation representable by a probability. Actually, we consider comparative probability, satisfying only de Finetti-Koopman qualitative additive axiom ([9], [21]) (only necessary for the representability by a probability, see [22]), and we prove that the upper envelope is a comparative plausibility.

Moreover, we obtain a comparative possibility if the two algebras are weakly logically independent.

These results contribute to the deepening of hybrid models involving probability, plausibility and possibility, which have been studied in many papers, e.g. [12,15,17,18,19,24]: our approach is essentially syntactic and emphasizes an inferential point of view in a comparative setting.

2   Preliminaries

Here we recall some definitions and results concerning the problem of extending a probability assessment. In particular, we focus on the properties of lower and upper envelopes of the class of probabilities extending the given probability.

2.1   Coherent Extensions

In probability theory it is well known the concept of coherence introduced by de Finetti [9] through a betting scheme, or its dual version consisting on the solvability of a linear system. In the coherent probability theory the most important result (known as fundamental theorem of probability) assures that, given a *coherent* assessment $p_i = P(E_i)$ (with $i = 1, 2, ..., n$) on an *arbitrary* finite family $\mathcal{E} = \{E_1, ..., E_n\}$ of events, it can be extended (possibly not in a unique way) to any set $\mathcal{E}'$; moreover, for each event $E \in \mathcal{E}'$ there exist two events E_* and E^* in the algebra spanned by $\mathcal{E}$ (possibly $E_* = \emptyset$ and $E^* = \Omega$) that are, respectively, the "maximum" and the "minimum" union of atoms A_r (generated by the initial family $\mathcal{E}$) such that

$$E_* \subseteq E \subseteq E^* .$$

If E is logical dependent on $\mathcal{E}$, then $E_* = E = E^*$.

Then, given the set $\{\tilde{P}\}$ of all possible extensions of P, coherent assessments of $\tilde{P}(E)$ are all real numbers of a closed interval $[p_*, p^*]$, with

$$p_* = p_*(E) = \inf \tilde{P}(E_*) = \inf \sum_{A_r \subseteq E_*} \tilde{P}(A_r) ,$$

$$p^* = p^*(E) = \sup \tilde{P}(E^*) = \sup \sum_{A_r \subseteq E^*} \tilde{P}(A_r) .$$

The values p_* and p^* can actually be computed by a linear programming problem [11,1,5].

If $\mathcal{E}'$ is an algebra, then $p_*(\cdot)$ and $p^*(\cdot)$ are, respectively, a lower and an upper probability on $\mathcal{E}'$. In particular, if also $\mathcal{E}$ is an algebra (or a partition), then $p_*(\cdot)$ and $p^*(\cdot)$ are, respectively, a belief and a plausibility (see [13]). When the algebras $\mathcal{E}$ and $\mathcal{E}'$ satisfy suitable logical conditions (see below), belief and plausibility reduce to necessity and possibility.

2.2 Weakly Logically Independent Partitions

We recall that two partitions $\mathcal{L}, \mathcal{L}'$ of Ω are logically independent if for every $E_i \in \mathcal{L}$ and $E'_j \in \mathcal{L}'$ one has $E_i \wedge E'_j \neq \emptyset$. Equivalently, $\mathcal{L}, \mathcal{L}'$ are logically independent if for every $E'_j \in \mathcal{L}'$, one has

$$\Omega = \bigvee_{E_i \wedge E'_j \neq \emptyset} E_i \; .$$

In [7] a "weak" form of logical independence (Definition 1 below) has been introduced. Let $\mathcal{L}, \mathcal{L}'$ be two partitions of Ω. For any $E'_j \in \mathcal{L}'$, we denote by A_j the minimal (with respect to the inclusion) event logically dependent on $\mathcal{L}$ containing E'_j, that is

$$A_j = \bigvee_{E_i \wedge E'_j \neq \emptyset} E_i \; .$$

Obviously, A_j is an element of the algebra $\mathcal{B}$ spanned by $\mathcal{L}$.

Given two partitions $\mathcal{L}, \mathcal{L}'$ of Ω, for any $E'_j \in \mathcal{L}'$, we consider the corresponding $A_j \in \mathcal{B}$.

Definition 1. *$\mathcal{L}'$ is weakly logically independent of $\mathcal{L}$ (in symbols, $\mathcal{L}' \perp\!\!\!\perp_w \mathcal{L}$) if, for any given $E'_i \in \mathcal{L}'$, every other $E'_k \in \mathcal{L}'$ ($k \neq i$) satisfies al leat one of the following conditions*
- *$E'_k \subseteq A_i$*
- *$E'_k \wedge E_j \neq \emptyset$ for any $E_j \subseteq A_i$.*

Clearly, if $\mathcal{L}, \mathcal{L}'$ are logically independent (i.e. every event of $\mathcal{L}$ is logically independent of all events of $\mathcal{L}'$), then $\mathcal{L}' \perp\!\!\!\perp_w \mathcal{L}$ (but the vice versa does not hold, see Example 1). For the intuitive meaning of weak logical independence, see [7]. Here we note that it requires that at least an event of $\mathcal{L}'$ has non empty intersection with all the events of $\mathcal{L}$ (i.e. it is logically independent of them). Moreover, no more than one event of $\mathcal{L}$ may include an event of $\mathcal{L}'$.

Example 1. Let us consider a set of incompatible and exhaustive symptoms $\mathcal{L} = \{S_1, ..., S_5\}$ and a set of incompatible and exhaustive diseases $\mathcal{L}' = \{D_1, ..., D_4\}$ and consider the following logical constraints: disease D_1 is compatible only with the symptom S_1, disease D_4 is compatible with all the symptoms, and it is implied by symptoms S_4 or S_5. Moreover for $i = 2, 3$ disease D_i implies $S_1 \vee ... \vee S_i$, and is incompatible with S_j for $j > i$.

The two partitions are not logically independent, but they are weakly logical independent.

As proved in [7], the notion of weakly logically independent partitions (i.e. $\mathcal{L}' \perp\!\!\!\perp_w \mathcal{L} \implies \mathcal{L} \perp\!\!\!\perp_w \mathcal{L}'$) is symmetric even if the definition is given in a nonsymmetric way.

We recall now some properties and a characterization of weakly logically independent partitions.

Proposition 1. *Let $\mathcal{L}, \mathcal{L}'$ be two partitions of Ω. If $\mathcal{L}' \perp\!\!\!\perp_w \mathcal{L}$, then the following statements hold:*

1. *for every $E_i', E_j' \in \mathcal{L}'$ either $A_j \subseteq A_i$ or $A_i \subset A_j$;*
2. *there exists $E_i' \in \mathcal{L}'$ such that $E_i' \wedge E_j \neq \emptyset$ for any $E_j \in \mathcal{L}$;*
3. *if there exist $E_i' \in \mathcal{L}'$ and $E_j \in \mathcal{L}$ such that $E_i' \subseteq E_j$, then, for every $E_r' \in \mathcal{L}'$, we have $E_r' \wedge E_j \neq \emptyset$.*
4. *there exists at most one $E_k \in \mathcal{L}$ such that $E_i' \subseteq E_k$ for some $E_i' \in \mathcal{L}'$.*

The previous proposition easily implies that if $\mathcal{L}$ is a refinement of $\mathcal{L}'$, then $\mathcal{L}' \not\perp\!\!\!\perp_w \mathcal{L}$.

Theorem 1. *Let $\mathcal{L} = \{E_1, ..., E_i, ..., E_n\}$ and $\mathcal{L}' = \{E_1', ..., E_j', ..., E_m'\}$ be two partitions of Ω. The following two conditions are equivalent:*

1. *$\mathcal{L}' \perp\!\!\!\perp_w \mathcal{L}$;*
2. *there exists a permutation of $\{1, ..., m\}$ such that the order induced by the inclusion on the corresponding events $A_{i_1}, ..., A_{i_m}$ is complete.*

2.3 Possibility Measures as Enlargement of a Coherent Probability

In [6] it has been proved that if $\mathcal{L}, \mathcal{L}'$ are two partitions of Ω and $\mathcal{B}'$ the algebra spanned by $\mathcal{L}'$, then if we assign a probability distribution on $\mathcal{L}$ and consider the family $\mathcal{P}$ of probabilities P_i extending P restricted to $\mathcal{L} \cup \mathcal{B}'$, the lower bound of $\mathcal{P}$ on $\mathcal{B}'$ is a belief function (and the upper bound a plausibility function). Vice versa for any belief function Bel on an algebra $\mathcal{B}'$ there exists a partition of Ω and a relevant probability distribution such that the lower bound of the class of probability extending P on $\mathcal{B}'$ coincides with Bel (similarly for a plausibility function).

These results are independent of any logical relation between the partition $\mathcal{L}$ and that constituted by the atoms of $\mathcal{B}'$. Obviously, the logical constraints rule the numerical values of the belief (or plausibility) function.

In [7] we proved that if two partitions are weakly logically independent, then the plausibility obtained as upper envelope of the class $\mathcal{P}$ is a possibility:

Theorem 2. *Let $\mathcal{L}, \mathcal{L}'$ be two partitions of Ω and $\mathcal{B}'$ the algebra spanned by $\mathcal{L}'$. Let P be a probability distribution on $\mathcal{L}$ and $\overline{P}$ the upper envelope of the class $\mathbf{P} = \{P'\}$ of all the probabilities extending P onto $\mathcal{L} \cup \mathcal{B}'$.*
If $\mathcal{L}' \perp\!\!\!\perp_w \mathcal{L}$, then $\overline{P}$ is a possibility measure on $\mathcal{B}'$.

As shown in [7], we can obtain a possibility also in the case that $\mathcal{L}' \not\perp\!\!\!\perp_w \mathcal{L}$, nevertheless the next result proves that this is not possible if the probability distribution is strictly positive.

Theorem 3. *Let $\mathcal{L}, \mathcal{L}'$ be two partitions of Ω and $\mathcal{B}'$ the algebra spanned by $\mathcal{L}'$. Let P be a strictly positive probability distribution on $\mathcal{L}$ and $\overline{P}$ the upper envelope of the class $\mathbf{P} = \{P'\}$ of all the probabilities extending P onto $\mathcal{L} \cup \mathcal{B}'$. If the restriction of $\overline{P}$ on $\mathcal{B}'$ is a possibility measure, then $\mathcal{L}' \perp\!\!\!\perp_w \mathcal{L}$.*

The next theorem (given in [7]) shows how weakly logically independent partitions not only rule the transition from probability to possibility but also the other way round.

Theorem 4. *Consider a possibility measure Π on an algebra $\mathcal{B}$ and let $\mathcal{L}$ be the set of atoms of $\mathcal{B}$. Then there exists an algebra $\mathcal{B}'$ generated by a partition $\mathcal{L}'$ and a probability on $\mathcal{B}'$ such that:*

1. *$\mathcal{L}' \perp\!\!\!\perp_w \mathcal{L}$,*
2. *the upper envelope $\overline{P}$ of the class $\mathbf{P} = \{P'\}$ of all the coherent probability assessments, extending P on $\mathcal{B}' \cup \mathcal{B}$ coincide on $\mathcal{B}$ with the possibility measure Π.*

This result is strictly related to that given in [16] concerning the connections between upper probability and possibility, where a characteristic property for a set of probabilities is given in order to its induced upper probability be a possibility measure (the upper probability induced by a set of lower bounds on events $A_1, ..., A_n$ is a possibility if the set $A_1, ..., A_n$ is nested, i.e. $A_1 \subseteq ... \subseteq A_n$).

Remark 1. In [7] we proved that, given two logically independent partitions $\mathcal{L}$ and $\mathcal{L}'$, the upper envelope of the extensions on $\mathcal{L} \cup \mathcal{B}'$ of a probability P on $\mathcal{L}$ is a possibility on $\mathcal{B}'$ and, for any $A \in \mathcal{B}' \setminus \emptyset$, $\overline{P}(A) = 1$.

It follows that if the partitions $\mathcal{L}$ and $\mathcal{L}'$ are logically independent, then the necessity N obtained as dual of the possibility Π (i.e., as lower probability of the class of probabilities extending any given probability distribution P on $\mathcal{L}$) is such that for any $A \in \mathcal{B}' \setminus \Omega$

$$N(A) = 1 - \Pi(A^c) = 0.$$

Thus, we get in this case the non informative necessity independently of the initial probability distribution.

3   Comparative Degree of Belief

Let $\preceq$ be a binary relation on an arbitrary set of events $\mathcal{F} = \{E_i, F_i\}_{i \in I}$ expressing the intuitive idea of being "no more believable than". The symbols $\sim$ and $\prec$ represent, respectively, the symmetric and asymmetric parts of $\preceq$: $E \sim F$ means (roughly speaking) that E is judged "equally believable" to F, while $E \prec F$ means that F is "more believed" than E.

The relation $\preceq$ expresses a qualitative judgement and it is necessary to set up a system of rules assuring the consistency of the relation with some numerical model. More precisely, given a numerical framework of reference (singled-out by a numerical measure of uncertainty), it is necessary to find conditions which are necessary and sufficient for the existence of a numerical assessment on the events representing a given ordinal relation.

We recall that a function f from $\mathcal{F}$ to $[0,1]$ *represents* (or *agrees* with) the relation $\preceq$ iff

$$E \preceq F \Longrightarrow f(E) \leq f(F),$$
$$E \prec F \Longrightarrow f(E) < f(F).$$

If we focus on the relations representable (or induced) by a capacity (i.e. a function monotone with respect to inclusion $\subseteq$), it is necessary that there is an extension of $\preceq$ on the algebra $\mathcal{B}$ spanned by $\mathcal{F}$ satisfying the following conditions:

(c1) $\preceq$ is a total preorder (reflexive, transitive, holding for all pairs $E, F \in \mathcal{B}$);
(c2) $\emptyset \preceq E$ for every $E \in \mathcal{B}$, and $\emptyset \prec \Omega$;
(c3) for every $E, F \in \mathcal{B}$, $E \subseteq F \Longrightarrow E \preceq F$.

In the following we call *comparative degree of belief* a binary relation on an algebra $\mathcal{B}$ satisfying $(c1), (c2), (c3)$.

When we specialize the numerical function f (probability, belief, lower probability, and so on) agreeing with a relation $\preceq$, then we need to require that there exists an extension of $\preceq$ satisfying a further characteristic condition.

The most known among these conditions is the "qualitative additivity" axiom (introduced by de Finetti [9] and Koopman [21]), which is a necessary (but not sufficient) condition for the the representability of $\preceq$ by a probability (as proved in [22]):

(p) for every $E, F, H \in \mathcal{B}$, with $(E \vee F) \wedge H = \emptyset$, the following conditions hold:

$$E \preceq F \Longrightarrow E \vee H \preceq F \vee H \tag{1}$$

$$E \prec F \Longrightarrow E \vee H \prec F \vee H. \tag{2}$$

Axiom (p) characterizes the comparative degree of belief representable by a weak $\oplus$-decomposable measure, with $\oplus$ strictly increasing (see [4]).

We need this result in the following, so we recall the definition of weak $\oplus$-decomposable measure.

Definition 2. *Given a function* $\varphi : \mathcal{B} \to [0,1]$ *and a commutative binary operation* $\oplus$ *on* $\{\varphi(A_i)\}_{A_i \in \mathcal{B}}$ *with* $\varphi(\emptyset)$ *neutral element,* φ *is a weakly $\oplus$-decomposable measure if the restriction of $\oplus$ to the pairs* $\{\varphi(A_i), \varphi(A_j)\}$*, with* $A_i \wedge A_j = \emptyset$ *is associative and increasing and moreover*

$$\varphi(A_i \vee A_j) = \varphi(A_i) \oplus \varphi(A_j).$$

The necessary and sufficient condition for the representability by a probability of a relation $\preceq$, defined on any finite set $\mathcal{F}$ of events, is the following (cp) condition (see [2]), which is the comparative version of de Finetti coherence condition and is equivalent, if $\mathcal{F}$ is an algebra, to those given in [22], [23]:

(cp) for any $A_i, B_i \in \mathcal{F}$ there exists $\lambda_i \geq 0$, $i = 1, ..., n$ such that $A_i \preceq B_i$

$$\sup \sum_{i=1}^{n} \lambda_i(|B_i| - |A_i|) \leq 0 \qquad \text{implies} \qquad A_i \sim B_i$$

where $|E|$ is the truth value of the event E and the supremum is taken over the set of atoms generated by A_i, B_i for $i = 1, ..., n$.

The next weaker qualitative additivity axioms have been introduced in [25,8]: the first one characterizes relations representable by a belief function and the second one relations representable by plausibility:

(b) if $E, F, H \in \mathcal{B}$, with $E \subseteq F$ and $F \wedge H = \emptyset$, then

$$E \prec F \Rightarrow (E \vee H) \prec (F \vee H)$$

(pl) if $E, F, H \in \mathcal{B}$, with $E \subseteq F$ and $F \wedge H = \emptyset$, then

$$E \sim F \Rightarrow (E \vee H) \sim (F \vee H)$$

Further conditions (PO), (NEC) introduced in [14], characterize relations representable by a possibility and a necessity respectively:

(PO) for every $A, G, H \in \mathcal{B}$

$$A \preceq G \Rightarrow (A \vee H) \preceq (G \vee H)$$

(NEC) for every $A, B, C \in \mathcal{B}$

$$A \preceq B \Longrightarrow (A \wedge C) \preceq (B \wedge C).$$

4   Extending Comparative Probabilities

We study the problem of extending a comparative degree of belief and we look for all the possible extensions. In particular, this problem has been treated for relations representable by a probability: it is known the following theorem [2].

Theorem 5. *Let $\mathcal{D}$ be a family of events and $\preceq$ an ordinal relation on $\mathcal{D}$; if $\preceq$ is an ordinal relation satisfying (cp), then there exists a (possibly not unique) extension $\preceq^*$ of $\preceq$ to an arbitrary family $\mathcal{D}'$ of events , with $\mathcal{D}' \supseteq \mathcal{D}$.*

In particular, if $\mathcal{D}' = \mathcal{D} \cup \{K\}$, there exist (uniquely defined) suitable subfamilies $\mathcal{C}_1, \mathcal{C}_2, \mathcal{C}_3, \mathcal{C}_4$ such that any coherent extension of $\preceq$ necessarily fulfils the following conditions $H' \prec K$ for every $H' \in \mathcal{C}_1$; $K \prec H''$ for every $H'' \in \mathcal{C}_2$; $H_* \preceq K$ for every $H_* \in \mathcal{C}_3$; finally $K \preceq H_{**}$ for every $H_{**} \in \mathcal{C}_4$ (any relation between K and H for $H \in (\mathcal{D} \setminus \cup_{i=1}^{4} \mathcal{C}_i)$).

The above result singles out for any new event K the events which must be no more probable than K, those no less probable than K in order to maintain condition (cp). Moreover, there is a set $\mathcal{D} \setminus \cup_{i=1}^{4} \mathcal{C}_i$ of events where the extension, mantaining (cp) is not univocally defined.

Now, we consider a comparative probability $\preceq$ (that is an ordinal relation satisfying (c1), (c2) and (p)) in the case that $\preceq$ is given on an algebra $\mathcal{B}$ and we need to extend it to an algebra $\mathcal{B}'$.

Theorem 6. *Let $\mathcal{B}$ be a finite algebra of events and $\preceq$ a comparative probability on $\mathcal{B}$. Then there exists a (possibly not unique) extension $\preceq^*$ of $\preceq$ to an algebra $\mathcal{B}'$ of events, with $\mathcal{B}' \supseteq \mathcal{B}$, which is a comparative probability on $\mathcal{B}'$.*

In particular, for any $K \in \mathcal{D}' \setminus \mathcal{D}$, there exist (uniquely defined) suitable subfamilies $\mathcal{C}_1^K, \mathcal{C}_2^K, \mathcal{C}_3^K, \mathcal{C}_4^K$ such that any extension of $\preceq$ necessarily fulfils the following conditions $H' \prec K$ for every $H' \in \mathcal{C}_1$; $K \prec H''$ for every $H'' \in \mathcal{C}_2^K$; $H_* \preceq K$ for every $H_* \in \mathcal{C}_3^K$; finally $K \preceq H_{**}$ for every $H_{**} \in \mathcal{C}_4^K$ (any relation between K and H for any $H \in \mathcal{C}_5^K = \mathcal{D} \setminus \cup_{i=1}^4 \mathcal{C}_i^K$).

Proof. From the results in [8] a comparative probability on a finite arbitrary set of events $\mathcal{D}$ (and in particular in the algebra $\mathcal{B}$) is represented by weakly $\oplus$-decomposable assessment on $\mathcal{B}$ [4]. Moreover, in the same paper it has been proved that an $\oplus$-decomposable assessment on an algebra $\mathcal{B}$ can be extended on any algebra $\mathcal{B}' \supset \mathcal{B}$. Any relation $\preceq'$ induced by such an extension is a comparative probability (see [8]) and its restriction to $\mathcal{B}$ coincides with $\preceq$.

Let us consider now the following sets:
- $\mathcal{C}_1^K$ is the set of events H' of $\mathcal{B}$ such that there exists $F \in \mathcal{B}$ with $H' \prec F$ and $F \subseteq K$.

- $\mathcal{C}_2^K$ is the set of events $H'' \in \mathcal{B}$ such that there exist $F \in \mathcal{B}$, with $F \prec H''$ and $K \subseteq F$.

- Let $\mathcal{C}_3^K$ and $\mathcal{C}_4^K$ be the sets defined as $\mathcal{C}_1^K$ and $\mathcal{C}_2^K$ respectively, with the conditions $H' \preceq F$ and $F \preceq H''$.

We need to prove that for every $H' \in \mathcal{C}_1^K$, $H'' \in \mathcal{C}_2^K$, $H_* \in \mathcal{C}_3^K$ and $H_{**} \in \mathcal{C}_4^K$ we have $H' \preceq H_* \preceq H_{**} \prec H''$.

We give a proof for the inequality $H' \prec H''$, the the proof of the other ones are similar. By definition of $\mathcal{C}_1^K$ and $\mathcal{C}_2^K$ there are $F_1, F_2 \in \mathcal{B}$ with $H' \prec F_1$, $F_2 \prec H''$ and $F_1 \subseteq K \subseteq F_2$. So (by monotonicity od $\preceq$ with respect to inclusion) $F_1 \preceq F_2$ and then $H' \prec H''$.

Notice that, due to the existence of $\mathcal{C}_5^K$, the extension of $\preceq$ to K is not unique.

The above result gives a method for extending a comparative probability to a set of events, and this can be done step–by–step. In particular, if we would extend $\preceq$ to the events $\{K_1, ..., K_n\}$, in a way that the extended $\preceq$ satisfies condition (p), then, for every event K_i, we must choose one of the possible extensions satisfying (p). Obviously the global extension strictly depends on the order of the events to which we extend $\preceq$; in fact every choice on $\mathcal{C}_5^{K_i}$ affects $\mathcal{C}_i^{K_{i+1}}$ and in particular makes a restriction on $\mathcal{C}_5^{K_{i+1}}$.

Nevertheless there is a different way to look at the extensions, consisting in computing $\mathcal{C}_j^{K_i}$, $(j = 1, ..., 5)$, independently for every K_i, and then consider the lower bound $\preceq_*$ and the upper bound $\preceq^*$ of the extensions.

Obviously $\preceq_*$ and $\preceq^*$ in general do not satisfy condition (p).

Note that, since any extension $\preceq'$ of $\preceq$ is a comparative probability, by monotonicity with respect to inclusion, it follows that for any $H \in \mathcal{B}'$, the following relation holds

$$H_* \preceq' H \preceq' H^*$$

where H_* (and H^*) is the maximal (minimal) event in $\mathcal{B}$ contained in (containing) H.

Then, we have the following results for the lower and upper extensions:

Theorem 7. *Let $\preceq$ be a comparative probability on the algebra $\mathcal{B}$. Given an algebra $\mathcal{B}'$, let $\Gamma = \{\preceq'\}$ be the set of comparative probability extensions of $\preceq$ on $\mathcal{B}'$ and let $\preceq_*$ and $\preceq^*$ be the lower and upper envelopes of Γ, respectively. Then for any $H, K \in \mathcal{B}^*$, one has*

$$H \preceq^* K \Longleftrightarrow H^* \preceq K^* \tag{3}$$

$$H \preceq_* K \Longleftrightarrow H_* \preceq K_*. \tag{4}$$

Proof. To prove relation (3) it is enough, for any $H \in \mathcal{B}'$, to look for a comparative probability $\preceq'$, extending $\preceq$ on the algebra $\mathcal{A}$ generated by $\mathcal{B} \cup \{H\}$, such that $H \sim' H^*$. Note that $\mathcal{A}$ is given by the events $H \wedge B$ and $H^c \wedge B$ for $B \in \mathcal{B}$.

Define $\preceq'$ on $\mathcal{A}$ as follows, for any $B \in \mathcal{B}'$:

- if $H \wedge B \neq \emptyset$, then $H \wedge B \sim' B$;
- if $H^c \wedge B \neq B$, then $H^c \wedge B \sim' \emptyset$.

Obviously, if $H \wedge B = \emptyset$, then $H \wedge B \sim' \emptyset$ and if $H^c \wedge B = B$, then $H^c \wedge B \sim' B$.

It is easy to check that $\preceq'$ is a comparative probability, which extends $\preceq$, so the thesis follows.

The proof for the relation (4) goes along the same lines.

Theorem 8. *Let $\preceq$ be a comparative probability on an algebra $\mathcal{B}$. The lower [upper] envelope $\preceq_*$ [$\preceq^*$] of the extensions of $\preceq$ on the algebra $\mathcal{B}'$ is a comparative belief [plausibility] on $\mathcal{B}'$.*

Proof. We prove the result for $\preceq_*$, the proof for $\preceq^*$ is similar.

Consider any $A, B, C \in \mathcal{B}'$ such that $A \subseteq B$ and $C \wedge B = \emptyset$. Since $A \subseteq B$, it follows $A_* \subseteq B_*$, and by Theorem 7 one has $A \prec_* B$ if and only if $A_* \prec B_*$. Moreover, since $C \wedge B = \emptyset$, one has $B_* \wedge C_* = \emptyset = A_* \wedge C_*$ and so, by condition (p), the inequality $A_* \prec B_*$ implies $A_* \vee C_* \prec B_* \vee C_*$.

Now, note that $A_* \vee C_*$ could be properly included in $(A \vee C)_*$, since there could be some element A_i of the partition of $\mathcal{B}$ which is included in $(A \vee C)_*$ but not in $A_* \vee C_*$. This means that $A_i \wedge A \neq \emptyset \neq A_i \wedge C$ and $A_i \subseteq A \vee C$. Analogously, for $B_* \vee C_*$ we obtain $A_i \wedge B \neq \emptyset \neq A_i \wedge C$ and $A_i \subseteq B \vee C$. Obviously, if there is an element $A_i^1 \not\subseteq A$ in the partition of $\mathcal{B}$ such that $A_i^1 \wedge A \neq \emptyset \neq A_i^1 \wedge C$ and $A_i^1 \subseteq A \vee C$, then $A_i^1 \wedge B \neq \emptyset \neq A_i^1 \wedge C$ (so $A_i^1 \not\subseteq B$) and $A_i^1 \subseteq B \vee C$. Such elements of the partition of $\mathcal{B}$ are denoted by $\mathcal{A}_A$. On the other hand there could be $A_i^2 \not\subseteq B$ in the partition of $\mathcal{B}$ such that $A_i^2 \wedge B \neq \emptyset \neq A_i^2 \wedge C$ and $A_i^2 \subseteq B \vee C$, but $A_i^2 \not\subseteq A \vee C$. Such elements of the partition of $\mathcal{B}$ are denoted by $\mathcal{A}_B^A$.

Note that if $A \subseteq B$ then, for any C with $C \wedge B = \emptyset$, $\mathcal{A}_A \subseteq \mathcal{A}_B$ and $\mathcal{A}_B = \mathcal{A}_A \bigcup \mathcal{A}_B^A$. Then, from $A_* \vee C_* \prec B_* \vee C_*$ it follows, by axiom (p)

$$A_* \vee C_* \vee D \prec B_* \vee C_* \vee D \preceq B_* \vee C_* \vee D \vee E$$

where $D = \bigvee_{A_i^1 \in \mathcal{A}_A} A_i^1$ and $E = \bigvee_{A_i^2 \in \mathcal{A}_B^A} A_i^2$ (possibly $D = \emptyset$ or $E = \emptyset$). Finally, since $(A \vee C)_* = A_* \vee C_* \vee D$ and $(B \vee C)_* = A_* \vee C_* \vee D \vee E$, by relation (4), $A \prec_* B$ implies $A \vee C \prec_* B \vee C$.

Thus $\preceq_*$ satisfies axiom (b), and so it is a comparative belief.

Theorem 9. *Let $\preceq$ be a comparative probability on an a finite algebra $\mathcal{B}$ and let $\mathcal{B}'$ be any finite algebra such that its set of atoms is weakly logically independent of that of $\mathcal{B}$. The lower [upper] envelope $\preceq_*$ [$\preceq^*$] of the extensions of $\preceq$ on the algebra $\mathcal{B}'$ is a comparative necessity [possibility] on $\mathcal{B}'$.*

Proof. We prove the result for $\preceq^*$, the proof for $\preceq_*$ goes along the same line.

We need to prove that, for $A, B, C \in \mathcal{B}'$, $A \preceq^* B$ implies $A \vee C \preceq^* B \vee C$.

Since the partition $\mathcal{E}$ of $\mathcal{B}$ is weakly logically independent of the partition $\mathcal{E}'$ of $\mathcal{B}'$, then from Theorem 1, for any pair A, B of events in $\mathcal{B}'$, one has either $A^* \subseteq B^*$ or $B^* \subseteq A^*$.

From relation (3), $A \preceq^* B$ if and only if $A^* \preceq^* B^*$. Thus, if $A^* \preceq^* B^*$, from the above considerations $A^* \subseteq B^*$.

Now, by considering any $C \in \mathcal{B}'$, for the corresponding event $C^* \in \mathcal{B}$, again from Theorem 1, one of the following situations occurs:

1. $C^* \subseteq A^*$;

2. $A^* \subseteq C^* \subseteq B^*$;

3. $B^* \subseteq C^*$.

Note that, for any $D \in \mathcal{B}'$ one has

$$(D \vee C)^* = \bigvee_{E_i \wedge (D \vee C) \neq \emptyset} E_i = \bigvee_{E_i \wedge D \neq \emptyset} E_i \vee \bigvee_{E_i \wedge C \neq \emptyset} E_i = D^* \vee C^*.$$

If $C^* \subseteq A^*$, then $(A \vee C)^* \subseteq A^* \subseteq B^*$ and so (by the monotonicity of a comparative probability) $(A \vee C)^* \preceq B^* \preceq (B \vee C)^*$ and again from relation (3), it follows $A \vee C \preceq^* B \vee C$.

If $A^* \subseteq C^* \subseteq B^*$, then $(A \vee C)^* = C^* \subseteq B^*$ and so

$$(A \vee C)^* \sim C^* \preceq B^* \preceq (B \vee C)^*$$

and so (3) implies $A \vee C \preceq^* B \vee C$.

If $B^* \subseteq C^*$, then $(A \vee C)^* = C^* \subseteq B^* \subseteq C^*$ and so $(A \vee C)^* \sim C^* \preceq (B \vee C)^*$ and again from relation (3), $A \vee C \preceq^* B \vee C$.

Note that even if an ordinal relation satisfying (p) on an algebra $\mathcal{B}$ is not necessarily representable by a probability, its upper ordinal relation $\preceq^*$ on $\mathcal{B}'$ is representable by a plausibility and, moreover, if $\mathcal{B} \perp_w \mathcal{B}'$, then $\preceq^*$ on $\mathcal{B}'$ is representable by a possibility.

Now we prove also the reverse result of Theorem 9, actually we prove it for comparative possibility:

Theorem 10. *Let $\preceq$ be a comparative possibility [necessity] on an algebra $\mathcal{B}$ and let $\mathcal{L}$ be the corresponding set of atoms. Then there is an algebra $\mathcal{B}'$ with set of atoms $\mathcal{L}'$ such that $\mathcal{L}'$ is weakly logically independent of $\mathcal{L}$, and there is a comparative probability $\preceq'$ on $\mathcal{B}'$ such that its upper [lower] envelope $\preceq^*$ $[\preceq_*]$ of the extensions of $\preceq'$ on the algebra $\mathcal{B}'$ coincides with the comparative possibility [necessity] $\preceq$.*

Proof. If $\preceq$ is a comparative possibility, then it is representable by a possibility Π on $\mathcal{B}$. From Theorem 4 there is a partition $\mathcal{L}'$ of Ω (and the spanned algebra $\mathcal{B}'$) weakly logically independent of $\mathcal{L}$ and there is a probability P on $\mathcal{B}'$ such that its upper extension on $\mathcal{B}$ coincides with Π. This probability P induces a comparative probability $\preceq'$ on $\mathcal{B}'$. From Theorem 9 the upper envelope $\preceq^*$ of the extensions of $\preceq'$ on $\mathcal{B}$ is a comparative possibility since $\mathcal{L}$ is weakly logically independent of $\mathcal{L}'$. We need to prove that $\preceq^*$ coincides with $\preceq$. From Theorem 7, $\preceq^*$ is such that $A \preceq^* B \implies A^* \preceq' B^*$. Since $\preceq'$ is induced by a probability P, it follows $P(A^*) \leq P(B^*)$, so from Theorem 2 we have $\Pi(A) \leq \Pi(B)$ and then $A \preceq B$.

5 Conclusion

The paper studies the connections between possibilistic and probabilistic frameworks from a comparative point of view. We show that starting with a comparative probability (that is a relation not necessarily representable by a probability) the upper envelope of its extensions on another algebra is a comparative plausibility. Moreover, when the two sets of atoms are weakly logically independent, the upper envelope of the extensions is a comparative possibility.

An open problem is to establish which is the upper envelope of a comparative relation satisfying conditions weaker than (p), for instance preorders which are only monotone with respect to inclusion.

References

1. Bruno, G., Gilio, A.: Application of the simplex method to the fundamental theorem for the probabilities in the subjective theory. Statistica 40, 337–344 (1980)
2. Coletti, G.: Coherent qualitative probability. Journal of Mathematical Psychology 34, 297–310 (1990)
3. Coletti, G.: Coherent numerical and ordinal probabilistic assessments. IEEE Trans. on Systems, Man, and Cybernetics 24, 1747–1754 (1994)
4. Coletti, G., Scozzafava, R.: From conditional events to conditional measures: a new axiomatic approach. Annals of Mathematics and Artificial Intelligence 32, 373–392 (2001)
5. Coletti, G., Scozzafava, R.: Probabilistic Logic in a Coherent Setting. In: Trends in Logic, vol. 15, Kluwer Academic Publishers, Dordrecht (2002)
6. Coletti, G., Scozzafava, R.: Toward a general theory of conditional beliefs. International Journal of Intelligent Systems 21, 229–259 (2006)

7. Coletti, G., Scozzafava, R., Vantaggi, B.: Possibility measures through a probabilistic inferential process. In: Proc. NAFIPS 2008, IEEE CN: CFP08750-CDR Omnipress (2008)
8. Coletti, G., Vantaggi, B.: Representability of ordinal relations on a set of conditional events. Theory and Decision 60, 137–174 (2006)
9. de Finetti, B.: Sul significato soggettivo della probabilità. Fundamenta Matematicae 17, 293–329 (1931)
10. de Finetti, B.: Sull'Impostazione Assiomatica del Calcolo delle Probabilità. Annali Univ. Trieste 19, 3–55 (1949) (Engl. transl.: Ch.5 in Probability, Induction, Statistics, Wiley, London, 1972)
11. de Finetti, B.: Teoria della probabilitá. Einaudi, Torino (1970) (Engl. Transl. (1974) Theory of probability vol.I,II, London: Wiley & Sons)
12. Delgado, M., Moral, S.: On the concept of possibility-probability consistency. Fuzzy Sets and Systems 21, 311–318 (1987)
13. Dennemberg, D.: Non-Additive Measure and Integral. Kluwer, Berlin (1997)
14. Dubois, D.: Belief structure, possibility theory and decomposable confidence measures on finite sets. Comput. Artificial Intelligence 5, 403–416 (1986)
15. Dubois, D., Nguyen, H.T., Prade, H.: Possibility theory, probability and fuzzy sets: misunderstandings, bridges and gaps. In: Dubois, D., Prade, H. (eds.) Fundamentals of Fuzzy Sets. The Handbooks of Fuzzy Sets Series, pp. 343–438. Kluwer, Boston (2000)
16. Dubois, D., Prade, H.: When upper probabilities are possibility measures. Fuzzy Sets and Systems 49, 65–74 (1992)
17. Dubois, D., Prade, H.: Qualitative possibility theory and its probabilistic connections. In: Grzegorzewski, P., et al. (eds.) Soft Methods in Probability, Statistics and Data Analysis, pp. 3–26. Physica Verlag, Heidelberg (2002)
18. Dubois, D., Prade, H., Smets, P.: A definition of subjective possibility. Operational Research and Decisions 4, 7–22 (2003)
19. Giles, R.: Foundations for a theory of possibility. In: Gupta, M.M., Sanchez, E. (eds.) Fuzzy Information and Decision Processes, pp. 183–195. North-Holland, Amsterdam (1982)
20. Halpern, J.: Reasoning about uncertainty. The MIT Press, Cambridge (2003)
21. Koopman, B.O.: The axioms and algebra of intuitive probability. Annals of Mathematics 41, 269–292 (1940)
22. Kraft, C.H., Pratt, J.W., Seidenberg, A.: Intuitive probability on finite sets. Annals of Mathematical Statistics 30, 408–419 (1959)
23. Scott, D.: Measurement structures and linear inequalities. Journal of Mathematical Psychology 1, 233–247 (1964)
24. Sudkamp, T.: On probability-possibility transformations. Fuzzy Sets and Systems 51, 311–318 (1992)
25. Wong, S.K.M., Yao, Y.Y., Bollmann, P., Burger, H.C.: Axiomatization of qualitative belief structure. IEEE Trans. Systems Man Cybernetics 21, 726–734 (1991)

Leximax Relations in Decision Making through the Dominance Plausible Rule

Franklin Camacho and Ramón Pino Pérez*

Departamento de Matemáticas
Facultad de Ciencias
Universidad de Los Andes
Mérida, Venezuela
{cfranklin,pino}@ula.ve

Abstract. In qualitative decision theory, a very natural way of defining preference relations $\succeq$ over the policies (acts) is by using the so called *Dominance Plausible Rule*. To do that, we need a relation $>$ over the consequences and a relation $\sqsupseteq$ over the events. Very interesting axiomatic characterizations, *à la* Savage, have been established for these decision relations [6,7]. Namely, when the relation $\sqsupseteq$ is a possibilistic relation. Unfortunately, this kind of decision relation is not discriminant enough. We have searched for decision rules that discriminate more than those defined through a possibilistic relation. In particular, in this work, we study decision relations defined by the Dominance Plausible Rule using a leximax relation $\sqsupseteq$. We give an axiomatic characterization of these decision relations.

Introduction

Given a set of states S and a set of consequences X, a policy (act) is a function $f : S \longrightarrow X$. We denote by X^S the set of policies. One of the most important problems in Decision Theory is to know which is the best policy. In order to decide which is the best policy when one has a probability over the events (sets of states) and a utility function $u : X \longrightarrow \mathbb{R}$, one can classify the policies via the expected value of the functions $u \circ f$ where f is a policy. The best policies are those maximizing the expected value. Thus, given a utility function u over X and a probability function p over S, we can define the *expected utility* of f as $EU(f) = \sum_{s \in S} p(s)u(f(s))$ (that is, the expected value of $u \circ f$). Then, we classify the policies in the following way $f \succeq g \Leftrightarrow EU(f) \geq EU(g)$ $(*)$.

Savage [12] proved that if the relation between the policies $\succeq$ satisfies some axioms, then there is a probability function p over S and also a utility function u over X such that the equivalence $(*)$ holds, *i.e.* the decision relation $\succeq$ over the policies can be defined via the expected utility when that relation obeys certain rationality criteria. Savage's framework makes sense for an infinite set of states. Now, when we consider a finite set of states, the archimedean axiom does not hold. Moreover, the expected utility is sensitive to small variations. For

* Thanks to the CDCHT-ULA for the financial support through the research project N° C-1451-07-05-A.

W. Liu (Ed.): ECSQARU 2011, LNAI 6717, pp. 569–581, 2011.

instance, suppose we have three states s_1, s_2 and s_3 where the states s_1 and s_2 are equally plausible and, in turn, more plausible than s_3. We must decide which policy between f_1 and f_2 is the best, and our decision will be done using the utility expected model. Suppose that $S = \{s_1, s_2, s_3\}$, $X = \{x_1, \ldots, x_6\}$, the policies f_1, f_2, the probabilities p_1 and p_2 over S and the utility function u for the consequences are defined as follows:

	s_1	s_2	s_3
f_1	x_1	x_3	x_2
f_2	x_5	x_6	x_4

	s_1	s_2	s_3
p_1	$\frac{2}{5}$	$\frac{2}{5}$	$\frac{1}{5}$
p_2	$\frac{9}{20}$	$\frac{9}{20}$	$\frac{1}{10}$

	x_1	x_2	x_3	x_4	x_5	x_6
u	10	60	36	50	20	30

If we classify the policies f_1 and f_2 using the expected utility with the probability p_1 and the utility function u, we have $EU(f_1) = 30.4$ and $EU(f_2) = 30$; thus $EU(f_1) > EU(f_2)$ and therefore $f_1 \succ f_2$. But if we calculate the expected utility using the probability p_2 and the utility function u, we have $EU(f_1) = 26.7$ and $EU(f_2) = 27.5$; thus $EU(f_1) < EU(f_2)$ and therefore $f_1 \prec f_2$.

The previous example shows that the quantitative framework is very sensitive to small variations in the inputs. This is one reason to look for pure qualitative frameworks which are more robust and more appropriate for the finite case. In this direction some recent works have been developed, for instance Dubois et al. [6,7].

One of the main contributions of the work of Dubois et al. is the axiomatic characterization à la Savage for the relations defined by the Dominance Plausible Rule (DPR) steaming from a preference relation over the consequences and a possibilistic relation over the events, a kind of plausibility relation (and more generally a relation over the events obtained as the intersection of a family of possibilistic relations).

More precisely, we have a relation $>$ over X and a relation $\sqsupseteq$ over $\mathcal{P}(S)$. Then we define $\succeq$ as follows: $f \succeq g \Leftrightarrow [f > g] \sqsupseteq [g > f]$ (**), where $[f > g]$ denotes the set $\{s \in S : f(s) > g(s)\}$. Usually $>$ is a modular[1] relation and $\sqsupseteq$ is a total pre-order[2].

The definition given by (**) tries to capture, in the finite case, the definition given by (*). The intended meaning of definition (**) is the following one: an agent should always choose action f over action g if she considers the event that f leads to a strictly preferable outcome than g more likely than the event that g leads to a strictly preferable outcome than f.

The definition given by (**) is quite natural and, in some cases (for instance when the relation $\sqsupseteq$ is the intersection of a family of possibilistic relations) there is an axiomatic characterization which is very similar to that of Savage's (see [6,7]).

However, this kind of preference relations $\succeq$ over the policies, when the relation $\sqsupseteq$ is the intersection of a family of possibilistic relations, is not

---

[1] Sometimes in the literature these relations are called *weak orders* (see for instance [10]). A relation R over X is modular iff R is transitive and if xRy and $\neg(yRz)$ and $\neg(zRy)$ then xRz.

[2] A total pre-order is a transitive and total relation.

discriminant enough. In order to see that, let's take the states S and the consequences X as in the previous example. We take a relation $\geq_X$ which is a total preorder over X (representing the utility) and a total preorder $\geq_s$ over S that we use to define a possibilistic relation $\sqsupseteq_\Pi$ (the possibilistic lifting of $\geq_s$) over $\mathcal{P}(S)$ in the following way: $A \sqsupseteq_\Pi B \Leftrightarrow \forall x \subset B \; \exists y \in A \; y \geq_s x$. Suppose $\geq_X$ and $\geq_s$ are defined by $x_2 >_X x_4 >_X x_3 >_X x_6 >_X x_5 >_X x_1$ and $s_1 \sim_s s_2 >_s s_3$ Let f_1 and f_2 be the policies defined by the previous table. Then it is easy to see that $[f_1 >_X f_2] = \{s : f_1(s) >_p f_2(s)\} = \{s_2, s_3\}$ and $[f_2 >_p f_1] = \{s : f_2(s) >_p f_1(s)\} = \{s_1\}$. Now, if we consider $\succeq$ defined by the Dominance Plausible Rule with the possibilistic relation $\sqsupseteq_\Pi$ and the relation $\geq_X$, i.e., $f \succeq g$ if and only if $[f >_X g] \sqsupseteq_\Pi [g >_X f]$, we get easily that $\{s_2, s_3\} \sqsupseteq_\Pi \{s_1\}$ and $\{s_1\} \sqsupseteq_\Pi \{s_2, s_3\}$. Thus, $f_1 \succeq f_2$ and $f_2 \succeq f_1$, i.e., f_1 and f_2 are indifferent for the relation $\succeq$.

However, in several natural contexts (extending the preferences $\geq_s$ over S to events) the event $\{s_2, s_3\}$ is strictly more plausible than the event $\{s_1\}$. This will be the case, when the the relation $\sqsupseteq$ considered is the leximax relation associated to $\geq_s$ (see section 1 for a precise definition of leximax relation[3]). Thus, in the particular previous example, if we put $\sqsupseteq$ the leximax relation associated to $\geq_s$ we would have $[f_1 >_X f_2] \sqsupseteq [f_2 >_X f_1]$ and then $f_1 \succ f_2$, that is, the policy f_1 has to be preferred over the policy f.

Our main concern will be to characterize the decision relations defined by DPR using a leximax relation. In order to do that, we need to have a good characterization of the leximax relations. Actually, Barberà et al. [2] give a characterisation of the leximax relation associated to $\geq_s$ when this last relation is a linear order. Our characterizations are different. We don't suppose that $\geq_s$ is a linear order. We only suppose that $\geq_s$ is a total preorder.

This work is organized as follows: Section 1 is devoted to define very precisely the concepts used throughout the paper. Section 2 is devoted to give three characterizations of the leximax relation. In Section 3 we give the axioms characterizing the decision relations defined by DPR via a leximax relation and establish our main representation theorem. Finally we make some concluding remarks in Section 4.

1   Preliminaries

Let W be a set and let $R \subset W \times W$ be a binary relation over W, generally interpreted like a preference relation between the objects in W. Thus, $(x, y) \in R$ means "x is at least as good as y". As usual we write xRy instead of $(x, y) \in R$. The strict preference relation P and the indifference relation I associated to R are defined by putting for any $x, y \in W$, xPy if and only if xRy and $\neg(yRx)$; xIy if and only if xRy and yRx. Remember that R is reflexive if and only if xRx for all $x \in W$. R is total (or complete) if and only if for any $x, y \in W$, xRy or yRx. Notice that every total relation is a reflexive relation. R is transitive if and only if for any $x, y, z \in W$, if xRy and yRz then xRz. R is antisymmetrical if and

---

[3] This leximax relation was defined in [5] but our definition is slightly different.

only if for any $x, y \in W$, if xIy then $x = y$. A total preorder is a relation which is transitive and total. A linear order is a total preorder which is antisymmetrical. R is symmetrical if and only if for any $x, y \in W$, $(xRy \Leftrightarrow yRx)$. R is said to be an equivalence relation if it is reflexive, transitive and symmetrical.

Let S be a finite set interpreted as a set of states (the states of the world). We denote by $\geq_s$ a preference relation over S. The relations $>_s$ and $\sim_s$ will denote the strict preference and the indifference relation respectively associated to $\geq_s$. Most of the time, we assume that $\geq_s$ is a total preorder over S. The elements of the set $\mathcal{P}(S)$ will be called events. If A is an event, the complementary event, $S \setminus A$, will be denoted A^c. The preference relations over the set of events will be generally denoted by $\sqsupseteq$ (with subindices when necessary). Most of the the times these relations will be called plausibility relations. The symbols $\sqsupset$ and $\simeq$ will denote the strict preference relation and the indifference relation associated to $\sqsupseteq$ respectively. Let X be a finite set interpreted as a set of consequences. The set of functions from S to X will be denoted X^S and its elements will be called policies (or acts). The preference relation over X^S will be denoted by the symbol $\succeq$. Its strict preference relation will be denoted $\succ$ and its indifference relation will be denoted $\curlyvee$.

Let f, g be policies in X^S let A an event in $\mathcal{P}(S)$. We denote by fAg the function taking the value $f(s)$ if $s \in A$ and $g(s)$ if $s \in A^c$. The policy taking a constant value x will be denoted f_x. Sometimes, if the context is non ambiguous, f_x will be denoted simply x. For instance, $f_x A f_y$ will be denoted simply xAy.

Let $\geq_X$ a preference relation over X with $>_X$ and $\sim_X$ the strict preference relation and the indifference relation associated respectively. If there exist $x, y \in X$ such that $x >_X y$, the relation $\geq_X$ is called *non trivial*. We define $[f >_X g] = \{s \in S : f(s) >_X g(s)\}$. Notice that the sets $[f >_X g]$, $[g >_X f]$ and $[f \sim_X g]$ are mutually disjoint and $[f \geq_X g] = [g >_X f]^c$.

Definition 1. *Let $\geq_X$ be a total pre-order over X and let $\sqsupseteq$ be a relation over $\mathcal{P}(S)$. The relation $\succeq$ over X^S is said to be defined by the Dominance Plausible Rule (DPR) with $(\geq_X, \sqsupseteq)$ when the following equivalence holds:*
$$f \succeq g \Leftrightarrow [f >_X g] \sqsupseteq [g >_X f]$$

It is easy to see that if $\sqsupseteq$ is a total pre-order over $\mathcal{P}(S)$, and if $\succeq$ is defined by DPR with $(\geq_X, \sqsupseteq)$ then $f \succ g \Leftrightarrow [f >_X g] \sqsupset [g >_X f$ and $f \curlyvee g \Leftrightarrow [f >_X g] \simeq [g >_X f]$.

When A is a set we denote by $|A|$ the cardinality of A (that is, the number of element of A when this set is finite). If $\boldsymbol{a}$ is a vector we denote by $|\boldsymbol{a}|$ the number of entries in the vector. Suppose $|S| = n$ and consider $V \downarrow$ the set of all vectors of size less or equal to n, the inputs of which are elements of S, there are not repetitions of the inputs and, finally, they are ordered in decreasing manner by $\geq_s$. That is, given $k \leq n$, $\boldsymbol{a} = (a_1, \cdots, a_k) \in V \downarrow$ iff, for all i, j such that $1 \leq i, j \leq k$ with $i \neq j$, $a_i \neq a_j$ and for all i such that $1 \leq i \leq k - 1$ $a_i \geq_s a_{i+1}$. Now, given $\boldsymbol{a}, \boldsymbol{a}' \in V \downarrow$ of length m with $m \leq n$, we define the following relation: $\boldsymbol{a} \equiv \boldsymbol{a}'$ if and only if $a_i \sim_s a_i'$ for all $i = 1, \cdots, m$. The relation $\equiv$ is an equivalence relation over $V \downarrow$. For each element $\boldsymbol{a} \in V \downarrow$ we denote by $[\boldsymbol{a}]$ its equivalence class.

Next we define $\succeq_{max}^{lex}$ over $V \downarrow$:

$$a \succeq_{max}^{lex} b \Leftrightarrow \begin{cases} a \equiv b \text{ or} \\ \exists k \in \{1, \cdots, min\{|a|, |b|\}\}, \text{ such that } \forall i < k \ a_i \sim_s b_i \text{ and } a_k >_s b_k \text{ or} \\ |a| > |b| \text{ and } \forall i \in \{1, \cdots, |b|\}, \ a_i \sim_s b_i. \end{cases}$$

Notice that the third clause in previous definition is lacking in Definition 9 of leximax given in [4]. Notice also that $a \sim_{max}^{lex} b \Leftrightarrow a \equiv b$.

It is easy to see that the relation $\succeq_{max}^{lex}$ is congruent with respect to the equivalent relation previously defined, i.e. if $a \equiv a'$ and $b \equiv b'$ then $a \succeq_{max}^{lex} b \Leftrightarrow a' \succeq_{max}^{lex} b'$. It is also quite easy to see that $\succeq_{max}^{lex}$ is a total preorder over $V \downarrow$.

Let $A \in \mathcal{P}(S)$ and suppose that $|A| = k$. The set of vectors in $V \downarrow$ of length k with inputs in A will be denoted by $R(A)$, that is $R(A) = \{a \in V \downarrow: |a| = k$ and the inputs of a are in $A\}$. For instance, if $A = \{a_1, a_2, a_3, a_4\}$ with $a_1 >_s a_2 \sim_s a_3 >_s a_4$ then $R(A) = \{(a_1, a_2, a_3, a_4), (a_1, a_3, a_2, a_4)\}$. If there are no indifferent elements in A, it is clear that $R(A)$ is a singleton.

Now we are ready to define the leximax relation[4] $\sqsupseteq_{max}^{lex}$ over $\mathcal{P}(S)$:

Definition 2. *Let $\geq_s$ be a total preorder over S. We define the relation $\sqsupseteq_{max}^{lex}$ over $\mathcal{P}(S)$ as follows: $A \sqsupseteq_{max}^{lex} B \Leftrightarrow \forall b \in R(B) \ \exists a \in R(A) \ a \succeq_{max}^{lex} b$.*

Notice that, by the previous definition, for every nonempty set A, we have $A \sqsupseteq_{max}^{lex} \emptyset$ and $\emptyset \not\sqsupseteq_{max}^{lex} A$. That is, $A \sqsupset_{max}^{lex} \emptyset$ for all A.

The relations over events having the previous property are called *non dogmatic* in the literature (see [6]). More precisely a relation $\sqsupseteq$ over $\mathcal{P}(S)$ is said to be non dogmatic if and only if $A \sqsupset \emptyset$ for all $A \in \mathcal{P}(S) \setminus \{\emptyset\}$.

It is also interesting to notice the following

Remark 1. *For all $A, B \in \mathcal{P}(S)$ $A \sqsupseteq_{max}^{lex} B \Leftrightarrow \forall a \in R(A)$ and $\forall b \in R(B)$, $a \succeq_{max}^{lex} b$ and when A and B are nonempty sets $A \sqsupseteq_{max}^{lex} B \Leftrightarrow \exists a \in R(A)$ and $\exists b \in R(B)$, $a \succeq_{max}^{lex} b$.*

These observations are very useful in order to prove the following proposition:

Proposition 1. *The relation $\sqsupseteq_{max}^{lex}$ is a total preorder on $\mathcal{P}(S)$.*

Now with the precise definition of $\sqsupseteq_{max}^{lex}$, let us come back to the example given in the Introduction. In this example we have to compare the events $[f_1 >_x f_2] = \{s_2, s_3\}$ and $[f_2 >_p f_1] = \{s_1\}$ using the leximax relation $\sqsupseteq_{max}^{lex}$ associated to the following total preorder over S: $s_1 \sim_s s_2 >_s s_3$. Since $(s_2, s_3) \succ_{max}^{lex} (s_1)$, we have $[f_1 >_x f_2] \sqsupset_{max}^{lex} [f_2 >_p f_1]$ and then $f_1 \succ f_2$.

2   Three Characterizations of Leximax

In this section we give three characterizations for the leximax relation. The first and the third characterization are purely ordinal, i.e., the axioms characterizing the leximax relation are given in terms of postulates concerning the relations $\sqsupseteq$

---

[4] This kind of relations were defined in [11].

over events. The second characterization is probabilistic, in a sense we will make precise below.

We begin with the most elementary of characterizations. In some way, it is very close to the definition of leximax relation. The main interest of this characterization is that it allows an easy intermediary representation to establish the other two characterizations.

The five axioms for our first characterization are *Extensionality*, *Monotony* and three axioms of *Left Independence* stated as follows:

Ext $\forall a, b \in S \ \ [a \geq_s b \Leftrightarrow \{a\} \sqsupseteq \{b\}]$
Mon $\forall A \in \mathcal{P}(S) \ \forall x \in S \setminus A \ \ A \cup \{x\} \sqsupset A$

Left Independence: $\forall A, B \in \mathcal{P}(S) \ \forall x, y \in S$ such that $\forall w \in A \ x \geq_s w$ and $\forall z \in B \ y \geq_s z$ we have:
LI1 $x >_s y \Rightarrow A \cup \{x\} \sqsupset B \cup \{y\}$
LI2 $[x, y \notin (A \cup B), x \sim_s y, A \sim B] \Rightarrow A \cup \{x\} \simeq B \cup \{y\}$
LI3 $[x, y \notin (A \cup B), x \sim_s y, A \sqsupset B] \Rightarrow A \cup \{x\} \sqsupset B \cup \{y\}$

Theorem 1. *Let $\geq_s$ be a total pre-order over S and let $\sqsupseteq$ be a total pre-order over $\mathcal{P}(S)$. The relation $\sqsupseteq$ satisfies the axioms* **Ext**, **Mon**, **LI1**, **LI2** *and* **LI3** *if only if $\sqsupseteq = \sqsupseteq_{max}^{lex}$.*

Proof: By Definition 2, it is easy to verify that the relation $\sqsupseteq_{max}^{lex}$ satisfies the axioms **Ext**, **Mon**, **LI1**, **LI2** and **LI3**.

For the converse, suppose that $\sqsupseteq$ is a total preorder satisfying **Ext**, **Mon**, **LI1**, **LI2** and **LI3**. We must show that $A \sqsupseteq_{max}^{lex} B \Leftrightarrow A \sqsupseteq B$. In order to do that it is enough to prove the following claim: $A \sqsupset_{max}^{lex} B \Rightarrow A \sqsupset B$ and $A \sim_{max}^{lex} B \Rightarrow A \simeq B$. The claim, of course, entails $A \sqsupseteq_{max}^{lex} B \Rightarrow A \sqsupseteq B$. For the converse implication, we reason by reductio. Suppose that $A \sqsupseteq B$ and $\neg(A \sqsupseteq_{max}^{lex} B)$. Since $\sqsupseteq_{max}^{lex}$ is a total preorder, we have $B \sqsupset_{max}^{lex} A$. Thus by the claim we have $B \sqsupset A$ which together with $A \sqsupseteq B$ is a contradiction.

Now we sketch the proof of the claim. Actually, we show how to prove the first part of the claim, that is $A \sqsupset_{max}^{lex} B \Rightarrow A \sqsupset B$; the other part is quite similar.

Suppose that $A \sqsupset_{max}^{lex} B$. Note that this assumption entails $A \neq \emptyset$. When $B = \emptyset$, we can obtain easily $A \sqsupset B$ by applying iteratively the postulate **Mon**. Thus, we may assume A and B nonempty sets. By Remark 1, $\exists \boldsymbol{a} \in R(A)$, $\exists \boldsymbol{b} \in R(B)$ such that $\boldsymbol{a} \succ_{max}^{lex} \boldsymbol{b}$. We can take $\boldsymbol{a} = (a_1, a_2, \cdots, a_n)$ and $\boldsymbol{b} = (b_1, b_2, \cdots, b_m)$ such that $[\forall i, \forall j (j > i, a_i \sim_s b_i \&, a_i \sim_s b_j \Rightarrow a_i \neq b_j \& b_i \neq a_j]$[5]. Now the proof proceeds by analyzing the cases in which $\boldsymbol{a} \succ_{max}^{lex} \boldsymbol{b}$. For space reasons, we illustrate only the following case: There is $k \in \{1, \cdots, min\{n, m\}\}$ such that $a_k >_s b_k$ and $\forall j < k, a_j \sim_s b_j$. Since $a_k >_s b_k$ and $\forall j[j > k \Rightarrow a_k \geq_s a_j \& b_k \geq_s b_j]$, by **LI1**, $\{a_k, a_{k+1}, \cdots, a_n\} \sqsupset \{b_k, b_{k+1} \cdots, b_m\}$. By our choice of $\boldsymbol{a}$ and $\boldsymbol{b}$ we have $a_{k-1}, b_{k-1} \notin (\{a_k, \cdots, a_n\} \cup \{b_k \cdots, b_m\})$ and by hypothesis $a_{k-1} \sim_s b_{k-1}$, then by **LI3**, $\{a_{k-1}, a_k, \cdots, a_n\} \sqsupset \{b_{k-1}, b_k \cdots, b_m\}$. Applying this procedure iteratively, we have $A = \{a_1, \cdots, a_n\} \sqsupset \{b_1, \cdots, b_m\} = B$.   ∎

---

[5] This is a technical fact, not very hard to see, which means we can choose the vectors $\boldsymbol{a}$ and $\boldsymbol{b}$ with the biggest number of common entries in the same position.

Now, we give the probabilistic representation. We begin by defining when a probability p over S represents a total preorder $\geq_s$ over S and a total preorder $\sqsupseteq$ over $\mathcal{P}(S)$.

Definition 3. *Let $\geq_s$, $\sqsupseteq$ and p be a relation over S, a relation over $\mathcal{P}(S)$ and a probability over events of S respectively. We say that p represents $\geq_s$ if and only if for all $x, y \in S$, $(x \geq_s y \Leftrightarrow p(\{x\}) \geq p(\{y\}))$. We say that p represents $\sqsupseteq$ if and only if for all $A, B \in \mathcal{P}(S)$, $(A \sqsupseteq B \Leftrightarrow p(A) \geq p(A))$.*

There is a kind of probability very well adapted to represent the leximax relations as we will see in the sequel. We call these probabilities, *big step probabilities*[6]. These probabilities are defined as follows:

Definition 4. *A probability p over events of S is said to be a big step probability if and only if $\forall x, \forall A \, (\forall y \in A \, (p(\{x\}) > p(\{y\})) \Rightarrow p(\{x\}) > p(A))$.*

The following result, which is quite easy to establish, is basic for the sequel.

Lemma 1. *Let $\geq_s$ be a total preorder over S. Then there is a big step probability p over S which represents $\geq_s$.*

Let p be a probability over $\mathcal{P}(S)$. As usual, we define a plausibility relation $\sqsupseteq_p$ associated to p over $\mathcal{P}(S)$ by putting $A \sqsupseteq_p B \Leftrightarrow p(A) \geq p(B)$. Now we can establish the following proposition:

Proposition 2. *Let $\geq_s$ and p be a total preorder over S and a big step probability representing $\geq_s$ respectively. Then $\sqsupseteq_{max}^{lex} = \sqsupseteq_p$.*

Proof: (Sketch) It is clear that $\sqsupseteq_p$ is a total preorder. Thus, by Theorem 1, it is enough to see that $\sqsupseteq_p$ satisfies **Ext**, **Mon**, **LI1**, **LI2** and **LI3**. This is a quite straightforward verification. ∎

Actually, if a probability represents a leximax relation, it has to be a big step probability. More precisely we have the following

Proposition 3. *Let $\geq_s$ and p be a total preorder over S and a probability over $\mathcal{P}(S)$ respectively. If $\sqsupseteq_{max}^{lex} = \sqsupseteq_p$ then p is a big step probability which represents $\geq_s$.*

Proof: (Sketch) That p represents $\geq_s$ follows directly from the hypothesis $\sqsupseteq_{max}^{lex} = \sqsupseteq_p$. Now suppose, towards a contradiction, that p is not a big step probability. Then there is $x \in S$ and $A \in \mathcal{P}(S)$ such that for all $a \in A$, $p(x) > p(a)$ but $p(A) \geq p(\{x\})$. Then $A \sqsupseteq_p \{x\}$, and therefore $A \sqsupseteq_{max}^{lex} \{x\}$. Notice that $A \neq \emptyset$, so $|A| = n \geq 1$. Thus, by Definition 2, there exists $\boldsymbol{a} = (a_1, \cdots, a_n) \in R(A)$ such that $(a_1, \cdots, a_n) \succeq_{max}^{lex} (x)$, that is $a_1 \geq_s x$, by the definition of $\succeq_{max}^{lex}$. Then $p(a_1) \geq p(x)$, a contradiction, because $a_1 \in A$. ∎

From Proposition 2 and Lemma 1 follows the probabilistic representation for the leximax relations. More precisely we have the following theorem:

Theorem 2. *Let $\geq_s$ be a total preorder over S. The relation $\sqsupseteq$ over $\mathcal{P}(S)$ can be represented by a big step probability that represents $\geq_s$ if and only if $\sqsupseteq = \sqsupseteq_{max}^{lex}$.*

Notice that this theorem is not new it appears in [4] without proof.

Using the previous representations we give now a very compact axiomatization for the leximax relations. This axiomatization will be very useful in order to give our main representation theorem for the decision relations defined through DPR via a leximax relation: Theorem 5.

The axioms to consider are the following ones:

(Lex1) $A \sqsupseteq B, C \sqsupseteq D$ and $A \cap C = \emptyset \Rightarrow A \cup C \sqsupseteq B \cup D$
(Lex2) $A \sqsupset B, C \sqsupseteq D$ and $A \cap C = \emptyset \Rightarrow A \cup C \sqsupset B \cup D$
(Lex3) $\{x\} \sqsupset A, \{x\} \sqsupset B$ and $x \notin (A \cup B) \Rightarrow \{x\} \sqsupset A \cup B$

When $\sqsupseteq$ is a total preorder over $\mathcal{P}(S)$ we say that this relation is a leximax relation if and only if it is the leximax relation associated to the relation $\geq_s$ obtained as the projection of $\sqsupseteq$ over the singletons of $\mathcal{P}(S)$. That is, $a \geq_s b$ if and only if $\{a\} \sqsupseteq \{b\}$

Theorem 3. *Let $\sqsupseteq$ be a total preorder over $\mathcal{P}(S)$ which is non dogmatic. Then $\sqsupseteq$ is a leximax relation if and only if $\sqsupseteq$ satisfies the postulates* **Lex1**, **Lex2** *and* **Lex3**.

Proof: Suppose $\sqsupseteq$ is the leximax relation associated with $\geq_s$, the projection of $\sqsupseteq$ over the singletons. By Theorem 2, the relation $\sqsupseteq$ can be represented by a big step probability p. From this, the axioms **Lex1**, **Lex2** and **Lex3** are deduced easily. For the converse, suppose that the relation $\sqsupseteq$ satisfies the axioms **Lex1**, **Lex2** and **Lex3**. By Theorem 2, it is enough to check that the relation $\sqsupseteq$ satisfies the axioms **Ext**, **Mon**, **LI1**, **LI2** and **LI3**. The axiom **Ext** is satisfied by the definition of $\geq_s$. In order to prove **Mon**, suppose that $x \notin A$. Since we have $\{x\} \sqsupset \emptyset$ because $\sqsupseteq$ is non dogmatic, $A \sqsupseteq A$, by reflexivity ($\sqsupseteq$ is a total preorder) and $\{x\} \cap A = \emptyset$, we can apply **Lex2** to conclude $\{x\} \cup A \sqsupset A$.

Now we check the axiom **LI1** (the proof for the axioms **LI2** and **LI3** is similar). Let A, B be elements of $\mathcal{P}(S)$ and let x, y be elements of S such that $\forall a \in A$, $x \geq_s a$, and $\forall b \in B$, $y \geq_s b$. Suppose $x >_s y$. We want to see that $A \cup \{x\} \sqsupset B \cup \{y\}$. Since $x >_s y$ and $\forall b \in B$, $y \geq_s b$, we have $\{x\} \sqsupset \{b\}$ for all $b \in B$; moreover $x \notin B \cup \{y\}$. Thus applying **Lex3** iteratively, we can conclude $\{x\} \sqsupset B \cup \{y\}$. We have also $A \setminus \{x\} \sqsupseteq \emptyset$ and $\{x\} \sqsupseteq \{x\}$, then by **Lex1**, $(A \setminus \{x\}) \cup \{x\} \sqsupseteq \{x\}$. But $(A \setminus \{x\}) \cup \{x\} = A \cup \{x\}$, so by transitivity, $A \cup \{x\} \sqsupset B \cup \{y\}$. ∎

Notice that preadditivity (see section 3) plus **Lex3** does not imply **Lex1** plus **Lex2**, because one can construct a relation satisfying preadditivity plus **Lex3** which is not a leximax relation.

3   Characterization for the Relations $\succeq$ Defined by DPR Using a Leximax

It is well known that Savage's axioms capturing exactly the expected utility model are not adequate to deal with the finite structures (see [7] for an excellent discussion). For finite structures it is quite natural adopting the model of the Dominance Plausible Rule (DPR) which we have described in the introduction. This model has essentially two parameters: the relation $\geq_X$ modelling the preferences over X (in some sense the utility) and the plausibility relation $\sqsupseteq$ modelling preferences over $\mathcal{P}(S)$, the events. The aim of this section is to study the behavior of the decision relations $\succeq$ defined via DPR using a plausibility relation $\sqsupseteq$ which is a leximax relation. We begin by recalling the first five axioms of Savage (those more relevant for the finite case) and a result of Dubois et al. [7], very important in order to obtain our main result.

We begin with some basic notions needed to establish Savage's Axioms: Let $\succeq$ be a relation over X^S. An event A is said to be null if and only if $\forall f, g, h \in X^S$, $fAh \sim gAh$. The preference conditioned to an event A is defined by putting $(f \succeq g)_A$ if and only if $\forall h \in X^S$, $fAh \succeq gAh$. We denote by $\geq_p$ the relation over X obtained as the projection of $\succeq$ over the constant policies, that is $x \geq_p y$ if and only if $f_x \succeq f_y$.

Now we can establish the first five axioms of Savage:

P1 The decision relation $\succeq$ over X^S is a total preorder.
P2 $\forall A \in \mathcal{P}(S), \forall f, g, h, h' \in X^S (fAh \succeq gAh \Leftrightarrow fAh' \succeq gAh')$
P3 $\forall A \in \mathcal{P}(S), [A$ not null $\Rightarrow [(f_x \succeq f_y)_A \Leftrightarrow f_x \succeq f_y]]$.
P4 $\forall A, B \in \mathcal{P}(S), \forall x, y, x', y' \in X, x >_p y \, \& \, x' >_p y' \Rightarrow (xAy \succeq xBy \Leftrightarrow x'Ay' \succeq x'By')$.
P5 $\exists x, y \in X$ such that $f_x \succ f_y$.

The most problematic of these axioms in the setting of the DPR model is **P1**. To ask of the relation $\succeq$ to be transitive is a very strong requirement. We will discuss this below. The totality requirement for $\succeq$ will not be a problem.

In order to define the postulate **OI**, presented by Dubois et al. [6,7] for capturing the essence of the RDP model, we need the following definition of pairs of policies *ordinally equivalent*: two pairs of policies (f, g) and (f', g') are said to be ordinally equivalent[7], denoted $(f, g) \equiv (f', g')$, if and only if $[f >_p g] = [f' >_p g']$ and $[g >_p f] = [g' >_p f']$. Now we can define the postulate of ordinal invariance **OI** as follows:

OI $(f, g) \equiv (f', g') \Rightarrow (f \succeq g \Leftrightarrow f' \succeq g')$

It is quite straightforward to verify that the decision relations defined by the DPR satisfy the postulate **OI**.

The monotonicity postulates (left monotonicity **LM** and right monotonicity **RM**, also proposed by Dubois et al. [7]) for the decision relation $\succeq$ are defined as follows:

---

[7] This definition is not the definition of pairs ordinally equivalent which appears in [6,7]. It is the fixed definition which appears in [8] and originally in [9].

LM If $\forall s \in A, f'(s) >_p f(s)$ then $f \succeq g \Rightarrow f'Af \succeq g$
RM If $\forall s \in A, g(s) >_p g'(s)$ then $f \succeq g \Rightarrow f \succeq g'Ag$

Let's recall two more concepts of [7]. The relation $\sqsupseteq$ over $\mathcal{P}(S)$ is *preadditive* if and only if for all $A, B, C \in \mathcal{P}(S)$, if $A \cap (B \cup C) = \emptyset$ then $B \sqsupseteq C$ iff $A \cup B \sqsupseteq A \cup C$. And the relation $\sqsupseteq$ is a *monotonic confidence relation* if and only if it is reflexive, $S \sqsupseteq \emptyset$ (non-triviality), for any $A \in \mathcal{P}(S)$, $S \sqsupseteq A$ (consistency) and the following two properties of monotony: for any $A, B, C \in \mathcal{P}(S)$, if $A \sqsupseteq B$ then $A \cup C \sqsupseteq B$ and if $A \sqsupseteq B \cup C$ then $A \sqsupseteq B$.

Now we can recall the following theorem of [7]:

Theorem 4 (Dubois et al. [7]). $\sqsupseteq$ *is a complete relation over constant acts, reflexive and it satisfies the postulates* **P5**, **OI**, **LM** *and* **RM** *if and only if there exists a non trivial and complete relation* $\geq_X$ *over* X *and a preadditive and monotonic confidence relation* $\sqsupseteq$ *over* $\mathcal{P}(S)$ *such that* $\succeq$ *is the relation defined by the DPR via* $\geq_X$ *and* $\sqsupseteq$.

Now we consider the following new postulates for all $x, y \in X$ such that $x >_p y$ and all $a \in S$:

D1 If $xAy \succeq xBy$, $xCy \succeq xDy$ and $A \cap C = \emptyset$ then $x(A \cup C)y \succeq x(B \cup D)y$
D2 If $xAy \succ xBy$, $xCy \succeq xDy$ and $A \cap C = \emptyset$ then $x(A \cup C)y \succ x(B \cup D)y$
D3 If $x\{a\}y \succ xAy$, $x\{a\}y \succ xBy$ and $a \notin (A \cup B)$ then $x\{a\}y \succ x(A \cup B)y$

We are ready to establish the main representation theorem of this work:

Theorem 5. *The relation* $\succeq$ *is a complete relation which is a total preorder over constant policies and* $\succeq$ *satisfies the postulates* **P5**, **OI**, **LM**, **RM**, **D1**, **D2** *and* **D3** *if and only if there exists a non trivial and total preorder* $\geq_X$ *over* X *and a leximax relation* $\sqsupseteq$ *over* $\mathcal{P}(S)$ *such that* $\succeq$ *is the relation defined by the DPR via* $\geq_X$ *and* $\sqsupseteq$, *i.e., for any* $f, g \in X^S$, $f \succeq g \Leftrightarrow [f >_X g] \sqsupseteq [g >_X f]$.

Sketch of proof: Our proof is based in our characterization theorems for leximax, Theorem 2 and Theorem 3, and Theorem 4 of Dubois et al.

In order to prove the *if* part, suppose that $\succeq$ is defined by DPR via a leximax relation $\sqsupseteq$ over $\mathcal{P}(S)$ and a total preorder $\geq_X$ over X. Since a leximax relation $\sqsupseteq$ has a probabilistic representation, Theorem 2, $\sqsupseteq$ satisfies preadditivity and the properties of a monotonic confidence relation. So, by Theorem 4, the relation $\succeq$ defined by DPR via a leximax relation $\sqsupseteq$ over $\mathcal{P}(S)$ and a total preorder $\geq_X$ over X, satisfies **P5**, **OI**, **LM** and **RM**. Moreover if the relation $\sqsupseteq$ is complete, necessarily the relation $\succeq$ is complete. This is enough to see that $\geq_p = \geq_X$, therefore $\geq_p$ is transitive. Thus $\succeq$ is a total preorder over the constant policies.

For this part, it remains to see that the postulates **D1**, **D2** and **D3** hold. This follows using the monotony of the relation $\sqsupseteq$ and the properties **Lex1**, **Lex2** and **Lex3** characterizing $\sqsupseteq$ after Theorem 3.

Now we outline the proof of the *only if* part. Thus, we suppose the relation $\succeq$ is a complete relation which is a total preorder over constant policies and, moreover, that the postulates **P5**, **OI**, **LM**, **RM**, **D1**, **D2** and **D3** hold. Again, by Theorem 4, there is a relation $\geq_X$ (actually the projection of $\succeq$ on the constant policies) over X and a relation $\sqsupseteq$ over $\mathcal{P}(S)$ (defined by $A \sqsupseteq B$ if and only if $xAy \succeq xBy$ with x, y such that $x >_p y$) which is preadditive and a monotonic confidence relation such that they define $\succeq$ via DPR. The fact that $\geq_X$ is a total preorder follows from the equality $\geq_X = \geq_p$ and the hypothesis that $\succeq$ is a total preorder over constant policies. It is important to notice that Theorem 3 tells us that $\sqsupseteq$ is a leximax relation if two conditions hold: the first of them is that the relation $\sqsupseteq$ has to be a total preorder. The second one is that the axioms **Lex1**, **Lex2** and **Lex3** have to be satisfied. We begin with the proof of the fact that $\sqsupseteq$ is a total preorder. We know, by hypothesis, that $\succeq$ is total, therefore $\sqsupseteq$ is also total. So, it remains to prove the transitivity. By definition of $\sqsupseteq$, the transitivity for this relation is equivalent to the transitivity of $\succeq$ restrained to the policies with values in the set $\{x, y\}$. We claim that this last affirmation is true. We use the following fact, the proof of which is easy using Theorem 4:

Fact 1. $\forall A, B \in \mathcal{P}(S)$, $xAy \succeq xBy \Leftrightarrow x(A \setminus (A \cap B))y \succeq x(B \setminus (A \cap B))y$.
Now we prove the claim that $\succeq$ restrained to the policies with values in the set $\{x, y\}$ is transitive. More precisely:

Claim 1. $\forall A, B, C \in \mathcal{P}(S)$, $xAy \succeq xBy$ & $xBy \succeq xCy \Rightarrow xAy \succeq xCy$. To prove the claim assume $xAy \succeq xBy$ & $xBy \succeq xCy$ and, towards a contradiction, $xAy \not\succeq xCy$. By completeness of $\succeq$, we have $xCy \succ xAy$. Then, by Fact 1, we have $x(A \setminus (A \cap B))y \succeq x(B \setminus (A \cap B))y$ and $x(C \setminus (A \cap C))y \succ x(A \setminus (A \cap C))y$. Notice that $A \setminus (A \cap B)$ and $C \setminus (A \cap C)$ are disjoint sets, then, by **D2**, we obtain
$x[(A \setminus (A \cap B)) \cup (C \setminus (A \cap C))]y \succ x[(B \setminus (A \cap B)) \cup (A \setminus (A \cap C))]y$

From this expression, using Fact 1, we obtain
$x[(C \setminus (A \cup B)) \cup ((A \cap C) \setminus B)]y \succ x[(B \setminus (A \cup C)) \cup ((A \cap B) \setminus C)]y$
and, using Fact 1 again, we obtain from the last expression $xCy \succ xBy$ contradicting our initial assumption $xBy \succeq xCy$. This concludes Claim 1's proof. Therefore the relation $\sqsupseteq$ is transitive. It remains to prove the postulates **Lex1**, **Lex2** and **Lex3**. This is quite straightforward using the definition of $\sqsupseteq$ and the postulates **D1**, **D2** and **D3**.   ∎

Once established the previous theorem, we can say which among Savage's axioms are satisfied by a decision relation $\succeq$ defined by DPR with the pair $\geq_X, \sqsupseteq$, where $\sqsupseteq$ is a leximax plausibility relation and $\geq_X$ is a non trivial total preorder over X. Actually, by results in [7], such a decision relation $\succeq$ satisfies **P2**, **P3**, **P4** and **P5**. The transitivity of $\succeq$ is not in general guaranteed. One can construct a counterexample or use a result in [3] characterizing the properties the relations $\sqsupseteq$ have to satisfy in order to have the relation $\succeq$ defined by DPR with the pair $\geq_X, \sqsupseteq$ be transitive. One of these properties is the property **T** stated as follows:

T: $A \sqsupseteq B$ & $C \sqsupseteq D$ & $A \cap B = \emptyset$ & $C \cap D = \emptyset \Rightarrow (A \cup C) \setminus (B \cup D) \sqsupseteq (B \cup D)$.
It is easy to construct leximax relations which do not satisfy property **T**. Even the strict relation associated to the leximax relation doesn't satisfy **T**. Thus, the relation $\succeq$ associated to this leximax relation via DPR will not be transitive and even more, the relation $\succ$ is not transitive.

Actually, for a non dogmatic relation $\sqsupseteq$, satisfying **T** is enough to have the transitivity of $\succeq$ defined by DPR with the pair $(\geq_X, \sqsupseteq)$. Thus, the relation $\succ$ associated to a non dogmatic possibilistic relation $\sqsupseteq$ via DPR, will be transitive because $\sqsupseteq$ satisfies **T**. But in general the possibilistic relations don't satisfy **T**. They do when the projection over S is a linear order. The same phenomena occurs for a leximax relation $\sqsupseteq$: when its projection over S is a linear order, then the relation $\succeq$ associated via DPR will be transitive.

4 Conclusion

The use of the Dominance Plausible Rule is very natural because in most cases the only information available is very rough: a preference relation over S and a preference relation over X. We can first lift the relation over S to a plausibility relation over $\mathcal{P}(S)$ and then we can combine the last two pieces of information via the DPR in order to have a mechanism for classifying policies.

The three characterizations of leximax relations we have established have been very useful in order to prove our main representation result: Theorem 5.

Let's say a word concerning a comparison between properties of $\succeq$ when it is defined by DPR with a possibilistic relation or a leximax relation both obtained by lifting a simply total preorder $\geq_s$ over S. We have seen that the decision relations defined with the leximax relation discriminate more than the decision relations defined with the possibilistic relation. The relation $\succ$ defined with the possibilistic is transitive but in general $\succ$ is not transitive when it is defined through a leximax relation.

Finally, when $\sqsupseteq$ is the leximax relation generated by a linear order $\geq_s$ over S, we have the transitivity of the relation $\succeq$ defined via DPR using $\sqsupseteq$.

References

1. Benferhat, S., Dubois, D., Lagrue, S., Prade, H.: A big-stepped probability approach for discovering default rules. International Journal of Uncertainty, Fuzziness and Knowledge- Based Systems (IJUFKS) 11, 1–14 (2003)
2. Barberà, S., Bossert, W., Pattanaik, P.K.: Ranking sets of objects. In: Barberà, S., Hammond, P.J., Seidl, C. (eds.) Handbook of Utility Theory. Kluwer Publisher, Dordrecht (2004)
3. Camacho, F., Pino Pérez, R.: Dominance plausible rule and transitivity. In: 9th Conference on Logic and the Foundations of Game and Decision Theory (LOFT 2010), Toulouse, France, July 5-7 (2010), http://loft2010.csc.liv.ac.uk/
4. Dubois, D., Fargier, H.: A Unified framework for order-of-magnitude confidence relations. In: Proceedings of the Twentieth Annual Conference on Uncertainty in Artificial Intelligence (UAI 2004), Arlington, Virginia, USA, pp. 138–145 (2004)
5. Dubois, D., Fargier, H., Prade, H.: Possibilistic likelihood relations. In: Proceedings of the 7th International Conference on Information, Processing and Management of Uncertainty in Knowledge-based Systems (IPMU 1998), Paris, Juillet, pp. 1196–1202. Editions EDK, Paris (1998)
6. Dubois, D., Fargier, H., Perny, P., Prade, H.: Qualitative Decision Theory: From Savage's Axioms to Nonmonotonic Reasoning. Journal of the ACM 49(4), 455–495 (2002)
7. Dubois, D., Fargier, H., Perny, P.: Qualitative decision theory with preference relations and comparative uncertainty: An axiomatic approach. Artificial Intelligence 148, 219–260 (2003)

8. Dubois, D., Fargier, H., Perny, P.: Corrigendum to "Qualitative decision theory with preference relations and comparative uncertainty: an axiomatic approach". Artificial Intelligence 171, 361–362 (2007); Artificial Intelligence 148(1-2), 219–260 (2003)
9. Fargier, H., Perny, P.: Qualitative models for decision under uncertainty without the commensurability hypothesis. In: Laskey, K.B., Prade, H. (eds.) Proc. 15th Conference on Uncertainty in Artificial Intelligence, Stockholm, Sweden, pp. 188–195. Morgan Kaufmann, San Mateo (1999)
10. Fishburn, P.: Utility theory for decision making. John Wiley & Sons Inc., New York (1970)
11. Moulin, H.: Axioms of cooperative decision making. Cambridge University Press, Cambridge (1988)
12. Savage, L.J.: The foundations of statistics. Dover, New York (1972)

Parameterized Uncertain Reasoning Approach Based on a Lattice-Valued Logic

Shuwei Chen, Jun Liu, Hui Wang, and Juan Carlos Augusto

School of Computing and Mathematics, University of Ulster at Jordanstown
Newtownabbey, BT37 0QB, Northern Ireland, UK
chen-s1@email.ulster.ac.uk,{j.liu,h.wang,jc.augusto}@ulster.ac.uk

Abstract. This paper presents a parameterized reasoning approach with uncertainty based on a lattice-valued logic system. In this uncertain reasoning approach, some parameters are used to represent uncertainty arising from different sources, which is a common phenomenon in rule-based systems. In our system, reasoning with different parameter values means reasoning with different levels of belief and consistency. Some methods are presented for selecting appropriate parameter values during the uncertain reasoning process which allow us to find suitable parameter values to meet the diverse practical and theoretical requirements.

Keywords: Parameterized reasoning, uncertainty, lattice-valued logic, rule-based systems.

1 Introduction

Rules are one of the most common forms for representing knowledge. Rule-based systems (or knowledge-based systems) using IF-THEN rules to represent knowledge and to reason with it, have been applied successfully in many areas [10]. A crucial issue in rule-based systems is to utilize all observations available and expert knowledge expressed by the rules to analyze the current situation, and infer the consequences which will lead to corresponding actions. Often, this is a process of uncertain reasoning, *i.e.*, inferring conclusions based on rules and new information under uncertainty.

Uncertainty may arise from different sources. For example, suppose that you are evaluating some cars to decide which one to buy from 4 aspects: price, safety, comfort and fuel economy, which will be discussed in more detail as an illustrative example in the paper. Uncertainty may arise from subjective judgment about a car, *e.g.*, "this car is quite safe", where "quite" depicts the truth degree of the judgment or evaluation about the safety of the car. There is also uncertainty on the belief degree of the experts on the rule, *e.g.*, "the rule is highly true". Uncertainty may also exist in the reasoning process from the observations of a car to the overall evaluation due to the subjective and ambiguous situations, such as, you think that it is "very" believable to get the overall evaluation of a car from the current observations and rules. Another source of uncertainty is inconsistency of observations or opinions about different aspects of a car.

W. Liu (Ed.): ECSQARU 2011, LNAI 6717, pp. 582–593, 2011.

Therefore it is necessary to consider all sources of uncertainty, represent them appropriately and aggregate them rationally by using uncertain reasoning to make sound decisions.

From the viewpoint of symbolism, the confidence and rationality of uncertain reasoning relies on non-classical logics [11], which are extensions of the classical logic. Zadeh [19] developed a theory of uncertain reasoning based on the notion of linguistic variable and fuzzy logic, which then inspired interests in the research of uncertain reasoning with strict logical foundation. Pavelka [9] and Novak [8] then laid the foundation for uncertain reasoning based on strict logic systems. Many researchers have made many important progress in this area [4], [5], [6], [15]. There is work in the literature that is related to reasoning with uncertainty from different sources. Larsen and Yager [7] presented a method for crisis recognition under uncertainty in the framework of possibility logic by using belief measure to reflect the type of uncertainty in the observations and knowledge base. Benferhat and Sossai [1] proposed a method for reasoning with multiple-source information by merging uncertain knowledge bases, provided by different sources, into a new possibilistic knowledge base in the framework of possibilistic logic. Zhou *et. al.* [20] gave a graded reasoning method in the framework of n-valued R_0-logic $\mathcal{L}_n^*$. Sottara *et. al.* [12] introduced an architecture based on a number of configuration parameters which could be set by the user, individually or as a whole for the entire rule base.

In this paper, we consider different sources of uncertainty, and propose to represent them by parameters in a unified uncertain reasoning framework based on lattice-valued logic [15], which is a type of non-classical logic. This parameterized uncertain reasoning method will have the advantage of direct reasoning with observed information, without the underlying numerical approximation needed by fuzzy set based methods.

The paper is organized as follows. First some related concepts and results about lattice-valued logic and lattice implication algebra are recalled and revised. Then, a review of the uncertain reasoning approach based on lattice-valued logic is given, followed by the introduction of methods for parameter selection when applying the uncertain reasoning approach in a specified lattice-valued logic system, $\mathscr{L}_{2nf}$. Finally, an example is given to illustrate the proposed method.

2   Lattice-Valued First-Order Logic

Lattice implication algebra [15] is a kind of lattice-valued logical algebra, which is the truth-value field of lattice-valued logic. It has been shown in [15], [18] that lattice implication algebra defines a residuated lattice [9], which possesses the common features in various fuzzy logical systems based on the different particular algebraic structures [13].

Definition 1. [15] *Let $(L, \vee, \wedge, O, I)$ be a bounded lattice with an order-reversing involution $\prime$, I and O the greatest and the smallest element of L respectively, and $\rightarrow: L \times L \rightarrow L$ be a mapping. $(L, \vee, \wedge, O, I)$ is called a lattice implication algebra (LIA) if the following conditions hold for any x, y, $z \in L$:*

$$(I_1) \quad x \to (y \to z) = y \to (x \to z); \tag{1}$$

$$(I_2) \quad x \to x = I; \tag{2}$$

$$(I_3) \quad x \to y = y' \to x'; \tag{3}$$

$$(I_4) \quad x \to y = y \to x = I \quad \text{implies} \quad x = y; \tag{4}$$

$$(I_5) \quad (x \to y) \to y = (y \to x) \to x; \tag{5}$$

$$(l_1) \quad (x \vee y) \to z = (x \to z) \wedge (y \to z); \tag{6}$$

$$(l_2) \quad (x \wedge y) \to z = (x \to z) \vee (y \to z). \tag{7}$$

In the following, we denote L as a lattice implication algebra (LIA) and L_{vfl} as the lattice-valued first-order logic based on L. The generalized quantifiers in L_{vfl} are denoted as $\mathbf{Q}_u$, where $u \in U$, U is an index set, which can be seen as the generalization of $\forall$ and $\exists$, such as "a few", "most". The set of all well-formed formulas (wffs), such as $\varphi \vee \psi$, $\varphi \wedge \psi$, $\varphi \to \psi$, $(\mathbf{Q}_u x)\varphi$, in L_{vfl} is denoted as $\mathcal{F}_f$. A well-formed formula is called a formula for short. In the car evaluation example, formulas φ, ψ will be used to represent the attributes of cars. For example, $\varphi_i(x)$ represents the i-th attribute, say comfort of car x. Let $\varphi, \psi \in \mathcal{F}_f$, we also denote $\varphi \leftrightarrow \psi = (\varphi \to \psi) \wedge (\psi \to \varphi)$, and $\varphi \otimes \psi = (\varphi \to \psi')'$.

An interpretation of wffs in L_{vfl} is a mapping $\mathscr{D}_{\mathcal{F}_f} : \mathcal{F}_f \longrightarrow L$, which is to assign wffs truth degrees, e.g., assign truth degrees to the attributes of cars in the car evaluation problem. The set of interpretations of wffs is denoted as

$$\mathcal{I}_h \subseteq \mathcal{I}_H \triangleq \{\mathscr{D}_{\mathcal{F}_f} | \mathscr{D}_{\mathcal{F}_f} \text{is an interpretation of wffs}\}.$$

In the following, we also call $\mathcal{I} \subseteq \mathscr{F}_L(\mathcal{F}_f)$ as the set of interpretations of wffs, where $\mathscr{F}_L(\mathcal{F}_f)$ is the set of all L-type fuzzy subsets on $\mathcal{F}_f$.

Definition 2. [15] *Let $D_n \subseteq \mathcal{F}_f^n$. A mapping $r_n : D_n \longrightarrow \mathcal{F}_f$ is called an n-ary partial operation of $\mathcal{F}_f$, where D_n is the domain of r_n, also denoted by $D_n(r_n)$.*

Definition 3. [15] *A mapping $t_n : L^n \longrightarrow L$ is said to be an n-ary truth-valued operation on L, if*
(1). $\alpha \to t_n(\alpha_1, \cdots, \alpha_n) \geq t_n(\alpha \to \alpha_1, \cdots, \alpha \to \alpha_n)$ holds for any $\alpha \in L$ and $(\alpha_1, \cdots, \alpha_n) \in L^n$.
(2). t_n is isotone in each argument.

We denote $R_n \subseteq \{r_n \mid r_n \text{ is an n-ary partial operation of } \mathcal{F}_f\}$,

$$T_n \subseteq \{t_n \mid t_n \text{ is an n-ary truth-valued operation on } L\},$$

$$\mathscr{R}_n \subseteq R_n \times T_n, \quad \mathscr{R} \subseteq \bigcup_{n=0}^{+\infty} \mathscr{R}_n.$$

If $(r, t) \in \mathscr{R}_n$, then (r, t) is called an *n-ary rule of inference* in L_{vfl}.

It can be seen that there are two parts for an inference rule in L_{vfl}, r is for the formal deduction of formulas, and t is for the transformation of truth values of these formulas. For car evaluation example, r is to describe the process from the attributes of a car to get the final evaluation, while t gives the truth degree transmission along with the process.

Definition 4. [15] *Let* $X \in \mathscr{F}_L(\mathcal{F}_f)$, $(r, t) \in \mathscr{R}_n$, $\alpha \in L$. *If*

$$X \circ r \supseteq \alpha \otimes (t \circ \prod^n X) \tag{8}$$

holds, then X *is said to be* α-I *type closed w.r.t.* (r, t). *If*

$$X \circ r \supseteq t \circ \prod^n (\alpha \otimes X) \tag{9}$$

holds, then X *is said to be* α-II *type closed w.r.t.* (r, t), *where* $\circ$ *means the composition of functions, and* $\prod$ *is Cartesian product.*

If for any $(r, t) \in \mathscr{R}$, X *is* α-i *type closed w.r.t.* (r, t), *then* X *is said to be* α-i *type closed w.r.t.* $\mathscr{R}$, $i =$I, II.

Definition 5. [15] *Let* $\alpha \in L$, $\mathscr{R}$ *is said to be* α-i *type sound w.r.t.* $\mathcal{I}$, *if* T *is* α-i *type closed w.r.t.* $\mathscr{R}$ *holds for any* $T \in \mathcal{I}$, $i =$I, II.

Here, α can be thought of as the level of soundness of the inference rule in lattice-valued logic, which can be interpreted as the belief degree of the decision rule in the rule base for car evaluation problem.

Definition 6. [15] *Let* $X, Y \in \mathscr{F}_L(\mathcal{F}_f)$, $\varphi \in \mathcal{F}_f$, α, $\beta \in L$, $i=$I, II. (1).

$$C_{\mathcal{I}} : \mathscr{F}_L(\mathcal{F}_f) \longrightarrow \mathscr{F}_L(\mathcal{F}_f),$$

$$C_{\mathcal{I}}^X(\varphi) \triangleq \bigwedge_{T \in \mathcal{I}} (\bigwedge_{\psi \in \mathcal{F}_f} (X(\psi) \to T(\psi)) \to T(\varphi)), \tag{10}$$

(2).

$$C_{(C_{\mathcal{I}}^\emptyset, \mathscr{R}(\alpha-i))}^\beta : \mathscr{F}_L(\mathcal{F}_f) \longrightarrow \mathscr{F}_L(\mathcal{F}_f),$$

$$C_{(C_{\mathcal{I}}^\emptyset, \mathscr{R}(\alpha-i))}^{\beta,X}(\varphi) \triangleq \bigwedge \{ Y(\varphi) \mid Y \supseteq \beta \otimes (C_{\mathcal{I}}^\emptyset \cup X), \\ Y \text{ is } \alpha\text{-i type closed w.r.t. } \mathscr{R} \}. \tag{11}$$

$C_{\mathcal{I}}$ is a semantic closure operator reflecting the transformation of truth values from X to $C_{\mathcal{I}}^X$ under interpretation set $\mathcal{I}$, which will be used to get the uncertain reasoning consequence. In the car evaluation problem, $C_{\mathcal{I}}^X$ gives the degree to which the evaluation X of a specified car can be included in or can reflect (that is what "$\to$" means) a general evaluation $\mathcal{I}$ of cars. β means the degree to which can we get the evaluation result from the observations of a car and established rules.

Definition 7. [15] *Let* $X \in \mathscr{F}_L(\mathcal{F}_f)$, $\varphi \in \mathcal{F}_f$, θ, α, $\beta \in L$. $(P^i, (n), X, (\varphi, \theta) - (\alpha, \beta))$ *is said to be an* (α, β)-i *type proof of* φ *from* X *with the truth-valued degree* θ *(shortly,* θ-(α, β)-i *type proof of* φ *from* X), *if the mapping*

$$P^i : (n) \longrightarrow \mathcal{F}_f \times L, \ (n) = \{1, 2, \cdots, n\}$$
$$j \longmapsto (\varphi_j, \theta_j),$$

satisfies:
(1). $(\varphi_n, \theta_n) = (\varphi, \theta)$ *and*
(2). $\theta_j = \beta \otimes C_{\mathcal{I}}^{\emptyset}(\varphi_j)$, *or*
(3). $\theta_j = \beta \otimes X(\varphi_j)$, *or*
(4). *there exist* $j_1, \cdots, j_k < j$, *and* $(r,t) \in \mathcal{R}_k$, *such that*

$$(\varphi_j, \theta_j) = (r(\varphi_{j_1}, \cdots, \varphi_{j_k}), \alpha \otimes t(\theta_{j_1}, \cdots, \theta_{j_k})), \; i = I,$$
$$(\varphi_j, \theta_j) = (r(\varphi_{j_1}, \cdots, \varphi_{j_k}), t(\alpha \otimes \theta_{j_1}, \cdots, \alpha \otimes \theta_{j_k})), \; i = II,$$

where n *is said to be the length of* θ*-*(α, β)*-i type proof of* φ *from* X *under* P^i, *and is denoted by* $l(P^i)$, $i = I, II$.

Definition 8. [15] *Let* $X \in \mathscr{F}_L(\mathcal{F}_f)$, $\tau \in L$, $i = I, II$. *If*

$$\bigvee \{C_{(C_{\mathcal{I}}^{\emptyset}, \mathscr{R}(\alpha-i))}^{\beta, X}(\varphi) \otimes C_{(C_{\mathcal{I}}^{\emptyset}, \mathscr{R}(\alpha-i))}^{\beta, X}(\varphi') | \varphi \in F_f\} \le \tau, \tag{12}$$

then X *is said to be* τ'*-i type consistent w.r.t.* $(\alpha, \beta, \mathcal{I})$.

τ' represents the level of consistency of X which can be antecedent or consequent in the inference rule. For example, there may be some conflicting observations of a car or conflicting rules in the rule-base, and τ' is used to represent the degree to which they are not conflicting, *i.e.*, consistent.

Theorem 9. [15] *Let* $X \in \mathscr{F}_L(\mathcal{F}_f)$, α, $\beta \in L$, *and the truth-valued operations in* $\mathscr{R}$ *satisfy the finite semicontinuity. Then for any* $\varphi \in F_f$, $i = I, II$,

$$C_{(C_{\mathcal{I}}^{\emptyset}, \mathscr{R}(\alpha-i))}^{\beta, X}(\varphi) = \bigvee \{\theta \mid \exists (P^i, (n), X, (\varphi, \theta) - (\alpha, \beta))\}, \tag{13}$$

where $(P^i, (n), X, (\varphi, \theta) - (\alpha, \beta))$ *is an* (α, β)*-i type proof of* φ *from* X *with the truth-valued degree* θ.

Theorem 10. [15] *Let* α, $\beta \in L$, *and for any* $X \in \mathscr{F}_L(\mathcal{F}_f)$, $\mathscr{R}$ *is* α*-i type sound w.r.t.* $\mathcal{I}$, *and* $C_{(C_{\mathcal{I}}^{\emptyset}, \mathscr{R}(\alpha-i))}^{\beta, X} \in \mathcal{I}$. *Then for* $i = I, II$,

$$C_{(C_{\mathcal{I}}^{\emptyset}, \mathscr{R}(\alpha-i))}^{\beta, X} = C_{\mathcal{I}}^{\beta \otimes X}. \tag{14}$$

Theorems 9 and 10 state the soundness and completeness of lattice-valued logic to some degree, *i.e.*, the compatibility between syntax and semantics in lattice-valued logic.

3   Uncertain Reasoning Approach Based on Lattice-Valued Logic L_{vfl}

We take the typical uncertain reasoning model to explain the uncertain reasoning approach based on lattice-valued logic L_{vfl}.

$$\begin{array}{r} Rule: \text{ If } X, \text{ then } Y, \\ Fact: \widetilde{X}, \\ \hline Conclusion: \widetilde{Y}, \end{array} \tag{15}$$

where $X, Y, \widetilde{X}, \widetilde{Y} \in \mathscr{F}_L(\mathcal{F}_f)$.

The inference rule shown in (15) is Modus Ponens when $\widetilde{X} = X$, and $\widetilde{Y} = Y$, and is always called Fuzzy Modus Ponens (FMP) when $\widetilde{X}$ does not exactly equal X. The task of uncertain reasoning is to find an appropriate output $\widetilde{Y}$.

An uncertain reasoning approach has been proposed in [2] based on the above model, and the corresponding uncertain reasoning consequence is expressed as:

$$\widetilde{Y} = C_{\mathcal{I}}^{\beta \otimes \widetilde{X}}, \tag{16}$$

where $C_{\mathcal{I}}$ is defined in Definition 6. Here, we need the uncertain reasoning model (15) to be $(\alpha, \beta, \tau, \mathcal{I})$-$i$ type regular [14], [2], i.e., there exist α, β, $\tau \in L$, $\mathcal{I} \subseteq \mathscr{F}_L(\mathcal{F}_f)$ and $\mathscr{R}$ such that $X, Y, \widetilde{X}$ is τ'-i type consistent w.r.t. $(\alpha, \beta, \mathcal{I})$, and $C_{\mathcal{I}}^X \supseteq \tau' \otimes Y$. Furthermore, if the above selected α, β, τ, $\mathcal{I}$ and $\mathscr{R}$ make $C_{(C_{\mathcal{I}}^{\beta}, \mathscr{R}(\alpha-i))}^{\beta, \widetilde{X}} \in \mathcal{I}$, then from Theorems 9 and 10, the uncertain reasoning consequence can also be obtained by a strict formal deduction in L_{vfl}, i.e., the uncertain reasoning consequence is not only semantically sound, but also syntactically provable to some degree.

It should be noticed that the above conditions for parameters are always satisfiable. For example, equation (12) always holds for $\tau = I$, i.e., any X is consistent at O level, this is of course useless. So, what we need to do is to choose reasonable values, according to practical and logical requirements, for these parameters under certain situations.

In [2], we have chosen a set of inference rules $\mathscr{R}^*$, including three special rules and five classes of rules, which can cover rules used frequently in most cases.

$$\begin{aligned}
\mathscr{R}^* &= \{(r_2^0, t_2^*), (r_2^*, t_2^*), (r_2^\triangle, t_2^*)\} \cup \{(r_1^{\theta_0}, t_1^{\theta_0}) \mid \theta_0 \in L\} \\
&\quad \cup \{(r_1^u, t_1) \mid u \in U\} \cup \{(r_2^u, t_1) \mid u \in U\} \\
&\quad \cup \{(r_3^u, t_1) \mid u \in U\} \cup \{(r_4^u, t_1) \mid u \in U\} \\
&\subseteq \mathscr{R},
\end{aligned} \tag{17}$$

where

$$\begin{aligned}
&r_2^0(\varphi, \varphi \to \psi) = \psi, \quad t_2^*(\theta, \beta) = \theta \wedge \beta, \\
&r_2^*(\varphi \to \gamma, \varphi \to \psi) = \varphi \to (\gamma \wedge \psi), \\
&r_2^\triangle(\varphi \to \psi, \psi \to \gamma) = \varphi \to \gamma, \\
&r_1^{\theta_0}(\varphi) = \theta_0 \to \varphi, \quad t_1^{\theta_0}(\alpha) = \theta_0 \to \alpha, \\
&r_1^u(\varphi) = (\mathbf{Q}_u x)\varphi, \quad t_1(\theta) = \theta, \\
&r_2^u(\varphi \to \psi) = \varphi \to (\mathbf{Q}_u x)\psi, \quad x \text{ is not free in } \varphi, \\
&r_3^u(\varphi \to \psi) = (\mathbf{Q}_u x)\varphi \to \psi, \quad x \text{ is not free in } \psi, \\
&r_4^u(\mathbf{Q}_u x)(\varphi \otimes \psi) = (\mathbf{Q}_u x)\varphi \otimes \psi, \quad x \text{ is not free in } \psi.
\end{aligned}$$

In the following, we use the set of inference rules $\mathscr{R}^*$ and the set of interpretations $\mathcal{I}_i$ for uncertain reasoning, where

$$\mathcal{I}_i = \{T \mid T \in \mathscr{F}_L(\mathcal{F}_f), T \text{ is } \alpha\text{-}i \text{ type closed w.r.t. } \mathscr{R}^*\}, \quad i = \mathrm{I}, \mathrm{II}.$$

The following theorem shows that such selected $\mathscr{R}^*$ and $\mathcal{I}_i$ can guarantee the soundness and completeness of lattice-valued logic according to Theorem 10.

Theorem 11. [2] *Given $\mathscr{R}$ and α. If*

$$\mathcal{I} = \{T \mid T \in \mathscr{F}_L(\mathcal{F}_f), T \text{ is } \alpha\text{-}i \text{ type closed w.r.t. } \mathscr{R}\},$$

then $C^{\beta,\tilde{X}}_{(C^0_{\mathcal{I}},\mathscr{R}(\alpha-i))} \in \mathcal{I}$, *i=I, II.*

As for the truth-value field L, it should be selected according to real requirements. In this paper, in order to provide some ideas for dealing with qualitative information which are widely used in real-life evaluation problems, we take the algebraic structure for modeling linguistic terms, linguistic truth-valued lattice implication algebra (L-LIA) [16], [17], as the truth-value field. L-LIA is constructed from the product of two finite Łukasiewicz chain. One is a Łukasiewicz chain with two elements which are meta truth values, "true" and "false", and the other chain is the set of some modifiers, also know as linguistic hedges [19] such as "very," "less," "possibly," and so on. The number of modifiers is always odd [16], [3], such 3, 5 or 9. For more information about L-LIA, please refer to [16].

So, suppose that there are two finite Łukasiewicz chain, $L_2 = \{b_1, b_2\}$ and $L_n = \{a_1, a_2, \cdots, a_n\}$, where $n \in \mathbb{N}^+$, an odd natural number. The product LIA produced by them is denoted as $L_{2n} = L_n \times L_2$, and the lattice-valued first-order logic whose truth-value field is L_{2n} is denoted as $\mathscr{L}_{2nf}$.

Then, there are three parameters, α, β and τ, whose values remain to be determined. From the properties of L_{vfl}, $\alpha \leq \bigwedge_{\theta \in L}(\theta \vee \theta')$ can generally guarantee that $\mathscr{R}^*$ is α-i type sound w.r.t. $\mathcal{I}_i$. So, in the following, we pay more attention to the selection of the values of parameters β and τ.

4   Parameter Selection

Because of the importance of $\bigwedge_{\theta \in L}(\theta \vee \theta')$ as a threshold for the soundness of inference rule, we firstly find its concrete value in L_{2n}.

Lemma 12. *In the product LIA L_{2n},*

$$\bigwedge_{\theta \in L_{2n}} (\theta \vee \theta') = \begin{cases} (a_{\frac{n+1}{2}}, b_2), & n \text{ is odd,} \\ (a_{\frac{n}{2}+1}, b_2), & n \text{ is even.} \end{cases}$$

Proof. In fact,

$$\bigwedge_{\theta \in L_{2n}} (\theta \vee \theta') = \bigwedge_{(a_i, b_j) \in L_{2n}} ((a_i, b_j) \vee (a'_i, b'_j))$$

$$= \bigwedge_{(a_i, b_j) \in L_{2n}} ((a_i \vee a'_i), (b_j \vee b'_j))$$

$$= (\bigwedge_{a_i \in L_n} (a_i \vee a'_i), \bigwedge_{b_j \in L_2} (b_j \vee b'_j))$$

$$= \begin{cases} (a_{\frac{n+1}{2}}, b_2), & n \text{ is odd,} \\ (a_{\frac{n}{2}+1}, b_2), & n \text{ is even.} \end{cases}$$

In the following, we determine the values of parameters β and τ by applying the uncertain reasoning process to some typical conditions.

Theorem 13. *For any $X \in \mathscr{F}_L(\mathcal{F}_f)$, assume that*

$$X(\varphi) = \begin{cases} \varphi, & \varphi \in L_{2n}, \\ O, & otherwise, \end{cases}$$

where $\varphi \in \mathcal{F}_f$. Then for any $\beta \in L_{2n}$, X is I-i (i.e., $\tau = 0$) type consistent w.r.t. $(\alpha, \beta, \mathcal{I}_i)$, where $\alpha \leq \bigwedge_{\theta \in L_{2n}} (\theta \vee \theta')$, $i = \mathrm{I}, \mathrm{II}$.

Proof. If $\alpha \leq \bigwedge_{\theta \in L_{2n}} (\theta \vee \theta')$, then it follows from the properties of L_{vfl} that $\mathcal{I}_H \subseteq \mathcal{I}_i$. So there exists $T_0 \in \mathcal{I}_H$, such that

$$C_{\mathcal{I}_i}^{\beta \otimes X}(\psi) = \bigwedge_{T \in \mathcal{I}_i} [(\bigwedge_{\varphi \in \mathcal{F}_f} (\beta \otimes X(\varphi) \to T(\varphi))) \to T(\psi)]$$

$$= \bigwedge_{T \in \mathcal{I}_i} [(\bigwedge_{(a_i, b_j) \in L} (\beta \otimes (a_i, b_j) \to T((a_i, b_j)))) \to T(\psi)]$$

$$\leq [\bigwedge_{(a_i, b_j) \in L} (\beta \otimes (a_i, b_j) \to T_0((a_i, b_j)))] \to T_0(\psi) = T_0(\psi).$$

Therefore, $C_{\mathcal{I}_i}^{\beta \otimes X}(\psi) \otimes C_{\mathcal{I}_i}^{\beta \otimes X}(\psi') \leq T_0(\psi) \otimes T_0(\psi') = O = I'$. Hence, X is I-i type consistent w.r.t. $(\alpha, \beta, \mathcal{I}_i)$, $i = \mathrm{I}, \mathrm{II}$.

Theorem 14. *For any $X \in \mathscr{F}_L(\mathcal{F}_f)$, assume that*

$$X(\varphi) = \begin{cases} \varphi, & \varphi \in L_{2n}, \\ \xi, & otherwise, \end{cases}$$

where $\varphi \in \mathcal{F}_f$, $\xi \in L_{2n}$. Then we can select $\beta = \xi'$, such that X is I-i type consistent w.r.t. $(\alpha, \beta, \mathcal{I}_i)$, where $\alpha \leq \bigwedge_{\theta \in L_{2n}} (\theta \vee \theta')$, $i = \mathrm{I}, \mathrm{II}$.

Proof. Because $\alpha \leq \bigwedge_{\theta \in L_{2n}} (\theta \vee \theta')$, then $\mathcal{I}_H \subseteq \mathcal{I}_i$. There exists $T_0 \in \mathcal{I}_H$, such that

$$C_{\mathcal{I}_i}^{\beta \otimes X}(\psi) = \bigwedge_{T \in \mathcal{I}_i} [(\bigwedge_{\varphi \in \mathcal{F}_f} (\xi' \otimes X(\varphi) \to T(\varphi))) \to T(\psi)]$$

$$= \bigwedge_{T \in \mathcal{I}_i} [(\bigwedge_{\mu \not\leq \xi} (\xi' \otimes \mu \to T(\mu))) \to T(\psi)]$$

$$\leq T_0(\psi).$$

Therefore,

$$C_{\mathcal{I}_i}^{\beta \otimes X}(\psi) \otimes C_{\mathcal{I}_i}^{\beta \otimes X}(\psi') \leq T_0(\psi) \otimes T_0(\psi') = O = I'.$$

Hence, X is I-i type consistent w.r.t. $(\alpha, \beta, \mathcal{I}_i)$, $i = \mathrm{I}, \mathrm{II}$.

If Y and $\widetilde{X}$ take the same forms as X in the above theorem, then we can get the following theorem.

Theorem 15. *Assume that in the uncertain reasoning model (15), X, Y, $\widetilde{X}$ are given in the following forms:*

$$X(\varphi) = \begin{cases} \varphi, & \varphi \in L_{2n}, \\ \xi_1, & otherwise, \end{cases}$$

$$Y(\varphi) = \begin{cases} \varphi, & \varphi \in L_{2n}, \\ \xi_2, & otherwise, \end{cases}$$

$$\widetilde{X}(\varphi) = \begin{cases} \varphi, & \varphi \in L_{2n}, \\ \xi_3, & otherwise, \end{cases}$$

where $\varphi \in \mathcal{F}_f$, $\xi_1, \xi_3, \xi_3 \in L_{2n}$. Let $\beta = \xi_1' \wedge \xi_2' \wedge \xi_3'$, $\tau = \bigwedge \{\eta \in L_{2n} \mid \eta' \otimes \xi_2 \leq \xi_1\}$, then the uncertain reasoning model (15) is $(\alpha, \beta, \tau, \mathcal{I}_i)$-i type regular, where $\alpha \leq \bigwedge_{\theta \in L_{2n}} (\theta \vee \theta')$, $i = \mathrm{I}, \mathrm{II}$. Then the uncertain reasoning consequence $\widetilde{Y} = C_{\mathcal{I}_i}^{\beta \otimes \widetilde{X}}$, which can also be obtained by a strict formal deduction in $\mathscr{L}_{2nf}$.

Furthermore, we can get the following theorem if X, Y, $\widetilde{X}$ take more general forms.

Theorem 16. *Assume that in the uncertain reasoning model (15), X, Y, $\widetilde{X}$ are given as:*

$$X(\varphi) = \begin{cases} c_1, & \varphi = \varphi_1, \\ \vdots \\ c_m, & \varphi = \varphi_m, \\ O, & otherwise, \end{cases} \quad Y(\psi) = \begin{cases} d_1, & \psi = \psi_1, \\ \vdots \\ d_l, & \psi = \psi_l, \\ O, & otherwise, \end{cases} \quad \widetilde{X}(\gamma) = \begin{cases} e_1, & \gamma = \gamma_1, \\ \vdots \\ e_s, & \gamma = \gamma_s, \\ O, & otherwise, \end{cases}$$

where $m, l, s \in \mathbb{N}^+$, φ, φ_i, ψ, ψ_j, γ, $\gamma_k \in \mathcal{F}_f$, c_i, d_j, $e_k \in L_{2n}$, $i = 1, \cdots, m$, $j = 1, \cdots, l$, $k = 1, \cdots, s$. Then we can choose $\beta_X = c_1' \wedge \cdots \wedge c_m'$, $\beta_Y = d_1' \wedge \cdots \wedge d_l'$, $\beta_{\widetilde{X}} = e_1' \wedge \cdots \wedge e_s'$, and $\beta = \beta_X \wedge \beta_Y \wedge \beta_{\widetilde{X}}$. If there exists $\tau \in L_{2n}$, such that $C_{\mathcal{I}}^X \supseteq \tau' \otimes Y$, then the uncertain reasoning model (15) is $(\alpha, \beta, \tau, \mathcal{I}_i)$-i type regular, where $\alpha \leq \bigwedge_{\theta \in L_{2n}} (\theta \vee \theta')$, $i = \mathrm{I}, \mathrm{II}$. Then the uncertain reasoning consequence $\widetilde{Y} = C_{\mathcal{I}_i}^{\beta \otimes \widetilde{X}}$, which can also be obtained by a strict formal deduction in $\mathscr{L}_{2nf}$.

5   An Illustrative Example

In this section, we will give a simple example of evaluation of cars to show how the proposed reasoning approach can be used in decision making with uncertainty.

Suppose that we are evaluating three kinds of cars: Benz (x_1), Toyota (x_2) and Ford (x_3), and there are four criteria or attributes: price (φ_1), safety (φ_2), comfort (φ_3) and fuel economy (φ_4). The truth-value field for modeling linguistic judgments is chosen as the L-LIA $L_{9 \times 2}$ in [16] with nine modifiers: slightly (a_1),

Table 1. Evaluation matrix of cars

	φ_1	φ_2	φ_3	φ_4
x_1	(a_6, b_1)	(a_7, b_2)	(a_7, b_2)	(a_3, b_1)
x_2	(a_3, b_2)	(a_2, b_1)	(a_3, b_2)	(a_7, b_2)
x_3	(a_2, b_2)	(a_2, b_2)	(a_2, b_2)	(a_2, b_2)

somewhat (a_2), rather (a_3), almost (a_4), exactly (a_5), quite (a_6), very (a_7), highly (a_8) and absolutely (a_9), and two prime terms: bad (b_1) and good (b_2). The judgment of each criterion for each kind of car is given in Table 1, by taking a simple standardization of these natural expressed evaluations. For example, the value of $\varphi_1(x_1)$ in Table 1 gives the evaluation "the price of Benz is quite bad", which really means "Benz is quite expensive".

The evaluation values in Table 1 for car x_1, x_2, and x_3 are expressed as $\widetilde{X}_1$, $\widetilde{X}_2$, $\widetilde{X}_3$ respectively, for example, that for x_1 is

$$\widetilde{X}_1(\varphi) = \begin{cases} (a_6, b_1), & \varphi = \varphi_1(x_1), \\ (a_7, b_2), & \varphi = \varphi_2(x_1), \\ (a_7, b_2), & \varphi = \varphi_3(x_1), \\ (a_3, b_1), & \varphi = \varphi_4(x_1), \\ O, & \text{otherwise}, \end{cases}$$

The decision rule is from our daily experience: "If the car is rather cheap, very safe, very comfortable and with quite good fuel economy, then the car is highly good", with a belief degree $\alpha = (a_5, b_2)$. Then the decision rule can be expressed as

$$\text{If } X \text{ then } Y,$$

where

$$X(\varphi) = \begin{cases} (a_7, b_2), & \varphi = (\forall x)\varphi_1(x), \\ (a_7, b_2), & \varphi = (\forall x)\varphi_2(x), \\ (a_7, b_2), & \varphi = (\forall x)\varphi_3(x), \\ (a_7, b_2), & \varphi = (\forall x)\varphi_4(x), \\ O, & \text{otherwise}, \end{cases}$$

$$Y(\psi) = \begin{cases} (a_8, b_2), & \psi = (\forall x)\psi_1(x), \\ O, & \text{otherwise}. \end{cases}$$

The consistency levels of X, Y, and $\widetilde{X}_i$ $(i = 1, 2, 3)$ are all $\tau' = (a_7, b_2)$, and the belief degree of the reasoning process is chosen to be $\beta = (a_7, b_2)$. By applying Theorem 16, we can get the overall evaluation result for car x_1,

$$\widetilde{Y}_1(\psi(x_1)) = C_{\mathcal{I}_i}^{\beta \otimes \widetilde{X}} = (a_3, b_1).$$

Similarly, we can get the overall evaluation results $\widetilde{Y}_2(\psi(x_2)) = (a_3, b_2)$, $\widetilde{Y}_3(\psi(x_3)) = (a_2, b_2)$, for x_2 and x_3.

These results can be retransformed into natural language: car x_1 is "rather bad", car x_2 is "rather good", car x_3 is "somewhat good". It can be seen that the "rather good" one, car x_2, *i.e.*, Toyota, is the best choice among the three cars according to the provided criteria and observations.

6   Conclusions

This paper proposed a parameterized uncertain reasoning approach with parameters representing uncertainty from different sources, which is a common phenomenon in many intelligent systems, based on a lattice-valued logic $\mathscr{L}_{2nf}$. We discussed some methods for selecting appropriate parameters during the uncertain reasoning process. Reasoning with different parameter values means reasoning with different degrees of belief and consistency. This proposed parameterized uncertain reasoning approach takes the advantage of direct reasoning with observed information, without the underlying numerical approximation needed by some other methods. An example for car evaluation was given to illustrate how the proposed uncertain reasoning approach works.

Acknowledgments. This paper has been partially supported by the research projects TIN2009-08286, P08-TIC-3548 and Feder Funds.

References

1. Benferhat, S., Sossai, C.: Reasoning with Multiple-Source Information in a Possibilistic Logic Framework. Information Fusion 7, 80–96 (2006)
2. Chen, S.W., Xu, Y.: Uncertainty Reasoning Based on Lattice-Valued First-Order Logic L_{vfl}. In: IEEE 2004 International Conference on Systems, Man, and Cybernetics, pp. 2237–2242. IEEE Press, New York (2004)
3. Chen, S., Xu, Y., Ma, J.: A Linguistic Truth-Valued Uncertainty Reasoning Model Based on Lattice-Valued Logic. In: Wang, L., Jin, Y. (eds.) FSKD 2005. LNCS (LNAI), vol. 3613, pp. 276–284. Springer, Heidelberg (2005)
4. Cignoli, R., D'Ottaviano, I., Mundici, D.: Algebraic Foundations of Many-Valued Reasoning. Kluwer, Dordrecht (2000)
5. Gottwald, S.: A Treatise on Many-Valued Logics. In: Studies in Logic and Computation, vol. 9. Research Studies Press Ltd., Baldock (2001)
6. Hájek, P.: Metamathematics of Fuzzy Logic. Kluwer Academic Publishers, Dordrecht (1998)
7. Larsen, H.L., Yager, R.R.: A Framework for Fuzzy Recognition Technology. IEEE Trans. Syst. Man Cybern. Part C 30, 65–76 (2000)
8. Novak, V., Perfilieva, I., Mojckojr, J.: Mathematical Principles of Fuzzy Logic. Kluwer Academic Publishers, Dordrecht (1999)
9. Pavelka, J.: On Fuzzy Logic I: Many-Valued Rules of Inference, II: Enriched Residuated Lattices and Semantics of Propositional Calculi, III: Semantical Completeness of Some Many-Valued Propositional Calculi. Zeitschr. F. Math. Logik und Grundlagend. Math. 25, 45–52, 119–134, 447–464 (1979)
10. Prado, R.P., Garcia-Galan, S., Munoz Exposito, J.E., Yuste, A.J.: Knowledge Acquisition in Fuzzy-Rule-Based Systems with Particle-Swarm Optimization. IEEE Trans. Fuzzy Syst. 18, 1083–1097 (2010)

11. Priest, G.: An Introduction to Non-Classical Logic, 2nd edn. Cambridge University Press, Cambridge (2008)
12. Sottara, D., Mello, P., Proctor, M.: A Configurable Rete-OO Engine for Reasoning with Different Types of Imperfect Information. IEEE Trans. Knowledge and Data Engineering 22, 1535–1548 (2010)
13. Turunen, E.: Algebraic Structures in Fuzzy Logic. Fuzzy Sets Syst. 52, 181–188 (1992)
14. Xu, Y., Ruan, D., Liu, J.: Approximate Reasoning Based on Lattice-Valued Propositional Logic L_{vpl}. In: Ruan, D., Kerre, E.E. (eds.) Fuzzy Sets Theory and Applications, pp. 81–105. Kluwer Academic Publishers, Dordrecht (2000)
15. Xu, Y., Ruan, D., Qin, K.Y., Liu, J.: Lattice-Valued Logic: An Alternative Approach to Treat Fuzziness and Incomparability. Springer, Berlin (2003)
16. Xu, Y., Chen, S.W., Ma, J.: Linguistic Truth-Valued Lattice Implication Algebra and Its Properties. In: IMACS 2006 Multiconference on "Computational Engineering in Systems Applications", pp. 1413–1418. IEEE Press, New York (2006)
17. Xu, Y., Chen, S.W., Liu, J., Ruan, D.: Weak Completeness of Resolution in a Linguistic Truth-Valued Propositional Logic. In: Melin, P., Castillo, O., Aguilar, L.T., Kacprzyk, J., Pedrycz, W. (eds.) IFSA 2007. LNCS (LNAI), vol. 4529, pp. 358–366. Springer, Heidelberg (2007)
18. Xu, Y., Liu, J., Ruan, D., Li, X.B.: Determination of α-Resolution in Lattice-Valued First-Order Logic LF(X). Inform. Sci. 181, 1836–1862 (2011)
19. Zadeh, L.A.: The Concepts of a Linguistic Variable and Its Applications to Approximate Reasoning, Part I, II, III. Inform. Sci. 8, 199–249, 301–357 (1975); 9, 43–80
20. Zhou, H.J., Wang, G.J., Zhou, W.: Consistency Degrees of Theories and Methods of Graded Reasoning in n-Valued R_0-Logic (NM-logic). Int. J. Approximate Reasoning 43, 117–132 (2006)

From Preference Relations to Fuzzy Choice Functions

Davide Martinetti, Ignacio Montes, and Susana Díaz

Dept. Statistics and O. R., University of Oviedo
{martinettidavide.uo,imontes,diazsusana}@uniovi.es

Abstract. This is a first approach to the study of the connection between fuzzy preference relations and fuzzy choice functions. In particular we depart from a fuzzy preference relation and we study the conditions it must satisfy in order to get a fuzzy choice function from it. We are particulary interested in one function: *G*-rationalization. We discuss the relevance of the completeness condition on the departing preference relation. We prove that not every non-complete fuzzy preference relation leads to a choice function.

Keywords: fuzzy preference relation, *G*-rational choice function, complete fuzzy relation.

1 Introduction

Life is a continuous choice and some of those choices are crucial. Given their relevance, choice problems have been studied since many years ago. They appear in very different disciplines such as economics or psychology. Basically, a choice problem involves a set of alternatives and an agent that has to make a choice among them. How to make such a choice in a rational way is a recurrent topic. Intuitively, choice processes are closely related to preferences and orderings. And the connection between both concepts, choice functions and preference relations, has been widely studied in the context of crisp preferences (see among others [1,7,9,10,11,12,13,14,15]).

In the crisp setting it is known that given a choice function, a preference relation among the alternatives, called revealed preference ([10]), can be defined. Conversely, when a preference relation is defined over the set of alternatives, it is possible to build a choice function.

In this contribution we focus on the second case. We depart from a preference relation and we handle an important function, related to the set of the greatest elements, defined from the preference relation. We intend to know for what preference relations this function is a choice function. However, we do not work with classical relations, but with fuzzy ones: those relations that allow the agent to express his/her preference by a value in an interval. Since [2] many authors have considered fuzzy sets to model choice functions (see for example [4,16]). A recent summary on the topic can be found in [17].

W. Liu (Ed.): ECSQARU 2011, LNAI 6717, pp. 594–605, 2011.
© Springer-Verlag Berlin Heidelberg 2011

The contribution is organized in four sections. After this introduction, in Section 2 we recall basic notions related to choice functions and preference relations. Results from both crisp and fuzzy contexts are recalled. Section 3 contains the main results and in Section 4 we address some conclusions and several open problems we find interesting.

2   Preliminaries

In this section we introduce the basic definitions, results and notations necessary to follow the contribution. We first provide a brief summary of the theory developed in the context of crisp relations. We finish the subsection with the result that inspires this contribution. In the second subsection we recall the generalization of the main definitions to the context in which intermediate degrees of preferences are allowed. The notations fixed in this subsection will be used along the paper.

2.1   Crisp Relations

We first recall the classical theory of choice functions based on $\{0, 1\}$-relations also known as crisp or classical relations.

Let X be a finite set of alternatives $\{x_1, x_2, \ldots, x_n\}$. An **available set**, usually denoted by S is any non-empty subset of X. It can also be identified with a mapping $S : X \rightarrow \{0, 1\}$ such that $S(x) = 1$, if $x \in S$ and $S(x) = 0$, otherwise.

Let $\mathcal{P}(X)$ be the set of subsets of X. A **choice space** is any pair (X, B) such that $B \subseteq \mathcal{P}(X) \setminus \{\emptyset\}$.

Definition 1. *Given a choice space (X, B), a **choice function** C is a mapping $C : B \rightarrow \mathcal{P}(X)$ such that for any $S \in B$, $C(S)$ verifies:*

- $C(S) \neq \emptyset$
- $C(S) \subseteq S$.

The first one of the previous conditions means that at least one alternative must be chosen in any subset S. The second one establishes that we cannot choose from one subset S an element that is not in the subset.

A classical or crisp binary relation Q can be identified with a subset of $X \times X$: $Q = \{(x, y) \in X \times X \mid xQy\}$. Also with a mapping $Q : X \times X \rightarrow \{0, 1\}$, such that $Q(x, y) = 1$ expresses that x is connected to y by Q, while $Q(x, y) = 0$ means that Q does not connect x to y. A classical relation is reflexive if xQx for every x in X, that is if it connects every alternative with itself. It is complete if for every pair of elements of X, x and y, at least xQy or yQx. It is transitive if for any three elements in X, x, y, z it holds that $(xQy \wedge yQz) \Rightarrow xQz$.

A **preference relation** is a reflexive binary relation [8]. It is usually denoted R and it is understood as follows:

aRb if and only if "a is at least as good as b"

Associated to any preference relation on a set of alternatives X, three binary relations are usually defined in the context of preference modelling (see among many others [3,6,8]): the *indifference relation*, denoted I and defined as $I = \{(x,y) \mid R(x,y) \wedge R(y,x)\}$; the *strict preference relation*, denoted P and defined as $P = \{(x,y) \mid R(x,y) \wedge \overline{R}(y,x)\}$ and the *incomparability relation*, denoted J and defined as $J = \{(x,y) \mid \overline{R}(x,y) \wedge \overline{R}(y,x)\}$, where $\overline{Q}$ is the complementary relation of the relation Q: $\overline{Q}(x,y) = 1 - Q(x,y)$. Because of the existence of a stronger preference relation, P, the preference relation R is sometimes called *weak preference relation* (see for example [3]).

In the setting of classical or crisp relations, every preference relation defined on a set of alternatives allows to build choice functions on the same set of alternatives. One classical choice function defined from a preference relation is based on the idea of optimality with respect to the preference relation R. An element $x \in S$ is said to be an R-greatest element of S, if for all $y \in S$, alternative x is at least as good as alternative y, according to the preference relation R.

Definition 2. *Given a set of alternatives X, a preference relation R on X and an available set S in X, the set of the R-**greatest elements** of S is denoted $G(S, R)$ and defined as*

$$G(S,R) = \{x \in S \mid (x,y) \in R, \forall y \in S\}.$$

Based on a preference relation R and on the idea of greatest elements in a set, a function on the choice space (X, B) is defined:

$$G_R : B \to \mathcal{P}(X)$$
$$S \mapsto G(S,R)$$

The set $G(S, R)$ is, by definition, a subsets of S. Then it only remains to ensure that it is a non-empty set for every available set S, to prove that G_R is actually a choice function. However, this last condition does not hold in general. Sen [11] provided a sufficient condition in order to ensure that G_R is a choice function.

Proposition 3. [11] *Let $(X, \mathcal{P}(X) \setminus \{\emptyset\})$ be a finite choice space. If R is a transitive and complete preference relation on X, then G_R is a choice function on (X, B).*

In the following section we discuss the generalization of this result to the case in which degrees of preferences are allowed.

2.2   Fuzzy Relations

Crisp relations only allow to determine if there is or not a connection between two alternatives. However, in many real life contexts, alternatives can be connected but the relation is not crisp or completely clear. In order to model in an accurate way those situations, fuzzy sets and fuzzy relations appeared.

The definitions given in the previous subsection in the context of crisp relations, can be extended to the more general context of fuzzy relations.

Let X be a finite set of alternatives $\{x_1, x_2, \ldots, x_n\}$. A fuzzy subset S of X is a mapping $S : X \to [0,1]$ that assigns to each element of X a membership degree $S(x) \in [0,1]$. An **available fuzzy subset** S of X is a fuzzy subset that verifies $S \neq \emptyset$, i.e., that assigns positive value $S(x)$ to at least one $x \in X$. The value $S(x)$ represents the degree up to which alternative x is available when the subset S of X is considered. The family of fuzzy subsets of X will be denoted by $\mathcal{F}(X)$. The pair $(X, \mathcal{B})$, where $\mathcal{B} \subseteq \mathcal{F}(X) \setminus \{\emptyset\}$, is called **fuzzy choice space**.

Definition 4. *A* **fuzzy choice function** *on* $(X, \mathcal{B})$ *is a function* $C : \mathcal{B} \rightarrow \mathcal{F}(X)$, *such that for every* $S \in \mathcal{B}$,

- $C(S)$ *is an available fuzzy subset of* X,
- $C(S)(x) \leq S(x)$, *for every* $x \in X$.

The outcome of $C(S)(x)$ for an element $x \in X$ represents the degree up to which this alternative is chosen when S is available, while the condition $C(S)(x) \leq S(x)$ simply means that an element cannot be more eligible than available.

It is important to remark that C is a fuzzy choice function if and only if, for every $S \in \mathcal{B}$, there exists at least one point $x \in X$, such that $C(S)(x) > 0$.

Example 5. Let us consider an agency that organizes different kinds of activities for groups of people on holidays. The available activities make up the finite set of alternatives. Most of those activities are developed outdoors so depending on the weather, some of them are more appropriate than others. Thus, for a "windy day" the set of available options can be modeled by an available fuzzy set S_W that assigns to each activity a value between 0 (not recomendable at all) and 1 (perfectly practicable). The available fuzzy sets are fixed by an expert in the agency. A fuzzy choice function assigns to each day (to each available fuzzy set) one or several activities (among the practicable ones).

A fuzzy binary relation on X is a relation $Q : X \times X \rightarrow [0,1]$, such that the value of $Q(x,y)$ represents the degree up to which the alternative x is connected to y by Q. If $Q(x,y) = 0$ then x is definitively not connected to y by Q, if $Q(x,y) = 1$, then x is absolutely connected to y by Q, while intermediate values of $Q(x,y)$ represent mild degrees of connection between x and y.

A fuzzy relation Q is said **reflexive** if $Q(x,x) = 1$ for all $x \in X$. As in the crisp sets context, a fuzzy relation Q is called **preference relation** if it is reflexive. We will denote it by R, as in the crisp case.

Example 6. In the previous example, the preference relation is established by the client who assigns a value between 0 and 1 to each pair of activities (a, b). This value indicates the degree of truth of the statement "I consider activity a at least as good as activity b".

The completeness property can be generalized too, but there is not a unique way. Different proposals can be found in the literature: a fuzzy relation Q is said **complete** if for all x and y in X, at least $Q(x,y) > 0$ or $Q(y,x) > 0$. It is said **weakly complete** if for all x and y in X, $Q(x,y) + Q(y,x) \geq 1$. It is said **strongly complete** if $\max(Q(x,y), Q(y,x)) = 1$ for all x and y in X. Obviously, strong completeness is a stronger condition than weak completeness. And this one is a stronger condition than the first definition.

We can also generalize the notion of transitivity. The usual way of extending this property to fuzzy relations is by means of a triangular norms.

Definition 7. *A triangular norm ∗ (t-norm for short) is a binary operator ∗ :* $[0,1] \times [0,1] \to [0,1]$ *such that, for any* $a, b, c \in [0,1]$, *the following axioms are verified:*

- $a * 1 = a$.
- $a * b = b * a$;
- $a * (b * c) = (a * b) * c$;
- *If* $a \leq b$ *then* $a * c \leq b * c$;

Among the most used t-norms, we can mention three examples:

- The **minimum or Gödel t-norm** that we will denote $*_M$,

$$a *_M b = \min(a, b) = a \wedge b;$$

- The **product t-norm** that we will denote $*_P$,

$$a *_P b = a \cdot b;$$

- The **Łukasiewicz t-norm** that we will denote $*_L$,

$$a *_L b = \max(a + b - 1, 0);$$

A t-norm ∗ is said to be **continuous** if it is continuous as a function on the unit interval. The three previous examples are continuous t-norms.

A value $x \in (0, 1)$ is said a **zero-divisor** of a t-norm ∗ if there exists another value $y \in (0, 1)$ such that $x * y = 0$. In that case the t-norm ∗ is said to admit or to have zero-divisors. If for a t-norm there is no $x \in (0, 1)$ such that it is a zero-divisor of ∗, then ∗ is said a t-norm without zero-divisors.

Among the examples given above, the minimum and the product are t-norms without zero-divisors, while the Łukasiewicz operator does admit zero-divisors. An exhaustive study of these operators can be found in [5].

A fuzzy relation Q is ∗-transitive if $Q(x, y) * Q(y, z) \leq Q(x, z)$ for any $x, y, z \in X$.

Associated to any continuous t-norm we can define an implication operator (or residuum).

Definition 8. *Let ∗ be a continuous t-norm. Then the implication operator associated to ∗ is a binary operator defined as* $\to: [0,1] \times [0,1] \to [0,1]$ *and such that:*

$$a \to b = \sup(c \in [0,1] | a * c \leq b).$$

Among the most used implication operators we find those ones that are associated to the most common t-norms:

- if the t-norm is the minimum operator, then $a \to_M b = \begin{cases} 1 \text{ if } a \leq b \\ b \text{ if } a > b \end{cases}$;
- if the t-norm is the product operator, then $a \to_P b = \begin{cases} 1 \quad \text{ if } a \leq b \\ b/a \text{ if } a > b \end{cases}$;
- if the t-norm is the Łukasiewicz operator, then $a \to_L b = \min(1, 1 - a + b)$.

Some properties of the implication operator are presented next:

Proposition 9. *Let $*$ be a continuous t-norm and $\to$ its associated implication operator. Then, for all a, b, c in $[0, 1]$ it holds that:*

1. $a * b \leq c \Leftrightarrow a \leq b \to c$;
2. $a * (a \to b) = \min(a, b)$;
3. $a \leq b \Leftrightarrow a \to b = 1$;
4. $a \to 1 = 1$;
5. $1 \to a = a$;
6. $a \to a = 1$;
7. $b \leq a \to b$;
8. *if $a \to b = 0$, then $b = 0$,*
9. $\to$ *is non-increasing in its first argument and non-decreasing in the second one.*

Once we have recalled t-norms and implicators, we can generalize the idea of R-greatest elements and the corresponding set.

Given an available set S and a fuzzy preference relation R, the following subset of S is defined:

$$G(S, R)(x) = S(x) * \bigwedge_{y \in X} [S(y) \to R(x, y)]. \tag{1}$$

And, based on it, a function is defined on the fuzzy choice space $(X, \mathcal{B})$:

$$G_R : \mathcal{B} \to \mathcal{F}(X)$$
$$S \hookrightarrow G(S, R)$$

In general, G_R is not a choice function, since it can lead to the empty set for some available set S, but when it is actually a fuzzy choice function, it is called G-rationalization of R.

It is interesting to prove if, under suitable conditions on R, it can be ensured that G_R is a fuzzy choice function. And this is the purpose of the next section.

3   From Complete Preference Relations to Fuzzy Choice Functions

In this section we discuss the conditions that the fuzzy preference relation must satisfy to ensure that the operator G_R defined above is a fuzzy choice function. As we will see, the completeness condition plays a key role.

The following proposition establishes a set of conditions on the preference relation R, in order to ensure that the generated G_R is a fuzzy choice function.

Proposition 10. *Let* $*$ *be a continuous t-norm without zero-divisors. Let* R *be a complete and* $*$-*transitive fuzzy preference relation on a finite set* X *and* $(X, \mathcal{B})$ *a fuzzy choice space. Then* G_R *is a fuzzy choice function on* $(X, \mathcal{B})$.

Let us note that the result holds in particular for two of the most employed t-norms: the Gödel and the product t-norms.

For the particular case of the Gödel t-norm, Georgescu [4] seems to have presented a more general result.

Proposition 11. [4] *Let* $*$ *be the Gödel t-norm, i.e. the minimum operator. Let* R *be a* $*$-*transitive fuzzy preference relation on a finite set* X *and* $(X, \mathcal{B})$ *a fuzzy choice space. Then* G_R *is a fuzzy choice function on* $(X, \mathcal{B})$.

This result concerning the particular case of the Gödel t-norm is more general than the one we have just presented. We can only assure the result under completeness. Georgescu's result does not impose such a condition. We have compared both results, we have studied whether completeness can be removed or not from the hypothesis and we have obtained the following counterexample that proves that the result in [4] is not true in general.

Remark 12. It is not difficult to provide a non-complete preference relation R such that G_R is not a fuzzy choice function. Consider for example the preference relation R_0 defined on the set of alternatives $X = \{a, b, c\}$:

R_0	a	b	c
a	1	0	0
b	0	1	0
c	0	0	1

It is clearly $*$-transitive with respect to any t-norm $*$, so, in particular, with respect to the Gödel t-norm. However, we can prove that the associated G_{R_0} function is not a fuzzy choice function. Without loss of generality, we can consider the family of available sets $\mathcal{B}$ composed by the power set of the set of alternatives $X = \{a, b, c\}$ excluding the empty set. It only contains crisp non-empty subsets of X. Using Eq. 1, we construct the set $G(S, R_0)$ for every S. If we consider $G(X, R_0)$, we get:

$$G(X, R_0)(a) = \min(X(a), \min_{y \in \{a,b,c\}}(X(y) \rightarrow_M R_0(a, y))) = \min(1, 1, 0, 0) = 0$$

$$G(X, R_0)(b) = \min(X(b), \min_{y \in \{a,b,c\}}(X(y) \rightarrow_M R_0(b, y))) = \min(1, 0, 1, 0) = 0$$

$$G(X, R_0)(c) = \min(X(c), \min_{y \in \{a,b,c\}}(X(y) \rightarrow_M R_0(c, y))) = \min(1, 0, 0, 1) = 0$$

so the function G_{R_0} is not a fuzzy choice function.

We have just proven that the completeness condition is not a trivial imposition. If we consider a non complete preference relation, as R_0, the associated function G_{R_0} is not a fuzzy choice function. It is interesting to remark that the preference relation considered in this counterexample R_0 is a crisp preference relation.

Next we prove that the other condition considered in Proposition 10 is not superfluous either. It does not hold that for every complete fuzzy preference relation which is $*$-transitive with respect to a t-norm **with** zero-divisors, the associated G_R function is a fuzzy choice function.

Remark 13. Let us consider the fuzzy binary relation defined on a set of three alternatives $X = \{a, b, c\}$ as follows

R	a	b	c
a	1	0	0.1
b	0.9	1	0
c	0	0.1	1

This relation is reflexive, therefore it is a preference relation. It is also complete and $*$-transitive w.r.t. the Łukasiewicz t-norm. Consider now the available set $S_0 = X$ and construct the operator G as illustrated in Eq. 1. Taking into account that $*$ is the Łukasiewicz t-norm:

$$G(S_0, R)(x) = S_0(x) *_L \bigwedge_{y \in X} (S_0(y) \to_L R(x, y))$$

$$= \max \left(S_0(x) + \bigwedge_{y \in X} (S_0(y) \to_L R(x, y)) - 1, 0 \right)$$

Since S_0 is the set of alternatives $\{a, b, c\}$, for any $x \in X$, $S_0(x) = 1$. It follows from here that $S_0(y) \to_L R(x, y) = 1 \to_L R(x, y) = R(x, y)$ for all $x, y \in X$. Then

$$G(S_0, R)(x) = \max \left(1 + \bigwedge_{y \in X} R(x, y) - 1, 0 \right)$$

$$= \bigwedge_{y \in X} R(x, y)$$

It is immediate to see that G_R is not a choice function, since it assigns membership function 0 to all points, when applied to the available set S_0, as we show below:

$$G(S_0, R)(a) = \bigwedge_{y \in X} R(a, y) = \min(1, 0, 0.1) = 0.$$

$$G(S_0, R)(b) = \bigwedge_{y \in X} R(b, y) = \min(0.9, 1, 0) = 0.$$

$$G(S_0, R)(c) = \bigwedge_{y \in X} R(c, y) = \min(0, 0.1, 1) = 0.$$

With this example we have proven that for a fuzzy preference relation $*$-transitive w.r.t. a t-norm with zero-divisors, it cannot be ensured that its G-rationalization is a choice function. The result presented in Proposition 10, cannot be automatically generalized to t-norms with zero-divisors.

However, we can also provide an example where we show that the fact that the t-norm has no zero-divisors is not a necessary condition in general.

Remark 14. There exist preference relations R such that they are complete (in the weakest sense) and $*$-transitive w.r.t. some t-norms with zero-divisors, as for example the Łukasiewicz t-norm, but not with respect to any t-norm without zero-divisors, which G-rationalization G_R is a choice function. Consider for example the preference relation

R	a	b	c
a	1	0.1	0
b	0	1	0.1
c	0.1	0.1	1

Clearly it is complete. It is easy to prove that it is $*$-transitive w.r.t. the Łukasiewicz t-norm, but not $*$-transitive w.r.t. any t-norm without zero-divisors, since

$$R(a,b) * R(b,c) = 0.1 * 0.1 \le R(a,c) = 0 \Leftrightarrow 0.1 \text{ is a zero-divisor.}$$

Now, by reductio ad absurdum, suppose that the G-rationalization of R is not a choice function, i.e. there exists a set $S \in \mathcal{B}$, such that $G(S,R)(x) = 0$, for all $x \in \{a,b,c\}$. This means that for the available set S, it holds that:

$$G(S,R)(a) = \max(S(a) + \bigwedge_{y \in X}(\min(1 - S(y) + R(a,y), 1)) - 1, 0) = 0$$

$$G(S,R)(b) = \max(S(b) + \bigwedge_{y \in X}(\min(1 - S(y) + R(b,y), 1)) - 1, 0) = 0$$

$$G(S,R)(c) = \max(S(c) + \bigwedge_{y \in X}(\min(1 - S(y) + R(c,y), 1)) - 1, 0) = 0$$

or equivalently

$$G(S,R)(a) = 0 \Leftrightarrow S(a) + \bigwedge_{y \in X}(\min(1 - S(y) + R(a,y), 1)) \le 1$$

$$G(S,R)(b) = 0 \Leftrightarrow S(b) + \bigwedge_{y \in X}(\min(1 - S(y) + R(b,y), 1)) \le 1$$

$$G(S,R)(c) = 0 \Leftrightarrow S(c) + \bigwedge_{y \in X}(\min(1 - S(y) + R(c,y), 1)) \le 1.$$

After some easy computations, the preceding conditions can be written as

$$\text{If } S(a) > 0 \text{ then } \min(S(a) - S(b) + 0.1, S(a) - S(c)) \le 0 \tag{2}$$
$$\text{If } S(b) > 0 \text{ then } \min(S(b) - S(a), S(b) - S(c) + 0.1) \le 0 \tag{3}$$
$$\text{If } S(c) > 0 \text{ then } \min(S(c) - S(a) + 0.1, S(c) - S(b) + 0.1) \le 0. \tag{4}$$

For every $S \in \mathcal{B}$, the triplet $(S(a), S(b), S(c))$ can assume seven different forms:

1. If $(S(a) > 0, S(b) = 0, S(c) = 0)$, then $\min(S(a) + 0.1, S(a)) > 0$, that contradicts Condition 2;
2. If $(S(a) = 0, S(b) > 0, S(c) = 0)$, then $\min(S(b), S(b) + 0.1) > 0$, that contradicts Condition 3;

3. If $(S(a) = 0, S(b) = 0, S(c) > 0)$, then $\min(S(c) + 0.1, S(c) + 0.1) > 0$, that contradicts Condition 4;

4. If $(S(a) > 0, S(b) > 0, S(c) = 0)$, then Conditions 2 and 3 become

$$\begin{cases} S(a) + 0.1 - S(b) \leq 0 \\ S(b) - S(a) \leq 0 \end{cases} \Rightarrow \begin{cases} S(a) \leq S(b) - 0.1 \\ S(b) \leq S(a) \end{cases}$$

hence $S(b) \leq S(a) \leq S(b) - 0.1$ that is clearly impossible;

5. If $(S(a) > 0, S(b) = 0, S(c) > 0)$, then Conditions 2 and 4 become

$$\begin{cases} S(a) \leq S(c) \\ S(c) \leq S(a) - 0.1 \end{cases}$$

hence $S(a) \leq S(c) \leq S(a) - 0.1$ that is clearly impossible;

6. If $(S(a) = 0, S(b) > 0, S(c) > 0)$, then Conditions 3 and 4 become

$$\begin{cases} S(b) \leq S(c) - 0.1 \\ S(b) \leq S(c) + 0.1 \end{cases}$$

hence $S(c) + 0.1 \leq S(b) \leq S(c) - 0.1$ that is clearly impossible.

7. Let us analyze the last case separately, i.e. when $(S(a) > 0, S(b) > 0, S(c) > 0)$. In this case, Conditions 2,3 and 4 are simultaneously verified, so:

$$\min(S(a) - S(b) + 0.1, S(a) - S(c)) \leq 0 \qquad (5)$$
$$\min(S(b) - S(a), S(b) - S(c) + 0.1) \leq 0 \qquad (6)$$
$$\min(S(c) - S(a) + 0.1, S(c) - S(b) + 0.1) \leq 0. \qquad (7)$$

Consider Condition 5:

- If $S(a) - S(b) + 0.1 \leq 0$, then it follows from Condition 6 that $S(c) \geq S(b) + 0.1$ and according to Condition 7, $S(b) + 0.1 \leq S(a)$. This is equivalent to

$$S(c) + 0.1 \leq S(a) \leq S(c) - 0.2$$

that is clearly impossible;

- If $S(a) \leq S(c)$, then it follows from Condition 7, $S(c) \leq S(b) - 0.1$ and so in Condition 6, $S(b) \leq S(a)$. This is equivalent to

$$S(b) \leq S(a) \leq S(c) \leq S(b) - 0.1$$

that is impossible.

We have finally proved that $G(S, R)(x)$ cannot assign 0 to every $x \in X$ without incurring into a contradiction and hence G_R is a choice function.

So it is clear that we can consider t-norms with zero-divisors and still obtain fuzzy choice functions. But it is also clear that in this case other properties must be imposed to the fuzzy preference relation to ensure a positive result. What other conditions are those? This is an interesting question for us that we will try to study in close future.

The following result is another possible generalization of the classical result of Sen [11]. A different version of Proposition 10.

Proposition 15. *Let R be a strongly complete and $*$-transitive preference relation on a finite set X. Let $(X, \mathcal{B})$ be a fuzzy choice space. Then G_R is a fuzzy choice function on $(X, \mathcal{B})$.*

In this last case we can assure that G_R is a fuzzy choice function for any t-norm we consider. In order to get the result extended to any t-norm, we have to impose the strongest completeness condition.

4   Conclusions

This work is the departing point of an interesting topic for us: the connection between fuzzy preference relations and fuzzy choice functions. In this first work we have studied a classical function that can be defined from a given fuzzy weak preference relation and we have obtained sufficient conditions to ensure that the associated function is a fuzzy choice function. We have not dealt only with the classical operator considered in the literature, the Gödel t-norm, but we have provided results for other important t-norms. Contrary to what can be found in the literature, the completeness of the weak preference relation appears as a key condition.

Given its relevance, one of the first open problems we want to tackle is the study of other definitions of completeness for fuzzy relations. We also consider interesting to handle other operators, apart from the classical minimum t-norm. In addition to this, we are interested in studying in depth a set of similar results to define a choice function from preference relations, inspired on another technique based on the concept of maximality.

Acknowledgements

The research reported on in this paper has been partially supported by Project MTM2010-17844, the Foundation for the promotion in Asturias of the scientific and technologic research grant BP10-090 and the Science and Education Ministry FPU grant AP2009-1034.

References

1. Arrow, K.J.: Rational choice functions and orderings. Economica 26, 121–127 (1959)
2. Banerjee, A.: Fuzzy choice functions, revealed preference and rationality. Fuzzy Sets and Systems 70, 31–43 (1995)
3. Fodor, J., Roubens, M.: Fuzzy Preference Modelling and Muticriteria Decision Support. Kluwer Academic Publishers, The Netherlands (1994)
4. Georgescu, I.: Fuzzy Choice Functions. Springer, Berlin (2007)
5. Klement, E.P., Mesiar, R., Pap, E.: Triangular Norms. Kluwer Academic Publishers, Boston (2000)
6. Orlovsky, S.A.: Decision-making with a fuzzy preference relation. Fuzzy Sets and Systems 1, 155–167 (1978)

7. Richter, M.K.: Revealed preference theory. Econometrica 34, 635–645 (1996)
8. Roubens, M., Vincke, P.: Preference modelling. LNEMS, vol. 76. Springer, Berlin (1985)
9. Samuelson, P.A.: Foundation of Economic Analysis. Harvard University Press, Cambridge (1947)
10. Samuelson, P.A.: Consumption theory in terms of revealed preference. Economica 15, 243–253 (1948)
11. Sen, A.K.: Collective Choice and Social Welfare. Holden-Day, San Francisco (1970)
12. Sen, A.K.: Choice functions and revealed preference. Review of Economic Studies 38, 307–317 (1971)
13. Sen, A. K.: Social choice theory: a re-examination. Econometrica 45, 53–89 (1977)
14. Suzumura, K.: Rational choice and revealed preference. Review of Economic Studies 46, 149–158 (1976)
15. Suzumura, K.: Houthakker's axiom in the theory of rational choice. Economic Theory 14, 284–290 (1977)
16. Wang, X.: A note on congruence conditions of fuzzy choice functions. Fuzzy Sets and Systems 145, 355–358 (2004)
17. Wang, X., Wu, C., Wu, X.: Choice Functions in Fuzzy Environment: An Overview. In: Cornelis, C., Deschrijver, G., Nachtegael, M., Schockaert, S., Shi, Y. (eds.) 35 Years of Fuzzy Set Theory, Studies in Fuzziness and Soft Computing, vol. 261, pp. 149–170. Springer, Heidelberg (2010)

Fuzzy Relational Inequations and Equations in the Framework of Control Problems

Jorge Jiménez[1], Susana Montes[1],
Branimir Šešelja[2], and Andreja Tepavčević[2]

[1] University of Oviedo, Gijón, Spain
{meana,montes}@uniovi.es
[2] University of Novi Sad, Novi Sad, Serbia
{seselja,andreja}@dmi.uns.ac.rs

Abstract. The paper deals with fuzzy relational inequations and equations connected with closed fuzzy sets under a fixed fuzzy relation over the same domain. Such formulas arise in the framework of control problems. We show that fuzzy sets being solutions of these inequations and corresponding equations form a descending sequence with particular lower bounds which are also analyzed. Our approach is based on complete lattices as structures of membership values, which makes this investigation more general then the classical, real-interval valued approach.

Keywords: fuzzy sets closed under fuzzy relations, fuzzy control.

1 Introduction

Fuzzy relations are known to have many applications in various fields like e.g., artificial intelligence, data bases, approximate reasoning, fuzzy automata and formal languages, fuzzy formal concept analysis and others. Many of these applications are presented in the book of Belohlavek ([1]), in papers by Bodenhofer, De Cock, Kerre ([2,3]), De Baets, Díaz, Montes ([4]), Fuentes-González ([5]), Ignjatović, Ćirić, Bogdanović ([7]), there are many others.

It is well known that fuzzy controllers are rule-based. They act on fuzzy input data and create the corresponding fuzzy output data, according to special rules. The Mamdani approach to fuzzy controllers starts from a fuzzy relation which is deduced from actual control process, and which from an input value creates an output value using a particular compositional rule of inference. In this context IF-THEN rules appear. In practical problems, it happens that output values are determined in advance by input value, and the problem is to find a fuzzy relation which performs such a transition.

What we consider here are some of the problems connected with fuzzy control that could be analyzed, investigated and successfully solved within the framework of fuzzy sets closed under fuzzy relations, with membership values in the complete lattice.

Namely, we deal with the problem of finding an input fuzzy set μ, which will be closed under composition of a fuzzy relation, i.e., which satisfy the following property, for any $y \in X$.

W. Liu (Ed.): ECSQARU 2011, LNAI 6717, pp. 606–615, 2011.

$$\bigvee_{x \in X} (\mu(x) \wedge R(x, y)) \leq \mu(y).$$

Using the properties of lattices, this is equivalent with the property that μ is closed under relation R, i.e., that for every $x, y \in X$,

$$\mu(x) \wedge R(x, y) \leq \mu(y).$$

This problem is closely related to the problem of finding appropriate solutions of the equation:

$$\bigvee_{x \in X} (\mu(x) \wedge R(x, y)) = \mu(y)$$

which has important role in stability problems in fuzzy control systems. This problem is also analyzed and partially solved here.

2 Preliminaries

Some basic notions and notations concerning fuzzy sets and binary relations that we use throughout the paper are as follows.

Let X be a non-empty set, $A \subseteq X$ its nonempty subset and $R \subseteq X^2$ a binary relation on X.

A subset A **is closed** with respect to the relation R, if from $x \in A$ and $(x, y) \in R$ it follows that $y \in A$.

A **poset** is an ordered pair $(X, \leq)$ where X is a nonempty set and $\leq$ an ordering (reflexive, antisymmetric and transitive) relation on X. A **sub-poset** of a poset $(X, \leq)$ is a poset $(Y, \leq)$ where Y is a nonempty subset of X and $\leq$ on Y is a set-intersection of Y^2 and $\leq$ on X. A **complete lattice** is a poset $(L, \leq)$ in which for every subset M there exist the greatest lower bound, infimum, meet, denoted by $\bigwedge M$, and the least upper bound, supremum, join, denoted by $\bigvee M$. In a complete lattice there is always the least element, bottom or zero, 0, and the greatest element, top, 1. Meet and join for a two-element set are binary operations on L, hence a complete lattice under the order $\leq$ can be denoted as an algebraic structure by $(L, \wedge, \vee, 0, 1)$.

A **fuzzy set** here is a mapping $\mu : X \to L$ from a nonempty set X into a complete lattice $(L, \wedge, \vee, 0, 1)$. L is the **set of membership values** of μ. If X and L are fixed, then by $\mathcal{F}(X)$ we denote the collection of all fuzzy sets on X with membership values in L:

$$\mathcal{F}(X) := \{\mu \mid \mu : X \to L\}.$$

It is known that the poset $(\mathcal{F}(X), \subseteq)$ *is a complete lattice under fuzzy inclusion* i.e., under a binary relation defined componentwise with respect to the lattice order $\leq$: for any $\mu, \nu : X \to L$

$$\mu \subseteq \nu \text{ if and only if for every } x \in X, \ \mu(x) \leq \nu(x).$$

3   Closedness of Fuzzy Sets Under a Fuzzy Relation

If $(L, \wedge, \vee, 0, 1)$ is a complete lattice, then $R : X^2 \to L$ is a **fuzzy relation** on X. A fuzzy relation on X is a fuzzy set on X^2.

The following definition is formulated in [3], it is a fuzzified version of the above property:

Let $\mu : X \to L$ be a fuzzy set and $R : X^2 \to L$ a fuzzy relation. Then μ is said to be **closed with respect to** R if for every $x, y \in X$

$$\mu(x) \wedge R(x, y) \le \mu(y).$$

The next result is implicitly proven in Bodenhofer [3], but we here provide a direct proof.

Theorem 1. *The collection of all fuzzy sets closed with respect to a fuzzy relation R on a set X is a complete lattice under inclusion of fuzzy sets.*

Proof. Fuzzy set $\iota : X \to L$, defined by $\iota(x) = 1$ for every $x \in X$ is a fuzzy set closed with respect to any fuzzy relation R on X.

Let $\{\mu_i \mid i \in I\}$ be a family of fuzzy sets closed with respect to R.

This means that for every $i \in I$, $\mu_i(x) \wedge R(x, y) \le \mu_i(y)$.

Now, consider the fuzzy set $\mu : X \to R$, defined by $\mu = \bigcap_{i \in I} \mu_i$. μ is the intersection of an arbitrary family of fuzzy sets closed under R, and we prove that it is closed under R as well. Indeed, for all $x, y \in X$,

$$\mu(x) \wedge R(x, y) = (\bigwedge_{i \in I} \mu_i(x)) \wedge R(x, y) =$$

$$\bigwedge_{i \in I} (\mu_i(x) \wedge R(x, y)) \le \bigwedge_{i \in I} \mu_i(y) = \mu(y).$$

Hence, the collection of all fuzzy sets closed under R is closed under set intersection and contains the greatest element. Therefore, it is a complete lattice. $\square$

In the following we denote by $\mathcal{S}_R$ the collection of all fuzzy sets closed under a fuzzy relation R on a universe X:

$$\mathcal{S}_R = \{\mu \in \mathcal{F}(X) \mid \mu(x) \wedge R(x, y) \le \mu(y) \text{ for any } x, y \in X\}.$$

By Theorem 1 the poset $(\mathcal{S}_R, \subseteq)$ is a complete lattice.

In a similar way we can prove that a collection of fuzzy sets satisfying the equation (2) is closed under intersections, but the fuzzy set $\iota : X \to L$, defined by $\iota(x) = 1$ does not satisfy this equation in general.

4   Closedness and Relational Inequations

Based on a control problem, we are interested in the identification of solutions μ of the inequation

$$\bigvee_{x \in X} (\mu(x) \wedge R(x, y)) \le \mu(y) \tag{1}$$

and of the equation

$$\bigvee_{x \in X} (\mu(x) \wedge R(x, y)) = \mu(y), \qquad (2)$$

where R is a given fuzzy binary relation on a universe X. The inequation and the equation are supposed to be fulfilled for any $y \in X$, and μ represents a fuzzy subset of X, that is, an element of $\mathcal{F}(X)$.

The empty fuzzy set is a trivial solution of both (the inequation and the equation) and the set X represented by its characteristic function, i.e, the fuzzy set having all values equal to 1 is always a solution of the inequation only (as we show by Theorem 1).

The inequation (1) is equivalent with the requirement that $\mu \in \mathcal{F}(X)$ fulfils the inequation

$$\mu(x) \wedge R(x, y) \leq \mu(y) \qquad (3)$$

for all $x, y \in X$.

Indeed, if we suppose that (1) is satisfied for $\mu \in \mathcal{F}(X)$, then for every $x \in X$,

$$\mu(x) \wedge R(x, y) \leq \bigvee_{x \in X} (\mu(x) \wedge R(x, y)) \leq \mu(y).$$

On the other hand if we suppose that for a $y \in X$, (3) is true for every $x \in X$, then by taking the supremum over x, we obtain (1).

It is straightforward to conclude that the *set of solutions of the inequation (1) is precisely the set of all the fuzzy subsets in $\mathcal{F}(X)$ which are closed with respect to R.* This set is in Section 3 denoted by $\mathcal{S}_R$. Therefore, we have

$$\mathcal{S}_R = \{\mu \in \mathcal{F}(X) \mid \mu(x) \wedge R(x, y) \leq \mu(y) \text{ for any } x, y \in X\}.$$

As it is known, the poset $(\mathcal{F}(X), \subseteq)$ is a complete lattice and by Theorem 1 the same holds for the poset $(\mathcal{S}_R, \subseteq)$.

Proposition 1. *Given a fuzzy binary relation R on X and $\mu \in \mathcal{S}_R$, define a new fuzzy subset μ_1 on X by*

$$\mu_1(x) = \bigvee_{z \in X} (\mu(z) \wedge R(z, x)).$$

Then, (i) $\mu_1 \subseteq \mu$ and (ii) $\mu_1 \in \mathcal{S}_R$.

Proof. To prove (i), observe that for any $x \in X$

$$\mu_1(x) = \bigvee_{z \in X} (\mu(z) \wedge R(z, x)) \leq \mu(x),$$

since $\mu \in \mathcal{S}_R$. Thus, $\mu_1 \subseteq \mu$.

Next, for any $x, y \in X$ we have that

$$\mu_1(x) \wedge R(x, y) \wedge R(x, y) \leq \mu(x) \wedge R(x, y) \leq \bigvee_{z \in X} (\mu(z) \wedge R(z, y)) = \mu_1(y).$$

which proves (ii).   □

Remark 1. *By induction, it is straightforward to prove that given a solution μ of inequation (1), that is, given an element $\mu \in S_R$, we have a chain of solutions of the same inequation:*

$$\mu \supseteq \mu_1 \supseteq \mu_2 \supseteq \cdots \supseteq \mu_{n-1} \supseteq \mu_n \supseteq \cdots$$

where $\mu_n \in S_R$ for every n, and $\mu_n(x) = \bigvee_{z \in X}(\mu_{n-1}(z) \wedge R(z,x))$ for every $x \in X$. If two members of this chain are equal, i.e., if for some n, $\mu_{n-1} = \mu_n$, then μ_n is a solution of the equation:

$$\bigvee_{x \in X}(\mu_n(x) \wedge R(x,y)) = \mu_n(y).$$

This solves the stability problem in case when the domain of the fuzzy set and the co-domain lattice are finite, which is formulated in the following proposition.

Proposition 2. *Let $R : X^2 \to L$ be a fuzzy binary relation R on a finite set X and let the lattice L be also finite. Then, there is a solution in $\mathcal{F}(X)$ of the equation:*

$$\bigvee_{x \in X}(\mu(x) \wedge R(x,y)) = \mu(y). \qquad \square$$

Next we present a simple example illustrating introduced notions and properties.

Example 1. Let $X = \{a,b\}$ and let the lattice L be as in Figure 1.

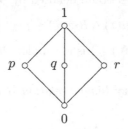

Fig. 1.

Further, let R be a fuzzy relation on X defined as follows.

$$R = \begin{bmatrix} p & q \\ q & q \end{bmatrix},$$

where we suppose that the upper left place in matrix is $R(a,a)$.

Let μ be a fuzzy set given by

$$\mu = \begin{pmatrix} a & b \\ 1 & p \end{pmatrix}.$$

We can easily check that μ does not satisfy the inequation (1), since (by symbolically represented computation in a lattice)

$$\begin{bmatrix} 1 & p \end{bmatrix} \wedge \begin{bmatrix} p & q \\ q & q \end{bmatrix} = \begin{bmatrix} p & q \end{bmatrix}.$$

For $y = b$ the inequation is not satisfied.

We can see that neither the fuzzy set

$$\mu_1 = \begin{pmatrix} a & b \\ 1 & 0 \end{pmatrix}$$

nor

$$\mu_2 = \begin{pmatrix} a & b \\ p & q \end{pmatrix}$$

satisfy the inequation.

We know that the set $X = \{a, b\}$, i.e., the fuzzy set

$$\begin{pmatrix} a & b \\ 1 & 1 \end{pmatrix}$$

is always (for any R) a solution of the inequation.

If we would like to find a solution of equation (2), then we start from this fuzzy set (X) and since both, domain and the lattice are finite, we obtain the solution in a finite number of steps.

$$\begin{bmatrix} 1 & 1 \end{bmatrix} \wedge \begin{bmatrix} p & q \\ q & q \end{bmatrix} = \begin{bmatrix} 1 & q \end{bmatrix}.$$

$$\begin{bmatrix} 1 & q \end{bmatrix} \wedge \begin{bmatrix} p & q \\ q & q \end{bmatrix} = \begin{bmatrix} 1 & q \end{bmatrix}.$$

Hence, a solution of equation (2) is the fuzzy set

$$\begin{pmatrix} a & b \\ 1 & q \end{pmatrix}.$$

Since we know that there is always a trivial solution, the empty fuzzy set, our aim is to find a non-trivial solution, that we really obtain in this case.   □

A detailed analysis about necessary and sufficient conditions for existence of a non-trivial solution is out of scope of this article. Let us mention that one sufficient condition is that there is $y \in X$ such that $\vee_{x \in X} R(x, y) = 1$.

In the following proposition another possible solution of the equation is described; the proof is technical.

Proposition 3. *Let R be a fuzzy binary relation on X and ν the fuzzy subset on X defined by*

$$\nu(x) = R(x, x).$$

Then, ν is a solution of the inequation (1) if and only if it is a solution of the equation (2).

Proposition 4. *Let μ be an element in $\mathcal{S}_R$ and let $\mathcal{S}_R^\mu$ be the subset of $\mathcal{S}_R$ defined by*

$$\mathcal{S}_R^\mu := \{\mu_n \in \mathcal{F}(X) \mid n \in \mathbb{N} \text{ and }$$
$$\text{for all } x \in X, \ \mu_n(x) = \bigvee_{z \in X} (\mu_{n-1}(z) \wedge R(z,x)), \text{ with } \mu_0 = \mu\}.$$

Then the fuzzy subset $\bar{\mu} \in \mathcal{F}(X)$ defined by

$$\bar{\mu}(x) = \mu(x) \wedge R(x,x) \text{ for every } x \in X$$

is a lower bound of $\mathcal{S}_R^\mu$ in the poset $(\mathcal{F}(X), \subseteq)$.

Proof. For every $i \in \mathbb{N}$, we define the fuzzy subset $\bar{\mu}_i$ of X by

$$\bar{\mu}_i(x) = \mu_i(x) \wedge R(x,x), \text{ for every } x \in X.$$

It is straightforward that for every $x \in X$, $\bar{\mu}(x) \leq \mu(x)$.
Further, we have that

$$\bar{\mu}(x) = \mu(x) \wedge R(x,x) \leq \bigvee_{z \in X} (\mu(z) \wedge R(z,x)) = \mu_1(x),$$

that is, $\bar{\mu} \subseteq \mu_1$. Analogously, we prove that for every i, $\bar{\mu}_i \subseteq \mu_{i+1}$.
On the other hand,

$$\bar{\mu}(x) = \mu(x) \wedge R(x,x) = \mu(x) \wedge R(x,x) \wedge R(x,x) \leq$$

$$\left(\bigvee_{z \in X} \mu(z) \wedge R(z,x) \right) \wedge R(x,x) = \mu_1(x) \wedge R(x,x) = \bar{\mu}_1(x),$$

and therefore $\bar{\mu} = \bar{\mu}_0 \subseteq \bar{\mu}_1$. Analogously, one can prove that for every i, $\bar{\mu}_i \subseteq \bar{\mu}_{i+1}$.
Thus, for every i we have that

$$\bar{\mu} = \bar{\mu}_0 \subseteq \bar{\mu}_{i-1} \subseteq \mu_i,$$

and therefore $\bar{\mu}$ is a lower bound of $\mathcal{S}_R^\mu$.   □

As commented above, the poset $(\mathcal{S}_R, \subseteq)$ is a complete lattice. As shown in [3], the set X represented by its characteristic function is closed under R, hence $X \in \mathcal{S}_R$.

Proposition 5. *Let R be a fuzzy binary relation on X and ν the fuzzy subset on X defined by*

$$\nu(x) = R(x,x).$$

Then, for any $\mu \in \mathcal{S}_R$, $\bar{\mu}$ belongs to $\mathcal{S}_R$ if and only if $\nu \in \mathcal{S}_R$.

Proof. Suppose that for any $\mu \in \mathcal{S}_R$, $\bar{\mu}$ belongs to $\mathcal{S}_R$. As mentioned above, $X \in \mathcal{S}_R$. Then by the present assumption, $\bar{X} \in \mathcal{S}_R$. But for every $x \in X$

$$\bar{X}(x) = X(x) \wedge R(x,x) = R(x,x) = \nu(x).$$

Thus, for any $x, y \in X$ we have that

$$\bar{X}(x) \wedge R(x,y) \leq \bar{X}(y)$$

or, which is equivalent,

$$\nu(x) \wedge R(x,y) \leq \nu(y).$$

Therefore, $\nu \in \mathcal{S}_R$.

Conversely, let us suppose that $\nu \in \mathcal{S}_R$. For any $\mu \in \mathcal{S}_R$ and any $x, y \in X$, we have that

$$\bar{\mu}(x) \wedge R(x,y) = \mu(x) \wedge R(x,x) \wedge R(x,y) = \mu(x) \wedge \nu(x) \wedge R(x,y).$$

As $\nu \in \mathcal{S}_R$, this is lower than or equal to

$$\mu(x) \wedge \nu(y) = \mu(x) \wedge R(y,y).$$

Thus, we have proven that

$$\bar{\mu}(x) \wedge R(x,y) \leq \mu(x) \wedge R(y,y).$$

Then,

$$\bar{\mu}(x) \wedge R(x,y) = \bar{\mu}(x) \wedge R(x,y) \wedge R(x,y) \leq \mu(x) \wedge R(x,y) \wedge R(y,y).$$

But $\mu \in \mathcal{S}_R$ and therefore,

$$\mu(x) \wedge R(x,y) \wedge R(y,y) \leq \mu(y) \wedge R(y,y) = \bar{\mu}(y).$$

Thus, for any $x, y \in X$ we have that

$$\bar{\mu}(x) \wedge R(x,y) \leq \bar{\mu}(y),$$

and therefore $\bar{\mu} \in \mathcal{S}_R$.   □

Corollary 1. *Let R be a fuzzy binary relation on X. For any $\mu \in \mathcal{S}_R$, we have that*

$$\bar{\mu} \in \mathcal{S}_R \text{ if and only if } \bar{X} \in \mathcal{S}_R.$$

Proof. Indeed, by the proof of Proposition 5, $\bar{X} = \nu$.   □

Corollary 2. *Let R be a fuzzy binary relation on X. For any $\mu \in \mathcal{S}_R$, we have that*

$$\bar{\mu} \in \mathcal{S}_R \text{ if and only if for all } x, y \in X, R(x,x) \wedge R(x,y) \leq R(y,y).$$

Proof. Straightforward by Proposition 5, since $R(x,x) \wedge R(x,y) \leq R(y,y)$ for all $x,y \in X$ is equivalent to require that $\nu \in \mathcal{S}_R$. $\square$

We are now able to describe some solutions of our inequations, which belong to the set of described lower bounds.

Corollary 3. *Let R be a fuzzy binary relation on X fulfilling the following weak-reflexivity condition:*

$$\text{For all } x,y \in X, \ R(x,y) \leq R(y,y).$$

Then, for any $\mu \in \mathcal{S}_R$, the lower bound $\bar{\mu}$ of $\mathcal{S}_R^\mu$ belongs to $\mathcal{S}_R$.

Proof. By weak-reflexivity R fulfils the condition imposed in Corollary 2. $\square$

Remark 2. Weak-reflexivity of R is a sufficient condition under which the lower bound $\bar{\mu}$ of $\mathcal{S}_R^\mu$ belongs to $\mathcal{S}_R$, but it is not necessary. Thus, for instance, the crisp binary relation

$$R = \begin{pmatrix} 0 & 1 \\ 1 & 0 \end{pmatrix}$$

is not weakly reflexive, but for $\mu \in \mathcal{S}_R$, we have that for every $x \in X$ $\bar{\mu}(x) = 0$ and therefore it belongs to $\mathcal{S}_R$.

Obviously, if R is reflexive, then it is weakly reflexive as well. Thus, reflexivity of R is another sufficient, but still not necessary condition under which $\bar{\mu} \in \mathcal{S}_R$ for any $\mu \in \mathcal{S}_R$.

Moreover, in this case for every $x \in X$, $\bar{\mu}(x) = \mu(x) \wedge R(x,x) = \mu(x)$. Thus, $\bar{\mu} = \cdots = \mu_n = \mu_{n-1} = \cdots = \mu_2 = \mu_1 = \mu$, that is, $\mathcal{S}_R^\mu = \{\mu\}$.

To sum up, we have shown that, dealing with inequation (1) and equation (2), we were able to find their solutions and a converging sequence of solutions, to prove existence of a solution in a finite case, and to connect solutions of both, equation and inequation. In addition, we have shown that there is an algorithm for the construction of a solution for the equality, and also we have given conditions under which some easy constructed bounds are solutions of the inequality in which the relation fulfils weak reflexivity.

It is possible to use our approach not only to deal with inequations, but also to find solutions of the equation (2) but this investigation is out of scope of this paper.

If we now switch to fuzzy controllers, then considering input and output values we get the following compositional rule of inference, which is obtained by the Mamdani approach:

$$\mu_{A \circ R}(y) = \bigvee_{x \in X} (\mu(x) \wedge R(x,y)). \tag{4}$$

Here the input values are represented by the fuzzy set μ, and the fuzzy relation R is deduced from the actual control process.

By our approach presented above, we can deal with this fuzzy control, by solving the inequations and equations appearing in this process. Obviously, every connected problem dealing with IF -THEN rules can be analyzed by our approach.

5   Conclusion

The paper deals with problems of solving particular inequations and equations, in the framework of fuzzy sets closed under a fuzzy relation on the same domain. This problem is closely connected with fuzzy control process. In this context, stability problems require further investigations of the solutions of relational equations we deal with. This is our task in the future.

Finally, using our approach we can deal with eigen fuzzy sets in the lattice valued framework (see, e.g., Sanches [11]). Applications of these are known in e.g., image analysis ([10]), which is also worth investigating by lattice-theoretic methods.

References

1. Bělohlávek, R.: Fuzzy Relational Systems. Kluwer Academic Publishers, Dordrecht (2002)
2. Bodenhofer, U.: A unified framework of opening and closure operators with respect to arbitrary fuzzy relations. Soft Computing 7, 220–227 (2003)
3. Bodenhofer, U., De Cock, M., Kerre, E.E.: Openings and closures of fuzzy pre-orderings: theoretical basics and applications to fuzzy rule-based systems. Int. J. General Systems. 32, 343–360 (2003)
4. Díaz, S., Montes, S., De Baets, B.: Transitive decomposition of fuzzy preference relations,: the case of nilpotent minimum. Kybernetika 40, 71–88 (2004)
5. Fuentes-González, R.: Down and up operators associated to fuzzy relations and t-norms: A definition of fuzzy semi-ideals. Fuzzy Sets and Systems 117, 377–389 (2001)
6. Gottwald, S.: Mathematical Fuzzy Control. A Survey of Some Recent Results. Logic Journal of IGPL 13(5), 525–541 (2005)
7. Ignjatović, J., Ćirić, M., Bogdanović, S.: On the greatest solutions to weakly linear systems of fuzzy relation inequalities and equations. Fuzzy Sets and Systems 161, 3081–3113
8. Jiménez, J., Montes, S., Šešelja, B., Tepavčević, A.: On lattice valued up-sets and down-sets. Fuzzy Sets and Systems 161, 1699–1710 (2010)
9. Klir, G.J., Yuan, B.: Fuzzy Sets and Fuzzy Logic. Prentice Hall, Upper Saddle River (1995)
10. Nobuhara, H., Bede, B., Hirota, K.: On various eigen fuzzy sets and their application to image reconstruction. Information Sciences 176, 2988–3010 (2006)
11. Sanchez, E.: Eigen Fuzzy Sets and Fuzzy Relations. Journal of Mathematical Analysis and Applications 81, 399–421 (1981)
12. Šešelja, B., Tepavčević, A.: Completion of Ordered Structures by Cuts of Fuzzy Sets, An Overview. Fuzzy Sets and Systems 136, 1–19 (2003)
13. Turunen, E.: Mathematics Behind Fuzzy Logic. Physica Verlag, Heidelberg (1999)

Fuzzy Autoepistemic Logic: Reflecting about Knowledge of Truth Degrees

Marjon Blondeel[1],[*], Steven Schockaert[2],[**],
Martine De Cock[2], and Dirk Vermeir[1]

[1] Dept. of Computer Science, Vrije Universiteit Brussel, Belgium
{mblondee,dvermeir}@vub.ac.be
[2] Dept. of Applied Mathematics and Computer Science, Ghent University, Belgium
{steven.schockaert,martine.decock}@ugent.be

Abstract. Autoepistemic logic is one of the principal formalisms for nonmonotonic reasoning. It extends propositional logic by offering the ability to reason about an agent's (lack of) knowledge or beliefs. Moreover, it is well known to generalize the stable model semantics of answer set programming. Fuzzy logics on the other hand are multi-valued logics, which allow to model the intensity with which a property is satisfied. We combine these ideas to a fuzzy autoepistemic logic which can be used to reason about one's knowledge about the degrees to which proporties are satisfied. In this paper we show that many properties from classical autoepistemic logic remain valid under this generalization and that the important relation between autoepistemic logic and answer set programming is preserved in the sense that fuzzy autoepistemic logic generalizes fuzzy answer set programming.

1 Introduction

Autoepistemic logic was introduced by Moore [16] as a way to reason about one's own beliefs. Later on (e.g. [15]), it was also seen as a tool to reflect about one's (lack of) knowledge. Consider for example my reason for believing that my sister smokes. If she smoked, I would have smelled it on her breath and I would believe she smoked: "smoke → breath" and "breath → B(smoke)", where B means "I believe". Now suppose I have never smelled anything, thus I do not believe that she smokes, then I can conclude that she does not smoke.

Since its introduction in the 1980s, autoepistemic logic has been one of the principal formalisms for nonmonotonic reasoning. It has also found important applications in logic programming. For example, Gelfond and Lifschitz [7] showed a connection between answer sets of logic programs and expansions of autoepistemic theories.

Fuzzy logics (e.g. [8]) are a class of logics, whose semantics are based on truth degrees that are taken from the unit interval [0, 1]. By admitting intermediary

---

[*] Funded by a joint Research Foundation-Flanders (FWO) project.
[**] Postdoctoral fellow of the Research Foundation-Flanders (FWO).

W. Liu (Ed.): ECSQARU 2011, LNAI 6717, pp. 616–627, 2011.

truth values between 0 and 1, the intensity with which some property holds can be encoded. From a practical point of view, fuzzy logics are thus useful to model knowledge of continuous domains in a logical way. For example, instead of saying that my sister smokes or not, a value between 0 and 1 can be given to specify how much she smokes. Reconsider the rule "smoke → breath", but in the setting of fuzzy logics. Then we may interpret this rule as "If she smoked a lot, her breath would smell often."

In this paper we combine the ideas of autoepistemic logic and fuzzy logics, which to the best of our knowledge, has not previously been considered. The resulting fuzzy autoepistemic logic is useful to reflect on one's beliefs (or knowledge) about the *degrees* to which some properties are satisfied. Consider for example my reason for not believing that my sister smokes *a lot*. If she smoked *a lot*, her breath would smell *often*. Since I do not smell it *often*, I do not believe she smokes *a lot*. Intuitively, if the truth value of $B\varphi$ is equal to c, this means that we only know that φ is true *at least* to degree c. Note in particular that the degrees of belief which we consider do not reflect strength of belief, but rather a Boolean form of belief in graded properties. Furthermore, note how this view generalizes the notion of belief from classical autoepistemic logic, in the sense that having $B\varphi$ false corresponds to having φ true to at least degree 0 and having $B\varphi$ true corresponds to having φ true at least to degree 1.

In this paper we show that many important proporties from classical autoepistemic logic remain valid when generalizing to fuzzy autoepistemic logic. We also prove that the relation between autoepistemic logic and answer set programming is preserved. In particular we show that the answer sets of a fuzzy answer set program correspond to the stable expansions of an associated fuzzy autoepistemic logic theory. The fact that this important relationship is preserved provides further insight into the nature of fuzzy answer set programming, and at the same time serves as a justification for the particular fuzzy autoepistemic logic we introduce in this paper.

The paper is structured as follows. In Section 2 the necessary background on autoepistemic logic and fuzzy logic is given. In Section 3 fuzzy autoepistemic logic is introduced, its properties are investigated and a motivating example is given. In Section 4, we briefly recall the basic notions of a fuzzy version of answer set programming which was recently proposed and we analyze the relation with fuzzy autoepistemic logic. We finish the paper by discussing related work and our conclusions in Sections 5 and 6.

2   Background

2.1   Autoepistemic Logic

The formulas of autoepistemic logic are built from a set of propositional atoms A using the usual propositional connectives and a modal operator B, interpreted as "is believed" (or "is known"). For example, if φ is a formula, then $B\varphi$ indicates that φ is believed. Also, $B(\neg\varphi)$ indicates that $\neg\varphi$ is believed and $\neg(B\varphi)$ that φ is not believed. We write L for the language of all propositional formulas over

A, and L_B for the extension of L with the modal operator B. As done in the literature (e.g. [13]), formulas from L are called *objective* and formulas from L_B are called *unimodal*. An *autoepistemic theory* is a set of unimodal formulas. We define $A' = A \cup \{B\varphi \mid \varphi \in L_B\}$, which is an infinite set, even if A is finite. For technical reasons, we sometimes treat A' as a set of atoms, and consider interpretations $I' \in \mathcal{P}(A')$, where $\mathcal{P}(X) = \{Y \mid Y \subseteq X\}$ for a set X. This trick allows us to deal with autoepistemic theories in a purely propositional fashion. For clarity, we will refer to the corresponding propositional language as L'.

The following definition was introduced by Moore [16] and is in line with Stalnaker's [20][1] view on the beliefs of a rational agent. For an arbitrary autoepistemic theory T, we can look for maximally conservative extensions which make it stable, in the sense that no more conclusions can be drawn from a stable theory than what is explicitly contained in it. Such extensions are called *stable expansions* of T.

Definition 1. *Suppose E and T are autoepistemic theories, then E is a stable expansion of T iff*

$$E = \mathrm{Cn}(T \cup \{B\varphi \mid \varphi \in E\} \cup \{\neg B\varphi \mid \varphi \notin E\}),$$

where $\mathrm{Cn}(X)$ denotes the set of propositional consequences of X w.r.t. the language L'.

Remark that Definition 1 says that a formula α is in E iff for each interpretation $I' \in \mathcal{P}(A')$ such that $I' \models T \cup \{B\varphi \mid \varphi \in E\} \cup \{\neg B\varphi \mid \varphi \notin E\}$ we have that $I' \models \alpha$. Moreover, the set of models of $T \cup \{B\varphi \mid \varphi \in E\} \cup \{\neg B\varphi \mid \varphi \notin E\}$ is exactly the set of models of E. By using Definition 1, the following proposition can be proved.

Proposition 1. *[14] Suppose T is a consistent autoepistemic theory. If all formulas in T are objective, then T has exactly one stable expansion.*

Autoepistemic logic can also be described in terms of models, more like a possible worlds semantics [17]. The relationship between this semantics and the one used in Definition 1 will become clear in Proposition 2. Suppose $I \in \mathcal{P}(A)$ is an interpretation on A and $S \subseteq \mathcal{P}(A)$ a set of interpretations on A. The corresponding satisfaction relation for unimodal formulas is defined inductively:

- For an atom p, $(I, S) \models p$ iff $p \in I$.
- For a unimodal formula φ, $(I, S) \models B\varphi$ iff for every $J \in S$, $(J, S) \models \varphi$.
- For unimodal formulas φ and ψ, the propositional connectives are handled in the usual way:
  - $(I, S) \models (\varphi \wedge \psi)$ iff $(I, S) \models \varphi$ and $(I, S) \models \psi$
  - $(I, S) \models (\varphi \vee \psi)$ iff $(I, S) \models \varphi$ or $(I, S) \models \psi$
  - $(I, S) \models (\neg\varphi)$ iff $(I, S) \not\models \varphi$
  - $(I, S) \models (\varphi \rightarrow \psi)$ iff $(I, S) \not\models \varphi$ or $(I, S) \models \psi$
  - $(I, S) \models (\varphi \leftrightarrow \psi)$ iff $(I, S) \models (\varphi \rightarrow \psi)$ and $(I, S) \models (\psi \rightarrow \varphi)$

---

[1] Article based on the unpublished manuscript (1980) to which Moore referred.

Intuitively, a unimodal formula φ is *believed* to be true, if it is true in every interpretation which is considered possible.

Definition 2. *Suppose T is an autoepistemic theory and S is a set of interpretations on A, then S is an* autoepistemic model *of T iff*

$$S = \{I \mid I \in \mathcal{P}(A), \forall \varphi \in T : (I, S) \models \varphi\}.$$

In other words, an autoepistemic model is a set of interpretations which model all formulas of T.

Definition 3. *Suppose S is a set of interpretations on A and T is an autoepistemic theory, then T is called the* (autoepistemic) theory *of S iff*

$$T = \{\varphi \mid \varphi \in L_{\mathrm{B}}, \forall I \in S : (I, S) \models \varphi\},$$

We will write $\mathrm{Th}(S)$ *to denote this set of formulas.*

The set $\mathrm{Th}(S)$ contains all formulas that are true in every interpretation in S. The following proposition describes the relation between stable expansions and autoepistemic models.

Proposition 2. *[17] Suppose T is an autoepistemic theory, then an autoepistemic theory E is a stable expansion of T iff $E = \mathrm{Th}(S)$ for some autoepistemic model S of T.*

We will now discuss the relationship between answer set programming [7] and autoepistemic logic. A brief refresher on answer set programming is provided in Appendix A. Gelfond and Lifschitz [7] proposed the following transformation from a program P to an autoepistemic theory $\lambda(P)$. For each rule $s \leftarrow a_1, \ldots, a_m, \mathrm{not}\ b_1, \ldots, \mathrm{not}\ b_n$ in P, the unimodal formula $a_1 \wedge \ldots \wedge a_m \wedge \neg \mathrm{B}b_1 \wedge \ldots \wedge \neg \mathrm{B}b_n \rightarrow s$ is added to $\lambda(P)$. The following result clarifies the relationship between the answer sets of P and the stable expansions of $\lambda(P)$.

Theorem 1. *[6],[7] A logic program P has an answer set[2] M iff $\lambda(P)$ has a stable expansion E such that $M = E \cap \mathcal{B}_P$.*

2.2 Fuzzy Logics

Fuzzy logics [8] are based on an infinite number of truth degrees, taken from the unit interval $[0, 1]$. We will consider fuzzy logics whose formulas are built from a set of atoms A, the truth constants in $[0, 1] \cap \mathbb{Q}$ and arbitrary n-ary connectives for each $n \in \mathbb{N}$. In particular, the semantics of logical conjunction can be generalized to $[0, 1]$ by a class of functions called *triangular norms* (short *t-norms*). These are mappings $\mathcal{T} : [0, 1]^2 \rightarrow [0, 1]$ which are symmetric, associative and increasing and which satisfy $\mathcal{T}(1, x) = x$ for all $x \in [0, 1]$.

---

[2] We refer to Appendix A for definitions and notations regarding answer set programming.

Given a t-norm $\mathcal{T}$, logical implication can be generalized by the *residuation* of $\mathcal{T}$, $x \rightarrow_{\mathcal{T}} y = \sup\{\lambda \mid \lambda \in [0,1] \text{ and } \mathcal{T}(x,\lambda) \leq y\}$. If $\mathcal{T}$ is a left-continuous t-norm we have the important property $x \rightarrow_{\mathcal{T}} y = 1$ iff $x \leq y$. By using the residuation it is possible to define a generalization of the logical equivalence $x \leftrightarrow_{\mathcal{T}} y = \min\{x \rightarrow_{\mathcal{T}} y, y \rightarrow_{\mathcal{T}} x\}$. Negation can be generalized by a decreasing map $\sim: [0,1] \rightarrow [0,1]$ satisfying $\sim 1 = 0$ and $\sim 0 = 1$. In what follows we will only use residual implicators based on left-continuous t-norms and if there is no confusion possible we will write $x \rightarrow y$ and $x \leftrightarrow y$.

An interpretation is a mapping $I : A \rightarrow [0,1]$, which is also called a *fuzzy set* on A. We can extend this interpretation as follows. Consider for each $n \in \mathbb{N}$ a finite set of n-ary connectives F_n and let $F = \cup F_n$. Each $f \in F_n$ is interpreted by a function $\mathbf{f} : [0,1]^n \rightarrow [0,1]$. We define $[f(\alpha_1,\ldots,\alpha_n)]_I = \mathbf{f}([\alpha_1]_I,\ldots,[\alpha_n]_I)$ for formulas α_i $(1 \leq i \leq n)$. For $c \in [0,1]$ we have $[c]_I = c$. If T is a set of formulas we say that I is a model of T iff $[\alpha]_I = 1$ for all $\alpha \in T$; we write this as $I \models T$.

In examples we will consider the connectives from Łukasiewicz logic, however all theorems can be proved for connectives $f \in F$. In the case of Łukasiewicz logic, the conjunction is defined as $x \otimes y = \max(x + y - 1, 0)$, which is a left-continuous t-norm. The disjunction is generalized by $x \oplus y = \min(x + y, 1)$. The implicator induced by the Łukasiewicz t-norm is $x \rightarrow_l y = \min(1, 1 - x + y)$ and for the negation we have $\neg x = 1 - x$.

3   Fuzzy Autoepistemic Logic

In this section, we combine the ideas of autoepistemic logic and fuzzy logics. This will provide us a tool to reason about one's beliefs about the degrees to which one or more properties are satisfied. Let us consider an example, for which we will use Łukasiewicz logic. Note that the main results in this section are valid for arbitrary connectives in F.

Example 1. Suppose we want to host a party for three persons. Since we do not know how much each guest will eat, it is not easy to determine how much food we need to order. Let us denote this latter amount by a variable a that ranges between ordering no food at all and ordering the maximum amount of food. Obviously, the correct value for a depends on the amount of food a_i $(i = 1,2,3)$ that we need to order for each individual guest. The variable a_i represents the proposition that person i eats a full portion. For an interpretation I, $I(a_i)$ denotes which percentage of a full portion person i eats. By appropriately rescaling the food quantities we can assume, without lack of generality, that $I(a_i) \in [0, \frac{1}{3}]$ for each graded interpretation I, such that it holds that $I \models a_1 \oplus a_2 \oplus a_3 \leftrightarrow_l a$ iff $I(a_1) + I(a_2) + I(a_3) = I(a)$. We thus consider the following formulas.

$$a_i \rightarrow_l \frac{1}{3} \tag{1}$$

$$a_1 \oplus a_2 \oplus a_3 \leftrightarrow_l a. \tag{2}$$

If no further information about the values a_i is known, it is best to make sure that everybody has enough food by ordering the maximum amount. By encoding additional beliefs we will try to refine this upper bound. Suppose we believe that everyone will eat at least a certain amount of food. We express this as

$$\mathrm{B}a_1 \leftrightarrow_l 0.1, \mathrm{B}a_2 \leftrightarrow_l 0.1, \mathrm{B}a_3 \leftrightarrow_l 0.05. \tag{3}$$

As in classical autoepistemic logic, we can treat formulas $\mathrm{B}\varphi$ as atoms. For each interpretation I, we then have that $I \models \mathrm{B}a_i \leftrightarrow_l c_i$ iff $[\mathrm{B}a_i]_I = c_i$. Later on, it will become more clear why including a formula such as $\mathrm{B}a_i \leftrightarrow_l c_i$ expresses a lower bound for the truth value of a_i. For each model I we have that $[\mathrm{B}a_i]_I = c_i$ implies $I(a_i) \geq c_i$.

Furthermore, we assume that if someone would eat an exceptional amount of food, we would have some information about this. For example, this could be the case if our friend brings her new boyfriend. If he would have an extreme appetite, we believe that she would have warned us. Insisting that we would know exactly how much each person would eat, i.e. $a_i \rightarrow_l \mathrm{B}a_i$, would be too strong. We may consider the following weaker variant however, which expresses that no guest will eat more than three times the amount mentioned in (3). We represent this meta-knowledge as follows:

$$a_i \rightarrow_l \mathrm{B}a_i \oplus \mathrm{B}a_i \oplus \mathrm{B}a_i. \tag{4}$$

Indeed, $I \models a_i \rightarrow_l \mathrm{B}a_i \oplus \mathrm{B}a_i \oplus \mathrm{B}a_i$ iff $I(a_i) \leq 3[\mathrm{B}a_i]_I$. In addition, we may be able to further decrease the amount of food that needs to be ordered if we know that some of the guests are on a diet. We will represent this by a variable d_i which represents the proposition that person i is on an extreme diet. If $I(d_i) = 0$, person i eats like he/she normally eats and if $I(d_i) = 1$, he/she will eat the amount mentioned in (3). Suppose we have information on d_2 and d_3, but no knowledge on d_1:

$$\mathrm{B}d_2 \leftrightarrow_l 0.95, \mathrm{B}d_3 \leftrightarrow_l 0.95. \tag{5}$$

If the lower bound for d_i increases, the upper bound for a_i should decrease. Consider for instance the meta-knowledge

$$\mathrm{B}d_i \rightarrow_l (a_i \rightarrow_l \mathrm{B}a_i). \tag{6}$$

Remark that this expression is equivalent to $a_i \rightarrow_l (\mathrm{B}d_i \rightarrow_l \mathrm{B}a_i)$, thus $I \models \mathrm{B}d_i \rightarrow_l (a_i \rightarrow_l \mathrm{B}a_i)$ iff $I(a_i) \leq 1 + [\mathrm{B}a_i]_I - [\mathrm{B}d_i]_I$.

In example 4, we will use fuzzy autoepistemic logic to determine an upper bound for $I(a)$ for a model I.

The formulas in fuzzy autoepistemic logic are built from a set A (atoms and constants in $[0,1] \cap \mathbb{Q}$), the set of connectives F with their corresponding functions $\mathbf{f} : [0,1]^n \rightarrow [0,1]$ $(n \in \mathbb{N})$ and a modal operator B, interpreted as "is believed". We will denote this language as $\overline{L}_{\mathrm{B}}$. Again, we will make the distinction between objective and unimodal formulas. An *autoepistemic theory in* $\overline{L_B}$ is a set of formulas in $\overline{L_B}$. As before, we define $A' = A \cup \{B\varphi \mid \varphi \in \overline{L_B}\}$. We write $\mathcal{F}(A')$ for the set of all fuzzy sets on A', i.e. the set of all graded interpretations I' over A'. We define a generalization of stable expansions (Definition 1).

Definition 4. *Suppose T is an autoepistemic theory in $\overline{L_B}$ and E is a fuzzy set on $\overline{L_B}$. E is a* fuzzy stable expansion *of T iff for each $\alpha \in \overline{L_B}$*

$$E(\alpha) = \inf\left\{[\alpha]_{I'} \mid I' \models T \cup \{B\varphi \leftrightarrow E(\varphi) \mid \varphi \in \overline{L_B}\}, I' \in \mathcal{F}(A')\right\}$$

In Definition 1, for each $I' \in \mathcal{P}(A')$ such that $I' \models T \cup \{B\varphi \mid \varphi \in E\} \cup \{\neg B\varphi \mid \varphi \notin E\}$ we had that $B\varphi \in I'$ iff $\varphi \in E$. To see the relation between Definitions 1 and 4, note that I' is a model of $B\varphi \leftrightarrow E(\varphi)$ iff $[B\varphi]_{I'} = E(\varphi)$.

Remark that for a fuzzy stable expansion E of T and $I', J' \in \{I' \mid I' \models T \cup \{B\varphi \leftrightarrow E(\varphi) \mid \varphi \in L_B\}, I' \in \mathcal{F}(A')\}$ we have that $[B\alpha]_{I'} = E(\alpha) \leq [\alpha]_{J'}$. Hence, $[B\alpha]_{I'} = 0.1$ intuively means that α is true to at least degree 0.1, instead of believing that α is true to exactly degree 0.1.

We can also generalize Definitions 2 and 3. First, we need to define another type of evaluation for unimodal formulas. Suppose $I \in \mathcal{F}(A)$ is an interpretation and $S \subseteq \mathcal{F}(A)$ is a set of interpretations.

- For an atom or a constant p: $[p]_{I,S} = I(p)$.
- For a unimodal formula α: $[B\alpha]_{I,S} = \inf_{J \in S}[\alpha]_{J,S}$.
- For unimodal formulas α_i $(1 \leq i \leq n)$ and $f \in F_n$:
  $[f(\alpha_1, \ldots, \alpha_n)]_{I,S} = f([\alpha_1]_{I,S}, \ldots, [\alpha_n]_{I,S})$.

Definition 5. *Suppose T is an autoepistemic theory in $\overline{L_B}$ and $S \subseteq \mathcal{F}(A)$ is a set of interpretations. S is a* fuzzy autoepistemic model *of T iff*

$$S = \{I \mid I \in \mathcal{F}(A), \forall \varphi \in T : [\varphi]_{I,S} = 1\}.$$

Example 2. Suppose $T = \{\neg(Ba) \rightarrow_l b, \neg(Bb) \rightarrow_l a\}$. We try to find a fuzzy autoepistemic model S of T. For the first formula of T we have for $S \subseteq \mathcal{F}(A)$ and $I \in S$ that $[\neg(Ba) \rightarrow_l b]_{I,S} = 1 \Leftrightarrow 1 - [Ba]_{I,S} \leq I(b) \Leftrightarrow 1 - I(b) \leq \inf_{J \in S} J(a)$. By symmetry we have $[\neg(Bb) \rightarrow_l a]_{I,S} = 1 \Leftrightarrow 1 - I(a) \leq \inf_{J \in S} J(b)$.

Hence, a set of interpretations S is a fuzzy autoepistemic model of T iff $S = \{I \mid I \in \mathcal{F}(A), 1 - I(b) \leq \inf_{J \in S} J(a)$ and $1 - I(a) \leq \inf_{J \in S} J(b)\}$. Moreover, we can show that the fuzzy autoepistemic models of T are all sets of the form $S_x = \{I \mid I \in \mathcal{F}(A), I(a) \geq x$ and $I(b) \geq 1 - x\}$, with $x \in [0, 1]$.

Definition 6. *Suppose $S \subseteq \mathcal{F}(A)$ is a set of interpretations. The* fuzzy autoepistemic theory *of S is the fuzzy set $\mathrm{Th}(S)$ on $\overline{L_B}$ such that for each unimodal formula φ*

$$\mathrm{Th}(S)(\varphi) = \inf_{I \in S}[\varphi]_{I,S}.$$

We can prove the following generalizations of Propositions 1 and 2.

Proposition 3. *Suppose T is an autoepistemic theory in $\overline{L_B}$. A fuzzy set E on $\overline{L_B}$ is a fuzzy stable expansion of T iff $E = \mathrm{Th}(S)$ with S a fuzzy autoepistemic model of T.*

Example 3. Reconsider the theory T from Example 2 and recall that all fuzzy autoepistemic models are of the form $S_x = \{I \mid I(a) \geq x \text{ and } I(b) \geq 1 - x\}$. Hence, for each $x \in [0,1]$ we have a fuzzy stable expansion E_x defined by $E_x(a) = \text{Th}(S_x)(a) = \inf_{I \in S_x} I(a) = x$ and $E_x(b) = \text{Th}(S_x)(b) = \inf_{I \in S_x} I(b) = 1 - x$.

Proposition 4. *Suppose T is a consistent set of objective formulas in $\overline{L_B}$, then there is exactly one fuzzy set E on $\overline{L_B}$ that is a fuzzy stable expansion of T.*

Example 4. Reconsider Example 1. Based on the formulas (2)-(6), an upper bound for $I(a)$ (I a model) can be derived. This is accomplished by determining the fuzzy autoepistemic models of the corresponding autoepistemic theory T. Suppose $S \subseteq \mathcal{F}(A)$, then we determine which conditions need to be satisfied for $I \in S$ such that S is a fuzzy autoepistemic model of T:

$$I(a_i) \leq \tfrac{1}{3}$$
$$I(a_1) + I(a_2) + I(a_3) = I(a)$$
$$[Ba_1]_{I,S} = 0.1, [Ba_2]_{I,S} = 0.1, [Ba_3]_{I,S} = 0.05$$
$$I(a_i) \leq 3[Ba_i]_{I,S}$$
$$[Bd_2]_{I,S} = 0.95, [Bd_3]_{I,S} = 0.95$$
$$[Bd_i]_{I,S} \leq 1 - I(a_i) + [Ba_i]_{I,S}$$

For example, let us compute the upper bound for $I(a_2)$. Without the knowledge about the diet, we know that $I(a_2) \leq 0.3$. If we include our beliefs about d_2, we get a much lower upper bound 0.15.

One can easily verify that there is exactly one fuzzy autoepistemic model

$$S = \{I \mid 0.1 \leq I(a_1) \leq 0.3, 0.1 \leq I(a_2) \leq 0.15, 0.05 \leq I(a_3) \leq 0.10,$$
$$I(d_1) \geq 0, I(d_2) \geq 0.95, I(d_3) \geq 0.95, 0.25 \leq I(a) \leq 0.55\}.$$

We thus believe that the amount of food that will be needed is between 0.25 and 0.55. Hence we will order 55% of the maximal order. Note that this means that we can express the lower bound on a as $E(Ba) = 0.25$ and the upper bound as $E(\neg B(\neg a)) = 0.55$, where $E = \text{Th}(S)$ is the unique stable expansion of T.

4   Relation between Fuzzy Answer Set Programming and Fuzzy Autoepistemic Logic

Let us briefly recall the basic notion of a fuzzy version of answer set programming, which was recently proposed [10]. Consider a set of atoms A. Here, a *literal* is either an atom $a \in A$ or an expression of the form not a, where $a \in A$ and not is the negation-as-failure operator. A rule over $[0,1]$ is an expression of the form $r : a \leftarrow f(b_1, \ldots, b_n)$ where $a \in A$, b_i $(1 \leq i \leq n)$ are literals, $\leftarrow$ corresponds to a residual implicator and $f \in F_n$. To assure the existence of a unique answer set we need to restrict to connectives f such that $\mathbf{f}$ is increasing in each argument. Typically $\mathbf{f}$ corresponds to the application of conjunctions and disjunctions in a given fuzzy logic. We will refer to the rule by its label r. The atom a is called the head of r and $f(b_1, \ldots, b_n)$ is the body. A *FASP program* over $[0,1]$ is a set of rules over $[0,1]$. We denote the set of atoms occurring in a FASP program as $\mathcal{B}_P$. An *interpretation* I of a FASP program P is a mapping $I : \mathcal{B}_P \to [0,1]$. We can extend this mapping as follows:

- $[c]_I = c$ for $c \in [0,1]$,
- $[\text{not } a]_I = \sim ([a]_I)$ for atoms a and a negator $\sim$,
- $[f(b_1, \ldots b_n)]_I = \mathbf{f}([b_1]_I, \ldots [b_n]_I)$ for bodies of rules,
- $[r]_I = ([r_b]_I \to I(r_h))$, for a rule $r : r_h \leftarrow r_b$.

For interpretations I_1 and I_2 we say that $I_1 \leq I_2$ iff $I_1(a) \leq I_2(a)$ for all $a \in \mathcal{B}_P$. An interpretation I is called a *model* of P iff $[r]_I = 1$ for all $r \in P$. Finally we say that a FASP program is *simple* if it contains no literals of the form not a. For such programs there exists a unique minimal model.

Definition 7. *[10] Consider a simple FASP program P. An interpretation I of P is called the* answer set *of P iff it is the minimal model of P.*

For programs which are not simple, answer sets are defined using a generalization of the Gelfond-Lifschitz reduct (see Appendix A). Specifically, let P be a FASP program and I an interpretation of P. The *reduct* of a literal l w.r.t. I is defined as follows. If l is an atom then $l^I = l$, if $l = \text{not } a$ then $l^I = [l]_I$. The reduct of a rule in P, $r : a \leftarrow f(b_1, \ldots, b_n)$ is defined as $r^I : a^I \leftarrow f(b_1^I, \ldots, b_n^I)$. The reduct of the program P is the set of rules $P^I = \{r^I \mid r \in P\}$.

Definition 8. *[10] Consider a FASP program P. An interpretation I of P is called an* answer set *of P iff I is the answer set of P^I.*

In this section we will show a correspondence between answer sets of a FASP program P and fuzzy stable expansions of an associated autoepistemic theory in $\overline{L}_\mathrm{B}$. From Theorem 1, we already know that such a correspondence exists between classical ASP and autoepistemic logic. Here we use a similar transformation. Suppose we have a FASP program P with rules of the form

$$r : a \leftarrow f(b_1, \ldots, b_n, \text{not } c_1, \ldots, \text{not } c_m),$$

where a, b_i and c_j are atoms $(1 \leq i \leq n), (1 \leq j \leq m)$ and $f \in F_{n+m}$. We define a set of implications in fuzzy autoepistemic logic. Specifically, for rule r we define the associated fuzzy autoepistemic formula $\lambda(r)$ as

$$f(b_1, \ldots, b_n, \sim_1 \mathrm{B}c_1, \ldots, \sim_m \mathrm{B}c_m) \to a.$$

We choose $\sim_i$ as the negator which is assumed for not c_i, thus for $I \in \mathcal{F}(\mathcal{B}_P)$, we have $[\text{not } c_i]_I = \sim_i (I(c_i))$. The resulting autoepistemic theory in $\overline{L}_\mathrm{B}$ is $\lambda(P) = \{\lambda(r) \mid r \in P\}$.

First, we provide a lemma that characterizes the relationship between stable expansions of $\lambda(P)$ and stable expansions of the autoepistemic theory corresponding to a specific reduct of the program P. Note that we use the notation $E_{|\mathcal{B}_P}$ for the restriction of the fuzzy set E on $\overline{L}_\mathrm{B}$ to $\mathcal{B}_P$.

Lemma 1. *Consider a FASP program P and a fuzzy set E on $\overline{L_\mathbf{B}}$. Then E is a fuzzy stable expansion of $\lambda(P)$ iff E is a stable expansion of $\lambda(P^{\bar{E}})$, where $\bar{E} = E_{|\mathcal{B}_P}$.*

Theorem 2. *Consider a FASP program P. M is an answer set of P iff $\lambda(P)$ has a fuzzy stable expansion E such that $E_{|\mathcal{B}_P} = M$.*

Example 5. Consider the logic program $P = \{b \leftarrow_l \text{ not } a, a \leftarrow_l \text{ not } b\}$. We will compute the answer sets by using the characterization from Theorem 2. We look for fuzzy stable expansions of $\lambda(P) = \{\neg \mathbf{B}a \rightarrow_l b, \neg \mathbf{B}b \rightarrow_l a\}$. Remark that this is the theory T we studied in Examples 2 and 3. Hence we know that for each $x \in [0,1]$ there is a fuzzy stable expansion $\text{Th}(S_x)$, with $S_x = \{I \mid I(a) \geq x \text{ and } I(b) \geq 1 - x\}$. Hence for each $x \in [0,1]$ there is an answer set M_x such that $M_x(a) = \text{Th}(S)(a) = \inf_{I \in S_x} I(a) = x$ and $M_x(b) = \text{Th}(S)(b) = \inf_{I \in S_x} I(b) = 1 - x$.

5 Related Work

Epistemic logic, the logic of epistemic notions such as knowledge and belief, is a major area of research in artifical intelligence. Von Wright's seminal work [22] is widely recognized as having initiated the formal study of epistemic logic as we know it today. Since then, various axiomatizations have been proposed, mainly in terms of possible-worlds semantics. An overview is given in [19]. Note that in general, epistemic logics may allow to model the beliefs of several agents, whereas autoepistemic logic is restricted to one's own beliefs. Autoepistemic logic has been important as an epistemic foundation for answer set set programming, which has also been studied from the angle of possibilistic logic [2], [4].

In recent years a variety of approaches to fuzzy answer set programming have been proposed, e.g. [3], [10], [21]. In [18] a fuzzy equilibrium logic was introduced, and a correspondence between fuzzy equilibrium logic models and answer sets of FASP programs was shown. Apart from this exception and our paper, it appears that little work has been done on nonmonotonic fuzzy logics nor about their relationship with fuzzy answer set programming.

We remark that fuzzy autoepistemic logic is also related to some work on fuzzy modal logics, see e.g. [9]. Another relevant paper is [1], where an epistemic modal logic is defined which is inspired by possibilistic logic. In this logic, interpretations are also sets of classical interpretations. Finally, there has also work been done on (finite) many-valued modal logics [11] and (finite) many-valued reflexive autoepistemic logic [12]. Instead of $[0,1]$, finite Heyting algebras are used for the space of truth values. Finitely-valued Gödel logic (truth values $\{0, \frac{1}{n}, \frac{2}{n}, \ldots 1\}$) is a particular case of such algebras.

6 Conclusions

In this paper we have introduced a fuzzy version of autoepistemic logic, which can be used to reason about one's beliefs about the degrees to which properties are satisfied. We have shown that important properties of classical autoepistemic logic are preserved and that the relation between answer set programming and autoepistemic logic remains valid when generalizing to fuzzy logics. These results lead to a better comprehension of how to interpret fuzzy answer sets.

In future work, it would be interesting to see whether the implementation of classical autoepistemic logic by using quantified boolean formulas [5] can be extended to fuzzy logics using multi-level linear programming. If this is indeed the case, it could be used as a basis to implement fuzzy autoepistemic logic reasoners, as well as fuzzy answer set programming solvers. The general theory of fuzzy autoepistemic logic is also useful for abductive reasoning about theories with gradual propositions.

References

1. Banerjee, M., Dubois, D.: A simple modal logic for reasoning about revealed beliefs. In: Proceedings of the 10th European Conference on Symbolic and Quantitative Approaches to Reasoning with Uncertainty, pp. 805–816 (2009)
2. Bauters, K., Schockaert, S., De Cock, M., Vermeir, D.: Possibilistic answer set programming revisited. In: Proceedings of the 26th Conference on Uncertainty in Artificial Intelligence (2010)
3. Damásio, C.V., Medina, J., Ojeda-Aciego, M.: Sorted multi-adjoint logic programs: termination results and applications. In: Proceedings of the 9th European Conference on Logics in Artificial Intelligence, pp. 260–273 (2004)
4. Dubois, D., Prade, H., Schockaert, S.: Règles et méta-règles dans le cadre de la théorie des possibilités et de la logique possibiliste. In: Rencontres Francophones sur la Logique Floue et ses Applications, pp. 115–122 (2010)
5. Egly, U., Eiter, T., Tompits, H., Woltran, S.: Solving advanced reasoning tasks using quantified boolean formulas. In: Proceedings of the Seventeenth National Conference on Artificial Intelligence and Twelfth Conference on Innovative Applications of Artificial Intelligence, pp. 417–422 (2000)
6. Gelfond, M.: On stratified autoepistemic theories. In: Proceedings of the Sixth National Conference on Artificial Intelligence, pp. 207–211 (1987)
7. Gelfond, M., Lifschitz, V.: The stable model semantics for logic programming. In: Proceedings of the Fifth International Conference and Symposiom on Logic Programming, pp. 1070–1080 (1988)
8. Hajek, P.: Metamathematics of Fuzzy Logic. Springer, Heidelberg (2001)
9. Hajek, P.: On fuzzy modal logics. Fuzzy Sets and Systems 161, 18 (2010)
10. Janssen, J., Schockaert, S., Vermeir, D., De Cock, M.: General fuzzy answer set programs. In: Proceedings of the International Workshop on Fuzzy Logic and Applications, pp. 353–359 (2009)
11. Koutras, C.D., Koletsos, G., Zachos, S.: Many-valued modal non-monotonic reasoning: Sequential stable sets and logics with linear truth spaces. Fundamenta Informaticae 38(3), 281–324 (1999)
12. Koutras, C.D., Zachos, S.: Many-valued reflexive autoepistemic logic. Logic Journal of the IGPL 8(1), 403–418 (2000)
13. Lifschitz, V., Schwarz, G.: Extended logic programs as autoepistemic theories. In: Proceedings of the Second International Workshop on Logic Programming and Nonmonotonic Reasoning, pp. 101–114 (1993)

14. Marek, W.: Stable theories in autoepistemic logic. Unpublished note, Department of Computer Science, University of Kentucky (1986)
15. Marek, W., Truszczynski, M.: Autoepistemic logic. Journal of the Association for Computing Machinery 38(3), 587–618 (1991)
16. Moore, R.C.: Semantical considerations on nonmonotonic logic. In: Proceedings of the Eighth International Joint Conference on Artificial Intelligence, pp. 272–279 (1983)
17. Moore, R.C.: Possible-world semantics in autoepistemic logic. In: Proceedings of the Non-Monotonic Reasoning Workshop, pp. 344–354 (1984)
18. Schockaert, S., Janssen, J., Vermeir, D., De Cock, M.: Answer sets in a fuzzy equilibrium logic. In: Proceedings of the 3rd International Conference on Web Reasoning and Rule Systems, pp. 135–149 (2009)
19. Sim, K.M.: Epistemic logic and logical omniscience: A survey. International Journal of Intelligent Systems 12, 57–81 (1997)
20. Stalnaker, R.: A note on non-monotonic modal logic. Artificial Intelligence 64(2), 183–196 (1993)
21. Straccia, U.: Annotated answer set programming. In: Proceedings of the 11th International Conference on Information Processing and Management of Uncertainty in Knowledge-Based Systems (2006)
22. von Wright, G.: An Essay in Modal Logic. In: Studies in Logic and the Foundations of Mathematics. North-Holland Pub. Co., Amsterdam (1951)

A   Answer Set Programming (ASP)

We define a literal as either an atom or an atom preceded by not, the *negation-as-failure* operator. Intuitively, we say that not a is true if there is no proof to support atom a. If X is a set of atoms, we define not $(X) = \{$not $a \mid a \in X\}$. A *normal rule* is an expression of the form $a \leftarrow (\alpha \cup$ not $(\beta))$, with a an atom and α and β sets of atoms. The atom a is called the *head* of the rule and $\alpha \cup$ not (β) (interpreted as conjunction) is the *body*.

A *normal program* P is a finite set of normal rules. The *Herbrand base* $\mathcal{B}_P$ of P is the set of atoms occuring in P. An *interpretation* I of P is any set of atoms $I \subseteq \mathcal{B}_P$. A *simple rule* is a normal rule without negation-as-failure. A *simple program* is a finite set of simple rules. If an interpretation I is the minimal model of P (i.e. the minimal interpretation such that $[r]_I = 1$ for each $r \in P$), then we say that I is the *answer set* of P. Thus, the answer set of a simple program P is the maximal set of atoms that can be deduced from P. For programs that are not simple, answer sets are defined using the Gelfond-Lifschitz reduct. Suppose P is a normal program, the *Gelfond-Lifschitz reduct* [7] of P w.r.t. the interpretation I is the set $P^I = \{a \leftarrow \alpha \mid (a \leftarrow (\alpha \cup$ not $(\beta)) \in P, \beta \cap I = \emptyset\}$, which is a simple program. We then say that I is an *answer set* of P iff I is the answer set of P^I.

Note that simple programs have exactly one answer set, while normal programs can have 0, 1 or more answer sets.

Belief Functions on MV-Algebras of Fuzzy Events Based on Fuzzy Evidence

T. Flaminio, L. Godo, and E. Marchioni

IIIA, Artificial Intelligence Research Institute
CSIC, Spanish National Research Council
Campus de la Univ. Autònoma de Barcelona s/n
08193 Bellaterra, Spain
{tommaso,godo,enrico}@iiia.csic.es

Abstract. Recently Kroupa has proposed a generalization of belief functions on MV-algebras, the latter being the chosen algebraic setting for fuzzy (or many-valued) events. However, Kroupa's belief functions evaluate the degree of belief in the occurrence of fuzzy events by taking into account (weighted) evidence on classical subsets. In other words, the focal elements, used in determining the degree of belief, are classical sets. Within the MV-algebraic setting, the aim of the present work is to introduce a generalization of Kroupa belief functions that allows to deal with fuzzy events supported by evidence on fuzzy subsets.

1 Introduction

Classical belief functions [18,20] are measures of uncertainty that represent our degree of confidence in the occurrence of some (classical) event taking into account the bodies of evidence that support our belief [18]. Such evidence plays a pivotal role in determining our belief. Indeed, the degree of belief is determined by those weights assigned to the different bodies of evidence. In Dempster-Shafer theory, such evidence is encoded by the focal elements, and their weight is given by a mass function (a probability distribution over the focal elements).

In the literature several attempts to extend belief functions on fuzzy events can be found. The first extension of Dempster-Shafer theory to the general framework of fuzzy set theory was proposed by Zadeh in the context of information granularity and possibility theory [24] in the form of an expected conditional necessity. After Zadeh, several further generalizations were proposed depending on the way a measure of *inclusion among fuzzy sets* is used to define the belief functions of fuzzy events based on fuzzy evidence. Indeed, given a mass assignment m for the bodies of evidence $\{A_1, A_2, \ldots\}$, and a measure $I(A \subseteq B)$ of inclusion among fuzzy sets, the belief of a fuzzy set B can be defined in general by the value: $Bel(B) = \sum_{A_i} I(A_i \subseteq B) \cdot m(A_i)$. We refer the reader to [13,21] for exhaustive surveys, and [1] for another approach through fuzzy subsethood. Different definitions were also introduced by Dubois and Prade [7] and by Denœux [4,5] to deal with belief functions ranging over intervals or fuzzy numbers.

W. Liu (Ed.): ECSQARU 2011, LNAI 6717, pp. 628–639, 2011.

More recently Kroupa [15] has proposed to define belief functions on semisimple MV-algebras [3], the latter being the chosen algebraic setting for fuzzy (or many-valued) events. However, Kroupa's belief functions evaluate the degree of belief in the occurrence of fuzzy events by taking into account (weighted) evidence on classical subsets. In other words, the focal elements used in determining the degree of belief are still classical sets.

In this work, we want to keep the MV-algebraic setting and generalize Kroupa belief functions to deal with fuzzy events with the support of evidence represented by fuzzy subsets. We rely on MV-algebras, because such structures are the equivalent algebraic semantics for the infinite valued Łukasiewicz logic, and hence, studying belief functions in this setting will be useful to develop a logical approach to extend and generalize that one proposed in [11].

This paper is organized as follows. In the next section, we provide basic background information on belief functions and MV-algebras. In Section 3, we introduce our generalized notion of a belief function and compare it to Kroupa's definition. In Section 4, we give an integral representation of belief functions in terms of both Choquet and Sugeno integrals, and in Section 5, we briefly deal with the combination of two belief functions. We end with some final remarks.

2   Preliminary Notions

2.1   Belief Functions on Boolean Algebras

Consider a finite set X whose elements can be regarded as mutually exclusive (and exhaustive) propositions of interest, and whose powerset $\mathcal{P}(X)$ represents all such propositions. The set X is usually called the *frame of discernment*, and every element $x \in X$ represents the lowest level of discernible information we can deal with.

Take now a frame of discernment X. A map $m : \mathcal{P}(X) \to [0, 1]$ is said to be a *basic belief assignment*, or a *mass assignment* whenever $m(\emptyset) = 0$ and $\sum_{A \in \mathcal{P}(X)} m(A) = 1$. Given a set X and a mass assignment m on $\mathcal{P}(X)$, for every $A \in \mathcal{P}(X)$, the *belief of A* is defined as

$$\mathbf{b}_m(A) = \sum_{B \subseteq A} m(B).$$

Every mass assignment m on $\mathcal{P}(X)$ is in fact a probability distribution on $\mathcal{P}(X)$ that naturally induces a probability measure P_m on $\mathcal{P}(\mathcal{P}(X))$. Consequently, the belief function $\mathbf{b}_m$ defined from m can be equivalently described as follows: for every $A \in \mathcal{P}(X)$, $\mathbf{b}_m(A) = P_m(\{B \in \mathcal{P}(X) : B \subseteq A\})$. Therefore, identifying the set $\{B \in \mathcal{P}(X) : B \subseteq A\}$ with its characteristic function on $\mathcal{P}(\mathcal{P}(X))$ defined by

$$\beta_A : B \in \mathcal{P}(X) \mapsto \begin{cases} 1 & \text{if } B \subseteq A \\ 0 & \text{otherwise,} \end{cases} \tag{1}$$

it is easy to see that, for every $A \in \mathcal{P}(X)$, and for every mass assignment $m : \mathcal{P}(X) \to [0, 1]$, we have $\mathbf{b}_m(A) = P_m(\beta_A)$. This easy characterization will be important when we discuss the extensions of belief functions on MV-algebras.

The following is a trivial observation about the map β_A that can be useful to understand our generalization: for every $A \in \mathcal{P}(A)$, β_A can be regarded as a map evaluating the (strict) inclusion of B into A, for every subset B of X.

A subset A of X such that $m(A) > 0$ is said to be a *focal element*. Every belief function is characterized by the value that m takes over its focal elements, and, therefore, the focal elements of a belief function $\mathbf{b}_m$ contain the pieces of evidence that characterize $\mathbf{b}_m$ itself. For every set X and for every mass assignment m, call $\mathfrak{F}_m$ the set of focal elements of $\mathcal{P}(X)$ with respect to m. It is well known that several subclasses of belief functions can be characterized just by the structure of their focal elements. In particular, when $\mathfrak{F}_m \subseteq \{\{x\} : x \in X\}$, it is clear that $\mathbf{b}_m$ is a probability measure. Moreover, if the focal elements are nested subsets of X, i.e. $\mathfrak{F}_m$ is a chain with respect to the inclusion relation between sets, then $\mathbf{b}_m$ is a *necessity measure* [7,18]; this means e.g. that in that case $\mathbf{b}_m(A_1 \cap A_2) = \min\{\mathbf{b}_m(A_1), \mathbf{b}_m(A_2)\}$.

2.2   MV-Algebras and States

An MV-algebra is a structure $M = (M, \oplus, \neg, 0)$ of type $(2, 1, 0)$ where M is a non-empty set, the reduct $(M, \oplus, 0)$ is an abelian monoid, and the following equations are satisfied: $\neg\neg x = x$, $x \oplus \neg 0 = \neg 0$, $\neg(\neg x \oplus y) = \neg(\neg y \oplus x)$.

The class of MV-algebras forms a variety that we denote by $\mathbb{MV}$. In every MV-algebra M, we define, as usual, the following operations: for all $x, y \in M$, $x \odot y = \neg(\neg x \oplus \neg y)$, $x \Rightarrow y = \neg x \oplus y$, $x \vee y = (x \Rightarrow y) \Rightarrow y$, $x \wedge y = \neg(\neg x \vee \neg y)$, and $1 = \neg 0$.

For every $x, y \in M$, $x \leq y$ if and only if $x \Rightarrow y = 1$. As a matter of fact, $\leq$ is a partial order on M, and M is said to be linearly ordered (or an MV-chain) whenever $\leq$ is a linear order.

Example 1. (1) Every Boolean algebra A is an MV-algebra and in every MV-algebra M the set $B(M) = \{x : x \oplus x = x\}$ of its idempotent elements is the domain of the largest Boolean subalgebra of M, called the *Boolean skeleton* of M.

(2) Take the following operations defined over $[0, 1]$: $x \oplus y = \min\{1, x + y\}$ and $\neg x = 1 - x$. Then, the structure $[0, 1]_{MV} = ([0, 1], \oplus, \neg, 0)$ is an MV-algebra called the *standard* MV-algebra. In this algebra $x \odot y = \max(0, x + y - 1)$, $x \Rightarrow y = \min(1, 1 - x + y)$, $x \wedge y = \min(x, y)$ and $x \vee y = \max(x, y)$. Chang Theorem (cf. [3]) shows that the algebra $[0, 1]_{MV}$ generates $\mathbb{MV}$.

For every finite set X, consider the MV-algebra $[0, 1]^X$ of all functions from X into $[0, 1]$, whose operations are defined by a pointwise application of those of $[0, 1]_{MV}$. These MV-algebras are the algebraic framework over which we will define belief functions. Adopting the same notation of [10], we call such algebras *finite domain MV-clans*. Notice that finite domain MV-clans are described, in algebraic terms, as those MV-algebras which are finite direct product of the standard MV-algebra $[0, 1]_{MV}$.

From now on, we will assume that, in any structure $M = [0, 1]^X$, the set X is finite, if not otherwise specified.

By a state [17] on an MV-algebra M, we mean a map $\mathbf{s} : M \rightarrow [0,1]$ satisfying the following properties:

(i) $\mathbf{s}(1) = 1$,
(ii) whenever $x \odot y = 0$, $\mathbf{s}(x \oplus y) = \mathbf{s}(x) + \mathbf{s}(y)$.

Mundici proved in [17] that every state $\mathbf{s}$ satisfies $\mathbf{s}(x \vee y) = \mathbf{s}(x) + \mathbf{s}(y) - \mathbf{s}(x \wedge y)$.

It is worth noticing that the restriction of every state $\mathbf{s}$ on M, to its Boolean skeleton $B(M)$, is a finitely additive probability. Moreover the following holds:

Theorem 1 ([14]). *Let be X be a non-empty (possibly infinite) set. For every state $\mathbf{s}$ on the MV-algebra of functions $M = [0,1]^X$ there exists a finitely additive probability measure μ on $\mathcal{P}(X)$ such that for each $a \in M$,*

$$\mathbf{s}(a) = \int_X a \, d\mu.$$

3   Belief Functions on Finite Domain MV-Clans

In [15], Kroupa provides a generalization of belief functions that are defined on finite domain MV-clans as follows. Let $M = [0,1]^X$ be a finite domain MV-clan, denote by $\mathcal{P}(X)$ the powerset of X, and consider, for every $a : X \rightarrow [0,1]$ the map $\hat{\rho}_a : \mathcal{P}(X) \rightarrow [0,1]$ defined as follows: for every $B \subseteq A$,

$$\hat{\rho}_a(B) = \min\{a(x) : x \in B\}. \tag{2}$$

Remark 1. Notice that $\hat{\rho}_a$ generalizes β_A in the following sense: whenever $A \in B(M) = \mathcal{P}(X)$, then $\hat{\rho}_A = \beta_A$. Namely, for every $A \in B(M)$, $\hat{\rho}_A(B) = 1$ if $B \subseteq A$, and $\hat{\rho}_A(B) = 0$ otherwise.

Definition 1. *We call a map $\hat{\mathbf{b}} : M \rightarrow [0,1]$ a Kroupa belief function whenever there exists a state $\hat{\mathbf{s}} : [0,1]^{\mathcal{P}(X)} \rightarrow [0,1]$ such that for every $a \in M$, $\hat{\mathbf{b}}(a) = \hat{\mathbf{s}}(\hat{\rho}_a)$.*

The state $\hat{\mathbf{s}}$ needed in the definition of $\hat{\mathbf{b}}$ is called the *state assignment* in [15]. Although $\hat{\mathbf{b}}$ has been directly introduced as a combination of $\hat{\rho}$ with the state assignment $\hat{\mathbf{s}}$, a notion of *mass assignment* can be introduced even for this generalized case. Indeed, since X is finite, it turns out that one can equivalently write

$$\hat{\mathbf{b}}(a) = \sum_{B \subseteq X} \hat{\rho}_a(B) \cdot \hat{\mathbf{s}}(B).$$

In particular, since $1 = \hat{\mathbf{b}}(X) = \sum_{B \subseteq X} \hat{\mathbf{s}}(B)$, the restriction of the state $\hat{\mathbf{s}}$ to $\mathcal{P}(X)$ (call it $\hat{m}$) is a classical mass assignment. Now, we are allowed to speak about *focal elements* of $\hat{\mathbf{b}}$ as those elements in $\mathcal{P}(X)$ that the mass assignment $\hat{m}$ maps into a non-zero value.

Notice that, although the arguments in Kroupa's definition of belief function are fuzzy sets, the mass assignments that characterize each of these belief functions are defined on crisp (i.e. Boolean) sets, and, therefore, the focal elements associated to every Kroupa belief function are crisp sets. In other words, every $\hat{b}$ is defined over crisp, and not fuzzy, pieces of evidence.

Kroupa's definition of belief function makes use (with the necessary modification in using a state instead of a probability measure as additive map to define $\hat{b}$), for every $a \in M$, of the map $\hat{\rho}_a$ which evaluates the degree of inclusion $\hat{\rho}_a(B)$ of a classical (i.e. crisp, Boolean) subset B of X, into the fuzzy set a. The definition that we introduce below generalizes Kroupa's definition by introducing, for every $a \in M$, a map ρ_a assigning to every fuzzy set $b \in M$ its degree of inclusion into a, cf. [1]. To be more precise, let $M = [0,1]^X$ be a finite domain MV-clan, and consider, for every $a \in M$ a map $\rho_a : M \to [0,1]$ defined as follows: for every $b \in M$,

$$\rho_a(b) = \min\{b(x) \Rightarrow a(x) : x \in X\}. \tag{3}$$

where $\Rightarrow$ denotes the Łukasiewicz implication function ($x \Rightarrow y = \min(1, 1 - x + y)$)[1].

Remark 2. In a sense, for every $a \in M$, ρ_a can be identified as the membership function of the fuzzy set of elements of M (and hence the fuzzy subsets of X) that are *included* in a. In particular one has $\rho_a(b) = 1$ whenever $b \leq a$ (for each point). Also notice that the Boolean skeleton $B(M)$ of any finite domain MV-clan $M = [0,1]^X$ coincides with $\mathcal{P}(X)$ and hence, as also shown by the following result, for every $a \in M$ the map ρ_a extends $\hat{\rho}_a$ in the domain.

Proposition 1. *(i) For all $a, a' \in M$, $\rho_{a \wedge a'} = \min\{\rho_a, \rho_{a'}\}$, and $\rho_{a \vee a'} \geq \max\{\rho_a, \rho_{a'}\}$.*

(ii) For every $a \in M$, the restriction of ρ_a to $B(M)$ coincides with the transformation $\hat{\rho}_a$ of equation (2).

(iii) For every $A \in B(M)$, the restriction of ρ_A to $B(M)$ coincides with the transformation β_A of equation (1)

Proof. (i) In every MV-chain, and in particular in the standard chain $[0,1]_{MV}$ the equation $\neg\gamma \oplus (\alpha \wedge \beta) = (\neg\gamma \oplus \alpha) \wedge (\neg\gamma \oplus \beta)$ holds:, i.e. $(\gamma \Rightarrow (\alpha \wedge \beta)) = (\gamma \Rightarrow \alpha) \wedge (\gamma \Rightarrow \beta)$. Therefore, for every $a, a', b \in M$,
$\rho_{a \wedge a'}(b) = \min\{b(x) \Rightarrow (a \wedge a')(x) : x \in X\} = \min\{b(x) \Rightarrow (a(x) \wedge a'(x)) : x \in X\} = \min\{(b(x) \Rightarrow a(x)) \wedge (b(x) \Rightarrow a'(x)) : x \in X\} = \min\{\rho_a(b), \rho_{a'}(b)\}$.
An easy computation shows that $\rho_{a \vee a'} \geq \max\{\rho_a, \rho_{a'}\}$.

(ii) For every $B \in B(M)$, $\rho_a(B) = \min\{B(x) \Rightarrow a(x) : x \in X\}$. Whenever $x \notin B$, $B(x) = 0$, and hence $B(x) \Rightarrow a(x) = 1$ for all those $x \notin B$. On the other hand for all $x \in B$, $B(x) = 1$, and so $B(x) \Rightarrow a(x) = 1 \Rightarrow a(x) = a(x)$ for all $x \in B$. Consequently, $\rho_a(B) = \min\{a(x) : x \in B\}$.

(iii) It trivially follows from (ii) and Remark 1. □

---

[1] Here the choice of $\Rightarrow$ is due to the MV-algebraic setting, but other choices could be made in other settings, see e.g. [1].

Definition 2. *Let* $M = [0,1]^X$ *be a finite domain MV-clan. A map* $\mathbf{b} : M \rightarrow [0,1]$ *is called a* belief function *if there exists a state* $\mathbf{s} : [0,1]^M \rightarrow [0,1]$ *such that for every* $a \in M$,

$$\mathbf{b}(a) = \mathbf{s}(\rho_a). \tag{4}$$

We denote the class of all belief functions over M *by* $Bel(M)$.

It is worth noticing that, in general, $\rho_\perp$ does not coincide with the bottom element of $M^{[0,1]}$. In fact, if, for instance, $a \in M$ is a function such that for no $x \in X$, $a(x) = 1$, then it immediately follows that $\rho_\perp(a) > 0$. Therefore, $\mathbf{b}(\perp) = 0$ does not hold in general.

It is clear from the definition that $Bel(M)$ is a convex set, since states are closed by convex combinations. Moreover, due to Theorem 1, for each belief function $\mathbf{b} : M \rightarrow [0,1]$ there exists a finitely additive probability measure μ on $\mathcal{P}(M)$ such that

$$\mathbf{b}(a) = \int_M \rho_a \, d\mu.$$

Proposition 2. *For every finite domain MV-clan* M, *and for every* $\mathbf{b} \in Bel(M)$, $\mathbf{b}$ *is totally monotone, i.e.* $\mathbf{b}$ *is monotone, and it satisfies: for all* $a_1, \ldots, a_n \in M$,

$$\mathbf{b}\left(\bigvee_{i=1}^{n} a_i\right) \geq \sum_{j=1}^{n} (-1)^{j+1} \cdot \mathbf{b}\left(\bigwedge_{k=1}^{j} a_i\right).$$

Proof. Since for every $a \in M$, ρ_a is monotone, and every state $\mathbf{s}$ is monotone, $\mathbf{b}$ is monotone as well. Moreover, for every n and for every $a_1, \ldots, a_n \in M$, from (4) and Proposition 1 (i):

$$\begin{aligned}
\mathbf{b}\left(\bigvee_{i=1}^{n} a_i\right) &= \mathbf{s}(\rho_{a_1 \vee \ldots \vee a_n}) \\
&\geq \mathbf{s}(\rho_{a_1} \vee \ldots \vee \rho_{a_n}) \\
&= \sum_{j=1}^{n} (-1)^{j+1} \cdot \mathbf{s}\left(\bigwedge_{k=1}^{j} \rho_{a_i}\right) \\
&= \sum_{j=1}^{n} (-1)^{j+1} \cdot \mathbf{s}\left(\rho_{a_1 \wedge \ldots \wedge a_j}\right) \\
&= \sum_{j=1}^{n} (-1)^{j+1} \cdot \mathbf{b}\left(\bigwedge_{k=1}^{j} a_i\right).
\end{aligned} \qquad \square$$

On Boolean algebras, total monotonicity is a property that characterizes belief functions. It is not known whether the same holds for MV-algebras.

For every belief function $\mathbf{b} : M \rightarrow [0,1]$ given by a state $\mathbf{s}$ on $[0,1]^M$, whenever $Supp(\mathbf{s}) = \{a \in M : \mathbf{s}(\{a\}) > 0\}$ is countable, we can introduce a notion of *mass assignment* that fully characterizes $\mathbf{b}$. Indeed define $m : M \rightarrow [0,1]$ such that, for every $a \in M$, $m(a) = \mathbf{s}(\{a\})$. Then we can define $Supp(m) = Supp(\mathbf{s})$ without danger of confusion. Notice that $\sum_{a \in Supp(m)} m(a) = 1$. It is well known that m defined as above characterizes $\mathbf{s}$ as follows: for every $f \in [0,1]^M$, $\mathbf{s}(f) = \sum_{a \in Supp(\mathbf{s})} f(a) \cdot m(a)$. In this case we get, for every $a \in M$,

$$\mathbf{b}(a) = \sum_{b \in Supp(\mathbf{s})} \rho_a(b) \cdot m(b).$$

Let us call *countably supported* those belief functions **b** given by a state **s** for which $Supp(\mathbf{s})$ is countable. In particular, whenever X is finite (as it is in our case), every Kroupa belief function is countably supported.

The focal elements in our definition of a countably supported belief function are elements of the MV-algebra $M = [0,1]^X$, and, hence, are not crisp sets in general. This supports the interpretation that the belief functions defined as in (4) differ from Kroupa definition by offering a more general setting for evidence theory. Indeed, the evidence that in our approach can be represented is not just limited to crisp subsets, but we can now deal with imprecise evidence within this framework.

Example 2. Let us revisit Smets' well-known story of the murder of Mrs. Jones [20]. There are 3 suspects of being her murderer: Peter, Paul and Mary. Consider the information provided by the janitor of the building where Mrs. Jones lives. He heard the victim yelling and saw *a small man* running. It turns out that Paul and Mary are not tall while Peter is taller ((Paul is 1.65 m. tall, Mary is 1.60 m tall and Peter is 1.85 m.). So, actually, the subset of small suspects of $X = \{Peter, Paul, Mary\}$ can be considered as a fuzzy set, with membership function, say,

$$\mu_{small}(Peter) = 0, \mu_{small}(Paul) = 0.7, \mu_{small}(Mary) = 0.9.$$

On the other hand, Mary has short hair, so she may be mistaken as a man at first sight, and hence, the subset of suspects looking like a man can be considered fuzzy as well, with membership function:

$$\mu_{man\text{-}like}(Peter) = 1, \mu_{man\text{-}like}(Paul) = 1, \mu_{man\text{-}like}(Mary) = 0.5.$$

The evidence supplied by the janitor may be represented by a mass assignment $m : [0,1]^X \rightarrow [0,1]$ such that $m(small \wedge man\text{-}like) = \alpha > 0$, $m(X) = 1 - \alpha$ and $m(f) = 0$ for any other $f \in [0,1]^X$. Here we interpret $\wedge$ by the min operator, so we have

$$\mu_{small \wedge man\text{-}like}(Peter) = 0, \mu_{small \wedge man\text{-}like}(Paul) = 0.7, \mu_{small \wedge man\text{-}like}(Mary) = 0.5$$

Suppose we are interested in computing the belief that the suspect is Paul. We then need to compute

$$\rho_{\{Paul\}}(small \wedge man\text{-}like) = \min_{x \in X} \mu_{small \wedge man\text{-}like}(x) \Rightarrow \mu_{Paul}(x)$$
$$= \min\{0 \Rightarrow 0, 1 \Rightarrow 1, 0.5 \Rightarrow 0\}$$
$$= \min\{1, 0.5\} = 0.5$$

and $\rho_{\{Paul\}}(X) = 0$. Finally, we have

$$\mathbf{b}(\{Paul\}) = \sum_{f \in Supp(m)} \rho_{\{Paul\}}(f) \cdot m(\{f\})$$
$$= \rho_{\{Paul\}}(small \wedge man\text{-}like) \cdot m(small \wedge man\text{-}like)$$
$$= 0.5 \cdot \alpha > 0$$

Hence, we get a positive belief degree on Paul being the murderer. This is in contrast with the results we would obtain with both the classical and Kroupa's models, where focal elements are only allowed to be classical subsets of X, in case we assume Mary can be mistaken as a man. Indeed, in that case, we would be forced to take as focal element, besides X itself, the set *small* $\wedge$ *man-like* = $\{Paul, Mary\}$, and since there would be no focal element included in $\{Paul\}$, we would get $\mathbf{b}(\{Paul\}) = 0$.

4   Belief Functions and Their Integral Representations

In [15], Kroupa belief functions are represented in terms of Choquet integrals: for any Kroupa belief function $\mathbf{b}$ on $M = [0,1]^X$ there exists a (classical) belief function β on 2^X such that $\mathbf{b}(f) = \oint f \, d\beta$, for every $f \in M$, where the Choquet integral is defined as $\oint a \, d\beta = \int_0^1 \beta(f^{-1}([t,1])) \, dt$.

However for the generalized belief functions specified in Definition 2, we have weaker integral representations that derive from the fact that the map $\rho_c : M \to [0,1]$ defined in (3) can be represented in two ways as an integral. This representation, in turn, allows us to offer two integral descriptions of belief functions on MV-algebras. In this section, we are going to address this issue.

Let us start recalling that, given a set X, a map $\pi : X \to [0,1]$ is called a *possibility distribution*, and π is said to be *normalized* if there is an $x \in X$ such that $\pi(x) = 1$. Given a possibility distribution π, the Sugeno integral of a function $a : X \to [0,1]$ with respect to π is defined as the value $\max_{x \in X}(\min(\pi(x), a(x)))$. When we replace the min operation by the Łukasiewicz t-norm (or even more in general by an arbitrary t-norm T), we obtain the so called *quasi Sugeno integral* [22,12]: for every $a : X \to [0,1]$, $\oint_X a \, d\pi = \max_{x \in X}(\pi(x) \odot a(x))$. The dual of the quasi Sugeno integral is defined as follows: for all $a : X \to [0,1]$,

$$\oint_X^* a \, d\pi = 1 - \oint_X (1 - a) \, d\pi = \min_{x \in X}(\pi(x) \Rightarrow a(x)). \tag{5}$$

Following [15], consider a function $a \in M = [0,1]^X$, and a monotone set function $\beta : \mathcal{P}(X) \to [0,1]$ such that $\beta(\emptyset) = 0$ and $\beta(X) = 1$ (also called capacity). Since we are only concerned with finite domain MV-clans, for every $a \in M$, the *Choquet integral* of a with respect to β, $\oint a \, d\beta = \int_0^1 \beta(a^{-1}([t,1])) \, dt$, exists and admits the following expression: letting $X = \{x_1, \ldots, x_n\}$ indexed in a way that $y_1 \geq y_2 \geq \ldots \geq y_n$ where $y_i = a(x_i)$ for $i = 1, \ldots, n$ and $y_{n+1} = 0$, and letting , $S_i = \{x_1, \ldots, x_i\}$, we have that

$$\oint a \, d\beta = \sum_{i=1}^{n}(y_i - y_{i+1})\beta(S_i).$$

Theorem 2. *For every finite domain MV-clan* $M = [0,1]^X$, *and for every* $\mathbf{b} \in Bel(M)$, *there exists a finitely additive probability measure* μ *on* $\mathcal{P}(M)$ *such that for every* $c \in M$:

1.

$$b(c) = \int_M \left(\oint_X^* (1-a) \ d\pi_c \right) \ d\mu(a),$$

where the possibility distribution π_c is defined as $\pi_c(x) = 1 - c(x)$.

2.

$$b(c) = \int_M \left(\oint a \Rightarrow c \ d\chi_X \right) \ d\mu(a),$$

where χ_X is the characteristic function of X over $\mathcal{P}(X)$.

For the case of countably supported belief functions, the above integral representations can be simplified as follows.

Corollary 1. *For every $M = [0,1]^X$, and every countably supported belief function $\mathbf{b}$ on M, there exists a mass assignment $m : M \to [0,1]$ such that, for every $c \in M$, the following hold:*

1. $\mathbf{b}(c) = \sum_{a \in Supp(s)} (\min_{x \in X}(a(x_i) \Rightarrow c(x_i))) \cdot m(a);$
2. $\mathbf{b}(c) = \sum_{a \in Supp(s)} (\sum_{i=1}^n (y_i - y_{i+1}) \cdot \chi_X(S_i)) \cdot m(a),$
   where $X = \{x_1, \ldots, x_n\}$ such that $y_i = a(x_i) \Rightarrow c(x_i)$, $y_{n+1} = 0$, with $y_1 \geq \ldots \geq y_n$, and $S_i = \{x_1, \ldots, x_i\}$ for all $i = 1, \ldots, n$.

In [21], Yen proposed a way to reduce belief functions over fuzzy focal elements to belief functions over crisp focal elements by considering α-cuts of fuzzy sets. A similar idea can be used to reduce a countably supported belief function $\mathbf{b}$ to an infimum of Kroupa belief functions. Indeed, for every $b \in [0,1]^X$, and every $\alpha \in [0,1]$, define $b_\alpha = \{x \in X \mid b(x) = \alpha\}$. Then, $\rho_a(b) = \inf_x b(x) \Rightarrow a(x) = \inf_{\alpha > 0} \inf_{x \in b_\alpha} \alpha \Rightarrow a(x) = \inf_{\alpha > 0} \hat{\rho}_{\alpha \Rightarrow a}(b_\alpha)$. Therefore:

$$\mathbf{b}(a) = \sum_{b \in Supp(s)} \rho_a(b) \cdot m(\{b\}) = \inf_{\alpha > 0} \sum_{b \in Supp(s)} \hat{\rho}_{\alpha \Rightarrow a}(b_\alpha) \cdot m(\{b\}) = \inf_\alpha \hat{\mathbf{b}}_\alpha(\alpha \Rightarrow a),$$

where $\hat{\mathbf{b}}_\alpha$ is the Kroupa belief function whose focal elements are the α-slices of those of $\mathbf{b}$, and its corresponding mass m_α is defined as $m_\alpha(\{b_\alpha\}) = m(\{b\})$.

Therefore, a countably supported belief function in our sense can be represented as well as an infimum of Choquet integrals.

5   Combining Belief Functions

In this section we present a natural way to generalize the well-known Dempster rule to combine the information carried by two belief functions $\mathbf{b}_1, \mathbf{b}_2 \in Bel(M)$, into a third $\mathbf{b}_{1,2} \in Bel(M)$. First of all let us introduce an easy result about the definition of states in a product space.

Proposition 3. *For every MV-algebra $M = [0,1]^X$, and for every pair of states $s_1, s_2 : M \to [0,1]$, there exists a state $s_{1,2} : M \times M \to [0,1]$ such that for every $(b, c) \in M \times M$, $s_{1,2}(b, c) = s_1(b) \cdot s_2(c)$.*

Let s_1, s_2 be two states on $[0,1]^M$ such that $\mathbf{b}_1(a) = s_1(\rho_a)$ and $\mathbf{b}_2(a) = s_2(\rho_a)$ for all $a \in M$. Furthermore, let $\mu_1, \mu_2 : \mathcal{P}(M) \to [0,1]$ be two probabilities such that for $i = 1, 2$, $s_i(f) = \int_M f \, d\mu_i$ as ensured by Theorem 1.

Take the mapping $\mu_{1,2} : \mathcal{P}(M \times M) \to [0,1]$ to be, as in the proof of Proposition 3, the product measure on the product space generated by $M \times M$ such that $\mu_{1,2}(b,c) = \mu_1(b) \cdot \mu_2(c)$ for all $(b,c) \in M \times M$. Then call $s_{1,2}$ that unique state on $[0,1]^{M \times M}$ defined by integrating on $\mu_{1,2}$. Since every $f \in [0,1]^{M \times M}$ is measurable in the product space generated by $M \times M$ with measure $\mu_{1,2}$, $s_{1,2}$ exists, and moreover notice that, if there exist $g, h : M \to [0,1]$ such that $f : (\overline{x}, \overline{y}) \mapsto g(\overline{x}) \cdot h(\overline{y})$, then by Proposition 3, $s_{1,2}(f) = s_1(g) \cdot s_2(h)$.

Finally, for every $a \in M$, consider the map $\rho_a^\wedge : M \times M \to [0,1]$ defined by $\rho_a^\wedge(b,c) = \rho_a(b \wedge c)$. Then we are ready to define the following combination of belief functions.

Definition 3. *(Generalized Dempster rule) Given* $\mathbf{b}_1, \mathbf{b}_2 \in Bel(M)$ *as above, define its* min-conjunctive combination $\mathbf{b}_{1,2} : M \to [0,1]$ *as follows: for all* $a \in M$,

$$\mathbf{b}_{1,2}(a) = s_{1,2}(\rho_a^\wedge). \tag{6}$$

From (6) we then obtain: for all $a \in M$,

$$\mathbf{b}_{1,2}(a) = \int_{M \times M} \rho_a^\wedge \, d\mu_{1,2} = \int_{M \times M} \rho_a(b \wedge c) \, d\mu_1(b) \, d\mu_2(c)$$

and in the case of countable support belief functions, this yields

$$\mathbf{b}_{1,2}(a) = \sum_{b,c \in M} \rho_a(b \wedge c) \cdot \mu_1(\{b\}) \cdot \mu_2(\{c\}).$$

Notice that the above expression reduces to $\mathbf{b}_{1,2}(a) = \sum_{d \in M} \sum_{b,c \in M, b \wedge c = d} \rho_a(d) \cdot (\mu_1(\{b\}) \cdot \mu_2(\{c\})) = \sum_{d \in M} \rho_a(d) \cdot \mu^*(\{d\})$, where $\mu^*(\{d\}) = \sum_{b,c \in M, b \wedge c = d} \mu_1(\{b\}) \cdot \mu_2(\{c\})$ is indeed a mass assignment and hence $\mathbf{b}_{1,2} \in Bel(M)$.

It is easy to check this combination of belief functions is well behaved.

Proposition 4. *The above defined operation of combination of belief functions with countable support satisfies the following properties:*

1. *is commutative, and associative;*
2. *the belief function* $\mathbf{b}_X$ *defined by the mass assignment* $\mu(X) = 1$, *and* $\mu(Y) = 0$, *for every* $Y \neq X$, *is its neutral element.*

Actually, the above min-conjunctive combination can be easily extended to well-known MV-operations on fuzzy sets, like e.g. the max-disjunction $\vee$, strong conjunction $\odot$ and strong disjunction $\oplus$, by defining $(b_1 \circledast b_2)(a) = s_{1,2}(\rho_a^\circledast)$, for $\circledast$ being one of these operations, and defining $\rho_a^\circledast(b,c) = \rho_a(b \circledast c)$. This generalizes classical conjuntive and disjunctive combination rules [8].

6   Conclusion and Future Work

In this paper we have introduced a generalization of belief functions on MV-algebras of fuzzy sets that further extends Kroupa definition (cf. [15]) by allowing focal elements to be fuzzy sets, and not just classical sets. Indeed focal elements play a central role in the (classical) theory of belief functions because they can be interpreted as those basic pieces of information that are probabilistically evaluated by the mass assignment to define the belief function we are considering. More than the foundational aspects, another important role of focal elements regards the fact that several particular belief functions (like probability measures, necessity and possibility measures) can be characterized by the fact that their focal elements satisfy a certain structural property.

In our future work we plan to investigate which further properties should a nested class of focal elements satisfy in order to characterize necessity and possibility measures on MV-algebras. Following the line of [16], we also plan to deepen the study on belief functions on more general MV-algebras than the ones considered in this paper where the notion of state is well developed and enjoy particularly nice properties (like the class of semi-simple MV-algebras, that can be represented as a certain class of continuous real-valued functions), as well as investigating their algebraic and geometrical properties, and axiomatic characterization. Moreover, following the line of [11], we also plan to introduce a multi-modal expansion of Łukasiewicz logic that could allow to treat both our as well as Kroupa definition of belief function on finite MV-algebras. Indeed, as a belief function on an MV-algebra is defined by combining a state s with the map $\rho : f \in [0,1]^X \mapsto \rho_f \in [0,1]^{[0,1]^X}$ (in our case, and the map $\hat{\rho} : f \in [0,1]^X \mapsto [0,1]^{\mathcal{P}(X)}$ in the case of Kroupa definition) that behaves like a necessity measure on $[0,1]^X$, we argue that a belief function on a finite MV-algebra can be axiomatized by combining the axioms of a state (cf. [9]) with the axioms for the two possible extensions of the modal logic K on finite MV-algebras as provided in [2] (i.e. the one relative to those Kripke frames with many-valued accessibility relation, and the one that is complete with respect to those particular frames whose accessibility relation is two-valued) to respectively characterize ρ and $\hat{\rho}$.

Acknowlegdments. The authors would like to thank Tomáš Kroupa for interesting discussions on the topic, as well as to the anonymous referees for their helpful remarks. They also acknowledge partial support from the Spanish projects TASSAT (TIN2010- 20967-C04-01), *Agreement Technologies* (CONSOLIDER CSD2007-0022, INGENIO 2010) and ARINF (TIN2009-14704-C03-03), as well as the ESF Eurocores-LogICCC/MICINN project (FFI2008-03126-E/FILO). Flaminio and Marchioni acknowledge partial support from the Juan de la Cierva Program of the Spanish MICINN.

References

1. Biacino, L.: Fuzzy subsethood and belief functions of fuzzy events. Fuzzy Sets and Systems 158(1), 38–49 (2007)
2. Bou, F., Esteva, F., Godo, L., Rodrìguez, R.: On the Minimum Many-Valued Modal Logic over a Finite Residuated Lattice. Journal of Logic and Computation (in press)
3. Cignoli, R., D'Ottaviano, I.M.L., Mundici, D.: Algebraic Foundations of Many-valued Reasoning. Kluwer, Dordrecht (2000)
4. Denœux, T.: Reasoning with imprecise belief structures. Int. J. Approx. Reasoning 20(1), 79–111 (1999)

5. Denœux, T.: Modeling vague beliefs using fuzzy-valued belief structures. Fuzzy Sets and Systems 116(2), 167–199 (2000)
6. Dubois, D., Prade, H. (with the collaboration of H. Farreny, R. Martin-Clouaire and C. Testemale). In: Possibility Theory. An Approach to Computerized Processing of Uncertainty, Plenum Press, New York (1988)
7. Dubois, D., Prade, H.: Evidence Measures Based on Fuzzy Information. Automatica 21(5), 547–562 (1985)
8. Dubois, D., Prade, H.: A Set-Theoretic View of Belief Functions: Logical Operations and Approximations by Fuzzy Sets. In: Classical Works of the Dempster-Shafer Theory of Belief Functions. Studies in Fuzziness and Soft Computing. Studies in Fuzziness and Soft Computing, vol. 219, pp. 375–410 (2008)
9. Flaminio, T., Godo, L.: A logic for reasoning about the probability of fuzzy events. Fuzzy Sets and Systems 158(6), 625–638 (2007)
10. Flaminio, T., Godo, L., Marchioni, E.: Geometrical aspects of possibility measures on finite domain MV-clans. In: Soft Computing (to appear)
11. Godo, L., Hájek, P., Esteva, F.: A Fuzzy Modal Logic for Belief Functions. Fundam. Inform. 57(2-4), 127–146 (2003)
12. Grabisch, M., Murofushi, T., Sugeno, M.: Fuzzy Measure of Fuzzy Events Defined by Fuzzy Integrals. Fuzzy Sets and Systems 50, 293–313 (1992)
13. Hwang, C., Yang, M.: Generalization of Belief and Plausibility Functions to Fuzzy Sets Based on the Sugeno Integral. International Journal of Intelligent Systems 22, 1215–1228 (2007)
14. Kroupa, T.: Every state on semisimple MV-algebra is integral. Fuzzy Sets and Systems 157(20), 2771–2782 (2006)
15. Kroupa, T.: From Probabilities to Belief Functions on MV-Algebras. In: Borgelt, C., et al. (eds.) Combining Soft Computing and Statistical Methods in Data Analysis. AISC, vol. 77, pp. 387–394. Springer, Heidelberg (2010)
16. Kroupa, T.: Extension of Belief Functions to Infinite-valued Events. Soft Computing (to appear)
17. Mundici, D.: Averaging the truth-value in Lukasiewicz logic. Studia Logica 55(1), 113–127 (1995)
18. Shafer, G.: A Mathematical Theory of Evidence. Princeton University Press, Princeton (1976)
19. Smets, P.: The degree of belief in a fuzzy event. Information Sciences 25(1), 1–19 (1981)
20. Smets, P.: Belief Functions. In: Smets, P., et al. (eds.) Nonstandard Logics for Automated Reasoning, pp. 253–277. Academic Press, London (1988)
21. Yen, J.: Computing Generalized Belief Functions for Continuous Fuzzy Sets. Int. J. Approx. Reasoning 6, 1–31 (1992)
22. Weber, S.: $\perp$-decomposable measures integrals for Archimedean t-conorms $\perp$. J. Math. Anal. Appl. 101, 114–138 (1984)
23. Zadeh, L.A.: Fuzzy sets as a basis for a theory of possibility. Fuzzy Sets and Systems 1, 3–28 (1978)
24. Zadeh, L.A.: Fuzzy sets and information granularity. In: Gupta, M., et al. (eds.) Advances in Fuzzy Sets Theory and Applications, pp. 3–18. North Holland, Amsterdam (1979)

Order Compatible Fuzzy Relations and Their Elicitation from General Fuzzy Partitions

Sandra Sandri and Flávia Toledo Martins-Bedé

INPE, Av. dos Astronautas, 1758, S. J. Campos, S.P., Brazil
sandri@lac.inpe.br, flavinha@dpi.inpe.br

Abstract. We study a special kind of fuzzy relations capable of modeling that two elements in the universe of discourse are similar to the extend that they are close to each other with respect to a given scale. These relations are reflexive and symmetric but not necessarily T-transitive. We study the requirements to construct such relations from a large class of fuzzy partitions that obey some useful but not severely constraining requirements. We give some formal results, including a lower bound (in terms of fuzzy sets inclusion) on the relations from this class that can be derived from the general class of fuzzy partitions.

Keywords: similarity relations, fuzzy partitions.

1 Introduction

Similarity relations were first defined as a generalization of equivalence relations in classical set theory. Lotfi Zadeh defined them as mappings $R : \Omega \times \Omega \to [0,1]$ that are reflexive, symmetric and transitive, with transitivity defined by means of the min operator (see [19]). Nowadays, transitivity in the fuzzy framework is usually given by T-transitivity, defined with the use of any T-norm operator and not just the min (see e.g. [17]). More recently, weaker forms of similarity relations have been considered, in which reflexivity and symmetry are required, but not necessarily T-transitivity [8][15][1].

Similarity relations and finite collections of fuzzy sets can both be used to describe some concepts in a given domain, e.g., the sweetness of cups of coffee [10]. Let us suppose we have a set of cups of coffee, ordered by the quantity of sugar poured into them, and that we are interested in grading their similarity according to their sweetness. One solution is to directly assign a number to each pair of cups that models the similarity between them. Another possibility is to derive parts of this relation from a previous classification of the cups of coffee (either in a crisp or fuzzy manner), as, say, "too-bitter","good" or "too-sweet". We know, for instance, that cups that fall in the same class of sweetness should be considered somewhat related, whereas cups from disjoint classes less so. Also, the closer a cup of coffee is to the most representative cup of the class, the

---

[1] Some authors call *tolerance relations* to fuzzy relations that are symmetric and that obey a weaker reflexivity property (see e.g. [3]).

W. Liu (Ed.): ECSQARU 2011, LNAI 6717, pp. 640–650, 2011.

more similar it is to that representative. Moreover, the similarity between a cup of coffee with one spoon of sugar and another with three spoons is certainly smaller than the similarity between either a cup with one spoon of sugar and another with two spoons or between a cup with two spoons of sugar and another with three spoons.

In classical set theory, a partition determines a unique equivalence relation and vice-versa. However, the problem of obtaining conversions between a fuzzy similarity relation and collections of fuzzy sets is not trivial, even though the two formalisms are closely related to each other. This problem has been very much addressed in what regards T-transitive similarity relations (see e.g. [17], [18] [4]) but not in what concerns similarity relations in which transitivity does not play a role, as in the coffee example.

Similarity relations that do not necessarily obey T-transitivity have been used in several applications, such as fuzzy control [5], molecular biology [16] and case-base reasoning [11] [7]. In these applications, the similarity relations in the real scale obey an extra property: two numbers are similar to the extend that they are close to each other with respect to the Euclidean distance [6] (see also [13]). Here we focus in this kind of relations but considering any total order, which we will call *order compatible fuzzy relations* (OCFR).

Several means can be devised to elicit order compatible fuzzy relations for an application. If the set of useful values in the application is discrete, the user can enter the similarity relation directly. In problems involving continuous domains, one way to obtain order compatible fuzzy relations is to select a family of parameterized similarity relations and then either learn the parameters from data or specify them directly. Here we are interested in yet another possibility: to derive the fuzzy similarity relation from a finite collection of fuzzy sets. Using fuzzy sets partitions, we are neither constrained to any fixed family of similarity relations, nor obliged to construct the relation as a look-up table, something impossible to do for continuous domains. Last but not least, the similarity relations can be learnt from samples, going through the intermediary step of learning a fuzzy sets partition.

In this work we study OCFRs and propose some reasonable requirements that should be obeyed by methods that transform partitions into relations in our context. Rather than proposing transformations between the two formalims, the goal of this paper is to lay a formal basis for such transformations. We address a large class of fuzzy partitions that can be used to derive the OCFRs but focus particularly in the so-called Ruspini partitions.

This paper is organized as follows. In the following section we give some basic definitions. In Section 3 we formally define a general class of fuzzy partitions and in Section 4 we define order gradual fuzzy relations. In Section 5 we propose properties to be obeyed when converting general fuzzy partitions into order gradual fuzzy relations and give a lower bound for these relations in the sense of fuzzy set inclusion. Finally, in Section 6 we conclude with some guidelines for future work.

2   Basic Definitions

A fuzzy set B on a domain Ω is a mapping $B : \Omega \rightarrow [0,1]$. It is said to be normalized when $\exists x_0 \in \Omega$ such that $B(x_0) = 1$. The core and support of a fuzzy set A_i are defined as $core(B) = \{x \mid x \in \Omega \wedge B(x) = 1\}$ and $supp(B) = \{x \mid x \in \Omega \wedge B(x) > 0\})$, respectively. The height of a fuzzy set B is given by $h(B) = \sup_{x \in \Omega} B(x)$. The α-level cut from B is defined as $[B]_\alpha = \{x \in \Omega \mid B(x) \geq \alpha\}$.

A fuzzy relation is a mapping from a multidimensional domain $\Omega_1 \times ... \times \Omega_n$ to $[0,1]$. Its normalization is defined as for fuzzy sets in one-dimensional domains. A binary fuzzy relation $S : \Omega \times \Omega \rightarrow [0,1]$ is a similarity relation on Ω when S is reflexive ($\forall x \in \Omega, S(x,x) = 1$) and symmetric ($\forall x, y \in \Omega, S(x,y) = S(y,x)$). Note that for some authors, similarity relations also have to obey T-transitivity: $\top(S(x,y), S(y,z)) \leq S(x,z)$ for all $x, y, z \in \Omega$, where $\top : [0,1]^2 \rightarrow [0,1]$, called a T-norm operator, is commutative, associative, monotonic and has 1 as neutral element. Given two similarity relations S and S', we say that S is *finer* than S' if $\forall x, y \in \Omega, S(x,y) \leq S'(x,y)$.

3   General Fuzzy Partitions

We introduce here the notion of a *general fuzzy partition with respect to a total order* (GFP) as a finite collection of normalized fuzzy sets that covers a given domain and is such that the cores of any pair of fuzzy sets in the partition are disjoint. Let $(\Omega, \preceq)$ be a total order and let $\mathbf{A} = \{A_1, ..., A_n\}$ be a collection of fuzzy sets in Ω. Formally, $\mathbf{A}$ is a GFP with respect to $\preceq$ if it obeys the following properties:

1. $\forall A_i \in \mathbf{A}, \exists x \in \Omega, A_i(x) = 1$ (normalization of fuzzy sets)
2. $\forall x, y, z \in \Omega, \forall A_i \in \mathbf{A}$, if $x \preceq y \preceq z$ then
   $\exists \alpha \in [0,1], A_i(y) \geq \alpha A_i(x) + (1 - \alpha)A_i(z)$ (convexity)
3. $\forall x \in \Omega, \exists A_i \in \mathbf{A}, A_i(x) > 0$ (domain covering)
4. $\forall A_i, A_j \in \mathbf{A}$, if $i \neq j$ then $core(A_i) \cap core(A_j) = \emptyset$
   (non-core intersection)

Note that every GFP obeys the non-inclusion property:

$$\forall A_i, A_j \in \mathbf{A}, \text{if } (\forall x \in \Omega, A_i(x) \leq A_j(x)) \text{ then } i = j \text{ (non-inclusion)}.$$

Let $GFP(\Omega, \preceq)$ denote the set of all general fuzzy partitions that can be derived considering total order $(\Omega, \preceq)$. We say that $\mathbf{A}$ is a *n-general fuzzy partition* (n-GFP) if it belongs to $GFP(\Omega, \preceq)$ and each element in Ω has non-null membership to at most n fuzzy sets in $\mathbf{A}$ ($n \geq 2$).

Some interesting properties that are worth of being considered for GFPs are:

- $\forall x \in \Omega, \sum_i A_i(x) = 1$ (additivity)
- $\bigcap_{A_i \in \mathbf{A}} supp(A_i) = \Omega$ (unique support)
- $\bigcup_{A_i \in \mathbf{A}} core(A_i) = \Omega$ (core covering)
- $\forall A_i, A_j \in \mathbf{A}$, if $i \neq j$ then $(\nexists \alpha \in [0,1], [A_i]_\alpha \subseteq [A_j]_\alpha)$
  (non-level-cut-inclusion)

The unique support property means that all fuzzy sets in a partition $\mathbf{A}$ on Ω share the same support, the universe of discourse itself; as a consequence, any element of domain Ω has positive membership to every fuzzy set in $\mathbf{A}$.

The most noteworthy fuzzy partitions are strong partitions [14], also known as Ruspini partitions, in which additivity also holds. Throughout this work, Ruspini partitions that are 2-GFP will be called 2-Ruspini. The fuzzy sets in Ruspini partitions are not always normalized, what makes sense in some applications. For instance, let us suppose we want to classify the pixels in a given image, where the classes are described by fuzzy sets in partition $\mathbf{C} = \{C_1, ..., C_n\}$, where $C_i : \Omega \to [0,1]$ and Ω is a set of gray levels. It is natural to expect the C_is to be normalized when they are furnished by an expert. But that does not usually happen when the partitions are learnt from data; for example, when fuzzy C-means clustering techniques are used [1], the clusters form Ruspini partitions whose fuzzy sets are usually non-normalized. GFPs could be used to model the first type of fuzzy partition but not the latter one.

An interesting kind of GFP is what we call a *crown partition*, which obeys the unique support and non-core-intersection properties. This kind of partition is useful to avoid inconsistencies in fuzzy rule bases that use residual implication operators (see e.g. [9]).

Another example of GFP, here called *core partition*, is defined using the core-covering and non-core-intersection properties. Together, these properties ensure that every element of the universe of discourse Ω has membership equal to 1 to exactly one fuzzy set in the partition; consequently, the cores of the fuzzy sets themselves form a crisp partition on Ω. A core partition where an element of the domain has positive membership to at most two fuzzy sets in $\mathbf{A}$ is a T-partition (see e.g. [4]) and will be called a 2-core partition throughout the text.

Ruspini and core partitions are such that no level cut of one fuzzy set is included in any of those of another fuzzy set in the same partition, described by the non-level-cut-inclusion property above. This property is much stronger than non-core-intersection and is not obeyed by crown partitions, for instance. Figure 1 illustrates a 2-Ruspini, a 2-core and a crown partition with three fuzzy sets (the central fuzzy set in each partition is highlighted).

Other GFPs are not so well-behaved (see Figure 2). The interest of these partitions is that, being less restricted than the more well-behaved GFPs, they can be closer to data, in case the partitions is learnt by clustering the samples in a given experiment.

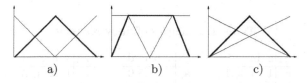

    a)   b)   c)

Fig. 1. Examples of 2-Ruspini (a), 2-core (b) and crown (c) triangular partitions

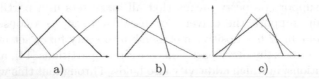

Fig. 2. Examples of triangular general fuzzy partitions

4 Orderly Gradual Fuzzy Relations

We introduce here the notion of an *order compatible fuzzy relation* (OCFR) as a similarity relation that is compatible with a given total order. Let $S : \Omega^2 \rightarrow [0,1]$ be a fuzzy binary relation and $(\Omega, \preceq)$ be a total order. Formally, S is an *OCFR with respect to* $\preceq$, denoted $OCFR_\preceq$, if it obeys the following properties:

- reflexivity and symmetry (see Section 2),
- If $a \preceq b \preceq c$, then $\min(S(a,b), S(b,c)) \geq S(a,c), \forall a,b,c \in \Omega$ (compatibility with total order $\preceq$).

The second property was proposed in [6] for $\Omega = \Re$, called *compatibility with the Euclidean distance*. It grasps the meaning of something being similar to something else as opposed of being distant, in the usual (Euclidean) sense (see also [13] for the same property in reciprocal preference relations context).

The T-transitivity and compatibility with total order properties are not mutually exclusive; for instance $S(x,y) = 1- \mid x-y \mid$ on $\Re$ is both T-transitive and compatible with total order $\leq$. Table 1 brings three fuzzy relations on Ω^2, where $\Omega = \{a, b, c, d\}$ and $(\Omega, \preceq)$ is a total order, with $a \prec b \prec c \prec d$. Relation S_1 is an $OCFR_\preceq$ and S_2 is compatible with $\preceq$ but is not an $OCFR_\preceq$ (it is neither reflexive nor symmetric). S_3 is T-transitive and is not an $OCFR_\preceq$ since it obeys neither compatibility with $\preceq$ nor symmetry.

Let $\top$ be a T-norm and let *weak anti-T-transitivity* be defined as $\forall x,y,z \in \Omega$, $S(x,z) < \top(S(x,y), S(y,z))$. It is easy to prove that when $(\Omega, \preceq)$ is a total order, weak anti-T-transitivity implies compatibility with total order, since for any T-norm $\top$ we have $\top(x,y) \leq min(x,y)$. The converse is however not true: any relation S such that $\exists \ x,y,z \in \Omega$, $S(x,y) = S(y,z)$ is not weak anti-T-transitive. S_2 is an example of a relation that is compatible with total order but not weak anti-T-transitive.

Table 1. Examples of fuzzy relations

S_1	a	b	c	d
a	1	.5	.5	.1
b	.5	1	.7	.3
c	.5	.7	1	.8
d	.1	.3	.8	1

S_2	a	b	c	d
a	.9	.5	.5	0
b	.3	1	.7	.3
c	.2	.4	1	.8
d	.1	.2	.3	1

S_3	a	b	c	d
a	1	.2	.1	.7
b	.2	1	.2	.2
c	1	.2	1	.6
d	.8	.2	..6	1

Note that although relation S_2 is not reflexive, it obeys a weak kind of reflexivity: $\forall x, y \in \Omega, S(x,x) > 0$ and $S(x,y) \leq S(x,x)$ (see [3]). Weak reflexivity does not imply compatibility with total order, but the converse holds when $\forall x, S(x,x) > 0$.

5 Generating OCFRs from GFPs

Transformations (called standard) were proposed in [18], between unrestricted collections of fuzzy sets and unrestricted fuzzy relations (called fuzzy partitions) on a finite domain Ω. The transformation from partitions to relations are given as follows.

- Let $\mathbf{A}=\{A_1,...A_k\}, k \leq |\,\Omega\,|$, be a partition on Ω. A relation S^* is obtained from $\mathbf{A}$ as

$$S^*(x,y) = \sup_i \min(A_i(x), A_i(y)).$$

Relation S^* can also be stated in terms of level cuts:

$$[S^*]_\alpha(x,y) = \begin{cases} 1, \text{if } \exists A_i \in \mathbf{A}, \exists \alpha \in]0,1], \text{ such that } x,y \in [A_i]_\alpha \\ 0, \text{otherwise} \end{cases}$$
$$S^*(x,y) = \sup_{\alpha \in [0,1]}[S^*]_\alpha(x,y)$$

Here we are only interested in obtaining an orderly general similarity relation from a general fuzzy partition, and the transformation above will serve as the basis for our transformations. But before moving further, let us verify an important property of S^*.

Proposition 1. *Let $(\Omega, \preceq)$ be a total order. Let $\mathbf{A}$ be a GFP wrt to $\preceq$ (i.e. the A_i's are convex wrt to $\preceq$). Then $S^* : \Omega \times \Omega \to [0,1]$ defined as*

$$S^*(a,b) = \sup_i \min(A_i(a), A_j(b))$$

is compatible with $\preceq$, i.e., if $a \preceq b \preceq c$, then $\min(S^*(a,b), S^*(b,c)) \geq S^*(a,c)$.

Proof. It is enough to check that, for each i, we have both $\min(A_i(a), A_i(b)) \geq \min(A_i(a), A_i(c))$ and $\min(A_i(b), A_i(c)) \geq \min(A_i(a), A_i(c))$. Indeed, since the A_i's are convex fuzzy sets, one has to only consider the following cases regarding the possible orderings among $A_i(a)$, $A_i(b)$ and $A_i(c)$:

1. $A_i(a) \leq A_i(b) \leq A_i(c)$
2. $A_i(a) \leq A_i(b), A_i(b) \geq A_i(c)$
3. $A_i(a) \geq A_i(b) \geq A_i(c)$

It is very easy now to check that in each of these cases the required conditions hold.

Let S be a generic reflexive and symmetric relation on Ω, $\mathbf{A}$ be a fuzzy partition on Ω and $S^*(a,b) = \sup_i \min(A_i(a), A_i(b))$. Let us examine the following properties:

- $\forall A_i \in \mathbf{A}, \forall c \in core(A_i), \forall x \in \Omega, S(c,x) = S(x,c) = A_i(x)$
  (core compatibility);
- $\forall a, b \in \Omega, S(a,b) \geq S^*(a,b) = \sup_i \min(A_i(a), A_i(b))$
  (support compatibility).

Core compatibility ensures that the "slice" from S, corresponding to an element at the core of a set A_i, is exactly the same as A_i. Support compatibility ensures that any two elements of Ω that belong to level cut $[A_i]_\alpha$ of a fuzzy set A_i in $\mathbf{A}$ will also belong to level cut $[S]_\alpha$ of relation S.

We say that a fuzzy relation S is *core-support compatible* with a fuzzy partition $\mathbf{A}$ defined in the same domain Ω, if S is core compatible and support compatible with $\mathbf{A}$. The following transformation is an example of a transformation that is support compatible but not core compatible:

$$S_{supp}(a,b) = \begin{cases} 1, \text{if } \exists A_i \in \mathbf{A}, a \in core(A_i) \\ S^*(a,b), \text{otherwise} \end{cases}$$

Let $(\Omega, \preceq)$ be a total order and $\mathbf{A} = \{A_1, ..., A_n\}$ be a 2-Ruspini partition. Moreover, let

$$- S_{id}(a,b) = \begin{cases} 1, \text{if } a = b \\ 0, \text{otherwise} \end{cases}$$

$$- S_i(a,c) = S_i(c,a) = \begin{cases} A_i(a), \text{if } \exists A_i \in \mathbf{A}, c \in core(A_i) \\ 0, \text{otherwise} \end{cases}$$

$$- S_p(a,b) = \bigcup_i S_i(a,b), \forall a, b \in \Omega$$
$$- S_f = S_{id} \bigcup S_p.$$

It is easy to prove that the finest reflexive and symmetric fuzzy relation that is core compatible with GFP$_\preceq$ $\mathbf{A}$ is given by S_f. This relation is not an OCFR$_\preceq$ because it is not compatible with total order $\preceq$. Figure 3.b illustrates S_f for $\mathbf{A} = \{A_1, A_2, A_3, A_4, A_5\}$, shown in Figure 3.a, with $A_1 = (0,0,2)$, $A_2 = (0,2,3)$, $A_3 = (2,3,4)$, $A_4 = (3,4,6)$, $A_5 = (4,6,6)$. We can see that this fuzzy relation is not support compatible with A; for instance, we have $\min(A_1(4.5), A_1(5)) > 0$ but $S_f(4.5, 5) = 0$. It is also not a OCFR$_\leq$, because $\min(S_f(4.5, 5), S_f(5, 6)) = 0$ but $S_f(4.5, 6) > 0$.

Proposition 2. *Let $(\Omega, \preceq)$ be a total order. The finest OCFR$_\preceq$ core-support compatible with a GFP $\mathbf{A}$ on Ω is given by $S_{id}^* = S^* \cup S_{id}$.*

Proof. By definition, S^* is obviously the finest symmetric fuzzy relation that is core-support compatible with $\mathbf{A}$. Its reflexive closure $S_{id}^* = S^* \cup S_{id}$ is an OCFR$_\preceq$ and therefore it is the finest core-support compatible one with $\mathbf{A}$.

Proposition 2 gives a lower bound on the core-support compatible OCFRs that can be derived from a GFP $\mathbf{A}$, considering a total order $(\Omega, \preceq)$. In particular,

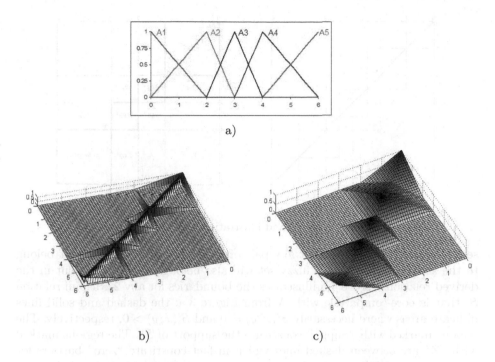

a)

b)   c)

Fig. 3. Example of a GFP **A** and its corresponding S_f and S^* relations

the support of any relation S that is core and support compatible with **A** must include the support of S^*, i.e., $supp(S^*) \subseteq supp(S)$.

Proposition 3. *Given a 2-Ruspini partition* **A** *on* Ω, *let* S *be any fuzzy binary relation that is core and support compatible with partition* **A**. *Then* $supp(S) = supp(S^*)$.

Proof. Since S^* is finer than S, i.e. $S \geq S^*$, we obviously have $supp(S^*) \subseteq supp(S)$. To show the other inclusion, suppose x, y are such that $S^*(x, y) = 0$. Since **A** covers Ω, there exists $A_i \in$ **A** such that $A_i(x) > 0$. But by definition of S^*, if $A_i(x) > 0$ then $A_i(y) = 0$. Since **A** is a 2-Ruspini partition, $A_i(x) = 1$. Therefore, $S(x, y) = A_i(y) = 0$.

Proposition 3 gives an upper bound for the support of a fuzzy relation S derived from a 2-Ruspini partition.

Figure 3.c depicts relation S^* derived from the Ruspini 2-GFP **A** shown in Figure 3.a. The projection of relation S^*_{id} for the same partition is shown in Figure 4.a; the thin solid lines represent the level cut at $\alpha = .5$, the dashed lines represent the support and the broad diagonal line represents the core. It is easy to see that, contrary to S^*_{id}, S^* is weak-reflexive but not reflexive.

In Figure 4.a, the upper right and lower left regions represent the complement of the support of both S^* and S^*_{id}. We can see that we obtain the original partition **A**, when we take a "slice" of the relation at the core of each fuzzy

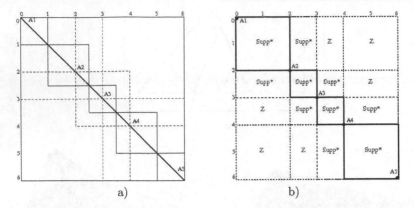

Fig. 4. Projection of S_{id}^* and illustration of of core compatibility

set. Moreover, we can see that any pair of elements of the domain that belong to the same α-level cut of a fuzzy set will also belong to the α-level cut in the derived relation. Figure 4.b illustrates the boundaries for any 2-Ruspini relation S' that is core-compatible with **A** from Figure 3.a: the dashed and solid lines indicate areas where necessarily $S'(x,y) = 0$ and $S'(x,y) > 0$, respectively. The regions marked with "Supp*" constitute the support of S^*. The regions marked with "Z" are between dashed lines which in fact constitute "zero" barriers for the core-compatibility property.

6   Conclusion

We proposed here some properties that we find reasonable for a type of fuzzy similarity relations, called order compatible fuzzy relations (OCFR), that are useful when any two elements in the universe of discourse are considered to be the more similar the closer they are with respect to a given total order. We also introduced a general class of collections of fuzzy sets, called general fuzzy partitions (GFP), and then proposed some compatibility properties that we consider reasonable when generating OCFRs from them. We gave some formal results; in particular, we calculated a lower bound on OCFRs that can be derived from a GFP, in the sense of fuzzy set inclusion.

As future work, we intend to extend our study to other specific classes of fuzzy partitions, such as crown partitions and core partitions. Also, we intend to investigate generators of OCFRs from GFPs. Several methods may be investigated, such as those involving min-max operations and/or interpolation schemes. One possible interpolation scheme consists in creating a fuzzy set A_a and A_b for each pair of elements (a, b) of the domain Ω and then making $S(a, b) = \min(A_b(a), A_a(b))$. Another one consists in creating a fuzzy set A_z for each element $z \in [a, b]$ and then making $S(a, b) = \sup_{z \in [a,b]} \min(A_z(a), A_z(b))$. Note that even though these methods appear costly at first sight, it is possible that they can be efficiently computed parting from a small set of relevant points in a partition **A**, e.g., those given by the support and core of the fuzzy sets in **A**.

In what regards which interpolation method to employ, there exists a plethora of choices in the literature, many of them addressed in [2] and [12]. The application of different pairs (interpolation method, approach) will certainly produce different results but it is also likely that for some specific types of OCFRs (e.g. Ruspini partitions), the results will be the same.

Acknowledgements

The authors are deeply indebted to Lluis Godo for helpful comments when preparing this manuscript. The authors would also like to thank Francesc Esteva and Bernard de Baets for pointing to pertinent literature, Ana Paula A. Castro for help with the figures and anonymous reviewers for their comments.

References

1. Bezdek, J.C.: Pattern Recognition with Fuzzy Objective Function Algoritms. Plenum Press, New York (1981)
2. Bouchon-Meunier, B., Esteva, F., Godo, L., Rifqi, M., Sandri, S.: A principled approach to fuzzy rule base interpolation using similarity relations. In: EUSFLAT-LFA Joint Conference, pp. 757–763 (2005)
3. Das, M., Chakraborty, M.K., Ghoshal, T.K.: Fuzzy tolerance relation, fuzzy tolerance space and basis. Fuzzy Sets and Systems 97(3), 361–369 (1998)
4. De Baets, B., Mesiar, R.: T-partitions. Fuzzy Sets and Systems 97(2), 211–223 (1998)
5. Drummond, I., Godo, L., Sandri, S.: Restoring Consistency in Systems of Fuzzy Gradual Rules Using Similarity Relations. In: Bittencourt, G., Ramalho, G.L. (eds.) SBIA 2002. LNCS (LNAI), vol. 2507, pp. 386–396. Springer, Heidelberg (2002)
6. Drummond, I., Godo, L., Sandri, S.: Learning fuzzy systems with similarity relations. In: De Baets, B., Kaynak, O., Bilgiç, T. (eds.) IFSA 2003. LNCS, vol. 2715, pp. 516–523. Springer, Heidelberg (2003)
7. Fanoiki, T., Drummond, I., Sandri, S.: Case-Based Reasoning Retreival and Reuse Using Case Resemblance Hypergraphs. In: WCCI 2010, pp. 864–870 (2010)
8. Godo, L., Sandri, S.: A similarity-based approach to deal with inconsistency in systems of fuzzy gradual rules. In: IPMU 2002, pp. 1655–1662 (2002)
9. Jones, H., Charnomordic, B., Dubois, D., Guillaume, S.: Practical Inference With Systems of Gradual Implicative Rules. IEEE Transaction On Fuzzy Systems 17(1), 61–78 (2009)
10. Luce, R.D.: Semi-Orders and a Theory of Utility Discrimination. Econometrica 24, 178–191 (1956)
11. Martins-Bedé, F.T., Godo, L., Sandri, S., Dutra, L.V., Freitas, C.C., Carvalho, O.S., Guimarães, R.J.P.S., Amaral, R.S.: Classification of Schistosomiasis Prevalence Using Fuzzy Case-Based Reasoning. In: Cabestany, J., Sandoval, F., Prieto, A., Corchado, J.M. (eds.) IWANN 2009. LNCS, vol. 5517, pp. 1053–1060. Springer, Heidelberg (2009)
12. Perfilieva, I., Dubois, D., Prade, H., Esteva, F., Godo, L., Hodáková, P.: Interpolation of fuzzy data: Analytical approach and overview. Fuzzy Sets and Systems (available online August 19, 2010) (in Press)

13. Rademaker, M., De Baets, B.: Aggregation of monotone reciprocal relations with application to group decision making. Fuzzy Sets and Systems (available online November 12, 2010) (in Press)
14. Ruspini, R.: A new approach to clustering. Information and Control 15, 177–200 (1969)
15. Slowinski, R., Vanderpooten, D.: A Generalized Definition of Rough Approximations Based on Similarity. IEEE Trans. KDE 12(2), 331–335 (2000)
16. Soldano, H., Viari, A., Champesme, M.: Searching for flexible repeated patterns using a non-transitive similarity relation. Pattern Recognition Letters 16(3), 233–246 (1995)
17. Soto, A., Recasens, J.: Modelling a linguistic variable as a hierarchical family of partitions induced by an indistinguishability operator. Fuzzy Sets and Systems 121(3), 427–437 (2001)
18. Thiele, H.: A characterization of arbitrary Ruspini partitions by fuzzy similarity relations. In: Sixth IEEE International Conference on Fuzzy Systems, pp. 131–134 (1997)
19. Zadeh, L.: Similarity relations and fuzzy orderings. Information Sciences 3(2), 177–200 (1971)

Web Services and *Incerta Spiriti*: A Game Theoretic Approach to Uncertainty*

Joaquim Gabarro[1], Maria Serna[1], and Alan Stewart[2]

[1] ALBCOM. LSI Dept. Universitat Politècnica de Catalunya, Barcelona
[2] School of Computer Science, The Queen's University of Belfast, Belfast
{gabarro,mjserna}@lsi.upc.edu, a.stewart@qub.ac.uk

Abstract. A web-service is a remote computational facility which is made available for general use by means of the internet. An orchestration is a multi-threaded computation which invokes remote services. In this paper game theory is used to analyse the behaviour of orchestration evaluations when underlying web-services are unreliable. *Uncertainty profiles* are proposed as a means of defining bounds on the number of service failures that can be expected during an orchestration evaluation. An uncertainty profile describes a strategic situation that can be analyzed using a zero-sum *angel-daemon* game with two competing players: an angel a whose objective is to minimize damage to an orchestration and a daemon $\eth$ who acts in a destructive fashion. An uncertainty profile is assessed using the value of its angel daemon game. It is shown that uncertainty profiles form a partial order which is monotonic with respect to assessment.

Keywords: Web orchestrations, zero-sum games, angel-daemon games, web incerta spiriti, uncertainty profile, assessment, partial order.

1 Introduction

Consider the behaviour of a set of services which have been made available for general use on a wide-area network. Demand for a particular service s can fluctuate – if the cost and quality of service (QoS) of s are attractive then s is likely to acquire additional users. If demand is excessive then s may fail to deliver its QoS (in an extreme situation s may fail).

Conventionally, probability is used to assess risk [5,6,7,14]. However, it is problematic to apply probabilistic techniques to the treatment of unreliable services due to the complexity of the interactions within a web environment. In [1] the term *uncertainty* refers to situations in which there are no objective standards upon which to construct a probabilistic theory. In this paper we treat the uncertainty associated with web-services by means of angel daemon games – the goal is to formulate a way of analysing the performance of service-based computations

---

* J. Gabarró and M. Serna are partially supported by TIN-2007-66523 (FORMAL-ISM), and SGR 2009-2015 (ALBCOM). Alan Stewart is partially supported by EP-SRC project EP/I03405X/1 (ECHO).

W. Liu (Ed.): ECSQARU 2011, LNAI 6717, pp. 651–662, 2011.

in a way that lies between over-optimism (all services behave as specified by their QoS specifications) and over-pessimism (all services are degraded, perhaps even broken). This angel-daemon approach can be applied to both single and multi-user web-service scenarios; in the former case a set of services are orchestrated to deliver a specified outcome while in the later a number of users compete for resources supplied by services [4]. In this paper the simpler orchestration scenario is used to derive basic properties of uncertainty profiles.

2   Orc and Uncertainty Profiles

An orchestration is a user-defined program that utilises web services. Typical examples of services might be: an eigensolver, a search engine or a database. A *service* accepts an argument and *publishes* a result value[1]. For example, a call to a search engine, *find*(s), may publish the set of sites which *currently* offer service s. A service is said to be *silent* if it does not publish a result when called. Service calls may induce *side effects*. A service call can publish *at most one response*. A service s may fail to respond when it is called in an unreliable environment. The orchestration language Orc [8] contains a number of inbuilt services: 0 is always silent whereas $1(x)$ always publishes x. The service $RTimer(t)$ returns a signal after t units of time – $RTimer$ is often used to program time-outs. *if*(b) publishes a signal if b is true and remains silent otherwise. An orchestration which composes a number of service calls into a complex computation can be represented by an Orc expression. The simplest kind of Orc expression is a service call. Two Orc expressions P and Q can be combined using the following operators:

- Sequence $P > x > Q(x)$: The orchestration P is evaluated: for each output v, published by P, an instance $Q(v)$ is invoked. If P publishes the stream of values, $v_1, v_2, \ldots v_n$, then $P > x > Q(x)$ publishes some interleaving of the set $\{Q(v_1), Q(v_2), \ldots, Q(v_n)\}$. The abbreviation $P \gg Q$ is used in situations where Q does not depend on x.
- Symmetric Parallelism $P \mid Q$: The independent orchestrations P and Q are executed in parallel; $P \mid Q$ publishes *some* interleaving of the values published by P and Q.
- Asymmetric parallelism $P(x) < x < Q$: The dependent orchestrations P and Q are evaluated in parallel; P may become blocked by a dependency on x. The first result published by Q is bound to x, the remainder of Q's evaluation is terminated and evaluation of the blocked residue of P is resumed. The abbreviation $P \ll Q$ is used in situations where P does not depend on x.

Example 1. Consider orchestrations which distribute digital newspapers by email.

$$Two\_Each = (CNN \mid BBC) > x > (EmailAlice(x) \mid EmailBob(x))$$

$$One\_Each = ((CNN > x > EmailAlice(x)) \mid (BBC > x > EmailBob(x)))$$

Two_Each delivers digital newspapers from both *CNN* and *BBC* to Alice and Bob. In *One_Each* only the *CNN* paper is delivered to Alice while only the *BBC* paper is delivered to Bob. □

---

[1] The words "publishes","returns" and "outputs" are used interchangeably.

Web environments are unreliable. Sites evolve and a user has little (or no) control over the execution environment. When a complex orchestration E is evaluated it is *unrealistic* to assume that all necessary services will be working.

> **Reliability assumption.** Service performance is variable and services can fail. A failed service remains silent when called. The behaviour of working service is always consistent with its specification.

Let E be an orchestration and $\alpha(E)$ be the set of sites that are called in E with $\alpha_+(E) = \alpha(E) \setminus \{0\}$. Let $\mathcal{F}$ denote a set a sites that are currently non-responsive. The effect of evaluating an orchestration E in such an environment is found by replacing all occurrences of services s, where $s \in \mathcal{F}$, by 0. An orchestration with multiple threads (and built-in redundancy) may still return partial results even if some services fail. Let $\mathsf{fail}_{\mathcal{F}}(E)$ denote the effect of evaluating E in an environment where services in $\mathcal{F}$ fail.

Definition 1 (resilience measure). *The behaviour of E in a failure environment $\mathcal{F}$ is denoted by $\mathsf{fail}_{\mathcal{F}}(E)$. The resilience of $\mathsf{fail}_{\mathcal{F}}(E)$ is $\mathsf{out}(\mathsf{fail}_{\mathcal{F}}(E))$, the number of outputs, out, published by E. Thus, $0 \leq \mathsf{out}(\mathsf{fail}_{\mathcal{F}}(E)) \leq \mathsf{out}(E)$.*

Definition 2 (non-blocking service). *A service s is* non-blocking *if the call $s(v_1, \ldots, v_n)$ publishes a result for all well-defined arguments $v_1, \ldots, v_n$; otherwise s is* potentially blocking.

For example, $Rtimer(t)$ is non-blocking while *if* is potentially blocking. The following Lemma is adapted from [3].

Lemma 1. *Given a non-blocking, well formed expression E and a failure set $\mathcal{F} \subseteq \alpha_+(E)$, the values $\mathsf{out}(E)$ and $\mathsf{out}(\mathsf{fail}_{\mathcal{F}}(F))$ can be computed in polynomial time with respect to the length of the expression E.*

Proof. By definition $\mathsf{out}(0) = 0$, $\mathsf{out}(1) = 1$. For a non-blocking service s it follows that $\mathsf{out}(s(v_1, \ldots, v_k)) = 1$ if all parameters are defined otherwise is similar site 0. Let E_1, E_2 be non-blocking well formed Orc expressions,

$$\mathsf{out}(E_1 | E_2) = \mathsf{out}(E_1) + \mathsf{out}(E_2), \; \mathsf{out}(E_1 > z > E_2(z)) = \mathsf{out}(E_1) * \mathsf{out}(E_2(z))$$

Finally $\mathsf{out}(E_1(z) < z < E_2) = \mathsf{out}(E_1(z))$ when $\mathsf{out}(E_2) > 0$, when $\mathsf{out}(E_2) = 0$ we have $\mathsf{out}(E_1(z) < z < E_2) = \mathsf{out}(E_1(\bot))$ otherwise. Here $E(\bot)$ denotes the behaviour of E when z is undefined; $E(\bot)$ is found by replacing all service calls with a z-dependency by 0. Therefore, given a non-blocking well formed Orc expression E, $\mathsf{out}(E)$, can be computed in polynomial time with respect to the length of the expression E. $\qquad\square$

Example 2. If no failures arise in Example 1 then $\mathsf{out}(Two\_Each) = 4$ and $\mathsf{out}(One\_Each) = 2$. If $\mathcal{F} = \{CNN\}$ then $\mathsf{out}(\mathsf{fail}_{\mathcal{F}}(Two\_Each)) = 2$. If $\mathcal{F} = \{CNN, EmailAlice\}$ then $\mathsf{out}(\mathsf{fail}_{\mathcal{F}}(Two\_Each)) = 1$. $\qquad\square$

From Lemma 1 it follows that

Lemma 2 (monotonicity). *Given a non-blocking, well formed expression* E *and* $\mathcal{F}, \mathcal{F}'$ *in* $\alpha_+(E)$ *such that* $\mathcal{F} \subseteq \mathcal{F}'$, *it holds* $out(fail_{\mathcal{F}'}(E)) \leq out(fail_{\mathcal{F}}(E))$.

The analysis of orchestration resilience is now extended from environments where the identity of potentially failing services is fixed *a priori* to untrusted environments where the identities of failing services are not specified in advance. The proposed approach models service failure in a way that lies between over-optimism (the only services that fail are those that do not adversely effect the evaluation of E) and over-pessimism (all critical services fail). In $\alpha_+(E)$ we consider two disjoint sets $\mathcal{A}$ (angelic services) and $\mathcal{D}$ (daemonic services) such that $\mathcal{A} \cup \mathcal{D} \subseteq \alpha_+(E)$. Sites in $\alpha_+(E) \backslash \{\mathcal{A} \cup \mathcal{D}\}$ are trusted. Resilience is analysed by assuming that service failures in $\mathcal{A}$ *cause the least amount of damage to* E whereas service failures in $\mathcal{D}$ *maximise damage to the application*. The notion of uncertainty profile is introduced to model the perception of orchestration resilience. A uncertainty profile defines $\mathcal{A}$, $\mathcal{D}$ together with the number of service failures that can be expected to occur within both $\mathcal{A}$ and $\mathcal{D}$ ($f_{\mathcal{A}}$, and $f_{\mathcal{D}}$, respectively):

Definition 3 (uncertainty profile). $\mathcal{U} = \langle E, \mathcal{A}, \mathcal{D}, f_{\mathcal{A}}, f_{\mathcal{D}} \rangle$ *is an uncertainty profile for orchestration* E *where* $\mathcal{A} \cup \mathcal{D} \subseteq \alpha_+(E)$, $\mathcal{A} \cap \mathcal{D} = \emptyset$, $f_{\mathcal{A}} \leq \#\mathcal{A}$ *and* $f_{\mathcal{D}} \leq \#\mathcal{D}$.

The set of all uncertainty profiles for E is:

$$\mathcal{U}(E) = \{\langle E, \mathcal{A}, \mathcal{D}, f_{\mathcal{A}}, f_{\mathcal{D}} \rangle \mid \mathcal{A} \cup \mathcal{D} \subseteq \alpha_+(E), \mathcal{A} \cap \mathcal{D} = \emptyset, f_{\mathcal{A}} \leq \#\mathcal{A}, f_{\mathcal{D}} \leq \#\mathcal{D}\}$$

An orchestration E can be analysed using a number of different profiles selected from $\mathcal{U}(E)$. For example, if t denotes the expected number of site failures that occur during the evaluation of E then the performance of E could be analysed using the profiles $\mathcal{U}_{best} = \langle E, \alpha(E), \{\}, t, 0 \rangle$, $\mathcal{U}_{worst} = \langle E, \{\}, \alpha(E), 0, t \rangle$ and $\mathcal{U}_{mixed} = \langle E, \mathcal{A}, \mathcal{D}, p, q \rangle$ where $\mathcal{A} \cup \mathcal{D} \subseteq \alpha(E)$ and $p + q = t$. In practice, mixed case analysis could be carried out using several profiles, for different choices of $\mathcal{A}$ and $\mathcal{D}$. One option may be to indentify the set $\mathcal{A}$ with sites whose behaviours are consistent with their SLAs and the set $\mathcal{D}$ with sites which are identified with more chaotic behaviour.

A more restrictive version of uncertainty profile (called a risk profile [3]) satisfies the stronger condition $\mathcal{A} \cup \mathcal{D} = \alpha_+(E)$. By relaxing this condition to $\mathcal{A} \cup \mathcal{D} \subseteq \alpha_+(E)$ it is possible to develop a partial order for profiles.

3 Angels and Daemons as Web Incerta Spiriti

Uncertainty profiles can be analysed using zero-sum games [11,12], as developed by John von Neumann and Oskar Morgenstern [10]. Here a class of zero-sum games called angel-daemon games [3] is used to provide a mixed analysis of uncertainty, lying between over-optimism and over-pessimism.

Definition 4 (angel-daemon game). *The profile* $\mathcal{U} = \langle E, \mathcal{A}, \mathcal{D}, f_{\mathcal{A}}, f_{\mathcal{D}} \rangle$ *has an associated zero-sum* angel-daemon game $\Gamma(\mathcal{U}) = \langle \{\mathfrak{a}, \mathfrak{d}\}, A_{\mathfrak{a}}, A_{\mathfrak{d}}, u_{\mathfrak{a}}, u_{\mathfrak{d}} \rangle$: *the players,* $\mathfrak{a}$ *and* $\mathfrak{d}$ *have the following sets of actions,*

- *The angel* $\mathfrak{a}$ *selects* f_A *distinct failing services from* $\mathcal{A}$. *Calls to remaining services in* $\mathcal{A} \setminus a$ *are successful. The actions are* $A_{\mathfrak{a}} = \{a \subseteq \mathcal{A} \mid \#a = f_A\}$.
- *The daemon* $\mathfrak{d}$ *selects* f_D *distinct failing services from* $\mathcal{D}$. *Calls to remaining services in* $\mathcal{D} \setminus d$ *are successful. The actions are* $A_{\mathfrak{d}} = \{d \subseteq \mathcal{D} \mid \#d = f_D\}$.

Sites which are not in either $\mathcal{A}$ *or* $\mathcal{D}$ *are assumed to be working. A strategy profile* $s = (a, d)$ *defines a set of failing sites* $a \cup d$. *The resilience of* E *under* s *is measured by the angel's utility* $u_{\mathfrak{a}}(s) = out(fail_{a \cup d}(E))$. *As the game is zero-sum:* $u_{\mathfrak{d}}(s) = -u_{\mathfrak{a}}(s)$.

Here $\mathfrak{a}$ and $\mathfrak{d}$ model "ambiguity or uncertainty" and represent *Web Incerta Spiriti* [1]. Angel-daemon games are zero sum because $u_{\mathfrak{a}}(a,d) + u_{\mathfrak{d}}(a,d) = 0$. As usual (in zero-sum games) all Nash equilibria (pure or mixed) are assessed using player 1's utility [10] (i.e. $\mathfrak{a}$'s utility). The value of this utility $\nu(\Gamma)$ is called the *value of* Γ. A player's choice of action can be defined probabilistically. A mixed strategy for player $\mathfrak{a}$ is a probability distribution $\alpha : A_{\mathfrak{a}} \to [0,1]$ and, similarly, a mixed strategy for $\mathfrak{d}$ is a probability distribution $\beta : A_{\mathfrak{d}} \to [0,1]$. A mixed strategy profile is a tuple (α, β) and $u_{\mathfrak{a}}(\alpha, \beta) = \sum_{(a,d) \in A_{\mathfrak{a}} \times A_{\mathfrak{d}}} \alpha(a)\beta(d)u_{\mathfrak{a}}(a,d)$. Let $\Delta_{\mathfrak{a}}$ and $\Delta_{\mathfrak{d}}$ denote the set of mixed strategies for $\mathfrak{a}$ and $\mathfrak{d}$, respectively. It is well known [10] that there is always a mixed saddle point (α, β) satisfying

$$\nu(\Gamma) = u_{\mathfrak{a}}(\alpha, \beta) = \max_{\alpha' \in \Delta_{\mathfrak{a}}} \min_{\beta' \in \Delta_{\mathfrak{d}}} u_{\mathfrak{a}}(\alpha', \beta') = \min_{\beta' \in \Delta_{\mathfrak{d}}} \max_{\alpha' \in \Delta_{\mathfrak{a}}} u_{\mathfrak{a}}(\alpha', \beta')$$

The set of saddle points (pure or mixed) coincides with the set of Nash equilibria (pure or mixed). The following property is adapted from Proposition 116.2 in [12]. A mixed strategy profile (α, β) is a mixed Nash equilibrium iff:

- for any $a \in A_{\mathfrak{a}}$ such such that $\alpha(a) > 0$ it holds $u_{\mathfrak{a}}(a, \beta) = u_{\mathfrak{a}}(\alpha, \beta)$,
- for any $d \in A_{\mathfrak{d}}$ such such that $\beta(d) > 0$ it holds $u_{\mathfrak{d}}(\alpha, d) = u_{\mathfrak{a}}(\alpha, \beta)$,
- for any $a \in A_{\mathfrak{a}}$ such such that $\alpha(a) = 0$ it holds $u_{\mathfrak{a}}(a, \beta) \leq u_{\mathfrak{a}}(\alpha, \beta)$,
- and, for any $d \in A_{\mathfrak{d}}$ such such that $\beta(a) = 0$ it holds $u_{\mathfrak{a}}(\beta, d) \leq u_{\mathfrak{a}}(\alpha, \beta)$.

Definition 5 (assessment). *The assessment* $\nu(\mathcal{U})$ *of an uncertainty profile* $\mathcal{U}$ *is defined to be the value of its associated angel-daemon* $\Gamma(\mathcal{U})$ *(i.e.* $\nu(\Gamma(\mathcal{U})))$.

Example 3. Let $E = A \mid B \mid ((C_1 \mid C_2 \mid \cdots \mid C_k) \ll (D \mid F))$, $k \geq 1$. Consider the uncertainly profile $\mathcal{U}_1 = \langle E, \{A\}, \{B, D\}, 1, 1 \rangle$. In $\Gamma(\mathcal{U}_1)$, the utilitites are $u_1(\{A\}, \{B\}) = out((0 \mid 0 \mid (C_1 \mid C_2 \mid \cdots \mid C_k) \ll (D \mid F))) = k$. Using the usual game representation $\Gamma(\mathcal{U}_1)$ is :

$$\mathfrak{d}$$

	$\{B\}$	$\{D\}$
$\mathfrak{a}\,\{A\}$	k	$k+1$

$$\Gamma(\mathcal{U}_1)$$

$$\mathfrak{d}$$

	$\{B\}$	$\{D\}$
$\mathfrak{a}\,\{A\}$	k	$k+1$
$\{F\}$	$k+1$	2

$$\Gamma(\mathcal{U}_2)$$

and $\nu(\mathcal{U}_1) = k$. Given $\mathcal{U}_2 = \langle E, \{A, F\}, \{B, D\}, 1, 1 \rangle$, the game $\Gamma(\mathcal{U}_2)$ has no PNE. Consider a mixed Nash equilibrium (α, β) such that $\alpha = (p, 1-p)$ and $\beta =$

$(q, 1 - q)$ with $0 < p, q < 1$. As $p > 0$ and $1 - p > 0$ it follows that $u_a(\{A\}, \beta) = u_a(\{F\}, \beta) = u_a(\alpha, \beta)$. As $u_a(\{A\}, \beta) = k + 1 - q$ and $u_a(\{F\}, \beta) = qk + 2 - q$ we obtain $q = (k - 1)/k$. Therefore $u_a(\{A\}, \beta) = u_a(\{F\}, \beta) = k + 1 - (k - 1)/k$.

As $q > 0$ and $1 - q > 0$ it also follows that $u_a(\alpha, \{B\}) = u_a(\alpha, \{D\}) = u_a(\alpha, \beta)$. As $u_a(\alpha, \{B\}) = k + 1 - p$ and $u_a(\alpha, \beta) = pk - p + 2$ we get $p = (k - 1)/k$. Thus $\Gamma(\mathcal{U}_2) = u_a(\alpha, \beta) = k + 1 - (k - 1)/k$ $(> k)$. □

Lemma 3. *If $\mathcal{U} = \langle E, A, D, p, q \rangle$ is an uncertainty profile then $0 \leq \nu(\mathcal{U}) \leq \text{out}(E)$. If $A \cup D = \alpha_+(E)$ and $p + q = \#\alpha_+(E)$ then $\nu(\mathcal{U}) = 0$. If $p + q = 0$ then $\nu(\mathcal{U}) = \text{out}(E)$.*

Proof. Let (α, β) a Nash equilibrium such that $u_a(\alpha, \beta) = \nu(\mathcal{U})$. For any (a, d) it holds that $\text{out}(\text{fail}_{a \cup d})(E) \leq \text{out}(E)$ by Lemma 2 we have:

$$u_a(\alpha, \beta) = \sum_{(a,d) \in A_a \times A_\partial} \alpha(a)\beta(d)u_a(a, d) = \sum_{(a,d) \in A_a \times A_\partial} \alpha(a)\beta(d)\text{out}(\text{fail}_{a \cup d})(E)$$

$$\leq \sum_{(a,d) \in A_a \times A_\partial} \alpha(a)\beta(d)\text{out}(E) = \text{out}(E) \sum_{(a,d) \in A_a \times A_\partial} \alpha(a)\beta(d) = \text{out}(E)$$

Case $\nu(\mathcal{U}) \geq 0$ is similar. When $A \cup D = \alpha_+(E)$ and $p + q = \#\alpha_+(E)$ it holds $\text{out}_{a \cup d}(E) = \text{out}_{\alpha_+(E)}(E) = 0$. When $p + q = 0$ as $p = 0$ and $q = 0$ it holds $\text{out}_{a \cup d}(E) = \text{out}_\emptyset(E) = \text{out}(E)$. □

4 Partial Order Sets

Given $\mathcal{U} = \langle E, A, D, p, q \rangle$ and $\mathcal{U}' = \langle E, A', D', p', q' \rangle$, $\mathcal{U}'$ is said to *be less risky than $\mathcal{U}$* (written as $\mathcal{U} \sqsubseteq \mathcal{U}'$) if all of the following conditions hold:

- the number of failures does not increase: $p \geq p'$ and $q \geq q'$.
- the angel has greater (or equal) freedom in $\mathcal{U}'$ compared to $\mathcal{U}$: i.e. $A \subseteq A'$.
- the daemon has reduced (or equal) freedom in $\mathcal{U}'$ compared to $\mathcal{U}$:: $D' \subseteq D$.

Ordering profiles in this way gives rise to a partial order $\sqsubseteq$ (see Theorem 1, see [2] for information about partial orders).

Definition 6. *Given $\mathcal{U} = \langle E, A, D, p, q \rangle$, $\mathcal{U}' = \langle E, A', D', p', q' \rangle$, we say $\mathcal{U} \sqsubseteq \mathcal{U}'$ if $A \subseteq A'$, $D' \subseteq D$ and $p' \leq p$, $q' \leq q$.*

Theorem 1. *Given E the set $\mathcal{U}(E)$ and the relation $\sqsubseteq$ form a partial order. The top is $\top_E = \langle E, \alpha_+(E), \emptyset, 0, 0 \rangle$ and $\nu(\top_E) = \text{out}(E)$. Given $\mathcal{U} = \langle E, A, D, p, q \rangle$ and $\mathcal{U}' = \langle E, A', D', p', q' \rangle$ the lub (least upper bound) is*

$$\mathcal{U} \sqcup \mathcal{U}' = \langle E, A \cup A', D \cap D', \min\{p, p'\}, \min\{q, q', \#(D \cap D')\} \rangle$$

An element $\mathcal{U}$ is minimal iff for any $\mathcal{U}'$ such that $\mathcal{U}' \sqsubseteq \mathcal{U}$ it holds $\mathcal{U}' = \mathcal{U}$. The set of minimal elements is $\min(E) = \{\langle E, A, D, \#A, \#D \rangle \mid A \cup D = \alpha_+(E)\}$ and the assessement of any $\mathcal{U} \in \min(E)$ verifies $\nu(\mathcal{U}) = 0$.

Proof. It is straightforward to prove that $\sqsubseteq$ is a partial order. Consider top. For any $\mathcal{U} \in \mathcal{U}(E)$ it holds $\mathcal{U} \sqsubseteq \top_E$ because $\mathcal{A} \subseteq \alpha_+(E)$ and $p \geq 0$, moreover $\emptyset \subseteq \mathcal{D}$ and $q \geq 0$. Direct application of Lemma 3 gives the asessement of top. Consider lub. To prove that $\mathcal{U} \sqcup \mathcal{U}' \in \mathcal{U}(E)$ we check

$$(\mathcal{A} \cup \mathcal{A}') \cap (\mathcal{D} \cap \mathcal{D}') = (\mathcal{A} \cap (\mathcal{D} \cap \mathcal{D}')) \cup (\mathcal{A}' \cap (\mathcal{D} \cap \mathcal{D}')) = \emptyset$$

Notice that $\mathcal{U} \sqsubseteq \mathcal{U} \sqcup \mathcal{U}'$ because $\mathcal{A} \subseteq \mathcal{A} \cup \mathcal{A}'$, $\min\{p, p'\} \leq p$, $\mathcal{D} \cap \mathcal{D}' \subseteq \mathcal{D}$ and $\min\{q, q', \#(\mathcal{D} \cap \mathcal{D}')\} \leq q$, similarly $\mathcal{U}' \sqsubseteq \mathcal{U} \sqcup \mathcal{U}'$. Finally, we prove that, for any $\mathcal{P} = \langle E, \mathcal{A}_\mathcal{P}, \mathcal{D}_\mathcal{P}, p_\mathcal{P}, q_\mathcal{P}, \rangle$ such that $\mathcal{U} \sqsubseteq \mathcal{P}$ and $\mathcal{U}' \sqsubseteq \mathcal{P}$ it holds $\mathcal{U} \sqcup \mathcal{U}' \sqsubseteq \mathcal{P}$. As $\mathcal{A} \subseteq \mathcal{A}_\mathcal{P}$ and $\mathcal{A}' \subseteq \mathcal{A}_\mathcal{P}$ it holds $\mathcal{A} \cup \mathcal{A}' \subseteq \mathcal{A}_\mathcal{P}$. As $p_\mathcal{P} \leq p$ and $p_\mathcal{P} \leq p'$ it holds $p_\mathcal{P} \leq \min\{p, p'\}$. As $\mathcal{D}_\mathcal{P} \subseteq \mathcal{D}$ and $\mathcal{D}_\mathcal{P} \subseteq \mathcal{D}'$ it holds $\mathcal{D}_\mathcal{P} \subseteq \mathcal{D} \cap \mathcal{D}'$. As $q_\mathcal{P} \leq q$ and $q_\mathcal{P} \leq q'$ and from definition or uncertainty profile $q_\mathcal{P} \leq \#\mathcal{D}_\mathcal{P} \leq \#(\mathcal{D} \cap \mathcal{D}')$ it holds $q_\mathcal{P} \leq \min\{q, q', \#(\mathcal{D} \cap \mathcal{D}')\}$. We conclude $\mathcal{U} \sqcup \mathcal{U}' \sqsubseteq \mathcal{P}$. Let us consider the minimal elements. Let $\mathcal{U} = \langle E, \mathcal{A}, \mathcal{D}, p, q \rangle$ be a profile such that $\mathcal{U} \in \min(E)$. It holds $p = \#\mathcal{A}$ otherwise $p < \#\mathcal{A}$ and it is possible to factor $\mathcal{A}$ as $\mathcal{A} = \mathcal{A}' \cup \mathcal{A}''$ such that $\#\mathcal{A}' = p$ and $\langle E, \mathcal{A}', \mathcal{D}, p, q \rangle \sqsubset \mathcal{U}$ (the inclusion is strict) and $\mathcal{U}$ is not minimal. Given a mininal element of the form $\mathcal{U} = \langle E, \mathcal{A}, \mathcal{D}, \#\mathcal{A}, q \rangle$ it holds $\#\mathcal{D} = q$ otherwise $\#\mathcal{D} > q$ and $\langle E, \mathcal{A}, \mathcal{D}, \#\mathcal{A}, q+1 \rangle \sqsubset \mathcal{U}$. Finally given $\mathcal{U} = \langle E, \mathcal{A}, \mathcal{D}, \#\mathcal{A}, \#\mathcal{D} \rangle$ we need $\mathcal{A} \cup \mathcal{D} = \alpha_+(E)$, otherwise $\mathcal{A} \cup \mathcal{D}$ is strictly included in $\alpha_+(E)$, exists $s \in \alpha_+(E) \setminus (\mathcal{A} \cup \mathcal{D})$ and $\langle E, \mathcal{A}, \mathcal{D} \cup \{s\}, \#\mathcal{A}, \#\mathcal{D} \rangle \sqsubset \mathcal{U}$. Let us prove the reverse. Let $\mathcal{U} = \langle E, \mathcal{A}, \mathcal{D}, \#\mathcal{A}, \#\mathcal{D} \rangle$, $\mathcal{A} \cup \mathcal{D} = \alpha_+(E)$ and $\mathcal{P} = \langle E, \mathcal{A}_\mathcal{P}, \mathcal{D}_\mathcal{P}, p_\mathcal{P}, q_\mathcal{P} \rangle$ be profiles such that $\mathcal{P} \sqsubseteq \mathcal{U}$. As constraints $\mathcal{A}_\mathcal{P} \subseteq \mathcal{A}$ and $p_\mathcal{P} \geq \#\mathcal{A}$ go in opposite directions we get $\mathcal{A}_\mathcal{P} = \mathcal{A}$, $p_\mathcal{P} = \#\mathcal{A}$ and $\mathcal{P} = \langle E, \mathcal{A}, \mathcal{D}_\mathcal{P}, \#\mathcal{A}, q_\mathcal{P} \rangle$. As restrictions $\mathcal{D} \subseteq \mathcal{D}_\mathcal{P}$, $q \leq q_\mathcal{P}$ go in the same direction we could, in principle, add $\mathcal{D}'$ elements to $\mathcal{D}$ get $\mathcal{D}_\mathcal{P} = \mathcal{D} \cup \mathcal{D}'$ and mark in $\mathcal{D}_\mathcal{P}$, $q_\mathcal{D}$ failures. However it is impossible because $\mathcal{D} \cup \mathcal{A} = \alpha_+(E)$ and there are "free" elements to enlarge $\mathcal{D}$. Lemma 3 gives $\nu(\mathcal{U}) = 0$ for $\mathcal{U} \in \min(E)$. □

From Theorem 1 we infer there is no glb (greather lower bound), Example 4 emphatizes that.

Example 4 (glb counterexample). Consider $\mathcal{U}_1 = \langle E, \{CNN\}, \emptyset, 1, 0 \rangle$ and $\mathcal{U}_2 = \langle E, \emptyset, \{CNN\}, 0, 1 \rangle$. Let us try to find $\mathcal{U} = \langle E, \mathcal{A}, \mathcal{D}, p, q \rangle$ such that $\mathcal{U} \sqsubseteq \mathcal{U}_1$ and $\mathcal{U} \sqsubseteq \mathcal{U}_2$. As the angelic sites increases in $\sqsubseteq$ we have $\mathcal{A} \subseteq \{CNN\}$ and $\mathcal{A} \subseteq \emptyset$. This forces $\mathcal{A} = \emptyset$. As $\mathcal{A} = \emptyset$ we have $p = 0$ and $\mathcal{U} = \langle E, \emptyset, \mathcal{D}, 0, q \rangle$. As the number of angelic failures decreases with $\sqsubseteq$ we need $p_{\mathcal{U}_1} \leq p$. We have a contradiction because $p_{\mathcal{U}_1} = 1$ and $p = 0$. If there is no lower bound there is glb. □

The intuitive notion of improvement described by the partial order ($\mathcal{U} \sqsubseteq \mathcal{U}'$) should match the notion of assessement given in Definition 5 (i.e. when the situation becomes less risky its the asessement should improve). Formally $\mathcal{U} \sqsubseteq \mathcal{U}' \implies \nu(\mathcal{U}) \leq \nu(\mathcal{U}')$. This section establishes this property (see Theorem 2).

Definition 7 (split strategy). *Given $\mathcal{A}$, $\mathcal{A}'$ such that $\mathcal{A} \subseteq \mathcal{A}'$, $f'_A \leq f_A$ and $\alpha \in \Delta_{\mathfrak{a}}$, the mapping* $\mathsf{split}(\alpha) : A'_{\mathfrak{a}} \to [0, 1]$ *is:*

$$\mathsf{split}(\alpha)(a') = \frac{1}{\binom{f_A}{f'_A}} \sum_{\{a \in A_{\mathfrak{a}} \mid a' \subseteq a\}} \alpha(a)$$

Observe that $\#\{a' \mid a' \subseteq a\} = \binom{f_A}{f'_A}$.

Example 5. Consider the case $\mathcal{A} = \{1, 2, 3, 4\}$ and $\mathcal{A}' = \mathcal{A} \cup \{5, 6, 7\}$ with $f'_A = 2$ and $f_A = 3$. The set of actions in both cases are:

$$A_a = \{\{1, 2, 3\}, \{1, 2, 4\}, \{1, 3, 4\}, \{2, 3, 4\}\}$$
$$A'_a = \{\{1, 2\}, \{1, 3\}, \{1, 4\}, \{1, 5\}, \{1, 6\}, \{1, 7\}, \{2, 3\}, \dots\}$$

As $\{a \in A_a \mid \{1, 2\} \subseteq a\} = \{\{1, 2, 3\}, \{1, 2, 4\}\}$, $\{a \in A_a \mid \{1, 5\} \subseteq a\} = \emptyset$ and $\binom{f_A}{f'_A} = 3$ we have $\mathsf{split}(\alpha)(\{1, 2\}) = 1/3(\alpha(\{1, 2, 3\}) + \alpha(\{1, 2, 4\}))$ and $\mathsf{split}(\alpha)(\{1, 5\}) = 0$.   □

Lemma 4. *Consider* $\mathcal{U} = \langle E, \mathcal{A}, \mathcal{D}, f_A, f_D \rangle$ *and* $\mathcal{U}' = \langle E, \mathcal{A}', \mathcal{D}, f'_A, f_D \rangle$ *such that* $\mathcal{A} \subseteq \mathcal{A}'$ *and* $f'_A \leq f_A$. *For any* $\alpha \in \Delta_a$ *it holds* $\mathsf{split}(\alpha) \in \Delta'_a$ *and* $u'_a(\mathsf{split}(\alpha), \beta) \geq u_a(\alpha, \beta)$. *The assessments of* $\mathcal{U}$ *and* $\mathcal{U}'$ *satisfy* $\nu(\mathcal{U}') \leq \nu(\mathcal{U})$.

Proof. Following we note $f_A = p$ and f'_A, then $p' \leq p$. First we prove that $\mathsf{split}(\alpha) \in \Delta'_a$. Observe that $0 \leq \mathsf{split}(\alpha)(a') \leq 1$, as α is a mixed strategy. Thus,

$$\sum_{a' \in A'_a} \mathsf{split}(\alpha)(a') = \sum_{a' \in A'_a} \frac{1}{\binom{p}{p'}} \sum_{\{a \in A_a \mid a' \subseteq a\}} \alpha(a) = \frac{1}{\binom{p}{p'}} \sum_{\{(a, a') \in A_a \times A'_a \mid a' \subseteq a\}} \alpha(a)$$

$$= \frac{1}{\binom{p}{p'}} \sum_{a \in A_a} \sum_{\{a' \in A'_a \mid a' \subseteq a\}} \alpha(a) = \sum_{a \in A_a} \alpha(a) \left(\frac{1}{\binom{p}{p'}} \sum_{\{a' \in A'_a \mid a' \subseteq a\}} 1 \right) = \sum_{a \in A_a} \alpha(a) = 1$$

For any $a' \in A'_a$, $a' \subseteq a$, and $d \in A_\partial$ it follows that $u_a(a, d) \leq u'_a(a', d)$ (since $\mathsf{out}(\mathsf{fail}_{a \cup d}(E)) \leq \mathsf{out}(\mathsf{fail}_{a' \cup d}(E))$). Applying this inequality to each a', where $a' \subseteq a$, we get

$$u_a(a, d) \leq \frac{1}{\binom{p}{p'}} \sum_{\{a' \mid a' \subseteq a\}} u'_a(a', d).$$

The inequality between u_a and u'_a is derived as follows:

$$u_a(\alpha, \beta) = \sum_{a \in A_a} \sum_{d \in A_\partial} \alpha(a) u_a(a, d) \beta(d)$$

$$\leq \sum_{a \in A_a} \sum_{d \in A_\partial} \frac{1}{\binom{p}{p'}} \sum_{\{a' \in A'_a \mid a' \subseteq a\}} \alpha(a) u'_a(a', d) \beta(d)$$

$$= \sum_{a' \in A'_a} \sum_{d \in A_\partial} \left(\frac{1}{\binom{p}{p'}} \sum_{\{a \in A_a \mid a' \subseteq a\}} \alpha(a) \right) u'_a(a', d) \beta(d)$$

$$= \sum_{a' \in A'_a} \sum_{d \in A_\partial} \mathsf{split}(\alpha)(a') u'_a(a', d) \beta(d) = u'_a(\mathsf{split}(\alpha), \beta)$$

Finally, the zero-sum game characterizations

$$\nu(\mathcal{U}') = \max_{\alpha' \in \Delta'_a} \min_{\beta \in \Delta_\partial} u'_a(\alpha', \beta), \quad \nu(\mathcal{U}) = \min_{\beta \in \Delta_\partial} \max_{\alpha \in \Delta_a} u_a(\alpha, \beta)$$

are used to establish that $\nu(\mathcal{U}') \leq \nu(\mathcal{U})$: As $u_a(\alpha, \beta) \leq u_{a'}(\text{split}(\alpha), \beta)$ for any α and β, choose a mixed strategy $\beta^*(\alpha)$ so that $u'_a(\text{split}(\alpha), \beta^*(\alpha)) = \min_\beta u'_a(\text{split}(\alpha), \beta)$. As $\min_\beta u'_a(\text{split}(\alpha), \beta) \leq \max_\alpha \min_\beta u'_a(\alpha, \beta) = \nu(\mathcal{U}')$ it follows that $u_a(\alpha, \beta^*(\alpha)) \leq u'_a(\text{split}(\alpha), \beta^*(\alpha)) \leq \nu(\mathcal{U}')$. Given the following set $\{(\alpha, \beta^*(\alpha)) \mid \alpha \in \Delta_a\}$, choose α^* such that $u_a(\alpha^*, \beta^*(\alpha^*)) = \max_\alpha u_a(\alpha, \beta^*(\alpha))$. As $\nu(\mathcal{U}) = \min_\beta \max_\alpha u_a(\alpha, \beta) \leq \max_\alpha u_a(\alpha, \beta^*(\alpha))$ it follows that $\nu(\mathcal{U}) \leq u_a(\alpha^*, \beta^*(\alpha^*))$ and $\nu(\mathcal{U}) \leq \nu(\mathcal{U}')$. $\square$

Example 6. Reconsider Example 3 where $\mathcal{U}_1 = \langle E, \{A\}, \{B, D\}, 1, 1 \rangle$, $\mathcal{U}_2 = \langle E, \{A, F\}, \{B, D\}, 1, 1 \rangle$ and $\mathcal{U}_1 \sqsubseteq \mathcal{U}_2$. Thus, from Lemma 4, $\nu(\mathcal{U}_1) \leq \nu(\mathcal{U}_2)$. The previous analysis showed that $\nu(\mathcal{U}_1) = k$, $\nu(\mathcal{U}_2) = k + 1 - (k-1)/k$. As $k \geq 1$, $1 - (k-1)/k \geq 0$ it follows that $\nu(\mathcal{U}_1) \leq \nu(\mathcal{U}_2)$. $\square$

Definition 8 (joint strategy). *Given $\mathcal{D}$, $\mathcal{D}'$ such that $\mathcal{D}' \subseteq \mathcal{D}$, $f'_\mathcal{D} \leq f_\mathcal{D}$ and $\beta' \in \Delta'_\eth$, the mapping $joint(\beta') : A_\eth \to [0,1]$ is:*

$$joint(\beta')(d) = \frac{1}{\binom{\#\mathcal{D} - f'_\mathcal{D}}{f_\mathcal{D} - f'_\mathcal{D}}} \sum_{\{d' \in A'_\eth \mid d' \subseteq d\}} \beta'(d')$$

Example 7. Consider the case $\mathcal{D}' = \{1, 2, 3, 4\}$ and $\mathcal{D} = \mathcal{D}' \cup \{5, 6, 7\}$ with $f'_\mathcal{D} = 2$ and $f_\mathcal{D} = 3$. The set of actions in both cases are:

$$A'_\eth = \{\{1, 2\}, \{1, 3\}, \{1, 4\}, \{2, 3\}, \{2, 4\}, \{3, 4\}\}$$
$$A_\eth = \{\{1, 2, 3\}, \{1, 2, 4\}, \{1, 2, 5\}, \ldots, \{5, 6, 7\}\}$$

As $\{d' \in A'_\eth \mid d' \subseteq \{1, 2, 3\}\} = \{\{1, 2\}, \{1, 3\}, \{2, 3\}\}$, $\{d' \in A'_\eth \mid d' \subseteq \{1, 2, 5\}\} = \{\{1, 2\}\}$, $\{d' \in A'_\eth \mid d' \subseteq \{5, 6, 7\}\} = \emptyset$ and $\binom{\#\mathcal{D} - f'_{\mathcal{D}'}}{f_\mathcal{D} - f'_{\mathcal{D}'}} = 5$ we have the following $joint(\beta')(\{1, 2, 3\}) = 1/5(\beta'(\{1, 2\}) + \beta'(\{1, 3\}) + \beta'(\{2, 3\}))$, $joint(\beta')(\{1, 2, 5\}) = \frac{1}{5}\beta'(\{1, 2\})$ and $joint(\beta')(\{5, 6, 7\}) = 0$. $\square$

Using a similar approach to the proof of Lemma 4 together with the inequality

$$u'_\eth(a, d') \geq \frac{1}{\binom{\#\mathcal{D} - f_{\mathcal{D}'}}{f_\mathcal{D} - f_{\mathcal{D}'}}} \sum_{\{d \in A_\eth \mid d' \subseteq d\}} u_\eth(a, d)$$

we obtain the following lemma.

Lemma 5. *Consider $\mathcal{U} = \langle E, \mathcal{A}, \mathcal{D}, f_\mathcal{A}, f_\mathcal{D} \rangle$ and $\mathcal{U}' = \langle E, \mathcal{A}, \mathcal{D}', f_\mathcal{A}, f'_\mathcal{D} \rangle$ such that $\mathcal{D}' \subseteq \mathcal{D}$ and $f'_\mathcal{D} \leq f_\mathcal{D}$. For any $\beta' \in \Delta'_\eth$ it holds $joint(\beta') \in \Delta_\eth$ and $u'_\eth(\alpha, \beta') \geq u_\eth(\alpha, joint(\beta'))$. The assessements verify $\nu(\mathcal{U}) \leq \nu(\mathcal{U}')$.*

Theorem 2. *$\mathcal{U} \sqsubseteq \mathcal{U}'$ implies $\nu(\mathcal{U}) \leq \nu(\mathcal{U}')$.*

Proof. Suppose $\mathcal{U} = \langle E, \mathcal{A}, \mathcal{D}, f_\mathcal{A}, f_\mathcal{D} \rangle$ and $\mathcal{U}' = \langle E, \mathcal{A}', \mathcal{D}', f'_\mathcal{A}, f'_\mathcal{D} \rangle$. As $\mathcal{U} \sqsubseteq \mathcal{U}'$ it holds $\mathcal{A} \subseteq \mathcal{A}'$, $\mathcal{D}' \subseteq \mathcal{D}$ and $f'_\mathcal{A} \leq f_\mathcal{A}$, $f'_\mathcal{D} \leq f_\mathcal{D}$. The profile $\mathcal{P} = \langle E, \mathcal{A}, \mathcal{D}', f_\mathcal{A}, f'_\mathcal{D} \rangle$ verifies $\mathcal{U} \sqsubseteq \mathcal{P}$, moreover by Lemma 5 we have $\nu(\mathcal{U}) \leq \nu(\mathcal{P})$. The profile $\mathcal{P}$ also verifies $\mathcal{P} \sqsubseteq \mathcal{U}'$, moreover by Lemma 4 we have $\nu(\mathcal{P}) \leq \nu(\mathcal{U}')$. By transitivity of the partial order we get the result. $\square$

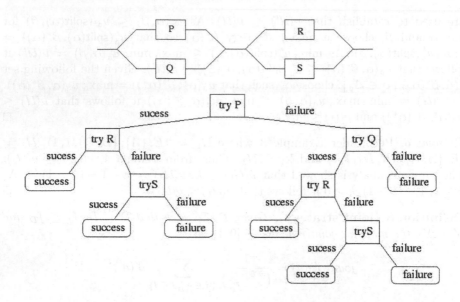

Fig. 1. Example of a contingency plan $C = C(P, Q, R, S)$. Either P or Q execute the first part of the job and either R or S execute the second part. The diagram is a schematic representation of possible evaluation paths of $C(P, Q, R, S)$.

5   Uncertainty and Risk

A risk-driven approach to software analysis associates every atomic service S with two costs [7]: a user U making a successful call to S pays amount $c(S)$ (to S); in the case of unsuccessful call, S pays amount $c_{df}(S)$ to U. Let $p(\overline{S})$ denote the probability of S failing to respond when called. In [7] *risk* is defined quantitatively as $r(S) = p(\overline{S})c_{df}(S)$.

Contingency plans (variant forms of orchestration) are used to compare the risk-based and game theoretic approaches to analysing the effects of service failure. A contingency plan specifies sub-computations to be launched in the case of failure. For example the plan $C = C(P, Q, R, S)$ is schematized in Figure 1 where the associated tree models the various execution paths, depending on the reliability of the underlying services[2]. Plan $C(P, Q, R, S)$ calls P first; if the call succeeds then R is called – otherwise the default service Q is invoked before R is called. Plan $C(P, Q, R, S)$ can also be associated with costs $c(C)$ and $C_{df}(C)$. Here we assume a *quid-pro-quo* approach to failure by letting $c(S) = c_{df}(S)$ and $c(C) = c_{df}(C)$.

The game theoretic approach to service-based computation can be adjusted by modifying the utilities to measure cost (rather than reliability). $C(P, Q, R, S)$ can be analysed using an uncertainty profile $\mathcal{U}$ where $\alpha(C)$ denotes the atomic

---

[2] Plan $C(P, Q, R, S)$ is different from $E = 1(y) < y < ((R(x)|S(x)) < x < (P|Q))$ which calls P and Q in parallel.

services appearing in C and $\Gamma(\mathcal{U})$ denotes a game which takes account of the execution cost of C:

Example 8. Consider plan $C(P, Q, R, S)$ (Figure 1). Assume that the probability of a service responding successfully is p (and that $q = 1 - p$ is the probability of a service defaulting). All atomic services are assumed to have cost c and $c(C) = \beta c$. The risk[3] $r(C)$ and the expected cost of the plan $E(C)$ are:

$$r(C) = c(pq^2(1 - \beta) + pq^3(2 - \beta) + q^2(2 - \beta))$$
$$E(C) = r(C) + c(p^2(\beta - 2) + 2p^2q(\beta - 1) + p^2q^2\beta)$$

The path "P succeeds"; "R fails" and "S fails" has probability pq^2 and cost $-c$ (payment to P) $+ 2c$ (payments from R and S) $-\beta c$ (cost of overall failure). The risk of this path is thus $pq^2c(1 - \beta)$. If all services are operational then C just calls P and then R with overall cost $c(-2 + \beta)$. Assigning $\beta = 3$ means that the overall cost of this successful path is c. Then $r(C) = c(-2pq^2 - pq^3 - q^2)$ and $E(C) = r(C) + c(p^2 + 4p^2q + 3p^2q^2)$. When $p = q = 1/2$, $r(C) = -9c/16$, $E(C) = -3c/8$.

Consider the uncertainty profile $\mathcal{U} = \langle C, \{P, Q\}, \{R, S\}, 1, 1 \rangle$ for the contingency plan. The utility $c_a(\{P\}, \{R\})$ involves P defaulting (P pays C an amount c), Q being called successfully (C pays Q an amount c), R defaulting and S being called successfully. The overall cost is: $c_a(\{P\}, \{R\}) = c(1 - 1 + 1 - 1 + \beta) = \beta c = 3c$. The game is assessed by:

$$\partial$$

		$\{R\}$	$\{S\}$
a	$\{P\}$	$\beta c = 3c$	$(\beta - 1)c = 2c$
	$\{Q\}$	$(\beta - 1)c = 2c$	$(\beta - 2)c = c$

In $\Gamma(\mathcal{U}_1)$, the strategy profile $(\{P\}, \{S\})$ is the only pure Nash equilibrium and the assessment is $\nu(\mathcal{U}) = 2c$.   □

6   Conclusions

In this paper we have presented a means of analysing the behaviour of service-based computations by means of game theory. Orchestrations such as $P > Q > R > S$ are susceptible to service failure. The assessment of this orchestration, using any profile with a single service failure, is 0 (as expected). On the other hand highly robust orchestrations, such as $1(x) < x < (Q|R|S)$, are assessed to give an output provided that at most two failures occur in the services $\{Q, R, S\}$. Complex orchestrations can be analysed using either best case behaviour (the daemon set is empty) for an expected number of service failures, worst case behaviour or even mixed behaviour (when the set of participating sites is partitioned over $\mathcal{A}$ and $\mathcal{D}$). In order to avoid contention about the service partition

---

[3] Risk can be defined as the expected cost of failing to deliver a service. In plan $C(P, Q, R, S)$ the risk can be found by following each failure path and multiplying the associated probability of the path by the cost of such a failure.

two (or more) different profiles could be used for mixed case analysis: the second profile could simply reverse the angel and daemon characteristics of the first. It has been shown that uncertainty profiles have expected monotonicity properties – indeed it is these properties that give confidence to the use of game theory as a means of analysing service-based computations. Finally, although we maintain that it is problematic to assign probabilities to service failures (due the the complexity of interactions in a web-environment), a comparison of a risk-driven approach to the proposed game-theoretic approach is given.

Acknowledgement

The authors are grateful to three anonymous referees for their comments which have led to significant improvements in the paper.

References

1. Akerlof, G., Schiller, R.: Animal Spirits. Princeton University Press, Princeton (2009)
2. Davey, B., Priestley, H.: Introduction to Lattices and Order. Cambridge University Press, Cambridge (2002)
3. Gabarro, J., García, A., Serna, M., Stewart, A., Kilpatrick, P.: Analysing Orchestrations with Risk Profiles and Angel-Daemon Games. In: Grid Computing Achievements and Propects, pp. 121–132. Springer, Heidelberg (2008)
4. Gabarro, J., Kilpatrick, P., Serna, M., Stewart, A.: Stressed Web Environments as Strategic Games: Risk Profiles and Weltanschauung. In: Wirsing, M., Hofmann, M., Rauschmayer, A. (eds.) TGC 2010, LNCS, vol. 6084, pp. 189–204. Springer, Heidelberg (2010)
5. Hull, J.: Risk Management and Finantial Institutions, 2nd edn. Pearson, London (2009)
6. Knight, F.: Risk, uncertainty and Profit (1921), Electronic access in: http://www.econlib.org/library/Knight/knRUP.html
7. Kokash, N., D'Andrea, V.: Evaluating Quality of Web Services: A Risk-Driven Approach. In: Abramowicz, W. (ed.) BIS 2007. LNCS, vol. 4439, pp. 180–194. Springer, Heidelberg (2007)
8. Misra, J., Cook, W.: Computation Orchestration: A basis for wide-area computing. Software and Systems Modeling 6(1), 83–110 (2007)
9. Moscibroda, T., Schmid, S., Wattenhofer, R.: When selfish meets evil: byzantine players in a virus inoculation game. In: PODC 2006, pp. 35–44 (2006)
10. von Neumann, J., Morgenstern, O.: Theory of Games and Economic Behavior, Princeton (1944)
11. Nisan, N., Roughgarden, T., Tardos, E., Vazirani, V.: Algorithmic Game Theory. Cambridge University Press, Cambridge (2007)
12. Osborne, M., Rubinstein, A.: A Course on Game Theory. MIT Press, Cambridge (1994)
13. Stewart, A., Clint, M., Harmer, T., Kilpatrick, P., Perrott, R., Gabarro, J.: Assessing the Reliability and Cost of Web and Grid Orchestrations. In: Conference on Availability, Reliability and Security, ARES 2008, pp. 428–443. IEEE, Los Alamitos (2008)
14. Verdon, D., McGraw, G.: Risk Analysis in Software Design. IEEE Security & Privacy 4, 79–84 (2004)

Underwater Archaeological 3D Surveys Validation within the Removed Sets Framework

Julien Hué[3], Mariette Sérayet[1], Pierre Drap[1], Odile Papini[1], and Eric Würbel[2]

[1] LSIS-CNRS 6168, Université de la Méditerranée, ESIL - Case 925, Av de Luminy,
13288 Marseille Cedex 9 France
{serayet,drap,papini}@esil.univmed.fr
[2] LSIS-CNRS 6168, Université du Sud Toulon -Var, BP 132,
83957 La Garde Cedex France
wurbel@univ-tln.fr
[3] CRIL-CNRS 8188, Université d'Artois, Rue Jean Souvraz SP 18,
62307 Lens Cedex France
hue@cril.univ-artois.fr

This paper presents the results of the VENUS european project aimed at providing scientific methodologies and technological tools for the virtual exploration of deep water archaeological sites. We focused on underwater archaeological 3D surveys validation problem. This paper shows how the validation problem has been tackled within the Removed Sets framework, according to Removed Sets Fusion (RSF) and to the Partially Preordered Removed Sets Inconsistency Handling (PPRSIH). Both approaches have been implemented thanks to ASP and the good behaviour of the Removed Sets operations is presented through an experimental study on two underwater archaeological sites.

1 Introduction

The VENUS European Project (Virtual ExploratioN of Underwater Sites, IST-034924)[1] aimed at providing scientific methodologies and technological tools for the virtual exploration of deep underwater archaeology sites. In this context, digital photogrammetry is used for data acquisition. The knowledge about the studied objects is provided by both archaeology and photogrammetry. One task of the project was to investigate how artificial intelligence tools could be used to perform reasoning with underwater archaeological 3D surveys. More specifically, this task focused on the validation problem of underwater artefacts 3D surveys. Within this project two different conceptual descriptions of the surveyed artefacts have been proposed leading to two different solutions both developed within the Removed Sets framework. This syntactic approach is more suitable than a semantic one, in order to pinpoint the errors that cause inconsistency. The present paper provides a synthesis of these two solutions. The first solution stems from the Entity Conceptual Model for modeling generic knowledge and uses instanciated predicate logic as representation formalism and Removed Sets Fusion (RSF) with *Sum* strategy for reasoning [9]. The second one is based on an application ontology for modeling generic knowledge and the belief base is represented in instanciated predicate logic equipped with a partial preorder

---

[1] http://www.venus-project.eu

W. Liu (Ed.): ECSQARU 2011, LNAI 6717, pp. 663–674, 2011.
© Springer-Verlag Berlin Heidelberg 2011

and Partially Preordered Removed Sets Inconsistency Handling (PPRSIH) for reasoning [17]. The paper is organized as follows. After describing in Section 2 the validation problem in the context of the VENUS project, Section 3 gives a brief synthetic presentation of the Removed Sets framework. Section 4 shows how the validation problem is expressed as a RSF problem while Section 5 shows that how the validation problem can be reduced to a PPRSIH problem. Finally, Section 6 discusses the results of the experimental study before concluding.

2   The Validation Problem in VENUS

In the context of the VENUS project, digital photogrammetry is used for data acquisition. Usual commercial photogrammetric tools only focus on geometric features and do not deal with the knowledge concerning the surveyed objects. The general goal is the integration of knowledge about surveyed objects into the photogrammetric tool ARPENTEUR [5] in order to provide more "intelligent" 3D surveys. In this project, we investigated how Artificial Intelligence tools can be used for representing and reasoning with 3D surveys information.

Within the context of underwater archaeological surveys, we deal with information of different nature. Archaeologists provide expert knowledge about artefacts, in most of the cases amphorae. Archaeological knowledge takes the form of a characterization of amphorae thanks to a typology hierarchically structured. For each type corresponds a set of features or attributes which we assign an interval representing the expected values for an amphora of this type.

The data acquisition process provides measures coming from the photogrammetric restitution of surveyed amphorae pictures on the underwater site (see ① in figure 1). These observations usually are uncertain, inaccurate or imprecise since the pictures are taken "in situ", their quality could not be optimal, because of the hostile environment: weather conditions, visibility, water muddying, site not cleaned, ... Moreover, errors could occur during the restitution step. For all these reasons, the archaeological knowledge (see ② in figure 1) and the data coming from the photogrammetric acquisition process could conflict. This special case of inconsistency handling is a validation problem because the measured values of attributes of a surveyed amphora "in situ", an instance, may not fit with the characterization of the amphorae type it is assumed to belong to. The VENUS project does not use image recognition. The generic knowledge is inserted in the system by the experts. There is no automatic image recognition since the experts recognise the objects in the image during the measuring step thanks to their a priori knowledge.

Example 1. We illustrate the validation problem with the Pianosa island site [12]. There are 8 types of amphorae: *Dressel20*, *Beltran2B*, *Gauloise_3*, ... and each type of amphorae is characterized by 9 attributes, *totalHeight*, *totalWidth*, *totalLength*, *bellyDiameter*, *internalDiameter*, ... [14]. However, the only measurable attributes are *totalHeight*, *totalLength*[2]. Default values for these attributes

---

[2] For amphorae the attributes *totalWidth* and *totalLength* have the same value since there are revolution objects.

take the form of a range of values $[v - v.t\%, v + v.t\%]$ centered around a typical value v (expressed in m.) where t is a tolerance threshold. For example, the default values for the attributes *totalHeight* and *totalLength* for the Dressel20 type are [0.5328, 0.7992] and [0.368, 0.552], while for a Beltran2B type they are [0.9008, 1.3512] and [0.3224, 0.4836]. Suppose, during the photogrammetric restitution process, the expert focuses on a given amphora, he recognizes as a *Beltran2B*. When the survey provides the values 1.13 as *totalHeight* and 0.27 as *totalLength*, the question is do these values fit with the characterization of the *Beltran2B*? When the values do not fit, the most probable reason is that the measures are incorrect due to bad conditions of acquisition.

In order to provide a qualitative representation of this validation problem, a conceptual description of archaeological knowledge is required (see ② in figure 1). Several conceptual descriptions have been used within the VENUS project. At the beginning of the project, we used a object oriented conceptual description, restricted form of the Entity Model approach [16]. The restricted Entity Model is denoted by $\mathcal{E} = \{\mathcal{C}, \mathcal{V}^d, \mathcal{C}^I\}$ where $\mathcal{C}$ is a concept (or a class), $\mathcal{V}^d$ is the set of default values for the attributes, $\mathcal{C}^I$ is a set of constraints on attributes. The concepts are the types of amphorae surveyed on the archaeological site. For each concept, that is each type of amphorae, we represent the measurable attributes. The default values for these attributes take the form of a range of values and $\mathcal{V}^d$ is a set of intervals, each interval corresponding to the possible values of attributes for a given type of amphorae. The set of constraints on the attributes $\mathcal{C}^I$ consists in integrity contraints, domain constraints and conditional constraints which express the compatibility of the measured values of attributes with the default values of attributes for a given type. The belief profile consists of the generic knowledge according to the restricted Entity Model provided by the `typology.xml` file and of the instances of amphorae provided by the `amphora.xml` file.

During the project, we constructed an application ontology [13] from a domain ontology which describes the vocabulary on the amphorae (the studied artefacts) and from a task ontology describing the data acquisition process. This ontology consists of a set of concepts, relations, attributes and constraints like domain constraints. The belief base contains the application and ontology, constraints and observations. The ontology represents the generic knowlegde which is preferred to observations. Due to the lack of space, we only consider a small part of the ontology (Figure 2).

3   The Removed Sets Framework

The Removed Sets framework provides a syntactic belief change approach for revision and fusion. When dealing with belief change operations since we deal with uncertain, incomplete, dynamic information, inconsistency can result. In order to provide a consistent result of the change operation, the Removed Sets approach focuses on the minimal set of formulae to remove, called *Removed sets*, in order to restore consistency. The Removed Sets operations have been proved to be equivalent to the ones based on maximal consistent subsets [15,4,1]. However, in the context of applications where few inconsistencies may occur, the Removed Sets approach seems to be more efficient when implementing large belief bases.

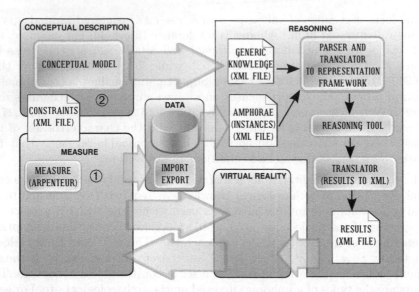

Fig. 1. General scheme

Initially, the Removed Sets approach has been proposed for revising propositional formulae in CNF (RSR [11,18]). It has then been generalized to arbitrary propositional formulae for revision and fusion (RSF [9]). The Removed Sets approach has been extended to totally preordered belief bases (PRSR [2]), (PRSF [8]) and more recently to partially preordered belief bases for revision (PPRSR [17]). A central notion is the one of potential Removed Set[3] which are sets of formulas whose removal restores consistency into the union of belief bases.

Definition 1. *Let* $E = \{K_1, \ldots, K_n\}$ *be a belief profile such that* $K_1, \ldots, K_n$ *are propotional belief bases and* $K_1 \sqcup \ldots \sqcup K_n$ *is inconsistent* ($\sqcup$ *denotes set union with accounting for repetitions*). $X \subseteq K_1 \sqcup \ldots \sqcup K_n$ *is a* potential Removed Set *of* E *if and only if* $(K_1 \sqcup \ldots \sqcup K_n) \backslash X$ *is consistent.*

The collection of potential Removed Sets of E is denoted by $\mathcal{PR}(E)$. Since the number of potential Removed Sets of E is exponential w.r.t. the number of formulae, we only consider the minimal potential Removed Sets w.r.t. set inclusion. Moreover belief change operations or belief change strategies are formalized in terms of total preorders or partial preorders on potential Removed Sets minimal w.r.t. set inclusion.

3.1   Removed Sets Fusion

For Removed Sets Fusion, the fusion strategies (*Card, Sum, Max, GMax*) are formalized thanks to a total preorder over $\mathcal{PR}(E)$. Let X and Y be two potential

---

[3] We give the definitions in the general setting of fusion where revision is a special case.

Removed Sets, for each strategy P a total preorder $\leq_P$ over the potential Removed Sets is defined. $X \leq_P Y$ means that X is preferred to Y according to the strategy P. We define $<_P$ as the strict total preorder associated to $\leq_P$ (i.e. $X <_P Y$ if and only if $X \leq_P Y$ and $Y \nleq_P X$).

Definition 2. *Let $E = \{K_1, \ldots, K_n\}$ be a belief profile such that $K_1 \sqcup \ldots \sqcup K_n$ is inconsistent. $X \subseteq K_1 \sqcup \ldots \sqcup K_n$ is a Removed Set of E according to the strategy P if and only if i) X is a potential Removed Set of E; ii) $\nexists X' \in \mathcal{PR}(E)$ such that $X' \subset X$; iii) $\nexists X' \in \mathcal{PR}(E)$ such that $X' <_P X$.*

The collection of Removed Sets of E according to the strategy P is denoted by $\mathcal{R}_P(E)$. The Removed Sets Fusion operation is defined by:

Definition 3. *Let $E = \{K_1, \ldots, K_n\}$ such that $K_1 \sqcup \ldots \sqcup K_n$ is inconsistent. The merging operation is defined by: $\Delta_P^{RSF}(E) = \bigcup_{X \in \mathcal{R}_P(E)} \{(K_1 \sqcup \ldots \sqcup K_n) \backslash X\}$.*

3.2 Partially Preordered Removed Sets Inconsistency Handling

Let K be a finite set of arbitrary formulae and $\preceq_K$ be a partial preorder on K. Restoring the consistency of a partially preordered belief bases involves the definition of a partial preorder on subsets of formulae, called comparators [3,19]. Several ways have been proposed for defining a preference relation on subsets of formulae of K, from a partial preorder $\preceq_K$. In the VENUS project, we focus on the lexicographic preference [19] which extends the lexicographic preorder initially defined for totally preordered belief bases to partially preordered belief bases. The belief base K is partitionned such that $K = E_1 \sqcup \ldots \sqcup E_n$ $(n \geq 1)$ where each subset E_i represents an equivalence class of K with respect to $=_K$ which is an equivalence relation. A preference relation between the equivalence classes E_i's, denoted by $\prec_s$ is defined by $E_i \prec_s E_j$ iff $\exists \varphi \in E_i, \exists \varphi' \in E_j$ such that $\varphi \prec_K \varphi'$. This partition can be viewed as a generalization of the idea of stratification defined for totally preordered belief bases. We rephrase the lexicographic preference defined in [19] as follows:

Definition 4. *Let $\preceq_K$ be a partial preorder on K, $Y \subseteq K$ and $X \subseteq K$. Y is said to be lexicographically preferred to X, denoted by $Y \trianglelefteq_\Delta X$, iff $\forall i, 1 \leq i \leq n$: if $|E_i \cap Y| > |E_i \cap X|$ then $\exists j, 1 \leq j \leq n$ such that $|E_j \cap X| > |E_j \cap Y|$ and $E_j \prec_s E_i$.*

Let $\mathcal{PR}(K)$ be the set of potential removed sets. Among them, we want to prefer the potential removed sets which allow us to remove the formulae that are not preferred according to $\preceq_K$. Therefore we generalize the notion of Removed Sets to subsets of partially preordered formulae. We denote by $\mathcal{R}_\Delta(K)$ the set of removed sets of K.

Definition 5. *Let K be an inconsistent belief base equipped with a partial preorder $\preceq_K$. $R \subseteq K$ is a removed set of K iff i) R is a potential removed set; ii) $\nexists R' \in \mathcal{R}_\Delta(K)$ such that $R' \subset R$; iii) $\nexists R' \in \mathcal{R}_\Delta(K)$ such that $R' \triangleleft_\Delta R$.*

Definition 6. *Let K be an inconsistent belief base equipped with a partial perorder $\preceq_K$. Restoring the consistency leads to a consistent belief base K' such that $K' = \bigcup_{X \in \mathcal{R}_\Delta(K)} \{K \backslash X\}$.*

3.3 ASP Implementation

In order to implement belief change operations within the Removed sets framework, we translate the belief change problem into a logic program with answer set semantics. This method proceeds in two stages. The first stage consists in the translation of E into a logic program Π_E and we have shown that the answer sets of Π_E correspond to the potential removed sets of E [9].

Let E be a belief profile[4]. Each propositional variable a occuring in E is represented by an ASP atom $a \in \mathcal{A}$ in Π_E. The set of all positive, (resp. negative) literals of Π_E is denoted by V^+, (resp. V^-). The set of rule atoms representing formulae is defined by $R^+ = \{r_f \mid f \in E\}$ and $F_O(r_f)$ represents the formula of E corresponding to r_f in Π_E, namely $\forall r_f \in R^+, F_O(r_f) = f$. This translation requires the introduction of intermediary atoms representing subformulae. We denote by ρ_f^j the intermediary atom representing f^j which is a subformula of $f \in E$. The first part of the construction has two steps:

1. We introduce rules in order to build a one-to-one correspondence between answer sets of Π_E and interpretations of V^+. For each atom, $a \in V^+$ two rules are introduced: $a \leftarrow not\ a'$ and $a' \leftarrow not\ a$ where $a' \in V^-$ is the negative atom corresponding to a.
2. We introduce rules in order to exclude the answer sets S corresponding to interpretations which are not models of $(E \backslash F)$ with $F = \{f \mid r_f \in S\}$. According to the syntax of f, the following rules are introduced: (i) If $f =_{def} a$ then $r_f \leftarrow not\ a$ is introduced; (ii) If $f =_{def} \neg f^1$ then $r_f \leftarrow not\ \rho_{f^1}$ is introduced; (iii) If $f =_{def} f^1 \vee \ldots \vee f^m$ then $r_f \leftarrow \rho_{f^1}, \ldots, \rho_{f^m}$ is introduced; (iv) If $f =_{def} f^1 \wedge \ldots \wedge f^m$ then it is necessary to introduce several rules: $\forall 1 \leq j \leq m,\ r_f \leftarrow \rho_{f^j}$.

This stage is common to any belief change operation while the next one depends on the chosen belief change operation.

In case of fusion the second stage provides, according to selected strategy P, another set of rules that leads to the program Π_E^P and we have shown [9] that the answer sets of Π_E^P correspond to the removed sets of E for a strategy P. In the validation problem since we have to minimize the number of formulae to remove, therefore the number of formulae occuring in a removed set, we select the Sum strategy. This strategy is expressed by the $minimize\{\}$ statement and the new logic progam $\Pi_E^{Sum} = \Pi_E \cup minimize\{r_f \mid r_f \in R^+\}$ is such that the answer sets of Π_E^{Sum} which are provided by the CLASP solver [7] correspond to the removed sets of $\Delta_{Sum}^{RSF}(E)$ [9].

In case of partially Preordered Removed Sets Inconsistency Handling the CLASP solver [7] gives the answer sets of Π_E. We then construct a partial preorder between them using the lexicographic comparator $\trianglelefteq_\Delta$. We have shown in [17] that the preferred answer sets according to $\trianglelefteq_\Delta$ correspond to the removed sets of E. We used a java program to partially preorder the answer sets to obtain the preferred answer sets. Since the lexicographic comparator satisfies the monotony property [19], it is sufficient to compare the answer sets which are minimal according to the inclusion. Moreover, the determination of the minimal

---

[4] In case of inconsistency handling the profile E is reduced to a belief base K.

answer sets according to this partial preorder does not increase the computa-
tionnal cost, since this cost is insignificant compared to the cost of answer sets
computation by CLASP.

4 The Validation Problem within RSF

In order to represent the validation problem within the RSF framework and to
implement it with ASP, we represented this problem with instanciated predicate
logic. The belief profile consists of two belief bases. The first one stems from
the restricted Entity Model conceptual description and represents the generic
knowledge. We introduce the predicates $type(x, y)$ and $cmp(z, y, x)$ where x is
an amphora, y is a type of amphorae and z is an attribute. $type(x, y)$ expresses
that an amphora x belongs to a type y and $cmp(z, y, x)$ expresses that an attribute z of an amphora x of type y has a value compatible with the possible
values for the type y, as specified in 2. The domain constraints specify that an
amphora must have one and only one type. For n types of amphorae, for each
amphora there is one disjunction $type(x, y_1) \lor \ldots \lor type(x, y_n)$ and $n(n-1)/$
2 mutual exclusion formulae $\neg type(x, y_i) \lor \neg type(x, y_j)$. The conditional constraints specify the compatibility of the attributes values with respect to the
type. For each amphora x, for each attribute z and for each type y, there is a
formula $type(x, y) \rightarrow cmp(z, y, x)$. Let m be the number of attributes, the in-
compatibility of type specifies that for each amphora and each type there is a
formula $\neg cmp(z_1, y, x) \land \ldots \land \neg cmp(z_m, y, x) \rightarrow \neg type(x, y)$. The second belief
base represents the instances of amphorae: the type the observed amphora be-
longs to (namely $type(x, y)$) and the compatible attributes with the type (namely
$cmp(z, y, x)$). We illustrate the RSF approach with the example 1.

Example 2. We limit ourselves to only two types of amphorae *Beltran2B* and
Dressel20, respectively denoted by $B2B$ and $D20$ thereafter, and to the survey of one observed amphora (denoted by 4 hereafter). Two attributes are
used: totalHeight (denoted by tH) and totalLength (denoted by tL). The
first belief base is automatically generated from the typology.xml file and
$K_1 = \{\neg type(4, B2B) \lor \neg type(4, D20), type(4, B2B) \lor type(4, D20), type(4, D20) \rightarrow$
$cmp(tH, D20, 4), type(4, D20) \rightarrow cmp(tL, D20, 4), type(4, B2B) \rightarrow cmp(tH, B2B, 4),$
$type(4, B2B) \rightarrow cmp(tL, B2B, 4), \neg cmp(tH, B2B, 4) \land \neg cmp(tL, B2B, 4) \rightarrow \neg type(4,$
$B2B), \neg cmp(tH, D20, 4) \land \neg cmp(tL, D20, 4) \rightarrow \neg type(4, D20) \}$. The second belief
base corresponding to the observed amphora is automatically generated from
typology.xml and amphora.xml files and $K_2 = \{type(4, B2B), cmp(tH, B2B, 4)\}$.
The operation $\Delta_{Sum, \top}^{RSF}(E)$ where $E = \{K_1, K_2\}$ is translated into Π_E^{Sum} as
follows:

$cmp(tH, B2B, 4).$ ⠀⠀⠀⠀⠀ $1 \{type(4, d20), type(4, B2B)\}\ 1.$
$r(x_0) \leftarrow not\ type(4, B2B).$ ⠀⠀⠀ $n\_type(4, B2B) \leftarrow r(x_0).$
$r(x_5) \leftarrow type(4, d20), not\ cmp(tH, d20, 4),$ ⠀ $\leftarrow n\_type(4, d20), type(4, d20).$
⠀⠀⠀⠀ $not\ cmp(tL, d20, 4).$
$r(x_1) \leftarrow type(4, d20), not\ cmp(tH, d20, 4).$ ⠀ $n\_cmp(tH, d20, 4) \leftarrow r(x_1).$

$$r(x_2) \leftarrow type(4, d20), not\ cmp(tL, d20, 4). \qquad n\_cmp(tL, d2, 4) \leftarrow r(x_2).$$
$$r(x_6) \leftarrow type(4, B2B), not\ cmp(tH, B2B, 4), \qquad \leftarrow n\_type(4, B2B), type(4, B2B).$$
$$not\ cmp(tL, B2B, 4).$$
$$r(x_3) \leftarrow type(4, B2B), not\ cmp(tH, B2B, 4). \quad n\_cmp(tH, B2B, 4) \leftarrow r(x_3).$$
$$r(x_4) \leftarrow type(4, B2B), not\ cmp(tL, B2B, 4). \quad n\_cmp(tL, B2B, 4) \leftarrow r(x_4).$$
$$minimize\ \{r(x_0), r(x_1), r(x_2), r(x_3), r(x_4)r(x_5), r(x_6)\}.$$

Note that the ASP translation uses some shortcuts compared to the translation scheme depicted in section 3.3. Thanks to the cardinality literals by recent ASP solvers, the unique type constraint is reduced to a single rule $1\ \{type(4, d20),$ $type(4, B2B)\}\ 1$. Also, the generation of the rule corresponding to $type(4, B2B)$ and the mutual exclusion between this atom and its classical negation are compacted into a single rule.

The only answer set of the above program is $\{cmp(tH, B2B, 4),$ $type(4, B2B),\ r(x_4),\ n\_cmp(tL, B2B, 4)\}$ which corresponds to the removed set $\{type(4, B2B) \rightarrow cmp(tL, B2B, 4)\}$ that pinpoints a bad measure for the total length attribute under the hypothesis of an amphora of type $Beltran2B$.

5   The Validation Problem within PPRSIH

The conceptual description in this approach is represented in terms of an application ontology and an extract is illustrated in Figure 2.

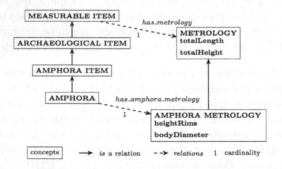

Fig. 2. Extract of the application ontology

The belief base consists of the application ontology, the constraints and the instances of amphorae represented in predicate logic. The introduced predicates are shown in an instanciated version in Table 1. The formulae corresponding to the extract of the ontology are given below where $amph, amph\_it, arch\_it, meas\_it,$ $metro, has\_metro, tL, tH, type$ denote $amphora, amphora\_item, archaeological\_item,$ $measurable\_item, metrology, has\_metrology, totalLenght, totalHeight, typology$ respectively: $\forall x\ arch\_it(x) \rightarrow meas\_it(x), \forall x\ amph\_it(x) \rightarrow arch\_it(x), \forall x\ amph(x) \rightarrow$ $amph\_it(x), \forall x\ meas\_it(x) \rightarrow \exists z\ has\_metro(x, z), \forall x\ \forall z\ has\_metro(x, z) \rightarrow metro(z),$ $\forall z\ metro(z) \rightarrow \exists l\ tL(z, l) \wedge \exists h\ tH(z, h), \forall x\ amph(x) \rightarrow amph\_it(x) \wedge (type(x, y_1) \vee \cdots \vee$ $type(x, y_n))$. The set of constraints consists in integrity constraints which specify that the value of attributes do not exceed a given value, domain constraints are specified by cardinality constraints within the application ontology and conditional constraints express the compatibility of the attribute values with respect to the type. The domain constraints are expressed like in Section 4 by one disjunction $\forall x\, type(x, y_1) \vee \cdots \vee type(x, y_n)$ and $n(n-1)/2$ mutual exclusion formulae $\neg type(x, y_i) \vee \neg type(x, y_j)$. The integrity constraints are expressed by the formulae: $\forall x\, meas\_it(x) \rightarrow \exists z \exists h(tH(z,h) \wedge cmpMItH(h,x))$, $\forall x\, meas\_it(x) \rightarrow \exists z \exists l(tL(z,l) \wedge cmpMItL(l,x))$, $\forall x\, arch\_it(x) \rightarrow \exists z \exists h(tH(z,h) \wedge cmpARItH(h,x))$, $\forall x\, arch\_it(x) \rightarrow \exists z\,\exists l\,(tL(z,l) \wedge cmpARItL(l,x))$, $\forall x\, amph\_it(x) \rightarrow \exists z \exists h(tH(z,h) \wedge cmpAItH(h,x))$, $\forall x\, amph\_it(x) \rightarrow \exists z \exists l(tL(z,l) \wedge cmpAItL(l,x))$. The conditional constraints are expressed by the formulae: $\forall x\, type(x, y_i) \rightarrow \exists z \exists h(tH(z,h) \wedge cmptH(h, y_i))$ $\forall x, type(x, y_i) \rightarrow \exists z \exists l(tL(z,l) \wedge cmptL(l, y_i))$. The formulae corresponding to the instances of amphorae are $amph(x)$, $type(x,y)$, $metro(z)$, $meas\_it(x)$, $arch\_it(x)$, $amph\_it(x)$, $has\_metro(x,z)$, $tL(z,l) \wedge cmpMItL(l,x) \wedge cmpARItL(l,x) \wedge cmpAItL(l,x) \wedge \neg cmptL(l, y_i)$ and $tH(z,h) \wedge cmpMItH(h,x) \wedge cmpARItH(h,x) \wedge cmpAItH(h,x) \wedge \neg cmptH(h, y_i)$. The belief base is equipped with a partial preorder which reflects the hierarchy of concepts in the ontology. Moreover constraints are preferred to the ontology which is preferred to the instances. We illustrate the PPRSIH approach thanks to example 1.

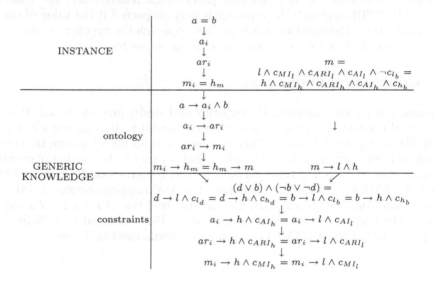

Fig. 3. Partial preorder on formulae of the belief base

Example 3. We limit ourselves to the amphorae types *Beltran2B* and *Dressel20* and to the survey of the observed amphora denoted by 4. Table 1 presents the instanciated predicates and Figure 3 illustrates the partially preordered belief base.

The validation problem is translated into a logic progam Π_E in the same spirit than the one presented in section 3.3. CLASP provides 1834 answer sets. However, if only focusing on the minimal answer sets with respect to inclusion we have to partially preorder 320 answer sets. According to the lexicographic

Table 1. Instanciated predicates and their corresponding proposition p

predicate	p	predicate	p	predicate	p
$meas\_it(4)$	m_i	$arch\_it(4)$	ar_i	$amph\_it(4)$	a_i
$amph(4)$	a	$metro(m)$	m	$type(4, Dressel20)$	d
$type(4, Beltran2B)$	b	$has\_metro(4,m)$	h_m	$tL(m,l)$	l
$tH(m,h)$	h	$cmpMItL(l,4)$	c_{MI_l}	$cmpARItL(l,4)$	c_{ARI_l}
$cmpAItL(l,4)$	c_{AI_l}	$cmpMItH(h,4)$	c_{MI_h}	$cmpARItH(h,4)$	c_{ARI_h}
$cmpAItH(h,4)$	c_{AI_h}	$cmptL(l, Dressel20)$	c_{l_d}	$cmptH(h, Dressel20)$	c_{h_d}
$cmptL(l, Beltran2B)$	c_{l_b}	$cmptH(h, Beltran2B)$	c_{h_b}	$amph(4)$	a
$type(4, Beltran2B)$	b	$metro(am)$	a_m		

comparator $\trianglelefteq_\Delta$, we obtain two uncomparable preferred answer sets S_1 and S_2 such that $F_O(S_1 \cap R^+) = \{a, b\}$ and $F_O(S_2 \cap R^+) = \{l \wedge c_{ARI_l} \wedge c_{AI_l} \wedge c_{MI_l} \wedge \neg c_{l_b}\}$. Therefore, there are two removed sets $R_1 = \{a, b\}$ and $R_2 = \{l \wedge c_{ARI_l} \wedge c_{ARI_l} \wedge c_{MI_l} \wedge \neg c_{l_b}\}$. The removed set R_1 pinpoints the typology while R_2 pinpoints that the value of TotalLength attribute may be wrong. This approach provides 2 removed sets while the RSF one only provides one removed set. The reason is that in PPRSIH approach the typology is only suspected if the value of one of the attributes is incompatible while in RSF approach the typology is suspected if the values of more than one attributes are incompatible.

6 Concluding Discussion

We now present the results of the experimental study, first on the full Pianosa survey which contains 40 amphorae then on the Port-Miou survey which contains 500 amphorae. We used 4 different tolerance thresholds t around the typical values of each type: 20%, 10%, 5% and 1% and N denotes the number of inconsistent amphorae. The CPU times $T1$, $T2$, $T3$ and T correspond to the translation from the XML files to the logic program, the ASP implementation of RSF, the translation from ASP to an XML file and the total time $T1 + T2 + T3$ respectively. The tests were conducted on a Centrino Duo cadenced at 1.73GHz and equipped with 2GB of RAM. The results are summarized in Table 2.

Table 2. CPU times (s) for RSF and PPRSIH on two surveys

(a) Pianosa survey (40 amphorae)

t	N	RSF T1	T2	T3	T	PPRSIH T1	T2	T3	T
20	5	0.05	0.62	0.95	1.62	0.24	1.12	0	1.36
10	26	0.05	0.60	0.64	1.29	0.27	5.13	0	5.40
5	30	0.05	0.61	0.45	1.11	0.29	5.87	0	6.16
1	36	0.05	0.60	0.33	0.98	0.31	6.91	0	7.22

(b) Port Miou survey (500 amphorae)

N	RSF T1	T2	T3	T	PPRSIH T1	T2	T3	T
44	0.43	5.26	0.14	5.83	0.68	9.38	0	10.06
65	0.43	5.06	0.04	5.53	0.75	13.69	0	14.44
72	0.43	4.99	0	5.42	0.81	15.03	0	15.84
81	0.43	5.06	0	5.49	0.88	16.80	0	17.68

Concerning the knowledge representation aspect the RSF approach stems from the Entity Model conceptual description and uses instanciated predicate logic. It creates a flat knowledge base, with numerous formulae, where all the objects are at the same level. In the full Pianosa survey involving 40 amphorae, the traduction of the problem requires 8462 formulae and 4160 atoms and in the full Port Miou involving 500 amphorae, the traduction of the problem requires 105775 formulae and 52000 atoms. Moreover, it only considers the intrinsic constraints between objects. However, the lack of expressivity and the high number of formulae are compensated by the good computational behaviour of the reasoning tasks expressed in this language. The PPRSIH approach stems from the application ontology and uses instanciated predicate logic equipped with a partial preorder. It creates a more structured belief base, involving less formulae than the first approach. In the full Pianosa survey involving 40 amphorae, the traduction of the problem requires 1080 formulae and 840 atoms and in the full Port-Miou survey involving 500 amphorae and the traduction requires 6021 formulae and 4683 atoms. It allows for representing the intrinsic constraints as well as the taxonomic relations between objects, and relations between objects. The partial preorder defined on the finite set of formulae expresses more structure than the first solution. This approach takes advantage of the good computational behaviour of instanciated predicate logic while expressing, in the same time, a more structured belief base.

Concerning the reasoning aspect, both implementations rely on CLASP which is one of the most efficient current ASP solver. The results obtained on Pianosa as well as on Port Miou survey given in Table 2 clearly show that both approaches deal with the full survey with a very good time. However, the first solution gives the best running times. Moreover, reducing the tolerance intervals increases the number of inconsistencies as illustrated in table 2 and the first solution seems to be not sensitive to this increasing while the running time of the second solution grows with the number of inconsistencies. The consuming task comes from the reading of the answer sets before partially ordering them in order to only select the preferred ones. In order to improve this approach we have to investigate how to directly encode the partial preorder on answer sets within the logic program. Another direction to follow in order to reach a trade-off between representation and reasoning could be to represent the validation problem in Description Logic, since the generic knowledge in expressed in terms of ontology. However, we have to study which low complexity Description Logic could be suitable. Moreover, we have to study to which extent the approach combining Description logic and ASP [6] could be used for implementation as well as the extended ASP solver to first order logic[10].

Acknowledgements

Work partially supported by the European Community under project VENUS (Contract IST-034924) of the "Information Society Technologies (IST) program of the 6th FP for RTD". The authors are solely responsible for the content of this paper. It does not represent the opinion of the European Community, and the European Community is not responsible for any use that might be made of data appearing therein.

References

1. Baral, C., Kraus, S., Minker, J., Subrahmanian, V.S.: Combining knowledge bases consisting of first order theories. In: Proc. of ISMIS, pp. 92–101 (1991)
2. Benferhat, S., Ben-Naim, J., Papini, O., Würbel, E.: An answer set programming encoding of prioritized removed sets revision: application to gis. Applied Intelligence 32(1), 60–87 (2010)
3. Benferhat, S., Lagrue, S., Papini, O.: Revision of partially ordered information: Axiomatization, semantics and iteration. In: Proc. of IJCAI 2005, Edinburgh, pp. 376–381 (2005)
4. Brewka, G.: Preferred sutheories: an extended logical framework for default reasoning. In: Proc. of IJCAI 1989, pp. 1043–1048 (1989)
5. Drap, P., Grussenmeyer, P.: A digital photogrammetric workstation on the web. Journal of Photogrammetry and Remote Sensing 55(1), 48–58 (2000)
6. Eiter, T., Ianni, G., Lukasiewicz, T., Schindlauer, R., Tompits, H.: Combining answer set programming with description logics for the semantic web. Artificial Intelligence 172(12-13), 1495–1539 (2008)
7. Gebser, M., Kaufmann, B., Neumann, A., Schaub, T.: *clasp*: A conflict-driven answer set solver. In: Baral, C., Brewka, G., Schlipf, J. (eds.) LPNMR 2007. LNCS (LNAI), vol. 4483, pp. 260–265. Springer, Heidelberg (2007)
8. Hue, J., Papini, O., Würbel, E.: Implementing prioritized merging with ASP. In: Hüllermeier, E., Kruse, R., Hoffmann, F. (eds.) IPMU 2010. CCIS, vol. 80, pp. 138–147. Springer, Heidelberg (2010)
9. Hué, J., Würbel, E., Papini, O.: Removed sets fusion: Performing off the shelf. In: Proc. of ECAI 2008, pp. 94–98 (2008)
10. Lefèvre, C., Nicolas, P.: A first order forward chaining approach for answer set computing. In: Erdem, E., Lin, F., Schaub, T. (eds.) LPNMR 2009. LNCS, vol. 5753, pp. 196–208. Springer, Heidelberg (2009)
11. Papini, O.: A complete revision function in propositionnal calculus. In: Neumann, B. (ed.) Proc. of ECAI 1992, pp. 339–343. John Wiley and Sons. Ltd., Chichester (1992)
12. Papini, O.: D3.1 archaeological activities and knowledge analysis. Technical report, Delivrable, VENUS project. january (2007), http://www.venus-project.eu
13. Papini, O., Curé, O., Drap, P., Fertil, B., Hué, J., Roussel, D., Sérayet, M., Seinturier, J., Würbel, E.: D3.6 reasoning with archaeological ontologies. technical report and prototype of software for the reversible fusion operations. Technical report, Delivrable, VENUS project (July 2009), http://www.venusproject.eu
14. Papini, O., Würbel, E., Jeansoulin, R., Curé, O., Drap, P., Sérayet, M., Hué, J., Seinturier, J., Long, L.: D3.4 representation of archaeological ontologies 1. Technical report, Delivrable, VENUS project (July 2008), http://www.venus-project.eu
15. Rescher, N., Manor, R.: On inference from inconsistent premises. Theory and Decision 1, 179–219 (1970)
16. Seinturier, J.: Fusion de connaissances: Applications aux relevés photogrammétriques de fouilles archéologiques sous-marines. PhD thesis, Université du Sud Toulon Var (2007)
17. Sérayet, M., Drap, P., Papini, O.: Extending removed sets revision to partially preordered belief bases. International Journal of Approximate Reasoning 52(1), 110–126 (2011)
18. Würbel, E., Papini, O., Jeansoulin, R.: Revision: an application in the framework of gis. In: Proc. of KR 2000, Breckenridge, Colorado, USA, pp. 505–516 (2000)
19. Yahi, S., Benferhat, S., Lagrue, S., Sérayet, M., Papini, O.: A lexicographic inference for partially preordered belief bases. In: Proc. of KR 2008, pp. 507–516 (2008)

Adaptive Dialogue Strategy Selection through Imprecise Probabilistic Query Answering

Ian O'Neill, Anbu Yue, Weiru Liu, and Phil Hanna

School of Electronics, Electrical Engineering and Computer Science,
Queen's University Belfast, Belfast BT7 1NN, UK
{i.oneill,a.yue,w.liu,p.hanna}@qub.ac.uk

Abstract. In a human-computer dialogue system, the dialogue strategy can range from very restrictive to highly flexible. Each specific dialogue style has its pros and cons and a dialogue system needs to select the most appropriate style for a given user. During the course of interaction, the dialogue style can change based on a user's response and the system observation of the user. This allows a dialogue system to understand a user better and provide a more suitable way of communication. Since measures of the quality of the user's interaction with the system can be incomplete and uncertain, frameworks for reasoning with uncertain and incomplete information can help the system make better decisions when it chooses a dialogue strategy. In this paper, we investigate how to select a dialogue strategy based on aggregating the factors detected during the interaction with the user. For this purpose, we use *probabilistic logic programming (PLP)* to model probabilistic knowledge about how these factors will affect the degree of freedom of a dialogue. When a dialogue system needs to know which strategy is more suitable, an appropriate query can be executed against the PLP and a probabilistic solution with a degree of satisfaction is returned. The degree of satisfaction reveals how much the system can trust the probability attached to the solution.

1 Introduction

There are many different ways in which a computer can talk to people. Often dialogue strategies can be categorized as finite-state or frame-based. Additionally, for very fluid, discursive dialogues, a free-form dialogue strategy is appropriate: this may be coupled to techniques for topic recognition as well as mechanisms for transferring to more structured or constrained dialogue once a known transaction context has been identified e.g., [PR03, OHSG].

This paper describes work undertaken by Queen's University Belfast as part of a 3-month collaborative research project commissioned by AUDI AG, Ingolstadt, Germany. While a business-strength solution would entail a functionally richer application and an extensive evaluation programme, the exploratory dialogue system that resulted from this short collaboration served to illustrate how a probabilistic logic program (PLP) might be used to drive a dialogue strategy selection mechanism based on uncertain observations and inputs.

W. Liu (Ed.): ECSQARU 2011, LNAI 6717, pp. 675–687, 2011.

In particular, we were interested in investigating how *probabilistic logic programming* might be able to draw together, into one decision-making process, dialogue-influencing inputs of quite disparate natures and modalities. A dialogue system capable of replicating a good human listener's sensitivity towards the needs and expectations of a dialogue partner, as well as replicating a human listener's awareness of her/his own limitations, might have to take into account a number of influencing factors. The research programme was not concerned in the first instance with how these factors might be measured or quantified, rather it is on how together these factors influence the selection of a dialogue strategy. The eight core dialogue factors, and the values they could take, are shown below.

Table 1. Dialogue-influencing factors

Factor	Values	Explanations
Experience (Proficiency)	high (2), med (1), low (0)	How effectively does the user interact with the system?
Recognition confidence	high (2), med (1), low (0)	How confident is the system that it has recognised what the user said?
Key values	multiple (2), one (1), none (0)	How many usable values does the user provide per turn?
Affect	good (2), ok (1), bad (0)	Is the user in a good or bad mood?
Response Type	good (3), talkative (2), thinking (1), wondering (0)	What is the relationship between speech and silence in the user's utterances?
Productivity t_0	yes (0), no (1)	A turn is productive if a keyword is provided incontext.
Productivity t_{-1}	yes (0), no (1)	A turn is productive if a keyword is provided incontext.
Productivity t_{-2}	yes (0), no (1)	A turn is productive if a keyword is provided incontext.

Productivity t_0 , Productivity t_{-1} , and Productivity t_{-2} , indicate whether or not usable keywords were identified by the system in the current dialogue turn (t_0), and in the two preceding turns (t_{-1} and t_{-2}). In the experiment, non-productivity (a failure in dialogue development) was regarded as more significant than productivity (normal dialogue flow). Non-productivity was therefore represented by '1', rather than the default assignment '0'.

For each of the factors indicated above, developers were able to suggest whether a high or low value would be a positive or negative influence on (i.e. should increase or decrease) the *degree of dialogue freedom* in the exchanges between system and user. A freer dialogue would be characterised by system turns that included minimal system prompts, similar to a frame-based dialogue (i.e. just ask the user for the information required, without setting out specific options), while a less-free dialogue would entail a high level of system guidance - to the extent of asking the user for a yes/no response to a very specific question. The role of the PLP was to calculate an overall *degree of dialogue freedom* based on these disparate input factors (which may be uncertain) and their supposed individual influences on the dialogue strategy. In turn the degree of freedom was used to determine the basic dialogue strategy. *Braking factors* were added to the *degree of freedom* calculation, so as to prevent too fast a transition from one dialogue strategy to another. In addition, a *manner* of system delivery (the particular form of words used to realize the dialogue strategy) was influenced by the user's own dialogue manner, perceived affective state, and the frequency with which they used the system. These additional influences on the precise form of the system utterance are not considered in this paper. Later, however, taking some simplified examples, we will examine the techniques used to calculate the degree of freedom itself.

Since these factors affecting the selection of a dialogue strategy can be modelled using conditional formulae with probabilistic intervals, our research and development is concerned with the appropriateness of using a PLP to help select a dialogue strategy.

Conditional probabilistic logic programming is a framework to represent and reason with imprecise (conditional) probabilistic knowledge. An agent's knowledge is represented by a *probabilistic logic program* (PLP) which is a set of (conditional) logical formulae with probability intervals. The impreciseness of the agent's knowledge is explicitly represented by assigning a probability interval to every logical formula (representing a conditional event) indicating that the probability of a formula will be in the given interval.

To intuitively explain how PLP can be used to model probabilistic knowledge, we take the common knowledge *typically Birds fly, magpies and penguins are birds, but penguins do not fly* as an example to illustrate the meanings of notations. Assume that based on common knowledge, we know that over 98% of birds can fly (so not all birds can fly), and we also know that every *magpie is a bird*. Then this knowledge can be modelled using a PLP as

$$\{(fly(X)|bird(X))[0.98, 1], (bird(X)|magpie(X))[1, 1]\}$$

which can be used to answer queries like *Can a magpie fly?* (e.g., $?(fly(t)|magpie(t))$).

Similarly, within the context of dialogue systems, the relationship between a factor and a dialogue strategy can be modelled using conditional probabilistic logical formulae too. For instance,

$$(dss(t1, free)|exp(t0, high), recog(t0, high))[0.85, 1]$$

states that when both a user's experience and the systems's recognition confidence are high, then the *degree of dialogue freedom* suggests that a *free dialogue strategy* should be chosen with a probability in the interval $[0.85, 1]$.

The main contributions of this paper are as follows. First, we designed a Dialogue Manager for an in-car dialogue system that choose a dialogue strategy dynamically considering factors observed during interaction with the user. With a freer dialogue, the user can provide 'over-informative answers' in response to a single question: however, with a more restricted dialogue, the user needs to answer the question directly. Second, since there is an exponentially large number of combinations of correlated properties in a dialogue, our system allows experts to use PLPs to state probabilistically how each individual property will affect the selection of the dialogue strategy. Third, our PLP *ignorance analysis* tool provides a mechanism that allows experts to judge the quality of the knowledge on which the choice of dialogue strategy is based. Finally, with the assistance of the *degree of satisfaction*, the user can easily configure this system to be freer or more restricted at any time.

This paper is organized as follows. After a brief review of probabilistic logic programming in Section 2, we discuss the role PLPs can play dialogue systems in Section 3. The experiment and simulated evaluations are discussed in Section 4. We compare our work with related research and conclude the paper in Section 5.

2 Preliminaries

We briefly review conditional probabilistic logic programming here [Luk98, Luk01, KIL04].

Let Φ be a finite set of *predicate symbols* and *constant symbols*, and V be a set of *variables*. An *event* or *logic formula* can be defined from $\Phi \cup V$ using none or any connectives $\neg, \wedge, \vee$ as usually done in first-order logics. We use ϕ, ψ, φ for events. For instance, let *Peter* be a person's name, then $man(Peter)$ is a logical formula saying that *Peter is a man* or let X be a variable, then $man(X)$ states that predicate man is applied to variable X. When reasoning, the variable can be bound to a constant. For instance, $man(Peter)$ can be considered as the result of assigning $Peter$ to X.

Given a PLP and a query against the PLP, traditionally, either a probability interval or a maximum entropy based probability (denoted as MEP below) is returned as the answer. An interval implies that the true probability of the query shall be within the given interval. However, when this interval is too wide, it provides no useful information. On the other hand, when the knowledge in a PLP is very imprecise, providing a single probability as the solution to a query can be misleading. In [YLH08, YLH10], we developed a new approach which can measure the degree of satisfaction of a single probability solution w.r.t the knowledge provided in a PLP.

A probability distribution Pr satisfies probabilistic formula $(\psi|\phi)[l, u]$ iff $Pr(\psi|\phi) \in [l, u]$. We say that a probabilistic formula $(\psi|\phi)[l, u]$ is a *consequence* of a PLP P, denoted as $P \models (\psi|\phi)[l, u]$, iff every probability distribution Pr that satisfies P also satisfies the probabilistic formula. A probabilistic formula $(\psi|\phi)[l, u]$ is a *tight consequence* of P, denoted as $P \models_{tight} (\psi|\phi)[l, u]$, iff $P \models (\psi|\phi)[l, u]$ and for all $[l', u'] \subset [l, u]$, $P \not\models (\psi|\phi)[l, u]$. For simplicity, if $P \models (\phi|\top)[0, 0]$, we denote $P \models_{tight} (\psi|\phi)[1, 0]$.

We use $me[P]$ to denote the probability distribution with maximum entropy among those that satisfy P. Let P be a PLP, we say that $(\psi|\phi)[l, u]$ is a *me-consequence* of P, denoted as $P \models^{me} (\psi|\phi)[l, u]$, iff P is unsatisfiable or $me[P] \models (\psi|\phi)[l, u]$. We say that $(\psi|\phi)[l, u]$ is a *tight me-consequence* of P, denoted as $P \models_{tight}^{me} (\psi|\phi)[l, u]$, iff one of the following conditions holds:

- $P \models (\phi|\top)[0, 0]$, $l = 1$, $u = 0$,
- $me[P](\phi) > 0$ and $me[P](\psi|\phi) = l = u$.

Example 1. Let PLP P be defined as follows:

$$P = \left\{ \begin{array}{l} (fly(X)|bird(X))[0.98, 1] \\ (bird(X)|penguin(X))[1, 1] \\ (penguin(X)|bird(X))[0.1, 1] \end{array} \right\}$$

Based on this knowledge base, a user can query the likelihood that *a penguin can fly*, e.g., $?(fly(t)|penguin(t))$.

The results of using our prediction tool based on this knowledge base is
$$P \models_{tight} (fly(t)|penguin(t))[0,1], \text{ and } P \models_{tight}^{me} (fly(t)|penguin(t))[0.98,0.98].$$

In [KIL04, Luk98, Luk01], approaches were provided to calculate the probability interval and probability with maximum entropy for any query. In [YLH08, YLH10], a formal method was provided to analyze the PLP and the maximum entropy principle as well as to calculate the degree of ignorance and degree of sastisfaction reviewed in this section.

First, an ignorance value is provided to evaluate the extent to which the answer given under maximum entropy is reliable. Second, a measure of the degree of satisfaction is provided to evaluate how reliable an interval is to serve as the answer of the query.

Definition 1 (Ignorance). *Let $\mathcal{PL}$ be the set of all PLPs and $\mathcal{E}$ be a set of conditional events. Function* $\mathsf{IG} : \mathcal{PL} \times \mathcal{E} \mapsto [0,1]$ *is called the* measure[1]*of ignorance, iff for any PLP P and conditional event $(\psi|\phi)$ it satisfies the following postulates*

[Bounded] $\mathsf{IG}(P, \psi|\phi) \in [0,1]$.
[Preciseness] $\mathsf{IG}(P, \psi|\phi) = 0$ *iff* $P \models_{tight} (\psi|\phi)[u,u]$ *or* $P \models \phi \rightarrow \bot$.
[Totally Ignorance] $\mathsf{IG}(\emptyset, \psi|\phi) = 1$, *if* $\not\models \phi \rightarrow \psi$ *and* $\not\models \phi \rightarrow \neg\psi$.
[Sound] *If* $\mathsf{IG}(P, \psi|\phi) = 1$ *then* $P \models (\psi|\phi)[0,1]$.
[Irrelevance] *If P and another PLP P' do not contain common syntaxes,*
   i.e. $\Phi \cap \Phi' = \emptyset$, *then* $\mathsf{IG}(P, \psi|\phi) = \mathsf{IG}(P \cup P', \psi|\phi)$.

If $P = \emptyset$, only tautologies can be inferred from P. Therefore, from any PLP P, $\mathsf{IG}_P(\psi|\phi) \leq \mathsf{IG}_\emptyset(\psi|\phi)$, which means that an empty PLP has the biggest ignorance value for any conditional event. When $\mathsf{IG}_P(\psi|\phi) = 0$, event $(\psi|\phi)$ can be inferred precisely from P, since a single precise probability for $(\psi|\phi)$ can be obtained from p. The ignorance measurement focuses on the knowledge about $(\psi|\phi)$ contained in P, which means that irrelevant knowledge does not provide a better understanding of this conditional event.

Definition 2 (Degree of Satisfaction). *Let $\mathcal{PL}$ be the set of all PLPs and $\mathcal{F}$ be a set of probabilistic formulae. Function* $\mathsf{SAT} : \mathcal{PL} \times \mathcal{F} \mapsto [0,1]$ *is called the measure of degree of satisfaction iff for any PLP P and ground probabilistic formula $\mu = (\psi|\phi)[l,u]$, it satisfies the following postulates:*

[Reflexive] $\mathsf{SAT}(P, \mu) = 1$, *iff* $P \models \mu$.
[Rational] $\mathsf{SAT}(P, \mu) = 0$ *if* $P \cup \{\mu\}$ *is unsatisfiable.*
[Monotonicity]
   $\mathsf{SAT}(P, \mu) \geq \mathsf{SAT}(P, (\psi|\phi)[l',u'])$, *if* $[l',u'] \subseteq [l,u]$.
   $\mathsf{SAT}(P, \mu) > \mathsf{SAT}(P, (\psi|\phi)[l',u'])$, *if* $[l',u'] \subset [l,u]$
   and $\mathsf{SAT}(P, (\psi|\phi)[l',u']) < 1$.

---

[1] In mathematical analysis, a measure m is a function, such that $m : 2^S \mapsto [0,\infty]$ and
1. $m(E_1) \geq 0$ for any $E \subseteq S$;
2. $m(\emptyset) = 0$;
3. If $E_1, E_2, \ldots$ is a countable sequence of pairwise disjoint subsets of S, the measure of the union of E_i's is equal to the sum of the measures of each E_i, that is, $m(\bigcup_{i=1}^{\infty} E_i) = \sum_{i=1}^{\infty} m(E_i)$.

[Cautious Monotonicity] *Let* $P' = P \cup \{(\psi|\phi)[l', u']\}$, *where* $P \models^{me} (\psi|\phi)[l', u']$
   If $1 \geq \text{SAT}(P, \mu) \geq 0$ *then* $\text{SAT}(P', \mu) \geq \text{SAT}(P, \mu)$.

The reflexive property says that every consequence is totally satisfied. The rational property says that 0 is given as the degree of satisfaction of an unsatisfiable probabilistic formula.

Monotonicity says that if we expect a more precise interval for a query, then the chance that the exact probability of the query is *not* in the interval is getting bigger. Cautious monotonicity says that, if P and P' are equivalent except for the bound of $(\psi|\phi)$, and if P' contains more knowledge about $(\psi|\phi)$, then the degree of satisfaction of μ under P' should be bigger than that of μ under P.

Example 2. Let P and query $?Q$ be the same as in Example 1. Then, the degree of satisfaction for the query answer $[0.7, 1]$ is 0.8.

If we require that the degree of satisfaction of a query answer must be above a threshold γ, then the PLP reasoning system can produce a tightest interval for which its degree of satisfaction is not less than γ. When $\gamma = 0.5$, the returned interval is [MEP, 1] (the upper bound is set to 1 in our system), so we obtain both an interval and the MEP value. This kind of consequence relation is an extension to $\models_{tight}$. Details about the calculation of degree of satisfaction are available in [YLH08, YLH10].

3   Dialogue Systems

A fully implemented spoken dialogue system requires a delicately balanced interaction between a number of main components. These typically include a speech recogniser, a semantic parser, a dialogue manager, a natural language generator, a speech synthesiser and an underlying database. More recently, components intended to capture and synthesise non-verbal interaction - affect recognisers, embodied conversational agents, and so on - may also feature in the configuration. In the experiment described here, we focus on the behaviour manifested by the Dialogue Manager, which takes a co-ordinating and decision-making role, determining how the system should ask the user questions and respond to the user's answers.

We were particularly interested in the degree of freedom that the Dialogue Manager should offer the user as they conducted their conversation. Thus the Dialogue Manager had at its disposal a number of dialogue strategies, ranging from several flavours of tightly system-led 'finite state' approaches, which required that the user choose just one of the options presented on a particular dialogue turn, to freer 'frame-based 'solutions, where, without being explicitly told the available options, the user could supply the system with one or more values needed to populate 'slots' in a notional enquiry frame.

3.1   Using Probabilistic Logic Programs to Represent Imprecise Data

The permutations of all dialogue-influencing factors are exponentially large in number and far exceed the experts' power to define a strategy for each of them. Developers can however provide PLP representations of the typical effect on dialogue style of key individual dialogue-influencing factors and of key combinations of these factors. Using this information the system can calculate degrees of dialogue freedom for all combinations of dialogue-influencing factors.

One problem in using traditional probabilistic logic programming [CPQC03, Luk01] is that, only a loose and uninformative interval or an unreliable single probability value can be extracted as the answer. However, by using PLP to model the domain knowledge and by then applying our reasoning method, we obtain more reliable intervals and single values in response to a query.

3.2 Observation vs. a Priori Facts

In PLPs, we use ground formulae to state a priori facts from statistics, i.e., something that must be true (statistically) is regarded as a fact. These facts are treated differently from observations about individuals. Observing an event (such as the total number of recognized keywords by a user) does not infer that the event would happen for sure. So, observations cannot be represented as formulae of the form $(\psi(a)|\top)[1, 1]$ in a PLP: doing so implies that we know $\psi(a)$ to be true even before it is observed. In other words, taking $\psi(a)$ as a probabilistic event, we cannot predict if $\psi(a)$ is true or false before we observe it. In dialogue systems, observations are very important for choosing dialogue strategies. In our framework, all observations are stored in a database (named OBS) that is separate from a PLP containing statistical knowledge. When querying $(\psi|\phi)[l, u]$ on PLP P, this observation database OBS is automatically called, with the effect that querying $(\psi|\phi)[l, u]$ is equivalent to querying $(\psi|\phi \wedge \bigwedge OBS)[l, u]$ on P.

4   The Experiment and Evaluation of Our Framework

4.1   Conducting the Experiment and Constructing a PLP

For each possible permutation of the values of the eight factors, the Dialogue Manager would use the answer to the query as its degree of dialogue freedom and would select its dialogue strategy accordingly. We interpret the answer to a query as: *With a given degree of satisfaction, what is the best estimation of the probability that a free dialogue strategy would be appropriate in these circumstances?* With a 0.5 degree of satisfaction, the result equals the Maximum Entropy Probability.

However, rather than have the Dialogue Manager generate degrees of dialogue freedom live (a computationally very intensive process), it acquired the answers for the queries from a look-up table, generated beforehand by the PLP Reasoner and Analyzer [YLH08, YLH10]. and covering all possible permutations of the values of the eight dialogue-influencing factors.

Thus, values generated off-line by our Reasoning Engine would subsequently be used live by the Dialogue Manager, as it selected its dialogue strategy. In the following example we concentrate on just a handful of dialogue-influencing factors, the PLP used by the Reasoning Engine, and the output generated by the Reasoning Engine. In the PLP, predicates *exp, recog,* and *key* are used to state respectively the user's experience

Table 2. Probability intervals for a free dialogue strategy given a selection of dialogue-influencing factors

	Level	Factor: User Experience			
		High	Medium	Low	
Factor:	High	[0.85, 1]	[0.80, 0.95]	[0.75, 0.85]	
Recognition	Medium	[0.65, 0.85]	[0.6, 0.8]	[0.55, 0.75]	Probability
Confidence	Low	[0.45, 0.65]	[0.4, 0.6]	[0.35, 0.55]	
Factor:	Multiple	[0.95, 1]	[0.90, 0.95]	[0.80, 0.95]	Interval
Number of	Single	[0.90, 1]	[0.85, 1]	[0.60, 0.90]	
Recognized Keywords	None	[0.80, 1]	[0.70, 0.90]	[0.20, 0.70]	

(strictly speaking, the user's *proficiency*: elsewhere we have used the term *experience* in a simpler sense to represent the number of times the user has interacted with the system); the system's recognition confidence; and the number of keywords recognized from the user's response. The sample probabilistic formulae below reflect these conventions. These formulae represent the effect of *combinations* of dialogue-influencing factors, and similar formulae are used to represent the typical effect on dialogue freedom of *individual* dialogue-influencing factors:

If the recognition confidence is high and user experience is high too, then the probability that a free dialogue strategy is appropriate is in the interval [0.8,1]. A PLP capturing this probabilistic knowledge can be created as follows.

$$
\begin{aligned}
&(dss(t1, free)|exp(t0, high), recog(t0, high)) && [0.85, 1] \\
&(dss(t1, free)|exp(t0, high), recog(t0, med)) && [0.65, 0.85] \\
&(dss(t1, free)|exp(t0, high), recog(t0, low)) && [0.45, 0.65] \\
&(dss(t1, free)|exp(t0, med), recog(t0, high)) && [0.80, 0.95] \\
&(dss(t1, free)|exp(t0, med), recog(t0, med)) && [0.60, 0.80] \\
&(dss(t1, free)|exp(t0, med), recog(t0, low)) && [0.40, 0.60] \\
&(dss(t1, free)|exp(t0, low), recog(t0, high)) && [0.75, 0.85] \\
&(dss(t1, free)|exp(t0, low), recog(t0, med)) && [0.55, 0.75] \\
&(dss(t1, free)|exp(t0, low), recog(t0, low)) && [0.35, 0.55] \\
&(dss(t1, free)|exp(t0, high), key(t0, multiple)) && [0.95, 1.00] \\
&(dss(t1, free)|exp(t0, high), key(t0, single)) && [0.90, 1.00] \\
&(dss(t1, free)|exp(t0, high), key(t0, none)) && [0.80, 1.00] \\
&(dss(t1, free)|exp(t0, med), key(t0, multiple)) && [0.90, 0.95] \\
&(dss(t1, free)|exp(t0, med), key(t0, single)) && [0.85, 1.00] \\
&(dss(t1, free)|exp(t0, med), key(t0, none)) && [0.70, 0.90] \\
&(dss(t1, free)|exp(t0, low), key(t0, multiple)) && [0.80, 0.95] \\
&(dss(t1, free)|exp(t0, low), key(t0, single)) && [0.60, 0.90] \\
&(dss(t1, free)|exp(t0, low), key(t0, none)) && [0.20, 0.70]
\end{aligned}
$$

The probability of $dss(t1, free)$ stands for the degree of freedom of the dialogue strategy at the next time point $t1$, while, for our initial trial, the values [min,max] represent the range within which developers believe dialogue freedom should lie, given the current level (high, medium, low, etc.) of the dialogue-influencing factor under consideration in the formula.

In order to facilitate reasoning, we need to include some background knowledge in this PLP for example, that the system's recognition confidence cannot be both high and medium simultaneously. This background knowledge is represented as the following additional probabilistic formulae:

$$recog(t0, high), recog(t0, med)[0, 0]$$
$$recog(t0, low), recog(t0, med)[0, 0]$$
$$recog(t0, high), recog(t0, low)[0, 0]$$
$$exp(t0, high), exp(t0, med)[0, 0]$$
$$exp(t0, low), exp(t0, med)[0, 0]$$
$$exp(t0, high), exp(t0, low)[0, 0]$$
$$key(t0, multiple), key(t0, single)[0, 0]$$
$$key(t0, multiple), key(t0, none)[0, 0]$$
$$key(t0, single), key(t0, none)[0, 0]$$

Now assume that we have a user, A, whose experience is *medium* at time point $t0$, assume also that keywords recognition is *multiple*, and recognition confidence is *low*. To determine which dialogue strategy is most suitable, we query

$$Q =?(dss(t1, free)|exp(t0, med), key(t0, multiple), recog(t0, low))$$

This can be executed against the PLP constructed above. For simplicity, let E be the conditional event in this query (i.e., $Q =?E$). For this query, we find $P \models_{tight} E[0, 1]$ and $P \models_{tight}^{me} E[0.8667, 0.8667]$. That is, we get a non-informative interval $[0, 1]$ and a precise probability 0.8667 as two possible answers to this query.

Note that the statistical (or, in the test system, heuristic) knowledge in the PLP states that for a user of medium experience, if the system's recognition confidence is low, then the next round of dialogue freedom should be relatively low ($[0.40, 0.60]$). However, if multiple keywords are recognized by the system then the freedom of the next round should be relatively high ($[0.80, 0.95]$). These two rules state two possible degrees of freedom for the next round, but how these two factors should be integrated, in order to determine the degree of freedom of next turn, remains unclear. The value 0.8667 given by the maximum entropy principle, suggests a degree of compromise.

Now, we examine the degree of satisfaction and ignorance of $?E[l, u]$. When $l = u = 0.8667$, the ignorance of this query is bigger than 0. Thus the value 0.8667 is possibly not a very accurate degree of dialogue freedom. To find a probabilistic interval within which the true probability might lie and to quantify our satisfaction with this interval, we assign different values to l and u and calculate the degree of satisfaction and ignorance for each pair l and u. Details of the calculation are given in Table 3. From this table, the system can choose a dialogue strategy based on these degrees of satisfaction. For instance, we have $p(Pr(E) \in [0.4, 1] = 0.8034$, which means the probability (that a degree of dialogue freedom of 0.4 in the next dialogue turn will be appropriate to this user) is 0.8034. From another perspective, it may be the case that there is a very high probability that the system has clearly recognised the user's response. If this is so, a strategy with freedom 0.4 may be too restrictive. Therefore, a dialogue system should choose a strategy that balances both the degree of satisfaction and the level of freedom that it affords the user. For a user who prefers a less restricted dialogue, the threshold of

Table 3. Probability interval for $?E$ and the degree of satisfaction of $Pr(E) \in [l, u]$

Probability interval	Degree of satisfaction	Probability interval	Degree of satisfaction
[0.1, 1]	0.9586	[0.2, 1]	0.9138
[0.3, 1]	0.8621	[0.4, 1]	0.8034
[0.5, 1]	0.7310	[0.6, 1]	0.6552
[0.7, 1]	0.5759	[0.8, 1]	0.5142
[0.81, 1]	0.5104	[0.82, 1]	0.5072
[0.83, 1]	0.5045	[0.84, 1]	0.5024
[0.85, 1]	0.5010	[0.86, 1]	0.5002

the degree of satisfaction can be low and for a user who prefers a system-led dialogue, the threshold can be higher.

4.2   Evaluating the Results

However, in our initial experiment we accepted the figure for MEP *at face value* and used it to help us select our dialogue strategy. We were particularly interested in the manner in which the precise probability, the MEP, changed according to the dialogue influencing factors that were input. Since we (and the system) take this precise value as answering the question *How probable is it that a free dialogue strategy would be appropriate in these circumstances?*, then, if the value turned out to be 1 (entirely probable), the Dialogue Manager would, if unchecked by any braking factor, chose the freest strategy; if the value were 0 (entirely improbable), it would choose the most restrictive strategy; and if somewhere between 0 and 1, it would choose a restrictive or non-restrictive strategy corresponding to the band within which the freedom value fell. In reality this *raw* freedom value was generally modified by a braking factor, which varied according to user proficiency, in order, as we have mentioned, to avoid jarringly rapid shifts between quite different dialogue strategies: thus a *raw* freedom value was converted by means of the appropriate braking factor, to a *current* freedom value and it was this that was used to select the dialogue strategy for the next turn. In future the braking factor might be replaced by an additional dialogue-influencing factor to be considered by the PLP Reasoner and Analyzer.

To judge the correctness of the *raw* system behaviour, we monitored the manner in which the unmodified MEP rose or fell depending on the combinations of dialogue influencing factors that were input. In the PLP for the experiment, some individual factors and some combinations of factors had been identified as placing raw *dialogue freedom* within particular ranges (probability intervals). In this way the PLP represented the developers', and by extension the Dialogue Manager's, basic decision-making heuristics or rules of thumb.

Table 4 illustrates the system's raw behaviour in one typical sequence of eight dialogue moves. Input to the system is shown for each move in the form of an eight-element feature vector. In each feature vector the input elements are ordered and have values as described previously in Table 1. Each feature vector is followed by the corresponding raw output MEP.

Table 4 represents eight moves in a dialogue with a proficient user. In user turns U1, U2 and U3 the dialogue is progressing well (raw freedom value 1). In user turns U4 and U5 there is no dialogue product (i.e. no usable user input) and the user's affective state worsens (the freedom value falls). In user turn U6 there is product and the user's affective state improves (the freedom value rises). In user turns U7 and U8 the user's affective state worsens again, and other dialogue factors are also sub-optimal (the freedom value falls again).

Table 4. The effect on MEP of different levels of dialogue-influencing factor across eight user-turns

User Turn	Dialogue-Influencing Factors								0.5 (MEP)
	1	2	3	4	5	6	7	8	
U1	2	2	2	2	3	0	1	1	1.00000
U2	2	2	2	2	3	0	0	1	1.00000
U3	2	2	2	2	3	0	0	0	1.00000
U4	2	0	0	2	3	1	0	0	0.82560
U5	2	0	0	1	3	1	1	0	0.62300
U6	2	1	1	2	3	0	1	1	0.83770
U7	2	0	0	1	1	1	0	1	0.70000
U8	2	1	1	0	0	0	1	0	0.64080
Level									

This scenario and others like it indicate that the degree of raw dialogue freedom, as represented by the generated MEP, is indeed a reasonable interpretation of the developers' rules of thumb for determining when freer dialogue strategies should be allowed, and when more restrictive system-led dialogue strategies should be considered.

5 Related Work and Conclusion

Related work: Logic programming is now a well established knowledge representation and reasoning formalism in artificial intelligence and deductive databases. The need for representing uncertainty in the logic programming framework is already reported by a great number of publications [Luk98, BGR04, BH07, RKT07, Fuh00], [DD04] etc.

Our PLP analytical and reasoning system [YLH08] is based on *conditional probabilistic logic programming* [CPQC03, Luk01], in which knowledge is represented by interval restrictions for probabilities on conditional events in the form of $(\psi|\phi)[l, u]$. In traditional probabilistic logic programming, the answer for a query is either a very uninformative wide interval or an unreliable probability value. In contrast, our method can provide an ignorance degree to evaluate how useful a PLP is to answer a query, and furthermore provide a reasoning method to give a more informative (narrower) interval as the answer that is acceptable to a user.

A few IT systems have been implemented that model and query probabilistic knowledge, for example, SPIRIT [RRK06] and PIT [SF97].

In order to manage imprecise probabilistic reasoning, an expert system shell, SPIRIT, was implemented which uses the principle of maximum entropy to avoid the request of precise probability distributions. Knowledge acquisition is performed by specifying probabilistic facts and rules on discrete variables in an extended propositional logic syntax. The shell generates the unique probability distribution which respects all facts and rules and maximizes entropy. After creating this distribution the shell is ready for answering simple and complex queries. System PIT (Probability Induction Tool) was implemented based on propositional logic, the probability calculus and the concept of model-quantification. The task of PIT is to deliver decisions under incomplete knowledge but to keep the necessary additional assumptions as minimal as possible.

In contrast, our system deploys a reasoning mechanism in conditional probabilistic logic programming, which is based on first order logic, rather than propositional logic.

From a dialogue perspective, the need to give a dialogue system the correct amount of user-led and system-led interaction is important. An experienced user will become frustrated, if in ideal conditions he or she is unduly restricted by the system, but so will an inexperienced user, if, in adverse conditions, the system does not curtail dialogue freedom (the paths along which the dialogue might progress) by providing assistance and guiding the dialogue more closely to a successful conclusion.

Conclusion: For the authors this has been a useful first exploration of the issues involved in PLP-based natural language dialogue management. Some advantages, and potential challenges, for live system development have emerged.

From a dialogue modelling perspective, the decision-making engine, the PLP, can be regarded as a black box. In other words, for those concerned with implementing a naturalistic dialogue, one which can at least pass as a reasonable sequence of spoken exchanges between system and user in pursuance of some task, it is immaterial how the figure representing the level of dialogue freedom is derived, so long as it might reasonably be regarded (by an external observer) as a sensible compromise between factors that individually pull towards greater dialogue restriction or push towards greater dialogue flexibility.

However in the longer term, logic programmers and dialogue modelers will have to embark on a demanding dialogue of their own, as they attempt to understand each others capabilities as knowledge engineers and meet each others requirements as providers of usable software systems.

Besides furthering this inter-disciplinary dialogue, future work will entail using more realistic, live inputs to represent the various factors that influence the human-computer dialogue. It will also involve attempting to assess how satisfied different categories of actual user are with the variety of dialogue styles that the system adopts in varied and evolving circumstances.

References

[BGR04]   Baral, C., Gelfond, M., Rushton, J.N.: Probabilistic reasoning with answer sets. In: Lifschitz, V., Niemelä, I. (eds.) LPNMR 2004. LNCS (LNAI), vol. 2923, pp. 21–33. Springer, Heidelberg (2003)

[BH07]   Baral, C., Hunsaker, M.: Using the probabilistic logic programming language p-log for causal and counterfactual reasoning and non-naive conditioning. In: IJCAI, pp. 243–249 (2007)

[CPQC03] Costa, V.S., Page, D., Qazi, M., Cussens, J.: CLP($\mathcal{BN}$): Constraint logic programming for probabilistic knowledge. In: UAI, pp. 517–524 (2003)

[DD04]   Dekhtyar, A., Dekhtyar, M.I.: Possible worlds semantics for probabilistic logic programs. In: Demoen, B., Lifschitz, V. (eds.) ICLP 2004. LNCS, vol. 3132, pp. 137–
148. Springer, Heidelberg (2004)

[Fuh00]   Fuhr, N.: Probabilistic datalog: Implementing logical information retrieval for advanced applications. JASIS 51(2), 95–110 (2000)

[KIL04]   Kern-Isberner, G., Lukasiewicz, T.: Combining probabilistic logic programming with
the power of maximum entropy. Artificial Intelligence 157(1-2), 139–202 (2004)

[Luk98]   Lukasiewicz, T.: Probabilistic logic programming. In: ECAI, pp. 388–392 (1998)

[Luk01]   Lukasiewicz, T.: Probabilistic logic programming with conditional constraints. ACM
Trans. Comput. Log. 2(3), 289–339 (2001)

[OHSG]   O'Neill, I.M., Hanna, P.J., Stewart, D.W., Gu, X.: Use of the quads architecture for
multimodal output generation

[PR03]   Pantic, M., Rothkrantz, L.J.M.: M. pantic and l.j.m. rothkrantz. In: IEEE, pp. 1370–
1390 (2003)

[RKT07]   De Raedt, L., Kimmig, A., Toivonen, H.: Problog: A probabilistic prolog and its
application in link discovery. In: IJCAI, pp. 2462–2467 (2007)

[RRK06]   Rödder, W., Reucher, E., Kulmann, F.: Features of the expert-system-shell spirit.
Logic Journal of the IGPL 14(3), 483–500 (2006)

[SF97]   Schramm, M., Fischer, V.: Probabilistic reasoning with maximum entropy - the system pit (system description). In: WLP (1997)

[YLH08]   Yue, A., Liu, W., Hunter, A.: Measuring the ignorance and degree of satisfac-
tion for answering queries in imprecise probabilistic logic programs. In: Greco, S.,
Lukasiewicz, T. (eds.) SUM 2008. LNCS (LNAI), vol. 5291, pp. 386–400. Springer,
Heidelberg (2008)

[YLH10]   Yue, A., Liu, W., Hunter, A.: Imprecise probabilistic query answering using measures of ignorance and degree of satisfaction. Annals of Mathematics and Artificial
Intelligence (2010) (accepted)

Statistical Estimations of Lattice-Valued Possibilistic Distributions

Ivan Kramosil* and Milan Daniel**

Institute of Computer Science***, Academy of Sciences of the Czech Republic
Pod Vodárenskou věží 2, CZ - 182 07 Prague 8, Czech Republic
{kramosil,daniel}@cs.cas.cz

Abstract. The most often applied non-numerical uncertainty degrees are those taking their values in complete lattices, but also their weakened versions may be of interest. In what follows, we introduce and analyze possibilistic distributions and measures taking values in finite upper-valued possibilistic lattices, so that only for finite sets of such values their supremum is defined. For infinite sets of values of the finite lattice in question we apply the idea of the so called Monte-Carlo method: sample at random and under certain conditions a large enough finite subset of the infinite set in question, and take the supremum over this finite sample set as a "good enough" estimation of the undefined supremum of the infinite set. A number of more or less easy to prove assertions demonstrate the conditions when and in which sense the quality of the results obtained by replacing non-existing or non-accessible supremum values by their random estimations tend to the optimum results supposing that the probabilistic qualities of the statistical estimations increase as demanded by Monte-Carlo methods.

Keywords: complete lattice, upper-valued semilattice, lattice-valued possibilistic distribution, random samples from upper-valued semilattices, probabilistic algorithms, Monte-Carlo methods.

1 Introduction

As soon as two years after publication of the Zadeh's pioneering paper on real-valued fuzzy sets [16], J. A. Goguen applied the basic ideas of fuzziness to partially ordered sets with non-numerical values, so arriving at complete lattices as the most often used support set for non-numerically valued fuzziness degrees [8]. As excellent theoretical survey of complete lattice-valued fuzzy sets can be found in [2]. The reader is supposed to be familiar with the basic ideas and results of

---

* This work was partly supported by the grant ICC/08/E018 of the Grant Agency of the Czech Republic (a part of ESF Eurocores-LogICCC project FP006 LoMoReVI),

** in part by the grant P202/10/1826 of the Grant Agency of the Czech Republic,

*** and in part by the Institutional Research Plan AV0Z10300504 "Computer Science for the Information Society: Models, Algorithms, Applications".

W. Liu (Ed.): ECSQARU 2011, LNAI 6717, pp. 688–699, 2011.

the papers [3] and [14] and with the most elementary stones of the formalized constructions from [11].

Shifting the fuzziness degrees from the real numbers in $[0, 1]$ to elements of a complete lattice we make these degrees much more freely defined and much more vaguely relating these degrees to corresponding non-numerical structures. But, at the same time, the space with this weakened assumptions becomes much more open for applications than that with the real-valued fuzziness degrees.

In this paper, we will go on with this paradigma when still more weakening the conditions imposed on the structure from which fuzziness takes its degrees, namely, instead complete lattice we will define that structure by an upper semi-lattice. Let us recall that a partially ordered set $\mathcal{T} = \langle T, \leq_T \rangle$ defines an upper semilattice, if for each *finite* set $A \subset T$ the supremum $\bigvee^T A$ (w.r.to $\leq_T$) is defined. If $\mathcal{T} = \langle T, \leq_T \rangle$ were a complete lattice (e.g., the standard unit interval $\langle [0, 1], \leq \rangle$), then each mapping $\pi : \Omega \to T$ defined on a nonempty set Ω for each $\omega \in \Omega$, defines a total set function $\Pi : \mathcal{P}(\Omega) \to T$. In other terms, the mapping π may be taken as a fuzzy or possibilistic distribution on the space Ω, implying uniquely the total fuzzy or possibilitic measure (set function) Π ascribing to each $A \subset \Omega$ the value $\bigvee^T_{\omega \in A} \pi(\omega) \in T$. When replacing real-valued or complete lattice-valued structure $\mathcal{T}$ by upper semilattice $\mathcal{T} = \langle T, \leq_T \rangle$, the set function Π will be defined only for finite (or π-finite, if elements $\omega \in \Omega$ with identical values $\pi(\omega)$ are also taken as identical) subsets of Ω, hence, if Ω is infinite, $\Pi : \mathcal{P}(\Omega) \to T$ will be a partial mapping. So, when $A \subset \Omega$ is an infinite set and $\bigvee_{\omega \in A} \pi(\omega)$ is not defined, we would like to find a finite sequence $\omega_1, \omega_2, \ldots, \omega_N$ of elements of A such that the finite (hence, defined) supremum $\bigvee^N_{i=1} \pi(\omega_i)$ would replace or approximate, in a reasonable sense, the undefined value $\Pi(A)$. However, such approximations are offered and reasonably founded and processed by probability theory and mathematical statistics, taking finite random samples of elements from A.

A similar situation arises for great finite Ω, when processing of all elements of Ω is expensive or time consuming in real applications, or when some of elements of Ω are not accessible for processing.

The values $\pi(\omega)$ ascribed to elements of the space Ω may be seen from two points of view: as the degrees of fuzziness or possibility degrees defined on the support set Ω of a fuzzy set or possibilistic distribution π, but also as a $\mathcal{T}$-valued function $\pi : \Omega \to T$. Supposing that Ω is completed to a probability space $\langle \Omega, \mathcal{A}, P \rangle$, π may be taken as $\mathcal{T}$-valued random variable. So, the value $\bigvee^T_{\omega \in A} \pi(\omega)$ may be approximated (if it is defined) or extended (if not defined) by the value approximating or extending the expected value $\Pi(A)$ of a probability density defined on $\mathcal{A}$ (cf. Section 2). Such a model enables to define the notions like statistical estimations related to the probability density, namely, statistical estimations which may be, within the framework of $\mathcal{T}$-valued possibilistic distributions, taken as reasonable approximations and completions of the values related to $\mathcal{T}$-distributions.

Let us introduce a motivation example before focusing to a precise formal theoretical presentation. (For simplicity, we will use great finite Ω.)

Example 1. Consider an urn schema with a great finite number of ballots numbered by positive integers. This enumeration is very general, some numbers may not be applied, on the other hand, more than one ballots may share the same numbers. Nevertheless, the supremum (the maximum, in this finite case) of the values ascribed to particular ballots is uniquely defined and our goal is to obtain or at least to approximate this maximum value.

However, our tools to reach the answer are rather poor and weak. We have at our disposal a sequence of statistically independent and identically distributed (i.i.d. sequence) random samples and we keep in mind the maximum value observed on the ballots sampled till now. Taking the next sample we compare the sampled value with the contemporary supremum and proceed as follows: if the newly sampled value is greater than the contemporary supremum, this last value is taken as the new contemporary supremum, otherwise the value of the contemporary supremum is not changed. Consider the most simple i.i.d. sequence with the same probability of sampling for each ballot at each sample, i.e., with the probalility equal to $1/|S|$ where $|S|$ is the number of ballots in the urn. Intuitively felt, the number of samples needed to arrive at a new actualization of the value of the contemporary supremum increases with the number of samples increasing. Hence, we take the step charged by the risk of error – if the number of samples taken without the change of the contemporary supremum exceeds some treshold value, we stop our searching and declare the last contemporary supremum as the (approximation) of the supremum over the whole urn schema.

The mathematical model explained in this paper enables to quantify explicitly the probability of error connected with this statistical decision algorithm and the dependence of statistical qualities of the algorithm on its parameters (e.g., on the number of steps for which we are waiting before the final decision).

Even if the extent of this contribution is rather limited, all the Section 2 is devoted to a formalized definition of statistical estimation of values of upper semilattice-valued measures in order to prove that this notion can be completely defined and processed within the standard framework of the axiomatic probability theory. Section 3 shows that statistical estimation of possibilistic distributions meets the basic paradigmatic property of standard statistical estimations according to which reasonably defined qualities of such estimations improve with their size increasing. Finally, Section 4 offers the notion of π-quasi-supremum as a useful, even if not generally acceptable substitution of the notion of supremum at least in some particular cases of incomplete upper semilattices. The section further presents some results on δ-statistical optimality.

2   Statistical Estimations of Lattice-Valued Possibility Degrees – a Formalized Model

Let T be a nonempty set, let $\leq_T$ be a partial ordering relation on T, so that $\mathcal{T} = \langle T, \leq_T \rangle$ defines a p.o.set. Suppose, moreover, that $\mathcal{T}$ meets the conditions imposed on *upper semilattice*, so that, for each *finite* set $A_0 \subset T$ the supremum

$\bigvee_{t \in A_0}^{T} t$ ($\bigvee^{T} A_0$ in abbreviation) is defined. As the empty subset of T is also finite, $\bigvee_{t \in \emptyset}^{T} t = \bigvee^{T} \emptyset$ is defined and denoted by $\mathbf{0}_T$ as it obviously plays the role of the minimum or zero element of T (obviously, if T is infinite, the supremum element $\bigvee_{t \in T}^{T} t = \bigvee^{T} T$ need not be defined).

Let Σ be a nonempty set, the elements of Σ will be denoted as η, η^*, η_i, and similarly. A mapping $\pi : \Sigma \to T$ is called a T-*(valued possibilistic) distribution* on Σ, if $\bigvee^{T} T$ (denoted also by $\mathbf{1}_T$) is defined and if $\bigvee_{t \in \Sigma}^{T} \pi(\eta) = \mathbf{1}_T$ holds. This is the case where the space Σ is π-*finite*, i.e., the set $\{\pi(\eta) : \eta \in \Sigma\}$ has finite cardinality (i.e., $card(\{\pi(\eta) : \eta \in \Sigma\} < \infty)$ holds); in this case all subsets of Σ are also π-finite, hence, the possibilistic measure $\Pi(A) = \bigvee_{\eta \in A}^{T} \pi(\eta)$ is defined for each $A \subset \Sigma$.

Our aim will be to replace or to extend the value $\bigvee_{\eta \in A}^{T} \pi(\eta)$ by the value $\bigvee_{i=1}^{T,N} \pi(\eta_i^*)$, (an abbreviation for $\bigvee_{\eta_i^* {}_{i=1}^{N}}^{T} \pi(\eta_i^*)$), where $\eta_1^*, \eta_2^*, \ldots \eta_N^*$ are "appropriately at random sampled" elements of the space Σ. The first formal notion needed in order to build the necessary mathematical construction is that of probability space.

Let Ω be a nonempty set, the elements of which are denoted by ω and are called *elementary random events*. Let $\mathcal{A} \subset \mathcal{P}(\Omega)$ be a non-empty system of subsets of Ω which defines a σ-*field*, so that, for each $E_1, E_2, \cdots \in \mathcal{A}$ also the sets $\Omega - E_i$ and $\bigcup_{i=1}^{\infty} E_i$ are in $\mathcal{A}$. Let $P : \mathcal{A} \to [0,1]$ be a mapping (set function on $\mathcal{A}$, as a matter of fact) such that $P(\Omega) = 1$ and $P(\bigcup_{i=1}^{\infty} E_i) = \Sigma_{i=1}^{\infty} P(E_i)$ for each sequence of mutually disjoint sets $E_1, E_2, \ldots$ from $\mathcal{A}$, i.e., $E_i \cap E_j = \emptyset$ for each $i \neq j$. Such a set function P is called σ-*additive probability measure* defined on *measurable space* $\langle \Omega, \mathcal{A} \rangle$ and the ordered triple $\langle \Omega, \mathcal{A}, P \rangle$ is called *probability space*.

Let $\langle \Omega, \mathcal{A}, P \rangle$ be a probability space, let $\mathcal{X} = \langle X, \mathcal{S} \rangle$ be a *measurable space*, i.e., X is a nonempty set and $\mathcal{S}$ is a nonempty σ-field of subsets of X. A mapping $f : \Omega \to X$ is called *random variable*, defined on the probability space $\langle \Omega, \mathcal{A}, P \rangle$, if for each set $S \subset X$, $S \in \mathcal{S}$, the relation $\{\omega \in \Omega : f(\omega) \in S\} \in \mathcal{A}$ holds, consequently, the probability $P(\{\omega \in \Omega : f(\omega) \in S\})$ is defined. A sequence $\{f_1, f_2, \ldots\}_{i=1}^{\infty}$ of random variables is called *independent and identically distributed sequence* of random variables (i.i.d. sequence, in abbreviation), if for each $A \in \mathcal{S}$ and each $j = 1, 2, \ldots$ the identity $P(\{\omega \in \Omega : f_j(\omega) \in A\}) = P(\{\omega \in \Omega : f_1(\omega) \in A\})$ holds and, moreover, if for each $1 \leq i, i \neq j$, and each $S_i, S_j \in \mathcal{S}$, the relation

$$P(\{\omega \in \Omega : f_i(\omega) \in S_i, f_j(\omega) \in S_j\}) =$$
$$= P(\{\omega \in \Omega : f_i(\omega) \in S_i\}) \cdot P(\{\omega \in \Omega : f_j(\omega) \in S_j\}) \qquad (2.1)$$

is valid.

Take the space Σ of elementary possibilistic events, take a nonempty σ-field $\mathcal{E}$ of subsets of Σ so that the pair $\langle \Sigma, \mathcal{E} \rangle$ defines a measurable space, take a probability space $\langle \Omega, \mathcal{A}, P \rangle$. Let $\eta^* : \Omega \to \Sigma$ be a mapping such that, for each $E \in \mathcal{E}$, $\{\omega \in \Omega : \eta^*(\omega) \in E\} \subset \mathcal{A}$ holds, so that the probability $P(\{\omega \in \Omega : \eta^*(\omega) \in E\})$ is defined. Hence, $\eta^*(\omega) \in \Sigma$ is an at random sampled element of the elementary possibilistic space Σ. Combining the mapping η^* with the mapping $\pi : \Sigma \to T$ we obtain the mapping $\pi(\eta^*(\cdot)) : \Omega \to T$. Supposing that $\mathcal{F} \subset \mathcal{P}(T)$ is a σ-field of subsets of T and that $\{\omega \in \Omega : \pi(\eta^*(\omega)) \in F\} \in \mathcal{A}$ holds for each $F \in \mathcal{F}$, the mapping $\pi(\eta^*(\cdot)) : \Omega \to T$ defines a random variable on the probability space $\langle \Omega, \mathcal{A}, P \rangle$ which takes its values in the measurable space $\langle T, \mathcal{F} \rangle$. Informally defined, $\pi(\eta^*(\omega))$ is the possibility degree ascribed by the mapping (possibilistic distribution on Σ, if it is the case) π to the at random sampled element $\eta^*(\omega)$ of the space Σ of elementary possibilistic events.

Let $A \subset \Sigma$ be given, let $\eta_1^*, \eta_2^*, \ldots$ be an infinite sequence of statistically independent and identically distributed random variables defined on the probability space $\langle \Omega, \mathcal{A}, P \rangle$, taking values in the measurable space $\langle \Sigma, \mathcal{E} \rangle$ and such that, for each $\omega \in \Omega$ and each $i = 1, 2, \ldots, \eta_i^*(\omega) \in A \subset \Sigma$ holds. Hence, for each integer $N \geq 1$, $\langle \eta_1^*(\omega), \eta_2^*(\omega), \ldots \eta_N^*(\omega) \rangle$ is a finite sequence of elements of A and $\langle \pi(\eta_1^*(\omega)), \pi(\eta_2^*(\omega)), \ldots, \pi(\eta_N^*(\omega)) \rangle$ is the corresponding sequence of their possibility degrees defined by the mapping $\pi : \Sigma \to T, T = \langle T, \leq_T \rangle$. Obviously, each $\pi(\eta_i^*(\omega)), i = 1, 2, \ldots, \omega \in \Omega$, is an element of the upper semilattice $T = \langle T, \leq_T \rangle$, consequently, the value $\bigvee_{i=1}^{T,N} \pi(\eta_i^*(\omega))$ is defined and belongs to T.

Supposing that $\bigvee_{i=1}^{T,N} \pi(\eta_i^*(\cdot)) : \Omega \to T$ defines a random variable which takes the probability space $\langle \Omega, \mathcal{A}, P \rangle$ into the measurable space $\langle T, \mathcal{F} \rangle$, i.e., if for each $F \in \mathcal{F}$ the relation $\{\omega \in \Omega : \bigvee_{i=1}^{T,N} \pi(\eta_i^*(\omega)) \in F\} \in \mathcal{A}$ holds, the mapping $\bigvee_{i=1}^{T,N} \pi(\eta_i^*(\omega)) : \Omega \to T$ is called the *statistical estimation* (if $\bigvee_{\eta \in A}^{T} \pi(\eta)$ is defined) or the *statistical extension* (if $\bigvee_{\eta \in A}^{T} \pi(\eta)$ is not defined) of the value of the partial T-valued possibilistic measure Π, induced by π, to the set $A \subset \Sigma$, let us denote it by $\Pi(A)$.

Before going on with the mathematical considerations, some comments may be of use, let us begin with the terms *statistical estimations* and *statistical extension*. As a rule, the term estimation is used when some value is correctly and precisely defined, but for some reasons this value cannot be explicitly specified. E.g., the expected value of a random variable may be defined as a function of empirical values, but in practice only more or less good averages of a series of values taken from repeated random samples may be used as a statistical estimation of the expected value in question. When modifying the definition of expected value in such a way that expected value of an integer-valued random variable must be also defined by an integer, then the expected number of points occurring on dice when tossing is not defined and the value 3.5 may be taken as extension, but not as the expected value of the number of points on the tossed dice.

The difference between the two notions is obvious when considering the problem how to measure the quality of statistical estimations and extensions. For estimations, the closer the estimation is to the estimated value, or the closer the probability, that these values are identical or sufficiently close to each other, is to 1, the better is the estimation. For extensions the situation is more difficult. If $\Pi(A) = \bigvee_{\eta \in A}^{T} \pi(\eta)$ is defined, then the statistical estimation $\bigvee_{i=1}^{T,N} \pi(\eta_i^*(\omega))$ is the best possible, if both the values are identical and in this case, with the probability one, the equality $\bigvee_{i=1}^{T,N} \pi(\eta_i^*(\omega)) = \bigvee_{i=1}^{T,N+1} \pi(\eta_i^*(\omega))$ holds. If

$\bigvee_{\eta \in A}^{T} \pi(\eta)$ is not defined, we may (and will) measure the quality of the extension $\Pi(A) = \bigvee_{i=1}^{T,N} \pi(\eta_i^*(\omega))$ by the criterion according to which the probability

$$
P\left(\left\{ \omega \in \Omega : \bigvee_{i=1}^{T,N+1} \pi(\eta_i^*(\omega)) > \bigvee_{i=1}^{T,N} \pi(\eta_i^*(\omega)) \right\}\right), \qquad (2.2)
$$

i.e., the probability that the value of the "supremum" of the values $\pi(\eta), \eta \in A$, will increase when taking into consideration one more sample from $A \subset \Sigma$ should be either 0 or as close to 0 as possible.

We have purposely formalized the notions of statistical estimation and extension at a rather general and abstract level with the aim to demonstrate that this problem can be defined and solved at the same level of description and processing as it is common in standard works on probability theory. However, in order to arrive at some more explicit results, let us assume the following simplifying conditions to hold. The space Σ is supposed to be infinite and countable, and the σ-field $\mathcal{E}$ of measurable subsets of Σ is defined by the power-set $\mathcal{P}(\Sigma)$. So, random variables η^* are defined on $\langle \Omega, \mathcal{A}, P \rangle$ as mapping ascribing to each $\omega \in \Omega$ the value $\eta^*(\omega)$. For each $\eta \in \Sigma$ the value $P(\{\omega \in \Omega : \eta^*(\omega) = \eta\})$ is defined (and denoted, if no misunderstanding menaces) by $p(\eta)$. Consequently, for each $A \subset \Sigma$, the value $P(A)$ is defined by $P(A) = \Sigma_{\eta \in A} p(\eta)$.

3   Asymptotic Properties of Statistical Estimations of Upper-Semilattice-Valued Possibilistic Degrees

Let $\langle \eta_1^*, \eta_2^*, \dots \rangle$ be an infinite sequence of statistically independent random variables distributed identically with η^*, let $N = 1, 2, \dots$, let $\eta^*(\omega) \in A$ for each $\omega \in \Omega$ hold. Define

$$
\Pi^N(\eta^*, \omega) = \bigvee_{i=1}^{T,N} \pi(\eta_i^*(\omega)). \qquad (3.1)
$$

The last supremum, hence, also the value $\Pi^N(\eta^*, \omega)$ is always defined. If $\Pi(A)$ is defined, then $\Pi^N(\eta^*, \omega)$ is called the *statistical estimation* of $\Pi(A)$, if $\Pi(A)$ is not defined, then $\Pi^N(\eta^*, \omega)$ is called the *statistical extension* of Π to A. In order to simplify our notation, we will use the term "statistical estimation of $\Pi(A)$" in both the cases, carefully keeping in mind the important differences staying behind both these approaches.

Lemma 1. *For each $A \subset \Sigma$, each $N = 1, 2, \dots$ and each $\omega \in \Omega$ the inequality $\Pi^N(\eta^*, \omega) \leq_T \Pi^{N+1}(\eta^*, \omega)$ holds.*

If $\Pi(A) = \bigvee_{\eta \in A}^{T} \pi(\eta)$ is defined, i.e., if A is a π-finite subset of Σ, then for each $N = 1, 2, \dots$, and each $\omega \in \Omega$ the relation $\Pi^N(\eta^*, \omega) \leq_T \Pi(A)$ holds.

Proof. Obvious.

Definition 1. *The statistical estimation* $\Pi^N(\eta^*, \omega)$ *of the value* $\Pi(A)$ *for* $A \subset \Sigma$ *is statistically optimal, if*

$$P(\{\omega \in \Omega : \Pi^{N+1}(\eta^*, \omega) = \Pi^N(\eta^*, \omega)\}) = 1 \qquad (3.2)$$

holds.

In a perhaps more intuitive setting, up to the cases with zero global probability P, the statistical estimation $\bigvee_{i=1}^{T,N} \pi(\eta_i^*(\omega))$ of $\Pi(A)$ cannot be improved, i.e., enlarged w.r.to the partial ordering $\leq_T$ on T, no matter how large finite number of samples made by random variables η_i^*, $i > N$, may be taken.

Lemma 2. *Let* $\Pi(A) = \bigvee_{\eta \in A}^{T} \pi(\eta)$ *be defined, let* $\Pi^N(\eta^*, \omega) = \Pi(A)$ *hold. Then* $\Pi^N(\eta^*, \omega)$ *is statistically optimal statistical estimation of the value* $\Pi(A)$.

Proof. Obvious.

Under some more conditions also an assertion inverse to that of Lemma 2 may be stated and proved.

Theorem 1. *Let* $A \subset \Sigma$ *be* π-*finite, let* Σ *be an infinite countable set, let* $\mathcal{E} = \mathcal{P}(\Sigma)$, *let* $\eta^* : \langle \Omega, \mathcal{A}, P \rangle \to \langle \Sigma, \mathcal{E} \rangle$ *be such that* $p(\eta) = P(\{\omega \in \Omega : \eta^*(\omega) = \eta\}) > 0$ *holds iff* $\eta \in A$, *let* $\langle \eta_1^*, \eta_2^*, \ldots \rangle$ *be an infinite sequence of statistically independent and identically distributed copies of the random variable* η^*. *Then the statistical estimation* $\bigvee_{i=1}^{T,N} \pi(\eta_i^*(\omega))$ *of the value* $\Pi(A) = \bigvee_{\eta \in A}^{T} \pi(\eta)$ *is statistically optimal iff the identity* $\bigvee_{i=1}^{T,N} \pi(\eta_i^*(\omega)) = \Pi(A)$ *holds.*

Proof. Due to Lemma 2, the only we have to prove is that if $\bigvee_{i=1}^{T,N} \pi(\eta_i^*(\omega)) \neq \Pi(A)$, i.e., if $\bigvee_{i=1}^{T,N} \pi(\eta_i^*(\omega)) <_T \Pi(A)$ is the case, then

$$P\left(\left\{\omega \in \Omega : \bigvee_{i=1}^{T,N+1} \pi(\eta_i^*(\omega)) >_T \bigvee_{i=1}^{T,N} \pi(\eta_i^*(\omega))\right\}\right) > 0 \qquad (3.3)$$

follows. Hence, we have to prove that if $\Pi^N(\eta^*, \omega) <_T \Pi(A)$ holds, then with a positive probability the statistical estimation $\Pi^N(\eta^*, \omega)$ of $\Pi(A)$ can be improved when taken one more random sample $\eta_{N+1}^*(\omega) \in A$.

As for each $\omega \in \Omega$ and each $i = 1, 2, \ldots$ holds that $\eta_i^*(\omega) \in A$ and $\{\pi(\eta_i^*(\omega)) : i = 1, 2, \ldots\} \subset \{\pi(\eta) : \eta \in A\}$, both with the probability one, the inequality $\bigvee_{i=1}^{T,N} \pi(\eta_i^*(\omega)) <_T \Pi(A)$ may happen only when there exists $\eta_0 \in A$ such that $\eta_0 \neq \eta_i^*(\omega), i = 1, 2, \ldots, N$, and $\bigvee_{i=1}^{T,N} \pi(\eta_i^*(\omega)) \vee \pi(\eta_0) > \bigvee_{i=1}^{T,N} \pi(\eta_i^*(\omega))$ hold together. In other words, $\bigvee_{i=1}^{T,N} \pi(\eta_i^*(\omega)) < \Pi(A)$ yields that there exists an element $\eta_0 \in A$ not sampled yet by the samples $\eta_1^*(\omega), \eta_2^*(\omega), \ldots, \eta_N^*(\omega)$ but such that the value $\pi(\eta_0)$ augments the value $\Pi^N(\eta^*, \omega) = \bigvee_{i=1}^{T,N} \pi(\eta_i^*(\omega))$. However, with the positive probability $p(\eta_0)$ the case $\eta_{N+1}^*(\omega) = \eta_0$ occurs, so that $\Pi^{N+1}(\eta^*, \omega) > \Pi^N(\eta^*, \omega)$ holds with probability $p(\eta_0) > 0$. Hence, $\Pi^N(\eta^*, \omega)$ is not statistically optimal statistical estimation of $\Pi(A)$ and the assertion is proved.

Theorem 2. *Let the notations and conditions of Theorem 1 hold with the only exception that the set A need not be π-finite. Let A_0 be finite subset of $A \subset \Sigma$ such that, for each $\eta_* \in A$, the relation*

$$\Pi(A_0) = \bigvee_{\eta \in A_0}^{\mathcal{T}} \pi(\eta) = \bigvee_{\eta \in A_0 \cup \{\eta_*\}}^{\mathcal{T}} \pi(\eta) = \Pi((A_0) \cup \{\eta_*\}) \qquad (3.4)$$

holds. Then $\Pi^N(\eta^*, \omega)$ tends to $\Pi(A_0)$ in probability P with N increasing, so that the relation

$$\lim_{N \to \infty} P(\{\omega \in \Omega : \Pi^N(\eta^*, \omega) = \Pi(A_0)\}) = 1 \qquad (3.5)$$

is valid.

Proof. Let $A_0 = \{\eta^1, \eta^2, \dots, \eta^K\} \subset \Sigma$. An easy combinatoric consideration yields that

$$P(\{\omega \in \Omega : \{\eta^1, \eta^2, \dots, \eta^K\} \not\subset \{\eta_1^*(\omega), \eta_2^*(\omega), \dots, \eta_N^*(\omega)\}\})$$

$$= P\left(\bigcup_{j=1}^{K} (\{\omega \in \Omega : \eta^j \notin \{\eta_1^*(\omega), \dots, \eta_N^*(\omega)\}\})\right) \le$$

$$\le \sum_{j=1}^{K} P(\{\omega \in \Omega : \eta^j \not\subset \{\eta_1^*(\omega), \eta_2^*(\omega), \dots, \eta_N^*(\omega)\}\}). \qquad (3.6)$$

For each $j = 1, 2, \dots, K$

$$P(\{\omega \in \Omega : \eta^j \notin \{\eta_1^*(\omega), \eta_2^*(\omega), \dots, \eta_N^*(\omega)\}\}) = (1 - p(\eta^j))^N \to 0 \qquad (3.7)$$

with $N \to \infty$ holds. Hence, given $\mathcal{E} > 0$, for each $j = 1, 2, \dots, K$ there exists $n_j \in \{1, 2, \dots\}$ such that for each $N \ge n_j$, $P(\{\omega \in \Omega : \eta^j \notin \{\eta_1^*(\omega), \dots, \eta_N^*(\omega)\}\}) < \mathcal{E}$ holds. Setting $N_0 \ge \max\{n_j : j \le K\}$, we obtain that $P(\{\omega \in \Omega : \eta^j \notin \{\eta_1^*(\omega), \dots, \eta_N^*(\omega)\}\}) < \mathcal{E}$ holds for each $j \le K$ supposing that $N \ge N_0$ is the case.

Consequently,

$$P(\{\omega \in \Omega : \{\eta^1, \dots, \eta^K\} \not\subset \{\eta_1^*(\omega), \dots, \eta_N^*(\omega)\}\}) \le$$

$$\le \sum_{i=1}^{K} P(\{\omega \in \Omega : \eta^j \notin \{\eta_1^*(\omega), \eta_2^*(\omega), \dots, \eta_N^*(\omega)\}\}) \le K\mathcal{E} \qquad (3.8)$$

follows, if $N \ge N_0$ is the case. As $\mathcal{E} > 0$ is arbitrary,

$$P(\{\omega \in \Omega : \{\eta^1, \dots, \eta^L\} \not\subset \{\eta_1^*(\omega), \dots, \eta_N^*(\omega)\}\}) \to 0 \qquad (3.9)$$

holds for each fixed L with $N \to \infty$, hence,

$$P(\{\omega \in \Omega : \{\eta^1, \dots, \eta^K\} \subset \{\eta_1^*(\omega), \dots, \eta_N^*(\omega)\}\}) \to 1 \qquad (3.10)$$

holds with $n \to \infty$. As $A_0 = \{\eta^1, \eta^2, \dots, \eta^K\}$, (3.10) yields that, for N increasing, with the probability increasing to 1 the relation

$$\Pi^N(\eta^*, \omega) = \bigvee_{i=1}^{\mathcal{T},N} \pi(\eta_i(\omega)) = \left(\bigvee_{j=1}^{\mathcal{T},K} \pi(\eta^j)\right) \vee^{\mathcal{T}} \left(\bigvee_{i=1}^{\mathcal{T},N} \pi(\eta_i^*(\omega))\right) =$$

$$= \Pi(A_0) \vee^{\mathcal{T}} (\pi(\eta_1^*(\omega)) \vee^{\mathcal{T}} \pi(\eta_2^*(\omega)) \vee^{\mathcal{T}} \cdots \vee^{\mathcal{T}} \pi(\eta_N^*(\omega))) = \Pi(A_0), \qquad (3.11)$$

as $\Pi(A_0) \vee^T \pi(\eta_*) = \Pi(A_0)$ due to the assumptions imposed on A_0 and the principle of finite mathematical induction is applied. Hence, the relation

$$\lim_{N \to \infty} P(\{\omega \in \Omega : \Pi^N(\eta^*, \omega) = \Pi(A_0)\}) = 1 \qquad (3.12)$$

holds and the assertion is proved.

4   Some More Results on Upper Semilattice-Valued Lattices

Let us reconsider, once more, the conditions of Theorem 2. If there exists a finite subset $A_0 \subset A$ meeting the condition (3.4), the value $\Pi(A_0)$ copies the properties of $\vee^T A$ (if defined) at least in the sense that no element of A, joined with A_0, is able to make the value $\Pi(A_0)$ larger. The notion of π-quasi-supremum of A tries to define this property explicitly.

Definition 2. *Under the notation introduced above, the value $\Pi(A_0) = \bigvee^T_{\eta \in A_0} \pi(\eta)$ is called the π-quasi-supremum of A and denoted by $Q^\pi(A)$, if A_0 is a finite subset of $A \subset \Sigma$ such that, for each $\eta_* \in A$, $\Pi(A_0 \cup \{\eta_*\}) = \Pi(A_0)$ holds. I.e., $\Pi(A_0)$ is the π-quasi supremum of A, if*

$$\bigvee_{\eta \in A_0}^{T} \pi(\eta) = \left(\bigvee_{\eta \in A_0}^{T} \pi(\eta) \right) \vee^T \pi(\eta_*) \qquad (4.1)$$

is valid for each $\eta_* \in A$ (in other notation, if $\pi(\eta_*) \leq_T \Pi(A_0)$ is the case).

We have to prove that the value $Q^\pi(A)$, if defined, is defined uniquely (like it is the case for the standard supremum and infimum operations). Let $A \subset \Sigma$ be given, let $A_0 \subset A, B_0 \subset A$ be finite subsets of A such that both $\Pi(A_0)$ and $\Pi(B_0)$ define π-quasi-suprema $Q^\pi_1(A)$ and $Q^\pi_2(A)$. In this case, however, the identity $Q^\pi_1(A) = Q^\pi_2(A)$ follows. Indeed, let $A_0 = \{a_1, a_2, \dots a_K\} \subset A$, let $B_0 = \{b_1, b_2, \dots, b_L\} \subset A$. Then, applying (4.1) we obtain that

$$\Pi(A_0) = \bigvee_{i=1}^{T,K} \pi(a_i) = \left(\bigvee_{i=1}^{T,K} \pi(a_i) \right) \vee^T \pi(b_1) = \left(\bigvee_{i=1}^{T,K} \pi(a_i) \right) \vee^T \pi(b_1) \vee^T \pi(b_2)$$

$$= \left(\bigvee_{i=1}^{T,K} \pi(a_i) \right) \vee^T (\pi(b_1) \vee^T \pi(b_2) \vee^T \cdots \vee^T \pi(b_2)) = \Pi(A_0) \vee^T \Pi(B_0).$$

$$(4.2)$$

Repeating this construction and consideration once more, but now starting from $\Pi(B_0)$ and adding, step by step, the values $\pi(a_1), \pi(a_2), \dots, \pi(a_K)$, we arrive at the equality $\Pi(B_0) = \Pi(B_0) \vee^T \Pi(A_0)$, hence, the identity $\Pi(A_0) = \Pi(B_0)$ follows, so that the π-quasi-supremum $Q^\pi(A)$ is defined uniquely supposing that it is defined.

On the other side, the π-quasi-supremum $Q^\pi(A)$ need not be defined in general, i.e., it is possible that there is no finite $A_0 \subset A$ meeting the conditions imposed on $Q^\pi(A)$. E.g., consider $\Sigma = \{\eta^1, \eta^2, \dots\}$ and $T = \{t_1, t_2, \dots\}$ together with binary relation $\leq_T$ such that $t_i <_T t_j$ holds iff $i < j$ is the case (obviously, $T = \mathcal{N} = \{1, 2, \dots\}$ and the standard linear ordering $\leq$ on $\mathcal{N}$ will do). The pair $\mathcal{T} = \langle T, \leq_T \rangle$ then defines the upper semilattice. Let $\pi : \Sigma \to T$ be defined by $\pi(\eta^i) = t_i$ for each $i \in \mathcal{N}$, let $A = \{\eta^{i_1}, \eta^{i_2}, \dots\}, i_1 < i_2 < \dots$ be any infinite subset of Σ. Then no finite subset $A_0 \subset A$ possesses the property that $\Pi(A_0) = \bigvee_{\eta \in A_0}^{\mathcal{T}} \pi(\eta)$ defines the π-quasi-supremum of A. Indeed, denote by $\alpha(A_0) \in \mathcal{N}$ the value $\alpha(A_0) = \max\{j \in \mathcal{N} : \eta^j \in A_0\}$. Then

$$\Pi(A_0) = \bigvee_{\eta \in A_0}^{\mathcal{T}} \pi(\eta) = \bigvee_{i=1, \eta^i \in A_0}^{\mathcal{T}, \alpha(A_0)} \pi(\eta^j) = \bigvee_{i=1}^{\mathcal{T}, \alpha(A_0)} t_i = t_{\alpha(A_0)}. \tag{4.3}$$

As the set A is infinite, there exists $j_0 \in \mathcal{N}$ such that $\eta^{j_0} \in A$ and $j_0 > \alpha(A_0)$ hold together. In this case, however, the relation $\pi(\eta^{j_0}) = t_{j_0} >_T t_{\alpha(A_0)} = \Pi(A_0)$ follows (cf. (4.3)), so that the inequality $\Pi(A_0) \vee^{\mathcal{T}} \pi(\eta^{j_0}) = \pi(\eta^{j_0}) >_T \Pi(A_0)$ holds. Hence, $\Pi(A_0)$ does not define the π-quasi-supremum of A.

It is perhaps worth being introduced explicitly, that the class of subsets $A \subset \Sigma$ for which π-quasi-supremum $Q^\pi(A)$ is defined is larger than the class of all π-finite subsets of Σ. Indeed, if A is π-finite, then there exists a finite set $A_0 \subset A$ such that $\pi(A_0) = \bigvee_{\eta \in A_0}^{\mathcal{T}} \pi(\eta) = \bigvee_{\eta \in A}^{\mathcal{T}} \pi(\eta)$, so that $\Pi(A_0)$ obviously defines the π-quasi-supremum of A. On the other side, when there exists a finite set $A_0 \subset A$ which defines the value $Q^\pi(A)$, it is possible that $A - A_0$ is an infinite set and the set of different values $\pi(\eta), \eta \in A - A_0$, is also infinite and for each $\eta \in A - A_0$ the relation $\pi(\eta) \leq_T \Pi(A_0)$ holds, hence, the set A is not π-finite.

Definition 3. *Let the notations and conditions of Definition 1 hold. The statistical estimation $\Pi^N(\eta^*, \omega)$ of the value $\Pi(A)$ for $A \subset \Sigma$ is δ-statistically optimal, where δ is a given real number from $(0, 1]$, if the relation*

$$P(\{\omega \in \Omega : \Pi^{N+1}(\eta^*, \omega) = \Pi^N(\eta^*, \omega)\}) > 1 - \delta \tag{4.4}$$

is valid.

Hence, $\Pi^N(\eta^*, \omega)$ is statistically optimal estimation of $\Pi(A)$ in the sense of Definition 1 iff $\Pi^N(\eta^*, \omega)$ is δ-statistically optimal in the sense of Definition 3 for every $\delta > 0$.

Theorem 3. *Let $\langle \Omega, \mathcal{A}, P \rangle$ be a probability space, let $\langle \Sigma, \mathcal{P}(\Sigma) \rangle$ be the complete measurable space over a countable set Σ of elementary possibilistic states. Let $\mathcal{T} = \langle T, \leq_T \rangle$ be an upper semilattice, let $\pi : \Sigma \to T$ be a mapping such that $\bigvee_{\eta \in \Sigma}^{\mathcal{T}} \pi(\eta) = \mathbf{1}_T = \bigvee_{\eta \in \Sigma}^{\mathcal{T}} \eta = \bigvee^{\mathcal{T}} T$ holds supposing that $\bigvee^{\mathcal{T}} T$ is defined. Let $A \subset T$ be given, let $\eta^* : \langle \Omega, \mathcal{A}, P \rangle \to \langle \Sigma, \mathcal{P}(\Sigma) \rangle$ be a random variable such that $P(\{\omega \in \Omega : \eta^*(\omega) = \eta\}) > 0$ is the case iff $\eta \in A$ holds.*

Let $\langle \eta_1^*, \eta_2^*, \dots \rangle$ be an infinite sequence of statistically independent random variables each of them being distributed identically with η^*, let $N = 1, 2, \dots$. Define

$$\Pi^N(\eta^*, \omega) = \bigvee_{i=1}^{\mathcal{T}, N} \pi(\eta_i^*(\omega)). \qquad (4.5)$$

Then, for each δ > 0, the assertion

$$\lim_{N \to \infty} P\left(\left\{\, \omega \in \Omega : \begin{array}{l} \Pi^N(\eta^*, \omega) \text{ defines a } \delta\text{-statistically optimal} \\ \text{statistical estimation of the value } \Pi(A) \end{array} \right\}\right) = 1 \quad (4.6)$$

holds.

Proof. Let $\delta > 0$ be given. According to the conditions imposed on η^* and consequently, on each $\eta_1^*, \eta_2^*, \ldots$, there exits a finite set $A_0 \subset \Sigma$ such that

$$P(A_0) = P(\{\omega \in \Omega : \eta^*(\omega) \in A_0\}) = P(\{\omega \in \Omega : \eta_i^*(\omega) \in A_0\}) =$$
$$= \sum_{\eta \in A_0} P(\{\omega \in \Omega : \eta_1^*(\omega) = \eta\}) > 1 - \delta \qquad (4.7)$$

holds. Hence, if $\Pi^N(\eta^*, \omega) \supset A_0$ is the case, then the inequality $\Pi^{N+1}(\eta^*, \omega) >_{\mathcal{T}} \Pi^N(\eta^*, \omega)$ may happen to be valid only when $\eta_{N+1}^*(\omega) \in A - A_0$ holds. However, the probability of this random event does not exceed δ, as proved in (4.7). As shown in Theorem 1, for each finite $A_0 \subset A$ the inclusion $\Pi^N(\eta^*, \omega) \supset A_0$ holds with the probability increasing to 1 with $N \to \infty$, the same limit assertion is valid for the probability that $\Pi^N(\eta^*, \omega)$ defines a δ-statistically optimal statistical estimation of the value $\Pi(A)$. The theorem is proved.

5   Conclusions

In this contribution we analyzed an alternative mathematical model of uncertainty quantification and processing which combines two qualitatively different approaches to the idea of uncertainty. The first one takes the uncertainty in the sense of fuzziness and vagueness formalized above by the notion of possibilistic space $\langle E, \mathcal{E} \rangle$, the other approach is that of randomness, formalized by the standard notion of probability space and probability algorithm. What may be perhaps of interest is the mutual relation of both the uncertainty processing tools which copies the structure of probability algorithms, well-known from numerous theoretical and practical procedures.

At least the two directions of further developing of the basic ideas of mixed uncertainty quantification and processing models might be considered. First, more sophisticated details of the probability algorithm sketched above and perhaps some of its interesting applications should be analyzed and discussed. Second, different combinations of various models of uncertainty quantification and processing should be considered. E.g., in the first step probability algorithm for classical real-valued quantification are applied, but the quality of the achieved results, e.g., the distance of these results from the ideally perfect masterpiece, are quantified in the terms of a possibilistic lattice-valued measure.

The authors hope to have a possibility, sometimes in the future, to return to these and related problems more closely.

Important note concerning the references: for the reader's convenience, the list of references contains not only the items namely referred in the text, but also some works thematically tightly close to the subject of this paper, so making its understanding more easy.

References

1. Birkhoff, G.: Lattice Theory, 3rd edn., Providence, Rhode Island (1967)
2. DeCooman, G.: Possibility theory I, II, III. International Journal of General Systems 25, 291–323 (1997); 325–351, 353–371
3. Dubois, D., Nguyen, H.T., Prade, H.: Possibility theory, probability theory and fuzzy sets: misunderstandings, bridges and gaps. In: Dubois, D., Prade, H. (eds.) The Handbook of Fuzzy Sets Series – Fundamentals of Fuzzy Sets, pp. 343–438. Kluwer Acadenic Publishers, Boston (2000)
4. Dubois, D., Prade, H.: A note on measures of specificity for fuzzy sets. International Journal of General Systems 10, 279–283 (1985)
5. Faure, R., Heurgon, E.: Structures Ordonnées et Algèbres de Boole. Gauthier-Villars, Paris (1971)
6. Fine, T.L.: Theories of Probability. In: An Examination of Foundarions, Academic Press, New York (1973)
7. Geer, J.F., Klir, G.J.: Discord in possibility theory. International Journal of General Systems 19, 119–132 (1991)
8. Goguen, J.A.: $\mathcal{L}$-fuzzy sets. Journal of Mathematical Analysis and Applications 18, 145–174 (1967)
9. Halmos, P.R.: Measure Theory. D. van Nostrand, New York (1950)
10. Kramosil, I.: Extensions of partial lattice-valued possibilistic measures from nested domains. International Journal of Uncertainty, Fuzziness and Knowledge-Based Systems 14, 175–197 (2006)
11. Loève, M.: Probability Theory. D. van Nostrand, New York (1960)
12. Miranda, E., Couso, I., Gil, P.: Relationship between possibilistic measures and nested random sets. International Journal of Uncertainty, Fuzziness and Knowledge-Based Systems 10, 1–15 (2002)
13. Miranda, E., Couso, I., Gil, P.: A random set characterization of possibility measures. Information Sciences 168, 51–75 (2004)
14. Shannon, C.E.: The mathematical theory of communication. The Bell Systems Technical Journal 27, 379–423 (1948); 623–656
15. Sikorski, R.: Boolean Algebras, 2nd edn. Springer, Berlin (1964)
16. Zadeh, L.A.: Fuzzy sets. Information and Control 8, 338–353 (1965)
17. Zadeh, L.A.: Probability measures of fuzzy events. Journal of Mathematical Analysis and Applications 23, 421–427 (1968)
18. Zadeh, L.A.: Fuzzy sets as a basis for a theory of possibility. Fuzzy Sets and Systems 1, 3–28 (1978)

Compiling Min-based Possibilistic Causal Networks: A Mutilated-Based Approach

Raouia Ayachi[1,2], Nahla Ben Amor[1], and Salem Benferhat[2]

[1] LARODEC, Institut Supérieur de Gestion Tunis, Le Bardo, Tunisie, 2000
raouia.ayachi@gmail.com, nahla.benamor@gmx.fr
[2] CRIL-CNRS, Université d'Artois, France, 62307
benferhat@cril.univ-artois.fr

Abstract. Qualitative causal possibilistic networks are important tools for handling uncertain information in the possibility theory framework. Despite their importance, no compilation has been performed to ensure causal reasoning in possibility theory framework. This paper proposes two compilation-based inference algorithms for min-based possibilistic causal networks. The first is a possibilistic adaptation of the probabilistic inference method [8] and the second is a purely possibilistic approach. Both of them are based on an encoding of the network into a propositional theory and a compilation of this output in order to efficiently compute the effect of both observations and interventions, while adopting a mutilation strategy.

1 Introduction

Possibilistic networks [2] provide efficient tools to deal with uncertain data. They compactly represent the prior background knowledge and efficiently reason in the presence of new information. While the quantitative (or product-based) possibilistic networks are very similar to probabilistic Bayesian networks, the qualitative (or min-based) ones, which are the focus of this paper, have significant differences. Emphasis has recently placed on inference in possibilistic networks [2,4], especially when it is dealt with *compilation* [1].

Causal possibilistic networks are updated in the presence of two types of information: *observations* which are the results of testing some variables and *interventions* which correspond to external actions forcing some variables to have some specific values. From a representational point of view, interventions are distinguished from observations using the concept of the 'do' operator [13,15]. From a reasoning point of view, an intervention on a variable A is represented using the so-called mutilation, by ignoring relations between the intervened variable A and its direct causes. Handling sets of observations and interventions is an important issue that can be useful where some variables are directly observed and/or forced to take some values by performing interventions.

In [1], we have proposed compilation-based inference methods for min-based possibilistic networks that only deal with observations. The idea in [1] consists in encoding the network using a propositional theory and then compiling the

W. Liu (Ed.): ECSQARU 2011, LNAI 6717, pp. 700–712, 2011.

resulting encoding to have a polytime possibilistic inference. However, there is no compilation that has been proposed for min-based possibilistic causal networks that takes into account the concept of interventions. In this paper, we will propose two mutilated-based approaches which deal with inference in min-based possibilistic causal networks under a compilation framework. Our objective is to ensure an efficient computation of the effect of both observations and interventions by avoiding a re-compilation of the network each time an intervention or an observation is taken place, which is considered intractable.

The remaining paper is organized as follows: Section 2 presents a brief refresher on possibility theory and compilation languages. Section 3 describes the inference process using the so-called mutilated Π-DNNFs (*Possibilistic Decomposable Negation Normal Form*). Inference using mutilated compiled possibilistic bases is presented in Section 4. Section 5 concludes the paper.

2   Basic Backgrounds on Possibility and Compilation

Let $V = \{X_1, X_2, ..., X_N\}$ be a set of variables. We denote by $D_{X_i} = \{x_1, .., x_n\}$ the domain associated with the variable X_i. By x_i we denote any instance of X_i. By x_{ij} we denote the jth instance of X_i. When there is no confusion we use x_i to mean any instance of X_i. Ω denotes the universe of discourse, which is the Cartesian product of all variable domains in V. Each element $\omega \in \Omega$ is called a state of Ω. $\omega[X_i] = x_i$ denotes an instantiation of X_i in ω.

2.1   Possibility Theory

One of the basic concepts in possibility theory (see [11] for more details) is the concept of possibility distribution, denoted by π. It is a mapping from Ω to the unit interval $[0, 1]$. In this paper, we consider the qualitative interpretation of this scale where only the ordering induced by degrees is important. Given a possibility distribution π, we can define a mapping grading the possibility measure of an event $\phi \subseteq \Omega$ by $\Pi(\phi) = max_{\omega \in \phi}\pi(\omega)$. Π has a dual measure which is the necessity measure defined by $N(\phi) = 1 - \Pi(\neg\phi)$.

Conditioning consists in modifying our initial knowledge, encoded by π, by the arrival of a new certain piece of information $\phi \subseteq \Omega$. The qualitative setting leads to the well known definition of min-conditioning [11]:

$$\Pi(\psi \mid \phi) = \begin{cases} \Pi(\psi \wedge \phi) \; if \; \Pi(\psi \wedge \phi) < \Pi(\phi) \\ 1 \qquad\qquad otherwise. \end{cases} \tag{1}$$

One of the well-used and developed compact representations of a possibility distribution is the concept of a possibilistic knowledge base [14]. Denoted by Σ, it is made up of a finite set of weighted formulas. Formally,

$$\Sigma = \{(\alpha_i, a_i), i = 1, .., n, a_i \neq 0\}. \tag{2}$$

Each possibilistic logic formula (α_i, a_i) expresses that the propositional formula α_i is certain to at least the level a_i, or more formally by $N(\alpha_i) \geq a_i$, where N is the necessity measure associated to α_i.

The following subsection represents another compact representation of possibility distribution that deals with both observations and interventions.

2.2 Possibilistic Causal Networks

A possibilistic causal network is a graphical way to represent uncertain information [4]. Over a set of variables V, a possibilistic causal network, denoted by ΠG_{min} is composed of:
- A *graphical component* that is a DAG where nodes represent variables and edges encode not only dependencies between variables but also direct causal relationships [4]. The parent set of any variable X_i, denoted by $U_i = \{U_{i1}, U_{i2}, ..., U_{im}\}$ where m is the number of parents of X_i, represents all direct causes for X_i. In what follows, we use x_i, u_i, u_{ij} to denote, respectively, possible instances of X_i, U_i and U_{ij}.
- A *numerical component* that quantifies different links. Uncertainty of each node in ΠG_{min} is represented by a local normalized possibility distribution in the context of its parents (i.e., $\forall u_i, max_{x_i} \Pi(x_i|u_i) = 1$).

The set of a priori and conditional possibility degrees in a ΠG_{min} induces a unique joint possibility distribution defined by the following min-based chain rule:

$$\pi(X_1, .., X_N) = \min_{i=1..N} \Pi(X_i \mid U_i). \tag{3}$$

Causal networks are updated in the presence of two types of information: set of *observations* (evidences) which are the results of testing some variables, and a set of *interventions* which represent external events, coming from outside the system and forcing some variables to take some specific values [15]. Interventions, denoted by $do(x_I)$ have a reasoning and a representational interpretations. This paper focuses on the reasoning aspect.

Mutilation. From a reasoning point of view, an intervention is handled by the so-called *mutilation* operation [15], which refers to altering the network structure by excluding all direct causes related to the variable of interest and maintaining the remaining variables intact [15]. The possibility distribution associated with the mutilated network ΠG_{mut} is denoted by π_m. The effect of $do(x_I)$ is to transform $\pi(\omega)$ into $\pi_m(\omega|x_I)$, which gives us [4]:

$$\forall \omega; \pi_m(\omega|x_I) = \pi(\omega|do(x_I)). \tag{4}$$

By mutilating the network, parents of X_I become independent of X_I. Moreover, the event that attributes the value x_I to X_I becomes sure after performing intervention $do(x_I)$. More formally, $\pi_m(x_I) = 1$ and $\forall x_i, x_i \neq x_I, \pi_m(x_i) = 0$. The effect of $do(x_I)$ on π is given as follows, $\forall \omega$:

$$\pi(\omega|do(x_I)) = \begin{cases} min_{i \neq I} \ \pi(x_i|u_i) \ if \ \omega[X_i] = x_I \\ 0 \qquad\qquad\qquad otherwise. \end{cases} \tag{5}$$

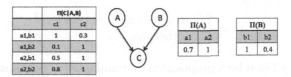

Fig. 1. A causal possibilistic network ΠG_{min}

Example 1. *Let us consider the ΠG_{min} of Figure 1. Let C be the variable in ΠG_{min} forced to take the value c_1 by the intervention $do(c_1)$. The possibility distribution $\pi_m(A, B, C)$ associated with ΠG_{mut} represents the effect of $do(c_1)$ on $\pi(A, B, C)$. The intervention $do(c_1)$ implies $\pi_m(c_1) = 1$ and $\pi_m(c_2) = 0$. For instance, $\pi(a_1, b_2, c_1 | do(c_1)) = \pi_m(a_1, b_2, c_1) = min(\pi_m(a_1), \pi_m(b_2), \pi_m(c_1)) = min(0.7, 0.4, 1) = 0.4$.*

The effect of interventions on the remaining network is defined by applying conditioning on the mutilated network after observation as follows:

Proposition 1. *Let ΠG_{min} be a min-based possibilistic causal network. Let $do(x_I)$ be an intervention forcing X_I to take the value x_I. Let ΠG_{mut} be the mutilated network obtained after mutilation. Then, $\forall \omega, \forall x_I \in D_{X_I}, \pi(\omega | do(x_I)) = \pi_m(\omega | X_I = x_I)$.*

2.3   Compilation Concepts

Knowledge compilation is an artificial intelligence area related to a mapping problem from intractable logical theories (typically, from propositional knowledge bases in a CNF form) into suitable target compilation languages. These latters are characterized by a *succinctness* criteria and a set of *queries* and *transformations* performed in polynomial time with respect to the size of compiled bases [6]. There are several compilation languages as it has been studied in the knowledge map of [10]. We are in particular interested in *Decomposable Negation Normal Form (DNNF)* [7] and *Valued Negation Normal Form (VNNF)* [12].

DNNF language. The *Negation Normal Form (NNF)* language represents the pivotal language from which a variety of target compilation languages give rise by imposing some conditions on it. For instance, the DNNF language is the set of all NNFs satisfying *decomposability*: conjuncts of any conjunction share no variables [7]. DNNF supports a rich set of polynomial-time operations which can be performed simply and efficiently. Our choice is especially motivated by the set of operations that supports and its succinctness [10].

DNNF supports several transformations and queries. We restrict our attention to conditioning and forgetting operations:

- *Conditioning*: Let α be a propositional formula. Let ρ be a consistent term, then conditioning α on ρ, denoted by $\alpha | \rho$ generates a new formula in which each propositional variable $P_i \in \alpha$ is set to:

$$P_i = \begin{cases} \top \text{ if } P_i \text{ is consistent with } \rho \ ^1 \\ \bot \text{ otherwise .} \end{cases} \tag{6}$$

- *Forgetting*: Let α be a propositional formula. Let P be a finite set of propositional variables P_i, then the forgetting of P from α, denoted by $\exists P.\alpha$ is equivalent to a formula that does not mention any variable P_i from P. It can be inductively defined as follows:

$$\exists P_i.\alpha = \alpha | P_i \vee \alpha | \neg P_i. \tag{7}$$

where $\alpha | P_i$ (resp. $\alpha | \neg P_i$) is the result of conditioning of α on P_i (resp. $\neg P_i$).

VNNF language. All subsets of NNFs, known as valuable representation languages for boolean functions, have been extended to represent an enriched class of functions ranging over an ordered scale, namely *Valued Negation Normal Forms (VNNFs)* [12]. The VNNF language is fully characterized by a *representation context* $\prec \varepsilon, Y, F \succ$ consisting of a *valuation structure* ε, a finite set Y of variables ranging on finite domains and a set F of primitive or local functions, i.e., functions representing preferences or plausibility degrees over assignments. By valuation structure, we mean a triple $\varepsilon = \prec E, \geq, OP \succ$ where $(E, \geq)$ is a set ordered by a relation $\geq$ and OP is the set of all binary operators $\otimes$ on E. OP may contain the operators $\vee$ and $\wedge$. When $\geq$ is a total order, min and max are alternative generalizations of the boolean connectives [12]. The VNNF framework supports a larger family of queries, such as *optimization*, etc. It also supports several transformations, namely $\otimes$-*variable elimination* (a generalization of classical forgetting by using $\otimes$ instead of $\vee$ in equation (7)).

Π-DNNF [1] is a possibilistic version of DNNF in which conjunctions and disjunctions are substituted by minimum and maximum operators, respectively. It is considered as a special case of VNNFs [12] in which $E = [0,1]$ and OP is restricted to min and max operators.

3   Causal Inference Using Π-DNNFs

In [1], we already proposed a possibilistic adaptation of the so-called arithmetic circuit method [8]. This adaptation requires the use of the Π-DNNF language [1] instead of the propositional DNNF language [7]. The main idea is based on encoding the possibilistic network using the CNF propositional language, then compiling it to infer in polytime (i.e., compute efficiently a posteriori possibility degrees given some evidence on a set of variables). The CNF encoding that we have used takes advantage of the structure exhibited by network parameters, known as *local structure*, which induces a reduction of the time and the size of factorization [9]. The question is whether this encoding can be adapted to deal with both observations and interventions. This section shows that the answer is yes. Of course, since we offer more flexibility, there is an extra-cost. In fact,

---

[1] P_i is consistent with ρ if there exists an interpretation that satisfies both P_i and ρ.

handling interventions requires that a unique variable should be assigned to each parameter, while when we only deal with observations, different parameters (degrees) may be encoded by the same propositional variable. This means that local structure is only allowed in the non-intervention strategy.

3.1   Did We First Mutilate the Network?

One simple way for handling sets of interventions consists in mutilating ΠG_{min}, encoding the resulting graph using a propositional theory and compiling it to offer a polynomial-time handling of queries. But, handling sets of interventions by this way is not efficient since it requires a re-compilation of the network each time an intervention is obtained, which is intractable. Our main contribution consists in allowing the treatment of both observations and interventions by avoiding the re-compilation of the network in case of sequences of observations or interventions are taken place. Handling interventions by mutilation is considered worthwhile since the initial network is vanished after mutilation, while we focus on computing the effect of both observations and interventions. For this reason, in the following subsection we will exhibit the appropriate trick that allows us to ensure such computation using only one compilation step.

3.2   Inference Process

Given a ΠG_{min}, we should first encode it using the CNF representation language. Using two types of propositional variables namely, *evidence indicators* λ_{x_i} for recording evidences and *network parameters* $\theta_{x_i | u_i}$ for recording possibility degrees, the CNF encoding is defined as follows [1]:

Definition 1. *Let ΠG_{min} be a possibilistic causal network, $\lambda_{x_{ij}}$, $(i = 1, .., N)$, $(j = 1, .., n)$ be the set of evidence indicators and $\theta_{x_i | u_i}$ be the set of parameter variables, then the encoding C_{min} should contain the following clauses:*

- $\forall\ X_i \in V$, C_{min} *contains the following two clauses (named indicator clauses):*

$$\lambda_{x_{i1}} \vee \lambda_{x_{i2}} \vee \cdots \lambda_{x_{in}} \tag{8}$$

$$\neg \lambda_{x_{ij}} \vee \neg \lambda_{x_{ik}}, j \neq k \tag{9}$$

- $\forall\ \theta_{x_i | u_i}$ *s.t* $u_i = \{u_{i1}, u_{i2}, ..., u_{im}\}$, C_{min} *contains the following clauses:*

$$\lambda_{x_i} \wedge \lambda_{u_{i1}} \wedge \ldots \wedge \lambda_{u_{im}} \to \theta_{x_i | u_i} \tag{10}$$

$$\theta_{x_i | u_i} \to \lambda_{x_i} \tag{11}$$

$$\theta_{x_i | u_i} \to \lambda_{u_{i1}}, \cdots, \theta_{x_i | u_i} \to \lambda_{u_{im}} \tag{12}$$

Note that Definition 1 handles n-ary variables. Clauses (8) and (9) state that indicator variables are exclusive, while clauses (10)-(12) encode network's structure. Once we have encoded ΠG_{min}, we compile C_{min} into DNNF (denoted by C_{DNNF}) as shown in Figure 2. The resulting compiled base is qualified to be symbolic since it does not take into consideration any parameter value while encoding the network.

Fig. 2. Encoding and compilation steps

Example 2. *Let us re-consider the network of Figure 1. According to Algorithm 3.2, we should first encode ΠG_{min} as follows: $C_{min} = (\lambda_{c_1} \vee \lambda_{c_2}) \wedge (\neg\lambda_{c_1} \vee \neg\lambda_{c_2}) \wedge (\lambda_{c_1} \wedge \lambda_{a_1} \wedge \lambda_{b_1} \rightarrow \theta_{c_1|a_1,b_1}) \wedge (\theta_{c_1|a_1,b_1} \rightarrow \lambda_{c_1}) \wedge (\theta_{c_1|a_1,b_1} \rightarrow \lambda_{a_1}) \wedge (\theta_{c_1|a_1,b_1} \rightarrow \lambda_{b_1}) \cdots$ For lack of space, we have only written evidence clauses of the variable C and $\theta_{c_1|a_1,b_1}$'s clauses. The full encoding contains 46 clauses.*

Computing efficiently the effect of observations in min-based possibilistic causal networks is ensured in the same spirit as the one given in [1]. While computing the effect of interventions as outlined Algorithm 3.2 requires a further step in which a simulation of mutilation is ensured under a compilation framework.

Let $do(x_I)$ be an intervention that forces the variable X_I to take the value x_I, and x an instantiation of some variables $X \subseteq V$, then computing $\Pi(x)$ given $do(x_I)$ is ensured by applying a fundamental function, i.e., *Computing* as follows:

1. Conditioning C_{DNNF} on x_I by setting $\theta_{x_i|u_i}$ of the variable of interest X_I to $\top$ or $\bot$ depending on $x_i = x_I$ or $x_i \neq x_I$, resp.,
2. Conditioning C_{DNNF} on x by setting each λ_{x_i} to:

$$\lambda_{x_i} = \begin{cases} \bot & \text{if } \exists \ x_j \in x \text{ s.t. } x_j \text{ and } x_i \text{ disagree on values (i.e., } x_i \nsim x) \\ \top & \text{otherwise (i.e., } x_i \sim x) \end{cases} \quad (13)$$

3. Decoding the mutilated and conditioned representation $C_{DNNF|x}^m$ to have a valued expression, denoted by $C_{\Pi-DNNF}^m$,
4. Computing $\Pi(x)$ by forgetting the remaining variables using the max operator (i.e., applying max-variable elimination).

The first step represents the mutilation phase under a compilation framework. Indeed, C_{DNNF} is conditioned on x_I, as if we assign $\pi_m(x_I) = 1$ and $\forall x_i, x_i \neq x_I, \pi_m(x_i) = 0$. The motivational factor behind such operation resides in the symbolic compiled base that does not take into account parameters values. In fact, given interventions, new possibility degrees are generated which results in a new compiled base associated with the mutilated network as illustrated by Figure 3.

In the second step, we should condition C_{DNNF} on x using evidence indicators. The third step consists in decoding the mutilated representation by replacing $\vee$ and $\wedge$ by max and min, respectively and substituting each $\top$ and $\bot$ by their values. In fact, each $\top$ (resp. $\bot$) related to evidence indicators or X_I's parameter variables is set to 1 (resp. 0), while each $\top$ corresponding to non X_I's parameter variables is set to its possibility degree. Finally, we compute $\Pi(x)$ using $C_{\Pi-DNNF}^m$ by forgetting the remaining variables using the max operator. This operation, which is called *max-variable elimination* is the key for ensuring

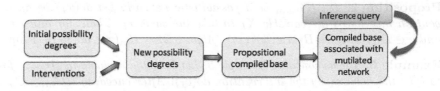

Fig. 3. The effect of interventions on compiled bases

linear-time inference since Π-DNNF, that is a special case of VNNF, supports max-variable elimination [12].

It is worth pointing out that our approach takes advantage from the fact that the compiled base is restricted to a set of symbols without regard to numerical values as shown in Figure 2. In particular, for any new intervention, we can re-use the same original encoding with a simple updating of parameters values as depicted Figure 3. Hence, we can conclude that our method does not depend on interventions, i.e., even if we grow the number of interventions, the complexity is not altered since the simulation of mutilation, which is a conditioning operation is ensured in polynomial time and the computation of the effect of interventions is also polynomial with respect to the size of the compiled base.

Nevertheless, such encoding requires one variable per parameter, which is not the case if observations occur since parameters are stationary. Indeed, the so-called *local structure* enhancement related to equal parameters, used to reduce the set of added variables cannot be explored in mutilated Π-DNNF. More precisely, we cannot attribute the same propositional variable even for equal parameters within CPTs as in [1]. For instance, assuming that we have $\theta_{c_1|a_1,b_2} = \theta_{c_2|a_1,b_1} = 0.7$. After performing intervention $do(c_1)$, $\theta_{c_1|a_1,b_2}$ (resp. $\theta_{c_2|a_1,b_1}$) should be set to 1 (resp. 0) which is infeasible if we use the same θ for both of $\theta_{c_1|a_1,b_2}$ and $\theta_{c_2|a_1,b_1}$.

A minor enhancement can be performed after mutilation, which consists in merging X_I's network parameters, i.e., each $\theta_{x_I|u_I}$, $\forall u_I$ can be replaced by θ_{x_I} since X_I and U_I are independent after mutilation.

Data: ΠG_{min}, instance of interest x, evidence e, intervention $do(x_I)$
Result: $\Pi_c(x|e, do(x_I))$
begin
    Let C_{min} be the CNF encoding obtained using equations (8)-(12)
    Let C_{DNNF} be the compilation result of C_{min}
    $\Pi_c(x, e, do(x_I)) \leftarrow Computing(C_{DNNF}, (x, e, do(x_I)))$
    $\Pi_c(e, do(x_I)) \leftarrow Computing(C_{DNNF}, (e, do(x_I)))$
    if $\Pi_c(x, e, do(x_I)) \prec \Pi_c(e, do(x_I))$ **then** $\Pi_c(x|e, do(x_I)) \leftarrow \Pi_c(x, e, do(x_I))$
    else $\Pi_c(x|e, do(x_I)) \leftarrow 1$
    return $\Pi_c(x|e, do(x_I))$
end

Algorithm 1.1. Inference in Mutilated Π-DNNFs

Proposition 2. *Let ΠG_{min} be a possibilistic network. Let $do(x_I)$ be an intervention that forces the variable X_I to take the value x_I. Then, for any $x \in D_X$ and $e \in D_E$, we have $\Pi_c(x|e, do(x_I))$ (Algo. 3.2) $= \Pi_m(x|e, do(x_I))$ (Prop. 1).*

Example 3. *Let us continue Example 3. Let C be the variable in ΠG_{min} forced to take the value c_1 by the intervention $do(c_1)$. After encoding ΠG_{min}, C_{min} is then compiled into C_{DNNF}, from which we will compute for instance the effect of $do(c_1)$ and a_1 on b_2, namely computing $\Pi_c(b_2|a_1, do(c_1))$. We need to compute both of $\Pi_c(b_2, a_1, do(c_1))$ and $\Pi_c(a_1, do(c_1))$. We start with $\Pi_c(b_2, a_1, do(c_1))$. First, we should set each $\theta_{c_1|u_i}$ (resp. $\theta_{c_2|u_i}$) to $\top$ (resp. $\bot$) $\forall u_i$ and condition C_{DNNF} on b_2, a_1 and $do(c_1)$. The resulting $C_{DNNF|b_2,a_1,do(c_1)}^m$ is then decoded into $C_{\Pi-DNNF}^m$ as depicted Figure 4. For lack of space, we apply Max-VariableElimination to an excerpt of $C_{\Pi-DNNF}^m = min(\theta_{a_1}, \theta_{b_2}, \theta_{c_1})$.*
Max-VariableElimination($C_{\Pi-DNNF}^m$, θ_{a_1}) $= max$ ($C_{\Pi-DNNF}^m|\theta_{a_1}$, $C_{\Pi-DNNF}^m|\neg\theta_{a_1}$) $= max(min(0.7, \theta_{b_2}, \theta_{c_1}), min(0, \theta_{b_2}, \theta_{c_1})) = min(0.7, \theta_{b_2}, \theta_{c_1})$,
$\Rightarrow$ Max-VariableElimination($min(0.7, \theta_{b_2}, \theta_{c_1})$, θ_{b_2}) $= min(0.7, 0.4, \theta_{c_1})$,
$\Rightarrow$ Max-VariableElimination($min(0.7, 0.4, \theta_{c_1})$, θ_{c_1}) $= min(0.7, 0.4, 1) = 0.4$.
This value corresponds exactly to the one computed in Example 1. $\Pi_c(a_1, do(c_1))$ is computed in the same spirit as $\Pi_c(b_2, a_1, do(c_1))$. Since $\Pi_c(b_2, a_1, do(c_1)) = 0.4$ $\prec \Pi_c(a_1, do(c_1)) = 0.7$, so $\Pi_c(b_2|a_1, do(c_1)) = 0.4$.

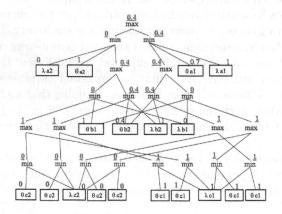

Fig. 4. Example of $C_{\Pi-DNNF}^m$

4   Causal Inference Using Compiled Possibilistic Bases

In [1], we proposed a purely possibilistic inference method which is not based on encoding probabilistic works grounded on compilation. The idea consists in transforming the binary network into a possibilistic knowledge base [3], encoding it into a CNF encoding by incorporating a set of additional variables corresponding exactly to the different weights of the base [5]. After that, a compilation step is required from which the inference query should be ensured in polynomial time. In this section, we will focus on how to enrich this method to compute efficiently the effect of both observations and interventions.

The key difference between handling only observations and handling both observations and interventions resides in the set of additional variables while encoding the possibilistic knowledge base. In fact, in a causal reasoning, even if we have the same degree for a set of formulae within the base, we cannot use the same propositional variable as we did for observations. In other terms, one variable per degree is used if we handle both observations and interventions as shown in the following proposition:

Proposition 3. *Let ΠG_{min} be a possibilistic causal network. Let Σ_{min} be its possibilistic knowledge base expressed by: $\Sigma_{min} = \Sigma_{X_1} \cup \Sigma_{X_2} \cup \cdots \cup \Sigma_{X_N}, \forall X_i \in V$ s.t. $\Sigma_{X_i} = \{(\neg x_i \vee \neg u_i, a_i) : a_i = 1 - \Pi(x_i|u_i) \neq 0\}$, then its CNF encoding is expressed by: $K_\Sigma = \{\alpha_i \vee A_i : (\alpha_i, a_i) \in \Sigma_{min}\}$ where A_i is a propositional variable associated to each degree a_i in Σ_{min}.*

It is important to note that even if we transform the network into a logic-based representation, causal links are not lost. Thanks to the parameters that allow us to encode network's structure.

Example 4. *Let us re-consider the ΠG_{min} of Figure 1. Its CNF encoding is expressed by: $K_\Sigma = \{(c_2 \vee a_2 \vee b_1 \vee A_1), (c_1 \vee a_2 \vee b_2 \vee A_2), (b_1 \vee A_3), (c_2 \vee a_1 \vee b_2 \vee A_4)), (a_2 \vee A_5), (c_2 \vee a_1 \vee b_1 \vee A_6)\}$ s.t. A_1, A_2, A_3, A_4, A_5 and A_6 are propositional variables associated to 0.9, 0.7, 0.6, 0.5, 0.3 and 0.2, respectively.*

Computing the effect of both observations and interventions requires a clausal deduction test and a conditioning transformation, hence the CNF encoding K_Σ should be compiled only once into the most succinct target compilation language that supports such operations. Our method is qualified to be flexible since it permits to exploit efficiently all the existing propositional compilers [1]. Given an instance of interest x, an evidence e and an intervention $do(x_I)$ performed on X_I, then computing $\Pi_c(x|e, do(x_I))$ using the compiled base K_c requires two steps as outlined Algorithm 1.2:

(i) K_c should be mutilated by assigning the degree 1 (resp. 0) to variables A_i corresponding to $\neg x_I$ (resp. x_I). The objective is to make the connection between mutilating ΠG_{min} and mutilating K_c as shown in Figure 3. After mutilation, variables A_i encoding equal degrees in K_c can be merged into the same variable B_j. The new set of variables is denoted by $B = \{B_1, \ldots, B_g\}$ where g represents the number of variables after merging.

(ii) We should first test if $K_c \not\models B_1 \vee \neg e \vee \neg x_I$. If this deduction is not satisfied, we condition K_c on $\neg B_1$ and then test if K_c entails $\neg x$. If this is the case, we compute $\Pi_c(x|e, do(x_I))$, else we move to the next B_j and we re-itere the same treatment. In the worst case, this computation is performed $g - 1$ times since the last variable B_g corresponds to the degree 0.

It is worth pointing out that before the mutilation step we can not attribute the same A_i even for equal degrees in Σ_{min}. For instance, assuming that we have the following formulae $(c_1 \vee a_1 \vee b_2, A_1)$ and $(c_2 \vee a_1 \vee b_1, A_1)$ such that A_1 encodes the degree 0.8. After performing intervention $do(c_1)$, we should set the degree 0 (resp. 1) to the A_i corresponding to $(c_2 \vee a_1 \vee b_1, 0.8)$ (resp. $(c_1 \vee a_1 \vee b_2, 0.8)$), which is infeasible if we use the same variable A_1. It is also crucial to note that our method does not depend on the number of interventions. Thanks to the symbolic compiled base that allows us to update parameters values linearly regardless of the number of interventions.

Data: ΠG_{min}, instance of interest x, evidence e, intervention $do(x_I)$
Result: $\Pi_c(x|e, do(x_I))$
begin

   Let Σ_{min} be the possibilistic base of ΠG_{min} using Proposition
   $K_\Sigma \leftarrow$ encoding(Σ_{min}, A, n) using Proposition   % A : the set of propositional
   variables, n: the number of A_i in A
   Let K_c be the compilation result of K_Σ
   Let A_k be the set of propositional variables A_i of $\neg x_i$
   foreach $A_i \in A_k$ **do** Degree of $A_i \leftarrow 1$
   Let A_c be the set of A_i of the variable of interest X_i except A_k
   foreach $A_i \in A_c$ **do** Degree of $A_i \leftarrow 0$
   Let $B = \{B_1, \ldots, B_g\}$ be the new set of variables after merging
   $i \leftarrow 1$, StopCompute $\leftarrow$ false, $\Pi_c(x|e, do(x_I)) \leftarrow 1$
   while $(K_c \nvDash B_i \vee \neg e \vee \neg x_I)$ **and** $(i \leq g-1)$ **and** *(StopCompute=false)* **do**
      $K_c \leftarrow$ condition $(K_c, \neg B_i)$ using equation (6)
      if $K_c \vDash \neg x$ **then**
         StopCompute $\leftarrow$ true
         Let *degree(i)* be the weight associated to B_i
         $\Pi_c(x|e, do(x_I)) \leftarrow 1\text{-}degree(i)$
      else $i \leftarrow i+1$
   return $\Pi_c(x|e, do(x_I))$
end

Algorithm 1.2. Inference in Mutilated Possibilistic Bases

Proposition 4. *Let ΠG_{min} be a possibilistic network. Let $do(x_I)$ be an intervention that forces the variable X_I to take the value x_I. Then, for any $x \in D_X$ and $e \in D_E$, we have $\Pi_c(x|e, do(x_I))$ (Algo. 1.2) $= \Pi_m(x|e, do(x_I))$ (Prop. 1).*

Example 5. *We continue with Example 5. Let C be the variable forced to take the value c_1 by the intervention $do(c_1)$, let a_1 be an observed evidence, then what is the effect of $do(c_1)$ and a_1 on b_2? First, we should compile K_Σ into DNNF as follows:*
$K_c = \{[(((c_2 \wedge A_2) \vee c_1) \wedge b_1) \vee ((b_2 \wedge A_3) \wedge (c_2 \vee (c_1 \wedge A_1)))) \wedge A_5 \wedge a_1]$
$\vee [a_2 \wedge ((b_1 \wedge (c_2 \vee (c_1 \wedge A_4))) \vee (b_2 \wedge A_3 \wedge (c_2 \vee (c_1 \wedge A_6))))]\}$. *Then, we should update the degree of $A_k=\{A_2\}$ from 0.7 to 1 and set the degree 0 for each variable in $A_c = \{A_1, A_4, A_6\}$. Merging variables gives us the new set of variables $B = \{B_1(1), B_2(0.6), B_3(0.3), B_4(0)\}$ which substitutes the set A in K_c as follows: $K_c = \{[(((c_2 \wedge B_1) \vee c_1) \wedge b_1) \vee ((b_2 \wedge B_2) \wedge (c_2 \vee (c_1 \wedge B_4)))) \wedge B_3 \wedge a_1] \vee [a_2 \wedge ((b_1 \wedge (c_2 \vee (c_1 \wedge B_4))) \vee (b_2 \wedge B_2 \wedge (c_2 \vee (c_1 \wedge B_4))))]\}$. We are now ready to compute $\Pi_c(b_2|a_1, do(c_1))$. The computation process requires two iterations which means that $\Pi_c(b_2|a_1, do(c_1)) = 1 - degree(2) = 1 - 0.6 = 0.4$ where $degree(2)$ designates the weight associated to B_2. This value corresponds exactly to the ones computed in Example 1 and Example 4.*

At this stage, a comparison study between the two proposed methods (i.e., mutilated Π-DNNFs and mutilated possibilistic bases) is crucial. It is clear that intuitively if we restrict our attention to the binary case, mutilated possibilistic bases are more compact than mutilated Π-DNNFs even if local structure is not exploited in both of them. In fact, mutilated possibilistic bases offer less variables and clauses since no formulae or clauses are associated to degrees equal to 1. Moreover, only one clause is encoded for each variable A_i which is not the case for each parameter $\theta_{x_i|u_i}$ in mutilated Π-DNNFs. This note deserves to be confirmed by an experimental study.

5 Conclusion

This paper proposed compilation-based inference algorithms for min-based possibilistic causal networks. First, we proposed a compilation-based approach from which we compute efficiently the effect of both observations and interventions using mutilated Π-DNNFs. Then, we developed a possibilistic inference method dealing with mutilated possibilistic bases. Our methods are qualified as flexible since we compute the effect of observations and interventions from an already compiled base without a re-compilation cost. However, the inherent cost of interventions is expensive since we introduce different variables even for equal degrees, which is not the case for observations. This is the price to be paid if interventions occur. We have also noticed that intuitively, if we focus on the binary case, mutilated possibilistic bases are more compact than mutilated Π-DNNFs. Our future work consists in studying the representational point of view of interventions under a compilation framework, then comparing mutilated-based approaches with both augmented-based approaches and the well known junction tree.

References

1. Ayachi, R., Ben Amor, N., Benferhat, S., Haenni, R.: Compiling possibilistic networks: Alternative approaches to possibilistic inference. In: Proceedings of 26th Conference on UAI, pp. 40–47. AUAI Press (2010)
2. Ben Amor, N., Benferhat, S., Mellouli, K.: Anytime propagation algorithm for minbased possibilistic graphs. Soft. Comput. 8(2), 150–161 (2003)
3. Benferhat, S., Dubois, D., Garcia, L., Prade, H.: On the transformation between possibilistic logic bases and possibilistic causal networks. IJAR 29(2), 135–173 (2002)
4. Benferhat, S., Smaoui, S.: Possibilistic causal networks for handling interventions: A new propagation algorithm. In: AAAI, pp. 373–378 (2007)
5. Benferhat, S., Yahi, S., Drias, H.: On the compilation of stratified belief bases under linear and possibilistic logic policies. IJAR, 2425–2430 (2007)
6. Cadoli, M., Donini, F.: A survey on knowledge compilation. AI Communications 10(3-4), 137–150 (1997)
7. Darwiche, A.: Decomposable negation normal form. Journal of the ACM 48(4), 608–647 (2001)
8. Darwiche, A.: A logical approach to factoring belief networks. In: Proceedings of KR, pp. 409–420 (2002)

9. Darwiche, A.: Modeling and Reasoning with Bayesian Networks, 1st edn. Cambridge University Press, New York (2009)
10. Darwiche, A., Marquis, P.: A knowledge compilation map. Journal of Artificial Intelligence Research 17, 229–264 (2002)
11. Dubois, D., Prade, H.: Possibility theory. In: Meyers, R.A. (ed.) Encyclopedia of Complexity and Systems Science, pp. 6927 6939. Springer, Heidelberg (2009)
12. Fargier, H., Marquis, P.: On valued negation normal form formulas. In: Proceedings of the 20th IJCAI, San Francisco, CA, USA, pp. 360–365 (2007)
13. Goldszmidt, M., Pearl, J.: Rank-based systems: A simple approach to belief revision, belief update, and reasoning about evidence and actions. In: KR, pp. 661–672 (1992)
14. Lang, J.: Possibilistic logic: complexity and algorithms. In: Handbook on Defeasible Reasoning and Uncertainty Management Systems, vol. 5, pp. 179–220 (2001)
15. Pearl, J.: Causality:models, reasoning, and inference. Cambridge Univ. Press, Cambridge (2000)

Possibilistic Evidence

Henri Prade[1] and Agnès Rico[2]

[1] Institut de Recherche en Informatique de Toulouse - IRIT
Université de Toulouse, 118, route de Narbonne, 31062 Toulouse Cedex 09, France
prade@irit.fr
[2] Equipe de Recherche en Ingénierie des Connaissances - ERIC
Université Claude Bernard Lyon 1, Lyon, France
agnes.rico@univ-lyon1.fr

Abstract. The paper investigates a qualitative counterpart of Shafer's evidence theory, where the basic *probability* assignment is turned into a basic *possibility* assignment whose weights have 1 as a maximum. The associated set functions, playing the role of belief, plausibility, commonality, and the dual of the latter, are now defined on a "maxitive", rather than on an additive basis. Although this possibilistic evidence setting has been suggested for a long time, and has a clear relation with the study of qualitative Möbius transforms, it has not been really systematically studied and considered for itself as a general qualitative representation framework. It can be viewed as defining imprecise possibilities, and encompasses standard possibilistic representations as a particular case. The paper particularly focuses on a generalized set-theoretic view of this setting and discusses the entailment relation between basic possibility assignments as well as combination rules.

Keywords: Dempster-Shafer evidence theory, possibility theory, knowledge representation.

1 Introduction

Many approaches to the handling of uncertainty and preference, including the classical ones, heavily rely on a quantitative / additive modeling. Additive structures are indeed at the basis of the classical approaches and of their generalizations for the representation of uncertainty (with probability theory and Shafer's evidence theory [14]), or in multiple criteria aggregation (with weighted averages, and more generally Choquet integrals). However, the processing of more qualitative information has also led to the emergence of "maxitive" settings such as possibility theory [19], or Sugeno integrals [15].

Shafer's evidence theory, which, mathematically speaking, includes both probability theory and possibility theory as particular cases, but also the classical set-based representation, provides a setting appropriate for representing imprecise and uncertain information, by means of a basic probability assignment from the power set of the referential to the unit interval. In this paper we investigate a qualitative (maxitive) counterpart to this framework, starting with a

W. Liu (Ed.): ECSQARU 2011, LNAI 6717, pp. 713–724, 2011.

basic *possibility* assignment. Such an assignment, whose weights no longer sum
to 1 but have 1 as a maximum, gives birth to a *possibilistic evidence* setting.
The idea of a basic possibility assignment dates back to a suggestion made in
[7,8]. This notion has been also empirically used in diagnosis contexts for nam-
ing different kinds of assignments, e.g. [17]. Other authors have been interested
in this qualitative counterpart. Thus, in [1] all fuzzy measures are proved to
be equal to a maximum of necessity measures and to a minimum of possibility measures. In [16], upper and lower possibilities and necessities are expressed
in terms of a basic possibility assignment or a necessity assignment. Moreover,
this qualitative counterpart is closely related to the study of qualitative Möbius
transforms in relation with Choquet and Sugeno integrals [4], and in particular
with the problem of refining qualitative multiple criteria evaluations [5]. Still,
the possibilistic evidence setting has never been much advocated as a general
representation setting worth of interest. This paper tries to remedy this state
of fact. It is organized as follows. Section 2 introduces the basic set functions
associated with a basic possibility assignment. Section 3 shows that this setting
can be understood in terms of imprecise possibilities just as Shafer's evidence
theory may be viewed as a particular imprecise probability system. Section 4
discusses the relation with qualitative Möbius transforms, showing that different basic possibility assignments can be associated with the same system of
set functions. Sections 5 presents an entailment relation between basic possibility assignments, and Section 6 studies conjunctive or disjunctive combination
rules. The concluding remarks briefly comment on the interest of the companion
"minitive" construct.

2   A Maxitive Weighted Subset Representation Framework

In evidence theory, given a universe $\Omega = \{1, \cdots, N\}$, called frame of discernment,
information is represented by means of a mapping m, called basic probability
assignment (or mass function) from 2^Ω to the unit interval $[0,1]$, which is such
that $\sum_{i=1}^{n} m(A_i) = 1$, where there is a finite set of focal elements A_i that are
such that $m(A_i) > 0$. If the information is consistent $m(\emptyset) = 0$ is assumed. $m(A)$
is the probability mass allocated to the subset A exactly. Attaching a mass to
a subset without dispatching it inside opens the door to the representation of
partial ignorance. A mass function m is associated to the following set functions:

$$\forall A \subseteq \Omega, \quad Bel(A) = \sum_{\emptyset \neq B \subseteq A} m(B); \quad \forall A \subseteq \Omega, \quad Pl(A) = \sum_{B \cap A \neq \emptyset} m(B);$$
$$\forall A \subseteq \Omega, \quad Q(A) = \sum_{A \subseteq B} m(B); \quad \forall A \subseteq \Omega, \quad \mathbb{O}(A) = \sum_{A \cup B \neq \Omega} m(B).$$

Bel is a belief function, *Pl* a plausibility function, and Q a commonality function.
$\mathbb{O}(A) = 1 - Q(\overline{A})$ is rarely considered ($\overline{A}$ denotes the complement of A).

2.1   Set Functions Associated with Possibilistic Evidence

In what can be termed *possibilistic evidence theory*, the basic building block is a
so-called basic *possibility* assignment which is a set function σ from a set 2^Ω (here

assumed to be a finite set) to $[0,1]$, such that $\bigvee_{A\subseteq\Omega}\sigma(A)=1$. As in Shafer's evidence theory setting, $\mathcal{F}_\sigma=\{A\,|\,\sigma(A)>0\}$ is called a body of evidence, and any element of $\mathcal{F}$ is called a focal element. σ may be also viewed as defining a normalized fuzzy set of subsets, i.e. a particular case of level 2-fuzzy set [18], or better as a possibility distribution over 2^Ω (just as m may be viewed as a probability distribution over 2^Ω). Moreover, a *normal* basic possibility assignment satisfies the additional condition $\sigma(\emptyset)=0$. In the following, *all the considered basic possibility assignments are normal.* As in evidence theory, a basic possibility assignment σ is associated with set functions now defined on a maxitive basis, in agreement with a qualitative setting:

Definition 1

$\forall A\subseteq\Omega,\ Bel^{pos}(A)=\bigvee_{B\subseteq A}\sigma(B),\ Bel^{pos}(\emptyset)=0,\ Bel^{pos}(\Omega)=1;$

$\forall A\subseteq\Omega,\ Pl^{pos}(A)=\bigvee_{\emptyset\neq A\cap B}\sigma(B),\ Pl^{pos}(\emptyset)=0,\ Pl^{pos}(\Omega)=1;$

$\forall A\subseteq\Omega,\ Q^{pos}(A)=\bigvee_{A\subseteq B}\sigma(B),\ Q^{pos}(\emptyset)=1,\ Q^{pos}(\Omega)=\sigma(\Omega);$

$\forall A\subseteq\Omega,\ \eth^{pos}(A)=\bigvee_{A\cup B\neq\Omega}\sigma(B),\ \eth^{pos}(\emptyset)=\bigvee_{B\neq\Omega}\sigma(B),\ \eth^{pos}(\Omega)=0.$

2.2 Duality Relations

In Shafer's evidence theory, the belief and plausibility functions Bel and Pl satisfy $\forall A\subseteq\Omega,\ Bel(A)\leq Pl(A)$. Moreover, they are related through the duality relation $\forall A\subseteq\Omega,\ Pl(A)+Bel(\bar{A})=1-m(\emptyset)$.

It is easy to see that the functions Bel^{pos} and Pl^{pos} are increasing and satisfy $\forall A,\ Bel^{pos}(A)\leq Pl^{pos}(A)$. Q^{pos} and $\eth^{pos}$ are decreasing. Having $\forall A,\ Q^{pos}(A)\leq\eth^{pos}(A)$ also requires $\sigma(\Omega)=0$. Moreover, a duality relation exists between Bel^{pos} and Pl^{pos} and between Q^{pos} and $\eth^{pos}$.

Proposition 1. $\forall A\subseteq\Omega,\ Pl^{pos}(A)\vee Bel^{pos}(\bar{A})=1,\ Q^{pos}(A)\vee\eth^{pos}(\bar{A})=1.$

Proof

$\bigvee_{B\cap A\neq\emptyset}\sigma(B)\vee\bigvee_{B\subseteq\bar{A}}\sigma(B)=\bigvee_{B\cap A\neq\emptyset}\sigma(B)\vee\bigvee_{B\cap A=\emptyset}\sigma(B)=\bigvee_{B\subseteq\Omega}\sigma(B)=1$

$\bigvee_{A\subseteq B}\sigma(B)\vee\bigvee_{B\cup\bar{A}\neq\Omega}\sigma(B)=\bigvee_{B\cup\bar{A}=\Omega}\sigma(B)\vee\bigvee_{B\cup\bar{A}\neq\Omega}\sigma(B)=\bigvee_{B\subseteq\Omega}\sigma(B)=1$

2.3 Particular Cases of Basic Possibility Assignment

Let us see how particular noticeable situations are represented in this setting.

Total imprecision: $\sigma(\Omega)=1$ and σ is 0 otherwise. Then, $\forall A\neq\Omega,\ Bel^{pos}(A)=0,\ \forall A\neq\emptyset,\ Pl^{pos}(A)=1$. Moreover, $\forall A,\ Q^{pos}(A)=1;\ \forall A,\ \eth^{pos}(A)=0$.

Partial imprecision: there exists $A\subseteq\Omega$, $|A|>1$ such that $\sigma(A)=1$ and for all $B\neq A$, $\sigma(B)=0$. Then,

$Bel^{pos}(B)=1$ if $A\subseteq B$ and 0 if $A\not\subseteq B$;

$Pl^{pos}(B)=1$ if $A\cap B\neq\emptyset$ and 0 if $A\cap B=\emptyset$;

$Q^{pos}(B)=1$ $B\subseteq A$ and 0 if $B\not\subseteq A$;

$\eth^{pos}(B)=1$ if $B\cup A\neq\Omega$.

Complete knowledge: There exists only one $\omega \in \Omega$ such that $\sigma(\{\omega\}) = 1$ and σ is equal to 0 otherwise. Then, $\forall A$, $Bel^{pos}(A) = Pl^{pos}(A) = 1$ if $\omega \in A$ and 0 if $\omega \notin A$. $Q^{pos}(A) = 1$ if $A = \{\omega\}$ and $0\ \forall A \neq \{\omega\}$; $Q^{pos}(A) = 1$ if $A \neq \{\Omega\}, \neq \overline{\{\omega\}}$.

Precise uncertainty: σ is a "Bayesian" possibility assignment if $\sigma(A) > 0$ implies that A is a singleton. Then $Bel^{pos}(A) = Pl^{pos}(A) = \bigvee_{\omega \in A} \sigma(\omega)$ is a possibility measure. $Q^{pos}(A) = 0$ for all A such that $|A| > 1$, $Q^{pos}(\{\omega\})) = \sigma(\{\omega\})$.

Possibilistic uncertainty: σ is not equal to 0 only for some A_i that are nested, i.e., $A_1 \subseteq \cdots \subseteq A_n$. In Shafer 's evidence theory, in such a case Pl is a possibility measure and Bel is a necessity measure. As shown below, we have the same result in our context. Moreover Q^{pos} and $\eth^{pos}$ are strong (or guaranteed) possibility and weak necessity measures respectively, as in bipolar possibility theory [10][2].

First let us introduce the following notations. For any set $A \subseteq \Omega$, $A_{min}^{\cap}$ denotes the minimum index i such that $A \cap A_i \neq \emptyset$, $A_{min}^{\subseteq}$ denotes the minimum index i such that $A \subseteq A_i$, and A_{max} denotes the maximum index i such that $A_i \subseteq A$.

Proposition 2

1. Bel^{pos} is a necessity measure, i.e. $Bel^{pos}(A \cap B) = Bel^{pos}(A) \wedge Bel^{pos}(B)$,
2. Pl^{pos} is a possibility measure, i.e. $Pl^{pos}(A \cup B) = Pl^{pos}(A) \vee Pl^{pos}(B)$,
3. $Q^{pos}(A \cup B) = Q^{pos}(A) \wedge Q^{pos}(B)$,
4. $\eth^{pos}(A \cap B) = \eth^{pos}(A) \vee \eth^{pos}(B)$.

Proof: Let A and B be two subsets of Ω.

1. The maximum index such that $A_i \subseteq (A \cap B)$ is the minimum of the indexes A_{max} and B_{max}. We have $Bel^{pos}(A \cap B) = \bigvee_{i \leq A_{max} \wedge B_{max}} \sigma(A_i) = \bigvee_{i \leq A_{max}} \sigma(A_i) \wedge \bigvee_{i \leq B_{max}} \sigma(A_i) = Bel^{pos}(A) \wedge Bel^{pos}(B)$.
2. The minimum index i such that $(A \cup B) \cap A_i \neq \emptyset$ is the minimum of the indexes $A_{min}^{\cap}$ and $B_{min}^{\cap}$. So $Pl^{pos}(A \cup B) = \bigvee_{i \geq A_{min}^{\cap} \wedge B_{min}^{\cap}} \sigma(A_i) = \bigvee_{i \geq A_{min}^{\cap}} \sigma(A_i) \vee \bigvee_{i \geq B_{min}^{\cap}} \sigma(A_i) = Pl^{pos}(A) \vee Pl^{pos}(B)$.
3. The minimum index i such that $A \cup B \subseteq A_i$ is the maximum of the indexes $A_{min}^{\subseteq}$ and $B_{min}^{\subseteq}$, so $Q^{pos}(A \cup B) = \bigvee_{i \geq A_{min}^{\subseteq} \vee B_{min}^{\subseteq}} \sigma(A_i) = Q^{pos}(A) \wedge Q^{pos}(B)$.
4. $\bar{A} \cup \bar{B} = \overline{A \cap B}$. The minimum index i such that $\bar{A} \cup \bar{B} \subseteq A_i$ is the maximum of the indexes $\bar{A}_{min}^{\subseteq}$ and $\bar{B}_{min}^{\subseteq}$ so $\eth^{pos}(A \cap B) = \bigvee_{i \leq \bar{A}_{min}^{\subseteq} \vee \bar{B}_{min}^{\subseteq}} \sigma(A_i) = \eth^{pos}(A) \vee \eth^{pos}(B)$.

3   Possibilistic Evidence as Imprecise Possibilities

A consistent probability assignment m defines an imprecise probability in the sense that m is compatible with any probability distribution p obtained by sharing the masses $m(A)$ between the elements ω in A (assuming Ω finite):

if $\forall A \in 2^{\Omega}, \exists k_A \in [0, 1]^A$ such that $m(A) = \sum_{\omega \in A} k_A(\omega)$, and $p(\omega) = \sum_{A \ni \omega} k_A(\omega)$.

Clearly $\sum_{A \neq \emptyset} m(A) = 1$ ensures that $\sum_{\omega \in \Omega} p(\omega) = 1$. Thus, viewing each $m(A)$ as a mass that can be shared and freely reallocated to the elements of A, m is associated to the family of probability distributions p that are compatible with m in the above sense. Then m models a particular imprecise probability system. Letting $P(A) = \sum_{\omega \in A} p(\omega)$, it can be checked that

$$Bel(A) = \sum_{\emptyset \neq B \subseteq A} m(B) \leq P(A) \leq Pl(A) = \sum_{B \cap A \neq \emptyset} m(B).$$

Indeed, $Bel(A) = \sum_{\emptyset \neq B \subseteq A} \sum_{\omega \in B} k_B(\omega) \leq \sum_{\omega \in A} \sum_{B \ni \omega} k_B(\omega) = P(A)$.

We may similarly try to define an imprecise possibility structure. Let us consider a basic possibility assignment σ and $\mathcal{U}_\sigma = \bigcup_{i | \sigma(A_i) > 0} A_i$. However, the situation is slightly more tricky than in the probabilistic case, if we want to interpret the $\sigma(A)$'s as providing an imprecise possibility specification. If it is so, there should exist a possibility distribution π and mappings $\kappa_A \in [0,1]^A$ such that such that $\sigma(A) = \max_{\omega \in A} \kappa_A(\omega)$, and $\pi(\omega) = \max_{B \ni \omega} \kappa_B(\omega)$. Note that $\Pi(A) = \max_{\omega \in A} \pi(\omega) = \max_{\omega \in A} \max_{B \ni \omega} \kappa_B(\omega) \geq \sigma(A)$. Note also that $\forall \omega \in \Omega - \mathcal{U}_\sigma, \pi(\omega) = 0$. Clearly $\max_{A \neq \emptyset} \sigma(A) = 1$ ensures that $\max_{\omega \in \Omega} \pi(\omega) = 1$. Thus, $\sigma(A)$ should be understood as a contribution to the specification of the possibility of A. Let us show that $Bel^{pos}(A) \leq \Pi(A) \leq Pl^{pos}(A)$.

Indeed, $Bel^{pos}(A) = \bigvee_{B \subseteq A} \sigma(B) \leq \bigvee_{B \subseteq A} \Pi(B) = \Pi(A)$. Let B_0 denote the set such that $A \cap B_0 \neq \emptyset$ and $\sigma(B_0) = \bigvee_{B \cap A \neq \emptyset} \sigma(B)$. For all $\omega \in A$, $\exists B_1$ such that $\omega \in B_1$ and $\pi(\omega) = \kappa_{B_1}(\omega)$. $\kappa_{B_1}(\omega) \leq \sigma(B_1) \leq \sigma(B_0)$ so $\forall \omega \in A$, $\pi(\omega) \leq \sigma(B_0)$ which entails $\Pi(A) \leq \sigma(B_0) = \bigvee_{B \cap A \neq \emptyset} \sigma(B) = Pl^{pos}(A)$.

Example. $\mathcal{F}_\sigma = \{A, \Omega\}$. Assume $\sigma(A) \geq \sigma(\Omega)$. Then $\sigma(A) = \max_{\omega \in A} \kappa_A(\omega)$, $\sigma(\Omega) = \max_{\omega \in \Omega} \kappa_\Omega(\omega)$, and $\pi(\omega) = \max(\kappa_A(\omega), \kappa_\Omega(\omega))$. By convention, $\kappa_A(\omega) = 0$ if $\omega \notin A$. Then $\Pi(A) = max(\sigma(A), \max_{\omega \in A} \kappa_\Omega(\omega)) = \sigma(A)$. But, $\Pi(\Omega) = max(\max_{\omega \in \Omega} \kappa_A(\omega), \sigma(\Omega)) = \sigma(A)$. If $\sigma(A) < \sigma(\Omega)$, $\sigma(A) \leq \Pi(A) \leq \sigma(\Omega) = \Pi(\Omega) = 1$.

4   Non Unicity of the Basic Possibility Assignment

A belief function Bel (or its dual Pl) is associated with only one mass function which is not tue in the maxitive setting as it can be seen in the following example:

	$\{1\}$	$\{2\}$	$\{3\}$	$\{1,2\}$	$\{1,3\}$	$\{2,3\}$	$\{1,2,3\}$
σ_1	1	0	1	0	0	0	1
σ_2	1	0	1	1	1	1	0
$Bel_1^{pos} = Bel_2^{pos}$	1	0	1	1	1	1	1

Moreover the equivalence $\forall A \subseteq \Omega$, $Bel_1(A) \leq Bel_2(A) \Leftrightarrow Pl_2(A) \leq Pl_1(A)$ is not true for the set functions Bel^{pos} and Pl^{pos}. For example if we consider

	$\{1\}$	$\{2\}$	$\{1,2\}$
σ_1	0	1	0
σ_2	1	1	1

we have $Bel_1^{pos} \leq Bel_2^{pos}$ and $Pl_1^{pos} \leq Pl_2^{pos}$.

Proposition 3. *Let Bel_1^{pos} and Bel_2^{pos} associated respectively with σ_1 and σ_2. If Bel_1^{pos} and Bel_2^{pos} are equal then σ_1 and σ_2 are equal on the singletons.*

In Shafer's evidence theory, the mass function associated to a belief function is computed with the Möbius transform. In our context, the qualitative Möbius transform [11,12,5] associates a possibilistic belief function $Bel^{pos} = v$ to an interval of basic possibility assignments, as stated in the following definition:

Definition 2. *Let $v : 2^\Omega \to [0,1]$ be an increasing set function, its qualitative Möbius transform is $\{\sigma | \forall A \subseteq \Omega \; v(A) = \bigvee_{B \subseteq A} \sigma(B)\} = \{\sigma | \sigma \in [\sigma_*, \sigma^*]\}$ where σ_* and σ^* are the basic possibility assignments defined as follows:*
$\forall A \subseteq \Omega, \; \sigma^*(A) = v(A),$
$\forall A \subseteq \Omega, \; \sigma_*(A) = 0 \text{ if } \exists B \subset A \text{ s.t. } v(B) = v(A) \text{ and } \sigma_*(A) = v(A) \text{ otherwise.}$

The sets A such that $\sigma_*(A) \neq 0$ are such that $\forall B \subset A$, $\sigma_*(B)$ is either 0 or $v(B)$ with $v(B) < v(A)$. So we have for all $B \subset A$, $\sigma_*(B) < \sigma_*(A)$. A can be viewed as the minimal set in the sense of inclusion satisfying $\sigma_*(A) = v(A)$. In the following, the sets A such that $\sigma_*(A) \neq 0$ are named the minimal sets of v.

Applying this result to the set function Bel^{pos} gives birth to an interval $[\sigma_*^B, \sigma^{B*}]$. Let us present an example.

	$\{1\}$	$\{2\}$	$\{3\}$	$\{1,2\}$	$\{1,3\}$	$\{2,3\}$	$\{1,2,3\}$
Bel^{pos}	1	0	1	1	1	1	1
σ^*	1	0	1	1	1	1	1
σ_*	1	0	1	0	0	0	0

Similarly the set function Pl^{pos} corresponds to an interval $[\sigma_*^P, \sigma^{P*}]$.

We have $\sigma_*^B \leq \sigma_*^P \leq \sigma^{B*} \leq \sigma^{P*}$. So if we know Bel^{pos} and Pl^{pos} everywhere σ is uniquely determined if and only if $\sigma_*^P = \sigma^{B*}$.

The set function Q^{pos} is not an increasing set function, but we can define an interval of basic possibility assignments associated with Q^{pos} as before, using a result proved for the "minitive" set function $\bigwedge_{A \subseteq B} \sigma(B)$ in [5].

Definition 3. *Let $v : 2^\Omega \to [0,1]$ be a decreasing set function, its transform is*
$\{\sigma | \forall A \subseteq \Omega \; v(A) = \bigvee_{B \subseteq A} \sigma(B)\} = \{\sigma | \sigma \in [\sigma_*, \sigma^*]\}$
where σ_* and σ^* are the basic possibility assignments defined as follows:
$\forall A \subseteq \Omega, \; \sigma^*(A) = v(A),$
$\forall A \subseteq \Omega, \; \sigma_*(A) = 0 \text{ if } \exists B \text{ s.t. } A \subset B \text{ and } v(B) = v(A); \; \sigma_*(A) = v(A)$
otherwise.

Similarly to the case where v was an increasing function, the sets A such that $\sigma_*(A) \neq 0$ can be viewed as the maximal sets in the sense of inclusion satisfying $\sigma_*(A) = v(A)$. In the following these sets are named the maximal sets of v.

Applying this result to the set functions Q^{pos} and $\eth^{pos}$ leads to the intervals $[\sigma_*^Q, \sigma^{Q*}]$ and $[\sigma_*^\eth, \sigma^{\eth*}]$.

When the four functions Bel^{pos}, Pl^{pos}, Q^{pos} and $\eth^{pos}$ are defined everywhere σ is unique if and only if the intersection of the four involved intervals is only one basic possibility assignment. This is not always the case. For example we can consider $\Omega = \{1, 2, 3\}$ and the following basic possibility assignments σ_1 and σ_2: σ_1 equal to 1 on $\{1\}$, $\{3\}$ $\{1, 2, 3\}$ and 0 on the other sets; σ_2 equal to 0 on $\{2\}$ and 1 on the other sets. In this example we have $Bel_1^{pos} = Bel_2^{pos}$, $Pl_1^{pos} = Pl_2^{pos}$, $Q_1^{pos} = Q_2^{pos}$ and $\mho_1^{pos} = \mho_2^{pos}$.

Using the previous results we can define two equivalence relations as follows.

Definition 4. $\sigma_1 \sim_{Bel^{pos}} \sigma_2$ if and only if $Bel_1^{pos} = Bel_2^{pos}$.
$\sigma_1 \sim_{Q^{pos}} \sigma_2$ if and only if $Q_1^{pos} = Q_2^{pos}$.

The first relation $\sigma_1 \sim_{Bel^{pos}} \sigma_2$ implies that $\sigma_{1*} = \sigma_{2*}$. So σ_1 and σ_2 have the same minimal sets. The second one $\sigma_1 \sim_{Q^{pos}} \sigma_2$ implies that σ_1 and σ_2 have the same maximal sets.

5   Entailment between Basic Possibility Assignments

Basic possibility assignments are generalized sets. This section deals with the notion of entailment between pieces of information represented by basic possibility assignments, viewed as an inclusion between these generalized sets.

5.1   Definitions

Taking lesson from the additive case [9], there are two points of view for defining that $\mathcal{F}_{\sigma_1}$ is included in $\mathcal{F}_{\sigma_2}$:

Definition 1. $\mathcal{F}_{\sigma_1} \subseteq \mathcal{F}_{\sigma_2} \Leftrightarrow Bel_2^{pos} \leq Bel_1^{pos}$ and $\mathcal{F}_{\sigma_1} \bar{\subseteq} \mathcal{F}_{\sigma_2} \Leftrightarrow Q_1^{pos} \leq Q_2^{pos}$.

Proposition 1

$\mathcal{F}_{\sigma_1} \subseteq \mathcal{F}_{\sigma_2} \Leftrightarrow \forall B \in \mathcal{F}_{\sigma_2} \exists A \in \mathcal{F}_{\sigma_1}$ such that $A \subseteq B$ and $\sigma_2(B) \leq \sigma_1(A)$
$\mathcal{F}_{\sigma_1} \bar{\subseteq} \mathcal{F}_{\sigma_2} \Leftrightarrow \forall A \in \mathcal{F}_{\sigma_1} \exists B \in \mathcal{F}_{\sigma_2}$ such that $A \subseteq B$ and $\sigma_1(A) \leq \sigma_2(B)$.

Proof: Let us prove the first equivalence.
If $\mathcal{F}_{\sigma_1} \subseteq \mathcal{F}_{\sigma_2}$ then for all $B \in \mathcal{F}_{\sigma_2}$, $Bel_2^{pos}(B) = \vee_{A \subseteq B} \sigma_2(A) \leq Bel_1^{pos}(B) = \vee_{A \subseteq B} \sigma_1(A)$ which implies $\sigma_2(B) \leq \vee_{A \subseteq B} \sigma_1(A)$ and $\exists A \subseteq B$ such that $\sigma_2(B) \leq \sigma_1(A)$.
Reciproquely, if $\forall B \in \mathcal{F}_{\sigma_2} \exists A \in \mathcal{F}_{\sigma_1}$ such that $A \subseteq B$ and $\sigma_2(B) \leq \sigma_1(A)$ then $\sigma_2(B) \leq \vee_{C \subseteq A} \sigma_1(C) = Bel_1^{pos}(A) \leq Bel_1^{pos}(B)$. So for all $B \in \mathcal{F}_{\sigma_2}$ $\sigma_2(B) \leq Bel_1^{pos}(B)$. It is true particularly for all $C \subseteq B$ so $\sigma_2(C) \leq Bel_1^{pos}(C) \leq Bel_1^{pos}(B)$ which implies $Bel_2^{pos}(B) = \vee_{C \subseteq B} \sigma_2(C) \leq Bel_1^{pos}(B)$ i.e. $\mathcal{F}_{\sigma_1} \subseteq \mathcal{F}_{\sigma_2}$.

The proof of the second equivalence is similar using that $\mathcal{F}_{\sigma_1} \bar{\subseteq} \mathcal{F}_{\sigma_2}$ implies for any A, $\sigma_1(A) \leq \vee_{A \subseteq B} \sigma_2(B)$.
Note that the first equivalence states that each element of $\mathcal{F}_{\sigma_2}$ contains an element of $\mathcal{F}_{\sigma_1}$ which is at least as good as it. The other one is to consider that each element of $\mathcal{F}_{\sigma_1}$ is included in an element of $\mathcal{F}_{\sigma_2}$ which is at least as good as it.

Hence it seems natural to state the following definition.

Definition 5. $\sigma_1 \models \sigma_2$ if and only if $Bel_2^{pos} \leq Bel_1^{pos}$ and $Q_1^{pos} \leq Q_2^{pos}$.

Note that in Shafer evidence theory Pl appears when defining inclusion since $\mathcal{F}_{\sigma_1} \subseteq \mathcal{F}_{\sigma_2} \Leftrightarrow \forall A \subseteq \Omega, [Bel_1(A), Pl_1(A)] \subseteq [Bel_2(A), Pl_2(A)]$. In our context it is not the case, since we do not have $Bel_2^{pos} \leq Bel_1^{pos} \Leftrightarrow Pl_1^{pos} \leq Pl_2^{pos}$. In case σ_1 and σ_2 are two consonant basic possibility assignments (i.e. their respective focal elements are nested), we have $\sigma_1 \vDash \sigma_2 \Rightarrow Pl_1^{pos}(\{\omega\}) \leq Pl_2^{pos}(\{\omega\})$, i.e. a fuzzy set inclusion holds between the contour functions.

We conclude this part by defining the core and the support of $\mathcal{F}_\sigma$.

Definition 6. $core(\sigma) = \{A \subseteq \Omega \,|\, \sigma(A) = 1 \text{ and } \forall B, \text{ s.t. } B \subset A, \ \sigma(B) \neq 1\}$.
$sup(\sigma) = \{A \subseteq \Omega \,|\, \sigma(A) = 1 \text{ and } \forall B \subseteq \Omega \text{ s.t. } A \subset B, \ \sigma(B) \neq 1\}$.

5.2   Behavior of Cores and Supports with Respect to Entailment

Let us study the behavior of this entailment on the core and the support We have the following results.

Proposition 4. *Let σ_1 and σ_2 be two basic possibility assignments.*
If $\sigma_1 \vDash \sigma_2$ then
$$\forall A \in core(\sigma_2) \ \exists B \ B \subseteq A \text{ and } B \in core(\sigma_1),$$
$$\forall A \in sup(\sigma_1) \ \exists B \ A \subseteq B \text{ and } B \in sup(\sigma_2).$$

Proof: If we consider $A \in core(\sigma_2)$ then $\sigma_2(A) = 1 \leq \bigvee_{B \subseteq A} \sigma_1(B)$, so there exits $B \subseteq A$ such that $\sigma_1(B) = 1$, so A contains a set which belongs to $core(\sigma_1)$.

If we consider $A \in sup(\sigma_1)$ then $\sigma_1(A) = 1 \leq \bigvee_{A \subseteq B} \sigma_2(B)$, so there exists $A \subseteq B$ such that $\sigma_2(B) = 1$, which entails that A is contained in a set which belongs to $sup(\sigma_2)$.   ∎

The following examples prove that we may have $\sigma_1 \vDash \sigma_2$ with $core(\sigma_2) \nsubseteq core(\sigma_1)$ or $sup(\sigma_1) \nsubseteq sup(\sigma_2)$.

Example: $\Omega = \{1,2\}$, σ_1 and σ_2 are defined as follows:

	$\{1\}$	$\{2\}$	$\{1,2\}$
σ_1	1	0	1
σ_2	0	0	1

we have $\{1,2\} \in core(\sigma_2)$ and $\{1,2\} \notin core(\sigma_1)$.

Example: $\Omega = \{1,2\}$, σ_1 and σ_2 are defined as follows:

	$\{1\}$	$\{2\}$	$\{1,2\}$
σ_1	1	1	0
σ_2	0	1	1

we have $\{2\} \in sup(\sigma_1)$ and $\{2\} \notin sup(\sigma_2)$.

Proposition 5. *Let σ_1, σ_2 be two basic possibility assignments such that $\sigma_1 \vDash \sigma_2$ and $\sigma_2 \vDash \sigma_1$, hence $core(\sigma_1) = core(\sigma_2)$ and $sup(\sigma_1) = sup(\sigma_2)$.*

Proof: We consider $A \in core(\sigma_1)$. According to the previous property, $\sigma_2 \vDash \sigma_1$ implies $\exists B \ B \subseteq A$ and $B \in core(\sigma_2)$. If $B \neq A$, then $\sigma_1 \vDash \sigma_2$ implies $\exists C \ C \subseteq B$ and $C \in core(\sigma_1)$. We have $C \subset A$ which contradicts $A \in core(\sigma_1)$. So $B = A$ which entails $core(\sigma_1) \subseteq core(\sigma_2)$. Similarly, according to the symmetry of the proposition we can prove $core(\sigma_2) \subseteq core(\sigma_1)$.

We consider $A \in sup(\sigma_1)$. According to the previous property, $\sigma_1 \vDash \sigma_2$ implies $\exists B \ A \subseteq B$ and $B \in sup(\sigma_2)$. If $B \neq A$, then $\sigma_2 \vDash \sigma_1$ implies $\exists C \ B \subseteq C$ and $C \in sup(\sigma_1)$. We have $A \subset C$ which contradicts $A \in sup(\sigma_1)$. So $B = A$ which entails $sup(\sigma_1) \subseteq sup(\sigma_2)$. Similarly, we can prove $sup(\sigma_2) \subseteq \sup(\sigma_1)$.   ∎

Proposition 6. *In the binary case, if σ_1, σ_2 are two basic possibility assignments such that $core(\sigma_1) = core(\sigma_2)$ and $sup(\sigma_1) = sup(\sigma_2)$ then $\sigma_1 \vDash \sigma_2$ and $\sigma_2 \vDash \sigma_1$.*

Proof: We consider a set A. If there is no $B \subseteq A$ such that $\sigma_1(B) = 1$ then A does not contain a set which is in $core(\sigma_1)$. So A does not contain a set that is in $core(\sigma_2)$, so $\forall B \subseteq A$, $\sigma_2(B) = 0$. In consequence $Bel_1^{pos}(A) = Bel_2^{pos}(A) = 0$.

If there exists $B \subseteq A$ such that $\sigma_1(B) = 1$ then A contains a set that is in $core(\sigma_1)$. So A contains a set which is in $core(\sigma_2)$ so $Bel_1^{pos}(A) = Bel_2^{pos}(A) = 1$.

Similarly using the supports instead of the cores we can prove that $Q_1^{pos}(A) = Q_2^{pos}(B)$.   ∎

Note that $\sigma_1 \vDash \sigma_2$ and $\sigma_2 \vDash \sigma_1$ is equivalent to $\sigma_1 \sim_{Bel^{pos}} \sigma_2$ and $\sigma_1 \sim_{Q^{pos}} \sigma_2$. So if two basic possibility assignments are in the same equivalence class with respect to Bel^{pos} and Q^{pos} then they have the same core and the same support.

6 Combination Laws

In Shafer's evidence theory, beside the well-known Dempster rule of combination [14] which corresponds to the conjunction of random sets, other combination laws have been proposed for fusing two mass functions. In particular, the disjunctive rule of combination appears to be another basic rule [9]. It has been shown that the Dempster rule of combination corresponds to the product of the commonality functions, while the disjunctive rule corresponds to the product of the belief functions. As shown below, these results have counterparts in the qualitative maxitive setting.

6.1 The Definitions

Thus, in our context, it is natural to define the following conjunctive and disjunctive combination laws.

Definition 7. *Let σ_1 and σ_2 be two basic possibility assignments.*

The combination rule is:
$(\sigma_1 \otimes \sigma_2)(\emptyset) = 0$ *and* $\forall A \subseteq \Omega$, $(\sigma_1 \otimes \sigma_2)(A) = \bigvee_{B \cap C = A \neq \emptyset} \sigma_1(B) \wedge \sigma_2(C)$.
The condition rule is:
$(\sigma_1 \oplus \sigma_2)(\emptyset) = 0$ *and* $\forall A \subseteq \Omega$, $(\sigma_1 \oplus \sigma_2)(A) = \bigvee_{B \cup C = A \neq \emptyset} \sigma_1(B) \wedge \sigma_2(C)$.

Note that the first combination rule was already suggested in [8].

The set function $\sigma_1 \otimes \sigma_2$ is a basic possibility assignment if and only if there exists B and C such that $B \cap C \neq \emptyset$ and $\sigma_1(B) = \sigma_2(C) = 1$. For example if either $\sigma_1 \vDash \sigma_2$ or $\sigma_2 \vDash \sigma_1$ then $\sigma_1 \otimes \sigma_2$ is a basic possibility assignment.

In our context $\sigma_1 \oplus \sigma_2$ is a basic possibility assignment because the basic possibility assignments are supposed to be normal.

6.2 Properties of the Combination Rule

Commutativity. Using the definition it is easy to see that $\otimes$ is commutative: $\sigma_1 \otimes \sigma_2 = \sigma_2 \otimes \sigma_1$ for all σ_1, σ_2.

Neutral element. Let σ_0 be the basic possibility assignment equal to 0 everywhere except on Ω. σ_0 is neutral with respect to $\otimes$ i.e. $\sigma_0 \otimes \sigma = \sigma$ for all σ: $\sigma_0 \otimes \sigma(A) = \bigvee_{B \cap C = A} \sigma_0(B) \wedge \sigma(C)$, if $B \neq \Omega$ then $\sigma_0(B) \wedge \sigma(C) = 0$ and if $B = \Omega$ then $\sigma_0(B) \wedge \sigma(C) = \sigma(C)$.

Associativity. We consider three basic possibility assignments σ_1, σ_2 and σ_3. We have to prove that for all A, $((\sigma_1 \otimes \sigma_2) \otimes \sigma_3)(A) = (\sigma_1 \otimes (\sigma_2 \otimes \sigma_3))(A)$. These two expressions are equal to $\bigvee_{B \cap C \cap D = A} \sigma_1(B) \wedge \sigma_2(C) \wedge \sigma_3(D)$.

We denote $Bel_1^{pos} \oplus Bel_2^{pos}$ the possibilistic belief associated to $\sigma_1 \oplus \sigma_2$ and $Q_1^{pos} \otimes Q_2^{pos}$ the possibilistic commonality function associated to $\sigma_1 \otimes \sigma_2$. The following properties which have counterparts in Dempster Shafer theory are still satisfied in our context.

Proposition 7. $Bel_1^{pos} \oplus Bel_2^{pos} = Bel_1^{pos} \wedge Bel_2^{pos}$.

Proof: First let us prove that $Bel_1^{pos} \oplus Bel_2^{pos} \leq Bel_1^{pos} \wedge Bel_2^{pos}$.

$$Bel_1^{pos} \oplus Bel_2^{pos}(A) = \bigvee_{B \subseteq A}(\sigma_1 \oplus \sigma_2)(B)$$
$$= \bigvee_{B \subseteq A} \bigvee_{C \cup D = B}(\sigma_1(C) \wedge \sigma_2(D))$$
$$= \bigvee_{C \cup D \subseteq A}(\sigma_1(C) \wedge \sigma_2(D))$$

If we consider C and D such that $C \cup D \subseteq A$. We have $\sigma_1(C) \leq \bigvee_{C \subseteq A} \sigma_1(C)$ and $\sigma_2(D) \leq \bigvee_{D \subseteq A} \sigma_2(D)$ so $\sigma_1(C) \wedge \sigma_2(D) \leq (\bigvee_{C \subseteq A} \sigma_1(C)) \wedge (\bigvee_{D \subseteq A} \sigma_2(D)) = Bel_1^{pos}(A) \wedge Bel_2^{pos}(A)$ which implies $Bel_1^{pos} \oplus Bel_2^{pos} \leq Bel_1^{pos} \wedge Bel_2^{pos}$.

Now let us prove that $Bel_1^{pos} \oplus Bel_2^{pos} \geq Bel_1^{pos} \wedge Bel_2^{pos}$.
$Bel_1^{pos}(A) \wedge Bel_2^{pos}(A) = (\bigvee_{C \subseteq A} \sigma_1(C)) \wedge (\bigvee_{D \subseteq A} \sigma_2(D)) = \sigma_1(C_0) \wedge \sigma_2(D_0)$ where $C_0 \cup D_0 \subseteq A$. We have $\sigma_1(C_0) \wedge \sigma_2(D_0) \leq \bigvee_{C \cup D \subseteq A}(\sigma_1(C) \wedge \sigma_2(D)) = Bel_1^{pos} \oplus Bel_2^{pos}(A)$. ∎

Proposition 8. $Q_1^{pos} \otimes Q_2^{pos} = Q_1^{pos} \wedge Q_2^{pos}$.

Proof: This proof is similar to the previous one.
$(Q_1^{pos} \otimes Q_2^{pos})(A) = \bigvee_{A \subseteq C \cap D}(\sigma_1(C) \wedge \sigma_2(D))$, if we consider C and D such that $A \subseteq C \cap D$ we have $\sigma_1(C) \wedge \sigma_2(D) \leq (\bigvee_{A \subseteq C} \sigma_1(C)) \wedge (\bigvee_{A \subseteq D} \sigma_2(D)) = Q_1^{pos}(A) \wedge Q_2^{pos}(A)$. So $Q_1^{pos} \otimes Q_2^{pos} \leq Q_1^{pos} \wedge Q_2^{pos}$.

For the other inequality, $Q_1^{pos}(A) \wedge Q_2^{pos}(A) = \sigma_1(C_0) \wedge \sigma_2(D_0)$ where $A \subseteq C_0 \cap D_0$. So we have $\sigma_1(C_0) \wedge \sigma_2(D_0) \leq \bigvee_{A \subseteq C \cap D}(\sigma_1(C) \wedge \sigma_2(D)) = (Q_1^{pos} \otimes Q_2^{pos})(A)$ which entails $Q_1^{pos} \wedge Q_2^{pos} \leq Q_1^{pos} \otimes Q_2^{pos}$. ∎

7 Concluding Remarks

In this paper, we have outlined a presentation of the basic properties of a qualitative representation setting that extends possibility theory by dealing, in a maxitive way, with possibility distributions on the power set of the frame of discernment. Then, a basic possibility assignment may be seen as a collection of a series of possibility qualifications [20] of events of interest. Here rather than selecting a particular possibility distribution that agrees with the qualification, we keep the specification has such, still being able to process it by computing measures associated to events, by defining entailments, and fusing information. This is certainly a very weak way of specifying information, but which may make sense especially in discrete universes.

This qualitative setting has been obtained by substituting the additive structure of Shafer's evidence theory with a maxitive structure. It is rather remarkable that while replacing the sum with the maximum, we preserve good structural properties that parallel the situation in the additive case. It is clear that we may have replaced the sum by the minimum, instead of the maximum, thus obtaining a minitive structure with quite similar properties, but with a different interpretation. For instance, considering $Bel^{nec}(A) = \bigwedge_{B \subseteq A} \sigma(B)$ clearly suggests that σ should be now understood as a necessity qualification. But here, in contrast with possibilistic logic [6] where the necessity measure is defined from a possibility distribution, it is only the pieces of knowledge that are explicitly stated through σ that are taken into account in the inference.

Beyond the results presented in this paper, many questions remain. Let us mention some of them. In Shafer's evidence theory the separable belief functions are decomposable in terms of simple support functions and this decomposition is unique. It seems also natural to define simple support functions in our context, but it is not clear if the decomposition will always be possible and unique. Another question is the counterpart in our setting (or in the minitive context) of the lower and upper additivity properties of belief and plausibility functions, which have been already shown to have a counterpart in a logic of incomplete information [3].

Besides, we have recently proposed a method to describe acceptable objects by means of Sugeno integral [13]. More precisely considering objects described by combinations of properties we have investigated the potential use of Sugeno integrals as a representation tool for these objects. The Sugeno integral was defined using the measure which is named Bel^{pos} in this paper. We expect that the entailment between the basic possibility assignments help us to better understand the entailment between the Sugeno integrals in order to understand how the objects are selected with the Sugeno integrals. Still another direction for further research is the use of the equivalence classes defined with the qualitative Möbius transform in order to propose a method with an acceptable complexity.

References

1. Banon, G.J.: Constructive decomposition of fuzzy measures in terms of possibility or necessity measures. In: Proc. 6th Int. Fuz. Syst. Ass. Cong., Sao Paulo, pp. 217–220 (1995)
2. Benferhat, S., Dubois, D., Kaci, S., Prade, H.: Modeling positive and negative information in possibility theory. Inter. J. of Intelligent Systems 23, 1094–1118 (2008)

3. Banerjee, M., Dubois, D.: A simple modal logic for reasoning about revealed beliefs. In: Sossai, C., Chemello, G. (eds.) ECSQARU 2009. LNCS, vol. 5590, pp. 805–816. Springer, Heidelberg (2009)
4. Calvo, T., De Baets, B.: Aggregation operators defined by k-order additive/maxitive fuzzy measures. Int. J. of Uncert., Fuzz. & Knowledge-Based Syst. 6, 533–550 (1998)
5. Dubois, D., Fargier, H.: Capacity refinements and their application to qualitative decision evaluation. In: Sossai, C., Chemello, G. (eds.) ECSQARU 2009. LNCS, vol. 5590, pp. 311–322. Springer, Heidelberg (2009)
6. Dubois, D., Lang, J., Prade, H.: Automated reasoning using possibilistic logic: semantics, belief revision and variable certainty weights. IEEE Trans. on Data and Knowledge Engineering 6, 64–71 (1994)
7. Dubois, D., Prade, H.: Upper and lower possibilities induced by a multivalued mapping. In: Proc. IFAC Symp. on Fuzzy Information, Knowledge Representation and Decision Analysis, Marseille, July 19-21, pp. 174–152 (1983); In: Sanchez, E. (ed.) Fuzzy Information, Knowledge Representation and Decision Analysis. Pergamon Press, Oxford (1984)
8. Dubois, D., Prade, H.: Evidence measures based on fuzzy information. Automatica 21, 547–562 (1985)
9. Dubois, D., Prade, H.: A set-theoretic view of belief functions. Logical operations and approximations by fuzzy sets. Int. J. General Systems 12, 193–226 (1986)
10. Dubois, D., Prade, H.: Possibility theory: qualitative and quantitative aspects. In: Gabbay, D., Smets, P. (eds.) Quantified Representation of Uncertainty and Imprecision. Handbook of Defeasible Reasoning and Uncertainty Management Systems, vol. 1, pp. 169–226. Kluwer Acad. Publ., Dordrecht (1998)
11. Grabisch, M.: The symmetric Sugeno integral. Fuzzy Sets and Systems 139, 473–490 (2003)
12. Grabisch, M.: The Moebius transform on symmetric ordered structures and its application to capacities on finite sets. Discrete Mathematics 287, 17–34 (2004)
13. Prade, H., Rico, A.: Describing acceptable objects by means of Sugeno integrals. In: Proc. 2nd IEEE International Conference of Soft Computing and Pattern Recognition (SoCPaR 2010), Cergy-Pontoise, December 7-10 (2010)
14. Shafer, G.: A Mathematical Theory of Evidence. Princeton Univ. Press, NJ (1976)
15. Sugeno, M.: Fuzzy measures and fuzzy integrals: a survey. In: Gupta, M., Saridis, G., Gaines, B. (eds.) Fuzzy Automata and Decision Processes, pp. 89–102. North-Holland, Amsterdam (1977)
16. Tsiporkova, E., De Baets, B.: A general framework for upper and lower possibilities and necessities. Inter. J. of Uncert., Fuzz. and Knowledge-Based Syst. 6, 1–34 (1998)
17. Yang, G., Wu, X.: Synthesized Fault Diagnosis Method Based on Fuzzy Logic and D-S Evidence Theory. In: Huang, D.-S., Heutte, L., Loog, M. (eds.) ICIC 2007. LNCS (LNAI), vol. 4682, pp. 1024–1031. Springer, Heidelberg (2007)
18. Zadeh, L.A.: Quantified fuzzy semantics. Information Sciences 3, 159–176 (1971)
19. Zadeh, L.A.: Fuzzy sets as a basis for a theory of possibility. Fuzzy Sets and Systems 1, 3–28 (1978)
20. Zadeh, L.A.: PRUF: A meaning representation language for natural languages. Int. J. of Man-Machine Studies 10, 395–460 (1978)

A Preference Query Model
Based on a Fusion of Local Orders

Patrick Bosc, Olivier Pivert, and Grégory Smits

Irisa – Enssat/IUT, University of Rennes 1
Technopole Anticipa 22305 Lannion Cedex France
{bosc,pivert}@enssat.fr, gregory.smits@univ-rennes1.fr

Abstract. In this paper, we define an approach to database preference queries based on the fusion of local orders. The situation considered is that of queries involving incommensurable partial preferences, possibly associated with scoring functions. The basic principle is to rank the tuples according to each partial preference, then to merge the local orders obtained, using a linear function for aggregating the local scores attached to the tuples. Basically, a local score expresses the extent to which a tuple is strictly better than many others and not strictly worse than many others with respect to the partial preference attached to a given attribute. This model refines Pareto order for queries of the Skyline type.

1 Introduction

Approaches to database preference queries may be classified into two categories according to their qualitative or quantitative nature [1]. In the latter, preferences are expressed quantitatively by a monotone scoring function (the overall score is positively correlated with partial scores). Representatives of this family of approaches are top-k queries [2], fuzzy-set-based approaches (e.g., [3]), and the model proposed in [4]. However, it is well known that scoring functions cannot represent all preferences that are strict partial orders [5], not even those that occur in database applications in a natural way [6]. Another issue is that devising the scoring function may not be simple. In the qualitative approach, preferences are defined through binary preference relations. Since binary preference relations can be defined in terms of scoring functions, the qualitative approach is more general than the quantitative one. Among the representatives of this second family of approaches, let us mention those relying on a dominance relation, e.g. Pareto order, as *Preference SQL* [7] and Skyline queries [8].

In [9], we introduced a preference query model inspired by the notion of outranking which was initially proposed in a decision-making context [10]. The approach assumes available a set of scoring functions which translate partial preferences that are supposed to be incommensurable. The proposal relies on an outranking measure $out(t, t')$ which aggregates the numbers of (weighted) partial preferences either concordant, discordant or indifferent with a given ordering between two tuples t and t'. Finally, the tuples are ordered on the basis of their global "quality", i.e., a tuple is all the more preferred as it outranks

W. Liu (Ed.): ECSQARU 2011, LNAI 6717, pp. 725–736, 2011.
© Springer-Verlag Berlin Heidelberg 2011

many other tuples (and is not outranked by many), and the mechanism proposed yields a total order (unlike Pareto-order based approaches). A variant of this model, which uses fuzzy concordance, discordance and indifference relations, is described in [11]. Both variants refine the (Pareto) order obtained while using regular Skyline queries. A drawback of the outranking-based preference query model is that queries have a data complexity in $\theta(n^2)$ since they involve pairwise tuple comparisons. On the other hand, recent works on Skyline queries show that their evaluation — whose data complexity is also quadratic if a straightforward evaluation method is used — can be significantly optimized using a strategy based on presorting [12,13].

In the present paper, we propose an approach which shares some concepts with the outranking-based model described in [9,11] — and which also refines Pareto order —, but leads to queries having a linear data complexity. The basic principle is to rank the tuples according to each partial preference, then to merge the local orders obtained, using a linear function for aggregating the local scores attached to the tuples. A local score does not correspond to a rank, but rather expresses the extent to which a tuple is strictly better than many others and not strictly worse than many others with respect to the partial preference attached to the considered attribute. This approach extends the well-known voting rule called Borda method in the following respects: i) it is able to deal with ties and "pseudo-ties" (i.e., ties defined according to an indifference relation), ii) it allows for a graded view of the notions "better" and "worse".

The remainder of this paper is structured as follows. Section 2 describes two related preference query models, namely that based on Pareto order and that based on the notion of outranking. Section 3 is devoted to three variants of the new approach we propose, which is based on the fusion of local orders. Section 4 deals with query evaluation, whereas Section 5 concludes the paper and outlines perspectives for future research.

2   Related Approaches

2.1   Pareto-Order-Based Approaches

Let us first recall the general principle of queries based on the use of Pareto order. Let $\{G_1, G_2, ..., G_n\}$ be a set of the atomic preferences. We denote by $t \succ_{G_i} t'$ (resp. $t \succeq_{G_i} t'$) the statement "tuple t satisfies preference G_i better than (resp. as least as good as) tuple t'". Using Pareto order, a tuple t dominates another tuple t' iff

$$\forall i \in \{1, ..., n\}, t \succeq_{G_i} t' \text{ and } \exists k \in \{1, ..., n\}, t \succ_{G_k} t'.$$

In other words, t dominates t' if it is at least as good as t' regarding every preference, and is strictly better than t' regarding at least one preference. The following example uses the syntax of the language *Preference SQL* [7], which is a typical representative of a Pareto-based approach.

Example 1. Let us consider a relation *car* of schema (*make, category, price, color, mileage*) whose extension is given in Table 1, and the query:

select * **from** *car* **where** *mileage* ≤ 20,000
preferring (*category* = 'SUV' **else** *category* = 'roadster') **and** (*make* = 'VW' **else** *make* = 'Ford' **else** *make* = 'Opel');

The idea is to retain the tuples which are not dominated in the sense of the *preferring* clause. Here, t_1, t_4, t_5, t_6 and t_7 are discarded since they are Pareto-dominated by t_2 and t_3. On the other hand, t_2 and t_3 are incomparable and the final answer is $\{t_2, t_3\}$.◊

Table 1. An extension of relation *car*

	make	category	price	color	mileage
t_1	Opel	roadster	4500	blue	20,000
t_2	Ford	SUV	4000	red	20,000
t_3	VW	roadster	5000	red	10,000
t_4	Opel	roadster	5000	red	8,000
t_5	Fiat	roadster	4500	red	16,000
t_6	Renault	sedan	5500	blue	24,000
t_7	Seat	sedan	4000	green	12,000

When the number of dimensions on which preferences are expressed gets high, many tuples may become incomparable. Several approaches have been proposed to define an order for two such tuples in the context of skylines, based on:

- the number of other tuples that each of the two tuples dominates (notion of k-representative dominance proposed by Lin *et al.* [14]) or
- some preference order of the attributes; see for instance the notions of k-dominance and k-frequency introduced by Chan *et al.* [15,16].

See also [17] where different fuzzy extensions of skyline queries are proposed and discussed.

2.2 Outranking-Based Approach

The approach proposed in [11] assumes that a scoring function is associated with each partial preference, but the preferences do not have to be commensurable. The outranking relation which is the basis of the approach relies on two basic notions, concordance and discordance. Concordance represents the proportion of preferences which validate the assertion "t is preferred to t'", denoted by $t \succ t'$, whereas discordance represents the proportion of preferences which contradict this assertion.

Let A_1, A_2, ..., A_n be the attributes concerned respectively by the set of preferences $G = \{G_1, G_2, ..., G_n\}$. Let g_1, g_2, ..., g_n be the scoring functions associated to preferences G_1, G_2, ..., G_n respectively.

Indifferent preferences: Each preference G_j may be associated with a threshold q_j. Preference G_j is indifferent with the statement "t is preferred to t'" iff $|g_j(t.A_j) - g_j(t'.A_j)| \leq q_j$. This notion makes it possible to take into account uncertainty or tolerance on the definition of the elementary preferences.

Concordant preferences: G_j is concordant with the statement "t is preferred to t'" iff $g_j(t.A_j) > g_j(t'.A_j) + q_j$.

Discordant preferences: Preference G_j is discordant with the statement "t is preferred to t'" iff $g_j(t'.A_j) > g_j(t.A_j) + q_j$.

We denote by $C(t, t')$ (resp. $I(t, t')$, resp. $D(t, t')$) the set of concordant (resp. indifferent, discordant) preferences from G w.r.t. $t \succ t'$. One may also attach a weight w_j to each preference G_j expressing its importance. It is assumed that the sum of the weights equals 1. Let us define:

$$conc(t, t') = \sum_{G_j \in C(t, t')} w_j,$$

$$disc(t, t') = \sum_{G_j \in D(t, t')} w_j, \text{ and}$$

$$ind(t, t') = \sum_{G_j \in I(t, t')} w_j$$

where w_j is the importance attached to preference G_j. The outranking degree attached to the statement $t \succeq t'$ (meaning "t is at least as good as t'"), denoted by $out(t, t')$, reflects the truth of the statement: most of the important criteria are concordant *or indifferent* with $t \succeq t'$ and few of the important criteria are discordant with $t \succeq t'$. It is evaluated by the following formula:

$$out(t, t') = conc(t, t') + ind(t, t') = 1 - disc(t, t'). \tag{1}$$

Let us denote by r the relation concerned. The tuples of r can be ranked on the basis of an aggregation of the outranking degrees:

1. for every tuple t, one computes the degree:

$$\mu(t) = \frac{\Sigma_{t' \in r \setminus \{t\}} out(t, t')}{|r| - 1}$$

   where $|r|$ denotes the cardinality of r. Degree $\mu_1(t)$ expresses the extent to which t is better to (or as good as) most of the other tuples from r, where the fuzzy quantifier *most* is assumed to be defined as

$$\mu_{most}(x) = x, \forall x \in [0, 1].$$

2. one ranks the tuples in increasing order of $\mu(t)$.

It is important to emphasize that the ranking obtained refines Pareto order when $\forall j, q_j = 0$, i.e., for Pareto-order-based queries.

Example 2. Let us consider the extension of the relation *car* from Table 1 and the preferences:

for make:

$1/\{VW\} \succ 0.8/\{Audi, BMW\} \succ 0.6/\{Seat\} \succ 0.4/\{Opel, Ford\} \succ 0.2/other;$

$q_{make} = 0.2; w_{make} = 0.2;$

for category:

$1/\{sedan\} \succ 0.7/\{roadster\} \succ 0.6/\{coupe\} \succ 0.4/\{SUV\} \succ 0.2/other;$

$q_{cat} = 0.2; w_{cat} = 0.3;$

for price:

$score(price) = 1$ if price ≤ 4000, 0 if price ≥ 6000, linear in-between;

$q_{pr} = 0.2; w_{pr} = 0.2;$

for color:

$1/\{blue, black\} \succ 0.8/\{red\} \succ 0.5/\{yellow, green\} \succ 0.3/\{white\};$

$q_{col} = 0.2; w_{col} = 0.1;$

for mileage:

$score(mileage) = 1$ if mileage $\leq 15,000$, 0 if mileage $\geq 20,000$, linear in-between;

$q_{mi} = 0.2; w_{mi} = 0.2;$

The satisfaction degrees associated with the data from Table 1 and related to the partial preferences are given in Table 2. The final result is:

$$0.87/t_7 > 0.77/t_5 > 0.73/t_4 > 0.67/t_3 > 0.6/\{t_1, t_6\} > 0.53/t_2. \quad \diamond$$

Table 2. Satisfaction degrees related to the partial preferences

	make	category	price	color	mileage
t_1	0.4	0.7	0.75	1	0
t_2	0.4	0.4	1	0.8	0
t_3	1	0.7	0.5	0.8	0.5
t_4	0.4	0.7	0.5	0.8	1
t_5	0.2	0.7	0.75	0.8	0.8
t_6	0.2	1	0.25	1	0
t_7	0.6	1	1	0.5	1

A variant of this approach is proposed in [9] where i) the comparison of tuples is based on discriminating preferences only ("strict" preference model), ii) the transition between the notions of concordance and indifference (resp. indifference and discordance) is fuzzy whereas it is crisp in [11].

A somewhat related approach, also based on a pairwise comparison of objects, is presented in [18]. The authors consider a voting problem where voters have expressed their preferences on a single set of objects, in the shape of *strict* partial order relations. Their approach aims at extracting a unique strict partial order relation corresponding to a social set of preferences, by determining the minimum number of votes a pairwise preferences should receive in order to qualify as a social pairwise preference. The main differences with respect to the approach presented further concern: i) the use of the number of votes instead of the number

of objects strictly preferred to a given object, as the central concept for building
the overall order, ii) the fact that the input partial order relations are *strict*
(which implies the absence of ties).

3   A New Approach Based on a Fusion of Local Orders

As mentioned before, the outranking-based approach assumes that a scoring
function is associated with each partial preference. In the order-based approach
proposed here, such an assumption is not necessary. In the basic version (cf.
Subsection 3.1), one only assumes available an ordering — which may include
ties — of the tuples for each partial preference. Therefore, this basic approach is
purely qualitative. If scoring functions are available (cf. Subsection 3.2), they do
not have to be commensurable (as in the outranking-based approach). Unlike the
outranking-based approach, however, the data complexity of query evaluation is
not in $\theta(n^2)$ but in $\theta(n)$ — indeed, we will see that the different ordered lists
do not even have to be constructed. The major difference with respect to the
outranking-based approach is that the evaluation is made column by column
(i.e., attribute by attribute) instead of relying on a pairwise comparison of the
rows (i.e., of the tuples).

Since rankings without scores are not very informative — they say nothing
about the "distance" (in terms of satisfaction) between two elements —, we
propose a gradual version of the model (cf. Subsection 3.3), which takes into
account the extent to which an attribute value is preferred to another one in the
computation of the scores (partial and global) attached to a tuple.

3.1   Basic Version

Let n be the number of tuples in relation r, and p the number of attributes
on which a preference is expressed in the query. Let $\{A_1, \ldots, A_p\}$ be these
attributes (i.e., a partial preference is associated with every A_i).

The algorithm is as follows:

1 **for every** tuple t **do**
2      $\sigma_1 \leftarrow 0$; $\sigma_2 \leftarrow 0$;
3   **for every** attribute A_i **do**
4          $\sigma_1 = \sigma_1 +$ number of tuples strictly before t on A_i;
5          $\sigma_2 = \sigma_2 +$ number of tuples strictly after t on A_i;
6   **done**;
7      $\sigma(t) = \frac{1}{2} \cdot \left(\frac{\sigma_2 - \sigma_1}{p \cdot (n-1)} + 1 \right)$
8 **done**;
9 rank the tuples in decreasing order of their σ value;

Remark 1. If $\sigma(t) = \frac{\sigma_2 - \sigma_1}{p \cdot (n-1)}$ were used instead, one would get a degree in
$[-1, 1]$ instead of $[0, 1]$, thus the normalization.

Remark 2. The final degree $\sigma(t)$ does not have the meaning of a satisfaction degree, but rather indicates the extent to which there are many tuples which are (partially) worse than t and few tuples better than it.

It is straightforward to prove that the order obtained refines Pareto order.

Proof. Let us consider a pair (t, t') such that t is better (dominates) t' in the sense of Pareto order. One thus have $\sigma_1(t) < \sigma_1(t')$ and $\sigma_2(t) > \sigma_2(t')$. Hence $\sigma(t) > \sigma(t')$. ∎

Example 3 (without scoring functions). Let r be a relation involving four attributes A_1, A_2, A_3, A_4 and six tuples $t_1 \ldots t_6$. Let us consider the partial preferences:

- $A_1 : \{t_1\} \succ \{t_4\} \succ \{t_2\} \succ \{t_3, t_6\} \succ \{t_5\}$
- $A_2 : \{t_4\} \succ \{t_3\} \succ \{t_1, t_6\} \succ \{t_5\} \succ \{t_2\}$
- $A_3 : \{t_5\} \succ \{t_1, t_3, t_4\} \succ \{t_6\} \succ \{t_2\}$
- $A_4 : \{t_4\} \succ \{t_2\} \succ \{t_6\} \succ \{t_1\} \succ \{t_5\} \succ \{t_3\}$.

One gets:

- for $t_1 : \sigma_1 = 0 + 2 + 1 + 3 = 6$, $\sigma_2 = 5 + 2 + 2 + 2 = 11$, $\sigma = 0.62$
- for $t_2 : \sigma_1 = 2 + 5 + 5 + 1 = 13$, $\sigma_2 = 3 + 0 + 0 + 4 = 7$, $\sigma = 0.35$
- for $t_3 : \sigma_1 = 3 + 1 + 1 + 5 = 10$, $\sigma_2 = 1 + 4 + 2 + 0 = 7$, $\sigma = 0.42$
- for $t_4 : \sigma_1 = 1 + 0 + 1 + 0 = 2$, $\sigma_2 = 4 + 5 + 2 + 5 = 16$, $\sigma = 0.85$
- for $t_5 : \sigma_1 = 5 + 4 + 0 + 4 = 13$, $\sigma_2 = 0 + 1 + 5 + 1 = 7$, $\sigma = 0.35$
- for $t_6 : \sigma_1 = 3 + 2 + 4 + 2 = 11$, $\sigma_2 = 1 + 2 + 1 + 3 = 7$, $\sigma = 0.4$

and the final result is: $0.85/t_4 \succ 0.62/t_1 \succ 0.42/t_3 \succ 0.4/t_6 \succ 0.35/\{t_2, t_5\}$.   ◇

Remark 3. Notice that in the absence of ties, this approach is equivalent to the Borda method since in this case σ_2 is the Borda count and $\sigma_1 + \sigma_2 = (n-1)p$.

3.2   Taking Scoring Functions into Account

In the case where one has available a scoring function associated with each partial preference, one may rewrite lines 4 and 5 of the algorithm Section 3.1 with:

$$\sigma_1 = \sigma_1 + |\{t' \in r \mid \mu_{A_i}(t') > \mu_{A_i}(t)\}|$$

$$\sigma_2 = \sigma_2 + |\{t' \in r \mid \mu_{A_i}(t') < \mu_{A_i}(t)\}|.$$

Example 4. Let us consider the relation represented in Table 3. One assumes that the scales used for the scores are:

- for A_1: $A \succ B \succ \ldots \succ E$
- for A_2: $100 \succ 99 \ldots \succ 0$
- for A_3: $20 \succ 19 \succ \ldots \succ 0$.

Table 3. Scores attached to the tuples of relation r

	μ_{A_1}	μ_{A_2}	μ_{A_3}
t_1	A	100	15
t_2	E	50	11
t_3	B	100	9
t_4	B	50	15

One gets:

- for t_1 : $\sigma_1 = 0 + 0 + 0 = 0$, $\sigma_2 = 3 + 2 + 2 = 7$, $\sigma = 0.89$
- for t_2 : $\sigma_1 = 3 + 2 + 2 = 7$, $\sigma_2 = 0 + 0 + 1 = 1$, $\sigma = 0.17$
- for t_3 : $\sigma_1 = 1 + 0 + 3 = 4$, $\sigma_2 = 1 + 2 + 0 = 3$, $\sigma = 0.44$
- for t_4 : $\sigma_1 = 1 + 2 + 0 = 3$, $\sigma_2 = 1 + 0 + 2 = 3$, $\sigma = 0.5$

and the final result is: $0.89/t_1 \succ 0.5/t_4 \succ 0.44/t_3 \succ 0.17/t_2$.   ◇

Remark 4. With a Pareto-order-based approach, one would get the result $\{t_1\}$.

One can refine the approach further by considering an indiscernability area instead of strict equality for defining ties (cf. the notion of indifference in the outranking-based approach). Besides, one may also generalize the approach by assigning an importance degree to each partial preference, and one then computes σ_1 and σ_2 by means of a weighted mean instead of a sum, thus lines 4 and 5 of the algorithm from Subsection 3.1 become:

$$\sigma_1 = \sigma_1 + |\{t' \in r \mid \mu_{A_i}(t') > \mu_{A_i}(t) + q_i\}| \times w_i$$

$$\sigma_2 = \sigma_2 + |\{t' \in r \mid \mu_{A_i}(t') + q_i < \mu_{A_i}(t)\}| \times w_i.$$

Example 5 (with indifference thresholds and importance weights). With the query from Example 2 and the data from Table 1, one gets:

- for t_1: $\sigma_1 = 1 \times 0.2 + 2 \times 0.3 + 2 \times 0.2 + 0 + 4 \times 0.2 = 2$
  $\sigma_2 = 0 + 1 \times 0.3 + 2 \times 0.2 + 1 \times 0.1 + 0 = 0.8$
  thus $\sigma = 0.43$,
- for t_2: $\sigma_1 = 2.8$, $\sigma_2 = 1.1$, $\sigma = 0.41$, etc

and the final result is:

$$0.66/t_7 > 0.52/\{t_3, t_5\} > 0.49/t_4 > 0.46/t_6 > 0.43/t_1 > 0.41/t_2.$$

Notice that this order is very similar to that obtained with the outranking-based approach (cf. Example 2), excepted for tuples t_4 and t_5 which get a slightly worse ranking as they are indifferently preferred to most of the other tuples.   ◇

The approach proposed here could also be used to merge the lists of documents produced by different search engines (or information retrieval systems) for a given query. Bordogna and Pasi also proposed an approach with such an objective and the same general philosophy [19], but they use a so-called Induced

Ordered Average (IOWA) operator to merge the ordered lists. Another important difference wrt our approach is that they aggregate the *positions* of the documents in the lists.

Another type of approach could consist in looking for the global order which has the highest average correlation degree (in the sense of the classical correlation indices, e.g., Kendall's τ or Spearman's indice, see, e.g., [20]) with the orders associated with the different partial preferences. However, such an approach is likely to be intractable.

3.3 Gradual Extension

An improvement of the previous approach is to refine σ_1 and σ_2 by taking into account a certain form of graduality in the interpretation of the notions "worse" and "better". Each scoring function μ_{A_i} may be associated with an ordinal scale $l_{i,1} \succ l_{i,2} \succ \ldots \succ l_{i,n_i}$. One defines: $\varphi(l_{i,j}, l_{i,k}) = max(k-j, 0)$. The computation of σ_1 (resp. σ_2) (cf. lines 4 and 5 of the algorithm from Subsection 3.1) can now be refined the following way:

$$\sigma_1 = \sigma_1 + \sum_{t' \in r \setminus \{t\}} \frac{\varphi(\mu_{A_i}(t'), \mu_{A_i}(t))}{n_i - 1}$$

$$\sigma_2 = \sigma_2 + \sum_{t' \in r \setminus \{t\}} \frac{\varphi(\mu_{A_i}(t), \mu_{A_i}(t'))}{n_i - 1}.$$

Example 6. With this new definition and the data from Table 3, one gets:

- for t_1 : $\sigma_1 = 0 + 0 + 0 = 0$, $\sigma_2 = \frac{1+1+4}{4} + \frac{50+50}{100} + \frac{4+6}{20} = 3$, $\sigma = 0.67$
- for t_2 : $\sigma_1 = \frac{4+3+3}{4} + \frac{50+50}{100} + \frac{4+4}{20} = 3.9$, $\sigma_2 = 0 + 0 + \frac{2}{20} = 0.1$, $\sigma = 0.29$
- for t_3 : $\sigma_1 = \frac{1}{4} + 0 + \frac{6+2+6}{20} = 0.95$, $\sigma_2 = \frac{3}{4} + \frac{50+50}{100} + 0 = 1.75$, $\sigma = 0.54$
- for t_4 : $\sigma_1 = \frac{1}{4} + \frac{50+50}{100} + 0 = 1.25$, $\sigma_2 = \frac{3}{4} + 0 + \frac{4+6}{20} = 1.25$, $\sigma = 0.5$

and the final result (which differs from that previously obtained) is:

$$0.67/t_1 \succ 0.54/t_3 \succ 0.5/t_4 \succ 0.29/t_2. \diamond$$

Remark 5. This approach still refines Pareto order.

4 Query Processing

The idea is the following:

- for each class L_{ij} — corresponding to a distinct score — of each partial preference P_i (associated with an attribute A_i), one runs a query in order to compute the number of tuples t from relation r such that $t.A_i \in L_{ij}$. In order to perform this step, either one has available an extended *group by* clause as that proposed in [21] (it is the ideal solution since a single query is then necessary to compute the cardinalities of all the classes associated with a given attribute), or one runs as many queries as there are classes associated with the attribute. This latter solution is used in the example hereafter. Notice that still another solution would be to build a temporary table containing the scores (but such a table can be very large). In the case where P_i is modelled by a fuzzy set, it is necessary to first discretize the degree in order to have a finite number of classes (one may take for instance $0.1 =]0, 0.1], 0.2 =]0.1, 0.2], \ldots, 1 =]0.9, 1]$).

- for each tuple t of the relation considered, one checks, for each attribute A_i concerned by a preference, which class L_{ij} the value $t.A_i$ belongs to. This makes it possible to compute σ_1 et σ_2 (on the basis of i) the cardinalities computed at the previous step, and ii) the ordering between the classes), thus, finally, the value of $\sigma(t)$.
- one ranks the t's in decreasing order of $\sigma(t)$.

This processing method is much more efficient than that aimed at outranking-based queries, since its data complexity is in $\theta(n)$ instead of $\theta(n^2)$. Notice that it is not necessary to effectively build the ordered lists to be merged.

Example 7. Let us use again the data from Table 3. Let us denote by $nbcl(i)$ the number of classes associated with attribute A_i. First, for every attribute A_i, one performs the following treatment:

for $j = 1$ **to** $nbcl(i)$ **do**
    select count(*) **as** $card_{ij}$ **from** r **where** A_i **in** L_{ij}
done.

These queries return:

- for attribute A_1:
  - L_{11} associated with score A: $card_{11} = 1$,
  - L_{12} associated with score B: $card_{12} = 2$,
  - L_{13} associated with score C: $card_{13} = 0$,
  - L_{14} associated with D: $card_{14} = 0$,
  - L_{15} associated with score E: $card_{15} = 1$.
- for attribute A_2 (representing only the nonempty classes):
  - L_{21} associated with score 100: $card_{21} = 2$,
  - L_{22} associated with score 50: $card_{22} = 2$.
- for attribute A_3 (representing only the nonempty classes):
  - L_{31} associated with score 9 : $card_{31} = 1$,
  - L_{32} associated with score 11 : $card_{32} = 1$,
  - L_{33} associated with score 15 : $card_{33} = 2$.

The scan of the relation leads to the following evaluations:

- tuple t_1
  - attribute A_1: since $t_1.A_1 = \text{`A'}$, one deduces from the previous cardinalities that there are $2 + 0 + 0 + 1 = 3$ tuples strictly worse than t_1, and 0 better. Thus $\sigma_1 = 0$ and $\sigma_2 = 3$.
  - attribute A_2: since $t_1.A_2 = 100$, one deduces from the previous cardinalities that there are 2 tuples strictly worse than t_1, and 0 better. Thus $\sigma_1 = 0 + 0 = 0$ and $\sigma_2 = 3 + 2 = 5$.

- attribute A_3: since $t_1.A_3 = 15$, one deduces from the previous cardinalities that there are $1 + 1 = 2$ tuples strictly worse than t_1, and 0 better. Thus $\sigma_1 = 0 + 0 = 0$ et $\sigma_2 = 5 + 2 = 7$.
- Finally $\sigma(t) = \frac{1}{2} \cdot \left(\frac{7-0}{3 \cdot (4-1)} + 1 \right) = \frac{8}{9} \approx 0.89$.

- tuple t_2: using the same principle, one gets: $\sigma_1 = 3 + 2 + 2 = 7$, $\sigma_2 = 0 + 0 + 1 = 1$, $\sigma = 0.17$,
- tuple t_3: using the same principle, one gets: $\sigma_1 = 1 + 0 + 3 = 4$, $\sigma_2 = 1 + 2 + 0 = 3$, $\sigma = 0.44$,
- tuple t_4: using the same principle, one gets: $\sigma_1 = 1 + 2 + 0 = 3$, $\sigma_2 = 1 + 0 + 2 = 3$, $\sigma = 0.5$.◇

Overall, the number of scans of the relation only depends on the total number of preference classes.

Taking into account indifference and importances does not raise any problem. Similarly, the impact of graduality on the evaluation method is very limited. One just has to take into account the "distance" between two classes during the computation of σ_1 and σ_2. Data complexity does not change.

5 Conclusion

In this paper, we have defined an approach to database preference queries which shares some concepts with the outranking-based model described in [9,11], but leads to queries having a linear data complexity. The situation considered is that of queries involving incommensurable partial preferences, possibly associated with scoring functions. The basic principle is to rank the tuples according to each partial preference, then to merge the local orders obtained, using a linear function for aggregating the local scores attached to the tuples. Basically, a local score expresses the extent to which a tuple is strictly better than many others and not strictly worse than many others with respect to the partial preference attached to a given attribute. In the graded version of this model, local scores also take into account the extent to which an attribute value is better (or worse) than another. As the outranking-based model, this model refines Pareto order for queries of the Skyline type. Considering its good data complexity and the fact that it yields a total order (unlike Pareto-order-based approaches), we think that it constitutes an interesting alternative to approaches such as Skyline or *Preference SQL* — which may produce a huge number of incomparable tuples.

Perspectives for future work concern (i) implementation aspects, (ii) experimentations and a user-study aimed notably at comparing the results obtained when using this approach with those produced by Skyline queries, outranking-based queries, and fuzzy queries (assuming that preferences are commensurable in this latter case and aggregated using, e.g., a weighted mean).

References

1. Hadjali, A., Kaci, S., Prade, H.: Database preferences queries – a possibilistic logic approach with symbolic priorities. In: Hartmann, S., Kern-Isberner, G. (eds.) FoIKS 2008. LNCS, vol. 4932, pp. 291–310. Springer, Heidelberg (2008)

2. Bruno, N., Chaudhuri, S., Gravano, L.: Top-k selection queries over relational databases: mapping strategies and performance evaluation. ACM Transactions on Database Systems 27(2), 153–187 (2002)
3. Bosc, P., Pivert, O.: SQLf: a relational database language for fuzzy querying. IEEE Trans. on Fuzzy Systems 3, 1–17 (1995)
4. Agrawal, R., Wimmers, E.L.: A framework for expressing and combining preferences. In: Proc. of SIGMOD 2000, pp. 297–306 (2000)
5. Fishburn, P.C.: Preferences structures and their numerical representation. Theoretical Computer Science 217, 359–383 (1999)
6. Chomicki, J.: Preference formulas in relational queries. ACM Transactions on Database Systems 28(4), 427–466 (2003)
7. Kießling, W., Köstler, G.: Preference SQL — design, implementation, experiences. In: Bressan, S., Chaudhri, A.B., Li Lee, M., Yu, J.X., Lacroix, Z. (eds.) CAiSE 2002 and VLDB 2002. LNCS, vol. 2590, pp. 990–1001. Springer, Heidelberg (2003)
8. Börzsönyi, S., Kossmann, D., Stocker, K.: The skyline operator. In: Proc. of the 17th IEEE Inter. Conf. on Data Engineering, pp. 421–430 (2001)
9. Bosc, P., Pivert, O., Smits, G.: A model based on outranking for database preference queries. In: Hüllermeier, E., Kruse, R., Hoffmann, F. (eds.) IPMU 2010. Communications in Computer and Information Science, vol. 81, pp. 95–104. Springer, Heidelberg (2010)
10. Roy, B.: The outranking approach and the foundations of ELECTRE methods. Theory and Decision 31, 49–73 (1991)
11. Bosc, P., Pivert, O., Smits, G.: A database preference query model based on a fuzzy outranking relation. In: Proc. of the 19th IEEE International Conference on Fuzzy Systems (FUZZ-IEEE 2010), Barcelona, Spain (2010)
12. Godfrey, P., Shipley, R., Gryz, J.: Maximal vector computation in large data sets. In: Proc. of VLDB 2005, pp. 229–240 (2005)
13. Bartolini, I., Ciaccia, P., Patella, M.: Efficient sort-based skyline evaluation. ACM Trans. Database Syst. 33(4), 1–49 (2008)
14. Lin, X., Yuan, Y., Zhang, Q., Zhang, Y.: Selecting stars: the k most representative skyline operator. In: Proc. of the ICDE 2007, pp. 86–95 (2007)
15. Chan, C.Y., Jagadish, H.V., Tan, K.L., Tung, A.K.H., Zhang, Z.: Finding k-dominant skylines in high dimensional space. In: Proc. of SIGMOD 2006, pp. 503–514 (2006)
16. Chan, C.Y., Jagadish, H.V., Tan, K.L., Tung, A.K.H., Zhang, Z.: On high dimensional skylines. In: Ioannidis, Y., Scholl, M.H., Schmidt, J.W., Matthes, F., Hatzopoulos, M., Böhm, K., Kemper, A., Grust, T., Böhm, C. (eds.) EDBT 2006. LNCS, vol. 3896, pp. 478–495. Springer, Heidelberg (2006)
17. Hadjali, A., Pivert, O., Prade, H.: On different types of fuzzy skylines. In: Proc. of the 19th International Symposium on Methodologies for Intelligent Systems (ISMIS 2011), Warsaw, Poland (2011)
18. Rademaker, M., De Baets, B.: A threshold for majority in the context of aggregating partial order relations. In: Proc. of the 19th IEEE International Conference on Fuzzy Systems (FUZZ-IEEE 2010), Barcelona, Spain, pp. 490–493 (2010)
19. Bordogna, G., Pasi, G.: A model for a soft fusion of information accesses on the web. Fuzzy Sets and Systems 148(1), 105–118 (2004)
20. Grzegorzewski, P.: Kendall's correlation coefficient for vague preferences. Soft Comput. 13(11), 1055–1061 (2009)
21. Bosc, P., Pivert, O.: On a fuzzy group-by clause in SQLf. In: Proc. of the 19th IEEE International Conference on Fuzzy Systems (FUZZ-IEEE 2010), Barcelona, Spain, pp. 2409–2414 (2010)

Approximate Achievability in Event Databases

Austin Parker*, Gerardo I. Simari**, Amy Sliva, and V.S. Subrahmanian

Department of Computer Science and UMIACS
University of Maryland College Park, College Park, MD 20742, USA

Abstract. An event DB is a database about states (of the world) and events (taken by an agent) whose effects are not well understood. Event DBs are omnipresent in the social sciences and may include diverse scenarios from political events and the state of a country to education-related actions and their effects on a school system. We consider the following problem: given an event DB $\mathcal{K}$ representing historical events (what was the state and what actions were done at various past time points), and given a goal we wish to accomplish, what "change attempts" can the agent make so as to "optimize" the potential achievement of the goal? We define a formal version of this problem and derive results on its complexity. We then present a basic algorithm that provably provides a correct solution to finding an optimal state change attempt, as well as an enhanced algorithm that is built on top of the well known trie data structure and is also provably correct. We show correctness and algorithmic complexity results for both algorithms and report on experiments comparing their performance on synthetic data.

1 Introduction

A large number of well known data sets in the social sciences have a tabular form. Each row refers to a period of time, and each column represents a variable that characterizes the state of some entity during a time period. These variables naturally divide into those actionable variables we can control (which we will call "action variables") and those we cannot (which we will call "state variables"). For example, data sets regarding school performance for various U.S. states contain "state variables" such as the graduation rate of students in the state and the student to staff ratio during some time frame, while the "action" variables might refer to the level of funding provided per student during that time frame, the faculty salary levels during that time period, etc. Clearly, a U.S. state can attempt to change the levels of funding per student and/or change the faculty salaries in an attempt to increase the graduation rate. In a completely different setting, political science data sets about the stability of a country (such as the data sets created by the well known Political Instability Task Force [2]) may have "state variables" such as the Gross Domestic Product (GDP) of a country during a time period, the infant mortality rate during the same time period and the number of people killed in political conflict in the country during that time period, while "action" variables might include information about the investment in hospitals or education during that time frame, the number of social workers available, and so forth. A government might want to see what actionable

---

* Current affiliation: Institute for Defense Analysis Center for Computer Science, MD, USA.
** Current affiliation: Computing Laboratory, Oxford University, United Kingdom.

W. Liu (Ed.): ECSQARU 2011, LNAI 6717, pp. 737–748, 2011.

policies it can attempt to achieve a certain goal (*e.g.*, bringing the infant mortality rate below some threshold).

These are just two examples of problems that are not easily solved using current algorithms for reasoning about actions in AI or by AI planning systems. The main reasons are the following (i) the relationships between the actions and their impact on the state are poorly understood, (ii) a set of actions, taken together, might have a cumulative effect on a state that might somehow be more than a naive combination of the effects of those actions individually—which of course are not known anyway, and (iii) the actions under consideration may not succeed—an attempt to raise hospital funding may be blocked for reasons outside of anyone's control.

In this paper, we first propose (Section 2) the notion of an *event DB* (this is not novel, but generalizes several social science data sets). Section 3 defines the concept of "state change attempts" (SCAs for short) and formulates the problem of finding "optimal" SCAs towards a given goal; we present results on the computational complexity of finding optimal SCAs. In Section 4, we first present a straightforward algorithm called DSEE_OSCA to compute optimal SCAs, and then develop a vastly improved algorithm called TOSCA based on tries in Section 5. Though tries are a well known data structure, the novelty of our work is rooted in how TOSCA uses tries to solve optimal SCA computation problems with lower computational complexity. Finally, in Section 6, we briefly describe an implementation of both algorithms, together with an experimental analysis to demonstrate that TOSCA is quite tractable on data sets of reasonable size.

2   Preliminaries on Event DBs

An event DB is a relational database whose rows correspond to some time period (explicit or implicit) and whose columns are of two types—*state attributes* and *action attributes*. Throughout this paper, we assume the existence of some arbitrary, but fixed set $\mathbf{A} = \{A_1, \ldots, A_n\}$ of action attributes, and another arbitrary, but fixed set $\mathbf{S} = \{S_1, \ldots, S_m\}$ of state attributes. As usual, each attribute (state or action) A has a domain $dom(A)$, which in this work we assume to be finite. A *tuple* w.r.t. $(\mathbf{A}, \mathbf{S})$ is any member of $dom(A_1) \times \cdots \times dom(A_n) \times dom(S_1) \times \cdots \times dom(S_m)$. We use $t(S_i)$ (resp. $t(A_j)$) in the usual way to denote the value assigned to attribute S_i (resp. A_j) by a tuple. An *event database* $\mathcal{K}$ is a finite set of tuples w.r.t. $(\mathbf{A}, \mathbf{S})$. We assume all attributes A have domain $dom(A) \subset \mathbb{R}$. We use $\mathcal{A}$ to represent the set $dom(A_1) \times \cdots \times dom(A_n)$ and $\mathcal{S}$ to represent the set $dom(S_1) \times \cdots \times dom(S_m)$. We say a tuple is an *action tuple* if it contains only values for the action attributes and that it is a *state tuple* if it contains only values for the state attributes.

Example 1. Throughout this paper, the "School" data set is a data set from the U.S. State Education Data Center about U.S. school performance. Figure 1 presents a small part of this data set; we call it the *school* event DB. The columns labeled $A_1, \ldots, A_4$ represent action attributes, while the columns labeled $S_1, \ldots, S_5$ represent state attributes.

The school dataset contains nine attributes explained at the bottom of Figure 1. Math and reading scores obtained from standardized tests are combined into one annual *proficiency score*. School administrators's have the goal of increasing proficiency and graduation percentages by certain amounts.

	A_1	A_2	A_3	A_4	S_1	S_2	S_3	S_4	S_5
t_1:	9,532	61.6	7.8	4.2	81.1	49.1	51.3	50.6	Yes
t_2:	9,691	63.2	7.8	5.7	82.3	52.1	54.6	53.3	No
t_3:	9,924	63.8	8.1	3.1	82.0	59.8	60.4	60.1	Yes
t_4:	10,148	64.2	7.6	3.4	83.4	60.5	64.2	63.3	Yes
t_5:	10,022	64.0	7.2	2.9	83.2	63.9	68.9	66.9	Yes

Fig. 1. Small instance of an event *DB* containing hypothetical school performance data. Action variables are A_1: Funding (\$/Student), A_2: Salaries (% of Total Funding), A_3: Student/Staff Ratio, A_4: Proficiency Increase Target; state variables are S_1: Graduation (%), S_2: Math Proficiency, S_3: Reading Proficiency, S_4: Proficiency Score, S_5: Target Reached.

3   Optimal State Change Attempts

In this section, we formalize the notion of a state change attempt (SCA). The idea is that when an SCA is successfully applied to a given tuple, it changes the action attributes with the hope of these changes resulting in a change in the state. For example, decreasing class size may lead to better proficiency scores.

Definition 1. *A simple SCA is a triple* (A_i, vf, vt) *where* $vf, vt \in Dom(A_i)$ *for some* $A_i \in \mathbf{A}$. *A (non-simple) SCA is a set* $\{(A_{i_1}, vf_1, vt_1), \ldots, (A_{i_k}, vf_k, vt_k)\}$ *of simple SCAs such that* $i_j \neq i_k$ *for all* $j \neq k$.

When clear from context, we will refer to these concepts as *simple changes* and *changes*, respectively. Intuitively, a *simple* SCA modifies one attribute, while a state change attempt may modify more than one.

Definition 2. *Given a tuple* t, *an action attribute* A_i, *and* $vf, vt \in Dom(A_i)$, *a simple SCA* (A_i, vf, vt) *is applicable w.r.t.* t *iff* $t(A_i) = vf$. *The result of applying a simple SCA that is applicable w.r.t.* t *is a tuple* t' *where* $t'(A_i) = vt$ *and* $t'(A_j) = t(A_j)$ *for all attributes (action and state)* $A_j \neq A_i$. *We use* $\gamma(t, (A_i, vf, vt))$ *to denote tuple* t'.

A state change attempt $SCA = \{A_{i_1}, vf_1, vt_1), \ldots, (A_{i_k}, vf_k, vt_k)\}$ *is applicable w.r.t.* t *iff all* (A_{i_j}, vf_j, vt_j) *for* $1 \leq j \leq k$ *are applicable to w.r.t.* t.

The application of *SCA* to t will be denoted with $\gamma(t, SCA)$; note that an SCA only changes action attributes.

Example 2. A simple SCA w.r.t. the school data from Example 1 could be the following: $a_1 = (A_1, 8700, 8850)$, *i.e*, funding is increased from \$8,700 to \$8,850 per student, or $a_2 = (A_2, 62.3, 65)$, *i.e.*, salaries are increased from 62.3% to 65% of the budget. Let $SCA = \{a_1, a_2\}$ be an SCA. If we assume that the values of the action attributes in the current environment are $t = (8700, 64, 7, 3.2)$, then a_1 is applicable w.r.t. t, but a_2 is not. The result of applying a_1 to t is $\gamma(t, (A_1, 8700, 8850)) = t' = (8850, 64, 7, 3.2)$.

The result of applying an SCA is therefore the result of applying each simple change. However, these changes do not occur without cost.

Definition 3. *Let* $a = (A_i, vf, vt)$ *be a simple state change attempt. The cost of attempting* a *is given by a real-valued function cost* : $\{A_1, \ldots, A_m\} \times \mathbb{R} \times \mathbb{R} \to \mathbb{R}$, *where* $cost(A_i, vf, vt)$ *is the cost of changing action attribute* A_i *from* vf *to* vt.

Cost functions will be highly dependent on the application domain, and we assume them to be provided by a user. The *cost* of an attempt, $cost(SCA) = \sum_{a \in SCA} cost(a)$, is the sum of the costs of the simple state change attempts in SCA.

Example 3. Let $a_1 = (A_1, 8700, 8850)$, $a_2 = (A_2, 62.3, 65)$ be the same simple changes from Example 2, and $a_3 = (A_4, 3.8, 3.9)$ be a third simple change (*i.e.*, increment the proficiency increase target from 3.8 to 3.9). A possible cost function could be defined in terms of monetary cost, in which: $cost(a_1) = 150 * s$ (where s is a constant set to the number of students affected), $cost(a_2) = 2.7 * A_1$, and $cost(a_3) = 0$.

Thus far, we have studied SCAs that are always successful. However, in general, we cannot expect this to be the case—the funding per student may not change simply because one attempted to change it. We will assume state change attempts are only probabilistically successful—they only induce the change attempted according to a specified probability. Further, we will assume that the probability of any simple change occurring successfully depends on the entire set of changes attempted.

Example 4. Consider the situation described in Example 3. Here the state change attempt a_2 increases teacher salaries from 62.3% to 65%. On its own, attempting this change may anger taxpayers (who would pay for the increase) and may only have a 10% probability of succeeding. Likewise, increasing per student funding might have a 15% chance of success. However, if the taxpayers are willing to increase teacher salaries, then they may also tend to approve per student funding increases, perhaps leading to a joint probability of 9% that both of these will occur when attempted together.

Let SCA and $SCA' \subseteq SCA$ be SCAs; let $pOccur(SCA'|SCA)$ denote the probability that only the actions in SCA' occur given that SCA is attempted. Such probabilities can either be derived from historical data or be explicitly stated by a user. When we say that a state change attempt SCA is "attempted" for a tuple t describing the current situation, this means that each $SCA' \subseteq SCA$ has the chance $pOccur(SCA'|SCA)$ of being successful, *i.e.*, of having $\gamma(t, SCA')$ be the resulting tuple.

Effect Estimators. The goal of this paper is to allow an end user to take an event DB $\mathcal{K}$ and a goal G (some desired outcome condition on state attributes) and find an SCA that "optimally" achieves goal G. We assume w.l.o.g. that goals are expressed as standard conjunctive selection conditions [8] on state attributes. We now define *effect estimators*.

Definition 4. *For action tuple t and goal G, an* effect estimator *is a function $\varepsilon(t, G) \rightarrow [0, 1]$ that maps a tuple and a goal to a probability $p \in [0, 1]$.*

Intuitively, $\varepsilon(t, G)$ specifies the conditional probability of goal G holding given that we are in a situation where the action attributes are as specified in t. This quantity can be estimated in many ways, some of which will be investigated below.

Probabilistic State Change Effectiveness. As mentioned above, we assume an environment where, just because an SCA is performed, it is not necessarily the case that all parts of the SCA will actually accomplish the attempted change. When one attempts to change the situation via SCA, any subset of SCA may succeed. For instance, if one tries to decrease the student/staff ratio and increase the funding per student, perhaps the student/staff ratio increases as expected, but that the funding per student remains the same. Thus to truly gauge the effectiveness of a state change attempt, we must consider the probability of each subset of the attempt occurring.[1]

Definition 5. *The probability of a state change attempt* $SCA = \{ (A_{i_1}, vf_1, vt_1), \ldots, (A_{i_k}, vf_k, vt_k) \}$ *satisfying goal G when applied to action tuple t is* $pEff(t, G, SCA, \varepsilon) = \sum_{SCA' \in \mathcal{P}(SCA)} pOccur(SCA'|SCA) \cdot \varepsilon(\gamma(t, SCA'), G)$, *where* $\mathcal{P}(SCA)$ *denotes the power set of* SCA.

$pEff(t, G, SCA, \varepsilon)$ is computed by summing over all the state changes that may occur given the attempt of SCA: since any subset can occur, this summation ranges over $SCA' \subseteq SCA$. For each SCA' that may occur, one multiplies its probability of occurring given that SCA was attempted $(pOccur(SCA'|SCA))$ times the effectiveness of the given attempt according to ε (recall that $\gamma(t, SCA')$ is the action tuple resulting from the application of SCA' to the original action tuple t). The following result shows that for arbitrary effect estimators, computing state change effectiveness is intractable.

Proposition 1. *For condition G, state change attempt SCA, action tuple t, and effect estimator* ε, *deciding if* $pEff(t, G, SCA, \varepsilon) > 0$ *is NP-hard w.r.t.* $|\mathbf{A}|$. *If* $\varepsilon(.)$ *can be computed in PTIME w.r.t.* $|\mathbf{A}|$, *the problem is NP-complete.*[2]

The Highest Probability SCA (HPSCA) Problem. Let $\mathbf{A} = \langle A_1, \ldots, A_n \rangle$ and $\mathbf{S} = \langle S_1, \ldots, S_m \rangle$, $\mathcal{K}$ be an event DB, t be an action tuple describing the current values of the action attributes, G be a goal over $\mathbf{S}$, *cost* and *pOccur* be the functions as mentioned earlier, and $p \in [0, 1]$ be a real number; does there exist a change attempt SCA such that $pEff(t, G, SCA, \varepsilon) \geq p$?

The above problem is stated as a decision problem; a search problem, to *find* such an SCA, can be analogously stated. We refer to any state change attempt that is a solution to this problem as an *optimal state change attempt* (OSCA, for short).

Theorem 1. *If the effect estimator used can be computed in PTIME, the Highest Probability SCA problem is #P-hard and in PSPACE w.r.t.* $|\mathbf{A}|$.

The #P-hard reduction uses #SAT (the language $\{\langle F, n \rangle\}$, where F is a formula with exactly n solutions), and membership in PSPACE is shown by giving algorithms.

A Basic Algorithm. We will now provide a basic algorithm to solve the HPSCA problem. It works by first enumerating each possible state change attempt with size at most h, then choosing the one that has the highest probability. Since there are only $O(|\mathbf{A}|^h)$ such state change attempts, this algorithm runs in $O(|\mathbf{A}|^h)$, which is PTIME with respect to the number of action attributes $|\mathbf{A}|$.

Proposition 2. *Algorithm 1 runs in time in* $O(|\mathbf{A}|^h)$, *and returns* (SCA, c, ef) *where* $|SCA| \leq h$, $c = cost(SCA)$ *and* $ef = pEff(t, G, SCA, \varepsilon)$, *such that there is no other* (SCA, c', ef') *with* $c' < c$ *and* $ef' > ef$.

To extend this technique to the non-limited, general version of the problem, one simply needs to solve the limited version of the problem with h equal to $|\mathbf{A}|$:

---

[1] In this work, we assume that each simple change attempt either succeeds or fails completely.

[2] NP-hardness is shown via reduction from subset sum.

Algorithm 1: solveHPSCA(t, G, ε, h, p)

1. Let $R = \emptyset$ // the set to be returned.
2. Add $(\emptyset, 0, pEff(t, G, \emptyset, \varepsilon))$ to R. // Initialize R with empty state change attempt.
3. For each $A_i \in \mathbf{A}$
4.   For each value $v \in dom(A_i)$
5.   **continue** if $v = t(A_i)$ // Go to next value, t won't be changed by this SCA.
6.   // iterate over all members of R, growing those which are small enough.
7.   For each $(SCA, c, ef) \in R$
8.   **continue** if $|SCA| = h$.
9.   Let $SCA' = SCA \cup \{(A_i, t(A_i), v)\}$.
10.   Let c' be the cost of SCA' and ef' be $pEff(t, G, SCA', \varepsilon)$.
11.   Add (SCA', c', ef') to R.
12. **return** $(SCA, c, ef) \in R$ s.t. $ef \geq p$ and $\nexists (SCA, c', ef') \in R$ with $c' < c$ and $ef' > ef$; false otherwise.

Fig. 2. Returns (SCA, c, ef), where c is the cost of state change attempt SCA and ef is the probability of effectiveness of SCA s.t. ef is highest and c is lowest

4   Different Kinds of Effect Estimators

In this section we introduce several effect estimators which specify the likelihood of a given action tuple satisfying a given goal condition G. An effect estimate answers the question: "if I succeed in changing the environment in this way, what is the probability that this new environment satisfies my goal?"

Learning Algorithms as Effect Estimators. We now show how to take any supervised learning algorithm (*e.g.*, neural nets, decision trees, etc.) and apply it to the event database $\mathcal{K}$ to get an effect estimator. We abstractly model a machine learning algorithm as a *learner*, which, given the appropriate information, will produce a *classifier*.

Definition 6. *For event DB $\mathcal{K}$ and goal condition G, a* classification algorithm *is a function* **learner** : $(\mathcal{K}, G) \mapsto$ **classifier**, *where* **classifer** *is a function from action tuples to the interval* $[0, 1]$. *Given a classification algorithm learner, a* learned effect estimator *is defined to be* $\varepsilon_{lrn}(learner, \mathcal{K})(t, G)$, *returning* $learner(\mathcal{K}, G)(t)$.

For instance, neural networks [7] fit this definition: we first define **learner** to be a function that generates a neural network with input nodes for each action attribute and exactly one output node with a domain of $[0, 1]$. The **learner** function then trains the network via backpropagation according to $\mathcal{K}$ and G. The resulting network is the **classifier** function, and will, given a set of values for the action attributes, return a value in the interval $[0, 1]$. We can use a classification algorithm to create a *learned effect estimator*.

Data Selection Effect Estimators. In this section we examine the special case of an effect estimator that uses selection operations in a database to create an estimation. For our purposes, selection operations will be denoted $\sigma_G(\mathcal{K})$, where $\mathcal{K}$ is an event DB and G is some goal condition on the state tuples. $\sigma_G(\mathcal{K})$ returns the subset of $\mathcal{K}$ satisfying the condition G.

Definition 7. *For goal G and action tuple t, a* data selection effect estimator *is a function that takes an event DB $\mathcal{K}$ as input and returns an effect estimator:* $\varepsilon^* : \mathcal{K} \mapsto$

$(t, G) \mapsto p$, where $p \in [0, 1]$. We require that ε^* be implemented with a fixed number of selection operations on $\mathcal{K}$ and that $\varepsilon^*(\mathcal{K})(t, G)$ be 0 if there is no tuple in $\mathcal{K}$ whose action attributes match t.

A data selection effect estimator differs from a normal effect estimator in that it depends explicitly on selection from event DB $\mathcal{K}$. While data selection effect estimators are limited to using only selection operators we will see that there are many ways to specify the relationship between G and the situation described by t using only selection operations. We abuse the notation used for selection operators in databases by writing $\sigma_t(\mathcal{K})$ to denote the selection of all the tuples in $\mathcal{K}$ that have the values described by t for the corresponding attributes.

Definition 8. *The* data ratio effect estimator *is defined:* $\varepsilon_r^*(\mathcal{K})(t, G) \stackrel{\text{def}}{=} \frac{|\sigma_{t \wedge G}(\mathcal{K})|}{|\sigma_t(\mathcal{K})|}$ *whenever* $|\sigma_t(\mathcal{K})| > 0$, *and zero otherwise.*

The data ratio effect estimator returns the marginal probability of G occurring given that the values specified by the action tuple t occur.

Example 5. Suppose we have a school metrics database containing only three columns: class size, teacher salary and graduation rate. The class size and teacher salary are action attributes, while the graduation rate is a state attribute. We want to determine from the data what fraction of the time a graduation rate is at least 95% for an average class size of 20 and an average teacher salary of $60,000. According to ε_r^*, this fraction is the fraction of tuples in the database with class size 20 and teacher salary $60,000 that have a graduation rate over 95% divided by the total number of tuples in the database with class size 20 and teacher salary $60,000.

One important feature of the data ratio effect estimator is that when there is no information on a given tuple, it assumes the tuple to be a negative instance. This allows it to quickly eliminate possibilities not contained in the database, and reduces the search space needed to compute optimal state change attempts. Further examples of data selection effect estimators include cautious or optimistic ratio effect estimators, which take the confidence interval into account.

Definition 9. *The* cautious ratio effect estimator *returns the probability of G given t to be the low end of the 95% confidence interval:* $\varepsilon_{c95}^* \mathcal{K}(t, G) \stackrel{\text{def}}{=} \varepsilon_r^*(\mathcal{K})(t, G) - 1.96 \cdot \sqrt{\frac{\varepsilon_r^*(\mathcal{K})(t,G)(1 - \varepsilon_r^*(\mathcal{K})(t,G))}{|\sigma_t(\mathcal{K})|}}$ *(if $\sigma_t(\mathcal{K})$ is empty, $\varepsilon_{c95}^*(\mathcal{K})(t, G)$ is defined to be zero).*

There is a whole class of cautious ratio effect estimators: one for every confidence level (90%, 80%, 99%, etc.). There are also optimistic ratio effect estimators which return the high end rather than the low end of the confidence interval.

Since data selection effect estimators are computed via a finite number of selection operations, effect estimators can always be computed in time in $O(|\mathcal{K}|)$. The complexity of finding SCAs changes when we insist on using data selection effect estimators. Problems that were NP-complete or $\#P$-hard w.r.t. the size of the action schema are polynomial in $|\mathcal{K}|$ when only data selection effect estimators are allowed.

```
Algorithm 2: DSEE_OSCA(DB K, Goal G, Action tuple env, p)
1. Let Dat1 = ∅ // Dat1 will contain state change attempts and their probability of occurrence.
2. // Iterate through all tuples satisfying G in K.
3. For t ∈ σ_G(K) do // Create SCA s.t. γ(env, SCA) equals t on action attributes.
4.      SCA = {(A, env(A), t(A)) | env(A) ≠ t(A)}
5.      If (SCA, ·) ∈ Dat1 then continue. // Already visited
6.      Let f = ε*_r(K)(t, G).
7.      Add (SCA, f) to Dat1.
8. Let Dat2 = ∅
9. For (SCA, f) ∈ Dat1 do
10.     Let nextF = pOccur(SCA|SCA) · f.
11.     For (SCA', f') ∈ Dat1 do
12.         If SCA' ⊊ SCA then
13.             nextF = nextF + pOccur(SCA'|SCA) · f'
14.     Add (SCA, ef) where (SCA, nextF) to Dat2.
15. Remove any (SCA, ef) from Dat2 where ef < p.
16. return arg min_(SCA,ef)∈Dat2 (cost(SCA)).
```

Fig. 3. A brute force algorithm for solving the HPSCA problem

Proposition 3. *For goal G, state change attempt SCA, action tuple t, and event DB K, if the effect estimator ε^* is a data selection effect estimator then deciding whether $pEff(t, G, SCA, \varepsilon^*(K)) > 0$ takes $O(|K|^2)$ time.*

Theorem 2. *If the effect estimator is a data selection effect estimator, then the HPSCA problem can be solved in $O(|K|^2)$ time.*

Computing OSCAs with Data Selection Effect Estimators. Using data selection effect estimators, we can devise algorithms to find optimal SCAs. In this section we use only the data ratio effect estimator (Definition 8). Figure 2 presents the DSEE_OSCA algorithm to solve the HPSCA problem.

Proposition 4. *Algorithm 2 computes SCA such that $pEff(env, G, SCA, \varepsilon^*_r(K)) \geq p$ and there is no other feasible state change attempt SCA' such that $cost(SCA') < cost(SCA)$ and $pEff(env, G, SCA', \varepsilon^*_r(K)) \geq p$.*

The DSEE_OSCA algorithm works by selecting all tuples in the event DB K satisfying the goal condition, then adding the pair (SCA, f) to a data structure $Dat1$ where f is the chance that SCA, when successful, results in a state satisfying the goal G (i.e., $\varepsilon^*_r(K)(t, G)$). In the next loop, two things happen: (i) f is multiplied by the probability that SCA is successful, and (ii) we iterate through all state change attempts and sum the probability of occurrence of each subset of SCA with that subset's probability of satisfying the goal G, adding the result to data structure $Dat2$. At this point $Dat2$ contains pairs (SCA, ef), where ef is the probability of effectiveness of SCA according to Definition 5. The algorithm then prunes all state change attempts without sufficiently high probabilities of effectiveness, and returns the one with the lowest cost.

Proposition 5. *Algorithm 2 runs in time $O(|K|^2)$.*

Alg. 3: TOSCA(Trie T, Goal G, Action tuple env, p)	Alg. 4: TOSCA-Helper(Trie T, Goal G, Action tuple env)
1. Let $Dat1 = $ TOSCA-Helper(T, G, env).	1. If T is a leaf node // Similar to Algorithm 2...
2. Let $Dat2 = \emptyset$.	2. Let $Dat = \emptyset$
3. For $(SCA, f) \in Dat1$ do	3. For $t \in \sigma_G(tuples(T))$
4. Let $nextF = pOccur(SCA\|SCA) \cdot f$.	4. // Create SCA s.t. $\gamma(env, SCA) = t$
5. For $(SCA', f) \in Dat1$ do	5. $SCA = \{(A, env(A), t(A))\|t(A) \neq env(A)\}$
6. If $SCA' \subsetneq SCA$ then	6. If $(SCA, \cdot) \in Dat$ then continue to next t
7. $nextF = nextF + pOccur(SCA'\|SCA) \cdot f'$	7. $f = \varepsilon_r^*(tuples(T))(t, G)$.
8. Add (SCA, ef) with $(SCA, nextF)$ to $Dat2$.	8. Add (SCA, f) to Dat.
9. Remove any (SCA, ef) from $Dat2$ where $ef < p$.	9. return Dat.
10. return arg $\min_{(SCA, ef) \in Dat2}(cost(SCA))$.	10. Else // Recursively call for all children of T.
	11. Let $(A, Edges) = T$.
	12. return the set
	$\bigcup_{(v^-, v^+, N) \in Edges} TOSCA\text{-}Helper(N, G, env)$

Fig. 4. Computes a state change attempt with minimal cost and probability of effectiveness at least p using a trie.

Fig. 5. Returns a set of (SCA, v) pairs, where SCA is a state change attempt and v is $\varepsilon^*(\mathcal{K})(G, Sit = \gamma(SCA, env))$.

5   Trie-enhanced Optimal State Change Attempt (TOSCA)

In this section, we present the TOSCA algorithm that uses tries [3] to improve the performance of finding an optimal state change attempt. In TOSCA, a trie is used to index the event DB to reduce the search space necessary for the data selection effect estimator in the DSEE_OSCA algorithm (Figure 3). An internal trie node is a pair $(Atr, Edges)$ where $Atr \in \mathbf{A} \cup \mathbf{S}$ is an attribute and $Edges$ contains (v^-, v^+, N) pairs, where v^- and v^+ are values from $Dom(Atr)$ with $v^- < v^+$ and N is another trie node. A leaf node in a trie maintained by TOSCA is simply a set of tuples from the DB, denoted $tuples(N)$. Tries have a unique root node.

A trie is *data correct* if for any leaf node N there is a unique path from the root $(Atr_1, Edges_1), \ldots, (Atr_{k-1}, Edges_{k-1}), N$ such that for all $t \in tuples(N)$ and all i between 1 and $k - 1$, there is $(v^-, v^+, (Atr_{i+1}, Edges_{i+1})) \in Edges_i$ such that $v^- \leq t(Atr_i) < v^+$. That is, the path to a leaf node determines which tuples are stored there. A trie is *construction correct* if for all sibling nodes (v_1^-, v_1^+, N_1) and (v_2^-, v_2^+, N_2), $v_1^- \geq v_2^+$ or $v_2^- \geq v_1^+$.

The *Trie-enhanced Optimal State Change Attempt* (TOSCA) algorithm uses tries to reduce the average case run time for computing optimal state change attempts. TOSCA is divided into the *base* and a *helper*, Algorithms 3 and 4 (Figures 4 and 5) respectively.

Example 6. In our example run of Algorithm 3, we use a simple database containing four tuples $\{(A_1 = 1, S_1 = 1), (A_1 = 2, S_1 = 1), (A_1 = 3, S_1 = 0), (A_1 = 3, S_1 = 1)\}$, and the trie T pictured in Figure 6. We use the tuple $(A_1 = 0)$ as the action tuple env, the goal condition $S_1 = 1$, and the threshold 0.7 as p. The first step of Algorithm 3 is to create $Dat1$ via Algorithm 4, which recursively traverses the trie, beginning at node A. At node B, Algorithm 4 recognizes a leaf node and selects tuples from that node that satisfy the goal condition, iterating through them in turn beginning with $(A_1 = 1, S_1 = 1)$. The state change attempt that changes the environment tuple

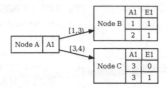

Fig. 6. The trie used in Example 6

$(A_1 = 0)$ to $(A_1 = 1, S_1 = 1)$ is $SCA = \{(A_1, 0, 1)\}$. The time saving step of the algorithm now occurs at line 7, where we run ε_r^* on the database $tuples(T)$ instead of the entire database (line 6 of Algorithm 2). Because there is only one tuple in $tuples(T)$ with $A_1 = 1$, and because that tuple also satisfies the goal condition, f is set to 1 and $(\{(A_1, 0, 1)\}, 1)$ is added to Dat. Similarly, $(\{A_1, 0, 2\}, 1)$ is added on the next tuple: $(A_1 = 2, S_1 = 1)$, finishing the call to node B.

The call to node C has slightly different results. The only member of $tuples(T)$ to satisfy the goal condition is $(A_1 = 3, S_1 = 1)$. Further, ε_r^* produces a result of $1/2$, as of the two tuples with value 3 for A_1, only one of them satisfies the condition that $S_1 = 1$. The returned set from this recursive call contains only $(\{(A_1, 0, 3)\}, 1/2)$.

After merging all recursive calls, the set $\{ (\{(A_1, 0, 3)\}, 1/2), (\{(A_1, 0, 2)\}, 1), (\{(A_1, 0, 1)\}, 1) \}$ is returned and labeled $Dat1$ by Algorithm 3. The next loop multiplies the second value of each member of $Dat1$ by the probability of the associated state change attempt occurring, which is provided by a user *a priori* and we will assume to be $3/4$ for all state change attempts. The inner loop then adds the probabilities associated with subsets of the state change attempt (of which there are none in this example). This results in the data structure $Dat2$ consisting of pairs $(SCA, pEff(env, S_1 = 1, SCA, \varepsilon_r^*))$, or $\{(\{(A_1, 0, 3)\}, 3/8), (\{(A_1, 0, 2)\}, 3/4), (\{(A_1, 0, 1)\}, 3/4)\}$.

At this point, those members of $Dat2$ with too low a probability of effectiveness are eliminated (only $(\{A_1, 0, 3\}, 3/8)$) and the SCA with lowest cost is returned.

Proposition 6. *Algorithm 3 computes SCA s.t. pEff(env, G, SCA, $\varepsilon_r^*(\mathcal{K})$) $\geq p$ and there is no other feasible state change attempt SCA' such that cost(SCA') < cost(SCA) and pEff(env, G, SCA', $\varepsilon_r^*(\mathcal{K})$) $\geq p$.*

The worse case time complexity of Algorithm 3 is $O(|\mathcal{K}|^2)$. However, the complexity of Algorithm 4 is $O(|\mathcal{K}| \cdot k)$, where k is the size of the largest leaf node in trie T. Since Algorithm 4 replaces the loop on line 9 of Algorithm 2 —a loop that takes time $O(|\mathcal{K}|^2)$ —we can expect speedup proportional to $k/|\mathcal{K}|$. Since, in the average case, k will be $|\mathcal{K}|/2^h$, (h is the trie's height) this speedup can be large.

While k is bounded by $|\mathcal{K}|$, it is usually much smaller: on the order of $|\mathcal{K}|/2^h$ for a trie of height h. We expect $Dat1$ to have size $O(|\mathcal{K}|)$, as it will be the same as $Dat1$ on line 9 of Algorithm 2. It was produced by at most $2 \cdot |\mathcal{K}|/k$ recursive calls to Algorithm 4 (there are at most $2 \cdot |\mathcal{K}|/k$ nodes in the trie). When given a leaf node, Algorithm 4 takes time in $O(k^2)$. Thus the run time of Algorithm 4 is in $O(|\mathcal{K}| \cdot k)$. The loop on line 3 then runs in time in $O(|\mathcal{K}|^2)$ (it is the same loop as in Algorithm 2), resulting in an overall run time in $O(|\mathcal{K}|^2)$. However, we will see that in practice, substantial speedup is achieved by using the $O(|\mathcal{K}| \cdot k)$ Algorithm 4 rather than $O(|\mathcal{K}|^2)$.

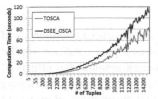 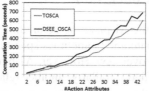 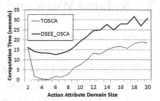

Fig. 7. Average running times for **DSEE_OSCA** and **TOSCA** over synthetic data, varying # of tuples

Fig. 8. Varying # of action attributes; Fixed: # of tuples at $8,000$

Fig. 9. Varying action attb. dom. size; Fixed: # tuples at $8K$, # sit. attb. at 4, and # event attb. at 3

6   Experimental Evaluation

We performed experiments to answer two main questions, with the following setup. We automatically generated k tuples with 4 action attributes and 3 state attributes. Each tuple's value for the action attributes was chosen randomly from $[0, 1]$. To generate the values for the state attribute, we generated random boolean formulas over the action attributes consisting of the operators $<, >, =, \neq$, and $\wedge$. We allowed at most three "$\wedge$" connectives in each formula. In a given tuple, each state attribute value is set to 1 if its associated formula is satisfied by the action attributes in that tuple, and set to 0 otherwise. Because we have the formula defining the state attributes, we can check the accuracy of the state change attempts returned by each algorithm. To do this, we apply the state change attempt and determine the state attribute values. The accuracy of a given algorithm will be the fraction of the time the resulting values for the state attributes satisfy the goal condition. Unfortunately, due to space limitations, we cannot include here experiments evaluating accuracy; we will provide a more comprehensive experimental analysis, including results on real world data, in future work.

Question 1: Which techniques scale best w.r.t number of tuples? We want to how **DSEE_OSCA** and **TOSCA** scale when presented with large amounts of data, *i.e.*, number of tuples. In these experiments, we provided the algorithms with $1,000$ to $10,000$ tuples. The results in Figure 7 show **TOSCA** to perform better than **DSEE_OSCA** as the database increases in size. Note that **TOSCA** does have a pre-computation step whose running time has been left out of these figures. However, the time needed to compute the trie is several orders of magnitude smaller than the running time of **TOSCA**, with only 91 ms to construct a trie with 10K tuples.

Question 2: Which techniques scale best w.r.t. number of attributes and their domain size? Figure 8 shows how **DSEE_OSCA** and **TOSCA** scale as the number of attributes increases in a database with $8,000$ tuples. This graph shows **TOSCA** outperforming **DSEE_OSCA**; it is important because the trie in **TOSCA** should lose efficiency as the number of attributes increases (the trie's depth equals the number of attributes). However, this shows that the decrease in the trie's efficiency does not affect the ability of the trie to offer **TOSCA** a speedup. Finally, Figure 9 shows **TOSCA** also outperforming **DSEE_OSCA** when the domain size of action attributes is varied.

7   Related Work and Conclusions

There is substantial work in the AI-planning community on discovering sequences of actions that lead to a given outcome (sometimes specified as a goal condition similar to this work), see [5] for an overview. However, AI planning assumes the effects of actions to be explicitly specified. Similarly, another related area is that of Reasoning about Actions [1,6]; work in this area generally assumes that descriptions of effects of actions on fluent predicates, causal relationships between such fluents, and conditions that enable actions to be performed are available. Our work approaches a similar problem in a fundamentally different and data-driven way, assuming *(i)* actions only change certain parameters in the system, *(ii)* all attempted changes succeed probabilistically depending on the set of attempted changes, and *(iii)* the effects of the changed parameters on the state can only be determined by appeal to past data. Finally, research within the Machine Learning community on the problem of classification [4] is also related to our endeavor. The main differences between that research and our own is that we are not only interested in classifying situations in past data (this is actually aided by the fact that goal conditions are provided), but in how to *arrive once again at similar situations*. As we have seen, this also involves analyzing costs of performing actions and their probabilities of success.

In this paper we have shown that determining optimal state change attempts is not an easy problem, since we prove that the optimization task belong to complexity classes widely believed to be intractable. However, we show that TOSCA is provably correct, and report preliminary experimental results on synthetic data showing that it is faster than a basic solution and tractable for reasonably sized inputs.

In future work, we will provide a more comprehensive empirical evaluation, including results on real world data and accuracy; finally, we will also investigate other interesting variants of the problem of finding optimal state change attempts.

Acknowledgements. The authors were funded in part by AFOSR grant FA95500610405 and ARO grant W911NF0910206. This work was also partially supported by the European Research Council under the EU's 7th Framework Programme (FP7/2007-2013)/ERC grant 246858 – DIADEM.

References

1. Baral, C., Tuan, L.-c.: Reasoning about actions in a probabilistic setting. In: AAAI 2002, pp. 507–512. AAAI Press, Menlo Park (2002)
2. Davies, J.L., Gurr, T.R.: Preventive Measures: Building Risk Assessment and Crisis Early Warning Systems. Rowman and Littlefield (1998)
3. Fredkin, E.: Trie memory. Communications of the ACM 3(9), 490–499 (1960)
4. Mitchell, T.M.: Machine Learning. McGraw-Hill, New York (1997)
5. Nau, D., Ghallab, M., Traverso, P.: Automated Planning: Theory & Practice. Morgan Kaufmann, San Francisco (2004)
6. Pearl, J.: Reasoning with cause and effect. AI Mag. 23(1), 95–111 (2002)
7. Rojas, R.: Neural Networks: A Systematic Introduction. Springer, Heidelberg (1996)
8. Ullman, J.D.: Principles of Database and Knowledge-Base Systems, vol. I. Computer Science Press, Rockville (1988)

A Probabilistic Interpretation for a Geometric Similarity Measure

Sebastian Lehrack and Ingo Schmitt

Brandenburg University of Technology Cottbus,
Institute of Computer Science,
Postfach 10 13 44, D-03013 Cottbus, Germany
`slehrack@informatik.tu-cottbus.de`
`schmitt@tu-cottbus.de`

Abstract. A Boolean logic-based evaluation of a database query returns
`true` on match and `false` on mismatch. Unfortunately, there are many
application scenarios where such an evaluation is not possible or does
not adequately meet user expectations about vague and uncertain conditions. Consequently, there is a need for incorporating impreciseness and
proximity into a logic-based query language. In this work we propose a
probabilistic interpretation for our query language CQQL which is based
on a geometric retrieval model. In detail, we show that the CQQL can
evaluate *arbitrary* similarity conditions in a probabilistic fashion. Furthermore, we lay a theoretical foundation for the combination of CQQL
with other probabilistic semantics.

1 Introduction

Evaluating a traditional *logic-based* database query against a data tuple yields
`true` on match and `false` on mismatch. Unfortunately, there are many application scenarios where such an evaluation is not possible or does not adequately
meet user needs about vague and uncertain conditions. Thus, there is a need
for incorporating the concepts of impreciseness and proximity into a logic-based
query language. An interesting approach is applying *similarity predicates* as
'*price about 100*' or '*location is close to Berlin*' within such a query language.
Data objects fulfill this kind of predicates to a certain degree which can be represented by a value out of the interval $[0, 1]$. Based on these *score values* a ranking
of all data objects is possible which distinguishes result items.

Our retrieval model presented in [10] incorporates score values into a logic-
based query language by exploiting a vector space model known from quantum mechanics and quantum logic [9]. Based on this model and a logic-based
weighting approach we developed the calculus query language CQQL, *Commut-
ing Quantum Query Language*, as an extension of the relational domain calculus
[8].

A popular probabilistic approach known from Information Retrieval expresses
a score value by a probability of relevance [12]: *What is the probability that a user
rates a data object as relevant?* In our adaption the underlying test criterion is

W. Liu (Ed.): ECSQARU 2011, LNAI 6717, pp. 749–760, 2011.
© Springer-Verlag Berlin Heidelberg 2011

embodied by a logic-based similarity condition. Consequently, we interpret the evaluation result of a similarity condition as a probability of relevance.

Besides those relevance probabilities *probabilistic databases* have been established as a challenging research field. In probabilistic databases a tuple may belong in the database with some amount of confidence. The semantics of such probabilistic databases are often given by the *possible-world-semantics* [2]. In this case several possible states of a given application system are managed in one integrated database.

Scenario: In order to demonstrate our ideas and concepts we use a running example and introduce a classification of different query types. The applied scenario represents a simple crime solver inspired by [13]. To be more precise, we work with a deterministic and a probabilistic table containing a record of registered criminals and a file of witness statements. In the deterministic table *criminals*, given in Figure (1) and abbreviated by *crim*, following attributes are stored: *name, status, sex, age* and *height*. Thereby, the domains for the attributes *status* and *sex* are given by {*free, jail, parole*} and {*female, male*}.

In addition, during an investigation it was possible to gather witness statements about a given crime. So, we can state that each witness saw one single person characterised by his/her sex (attribute *obs_ sex*) and an estimated age (attribute *obs_ age*) annotated by a confidence value (see Figure (2)).

Criminals (crim)				
TID	name	status	sex	age	height
t_1	Bonnie	free	female	36	170
t_2	Clyde	jail	male	44	188
t_3	Al	parole	male	47	190

Observation (obs)				
TID	witness	obs_sex	obs_age	Pr
t_4	Amber	male	30	0.3
t_5	Mike	female	20	0.7
t_6	Carl	female	30	0.9

Fig. 1. Registered criminals   **Fig. 2.** Witness statements

Classification: For specifying a classification of different query types we identify two significant criteria concerning query language expressiveness and the underlying relational data basis: (i) incorporating the concepts of impreciseness and proximity in terms of similarity predicates and (ii) modeling different possible database states.

We denote the fulfilling of one of these criteria by the term *uncertain*. That means, we apply certain or uncertain queries on certain or uncertain relation data. Please be aware that the terms certain and uncertain can be used in different meanings. In our model we use the term *uncertain* on the data modeling aspect. So, a user, for example, does not know which is the correct instance of his/her data. Consequently, the user annotates his/her data by a confidence value expressing a probability of occurrence.

Next we present four query classes which are built by applying the two classification criteria orthogonally. Additionally, we give a characteristic example query referring to our running scenario for each class.

(i) Certain queries on certain data CQonCD: The class CQonCD contains queries formed by Boolean conditions on deterministic relational data. According to our scenario a typical query of CQonCD is given by *"Determine all criminals who have the status free"*. The corresponding expression $\pi_{name}(\sigma_{st=f}(crim))$ is formulated in relational algebra.

(ii) Uncertain queries on certain data UQonCD: The class UQonCD stands for queries which supports impreciseness and proximity by integrating similarity predicates. A UQonCD-query is given by *"Determine all criminals who have the status free or parole and his/her age is around 30 and his/her body height is about 180 cm"*. A corresponding CQQL similarity condition can be expressed as '$(st = f \lor st = p) \land age \approx 30 \land hei \approx 180$'.

(iii) Certain queries on uncertain data CQonUD: The queries of the class CQonUD are typical for probabilistic databases with possible-world-semantics. As an example query we examine *"Determine all criminals who were possibly observed. That means, his/her age is within an interval of 10 years around an observed age and his/her observed sex is matching"*. For formalising this CQonUD-query we use the PRA algebra developed by Fuhr et. al [5]: $\pi_{name}(crim \bowtie_{F_B} obs)$, whereby the join condition $F_B \equiv (sex = obs\_sex \land age \in [obs\_age - 5, obs\_age + 5])$ is evaluated as Boolean condition.

(iv) Uncertain queries on uncertain data UQonUD: If we augment possible-world-semantics by similarity conditions, a query class with an expanded expressiveness is emerging. That means, in the class UQonUD we apply similarity conditions on data objects which are given in a specific possible database state. The class UQonUD obviously subsumes the first three classes. As an example query for UQonUD we give a variant of the last CQonUD-query: *"Determine all criminals who were possibly observed. That means, his/her age is similar to an observed age and his/her observed sex is matching"*. In order to exemplify this query we extend the PRA algebra by similarity conditions evaluated by CQQL: $\pi_{name}(crim \bowtie_{(sex=obs\_sex \land age \approx obs\_age)} obs)$.

The main motivation of our research is the development of a unifying probabilistic query framework called *ProQua* which comprehends all four query classes. The underlying idea of *ProQua* is the combination of relevance probabilities known from Information Retrieval and possible-world-semantics applied in probabilistic databases.

As an essential step we connect our geometric retrieval model to probability theory by presenting a probabilistic interpretation in this paper. After defining an appropriate probability space we will be able to build a unifying data and query model for UQonUD-queries. Therefore, the main contributions of this work are twofold: (i) adapting and tailoring our CQQL retrieval model for a probabilistic interpretation in Section (3) and (ii) developing a probability interpretation of CQQL by building a probability space covering *arbitrary* UQonCD-queries in Section (4).

As a further result we lay a theoretical foundation for combining vector space-based retrieval approaches (e.g. term vector model, latent semantic analysis, support vector machines, etc.) with probabilistic databases.

2   Related Work

In the last decade a huge amount of probabilistic relational database approaches as [2,1,4,5,3,7,13] have been proposed. They all support the processing of probabilistic relational data, i.e., queries from class CQonUD.

Besides computation complexity the expressiveness of the applied query languages is a significant comparison criterion. Especially, the groundbreaking papers [5] and [3] explicitly discuss the integration of similarity predicates, i.e., the additional support of UQonCD-queries.

Fuhr and Roellecke [5] propose to model similarity predicates as built-in predicates. That means, the corresponding scoring functions are encoded as usual probability relations. Unfortunately, in this case it is not allowed to apply algebra operations arbitrarily any more. Contrarily, Dalvi and Suciu [3] suggest to calculate the score values of all similarity predicates in advance. After such a pre-processing step the calculated score values are getting integrated in a probabilistic relation as occurrence probabilities. This method is restricted to the set of conjunctive queries, because the defined join operation for probabilistic relations always aggregates probabilities conjunctively. Further approaches as [13,7] offer the opportunity to model uncertainty on attribute level. In this case the evaluation of a similarity predicate could be encoded in the corresponding uncertain attribute. But once again this approach is only working for conjunctive queries, because the probability for an entire tuple is always combined by a conjunctive join operation.

We can summarise that the discussed approaches [5], [3], [7] and [13] are not supporting *arbitrary* logic-based similarity queries from UQonCD or UQonUD. As we see in Section (4) the probabilistic interpretation of CQQL can process arbitrary UQonCD-queries. If we combine CQQL with the possible-world-semantics, we are also able to handle queries from UQonUD.

In contrast to established probabilistic systems, fuzzy databases as [6] support arbitrary UQonCD- and UQonUD-queries using fuzzy logic [14]. However, fuzzy databases are not based on probabilistic semantics and the result of a query evaluated by fuzzy logic does not meet user expectations adequately. Especially, the result of the *minimum* function, which is the *only* t-norm with the logic properties idempotence and distributivity, depends only on one input parameter (dominance problem) [11].

3   CQQL Retrieval Model

In this section we tailor the underlying theoretical model of CQQL in order to provide the foundation of our probabilistic interpretation presented in the next section. For this purpose we use the introduced UQonCD-condition '$(st = f \vee st = p) \wedge age \approx 30 \wedge hei \approx 180$' applied on the table *criminals* as a running example. Thereby, the example subconditions '$(st = f \vee st = p)$', '$age \approx 30$' and '$hei \approx 180$' are abbreviated by sc_1, sc_2 and sc_3.

In general, the CQQL model enables the logic-based construction of queries out of Boolean and similarity predicates. The underlying idea is to apply the

Table 1. Correspondences between query processing and the model of CQQL

query processing		CQQL model
value domain	$\leftrightarrow$	vector space
$Dom(t)$	$\leftrightarrow$	$\mathbf{H}$
tuple to be queried	$\leftrightarrow$	tuple vector
t	$\leftrightarrow$	$\vec{t}$
condition	$\leftrightarrow$	condition space
c	$\leftrightarrow$	$\mathbf{cs}[c]$
evaluation	$\leftrightarrow$	squared cosine of the angle
		between $\vec{t}$ and $\mathbf{cs}[c]$
$eval^t(c)$	$\leftrightarrow$	$cos^2(\angle(\vec{t}, \mathbf{cs}[c]))$

theory of vector spaces, also known from quantum mechanics and quantum logic, for query processing. Table (1) gives analogies between query processing concepts and the vector space model of CQQL.

Before we go into more detail, we summarise the basic idea of evaluating a single tuple t against a given CQQL condition c. We start by considering a vector space $\mathbf{H}$ being the domain of tuple t. All attribute values of a tuple t are embodied by the direction of a tuple vector $\vec{t}$ of *length one*. A condition c itself corresponds to a vector *sub*space of $\mathbf{H}$ denoted as $\mathbf{cs}[c]$. For distinguishing the subspace $\mathbf{cs}[c]$ from the containing vector space $\mathbf{H}$ we call $\mathbf{cs}[c]$ as *condition space* of c.

The evaluation result $eval^t(c)$ is determined by the minimal angle between tuple vector $\vec{t}$ and condition space $\mathbf{cs}[c]$ denoted as $\angle(\vec{t}, \mathbf{cs}[c])$. The squared cosine of this angle, i.e., $cos^2(\angle(\vec{t}, \mathbf{cs}[c]))$, is a value out of the interval $[0, 1]$ and can therefore be interpreted as a similarity measure as well as a score value.

For instance, if the tuple vector belongs to the condition space, i.e., $\angle(\vec{t}, \mathbf{cs}[c]) = 0°$, then we interpret the condition outcome as a complete match: $cos^2(0°) = 1$. Contrarily, a right angle of 90° between $\vec{t}$ and $\mathbf{cs}[c]$ leads to a complete mismatch: $cos^2(90°) = 0$.

In order to construct the elements $\mathbf{H}$, $\vec{t}$ and $\mathbf{cs}[c]$ of Table (1) we employ a typical bottom-up strategy which is built on the logical structure of condition c. In this composition predicates (denoted as pr) are the smallest evaluable entities which are getting combined by the logical connectors $\wedge$, $\vee$ and $\neg$. We exploit this construction principle (going from single predicates over combined subconditions to a final condition) in order to deploy the required elements $\mathbf{H}$, $\vec{t}$ and $\mathbf{cs}[c]$.

According to their semantics predicates can be classified into two different main types: Boolean and similarity predicates. For instance, our running example condition includes four predicates '$st = f$', '$st = p$', '$age \approx 30$' and '$hei \approx 180$', whereby the first and second are classified as Boolean predicates and the last two conditions are typical similarity predicates.

In order to preserve the character of a Boolean algebra we need the following restriction in CQQL [8]: In a valid condition any attribute must not be queried by more than one constant in different similarity predicates. Consequently, the

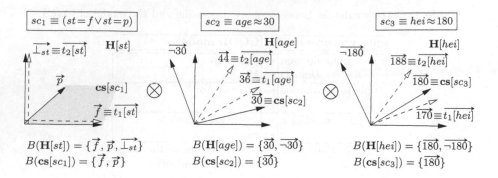

$$B(\mathbf{H}[st]) = \{\vec{f}, \vec{p}, \overrightarrow{\perp_{st}}\}$$
$$B(\mathbf{cs}[sc_1]) = \{\vec{f}, \vec{p}\}$$

$$B(\mathbf{H}[age]) = \{\overrightarrow{30}, \overrightarrow{\neg 30}\}$$
$$B(\mathbf{cs}[sc_2]) = \{\overrightarrow{30}\}$$

$$B(\mathbf{H}[hei]) = \{\overrightarrow{180}, \overrightarrow{\neg 180}\}$$
$$B(\mathbf{cs}[sc_3]) = \{\overrightarrow{180}\}$$

Fig. 3. Basic modules for the running example condition

condition '$age \approx 30 \wedge age \approx 35$' is not allowed in CQQL. However, the condition '$(age \approx 30 \wedge sex = f) \vee (age \approx 30 \wedge sex = m)$' is valid, because age is queried by the same constant 30. We emphasise that this restriction corresponds to the independence assumption of tuple-independent and block-independent probabilistic databases (see Section (2)). In fact, the similarity predicates '$age \approx 30$' and '$age \approx 35$', for example, cannot be evaluated to 1 (complete fulfilling) for a certain person at the same time. In this sense they are not independent and violates therefore the constraint of independence.

As the first construction step we set up a *separate* vector space $\mathbf{H}[A]$ for *each* queried attribute A of tuple t. In the case of our example condition we achieve three initial vector spaces: $\mathbf{H}[st]$, $\mathbf{H}[age]$ and $\mathbf{H}[hei]$. Such vector spaces possess the character of *basic modules* for the final vector space $\mathbf{H}$.

There are two types of information entities which have to be encoded in a basic module $\mathbf{H}[A]$. On one hand, we have to deal with the value of the queried tuple attribute. For example, considering tuple t_1 of *criminals*. So, the tuple vector $\overrightarrow{t_1[st]}$ must express the value *free* by its direction. On the other hand, the comparison constant of the querying predicate (denoted by $con_1(pr)$) must be integrated as condition space $\mathbf{cs}[pr]$. Taking the predicate '$st = f$' as example, we get the value *free* as condition constant which has to be embodied in the condition space $\overrightarrow{\mathbf{cs}}[st = f]$.

Boolean basic modules: For a Boolean attribute (queried by a Boolean predicate and denoted by BA) each comparison constant querying BA constitutes a single base vector of $\mathbf{H}[BA]$. So, we define the basis $B(\mathbf{H}[BA])$ for a Boolean module as $B(\mathbf{H}[BA]) := \{\overrightarrow{bv} \mid val(\overrightarrow{bv}) \in con_2(BA)\} \cup \{\overrightarrow{\perp_{BA}}\}$, whereby $con_2(BA)$ returns all comparison constants regarding BA and $val(\vec{v})$ gives the encoded value of $\vec{v}$, e.g., $con_2(st) = \{free, parole\}$ and $val(\vec{f}) = f$. The vector $\overrightarrow{\perp_{BA}}$ represents all domain values which do not occur as comparison constant in the given condition. The constructed base vectors must always form an orthonormal[1] basis.

---

[1] Two vectors are orthonormal, if they are both of unit length and perpendicular, i.e., they enclose a right angle.

For instance, a 3-dimensional Boolean basic module $\mathbf{H}[st]$ is built for the attribute $\underline{status}$, whereby the base vectors are given by $\vec{f} \equiv (1,0,0)^t$, $\vec{p} \equiv (0,1,0)^t$ and $\overrightarrow{\perp_{st}} \equiv (0,0,1)^t$.

In order to encode the attribute value $t[A]$ and the condition constant $con_1(pr)$ we map the corresponding elements $\overrightarrow{t[A]}$ and $\mathbf{cs}[pr]$ to a base vector embodying the corresponding domain value or $\overrightarrow{\perp_{BA}}$, respectively. Figure (3) depicts the Boolean basic module for the attribute $\underline{status}$.

Similarity basic modules: A similarity basic module for a similarity attribute (queried by a similarity predicate pr and denoted by SA) has in its simplest form two dimensions. So, the attribute value and the condition constant are represented by not necessarily orthogonal vectors embedded in the 2-dimensional vector space $\mathbf{H}[SA]$ (see Figure (3)).

The embedding of $\overrightarrow{t[SA]}$ and $\mathbf{cs}[p]$ in $\mathbf{H}[SA]$ is determined by a scoring function $SF_{SA} : Dom(SA) \times Dom(SA) \rightarrow [0,1]$ which calculates $cos^2(\overrightarrow{t[SA]}, \mathbf{cs}[pr])$ as $SF_{SA}(t[SA], con_1(pr))$. This scoring function expresses a similarity measure. In general, any set of similarity values which can be produced by the squared scalar product is supported. That is, the similarity values must form a semi-positive definite correlation matrix. Please notice that in a basic module a condition space $\mathbf{cs}[pr]$ only spans one dimension and is therefore equivalent to a single vector.

Combining modules: In order to handle *multi*-attribute tuples and *complex* conditions we combine basic modules, tuple vectors and condition spaces by means of the *tensor product* denoted as $\otimes$. This algebraic operation is motivated by the 4th postulate of quantum mechanics [9]. This postulate defines how to assemble various quantum systems (in our case basic modules) to one system. The base vectors of the composed system are here constructed by applying the tensor product to base vectors of the respective subsystems.

Precisely, the tensor product of two 2-dimensional vectors $\vec{x}$ and $\vec{y}$ is defined as: $\vec{x} \otimes \vec{y} \equiv \vec{x}\,\vec{y} := (x_1, x_2)^t \otimes (y_1, y_2)^t \equiv (x_1 y_1, x_1 y_2, x_2 y_1, x_2 y_2)^t$. Additionally, we extend the tensor product of two vectors to two *sets of vectors* as $\{\vec{x_1}, \ldots, \vec{x_n}\} \otimes \{\vec{y_1}, \ldots, \vec{y_m}\} := \{\vec{x_1}\vec{y_1}, \ldots, \vec{x_1}\vec{y_m}, \vec{x_2}\vec{y_1}, \ldots, \vec{x_2}\vec{y_m}, \ldots, \vec{x_n}\vec{y_1}, \ldots, \vec{x_n}\vec{y_m}\}$.

For applying the 4th postulate of quantum mechanics we have to deal with *orthonormal bases* for basic modules (denoted as $B(\mathbf{H}[A])$) and condition spaces (denoted as $B(\mathbf{cs}[c])$). These base vector sets span the whole corresponding vector and condition spaces. Hence, we use base vector sets to identify and combine vector and condition spaces.

(i) Combining modules $\mathbf{H}[A]$: For combining two arbitrary modules $\mathbf{H}[A_1]$ and $\mathbf{H}[A_2]$ we apply the tensor product on the respective base vector sets, i.e., $B(\mathbf{H}[A_1, A_2]) := B(\mathbf{H}[A_1]) \otimes B(\mathbf{H}[A_2])$. Thus, the base vector sets for the merged modules $\mathbf{H}[st, age]$ is given by $\{\vec{f}\,\vec{30}, \vec{f}\,\vec{30}, \vec{p}\,\vec{30}, \vec{p}\,\vec{30}, \overrightarrow{\perp_{st}}\vec{30}, \overrightarrow{\perp_{st}}\vec{30}\}$.

(ii) Combining tuple vectors $\overrightarrow{t[A]}$: We merge two tuple vectors $\overrightarrow{t[A_1]}$ and $\overrightarrow{t[A_2]}$ by applying the tensor product on vectors directly: $\overrightarrow{t[A_1, A_2]} := \overrightarrow{t[A_1]} \otimes \overrightarrow{t[A_2]}$. Please notice that $\overrightarrow{t[A_1, A_2]}$ is still normalised. The tuple vectors for t_1 and t_2 are given by $\vec{f}\,\overrightarrow{36170}$ and $\overrightarrow{\perp_{st}}\overrightarrow{44188}$.

(iii) **Combining condition spaces** $\mathbf{cs}[c]$: The combination of two condition spaces $\mathbf{cs}[c_1]$ and $\mathbf{cs}[c_2]$ is realised in two steps:

(a) transferring $\mathbf{cs}[c_1]$ and $\mathbf{cs}[c_2]$ into the merged module vector space $\mathbf{H}[attr(c_1), attr(c_2)]$ by applying the tensor product on the basis of a condition space and the basis of the opposite module vector space, i.e., $B(\mathbf{cs}[c_1])' := B(\mathbf{cs}[c_1]) \otimes B(\mathbf{H}[attr(c_2)])$ and $B(\mathbf{cs}[c_2])' := B(\mathbf{H}[attr(c_1)]) \otimes B(\mathbf{cs}[c_2])$, whereby the auxiliary function $attr(c)$ returns the queried attributes of condition c, and

(b) applying the corresponding set operations $(\wedge \leftrightarrow \cap, \vee \leftrightarrow \cup, \neg \leftrightarrow \setminus)$ on the transferred base vector sets, i.e., $B(\mathbf{cs}[c_1 \wedge c_2]) := B(\mathbf{cs}[c_1])' \cap B(\mathbf{cs}[c_2])'$, $B(\mathbf{cs}[c_1 \vee c_2]) := B(\mathbf{cs}[c_1])' \cup B(\mathbf{cs}[c_2])'$ and $B(\mathbf{cs}[\neg c]) := B(\mathbf{H}[attr(c)]) \setminus B(\mathbf{cs}[c])$. The combined base vector set $B(\mathbf{cs}[sc_1 \wedge sc_2])$ is computed as
$(B(\mathbf{cs}[sc_1])' \otimes B(\mathbf{H}[age])) \cap (B(\mathbf{H}[st]) \otimes B(\mathbf{cs}[sc_2])') = \{\vec{f}\,\vec{30}, \vec{p}\,\vec{30}\}$.

Geometric evaluation: Referring to the law of cosine[2] the squared cosine of the minimum angle between $\vec{t}$ and $\mathbf{cs}[c]$ can be computed by using the scalar product between $\vec{t}$ and an orthonormal basis for $\mathbf{cs}[c]$, i.e., $eval^t(c) := cos^2(\sphericalangle(\vec{t}, \mathbf{cs}[c])) = \sum_{\vec{bv} \in B(\mathbf{cs}[c])} (\vec{t} * \vec{bv})^2$. In the remainder we denote the scalar product of two vectors as a star ($*$) and the multiplication of two numbers as a centered dot ($\cdot$).

4   Probabilistic Interpretation

In this section we develop a probabilistic interpretation for the CQQL retrieval model presented in the last section. The main idea of our probabilistic interpretation is a mapping between elements of the CQQL retrieval model and a discrete probability space $(\Omega, \mathcal{F}, P^t)$. This mapping, given in Table (2), guarantees the same results for the geometric and probabilistic evaluation.

Next we define probability spaces $(\Omega, \mathcal{F}, P^t)$ for each queried tuple t and specify the semantics of a CQQL condition c as an event $E[c]$ out of $\mathcal{F}$. Based on the events $E[c]$ we are able to evaluate a given tuple t against a CQQL condition c as $eval^t(c) := P^t(E[c])$.

Generally, the definition of a probability space requires three steps: (i) defining a sample space Ω, a σ-algebra $\mathcal{F}$ and a probability measure P^t, (ii) proving that σ-additivity holds for P^t and (iii) verifying that $P^t(\Omega)$ sums up to 1.

We tailored our CQQL retrieval model in a way that all constructed sample spaces are countable, despite the underlying attribute domains can be continuous. So, we can comfortably define $\mathcal{F}$ as the power set of Ω: $\mathcal{F} := \mathcal{P}(\Omega)$. Thus, σ-additivity holds for each P^t, if we declare the probability measure $P^t : \mathcal{P}(\Omega) \to [0,1]$ pointwise by a probability function $p^t : \Omega \to [0,1]$. That means, $P^t(E) := \sum_{\omega \in E} p^t(\omega)$. Consequently, in our case we have only to define Ω and p^t and prove that $P^t(\Omega)$ equals 1.

For building $(\Omega, \mathcal{F}, P^t)$ we basically use our bottom-up strategy generating $\mathbf{H}$, $\vec{t}$ and $\mathbf{cs}[c]$. Therefore, at the beginning we define a probability space for

---

[2] Law of cosine: $\vec{x_1} * \vec{x_2} = ||\vec{x_1}|| \cdot ||\vec{x_2}|| \cdot cos(\sphericalangle(\vec{x_1}, \vec{x_2}))$.

Table 2. Analogies between the CQQL model and its probabilistic interpretation

CQQL model	prob. interpretation
vector space $\leftrightarrow$	sample space
basis of $\mathbf{H}$ $\leftrightarrow$	Ω
tuple vector $\leftrightarrow$	probability function
$\vec{t}$ $\leftrightarrow$	$p^t(\omega), \omega \in \Omega$
condition space $\leftrightarrow$	event
$\mathbf{cs}[c]$ $\leftrightarrow$	$E[c] \subset \Omega$
evaluation by angle $\leftrightarrow$	probability measure
$cos^2(\angle(\vec{t}, \mathbf{cs}[c]))$ $\leftrightarrow$	$P^t(E[c])$

each basic module in a similar way to the construction of separate vector spaces in Section (3).

Boolean basic modules: For specifying the sample space Ω_{BA} for a Boolean attribute BA we use the base vector set $B(\mathbf{H}[BA])$, i.e., $\Omega_{BA} := B(\mathbf{H}[BA])$. So, the sample space Ω_{st} is given by $B(\mathbf{H}[st]) = \{\vec{f}, \vec{p}, \vec{\perp}_{st}\}$. The respective probability function p^t_{BA} is built in two steps. First we define $\forall \overrightarrow{bv} \in (\Omega_{BA} \setminus \{\vec{\perp}_{BA}\})$: $p^t_{BA}(\overrightarrow{bv}) := cos^2(\angle(\overrightarrow{t[BA]}, \mathbf{cs}[BA = val(\overrightarrow{bv})])) = (\overrightarrow{t[BA]} * \overrightarrow{bv})^2$. This part sets the connection between the geometric and the probabilistic evaluation. Particularly, it means that p^t_{BA} equals 1, if $t[BA] = val(\overrightarrow{bv})$, and $p^t_{BA}(\overrightarrow{bv}) = 0$ otherwise, because we compute the squared scalar product of two vectors of an orthonormal basis. Secondly, we set $p^t_{BA}(\vec{\perp}_{BA}) := 1$, if $t[BA] \notin con_2(BA)$, and $p^t_{BA}(\vec{\perp}_{BA}) := 0$ otherwise.

Lemma 1. *The triple $(\Omega_{BA}, \mathcal{P}(\Omega_{BA}), P^t_{BA})$ based on a Boolean predicate pr querying BA and a tuple t is a probability space.*
Proof.
<u>Case 1:</u> $t[BA] \in con_2(BA) \Rightarrow \Omega_{BA} = \{\overrightarrow{t[BA]}\} \cup (\Omega_{BA} \setminus \{\overrightarrow{t[BA]}\}) \Rightarrow P^t_{BA}(\Omega_{BA}) = p^t_{BA}(\overrightarrow{t[BA]}) + \sum_{\substack{\overrightarrow{bv} \in \\ (\Omega_{BA} - \{\overrightarrow{t[BA]}\})}} p^t_{BA}(\overrightarrow{bv}) = 1 + 0 = 1.$

<u>Case 2:</u> $t[BA] \notin con_2(BA) \Rightarrow \Omega_{BA} = \{\vec{\perp}_{BA}\} \cup (\Omega_{BA} \setminus \{\vec{\perp}_{BA}\}) \Rightarrow P^t_{BA}(\Omega_{BA}) = p^t_{BA}(\vec{\perp}_{BA}) + \sum_{\substack{\overrightarrow{bv} \in \\ (\Omega_{BA} - \{\vec{\perp}_{BA}\})}} p^t_{BA}(\overrightarrow{bv}) = 1 + 0 = 1.$

Similarity basic modules: Again we specify the sample space Ω_{SA} of a similarity attribute SA by the corresponding base vector set, i.e., $\Omega_{SA} := B(\mathbf{H}[SA]) = \{\overrightarrow{con_1(pr)}, \overrightarrow{\neg con_1(pr)}\}$, whereby pr is the predicate querying SA. Then Ω_{age} is given by $\{\overrightarrow{30}, \overrightarrow{\neg 30}\}$.

The probability function p^t_{SA} is derived from the geometric evaluation of '$SA \approx con_1(pr)$'. So, we obtain

$$p_{SA}^t(\overrightarrow{bv}) := \begin{cases} cos^2(\sphericalangle(t[\overrightarrow{SA}], \mathbf{cs}[SA \approx val(\overrightarrow{bv})])) & \text{if } \overrightarrow{bv} \text{ is not negated} \\ cos^2(\sphericalangle(t[\overrightarrow{SA}], \mathbf{cs}[\neg(SA \approx val(\overrightarrow{bv}))])) & \text{if } \overrightarrow{bv} \text{ is negated} \end{cases}$$

$$= \begin{cases} SF_{SA}(t[SA], val(\overrightarrow{bv})) & \text{if } \overrightarrow{bv} \text{ is not negated} \\ 1 - SF_{SA}(t[SA], val(\overrightarrow{bv})) & \text{if } \overrightarrow{bv} \text{ is negated.} \end{cases}$$

Thus, for setting p_{SA}^t we use the score function SF_{SA} which produces a similarity value (see Section (3)). This similarity value is here interpreted as relevance probability for a similarity predicate.

Lemma 2. *The triple* $(\Omega_{SA}, \mathcal{P}(\Omega_{SA}), P_{SA}^t)$ *based on a similarity predicate pr querying SA and a tuple t is a probability space.*
Proof. $P_{SA}^t(\Omega_{SA}) = p_{SA}^t(\overrightarrow{con_1(pr)}) + p_{SA}^t(\overrightarrow{\neg con_1(pr)}) = SF_{SA}(t[SA], con_1(pr)) + (1 - SF_{SA}(t[SA], con_1(pr))) = 1$

Combined probability space: In order to generate a probability space which is corresponding to the combined vector space $\mathbf{H}$ we build a product probability space. For the sake of clarity, we order the attributes of a tuple t as $t \equiv t[BA_1, \ldots, BA_n, SA_1, \ldots, SA_m]$ abbreviated by $t[BA_1, \ldots, SA_m]$. Then we define the product sample space Ω as cartesian product of the basic sample spaces, i.e., $\Omega := \Omega_{BA_1} \times \ldots \times \Omega_{BA_n} \times \Omega_{SA_1} \times \ldots \times \Omega_{SA_m}$.

The probability function p^t is defined as $p^t((\overrightarrow{bv}_{BA_1}, \ldots, \overrightarrow{bv}_{SA_m})) :=$ $cos^2(\sphericalangle(t[\overrightarrow{BA_1, \ldots, SA_m}], \mathbf{cs}[c_1 \wedge \ldots \wedge c_{n+m}]))$, whereby c_i is a predicate or a negated predicate. The structure of c_i depends on the predicate type, i.e., $\forall i = 1, \ldots, n$: $c_i \equiv (BA_i = val(\overrightarrow{bv}_{BA_i}))$ and $\forall j = n+1, \ldots, n+m$ the condition c_j is given by $c_j \equiv SA_j \approx val(\overrightarrow{bv}_{SA_j})$, if $\overrightarrow{bv}_{SA_j}$ is not negated and $c_j \equiv \neg(SA_j \approx val(\overrightarrow{bv}_{SA_j}))$ if $\overrightarrow{bv}_{SA_j}$ is negated.

The condition space $\mathbf{cs}[c_1 \wedge \ldots \wedge c_{n+m}]$ expresses a conjunction of disjoint attribute constraints. So, each basic probability space $\Omega_{BA_1}, \ldots, \Omega_{SA_m}$ is bijectively restricted by a condition of $c_1, \ldots, c_{n+m}$. Therefore, we achieve a single base vector for the condition space $\mathbf{cs}[c_1 \wedge \ldots \wedge c_{n+m}]$ as $\overrightarrow{bv}_{BA_1} \cdots \overrightarrow{bv}_{SA_m}$. Using this single base vector and the equivalence

$$\overrightarrow{t_1[A_1, \ldots, A_n]} * \overrightarrow{t_2[A_1, \ldots, A_n]} = (\overrightarrow{t_1[A_1]} * \overrightarrow{t_2[A_1]}) \cdot \ldots \cdot (\overrightarrow{t_1[A_n]} * \overrightarrow{t_2[A_n]})$$

we can compute p^t by multiplying the probability functions $p_{BA_1}^t, \ldots, p_{SA_m}^t$:

$$p^t((\overrightarrow{bv}_{BA_1}, \ldots, \overrightarrow{bv}_{SA_m})) := cos^2(\alpha(t[\overrightarrow{BA_1, \ldots, SA_m}], \mathbf{cs}[c_1 \wedge \ldots \wedge c_{n+m}]))$$
$$= (t[\overrightarrow{BA_1, \ldots, BA_n}] * \overrightarrow{bv}_{BA_1} \cdots \overrightarrow{bv}_{SA_m})^2$$
$$= (t[\overrightarrow{BA_1}] * \overrightarrow{bv}_{BA_1})^2 \cdot \ldots \cdot (t[\overrightarrow{SA_m}] * \overrightarrow{bv}_{SA_m})^2$$
$$= p_{BA_1}^t(\overrightarrow{bv}_{BA_1}) \cdot \ldots \cdot p_{SA_m}^t(\overrightarrow{bv}_{SA_m})$$

Theorem 1. *The triple* $(\Omega, \mathcal{P}(\Omega), P^t)$ *based on a CQQL condition* c *and a tuple* t *is a probability space.*

Proof.

$$P^t(\Omega) = \sum_{(\overrightarrow{bv}_{BA_1}, \ldots, \overrightarrow{bv}_{SA_m}) \in \Omega} p^t((\overrightarrow{bv}_{BA_1}, \ldots, \overrightarrow{bv}_{SA_m})) = \sum_{(\overrightarrow{bv}_{BA_1}, \ldots, \overrightarrow{bv}_{SA_m}) \in \Omega} (p^t_{BA_1}(\overrightarrow{bv}_{BA_1}) \cdot \ldots \cdot p^t_{SA_m}(\overrightarrow{bv}_{SA_m}))$$

$$= \sum_{\overrightarrow{bv}_{BA_1} \in \atop \Omega_{BA_1}} p^t_{BA_1}(\overrightarrow{bv}_{BA_1}) \cdot \ldots \cdot \sum_{\overrightarrow{bv}_{SA_m} \in \atop \Omega_{SA_m}} p^t_{SA_m}(\overrightarrow{bv}_{SA_m}) = 1 \cdot \ldots \cdot 1 = 1$$

Probabilistic evaluation: After verifying the probability space $(\Omega, \mathcal{P}(\Omega), P^t)$ we investigate the evaluation of a tuple t against a condition c. Respecting the probabilistic interpretation a condition c represents an event $E[c]$ out of $\mathcal{P}(\Omega)$. In order to calculate the probability of such an event we use the defined probability measure P^t.

First we set $E[pr]$ for a predicate pr to $E[pr] := \{(\overrightarrow{bv}_{BA_1}, \ldots, con_1(pr), \ldots, \overrightarrow{bv}_{SA_m}) \mid \overrightarrow{bv}_{BA_i} \in \Omega_{BA_i}, \overrightarrow{bv}_{SA_j} \in \Omega_{SA_j}, BA_i \neq attr(pr), SA_j \neq attr(pr)\}$. Thus, for the predicate '$st = f$' we generate $\{(\overrightarrow{f}, \overrightarrow{30}, \overrightarrow{180}), (\overrightarrow{f}, \overrightarrow{30}, \overrightarrow{\neg 180}), (\overrightarrow{f}, \overrightarrow{\neg 30}, \overrightarrow{180}), (\overrightarrow{f}, \overrightarrow{\neg 30}, \overrightarrow{\neg 180})\}$.

Events expressing combined conditions can be constructed by applying the corresponding set operations: $E[c_1 \wedge c_2] := E[c_1] \cap E[c_2]$, $E[c_1 \vee c_2] := E[c_1] \cup E[c_2]$ and $E[\neg c] := \Omega \setminus E[c]$.

In general, we can calculate $P^t(E[c])$ by enumerating the elementary events of $E[c]$: $eval^t(c) := P^t(E[c]) = \sum_{\omega \in E[c]} p^t(\omega)$. This method equals the evaluation formula for the geometric evaluation of Section (3), but now we are able to exploit characteristics of the defined probability space. Thus, we can apply following standard evaluation rules provided the events $E[c_1]$ and $E[c_2]$ are independent:

$$eval^t(pr) := P^t(E[pr])$$
$$= SF_{attr(pr)}(t[attr(pr)], con_1(pr)) \text{ if } pr \text{ is a predicate}$$
$$eval^t(c_1 \wedge c_2) := P^t(E[c_1] \cap E[c_2]) = P^t(E[c_1]) \cdot P^t(E[c_2])$$
$$eval^t(c_1 \vee c_2) := P^t(E[c_1] \cup E[c_2]) = P^t(c_1) + P^t(c_2) - P^t(c_1) \cdot P^t(c_2)$$
$$eval^t(\neg c) := P^t(\Omega \setminus E[c]) = 1 - P^t(c).$$

Because of the separate construction of the underlying basic modules (see Section (3)) it can be proved that events $E[pr_1], \ldots, E[pr_n]$ generated by CQQL predicates are independent. Two complex events $E[c_1]$ and $E[c_2]$ are independent, if the underlying conditions c_1 and c_2 do not contain overlapping similarity predicates. For instance, we must not use the evaluation rules on the condition '$(age \approx 30 \wedge age \approx 30)$'.

For conditions including overlapping similarity predicates we apply the well-known sieve formula after performing two transformation steps: (i) building the equivalent disjunctive normal form $DNF(c)$ of condition c and then (ii) simplifying the generated conjuncts K_i of $DNF(c)$ by the logical laws of idempotence, complement and absorption (denoted as K_i'):

$$eval^t(c) := P^t(E[simpl(DNF(c))]) = \sum_{i=1}^{n}(-1)^{i-1}\sum_{1\leq j_1<...<j_i\leq n}eval^t(K'_{j_1})\cdot...\cdot eval^t(K'_{j_i})$$

5 Conclusion and Outlook

In this work we have developed a probabilistic interpretation for a quantum logic-based retrieval model. It provides an important milestone for the development of our unifying probabilistic query framework called *ProQua* which combines possible-world-semantics with relevance probabilities.

Acknowledgment. Sebastian Lehrack was supported by the German Research Foundation grant SCHM 1208/11 − 1.

References

1. Barbar, D., Garcia-Molina, H., Porter, D.: The management of probabilistic data. IEEE Trans. Knowl. Data Eng. 4(5), 487–502 (1992)
2. Cavallo, R., Pittarelli, M.: The theory of probabilistic databases. In: Stocker, P.M., Kent, W., Hammersley, P. (eds.) VLDB, pp. 71–81. Morgan Kaufmann, San Francisco (1987)
3. Dalvi, N., Suciu, D.: Efficient query evaluation on probabilistic databases. VLDB J. 16(4), 523–544 (2007)
4. Dey, D., Sarkar, S.: A probabilistic relational model and algebra. ACM Trans. Database Syst. 21(3), 339–369 (1996)
5. Fuhr, N., Roelleke, T.: A probabilistic relational algebra for the integration of information retrieval and database systems. ACM Trans. Inf. Syst. 15(1), 32–66 (1997)
6. Galindo, J., Urrutia, A., Piattini, M.: Fuzzy Databases: Modeling, Design and Implementation. Idea Group Publishing, Hershey (2006)
7. Koch, C.: MayBMS: A System for Managing Large Uncertain and Probabilistic Databases. In: Managing and Mining Uncertain Data, ch. 6. Springer, Heidelberg (2008)
8. Lehrack, S., Schmitt, I., Saretz, S.: CQQL: A Quantum Logic-Based Extension of the Relation Domain Calculus. In: Proceedings of the International Workshop Logic in Databases (LID 2009) (October 2009)
9. Nielson, M.A., Chuang, I.L.: Quantum Computation and Quantum Information. Cambridge University Press, Cambridge (2000)
10. Schmitt, I.: QQL: A DB&IR Query Language. VLDB J. 17(1), 39–56 (2008)
11. Schmitt, I., Nuernberger, A., Lehrack, S.: On the relation between fuzzy and quantum logic. In: Seising, R. (ed.) Views on Fuzzy Sets and Systems from Different Perspectives. STUDFUZZ, vol. 243, pp. 417–438. Springer, Heidelberg (2009)
12. van Rijsbergen, C.J.: Information Retrieval, Butterworth (1979)
13. Widom, J.: Trio: A system for data, uncertainty, and lineage. In: Managing and Mining Uncertain Data, pp. 113–148. Springer, Heidelberg (2008)
14. Zadeh, L.A.: Fuzzy logic. IEEE Computer 21(4), 83–93 (1988)

Author Index

Alonso-Barba, Juan I.   194
Amgoud, Leila   86
Ammar, Sourour   229
Augusto, Juan Carlos   582
Ayachi, Raouia   700

Baioletti, Marco   239
Ben Amor, Nahla   182, 700
Benferhat, Salem   700
Ben Messaoud, Montassar   182
Besnard, Philippe   532
Blondeel, Marjon   616
Bodlaender, Hans L.   170
Boella, Guido   74
Bosc, Patrick   725
Bounhas, Myriam   434
Broersen, Jan   521
Burger, Thomas   275
Busanello, Giuseppe   239
Butz, Cory J.   110

Camacho, Franklin   569
Cano, Andrés   217
Chen, Shuwei   582
Chen, Tao   410
Cholvy, Laurence   386
Cohen, Andrea   50
Coletti, Giulianella   557
Confalonieri, Roberto   485, 509
Couceiro, Miguel   545
Cuzzolin, Fabio   287

Daniel, Milan   688
de Campos, Cassio P.   158
De Cock, Martine   616
de la Ossa, Luis   194
Destercke, Sebastien   263
Díaz, Susana   594
Doder, Dragan   459
Doré, Pierre-Emmanuel   350
Drap, Pierre   663
Dubois, Didier   1

Elouedi, Zied   314
Evers, Sander   251

Feelders, Ad   422
Fisseler, Jens   447
Flaminio, Tommaso   628

Gabarro, Joaquim   651
Gabbay, Dov M.   19, 74
Gaggl, Sarah Alice   38
Gámez, Jose A.   194
García, Alejandro J.   50
Gilio, Angelo   497
Godo, Lluis   628
Gómez-Olmedo, Manuel   217
Grant, John   362
Grégoire, Éric   532

Halpern, Joseph Y.   36
Hanna, Phil   675
Hué, Julien   663
Hunter, Anthony   362

Ji, Qiang   158
Jiménez, Jorge   606
Jousselme, Anne-Laure   350

Kaci, Souhila   62
Kern-Isberner, Gabriele   447
Kessentini, Yousri   275
Koutras, Costas D.   374
Kramosil, Ivan   688

Labreuche, Christophe   62, 338
Lefèvre, Éric   314
Lehrack, Sebastian   749
Leray, Philippe   182, 229
Lín, Václav   206
Liu, Jun   582
Liu, Weiru   675
Lucas, Peter J.F.   251

Madsen, Anders L.   110
Marchioni, Enrico   628
Martin, Arnaud   350
Martinetti, Davide   594
Masegosa, Andrés R.   217
Mata Díaz, Amílcar   398
Maupin, Patrick   350

Mellouli, Khaled   434
Mercier, David   314
Montes, Ignacio   594
Montes, Susana   606
Moral, Serafín   217

Nieves, Juan Carlos   509

Ognjanović, Zoran   459
O'Neill, Ian   675
Osswald, Christophe   350

Papini, Odile   663
Paquet, Thierry   275
Parker, Austin   737
Perović, Aleksandar   459
Pieters, Barbara F.I.   422
Pino Pérez, Ramón   398, 569
Pivert, Olivier   725
Poon, Leonard K.M.   410
Pouly, Marc   299
Prade, Henri   434, 485, 509, 713
Puerta, Jose M.   194

Ramasso, Emmanuel   326
Ramon, Sébastien   532
Rico, Agnès   713
Rietbergen, Merel T.   134

Saad, Emad   472
Sandri, Sandra   640
Sanfilippo, Giuseppe   497
Savéant, Pierre   338
Schmitt, Ingo   749
Schockaert, Steven   616
Scozzafava, Romano   557
Sérayet, Mariette   663
Serir, Lisa   326
Serna, Maria   651

Serrurier, Mathieu   434
Šešelja, Branimir   606
Shenoy, Prakash P.   98
Simari, Gerardo I.   737
Simari, Guillermo R.   50
Sliva, Amy   737
Smits, Grégory   725
Soubaras, Hélène   338
Stewart, Alan   651
Subrahmanian, V.S.   737

Tepavčević, Andreja   606
Thimm, Matthias   447
Toledo Martins-Bedé, Flávia   640

van der Gaag, Linda C.   122, 134, 170, 422
van der Torre, Leendert   74
van Engelen, Robert   146
Vantaggi, Barbara   239, 557
Vermeir, Dirk   616
Vesic, Srdjan   86
Villata, Serena   74

Waldhauser, Tamás   545
Wang, Hui   582
Wang, Yi   410
Williams, Kevin   110
Woltran, Stefan   38
Woudenberg, Steven P.D.   122
Würbel, Eric   663

Yu, Haohai   146
Yue, Anbu   675

Zerhouni, Noureddine   326
Zhang, Nevin L.   410
Zikos, Yorgos   374